CHURCH LAW & TAX REPORT

CHURCH & CLERGY TAX GUIDE

1998 EDITION

The most comprehensive and authoritative
tax guide available for both churches and clergy
Updated Annually!

Richard R. Hammar, J.D., LL.M., CPA

CHURCH LAW & TAX REPORT
CHURCH AND CLERGY TAX GUIDE
1998 Edition

ISBN 1-880562-31-6

This publication is designed to provide accurate and authoritative information in regard to the subject matter covered. It is sold with the understanding that the publisher is not engaged in rendering legal, accounting, or
other professional service. If legal advice or other expert assistance is
required, the services of a competent professional person should be sought.
"From a Declaration of Principles jointly adopted by a Committee of the
American Bar Association and a Committee of Publishers and Associations."

Every effort has been made to make the materials in this text current as
of the date of publication. Federal tax law, however, is subject to change.
Congress can modify the law, as it has on numerous occasions over the past
few years. Also, court decisions and IRS rulings can significantly affect the
application of federal tax laws to individual circumstances. Such changes
may affect the accuracy of this book. These changes are updated in our
bimonthly publication *Church Law & Tax Report*. Also note that tax forms
can change. Always be certain to use the most recent copy of any tax form.

Published by
Christian Ministry Resources
PO Box 2301
Matthews, NC 28106
(704) 841-8066
(704) 841-8039 (Fax)

Printed in the U.S.A.

TABLE OF CONTENTS

Introduction 7

Summary of Important Tax Changes Occurring in 1997 8

Explanation of Legal Terms 24

Chapter 1: The Income Tax Return 26

Chapter Highlights 26

Section A: Filing Your Return 27
1.   Must ministers pay federal income taxes? 27
2.   Who must file a return? 27
3.   Which form to use 28
4.   Recordkeeping 29
5.   How to figure your tax 29
6.   When to file 30
7.   Extensions of time to file 30
8.   Refunds 30
9.   If you owe additional taxes 30
10.   Amended returns 30
11.   Audit risk 31
12.   Penalties 31
13.   Limitations periods 34
14.   Should you prepare your own tax returns? 34

Section B: Filing Status 35

Section C: Personal Exemptions and Dependents 35

Section D: Tax Withholding and Estimated Tax 36
1.   Withholding 36
2.   Estimated tax 38

Section E: If Your Return Is Examined 40

Section F: "Offers in Compromise" 41

Section G: The "Taxpayer Bill of Rights" ... 42

Section H: Right to Minimize Taxes 46

Section I: Notifying the IRS of a Change of Address 46

Illustration 1-1: Income Tax Appeal Procedure 48

Chapter 2: Are Clergy and Church Staff Employees or Self-Employed? 49

Chapter Highlights 49

Section A: Ministers 49
1.   In general 49
2.   Selecting the correct status—4 tests 51
Illustration 2-1: Sample clause characterizing a minister as self-employed 53
3.   Court decisions and IRS rulings 55
4.   IRS Tax Guide for Churches 66
5.   IRS audit guidelines for ministers 66
6.   How ministers should determine their correct reporting status 68
7.   Additional considerations 68

Section B: Nonminister Staff 71

Appendix 1: A Summary of Cases 72

Chapter 3: Eligibility of Clergy and Church Workers for Housing Allowances and Other Special Tax Provisions 73

Chapter Highlights 73

Section A: Introduction 73

Section B: Ministers Serving Local Churches 75
1.   Minister 75
2.   Services performed in the exercise of ministry 86

Section C: Ministers Employed by Integral Agencies or on Assignment 94

Section D: Religious Orders 98

Chapter 4: Income 100

Chapter Highlights 100

Section A: Wages, Salaries, and Earnings 101
1.   Bonuses 106
2.   Christmas and other special occasion gifts 106
3.   Retirement gifts 109
4.   Property purchased from an employer 112
5.   Sick pay 113
6.   Social security tax paid by the church 113
7.   Taxable fringe benefits 113
8.   Personal use of a church provided car 114
9.   Below-market interest loans 117
10.   "In kind" transfers of property 118
11.   Assignments of income 118
12.   Refusal to accept full salary 118
13.   Discretionary funds 119
14.   Nonaccountable business expense reimbursements 120
15.   Employer reimbursements of a spouse's travel expenses 121
16.   Forgiveness of debt 121
17.   Severance pay 122
18.   Trips to the Holy Land 124
19.   Payment of personal expenses 125
20.   Frequent flier miles 125
21.   Sabbatical pay 126

Section B: Fees for Performing Marriages, Funerals, and Baptisms 126

Section C: Interest and Dividend Income 126

Section D: Rental Income and Expenses 127

Section E: Retirement Plans, Pensions, and Annuities 128

Section F: Social Security Benefits 128

Section G: Other Income 129

Section H: Gains and Losses 130
1.   Sale of investment property 130
2.   Selling your home 131

Section I: **Splitting Income Between Spouses** 132

Chapter 5: Exclusions from Gross Income 135

Chapter Highlights 135

Section A: **Gifts and Inheritances** 136

Section B: **Life Insurance Proceeds** 136

Section C: **Scholarships and Fellowship Grants** 137

Section D: **Medical Insurance Premiums** 137

Section E: **Amounts Received under Accident and Health Plans** 139

Section F: **Medical Savings Accounts (MSAs)** 140

Section G: **Group Term Life Insurance** ... 141

Section H: **Certain Fringe Benefits** 142

Section I: **Reporting Requirements** 149

Chapter 6: Ministers' Housing and Parsonage Allowances 150

Chapter Highlights 150

Section A: **Parsonages** 151

Illustration 6-1: Parsonage Allowance Designation for Ministers Who Live in a Church-Owned Parsonage 152

Section B: **Owning or Renting Your Home** 156

Illustration 6-2: Housing Allowance Designation for Ministers Who Own or Rent Their Homes 159

Section C: **Reporting of Housing Allowances** 165

Illustration 6-3: Housing Allowance Expense Form for Clergy Who Own Their Home 168
Illustration 6-4: Housing Allowance Expense Form for Clergy Who Rent Their Home 169
Illustration 6-5: Parsonage Allowance Expense Form for Clergy Who Live in a Church-Owned Parsonage 170

Chapter 7: Adjustments, Deductions, and Credits 171

Chapter Highlights 171

Section A: **Adjustments to Gross Income** 172

Section B: **Deductions—Introduction** 173

Section C: **Business and Professional Expenses** 173

1.   Transportation expenses 175
2.   Travel expenses 182
3.   Entertainment expenses 190
4.   Business gifts 192
5.   Educational expenses 192
6.   Subscriptions and books 193
7.   Personal computers 194
8.   Clothing and laundry 195
9.   Office in the home 196
10. Moving Expenses 199
11. Telephone expenses 200
12. Club dues 200
13. Financial support by clergy to local churches and denominational agencies 201

Section D: **Business and Professional Expenses—How to Report Them** 204

Illustration 7-1: Full Accountable Reimbursement Policy 207

Section E: **Business and Professional Expenses—Substantiation and Recordkeeping Requirements** 218

Section F: **Business and Professional Expenses— the Deason Rule** 222

Section G: **Itemized Deductions** 224

1. Medical expenses 224
2. Taxes 225
3. Interest 225
4. Charitable contributions 226
5. Casualty and theft losses 226
6. Moving expenses 226
7. Miscellaneous deductions 228

Section H: **Tax Credits** 228

1. Child and dependent care credit 228
2. Earned income credit 229
3. Adoption credit 230
4. Child Tax Credit 230
5. HOPE Scholarship Tax Credit 230
6. Lifetime Learning Credit 232
Illustration 7-2: Daily Business Mileage and Expense Log 233
Illustration 7-3: Weekly Traveling Expense and Entertainment Record 233

Chapter 8: Charitable Contributions 234

Chapter Highlights 234

Section A: **Introduction** 235

1. Gift of cash or property 235
2. Time of contribution 239
3. Unconditional and without personal benefit 240
4. Contribution made to or for the use of a qualified organization 244
5. Amount deductible 245
6. Substantiation 247

Section B: **Designated Contributions** 248

1. Missionaries 249
2. Benevolence funds 252
Illustration 8-1: Benevolence Fund Policy 252
3. Scholarship gifts 257
4. Gifts that designate clergy 261

Section C: **Substantiation of Charitable Contributions** 262

1. Contributions of cash 263
Illustration 8-2: Sample Receipt 272
2. Contributions of noncash property 272

Section D: How to Claim
the Deduction 278

Illustration 8-3: Sample receipt: cash
contributions 280
Illustration 8-4: Sample receipt: property
and quid pro quo contributions 281
Illustration 8-5: Sample receipt: cash,
property, and quid pro quo contributions 282

Chapter 9: Social Security for Ministers 286

Chapter Highlights 286

Section A: Introduction 287

Section B: Ministers Deemed
Self-Employed 287

Section C: Exemption of Ministers from
Social Security Coverage 288

Section D: Services to which
Exemption Applies 296

Section E: Computation of Tax 297

Section F: Working After You Retire 299

Section G: Exemption of Members of
Certain Religious Faiths..........299

Section H: Is Social Security a
"Good Investment?" 300

Chapter 10: Retirement Plans 302

Chapter Highlights 302

Section A: Introduction 302

Section B: Individual
Retirement Accounts 303

Section C: Simplified Employee
Pensions (SEPs).....................309

Section D: Keogh Plans 309

Section E: Deferred Compensation
Plans 310

Section F: Tax-Sheltered Annuities 312

Section G: Church Retirement Income
Accounts 318

Section H: Qualified Pension Plans..........318

Section I: 401(k) plans ("cash or
deferred arrangements").........319

Section J: Denominational Plans 319

Section K: Housing Allowances 320

Section L: Retirement Distributions not
Pursuant to a Formal Plan.....323

Section M: "SIMPLE" Retirement Plans ..324

The IRS Model Rabbi
Trust Agreement 325

Chapter 11: Church Reporting Requirements 330

Chapter Highlights 330

Introduction 331

Section A: Payroll Tax Procedures
for 1998 331
1. Why church leaders should take the
payroll tax reporting rules seriously................331
2. Application of the payroll reporting rules
to clergy........................335
3. Mandatory church compliance with the
payroll reporting rules does not violate
"separation of church and state" 337
4. The "10-step" approach to compliance
with federal payroll tax reporting obligations....337
5. Taxpayer Bill of Rights 2 346

Section B: Social Security Taxes 349

Section C Unemployment Taxes 353

Section D: Form 990 (Annual Information
Returns) 355

Section E: Proof of Racial
Nondiscrimination.....................356

Section F: Application for Recognition
of Tax-Exempt Status
(Form 1023) 356

Section G: Unrelated Business
Income Tax Return...................359

Section H: Charitable Contributions 362

Section I: Illustration
#1 of Tax Withholding and
Reporting Requirements 363

Section J: Illustration
#2 of Tax Withholding and
Reporting Requirements 373

Section K: Illustration
#3 of Tax Withholding and
Reporting Requirements 378

Chapter 12: Comprehensive Illustration of Clergy Tax Reporting........................379

Tax Tables 393

Index........................399

Resources 403

Discount Order Form 404

INTRODUCTION

Long ago, an eminent judge observed:

> In my own case the words of such an act as the income tax . . . merely dance before my eyes in a meaningless procession: cross-reference to cross-reference, exception upon exception—couched in abstract terms that offer no handle to seize hold of—leaving in my mind only a confused sense of some vitally important, but successfully concealed purport, which it is my duty to extract, but which is within my power, if at all, only after the most inordinate expenditure of time. I know that these monsters are the result of fabulous industry and ingenuity, plugging up this hole and casting out that net, against all possible evasion . . . that they were no doubt written with a passion of rationality; but that one cannot help wondering whether to the reader they have any significance save that the words are strung together with syntactical correctness. I. Dillard, *The Spirit of Liberty: Papers and Addresses of Learned Hand* 213 (1960).

Sound familiar? Few persons have more ably described the frustrations created by the federal income tax. Our tax law is so complex that it is incomprehensible to most taxpayers. A small and declining number of taxpayers are able to complete a Form 1040. And, as if this were not enough, the tax law is ever-changing. Ministers' taxes are especially frustrating, since a number of unique rules apply to the reporting of ministers' federal income and social security taxes. For example, ministers are permitted to exclude (for income tax purposes) the cost of owning or renting a home; they are always treated as self-employed for social security purposes with respect to services performed in the exercise of ministry; their compensation is exempt from tax withholding; they are permitted to exempt themselves from social security taxes if they satisfy several requirements; and they often are eligible for favorable tax-sheltered annuities (TSAs) under section 403(b) of the Internal Revenue Code. The reporting of ministers' income taxes also involves a number of complex and sometimes controversial issues. To illustrate, a debate has raged for years over the question of whether a minister should report his or her federal income taxes as an employee or as a self-employed person.

With so many unique and complex rules applying to ministers, it is no wonder that there is such confusion among tax practitioners, the courts, and even within the IRS regarding the application of tax law to ministers. Let me give one example of this confusion that is especially revealing. In a recent edition of Publication 517 ("Social Security for Members of the Clergy and Religious Workers"), the IRS gives an example of how ministers should report their taxes. The example describes a minister who has social security earnings both as an employee and as a self-employed person. The only problem with this statement is that ministers are *never* taxed as employees (the "FICA" tax) for social security purposes with respect to compensation earned in the exercise of

ministry. The same error has been repeated in several editions of Publication 517 though the IRS has acknowledged the mistake and agreed to correct it. The point is this—even the IRS is confused over the correct reporting of ministers' taxes!

This book has two objectives. First, to help ministers (1) understand the many unique features of our tax laws that apply to them; (2) correctly report their federal income taxes; (3) understand the basis for exempting themselves from social security (and why it does not apply to most ministers); (4) correctly report social security taxes (if not exempt); and (5) reduce income tax and social security liability as much as possible. A second objective of this book is to help church treasurers, board members, bookkeepers, attorneys, CPAs, and tax practitioners understand (1) the definition of "income" in the church environment; (2) how to handle and report employee business expenses; (3) the substantiation rules that apply to charitable contributions; (4) the handling of designated contributions; and (5) the federal tax reporting requirements that apply to churches and church employees.

Most tax guides lose most if not all of their relevance after April 15. This book is different—it was designed to have direct and immediate relevance to ministers, churches, and their advisers *throughout the year*. For example, there are *entire chapters* devoted to charitable contributions, clergy retirement plans, social security, and church reporting requirements. Other chapters contain vital information of continuing relevance, such as the mechanics of the housing allowance and a business expense reimbursement policy. A generous supply of illustrations and legal forms makes this a resource that you will refer to again and again *throughout the year*.

Because tax laws change from year to year, this book is republished each year to provide readers with information that is as up-to-date and accurate as possible. This edition addresses all of the important tax developments that occurred during 1997.

Of course, I welcome your suggestions for future editions. Please send your ideas to *Church Law & Tax Report*, P.O. Box 1098, Matthews, North Carolina 28106. My objective is to make this resource the most helpful, accurate, and comprehensible guide available.

Richard R. Hammar, J.D., LL.M., CPA
October 15, 1997

SUMMARY OF IMPORTANT TAX CHANGES EFFECTIVE IN 1997

✎ **Key point.** Congress enacted sweeping tax law changes in 1997 that will directly impact ministers and churches. In addition, a number of court decisions and IRS rulings provided clarification on a number of tax issues. All of the important changes and clarifications are summarized in this introductory chapter, and addressed in relevant sections of this text.

TAX CHANGES OF INTEREST TO MINISTERS

1. Tax rate adjustments. For 1997, the income tax rates for **married couples filing jointly** are 15% for the first $41,200 of taxable income, 28% for taxable income from $41,200 to $99,600, 31% for taxable income from $99,600 to $151,750, 36% on taxable income from $151,750 to $271,050, and 39.6% on taxable income in excess of $271,050. For 1997, the income tax rates for **single individuals** are 15% for the first $24,650 of taxable income, 28% for taxable income from $24,650 to $59,750, 31% for taxable income from $59,750 to $124,650, 36% on taxable income between $124,650 and $271,050, and 39.6% on taxable income in excess of $271,050. The new income tax rate structure is summarized in the following two tables.

TABLE 1 — 1997 INCOME TAX RATES MARRIED PERSONS FILING JOINTLY

taxable income		pay	plus the following percent	of taxable income exceeding
over	but not over			
$0	$41,200	$0	15%	$0
$41,200	$99,600	$6,180	28%	$41,200
$99,600	$151,750	$22,532	31%	$99,600
$151,750	$271,050	$38,698	36%	$151,750
$271,050		$81,646	39.6%	$271,050

TABLE 2 — 1997 INCOME TAX RATES SINGLE PERSONS

taxable income		pay	plus the following percent	of taxable income exceeding
over	but not over			
$0	$24,650	$0	15%	$0
$24,650	$59,750	$3,697	28%	$24,650
$59,750	$124,650	$13,525	31%	$59,750
$124,650	$271,050	$33,644	36%	$124,650
$271,050		$86,348	39.6%	$271,050

☞ **Example.** Rev. B is married and for 1997 has gross income of $45,000 from his services as senior minister of his church. He and his wife file a joint income tax return. His taxable income, after deducting his itemized deductions, personal exemptions, and housing allowance, is $35,000. According to Table 1, he will pay an income tax rate of 15% on his entire taxable income, since it is below $41,200.

☞ **Example.** Same facts as the previous example, except that Rev. B's gross income for 1997 is $60,000, and his taxable income is $45,000. According to Table 1, some of his taxable income will be subject to the higher 28% tax rate. He computes his income taxes as follows: (1) $6,180 in taxes on the first $41,200 of taxable income (taxed at 15%); and (2) a 28% tax on taxable income between $41,200 and $99,600, or $1,064 ($45,000 - $41,200 x 28%). The combination of these amounts is $7,244. This is in addition to Rev. B's self-employment tax, which is an additional 15.3% multiplied times his net earnings from self employment (note that this amount will include his housing allowance).

2. Increase in earnings subject to the self-employment tax. The self-employment tax rate (15.3%) did not change in 1997. However, the amount of earnings subject to tax increased. The 15.3% tax rate consists of two components: (1) a Medicare hospital insurance (HI) tax of 2.9%, and (2) an "old-age, survivor and disability" (OASDI) tax of 12.4%. There is no maximum amount of self-employment earnings subject to the Medicare hospital insurance (the 2.9% "HI" tax rate). The tax is imposed on all net earnings regardless of amount. For 1997, the maximum earnings subject to the "old-age, survivor and disability" (OASDI) portion of self-employment taxes (the 12.4% amount) increases to $65,400—up from $62,700 in 1996. Stated differently, persons who receive compensation in excess of $65,400 in 1997 will pay the 15.3% tax rate for net self-employment earnings up to $65,400, and the "HI" tax rate of 2.9% on all earnings above $65,400. These rules directly impact ministers, who always are considered self-employed for social security purposes with respect to their ministerial services. *Ministers should take these rules into account in computing their quarterly estimated tax payments.*

☞ **Example.** Rev. L has net earnings from self-employment for 1997 of $65,400 (the maximum amount subject to the self-employment tax). His self-employment tax will be $10,006. Note that the housing allowance is not excluded when computing this tax.

3. Inflation adjustments. One of the major "tax reforms" to take effect in 1990 was the introduction of annual "inflation adjustments" for tax brackets, the personal exemption amount, and the standard deduction. This is good news for taxpayers. In the past, as inflation increased your income, you often wound up with little if any additional income. Why? Because the added income boosted you to a higher tax rate bracket that increased your taxes. Also, the "standard deduction" (the amount you can deduct if you cannot itemize your deductions) either remained level or did not keep up with inflation, meaning that its real value decreased each year, exposing more and more of your income to tax. This was unfair, since your higher income was often offset by higher tax rates and decreasing deductions. While this was unfair to taxpayers, it provided the federal government with automatic "tax increases." Congress could raise additional taxes each year simply by not adjusting the tax brackets and various deductions for inflation. This was unfair, and Congress has taken a big step to address the problem. For 1997, the following three "inflation adjustments" took effect:

•**Tax rates.** The amounts of income you need to earn to boost you to a higher tax rate were adjusted for inflation. This means that additional income you earn due to inflation will not automatically put you in a higher tax rate bracket. You will begin to keep more of your annual pay increases. This will be good news for many taxpayers. To illustrate, married persons filing jointly do not move from the 15% to the 28% tax rate in computing their 1997 taxes until they have at least $41,200 of taxable income (up from $40,100 in 1996). Single persons do not move from the 15% to the 28% tax rate until they have $24,650 of taxable income (up from $24,000 in 1996). As noted elsewhere in this summary, additional tax rates apply to higher income taxpayers in 1997.

• **Personal exemptions.** The "personal exemption amount" (the amount you can deduct for yourself, your spouse, and each dependent) was adjusted for inflation. For 1997, the amount increased to $2,650 per person (up from $2,550 in 1996).

• **Standard deduction.** The "standard deduction" (the amount you can deduct if you cannot itemize your deductions) was adjusted for inflation. The standard deduction increases to $6,900 for married couples filing jointly (up from $6,700 in 1996). It increases to $4,150 for single taxpayers (up from $4,000 in 1996). Single taxpayers who are 65 years of age or older, or blind, get a $1,000 increase in their standard deduction for 1997 (the same amount as in 1996). Married taxpayers who are 65 years of age or older, or blind, get a $800 increase in their standard deduction for 1997 (the same amount as in 1996).

4. Child tax credit. Congress enacted legislation in 1997 creating a new "child tax credit." If you have one or more children under 17 years of age, and you earn less than a specified amount of income, then you will be able to claim a $400 credit on your 1998 tax return for each child. The credit increases to $500 in 1999 and thereafter. To qualify for the credit, you must have a child who (1) is under 17 years of age; (2) is your child, descendent, stepson or stepdaughter, or foster child; and (3) is claimed by you as a dependent on your tax return. The child care credit is reduced by $50 for each $1,000 of adjusted gross income in excess of $110,000 for married couples filing jointly. For single persons, the credit is reduced by $50 for each $1,000 of adjusted gross income in excess of $75,000. These amounts are not adjusted for inflation. The child tax credit is in addition to the

personal exemption amount ($2,650 for 1997) that can be claimed for each dependent child.

5. Home office expenses. Many ministers and church staff members maintain an office in their home, and perform some of their duties in their home office. In the past, it has been very difficult to treat expenses associated with a home office as a tax-deductible business expense. Congress enacted legislation in 1997 that will make it easier to qualify for a home office deduction—beginning in 1999. The new law permits some taxpayers to claim a home office deduction if they use their home office for largely administrative tasks—even if their income-generating activities occur at another location. As before, the home office must be used regularly and exclusively for business purposes.

6. Health insurance deduction for the self-employed. Under current law, self-employed persons can deduct health insurance costs for themselves (and their spouse and children) as follows: 40 percent in 1997; 45 percent in 1998 through 2002; 50 percent in 2003; 60 percent in 2004; 70 percent in 2005; and 80 percent in 2006 and thereafter. This deduction is not allowed in any year in which the self-employed person is eligible to participate in a subsidized health plan maintained by an employer of either the self-employed person or his or her spouse. Congress enacted legislation in 1997 that accelerates the health insurance deduction for self-employed workers as follows: 40 percent in 1997; 45 percent in 1998 and 1999; 50 percent in 2000 and 2001; 60 percent in 2002; 80 percent in 2003 through 2005; 90 percent in 2006; and 100 percent in 2007 and thereafter.

7. Real estate reporting requirements. Under current law, persons who close real estate transactions are required to file an information return (Form 1099S) with the IRS. This return reports the details of the transaction, and is designed to disclose persons who may owe capital gains tax. Congress enacted legislation in 1997 that exempts sales of personal residences with a gross sales price of $500,000 or less ($250,000 or less for single taxpayers) from this reporting requirement, beginning after May 6, 1997. The purpose of this change is to relieve taxpayers of the reporting requirement on transactions that will be exempt from the capital gains tax under new rules (explained below) that took effect after May 6, 1997. To qualify for this exemption, a home seller must provide the buyer with written assurance that no capital gain tax will be payable on the transaction. The IRS will issue further guidance on this requirement.

8. "Continuous levy" authority of the IRS extends to social security payments. Under current law, taxpayers who do not pay a tax within 10 days of notice and demand by the IRS are subject to "levy." A levy is a procedure the IRS uses to collect the tax deficiency. It permits the IRS to seize property owned by the taxpayer. Generally, a levy does not apply to property acquired after the date of the levy—with one exception. A levy on wages is "continuous" from the date it is first made until the debt is paid in full. Congress enacted legislation in 1997 that permits the IRS to impose a continuous levy on federal payments for which eligibility is not based on the income or assets of the taxpayer. To illustrate, the IRS will now be able to treat social security checks like wages. This means that a levy against such payments will "continue" until the tax deficiency is paid. The new law specifies that such levies can attach up to 15 percent of any payment due the taxpayer. This provision took effect on August 6, 1997.

9. Earned income credit modifications. Certain low-income workers are entitled to claim a refundable earned income credit (EIC) on their tax return. A refundable credit is a credit that not only reduces income taxes, but allows a refund to taxpayers whose credit exceeds their tax liability. The amount of the credit depends on the number of children the taxpayer has, and it is phased out for taxpayers with adjusted gross income above certain limits. Congress enacted legislation in 1997 that makes certain changes to the earned income credit, including the following:

- *Fraud or recklessness.* A taxpayer who fraudulently claims an EIC is ineligible to claim the EIC for the next 10 years. A taxpayer who erroneously claims the EIC due to reckless or intentional disregard of the law is ineligible to claim the credit for the next 2 years. This provision took effect January 1, 1997.

- *Definition of adjusted gross income.* The EIC is phased out for taxpayers with adjusted gross income above specified levels. The new law provides that tax-exempt interest and nontaxable distributions from pensions, annuities, and IRAs (if not rolled over into similar tax-favored products) are not counted in computing adjusted gross income for purposes of determining eligibility for the EIC. This provision takes effect in 1998.

10. Foreign earned income credit. United States citizens generally are subject to federal income tax on all their income, whether derived in the United States or in a foreign country. However, citizens working in foreign countries may be eligible to exclude from their income for federal income tax purposes certain foreign earned income and housing costs. To qualify for these exclusions, the individual must either (1) be a resident of the foreign country for an uninterrupted period that includes the entire tax year, or (2) be present overseas for 330 days out of any 12 consecutive month period. The maximum exclusion for foreign earned income under current law is $70,000 per year. Congress enacted legislation in 1997 that increases the $70,000 annual foreign earned income exclusion by $2,000 per year beginning in 1998, until it reaches a maximum of $80,000 in the year 2002. In addition, the credit will be indexed for inflation beginning in 2008. This credit is claimed by many American missionaries serving in foreign countries.

11. Increase in standard deduction of dependents. Under current law, the standard deduction of a taxpayer who is claimed as a dependent on another's tax return cannot exceed the lesser of (1) the standard deduction for an individual ($4,150 for 1997), or (2) the greater of $500 (indexed for inflation) or the dependent's earned income. In other words, a minor child who works outside the home, and who is claimed as a dependent on his parents' tax return, is eligible for a reduced standard deduction based on this formula. Congress enacted legislation in 1997 that increases the standard deduction for a taxpayer who is claimed as a dependent on another's tax return to the lesser of (1) the standard deduction for individuals, or (2) the greater of (a) $500 (indexed for inflation), or (b) the individual's earned income plus $250. The $250 amount will be indexed for inflation after 1998. The new standard deduction rules take effect in 1998.

12. Estimated tax penalties. Taxpayers are subject to an "addition to tax" for any underpayment of estimated taxes. This penalty is not assessed if the total tax liability for the year (reduced by any withheld tax and estimated tax payments) is less than $500. Congress enacted legislation in 1997 that increases this amount to $1,000, beginning in 1998. This provision is relevant to ministers, who always pay estimated taxes because their wages are exempt from tax withholding (unless they elect voluntary tax withholding).

13. Estimated tax requirements. Under current law, a taxpayer is subject to a penalty for underpayments of estimated taxes. The penalty is avoided if a taxpayer makes timely estimated tax payments at least equal to (1) 100 percent of the previous year's tax liability, or (2) 90 percent of the current year's tax liability. The 100 percent of last year's tax liability exception is increased to 110 percent for individuals with adjusted gross income of more than $150,000 for the previous year. Congress enacted legislation in 1997 that changes the 110 percent of last year's tax liability rule to 100 percent of the previous year's tax liability in 1998; 105 percent of the previous year's tax liability in 1999, 2000, and 2001; and 112 percent of the previous year's tax liability in 2002.

14. HOPE scholarship tax credit. Congress enacted legislation in 1997 that provides welcome relief to families with children in college or vocational training. Beginning in 1998, taxpayers can claim a "HOPE" credit against federal income taxes of up to $1,500 per student per year for 50 percent of qualified tuition and related expenses (not including room, board, and books) paid during the first two years of the student's postsecondary, undergraduate education in a degree or certificate program. This new credit is explained in chapter 7 of this text.

15. Lifetime learning credit. Congress enacted legislation in 1996 that allows taxpayers to claim a "lifetime learning credit" against federal income taxes equal to 20 percent of tuition and academic fees incurred during a year on behalf of the taxpayer, or the taxpayer's spouse or dependent child. This credit applies to tuition expenses incurred after June 30, 1998, for education furnished in academic periods beginning after such date. The credit is available for tuition expenses incurred by a taxpayer, or the taxpayer's spouse or dependent child. The credit is 20 percent of the first $5,000 of tuition and academic fees This means that the maximum credit will be $1,000 per year. However, for expenses paid after

December 31, 2002, up to $10,000 of tuition and academic fees will be eligible for the 20 percent lifetime learning credit. This means that the maximum credit will increase to $2,000 per year. Unlike HOPE credits, the lifetime learning credit is not limited to the first two years of postsecondary, undergraduate education. It can be claimed for an unlimited number of years. The lifetime learning credit can be claimed in any one year on behalf of any number of eligible students. The lifetime learning credit is available to students at both undergraduate and graduate educational institutions (and postsecondary vocational schools). In addition, students need not be enrolled half-time or full-time. If a taxpayer claims a HOPE credit with respect to a student then the lifetime learning credit will not be available with respect to that same student for the year, although the lifetime learning credit may be available with respect to that student for other years. This new credit is explained in chapter 7 of this text.

16. Education IRAs. Taxpayers are given yet another break for education expenses under legislation enacted by Congress in 1997—they can contribute up to $500 each year to an "education IRA." Here is how it works. A taxpayer establishes an education IRA and designates a "beneficiary" (usually, the taxpayer's child). The taxpayer contributes up to $500 each year into the account, up until the beneficiary's 18th birthday. Earnings on an education IRA generally accumulate tax-free—provided they are distributed for the post-secondary educational expenses of the beneficiary. Parents can begin contributing to education IRAs on or after January 1, 1998. In any year in which an exclusion is claimed for a distribution from an education IRA, neither a HOPE credit nor a lifetime learning credit may be claimed with respect to educational expenses incurred during that year on behalf of the same student. The HOPE credit and lifetime learning credit may be available in other years with respect to that beneficiary. Education IRAs are explained in chapter 10 of this text.

17. Penalty-free withdrawals from an existing IRA to pay for educational expenses. Congress enacted legislation in 1997 permitting taxpayers, beginning in 1998, to make early withdrawals from an IRA to pay for qualified higher education expenses of the taxpayer or the taxpayer's spouse, child, or grandchild—without triggering the 10 percent penalty that applies to early distributions from an IRA. This new rule is explained in chapter 10.

18. Extension of employer-provided educational assistance exclusion. In the past, an employee's taxable income did not include amounts paid by an employer for educational assistance if such amounts were paid pursuant to an educational assistance program that met certain requirements. This exclusion was limited to $5,250 of educational assistance per employee during a calendar year, and applied whether or not the education was job related. The exclusion expired for graduate education beginning after June 30, 1996, and for undergraduate education beginning after June 30, 1997. Congress enacted legislation in 1997 that extends this exclusion for undergraduate education for courses beginning before June 1, 2000. The exclusion does not apply to graduate-level courses.

19. Increase IRA phaseout limits. Under current law, if an individual (or his or her spouse) is an active participant in an employer-sponsored retirement plan, the $2,000 IRA deduction limit is phased out over the following levels of adjusted gross income: (1) $25,000 to $35,000 for single persons; and (2) $40,000 to $50,000 for married persons filing jointly. Congress enacted legislation in 1997 that makes two important modifications to these rules, beginning in 1998: (1) An individual will not be considered to be an active participant in an employer-sponsored retirement plan merely because his or her spouse is an active participant in such a plan; and (2) the deductible IRA phaseout ranges are increased. These changes are explained in chapter 10.

20. "Roth" ("backloaded") IRAs. Congress enacted legislation in 1997 creating another new type of IRA—the so-called "Roth" or "backloaded" IRA. Beginning in 1998, taxpayers can make annual *nondeductible* contributions of up to $2,000 to a Roth IRA, and distributions from such an IRA are not taxed if they are made after a five year holding period, and are made as a result of the account holder's attaining age 59 and 1/2 or older, death, disability, or purchase of a first home. Further, earnings on Roth IRAs accumulate tax-free. Roth IRAs are explained further in chapter 10.

21. No penalty for early IRA withdrawals by first-time homebuyers. Under current law, a 10 percent "additional tax" applies to distributions from an IRA prior to age 59 and 1/2. Congress enacted legislation in 1997 that permits taxpayers to withdraw up to $10,000 from their IRA prior to age 59 and 1/2 for "first-time homebuyer expenses" without triggering the 10 percent penalty. The expenses must be incurred to buy or build a principal residence for yourself, or a child or grandchild. This new rule takes effect in 1998, and is explained further in chapter 10.

22. Repeal of 15 percent tax on excess distributions from a retirement plan. Under current law, a 15 percent tax is imposed on excess distributions from most types of retirement plans (including IRAs and tax-sheltered annuities). Excess distributions generally are those in excess of $160,000 for 1997, or $800,000 in the case of a lump-sum distribution. Congress suspended this tax for the years 1997 through 1999. Congress enacted legislation in 1997 that repeals it permanently.

23. Modification of section 403(b) exclusion allowance. Under current law, annual contributions to a 403(b) annuity cannot exceed the "exclusion allowance." In general, the exclusion allowance is the excess (if any) of (1) 20 percent of the employee's "includible compensation" multiplied times his or her years of service, over (2) the total employer contributions for an annuity excluded for prior years. Congress enacted legislation in 1997 providing that the term "includible compensation" shall not include elective deferrals (by salary reduction agreement) into a 403(b) annuity or a cafeteria plan. The effect of this change, which takes effect in the year 2000, will be to increase the amount that some employees can contribute to their 403(b) annuity.

24. Capital gains tax rate reduction. Under current law, gain or loss in the value of an asset is not recognized for income tax purposes until a taxpayer disposes of the asset. On the sale or exchange of a "capital asset," the "capital gain" is taxed at ordinary income tax rates, except that individuals are subject to a maximum rate of 28 percent on the net capital gain. A capital asset generally means any property, with some exceptions (including depreciable real estate used in a taxpayer's trade or business, and property held for sale to customers). Common examples include real personal residences and investments. Congress enacted legislation in 1997 containing the following modifications: (1) The maximum rate of tax on net capital gain of individuals is reduced from 28 percent to 20 percent. This means that taxpayers who are in the 28 percent (or higher) income tax bracket will pay a capital gains tax of 20 percent. Lower-income taxpayers whose ordinary income is taxed at the 15 percent rate will pay a capital gains tax of 10 percent. (2) Beginning in the year 2001, the maximum capital gains rates for assets which are held for more than 5 years are 18 percent (for persons in the 28 percent or higher ordinary income tax bracket) and 8 percent (for persons in the 15 percent ordinary income tax bracket). The 18 percent rate applies only to assets that are acquired on or after January 1, 2001.

25. Sales of personal residences. Under current law, no gain is recognized on the sale of a principal residence if (1) a new residence is purchased that is at least equal in cost to the sales price of the old residence, and (2) the new residence is used as a principal residence of the taxpayer at some point within a "replacement period" that begins two years prior to the sale of the old residence and ends two years after the sale. Also, under present law an individual can exclude on a one-time basis up to $125,000 of gains from the sale of a principal residence if the taxpayer (1) has attained age 55 before the sale, and (2) has owned the property and used it as a principal residence for 3 or more of the 5 years preceding the sale. Congress enacted legislation in 1997 that eliminates these rules for sales of principal residences occurring after May 6, 1997. The new rules are much more liberal, and will greatly benefit many taxpayers.

Most importantly, after May 6, 1997 a married couple (who file a joint return) can exclude up to *$500,000* of gain from the sale or exchange of a principal residence. Single taxpayers can exclude up to $250,000. To qualify for the full exclusion, a taxpayer must have owned and occupied the residence as a principal residence for at least 2 of the 5 years prior to the date of sale or exchange. But, unlike the former law, the tax benefit may not be lost completely if this "holding period" is not satisfied. Taxpayers who sell a home without meeting this requirement get a partial benefit if they had to sell their home on account of a change of place of employment, health, or other unforeseen circumstances. The partial benefit is the fraction of $500,000 (or $250,000 for single taxpayers) equal to the fraction of 2 years that the home

was owned and occupied as a principal residence. The old rule that permitted only one exclusion of up to $125,000 for taxpayers at least 55 years of age is out the window. Taxpayers can claim the $500,000 exclusion every two years, and there is no minimum age requirement.

26. Estate tax relief. Some people unexpectedly find themselves subject to federal estate taxes because of insurance proceeds, successful investments, and inheritances. The estate tax is substantial—it begins at a 37 percent rate. Fortunately, there are ways to reduce it. Under current law, estates of less than $600,000 are exempt from tax (unchanged since 1987). Congress enacted legislation in 1997 that increases this amount to $1 million between 1998 and 2006. Some estates that include a family-owned business are eligible for a $1.3 million exemption amount beginning in 1998.

27. Annual gift exclusion. Under current law, a taxpayer can exclude up to $10,000 in gifts made to each donee during a calendar year without affecting the $600,000 lifetime exemption from estate taxes described above. Gifts of more than this amount reduce the $600,000 estate exemption. For married couples, the exclusion is available to each spouse. To illustrate, a couple with three children can give up to $60,000 each year ($20,000 to each child), without affecting their exemption from estate taxes. Many couples have used this technique to reduce estate taxes by reducing the size of their estate that will be distributed at death. The $10,000 annual gift exclusion has remained unchanged for several years, meaning that its real value has been steadily eroded by inflation. Congress enacted legislation in 1997 that indexes the $10,000 annual gift exclusion for inflation beginning in 1999 (rounded to the next lowest multiple of $1,000).

28. The Tax Court ruled that an Assemblies of God foreign missionary was self-employed for income tax reporting purposes. The missionary, who lived in Bangladesh, reported his income taxes as self-employed. He was audited by the IRS and informed that he was in fact an employee. The IRS transferred his business expenses from Schedule C to Schedule A, resulting in additional taxes. The missionary appealed to the Tax Court, which ruled that he was self-employed. The Tax Court listed eight factors to be considered in deciding whether a worker is an employee or self-employed for federal income tax reporting purposes:

(1) the degree of control exercised by the [employer] over the details of the work; (2) which party invests in the facilities used in the work; (3) the taxpayer's opportunity for profit or loss; (4) the permanency of the relationship; (5) the [employer's] right of discharge; (6) whether the work performed is an integral part of the [employer's] business; (7) what relationship the parties believe they are creating; and (8) the provision of benefits typical of those provided to employees. No one factor is determinative; rather, all the incidents of the relationship must be weighed and assessed.

The court concluded that the missionary was self-employed on the basis of these eight factors. It relied on a number of factors in reaching this conclusion, including the following: (1) the national church provided no professional training for the missionary; (2) the national church did not assign the missionary to a particular country; (3) the missionary chose the type of duties he would perform; (4) the missionary determined his own work days and hours; (5) the missionary used vacation and sick leave without notifying or seeking permission from the national church; (6) apart from filing periodic expense and activity reports, the missionary and the national church did not communicate regularly; and (7) the missionary was not directly supervised or evaluated by anyone. *Greene v. Commissioner, T.C. Memo. 1996-531 (1996).*

29. A federal appeals court ruled that an Assemblies of God pastor was self-employed rather than an employee for federal income tax reporting purposes. In reaching this conclusion, the court applied a test set forth in a 1992 Supreme Court decision:

> [Besides considering] the hiring party's right to control the manner and means by which the product is accomplished, [a court must also look at] the skill required; the source of the instrumentalities and tools; the location of the work; the duration of the relationship between the parties; whether the hiring party has the right to assign additional projects to the hired party; the extent of the hired party's discretion over when and how long to work; the method of payment; the hired party's role in hiring and paying assistants; whether the work is part of the regular business of the hiring party; whether the hiring party is in business; [and] the provision of employee benefits.

The appeals court concluded, on the basis of this test, that the pastor was self-employed rather than an employee for federal income tax reporting purposes. It observed: "For the most part [the pastor] set his own schedule (except of course for regularly scheduled church services). He was free to perform weddings, funerals, and revivals for a fee, and was not required to pay over any of the fees to the church. He was not expected to pay for a substitute pastor if one was necessary. [He] arranged for evangelists or special speakers at [his church], and contributed to special collections taken for them." *Alford v. United States, 1997 WL 336105 (8th Cir. 1997).*

30. Tax Court ruled that a Methodist minister was an employee rather than self-employed for income tax reporting purposes. The court mentioned the following facts suggesting that the pastor. Rev. Radde, was an employee: (1) Rev. Radde agreed to abide by and practice the precepts contained in the Book of Discipline of the United Methodist Church (the Discipline), which sets forth guidelines and specific duties that he was required to follow in order to retain his position as a minister; (2) under the Discipline, bishops were authorized to and did appoint petitioner to various positions within the church; (3) Rev. Radde was required to accept the appointments in order to retain his position as a mini-

ster; (4) for the first 5 months of 1990, Rev. Radde was appointed and served as senior pastor of a church in Texas; (5) as senior pastor he conducted worship services, preached, visited and counseled parishioners, performed baptisms, weddings, and funerals, and oversaw the general welfare of the church; (6) he reported to and was supervised by a district superintendent and submitted reports to the district superintendent regarding the number of baptisms, number of new members, attendance, finances, and other church matters; (7) while Rev. Radde was not required to be in the church during specific hours, he was required to follow the guidelines set forth in the Discipline as to the doctrine he preached and as to the many duties he performed; (8) while Rev. Radde was allowed to select specific topics for weekly sermons, he was required to preach the theology of the United Methodist Church; (9) the majority of his duties were performed in the church or in an office provided to him, although some duties were performed in a house that was provided by the church as a parsonage. From June 1990 through 1991, Rev. Radde was appointed and served as district superintendent for a district in Texas. As district superintendent he supervised 56 local Methodist churches and more than 40 pastors, made periodic reports to the supervising bishop, handled administrative duties associated with the district, occasionally preached at a local Methodist church, and counseled parishioners. The majority of his duties as district superintendent were performed in the district office, in a local Methodist church, and in the supervising bishop's office. Occasionally, some of his duties were performed in a home that was provided to him as a parsonage.

The IRS audited Rev. Radde's 1990 and 1991 tax returns, and determined that he was an employee of the United Methodist Church and not as a self-employed minister. It therefore disallowed his Schedule C business expenses and concluded that these expenses could be deducted only as miscellaneous expenses on Schedule A to the extent they exceed 2 percent of his adjusted gross income.

Rev. Radde appealed the case to the Tax Court. The court applied the same 7 factor test that it used in a 1994 case in which a Methodist minister was determined to be an employee. *Weber v. Commissioner, 103 T.C. 378, 386 (1994), affirmed 60 F.3d 1104 (4th Cir. 1995).* Rev. Radde argued that the *Weber* case should not be applied retroactively to his 1990 and 1991 tax returns. He stressed that he set his own hours and was not required to account for his time or to submit detailed reports of his activities. The court disagreed. It acknowledged that "the structure of the United Methodist Church provides several levels of supervision for its ministers," but it concluded that while serving as a senior pastor in 1990 Rev. Radde was supervised by a district superintendent and was required to abide by the Discipline and to report statistics concerning his congregation." Further, when he served as a district superintendent "his duties involved those typically associated with an employee. [He] supervised 56 churches and more than 40 pastors and reported directly to the Conference bishop. As a minister of the United Methodist Church, [he] agreed to abide by the duties set forth in the Discipline. In giving sermons [he] was required to preach the doctrine of the United Methodist Church. [He] was appointed by a bishop to positions he held. Under the Discipline, in order to remain a Methodist minister [he] was required to accept such positions." The court concluded that Rev. Radde had failed to distinguish his case from the *Weber* ruling. *Radde v. Commissioner, T.C. Memo. 1997-490 (1997).*

31. The Tax Court ruled that the fair rental value of a parsonage should not be reduced by the amount of a parsonage allowance in computing the self-employment tax. A minister was provided with a parsonage and in addition a portion of his annual compensation was designated a parsonage allowance to assist him in paying utilities, furnishings, and other miscellaneous expenses. The fair rental value of a parsonage is taxable in computing a minister's self-employment (social security) tax. The minister claimed that this amount "includes" any parsonage allowance designated by the church. As a result, he reduced his parsonage's fair rental value by the parsonage allowance designated by his church in computing his self-employment tax. The Tax Court ruled that this was improper, noting that the minister had "not proven that the stipulated fair rental value of the parsonage already includes amounts designated or received in cash relating to the utility and other household expenses of the parsonages." *Radde v. Commissioner, T.C. Memo. 1997-490 (1997).*

32. The Tax Court ruled that an administrator of a Jewish synagogue was not eligible for a housing allowance since he was not ordained, commissioned, or licensed, and there was no evidence that a housing allowance had been properly designated for him. In ruling that the administrator was not a "minister" and therefore was not eligible for a housing allowance, the court made a number of important observations: (1) While the tax code limits housing allowances to ministers of the gospel, neither the code nor the income tax regulations define this term. (2) The income tax regulations do define "what a minister does." They list the following functions: the performance of sacerdotal functions; the conduct of religious worship; and the performance of services in control, conduct, and maintenance of religious organizations. (3) In deciding whether or not an individual performs the functions of a minister, consideration must be given not only to the religious duties the individual performs, but also to the religious duties that are not performed. (4) The performance of some religious functions is not enough to make one a minister for federal tax purposes. The administrator in this case performed a number of religious functions, but these were largely administrative in nature. More importantly, he performed few of the duties of an ordained, commissioned, or licensed minister. (5) The court stressed that no one can be a "minister" for federal tax purposes who is not, at a minimum, "ordained, commissioned, or licensed." (6) The court referred to the fact that the administrator had no seminary training.

The court concluded that even if the administrator were a "minister" for federal tax purposes, he would still be ineligible for a housing allowance since there was no evidence that a housing allowance had ever been properly designated for him. *Haimowitz v. Commissioner, T.C. Memo. 1997-40 (1997).*

33. The IRS ruled that a full-time chaplain employed by a retirement home was eligible for a housing allowance, even though the home was not affiliated with any church or denomination. The home existed to provide services to senior citizens in a Christian environment and based upon Christian principles. To provide for the spiritual needs of its residents, a chaplain was employed. During a typical week the chaplain prepares for and conducts four worship services. He visits sick residents of the community either at the community or at a local hospital and he counsels residents and staff. He holds a communion service monthly and when requested by a resident, performs baptisms, weddings and funerals. The IRS noted that it ruled in 1971 that "duly ordained, commissioned or licensed ministers of various churches employed as chaplains by church-related hospitals and health and welfare institutions, at private nonprofit hospitals (not church-related) who conducted worship, ministered sacerdotal functions and provided spiritual counseling services were performing services in the exercise of their ministry." As a result, the IRS concluded that such chaplains were entitled to a housing allowance, and in all other respects should be treated as ministers. *Revenue Ruling 71-258.* The IRS considered this precedent to be applicable in the present case, and as a result concluded that the chaplain in question could be treated as a minister for federal tax purposes. *IRS Letter Ruling 9743037.*

34. Increase in charitable mileage rate. Under current law, taxpayers can deduct out-of-pocket expenses incurred in performing services on behalf of a church or other charity. Since 1984, taxpayers have been permitted to value the use of a car while performing charitable services at a "standard charitable mileage rate" of 12 cents per mile. Congress enacted legislation in 1997 that increases this rate to 14 cents per mile for miles driven on or after January 1, 1998. The new rate is not indexed for inflation.

35. Contributions on behalf of self-employed ministers to church retirement plans. Congress enacted legislation in 1997 clarifying that in the case of contributions made on behalf of a minister who is self-employed to a church plan, the contribution is nontaxable to the extent that it would be if the minister were an employee of a church and the contribution were made to the plan. This provision takes effect in 1998.

36. A bill introduced in Congress would permit ministers who have opted out of social security to revoke their exemption. Representative English of Pennsylvania has introduced House Bill 939, which provides, in part:

> [A]ny exemption which has been received . . . by a duly ordained, commissioned, or licensed minister of a church . . . and which is effective for the taxable year in which this Act is enacted, may be revoked by filing an application therefor (in such form and manner, and with such official, as may be prescribed in regulations . . .), if

such application is filed no later than the due date of the federal income tax return (including any extension thereof) for the applicant's second taxable year beginning after December 31, 1997. Any such revocation shall be effective . . . as specified in the application, either with respect to the applicant's first taxable year beginning after December 31, 1997, or with respect to the applicant's second taxable year beginning after such date, and for all succeeding taxable years; and the applicant for any such revocation may not thereafter again file application for an exemption . . . . If the application is filed after the due date of the applicant's federal income tax return for a taxable year and is effective with respect to that taxable year, it shall include or be accompanied by payment in full of an amount equal to the total of the taxes that would have been imposed by . . . the Internal Revenue Code of 1986 with respect to all of the applicant's income derived in that taxable year which would have constituted net earnings from self-employment . . . except for the exemption . . . .

37. The IRS ruled that employee contributions to a nonprofit hospital's benevolence fund were tax-deductible. The IRS noted that the fund was established to assist financially needy persons who suffer economic hardship due to accident, loss, or disaster. Persons eligible for assistance include current employees of the hospital, retirees, former employees, volunteers and the spouses and children of such persons. It emphasized that employee contributions did not earmark specific recipients. Rather, all distributions from the fund were made by a committee consisting of employees of the hospital. The committee reviews a potential beneficiary's application to determine the need for emergency financial assistance and the availability of resources in the fund to meet that need. The IRS concluded that employee contributions to the fund were tax-deductible since the purpose of the fund was consistent with the hospital's charitable purposes and the class of potential beneficiaries was sufficiently large: "All awards of the fund are payable only after a determination of need in the discretion of the committee. Contributions may not be earmarked and there is no guarantee that funds will even be available for past contributors should they have a need arise and apply to the fund for assistance. Thus, contributions cannot be made to the fund with an expectation of procuring a financial benefit. The fund derives its income from voluntary contributions and no part of its income inures to the benefit of any individual. The class of potential beneficiaries consists of several thousand employees . . . . Such a class of beneficiaries is not so limited in size that the donee organization is considered to benefit specified individuals. Accordingly, we rule that contributions to the fund are deductible as charitable contributions . . . . The IRS cautioned that the hospital needed to comply with various recordkeeping requirements: "[A]dequate records and case histories should be maintained to show the name and address of each recipient, the amount distributed to each, the purpose for which the aid was given, the manner in which the recipient was selected and the relationship, if any, between the recipient and members, officers, or trustees of the organization, in order that any or all distributions made to individuals can be substantiated upon request by the IRS." Revenue Ruling 56-304 . *IRS Letter Ruling 9741047.*

38. The standard mileage rate for business miles increased to 31.5 cents per mile in 1997 (up from 31 cents in 1996). The standard mileage rate can be used to compute the cost associated with the business use of a car, provided that it is used in the first year the car is used for business purposes. In addition, employers can use the standard mileage rate to reimburse clergy and church workers for their business use of a car. Of course, clergy are free to deduct the actual costs associated with the business use of a car. Most do not use the "actual cost method, since it is much more time-consuming and inconvenient. The new standard mileage rate applies to all business miles driven in 1997.

39. The IRS addressed the use of employer-provided credit cards to pay for employee business expenses. It ruled that an employer's business expense reimbursement arrangement is "accountable" if it meets the following three requirements: (1) only those expenses with a "business connection" are reimbursed; (2) only those expenses that are properly substantiated (as to amount, date, location, and business purpose) are reimbursed; and (3) employees are required to return to the employer within sixty days any reimbursements in excess of substantiated expenses. The IRS noted that reimbursements paid under an accountable plan are not reportable by the employer or employee as taxable income. This means that the reimbursements are not reported by the employer on the employee's W-2, or on Form 941. Further, the employee does not report the reimbursements as income on his or her income tax return. The IRS cautioned that if an arrangement does not satisfy one or more of the three requirements of an accountable plan, then all amounts paid under the arrangement are treated as paid under a "nonaccountable plan" and must be reported as income on the employee's W-2 and Form 1040, and the employer's Form 941. Further, such reimbursements would be subject to tax withholding for ministers who have elected voluntary withholding, and nonminister employees. This ruling provides useful guidance to any church that provides credit cards to ministers or other staff members. *IRS Letter Ruling 0706018*

40. IRS accepting more "offers in compromise." The IRS announced in 1997 that it had accepted a record 27,673 offers in compromise in 1996—up from 1,995 in 1991. These offers settled $2.2 billion of tax liabilities for $287 million. About half of all offers are accepted, an IRS official disclosed. The IRS has issued new forms and instructions that taxpayers can use to submit an offer in compromise. The new forms and instructions can be obtained by calling the IRS toll-free at 1-800-829-3676.

41. The IRS can garnish social security checks to recover tax debts. So said a federal court in Connecticut. A retired taxpayer owed the IRS a large amount of back taxes. The IRS sent a notice to the Social Security Administration, garnishing half of each social security retirement check sent to the taxpayer. The taxpayer challenged the IRS action, and a court ruled in favor of the IRS. The court noted that federal law permits the IRS to garnish any kind of payment to collect back taxes, subject to limited exceptions. There is no exception that applies to social security checks. As a result, the court concluded that the IRS "may garnish the [taxpayer's] monthly social security benefits until the outstanding federal income tax liability and assessed penalties are paid."

42. Update on intermediate sanctions. Congress enacted legislation in 1996 that permits the IRS to assess "intermediate sanctions" against exempt organization employees who are paid excessive compensation. The sanctions include an excise tax that can be assessed against the employee in the amount of 25 percent of the amount of compensation that exceeds a reasonable amount. If the excess compensation is not "corrected" (that is, returned) within a specified time, the employee can be assessed an additional excise tax in the amount of 200 percent of the amount of compensation that is unreasonable. In addition, "managers" (board members) who authorized the compensation package can be assessed an additional 10 percent tax. Clearly, church treasurers need to be familiar with these new sanctions. Marcus Owens, director of the IRS Exempt Organization Division, addressed intermediate sanctions at a tax conference in Washington, DC, in 1997, and made the following observations: (1) The IRS will impose intermediate sanctions only in extreme cases. He referred to the "front page test," meaning that sanctions will be assessed in cases of compensation that are so excessive that they would make the front page of the local newspaper. (2) He stressed that the new sanctions were intended to change the behavior of nonprofit boards by encouraging them to take seriously the task of establishing compensation packages. (3) He encouraged nonprofit boards to maintain records documenting how they determined the compensation of higher paid employees. (4) He estimated that intermediate sanctions will result in $33 million of excise taxes over the next five years.

43. Tax Court warns that car and computer expenses cannot be "estimated." Church staff members who use their own car or a computer in their work should be aware of an important rule of tax law—the amount of the business use of cars and computers cannot be estimated. Records must be maintained proving the actual expenses corresponding to the business use of such items. The Tax Court applied this rule in a recent case. An employee claimed a business expense deduction in the amount of $8,400 for the business use of her car, plus an additional $1,100 for the business use of her computer. The IRS disallowed both deductions since the taxpayer was unable to prove that she incurred actual expenses in these amounts. The Tax Court agreed. It acknowledged that taxpayers can "estimate" the amount of some business expenses. But it pointed out that this principle does not apply to other business expenses, including travel, transportation, entertainment, and computers. For these expenses a taxpayer must produce records substantiating the actual expenses incurred. The employee in this case insisted that her car was used 95% of the time

for business purposes, and she multiplied her total car expenses for the year times this percentage. The court concluded that she failed to produce any records or evidence demonstrating that she used the car 95% of the time for business purposes. Without such proof she could not claim a business expense deduction for her actual car expenses. The court also ruled that the employee could not claim any deduction for the business use of her personal computer since she failed to maintain any records demonstrating the percentage of total use that was for business purposes. *Kelly v. Commissioner, T.C. Memo. 1997-185*

44. Amended regulations address substantiation of business expenses. In 1997 the IRS released amended regulations addressing the substantiation of business expenses under an employer's expense reimbursement arrangement. The amended regulations contain a number of provisions that will affect the way churches reimburse business expenses. The amended regulations address the following issues: (1) retaining documentary evidence substantiating employee business expenses; (2) maintaining records in electronic form; (3) credit card charges; (4) oral substantiation of expenses; (5) employer verification procedures; and (6) a "de minimis" exception to the substantiation requirements. The amended regulations are addressed in chapter 7.

45. Sabbatical pay is taxable income. So said the Tax Court in a 1997 ruling. A professor was given a year off to pursue studies overseas. He was paid $27,000 during his sabbatical, and he treated this entire amount as a tax-free scholarship. The IRS ruled that the sabbatical income represented taxable income, and the Tax Court agreed The court noted that scholarships are nontaxable only if certain conditions are met. The recipient must be "a candidate for a degree at an educational organization" and the scholarship must be used for qualified tuition. The court noted that the professor's sabbatical income was not a nontaxable scholarship since he was not a candidate for a degree and failed to prove that he used any portion of the income for qualified tuition expenses. This ruling will be useful to church treasurers in evaluating the tax status of sabbatical income provided to pastors or other staff members. *Kant v. Commissioner, T.C. Memo. 1997-217.*

46. Still plenty of room. In 1996 Congress authorized medical savings accounts (MSAs). MSAs are similar to IRAs, except that they are used to pay for medical expenses. Contributions made to an MSA by an "eligible individual" are tax-deductible; employer contributions are excluded from an eligible individual's taxable income; and, earnings on an MSA are not currently taxable. There are restrictions. They are available only to self-employed workers or employees of employers with fewer than 50 employees. Participants must be covered under a "high deductible" health plan. And, MSAs are available to only 750,000 persons through the year 2000. How many people have enrolled in an MSA during the first year? The IRS reported recently that only 7,383 MSAs have been created as of April 30, 1997.

47. IRS announces moving expense changes for 1998. Churches often reimburse moving expenses incurred by new staff. Church leaders should be familiar with the following changes in moving expense reporting that take effect in 1998: (1) Form 4782, which is used by employers to report moving expense reimbursements made to employees, will be eliminated; (2) qualified moving expenses an employer pays to a third party on behalf of the employee (e.g. to a moving company) will not be reported on Form W-2; (3) qualified moving expenses reimbursements an employer pays directly to an employee will be reported in Box 13 of Form W-2 and will be identified using Code P (currently, all qualified moving expense reimbursements are identified with Code P, regardless of whether or not they were paid directly to the employee); (4) other moving expense reimbursements (nonqualified expenses) will continue to be included in wages (Form W-2, box 1) and are subject to income tax withholding and social security and Medicare taxes.

48. No change in IRS audit rate. The IRS audited the same percentage of tax returns in 1996 as it did in 1995, according to IRS statistics published in 1997. The audit rate for 1996 was 1.67% of individual income tax returns—the same rate as 1995.

49. Projected inflation adjustments for 1998. The "personal exemption amount" (the amount you can deduct for yourself, your spouse, and each dependent) is projected to increase to $2,700 in 1998—up from $2,650 in 1997. The "standard deduction" (the amount you can deduct if you cannot itemize your deductions) is expected to increase to $7,100 for married couples filing jointly—up from $6,900 in 1997. It increases to $4,250 for single taxpayers—up from $4,150 in 1997. For married persons filing jointly, the 28% income tax bracket will start at $42,350 in 1998. For single persons, the 28% income tax bracket will start at $25,350. The luxury auto tax will be triggered in 1998 if you purchase a car for $36,000 or more.

50. Eliminating the "marriage tax." Some married couples pay more taxes than they would if they were single. Two bills have been introduced in Congress to change this. HR 2462 and HR 2456 would give married couples the option of filing their taxes as single persons. This would enable each spouse to claim the standard deduction for single persons (currently $4,150), for a combined standard deduction of $8,300—or $1,400 more than the current standard deduction for married couples filing jointly. More than 170 members of Congress have cosponsored HR 2456, which was introduced by Rep. Weller (R-Ill.).

51. Self-employed ministers can participate in 403(b) tax-sheltered annuities. Congress enacted legislation in 1996 permitting self-employed ministers to participate in qualified retirement plans including 403(b) tax-sheltered annuities. This resolves a question that has plagued church plans for many years. In the past, there was much confusion over the eligibility of self-employed ministers and other church workers to participate in church retirement plans including 403(b) tax-sheltered annuities. This provision took effect in 1997.

52. Participation in tax-sheltered annuities by ministers employed by non-exempt organizations. Another question that has arisen under 403(b) tax-sheltered annuities is whether they are available to ministers employed by organizations that are not exempt from tax under section 501(c)(3) of the tax code. Section 403(b) of the tax code limits participation in tax-sheltered annuities to employees of an employer "described in section 501(c)(3) which is exempt from tax." This includes religious, charitable, and educational organizations (and some others), but does not include government agencies and secular businesses. As a result, ministers employed by the government or a secular business (for example, as chaplains) generally have been deemed to be ineligible to participate in 403(b) tax-sheltered annuities. Congress enacted legislation in 1996 changing this rule—beginning in 1997. Ministers who are employed by a non-exempt organization are eligible to participate in a tax-sheltered annuity so long as their duties consist of the exercise of ministry.

53. Spousal IRAs. An IRA is an attractive way to shelter income from tax while at the same time deferring tax on earnings. Taxpayers can contribute up to the lesser of $2,000 or 100 percent of compensation each year into an IRA, claim a tax deduction for the amount of their contribution (this deduction may be reduced or eliminated in some cases), and defer taxes on earnings generated by their IRA until they retire. Unfortunately, in the past persons who have chosen to remain at home to care for children have been ineligible to participate fully in an IRA since they have no "compensation" from which to make contributions. This rule ignored the value of services rendered by these individuals, and in 1996 Congress recognized this inequity and enacted legislation allowing married persons who receive no compensation to contribute up to $2,000 annually to an IRA—if the compensation of their spouse is at least as much as the combined amount of their IRA contributions. This provision took effect in 1997.

54. Simplified definition of "highly compensated employee." A number of tax-favored rules do not apply if there is discrimination in favor of "highly compensated employees." These include (1) simplified employee pensions (SEPs); (2) 403(b) tax-sheltered annuities (churches and qualified church-controlled organizations are exempt from this nondiscrimination rule); (3) qualified employee discounts; (4) cafeteria plans; (5) flexible spending arrangements; (6) qualified tuition reductions; (7) employer-provided educational assistance; and (8) dependent care assistance. Unfortunately, the definition of a "highly compensated employee" has been complex, and has often led to absurd results. Congress enacted legislation in 1996 making the definition of the term "highly compensated employee" much simpler and fairer. Beginning in 1997, a highly compensated employee is one who (1) was a 5 percent owner of the employer at any time during the current or prior year (this definition will not apply to churches), or (2) had compensation for the previous year in excess of $80,000, and, if an employer elects, was in the top 20 percent of employees by compensation. The new definition repeals the previous rule requiring the highest paid officer to be treated as highly compensated, no matter how little he or she was paid.

55. Increase in "section 179" deduction. It is a basic principle of tax law that if a product is purchased for business use and has a useful life of more than one year, the full cost may not be deducted in the year of purchase but rather must be allocated over the useful life of the product and an annual "depreciation" deduction claimed each year. Section 179 of the Code, however, permits taxpayers to elect to deduct most if not all of the cost of business property in the year of purchase if certain conditions are satisfied. Over the past few years the section 179 deduction could not exceed $17,500 in any one year. Beginning in 1997, this amount is increased as follows:

taxable year beginning in	maximum section 179 deduction
1997	$18,000
1998	$18,500
1999	$19,000
2000	$20,000
2001	$24,000
2002	$24,000
2003	$25,000

56. Adoption expenses. Congress enacted legislation in 1996 giving taxpayers a maximum nonrefundable credit against income tax liability of $5,000 per child ($6,000 for children with special needs) for qualified adoption expenses paid or incurred by the taxpayer. Qualified adoption expenses are reasonable and necessary adoption fees, court costs, attorneys fees and other expenses that are directly related to the legal adoption of an eligible child. In the case of an international adoption, the credit is not available unless the adoption is finalized. In that case the credit is allowed for all prior qualified expenses in the year that the adoption becomes final. An eligible child is an individual (1) who has not attained age 18 as of the time of the adoption, or (2) who is physically or mentally incapable of caring for himself or herself. No credit is allowed for expenses incurred (1) in violation of state or federal law, (2) in carrying out any surrogate parenting arrangement, or (3) in connection with the adoption of a child of the taxpayer's spouse. The credit is phased out for taxpayers with modified adjusted gross income (AGI) above $75,000, and is fully phased out at $115,000 of modified AGI.

The $5,000 limit is a per child limit, not an annual limitation. For example, in the case of a domestic adoption if a taxpayer pays or incurs $3,000 of otherwise allowable qualified adoption expenses with respect to a child in year one and $3,000 of otherwise allowable qualified adoption expenses with respect to that same child in year two, then the taxpayer would receive a $3,000 credit with respect to year one and a $2,000 credit with respect to year two. The credit may be less than $5,000 because of other limitations.

The credit for adoption expenses took effect in 1997. The credit for non-special needs adoptions is repealed for expenses paid or incurred after December 31, 2001.

57. Extend the phaseout of the luxury tax on automobiles. Under present law, an excise tax is imposed on the sale of a "luxury automobile" whose price exceeds a threshold amount ($34,000 in 1996). The excise tax is imposed at a rate of 10 percent on the excess of the sales price above the threshold amount. The tax applies to sales prior to January 1, 2000. Congress enacted legislation in 1996 that both extends and phases out the luxury tax on automobiles. The new tax rate is reduced by one percentage point per year beginning in 1996. The tax rate for sales occurring within seven days of enactment of the new law in 1996 is 9 percent. The tax rate for sales in 1997 is 8 percent. The tax rate for sales in 1998 is 7 percent. The tax rate for sales in 1999 is 6 percent. The tax rate for sales in 2000 is 5 percent. The tax rate for sales in 2001 is 4 percent. The tax rate for sales in 2002 is 3 percent. The tax expires after December 31, 2002.

58. Senior Citizens' Right to Work Act. The amount of annual income that retired persons (from age 65 to 70) may earn without losing some of their social security benefits was increased as a result of the Senior Citizens' Right to Work Act, enacted by Congress in 1996. This is good news for those churches that employ retired persons and would like to compensate them adequately without reducing their social security benefits. Under the new law, workers from age 65 to 70 may earn up to $13,500 in 1997 without a reduction in their social security benefits. Workers can earn $14,500 in 1998 without a reduction in benefits; $15,500 in 1999; $17,000 in 2000; $25,000 in 2001; and $30,000 in 2002 and later years. These tests apply only to workers who are 65 to 70 years old. Social security benefits are reduced by $1 for every $3 of income above these limits.

Workers 62 to 65 years of age were not addressed by the new law. For 1997, they can earn only $8,640 without a reduction in social security benefits (a $1 reduction for every $2 of income in excess of the limit). This amount is indexed for inflation in future years. There is no earnings limit for workers who have reached age 70.

59. "Luxury car" limits adjusted for inflation. Ministers who use the "actual expense" method of computing their car expenses can claim a deduction for depreciation. There are limits on the amount of depreciation that you can claim in any given year. These limits are known as the "luxury car" limits. The 1997 limits are summarized in table below, along with the limits for 1996 (for comparison purposes).

"Luxury car" depreciation limits

tax year	maximum depreciation deduction for cars first placed in service in 1996	maximum depreciation deduction for cars first placed in service in 1997
first	$3,160	$3,060

second	5,000	4,900
third	3,050	2,950
each succeeding year	1,775	1,775

60. The IRS continues to target "self-employed" taxpayers. The IRS continues to target self-employed taxpayers for audits. Particularly vulnerable are persons who receive only one or two 1099 forms each year. Why all the attention on self-employed persons? A joint IRS and General Accounting Office study concluded that most taxpayers who report as self-employed, but who receive only one or two 1099 forms each year, are actually employees. Reclassifying self-employed persons as employees results in higher tax revenues for the IRS, since employees are subject to tax withholding and they often are not allowed to deduct their business expenses (unless their employer has adopted an accountable reimbursement plan). Also, the employer of a self-employed person who is reclassified as an employee by the IRS is subject to a special penalty under the tax code. Clergy who report their income taxes as self-employed are "prime targets" for IRS examination, since most of them will "fit the profile" of receiving only one or two 1099 forms. Our recommendation—most clergy should report their income taxes as employees, not self-employed. This is one very good reason. See chapter 2 for complete details.

61. Phase-out of personal exemption for high-income taxpayers. As noted elsewhere in this summary, the personal exemption deduction (that you can claim for yourself and each dependent) increased to $2,650 in 1997 (up from $2,550 in 1996). In 1997, the personal exemption amounts are phased out for certain high-income taxpayers. For married taxpayers filing jointly, the phase-out begins when adjusted gross income exceeds $181,800. For single taxpayers, the phase-out begins when adjusted gross income exceeds $121,200.

62. New per diem rates for substantiating the amount of travel expenses incurred in 1997 released by the IRS. The IRS allows taxpayers to substantiate the *amount* of their business expenses by using "per diem" (daily) rates. Taxpayers still must have records substantiating the date, place, and business purpose of each expense. There are separate rates for meals and lodging, and separate rates for "high-cost localities" and all other communities. The rates for 1997 are summarized in the table below.

**Per Diem Rates
1997**

locality (destination of overnight travel)	lodging per diem rate	meals and incidental expense per diem rate	maximum per diem rate
high-cost localities	$126	$40	$166
all other localities	$77	$32	$109

In some cases using the per diem rates will simplify the substantiation of meals and lodging expenses incurred while engaged in business travel. However, a number of restrictions apply, and these are explained in chapter 7.

63. Extend the phaseout of the luxury tax on automobiles. An excise tax is imposed on the sale of a "luxury automobile" whose price exceeds a threshold amount ($36,000 in 1997). The excise tax is imposed at a rate of 8 percent on the excess of the sales price above the threshold amount. The tax rate for sales in 1998 drops to 7 percent. The tax rate for sales in 1999 is 6 percent. The tax rate for sales in 2000 is 5 percent. The tax rate for sales in 2001 is 4 percent. The tax rate for sales in 2002 is 3 percent. The tax expires after December 31, 2002.

64. A charitable contribution deduction of property may be denied if no qualified appraisal is obtained. The Tax Court ruled that a donor who contributed more than $10,000 of nonpublicly traded stock to a church was not eligible for a charitable contribution deduction, even though there was no dispute as to the value of the stock, because he failed to attach a qualified appraisal summary (Form 8283) to the tax return on which the contribution was claimed. *Hewitt v. Commissioner, 109 T.C.12 (1997).*

65. Impact of tax simplification. A number of tax proposals currently being discussed would cause fundamental changes in the way taxes are reported. We will be closely monitoring these developments, and will report fully any changes in the next issue of this tax guide.

TAX CHANGES OF INTEREST TO CHURCHES

1. Increase in wages subject to FICA tax. The FICA tax rate (7.65% for both employers and employees, or a combined tax of 15.3%) did not change in 1997. However, the amount of earnings subject to tax increased. The 7.65% tax rate is comprised of two components: (1) a Medicare hospital insurance (HI) tax of 1.45%, and (2) an "old-age, survivor and disability" (OASDI) tax of 6.2%. There is no maximum amount of wages subject to the Medicare hospital insurance (the 1.45% "HI" tax rate). The tax is imposed on all wages regardless of amount. For 1997, the maximum wages subject to the "old-age, survivor and disability" (OASDI) portion of self-employment taxes (the 6.2% amount) increases to $65,400—up from $62,700 in 1996. Stated differently, employees who receive wages in excess of $65,400 in 1997 will pay the full 7.65% tax rate for wages up to $65,400, and the "HI" tax rate of 1.45% on all earnings above $65,400. Employers pay an identical amount.

2. Intent to make a charitable contribution. For many years, the IRS has ruled that persons who receive goods or services in exchange for a payment to a charity are eligible for a charitable contribution deduction only with respect to the amount by which their payment that exceeds the fair rental value of the goods or services they received. Regulations issued by the IRS in 1997 add an additional condition—

donors may not claim a charitable contribution in such a case unless they intended to make a payment in excess of the fair market value of the goods or services. How will church treasurers know when donors intend to make a payment in excess of goods or services received in exchange? The final regulations aren't of much help here. They simply state that "the facts and circumstances" of each case must be considered. One rule of thumb may help—the greater the amount by which a payment exceeds the market value of goods or services received in exchange, the more likely the donor intended to make a charitable contribution. The regulations are addressed in chapter 8.

3. Refusal of benefits. What if a member purchases a $100 ticket to a church's missions banquet but has no intention of attending the banquet? Is the member entitled to a charitable contribution deduction of $100, or $100 less the value of the meal? In other words, must a charitable contribution be reduced by the amount of goods or services that a donor refuses to accept? The IRS addressed this issue in regulations issued in 1997. The regulations specify that "a taxpayer who has properly rejected a benefit offered by a charitable organization may claim a deduction in the full amount of the payment to the charitable organization." How does a donor reject a benefit? The IRS suggested that charities create a form containing a "check-off box" that donors can check at the time they make a contribution if they want to refuse a benefit. The regulations are addressed in chapter 8.

4. Timely receipts. The new rules for substantiating charitable contributions that took effect in 1994 deny a deduction for individual contributions of $250 or more unless the donor receives a receipt from the charity that complies with several requirements. One of those requirements is that the donor must receive a "contemporaneous" or timely receipt from the charity. This means that the receipt acknowledging the contribution must be *received by the donor* on or before the *earlier* of the following two dates: (1) the date the donor files a tax return claiming a deduction for the contribution, or (2) the due date (including extensions) for filing the return. Will the IRS actually deny a charitable contribution deduction to a donor simply because she did not receive a timely receipt from the charity? The official comments to IRS regulations issued in 1997 leave no doubt that a deduction may be denied in such cases. The regulations state that a donor who files a return *before* receiving a receipt from a charity cannot "correct" this situation by filing an amended tax return since "a written acknowledgment obtained after a taxpayer files the original return for the year of the contribution is not contemporaneous within the meaning of the statute." The regulations are addressed in chapter 8.

5. Multiple contributions. Assume that Don makes ten separate contributions to his church during 1997 of $250 or more. Must the church issue a written receipt that lists each of these contributions separately, or can the ten contributions be lumped together as one amount? The official comments to regulations issued by the IRS in 1997 contain the following statement: "[F]or multiple contributions of $250 or more to one charity, one [receipt] that reflects the

total amount of the taxpayer's contributions to the charity for the year is sufficient." In other words, the church is free to lump all of Don's contributions together as one amount on its receipt. The regulations are addressed in chapter 8.

6. Out-of-pocket expenses. Let's say that Greg, a member of First Church, participates in a short-term missions project and in the process incurs $300 of unreimbursed out-of-pocket travel expenses. The IRS has long acknowledged that such expenses are deductible as a charitable contribution. But what about the new rules for substantiating charitable contributions of $250 or more? Do they apply to this kind of contribution? Is the church responsible for keeping track of Greg's travel expenses in order to determine if they are $250 or more? Must it issue a receipt that states the amount of travel expenses incurred? Regulations issued by the IRS in 1997 specify that when a taxpayer incurs unreimbursed expenses in the course of performing services for a charitable organization, the expenses may be substantiated by an "abbreviated written acknowledgment" provided by the charity containing the following information: (1) a description of the services provided by the donor; (2) whether or not the charity provided any goods or services in return; and (3) if the charity provided any goods or services, a description and good faith estimate of the fair market value of those goods or services. In addition, the abbreviated written acknowledgment must be received by the taxpayer before the earlier of the date he or she files a tax return claiming the contribution deduction, or the due date (including extensions) for the tax return for that year. In response to several comments, the final regulations drop the requirement that the abbreviated acknowledgment include the dates on which the volunteer services were performed.

7. Sale of charity-owned property not subject to the unrelated business income tax. So ruled the IRS. A school was given land by a donor with the understanding that it would use the land for school purposes and not sell it unless absolutely necessary. The school attempted to lease the property for many years, but the school's trustees eventually decided that the land had to be sold. The school asked the IRS if the sales proceeds would be subject to the unrelated business income tax (UBIT). The IRS said no. UBIT is imposed on earnings generated by exempt organizations from an "unrelated trade or business" that is regularly carried on. There are a number of exceptions. For example, the tax code specifically exempts from this tax "all gains from the sale of property" other than "property held primarily for sale to customers in the ordinary course of the trade or business." The IRS ruled that taxable income would not result "*unless a sales purpose is dominant.*" The IRS concluded that this standard had not been met in this case because of the following factors: (1) the land was held for "a significant period of time" before it was sold (contrary to the "short turn around period experienced by a typical buyer and seller of property"); (2) the school did not "regularly sell real estate"; (3) the school's "management activities with respect to the property have been minimal," and have consisted of collecting rents and providing routine maintenance and repairs; and (4) the school had not been "involved in any way with improving the land or providing services to tenants". The IRS concluded that "these facts distinguish [this sale] from the sale of property held primarily for sale to customers in the ordinary course of business." Therefore "income from the sale of this property is excluded from the computation of unrelated business taxable income." *IRS Letter Ruling 9651014.*

8. IRS addresses a church's sale of "coupon books." In order to raise funds for its school, a church sold "scrip coupon books" containing coupons that are redeemable at various businesses. The church purchases the scrip from the scrip vendor and distributes it to parents who sell it and return the proceeds to the school. Do revenues earned from this program represent taxable "unrelated business income"? No, ruled the IRS. It noted that the sale of scrip by a church solely to raise funds for an exempt purpose is an unrelated "trade or business" since it is an activity "carried on for the production of income from the sale of goods." Such sales "do not themselves have a substantial causal relationship to the exempt purposes of the school." However, the IRS noted that the tax code exempts from the definition of an unrelated trade or business "any trade or business in which substantially all the work in carrying on such trade or business is performed for the organization without compensation." Such was the case here, since the scrip program was administered by a volunteer parent who received no compensation for her services, and she was assisted by other volunteer parents who also served without compensation. The IRS noted that a compensated school employee wrote the checks to purchase the coupon books and another employee deposited the proceeds of the scrip sales. However, the IRS concluded that the involvement of these two employees did not affect the exclusion since "the amount of time spent by these employees on the scrip program is insubstantial." *Letter Ruling 9704012.*

9. Fund-raising concerts may trigger tax on unrelated business income. So said the IRS in a recent ruling. Tax-exempt organizations, including churches, must pay this tax on net earnings from a business activity that is regularly carried on—if the activity is not substantially related to the organization's exempt purposes. The fact that income from the activity is devoted to an exempt use does not matter. It is the nature of the activity that counts. A charity conducted two concerts each year to raise funds. The concerts in no way furthered the charity's exempt purposes, other than the raising of revenue. The IRS acknowledged that "intermittent" activities are not "regularly carried on," and therefore cannot be a taxable unrelated trade or business. However, it insisted that the "preparatory time for an event must be taken into account in determining whether an activity is regularly carried on." Since the charity in this case spent up to six months preparing for each concert, the concerts were "regularly carried on." *IRS Letter Ruling 9712001.*

10. Authority of bankruptcy trustees to recover charitable contributions. Some bankruptcy trustees have asked churches to return contributions made by a bankrupt donor. Federal law gives bankruptcy trustees the power to "set aside" transfers by bankrupt debtors for less than fair value during the twelve months preceding the filing of a bankruptcy petition. A federal appeals court ruled in 1996 that the first amendment guaranty of religious freedom did not prevent bankruptcy trustees from recovering contributions made by bankrupt donors to a church. However, the court ruled that allowing trustees to recover contributions would violate the Religious Freedom Restoration Act with respect to those donors for whom giving to their church was an important religious practice. *In re Young, 82 F.3d 1407 (8th Cir. 1996).* In 1997, the United States Supreme Court struck down the Religious Freedom Restoration Act on the ground that Congress exceeded its authority in enacting the law. This decision has the effect of repealing the *Young* case. Contributions made by church members to their church within a year before filing a bankruptcy petition are now subject to recovery by a bankruptcy court. In summary, there is little chance that a church or donor could successfully challenge a bankruptcy trustee's efforts to recover contributions made by the donor within one year of filing a bankruptcy petition.

11. Rental income not taxable, says IRS. A charity rented a portion of its premises to another charity with similar purposes. The IRS ruled that the rental income was not subject to the "unrelated business income tax" (UBIT), even though the property was "debt-financed," since the rental arrangement was "substantially related" to the charity's exempt purposes. The IRS noted that rental income received by a charity from "debt-financed" property generally is subject to UBIT. However, an exception applies to rental agreements that are substantially related to the charity's exempt purposes. The IRS noted that "an organization's leasing of its property to others may be substantially related to the performance of its exempt function." This test was met, the IRS concluded, because the rental agreement "will contribute importantly to the accomplishment of [the charity's] purposes" and will help further its "charitable goals." The IRS noted that a rental agreement will be "substantially related" to a charity's exempt purposes if it meets any one or more of the following conditions: (1) it has a "causal relationship to the achievement of exempt purposes (other than through the production of income)"; (2) it contributes importantly to the accomplishment of those purposes; (3) the entire property is devoted to the charity's exempt purposes at least 85 percent of the time, or (4) at least 85 percent of the property (in terms of physical area) is used for the charity's exempt purposes. *IRS Letter Ruling 9726005.*

12. Delay in penalty for failure to deposit payroll taxes electronically. In 1993 Congress enacted legislation requiring the IRS to develop a system for the electronic filing of payroll taxes. Congress wanted a simple, "paperless" way for employers to deposit their payroll taxes. In response the IRS came up with the Electronic Federal Tax Payment System (or EFTPS). The new electronic system is phased in over a period of years by increasing the percentage of total taxes subject to the new EFTPS system each year. For 1997, the target percentage was to be achieved by requiring all employers that deposited more than $50,000 in payroll taxes in 1995 to begin using EFTPS by January 1, 1997. Congress later postponed this deadline until July 1, 1997, and the IRS announced in 1997 that it would not impose penalties for non-compliance through the end of 1997—for employers that make timely deposits using paper forms while converting over to the EFTPS system. Congress enacted legislation in 1997 providing that no penalties will be assessed for failure to use the EFTPS system to deposit payroll taxes prior to July 1, 1998.

13. Corporate sponsorship payments. Many churches produce pictorial directories of members, and sponsor concerts or other events. In some cases, churches seek financing for these projects from local businesses. For a fee, a business can have its name appear as a sponsor in the pictorial directory, or in a printed program distributed at the concert or other event. Are these fees subject to the federal unrelated business income tax (UBIT)? Congress enacted legislation in 1997 that addresses this issue directly. Here are the new rules, which take effect in 1998:

- "Qualified sponsorship payments" received by a church or other charity will not be subject to UBIT. A qualified sponsorship payment is defined as a payment made by a business to a charity in exchange for the use of the business's name or logo by the charity.

- This exception will not apply to any payment which entitles a company to advertise its name or logo "in regularly scheduled and printed material" published by the charity—unless "related to and primarily distributed in connection with a specific event conducted by" the charity.

14. Eliminate gift tax filing requirements for gifts to charity. Persons who donate more than $10,000 to any one person or organization in the same year are required to file a federal gift tax return with the IRS. Gifts to churches and other charities are exempted from this requirement. Congress enacted legislation in 1997 clarifying that this exemption applies only to gifts of a donor's *entire* interest in property to the church or charity. It does not apply to a gift of a *partial* interest in property. This provision applies to gifts made after August 5, 1997. This development is addressed further in chapter 8.

15. Church plan exception to group health coverage. Legislation enacted in 1996 prohibits group health plans from excluding an employee on account of his or her health or medical condition. Congress enacted legislation in 1997 providing that a church plan does not violate this nondiscrimination requirement merely because the plan requires evidence of good health in order for an individual to enroll in the plan. However, this exception only applies with respect to individuals (1) who are employees of an employer with 10 or fewer employees, or self-employed, or (2) who enroll after the first 90 days of eligibility under the plan. Further, this exception applies to a church for a particular year only if the health plan required evidence of good health as of July 15, 1997, and at all times thereafter.

16. Religious schools exempt from federal unemployment tax. Since 1970, all work performed for nonprofit organizations is subject to federal unemployment tax and must be covered by state unemployment law, unless specifically exempted by law. Exemptions have included work performed for a church (or convention or association of churches), or an organization "which is operated primarily for religious purposes and which is operated, supervised, controlled, or principally supported by a church or convention or association of churches." Congress enacted legislation in 1997 that expands this list of exceptions to include work performed in an elementary or secondary school that is operated primarily for religious purposes, even if it is not operated, supervised, controlled, or principally supported by a church or a convention or association of churches.

17. New W-4s. The comprehensive Taxpayer Relief Act, enacted by Congress in 1997, does what its title suggests—it provides significant tax relief to many taxpayers. The biggest winners are lower and middle income taxpayers. As a result, many church staff members will be paying less taxes in 1998. Church treasurers should encourage all staff members to consider filing new and updated W-4 forms for 1998—to reduce their income tax withholdings.

18. The IRS addressed "designated contributions" to charity in an important ruling. Every church has received contributions designating a specific project or use. It is important for church treasurers to understand the tax implications of such gifts. Are they tax-deductible? Should the church issue the donor a receipt acknowledging the contribution? Can the donor claim a tax deduction on his or her tax return? A 1997 IRS ruling addressed this important topic. While the case involved a university, it is directly relevant to churches. The IRS ruled that contributions to a university for the renovation of designated fraternity houses were tax-deductible since (1) the university assured donors that it would "attempt" to honor their designations; and (2) the university made it clear to donors that it accepted their designated gifts with the understanding that the designations would not restrict or limit the university's full control over the contributions, and that the university could use the designated contributions for any purpose. The IRS cautioned that for a designated gift to be a tax-deductible charitable contribution, it

> must be in reality a gift to the college and not a gift to the fraternity by using the college as a conduit. The college must have the attributes of ownership in respect of the donated property, and its rights as an owner must not, as a condition of the gift, be limited by conditions or restrictions which in effect make a private group the beneficiary of the donated property. In addition . . . the college should, as an owner, be free to use the property acquired with the gift as its future policy suggests or requires. . . . [The] university will accept gifts designated for the benefit of a particular fraternity only with the understanding that such designation will not restrict or limit university's full ownership rights in either the donated property or property acquired by use of the donated property. *Private Letter Ruling 9733015.*

19. Increased IRS scrutiny of 403(b) plans. A top IRS official announced in 1997 that the IRS will be conducting more exams of 403(b) plans to ensure compliance with federal law. The main target—contributions that exceed the complex limits imposed by law. The remarks were made by Robert Architect, an employee of the IRS Employee Plans Division, at a recent American Bar Association conference in Washington, DC.

20. Application of pre-ERISA nondiscrimination rules to church plans. Church retirement plans are exempt from various requirements imposed by the Employee Retirement Income Security Act of 1974 ("ERISA") upon pension plans. For example, church plans are not subject to ERISA's vesting, coverage, and funding requirements. However, according to a comment in the conference committee's official report to the Small Business Job Protection Act of 1996, "in some cases" church plans will be "subject to provisions in effect before the enactment of ERISA" and that under these rules a church plan "cannot discriminate in favor of officers . . . [or] persons whose principal duties consist in supervising the work of other employees, or highly compensated employees." The Act clarifies that church plans subject to these pre-ERISA nondiscrimination rules may not discriminate in favor of "highly compensated employees" as defined under the new and simplified definition of that term contained in the Act, and this single nondiscrimination rule replaces the pre-ERISA rule banning discrimination in favor of officers or persons whose principal duties consist in supervising the work of other employees (unless they also satisfy the new definition of a highly compensated employee). As noted in another paragraph in this summary, the new definition of a highly compensated employee includes an employee who had compensation for the previous year in excess of $80,000, and, if an employer elects, was in the top 20 percent of employees by compensation. This provision took effect in 1997.

21. Churches permitted to establish 401(k) retirement plans. A 401(k) retirement plan (also known as a "qualified cash or deferred arrangement") is one of the most popular forms of retirement plan in use today. They have not been available to churches and other tax-exempt organizations since 1986, but this has not been a problem since these organizations can establish "tax-sheltered annuities" which contain many of the same features including generous employee contributions through tax-deferred "salary reduction agreements," and employer contributions. Prior to 1996, tax-sheltered annuities have been more attractive than 401(k) plans, since an employee could contribute a slightly larger amount to a tax-sheltered annuity than to a 401(k) plan. The two kinds of plans are nearly identical today in terms of tax advantages, and so it is doubtful that many churches will create 401(k) plans as an alternative to tax-sheltered annuities. This provision took effect in 1997.

22. The IRS expresses concern over widespread failure by donors to properly substantiate their contributions of noncash property to charity. The IRS continues to express concern over the widespread lack of compliance with the substan-tiation requirements that apply to charitable contributions of noncash property valued by the donor at $500 or more (note that these rules are in addition to the new substantiation rules that took effect on January 1, 1994). Any donor who contributes non-cash property (i.e., homes, land, vehicles, equipment, jewelry) to a church or other charity, and who claims a deduction of $500 or more, must complete IRS Form 8283 and enclose it with the Form 1040 on which the deduction is claimed. If property valued at more than $5,000 is donated, then additional requirements apply. The donor must obtain a qualified appraisal and enclose an appraisal summary with the Form 1040 on which the deduction is claimed. These important requirements are discussed fully in chapter 8. Church treasurers should be familiar with these rules.

23. Corporate sponsorship payments. Congress enacted legislation in 1997 specifying that "qualified sponsorship payments" received by a tax-exempt organization will not be subject to the unrelated business income tax (UBIT). A qualified sponsorship payment is defined as a payment made by a business to a charity in exchange for the use of the business's name or logo by the charity. The new law cautions that this exception will not apply to: (1) Advertising of a company's products or services "including messages containing qualitative or comparative language, price information, or other indications of savings or value, an endorsement, or an inducement to purchase, sell, or use such products or services." (2) Any payment which entitles a company to advertise its name or logo "in regularly scheduled and printed material" published by the charity—unless "related to and primarily distributed in connection with a specific event conducted by" the charity. (3) Any payment made in connection with any qualified convention or trade show activity. This provision applies to payments made or received on or after January 1, 1998.

24. A federal court in Rhode Island ruled that the exemption of churches from unemployment tax did not violate the first amendment's nonestablishment of religion clause. The Salvation Army dismissed an employee for budgetary reasons. The employee applied for unemployment benefits, and was informed that she was not eligible since her former employer was a religious organization that was exempt from unemployment tax. The employee filed a lawsuit claiming that the exemption of religious organizations from the unemployment law violated the first amendment. A federal court disagreed in an important decision that reaffirms the historic exemption of churches from unemployment taxes. *Rojas v. Fitch, 928 F. Supp. 155 (D.R.I. 1996).*

25. The IRS ruled that income generated by a charity from various "vocational training" programs was not subject to the unrelated business income tax (UBIT). A charity operates a residential program for troubled boys ages 12 through 18. Children are referred to the charity by government agencies and school districts. The charity provides both academic and limited vocational training, both of which it considers essential to its goals of developing improved social skills, more meaningful interpersonal relationships, and the development of self control, honesty, and self-esteem. Staff members provide individual, group, and vocational therapy for the residents. The charity is located on a farm which serves as a training ground for residents. It also provides residents with opportunities to learn the basics of various trades and crafts, including automotive and heavy equipment repair, printing, and upholstery. Vocational training is secondary to the primary goal of social reintegration into the community. Most residents have never been employed. In order to give residents retail sales experience and other work-related experiences, the organization proposes to erect a shed alongside a highway which crosses its property, and to conduct in that facility the following three activities using residents who would be paid minimal wages and who voluntarily agree to participate: (1) sales of produce from farming activities; (2) sales of furniture built by students; and (3) operation of a golf driving range. Each activity will charge prices competitive with for-profit businesses in the area, although anticipated profits will be minimal. The primary goal of these sales operations is to give residents the experience of operating a business, to learn general business principles and judgment, and to enhance their social skills in a public environment. The charity will employ no special personnel for this program.

The charity asked the IRS if the earnings from these activities would be subject to the unrelated business income tax (UBIT). The IRS said no. It noted that an "unrelated trade or business" is any trade or business of an exempt organization that is not substantially related (aside from the need of such organization for income) to the organization's exempt functions. The IRS noted that the income tax regulations specify that a trade or business is related to exempt purposes when the conduct of the business activity has a direct and substantial relationship to the achievement of an exempt purpose, and contributes importantly to the accomplishment of those purposes. The IRS concluded that the charity's proposed activities "are being undertaken to further the goals of the existing programs for residents, and not for the production of income. The proposed activities are a natural extension of existing programs for residents. The scale of the operations is no larger than is necessary for the organization to accomplish its charitable purposes. This is evidenced by the fact that the individuals providing labor for these facilities are residents who are employed as part of your rehabilitation program, and your staff. Supervision will be provided by members of your staff who will not receive additional pay for performing this duty." Therefore, income generated from the sale of products is not subject to UBIT. *IRS Letter Ruling 9718034.*

26. Impact of tax simplification. A number of sweeping proposals for tax reform have been proposed in Congress over the past few years. Some "flat tax" proposals would eliminate most deductions, including a deduction for charitable contributions, in exchange for a flat income tax rate. How would such a tax impact churches and other charities? Would donations decline because of the loss of a contribution deduction? Two factors suggest that they would not. First—71% of all taxpayers can't deduct their contributions under present law, because they cannot itemize deductions on Schedule A. A "flat tax" that eliminated charitable contribution deductions would only affect the remaining 29% of taxpayers that currently can deduct their contributions. Second—when the partial deduction of charitable contributions by nonitemizers expired in 1986, there was no decrease in charitable giving. We will be closely following the continuing debate in Congress over tax reform. If any new laws emerge, we will let you know the details in future editions of this text.

EXPLANATION OF LEGAL TERMS

A few legal terms are used occasionally in this book. They are listed below, along with definitions to assist you in understanding the text.

Internal Revenue Code (the "Code" or "IRC"). The federal tax law enacted by Congress. It covers several subjects, including federal income taxes, social security taxes, and withholding and estimated tax procedures. It is important to recognize that Congress, not the IRS, enacts federal tax laws. The IRS is an administrative agency established by Congress to assist in the administration of the tax laws enacted by Congress.

Regulations (or "Treas. Reg."). Regulations are interpretations of the Internal Revenue Code issued by the Treasury Department. They provide taxpayers with guidance as to the meaning and application of the Code. They are inferior to and may never contradict the Code itself.

Internal Revenue Service (IRS). An administrative agency that is part of the Treasury Department. It was created by Congress, and exists to administer and enforce federal tax laws. It is subordinate to Congress, and has no authority to make law.

Revenue Rulings ("Rev. Rul.") and Revenue Procedures ("Rev. Proc."). Official pronouncements of the national office of the IRS. Like regulations, they are designed to provide guidance on tax issues. Usually, they pertain to a specific issue. They are inferior in authority to both the Code and regulations.

IRS Private Letter Rulings ("IRS Letter Rulings"). IRS responses to individual tax questions submitted by taxpayers. These letters can be relied upon only by the taxpayers to whom they are specifically directed. They cannot be cited or used as precedent by other taxpayers in similar circumstances.

Court decisions. A number of federal court decisions are referred to in the text. The initials "S. Ct." or "U.S." refer to a United States Supreme Court decision. The initials "F.2d" refer to a federal appeals court decision. The initials "F. Supp." refer to a federal district court decision. The initials "T.C." or "T.C.M." refer to a decision of the United States Tax Court. However, note that the initials "T.C." refer to a ruling by all 34 judges comprising the full United States Tax Court, while the initials "T.C.M." refer to a "memorandum" decision by only one Tax Court judge. Tax Court decisions rendered by all 34 judges ("T.C.") have much more precedential value than memorandum decisions. Supreme Court rulings are binding in all state and federal courts. Federal appeals court rulings are binding in all federal courts in the respective federal circuit (there are 11 geographical circuits). Federal district court and tax court decisions ordinarily are not binding on any other court. Any federal court has the authority to interpret contested provisions of the Code.

Chapter 1

THE INCOME TAX RETURN

Chapter Highlights

- **Clergy not exempt from taxes.** Clergy are not exempt from paying federal taxes.

- **Filing a tax return.** Clergy are required to file a federal income tax return if they have earnings of $400 or more (if they are not exempt from social security).

- **Form 1040.** Most clergy must use Form 1040 (rather than Form 1040A or 1040EZ).

- **Penalties.** Clergy are subject to substantial penalties for not filing a tax return (if one is required), and for reporting inaccurate information on a tax return.

- **Audit risk.** The risk of being audited is small. But it is much higher for self-employed persons, and even higher for self-employed persons who receive only one or two 1099 forms (as is true for many clergy who report their federal income taxes as self-employed).

- **Exemption from income tax withholding.** Clergy are exempt from federal tax withholding, whether they report their income taxes as employees or as self-employed. However, if they report their income taxes as an employee, they may request "voluntary withholding" of their income taxes and   self-employment taxes.

- **Estimated taxes.** Since clergy are exempt from federal tax withholding, they must prepay their income taxes and self-employment taxes by using the estimated tax reporting procedure. The only exception would be clergy who report their income taxes as employees and who elect voluntary withholding of both income taxes and self-employment taxes. Estimated taxes must be paid in quarterly installments. Use IRS Form 1040-ES.

- **Taxpayer Bill of Rights.** The "taxpayer bill of rights" gives taxpayers several important protections, including (1) mandatory IRS disclosure of taxpayer rights prior to an audit; (2) the right to tape-record IRS interviews; (3) the right to suspend an audit in order to consult with an attorney or CPA; (4) the elimination of any penalty for taxpayer reliance on written IRS advice that proves to be incorrect; (5) IRS employees cannot be evaluated on the basis of the amount of taxes they collect; (6) the IRS must use greater clarity in preparing taxpayer notices of taxes due; (7) taxpayers are permitted to pay delinquent taxes in installments in some cases; (8) the amount of taxpayer wages and property that is exempt from IRS seizure is increased; and (9) taxpayers now have the right to sue the IRS (up to $100,000) if an agent takes a position that intentionally or recklessly disregards a provision in the Code or regulations.

- **Taxpayer Bill of Rights 2.** In 1996 Congress enacted the Taxpayer Bill of Rights ("TBOR2"). TBOR2 includes several provisions that will be of interest to ministers and other church leaders, including the following: (1) creation of the office of taxpayer advocate; (2) the IRS must notify taxpayers 30 days before modifying or terminating any installment agreement for the payment of back taxes; (3) the IRS is authorized to reduce or eliminate the penalty that otherwise would apply to employers that fail to make their first deposit of payroll taxes on time (for example, because they sent the withheld taxes directly to the IRS instead of depositing them with a bank); (4) offers in compromise must have the approval of the IRS chief counsel only the amount of unpaid taxes is $50,000 or more (up from $500 under prior law); (5) employers who issue fraudulent 1099 or W-2 forms may be sued by the person who receives them; (6) in any court proceeding, if a taxpayer asserts a reasonable dispute with respect to any item of income reported on an information return (Form 1099 or Form W-2) filed by an employer and the taxpayer has fully cooperated with the IRS, then the government has the burden of proving the deficiency (with evidence in addition to the information return itself); (7) it is much easier for taxpayers to collect their attorney's fees in disputes with the IRS; (8) increases the maximum IRS liability for taking a position that recklessly or intentionally disregards the tax law from $100,000 to $1 million; (9) provides limited relief to uncompensated board members of churches and other nonprofit organizations from penalties for failure to withhold payroll taxes or pay them to the government; (10) all 1099 forms issued after December 31, 1996, must contain the name, address, and telephone number of a "contact person" who can answer questions the recipient may have about the form; (11) the IRS can assess "interim sanctions" (an excise tax) against churches and other exempt organizations that pay unreasonable compensation to an officer or director.

A. Filing Your Return

1. Must ministers pay federal income taxes?

✎ **Key point: clergy are not exempt from paying federal taxes**

The United States Supreme Court has ruled that the first amendment guaranty of religious freedom is not violated by subjecting ministers to the federal income tax. *Murdock v. Pennsylvania, 319 U.S. 105 (1943).* The courts have rejected every attempt by clergy (many with only mail-order credentials) to claim that they are "exempt" from the payment of income taxes. Note the following examples of arguments that have been summarily rejected by the courts:

• A minister claimed that his income was not taxable since he was "a minister of the gospel of Jesus Christ living by the grace and mercy of God, and not by receipt of worldly income."

• A minister attempted to avoid income taxes by characterizing his compensation as "remuneration received for assigned services as an agent of the church, and not income or wages."

• A minister claimed that the religious tenets of his church forbade members to pay income taxes, and therefore it would violate the first amendment guaranty of religious freedom for him to be required to pay taxes. A federal court summarily rejected this argument, noting that "imposing income taxes on individuals whose religious tenets forbid the payment of those taxes does not violate the first amendment," and that "while the minister's religious beliefs may be sincerely held, the payment of income taxes is not voluntary." *United States v. Gonzalez, 91-1 USTC ¶ 50,100 (D. Colo. 1991).*

• A minister stopped filing tax returns when his study of the Bible led him to the conclusion that he was a "one-man church." The court in the last case concluded that if such claims were ever recognized, "there would likely be an overabundance of one-person churches paying no income taxes, and leaving to the rest of us the payment of their fair share of the expense of running the government. That attitude hardly seems like an act of churchly charity to one's neighbors."

All of these claims, and many like them, are treated as frivolous by the IRS and the courts. Often, such ministers are required to pay substantial penalties in addition to back taxes and interest.

Tax protestors. Lamentably, many "tax protestors" use religion in their futile attempts to excuse the non-payment of taxes. Some argue that payment of income taxes violates their constitutional right to freely exercise their religion, and a rapidly growing number of protestors attempt to escape taxes through the creation of "mail order churches." Unfortunately, such cases, along with the celebrated televangelist scandals and excesses of recent years, have encouraged a governmental cynicism toward churches and clergy.

Other popular "tax protestor" arguments—all of which have been rejected repeatedly by the courts—include the following:

• the Constitution prohibits the assessment of income taxes (ignoring the 16th amendment)

• income taxes violate the Constitution's ban on involuntary servitude and self-incrimination

• the United States Tax Court is unconstitutional

• income received in the form of paper currency (Federal Reserve notes) is not "legal tender" since it is not redeemable in gold or silver, and is not taxable as income until paid in gold or silver

• claiming deductions or "tax credits" to avoid supporting war, defense, or abortion

• claiming excessive withholding allowances on Form W-4

• characterizing wages as a nontaxable exchange for services rendered rather than as taxable income

Tax protestors are active in presenting seminars and publishing defenses of their positions, and often appear convincing to the uninformed. Congress has enacted legislation designed to discourage the use of tax protestor schemes. Besides the normal penalties for failure to pay taxes (including potential criminal penalties for willfully evading taxes or refusing to file a return), tax protestors face an array of additional penalties, including a $500 penalty for claiming a "frivolous" position on a tax return and a $25,000 penalty for maintaining a frivolous tax position (or a position designed solely for delay) before the Tax Court. *IRC 6702, 6673.*

Members of religious or apostolic associations. Clergy who are members of religious or apostolic associations having a common treasury do not have to report any income received in connection with duties required by the association if they have taken a vow of poverty and no portion of the net income of the association is distributable to them. *Revenue Procedure 72-5, IRC 501(d).* If a member of an association has a share in its net income, then he or she must include such share (whether distributed or not) in gross income as a dividend received. The association should file a partnership return (Form 1065) each year.

2. Who must file a return?

Not everyone is required to file an individual federal income tax return (Form 1040). For 1997, a federal income tax return (with appropriate schedules) must be filed only if your gross income exceeds your applicable standard deduction plus personal exemptions (there is an exception for married taxpayers filing separately). The following table illustrates the filing requirements for most individuals:

❖ **New in 1997. The standard deduction amounts increase.**

Table 1-1
Filing Requirements for 1997

filing status	standard deduction	personal exemptions	file if gross income exceeds
single	$4,150	$2,650	$6,800
married filing jointly	$6,900	$5,300	$12,200
married filing separately	$3,450	$2,650	$2,650
head of household	$6,050	$2,650	$8,700
surviving spouse	$6,900	$2,650	$9,550

For 1997, the standard deduction amount (listed in Table 1-1) increases by $1,000 for single persons if either age 65 or older or blind ($2,000 if both) and $800 for married persons filing jointly if either spouse is age 65 or older or blind ($1,600 if a spouse is both age 65 and blind). This adjustment in the standard deduction amount will affect the filing requirements of some taxpayers, as illustrated in Table 1-2.

☞ *Example. Rev. L is 67 years of age. His spouse is 66. Rev. L filed an application for exemption from social security coverage that was approved by the IRS in 1976. For 1997, Rev. L and his spouse file a joint return. Their standard deduction for 1997 is $8,500 ($6,900 basic standard deduction plus an additional $800 for each spouse because each is at least 65 years of age). Since Rev. L and his spouse are each entitled to a personal exemption of $2,650, they need not file a return for 1997 unless their income exceeds $13,800.*

❖ **New in 1997. The amount of income needed to file a federal tax return increased in 1997 for most taxpayers.**

Table 1-2
Adjusted Filing Requirements for 1997

filing status	file if gross income exceeds
joint return, one spouse age 65 or older	$13,000
joint return, both spouses age 65 or older	$13,800
single, age 65 or older	$7,800
head of household, age 65 or older	$9,700
surviving spouse, age 65 or older	$10,350

These basic filing requirements are subject to an important exception—any taxpayer who has **net earnings from self-employment of $400 or more** must file

an income tax return even if his or her gross income is less than the minimum amounts discussed above. This exception can apply to ministers in either of two ways:

• **Ministers who report their income taxes as employees.** Ministers always are treated as self-employed for social security purposes with respect to services performed in the exercise of their ministry even if they report their federal income taxes as an employee. As a result, ministers who report their income taxes as an employee must file a tax return for 1997 if they had net church or other ministerial compensation of $400 or more. However, ministers who report their income taxes as an employee and who have applied for and received IRS recognition of exemption from self-employment (social security) taxes are subject to the higher filing requirements discussed above unless they have net self-employment earnings of $400 or more from some other source. Such sources can include secular self-employment activities, guest speaking appearances in other churches, or fees received directly from church members for performing personal services such as funerals, weddings, and baptisms. See chapter 9 for details regarding the exemption from self-employment taxes.

• **Ministers who report their income taxes as self-employed.** Ministers who report their federal income taxes as self-employed, and who receive net earnings of at least $400 from the performance of ministerial (or secular) duties, must file a federal tax return whether or not they are exempt from social security coverage.

✎ **Key point: clergy are required to file a federal income tax return if they have net self-employment earnings of $400 or more from any source.**

☞ *Example. Rev. T has never exempted himself from social security coverage. He is single, works part-time at First Church, and receives $5,000 in compensation from the church in 1997. He has no other income. Rev. T must file an income tax return. While single persons ordinarily are not required to file a return if they earn less than $6,800, they must file if they have net earnings from self-employment of $400 or more. Since Rev. T is considered to be self-employed for social security purposes with respect to services performed in the exercise of his ministry at First Church, he must file a return if he has net earnings of $400 or more.*

3. Which form to use

✎ **Key point: most clergy must use Form 1040 (rather than Form 1040A or Form 1040EZ)**

You **must use Form 1040** if you meet any one of several conditions, including any one or more of the following:

• taxable income of $50,000 or more

• you had income from an annuity, gain from the sale of a home, or self-employment

• you itemize your deductions

• you deduct half your self-employment tax as an "adjustment" in computing your gross income (see chapter 9 for details)

• you pay self-employment taxes (reported on Schedule SE)

✎ **Key point: nonminister employees of a church that elected to exempt itself from the employer's share of FICA taxes by filing a timely Form 8274 with the IRS must use Form 1040 if they receive wages of $108.28 or more.**

Most ministers must use Form 1040 since they will have income from self-employment (remember that ministers always are treated as self-employed for social security purposes with respect to their ministerial services). It is possible, however, for ministers to qualify for the simpler **Form 1040A** if they (1) have applied for and received IRS recognition of exemption from self-employment taxes, (2) report their income taxes as an employee, (3) have no self-employment earnings from any source (ministerial or secular), (4) have less than $50,000 in taxable income, and (5) do not itemize deductions. Obviously, such cases will be rare.

☞ *Example. Rev. A is senior minister at First Church. He has exempted himself from self-employment (social security) taxes, earns $45,000 in 1997 from the church (his only source of income), and does not plan to itemize deductions. Rev. A may be eligible to use the simpler Form 1040A. However, he must use Form 1040 if he satisfies any one of several conditions, including the following: he is not exempt from self-employment (social security) taxes, he has taxable income of $50,000 or more, he reports his income taxes as a self-employed person, or he itemizes deductions.*

4. Recordkeeping

You must keep records so that you can prepare a complete and accurate income tax return. The law does not require any special form of records. However, you should keep all receipts, canceled checks, and other evidence to prove amounts you claim as deductions, exclusions, or credits. Records should be retained for as long as they are important for any income tax law. In general, you should keep records that support an item of income or a deduction appearing on a return until the statute of limitations (the period during which the IRS can audit your return) runs out. Usually this is three years after the date a return was filed (or three years after the due date of the return, if later). However, in some cases it is wise to keep records for a longer period of time, since a six year limitations period applies in some situations, and in others (e.g., no return was filed, or a return was fraudulent) there is no time limitation on the authority of the IRS to begin an audit. The time limitation rules are summarized later in this book.

Specific recordkeeping requirements with respect to the following exclusions and deductions are discussed later in this tax guide:

✓ housing allowances (chapter 6)

✓ business expenses (chapter 7)

✓ contributions (chapter 8)

Records of transactions affecting the basis (cost) of some assets should be retained until after the expiration of the limitations period for the tax year in which the asset is sold. Taxpayers who have excluded or postponed gain from the sale of a residence should keep a copy of Form 2119 indefinitely.

✎ **Key point: churches have recordkeeping requirements too. They are discussed in chapter 11.**

5. How to figure your tax

If you file Form 1040 (rather than Form 1040A), you must find your gross income, adjusted gross income, and taxable income before you can figure your tax. **Gross income** is your income after deducting all exclusions allowed by law. It is the starting point for determining your tax liability, and its various components are reported directly on Form 1040 (lines 7-22). Since gross income is net of any exclusions, *no exclusions are reported on Form 1040.* Exclusions are discussed fully in chapters 5 and 6 of this tax guide.

☞ *Example. Rev. M rents his home, and his church provides him with a rental allowance of $7,000 for 1997. Assuming that Rev. M's actual expenses in renting his home equal or exceed $7,000 in 1997, his gross income should not reflect the $7,000 allowance since it is an exclusion from gross income. This means that Rev. M's Form W-2 (box 1) or 1099 (box 7) should report his church compensation less the $7,000. And, Rev. M should report his church compensation less the $7,000 as wages on line 7 of Form 1040 (or on Schedule C if self-employed). This is the approach taken by the IRS in Publication 517. Note, however, that the housing allowance is an exclusion for federal income tax purposes only. It must be included in Rev. M's self-employment earnings (Schedule SE of Form 1040) for purposes of computing his social security tax liability (assuming he has not exempted himself from social security coverage).*

Adjusted gross income is gross income minus various adjustments that are reported on Form 1040, lines 23-30. If you do not itemize deductions, your **taxable income** is your adjusted gross income less the standard deduction ($4,150 for single persons and $6,900 for married persons filing jointly) and less the deduction for your exemptions. If you itemize your deductions, your taxable income is your adjusted gross income less your itemized deductions and less your deduction for your exemptions. If you *must* itemize your deductions (this rule applies to various categories of taxpayers, including a married person filing a separate return if his or her spouse itemizes deductions), then you should refer to the instructions accompanying Form 1040 for the more complicated rules that apply in such a case. The rules described above are all discussed in much greater detail in the chapters that follow. They are summarized in table 1-3.

Tax liability is determined by taking your income tax liability (ordinarily computed from a table) less any credits (Form 1040, lines 40-46), plus any other taxes (Form 1040, lines 47-53, including self-employment taxes), and minus payments already made (Form 1040, lines 54-60) through withholding or estimated tax payments.

6. When to file

The deadline for filing your 1997 federal tax return is April 15, 1998.

Your return is filed on time if it is properly addressed and postmarked no later than the due date. The return must have sufficient postage. If you do not file your return by the due date, you may have to pay a failure-to-file penalty. The **failure-to-file penalty** currently is 5% of your unpaid taxes for each month, or part of a month, after the due date that the tax is not paid—but ordinarily not more than 25% of your tax (if fraudulent, 15% per month, with a maximum of 75% of your tax). The penalty is waived if you can show reasonable cause for not filing your return on time.

TABLE 1-3

	where reported on Form 1040	where covered in this handbook
Total income	not reported	Chapter 4
- Exclusions	not reported	Chapter 5-6
= Gross income	Form 1040, lines 7-22	Chapter 4
- Adjustments	Form 1040, lines 23-30	Chapter 7
= Adjusted gross income	Form 1040, lines 32 and 33	Chapter 7

Option 1

- Standard deduction	Form 1040, line 35	Chapter 7
- Personal exemptions	Form 1040, line 37	Chapter 1
= Taxable income	Form 1040, line 38	Chapter 7

Option 2

- Itemized deductions	Form 1040, line 34	Chapter 7
- Personal exemptions	Form 1040, line 36	Chapter 1
= Taxable income	Form 1040, line 37	Chapter 7

7. Extensions of time to file

Taxpayers can obtain an automatic four-month extension (from April 15 to August 15, 1998) of time to file their 1997 Form 1040. To get the automatic extension, you must file a Form 4868 by April 15, 1998 with the IRS service center for your area. Your Form 1040 can be filed at any time during the four-month extension period. It is important to recognize that the extension only relieves you from the obligation to *file your return*; it is *not an extension of the obligation to pay your taxes.* Therefore, you must make an estimate of your tax for 1997 and pay the estimated tax with your Form 4868. When you file your Form 1040, you list the estimated payment made with your Form 4868 as a prior payment of taxes on line 57. If your actual tax liability for 1997 is more than the amount you estimated and enclosed with your Form 4868, you may have to pay an underpayment penalty.

Extensions of time beyond the automatic four-month extension are granted only for very good reasons. An extension of more than six months will not be granted if you are in the United States. Additional extensions are requested by filing a Form 2688.

8. Refunds

If you overpay income or social security taxes, you can get a refund of the amount you overpaid. Or, you may choose to apply all or a part of the overpayment to your next year's estimated tax (if applicable). If you are due a refund, no interest will be paid if the refund is made within 45 days of the due date of the return. If the refund is not made within this 45-day period, interest will be paid from the due date of the return or from the date you filed, whichever is later.

9. If you owe additional taxes

If your tax liability exceeds the amount of taxes that have been withheld or the amount of your estimated tax payments (or other payments), then you should enclose a check for the additional tax with your return. In addition, you may be liable for an underpayment penalty (discussed in Chapter 1, Section D.2) and interest.

10. Amended returns

If, after filing your return, you find that you did not report some income, you claimed deductions or credits you should not have claimed, or you did not claim deductions or credits that you could have claimed, you should correct your return. Form 1040X is the form to use to correct the Form 1040 or Form 1040A that you previously filed. The amended return should be filed within three years from the date you filed your original return (including extensions), or within two years from the time you paid your tax, whichever is later. A return filed early is considered filed on the due date.

11. Audit risk

✎ **Key point: the risk of being audited is small, but is much higher for self-employed persons (especially if they only receive one or two 1099 forms)**

The IRS "Annual Report" for 1996 contains some interesting information about "audit risk." Only 1.67% of personal income tax returns were audited in 1996. However, the actual audit rate varied significantly depending on the IRS region involved and the amount of income reported, as noted below.

region	returns audited
Western	309,000
Southeast	232,000
Midstates	210,000
Northeast	193,000

The 1996 IRS Annual Report confirms that persons with higher incomes have a higher audit risk, as noted below:

Percentage of returns examined

type of return	1994	1995
1040A; income under $25,000	1.04	1.9
1040; income under $25,000	0.88	1.30
1040; income $25,000 to $50,000	0.53	0.90
1040; income $50,000 to $100,000	0.72	1.05
1040; income $100,000 and over	2.94	2.79
Schedule C; income under $25,000	4.39	5.85
Schedule C; income $25,000 to $100,000	3.01	3.08
Schedule C; income $100,000 and over	3.57	3.47

This data demonstrates two important points. First, audit risk increases as income increases; and second, audit risk is much higher for self-employed persons than for employees. In the table, self-employed persons are identified as those persons who report their income on Schedule C. Employees are identified as those persons who report income on Form 1040 (or 1040A).

Some taxpayers have a much higher risk of being audited because of a number of additional considerations including unusually large itemized deductions, and the existence of moving or education expenses. Itemized deductions that exceed ranges established by the IRS also increase your audit risk. While the IRS does not publish its audit criteria, it does publish the average itemized deductions claimed by taxpayers based on the amount of their income. This information is helpful in comparing the size of your deductions with the average amounts claimed. The most recent data (for 1995 returns) is reproduced below.

Success on appeal. How successful are taxpayers in appealing adverse IRS determinations in court? The most recent available data suggests that they do very poorly and in most cases would be better off not wasting their time and money. Only 4% won their cases in the Tax Court; 23.2% won their cases in federal district courts; and 19% won their cases in federal appeals courts. Taxpayers should bear these statistics in mind before paying potentially substantial legal fees to appeal an adverse IRS ruling to the courts.

12. Penalties

✎ **Key point: clergy are subject to substantial penalties for not filing a tax return (if one is required) and for reporting inaccurate information on a tax return**

Some taxpayers view the risk of being audited as so low that they deliberately underreport income, overstate expenses, or adopt very questionable interpretations of the tax laws. Ministers should bear in mind the following penalties before adopting questionable interpretations of the tax laws.

a. "Accuracy-related penalties". Penalties are imposed for various inaccuracies in tax returns, as noted below.

✎ **Key point: the penalty for underpayment of tax due to negligence no longer can be avoided through "adequate disclosure" of a taxpayer's "reasonable" position on IRS Form 8275.**

average itemized deductions (1995 returns)				
adjusted gross income (thousands)	medical expenses	taxes	interest	contributions
$ 15-20	$5,246	$1,922	$5,355	$1,416
$ 20-25	4,513	2,049	4,556	1,150
$ 25-30	3,247	2,374	5,478	1,414
$ 30-40	3,147	2,717	5,546	1,217
$ 40-50	4,123	3,287	6,020	1,688
$ 50-75	6,003	4,424	6,437	1,685
$ 75-100	10,116	6,312	8,309	2,142
$ 100-200	21,250	9,772	11,305	4,017
$ 200 and over	——	36,443	21,997	12,189

Negligence or disregard. If an underpayment of tax is due to negligence or a disregard of tax law, a "negligence penalty" is imposed. This penalty is computed by multiplying 20% times the amount of the underpayment of taxes that is due to negligence or disregard. "Negligence" includes (1) a failure to make a reasonable attempt to comply with the tax law; (2) a failure to exercise reasonable care in the preparation of a tax return; or (3) a failure to keep adequate records or to substantiate items properly. The term "disregard" includes any careless, reckless, or intentional disregard of federal tax law.

Reliance on the advice of a tax adviser does not relieve a minister of liability for either the negligence or disregard penalties. Taxpayers can avoid the negligence penalty only "with respect to any portion of an underpayment if it is shown that there was a reasonable cause for such portion and that the taxpayer acted in good faith with respect to such portion." IRC 6664(c).

Substantial understatement. Taxpayers who "substantially understate" their income tax are subject to a "substantial understatement" penalty. This penalty is computed by multiplying 20% times the portion of an underpayment of income taxes that is due to a substantial understatement. A substantial understatement of income taxes exists if an understatement exceeds the greater of (1) 10% of the actual income taxes that should have been paid, or (2) $5,000. However, the amount of an understatement is reduced by either of the following:

• Any portion of an understatement that is due to taxpayer reliance on "substantial authority"—including the tax code, income tax regulations, most IRS rulings and published materials, court cases, and the "blue book" (a general explanation of tax legislation prepared by the Congressional Joint Committee on Taxation).

• Any portion of an understatement for which the taxpayer includes an "adequate disclosure" of his or her "reasonable position" in a statement attached to the tax return. A congressional committee observed that a "reasonable position" is "a relatively high standard" that means more than "not patently improper." It is higher than the "not frivolous" standard that applied before 1994. Disclosures should be made on IRS Form 8275. Form 8275-R is used to disclose a position that is contrary to the income tax regulations (Form 8275 should not be used in such cases).

☞ **Example.** Rev. S failed to properly report several items, including a salary he paid his wife for performing duties at the church, without satisfactory explanation. He also failed to prove that man of his business expense deductions (claimed on Schedule C) were for business purposes and failed generally to keep adequate books and records to support the amounts claimed on his tax returns. Rev. S explained only that he was too busy to keep records. The Tax Court upheld an IRS assessment of a negligence penalty. The court defined negligence as "as the lack of due care, or the failure to do what a prudent person

would do under the circumstances." Shelley v. Commissioner, T.C. Memo. 1994-432 (1994).

☞ **Example.** Same facts as the previous example. The Tax Court also ruled that Rev. S would be liable for the penalty for substantially understating his tax liability if the understatement exceeded the greater of 10% of his actual income taxes or $5,000. The court noted that this penalty is not available if "there was substantial authority for the taxpayer's treatment of the items in issue or if the relevant facts relating to the tax treatment were adequately disclosed on the returns." However, the court concluded that "the record does not demonstrate that either exception applies."

☞ **Example.** The Tax Court upheld an IRS assessment of a negligence penalty against a pastor who attempted to deduct commuting expenses as a business expense. The Court concluded that "the record in this case is replete with examples of [the pastor's] negligence. [He] claimed deductions for numerous items which in many cases are either nondeductible or lack substantiation. Accordingly, we find that [the pastor is] subject to the addition to tax for negligence for all the years at issue." Clark v. Commissioner, 67 T.C.M. 2458 (1994).

Substantial valuation overstatement. Taxpayers who understate their income taxes in any year by $5,000 or more because they overstated the value of property on their tax return are subject to a penalty. The penalty only applies if the overstated value is at least 200% of its actual value. The penalty is computed by multiplying 20% times the amount of the underpayment of income taxes (the penalty rate increases to 40% if the overstated value is at least 400% of its actual value). A common example of valuation overstatements involves overvaluations of properties donated to charity. Such overvaluations result in inflated charitable contribution deductions and a corresponding understatement of income taxes. However, the Code clarifies that taxpayers who comply with the substantiation requirements that apply to contributions of noncash property valued by the donor in excess of $5,000 are not subject to this penalty even if there is an overvaluation. These requirements include a qualified appraisal of the donated property, and the inclusion of a "qualified appraisal summary" (IRS Form 8283) with the donor's tax return on which the contribution is claimed. See chapter 8 for complete details.

Property overvaluations that are not enough to trigger this penalty may still be subject to the negligence or substantial understatement penalties discussed previously.

✎ **Key point: the Code specifies that no accuracy-related penalty (including negligence and substantial understatement) shall be imposed with respect to any underpayment of taxes *if the taxpayer had reasonable cause for the underpayment and acted in good faith.***

b. Fraud. The fraud penalty, which is imposed at a rate of 75%, applies to the portion of any underpayment of income taxes that is due to fraud. If the IRS establishes by "clear and convincing evidence" that any portion of an underpayment of income taxes is due to fraud, then the entire underpayment is treated as fraudulent except for any portion that the taxpayer can prove (by a "preponderance of the evidence") is not based on fraud. Note that the IRS must establish fraud initially by a high standard (clear and convincing evidence); and that once it does so the taxpayer can rebut the presumption of fraud by a lesser standard of proof (a preponderance of the evidence). No "accuracy-related penalty" (defined above) can apply to any portion of an understatement of income taxes on which the fraud penalty is imposed. However, an accuracy-related penalty can be assessed against any portion of an underpayment that is not due to fraud.

c. Sanctions and costs. The Tax Court can impose a penalty of up to $25,000 if a taxpayer (1) initiates an action primarily for delay, (2) takes a position that is frivolous, or (3) unreasonably fails to pursue available administrative remedies within the IRS. This penalty is designed to reduce the large numbers of lawsuits brought by taxpayers who claim frivolous positions. The Tax Court also can require a taxpayer's attorney to pay the costs of litigating a frivolous lawsuit (including court costs, and attorneys' fees incurred by the government).

e. Failure-to-file penalty. If you do not file your return by the due date, you may have to pay a failure-to-file penalty. The failure-to-file penalty currently is 5% of your unpaid taxes for each month, or part of a month, after the due date that the tax is not paid—but ordinarily not more than 25% of your tax (if fraudulent, 15% per month, with a maximum of 75% of your tax). The penalty is waived if you can show reasonable cause for not filing your return on time.

f. Frivolous income tax return. Taxpayers can be assessed a penalty of $500 for filing a "frivolous" return that does not include enough information to figure the correct tax, or a return that contains information that shows on its face that the tax shown on the return is substantially incorrect, if the return was filed due to a frivolous position or out of a desire to delay or interfere with the administration of the federal tax laws. This penalty is in addition to any other penalty allowed by law.

g. Criminal penalties. In addition to the civil penalties discussed above, a taxpayer can be subject to criminal penalties for a willful attempt to evade taxes. Criminal liability requires an affirmative act (typically filing a false return). Omission of an act is insufficient. Tax evasion is a felony punishable by a fine of not more than $100,000 or a prison sentence of up to five years, or both.

✎ **Key point: In 1991, the United States Supreme Court ruled that taxpayers cannot be guilty of a criminal violation of the tax law for taking positions based on ignorance or a misunderstanding of the law, or a sincere belief that they are not violating the law. A taxpayer who failed to pay taxes or file** returns for several years was prosecuted on several counts of willfully violating the law. He maintained that he could not be convicted of willfully violating the law since he had a good faith belief that he was not a taxpayer and that wages are not taxable. The taxpayer's beliefs arose from his own study of the constitution and federal tax law, and from information he received while attending several seminars sponsored by a tax protestor group. In a surprise ruling, the Supreme Court agreed with the taxpayer that he could not be convicted of willfully violating the law if he sincerely believed that wages are not taxable, even if this belief was not "objectively reasonable." *Cheek v. United States, 111 S. Ct. 604 (1991).*

☞ *Example. Rev. O claimed on his 1997 income tax return a deduction for a contribution he made in 1996 but forgot to claim, and an unallowable deduction for the education expenses incurred by his dependent children in attending a private school. He sincerely believed he was legally entitled to claim both deductions on his 1997 return. Rev. O's taxes were underpaid by $4,000 because of these deductions. Such conduct amounts to negligent disregard of the tax laws, and subjects Rev. O to a penalty of 20% of the amount of the underpayment (a total penalty of $800, excluding interest). Of course, Rev. O also will have to pay the full $4,000 of underpaid taxes.*

☞ *Example. Rev. W believes that ministers should not pay taxes. He bases his belief on his interpretation of the Bible. In 1997, Rev. W had church income of $30,000. Assume that Rev. W should have paid federal taxes of $5,000. In addition to having to pay the $5,000 tax deficiency, Rev. W will be subject to a "delinquency" penalty for fraudulently failing to file a tax return. The penalty is 15% of the net amount of tax due for each month that the return is not filed (up to a maximum of 5 months or 75%—a total of $3,750 in this case). The IRS has the burden of proving that the taxpayer fraudulently failed to file a return. Rev. W also may be liable for criminal penalties on the basis of a willful attempt to evade taxes. However, the likelihood of a criminal conviction under these circumstances is reduced by the Supreme Court's decision in the Cheek case (discussed above).*

☞ *Example. Rev. J's church failed to designate a portion of his 1997 compensation as a housing allowance. In January of 1998, Rev. J had his church board retroactively designate a 1997 housing allowance although he knew that retroactive housing allowances are not excludable in computing income taxes. He claims a housing allowance exclusion on his 1997 tax return which results in a $4,000 understatement of his tax liability. Rev. J may be subject to any of the following penalties: (1) the negligence penalty, which would be 20% of the underpayment of*

$4,000 (for a total penalty of $800); (2) a substantial understatement penalty, which would be 20% of the underpayment of $4,000 (for a total penalty of $800); (3) if the IRS could establish that Rev. J acted fraudulently, it could assess the fraud penalty, which would be 75% of the underpayment of $4,000 (for a total penalty of $3,000). These penalties are in addition to Rev. J's obligation to pay the $4,000 tax deficiency (plus interest).

☞ *Example.* Rev. G purchases a home in 1997, and makes a large down payment of $25,000. Other housing expenses for the year amount to an additional $15,000. Rev. G's total church compensation for the year is $50,000, of which $40,000 was designated as a housing allowance. Rev. G is aware that in 1971 the IRS ruled that a housing allowance exclusion may never exceed the fair rental value of a home (furnished, including utilities). The fair rental value of Rev. G's home is $15,000. Nevertheless, he claims a housing allowance exclusion of the full $40,000 in computing his income taxes. This results in an understatement of his income taxes of $6,000. Under these facts, Rev. G may be subject to any one of the following penalties (in addition to having to pay the tax deficiency of $6,000): (1) the negligence penalty, which would be 20% of the underpayment of $6,000 (for a total penalty of $1,200); (2) a substantial understatement penalty, which would be 20% of the underpayment of $6,000 (for a total penalty of $1,200); (3) if the IRS could establish that Rev. G acted fraudulently, it could assess the fraud penalty, which would be 75% of the underpayment of $6,000 (for a total penalty of $4,500).

☞ *Example.* Same facts as the preceding example, except that Rev. G makes an "adequate disclosure" of his position by including a properly completed IRS Form 8275 with his Form 1040. Such a disclosure may avoid the penalty for substantial understatement of tax—at the cost of disclosing to the IRS the questionable position that is being asserted. To avoid the penalty, Rev. G's disclosed position must be reasonable. Note that even if Rev. G does not file the Form 8275 disclosure statement, he may avoid the substantial understatement penalty if he can demonstrate that he had "reasonable cause" for his position. This may be possible under these facts, since the reasonableness of the "fair rental value" limitation imposed by the IRS in 1971 is itself questionable (see chapter 6 for more details).

13. Limitations periods

For how many years can the IRS question or audit your income tax returns? Consider the following 3 rules:

3 years. In general, the IRS may audit your returns to assess any additional taxes within 3 years after the date a return is filed (or within three years after the due date of the return if later).

☞ *Example.* Rev. W filed his 1994 tax return on April 10, 1995. The IRS ordinarily may audit Rev. W's 1994 return only if it does so by April 15, 1998.

6 years. The 3-year period during which the IRS may audit your returns is expanded to 6 years if you omit from gross income an amount greater than 25% of the amount reported on your return.

No limit. The IRS can audit returns without any time limitation in any of the following situations: (1) a false or fraudulent return is filed with the intent to evade tax; (2) a taxpayer engages in a willful attempt in any manner to defeat or evade tax; or (3) a failure to file a tax return. *IRC 6501(c).*

14. Should you prepare your own tax returns?

There is no reason why most ministers cannot prepare their own tax returns. While clergy taxes present several unique rules, these rules are not complex. Unfortunately, many persons confuse uniqueness with complexity. With a little effort, most ministers should be able to comprehend these rules sufficiently to prepare their own tax returns. The information provided in this tax guide, together with IRS Publication 17 ("Your Federal Income Tax"), should be all the information needed in most cases. Of course, some ministers will prefer, for a variety of reasons, to have someone else prepare their tax returns. If that is your choice, be sure that you select someone with experience in the preparation of ministers' tax returns (preferably a tax attorney or a CPA). You may wish to share a copy of this book with the person you select.

Before deciding to have someone else prepare your tax return, consider the following:

• First, over half of all income tax returns prepared by "paid preparers" contain errors, according to an IRS study. What were the most common mistakes? Failing to claim the standard deduction; entering dollars and cents in the area for dollars; failing to claim (or incorrectly stating) the amount of a refund; failing to total the multiple entries on Schedule C; filing a Schedule SE though net self-employment earnings are less than $400; using the wrong filing status (joint, head-of-household, etc.); and failing to check the age/blind box.

• Second, "paid preparers" are subject to a penalty of $250 per return for any understatement in taxes that is due to a position for which there is "not a realistic possibility of being sustained on the merits," unless they adequately disclose the position on the tax return. *IRC 6694(a).* The penalty increases to $1,000 if the understatement in taxes is due to "a willful attempt to understate the liability for tax" or "any reckless or intentional disregard of rules or regulations." *IRC 6694(b).* As a result, competent paid preparers (i.e., most attorneys and CPAs) often "play it safe" by taking conservative positions when completing clergy tax returns.

• Third, the IRS has established a "Return Preparers Program" that can trigger audits of *all returns prepared by certain return preparers who intentionally or negligently disregard federal tax law (Code, regulations, and rulings).* To illustrate, hundreds of clergy tax returns prepared by one self-proclaimed clergy tax "authority" (he was neither an attorney nor a CPA) were pulled for audit by the IRS because the Return Preparers Program indicated a pattern of noncompliance with federal tax law. Clergy and church staff should be extremely cautious when dealing with nonprofessional or "mail-order" return preparers, especially those who promise significant tax savings or are not attorneys or CPAs.

Tips on Selecting a Tax Preparer

Let's assume you have decided to have your tax return prepared by a professional. The next step is to find someone who is experienced and competent in the preparation of clergy tax returns. Here are some tips to help you find such a person:

• If possible, stick with a CPA or tax attorney.

• Try to use someone local or nearby.

• Find other clergy in your community who have their tax returns prepared by a professional. Who do they use? Are they pleased? What is the cost? How many clergy tax returns does the person prepare?

• Call CPAs listed in your telephone directory, and ask them if they prepare clergy tax returns. If they do, ask how many they prepare.

• When you find one or more possible candidates, consider asking a few simple questions that should easily be answered by anyone with any experience in handling clergy tax returns. Here are a few examples: *(1) Are ministers employees or self-employed for social security purposes?* Of course, clergy always are self-employed for social security purposes with respect to their ministerial income. *(2) Can I claim my housing allowance exclusion in computing my self-employment taxes?* Absolutely not—ever. *(3) If I report my church wages as an employee, are my wages subject to FICA taxes?* The answer is never. *(4) If I report my church wages as an employee, are my wages subject to income tax withholding?* The answer is no, unless a minister elects voluntary withholding. *(5) What is the minister's housing allowance?* Persons with some familiarity with clergy taxes should be able to answer this question.

B. Filing Status

1. In general

Single. You must file as single if on the last day of last year you were unmarried or separated from your spouse either by divorce or separate maintenance decree and you do not qualify for another filing status. State law governs whether you are married, divorced, or legally separated.

Married. If you were married as of the last day of last year, you and your spouse may be able to file a joint return or you may choose to file separate returns. You are considered to be married even if you are living separate and apart provided that you and your spouse were not legally separated under a decree of divorce or separate maintenance (as noted below, you may be able to report your taxes as a head of household under these circumstances if you meet certain requirements). If your spouse died during the year, you are considered married for the whole year. If you and your spouse both have income, you should figure your tax both on a joint return and on separate returns to see which way gives you the lower tax. In most cases, you will pay more taxes if you file separately. If you do file separately, and one spouse itemizes deductions, the other spouse ordinarily should itemize deductions too since he or she cannot take the standard deduction.

Qualifying widows and widowers. The last year for which you may file a joint return with your deceased spouse is the year of your spouse's death. However, for the two years following the year of death, you may be able to figure your tax using the joint rates. These rates are lower than the rates for single or head of household status. To use the joint rates, you must file as a qualifying widow or widower and meet all of the following conditions: (1) you were entitled to file a joint return with your spouse for the year your spouse died; (2) you did not remarry before the end of the current year; (3) you have a child who qualifies as your dependent for the year; and (4) you paid more than half the cost of keeping up your home, which is the principal home of that child for the entire year.

☞ *Example. Rev. B died in 1995. His surviving spouse has not remarried and has continued during 1996 and 1997 to keep up a home for herself and her 2 dependent children. For 1995 Rev. B's surviving spouse was entitled to file a joint return for herself and her deceased husband. For 1996 and 1997 she may use the joint rates because she is a widow with dependent children.*

Head of household. You may be eligible to file as head of household for 1997 if you were unmarried on the last day of the year. You must also have paid more than half the cost of keeping up a home that was the principal home for more than half the year for you *and* any one or more of a long list of eligible relatives (consult the instructions to Form 1040). More restrictive rules apply if the dependent relative is a parent.

C. Personal Exemptions and Dependents

Taxpayers may deduct an amount for each available personal or dependent exemption in computing taxable income. For 1997, each exemption is worth $2,650. This is an increase of $100 over the 1996 amount. You may claim an exemption for *yourself* and one for your *spouse.* For 1997, the standard deduction amount increases by $1,000 for single persons if either age 65 or older or blind ($2,000 if both) and $800 for married persons filing jointly if either spouse is age 65 or older or blind ($1,600 if a spouse is both age 65 and blind).

You may also claim an exemption for each *dependent* who meets *all five* of the following dependency tests: (1) the dependent must live with you for the entire year as a member of your household or be related to you; (2) the dependent must be a U.S. citizen or resident, or a resident of Canada or Mexico, for some part of the calendar year; (3) the dependent must not file a joint income tax return; (4) the dependent must not have gross income (less social security benefits in most cases) in excess of $2,650 for the year (this test does not apply if the person is a child of yours under age 19 at the end of 1997, or under 24 years of age if a student); and (5) the dependent received more than half of his or her total support during the calendar year from you. Special rules apply for children of divorced or separated parents. For additional discussion of these requirements, see the instructions to Form 1040.

✎ **Key point:** Persons who claim personal exemptions for dependents and the dependent care credit must include on their tax return the name and social security number of each dependent. The IRS can deny a dependency exemption and dependent care credit to any taxpayer who fails to provide the correct social security number of a dependent on his or her tax return. If a person who you expect to claim as a dependent does not have a social security number, either you or that person should apply for one as soon as possible. You can apply for a number by filing IRS Form SS-5 with the Social Security Administration. You can obtain a Form SS-5 from any IRS or social security office. A penalty will not be applied for a failure to list a dependent's social security number on your 1997 tax return if the dependent was born after November 30, 1997.

❖ **New in 1997.** The phaseout of the personal exemption for high-income taxpayers begins at a higher amount of income in 1997.

Phase-out of personal exemption for high-income taxpayers. The amount claimed as a deduction for personal exemptions is phased out for certain high-income taxpayers. For 1997, the phaseout applies to (1) married taxpayers filing jointly and having at least $181,800 of adjusted gross income, and (2) single taxpayers having at least $121,200 of adjusted gross income. The instructions to Form 1040 (line 37) explain how to reduce the personal exemption amount for taxpayers in these categories.

❖ **New in 1998.** Under current law, the standard deduction of a taxpayer who is claimed as a dependent on another's tax return cannot exceed the lesser of (1) the standard deduction for an individual ($4,150 for 1997), or (2) the greater of $500 (indexed for inflation) or the dependent's earned income. In other words, a minor child who works outside the home, and who is claimed as a dependent on his parents' tax return, is eligible for a reduced standard deduction based on this formula. Congress enacted legislation in 1997 that increases the standard deduction for a taxpayer who is claimed as a dependent on another's tax return to the lesser of (1) the standard deduction for individuals, or (2) the greater of (a) $500 (indexed for inflation), or (b) the individual's earned income plus $250. The $250 amount will be indexed for inflation after 1998. The new standard deduction rules take effect in 1998.

D. Tax Withholding and Estimated Tax

The federal income tax is a "pay-as-you-go" tax. You must pay your tax as you earn or receive income during the year. There are two ways to pay as you go—tax withholding and quarterly estimated tax payments. These two procedures will be summarized in this section.

1. Withholding

✎ **Key point:** clergy are exempt from income tax withholding whether they report their income taxes as employees or as self-employed

✎ **Key point:** clergy who report their income taxes as employees can elect voluntary withholding

Since 1943, Congress has required most employers to withhold federal income taxes from employees' wages as they are paid. However, Congress specifically exempted "services performed by a duly ordained, commissioned, or licensed minister of a church in the exercise of his ministry." *IRC 3401(a)(9)*. As a result, a church is *not* required to withhold income taxes from wages paid to ministers who report and pay their income taxes as employees. This exemption of clergy only applies to services performed in the exercise of ministry. It does not apply to nonminister church employees. To illustrate, one federal court ruled that the services of a church secretary, organist, custodian, and choir director were not covered by the exemption, and accordingly the church was required to withhold taxes from the wages of such workers (all of whom were treated as employees by the church). *Eighth Street Baptist Church, Inc. v. United States, 295 F. Supp. 1400 (D. Kan. 1969)*. A church's withholding obligations with respect to nonminister employees are covered in chapter 11. Again, the exemption of clergy wages from income tax withholding applies only with respect to "services performed in the exercise of ministry." This significant term is defined fully in chapter 3.

Ministers who are self-employed for income tax purposes report and prepay their income taxes and social security taxes by means of the estimated tax procedure (discussed below). Self-employed persons are not subject to tax withholding.

IRS "Tax Guide for Churches". In 1994 the IRS released a "Tax Guide for Churches" (Publication 1828) that contains the following paragraph on the application of tax withholding to ministers:

The remuneration that a church pays to its duly ordained, commissioned, or licensed minister(s) for their services is not subject to mandatory Federal income tax withholding, nor is it subject to the Federal Insurance Contribution Act (FICA). However, a church is still required to report a minister's compensation to the IRS on a Form W-2. The earnings that a minister earns in the performance of his or her ministry are generally subject to self-employment taxes under the Self-Employment Contributions Act (SECA). A minister may voluntarily request that a church withhold income taxes from the amounts paid him or her. This is accomplished by having the minister furnish the church with a completed Form W-4, Employee's Withholding Allowance Certificate. These withheld amounts would then be reflected on the minister's Form W-2.

IRS audit guidelines for ministers. In 1995 the IRS published audit guidelines for use by its agents in auditing ministers. The guidelines contain the following statement regarding the application of tax withholding to ministers: "Although they are generally considered employees under the common law rules, payment for services as a minister is considered income from self employment and is not subject to FICA taxes or income tax withholding (if the employer and employee agree, an election can be made to have income taxes withheld)."

voluntary withholding

A church and its minister (who reports his or her income taxes as an employee) can voluntarily agree to subject the minister's compensation to income tax withholding. Some ministers find *voluntary withholding* attractive since it avoids the additional work and discipline associated with the estimated tax procedure. A minister who elects to enter into a voluntary withholding arrangement with his or her church need only file a completed IRS Form W-4 (employee's withholding allowance certificate) with the church. The filing of this form is deemed to be a request for voluntary withholding. Voluntary withholding arrangements may be terminated at any time by either the church or minister individually, or by mutual consent of both. Alternatively, a minister can stipulate that the voluntary withholding arrangement terminates on a specified date. Of course, a voluntary withholding arrangement will affect the church's quarterly Form 941 (see chapter 11).

Remember that ministers are always deemed to be self-employed for social security purposes with respect to services performed in the exercise of ministry. Therefore, a church whose minister elects voluntary withholding is only obligated to withhold the minister's federal income tax liability. The minister is still required to use the estimated tax procedure to report and prepay his or her self-employment tax (the social security tax on self-employed persons). Such a result is unsatisfactory since it still requires the minister to file quarterly estimated tax payments (Form

---

Only 29 percent (about 3 out of 10) taxpayers are able to itemize deductions on Schedule A

This interesting statistic is buried in the *Statistics of Income Bulletin* issued by the IRS in June of 1994. What is the relevance of this statistic? *It demonstrates that 7 out of 10 ministers and lay church workers who report their federal income taxes as employees (or who are reclassified as employees by the IRS) will be unable to deduct either their unreimbursed business expenses or business expenses reimbursed under a nonaccountable arrangement.* Here's why. Employees can claim unreimbursed business expenses (including travel and transportation expenses), and business expenses reimbursed by their church under a nonaccountable arrangement, only as miscellaneous itemized deductions on Schedule A. Employees who cannot itemize deductions will not be able to deduct any of these expenses. This is particularly unfortunate for employees whose business expenses are reimbursed under a *nonaccountable* plan, since they must include the full amount of all the expense reimbursements as taxable income but they are denied any deduction of their expenses. Reimbursed expenses are nonaccountable if the employee was not required to or did not "account" to the employer for the expenses *or* was not required to or did not return any "excess reimbursements" (employer reimbursements in excess of substantiated expenses) to the employer. The most common form of nonaccountable reimbursement is a monthly car allowance paid to a church employee without any requirement that actual business expenses be substantiated. Other examples of nonaccountable arrangements include: (1) a church reimburses business expenses without requiring adequate written substantiation (with receipts for all expenses of $75 or more) of the amount, date, place, and business purpose of each expense; (2) a church only reimburses business expenses once each year; or (3) a church provides clergy or lay staff with travel advances and requires no accounting for the use of these funds. In addition, most miscellaneous expenses (including unreimbursed and unsubstantiated reimbursed employee business expenses) are deductible on Schedule A only to the extent they exceed 2% of adjusted gross income (only 50% of business meals and entertainment are counted).

1040-ES). Ministers who report their income taxes as employees (and who are not exempt from social security) should file an amended W-4 form (withholding allowance certificate), indicating on line 6 an additional amount of cash to be withheld from each pay period that will be sufficient to pay the estimated self-employment tax liability by the end of the year. IRS Publication 517 specifically states that "if you perform your services as an employee of the church (under the common law rules), you may be able to enter into a voluntary withholding agreement with your employer, the church, to cover any income *and self-employment tax* that may be due" (emphasis added).

A church whose minister has elected voluntary withholding (and who is not exempt from social security taxes) simply withholds an additional amount from each paycheck to cover the minister's estimated self-employment tax liability for the year, and then reports this additional amount as additional *income tax* (not "FICA" tax) withheld on its quarterly 941 forms. The excess income tax withheld is a credit against tax that the minister claims on his or her federal income tax return (Form 1040, line 54), and it in effect is applied against the minister's self-employment tax liability. Since any tax paid by voluntary withholding is deemed to be timely paid, a minister paying his or her self-employment tax through this procedure will not be liable for any underpayment penalty (assuming that a sufficient amount of taxes are in fact withheld). Clergy who report their income taxes as employees should seriously consider the convenience of voluntary withholding (with respect to *both* income taxes and self-employment taxes).

A self-employed minister is free to enter into an "unofficial" withholding arrangement whereby the church withholds a portion of his or her compensation each week and deposits it in a church account, and then distributes the balance to the minister in advance of each quarterly estimated tax payment due date. No W-4 forms should be used, and the "withholdings" are not reported on Form 941.

A church's withholding obligations under federal law are explained (and illustrated) fully in chapter 11.

2. Estimated tax

✎ **Key point: clergy compensation is exempt from federal income tax withholding, whether clergy report their income taxes as employees or as self-employed**

✎ **Key point: clergy must prepay their income taxes and self-employment taxes using the estimated tax procedure (unless they elect voluntary withholding)**

Since compensation paid to clergy who report and pay their federal income taxes as employees ordinarily is exempt from withholding (see above), minister-employees must report and prepay their federal income taxes by means of the estimated tax procedure if they do not request voluntary withholding. Self-employed ministers are similarly exempt from tax withholding, and accordingly should report and prepay their federal income taxes by means of the estimated tax procedure. In addition, since *all* ministers always are treated as self-employed for social security purposes with respect to services performed in the exercise of ministry, they ordinarily must use the estimated tax procedure to report and prepay their social security taxes (assuming they are not exempt)—unless they have entered into a voluntary withholding arrangement with their employing church that includes the withholding of self-employment taxes, as described earlier in this section. Estimated taxes are computed and reported on IRS Form 1040-ES. The exemption of ministers from income tax withholding, coupled with an unfamiliarity with the es-

timated tax requirements, has induced many younger and inexperienced ministers to refrain from reporting or paying their taxes. It is essential that ministers be familiar with the rules discussed below.

Generally, you should make estimated tax payments for 1998 if your estimated tax for 1998 will be $1,000 or more and the total amount of income tax that will be withheld from your 1998 income will be less than the lesser of (1) 90% of the tax to be shown on your 1998 income tax return, or (2) 100% of the tax shown on your 1997 income tax return (if your 1997 return covered all twelve months of the year). If you are required to pay estimated taxes, but fail to do so, you will be subject to an "underpayment penalty". Since the penalty is figured separately for each quarterly period, you may owe a penalty for an earlier payment period even if you later paid enough to make up the underpayment. If you did not pay enough tax by the due date of each of the payment periods, you may owe a penalty even if you are due a refund when you file your income tax return!

✎ **Key point: stated differently, if your estimated taxes for the current year will be $500 or more (after subtracting any tax withholdings and credits), then you will owe a penalty for not paying quarterly estimated taxes to the IRS. But, the penalty is avoided if the estimated taxes that you pay this year are at least (1) 90% of your tax liability for the current year, or (2) 100% of your tax liability for the previous year (if your tax return covered the entire year).**

❖ **New in 1998. Taxpayers are subject to an "addition to tax" for any underpayment of estimated taxes. In the past, this penalty was not assessed if the total tax liability for the year (reduced by any withheld tax and estimated tax payments) was less than $500. Congress enacted legislation in 1997 that increases this amount to $1,000, beginning in 1998.**

☞ *Example. Rev. T's 1997 income tax return (which was for the entire calendar year) showed a tax of $7,000. Rev. T projects that the tax to be shown on her 1998 return will be $7,500. She also anticipates that no taxes will be withheld from her 1998 income as a minister (her only source of income). Rev. T is exempt from social security taxes. Under these facts, Rev. T's estimated tax will be $7,500 (tax liability of $7,500 with no withholding). Since Rev. T's estimated tax will be at least $500, and none of it will be subject to withholding, she must make estimated tax payments for 1998.*

☞ *Example. Same facts as the preceding example, except that Rev. T has entered into a voluntary withholding agreement with her church, and estimates that $6,500 will be withheld from her compensation in 1998. Must she make estimated tax payments? Yes, since the total amount of income taxes to be withheld from her compensation in 1998* *is less than the lesser of (1) 90% of her estimated total tax liability for 1998 (90% x $7,500 = $6,750), or (2) 100% of the tax shown on her 1997 return ($7,000). If she fails to pay estimated taxes, she will be subject to a penalty (as explained below).*

estimated tax procedure for 1998

The 4-step procedure for reporting and prepaying estimated taxes for 1998 is summarized below:

Step 1. Obtain a copy of IRS Form 1040-ES. Obtain a copy of IRS Form 1040-ES prior to April 15, 1998. You will note that Form 1040-ES consists of a worksheet, instructions, and four dated "payment vouchers." You can obtain a copy from any IRS office, many public libraries, or by calling the toll-free IRS forms "hotline" at 1-800-TAX-FORM (1-800-829-3676).

Step 2. Compute estimated taxes for 1998. Compute your estimated tax for 1998 on the Form 1040-ES worksheet. This is done by estimating adjusted gross income and then subtracting estimated adjustments, deductions, exemptions, and credits. Using the data set forth on your previous year's tax return is a helpful starting point. To determine your estimated taxes for 1998, estimated taxable income is multiplied by the applicable tax rate contained in the Tax Rate Schedule reproduced on Form 1040-ES. Remember to include your estimated social security tax on the worksheet if you are not exempt, and to include your housing allowance exclusion in computing your estimated earnings subject to the self-employment tax (the housing allowance is excluded from income only in computing your income tax liability, not your self-employment tax).

Step 3. Pay estimated taxes in quarterly installments. If estimated taxes (federal income taxes and self-employment taxes) are more than $1,000 for 1998, and the total amount of taxes to be withheld from your compensation is less than the lesser of (1) 90% of the total taxes (income and social security) to be shown on your actual 1998 tax return, or (2) 100% of the total taxes (income and social security) shown on your 1997 return, then you must pay one-fourth of your total estimated taxes for 1998 in four quarterly installments as follows:

For the Period	Due Date
Jan. 1 - Mar. 31	April 15, 1998
April 1 - May 31	June 15, 1998
June 1 -Aug. 31	September 15, 1998
Sep. 1 - Dec. 31	January 15, 1999

If the due date for making an estimated tax payment falls on a Saturday, Sunday, or legal holiday, the payment will be on time if you make it on the next day that is not a Saturday, Sunday, or legal holiday.

You must send each payment to the IRS, accompanied by one of the four payment vouchers contained in Form 1040-ES. If you paid estimated taxes last year, you should receive a copy of your 1998 1040-ES in the mail with payment vouchers preprinted with your name, address, and social security number. If you did not pay estimated taxes last year, you will have to get a copy of Form 1040-ES from the IRS. After you make your first payment (April 15, 1998), you should receive a Form 1040-ES package in your name with the preprinted information. There is a separate payment voucher for each of the four quarterly payment periods. Each one has the due date printed on it. Be sure to use the correct payment voucher.

A minister may become liable for estimated tax payments midway through a year. For example, a minister may begin his or her first pastoral assignment during the summer of 1998, or a minister may change churches midway through a year, leaving a church that voluntarily withheld taxes and going to another church that does not withhold taxes. In such a case, the minister should submit a payment voucher by the next filing deadline accompanied by a check for a prorated portion of the entire estimated tax liability for the year.

☞ *Example. Rev. K graduates from seminary in May of 1998, and assumes the position of associate pastor of First Church on July 20, 1998. Rev. K had no income for the year until he began working for First Church. Rev. K estimates his total tax liability for 1998 to be $5,000. He should obtain a Form 1040-ES, and submit the third payment voucher on or before September 15, 1998 along with a check for one-half of the total tax (i.e., $2,500). He should send the remaining half with his January 15, 1999 payment voucher.*

After making your first or second estimated tax payment, changes in your income, deductions, credits, or exemptions may make it necessary for you to refigure your estimated tax and adjust your remaining quarterly payments accordingly.

☞ *Example. Rev. H is senior minister at First Church. His church board fails to designate a housing allowance for 1998 until May 1, 1998. Rev. H's April 15th estimated tax payment was based on his annual earnings less an anticipated housing allowance exclusion. The delayed designation of a housing allowance will almost certainly affect Rev. H's estimated taxes for 1998, and accordingly his remaining quarterly payments should be recalculated so that an underpayment penalty is avoided.*

Step 4. Compute actual taxes at the end of the year. After the close of 1998, compute your actual tax liability on Form 1040. Only then will you know your actual income, deductions, exclusions, and credits. Estimated tax payments rarely reflect actual tax liability. Most taxpayers' estimated tax payments are either more or less than actual taxes as computed on Form 1040. The consequences of overpayment and underpayment of estimated taxes is summarized below.

• **Overpayment (estimated tax payments exceed actual tax liability).** If you overpaid your estimated taxes (i.e., your estimated tax payments plus any withholding were *more* than your actual taxes computed on Form 1040) you can elect to have the overpayment credited against your first 1999 quarterly estimated tax payment or spread out in any way you choose among any or all of your next four quarterly installments. Alternatively, you can request a refund of the overpayment.

• **Underpayment (estimated tax payments were less than actual tax liability).** If you underpaid your estimated taxes (i.e., your estimated tax payments plus any withholding were *less* than your actual taxes computed on Form 1040) you may have to pay a **penalty**. In general, you may owe a penalty for 1998 if you do not pay at least the smaller of (1) 90% of your 1998 actual taxes, or (2) 100% of your 1997 actual taxes (your 1997 return must cover a 12-month period). The penalty is computed separately for each quarterly payment period. You will not have an underpayment for any quarter in 1998 in which your estimated tax payment is paid by the due date for that quarter and equals or exceeds the lesser of 22.5% of the tax shown on your 1998 return or 25% of the tax shown on your 1997 return (if your 1997 return covered all twelve months of the year). The penalty is figured separately for each quarterly payment period, so you may owe the penalty for an early period even if you later pay enough to make up the underpayment. Contrary to popular belief, payment of your entire 1998 estimated tax liability by January 15, 1999, or by April 15, 1999, will *not* relieve you of the penalty if you did not pay the estimated income tax due earlier in your tax year. Waiting until the end of the year to pay the full amount of estimated taxes will result in an underpayment penalty for the three preceding quarters. *Veis v. United States, 88-2 USTC ¶ 9616 (D. Mont. 1988).* If, however, you file your 1998 Form 1040 and pay the actual taxes due by *January 31, 1999*, you will have no penalty for the payment due on January 15, 1999 if you failed to make your fourth quarterly payment by that date.

☞ *Example. Rev. J does not elect voluntary withholding of any taxes, and does not use the estimated tax procedure. Instead, he simply computes his taxes for the year and sends in a check with his Form 1040. Rev. J will be assessed a penalty for failure to pay each of the four quarterly payments that he missed. This is not a recommended practice since Rev. J will needlessly pay penalties and interest in addition to his tax liability.*

☞ *Example. Rev. K estimates that his taxes for 1998 will be $8,000. He pays his first quarterly installment of $2,000 on April 15, 1998, but only pays $1,000 for his second quarterly installment on June 15, 1998 and another $1,000 for his third quarterly installment on September 15, 1998. He "makes up the difference" by paying a fourth quarterly installment of $4,000 on January 15, 1999. While Rev. K has paid his entire estimated tax of $8,000, he will be assessed an underpayment penalty for failure to pay his full second and third installments on time.*

✎ **Key point: higher-income taxpayers need to estimate their taxes accurately to avoid the underpayment penalty.**

Form 2210. You can use Form 2210 to see if you owe a penalty and to figure the amount of the penalty. If you owe a penalty and do not attach Form 2210 to your Form 1040, the IRS will compute your penalty and send you a bill. You do not have to fill out a Form 2210 or pay any penalty if either of two conditions apply: (1) your total tax less income tax withheld is less than $1,000, or (2) you had no tax liability last year and you were a United States citizen or resident for the entire year.

The IRS can waive the underpayment penalty if the underpayment was due to casualty, disaster, or other unusual circumstance and it would be inequitable to impose the penalty.

For further information, obtain a copy of IRS Publication 505 ("Tax Withholding and Estimated Tax").

Special rule for high-income taxpayers. High-income taxpayers no longer can avoid the underpayment penalty by paying estimated taxes for the current year of at least 100% of last year's tax. A high-income taxpayer is one with adjusted gross income for the previous year of at least $150,000. For such persons, the 100% rule is replaced with a 110% rule, meaning that they will be subject to an underpayment penalty unless they have paid estimated taxes for the current year of at least the lesser of (1) 90% of the current year's actual tax liability, or (2) 110% of last year's actual tax liability. For persons who are not high-income taxpayers, the 90% and 100% rules described above continue to apply.

❖ **New in 1998. Congress enacted legislation in 1997 that changes the 110 percent of last year's tax liability rule (for high-income taxpayers) to 100 percent of the previous year's tax liability in 1998; 105 percent of the previous year's tax liability in 1999, 2000, and 2001; and 112 percent of the previous year's tax liability in 2002.**

E. If Your Return Is Examined

Tax returns are examined to verify the correctness of your reported taxes. An IRS computer program selects most returns that are examined. Under this program (called the discriminant function system) selected entries on your return are evaluated and the return is given a score. Returns are then screened by IRS personnel. Those returns having the highest probability for error are selected for examination. Some returns are randomly selected for a comprehensive audit under the taxpayer compliance measurement program (TCMP). Other returns are selected because of discrepancies among forms (i.e., stated compensation differs from amounts reported on W-2 or 1099-MISC forms). An examination of your return does not suggest a suspicion of dishonesty. It may not even result in more tax. Many audits are closed without any change in your reported tax, and in others taxpayers receive refunds.

The examination (or "audit") may be conducted by correspondence, or it may take place in your home or place of business, an IRS office, or the office of your attorney or accountant. The place and method of examination is determined by the IRS, but your wishes will be considered. You may act on your own behalf or you may have someone represent you or accompany you. An attorney, CPA, "enrolled agent" (someone other than an attorney or CPA who is enrolled to practice before the IRS), or the person who prepared your return and signed it as the preparer may represent or accompany you. You must furnish your representative (if any) with a power of attorney (Form 2848).

If your return is selected for examination, you will be contacted by the IRS and asked to assemble records supporting the items on your return that are being investigated. When the examination is completed, you will be advised of any proposed change in your taxes and the reasons for any such change. If you agree with the findings of the examiner, you will be asked to sign an agreement form. By signing the form, you indicate that you agree with the changes. If you owe any additional tax, you may pay it when you sign the agreement.

If you do not agree with changes proposed by the examiner, the examiner will explain your appeal rights. This includes your right to request an immediate meeting with a supervisor to explain your position if your examination takes place in an IRS office. If agreement is reached, your case will be closed. If agreement is not reached at this meeting, or if your examination occurs outside of an IRS office, you will be sent: (1) a letter notifying you of your right to appeal within 30 days; (2) a copy of the examination report explaining the proposed adjustments; (3) an agreement or waiver form; and (4) a copy of IRS Publication 5 (which explains your appeal rights in detail). If after receiving the examiner's report you decide to agree with it, simply sign the agreement or waiver form and return it to the examiner. If you decide not to agree with the examination report, you may appeal your case within the IRS or take it immediately to the federal courts. For a complete explanation, obtain a copy of IRS Publication 556. These procedures are summarized in Illustration 1-1.

Taking your dispute with the IRS to court. Have you ever wondered what your chances are if you appeal an adverse IRS decision? The most recent IRS data indicates that taxpayers who challenged IRS audit findings in court did very poorly. Only 4% won their cases in the Tax Court; 23.2% won their cases in federal district courts; and 19% won their cases in federal appeals courts. Taxpayers should bear these statistics in mind before incurring potentially substantial legal fees to appeal adverse IRS rulings to the courts.

F. "Offers in Compromise"

Are any options available to clergy who cannot afford to pay their taxes? This is an important question. Many clergy have been audited by the IRS and assessed several thousands of dollars of taxes and penalties, without any prospect for paying their bill. In

some cases, they incorrectly claimed a housing allowance exclusion in computing both their income taxes and self-employment taxes (it is an exclusion only in computing income taxes). In other cases, clergy who have reported their income taxes as self-employed are reclassified as employees by the IRS, which often results in hundreds if not thousands of dollars in additional taxes (since business expenses are shifted from Schedule C to Schedule A, where they are not deductible by clergy who cannot itemize their expenses). Some clergy have incorrectly assumed that they are exempt from social security, though they have never received IRS confirmation of their exempt status. Obviously, these ministers often face many thousands of dollars in taxes and penalties. For whatever reason, clergy sometimes face enormous tax liabilities without any reasonable prospect of payment. In many cases, these liabilities are due to the complex and confusing tax rules that apply to clergy. What can be done in such cases? Some will appeal the IRS determination in court. This will take time, and the cost can be significant. There is another option that is available in some cases—the "offer in compromise." This can be a simple, quick, and relatively inexpensive alternative to the courts. An offer in compromise is an agreement between a taxpayer and the IRS to settle an outstanding tax obligation if there is no reasonable possibility that it can be fully paid. In 1992, the IRS announced new rules for evaluating offers in compromise. The new rules are summarized below:

• The IRS will accept an offer in compromise "when it is unlikely that the tax liability can be collected in full and the amount offered reasonably reflects collection potential." The new rules further specify: "In cases where an offer in compromise appears to be a viable solution to a tax delinquency, the IRS employee assigned the case will discuss the compromise alternative with the taxpayer and, when necessary, assist in preparing the required forms. The taxpayer will be responsible for initiating the first specific proposal for compromise. . . . Taxpayers are expected to provide reasonable documentation to verify their ability to pay. The ultimate goal is a compromise which is in the best interest of both the taxpayer and the IRS. Acceptance of an adequate offer will also result in creating, for the taxpayer, an expectation of and a fresh start toward compliance with all future filing and payment requirements."

• When an analysis of the taxpayer's assets, liabilities, income and expenses shows that a tax liability cannot be realistically collected in full, the

---

IRS Expresses Concern over Offers in Compromise Program

A high-level IRS officer has noted that the IRS is pleased with the popularity of the program, but she expressed concern whether the program is achieving its objectives of increased tax compliance and collections. She added, "the program's growth may strain the IRS's collection resources and . . . adversely affect voluntary compliance if taxpayers believe the program is too liberal."

possibility of an offer in compromise will be discussed with the taxpayer. The taxpayer will be advised what an offer is, what the IRS procedures and policies are with respect to offers, what forms must be completed, and what benefits the taxpayer will receive from an offer acceptance. Taxpayers will also be advised that collection will normally be withheld unless it is determined that the offer is a delaying tactic and collection is in jeopardy. Before an offer is submitted, the taxpayer will not be told what specifically to offer. The taxpayer will be responsible for initiating the first specific proposal for compromise. However, the taxpayer should be advised that the proposal should not be a "fishing expedition" but a legitimate compromise proposal based on the ability to pay. The taxpayer will be advised that the service does not operate on the theory that "something is better than nothing."

• Submission of an offer does not constitute acceptance. No offer is accepted until the appropriate delegated official approves acceptance and the taxpayer is notified by letter that the offer has been accepted.

Preparation of the offer. An offer in compromise is made by the taxpayer and submitted to the IRS. The taxpayer must take the initiative. The offer is made on IRS Form 656. The offer must contain the following information: (1) The name, address, and social security number of the taxpayer. (2) A listing of all unpaid tax liabilities sought to be compromised (including the type of tax and year of tax). (3) The amount offered by the taxpayer in compromise of the listed tax liabilities. (4) Whether the offer is a lump sum cash offer, or a "deferred payment" offer (paid in installments). (5) An explanation of why the taxpayer's offer should be accepted. If the offer is based only on *doubt as to collectability,* the taxpayer must submit a detailed financial statement which describes why the IRS cannot collect more than the amount offered from his or her assets and present and future income (taking into account the fact that the IRS generally has 10 years to collect the liability). The financial statement is prepared on IRS Form 433-A. (6) The offer must be signed by the taxpayer.

IRS response. The IRS ordinarily will suspend all collection activity while considering a taxpayer's offer in compromise. Further, within 30 calendar days from receipt of the offer, the IRS examining officer should contact the taxpayer. The taxpayer should be notified of any information that the examiner needs to make a decision. The new rules specify: "In evaluating a taxpayer's offer, the starting point in the consideration of an offer submitted based on doubt as to collectability is the value of the taxpayer's assets less encumbrances which have priority over the federal tax lien. . . . The Service also takes into consideration the amount that can be collected from the taxpayer's future income. In evaluating those future prospects, the taxpayer's education, profession or trade, age and experience, health, past and present income will be considered. In evaluating future income potential an evaluation must be made of the likelihood that any increase in real income will be available to pay the delinquent taxes. The IRS needs to take into consideration the increasing cost of living as a factor in determining amounts potentially collectible from future

income." Finally, the new rules provide: "The examining officer should determine what would be an acceptable offer. The taxpayer will be given an opportunity to increase the offer. Because asset values are generally not carved in stone, offer examiners should remain flexible towards negotiating an offer that, considering all factors, would be in the government's best interests."

The new rules further provide that "if an offer in compromise appears to be a viable solution to a tax delinquency, the IRS employee assigned the case will discuss the compromise alternative with the taxpayer and, when necessary, assist in preparing the required forms. The taxpayer will be responsible for initiating the first specific proposal for compromise."

The offer in compromise is an option that is available to clergy facing substantial tax liabilities without any reasonable prospect of payment.

❖ **New in 1997. The IRS announced in 1997 that it had accepted a record 27,673 offers in compromise in 1996—up from 1,995 in 1991. These offers settled $2.2 billion of tax liabilities for $287 million. About half of all offers are accepted, an IRS official disclosed.**

✎ **Key point: in the past, the success of offers in compromise has been stifled by the requirement that the IRS chief counsel approve all such offers if the amount of unpaid tax is $500 or more. This low threshold meant that the IRS chief counsel had to personally approve the vast majority of offers in compromise. In many cases, offers that were approved at lower levels of the IRS were denied by the chief counsel. The Taxpayer Bill of Rights 2, enacted by Congress in 1996, addressed this problem and requires IRS chief counsel approval of offers in compromise only if the amount of unpaid tax is $50,000 or more.**

✎ **Key point: the IRS in some cases enters into installment agreements with taxpayers who are unable to pay a tax liability in a lump sum. The Taxpayer Bill of Rights 2, enacted by Congress in 1996, requires the IRS to notify taxpayers 30 days before modifying or terminating any installment agreement for any reason other than that the collection of tax is in jeopardy. The IRS must include in the notification an explanation of why it intends to take this action.**

G. The "Taxpayer Bill of Rights"

In 1988 Congress enacted the first "Taxpayer Bill of Rights." This legislation provided taxpayers with a number of important protections. In 1996 Congress enacted a second Taxpayer Bill of Rights that builds on what was done in 1988. The new law contains more than 40 provisions. The key provisions in both laws are summarized below.

Taxpayer Bill of Rights 1

1. Disclosure of rights. Previously, there has been no legal requirement that a taxpayer who is being audited by the IRS be provided with a written statement of his or her rights and the obligations of the IRS during the audit process. Under taxpayer bill of rights, when the IRS contacts a taxpayer concerning the "determination or collection" of any tax, it is required to provide a written statement of the rights of the taxpayer and the obligations of the IRS during the audit, appeals, refund, and collection processes. In addition, the IRS is required to take action to ensure that taxpayers are not sent *multiple statements* as a result of a single audit. Congress must approve the written statement of taxpayer rights before it is used.

2. Taxpayer interviews. The IRS typically interviews taxpayers whose returns are being audited. However, a number of questions have arisen over the years regarding taxpayer interviews. For example, how does the IRS determine the time and place of such interviews? Are taxpayers allowed to tape-record the interview? Who can the taxpayer take with him or her to the interview? Under the taxpayer bill of rights, the IRS is required to publish regulations listing standards for determining the selection of a reasonable time and place for taxpayer interviews. The taxpayer bill of rights also permits taxpayers, upon advance notice to the IRS, to make an **audio recording** of any in-person IRS interview at the taxpayer's expense and with the taxpayer's own equipment. IRS employees are also authorized to tape-record interviews, but only if the taxpayer is notified in advance and is supplied a copy of a transcript of the recording upon request (the taxpayer must pay for the transcript). This is a significant provision, since in the past many clergy have been unsure whether they could tape-record interviews with IRS agents. Note that the making of audio recordings is allowed only after the taxpayer gives advance notice to the IRS. The law does not specify how far "in advance" the notice must be made, so presumably a taxpayer could notify an IRS agent immediately before the interview begins of his or her intention to record it. The IRS does not have the authority to deny a taxpayer's right to record the interview, provided that the recording is made at the taxpayer's expense, on the taxpayer's equipment, and following advance notice of the intent to record. The IRS has released guidelines for audio recording of interviews by taxpayers. The guidelines are quoted below in their entirety:

(1) Requests by taxpayers of their authorized representatives to make audio recordings of examination or collection proceedings, will be approved by the IRS official or employee conducting the interview under the following conditions: (a) the taxpayer or authorized representative supplies the recording equipment; (b) the IRS may produce its own recording of the proceedings; (c) the recording takes place in a suitable location, ordinarily in an Internal Revenue Service office where equipment is available to produce the Service's recording; and (d) all participants in the proceeding other than IRS personnel must consent to the making of the audio recording and all participants must identify themselves and their roles in the proceeding.

(2) Requests by taxpayers or authorized representatives to make audio recordings of examination proceedings or collection proceedings must be addressed to the officer or employee of the IRS who is conducting the interview and must be received by the IRS no later than 10 calendar days prior to the interview that is to be recorded. If 10 calendar days' advance notice of intent to record is not given, the IRS may, in its discretion, conduct the interview as scheduled or set a new date. (3) When the IRS intends to record a taxpayer interview that is part of an examination or collection proceeding, it will so inform the taxpayer or authorized representative no later than 10 calendar days prior to the interview that is to be recorded. This requirement does not apply where the taxpayer has already submitted a request to make a recording and the IRS is merely seeking to make its own recording. (4) Requests by taxpayers or their authorized representatives for a copy or transcript of an audio recording procured by the IRS must be addressed to the official or representative conducting the interview and must be received by the IRS no later than 30 calendar days after the date of the recording. However, the IRS will attempt to accommodate requests received at a later date. All requests must be accompanied by payment of the costs of duplication or transcription. (5) At the outset of the recording, the official or employee conducting an examination or meeting that is to be recorded will identify himself or herself, the date, the time, the place, and the purpose of the proceeding. (6) When written records are presented or discussed during the proceeding, they must be described in sufficient detail to make the audio recording a meaningful record when matched with the other documentation contained in the case file. (7) At the conclusion of the proceeding, the IRS official or employee will state that the proceeding has been completed and that the recording is ended. *IRS Notice 89-51.*

Prior to the initial in-person audit interview, the IRS must explain to taxpayers the audit process and the taxpayer's rights.

As under prior law, a taxpayer may be represented during a taxpayer interview by any attorney, CPA, or enrolled agent, provided that such representative has a properly executed "power of attorney" (IRS Form 2848) from the taxpayer. The taxpayer bill of rights clarifies, however, that a taxpayer need not be present at an interview at which the taxpayer's authorized representative is present (the IRS ordinarily can only request that taxpayers voluntarily attend). Further, if a taxpayer appears without his or her representative during an IRS interview, and during the interview clearly states that he or she wishes to consult with the authorized representative, the *interview must be suspended* to afford the taxpayer a reasonable opportunity to consult with the representative. However, the IRS is permitted to issue a summons requiring the presence of both parties in the event that the taxpayer repeatedly suspends an interview to consult with representatives not present at the interview.

The taxpayer interview provisions do not apply to criminal investigations. They apply to interviews conducted on or after the 90th day after the date of the new tax law's enactment.

3. Taxpayer reliance on IRS written advice. The IRS is required to eliminate any penalty or addition to tax that is attributable to erroneous written advice furnished to a taxpayer by the IRS pursuant to a written request by the taxpayer that included adequate and accurate information. The IRS is not required to furnish written advice to taxpayers, but when it does so, taxpayers will now be able to place greater reliance on that advice.

4. Basis for evaluating IRS employees. There is a common perception that the evaluation and promotion of IRS employees is based on the amount of taxes that they collect during taxpayer audits, and that this system encourages auditors to take unreasonable positions in an effort to collect the most taxes. Many clergy who have been audited will share this belief. Congress also is aware of this perception, and to ensure that IRS employees are not evaluated on the basis of the amount of taxes they collect, the taxpayer bill of rights *prohibits the IRS from evaluating employees on the basis of taxes collected or production quotas or goals.* This restriction applies only to the evaluation of IRS employees directly involved in tax collection activities, and their immediate supervisors. This provision took effect on January 1, 1989. Clergy now will have the assurance that IRS auditors will not have a vested interest in taking unreasonable positions in an attempt to exact the most taxes.

5. Tax deficiency notices. Under the new law, all notices of tax deficiencies must contain an identification of taxes due, interest, additions to tax, and penalties, along with an explanation of the basis for such amounts. Congress emphasized that all IRS correspondence should be sufficiently clear as to enable a taxpayer to understand an IRS question about a tax return as well as any adjustments or penalties assessed.

6. Installment payment of tax liability. Many clergy have been faced with huge amounts of delinquent taxes, often because of bad advice from a tax preparer, and are faced with the dilemma of how to pay the taxes. For example, many clergy do not pay self-employment taxes (social security taxes for self-employed persons) because they think that they filed a timely exemption application (Form 4361) with the IRS. However, federal law does not recognize the validity of such an exemption application until it has been officially approved by the IRS and one of the three copies of the Form 4361 (it is filed in triplicate) returned by the IRS to the minister marked "approved". Many clergy who have filed a timely exemption application have never received back an approved copy from the IRS, meaning that they are not exempt from self-employment taxes. Occasionally, such a minister will be audited, and the IRS will assess many thousands of dollars of back taxes. How does the minister pay such a staggering liability? Prior to the taxpayer bill of rights, the IRS was not required to enter into "installment payment" agreements with taxpayers. This obviously led to serious problems for many clergy. Under the taxpayer bill of rights, the IRS is given the authority to enter into installment agreements with taxpayers if the IRS determines that such an agreement will facilitate the collection of the tax owed. Any such installment agreement can be canceled by the IRS if the taxpayer furnished inaccurate or incomplete information, the taxpayer fails to pay an installment when due, or the taxpayer fails to respond to an IRS request for updated financial information. In addition, the IRS may alter an installment agreement if it determines that the financial condition of a taxpayer has changed significantly. Another option that is available to clergy facing huge tax liabilities is the "offer in compromise." This option is discussed earlier in this chapter.

7. Taxpayer property subject to IRS seizure and sale. The amount of property and wages exempt from IRS seizure is increased. For example, the amount of a taxpayer's wages exempt from IRS seizure is the taxpayer's standard deduction amount plus personal exemptions allowed for the year in question, divided by 52. Generally, this amount is greater than previously allowed.

8. Liability of IRS for certain unauthorized actions of employees. Prior to the taxpayer bill of rights, taxpayers did not have a specific right to sue the government for damages sustained because of unreasonable actions taken by IRS employees. Under the new law, taxpayers are granted the right to sue the federal government in federal court for damages suffered due to reckless or intentional disregard of the Internal Revenue Code (and income tax regulations) by IRS employees engaged in tax collection activities. *IRC 7433.* The lawsuit must be brought within two years after an incident, and the taxpayer is permitted to recover legal expenses and actual direct economic damages up to $100,000. This remedy will equip taxpayers with an important weapon.

Taxpayer Bill of Rights 2

The Taxpayer Bill of Rights 2 (TBOR2) contains a number of additional protections. Note, however, that it also contains some penalties.

1. Taxpayer advocate. TBOR2 establishes a new position, Taxpayer Advocate, within the IRS. This replaces the position of Taxpayer Ombudsman. The Taxpayer Advocate is appointed by and reports directly to the Commissioner. TBOR2 also establishes the Office of Taxpayer Advocate within the IRS. The functions of the office are (1) to assist taxpayers in resolving problems with the IRS; (2) to identify areas in which taxpayers have problems in dealings with the IRS; (3) to propose changes in the administrative practices of the IRS that will reduce those problems; and (4) to identify potential legislative changes that may reduce those problems. The Taxpayer Advocate is given broad authority to affirmatively take any action with respect to taxpayers who would otherwise suffer a significant hardship as a result of the manner in which the IRS is administering the tax laws.

2. Installment agreements. The IRS in some cases enters into installment agreements with taxpayers who are unable to pay a tax liability in a lump sum. TBOR2 requires the IRS to notify taxpayers 30 days before modifying or terminating any installment agreement for any reason other than that the collection of tax is in jeopardy. The IRS must include in the notification an explanation of why it intends to take this action.

3. Abatement of penalty for failure to deposit payroll taxes. Section 6656 of the tax code imposes a penalty on employers that fail to deposit payroll taxes on time. The penalty is 2 percent of the amount of the underpayment if the deposit is late by less than 5 days; 5 percent if the deposit is late by more than 5 days but not more than 15 days; and 10 percent if the deposit is late by more than 15 days. The penalty goes to 15 percent if the deposit is not made within 10 days of the date of the first delinquency notice sent by the IRS. TBOR2 provides that the IRS may waive these penalties with respect to an inadvertent failure to deposit any employment tax if: (a) the employer's net worth is less than $7 million; (b) the failure to deposit occurs during the first quarter that the employer was required to deposit any employment tax; and (c) the return for the employment tax was filed on or before the due date. TBOR2 also provides that the IRS may abate any penalty for failure to make deposits for the first time an employer makes a deposit if it inadvertently sends the deposit to the IRS instead of to the required government depository (ordinarily a bank).

4. Offers in compromise. Offers in compromise have become increasingly popular with taxpayers over the past few years, and many taxpayers have obtained significant relief. In many cases, however, the success of offers in compromise has been stifled by the requirement that the IRS chief counsel approve all such offers if the amount of unpaid tax is $500 or more. This low threshold meant that the IRS chief counsel had to personally approve the vast majority of offers in compromise. In many cases, offers that were approved at lower levels of the IRS were denied by the chief counsel. TBOR2 addressed this problem and requires IRS chief counsel approval of offers in compromise only if the amount of unpaid tax is $50,000 or more.

5. Civil damages for filing fraudulent 1099 forms. TBOR2 permits employers who issue fraudulent 1099 or W-2 forms to be sued by the person who receives them. Damages are the greater of $5,000, or actual damages plus attorney's fees.

6. IRS must investigate disputed W-2s and 1099 forms. TBOR2 provides that, in any court proceeding, if a taxpayer asserts a reasonable dispute with respect to any item of income reported on an information return (Form 1099 or Form W-2) filed by an employer and the taxpayer has fully cooperated with the IRS, then the government has the burden of proving the deficiency (in addition to the information return itself). Fully cooperating with the IRS includes (but is not limited to) the following: bringing the reasonable dispute over the item of income to the attention of the IRS within a reasonable period of time, and providing (within a reasonable period of time) access to and inspection of all witnesses, information, and documents within the control of the taxpayer (as reasonably requested by the IRS).

7. Collecting litigation costs from the IRS. Under prior law, taxpayers could sue the IRS for attorney's fees if they prevailed in a lawsuit with the IRS and they proved that the IRS was not "substantially justified" in its position. TBOR2 makes it much easier for taxpayers to collect their attorney's fees in such cases by switching the burden of proof to the IRS. Under the new law (which is effective immediately) taxpayers who prevail in lawsuits with the IRS will receive an award of attorney's fees unless the IRS can prove that it was substantially justified in maintaining its position against the taxpayer. TBOR2 also establishes a rebuttable presumption that the position of the government was not substantially justified if the IRS did not follow (1) its published regulations, revenue rulings, revenue procedures, information releases, notices, or announcements, or (2) a private letter ruling, determination letter, or technical advice memorandum issued to the taxpayer. This provision only applies to the version of IRS guidance that is most current.

8. $1 million damage cap. As noted above, the first Taxpayer Bill of Rights gave taxpayers the right to sue the federal government for damages suffered due to reckless or intentional disregard of federal tax law by IRS employees engaged in tax collection activities. The lawsuit must be brought within two years after an incident, and the taxpayer is permitted to recover legal expenses and actual direct economic damages up to $100,000. TBOR2 increases the damages limit to $1 million.

9. Penalty for failure to pay withheld payroll taxes. Federal law currently provides that any corporate officer, director, or employee who is responsible for withholding taxes and paying them over to the government is liable for a penalty in the amount of 100% of such taxes if they are either not withheld or not paid over to the government. This penalty is of special relevance to church leaders, given the high rate of noncompliance by churches with the payroll reporting procedures. TBOR2 contains four important limitations on the application of this penalty:

1. Notice requirement. The IRS must issue a notice to an individual the IRS had determined to be a responsible person with respect to unpaid payroll taxes at least 60 days prior to issuing a notice and demand for the penalty.

2. Disclosure of information if more than one person subject to penalty. TBOR2 requires the IRS, if requested in writing by a person considered by the IRS to be a responsible person, to disclose in writing to that person the name of any other person the IRS has determined to be a responsible person with respect to the tax liability. The IRS is required to disclose in writing whether it has attempted to collect this penalty from other responsible persons, the general nature of those collection activities, and the amount (if any) collected. Failure by the IRS to follow this provision does not absolve any individual from any liability for this penalty.

3. Contribution from other responsible parties. If more than one person is liable for this penalty, each person who paid the penalty is entitled to recover from other persons who are liable for the penalty an amount equal to the excess of the amount paid by such person over such person's proportionate share of the penalty. This proceeding is a federal cause of action and is separate from any proceeding involving IRS collection of the penalty from any responsible party.

4. Volunteer board members of churches and other charities. TBOR2 clarifies that the responsible person penalty is not to be imposed on volunteer, unpaid members of any board of trustees or directors of a tax-exempt organization to the extent such members are solely serving in an honorary capacity, do not participate in the day-to-day or financial activities of the organization, and do not have actual knowledge of the failure. However, this provision cannot operate in such a way as to eliminate all responsible persons from responsibility.

10. Including telephone numbers on 1099 forms. All 1099 forms issued after December 31, 1996, must contain the name, address, and telephone number of a "contact person" who can answer questions the recipient may have about the form. The purpose of this new requirement is to give recipients of 1099 forms the ability to contact a person who was responsible for preparing the form and who presumably has the ability to answer any questions the recipient may have. For many churches, the "contact person" will be the church treasurer. This means that all 1099 forms issued by the church must contain the name, address, and telephone number of the treasurer. In other churches, the contact person will be a business administrator.

11. Use of private mailing services. A federal court ruled in 1995 that tax returns and other documents are deemed to be filed on the date they are mailed only if they are sent via the postal service. The Taxpayer Bill of Rights 2, enacted by Congress in 1996, authorizes the IRS to permit document sent via private delivery services to be treated in the same way. The IRS may designate a delivery service only if it meets the following criteria: (1) it is available to the general public; (2) it is at least as timely and reliable on a regular basis as the United States mail; (3) it satisfies recordkeeping criteria; and (4) it meets any additional criteria the IRS may prescribe. The provision also gives the IRS similar authority with respect to equivalents for United States certified or registered mail.

12. Interim sanctions. TBOR2 contains a provision allowing the IRS to assess "intermediate sanctions" (an excise tax) against exempt organizations in lieu of outright revocation of exempt status. The intermediate sanctions may be assessed only in cases of "excess benefit transactions," meaning one or more transactions that provide unreasonable compensation to an officer or director of the exempt organization. A person who benefits from an excess benefit transaction is subject to a penalty tax equal to 25 percent of the amount of the excess benefit. An exempt organization's managers who participate in an excess benefit transaction knowing that it is an improper transaction are subject to a penalty tax of 10 percent of the amount of the excess benefit (up to

a maximum penalty of $10,000). It is possible that the IRS will assess this penalty against church board members who participate in an excess benefit transaction involving a pastor or other church employee.

☞ *Example. Rev. A's 1996 income tax return is audited by the IRS. An IRS auditor insists that a church's reimbursements of a minister's business expenses must be reported as income on the minister's W-2 and 1040. The church reimbursed Rev. A's business expenses under an "account-able" reimbursement plan that satisfied the requirements of the income tax regulations. Reimbursements paid under such a plan do not need to be included on an employee's W-2 or 1040, and so the auditor's position was in clear violation of the regulations. Rev. A can bring a lawsuit in federal court seeking money damages against the IRS for the auditor's intentional and reckless disregard of federal law. Rev. A will be permitted to recover legal costs and any direct economic damages that he can prove, up to $1,000,000. No "punitive" damages are available.*

H. Right to Minimize Taxes

While *evasion* of taxes will subject a taxpayer to civil and possibly criminal penalties, every taxpayer has the legal right to *avoid* or *minimize* taxes. As Judge Learned Hand remarked: "Over and over again the courts have said that there is nothing sinister in so arranging one's affairs as to keep taxes as low as possible. Everybody does so, rich or poor; and all do right, for nobody owes any public duty to pay more tax than the law demands; taxes are enforced exactions, not voluntary contributions." *Newman v. Commissioner, 159 F.2d 848 (2d Cir. 1947).* Similarly, another federal appeals court judge has observed that "it is a well-settled principle that a taxpayer has the legal right to decrease the amount of what otherwise would be his taxes, or to avoid them altogether, by means which the law permits." *Jones v. Grinnell, 179 F.2d 873 (10th Cir. 1950).*

I. Notifying the IRS of a Change of Address

The IRS has explained how to notify it of a change in address. Many taxpayers are surprised to learn that IRS notices are legally effective even if never received, so long as they are mailed to a taxpayer's "last known address." The Tax Court has ruled that the address listed on a taxpayer's most recent federal tax return is his or her "last known address," *unless* the taxpayer has given the IRS "clear and concise notification" of a different address. To effectively notify the IRS of a change in address a taxpayer must send a change of address notification to the IRS Service Center serving the taxpayer's old address, or to the Chief, Taxpayer Service Division, in the local IRS district office. The IRS has developed a form (Form 8822) that is designed specifically to notify it of a change of address. A copy is reproduced at the end of this chapter. Taxpayers are encouraged to use this form in notifying the IRS of any change in their address, since it will satisfy the "clear and concise notification" requirement, and will identify the specific IRS office to which the notification should be sent.

The IRS has stated that informing the Postal Service of a change of address will *not* constitute clear and concise notification to the IRS. Predictably, the IRS Form 8822 is seldom used by taxpayers to notify the IRS of a change of address.

✎ **Key point: the IRS is looking for thousands of taxpayers who have not yet received their 1996 refund checks. These undelivered refunds total nearly $100 million. The Postal Service returned these refunds checks to the IRS because they could not deliver them. Thousands of checks are returned because the names or addresses on the checks are incorrect.**

Form **8822**	**Change of Address**	OMB No. 1545-1163
(Rev. May 1994)	▶ **Please type or print.**	Expires 5-31-95
Department of the Treasury Internal Revenue Service	▶ **See instructions on back.** ▶ **Do not attach this form to your return.**	

Part I   Complete This Part To Change Your Home Mailing Address

Check **ALL** boxes this change affects:

1 ☐ Individual income tax returns (Forms 1040, 1040A, 1040EZ, 1040NR, etc.)
　▶ If your last return was a joint return and you are now establishing a residence separate
　from the spouse with whom you filed that return, check here . . . . ▶ ☐

2 ☐ Employment tax returns for household employers (Forms 942, 940, and 940-EZ)
　▶ Enter your employer identification number here . . . . ▶ _____

3 ☐ Gift, estate, or generation-skipping transfer tax returns (Forms 706, 709, etc.)
　▶ For Forms 706 and 706-NA, enter the decedent's name and social security number below.

▶ Name　　　　　　　　　　　　　　　　　　　▶ Social security number

4a Your name (first name, initial, and last name)	4b Your social security number
5a Spouse's name (first name, initial, and last name)	5b Spouse's social security number

6　Prior name(s). See instructions.

7a Old address (no., street, city or town, state, and ZIP code). If a P.O. box or foreign address, see instructions.	Apt. no.
7b Spouse's old address, if different from line 7a (no., street, city or town, state, and ZIP code). If a P.O. box or foreign address, see instructions.	Apt. no.
8 New address (no., street, city or town, state, and ZIP code). If a P.O. box or foreign address, see instructions.	Apt. no.

Part II   Complete This Part To Change Your Business Mailing Address or Business Location

Check **ALL** boxes this change affects:

9 ☐ Employment, excise, and other business returns (Forms 720, 941, 990, 1041, 1065, 1120, etc.)
10 ☐ Employee plan returns (Forms 5500, 5500-C/R, and 5500-EZ). See instructions.
11 ☐ Business location

12a Business name	12b Employer identification number
13 Old address (no., street, city or town, state, and ZIP code). If a P.O. box or foreign address, see instructions.	Room or suite no.
14 New address (no., street, city or town, state, and ZIP code). If a P.O. box or foreign address, see instructions.	Room or suite no.
15 New business location (no., street, city or town, state, and ZIP code). If a foreign address, see instructions.	Room or suite no.

Part III   Signature

Daytime telephone number of person to contact (optional) ▶ (   )

Please Sign Here

▶ _____		▶ _____	
Your signature	Date	If Part II completed, signature of owner, officer, or representative	Date
▶ _____		▶ _____	
If joint return, spouse's signature	Date	Title	

Illustration 1-2

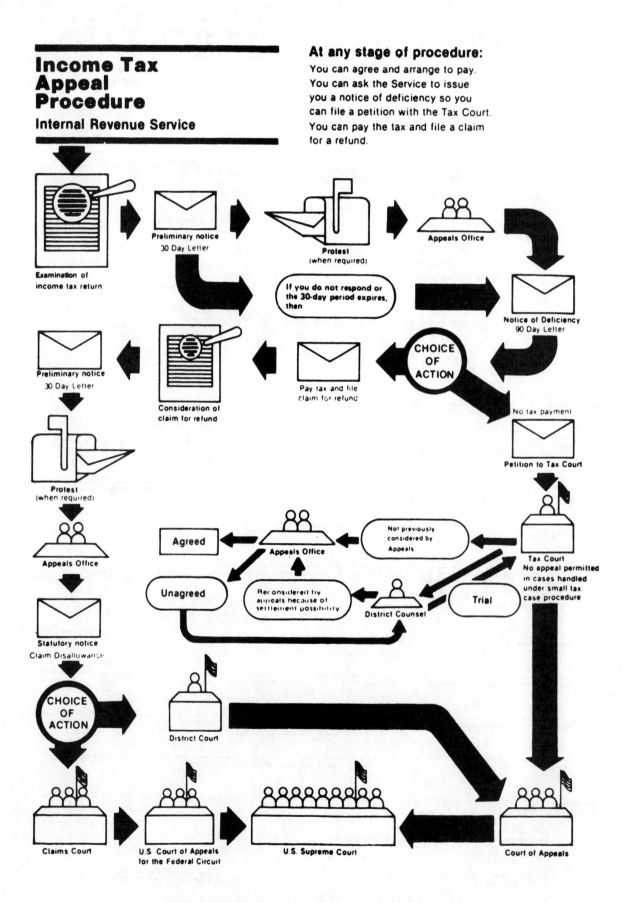

Income Tax Appeal Procedure
Internal Revenue Service

At any stage of procedure:
You can agree and arrange to pay.
You can ask the Service to issue
you a notice of deficiency so you
can file a petition with the Tax Court.
You can pay the tax and file a claim
for a refund.

Examination of income tax return

Preliminary notice 30 Day Letter

Protest (when required)

Appeals Office

If you do not respond or the 30-day period expires, then

Notice of Deficiency 90 Day Letter

CHOICE OF ACTION

Pay tax and file claim for refund

No tax payment

Consideration of claim for refund

Preliminary notice 30 Day Letter

Petition to Tax Court

Protest (when required)

Appeals Office

Statutory notice Claim Disallowance

Agreed

Appeals Office

Not previously considered by Appeals

Tax Court No appeal permitted in cases handled under small tax case procedure

Unagreed

Reconsidered by appeals because of settlement possibility

District Counsel

Trial

CHOICE OF ACTION

District Court

Claims Court

U.S Court of Appeals for the Federal Circuit

U.S. Supreme Court

Court of Appeals

Chapter 2

ARE CLERGY AND CHURCH STAFF EMPLOYEES OR SELF-EMPLOYED?

Chapter Highlights

- **Reporting income taxes as an employee.** Most clergy should report their federal income taxes as employees, because they will be considered employees under the test currently used by the IRS. Most clergy will be "better off" reporting as employees, since (1) the value of various fringe benefits will be excludable, including the cost of employer-paid health insurance premiums on the life of the minister, (2) the risk of an IRS audit is substantially lower, and (3) reporting as an employee avoids the additional taxes and penalties that often apply to self-employed clergy who are audited by the IRS and reclassified as employees.

- **Ministers have a "dual tax status."** While most ministers are employees for federal income tax reporting purposes, they all are self-employed for social security purposes (with respect to services they perform in the exercise of their ministry). This means that ministers are not subject to "FICA" taxes, even though they report their income taxes as employees and receive a W-2 from their church. Rather, they pay the "self-employment tax."

- **Nonminister church workers.** The IRS and the courts will apply the same tests used in determining the correct reporting status of ministers to determine the reporting status of nonminister church workers for income tax reporting purposes.

- **Tests for determining employee status.** There are at least 4 recognized tests for determining whether a minister or lay worker is an employee or self-employed for federal income tax reporting purposes. These include: (1) the "common law employee" test set forth in the income tax regulations; (2) the "20 factor" test announced by the IRS in 1987; (3) the "7 factor" test announced by the United States Tax Court in 1994 in 2 cases addressing the correct reporting status of ministers; and (4) a "12 factor" test developed by the United States Supreme Court and used by a federal appeals court in a 1997 case addressing the correct reporting status of a minister.

Whether or not a minister or nonminister staff member is an employee or self-employed is an important question. Unfortunately, it also can be a complex and at times confusing question. This chapter will address this question on the basis of the most recent legal precedent.

The focus of this chapter will be on the correct reporting status of ministers and nonminister staff members for *federal income tax* reporting purposes. The correct reporting status of these individuals for *social security* purposes is also addressed in this chapter, but this issue occupies much less attention. The reason is simple—ministers always are treated as self-employed for purposes of social security with respect to services they perform in the exercise of their ministry. The difficulty in determining the correct reporting status of ministers therefore is associated with income tax reporting, and not social security. Similarly, for nonminister staff members, their reporting status for federal income tax purposes generally determines their reporting status for social security. In summary, the focus of this chapter will be on the correct reporting status of ministers and nonminister staff members for income tax purposes.

A. Ministers

1. In general

✎ **Key point: are ministers employees or self-employed for federal income tax reporting purposes? This is an important question. In fact, the "audit guidelines for ministers" released by the IRS in 1995 inform agents that "the first issue that must be determined is whether the minister is an employee or an independent contractor."**

✎ **Key point: most clergy should report their federal income taxes as employees, since (1) the value of various fringe benefits will be non-taxable, (2) audit risk is much lower, (3) reporting as an employee avoids the additional taxes and penalties that often are assessed against clergy who are reclassified as employees by the IRS, (4) the IRS considers most clergy to be employees, (5) most clergy are employees under the tests applied by the IRS and the courts**

✎ **Key point: while most clergy are employees for federal income tax reporting purposes, all clergy are self-employed for social security purposes with respect to services performed in the exercise of ministry (they have a "dual tax status")**

The question of whether ministers should report their federal income taxes as an employee or as a self-employed person has generated a good deal of controversy. It is a significant question for many reasons, including the following:

(1) Reporting compensation. Employees report their compensation directly on Form 1040 (line 7—wages), and deduct unreimbursed (and "nonaccountable" reimbursed) business expenses on Schedule A only if they itemize deductions *and* only to the extent that such expenses exceed 2% of adjusted gross income (only 50% of business meals and entertainment expenses are counted). Self-employed persons report compensation and business expenses on Schedule C. Business expenses are in effect deductible whether or not the minister itemizes deductions, and are not subject to the 2% floor.

(2) Adjusted gross income. Adjusted gross income ordinarily will be higher if a minister reports as an employee, since unreimbursed (and "nonaccountable" reimbursed) business expenses are deductions *from* adjusted gross income. Self-employed persons deduct business expenses in computing adjusted gross income. Adjusted gross income is a figure that is important for many reasons. For example, the percentage limitations applicable to charitable contributions and medical expense deductions are tied to adjusted gross income.

(3) W-2 or 1099? Ministers working for a church or church agency should receive a Form W-2 each year if they are employees, and a Form 1099-MISC if they are self-employed (and receive at least $600 in compensation).

(4) Tax-deferred annuities. Favorable "tax-deferred annuities" (also known as "403(b) annuities") offered by nonprofit organizations (including churches) may only be available to employees. This issue is discussed in further detail later in chapter 10.

❖ **New in 1997. Congress enacted legislation in 1996 permitting self-employed ministers to participate in qualified retirement plans including 403(b) tax-sheltered annuities. This resolves a question that has plagued church plans for many years. In the past, there was much confusion over the eligibility of self-employed ministers and other church workers to participate in church retirement plans including 403(b) tax-sheltered annuities. . . ."** This provision took effect in 1997.

❖ **New in 1998. Congress enacted legislation in 1997 clarifying that in the case of contributions made on behalf of a minister who is self-employed to a church plan, the contribution is nontaxable to the extent that it would be if the minister were an employee of a** church and the contribution were made to the plan. This provision takes effect in 1998.

(5) Tax treatment of various fringe benefits. Certain fringe benefits provided by a church on behalf of a minister are excludable from the minister's income only if he or she is an employee. Examples include medical insurance premiums paid by a church on behalf of its minister; group term life insurance (up to $50,000) provided by a church on behalf of a minister; amounts payable to employees on account of sickness, accident, or disability pursuant to an employer-financed plan; employer-sponsored "cafeteria plans" which permit employees to choose between receiving cash payments or a variety of fringe benefits.

(6) Audit risk. Self-employed persons face a much higher risk of having their tax returns audited. Why? IRS data reveals that the "voluntary reporting percentage" (i.e., persons who voluntarily report the correct amount of income) is 99.5% for employees covered by mandatory income tax withholding, but is only 13% for persons not covered by mandatory withholding and for whom no 1099 or W-2 forms are filed. As a result, the IRS scrutinizes the tax returns of self-employed persons (who are not subject to tax withholding) much more closely than those of employees. It is also relevant to note that the IRS has been concerned for a number of years with the problem of persons reporting their income taxes as self-employed when in fact they are more properly characterized as employees. The IRS and General Accounting Office conducted a joint study to determine whether 1099-MISC forms (annual information returns issued to self-employed workers) may reveal workers more properly classified as employees. The study revealed a "universe" of self-employed persons who received *all* of their business income (reported on Schedule C of Form 1040) *from a single employer.* The IRS is in the process of determining whether such a relationship is an indication of a misclassification of employees as self-employed. This is a significant issue for clergy, many of whom continue to report their federal income taxes as self-employed. In many cases, all of the Schedule C earnings of such clergy are attributable to their employing church, and are reported on a single 1099-MISC form. The IRS study concluded that the receipt of a single 1099-MISC form reporting self-employment income from a single source indicates that a worker is improperly reporting his or her federal income taxes as self-employed. As a result, self-employed clergy may wish to re-evaluate their status for federal income tax reporting purposes. *Internal Revenue Manual update MT 5(10)00-2.*

✎ **Key point: the IRS estimates that 70% of workers who should be treated as employees but who report their income taxes as self-employed file no income tax returns.**

(7) Consequences of being reclassified as an employee. Clergy who report as self-employed face a significant risk of additional taxes and penalties if they are audited by the IRS and reclassified as employees. This is because many clergy who report as self-employed deduct their unreimbursed (and "nonaccountable" reimbursed) business expenses as a deduction on Schedule C. If they are reclassified by the IRS as employees, their business expense deduction will be allowable only as an itemized deduction on Schedule A, and then only to the extent that the expenses exceed 2% of adjusted gross income. Clergy who are not able to itemize end up with no deduction for their business expenses. This can result in a substantial increase in taxable income.

The primary **disadvantage** of employee status is that most business expenses are deductible only as itemized deductions on Schedule A (i.e., the minister must be able to itemize deductions in order to deduct them), and they are deductible only to the extent that they exceed 2% of adjusted gross income. As we will see in chapter 7, this "disadvantage" can be overcome simply by having your employing church adopt an *accountable reimbursement policy* under which the church reimburses you for those business expenses that you periodically substantiate.

2. Selecting the correct status—4 tests

So much for the consequences of reporting as an employee or a self-employed person. Now let's consider how to determine which status applies. For many years, most ministers reported their income taxes as self-employed persons. This was consistent with the treatment of *all* ministers as self-employed for social security purposes (with respect to services performed in the exercise of ministry). However, it is important for clergy to realize that they have a "dual" tax status—they are considered self-employed for social security purposes (they pay the self-employment tax rather than FICA taxes), but they may be employees or self-employed for federal income tax purposes depending upon a variety of circumstances outlined below.

Table 2-1
Employee or Self-Employed — What Difference Does it Make?

issue	employee	self-employed
where to report income and expenses	Form 1040 (line 7) and Schedule A	Schedule C
annual information return issued by church to the minister	W-2	1099-MISC
tax-free fringe benefits (employer-paid medical insurance; employer-paid group term life insurance; etc.)	tax free (not reported as income on Form 1040 or W-2)	taxable; must be reported on 1099 and Schedule C
audit risk	low (99.5% compliance rate)	(1)high (13% compliance rate); (2) shifting expenses from Schedule C to Schedule A results in loss of any deduction for many
unreimbursed business expenses	Schedule A itemized deduction (if you itemize), and then only to the extent that the expenses exceed 2% adjusted gross income	Schedule C deduction whether you can itemize deductions on Schedule A or not
nonaccountable reimbursed expenses (e.g., monthly car allowance)	(1) Schedule A itemized deduction (if you itemize), and then only to the extent that the expenses exceed 2% AGI; (2) all reimbursements must be reported as income (W-2 and 1040)	(1) Schedule C deduction whether you can itemize deductions on Schedule A or not; (2) all reimbursements must be reported as income (Schedule C and 1040)
accountable reimbursed expenses (e.g., only substantiated expenses reimbursed; excess reimbursements must be returned to employer)	(1) no expenses to deduct; (2) reimbursements are not reported as income on either W-2 or 1040	(1) no expenses to deduct; (2) reimbursements are not reported as income on either W-2 or 1040
income tax withholding	exempt (with respect to service performed in the exercise of ministry)	not applicable (use the quarterly estimated tax procedure)
social security	ministers are never treated as employees for social security purposes with respect to service performed in the exercise of ministry (they do not pay FICA taxes)	ministers always are treated as self-employed for social security purposes with respect to service performed in the exercise of ministry (they pay the "self-employment tax," not FICA taxes)
housing allowance	available	available

Beginning in 1978, the IRS began making statements that were interpreted by some to *require* ministers to report their income taxes as employees. For example, in Revenue Ruling 80-110, the IRS held that a minister who is "an employee of a church" may not deduct unreimbursed business expenses on Schedule C but rather must use Schedule A. *See also Revenue Ruling 79-78.* In Publication 517 ("Social Security for Members of the Clergy and Religious Workers"), the IRS lists a comprehensive example demonstrating how a minister who is "an employee of the church" should report his income and business deductions. These pronouncements led some tax advisors to conclude that the IRS now views *all* ministers serving local churches as employees rather than as self-employed. Reliance has also been placed on section 3401(a)(9) of the Internal Revenue Code which states that ministers who are employees of a church are exempt from tax withholding.

Your author has always taken the position that the IRS pronouncements mentioned above merely stated the appropriate manner of reporting income and deductions *if employee status was assumed,* and were not IRS directives requiring all ministers to report their taxes as employees. Publication 517 itself recognizes that it is possible for ministers who are employees of their churches to be self-employed with respect to certain services (baptisms, marriages, funerals, etc.). And, no one seriously questions that full-time evangelists are self-employed for income tax purposes. It is therefore difficult to support sweeping generalizations that all ministers are employees for income tax purposes. Further, Publication 517 states that a minister "*may* be treated as an employee" for income tax purposes, and that the common law rules (discussed below) apply in determining whether a particular minister is an employee or a self-employed person for income tax purposes. This language certainly is not consistent with the conclusion that all clergy must report their federal income taxes as employees.

The IRS and the courts have applied a variety of tests to determine whether or not a particular worker is an employee or self-employed for income tax reporting purposes. These include the so-called common law employee test and the "20 factor test" adopted by the IRS in 1987. In addition, the Tax Court applied a 7-factor test in two cases involving the correct reporting status of ministers, and a federal appeals court applied a 12-factor test in concluding that a minister was self-employed rather than an employee for federal income tax reporting purposes. Each of these tests is summarized below.

test #1 — the "common law employee" test

The income tax regulations contain the following "common law employee" test for determining whether a worker is an employee or self-employed. This test is used frequently by the IRS and the courts.

Generally the relationship of employer and employee exists when the person for whom services are performed has the right to control and direct the individual who performs the services, not only as to the result to be accomplished by the work but also as to the details and means by which that result is accomplished. That is, an employee is subject to the will and control of the employer not only as to what shall be done but how it shall be done. In this connection, it is not necessary that the employer actually direct or control the manner in which the services are performed; it is sufficient if he has the right to do so. The right to discharge is also an important factor indicating that the person possessing that right is an employer. Other factors characteristic of an employer, but not necessarily present in every case, are the furnishing of tools and the furnishing of a place to work to the individual who performs the services. In general, if an individual is subject to the control or direction of another merely as to the result to be accomplished by the work and not as to the means and methods for accomplishing the result, he is not an employee. Generally, physicians, lawyers, dentists, veterinarians, contractors, subcontractors, public stenographers, auctioneers, and others who follow an independent trade, business, or profession, in which they offer their services to the public, are not employees. *Treas. Reg. 31.3401(c)-1(b)-(c). See also* Publication 517.

test #2 — the IRS "20 factor" test

Determining a taxpayer's correct reporting status under the common law employee test is often difficult. In 1987, the IRS developed a list of 20 factors to be used "as an aid in determining whether an individual is an employee under the common law rules." *Revenue Ruling 87-41.* The factors were "developed based on an examination of cases and rulings considering whether an individual is an employee." The IRS cautioned that "[t]he degree of importance of each factor varies depending on the occupation and the factual context in which the services are performed," and that "if the relationship of employer and employee exists, the designation or description of the relationship by the parties as anything other than that of employer and employee is immaterial." The 20 factors are set forth below. Clergy who report their income taxes as self-employed should carefully consider these factors to determine if they have a substantial basis for reporting as self-employed.

(1) **Instructions.** A person who is required to comply with instructions about when, where, and how to work is ordinarily an employee.

(2) **Training.** Training of a person by an experienced employee or by other means is a factor of control and indicates that the worker is an employee.

(3) **Integration.** Integration of a person's services into the business operations generally shows that the person is subject to direction and control and accordingly is an employee.

(4) **Services rendered personally.** If the services must be rendered personally by the individual employed, it suggests an employer-employee relationship. Self-employed status is indicated when

an individual has the right to hire a substitute without the employer's knowledge.

(5) Hiring, supervising, and paying assistants. Hiring, supervising, and payment of assistants by the employer generally indicates that all workers on the job are employees. Self-employed persons generally hire, supervise, and pay their own assistants.

(6) Continuing relationship. The existence of a continuing relationship between an individual and the organization for whom the individual performs services is a factor tending to indicate the existence of an employer-employee relationship.

(7) Set hours of work. The establishment of set hours of work by the employer is a factor indicating control and accordingly the existence of an employer-employee relationship. Self-employed persons are "masters of their own time."

(8) Full time required. If the worker must devote full time to the business of the employer, he or she ordinarily will be an employee. A self-employed person on the other hand may choose for whom and when to work.

(9) Doing work on employer's premises. Doing the work on the employer's premises may indicate that the worker is an employee, especially if the work could be done elsewhere.

(10) Order or sequence of work. If a worker must perform services in an order or sequence set by the organization for whom he or she performs services, this indicates that the worker is an employee.

(11) Oral or written reports. A requirement that workers submit regular oral or written reports to the employer is indicative of an employer-employee relationship.

(12) Payment by hour, week, month. An employee usually is paid by the hour, week, or month, whereas a self-employed person usually is paid by the job on a lump sum basis (although the lump sum may be paid in intervals in some cases).

(13) Payment of business expenses. Payment by the employer of the worker's business or travel expenses suggests that the worker is an employee. Self-employed persons usually are paid on a job basis and take care of their own business and travel expenses.

(14) Furnishing of tools and materials. The furnishing of tools and materials by the employer indicates an employer-employee relationship. Self-employed persons ordinarily provide their own tools and materials.

(15) Significant investment. The furnishing of all necessary facilities (equipment and premises) by the employer suggests that the worker is an employee.

(16) Realization of profit or loss. Workers who are in a position to realize a profit or suffer a loss as a result of their services generally are self-employed, while employees ordinarily are not in such a position.

(17) Working for more than one firm at a time. A person who works for a number of persons or organizations at the same time is usually self-employed.

(18) Making services available to the general public. Workers who make their services available to the general public are usually self-employed. Individuals ordinarily hold their services out to the public by having their own offices and assistants, hanging out a "shingle" in front of their office, holding a business license, and by advertising in newspapers and telephone directories.

(19) Right to discharge. The right to discharge is an important factor in indicating that the person possessing the right is an employer. Self-employed persons ordinarily cannot be fired as long as they produce results which measure up to their contract specifications.

(20) Right to terminate. An employee ordinarily has the right to end the relationship with the employer at any time he or she wishes without incurring liability. A self-employed person usually agrees to complete a specific job and is responsible for its satisfactory completion or is legally obligated to make good for failure to complete the job.

Another factor, not mentioned in the above list, is the parties' own characterization of their relationship. For example, if a church and its minister enter into a written contract that specifically characterizes the minister as self-employed, this would be an additional factor to consider. Illustration 2-1 presents a clause that may be used by a church wishing to characterize its minister as self-employed rather than as an employee. The clause could be inserted in the contract of employment, or simply adopted as a resolution by the church board and included in the board's official minutes. Keep in mind that such a clause by itself, as the IRS observed in Revenue Ruling 87-41, will have little if any relevance and will never result in a minister being characterized as self-employed if he or she failed the "common law employee test" or a

---

Illustration 2-1

**Sample clause characterizing
a minister as self-employed**

The church board and Rev. L agree and intend that Rev. L's status shall be that of a self-employed person rather than that of an employee in view of the board's determination, based on its review and consideration of all the facts and circumstances, that Rev. L does not satisfy the "common law employee" test. In particular, it is the board's conclusion that it does not have the authority to control the methods or means by which Rev. L conducts his services on behalf of the church.

majority of the twenty factors. It is merely one factor that will be considered, but one that could be given considerable weight in a close case. Of course, a church will offset the effect of such a clause by issuing its minister a W-2 instead of a 1099-MISC form at the end of each year.

✎ **Key point:** the IRS released a worker classification training guide in 1996 to assist its agents in evaluating whether or not workers are employees or self-employed. The guide relies heavily on the common law employee test and the 20 factor test developed by the IRS in 1987 to assist in properly classifying workers. The guide emphasizes that an employer's right to "control" the means by which a worker performs his or her duties is the critical characteristic of an employer-employee relationship. However, with respect to "occupations for highly trained professionals" (including ministers) the guide notes that "because the ability, and in some cases the right, to direct and control the details of how a professional or skilled worker performs a task is limited, evidence of control over the financial aspects of how the task is performed tends to be especially important in these cases." Financial aspects indicating an employer-employee relationship include: (1) the worker has made no significant investment in his or her job; (2) the employer reimburses the worker's business expenses; (3) the worker is employed by one employer and does not offer his or her services to the public; (4) the worker is paid a salary rather than "by the job"; (5) the worker has no risk of realizing a profit or loss as a result of his or her services.

test #3 — the Tax Court's "7 factor" test

In 1994 the United States Tax Court issued two rulings addressing the correct tax reporting status of ministers. In one case the court found that a Methodist minister was an employee for federal income tax reporting purposes. *Weber v. Commissioner, 103 T.C. 378 (1994).* In the second case the court concluded that a Pentecostal Holiness pastor was self-employed for income tax reporting purposes. *Shelley v. Commissioner, T.C. Memo. 1994-432 (1994).* These cases are summarized later in this section. While the court reached different conclusions in these two cases, it applied the same test for determining the correct tax status of ministers. The test, along with an explanation of each factor, is set forth in Table 2-2.

There are two additional points the court made that should be considered in applying this test: (1) "No one factor dictates the outcome. Rather, we must look at all the facts and circumstances of each case." (2) "The threshold level of control necessary to find employee status is generally lower when applied to professional services than when applied to non-professional services."

✎ **Key point:** the Tax Court did not refer to the 20 factor test announced by the IRS in 1987 (discussed above). Ministers who report their income taxes as self-employed probably will have a higher chance of prevailing under the 7 factor test than under the more restrictive 20 factor test.

Table 2-2
The Tax Court's "7 Factor" Test

factor	explanation
(1) the degree of control exercised by the employer over the details of the work	the more control exercised by an employer over the details of the work, the more likely the worker is an employee
(2) which party invests in the facilities used in the work	workers employed by an employer who provides the facilities used in the work are more likely to be employees
(3) the opportunity of the individual for profit or loss	employees generally do not realize profits or losses as a result of their work (they are paid a salary); self-employed workers often do realize profits or losses
(4) whether or not the employer has the right to discharge the worker	if the employer can discharge a worker, this indicates that the worker is an employee
(5) whether or not the work is part of the employer's regular business	workers who are furthering the employer's regular or customary business are more likely to be employees
(6) the permanency of the relationship	the more permanent the relationship, the more likely the worker is an employee
(7) the relationship the parties believe they are creating	ordinarily, the parties assume that a worker is an employee who is issued a W-2 and who receives several fringe benefits

test #4 — the Supreme Court's "12 factor" test

In 1992 the Supreme Court listed 12 factors to be considered in deciding if a worker is an employee or self-employed. *Nationwide Mutual Insurance Company v. Darden, 503 U.S. 318 (1992).* The Court observed that each factor must be considered, and that none is decisive. The 12 factors, along with an explanation of whether they support employee or self-employed status, are summarized in Table 2-3.

Table 2-3
The Supreme Court's "12 Factor" Test

factor	explanation
(1) the hiring party's right to control the manner and means by which the product is accomplished	indicates a worker is an employee
(2) the skill required	the more skill that is required, the more likely a worker is self-employed

(3) the source of the instrumentalities and tools	workers who provide their own are more likely self-employed
(4) the location of the work	if the work occurs on the employer's premises, this indicates the worker is an employee
(5) the duration of the relationship between the parties	the longer the relationship, the more likely a worker is an employee
6) whether the hiring party has the right to assign additional projects to the hired party	(indicates a worker is an employee
(7) the extent of the hired party's discretion over when and how long to work	the more discretion, the more likely the worker is self-employed
(8) the method of payment	employees are paid by the hour or week; self-employed workers are paid by the job
(9) the hired party's role in hiring and paying assistants	self-employed workers hire and pay their own assistants; employees do not
(10) whether the work is part of the regular business of the hiring party	an employee's work is part of the regular business of the employer
(11) whether the hiring party is in business	employers are more likely to work for organizations that provide services or products to the public
(12) the provision of employee benefits	employees are more likely to receive fringe benefits

3. Court decisions and IRS rulings

✎ **Key point: four court decisions and one IRS ruling address the correct reporting status of ministers for federal income tax reporting purposes. They are summarized in Appendix 1.**

Four court decisions and one IRS ruling have addressed the question of whether a minister is an employee or self-employed for federal income tax reporting purposes. These five rulings are discussed below, and they are summarized in Appendix 1 at the end of this chapter.

Alford v. United States, 116 F.3d 334 (8th Cir. 1997)

A federal appeals court ruled that an Assemblies of God minister was self-employed rather than an employee for federal income tax reporting purposes. The court used a "12 factor" test in reaching this result that was announced by the United States Supreme Court in 1992 (summarized in Table 2-3).

The facts of the case can be quickly summarized. Rev. James Alford is an ordained Assemblies of God minister who served as pastor of an Assemblies of God church in Hampton, Arkansas for several years. He reported his income taxes as a self-employed person while serving as pastor of the church. The IRS audited Rev. Alford's 1986, 1987, and 1988 tax returns and determined that he should have reported his income taxes as an employee rather than as self-employed. As a result, all of Rev. Alford's business expenses were shifted from Schedule C to Schedule

A, and were deductible only to the extent they exceeded 2 percent of his adjusted gross income.

Rev. Alford paid the additional taxes assessed by the IRS, and then filed a lawsuit in a federal district court in Arkansas seeking a refund. The district court rejected Rev. Alford's request for a refund. It agreed with the IRS that he was an employee and that the IRS had correctly assessed the additional taxes. The district court concluded, however, that Rev. Alford was not an employee of the local Arkansas church that he served. But it found that "an extremely close relationship exists" among the national and regional Assemblies of God agencies and the local church that Rev. Alford served, and that "the control exercised by each of them should be considered together." The district court concluded that Rev. Alford was an employee because of the "significant control by [his church] through its supervision by the District Council and the National Church, over the manner in which [he] performed his work."

Rev. Alford appealed the district court's ruling to the eight circuit court of appeals (its decisions are binding in the states of Arkansas, Iowa, Minnesota, Missouri, Nebraska, North Dakota, and South Dakota). The court reversed the district court's decision, and concluded that Rev. Alford was self-employed rather than an employee for income tax reporting purposes. As a result, it ordered the IRS to refund to Rev. Alford the additional taxes he paid because of the erroneous decision by the IRS that he was an employee.

Was Rev. Alford an employee of his local church? The court began its opinion by selecting the test to apply in deciding whether Rev. Alford was an employee or self-employed. It adopted a test set forth in a Supreme Court decision in 1992:

[Besides considering] the hiring party's right to control the manner and means by which the product is accomplished, [a court must also look at] the skill required; the source of the instrumentalities and tools; the location of the work; the duration of the relationship between the parties; whether the hiring party has the right to assign additional projects to the hired party; the extent of the hired party's discretion over when and how long to work; the method of payment; the hired party's role in hiring and paying assistants; whether the work is part of the regular business of the hiring party; whether the hiring party is in business; [and] the provision of employee benefits. *Nationwide Mutual Insurance Company v. Darden, 503 U.S. 318 (1992).*

The Supreme Court clarified that "all of the incidents of the relationship must be assessed and weighed with no one factor being decisive."

The appeals court concluded, on the basis of this test, that Rev. Alford was not an employee of the local church he served:

We begin our analysis with Alford's relationship with the Hampton Church. Alford was pastor at the church for a total of about ten years. The local church hired Alford and paid him a salary of

$24,400 in 1986, $23,425 in 1987, and $22,100 in 1988. The salary was negotiated by Alford and the church and, although it was not calculated as a percentage of the revenues of the Hampton Church, it was dependent in part upon local church revenue. The church paid Alford a $4000 housing allowance and he did not pay rent when he lived in the parsonage. The church paid Alford an additional $250 each quarter so that he could pay his social security taxes; paid for his health insurance; paid into a retirement fund set up by the national church; and provided Alford a credit card for gasoline, on which he charged up to $520 a year. He received an annual $750 Christmas gift from the congregation, in addition to his salary. The church provided a desk, chair, and copy machine for the pastor's use, but Alford used his own desk and chairs, and in addition provided and used for the benefit of the church his own car, typewriter, computer, and library. Alford signed a contract with the church and paid his own self-employment taxes.

For the most part, Alford set his own schedule (except of course for regularly scheduled church services). He was free to perform weddings, funerals, and revivals for a fee, and was not required to pay over any of the fees to the church. He was not expected to pay for a substitute pastor if one was necessary. Alford arranged for evangelists or special speakers at the Hampton Church, and contributed to special collections taken for them.

Table 2-4
The Alford Case

facts suggesting employee	facts suggesting self-employed
Rev. Alford's salary, though not based on percentage of church income, was dependent on church revenue	Rev. Alford provided his own furniture
church paid several fringe benefits, including (1) a portion of his self-employment tax (2) housing allowance; (3) health insurance	he used his own car, computer, and library in the performance of his duties
church provided a credit card to purchase gasoline	he set his own schedule
church provided an annual Christmas gift of $750	he was free to perform weddings, funerals, and revivals for a fee, and was not required to pay over any of the fees to the church.
church provided a desk, chair, and copy machine	he was not expected to pay for a substitute pastor if one was necessary
	he arranged for evangelists or special speakers, and contributed to special collections taken for them.

✎ **Key point.** The IRS conceded that Rev. Alford was not an employee of the local church. But, it insisted that if the authority of the regional and national churches to "control" him were considered, then the "combined" authority of the local, regional, and national churches was sufficient to make Rev. Alford an employee. As a result, the IRS itself contributed to the

result in this case. When the court concluded that the combined control exercised over Rev. Alford by the local, regional, and national church bodies was insufficient to make him an employee, the only alternative was to treat him as self-employed.

Was Rev. Alford an employee of the "combination" of his local, regional, and national churches? The IRS conceded that Rev. Alford was not an employee of his local church. But it insisted that he was an employee of the "combination" of the local, regional, and national churches. The trial court agreed on the ground that "[a]n extremely close relationship exists" among the local, regional, and national church entities and "thus, the control exercised by each of them should be considered together." The trial court concluded that Rev. Alford was an employee because of the "significant control by the Hampton Church, through its supervision by the District Council and the National Church, over the manner in which [he] performed his work."

Ironically, it was this conclusion that resulted in an appeal of the case by the national church. The national church was concerned over the trial court's novel and sweeping conclusion that the relationship between local and regional churches with the national church was so "interconnected" that Rev. Alford had to be viewed as an employee of them all. Such a conclusion exposed the national church to a far greater risk of litigation and liability for the actions and obligations of local churches, clergy, and church workers.

The appeals court rejected the conclusion of both the IRS and the trial court that the authority of the local, regional, and national church bodies over Rev. Alford should be combined:

The [trial court] concluded, and the [IRS] does not dispute, that under these circumstances . . . Alford cannot be considered to have been an employee of the Hampton Church . . . . The question now, however, is whether Alford was indeed an employee when we consider, in addition, the regional and national churches' right to control him in the performance of his duties as pastor of the Hampton Church. We note that the [Supreme Court's 12-factor test summarized above] becomes less relevant to this part of our analysis, because most of those factors concern the services the individual in question actually rendered, and Alford clearly did no work for the regional or national offices during the tax years at issue (yet another reason, we might add, that the [trial court's] aggregation of the control of the three entities is questionable). Further, it is important to remember that we look at the district and national entities' right to control Alford, the putative employee, in the performance of his duties, not at any right they may have had to control the Hampton Church.

The General Council's and District Council's right to control Alford during the relevant years extended primarily to their function in awarding credentials to ministers like himself. Generally, the church has established certain criteria that must be met for an individual such as Alford to obtain credentials initially and to renew that status annually. There are standards for the education a minister must acquire (which he must obtain and pay for himself) and for his performance on certain tests. Other requirements include subscribing to the doctrinal statement of the Assemblies of God, which sets forth the religious beliefs of the church, its ministers, and its members, and to the form of church government. Ordained ministers must preach thirteen times a year, but topics are not decreed by the regional or national organizations. Ministers holding credentials cannot preach in churches other than Assemblies of God churches without permission of the District Council. Ministers may be disciplined for what the church considers failure to follow church doctrine and for lapses in personal conduct, and may, in fact, have their credentials revoked. With some exceptions not relevant here, a minister must tithe to both the regional and national organizations. Attendance at certain meetings is expected, but not required. Thus it is apparent that, while the regional and national churches had doctrinal authority to exercise considerable control over Alford as regards his beliefs and his personal conduct as a minister of the church, they did not have "the right to control the manner and means by which the product [was] accomplished."

The [trial court] and the United States make much of the fact that Alford, as a minister holding credentials, was "amenable" to the General Council and to the District Council in matters of doctrine and conduct. But this is not unusual in such a profession, and actually is merely a shorthand way of describing the parent church's doctrinal and disciplinary control discussed above. The control exercised by the regional and national organizations, and their right to control Alford, was no more nor less than most professions require of individuals licensed or otherwise authorized to work in the profession. State bar associations, for example, have certain education requirements and demand a certain level of performance on a bar examination before an individual can be licensed to practice law. On an annual basis, such associations require the payment of dues and often the completion of continuing legal education in order for an attorney to retain his license. State bar associations are empowered to monitor attorneys' behavior and to discipline them as they see fit, including the revocation of an attorney's license to practice law (disbarment). Yet no one would suggest that, by virtue of this right to control an attorney's working life, the bar association is his employer, or even one of his employers.

Further, we are somewhat concerned about venturing into the religious arena in adjudicating cases such as this one, and interpreting what really are church matters as secular matters for purposes of determining a minister's tax status. The doctrinal and disciplinary control exercised by the General and District Councils, or available for their exercise, "is guided by religious conviction and religious law, not by employment relationships, and . . . should be considered impermissible or immaterial in determining the employment status of a religious minister."

Perhaps more telling in this case are the aspects of Alford's work for the Hampton Church that the General and District Councils had no right to control during the years in question. They did not locate the job at the Hampton Church for Alford nor could they have "placed" him as pastor there. They did not and could not have negotiated his salary and benefits. They could neither have guaranteed him a job (with the Hampton Church or any other local church) nor could they have guaranteed his salary. The regional and national churches could not have fired him from the job as pastor of the Hampton Church (although if he had lost his credentials the Hampton Church would have lost its affiliate status if it had kept him on as pastor). They could not have required him to retire. They did not observe or grade his performance at the Hampton Church to determine if his credentials should be renewed, nor did they regularly evaluate him. Clearly the national and regional entities had little if any control over—or right to control—the "manner and means" Alford employed in accomplishing his duties as pastor at the Hampton Church during 1986, 1987, and 1988.

The court concluded that "the General and District Councils' right to control Alford, in combination with the common law agency factors present in Alford's relationship with the Hampton Church that weigh in favor of employee status, do not suffice to render Alford an employee within the meaning of the relevant provisions of the tax code."

The *Alford* case will insure that the correct reporting status of ministers for income tax purposes will remain ambiguous.

Binding precedent. The court's decision will be binding only in the eighth federal circuit, which covers the following states: Arkansas, Iowa, Minnesota, Missouri, Nebraska, North Dakota, South Dakota. The decision will be persuasive, but not binding, in other states.

Application to multi-staff churches. Perhaps the most significant fact in the *Alford* case was that Rev. Alford was the only employee of his church. Under such circumstances, a minister often will have a greater degree of autonomy and be subject to less "control" by the church. It is doubtful that ministers in larger churches employing several full-time staff members will be able to support self-employed status on the basis of the *Alford* decision.

Greene v. Commissioner, T.C. Memo. 1996-531 (1996)

In 1997 the Tax Court ruled that an Assemblies of God foreign missionary who resided in Bangladesh was self-employed rather than an employee for federal income tax reporting purposes. The court listed eight factors to be considered in deciding whether a worker is an employee or self-employed for federal income tax reporting purposes:

(1) the degree of control exercised by the [employer] over the details of the work; (2) which party invests in the facilities used in the work; (3) the taxpayer's opportunity for profit or loss; (4) the permanency of the relationship; (5) the [employer's] right of discharge; (6) whether the

work performed is an integral part of the [employer's] business; (7) what relationship the parties believe they are creating; and (8) the provision of benefits typical of those provided to employees. No one factor is determinative; rather, all the incidents of the relationship must be weighed and assessed.

The court concluded that the missionary was self-employed on the basis of these eight factors. Its conclusions are summarized below:

Factor #1 — degree of control. The court noted that an employer's right to control the manner in which a person's work is performed "is ordinarily the single most important factor" in determining whether that person is an employee. The more control, the more likely the worker is an employee. The court mentioned three additional factors to be considered in applying this test: (1) A sufficient degree of control for employee status does not require the employer to "stand over the taxpayer and direct every move made by that person." (2) "The degree of control necessary to find employee status varies according to the nature of the services provided." (3) "[W]e must consider not only what actual control is exercised, but also what right of control exists as a practical matter."

facts indicating control

The IRS insisted that the following facts demonstrated a sufficient degree of control for the missionary to be considered an employee:

✓ Missionaries qualify as professionals who require little supervision and therefore the absence of actual control should not be confused with an absence of the right to control.

✓ The Assemblies of God Division of Foreign Missions (DFM) maintained control over the missionary through its missions manual that dictated the manner in which he was to conduct his "deputational" and foreign ministry. Deputational ministry refers to the practice of Assemblies of God of missionaries raising their own financial support by visiting local churches.

✓ The national Assemblies of God organization (the "National Church") exercised control, or had the right to exercise control, over the missionary's ministerial credentials to such a degree that he was an employee. For example, the National Church: (1) maintains specific requirements for ministerial licensing and ordination; (2) has the authority to discipline ministers based on their behavior and conduct; and (3) has the authority to withdraw ministerial credentials.

facts indicating a lack of control

The court pointed to the following facts in concluding that there was no sufficient control exercised over the missionary to treat him as an employee:

✓ Neither the National Church nor DFM provided any type of professional training for the missionary.

✓ The DFM did not assign the missionary to minister in a particular country. The missionary himself selected Bangladesh, despite some reservations expressed by the DFM.

✓ The DFM did not direct the missionary to work on a particular project in Bangladesh. Rather, the missionary independently chose to become involved in student ministry. He decided to expand his foreign ministry to include a drug-rehabilitation program. He was able to make this decision without seeking permission from the DFM. In fact, it appears that the DFM was not even aware of the missionary's plans to initiate a drug-rehabilitation clinic in Bangladesh.

✓ The missionary determined his own work days and hours.

✓ The missionary used vacation and sick leave without notifying or seeking permission from the DFM.

✓ The missionary decided to return from his foreign ministry after only three years in the foreign field. He made this decision considering the needs of his school-aged children and the schedules of the other missionaries in his area. It appears that the DFM played little or no role in his field departure date.

✓ The missionary decided when his "personal allowance" (a monthly distribution for living expenses) would begin, and he had the power to designate the amount of his personal allowance up to the limit imposed by the DFM.

✓ The missionary was required to attend only one meeting every five years.

✓ Apart from filing periodic expense and activity reports, the missionary and the DFM did not communicate regularly. Specifically, the DFM did not contact him at all during his year of "deputational ministry" (when he visited churches in the United States raising support). Likewise, the DFM communicated with the missionary infrequently while he served in the foreign field.

✓ The missionary was not directly supervised or evaluated by anyone.

✓ The court acknowledged that the DFM missions manual contains extensive information with respect to foreign ministry. However, it concluded that "the missions manual was intended by the DFM to be an informational reference for missionaries, not a set of rules controlling their day-to-day conduct."

✓ The court concluded that the IRS's emphasis on the National Church's control of the missionary's ministerial credentials was misplaced for two reasons. First, although the missionary was an ordained Assemblies of God minister, he worked as a missionary. The court observed that "the National Church's requirements for ministerial licensing and ordination, as well as its authority to discipline [the missionary] and withdraw his ministerial credentials, have little or no bearing as to the details and means by which [he] performed his duties as a missionary." Second, the court concluded that the "control test" is not satisfied "where the manner in which a service is performed is controlled by the threat of the loss of professional credentials. Carried to its logical extreme, this argument would serve to classify all ordained ministers as employees of the National Church, regardless of the type of service performed."

The Tax Court noted that the missionary's circumstances in this case "are very different" from those of a pastor of a local church:

[The taxpayer in this case] was employed as a foreign missionary, not a pastor. We think that the National Church's authority over the manner in which a pastor performs his or her duties is not highly probative in analyzing the National Church's control over the daily activities of a foreign missionary. This is because pastoring a local church and engaging in foreign mission work are two different jobs involving different qualifications, duties, and bodies of authority. Pastors are subject to the controls of a local church whereas missionaries are subject to the authority of the DFM. As previously discussed, the DFM exerted very little control over petitioner.

The court concluded:

In summary, the DFM lacked the control and lacked the right to control the manner and means by which [the taxpayer] performed his duties as a foreign missionary. Rather, the DFM facilitates foreign ministry by processing a missionary's collections and pledges and providing useful information to missionaries through the missions manual and a proposed foreign living budget. In other words, we view the DFM as a service provider relieving endorsed missionaries from the administrative burdens of collecting and processing their pledges and obtaining information regarding their country of service.

Factor #2 — investment in facilities and equipment. The second factor in the Tax Court's eight factor test is "which party invests in the facilities used in the work"? If the employer invests in the facilities, it is more likely that the worker is an employee. The court observed:

[The taxpayer's] sole compensation as a missionary was in the form of a "personal allowance" secured from funds that he raised during his deputational ministry. In this regard, we observe that if a donor fails to remit a pledged amount, the DFM makes no effort to contact the donor, much less obtain the donation. Additionally, the National Church does not guarantee missionaries minimum compensation or support. [The taxpayer] used his personal car and telephone to raise funds during his deputational ministry. [He] occasionally hired assistants at his own discretion and accepted responsibility for paying those assistants.

The IRS pointed out that the missionary was reimbursed for his expenses when he withheld costs from the offerings remitted to the DFM. The court did not find this relevant: "Even if [he] were regarded as receiving reimbursement for his expenses, this matter is more than outweighed by other evidence probative of his being an independent contractor, e.g.,

petitioner's efforts in securing the funding for his foreign ministry and his investment in his automobile and telephone." The court concluded that the second factor supported self-employed status.

Factor #3 — opportunity for profit or loss. The third factor in the Tax Court's eight factor test is "the taxpayer's opportunity for profit or loss." The court noted that the National Church does not guarantee missionaries minimum compensation. Rather, compensation received by missionaries is in the form of a personal allowance, the amount of which depends on the total amount of funding that missionaries are able to secure during their deputational ministry. Additionally, upon resignation, missionaries forfeit any account balance they may have with the DFM and must reallocate their funds to another ministry. The court concluded that the third factor supported self-employed status.

Factor #4 — permanency of the relationship. The fourth factor in the Tax Court's eight factor test is the permanency of the relationship. The more permanent the relationship, the more likely the individual is an employee. The taxpayer conceded that missionary service is a lifetime career. Therefore, the court concluded that the fourth factor supported employee status.

Factor #5 — DFM's right of discharge. The fifth factor in the Tax Court's eight factor test is whether or not the employer has the right to discharge the worker. If such a right exists, it is more likely that the worker is an employee. The court noted that the DFM did not have the power to prevent the taxpayer from serving as an Assemblies of God missionary in Bangladesh:

The DFM's most extreme form of discipline is the withdrawal of a missionary's endorsement. For a missionary, the practical consequence of losing the DFM's endorsement is one of administrative inconvenience, namely, that the missionary must collect and process pledges without the assistance of the DFM. In any event, unendorsed Assemblies of God missionaries can and do serve in the foreign field.

The IRS insisted that because the missionary is an Assemblies of God minister, the National Church has the right to revoke his ministerial credentials, and therefore the National Church can effectively discharge him. The court disagreed:

Indeed, the credentials committee [of the National Church] has the authority to withdraw the approval and recommend the recall of ministerial credentials. Although [the taxpayer] is an Assemblies of God minister subject to the disciplinary proceedings in the constitution and bylaws, he presently serves in the capacity of a foreign missionary. Thus, we think the more appropriate analysis considers the DFM's right to discharge [him] in his capacity as a missionary, rather than the National Church's right to recall [his] ministerial credentials.

The court concluded that the fifth factor supported self-employed status.

Factor #6 — integral part of business. The sixth factor in the Tax Court's eight factor test is whether or not the work performed is an integral part of the employer's business. The court noted that the DFM's primary mission is world evangelism and that the taxpayer's work as an Assemblies of God missionary was directly related to the accomplishment of that mission. Therefore the court concluded that the sixth factor supported employee status.

Factor #7 — relationship the parties believe they have created. The seventh factor in the Tax Court's eight factor test is the relationship the parties believe they have created. That is, did the DFM and its missionaries believe that their relationship was that of employer and employee, or did they believe that their relationship was that of an employer and self-employed workers? The court concluded that the parties believed that missionaries were self-employed, based on the following factors: (1) the financial comptroller of the DFM testified that the DFM considered its missionaries to be self-employed; (2) the National Church issued the taxpayer a 1099 form each year reflecting nonemployee compensation for services rendered; (3) federal income tax was not withheld from the missionary's compensation (the court apparently was unaware of the fact that the compensation of ministers and missionaries is exempt from federal income tax withholding whether they report their income taxes as employees or as self-employed); and (4) the taxpayer thought he was self-employed as evidenced by the fact that he reported his foreign ministry income and expenses on Schedule C. The court concluded that the seventh factor supported self-employed status.

Factor #8 — employee-type benefits. The eighth factor in the Tax Court's eight factor test is whether or not the employer provides "employee-type benefits" to the worker. The court noted that the DFM provided its missionaries with the following fringe benefits: (1) access to the National Church's retirement plan, and (2) access to the National Church's health insurance plan. On the other hand, the DFM has no policy regarding sick leave and does not maintain records reflecting either vacation or sick leave taken by missionaries. The court concluded that "although the matter is not free from doubt, we think that these facts support a finding that [the taxpayer] was an employee, not [self-employed]."

The court concluded its analysis of the eight factors by observing:

> Some aspects of the relationship between [the missionary] and the National Church indicate that [he] was an employee, whereas other aspects of the relationship indicate that he was [self-employed]. After weighing the above factors, giving particular weight to the lack of control and the lack of the right to control that the National Church and the DFM had over endorsed missionaries, we conclude that [the taxpayer] was [self-employed], and not an employee . . . .

Weber v. Commissioner, 103 T.C. 378 (1994), aff'd 60 F.3d 1104 (4th Cir. 1995)

The Tax Court concluded that a Methodist minister was an employee and not self-employed for federal income tax reporting purposes. The court began its opinion by asserting that Rev. Weber, "a United Methodist Minister, is an employee for federal income tax purposes." What factors led the court to reach this conclusion, and how will the ruling affect other ministers? These are critical questions.

The court noted that Rev. Weber had the burden of proving that he was in fact self-employed for federal income tax purposes and not an employee. The court conceded that the tax code contains no definition of the term "employee". Whether an employer-employee relationship exists in a particular situation "is a factual question" to be decided on a case-by-case basis. How is this determination made? The court referred to "common law rules" that are applied in making such a decision. These common law rules are set forth in the income tax regulations, and also in court decisions. The court quoted the income tax regulations' definition of an employer-employee relationship (quoted above as "test 1—the common law employee test").

✎ **Key point: the Tax Court announced a 7 factor test in 1994 for determining whether a minister is an employee or self-employed for federal income tax reporting purposes.**

The 7 factor test. The court then referred to 7 factors the courts consider in deciding if a particular worker is an employee or self-employed. The court emphasized that "[n]o one factor dictates the outcome . . . [r]ather we must look at all the facts and circumstances of each case." Here are the 7 factors:

> Courts consider various factors to determine an employment relationship between the parties. Relevant factors include:
>
> (1) the degree of control exercised by the employer over the details of the work
>
> (2) which party invests in the facilities used in the work
>
> (3) the opportunity of the individual for profit or loss
>
> (4) whether or not the employer has the right to discharge the individual
>
> (5) whether the work is part of the employer's regular business
>
> (6) the permanency of the relationship
>
> (7) the relationship the parties believe they are creating

✎ **Key point: the Court adopted a "7 factor test" for determining whether or not a minister or other worker is an employee or self-employed for income tax reporting purposes.**

The importance of this test cannot be overemphasized. The Tax Court totally ignored the 20 factor test adopted by the IRS in 1987 (discussed above), and substituted a 7 factor test. The court discussed each of the 7 factors as follows:

Factor #1—the degree of control exercised by the employer over the details of the work. The court emphasized that the "right-to-control" test is "the crucial test to determine the nature of a working relationship." The more control exercised by an employer over the details of a worker's job, the more likely the worker is an employee rather than self-employed. The court noted that the degree of actual control over a worker is important but it is not exclusive, since "we must examine not only the control exercised by an alleged employer, but also the degree to which an the alleged employer may intervene to impose control." The court observed that "[i]n order for an employer to retain the requisite control over the details of an employee's work, the employer need not stand over the employee and direct every move made by that employee." Further, and this is a point the court stressed repeatedly, "the degree of control necessary to find employee status varies according to the nature of the services provided." In particular, "[t]he threshold level of control necessary to find employee status is generally lower when applied to professional services than when applied to non-professional services." Therefore, less evidence of control (whether exercised or potential) is required to support a finding that a minister (or other professional) is an employee for income tax reporting purposes. The court quoted from a federal appeals court ruling: "From the very nature of the services rendered by . . . professionals, it would be wholly unrealistic to suggest that an employer should undertake the task of controlling the manner in which the professional conducts his activities."

The court then itemized several factors that demonstrated sufficient control over Rev. Weber to establish employee status. These are listed below:

• A Methodist bishop testified at trial that the church is "very proactive" and none of its members work without supervision.

• As a minister of the United Methodist Church, Rev. Weber was required to perform the numerous duties set forth in the Discipline. He agreed to perform those duties.

• Rev. Weber had to explain the position of the Discipline on any topic he chose to present in his sermons.

• Rev. Weber admitted that he followed the United Methodist theology in his sermons.

• Rev. Weber does not have the authority to unilaterally discontinue the regular services of a local church.

• Under the itinerant system of the United Methodist Church, Rev. Weber was appointed by the bishop to the positions he held. A bishop of the North Carolina Annual Conference determined where Rev.

Weber would preach. Rev. Weber had no right ultimately to refuse the appointment.

• Rev. Weber could not establish his own church.

• Rev. Weber was bound by the rules stated in the Discipline regarding mandatory retirement at age 70 and involuntary retirement.

• Rev. Weber was required to obtain the approval of the relevant bishop before he transferred from one Annual Conference to another.

• The Annual Conference limits the amount of leave ministers can take during a year.

• Methodist ministers are required by the Discipline to be "amenable" to the Annual Conference in the performance of their duties in the positions to which they are appointed. The court noted that "[t]he requirement that [Rev. Weber] be amenable to the Annual Conference is another indication of the control the Annual Conference had over [him]."

• A bishop testified at trial that ineffectiveness or unfitness ultimately may result in the termination of a minister's membership in the Annual Conference. A minister may be subject to termination from membership in the Annual Conference for the use of materials that do not conform to the United Methodist faith. Furthermore, one of the district superintendent's responsibilities is to establish a clearly understood process of supervision for clergy.

The court concluded its discussion of the first factor in its 7 factor test by noting:

Normally the control factor is the most persuasive factor in determining whether an employment relationship exists. We are mindful, however, that where professional individuals are involved this control "must necessarily be more tenuous and general than the control over nonprofessional employees." Nevertheless, it is clear that [Rev. Weber] is subject to significant control.

Factor #2—which party invests in the facilities used in the work. The court then turned to the second factor in its 7 factor test. This factor asks which party (employer or worker) invests in the facilities used in the work. If the employer invests in or provides the facilities used by the worker to perform the work, this suggests an employer-employee relationship. The court observed:

[Rev. Weber] was not required to invest in the work facilities. The local churches provided him with a home. The local churches provided the church in which [he] gave his sermons, and which contained office space for performing his duties. The local churches bought religious materials for his ministry.

The court dismissed the relevance of Rev. Weber's assertion that he prepared the weekly church bulletin at home, used his own computer for church work, and purchased some of his own vestments and a personal library. The court noted that "[h]is choice to work at home does not negate the fact that the local churches provided him with an office. [He] purchased computer equipment to make his work easier and to perform better. It does not prove that he was required to provide office equipment." With regard to Rev. Weber's assertion that he purchased his own vestments the court observed that "[v]estments were not required by the local churches, nor were they necessary for him to perform his duties. [His] choice was merely his own preference." Finally, the court pointed out that many professionals acquire their own libraries "whether they are employees or independent contractors."

Factor #3—the opportunity of the individual for profit or loss. The third factor is whether a worker has an opportunity to realize a profit or suffer a loss as a result of his or her services. Workers who are in a position to realize a profit or suffer a loss as a result of their services generally are self-employed, while employees ordinarily are not in such a position. The court concluded that this factor supported employee status in this case. It observed:

[Rev. Weber] was paid a salary, and provided with a parsonage, a utility expense allowance, and a travel expense allowance from each local church. Furthermore, if [he] was not assigned to a local church, the Annual Conference would pay him a minimum guaranteed salary, or if he were in special need, the Annual Conference could give him [special support]. Aside from minimal amounts earned for weddings and funerals and amounts spent on utilities and travel, [Rev. Weber] was not in a position to increase his profit, nor was he at risk for loss.

Factor #4—whether or not the employer has the right to discharge the worker. The authority of an employer to discharge a worker generally indicates that the worker is an employee rather than self-employed. The court concluded that Rev. Weber was subject to dismissal, and accordingly this factor supported employee status. The court observed:

The Annual Conference had the right to try, reprove, suspend, deprive of ministerial office and credentials, expel or acquit, or locate [Rev. Weber] for unacceptability or inefficiency. The clergy members of the executive session of the Annual Conference had the authority to discipline and fire [Rev. Weber]. These are other strong factors indicating that [Rev. Weber] was an employee rather than [self-employed].

Factor #5—whether the work is part of the employer's regular business. The fifth factor addresses the nature of the worker's services. Is the worker furthering the employer's regular or customary business? If so, this indicates an employer-employee relationship. Again, the court concluded that this factor supported a finding that Rev. Weber was an employee:

[Rev. Weber's] work is an integral part of the United Methodist Church. A minister has the responsibility to lead a local church in conformance with the beliefs of the United Methodist Church, to give an account of his or her pastoral ministries to the Annual Conference according to

prescribed forms, and to act as the administrative officer for that church.

A bishop confirmed the integral part played by ministers in the mission of the Methodist Church. When asked "and with respect to the pastor of the local church, would you also agree that to further the local church's integral role in the mission of the United Methodist Church, the pastor must perform his or her responsibilities and duties in conformance with this mission in mind," the bishop responded, "yes, sir."

Factor #6—the permanency of the relationship. The sixth factor focuses on the permanency of the relationship between the employer and a worker. The more permanent the relationship, the more likely the worker is an employee. The court concluded that this factor suggested that Rev. Weber was an employee. The relationship between Methodist ministers and the United Methodist Church is "intended to be permanent as opposed to transitory." Rev. Weber

has been an ordained United Methodist minister since 1978. [He] has conceded . . . that he is likely to remain a minister for his entire professional religious career, and that he is likely to remain affiliated with the North Carolina Annual Conference. The Annual Conference will pay a salary to a minister even when there are no positions with a local church available. The fact that ministers are also provided with retirement benefits indicates that the parties anticipate a long-term relationship. An independent contractor would not normally receive such benefits from a customer or client.

Further, Rev. Weber "does not make his services available to the general public, as would an independent contractor." He "works at the local church by the year and not for individuals 'by the job'". The court also noted that Rev. Weber "was required to work at the church to which he was assigned, and was required to attend meetings."

Factor #7—the relationship the parties believe they are creating. The final factor asks what kind of relationship the parties themselves thought they were creating. Did they intend for the worker to be an employee or self-employed? The court again ruled that this factor supported its conclusion that Rev. Weber was an employee rather than self-employed:

Because there was no withholding of income taxes and no Form W-2, we assume that [Rev. Weber] and his supervisors believed that ministers such as [Rev. Weber] were independent contractors. We give this factor little weight.

The court noted that the parties' characterization of their relationship was completely negated by the volume of "fringe benefits" made available to Rev. Weber. The court concluded that these fringe benefits demonstrated, far more strongly than the parties' outward intentions, that Rev. Weber was an employee rather than self-employed since the level of benefits was virtually unknown to self-employed workers. The court observed:

[Rev. Weber] received many benefits that we find are typical of those provided to employees rather than independent contractors, some of which follow. Each local church made contributions on [his] behalf . . . to a pension plan. [Rev. Weber] continued to receive his salary while on vacation. If needed, [he] would have been entitled to disability leave and paternity leave. If he could not be assigned to a local church, he would receive a guaranteed salary from the Annual Conference. If he were needy, he might be able to get [special relief] from the Annual Conference. A portion of the cost of [his] life insurance was paid by the local churches. The local churches paid a portion of the death benefit plan premiums, and [he] paid a portion. The local churches paid 75 percent of [his] 1988 health insurance premiums.

The court noted simply that "[t]hese enumerated benefits also indicate that [Rev. Weber] is an employee rather than self-employed."

Conclusion. The court concluded its lengthy analysis of the facts of this case by observing:

After considering all the facts and circumstances present in this case, we conclude that the factors that indicate [that Rev. Weber] was an employee outweigh those factors that indicate that he was self-employed. Accordingly, we hold that [his] ordinary and necessary trade or business expenses paid in 1988 were not properly listed on Schedule C, but are allowable as miscellaneous itemized deductions on Schedule A, subject to the 2% floor.

Who is Rev. Weber's employer? Amazingly, having concluded its lengthy discourse on the reasons why Rev. Weber was an employee rather than self-employed, the court refused to identify his employer! The court simply noted that "[t]he parties have stipulated that the only issue in dispute is whether [Rev. Weber] was an employee or was self-employed. We need not decide which part of the United Methodist Church is the employer." Unfortunately, the court left unanswered a fundamental question. Was Rev. Weber's employer the annual conference, the local church, or some other entity within the Methodist Church? While the 7 factor test may clearly support employee status for Rev. Weber, it is not so clear in identifying his employer. Some of the factors suggest that the annual conference is the employer while others point to the local church. Rev. Weber contended that no one agency within the Methodist Church exercised sufficient control over him to be his employer, and therefore an employer-employee relationship could not exist. The court responded to this argument as follows:

[Rev. Weber] contends that an employee-employer relationship cannot exist because there is no entity which exercised sufficient control over [him] so that he may be classified as an employee. He claims that the control over a minister is deliberately spread in a way that ensures that the minister has the maximum freedom to be the man or woman of God, which the United Methodist Church believes the ministry is all about. We do not question this polity for religious purposes. However, we disagree with [Rev. Weber's] contention when we analyze this case by application of the relevant court decisions and regulations. We acknowledge that an important religious purpose is served by the organizational structure. Nonetheless, we find that there is sufficient control over [Rev. Weber] as well as several other factors which establish that he was an employee.

The identification of Rev. Weber's employer is not an academic question. It will determine a number of important issues, including payroll tax reporting issues and the availability of various fringe benefits. One can only wonder if the court's refusal to address this issue was based on the difficulty of answering it and the inconsistency of any answer with the court's decision. Perhaps this also explains why the court took so long to announce its decision.

The Tax Court's decision does not apply to all ministers. While the Tax Court's decision was considered a "test case" by several Methodist ministers, it is not a "test case" for ministers in other denominations. While the court's 7 factor test can now be used to evaluate the correct reporting status of other ministers, the court did not decide that all ministers are employees for income tax reporting purposes. Quite to the contrary, the Tax Court ended the *Weber* case with the following comment: "We recognize that there may be differences with respect to ministers in other churches or denominations, and the particular facts and circumstances must be considered in each case."

✎ **Key point: the Tax Court ended the *Weber* case by noting that "there may be differences with respect to ministers in other churches or denominations, and the particular facts and circumstances must be considered in each case." In other words, the Tax Court was not addressing the correct reporting status of all ministers.**

Relevance of religious considerations. Some ministers point to theological considerations in sup-

---

Why Most Clergy Are "Better Off" Reporting Their Federal Income Taxes As Employees

Most clergy will be "better off" reporting their federal income taxes as employees, since

✓ the value of various fringe benefits will be excludable, including the oftentimes significant cost of employer-paid health insurance premiums on the life of the minister and his or her dependents

✓ the risk of an IRS audit is substantially lower

✓ they avoid the additional taxes and penalties that often apply to self-employed clergy who are audited by the IRS and reclassified as employees. Most clergy would be employees under the "common law employee test."

port of their self-employed status. For example, some say that they are theologically opposed to the notion that they are "controlled" by their church. The Tax Court was not sympathetic to this view. It observed:

> [Rev. Weber's] basic position appears to be that because he is a minister in a unique religious order he cannot be an employee. While we have great respect for [his] religious dedication, religion is not the question before us.

> [Rev. Weber] is seeking a business benefit. He wants to file a Schedule C . . . and to claim business expenses on it. It is he who has cast this case in business terms.

The court also noted: "[Rev. Weber] contends that no one had the right to control either the method or the means by which he conducted his ministry. We do not agree."

The Tax Court's decision is upheld on appeal. In 1995, a federal appeals court upheld the Tax Court's decision in the *Weber* case. It adopted the Tax Court's decision as its own. *Weber v. Commissioner, 60 F.3d 1104 (4th Cir. 1995).*

✎ **Key point: the Tax Court's decision in the Weber case was upheld by a federal appeals court in 1995 by a 2-1 vote. This elevates the significance of this ruling, and makes it more likely that the IRS will assert that ministers are employees for federal income tax reporting purposes.**

✎ **Key point: the *Weber* case was a regular opinion of the Tax Court, meaning that it was a decision by all 34 judges. On the other hand, the *Shelley* case was a memorandum decision of the Court, meaning that it was a ruling by only 1 judge. Regular opinions, such as the *Weber* case, have much greater precedential value than memorandum opinions, since they are decisions by the full Court. This conclusion is reinforced by the fact that the *Weber* case was affirmed by a federal appeals court.**

❖ **New in 1997. Tax Court ruled that a Methodist minister was an employee rather than self-employed for income tax reporting purposes. The court applied the same 7 factor test it used in the Weber case, and concluded that there was no basis for distinguishing between the two cases. The minister in question had served as both a senior pastor and a denominational official for the years under audit. *Radde v. Commissioner, T.C. Memo. 1997-490 (1997).***

Shelley v. Commissioner, T.C. Memo. 1994-432

Moments after issuing its decision in the *Weber* case, the Tax Court released a second opinion finding that a Pentecostal Holiness minister was self-employed rather than an employee for federal income tax reporting purposes. This second decision confirms that the Tax Court did not intend by its *Weber* decision to find all ministers to be employees. It also assures that the correct reporting status of individual ministers will be a continuing source of confusion and controversy!

The Tax Court applied the same 7 factor test that it applied in the *Weber* case, but it concluded that Rev. Shelley was self-employed rather than an employee for federal income tax reporting purposes. Here is how the court analyzed the 7 factors:

Factor #1—the degree of control exercised by the employer over the details of the work. The court concluded that this factor supported a finding that Rev. Shelley was self-employed for income tax reporting purposes, since his employing church exercised insufficient control over the details of his work. Here are some of the factors the court mentioned in reaching its conclusion:

• Rev. Shelley was hired by the church because of his specialized skills and his particular style of ministry.

• He was free to use his own methods and style in the day-to-day conduct of his activities.

• He was chairman of the church board.

• He had the power to appoint and remove members of the church board. He also appointed members of the board to the various church committees.

• He was not supervised by anyone, and was not evaluated regularly.

• He could hire, supervise, and fire assistants as he saw fit.

• He could delegate his duties to the church's associate pastor.

• He had the power to adjust his own salary, and did so on occasion.

• He performed services for the church both on and off the Church's premises.

• He was not restricted to performing services solely for his own congregation.

• He determined his own work hours.

• He was not subject to a mandatory retirement age.

• He was encouraged, but not required, to participate in continuing education.

• He was free to go on missions when he felt called to do so, and there was no requirement that he request permission for a leave of absence.

• He was not assigned to the church by the state conference of the Pentecostal Holiness Church (the denomination that ordained him and with which his church was affiliated).

• He was free to establish his own church within the denomination, and could serve temporarily as pastor of a church not affiliated with the Pentecostal Holiness Church.

• His state conference will not evaluate a pastor until approached with a problem by a church that the church board and congregation have been unable to resolve. Once involved, the conference's primary responsibility is to provide spiritual guidance and counseling to the pastor and the church. The denomination's Manual states that if serious conflicts that cannot be resolved develop between a pastor and the quadrennial conference (a regional denominational body), the quadrennial conference has the right to place the pastor on probation or revoke his ordination certificate. However, these measures would not be used unless the pastor was unable to accomplish the basic goals for which he was hired, "to lead in worship, to lead in the nurture of believers, and to win the lost to Christ", in a manner consistent with church doctrines. At no point would a quadrennial conference official step in and specifically tell the pastor how to run his church.

The court acknowledged that the denominational Manual specified that ministers are "amenable to the quadrennial conference and the conference board." However, this did not alter its conclusion that insufficient control was exercised over Rev. Shelley by either his church or denomination to render him an employee for income tax reporting purposes. The court concluded:

After considering all the facts and circumstances affecting the issue of control, we are persuaded that [Rev. Shelley] was "subject to the control or direction of another merely as to the result to be accomplished by the work and not as to the means and methods for accomplishing the result". *Treas. Reg. 31.3401(c)-1(b).* [His] primary responsibility was to help the church thrive. The record does not reflect that the church or the [state conference] retained any significant rights to control [his] efforts to accomplish this goal.

Factor #2—which party invests in the facilities used in the work. The court noted simply that while Rev. Shelley was not required to invest in the basic work facilities he used as a pastor, he did pay for the collection of his own substantial library (which he used in his ministry) and he regularly paid a portion of the expenses associated with continuing education courses and other church- related travel.

Factor #3—the opportunity of the individual for profit or loss. The court did not consider this factor relevant under the circumstances of this case since "[w]e do not believe that the normal business risks of profit and loss are particularly applicable" to a minister. However, it observed that "[t]o the extent that this factor has any bearing, we note that [Rev. Shelley] had no guarantee from the [state conference] or the church that his salary would be maintained if the church was not successful or if he left the church and could not find another ministry within the [denomination]. In this sense, [he] did have some risk of loss."

Factor #4—whether or not the employer has the right to discharge the worker. The IRS insisted that the fact that there are procedures available to remove a Pentecostal Holiness minister from a church or to revoke minister's ordination certificate mandates a finding that Rev. Shelley was an employee. The Tax Court disagreed

[Rev. Shelley] could not be fired at will by either the church board, the [state conference], or any other body within the [denomination]. Discharge of a pastor typically requires the involvement of the church board, the congregation, and the [state conference] board. According to the Manual, it is possible for the church board to vote to request that the congregation hold a vote of confidence with respect to a pastor. However, this possibility must be considered in conjunction with the fact that the pastor has the power to appoint and remove members of the church board. As stated above, the testimony offered at trial made clear that the [state conference] board will not evaluate a pastor or a minister until approached by a church with a problem that the church board and congregation have been unable to resolve. The procedures delineated in the Manual and by witnesses for dealing with dissension within the church are oriented more toward conflict resolution than termination, and differ from what we would expect to find in a typical employer-employee relationship. In the context of this case, we do not believe that the remote possibility that [Rev. Shelley] could be forced to leave the church or could have his ordination certificate withdrawn indicates that [he] was an employee rather than an independent contractor.

Factor #5—whether the work is part of the employer's regular business. The court conceded that Rev. Shelley's work "was part of both the church's and the [denomination's] regular business." It noted that this "may tend to suggest that [he] was an employee; however, [it is] not significant enough to outweigh the conclusion we draw from the record that [Rev. Shelley] was an independent contractor [self-employed]."

Factor #6—the permanency of the relationship. The court conceded that Rev. Shelley's relationship with the church and the denomination was reasonably permanent. It noted that this "may tend to suggest that [he] was an employee; however, [it is] not significant enough to outweigh the conclusion we draw from the cord that [Rev. Shelley] was an independent contractor [self-employed]."

Factor #7—the relationship the parties believe they are creating. The court noted that there was no written agreement between Rev. Shelley and his church or state conference disclosing the type of relationship the parties believed they were creating. However, the court noted that Rev. Shelley "did not have any income tax withheld from his salary and did not receive any Forms W-2 from the church, the [state conference], or any other body in the [denomination]. We assume, therefore, that petitioner and the other parties involved believed that petitioner was an independent contractor." The court rejected the assertion of the IRS that the church provided fringe benefits to Rev. Shelley that ordinarily are provided only to employees. As examples the IRS cited a biweekly salary, a health insurance plan provided by the state conference, disability leave, and vacation pay. The court observed:

> While these benefits are more likely to be found in an employer-employee relationship, their presence does not eliminate the possibility that the taxpayer is an independent contractor, particularly in situations where the taxpayer maintains a relationship with a particular institution over a long period of time. . . . [Rev. Shelley] received some benefits typical of an employer-employee relationship. Nevertheless, considering [his] long-term relationship with the [denomination] we find it significant that there is no evidence that [he] received life insurance coverage or any retirement benefits through the [denomination, state conference] or the church.

Conclusion. The Tax Court concluded: "Based on the application of the enumerated factors to the facts and circumstances present in this case, we conclude that, during the years in issue, [Rev. Shelley] was an independent contractor and must report his business income and expenses on Schedules C." The court added: "We are aware that *Weber v. Commissioner, 103 T.C. 378 (1994)*, involving a United Methodist minister, shares certain similarities with the instant case but holds that the taxpayer was an employee. We find that the [Pentecostal Holiness Church] did not have the same type of relationship with [Rev. Shelley] that the United Methodist Church does with its ministers. Accordingly, we conclude that the facts and circumstances present in this case warrant our reaching a different conclusion than that reached in *Weber.*"

IRS appeals the Shelley case. The IRS appealed the *Shelley* decision to the federal court of appeals for the eleventh circuit. The case was settled out of court while the appeal was pending.

IRS Letter Ruling 9414022 (1994)

In 1994 the IRS ruled that a youth pastor was an employee rather than self-employed for federal income tax reporting purposes. The youth pastor was responsible for the church's youth ministry and was qualified to carry out all the ordinances of the church when necessary, including baptisms and communion; he received instructions from the senior pastor; the senior pastor supervised him and retained the right to change the methods used in the performance of his duties; he was hired for an indefinite period of time and was required to follow a schedule established by the church; he performed his services at the church's location and the church provided him with the materials, equipment and supplies and reimbursed him for expenses incurred in performing his services; he received a salary for his services plus a housing allowance; he received paid vacation; the church did not carry worker's compensation for the youth pastor and did not deduct social security or federal income taxes from his pay; the church reported the youth pastor's income to the IRS on form W-2; the youth pastor performed his services on a full-time basis, at least 8 hours a day; the church retained the right to discharge the youth pastor at any time while he retained the right to terminate his services at any time without either party incurring any liability; the youth pastor performed his services under the church's name and did not represent himself to the public as being in the business to perform such services for others; he did not have a financial investment in the church and did not assume the risk of realizing a profit or suffering a loss. The IRS, applying the 20 factor test for determining a taxpayer's correct reporting status, concluded that the youth pastor was an employee for income tax reporting purposes. The IRS concluded that "the church has the right to and does, in fact, exercise the degree of direction and control necessary in establishing an employer-employee relationship. Accordingly, we conclude that the [youth pastor] is an employee of the church." The IRS correctly pointed out that the youth pastor, like any minister, is self-employed for social security purposes with respect to services performed in the exercise of ministry.

4. IRS Tax Guide for Churches

In 1994 the IRS published a "tax guide for churches" that addresses the correct reporting status of ministers by simply noting that "in determining the church's responsibilities for employment tax, the determination of whether a particular worker is an employee is important. The facts will determine whether there is an actual employer-employee relationship." The tax guide refers to IRS Publication 937 ("Employment Taxes and Information Returns"), which discusses the "20 factor test" for determining a taxpayer's correct reporting status.

5. IRS audit guidelines for ministers

In 1995 the IRS released its long-awaited audit guidelines for ministers. These guidelines were issued pursuant to the IRS "Market Segment Specialization Program" (MSSP), and are intended to promote a higher degree of competence among those agents who audit ministers. The guidelines state that "the first issue that must be determined is whether the minister is an employee or an independent contractor."

✎ **Key point. IRS agents are informed, by the new audit guidelines, that the very first issue to be resolved in auditing a minister's tax return is whether or not the minister is an employee or self-employed for income tax reporting purposes.**

✎ **Key point: the audit guidelines will instruct IRS agents in the examination of ministers' tax returns. They alert agents to the key questions to ask, and provide background information along with the IRS position on a number of issues. It is therefore of utmost importance that ministers be familiar with these guidelines.**

The guidelines provide IRS agents with the following information regarding this important issue:

• This is a factual question that will depend on the circumstances of each case.

• The distinction between an employee and self-employed person "must be made on common law grounds."

• Ministers "are generally considered employees under the common law rules."

⊃ **Observation. The guidelines do not say that all ministers are employees for federal income tax reporting purposes. Rather, they state that ministers "are generally considered employees." This flexible approach leaves open the possibility that some ministers will not be employees under the so-called "common law employee test. Note, however, that self-employed status will be the exception, and that any minister reporting income taxes as self-employed must expect to have his or her status challenged if audited.**

• In determining whether a worker is an employee, "employer control over the manner in which the work is performed, either actual or the right to it, is the basic test." Actual control "need not be exercised by the employer, provided the employer has the right to control the employee when it is appropriate and necessary."

• The control test must be applied only after taking into account the nature of the work to be performed. "When the worker is a professional, such as a minister, the extent of control necessary for the professional to qualify as an employee is less than that necessary for a nonprofessional worker performing routine and mechanical duties."

• The absence of the need to control the manner in which the minister conducts his or her duties should not be confused with the absence of the right to control. The right to control contemplated by the common law as an incident of employment requires only such supervision as the nature of the work requires.

• The guidelines specify that "even though a minister may receive a Form 1099-MISC for the performance of services, he or she may be a common law employee and should in fact be receiving a Form W-2. In those very limited cases in which a minister is an independent contractor, such as in the case of a traveling evangelist, the issuance of a Form 1099-MISC is appropriate."

• The guidelines refer to the following authorities in support of these conclusions:

(1) McGuire v. United States of America, 349 F.2d 644 (9th Cir. 1965). A federal appeals court ruled that loaders employed by motor freight carriers engaged in hauling fruit between the Yakima Valley in Washington and the Los Angeles area were employees rather than self-employed. The court found that "evidence of actual supervision [of the loaders] was minimal, but little supervision was required because the nature of the work was uncompli-

cated and because unloaders were generally familiar with the procedures of the job."

(2) James v. Commissioner, 25 T.C. 1296 (1956). The Tax Court ruled that a pathologist who worked at a hospital was an employee. The court noted that "the control of an employer over the manner in which professional employees shall conduct the duties of their positions must necessarily be more tenuous and general than the control over non-professional employees. Yet, despite this absence of direct control over the manner in which professional men shall conduct their professional activities, it can not be doubted that many professional men are employees."

(3) United States v. Webb, 397 U.S. 179 (1970). The United States Supreme Court ruled that standards of maritime law, rather than common-law standards relating to land-based occupations, applied in determining whether captains and crewmen of fishing boats were employees of boat owners for federal tax purposes.

(4) Regulation 31.3121(d)-1(c). This regulation is quoted earlier in this chapter.

(5) Regulation 31.3401(c)-1. This regulation is substantially the same as 31.3121(d)-1(c), quoted above.

(6) Code section 3121(d)(2). This section of the Internal Revenue Code specifies that the term "employee" means "any individual who, under the usual common law rules applicable in determining the employer-employee relationship, has the status of an employee."

⊃ **Observation. The guidelines provide IRS agents with inadequate information to decide consistently and correctly whether ministers are employees or self-employed. Reliance on cases involving fishing captains, freight loaders, and pathologists provide little practical guidance.**

⊃ **Observation. Surprising, the guidelines do not refer to the "20 factor test" announced by the IRS in 1987 (Revenue Ruling 87-41). This is good news, since the 20 factor test has been widely criticized as being too biased in favor of employee status.**

⊃ **Observation. It is also surprising that the guidelines do not refer to either the Weber or Shelley cases (both were decided before the guidelines were released). Both cases involved the application of a 7 factor test for deciding whether a worker is an employee or self-employed for income tax reporting purposes. It is difficult to see why the guidelines omit any reference to these cases and instead refer to cases involving fishing captains, freight loaders, and pathologists. There is little question which cases the federal courts will consider most relevant.**

6. How ministers should determine their correct reporting status

Our recommendation is that ministers review the 4 tests described in this chapter in determining their correct reporting status for federal income tax reporting purposes. Any of the tests can be used. The tests should be applied in light of the court decisions and IRS ruling summarized above.

7. Additional considerations

Finally, note the following additional considerations.

(1) The IRS has a definite bias in favor of treating taxpayers as employees. The reason is simple—employees are subject to income tax withholding, and accordingly there is a much greater likelihood that a person's taxes will be paid if he or she is an employee rather than self-employed. This consideration has no application to clergy, however, whose income is exempt by law from income tax withholding even if they are employees for income tax purposes. *IRC 3401(a)(9).*

(2) Ministers who may be self-employed for income tax reporting purposes. There are a number of situations in which a minister is more likely to be self-employed for federal income tax reporting purposes. These include:

• **Itinerant evangelists.** Itinerant evangelists, who conduct services in several different churches during the course of a year, ordinarily would be considered self-employed for purposes of both income taxes and social security taxes. They ordinarily would not be considered employees under either the Tax Court's 7 factor test of the IRS 20 factor test.

• **Guest speaking.** Many ministers are called upon to conduct worship services in other churches on an occasional basis. To illustrate, Rev. D, who serves as senior minister at First Church, is invited to conduct a service at a church in another community. Clergy generally will be considered to be self-employed with respect to such occasional guest speaking commitments.

• **Supply pastors.** Many ministers serve temporary assignments in local churches until a permanent minister can be selected. In some cases, these ministers will be self-employed with respect to such an assignment. This will depend on an application of the Tax Court's 7 factor test (or the IRS 20 factor test). In general, the shorter the assignment the more likely that the minister will be considered self-employed.

• **Direct services.** IRS Publication 517 recognizes that it is possible for ministers who are employees of their churches for income tax reporting purposes to be self-employed for certain services (such as baptisms, marriages, and funerals) that are performed directly for individual members who in turn pay a fee or honorarium to the minister.

• **Church polity.** In some cases a church's polity may suggest that ministers are self-employed rather than employees for income tax reporting purposes. For example, ministers who are not associated with a regional or national religious body that exercises control over their activities will find it easier in some cases to argue that they are self-employed for income tax reporting purposes. It is significant that the Tax Court ended the *Weber* case with the following comment: "We recognize that there may be differences with respect to ministers in other churches or denominations, and the particular facts and circumstances must be considered in each case."

(3) Ministers may obtain an official determination of their reporting status by filing a Form SS-8 with the IRS. This can be a time-consuming and involved process, however, and the IRS demonstrates a decidedly pro-employee bias in its rulings. In other words, a minister wanting to report his or her income taxes as a self-employed person ordinarily will not be successful in obtaining IRS confirmation in response to an SS-8 application.

(4) Some clergy insist on reporting their income taxes as self-employed for theological reasons. That is, they consider themselves to be under the control or authority of Jesus Christ rather than a local church or church board. Such persons feel that they would be compromising their biblical authority by reporting as an employee since it would amount to an acknowledgment of subordination to local church authority. Such a view, if corroborated by appropriate language in the church's charter or bylaws, might support self-employed status for income tax reporting purposes *if in fact the church does not exercise meaningful control over the minister.* Note, however, that an IRS auditor might well want to determine whether or not the church board shares the minister's "theology" on this point. If church board members do not agree that they lack any meaningful control over the minister, then it is highly unlikely that this argument will be of any relevance. Also, note that the Tax Court dismissed the relevance of theological considerations in the *Weber* case by observing

[Rev. Weber's] basic position appears to be that because he is a minister in a unique religious order he cannot be an employee. While we have great respect for [his] religious dedication, religion is not the question before us.

[Rev. Weber] is seeking a business benefit. He wants to file a Schedule C . . . and to claim business expenses on it. It is he who has cast this case in business terms.

The court also noted: "[Rev. Weber] contends that no one had the right to control either the method or the means by which he conducted his ministry. We do not agree."

(5) Clergy who report their federal income taxes as employees do not lose the housing allowance exclusion. There is a common misconception that clergy who report their income taxes as employees will lose the housing allowance exclusion. This is not so. The housing allowance is available to clergy whether they report their income taxes as an employee or as self-employed. However, as noted above, certain fringe benefits provided by a church on behalf of a minister are excludable from the minister's income only if he or she is an employee for federal income tax reporting purposes. Examples include medical insurance premiums paid by a church on behalf of its minister; group term life insurance (up to $50,000) provided by a church on behalf of a minister; amounts payable to employees on account of sickness, accident, or disability pursuant to an employer-financed plan; and employer-sponsored "cafeteria plans" which permit employees to choose between receiving cash payments or a variety of fringe benefits.

(6) "Section 530" of the Revenue Act of 1978. In the late 1960s, the IRS began vigorously challenging employer attempts to classify workers as self-employed rather than as employees. In many cases, employers were assessed large penalties for improperly classifying some workers as self-employed. Congress responded to these developments by enacting "section 530" of the Revenue Act of 1978. Section 530 was designed to provide *employers* with relief from hostile IRS attempts to reclassify workers as employees. If employers meet certain requirements set forth in section 530, they are relieved of penalties that otherwise might apply because of their treatment of workers as self-employed. The IRS has interpreted section 530 in ways that seriously undermine the protections it was designed to create. Congress responded to these IRS efforts by enacting legislation in 1996 repudiating most of the schemes the IRS has used over the years to avoid section 530. This is an important development for churches and other employers. It is discussed more fully in chapter 11 of this text. For purposes of this chapter, the important point to note is that section 530 only relieves *employers* of penalties for improperly classifying a worker as self-employed. It provides no relief to such workers in defending their self-employed status for purposes of their individual income tax returns.

(7) Generally, an employer is legally accountable for the misconduct of employees (but not the misconduct of self-employed persons). Most courts have reached the conclusion that clergy serving local churches are employees rather than self-employed for purposes of deciding whether or not the employing church is legally responsible for their conduct. For example, a federal appeals court concluded that a Methodist church was legally responsible for the copyright infringement of a minister of music since "the only inference that reasonably can be drawn from the evidence is that in selecting and arranging the song . . . for use by the church choir [the minister] was engaged in the course and scope of his employment by the church." *Wihtol v. Crow, 309 F.2d 777 (8th Cir. 1962).* Many other cases have involved accidents involving motor vehicles driven by clergy in the course of church work. Such cases support the treatment of clergy as employees for income tax purposes, since the legal considerations employed in determining whether or not a minister is an employee for church liability purposes are substantially the same as those used in determining whether or not a

minister is an employee for income tax purposes. Note, however, that some courts have not agreed with these rulings. To illustrate, the Kansas Supreme Court concluded that a Catholic priest was self-employed for purposes of determining the legal liability of his diocese for his misconduct even though the diocese "followed the majority of dioceses in issuing a W-2 form to each priest." *Brillhart v. Sheier, 758 P.2d 219 (Kan. 1988).*

(8) Workers compensation. Ministers who report their federal income taxes as self-employed are not necessarily self-employed for workers compensation purposes. The term "employee" generally is defined more broadly under workers compensation laws than under federal tax law.

(9) Penalties. As noted in chapter 11, a church can be assessed penalties for reporting as self-employed a worker who the IRS later determines to be an employee.

(10) The Cosby case. In 1987 the Tax Court ruled that a Methodist minister was *not an employee of his local church* but rather was self-employed, and accordingly could report his church income and all business expenses on Schedule C. The court acknowledged that the "common law employee test" had to be applied in reaching a determination as to the minister's status, and referred to most of the 20 factors discussed above as helpful guidelines. The court relied upon the following considerations in reaching its conclusion: (1) the minister was "free to use his own methods and style in the day-to-day conduct of his activities" and was clearly "his own man and operated free from any substantial control"; (2) the procedures that existed for terminating the minister's services did "not at all approximate the type of day-to-day supervision and control which is characteristic of an employer-employee relationship" and did not enable the church to "control or direct the details and means by which the desired result was to be accomplished"; (3) the minister's seminary education represented a substantial capital investment in his profession; (4) the minister's profession requires considerable skill; and (5) the minister and his church regarded him as self-employed rather than as an employee. The court observed that its conclusion was "bolstered by the fact that neither party, nor our own research, *disclosed a single case in which a member of the clergy . . . was held to be an employee of either his or her local congregation* or of the hierarchical structure of his or her denomination."

The *Cosby* decision was a "small tax court case," meaning that it involved less than $10,000 and the taxpayer elected to pursue an expedited and simplified procedure authorized by section 7463 of the Internal Revenue Code. While small tax court cases are more quickly resolved, there is a trade-off—section 7463 specifies that "a decision entered in any case in which the proceedings are conducted under this section shall not be reviewed by any other court and shall not be treated as precedent for any other case." In other words, the decision of the Tax Court in the *Cosby* case was final, and it cannot be cited as precedent in other cases. Obviously, this greatly limits the impact of the case. Further, while the Tax Court did not refer to the *Cosby* case in the *Weber* ruling, it is likely that the *Weber* case overruled the *Cosby* decision (meaning that the *Cosby* case has no relevance whatever). *Cosby v. Commissioner, T.C. Sum. Op. 1987-141 (unpublished, small Tax Court case).*

✎ **Key point: the importance of the distinction between employee and self-employed status for purposes of computing business expense deductions is fully in chapter 7.**

☞ *Example. Rev. P is a retired minister who serves as an interim minister for churches in a given geographical region that are temporarily in need of ministerial services. Rev. P typically spends no more than three months with any particular congregation, is given great freedom with respect to the duties he performs and the manner or method of performance, and is issued a 1099-MISC form by each church. These facts suggest that Rev. P could report his income and business expenses as a self-employed person on Schedule C.*

☞ *Example. Rev. L is a minister of education at First Church. She has a specific job description, her services are under the direct supervision and control of her senior pastor, she is issued a W-2 form each year, and is required to follow prescribed methods in the performance of her duties. These facts strongly suggest that Rev. L is an employee for income tax reporting purposes.*

☞ *Example. Rev. G serves as pastor of a small congregation that has no other employees. He performs his duties free from any control or supervision by the church. Much of his work is performed off of church premises. He is issued a 1099-MISC form each year, and his work agreement with the church characterizes him as self-employed. Under these facts, the federal appeals court's decision in the Alford case (discussed above) suggests that Rev. G may be a self-employed person for income tax reporting purposes. However, Rev. G should carefully evaluate the following three advantages of employee status before continuing to report as self-employed: (1) the value of various fringe benefits will be excludable, including the often-times significant cost of employer-paid health insurance premiums on the life of the minister and his or her dependents, (2) the risk of an IRS audit is substantially lower, and (3) as an employee, he would avoid the additional taxes and penalties that often apply to self-employed clergy who are audited by the IRS and reclassified as employees.*

☞ *Example. Same facts as the previous example, except that Rev. G is senior minister of a church with 2 other ministers and 10 lay employees. It is less likely that Rev. G will be able to use the Alford case to support his self-employed status, because ministers in larger churches tend to be subject to more control with respect to the manner in which they perform their duties.*

☞ *Example. Rev. M works in an administrative capacity for a church agency. Ordinarily, ministers who work in such a capacity will satisfy the definition of a common law employee since they are subject to a greater degree of control and supervision with respect to the details and performance of their duties, and accordingly should report their income taxes as employees. The income tax regulations specify that "generally, an officer of a corporation is an employee of the corporation." Treas. Reg. 31.3401(c)-1(f).*

☞ *Example. Rev. H is a youth minister at First Church. Ordinarily, ministers who work in such a capacity will satisfy the definition of a common law employee since they are subject to a greater degree of control and supervision with respect to the details and performance of their duties, and accordingly should report their income taxes as employees. IRS Letter Ruling 9414022.*

☞ *Example. Rev. H has been the senior minister at First Church since 1981. He reports his income taxes as a self-employed person on Schedule C (Form 1040). First Church issues Rev. H a W-2 form at the end of each year, and includes his compensation on its quarterly 941 returns. Rev. H's predecessor was Rev. N, who reported his income taxes as an employee. The fact that the church issues Rev. H a W-2 form rather than a 1099-MISC, and includes his compensation on its quarterly employer's tax returns (941 forms), would probably result in a determination that he is an employee for income tax reporting purposes in the event that his return is audited by the IRS. Further, while Revenue Procedure 85-18 is not directly relevant to clergy, it may support the conclusion that Rev. H should be treated as an employee.*

☞ *Example. Rev. W has reported his federal income taxes as a self-employed person for many years. In 1997, he decides to report his taxes as an employee. His employing church withholds FICA taxes from his pay throughout 1997, and in addition pays the employer's share of FICA taxes. Clergy are always deemed self-employed for social security purposes with respect to services performed in the exercise of their ministry, and accordingly they are never subject to FICA taxes with respect to such services. Rev. W's decision to report his income taxes as an employee did not change his self-employed status for social security purposes. The church is incorrectly treating Rev. W as an employee for FICA purposes. He should continue to pay the self-employment tax (the social security tax for self-employed persons).*

☞ *Example. Rev. T, senior minister of First Church, reports his income taxes as a self-employed person (using Schedule C). His church compensation for 1997 was $35,000. In addition, the church paid the annual premium ($2,500) on a health insurance policy for Rev. T and his family. Since Rev. T considers himself to be self-employed for federal income tax reporting purposes, he is not eligible for the exclusion of employer-paid health insurance premiums. Accordingly, the church must list the full $2,500 premium as income on Rev. T's Form 1099-MISC.*

☞ *Example. Rev. O reports her income taxes as a self-employed person. She has $4,000 of business expenses in 1997 that were not reimbursed by his church. She deducted all of them on Schedule C. She did not have enough expenses to itemize deductions on Schedule A. Rev. O is later audited by the IRS, and she is reclassified as an employee. She will not be able to deduct any of the $3,500 of business expenses since they are deductible, by an employee, only as an itemized deduction on Schedule A. This harsh result can be avoided by the church adopting an accountable reimbursement plan (see chapter 7 for full details).*

☞ *Example. Rev. T is an associate pastor under the supervision of the senior pastor and has primary responsibilities for the music, arts, drama, and missions program of his church. His responsibilities include working with the music, arts, drama and missions committees and assisting the lead pastor and congregation in all phases of the ministry. He serves as the resource person, motivator and administrator of various church activities. The church requires the associate pastor to perform services during regular working hours. His services are supervised and reviewed by the church, and he receives instructions from the church. His day-to-day activities are reviewed almost weekly by the senior pastor. He is required to attend a workshop of a general informative nature and his budget includes funds for one week of formalized training per year. All of the associate pastor's duties must be performed by him personally and cannot be delegated by him to others. The church makes contributions toward hospital or medical insurance for the associate pastor, and provides him with an office in the church building. The associate pastor is paid an annual rate on a bi-weekly basis. He is also provided with lump sum amounts for automobile and housing expenses. His services may be terminated for unsatisfactory performance. He has the right to terminate his services at any time. Under these facts, the IRS ruled that the associate pastor was an employee and not self-employed for federal income tax reporting purposes. It noted that "it is clear that [the church has] the right to direct and control the associate pastor to the degree necessary to create an employer-employee relationship." IRS Letter Ruling 8333107.*

B. Nonminister Staff

Many churches employ staff members other than ministers. In general, the same tests for determining whether or not a minister is an employee or self-employed for federal income tax reporting purposes will apply in evaluating the correct reporting status of nonminister staff. There are a few differences, however, that should be noted:

• **Social security.** Nonminister staff, unlike ministers, are not always treated as self-employed for social security. Nonminister staff who are employees for income tax reporting purposes under the tests discussed in this chapter generally must be treated as employees for social security. This means that they will be subject to FICA taxes. There is one exception—nonminister staff employed by a church that exempted itself from payment of the employer's share of FICA taxes by filing a timely Form 8274 (discussed in chapter 11) are treated as self-employed for social security.

• **Withholding.** Nonminister staff who are employees for income tax reporting purposes are subject to income tax and FICA withholding.

☞ *Example. A church employed a worker to serve as church custodian, under the following terms and conditions: (1) The position of church custodian is advertised for bids on a yearly basis; (2) the custodian is required to follow guidelines established by the church; (3) the custodian's duties include the cleaning of the church building and, when necessary, snow removal; (4) the custodian works at the church once each week; (5) the custodian is not required to perform services during regular working hours, but rather performs his duties at his own discretion; (6) the church reviews the custodian's services only to the extent necessary to ensure that they are completed in accordance with church guidelines; (7) equipment and supplies are furnished to the custodian at no cost (the custodian purchases the necessary supplies and is reimbursed by the church treasurer)' (8) the custodian is paid on a monthly basis; (9) the church assumes that the custodian will perform his services personally; (10) the custodian does not engage helpers to assist in the work; (11) the custodian is not eligible for bonuses, pensions, sick pay, or other fringe benefits; (12) the church does not make contributions toward hospital or medical insurance for the custodian; (13) no formal guidelines have been established for termination, however, the custodian could be terminated for gross negligence; (14) the custodian can terminate his services at any time; (15) the custodian does not perform similar services for others. It is the church's belief that the custodian is self-employed rather than an employee, and accordingly it has not withheld FICA taxes or income taxes from the custodian's compensation. The IRS disagreed, concluding that the custodian was an employee. The IRS observed:*

Careful consideration has been given to the information submitted in this case. The facts show that the [custodian is] subject to certain restraints and conditions that are indicative of the church's control over [him]. The [custodian] performs personal services for the church on its premises and property. [He performs his] services according to guidelines established by the church. He renders his services personally and does not engage any helpers or assistants. The church provides him with the use of equipment and supplies in the performance of services at no cost. His services are supervised and reviewed. His services are necessary and incident to the church's operation. He is not engaged in an independent enterprise in which he assumes the usual business risks. He has a continuous relationship with the church as opposed to a single transaction. Both parties could terminate the agreement at any time. IRS Letter Ruling 8505023.

APPENDIX 1

ARE MINISTERS EMPLOYEES OR SELF-EMPLOYED?
A SUMMARY OF ALL CASES AND RULINGS

Case	IRS Letter Ruling 94140)622 (1994)	Shelley v. Commissioner, (Tax Court, 1994)	Weber v. Commissioner (federal appeals court, 1995)*	Greene v. Commissioner (Tax Court, 1997)	Alford v. United States (federal appeals court, 1997)
Church	not disclosed	Pentecostal Holiness	Methodist	Assemblies of God	Assemblies of God
Test	1) employer controls how an employee does job	X	X	X	X
	2) employees more likely to be trained on job				
	3) employees' work is part of employer's operations	X	X	X	X
	4) self-employed workers hire and pay substitutes; employees do not				
	5) self-employed workers hire and pay assistants; employees do not				X
	6) employees more likely to have a continuing relationship with their employer	X	X	X	X
	7) employees more likely to work set hours				X
	8) employees more likely to work full-time				
	9) employees more likely to do work on employer's premises				X
	10) employees more likely to perform work in a sequence set by employer				
	11) employees more likely to submit oral or written reports to employer				
	12) employees paid by hour or week; self-employed paid by the job				X
	13) employees more likely to have their business expenses paid by employer				
	14) self-employed more likely to provide their own tools and materials				X
	15) employees more likely to have equipment and facilities provided by employer	X	X	X	
	16) self-employed more likely to realize a profit or loss from their work	X	X		
	17) self-employed work for more than one employer at same time				
	18) self-employed promote their services to the public				
	19) employees can be dismissed	X	X	X	
	20) employees can quit at any time				
		the relationship the parties believe they are creating (fringe benefits indicate an employment relationship)	X	X	
				whether fringe benefits are typical of those given to employees	X
					self-employed workers likely to be more skilledemployees more likely to be assigned added tasks
					employers are more likely to work for organizations that provide services or products to the public
Conclusion	youth pastor was an employee	senior pastor was self-employed	senior pastor was an employee	missionary was self-employed	senior pastor was self-employed

* The Tax Court reached the same result in a 1997 ruling involving a Methodist minister who served as a senior pastor and a denominational official. *Radde v. Commissioner, T.C. Memo. 1997-490 (1997).*

Chapter 3

ELIGIBILITY OF CLERGY AND CHURCH WORKERS FOR HOUSING ALLOWANCES AND OTHER SPECIAL TAX PROVISIONS

Chapter Highlights

- **4 special tax rules.** "Ministers" are eligible for the following 4 special tax rules with respect to services they perform in the exercise of their ministry:

  ✓ the housing allowance

  ✓ exemption from social security coverage (if several conditions are met)

  ✓ self-employed status for social security purposes (if not exempt)

  ✓ exemption from income tax withholding

- **Consistency.** Persons who qualify as a minister must be consistent with respect to the four special tax rules. For example, not only are they eligible for a housing allowance, but they are also self-employed for social security, they are exempt from income tax withholding, and the "two year" time limit for filing an exemption from social security coverage has begun.

- **Importance of ministerial services.** Persons who qualify as "ministers" for federal tax purposes will be eligible for the four special tax rules only with regard to *services that they perform in the exercise of their ministry.* For example, a minister is not eligible for a housing allowance with respect to secular earnings. And, a minister who has obtained exemption from social security coverage is not exempt with respect to income from secular employment. Services performed in the exercise of ministry include conducting religious worship, administering sacraments, and performing management functions for a church, a denomination, or an "integral agency" of a church or denomination (such as some religious colleges). Further, working for a secular organization can constitute the exercise of one's ministry if the work is done pursuant to a valid assignment by one's church or denomination (and the work furthers the purposes of the church or denomination).

- **Who is a minister for federal tax purposes?** In deciding if a person is a "minister" for federal tax purposes, the following five factors must be considered: (1) the person must be ordained, commissioned, or licensed; (2) administration of sacraments; (3) conduct of religious worship; (4) management responsibilities in the local church or a parent denomination; (5) considered to be a religious leader by the church or parent denomination. It is not clear how many of these factors must be satisfied in order for one to be a "minister" for federal tax purposes. Some Tax Court decisions and IRS rulings suggest that all 5 five factors must be satisfied, while others suggest that a more flexible "balancing" test may be applied (under which some of the factors need not be satisfied).

- **The IRS may not recognize the ministerial status of some ministers.** The IRS probably will not recognize the ministerial status of one who receives ministerial credentials from a local church if (1) the church is affiliated with a parent denomination that does not recognize the local church's action; (2) the local church's charter or bylaws do not authorize it to confer ministerial credentials; (3) the church does not have an established history and practice of conferring ministerial credentials; and (4) the ministerial credentials result in no change in job description or duties.

- **Ministerial status conferred to obtain tax benefits.** Any attempt to confer ministerial credentials upon persons solely to qualify them for "tax benefits," without changing their duties or responsibilities in any way, probably will not be recognized by the IRS or the courts.

A. Introduction

✎ **Key point:** "ministers" are eligible for the following 4 special tax rules with respect to services they perform in the exercise of their ministry:

- housing allowance exclusion (and the exclusion of the fair rental value of a church-owned parsonage)

- exemption from self-employment taxes (if several conditions are met)

- **self-employed status for social security purposes (if not exempt)**

- **wages exempt from federal income tax withholding**

✎ **Key point: persons who qualify as "ministers" for federal tax purposes must be consistent with regard to these 4 special tax rules—if one applies, then they all apply**

✎ **Key point: to be eligible for these 4 special tax provisions, a person must satisfy 2 requirements:**

- **qualify as a minister for federal tax purposes**

- **be engaged in service performed in the exercise of ministry**

A number of provisions in the Internal Revenue Code (our federal tax law) apply specifically to ministers. However, four of these provisions are unique in that they use identical language in defining which persons are eligible for the special treatment. These four provisions include: (1) the exclusion (for income tax purposes) of housing allowances and the fair rental value of church-owned parsonages provided to clergy rent-free; (2) the exemption of some clergy from self-employment taxes (e.g., social security taxes for the self-employed) if several conditions are met; (3) treatment of clergy (who are not exempt) as self-employed for social security tax purposes with respect to ministerial services; and (4) exemption of clergy wages from income tax withholding.

Let's illustrate the significance of this subject with an example. Assume that First Church has an ordained senior minister, a licensed associate minister, an unordained youth minister, an unordained music minister, a business administrator, four office secretaries, and two custodians. How many of these persons are eligible for a housing allowance? How many should be treated as self-employed for social security purposes (and pay the self-employment tax rather than FICA taxes)? How many are eligible for exemption from social security coverage (assuming they meet all of the other conditions)? How many are exempt from income tax withholding? These are questions that many churches are asking. This chapter is designed to provide helpful guidance in resolving the same or similar issues in your church or organization on the basis of the most recent legal precedent.

Income tax regulations

As noted above, all four special tax provisions are unique in that they use identical language in defining which persons are eligible for the special treatment. The housing allowance exclusion, exemption from social security coverage, exemption from income tax withholding, and self-employed status for social security purposes (if not otherwise exempt), are available only to *ordained, commissioned, or licensed ministers of a church with respect to service per-*

formed in the exercise of ministry. This critical terminology is defined in the income tax regulations as follows:

Service performed by a minister in the exercise of his ministry includes the ministration of sacerdotal functions and the conduct of religious worship, and the control, conduct, and maintenance of religious organizations . . . under the authority of a religious body constituting a church or church denomination. The following rules are applicable in determining whether services performed by a minister are performed in the exercise of ministry:

(i) Whether service performed by a minister constitutes the conduct or religious worship or the ministration of sacerdotal functions depends on the tenets and practices of the particular religious body constituting his church or church denomination.

(ii) Services performed by a minister in the control, conduct, and maintenance of a religious organization relates to directing, managing, or promoting the activities of such organization. Any religious organization is deemed to be under the authority of a religious body constituting a church or church denomination if it is organized and dedicated to carrying out the tenets and principles of a faith in accordance with either the requirements or sanctions governing the creation of institutions of the faith. . . .

(iii) If a minister is performing service in the conduct of religious worship or the ministration of sacerdotal functions, such service is in the exercise of his ministry whether or not it is performed for a religious organization.

(iv) If a minister is performing service for an organization which is operated as an integral agency of a religious organization under the authority of a religious body constituting a church or church denomination, all service performed by the minister in the conduct of religious worship, in the ministration of sacerdotal functions, or in the control, conduct, and maintenance of such organization is in the exercise of his ministry.

(v) If a minister, pursuant to an assignment or designation by a religious body constituting his church, performs service for an organization which is neither a religious organization nor operated as an integral agency of a religious organization, all service performed by him, even though such service may not involve the conduct of religious worship or the ministration of sacerdotal functions, is in the exercise of his ministry.

If a minister is performing service for an organization which is neither a religious organization nor operated as an integral agency of a religious organization and the service is not performed pursuant to an assignment or designation by his ecclesiastical superiors, then only the service performed by him in the conduct of religious worship or the ministration of sacerdotal functions is in the exercise of his ministry.

Only ministers satisfying the above definition of "service by a minister in the exercise of his ministry" may exclude from gross income a housing allowance or apply for exemption from social security coverage, be exempt from income tax withholding, or be conclusively presumed to be self-employed for social security purposes. Note that this chapter is not intended to describe in detail these various special provisions. Rather, the focus is on the question of which ministers and church workers are eligible for special treatment under these four provisions assuming that all other requirements are satisfied.

B. Ministers serving local churches

The regulation quoted above makes the four special tax provisions discussed in this chapter available to persons who satisfy two requirements:

• they must be **ministers**, and

• the special treatment only applies with respect to **service performed in the exercise of ministry**

These two requirements will be discussed below in light of the income tax regulations and Tax Court interpretations.

1. Minister

Tax Court decisions

Unfortunately, Tax Court decisions have not always been helpful in deciding whether or not a particular minister or church worker was eligible for a housing allowance or any of the other three special tax provisions discussed in this chapter. Consider the following cases.

Salkov v. Commissioner, 46 T.C. 190 (1966). The Court ruled that a Jewish cantor was eligible for a housing allowance since he was the equivalent of a "commissioned minister" and was recognized as a religious leader by his congregation. The Court observed that the cantor satisfied all three types of religious services described in the regulations (ministration of sacerdotal functions, conduct of religious worship, and the control, conduct, and maintenance of a religious organization), and accordingly he had to be regarded as a minister. The Court reasoned that neither the Code nor the regulations "attempt to say what a minister is, but only what a minister does." The Court left unclear the question of whether a minister must satisfy all three kinds of religious activities mentioned in the regulations to qualify as a minister for tax purposes. A similar result was reached by the Court a few years later in the case of Silverman v. Commissioner, 57 T.C. 727 (1972).

Lawrence v. Commissioner, 50 T.C. 494 (1968). The Tax Court ruled that a nonordained but commissioned minister of education in a Southern Baptist church was not eligible for a housing allowance since he was not a "minister of the gospel." The court emphasized that the minutes of the meeting at which the "minister" had been "commissioned" indicated that he had been commissioned a "minister of the gospel in religious education so that he may receive benefits of laws relative to the Social Security Act and Internal Revenue Service [sic]." The Court called such a com-

missioning "nothing more than a paperwork procedure designed to help him get a tax benefit . . . without giving him any new status." It noted that his duties were in no way changed by the commissioning. Such evidence convinced the Court that the individual was not "recognized by his church as a minister of the gospel," and therefore could not be considered a minister for tax purposes. The Court rejected the individual's argument that he qualified as a minister since he "performed the duties of a minister of the gospel." The Court observed that "even if it be thought that the status of a minister of the gospel in the Baptist religious could be established by proof of services performed, the evidence falls far short of showing the prescribed duties of a minister of education are equivalent to the services performed by a Baptist minister."

In particular, the Court noted that "it is more important to note the religious rites and ceremonies which [the taxpayer] did not perform," including the only two "ordinances" of the Baptist faith—baptism and the Lord's Supper. The taxpayer admitted that he never administered either ordinance or assisted the regular pastor in their administration. This case seemed to require that a minister satisfy all three kinds of religious services described in the regulations, despite the fact that the regulations specifically state that "if a minister is performing service in the conduct of religious worship *or* the ministration of sacerdotal functions, such service is in the exercise of his ministry whether or not it is performed for a religious organization."

Wingo v. Commissioner, 89 T.C. 922 (1987). The Tax Court defined the term *minister* as follows: "In determining whether [one] is a minister, we must look at whether he performed the duties and functions of a minister within the three types of services set out in the regulations. In making that determination, we will also consider the additional factors as to whether he was ordained, or commissioned, or licensed, and whether [his church] considered him to be a religious leader." This language, along with other statements in the Court's opinion, clearly indicates that to be a minister for tax purposes one must satisfy all three types of religious services mentioned in the regulations. To illustrate, the Court noted that "the regulations . . . describe *three types of services that a minister in the exercise of his ministry performs,*" and that "*when a person performs all three types of services set forth in the regulations,* and is recognized as a minister or religious leader by his denomination, that person is a minister . . . ."

The *Wingo* case was disturbing for two reasons. First, it was contrary to the specific wording of the regulations, which provide that "if a minister is performing service in the conduct of religious worship *or* the ministration of sacerdotal functions, such service is in the exercise of his ministry whether or not it is performed for a religious organization." This language certainly recognizes that not all three types of services are essential. The IRS itself recognized this in a 1978 ruling in which it ruled that licensed or commissioned clergy need not perform *all* the religious functions of ordained clergy in order to qualify for a housing allowance (or any of the other special tax provisions), but rather need only perform *"substantially all"* of such functions. The IRS also recognized that "when the individual's regular, full-time duties to the congregation are spiritual or religious in nature, such as leading the worship service, those duties are in the exercise of ministry." *Revenue Ruling 78-301.* The *Wingo* case was also disturbing because it implied that only those clergy who work for churches or church-controlled organizations were eligible for the housing allowance and other special tax provisions since only such clergy satisfied the third type of service mentioned in the regulations (the control, conduct, and maintenance of a religious organization "under the authority of a religious body constituting a church or church denomination"). This was clearly contrary to the regulations quoted above, which specifically recognize that "if a minister is performing service in the conduct of religious worship *or* the ministration of sacerdotal functions, *such service is in the exercise of his ministry whether or not it is performed for a religious organization.*"

Knight v. Commissioner, 92 T.C. 199 (1989). The Tax Court's decisions, and in particular its 1987 decision in the *Wingo* case, demanded correction and clarification. The needed response occurred, fortunately, in 1989 in the *Knight* decision. The *Knight* case presented the question of whether or not a "licentiate" minister in the Cumberland Presbyterian Church (CPC) was a minister for tax purposes. Here are the facts. The taxpayer was presented as a candidate for ministry in the CPC in 1980, and became a "licentiate" in 1981. Becoming a licentiate in the CPC is a solemn occasion and a necessary step toward ordination. A licentiate (or licensed minister) is authorized to preach and perform certain other functions of the ministry. In 1984, the taxpayer was called by a local CPC church to serve as its minister, and he remained at the church during 1984 and 1985 during which time he preached, conducted worship services, visited the sick, performed funerals, and ministered to the needy. Because he was not ordained, he was not able to vote in the "session" (the local church's governing body), administer the sacraments (the Lord's Supper and baptism), or solemnize marriages. The taxpayer reported his income as a self-employed minister in 1984 and 1985 (using Schedule C), and never filed an application for exemption from social security taxes (Form 4361). The local church issued the taxpayer a 1099 (rather than a W-2), and did not withhold taxes from his wages. The taxpayer was audited, and the IRS asserted that he owed self-employment taxes (i.e., social security taxes for self-employed persons) for 1984 and 1985. The taxpayer argued, somewhat inconsistently, that while he reported his income taxes as a self-employed person, he was an employee for social security purposes and accordingly was not subject to the self-employment tax for 1984 or 1985.

The Tax Court noted that section 1402 of the Code specifies that a "duly ordained, commissioned, or licensed minister of a church in the exercise of his ministry" is always self-employed for social security purposes (unless a timely exemption application is filed that is subsequently approved by the IRS), and accordingly is subject to the self-employment tax. The question in this case, therefore, was whether the taxpayer was a "duly ordained, commissioned, or licensed minister of a church in the exercise of his ministry."

The taxpayer, relying on the *Lawrence* case (discussed above), argued that he was not a minister for tax purposes since he had not been formally ordained by the CPC, and could not participate in church government or administer the sacraments. The IRS maintained that he was a minister for tax purposes, and that he should have paid self-employment taxes for 1984 and 1985.

The Court reviewed its earlier decisions, and interpreted them to mean that "the phrase 'ordained, commissioned, or licensed' is applicable to various classes of ministry within a particular religious body." The Court acknowledged that the taxpayer could not administer the sacraments, and that this same fact had led it to conclude in the *Lawrence* case that the taxpayer was *not* a minister for tax purposes. The Court repudiated *Lawrence* to the extent that it precludes ministerial status to those clergy who are not authorized to administer sacraments. The Court announced a new test for determining whether or not a particular individual is a minister: "Five factors [must be] analyzed. Those factors are whether the individual (1) administers sacraments, (2) conducts worship services, (3) performs services in the 'control, conduct, or maintenance of a religious organization,' (4) is 'ordained, commissioned, or licensed,' and (5) is considered to be a spiritual leader by his religious body." The Court claimed to base its new test on the *Wingo* case as well as the regulations quoted above. Surprisingly, the Court claimed that the *Wingo* case never implied that "all of the ecclesiastical functions mentioned [in the regulations] must be performed" in order for one to be a minister for tax purposes. Such a statement is not supported by a careful reading of *Wingo* (as noted above).

The Court concluded that the taxpayer (1) did *not* administer the CPC sacraments, (2) did conduct religious worship, (3) did *not* participate in the conduct, control, or maintenance of his church or denomination, (4) was duly licensed (though not ordained), and (5) was considered to be a religious leader by the CPC. Thus, three of the five factors were present and accordingly the taxpayer satisfied the definition of a minister for tax purposes and was subject to the self-employment tax. The Court emphasized that its new test for ministerial status "is not an arithmetical test but a balancing test. Failure to meet one or more of these factors must be weighed by the court in each case." It did acknowledge that one of the five factors must be present in every case—the requirement that the individual be an ordained, commissioned, or licensed minister. The Court further observed that in weighing the significance of the limitations upon the taxpayer's ministry, "it appears that [his] incapacity to perform the Lord's Supper, baptism, marriage or to moderate the church session or otherwise participate in church government did not diminish the ministry that [the taxpayer] did perform. [He] preached, conducted worship, visited the sick, performed funerals, and ministered to the needy in the exercise of his ministry. [He] did perform one of the three significant ecclesiastical functions described [in the regulations]—the conduct of religious worship." Therefore, the taxpayer satisfied the definition of the term minister "notwithstanding that the CPC constitution provides for the ordination of a minister with higher authority and greater ministry."

Reeder v. Commissioner, T.C. Memo. 1993-287. Unfortunately, the most recent ruling of the Tax Court (in 1993) reaffirms the *Wingo* case under which all 5 factors are required. Fortunately, the *Reeder* case is a "memorandum" decision by the Tax Court, meaning that it is a ruling by only 1 judge. Such rulings have far less precedential value than full Tax Court decisions rendered by all 34 Tax Court judges. Both the *Wingo* and *Knight* decisions were full Tax Court decisions, and as such they are entitled to considerably more weight than the *Reeder* case. The minister in the *Reeder* case became a licensed Assemblies of God minister in 1971. During 1973 and 1974, he served as senior pastor of a local church. He left the church to pursue further seminary training, and he was ordained in 1980. On December 23, 1980, the minister filed an application for exemption from self-employment taxes (IRS Form 4361). The minister represented on the application for exemption that he was licensed in 1971 and ordained in 1980, and that 1973 and 1974 were the first years that he had received ministerial earnings subject to social security tax. The minister's application for exemption was denied in 1981. The IRS noted that under federal law, an application for exemption must be filed no later than the due date of the federal tax return (Form 1040) for the second year in which a minister earns $400 or more in self-employment earnings, any portion of which comes from ministerial services. The IRS reasoned that the taxpayer became a minister when he was licensed in 1971, and accordingly the exemption application was due no later than April 15, 1973.

In 1983 the minister submitted a second Form 4361, but this time he stated that he was ordained in 1980 and did not refer to the date he was licensed. This second application was also denied. The IRS again reasoned that the taxpayer became a minister in 1971 when he was licensed, and that the exemption application accordingly was due no later than April 15, 1973. The minister appealed this denial to the Tax Court. He argued that he was not a "minister" until he was ordained in 1980, and therefore his application was filed on time. He acknowledged that he had been licensed in 1971, and had served as a pastor of a local church in 1973 and 1974. However, he insisted that his church was a dependent Assembly under the direct supervision of his District, and that only upon ordination was he able to participate in the governance of his church organization at a higher level than the local church.

The Tax Court agreed with the IRS that the taxpayer had become a "minister" for federal tax purposes when he was licensed in 1971, and accordingly both of his applications for exemption were filed too late. The Court noted that one of the requirements for exemption from self-employment taxes is that the applicant must be an "ordained, commissioned, or licensed minister." While this term is not

---

Who Is A Minister for Federal Tax Purposes— The Tax Court's 5-Factor Test

Who is a minister for federal tax purposes? The Tax Court ruled in 1987 that a minister is one who satisfies all 5 of the following factors:

• administers sacraments

• conducts religious worship

• management responsibility in a local church or religious denomination ("control, conduct, or maintenance of a religious organization")

• ordained, commissioned, or licensed

• considered to be a religious leader by one's church or denomination

In 1989, the Tax Court ruled that only the fourth factor is required (ordained, commissioned, or licensed) and that a balancing test should be applied with respect to the remaining factors. This more flexible and enlightened test was ignored by the Tax Court in its most recent decision in 1993, in which it applied its more strict 1987 ruling. The IRS, in its most recent rulings, applies the Tax Court's 1987 test, requiring that all 5 factors apply for one to be considered a minister for federal tax purposes. In summary, there are two conflicting definitions of the term *minister*. The Tax Court's rigid 1987 decision (all 5 factors are required) or its more flexible 1989 decision.

---

defined in the tax code or regulations, the Court did note that it had ruled in a previous case that whether or not an individual is an "ordained, commissioned, or licensed minister" depends on whether or not he or she performs the duties and functions of a minister. The Court referred to its previous 1987 ruling in *Wingo v. Commissioner*, 89 T.C. 922, 930 (1987), in which it addressed the question of whether a licensed local pastor of a church was a minister for federal tax purposes. In the *Wingo* case, the Court pointed out that the income tax regulations describe three types of services that a minister in the exercise of his ministry performs: "(1) the ministration of sacerdotal functions; (2) the conduct of religious worship; and (3) service in the control, conduct, and maintenance of religious organizations (including the religious boards, societies, and other integral agencies of such organizations), under the authority of a religious body constituting a church or church denomination." The Court concluded in this case that the Assemblies of God minister became an "ordained, commissioned, or licensed minister" when he was licensed in 1971, since he satisfied all three of these conditions.

First, with respect to the ministration of sacerdotal functions, the Court observed:

As to the sacerdotal functions, [the minister's] own testimony is that while he was the pastor of the [local church] during 1973 and 1974, he could have performed a marriage or performed funeral services with permission or performed services with respect to the dedication of infants, and he did in fact perform the ministry functions of preaching and teaching, baptism, and communion. There is no requirement that to qualify as a "duly ordained, commissioned, or licensed minister" . . . an individual must be qualified to perform and actually perform every sacrament or rite of the religion.

Second, as to the conduct of religious worship, the Court noted that "there is no dispute here that [the taxpayer] conducted the religious services of the church . . . during 1973 and 1974."

Third, as to the question of service in the control, conduct, and maintenance of the religious organization, the Court observed:

[The taxpayer] points out that during 1973 and 1974 he was the pastor of a local church which was a dependent church and subject to supervision under the constitution and bylaws of the [District]. [The taxpayer] argues that only upon ordination was he able to participate in the governance of his church organization at a higher level than the local church. In response to a similar argument, in Wingo v. Commissioner, we stated: "To perform services in the control, conduct, and maintenance of the church or organizations within the church, the minister need only have some participation in the conduct, control, and maintenance of the local church or the denomination."

The *Reeder* case is unfortunate since the Tax Court reaffirmed the rigid *Wingo* case that it repudiated in the more enlightened *Knight* ruling in 1989. There are a few positive aspects of this decision. First, the Court clarified that "there is no requirement that to qualify as a 'a duly ordained, commissioned, or licensed minister' . . . an individual must be qualified to perform and actually perform every sacrament or rite of the religion." Second, the Court clarified that "[t]o perform services in the control, conduct, and maintenance of the church or organizations within the church, the minister need only have some participation in the conduct, control, and maintenance of the local church or the denomination." And finally, the Court did not reverse or overrule the *Knight* decision. On the contrary, it did not even mention it. As a result, the *Knight* case can still be relied upon as precedent. However, such reliance will be a more aggressive position in light of the *Reeder* case.

Other legal precedents

IRS Technical Advice Memorandum 8915001. In a 1989 Technical Advice Memorandum (released prior to the *Knight* decision), the IRS national office addressed the question of who is a minister for tax purposes. Specifically, the IRS was addressing the question of whether a minister had filed a timely application for exemption from social security taxes (Form 4361). The individual had been licensed in 1971 and ordained in 1980, and had submitted an application for exemption from social security taxes (Form 4361) in 1980. The parties conceded that if the individual became a minister for tax purposes at the time he was licensed, then the exemption application was properly rejected since it was too late, but if he became a minister for tax purposes upon his ordination in 1980, then the application was timely. The IRS, applying the *Wingo* test, concluded that the individual became a minister for tax purposes in 1971 (when he was licensed) since at that time he performed all three kinds of ministerial services described in the regulations and mandated by the *Wingo* decision. The IRS observed that in determining whether an individual is a minister for tax purposes, "the courts have consistently examined *whether the individual has performed the three types of ministerial services set forth in . . . the regulations.*" In summary, the IRS reached the right result for the wrong reasons. There is no doubt that the individual satisfied the 5-part test of ministerial status announced a few weeks later in the *Knight* decision. It is unfortunate that the IRS reached its conclusion by relying on the much more restrictive test announced in the *Wingo* decision—a test repudiated in the *Knight* decision. The reliance by the IRS on the *Wingo* case in this ruling can be explained by the fact that it was released prior to the Tax Court's decision in the *Knight* case.

IRS Letter Ruling 9221025. The IRS addressed the question of whether commissioned ministers in a denomination that both commissions and ordains ministers are eligible for a housing allowance. A Protestant denomination (the "Church") with more than 5,900 congregations located throughout the United States recognizes two levels of ministry—commissioned and ordained. Generally, a candidate for commissioned minister completes four years of study at a college operated by the Church where the curriculum centers around courses in religion. Upon completion of the required education, the college faculty, on behalf of the Church, certifies that the candidate is fit for the position of commissioned minister. The certificate of fitness assures that the candidates are academically, theologically and morally fit to have the status and authority of commissioned minister. The certified candidate is then "called" by a congregation, and after accepting the call, the candidate is installed as a commissioned minister in a formal ceremony. Occasionally an individual may become a commissioned minister through a "colloquy", which requires the candidate to have achieved equivalent academic, religious, educational, and personal life qualifications. In addition, a colloquy candidate must pass oral and written examinations. Commissioned ministers serve God and the Church by performing full-time public ministry functions including: classroom teaching; evangelism; counseling individuals; leading Bible study groups; leading devotions; worship services for youth; music ministry; giving the children's sermon at the regular Sunday worship service; addressing the congregation in a worship service on a subject in which the commissioned minister has expertise; coordinating lay church workers; administering or guiding a congregation's youth ministry; coordinating family ministry events; participating in ministries to those with special needs; and, caring spiritually for the sick and imprisoned and their families. The Church regards teaching of the faith to the children and youth of the flock as a major duty of the pastoral office. Upon acceptance of a call and installation into a ministry position, a commissioned minister becomes a "member" of the Church.

The majority of commissioned ministers are called directly by local churches to serve in church-controlled parochial schools. The schools, for the most part are not separate organizations from the churches. However, some of the schools are incorporated separately from a member congregation, but each such school is an integral agency of a member congregation. A commissioned minister also may be called by a congregation to be a deaconess or director of Christian education. In contrast, *ordained ministers* of the Church officiate in the public administration of the sacraments and lead in public worship. In certain situations, a commissioned minister may lead in prayer, read the Scriptures in a church service, or perform a baptism. Under the doctrine of the Church, baptism is a sacrament. The IRS national office concluded that commissioned ministers are eligible for a housing allowance. The IRS based its decision on a 1978 "revenue ruling" in which it stated that "if a church or denomination ordains some ministers of the gospel and licenses or commissions other ministers, the licensed or commissioned minister must perform substantially all the religious functions within the scope of the tenets and practices of his religious denomination to be treated as a minister of the gospel." *Revenue Ruling 78-301.* However, the IRS also relied squarely on the *Wingo* case. The IRS, applying the *Wingo* 5-part test, concluded that the commissioned ministers were "ministers" for federal tax purposes since they satisfied all 5 of the conditions set forth in that decision.

Eade v. United States, (unpublished opinion, W.D. Va. 1991). A federal court in Virginia ignored the *Knight* test and applied the *Wingo* ruling. The court ruled that a minister was entitled to exemption from self-employment taxes. In reaching its decision, the court concluded that the individual satisfied the definition of *minister* since he met all 5 of the factors required by the *Wingo* decision. It observed:

> The minister testified that he performed ministerial functions for the [church] beginning in March of 1985, that he conducted religious worship, and that the church was an independent Baptist church under the authority of a religious body comprised of deacons drawn from members of the church congregation. As to his qualifications for the ministry, the minister testified, without contradiction, that he received a B.A. in Bible Studies from a Tennessee Bible college, an M.A. in sacred literature from Liberty Baptist University, had earned credits toward a Ph.D. in church administration, and had been ordained a minister in the Baptist faith on January 26, 1985 after nomination by the ordination committee of the [church]. At that time the minister received a certificate of ordination. Thereafter, [the church], comprised of some 300-350 active members, issued a call for him to become their pastor, which call he accepted, assuming his pastoral duties in April of 1985.

Applying the *Wingo* factors and the income tax regulations criteria, I find that the minister meets [all 5 requirements]. I find that he performs in accordance with his denomination's requirements for sacerdotal function, that he conducts religious worship and provides service that is under the control, conduct and maintenance of an organized and recognized religious body constituting an independent church belonging to that denomination widely known as Baptist. Further, I find that he is an ordained minister and that Colonial Baptist Church recognizes him as its religious leader by paying him a salary to minister to the needs of its congregants.

Ballinger v. Commissioner, 728 F.2d 1287 (10th Cir. 1984). A federal appeals court ruled that a person who functioned as a minister could file an application for exemption from self-employment taxes despite the fact that he had not been ordained! The court observed:

> Not all churches or religions have a formally ordained ministry, whether because of the nature of their beliefs, the lack of a denominational structure or a variety of other reasons. Courts are not in a position to determine the merits of various churches nor an individual's conversion from one church to another. Thus, we cannot hold that an individual who functions as a minister in a church which does not ordain, license or commission that individual in a traditional or legally formal manner is not entitled to the exemption. Nor can we hold that an individual who has a change of belief accompanied by a change to another faith is not entitled to the exemption. We interpret Congress' language providing an exemption for any individual who is "a duly ordained, commissioner or licensed minister of a church" to mean that the triggering event is the assumption of the duties and functions of a minister.

This language suggests that the court was limiting its conclusion to churches that do not formally ordain, commission, or license clergy. However, the case before the court involved a church that eventually did ordain the minister. As a result this case would support the treatment of a person as a "minister" for federal tax purposes who performs the functions of a minister though the person has not been formally ordained, commissioned, or licensed—whether or not he or she is associated with a church that credentials ministers. No other court has reached this rather questionable conclusion, and so it should not be relied upon without the advice of a tax attorney or CPA.

Haimowitz v. Commissioner, T.C. Memo. 1997-40 (1997). The Tax Court ruled that an administrator of a Jewish synagogue was not eligible for a housing allowance since he was not ordained, commissioned, or licensed, and there was no evidence that a housing allowance had been properly designated for him. In ruling that the administrator was not a "minister" and therefore was not eligible for a housing allowance, the court made a number of important observations: (1) While the tax code limits housing allowances to ministers of the gospel, neither the code nor the income tax regulations define this term. (2) The income tax regulations do define "what a minister does." They list the following functions: the performance of sacerdotal functions; the conduct of religious worship; and the performance of services in control, conduct, and maintenance of religious organizations. (3) In deciding whether or not an individual performs the functions of a minister, consideration must be given not only to the religious duties the individual performs, but also to the religious duties that are not performed. (4) The performance of some religious functions is not enough to make one a minister for federal tax purposes. The administrator in this case performed a number of religious functions, but these were largely administrative in nature. More importantly, he performed few of the duties of an ordained, commissioned, or licensed minister. (5) The court stressed that no one can be a "minister" for federal tax purposes who is not, at a minimum, "ordained, commissioned, or licensed." (6) The court referred to the fact that the administrator had no seminary training.

The court concluded that even if the administrator were a "minister" for federal tax purposes, he would still be ineligible for a housing allowance since there was no evidence that a housing allowance had ever been properly designated for him.

The IRS Tax Guide for Churches

In 1994 the IRS published a "tax guide for churches" that briefly addresses the definition of the term "minister". Regrettably, the IRS tax guide perpetuates rather than clarifies the substantial confusion that presently exists regarding the definition of the term *minister*, by defining the term as follows:

> A minister is an individual who is duly ordained, commissioned, or licensed by a religious body constituting a church or church denomination. A minister has the authority to conduct religious worship, perform sacerdotal functions, and administer ordinances or sacraments according to the prescribed tenets and practices of that church or denomination. A minister is considered to be a religious leader by his or her church or denomination. Generally, an individual who is a minister of music or education is not considered to be a minister for Federal tax purposes. As used in this booklet, the term includes priests, rabbis, imams, and similar members of the clergy.

This language confuses the terms *minister* and *services performed in the exercise of ministry*. To illustrate, while some ministers of music or education may not be "ministers" for federal tax purposes, this ordinarily is due to the fact that they are not engaged in performing the kinds of pastoral functions included within the definition of the term *service performed in the exercise of ministry* and not because they are not ministers. Quite to the contrary, many of them are ordained or licensed, and as a result it is nonsensical to conclude that they are not "ministers" for federal tax purposes. By confusing the terms *minister* and *service performed in the exercise of ministry*, the term *minister* is unnecessarily narrowed.

✎ **Key point: the definition of "minister" contained in the IRS tax guide for churches, and in a number of IRS and Tax Court rulings, assumes that a minister is engaged in pastoral ministry. This is an unreasonably narrow definition for it fails to recognize that many bona fide ministers are not engaged in pastoral ministry—they are employed by denominational agencies, seminaries and other religious schools, parachurch ministries, or as support staff in local congregations.**

✎ **Key point: there is one aspect of the IRS tax guide's definition that is potentially significant. The tax guide states that a minister is one who "has the authority" to conduct religious worship, perform sacerdotal functions, and administer ordinances or sacraments. The tax guide does not say that a minister in fact must perform these duties, but rather that the minister has the authority to do so. This is a potentially significant concession, for it means that many ordained, commissioned, or licensed ministers will satisfy the definition of a "minister" for federal tax purposes even though they do not in fact conduct worship services or administer sacraments or perform sacerdotal functions—so long as they have the ecclesiastical authority to perform such tasks.**

The IRS audit guidelines for ministers

In 1995 the IRS released audit guidelines for ministers. These guidelines were issued pursuant to the IRS "Market Segment Specialization Program" (MSSP), and are intended to promote a higher degree of competence among those agents who audit ministers. The guidelines state that "the first issue that must be determined is whether the minister is an employee or an independent contractor."

✎ **Key point: In 1995 the IRS issued audit guidelines for its agents to follow when auditing ministers. The guidelines cover a range of issues, including the definition of the term "minister" for federal tax purposes.**

✎ **Key point: the audit guidelines will instruct IRS agents in the examination of ministers' tax returns. They alert agents to the key questions to ask, and provide background information along with the IRS position on a number of issues. It is therefore of utmost importance that ministers be familiar with these guidelines.**

The guidelines provide IRS agents with the following assistance in defining the critical term "minister":

• The income tax regulations require that an individual be a "duly ordained, commissioned, or licensed minister of a church."

• The Tax Court, in *Salkov v. Commissioner, 46 T.C. 190 (1966)*, ruled that the phrase "duly ordained, commissioned, or licensed minister of a church" must be interpreted "disjunctively." By this it meant that a person qualifies as a minister for tax purposes if he or she meets any of these three categories. Ordained status, therefore, is not required.

• The guidelines add that "[t]he duties performed by the individual are also important to the initial determination whether he or she is a duly ordained, commissioned, or licensed minister. Because religious disciplines vary in their formal procedures for these designations, whether an individual is duly ordained, commissioned, or licensed depends on these facts and circumstances."

• The guidelines then refer to the following legal authorities:

(1) Salkov v. Commissioner (discussed above) and Silverman v. Commissioner, 57 T.C. 727 (1972). The guidelines note that the Tax Court, in holding that a cantor of the Jewish faith was a duly ordained, commissioned, or licensed minister, looked to "the systematic manner the cantor was called to his ministry and the ecclesiastical functions he carried out in concluding that he was a minister . . . ."

(2) Revenue Ruling 78-301 (discussed above). The IRS followed the Tax Court decisions in Salkov and Silverman and held that a Jewish cantor who is not ordained but has a bona fide commission and is employed by a congregation on a full-time basis to perform substantially all the religious worship, sacerdotal, training, and educational functions of the Jewish denomination's religious tenets and practices is a minister of the gospel for federal tax purposes. The audit guidelines state that this ruling "revoked and modified prior revenue rulings to the extent that they required that an individual must be invested with the status and authority of an ordained minister fully qualified to exercise all of the ecclesiastical duties of a church denomination to be considered ministers . . . ."

(3) Knight v. Commissioner 92 T.C. 199 (1989) (discussed above). The guidelines, in commenting on the Knight case, note:

The Tax Court considered whether a licentiate of the Cumberland Presbyterian Church (a status that was less than full ordination), who had not filed a timely exemption from self-employment tax, was a duly ordained, commissioned, or licensed minister in the exercise of required duties who was thus liable for self-employment tax. The petitioner argued that he was not formally ordained as a minister and could not administer church sacraments or participate in church government. Thus, he could not be a minister subject to [self-employment taxes]. The court rejected this view, and looked at all the facts. In concluding that he was a licensed minister, it cited the facts that he was licensed by the church, he conducted worship services, and he was considered by the church to be a spiritual leader.

⊃ Observation. The guidelines' reference to the Knight case is very significant. The Knight case contains perhaps the best analysis of the terms "minister" and "exercise of minis-

try." The court applied a "balancing test," noting that a minister need not actually perform every category of ministerial service described in the income tax regulations. In recent rulings the IRS has omitted any reference to this important decision. The guidelines take a different view. IRS agents will now consider this important ruling. As a result, more bona fide ministers will in fact be considered "ministers" for tax purposes. This is an important clarification, and one of the most important aspects of the guidelines.

(4) Lawrence v. Commissioner, 50 T.C. 494 (1968) (discussed above). The guidelines, in commenting on the Lawrence case, note the Tax Court found that

a "minister of education" in a Baptist church was not a "duly ordained, commissioned, or licensed" minister for purposes of [eligibility for a housing allowance]. The petitioner held a Master's Degree in Religious Education from a Baptist Theological Seminary, but was not ordained. Although his church "commissioned" him after he assumed the position, the court interpreted the commissioning to be for tax purposes, as it did not result in any change in duties. Most significant, however, was the court's analysis of petitioner's duties or rather, the duties he did not perform. He did not officiate at Baptisms or the Lord's Supper, two Ordinances that closely resembled sacraments, nor did he preside over or preach at worship services. The court concluded that the evidence did not establish that the prescribed duties of a minister of education were equivalent to the duties of a Baptist minister.

⊃ Observation. The guidelines contain no reference to the Tax Court's decision in Wingo v. Commissioner, 89 T.C. 922 (1987). In the Wingo case, the Court adopted the totally untenable conclusion that a "minister" is one who must satisfy all of the following 5 conditions: (1) administer sacraments, (2) conduct worship services, (3) perform services in the "control, conduct, or maintenance of a religious organization," (4) be ordained, commissioned, or licensed, and (5) be considered a spiritual leader by one's religious body. This test was so narrow that it denied ministerial status to many bona fide ministers who worked for seminaries, parachurch ministries, or as associate pastors within local congregations. Happily, the guidelines do not even mention this unfortunate ruling (despite the fact that the IRS has relied on it in recent rulings). This is good news, and makes it more likely that IRS agents will consider those claiming to be ministers to be ministers for federal tax purposes.

⊃ Observation. Unfortunately, the guidelines do not adequately distinguish between the terms "minister" and "service performed in the exercise of ministry." The failure to distinguish between these key terms has produced much confusion, and the guidelines provide little assistance. **This will mean that agents auditing ministers' tax returns will continue to experience confusion. The guidelines' disregard of the *Wingo* case will help.**

Conclusions

What conclusions can be drawn from these rulings? Consider the following:

1. There are 2 competing definitions of the term "minister" for federal tax purposes.

• **The *Knight* definition of "minister."** This is now the preferred definition since it was adopted by the IRS in its audit guidelines for ministers in 1995. It is likely that this is the only test that IRS agents will apply when auditing persons who claim to be ministers. Under this test, the following 5 factors must be considered in deciding whether or not a person is a minister for federal tax reporting purposes: (1) does the individual administer the "sacraments", (2) does the individual conduct worship services, (3) does the individual perform services in the "control, conduct, or maintenance of a religious organization" under the authority of a church or religious denomination, (4) is the individual "ordained, commissioned, or licensed," and (5) is the individual considered to be a spiritual leader by his or her religious body? Only the fourth factor is required in all cases (the individual *must* be ordained, commissioned, or licensed). The remaining 4 factors need *not* all be present for a person to be considered a minister for tax purposes. The Tax Court in the *Knight* case did not say how many of the remaining 4 factors must be met. It merely observed that "failure to meet one or more of these factors must be weighed . . . in each case." The Court concluded that the taxpayer in question *was* a minister despite the fact that he only satisfied 3 of the 5 factors.

It may reasonably be assumed, however, that persons who claim to be "ministers" solely on the basis of the final 3 factors mentioned in the *Knight* case will *not* be deemed ministers by the IRS or the courts unless they can demonstrate that they are entitled to ministerial status on the basis of other considerations. After all, if a church is willing to ordain its bookkeeper and secretary, these persons could argue that they satisfy the final 3 factors in the *Knight* case (management responsibilities, ordination, and a "religious leader"). There is no doubt that the IRS and the courts will not accept such a conclusion. Considerations that suggest ministerial status, even if the first 2 *Knight* factors are not satisfied, would include (1) ordination to the pastoral ministry, and actual pastoral experience in the past, and (2) formal theological training.

• **The *Wingo* definition of the term "minister."** As noted above, this definition has been applied by the IRS in 2 rulings, and by 2 federal courts in addition to two Tax Court rulings. However, all of these rulings occurred prior to the issuance of the IRS audit guidelines for ministers in 1995. The audit guidelines not only fail to even mention the *Wingo* definition, but they specifically endorse the *Knight* definition discussed above. To be a minister under the *Wingo* test,

one must satisfy *all 5* of the factors mentioned in the *Knight* decision. The *Wingo* definition is overly restrictive and results in the denial of ministerial status to many persons who clearly are ministers. Examples include ministers of music, ministers of education, ministers of youth, and other associate ministers who often will not satisfy all 5 factors announced by the Tax Court in the *Wingo* decision. Ministers employed by parachurch organizations also may be adversely affected, particularly if their organization is not under the direct control of a church or religious denomination. The reason for this result is that one of the 5 factors required in all cases under the current IRS test is "the control, conduct, and maintenance of religious organizations . . . *under the authority of a religious body constituting a church or church denomination.*" Even ordained ministers teaching at church-operated seminaries would be adversely affected by a literal application of the *Wingo* decision, to the extent that they do not satisfy all 5 of the factors for ministerial status.

✎ **Key point: happily, the IRS did not even mention the *Wingo* case in its audit guidelines for ministers. It is unlikely that the *Wingo* case will be applied by IRS agents when auditing ministers' tax returns. This indicates a preference by the IRS for the *Knight* definition of "minister."**

✎ **Key point: it now appears that the *Knight* definition is the preferred definition of the term "minister." This conclusion is based on the following 2 considerations: (1) The audit guidelines for ministers released by the IRS in 1995 refer to the *Knight* definition but do not even mention the *Wingo* case. (2) The most recent decision by the full Tax Court was the *Knight* case in 1989. While the *Reeder* case (which followed the *Wingo* definition) was decided in 1993, it was a Tax Court "memorandum" decision, meaning that it was a ruling by only 1 of the Court's 34 judges and has minimal precedential value. The IRS often ignores Tax Court memorandum decisions. By comparison, the *Knight* case was a decision by the full Tax Court and has a much higher precedential value.**

The following examples illustrate the application of these 2 definitions.

☞ ***Example.*** *Rev. J is an ordained minister who serves as a minister of education at his church. He does not preach or conduct worship services, and never administers the sacraments. He does have management responsibility in his local church and at regional and national meetings of his denomination. His duties include overseeing the educational program of his church, occasional counseling, and hospital visitation.*

• *Under the Wingo test Rev. J would not be a "minister" for federal tax purposes, since he does not meet all 5 factors. Specifically, he does not conduct religious worship or administer sacerdotal functions.*

• Under the IRS tax guide test it is possible that Rev. J would be considered to be a minister for federal tax purposes so long as he has the ecclesiastical authority to conduct worship, administer sacraments, and perform sacerdotal functions—even though he does not perform any of these tasks.

• Under the IRS audit guidelines for ministers it is likely that Rev. J would be considered to be a minister for federal tax purposes so long as he is a minister under the Knight definition.

• Under the Tax Court's decision in the Knight case it is probable that Rev. J would be considered a minister for federal tax purposes.

Rev. J must now decide whether or not to follow the Knight decision, or the Wingo test. For the reasons stated above, the Knight definition of the term "minister" is now the preferred definition.

☞ **Example.** Rev. B is minister of music at his church. He is not ordained, commissioned, or licensed. Rev. B is not a minister for federal tax purposes, under either the Wingo or Knight cases since he is not ordained, commissioned, or licensed.

☞ **Example.** Rev. C is minister of music at her church. She is licensed, and her duties include leading religious worship and administering all of the music programs and activities of the church. However, Rev. C does not administer sacraments or engage in sacerdotal functions. Rev. C would not be a minister for federal tax purposes under the Wingo test, but she may be under the Knight test and the IRS audit guidelines. Further, if Rev. C's status as a licensed minister invests her with the ecclesiastical authority to conduct worship, administer sacraments, and perform sacerdotal functions, she may satisfy the IRS tax guide's test even though she does not actually perform some or all of these tasks.

☞ **Example.** Same facts as the previous example, except that Rev. C occasionally assists the senior pastor in administering communion. This limited performance of a sacerdotal function increases the likelihood that Rev. C will be considered to be a minister for federal tax purposes. The Tax Court noted in the Reeder case that "there is no requirement that to qualify as a 'a duly ordained, commissioned, or licensed minister' . . . an individual must be qualified to perform and actually perform every sacrament or rite of the religion." However, the performance of only one sacerdotal function on an occasional basis will not necessarily make Rev. C a minister for federal tax purposes, and probably would be of limited relevance.

☞ **Example.** Rev. G, an ordained minister with 25 years of pastoral experience, is now employed as a full-time seminary professor. Rev. G does not preach or administer sacraments, and accordingly

would not be considered a minister under the Wingo case. This is an unreasonable result. Such a person clearly is a minister, even though not presently serving in a traditional pastoral ministry. It is possible that Rev. G would be a minister under the Knight test and the IRS audit guidelines. Further, if Rev. G's status as an ordained minister invests him with the ecclesiastical authority to conduct worship, administer sacraments, and perform sacerdotal functions, he may satisfy the IRS tax guide's test even though he does not actually perform some or all of these tasks.

☞ **Example.** Rev. K is employed by a parachurch ministry that is not controlled by a church or denomination. His duties are primarily administrative. His job description does not include the conduct of religious worship or the performance of sacerdotal functions. It is very doubtful that Rev. K would be considered a minister for federal tax purposes under either the Wingo or Knight rulings.

☞ **Example.** Rev. G is an ordained minister who is employed full-time by a parachurch ministry that is not controlled by a church or religious denomination. His job includes conducting religious services. He would be considered to be a minister under the Knight definition, and possibly under the definition adopted by the IRS audit guidelines for ministers, but would not be a minister under the Wingo definition since he does not satisfy at least one of the 5 factors identified in that decision (he is not engaged in the "control, conduct, or maintenance" of a religious organization under the authority of a religious body constituting a church or church denomination). Accordingly, he would be a minister and therefore eligible for the 4 special tax rules discussed in this chapter only under the Knight definition, and not the prevailing Wingo definition.

☞ **Example.** M is a teacher at a private religious school operated by First Church. She is not a minister, and accordingly she is not eligible for a housing allowance exclusion. Assume further that M asks the church to "commission" her in order to render her eligible for a housing allowance. Even if the church complies with such a request, it is doubtful, based on the Lawrence decision, that she will become eligible for the housing allowance exclusion. Recall that the Tax Court in the Lawrence decision called Rev. Lawrence's commissioning "nothing more than a paperwork procedure designed to help him get a tax benefit . . . without giving him any new status." It emphasized that his duties were in no way changed by the commissioning. Such evidence convinced the Court that the individual was not "recognized by his church as a minister of the gospel," and therefore could not be considered a minister for tax purposes. The following factors would further support this conclusion: (1) the local church's charter does not specifically authorize it to "commission" ministers; (2) the church in fact has never before commissioned a minister; (3) the church is affiliated with a denomination that will not recognize the ministerial status of M.

☞ **Example.** Rev. K is ordained to the pastoral ministry following a formal theological education. After serving for a number of years as a pastor, Rev. K elects to become a teacher at a church-operated school. His duties include teaching and administration. He occasionally conducts religious services, but does not administer sacraments. Rev. K would qualify as a minister for federal tax purposes under the Knight test, since he certainly satisfies the final 3 factors mentioned in that case, and this should be enough in light of his previous ordination to the pastoral ministry, his prior pastoral experience, and his theological training. His status is in doubt under the Wingo definition of minister.

☞ **Example.** The IRS ruled that full-time male and female teachers employed by parochial schools of a particular church denomination qualified as "duly ordained, commissioned, or licensed ministers of a church" for purposes of federal tax law. The teachers were graduates of a theological college conducted under the auspices of a church denomination for the express purpose of training full-time church workers. Upon graduation, teachers are recommended as candidates for the teaching ministry in the congregations of the church, and in its parochial schools. Although not ordained as pastors, the male teachers' duties as full-time teachers in the parochial schools include the teaching and preaching of the religious principles of the church to the children and youth of the various congregations and the conducting of the musical portion of their religious services. They may also be called upon to function in the place of a pastor during his absence or together with him as the needs for the ministrations of the pastor increase. The female teachers' duties include all of the above-prescribed functions except that they are never called upon to preach, or to take the place of, or assist a pastor in the conduct of religious services. Both the male and female teachers are called to their respective offices for life. Teachers may be removed from office only for the same reasons that apply to pastors. Under these facts, the IRS concluded that "the male teachers, although not duly ordained as pastors, are, in performing full-time services for the church by teaching, preaching, and, when needed, acting for or assisting an ordained pastor in the conduct of religious services, "duly ordained, commissioned, or licensed ministers of a church" for purposes of [federal tax law], and that their services are performed in the exercise of their ministry. . . . The female teachers whose services appear to be restricted to the teaching of the religious principles of the church and to the direction of the musical portion of the church services, do not qualify as "duly ordained, commissioned, or licensed ministers of a church." Revenue Ruling 57-107. See also IRS Letter Ruling 7939023. But compare IRS Letter Ruling 8614010.

☞ **Example.** The IRS ruled that a "minister of administration" who was licensed by a denomination that also ordained ministers was not a "minister" for federal tax purposes since he did not "perform substantially all the religious functions within the scope of the tenets and practices of his religious denomination." The IRS noted that the minister acknowledged that he had never conducted worship services, preached a sermon, conducted a funeral, performed a baptism, or administered communion, and had no intention of performing any of these activities. The IRS concluded that because the minister had "not performed substantially all the religious functions within the scope of the tenets and practices of [his] religious denomination," he was not a minister of the gospel for federal tax purposes. IRS Letter Ruling 8442130.

☞ **Example.** In a 1955 ruling, the IRS clarified that "there is no requirement that a minister must exercise his sacerdotal functions in a church of his faith. So long as he exercises that function, its exercise anywhere meets the test. Special Ruling, September 1, 1955.

2. Any future reliance on the *Wingo* decision by either the IRS or the courts will result in the denial of ministerial status to many persons who clearly are ministers under the *Knight* test. For example, the minister in the *Knight* case did not administer sacraments, and he had no authority to participate in the control, conduct, and maintenance (e.g., "directing, managing, or promoting") of his church. He clearly would have failed 2 of the 5 factors required by the court in *Wingo*, yet the Tax Court ruled that he was a minister under its more liberal and enlightened "balancing test." Persons who would be adversely affected by an application of the *Wingo* definition would include associate ministers and licensed ministers. Examples include ministers of music, ministers of education, ministers of youth, and other associate ministers who often will not satisfy all 5 factors announced by the Tax Court in the *Wingo* decision. Ministers employed by parachurch organizations also would be adversely affected, particularly if their organization is not under the direct control of a church or religious denomination. The reason for this result is that one of the 5 factors required in all cases under the current IRS test is "the control, conduct, and maintenance of religious organizations . . . under the authority of a religious body constituting a church or church denomination." Even ordained ministers teaching at church-operated seminaries would be adversely affected by a literal application of the *Wingo* decision, to the extent that they do not satisfy all 5 of the factors for ministerial status.

✎ **Key point: any attempt to confer ministerial credentials upon persons solely to qualify them for "tax benefits," without changing their duties or responsibilities in any way, probably will not be recognized by the IRS or the courts**

3. Those seeking to be ordained, commissioned, or licensed by their local church should bear in mind several additional considerations.

• If the church is affiliated with a denomination that ordains, commissions, or licenses clergy, then it is less likely that the IRS will recognize an attempt by a local church to perform the same function (particularly if the national church will not recognize the validity of the ministerial credentials conferred by the local church).

• It is doubtful that the IRS will recognize an attempt by a local church to ordain, commission, or license a minister unless the charter or bylaws of the local church specifically authorizes such a practice. If such documents are silent regarding the authority of the local church to confer ministerial credentials, then the IRS likely would conclude that the conferring of ministerial credentials is "nothing more than a paperwork procedure designed to help [the individual] get a tax benefit . . . without giving him any new status."

• Does the church have a history or practice of ordaining, commissioning, or licensing ministers? If not, it is more likely that a present attempt to do so will be viewed as an attempt to confer tax benefits rather than ministerial credentials.

• Have the duties of the "minister" changed since he or she was ordained, commissioned, or licensed by the church?

• Did the "minister" have any formal theological training prior to being ordained, commissioned, or licensed by the church? If not, it is more likely that the granting of ministerial status will be viewed solely as an attempt to confer tax benefits.

• Did the "minister" have any pastoral experience in a local church following his or her ordination, commissioning, or licensing (including conducting worship and administration of sacerdotal functions)?

✎ **Key point: the IRS probably will not recognize the ministerial status of one who receives ministerial credentials from a local church if (1) the church's charter does not authorize the conferring of ministerial credentials; (2) the church has never issued ministerial credentials in the past; or (3) the church is affiliated with a denomination that will not recognize the credentials issued by the church**

4. It is not necessarily true that a church worker will be "better off" for tax purposes by becoming a minister. For example, assume that a layperson serving as "youth minister" is debating whether or not to have the church license or ordain him as a minister. Assume further that the person is earning $30,000. By becoming a minister, the individual will have the "benefit" of a housing allowance exclusion in computing his federal income taxes. On the other hand, his social security tax rate increases from 7.65% (the employee's share of FICA taxes) to 15.3% (the self-employment tax). In other words, whether or not he will be "better off" for tax purposes

depends on whether the housing allowance exclusion offsets the additional $2,295 in social security taxes. As a result, church workers should not assume that they automatically will be "better off" for tax purposes if their church ordains, commissions, or licenses them. In many cases, they will not be. Of course, many persons seek ministerial credentials not only for the housing allowance, but also so they can exempt themselves from social security. As noted in chapter 9, very few ministers qualify for this special exemption. Further, even for those few that do, the extreme financial hardships often associated with such a decision makes the avoidance of social security taxes a dubious "benefit."

☞ *Example. J is youth pastor at First Church. He is married and has one dependent child. He is not ordained, commissioned, or licensed. He receives a salary of $20,000 and a housing allowance of $10,000. Since J is not ordained, commissioned, or licensed, he is a "minister" for tax purposes. As a result, he is not eligible for a housing allowance exclusion and is an employee for FICA purposes. How much taxes will J pay in 1997? Taking into account only three personal exemptions (at $2,650 each) and the standard deduction ($6,900) for the sake of simplicity, J's taxable income will be $15,150. At the 15% tax rate J will pay $2,272 in federal income taxes. Note that his taxable income is not reduced by a housing allowance. However, as a nonminister employee, J pays the employee's share of FICA taxes, which amounts to $2,295 ($30,000 times 7.65%), rather than the self-employment tax. J's total tax bill for 1997 is $4,567 (income taxes plus FICA taxes).*

☞ *Example. Same facts as the preceding example, except that J is licensed and is a minister for tax purposes. His taxable income for income tax purposes is reduced by the housing allowance ($10,000), assuming that his housing expenses are at least this much. This leaves taxable income of only $5,150. This amount is reduced further by half of J's self-employment tax (or $2,119, as computed below), for taxable income of $3,031 and a tax of only $455. J has saved a substantial amount in income taxes by being classified as a minister for tax purposes. However, as a minister J pays the self-employment tax, which will be $4,238 (salary plus housing allowance less 7.65% multiplied times the self-employment tax rate of 15.3%). J's total tax bill for 1997 as a minister will be $4,693. In summary, J pays $126 more in taxes by being treated as a minister.*

5. Confusing status and function. Part of the reason the IRS and Tax Court struggle to define the term *minister* is that they confuse the status and functions of a minister. Both the IRS and the Tax Court refer to the income tax regulations' definition of *service performed in the exercise of ministry* in attempting to define the term *minister*. But the Code and regulations treat the concepts of minister and *service performed in the exercise of ministry* separately.

6. Finally, persons seeking ministerial credentials solely to qualify for tax benefits should recognize the legal and theological deficiencies of their position. Consider the following:

a. As the Tax Court recognized in the *Lawrence* decision (discussed above), a "commissioning" of a minister solely to qualify him for tax benefits is "nothing more than a paperwork procedure designed to help him get a tax benefit . . . without giving him any new status." Such a "minister," the court concluded, generally should *not* be treated as a minister for tax purposes since he is not "recognized by his church as a minister of the gospel."

b. Because of the televangelist scandals and the proliferation in the numbers of "tax protestors" seeking to avoid paying taxes through the acquisition of "mail order" credentials, the IRS has become more aggressive in its dealings with clergy—particularly those who appear to have obtained ministerial credentials solely for tax benefits.

c. I Kings 13:33 states that "after this thing Jeroboam returned not from his evil way, but made again of the lowest of the people priests of the high places; whosoever would, he consecrated him, and he became one of the priests of the high places. And this thing became sin unto the house of Jeroboam, even to cut it off, and to destroy it from the face of the earth."

2. Service performed in the exercise of ministry

✎ **Key point: persons who qualify as ministers for federal tax purposes will qualify for the 4 special tax provisions only with respect to services they perform in the exercise of their ministry**

An individual who satisfies the definition of a minister, as described above, is eligible for the four special tax provisions discussed in this chapter. However, it must be stressed that the special tax treatment will only apply with respect to **service performed in the exercise of ministry.** In other words, the fact that Rev. Smith is in fact a minister does not mean that he automatically is eligible for a housing allowance exclusion. The exclusion is available only with respect to compensation received by Rev. Smith from the performance of services in the exercise of ministry. If he works part-time in secular employment, the housing allowance benefit will not apply to such work, since it is not service performed in the exercise of ministry (even though Rev. Smith is a minister). With respect to clergy serving in local churches, the regulations state that "[i]f a minister is performing service in the conduct of religious worship or the ministration of sacerdotal functions, such service is in the exercise of ministry whether or not it is performed for a religious organization." Similarly, the IRS noted in Revenue Ruling 78-301 that "when the individual's regular, full-time duties to the congregation are spiritual or religious in nature, such as leading the worship service, those duties are in the exercise of ministry."

the income tax regulations

As noted above, the income tax regulations define **service performed in the exercise of ministry** as follows:

> *Service performed by a minister in the exercise of his ministry includes the ministration of sacerdotal functions and the conduct of religious worship, and the control, conduct, and maintenance of religious organizations . . . under the authority of a religious body constituting a church or church denomination. The following rules are applicable in determining whether services performed by a minister are performed in the exercise of ministry:*

The regulations provide the following examples:

> Examples of specific services the performance of which will be considered duties of a minister . . . include the performance of sacerdotal functions, the conduct of religious worship, the administration and maintenance of religious organizations and their integral agencies, and the performance of teaching and administrative duties at theological seminaries. Also, the service performed by a qualified minister as an employee of the United States (other than as a chaplain in the Armed Forces, whose service is considered to be that of a commissioned officer in his capacity as such, and not as a minister in the exercise of his ministry), or a State, Territory, or possession of the United States, or a political subdivision of any of the foregoing, or the District of Columbia, is in the exercise of his ministry provided the service performed includes such services as are ordinarily the duties of a minister. *Treas. Reg. § 1.107-1(a).*

The regulations list 3 examples of services performed by ministers in the exercise of their ministry:

• the ministration of sacerdotal functions

• the conduct of religious worship, and

• the control, conduct, and maintenance of religious organizations under the authority of a religious body constituting a church or church denomination

⟳ **Observation. It is very significant that the IRS audit guidelines for ministers do not require that all three categories of ministry described in the regulations be met in order for one to be a minister for tax purposes or engaged in the performance of services in the exercise of ministry. This is a potentially significant admission by the IRS. Many bona fide ministers do not satisfy all three categories of ministry, and to suggest (as the IRS and Tax Court have in the past) that all three are required is inappropriate and naive.**

These 3 examples of services performed by ministers in the exercise of their ministry are illustrated below:

Sacerdotal functions. The term *sacerdotal functions* generally includes baptisms, communion, marriages, funerals, and prayer for the sick. The Tax Court, in the *Reeder* decision (discussed above), made the following comment regarding the performance of sacerdotal functions:

> As to the sacerdotal functions, [the minister's] own testimony is that while he was the pastor of the [local church] during 1973 and 1974, he could have performed a marriage or performed funeral services with permission or performed services with respect to the dedication of infants, and he did in fact perform the ministry functions of preaching and teaching, baptism, and communion. There is no requirement that to qualify as a "duly ordained, commissioned, or licensed minister" . . . an individual must be qualified to perform and actually perform every sacrament or rite of the religion.

The income tax regulations (quoted above) clarify that "[w]hether service performed by a minister constitutes the . . . ministration of sacerdotal functions depends on the tenets and practices of the particular religious body constituting his church or church denomination." The regulations also specify that "[i]f a minister is performing service in . . . the ministration of sacerdotal functions, such service is in the exercise of his ministry whether or not it is performed for a religious organization."

The IRS has recognized that sacerdotal functions include, but are not limited to, baptism, holy communion, and the performance of marriage and funeral ceremonies. *IRS Letter Ruling 8915001.*

Religious worship. The income tax regulations (quoted above) clarify that "[w]hether service performed by a minister constitutes the conduct of religious worship . . . depends on the tenets and practices of the particular religious body constituting his church or church denomination." The regulations also specify that "[i]f a minister is performing service in the conduct of religious worship . . . such service is in the exercise of his ministry whether or not it is performed for a religious organization."

How much religious worship is necessary to satisfy this test? This is an interesting question. The IRS has ruled on a few occasions that the religious worship must be part of a minister's regular duties. In one case, the IRS ruled that an ordained minister who served as administrator of a religious school was not engaged in services performed in the exercise of ministry despite the fact that his duties included conducting worship services three times each week for the students. The IRS noted that while the administrator performed religious services and sacerdotal functions on occasion, his "regular, full-time duties were administrative duties." *IRS Letter Ruling 8646018.* Similarly, in 1968 the IRS ruled that an ordained minister employed by a charitable organization as its Director of Special Services was not

engaged in the performance of services in the exercise of ministry despite the fact that he occasionally performed certain sacerdotal duties including the conduct of worship service. The IRS acknowledged that while the minister occasionally performed worship and some sacerdotal duties, his overall duties were not basically the conduct of religious worship or the ministration of sacerdotal functions as contemplated by the regulations. *Revenue Ruling 68-68.*

On the other hand, the Tax Court has ruled that a minister employed by a parachurch ministry was engaged in services performed in the exercise of ministry because he conducted staff devotions, despite the fact that his "regular, full-time duties were administrative duties." *Mosley v. Commissioner, T.C. Memo. 1994-457 (1994).* The Court observed:

> Daily worship services are conducted at [the parachurch ministry]. Apparently, they were conducted during the years in question. [The minister] conducts those services. They are conducted for employees engaged in [the organization's] marketing efforts. On occasion, the Lord's Supper is administered at those services. . . . [I]t seems clear that his activity in conducting worship services was known to, and approved by, the board of directors of the corporation. We think that his conduct of those services constitutes the conduct of religious services within the meaning of [the regulations]. . . . Clearly, [his] preaching and conduct of religious services constituted only a portion of [his] duties on behalf of [the organization].

The control, conduct, and maintenance of religious organizations. The regulations include the *control, conduct, and maintenance of religious organizations* in the definition of service performed by a minister in the exercise of ministry. The regulation quoted above defines this term as "directing, managing, or promoting the activities of such organization." This terminology is admittedly confusing.

The Tax Court in the *Wingo* decision, in interpreting this language, noted that "the fact that [a minister] was not permitted to do all that [an ordained minister] could do does not mean that he performed no services in the control, conduct, and maintenance of his church or denomination. To perform services in the control, conduct, and maintenance of the church or organization within the church, the minister need only have some participation in the conduct, control, and maintenance of the local church or denomination." The *Wingo* court also noted that a minister can be engaged in the control, conduct, or maintenance of *either* a local church or a denomination. To illustrate, the fact that a minister has the right to vote at national conventions of his or her denomination will constitute sufficient control, even if the minister possesses little if any control over a local church. This is often true of ordained youth pastors—they have the right to vote at national conventions (and thereby they are engaged in the control, conduct, and maintenance of their denomination) even though they possess little if any authority in their own congregation.

The Tax Court, in the *Reeder* decision (discussed above), made the following comment regarding the question of service in the control, conduct, and maintenance of the religious organization:

> [The taxpayer] points out that during 1973 and 1974 he was the pastor of a local church which was a dependent church and subject to supervision under the constitution and bylaws of the [District]. [The taxpayer] argues that only upon ordination was he able to participate in the governance of his church organization at a higher level than the local church. In response to a similar argument in Wingo v. Commissioner, we stated: "To perform services in the control, conduct, and maintenance of the church or organizations within the church, the minister need only have some participation in the conduct, control, and maintenance of the local church or the denomination."

The income tax regulations (quoted above) further clarify that

> [s]ervices performed by a minister in the control, conduct, and maintenance of a religious organization relates to directing, managing, or promoting the activities of such organization. Any religious organization is deemed to be under the authority of a religious body constituting a church or church denomination if it is organized and dedicated to carrying out the tenets and principles of a faith in accordance with either the requirements or sanctions governing the creation of institutions of the faith.

The IRS has recognized that services in the "control, conduct, and maintenance" of a religious organization can occur at either the local congregational level or in the context of a regional or national denomination. To illustrate, in one ruling the IRS noted that a minister satisfied this test because "[h]e was directly responsible for the local church as its administrative head or overseer, and he was chairman of the official board of the church. Thus, he was in charge of all the organizational concerns of his own congregation." The IRS also noted that the minister was a member of a regional body of his denomination and in that role was part of the voting constituency of that body. As a voting member "he had the opportunity to influence the conduct, control, and maintenance of the governing body of his church in [his denomination]. Also, [his] denomination recognized the taxpayer as a minister or religious leader, by licensing him as a minister. *IRS Letter Ruling 8915001.*

the IRS audit guidelines for ministers

In 1995 the IRS released audit guidelines for ministers. These guidelines were issued pursuant to the IRS "Market Segment Specialization Program" (MSSP), and are intended to promote a higher degree of competence among those agents who audit ministers. The guidelines state that "the first issue

that must be determined is whether the minister is an employee or an independent contractor."

✎ **Key point: in 1995 the IRS issued audit guidelines for its agents to apply when auditing ministers. The guidelines cover a range of issues, including the definition of the term "service performed in the exercise of ministry."**

The guidelines inform IRS agents that the income tax regulations define the term "service performed by a minister in the exercise of the ministry" to include:

• ministration of sacerdotal functions

• conduct of religious worship

• control, conduct, and maintenance of religious organizations (including the religious boards, societies, and other integral agencies of such organizations), under the authority of a religious body constituting a church or denomination

The guidelines further instruct agents that the income tax regulations specify that whether service performed by a minister constitutes conduct of religious worship or ministration of sacerdotal functions depends on the tenets and practices of the particular religious body constituting the church or denomination.

The guidelines, referring again to the regulations, provide the following examples of specific services considered duties of a minister:

• performance of sacerdotal functions

• conduct of religious worship

• administration and maintenance of religious organizations and their integral agencies

• performance of teaching and administrative duties at theological seminaries

⊃ **Observation.** *This list does not suggest or require that a person satisfy all of the categories to be a minister or be engaged in service performed in the exercise of ministry. To illustrate, a theology professor at a seminary who seldom if ever conducts religious worship or performs sacerdotal functions would still be considered a minister engaged in ministry under the approach taken both in the regulations and the guidelines. This is an important clarification, since some previous IRS and Tax Court rulings have suggested that all categories of ministerial services must be performed.*

IRS Publication 517

IRS Publication 517, which addresses tax reporting for ministers, refers to "service performed in the exercise of ministry" as "qualified services," and describes this term as follows:

Most services you perform as a minister, priest, rabbi, etc., are qualified services. These services include:

1) Performing sacerdotal functions,

2) Conducting religious worship, and

3) Controlling, conducting, and maintaining religious organizations, boards, societies, and other integral agencies that are under the authority of a religious body that is a church or denomination.

You are considered to control, conduct, or maintain a religious organization if you direct, manage, or promote the organization's activities. A religious organization is under the authority of a religious body that is a church or denomination if it is organized for and dedicated to carrying out the principles of a faith according to the requirements governing the creation of institutions of the faith.

Services for nonreligious organizations. Your services for a nonreligious organization are qualified services if the services are assigned or designated by your church. Assigned or designated services qualify even if they do not involve performing sacerdotal functions or conducting religious worship.

Ordinarily, your services are not considered assigned or designated by your church if you are in any of the following categories:

1) You perform services for an organization that did not arrange with your church to receive them.

2) You perform the same services for an organization that other undesignated employees perform.

3) You perform the same services before and after the designation.

If your services are not assigned or designated by your church, they are qualified services only if they involve performing sacerdotal functions or conducting religious worship.

Services that are not part of your ministry. The following are not qualified services. Your income from these services is generally subject to FICA (and not SECA) taxes under the rules that apply to workers in general.

1) Services that you perform for nonreligious organizations other than the services stated earlier.

2) Services that you perform as a duly ordained, commissioned, or licensed minister of a church as an employee of the United States, the District of Columbia, a foreign government, or any of their political subdivisions. This is true even if you are performing sacerdotal functions or conducting religious worship. (For example, if you perform services as a chaplain in the Armed Forces of the United States, the services are not qualified services.)

3) Services that you perform in a government-owned and operated hospital are considered performed by a government employee, not by a minister as part of the ministry. However, services that you perform at a church-related hospital or health and welfare institution are considered to be part of the ministry.

Books or articles. Writing religious books or articles is considered to be in the exercise of your ministry. Royalty income from the sale of books or articles is self-employment income.

Ministers engaged in pastoral ministry in local congregations

The courts and the IRS have had little difficulty in deciding that a minister engaged in pastoral ministry in a local congregation is performing services in the exercise of ministry. As the IRS noted in Revenue Ruling 78-301, "when the individual's regular, full-time duties to the congregation are spiritual or religious in nature, such as leading the worship service, those duties are in the exercise of ministry." Further, the income tax regulations (quoted above) clarify that "[i]f a minister is performing service in the conduct of religious worship or the ministration of sacerdotal functions, such service is in the exercise of his ministry whether or not it is performed for a religious organization."

Consider the following examples:

☞ *Example. Rev. R is an ordained minister of youth at First Church. He regularly performs sacerdotal duties and conducts religious worship. He would be considered to be a minister under the Knight definition, and possibly under the Wingo definition (if he is engaged in the "control, conduct, or maintenance" of his church, and is considered to be a religious leader). As a minister, he is eligible for the four special tax provisions discussed in this chapter (assuming that he otherwise qualifies), with respect to his services on behalf of the church.*

☞ *Example. Ms. R is the minister of music at First Church. She has not been ordained, commissioned, or licensed by her church or denomination, and she does not perform any sacerdotal duties. Her duties include directing the church choir, overseeing the music program at the church, and playing the organ during church services. She will not qualify for any of the four special provisions discussed above, since she is not ordained, commissioned, or licensed (according to both the Knight and Wingo definitions, one must be ordained, commissioned, or licensed in order to be a minister for federal tax purposes). This means that she is not eligible for a housing allowance exclusion or exemption from either so-*

cial security taxes or income tax withholding. Revenue Ruling 59-270.

☞ **Example.** Mr. B retired from a secular job, and began working at First Church as a "minister of visitation." His responsibilities include hospital visitation and visiting new and prospective members. He is not ordained, commissioned, or licensed, and performs no sacerdotal functions or religious worship. He does not qualify for the four special tax provisions discussed in this chapter (under either the Knight or Wingo definition of the term minister), since he is not an ordained, commissioned, or licensed minister, and he performs neither sacerdotal duties nor religious worship.

☞ **Example.** Pastor P is the senior minister at First Church. The church is not affiliated with any sect or denomination. Pastor P has never been ordained or licensed. He is not eligible for any of the special tax provisions discussed in this chapter (including a housing allowance) under either the Knight or Wingo definition of the term minister. Of course, his church is free to ordain or commission Pastor P, and this may entitle him to the special tax provisions. However, note that the Tax Court in the Lawrence decision warned that an individual would not qualify for such special tax provisions if he or she was ordained or commissioned solely for tax savings purposes. Further, the court noted in the Salkov case that an individual cannot become eligible for the special tax provisions by "ordaining" himself or herself.

☞ **Example.** B serves as business administrator of First Church. The church "licenses" her as a "minister of administration" in order to make her eligible for a housing allowance. B performs no sacerdotal functions and does not conduct religious worship. She has no formal theological training, and her duties were in no way affected by her "license." The act of licensing B probably will not make her eligible for a housing allowance, according to the legal precedent cited above, since it is doubtful that she will satisfy a majority of the 5 criteria mentioned in the Knight case. Again, persons seeking special tax benefits through licensing or commissioning should pay special heed to the Tax Court's decision in Lawrence (discussed above).

Ministers not engaged in pastoral ministry in local congregations

It is often difficult to determine if a minister is engaged in service performed in the exercise of ministry with respect to **services performed outside of the context of a local church.**

The following examples, based on actual cases, will be instructive:

☞ **Example.** The IRS ruled that an ordained Presbyterian minister employed full-time by a nonprofit pastoral counseling center was not eligible for a housing allowance. The minister spent 50% of his working hours providing "spiritual and pastoral counsel to individuals about a variety of issues, including marital difficulties, depression, anxiety, sexual problems, eating disorders and gender identity." His counseling approach was based on "applying Biblical principles of human nature and behavior" to the problems of patients. He spent 35% of his time preparing for and leading three small Bible studies groups and two discussion groups of other ordained ministers; 10% of his time was spent preparing for and teaching Sunday School classes in nearby congregations; and 5% of his time was spent on preaching, leading worship services, officiating at weddings and administering the sacraments. Less than 5% of his was taken up with administrative duties. The counseling center's board of directors designated a portion of the minister's compensation as a housing allowance. This practice was questioned by the IRS, and guidance was sought from the IRS national office. The IRS national office concluded that the minister was not entitled to a housing allowance. It conceded that the taxpayer was a minister, but it concluded that he was not engaged in service performed in the exercise of his ministry and therefore he was not eligible for a housing allowance with respect to his employment by the counseling center. It observed: "In the present case, the facts indicate that only 5% of the taxpayer's working hours are spent performing duties such as the conduct of religious worship or the performance of sacerdotal functions that are described in the income tax regulations as constituting service performed by a minister in the exercise of his ministry. Therefore, we conclude that the duties performed by the taxpayer for [the counseling center] are not service performed in the exercise of his ministry pursuant to . . . the income tax regulations." This ruling is unique in the sense that the IRS limited its analysis to the percentage of the minister's time that was spent performing worship or sacerdotal functions. Such an approach is questionable, since most pastoral ministers (like the pastoral counselor in this case) spend no more than 5% of their time conducting worship or administering the sacraments and they spend a substantial amount of time engaged in counseling. Clearly, there is a need for the IRS to come up with a better justification for the result reached in this private letter ruling. IRS Letter Ruling 9124059.

☞ **Example.** An ordained minister was a full-time counselor for an organization that promoted recovery from addictive disorders, such as alcoholism and drug addiction, through spiritual ministration and counseling. Many of the organization's patients were referred by churches. The minister spent 75% of his time engaged in spiritual counseling; 20% in administration; and 5% in performing weddings and funerals, prayer services, and adult religious education classes. Under these circumstances, the IRS concluded that the minister was not eligible for a housing allowance since "the facts indicate that only 5% of the minister's working hours are spent performing duties such as the conduct of religious worship or the performance of sacerdotal functions that are described in [the income tax regulations] as constituting service performed by a minister in the exercise of his ministry." IRS Letter Ruling 9231053.

☞ **Example.** Rev. B is an ordained minister who is employed as a counselor by a nonprofit religious organization not associated with any particular church. His employment includes the following services—teaching Bible classes, performing spiritual counseling, conducting seminars and workshops, speaking at churches, acting as a liaison with area churches, preaching, attending ministerial alliance meetings, and conducting staff devotions. Rev. B requested a ruling from the IRS that his services were in the exercise of his ministry and accordingly that he was eligible for a housing allowance exclusion (and the other special tax provisions available to ministers). The IRS concluded that Rev. B was engaged in the performance of services in the exercise of his ministry, and accordingly was eligible for a housing allowance and the other special tax provisions. It relied on the regulation (quoted above) which specifies that "if a minister is performing service in the conduct of religious worship or the ministration of sacerdotal functions, such service is in the exercise of his ministry whether or not it is performed for a religious organization." The IRS concluded that the services performed by Rev. B were "clearly ministerial in nature" and accordingly that the services he performed on behalf of his employer were in the exercise of his ministry. This case suggests that a minister serving in a parachurch ministry may be engaged in service performed in the exercise of ministry if his or her job description is amended to reflect the following responsibilities: (1) weekly worship service; (2) weekly religious education classes; (3) religious counseling with employees or supporters as desired; (4) administration of sacraments or sacerdotal functions to employees or supporters as desired; (5) liaison with area churches; (6) staff devotions; and (7) representation of the ministry at ministerial alliance meetings. IRS Letter Ruling 8825025.

☞ **Example.** An ordained rabbi is employed full-time as a religious instructor by a synagogue-controlled private school. In this capacity, the rabbi teaches Judaic studies, leads daily worship services with the students in the school, trains students to conduct religious services, teaches students to read the Torah, assists with Bar Mitzvah training, and provides consultation to students, faculty and administrators of the school with respect to Jewish religious practices. The rabbi also instructs students on the subjects of Jewish law, liturgy, holidays, customs, ethics and values. The rabbi is a minister, and he is engaged in service performed in the exercise of ministry. Accordingly, he is eligible for a housing allowance. IRS Letter Ruling 9126048.

☞ **Example.** Rev. C performs services as an employee of a nonprofit organization that was formed to provide a chaplaincy ministry of pastoral and theological care for and to hospitalized patients, including counseling and guidance of patients and their families, outpatients, staff and medical personnel, who may be connected with local hospitals and health organizations. The organization receives its operating funds from contributions by local churches. Rev. C is an ordained minister, and was employed to perform services for the organization as director of pastoral care at a public hospital. His daily duties include: (1) spiritual and emotional counseling of patients and their families referred by the nursing staff and physicians (this counseling occupies approximately 40% of his working hours); (2) performing religious rituals at the time of death for patients who pass away while in the hospital (15%); (3) spiritual crisis counseling and notification of patients' ministers in emergency situations (15%); (4) pastoral counseling to the hospital staff and student nurses in time of stress (5%); (5) performing funeral services, wedding services, and bedside communion services (5%); (6) speaking in the hospital chapel at various community and church group gatherings on the hospital chaplaincy program and performing devotional programs (5%). The IRS ruled that Rev. C is a minister and that his work constitutes service performed in the exercise of ministry and accordingly he should be treated as a minister for federal tax purposes. It noted that "his services are principally spiritual counseling and the ministration of sacerdotal functions." IRS Letter Ruling 8519004.

☞ **Example.** Rev. N is an ordained minister who teaches theology at a church-operated seminary. He rarely conducts religious worship or administers sacerdotal functions. Is he a minister engaged in service performed in the exercise of ministry? The answer is yes. As noted above, the income tax regulations specify that "[e]xamples of specific services the performance of which will be considered duties of a minister . . . include . . . the performance of teaching and administrative duties at theological seminaries." Treas. Reg. § 1.107-1(a).

☞ **Example.** Rabbi L was hired by the United Jewish Appeal (UJA) to serve as its Director of the Rabbinic Advisory Council. The placement bureau of the Rabbinical Assembly, an organization of conservative rabbis, assisted the rabbi in securing this position. Prior to his employment with the UJA, Rabbi L served as a rabbi of various congregations, and was provided housing by these congregations. The services Rabbi L performed with the UJA were in substantial part rabbinic in nature. He served as a consultant to the UJA and its staff regarding matters of Jewish law and practices. He functioned as staff chaplain providing rabbinic counseling to staff and conducting services at meetings. He performed sacerdotal functions, conducting weddings and funerals for the staff and families. He directed religious services and observances at all UJA conferences and meetings and conducted study sessions on Jewish customs and practices for the executive staff of the UJA. He communicated to rabbis around the world regarding the importance of the concept of charity and enlisted their support for programs sponsored by the UJA. In this respect, he conducted seminars for various rabbinic groups and delivered Sabbath sermons to various congregations. The Tax Court concluded that Rabbi L was engaged in service performed in the exercise of ministry and accordingly was eligible for a housing allowance. It observed: "The services petitioner performed with the UJA, though different than that of a rabbi of a specific congregation, were clearly rabbinic or 'ministerial' in nature. . . . [Rabbi L] performed many religious or sacerdotal functions similar to those performed by a rabbi with a defined congregation. [He] served as staff chaplain to the UJA and its staff, explaining matters of Jewish law and practices and conducting weddings and funerals for the staff and families upon their request. In addition, he directed religious services and observances at all conferences and meetings and conducted study sessions on Jewish customs and practices for the executive staff of the UJA. Thus, based on the entire record, we are convinced that the services petitioner performed for the UJA were in the exercise of his ministry within the meaning of the regulations. Libman v. Commissioner, 44 TCM 370 (1982).

☞ *Example.* An ordained Baptist minister established an exempt organization to produce videotapes to promote world missions. The minister was responsible for the "message" conveyed on the tapes. His other duties included preaching in local church missions conventions and marketing the tapes. He conducts daily worship services for employees of the organization to emphasize the importance of their work, and performs sacerdotal duties (communion) on occasion. More than 30,000 churches have purchased or used the organization's videos. The organization designated a portion of the minister's compensation as a housing allowance. The IRS audited the minister and determined that he was not eligible for a housing allowance since his services did not constitute the exercise of ministry. The minister appealed, and the Tax Court ruled that the minister's duties were in the exercise of his ministry and that he qualified for a housing allowance. The court noted that the regulations specify that a minister employed by a separate organization can be engaged in ministerial services (and eligible for a housing allowance) under any of 3 circumstances: (1) the minister is assigned to the position by a church or denomination, (2) the minister is engaged in the "control, conduct, and maintenance" of a religious organization under the control of a church or denomination, or (3) the minister conducts religious worship or performs sacerdotal functions. The court concluded that the minister did not qualify under the first 2 tests, but that he did under the third test. It emphasized that the minister conducted daily worship services for the employees of the organization, and occasionally

administered communion. In addition, he preached at local church missions conventions on behalf of the organization. The court acknowledged that these activities comprised only a portion of the minister's duties, but it concluded that this did not matter since these activities were the minister's principal duties. The court relied in part on the testimony of a Baptist professor who testified that some ministers, such as the minister in this case, broaden their ministries beyond the local church to proclaim the Gospel through other means (such as videotapes and other media). The professor testified that Baptist churches consider an ordained minister who "seeks to proclaim the Gospel in any fashion to any person or group of persons, or who provides church-related services to congregations," to be functioning as a minister in accordance with the overall purpose of his ordination. The court concluded that the minister in this case was fulfilling his ministry through his organization by producing missions tapes for local congregations. Mosley v. Commissioner, T.C. Memo. 1994-457 (1994).

☞ *Example.* The IRS ruled that teachers and administrators employed by an "interdenominational" seminary, that was not an integral agency of a particular church or denomination, were not engaged in the exercise of ministry and accordingly were not eligible for a housing allowance. The IRS acknowledged that the income tax regulations define "service performed in the exercise of ministry" to include "the performance of teaching and administrative duties at theological seminaries." It further acknowledged that the regulations provide that "services rendered by an ordained minister in the conduct of religious worship or the ministration of sacerdotal functions are considered services in the exercise of a ministry whether or not it is performed for a religious organization or an integral agency thereof." However, the IRS concluded: "[T]he information submitted does not show which religious activities qualify in accordance with the tenets and practices of a particular religious body constituting a church or church denomination. Since the employer is an interdenominational seminary, it is difficult to envision how the duties of the faculty could in any significant amount be said to constitute the conduct of religious worship or the ministration of sacerdotal functions of a particular denomination." IRS Letter Ruling 7833017.

☞ *Example.* The IRS ruled that an ordained minister who was fully qualified to perform all of the sacerdotal functions of his church, and who served as the canon/administrator of his local church, was engaged in the exercise of ministry and accordingly was eligible for a housing allowance. His duties included supervising all aspects of the church's finances, fund raising program, plant and equipment, kitchen operations and housekeeping. The IRS noted that "examples of specific services the performance of which will be considered duties of a minister for purposes of [the housing allowance] include the performance of sacerdotal functions, the conduct of religious worship, the administration and maintenance of religious organizations and their integral agencies." The IRS concluded that "the regulations are specific concerning ministers who serve as administrators of religious organizations. Accordingly, we have concluded that you are performing services that are ordinarily the duties of a minister of the gospel and, as such, are eligible to receive a rental allowance exclusion." *IRS Letter Ruling 8142076.*

☞ **Example.** *The IRS ruled that ordained ministers of the gospel who are employed as teachers and administrators by a seminary that is not an integral agency under the authority of a religious body constituting a church or church denomination are not engaged in the exercise of ministry and accordingly are not eligible for a housing allowance (unless they serve by virtue of an assignment from their church or denomination, as explained in the next section of this chapter). Revenue Ruling 63-90. See also IRS Letter Ruling 7833017.*

☞ **Example.** *The IRS ruled that a "licensed minister" in a denomination that both ordains and licenses its ministers was a "minister" for federal tax purposes since he performed substantially all the functions of an ordained minister. The minister was licensed in 1971, and as a licensed minister he pastored a church, administered the ordinances of baptism and holy communion, preached sermons, and performed the services of marriage, burial and membership reception. He also was responsible for ministering to the needs of the people of the church, which included instructing candidates for membership and receiving them into the church, and counseling troubled or bereaved families. The minister was ordained in 1980, and filed an application for exemption from self-employment tax (Form 4361) in 1980. The IRS ruled that the minister qualified as a minister for tax purposes when he was licensed in 1971, and accordingly the Form 4361 was filed too late. The IRS noted that the minister performed all 3 of the kinds of ministerial services described in the income tax regulations (sacerdotal functions, conduct of worship, and the "control, conduct, and maintenance" of a religious organization): "The taxpayer was heavily involved in all three of the types of services in his capacity as a licensed minister and pastor of a local church . . . . With respect to the first type of ministerial services, he was authorized to and in fact did administer sacerdotal functions. He administered the ordinances of baptism and holy communion, and presided at marriage and funeral ceremonies. Secondly, he conducted religious worship on a regular basis in his capacity as pastor of a local church. Thirdly, in his role as pastor of a local church he was involved in the control, conduct, and maintenance of religious organizations under the authority of a religious body. He was directly responsible for the local church as its administrative head or overseer, and he was chairman of the official board of the church. Thus, he was in charge of*

all the organizational concerns of his own congregation . . . . He was also a member of the District Council and in that role was part of the voting constituency of the District Council. As a voting member of the District Council, he had the opportunity to influence the conduct, control, and maintenance of the governing body of his church in [his] District. Also, [his] denomination recognized the taxpayer as a minister or religious leader, by licensing him as a minister. IRS Letter Ruling 8915001.

☞ **Example.** *The IRS ruled that a minister who was employed as an administrator at a religious school was not a "minister" for federal tax purposes since the school was not an integral agency of a church. A group of concerned parents joined together for the purpose of establishing a religious school. The articles of incorporation of the school specify that the school is independent and autonomous and not subject to ecclesiastical control from any convention, conference, association, council, group, church, or individual. The administrator's duties included conducting worship services three times each week for the students, ministering to the spiritual needs of parents and students through counseling, preaching in various churches as a representative of the school, attending ministerial meetings as the head of the school, establishing programs for the spiritual, mental, and physical development of students, disciplining the students, and acting as the business agent for the school. The IRS concluded that the school was not an integral agency of a church, and accordingly the administrator was not engaged in the performance of services in the exercise of ministry. The IRS acknowledged that the income tax regulations specify that if a minister is performing service in the conduct of religious worship or the ministration of sacerdotal functions, such service is in the exercise of his ministry whether or not it is performed for a religious organization. However, the IRS noted that while the administrator performed religious services and sacerdotal functions on occasion, his "regular, full-time duties were administrative duties." IRS Letter Ruling 8646018. But see Mosley v. Commissioner, T.C. Memo. 1994-457 (1994).*

☞ **Example.** *An ordained minister was employed by a charitable organization as its Director of Special Services. The organization was neither a religious organization nor an integral agency of a religious organization. As Director of Special Services the minister's basic functions were the directorship of the organization's advisory council and the coordination of its cultural programs. In connection with his position, he occasionally performed certain sacerdotal duties including the conduct of worship service. The IRS ruled that since the charitable organization was neither a religious organization nor an integral agency of one, the minister's duties did not qualify as those in the administration or maintenance of a religious organization or an integral agency. The IRS acknowledged that while the minister oc-*

casionally performed sacerdotal duties, his overall duties were not basically the conduct of religious worship or the ministration of sacerdotal functions as contemplated by the regulations. Revenue Ruling 68-68. But see Mosley v. Commissioner, T.C. Memo. 1994-457 (1994).

☞ **Example.** The IRS ruled that ordained ministers serving as chaplains in government owned and operated hospitals are not engaged in service performed in the exercise of ministry for purposes of social security, and accordingly they are employees for FICA purposes (and, if exempt from self-employment taxes, the exemption does not apply). However, the chaplains are engaged in the exercise of ministry for purposes of the housing allowance, and accordingly are eligible for this exclusion. The services performed by the chaplains included the conduct of religious worship, the ministration of sacerdotal functions, and spiritual counseling. The IRS noted that service performed by a duly ordained, commissioned, or licensed minister of a church "as an employee of the United States, a State, Territory, or possession of the United States, the District of Columbia, a foreign government, or a political subdivision of any of the foregoing," is not considered to be "in the exercise of his ministry" even though such service may involve the ministration of sacerdotal functions or the conduct of religious worship. Such service is considered to be performed in his capacity as an employee of the government and not by a minister "in the exercise of his ministry." Treas. Reg. § 1.1402(c)-5. Accordingly, service of the type described above performed by a minister as a chaplain at a government owned and operated hospital is not considered to be "in the exercise of his ministry," for social security purposes, and compensation paid by such hospitals to their minister-employees is subject to income tax withholding. On the other hand, the income tax regulations specify that "service performed by a qualified minister as an employee of the United States (other than as a chaplain in the Armed Forces, whose service is considered to be that of a commissioned officer in his capacity as such, and not as a minister in the exercise of his ministry), or a State, Territory, or possession of the United States, or a political subdivision of any of the foregoing, or the District of Columbia, is in the exercise of his ministry provided the service performed includes such services as are ordinarily the duties of a minister." Treas. Reg. 1.107-1(a). Accordingly, chaplains employed by government owned and operated hospitals are eligible for a housing allowance. Revenue Ruling 71-258. See also IRS Letter Rulings 7727019, 7809092, 8004046, 8138184, 8519004, and 9743037.

☞ **Example.** Ordained ministers employed as chaplains by state prisons are not engaged in the exercise of ministry for social security purposes. As a result, they are subject to FICA taxes. If they exempted themselves from self-employment taxes, the exemption does not apply. This result is based on the income tax regulations, which

specify that service performed by a duly ordained, commissioned, or licensed minister of a church "as an employee of the United States, a State, Territory, or possession of the United States, the District of Columbia, a foreign government, or a political subdivision of any of the foregoing," is not considered to be "in the exercise of his ministry" even though such service may involve the ministration of sacerdotal functions or the conduct of religious worship. The regulations specify that "service performed by an employee of a state as a chaplain in a state prison is considered to be performed by a civil servant of the state and not by a minister in the exercise of his ministry." Treas. Reg. § 1.1402(c)-5. On the other hand, the regulations specify that, for purposes of determining the eligibility of a chaplain for a housing allowance, "service performed by a qualified minister as an employee of the United States . . . or a State, Territory, or possession of the United States, or a political subdivision of any of the foregoing, or the District of Columbia, is in the exercise of his ministry provided the service performed includes such services as are ordinarily the duties of a minister." Treas. Reg. 1.107-1(a).

C. Ministers Employed by Integral Agencies or on Assignment

The income tax regulations (quoted above) give a special definition to the critical phrase service performed in the exercise of ministry in two situations. These two special situations are explained below.

integral agencies of a church or denomination

If a minister is performing service for an organization which is operated as an integral agency of a religious organization under the authority of a religious body constituting a church or church denomination, all service performed by the minister in the conduct of religious worship, in the ministration of sacerdotal functions, or in the control, conduct, and maintenance of such organization is in the exercise of his ministry. What is an integral agency of a church or religious denomination? The IRS (in Revenue Ruling 72-606) has listed eight criteria to be considered in determining whether a particular "institution" is an integral agency of a "religious organization":

(1) whether the religious organization incorporated the institution;

(2) whether the corporate name of the institution indicates a church relationship;

(3) whether the religious organization continuously controls, manages, and maintains the institution;

(4) whether the trustees or directors of the institution are approved by or must be approved by the religious organization or church;

(5) whether trustees or directors may be removed by the religious organization or church;

(6) whether annual reports of finances and general operations are required to be made to the religious organization or church;

(7) whether the religious organization or church contributes to the support of the institution; and

(8) whether, in the event of dissolution of the institution, its assets would be turned over to the religious organization or church.

☞ *Example. Rev. T is an ordained minister employed in an administrative capacity by a nursing home. The institution is affiliated with, but not controlled by, a religious denomination. Although the old age home had a corporate name which implied a church relationship and its articles of incorporation directed that upon dissolution all assets would be turned over to the sponsoring denomination, these facts were not sufficient to support a finding that the home was an integral agency of the denomination. Rev. T's administrative services in the control, conduct, and maintenance of the institution are not service performed in the exercise of ministry. Accordingly, he does not qualify for a housing allowance or any of the other special rules summarized above. Revenue Ruling 72-606. See also IRS Letter Ruling 8329042.*

☞ *Example. A college was ruled to be an integral agency of a church because of the following factors: (1) the board of directors of the college was indirectly controlled by the church because each board member had to be a member in good standing of the congregation; (2) every teacher was a member in good standing of the congregation; (3) the majority of students were members of the church; (4) all subjects taught at the college, whether in natural science, mathematics, social science, languages, etc., were taught with emphasis on religious principles and religious living; (5) the college had a department which performed all the functions for ministerial training that a seminary offers. Accordingly, ordained ministers employed in teaching or administrative positions at the college were engaged in the exercise of ministry and were eligible for the special benefits (including a housing allowance) discussed above. Revenue Ruling 70-549. See also IRS Technical Advice Memorandum 9033002, and IRS Letter Rulings 7907160, 8004087, 80929145, 8922077, 9144047, and 9608027.*

☞ *Example. Rev. F is an ordained minister who serves as a professor of religion at Texas Christian University. He occasionally officiates at weddings, preaches sermons, and performs other sacerdotal functions, but these activities are not part of his employment at the University. The University has a close relationship with the Christian Church (Disciples of Christ), but the Church does not control or manage the University either*

directly or indirectly. In fact, the University only satisfies the last of the 5 factors listed in Revenue Ruling 70-549 (see preceding example). In addition, the University satisfies only two of the eight criteria cited in Revenue Ruling 72-606 (quoted above). Accordingly, the University is not an integral agency of the Church, and Rev. F is not eligible for any of the special provisions discussed above (including a housing allowance). Since he was not working for an integral agency of a church, he had to satisfy all three elements of the definition of "service performed by a minister in the exercise of his ministry" in order to qualify. He failed to satisfy all three elements with respect to his employment by the University. Flowers v. Commissioner, 82-1 USTC para. 9114 (N.D. Tex. 1981).

☞ *Example. Rev. B, a duly ordained minister, is engaged by a public university to teach history. She performs no other service for the university, although from time to time she performs marriages and conducts funerals for relatives and friends. The university is neither a religious organization nor operated as an integral agency of a religious organization. Rev. B is not performing services for the university pursuant to an assignment or designation by her ecclesiastical superiors. The service performed by Rev. B for the university is not in the exercise of ministry. However, service performed by Rev. B in performing marriages and conducting funerals is in the exercise of ministry. Only as to the later kinds of services will the four special tax provisions apply.*

☞ *Example. Rev. W works in an administrative capacity for the headquarters of his religious denomination. Such employment constitutes service performed in the exercise of ministry even if Rev. W does not perform sacerdotal functions or conduct religious worship as part of his employment, since he is engaged in the control, conduct, and maintenance of a church organization. Revenue Ruling 57-129.*

assignments

As noted above, the income tax regulations specify that

> if a minister, pursuant to an assignment or designation by a religious body constituting his church, performs service for an organization which is neither a religious organization nor operated as an integral agency of religious organization, all service performed by him, even though such service may not involve the conduct of religious worship or the ministration of sacerdotal functions, is in the exercise of his ministry.

The regulations further provide that "if a minister is performing service for an organization which is neither a religious organization nor operated as an integral agency of a religious organization and the service is not performed pursuant to an assignment or designation by his ecclesiastical superiors, then only the service performed by him in the conduct of religious worship or the ministration of sacerdotal functions is in the exercise of his ministry."

The regulations contain the following two examples:

☞ *Example. M, a duly ordained minister, is assigned by X, the religious body constituting his church, to perform advisory service to Y Company in connection with the publication of a book dealing with the history of M's church denomination. Y is neither a religious organization nor operated as an integral agency of a religious organization. M performs no other service for X or Y. M is performing service in the exercise of his ministry.*

☞ *Example. M, a duly ordained minister, is engaged by N University to teach history and mathematics. He performs no other service for N although from time to time he performs marriages and conducts funerals for relatives and friends. N University is neither a religious organization nor operated as an integral agency of a religious organization. M is not performing the service for N pursuant to an assignment or designation by his ecclesiastical superiors. The service performed by M for N University is not in the exercise of his ministry. However, service performed by M in performing marriages and conducting funerals is in the exercise of his ministry.*

The IRS and the courts have addressed "assignments" of ministers in a few rulings that are summarized below:

Boyer v. Commissioner, 69 T.C. 521 (1977). The *Boyer* case is the leading judicial interpretation of the assignment language in the regulations. In the Fall of 1969 Rev. Boyer, a Methodist minister, began teaching data processing at a community college having no affiliation with the United Methodist Church. At the end of his first year of teaching at this college, Rev. Boyer had the college send his ordaining body (Annual Conference) a letter requesting that he be "assigned" to the college as a professor. The Conference sent the college a letter "appointing" Rev. Boyer as professor, but did not negotiate with college as to Rev. Boyer's salary or duties and paid no portion of his compensation. The purpose of this appointment was to qualify Rev. Boyer for a housing allowance. The Tax Court, in rejecting Rev. Boyer's eligibility for a housing allowance, remarked:

[Rev. Boyer] began teaching at [the college] in 1969; [the college] requested his assignment . . . in May, 1970, after he had completed an academic year at the institution. His assignment . . . was virtually pro forma—the ratification by the church of employment previously begun. In contrast, we believe that the "assignment" referred to in the regulations must be significant, in that the minister must have been assigned by the church for reasons directly related to the accomplishment of purposes of the

church. Unless we read these regulations to require a genuine church-related purpose in the church's assignment of the minister, bootstrapping of the type attempted here by petitioner would enable any ordained minister, merely by obtaining a pro forma "assignment" after he secures secular employment, to qualify for the ministerial rental exclusion. The special benefits of section 107 would follow him through a purely secular career. We do not believe that Congress intended any such result. More is required than mere ordained status and the perfunctory ratification by religious authority of secular employment obtained by the minister for non-church-related reasons.

The court further concluded that the regulations "contain an implicit requirement that the assignment by the church must be to further the purposes of the church," and that Rev. Boyer's assignment to the college "did not qualify as an assignment which transformed his secular duties at a state university school into service in the exercise of his ministry."

This case suggests that an assignment of a minister by his or her ordaining body, to satisfy the requirements of the regulations, must satisfy 2 requirements: (1) the assignment must precede and initiate the minister's new work assignment; and (2) the assignment must be directly related to the accomplishment of the purposes of the church or other ordaining body. "Retroactive" assignments, occurring after a minister has served for a period of time in a new position, do not fulfill these requirements. As the court noted, more is required than "pro forma" assignments involving little more than "perfunctory ratification by religious authority".

Tanenbaum v. Commissioner, 58 T.C. 1 (1972). A rabbi was employed by the American Jewish Committee as its National Director of Interreligious Affairs. The Tax Court ruled that he was not eligible for a housing allowance since his duties did not involve the conduct of religious worship of the performance of sacerdotal functions. The court made the following comments regarding assignment:

In addition, the [rabbi] was not assigned to the American Jewish Committee by any religious body constituting his "church." In accepting his position with the American Jewish Committee, he functioned as an independent contractor, separate and apart from any association with a religious group.

The [rabbi] argues that the [assignment] test cannot be met by him because the Jewish faith does not have a hierarchical order, and consequently, does not assign rabbis to occupy positions such as his. He contends that this test focuses primarily upon the type of activity involved and that his work with the American Jewish Committee is of a type covered by the regulation. We cannot agree. The [assignment] test unequivocally requires that the [minister] be working "pursuant to an assignment or designation by a religious body constituting his church"

. . . and in the instant case the [rabbi] clearly was not.

This case demonstrates that an "assignment" is not effective unless a religious body in fact has the authority to assign a minister to a position in furtherance of its mission and in fact does so on its own initiative (rather than merely ratifying a position the minister unilaterally secures). Many Protestant churches and denominations have no legal or ecclesiastical authority to "assign" ministers to any position, and any attempt by them to do so would be ineffective. The organizational documents of a church or denominational agency should be reviewed carefully to determine whether or not it has the authority to assign ministers. Further, the practice of the church or denominational agency should be studied. Does it have an established practice of assigning ministers to their positions? If not, it is very unlikely that any assignment would be recognized by the courts or by the IRS.

Libman v. Commissioner, 44 T.C.M. 370 (1982). The Tax Court ruled that a rabbi employed by the United Jewish Appeal was eligible for a housing allowance because he performed ministerial duties and not because of any assignment. The court rejected the validity of a purported "assignment" of the rabbi by his "Rabbinical Assembly," since it lacked any authority to assign rabbis. The court observed that "since the Jewish faith does not have a hierarchical order and consequently does not assign rabbis to occupy positions such as this (although rabbinic organizations may assist in placement), under a strict reading of the regulation it is difficult for [the rabbi] or someone similarly situated to pass this test."

Once again, the implication is clear—religious bodies cannot "assign" clergy in order to qualify them for a housing allowance unless they have the ecclesiastical authority to do so and this authority is validated by actual practice.

Letter Ruling 8520043. The IRS concluded that a purported assignment of a minister by his church to teach at a college was not effective and did not qualify the minister for a housing allowance. The minister found and accepted his position as a teacher at the college before he was ordained. Shortly after accepting the teaching position the minister was ordained. His ordaining body approved of his work at the college and gave him annual permission to continue. The IRS observed:

The assignment envisaged in the regulations is more than a formality. In the case of Boyer v. Commissioner, 69 T.C. 521 (1977), a minister found employment as a teacher at a university on his own and later received an "assignment" from his church to that position. In concluding that the "assignment" was not of the type envisaged by the regulations, the court stated as follows:

His assignment . . . was virtually pro forma—the ratification by the church of employment previously began. In contrast, we believe that the "assignment" referred to in the regulations must be significant, in that the minister must have

been assigned by the church for reasons directly related to the accomplishment of purposes of the church. . . . More is required than mere ordained status and the perfunctory ratification by religious authority of secular employment obtained by the minister for non-church-related reasons.

From the facts submitted it is apparent that [your church's] approval or ratification of your work at the college is not an assignment within the meaning of . . . the regulations.

This ruling represents another example of a purported assignment of a minister to a position that the minister previously secured on his own initiative. This does not meet the requirement of the regulations that the assignment must establish the minister's new position rather than ratify it after the minister on his or her own initiative has already secured it.

Letter Ruling 8826043. The IRS ruled that a pastoral counselor employed by a counseling center was not eligible for a housing allowance despite a purported "assignment" by his ordaining church. The church, in a letter to the minister, expressed its support of the minister's counseling practice; expressed its desire to support the minister in his counseling; and "endorsed" him as a counselor through the counseling practice in order to further the efforts and mission of the church. The IRS observed:

Applying the regulations as interpreted in Boyer v. Commissioner to the facts in this situation, we conclude that the services the minister performs through his counseling practice do not qualify as services in the performance of his ministry. [The regulations require] that services that are not performed for a religious organization be performed pursuant to an assignment or designation by the church. In your case, we find that the counseling services the minister performs are not pursuant to an assignment or designation by the church. Although the church states it commissions and endorses the minister in his counseling practice, this does not constitute an assignment or designation by the church. *The church is supportive of the minister's counseling practice, but we find no evidence to suggest that the church specifically assigned the minister to perform such counseling services on its behalf.* Also, it does not appear that the counseling services the minister performs are to directly further the purposes of the church. *The minister performs his services free from the church's control,* and he states his purpose is to meet human needs as effectively as possible, using the principles and teachings of his church. The intent of the counseling services is not to further any of the church's purposes (although the church may benefit from the minister's counseling). While the minister may provide his counseling services based on his church's religious beliefs, this does not meet the requirement that the minister be assigned to perform his services in order for them to qualify as services performed in the exercise of his ministry. (emphasis added)

In this ruling, the IRS interpreted the assignment language of the regulations to require that (1) the assignment must result in services being performed by the minister "on behalf of" the assigning church; (2) the assignment must "directly further the purposes of the church"; (3) the assigned minister, in the performance of his or her duties, must intend to further the church's purposes; and (4) the assigned minister's services must remain subject to the assigning church's control.

Letter Ruling 8930038. The IRS reaffirmed its ruling in Letter Ruling 8826043 (summarized above), and rejected the minister's claim that a valid assignment can be "inferred" from the actions of his church. The IRS, in rejecting this view, observed:

> Furthermore, the information provided states that counseling practice was originally associated with the church until the minister established the counseling practice as a sole proprietorship. As stated in a letter from the church to the minister, it was a shared goal of the church and the minister to make the counseling practice an independent counseling ministry in which the minister performs his services free from the church's control. The minister states that as a matter of religious doctrine, the church does not assign or designate its ministers to any particular work. However, while counseling may be viewed as an integral element by the church of its mission for the community, the services are performed for the general public as well as for church members and in this case is also conducted for purposes of financial independence.

Conclusions. Based on the legal precedent reviewed above, a minister's eligibility for a housing allowance should not be based on an "assignment" unless the assignment satisfies the following conditions:

1. The church or denominational agency that assigned the minister has the authority, by virtue of its organizational documents, to assign ministers to their positions.

2. The church or denominational agency that assigned the minister has a history of assigning ministers to their positions.

3. The church or denominational agency assigned the minister to a particular position solely on its initiative.

4. The assignment establishes the employment relationship between the minister and his or her employer.

5. The assignment results in services being performed by the minister "on behalf of" the assigning church or denominational agency.

6. The assigned minister, in the performance of his or her duties, intends to further the purposes of the assigning church or denominational agency.

7. The assignment directly furthers the purposes of the assigning church or denominational agency.

8. The assigned minister's services are subject to the control of the church or denominational agency that assigned him or her.

☞ ***Example.*** *Rev. C, a duly ordained minister, is assigned by his religious denomination to perform advisory service to a publishing company in connection with the publication of a book dealing with the history of the denomination. The publisher is neither a religious organization nor operated as an integral agency of a religious organization. Rev. C performs no other service for his denomination or the publisher. He is performing service in the exercise of ministry, and accordingly he is eligible for all of the four special tax provisions discussed in this chapter. To summarize, this means that (1) he is eligible for a housing allowance exclusion; (2) he must pay self-employment taxes (the social security tax for self-employed individuals) rather than FICA taxes, assuming that he is not exempt; (3) if he is exempt from social security taxes (because his timely exemption application was approved by the IRS), then he pays no self-employment tax on compensation received from the publisher; and, (4) his wages are not subject to federal income tax withholding, meaning that he must report and pay his income taxes (and self-employment taxes, if applicable) using the estimated tax procedure (Form 1040-ES).*

D. Religious Orders

The Internal Revenue Code exempts from social security taxes and income tax withholding "services performed . . . by a member of a religious order in the exercise of duties required by such order." Neither the Code, nor the income tax regulations, defines the term *religious order*. To provide some certainty regarding the definition of a religious order, the IRS (in 1991) published 7 characteristics that traditionally have been associated with religious orders. *IRS Revenue Procedure 91-20.* The IRS came up with this list by reviewing the court decisions that have addressed the issue. From now on, the IRS will use the following characteristics in determining whether or not an organization is a religious order:

> (1) The organization is described in section 501(c)(3) of the Code. (2) The members of the organization vow to live under a strict set of rules requiring moral and spiritual self-sacrifice and dedication to the goals of the organization at the expense of their material well-being. (3) The members of the organization, after successful completion of the organization's training program and probationary period, make a long-term commitment to the organization (normally, more than two years). (4) The organization is, directly or indirectly, under the control and supervision of a church or convention or association of churches, or is significantly funded by a church or convention or association of churches. (5) The members of the organization nor-

mally live together as part of a community and are held to a significantly stricter level of moral and religious discipline than that required of lay church members. (6) The members of the organization work or serve full-time on behalf of the religious, educational, or charitable goals of the organization, (7) The members of the organization participate regularly in activities such as public or private prayer, religious study, teaching, care of the aging, missionary work, or church reform or renewal.

The IRS has stated that "generally, the presence of all the above characteristics is determinative that the organization is a religious order" and that "the absence of one or more of the other enumerated characteristics is not necessarily determinative in a particular case. Generally, if application of the above characteristics to the facts of a particular case does not clearly indicate whether or not the organization is a religious order, the [IRS] will contact the appropriate authorities affiliated with the organization for their views concerning the characteristics of the organization and their views will be carefully considered." *Revenue Ruling 91-20. See also IRS Letter Ruling 9219012* (an organization was a religious order though it did not satisfy one of the 7 criteria) and *IRS Letter Rulings 9418012 and 9630011* (evangelical organizations were religious orders though they were not directly or indirectly under the control and supervision of a church or convention or association of churches or significantly funded by a church or convention or association of churches).

It is interesting that one of the cases the IRS relied on involved a claim by a Baptist church that the services of its church secretary, organist, custodian, and choir director were exempt from tax withholding since the church was a "religious order." In rejecting the church's claim, the court defined a "religious order" as "a religious body typically an aggregate of separate communities living under a distinctive rule, discipline or constitution; a monastic brotherhood or society." *Eighth Street Baptist Church, Inc. v. United States, 295 F. Supp. 1400 (D. Kan. 1969).*

Under the new IRS definition, there will be very few organizations that will be able to justify an exemption from FICA or tax withholding on the ground that they are "religious orders." Organizations that currently are relying upon an exemption from FICA coverage or the income tax withholding rules on the basis of "religious order" status should carefully review the new IRS definition to assess its impact.

Chapter 4

INCOME

Chapter Highlights

- **Clergy income.** Clergy "income" includes much more than a church salary.

- **Fringe benefits.** Besides a salary, clergy "income" may include several additional items, such as the following:

  - bonuses
  - Christmas and special occasion offerings
  - retirement "gifts"
  - the portion of a minister's social security tax paid by a church
  - the personal use of a church-provided car
  - purchases of church property for less than fair market value
  - rental income
  - interest income
  - some forms of pension income
  - some reimbursements of a spouse's travel expenses
  - forgiven debts
  - severance pay
  - church-paid trips to the Holy Land
  - nonaccountable reimbursements of a minister's business expenses

- **Unreasonable compensation.** Churches that pay "unreasonable compensation" to a minister jeopardize their tax-exempt status.

- **Social security income.** Clergy who are retired and who earn more than a specified amount of income may be taxed on some of their social security benefits.

- **Loans to ministers.** Churches that make low-interest or no-interest loans to clergy may be violating state nonprofit corporation law. These kinds of loans also result in taxable income to the minister.

- **Discretionary funds.** Many churches have established a fund that can be distributed by a minister in his or her sole discretion. Such "discretionary funds" can inadvertently result in taxable income to the minister if they are unrestricted.

- **Reimbursement of spouse's travel.** Church reimbursements of a spouse's travel expenses incurred while accompanying a minister on a business trip represent income to the minister unless the spouse's presence serves a legitimate business purpose and the spouse's expenses are reimbursed under an accountable arrangement.

- **"Splitting" income with a spouse.** Many ministers have attempted to shift their church income to a spouse in order to achieve a tax benefit. These benefits include (1) reducing the impact on the minister of the "annual earnings test" that reduces the social security benefits of individuals between 62 and 70 years of age who earn more than specified amounts of annual income; and (2) lower tax rates. Income shifting often does not work, because there is no "economic reality" to the arrangement. Ministers who have engaged in income shifting, or who are considering doing so, should carefully evaluate their circumstances in light of this ruling.

Your Form 1040 begins (lines 7-22) with the reporting of **gross income**. This chapter will summarize those items of gross income that are of greatest relevance to ministers. There are several items that the Internal Revenue Code excludes from gross income. These **exclusions** (including the housing allowance) will be considered in chapters 5-6. Exclusions are not reported on your tax return. Finally, after you compute your gross income, you are permitted to claim certain **adjustments** that reduce gross income. Gross income less the total of all available adjustments yields **adjusted gross income**. Adjusted gross income is an important figure for several reasons. Adjusted gross income, and the various adjustments of greatest relevance to ministers, are discussed in chapter 7.

It is beyond question that clergy must report and pay federal income taxes on their taxable compensation. A number of clergy have attempted, unsuccessfully, to evade taxes through reliance on a variety of theories. Many of these theories are reviewed in chapter 1, section A.1. The penalties for refusing to file income tax returns are reviewed in chapter 1, section A.12.

A. Wages, Salaries, and Earnings

The most significant component of income for most ministers is compensation received from a church or church agency for personal services. Church compensation of ministers who are employees for income tax purposes constitutes wages and is reported on Form 1040, line 7. Church compensation of ministers who are self-employed for income tax purposes constitutes self-employment earnings and is reported on Schedule C (Form 1040). As we will see later (in chapters 5-7), some items of income are *not* included on Form 1040, line 7, or Schedule C. These include a properly designated housing allowance, a church's reimbursements of a minister's business expenses under an "accountable" reimbursement plan, and various fringe benefits.

Whether an employee or self-employed, a minister's total church compensation ordinarily consists of several items (discussed below) besides a weekly paycheck, all of which must be included on the minister's W-2 or 1099 form at year end.

Unreasonable Compensation

✎ **Key point: churches that pay "unreasonable compensation" to a minister jeopardize their tax-exempt status**

In order for a church to maintain its exemption from federal income taxes under section 501(c)(3) of the Internal Revenue Code, it must not pay **unreasonable compensation** to any worker. A church will jeopardize its tax-exempt status if it pays unreasonable compensation to a minister. Loss of a church's exempt status would have a variety of negative consequences, including (1) the church's net income would be subject to federal (and possibly state) income taxation; (2) donors no longer could deduct contributions to the church; (3) ineligibility to establish "403(b)" tax-sheltered annuities; (4) possible loss of property and sales tax exemptions; (5) loss of preferential mailing rates; (6) possible loss of a housing allowance exclusion for ministers serving the church; (7) possible inapplicability of a minister's exemption from self-employment (social security) taxes to compensation received from the church; and (8) clergy compensation might not be exempt from federal income tax withholding. Clearly, any activity that jeopardizes a church's exemption from federal income taxation, and correspondingly the benefits summarized above, is a matter that must be taken very seriously.

Unfortunately, there is very little guidance currently available to help in determining how much income is "reasonable" and therefore appropriate. Summarized below are a few of the key cases.

Church of Scientology v. Commissioner of Internal Revenue, 823 F.2d 1310 (9th Cir. 1987). One federal appeals court concluded that combined annual income of $115,680 paid by a religious organization to its founder and his wife was not excessive. Unreasonable compensation sometimes is associated with payment of clergy compensation based on a percentage of church income. For example, a small church with annual income of $20,000 agrees to pay its minister "one-half" of the church's annual compensation. This amount is certainly reasonable. However, assume that within a few years the church experiences substantial growth and its annual income increases to $500,000. If the church has not changed its method of paying its minister (i.e., the minister now receives annual compensation of $250,000), the IRS (and the courts) would almost certainly conclude that this amounts to unreasonable compensation.

Heritage Village Church and Missionary Fellowship, Inc., 92 B.R. 1000 (D.S.C. 1988). The bankruptcy court in the "PTL" case also addressed the critical issue of what constitutes "reasonable compensation" for a minister. The bankruptcy court ruled that *reasonable compensation* for Jim Bakker would have been $133,100 in 1984, $146,410 in 1985, $161,051 in 1986, and $177,156 in 1987. These are the same figures computed by the IRS, and the court openly expressed its reliance upon the IRS calculations. The court found that Bakker's actual compensation for the four years in question amounted to more than $7.3 million, and that much of this was in the form of "bonuses" and fringe benefits. To illustrate, Bakker's "salary" (as determined by the court) for the years in question was $228,500 in 1984, $291,500 in 1985, $265,000 in 1986, and $265,000 in 1987. However, the total amount of compensation and benefits attributable to Bakker for the same years was $1.2 million in 1984, $1.6 million in 1985, $1.9 million in 1986, and $2.7 million in 1987.

How did the court in the PTL case determine what "reasonable compensation" was for Jim Bakker? This is both an interesting and highly relevant question, since the IRS and the courts have provided so little guidance in defining this significant term. In answering this question, the court noted that "the highest paid head of a government agency in the State of South Carolina with a salary approved by the legislature is the president of the University of South Carolina who, for the years in question, had a salary under $100,000" (the court undoubtedly overlooked the compensation paid to certain university football and basketball coaches—who also could be considered government employees). The court also referred to the testimony of "expert witnesses" who had testified that normal salary of the highest compensated clergy "would run from $75,000 to $120,000," and that "bonuses were almost unheard of in the religious field, although fringe benefits would amount to about 30% of the salary." In responding to the view of one of Bakker's witnesses that the Bible mandates that a minister should get 10% of all donations and a "high priest" should receive 20%, the court commented that such a view "defies common sense and rational judgment."

In conclusion, clergy compensation in excess of $100,000 should be carefully reviewed to determine its reasonableness. It would be very appropriate for churches and religious organizations to condition the payment of compensation in excess of $100,000 upon the receipt of a legal opinion (from a tax attorney) certifying that in his or her opinion the level of suggested compensation is not unreasonable. Again, as noted above, the negative consequences of clergy compensation being classified by the IRS as "unreasonable" are so severe that precautionary measures are warranted. In calculating whether or not a minister's compensation exceeds $100,000, it is important to include *all* components of compensation (bonuses, canceled debts, personal expenses paid by the church either by check or credit card, personal use of church vehicles, etc.).

✎ **Key point: clergy compensation in excess of $100,000 should be reviewed by a tax attorney to determine its reasonableness**

The bankruptcy court's ruling in the PTL case is also relevant because it helps to clarify the meaning of ministerial compensation. Clergy sometimes find it difficult to determine what benefits are includable in their income for tax purposes. The PTL bankruptcy court concluded that following items were properly included in the income of Jim Bakker: (1) salary; (2) "bonuses" (note that the court found that bonuses were "almost unheard of in the religious field"); (3) personal use of a PTL vehicle (e.g., the corporate jet); (4) PTL contributions to Bakker's retirement fund; (5) utilities paid by PTL on Bakker's parsonage "notwithstanding the fact that Jim Bakker also received a housing allowance during the entire period of not less than $2,000 per month"; (5) Bakker's housing allowance of $2,000 per month (since he lived in a PTL-owned "parsonage" rent-free); (6) numerous expenditures from the PTL general checking account for the use and benefit of Bakker for which there was not sufficient documentation to justify their classification as a business expense; (7) charges made on PTL credit cards on Bakker's behalf for which there was not sufficient documentation to justify their classification as business expenses; and (8) cash advances to Bakker that had been "written off" by PTL. The IRS reached these same conclusions, but it added several additional items to Bakker's compensation, including personal use of PTL automobiles; the fair rental value of Bakker's "parsonage"; a "housekeeping and maintenance allowance of $28,000 each year; the fair rental value of a PTL-owned condominium in Florida; and, personal use by Bakker of the presidential suite in the Heritage Grand Hotel.

There are several important lessons here.

• Clergy should recognize that bonuses, and many kinds of fringe benefits, are includable in compensation. They are not tax-free "gifts."

• Clergy who live in a church-owned parsonage without having to pay rent are free to exclude from income (for income tax purposes) the fair rental value of the parsonage. They may also exclude that part of their compensation that is designated by their employing church as a "parsonage allowance" to the extent that it is actually used to pay parsonage-related expenses. Bakker's problem was that he not only lived in a parsonage without paying rent, but also received a "housekeeping and maintenance allowance" (of about $28,000 each year) and a housing allowance (of $24,000 each year) despite the fact that PTL paid all of his housing expenses. Such payments clearly were above any reasonable parsonage-related expenses, in the court's judgment.

• Church payments of clergy expenses (whether by check or credit card charge) generally are includable in clergy compensation unless the payments are made pursuant to an "accountable" reimbursement arrangement. As discussed fully in chapter 7, under an accountable arrangement, a church reimburses a minister only for those business expenses that are adequately substantiated. Reimbursements of business expenses without sufficient substantiation constitute "nonaccountable" reimbursements, and they are fully includable in a minister's income for tax reporting purposes. Further, any employer reimbursements of an employee's purely personal expenses constitute taxable income. PTL reimbursed many of Bakker's personal expenses, and failed to report these reimbursements as taxable income.

• A minister who uses a church vehicle for personal reasons has received a material benefit that must be valued and included in his or her compensation. Again, this is not a tax-free "gift."

✎ **Key point: clergy "income" includes much more than a church salary**

Truth Tabernacle, Inc. v. Commissioner of Internal Revenue, T.C. Memo. 1989-451. The United States Tax Court addressed the issue of "unreasonable compensation" paid to clergy in an important decision. Truth Tabernacle was incorporated as an independent church in 1978. The church was a fundamentalist Christian congregation, and its doctrine included a belief in "the death, burial, and resurrection of the Lord Jesus Christ . . . the sovereignty of the Church of God . . . Jesus Christ as the head of the church . . . resurrection of the dead . . . and Jesus Christ coming back again to reign as King of Kings and Lord of Lords over all the earth." The church, which consisted of about 40 members, conducted worship services three times each week. Regular men's and women's Bible classes were held two or three times each month. Sunday School classes were held every Sunday. Saturday night prayer services were conducted each week. The church's pastor (who was an ordained minister) performed sacerdotal functions, including dedications of children, baptisms, funerals, and marriages.

The IRS audited the church in 1986 (the audit covered the years 1983, 1984, and 1985). At the conclusion of the audit, the IRS revoked the church's tax-exempt status retroactively. The IRS alleged that (1) the church was not operated exclusively for religious purposes, and (2) the church paid "unreasonable compensation" to its minister. The Tax Court rejected the IRS position, and ruled in favor of the church. In rejecting the IRS claim that the church was not acted exclusively for religious purposes, the Court observed: "Petitioner was a small church operating on a modest budget provided by the weekly contributions of its members. Essentially all of its contributions during the audit years were used to pay the mortgage, utility and maintenance expenses on the church building. Its activities primarily consisted of various worship services conducted in the church building and the performance of sacerdotal rites. In our view the [church is operated exclusively for religious purposes]."

The Court noted that in 1983, the church received contributions of $10,700 and incurred expenses of $12,200. In 1984 it had contributions of $13,700 and expenses of $13,500. In 1985 it had contributions of $16,200 and expenses of $16,200. The major expenses each year were the mortgage payments, utilities, and repairs on the church building. The mortgage alone amounted to $5,000 of the church's annual budget. In rejecting the IRS claim that the church paid "unreasonable compensation" to its minister, the Court noted that the pastor was provided a car and an apartment free of charge (a custodian and a caretaker received rent-free apartments on the church's property in exchange for 20 hours of service each week), but otherwise received no salary. The Court observed that

> "[in determining] whether compensation is reasonable or excessive . . . one factor to consider is whether comparable services would cost as much if obtained from an outside source in an arm's-length transaction. Applying that standard to the present case, and considering the meager benefits received by the [church's] minister and grounds keepers in return for services that they performed, we find that the benefits were within the bounds of reasonable compensation for those services. Accordingly, there was no inurement of [the church's] net earnings to any private individual . . . ."

It is difficult to comprehend why the IRS challenged the tax-exempt status of a church that so clearly qualified for exempt status. Clearly, if the exempt status of Truth Tabernacle could be challenged, then few churches are beyond challenge. The Tax Court's decision will be a useful tool in combating similar efforts in the future.

Can Churches Pay Ministers a Percentage of Revenue?

A number of churches pay their minister a percentage of church revenue. Are such compensation arrangements legally permissible? The Tax Court addressed this issue in a 1980 ruling. *People of God Community v. Commissioner, 75 T.C. 127 (1980).* The Tax Court, in the *People of God Community* case, revoked the exempt status of a religious organization on the grounds that it paid its three ministers a percentage of gross revenue. However, the circumstances of this case reveal that payments to the three ministers were unreasonable apart from the percentage arrangement. The ministers' salaries made up 86% of the organization's budget, and in addition the ministers received no-interest loans. Further, the amount of the salaries paid to the ministers

was well in excess of the average salary of comparable ministers. As a result, this case should not be interpreted as an absolute prohibition of all compensation arrangements for clergy based on a percentage of income. Churches are free to pay their ministers reasonable compensation for services rendered. Compensation packages based on a percentage of income are "reasonable" and appropriate so long as the amount of compensation paid to a minister under such an arrangement is in fact reasonable in amount.

An absolute rule characterizing all "percentage of income" compensation arrangements as "unreasonable" would lead to absurd results. For example, many ministers serve small congregations and receive all of the church's income. In many cases, these arrangements result in compensation of less than $10,000 per year to a minister. There can be no doubt that such an arrangement is reasonable and permissible under these circumstances. Such arrangements are very common, and neither the IRS nor any federal court has addressed the propriety of this specific issue.

On the other hand, there is no doubt that compensation arrangements based on a percentage of income would be impermissible and jeopardize a church's exempt status to the extent they result in excessive or unreasonable compensation. To illustrate, assume that Rev. B begins a new church with a few people and agrees to be paid 50% of annual church revenue. For a few years, this arrangement results in very modest income to the pastor. However, the church prospers, and after a number of years the pastor is paid in excess of one million dollars per year. There is no doubt that this constitutes unreasonable compensation, and jeopardizes the exempt status of the church. This is not because of the percentage arrangement, but rather because of the amount of compensation.

In summary, until the IRS and the courts directly address this question in the context of legitimate churches paying reasonable amounts to clergy on the basis of a percentage arrangement, there is no reason to assume that all percentage arrangements are impermissible. The Court in the *People of God Community* case suggested that percentage arrangements would be permissible if they were subject to "an upper limit." Such a condition is simply not needed in the vast majority of cases in which the amount of compensation paid to ministers under a percentage arrangement is minimal to modest.

✎ **Key point: the IRS will be releasing regulations in the near future specifying when compensation based on a percentage of a charity's income constitutes an "excess benefit transaction" triggering intermediate sanctions**

Intermediate Sanctions

✎ **Key point: the IRS can impose an excise tax against a "disqualified person," and in some cases against church board members in-**

dividually, if excessive compensation is paid to the disqualified person. Pastors ordinarily will be disqualified persons.

The Taxpayer Bill of Rights 2 (TBOR2), enacted by Congress in 1996, contains a provision allowing the IRS to assess "intermediate sanctions" (an excise tax) against "disqualified persons" in lieu of outright revocation of an organization's exempt status. The intermediate sanctions may be assessed only in cases of "excess benefit transactions," meaning one or more transactions that provide unreasonable compensation to an officer or director of the exempt organization. An excess benefit transaction is defined as:

• any transaction in which an economic benefit is provided to a "disqualified person" (someone in a position to exercise substantial influence over the affairs of the organization) if the value of the benefit exceeds the value of the services provided by the disqualified person, or

• to the extent provided in IRS regulations (to be released soon), any transaction in which the amount of an economic benefit provided to a disqualified person is based on the revenues of the organization, if the transaction results in unreasonable compensation being paid

The payment of personal expenses and benefits to or for the benefit of disqualified persons, and non-fair-market-value transactions benefiting such persons, would be treated as compensation only if it is clear that the organization intended and made the payments as compensation for services. In determining whether such payments or transactions are, in fact, compensation, the relevant factors include whether the appropriate decision-making body approved the transfer as compensation in accordance with established procedures and whether the organization and the recipient reported the transfer (except in the case of nontaxable fringe benefits) as compensation on the relevant forms (i.e., the organization's Form 990, the Form W-2 or Form 1099 provided by the organization to the recipient, the recipient's Form 1040, and other required returns).

The presumption of reasonableness. A committee report to the new law clarifies that the parties to a transaction are entitled to rely on a presumption of reasonableness with respect to a compensation arrangement with a disqualified person if such arrangement was approved by a board of directors (or committee of the board) that: (1) was composed entirely of individuals unrelated to and not subject to the control of the disqualified person involved in the arrangement; (2) obtained and relied upon objective "comparability" information, such as (a) compensation paid by similar organizations, both taxable and tax-exempt, for comparable positions, (b) independent compensation surveys by nationally recognized independent firms, or (c) actual written offers from similar institutions competing for the services of the disqualified person; and (3) adequately documented the basis for its decision.

✎ **Key point: The new law creates a presumption that a minister's compensation package is reasonable if approved by the church board who relied upon objective "comparability" information, including independent compensation surveys by nationally recognized independent firms. The most comprehensive compensation survey for church workers is the annual** *Compensation Handbook for Church Staff*, **written by Richard Hammar and James Cobble, and available from the publisher of this tax guide.**

A similar presumption arises with respect to the reasonableness of the valuation of property sold by an organization to a disqualified person if the sale is approved by an independent board that uses appropriate comparability data and adequately documents its determination.

Penalties. The intermediate sanctions that the IRS can impose, in lieu of revocation of a charity' exempt status, include the following:

1. Tax on disqualified persons. A disqualified person who benefits from an excess benefit transaction is subject to a penalty tax equal to 25 percent of the amount of the "excess benefit" (the amount by which actual compensation exceeds the fair market value of services rendered). This tax is paid by the disqualified person directly, not his or her employer.

2. Additional tax on disqualified persons. If the 25% excise tax is assessed against a disqualified person, and he or she fails to "correct" the excess benefit within the "taxable period," the IRS can assess an additional tax of 200% of the excess benefit. The new law states that the disqualified person can "correct" the excess benefit transaction by "undoing the excess benefit to the extent possible, and taking any additional measures necessary to place the organization in a financial position not worse than that in which it would be if the disqualified person were dealing under the highest fiduciary standards." The "correction" must occur by the earlier of the date the IRS mails a notice informing the disqualified person that he or she owes the 25% tax, or the date the 25% tax is actually assessed.

3. Tax on organization managers. If the IRS assesses the 25% tax against a disqualified person, it is permitted by the new law to impose an additional 10% tax on any "organization manager" (any officer, director, or trustee) who participates in an excess benefit transaction knowing it is such a transaction, unless the manager's participation "is not willful and is due to reasonable cause." This tax is limited to a maximum of $10,000 per manager.

❖ **New in 1997. Recent clarifications from the IRS: (1) the IRS will impose intermediate sanctions only in extreme cases meeting a "front page test"; (2) the new sanctions were intended to change the behavior of nonprofit boards by encouraging them to take seriously the task of establishing compensation packages; (3) nonprofit boards are encouraged to maintain records documenting how they** determined the compensation of higher paid employees; and (4) intermediate sanctions will result in an estimated $33 million of excise taxes over the next five years.

☞ *Example.* Many years ago, a church board adopted a resolution agreeing to pay its pastor "one-half of all revenues." For the first several years, this formula resulted in modest compensation. But in recent years, the church has grown and the compensation paid to the pastor has increased dramatically. In 1997 the church received revenues of $500,000 and paid its pastor $250,000. How would the new law apply to this situation? Consider the following: (1) The level of compensation paid to the pastor is almost certainly unreasonable. As a result, it is possible that the IRS, if it learns of the amount of compensation paid by the church to its pastor, will revoke the church's exempt status. This would have very negative consequences to the pastor, the church, and its membership. (2) Under the new law, the IRS has the option of applying "intermediate sanctions" against the church in lieu of outright revocation of its exempt status, if it establishes that the pastor is a "disqualified person" who was paid benefits in excess of the fair market value of his services. Sanctions available to the IRS include: (a) An excise tax of 25% of the amount of the pastor's compensation that exceeds the fair market value of his services. If the IRS concludes that the maximum reasonable compensation under these circumstances would be $100,000, then the pastor was paid an "excess benefit" of $150,000, and the excise tax would be $37,500 for 1997 (25% x $150,000). This tax is paid by the pastor directly, not the church. (b) If the 25% excise tax is assessed against the pastor, and he fails to "correct" the excess benefit within the "taxable period," the IRS can assess an additional tax of 200% of the excess benefit. In this case, this would amount to an additional $300,000! The new law states that the pastor can "correct" the excess benefit transaction by "undoing the excess benefit to the extent possible, and taking any additional measures necessary to place the organization in a financial position not worse than that in which it would be if the disqualified person were dealing under the highest fiduciary standards." The "correction" must occur by the earlier of the date the IRS mails a notice informing the pastor that he owes the 25% tax, or the date the 25% tax is actually assessed. (3) If the IRS assesses the 25% tax against the pastor, it is permitted by the new law to impose an additional 10% tax on any "organization manager" (any officer, director, or trustee) who participates in an excess benefit transaction knowing it is such a transaction, unless the manager's participation "is not willful and is due to reasonable cause."

☞ *Example.* A small rural church with total income of $20,000 in 1998 pays its pastor "75% of gross income." It is doubtful that this arrangement will trigger intermediate sanctions, even though compensation is based on a percentage of church income, since the resulting compensation paid to the pastor is minimal.

☞ *Example.* A pastor retires in 1998 after serving for 30 years in the same church. The church board authorizes a retirement gift of $100,000. Assume that the pastor also receives a salary of $50,000 for 1998. Assume that the IRS determines that the maximum "reasonable compensation" for this pastor for 1998 would be $100,000. This may expose the pastor to intermediate sanctions, beginning with a 25% excise tax applied to the amount of the pastor's total compensation for 1998 that exceeds what the IRS has determined to be "reasonable." This would yield a tax of $12,500 (25% x $50,000). If the excess compensation ($50,000) is not refunded to the church by the time the 25% tax is assessed, then the pastor can be assessed an additional excise tax of 200% times the amount of the excess compensation (for a total tax of $100,000). This is in addition to the 25% tax. In addition, members of the board may be assessed a tax in the amount of 10% times the excess compensation amount (or $5,000). The threat of intermediate sanctions could be reduced or eliminated under these circumstances if the board distributed the retirement gift over more than one year, so that the total compensation received by the pastor in any one year is reduced below what the IRS might consider to be unreasonable or excessive. Any such multi-year arrangement must avoid the "constructive receipt" rule (discussed in chapter 10. section E).

☞ *Example.* A pastor lives in a church-owned parsonage for 25 years. The parsonage has a current value of $100,000, and is debt-free. The church board authorizes a gift of the parsonage to the pastor. This transaction may trigger intermediate sanctions. The analysis in the previous example should be reviewed.

Intermediate sanctions apply to excess benefit transactions occurring on or after September 14, 1995.

Miscellaneous Forms of Compensation

✎ **Key point:** In 1995 the IRS issued audit guidelines for its agents to follow when auditing ministers. The guidelines cover a range of issues, including sources of ministerial income. The guidelines list the following sources of taxable income (this list, of course, is not exhaustive):

• compensation

• bonuses

• "special gifts"

• **fees paid directly from parishioners for performing weddings, funerals, baptisms and masses**

• **expense allowances for travel, transportation, or other business expenses received under a nonaccountable plan**

• **amounts paid by a church in addition to salary to cover the minister's self-employment tax or income tax**

Generally, items that are a part of a minister's church compensation include the following:

1. Bonuses

Bonuses paid to a minister for outstanding work or other achievement are income and must be included as part of his or her church compensation on Form W-2 (if an employee) or Form 1099 (if self-employed). *Treas. Reg. 1.61-2(a)(1).* Note that the bankruptcy court in the PTL case (discussed above) remarked that "bonuses [are] almost unheard of in the religious field."

2. Christmas and other special occasion gifts

Clergy often receive special occasion gifts during the course of the year. Examples include Christmas, birthday, and anniversary gifts. Church leaders often do not understand how to report these payments for federal tax purposes. Section 102 of the Internal Revenue Code specifies that "gross income does not include the value of property acquired by gift." This means that the value of gifts are not included in taxable income by the recipient. Are special occasion "gifts" made to a minister tax-free gifts? Or, are they taxable compensation for services rendered? The United States Supreme Court, in an important ruling, freely admitted the difficulty of distinguishing between tax-free gifts and taxable compensation. The Court did attempt to provide some guidance, however, by noting that

> a gift in the statutory sense . . . proceeds from a detached and disinterested generosity . . . out of affection, respect, admiration, charity, or like impulses . . . . The most critical consideration . . . is the transferor's intention. *Commissioner v. Duberstein, 363 U.S. 278, 285 (1960).*

The Court added that "it doubtless is the exceptional payment by an employer to an employee that amounts to a gift," and that the church's characterization of the distribution as a "gift" is "not determinative—there must be an objective inquiry as to whether what is called a gift amounts to it in reality."

In another ruling (not involving retirement gifts to a minister) the Supreme Court attempted to provide further guidance in distinguishing between a tax-free gift and taxable compensation: "What controls is the intention with which payment, however voluntary, has been made. Has it been made with the intention that services rendered in the past shall be requited more completely, though full acquittance has been given?

If so, it bears a tax. Has it been made to show good will, esteem, or kindliness toward persons who happen to have served, but who are paid without thought to make requital for the service? If so, it is exempt." *Bogardus v. Commissioner, 302 U.S. 34, 45 (1936).*

Also relevant in this discussion is section 102(c) of the Internal Revenue Code, which was added by the Tax Reform Act of 1986. Section 102(c) specifies that the definition of the term *gift* shall not include "any amount transferred by or for an employer to, or for the benefit of, an employee." The Code does permit employees to exclude from income certain "employee achievement awards" if the award is based on length of service or safety achievement, consists of tangible personal property valued at less than $400, and qualifies as a deductible business expense by the employer (bona fide churches will never satisfy this requirement). *IRC 74(c).* Employees (including ministers) are still permitted to exclude from gross income (as a "de minimis" fringe benefit) the value of any gift received from an employer if the value is so insignificant that accounting for it would be unreasonable or administratively impracticable. *IRC 132(e).* To illustrate, a traditional employer holiday gift of low fair market value (a turkey, fruitcake, etc.) will continue to be excludable from an employee's income.

Finally, the income tax regulations specify that "Christmas bonuses" paid by an employer are taxable income to the recipient. *Treas. Reg. 1.61-2(a)(1).*

All of this legal precedent can be reduced to the following general principles:

• Special occasion "gifts" made to a minister by the church out of the general fund should be reported as taxable compensation and included on the minister's W-2 or 1099, and Form 1040.

• Members are free to make personal gifts to clergy, such as a card at Christmas accompanied by a check or cash. Such payments may be tax-free gifts to the minister (though they are not deductible by the donor).

• Special occasion "gifts" to a minister funded through members' contributions to the church (i.e., the contributions are entered or recorded in the church's books as cash received and the members are given charitable contribution credit), should be reported as taxable compensation and included on the minister's W-2 or 1099, and Form 1040. Of course, the same result applies to any non-minister church worker.

• Members who contribute to special occasion offerings may deduct their contributions if (1) the contributions are to the church and are entered or recorded in the church's books as cash received, and (2) they are able to itemize deductions on Schedule A (Form 1040).

• A church can collect an all-cash special occasion offering, with the express understanding that the entire proceeds will be paid directly to the minister and that no contributions will be tax-deductible. It is possible that in some cases such direct "member to minister" transfers would satisfy the definition of a gift set forth in the Supreme Court's *Duberstein* decision (mentioned above). Members wishing to contribute checks in such an offering should be advised to issue their checks payable to the pastor and not the church. All donors should be further advised that no contributions to the offering will be tax-deductible. In such cases, the critical question, as the Supreme Court observed in its *Bogardus* decision (mentioned above), is whether the donors intended that "services rendered in the past shall be requited more completely, though full acquittance has been given." Or, did the donors intend simply to "show good will, esteem, or kindliness toward persons who happen to have served, but who are paid without thought to make requital for the service"? If so, the contributions are tax-free gifts.

The reason for these rules is that churches, being nonprofit and tax-exempt organizations, may not make any distribution of their funds other than as reasonable compensation for services rendered or as payments in direct furtherance of their exempt purposes. They cannot make "gifts" to ministers. Therefore, to avoid any jeopardy to a church's tax-exempt status, it is imperative that special occasion distributions from a church to its minister be characterized as compensation for services rendered and reported on the minister's W-2 or 1099 form. *IRC 501(c)(3).*

The *Banks* case. These principles were illustrated in a 1991 decision of the Tax Court. *Banks v. Commissioner, 62 T.C.M. 1611 (1991).* In the *Banks* case, the Court ruled that special offerings made to a minister on her birthday, Mother's Day, the church's anniversary, and Christmas, were taxable compensation for services rendered rather than nontaxable gifts. Members of a local church transferred cash to their minister on these four "special" days each year. The offerings were in addition to the pastor's salary. The offerings accumulated to more than $40,000 annually. The minister considered them to be tax-free gifts, and did not report any of them as income on her income tax returns. The IRS audited the minister, and determined that the special offerings were personal income and not tax-free gifts. The Tax Court agreed. It based its decision entirely on the Supreme Court's definition of the term *gift* announced in its *Duberstein* decision (mentioned above).

The Tax Court concluded that there simply was no way that the special occasion offerings in this case could be characterized as a gift under the *Duberstein* test, since: (1) There was ample testimony from church members that they contributed to the special occasion offerings in order to show their appreciation to the minister for the excellent job that she had done. This testimony clearly demonstrated that the offerings were compensation for services rendered (and therefore taxable), rather than a tax-free gift proceeding from a "detached and disinterested generosity." (2) Further, the offerings were not spontaneous and voluntary, but rather were part of a "highly structured program" for transferring money to the minister on a regular basis. Church members met to discuss the amounts of the four special occasion offerings, and most members made donations or

"pledges" of a suggested amount and were pressured into honoring their pledges. The existence of such a program suggested that the transfers were not the product of a "detached and disinterested generosity" but, instead, were designed to compensate the minister for her service as a minister. (3) The church substantially increased the minister's salary following the discontinuance of the four special occasion offerings so that the minister's total compensation remained basically the same.

The *Goodwin* case. A federal appeals court ruled that congregational offerings that were collected on four special days each year and presented to a pastor represented taxable compensation rather than tax-free gifts. *Goodwin v. United States, 67 F.3d 149 (8th Cir. 1995).* About 2 weeks before each "special occasion," the associate pastor made an announcement prior to the commencement of a church service that he would be collecting money for the "special occasion" gift. The pastor and his wife were not present in the sanctuary during this announcement. People wishing to donate placed money in an envelope and gave it to the associate pastor or one of the deacons. The money was never placed in the offering plates passed during the services. Any checks received were returned in order to maintain anonymity. The money was never counted, and was not recorded in the church book or records. The congregation was advised that their "contributions" would not be receipted by the church and were not tax-deductible. The IRS audited the pastor's tax returns for 1987 through 1989, and determined that the special occasion gifts were in fact taxable compensation to the pastor. The congregational "gifts" to the pastor amounted to $12,750 in 1987, $14,500 in 1988, and $15,000 in 1989. The pastor's salary (not counting the special occasion gifts) was $7,800 in 1987, $14,566 in 1988, and $16,835 in 1989.

Despite the church members' belief that they were giving to their pastor out of "love, respect, admiration and like impulses," the court concluded that the payments constituted taxable compensation to the pastor. The court based its decision on the *Duberstein* case (discussed above), from which it derived the following principles: (1) the donor's intent is "the most critical consideration," and (2) "there must an objective inquiry" into the donor's intent. The court concluded that the facts of the case demonstrated that the donors' intent was to more fully compensate their pastor and accordingly the "gifts" represented taxable compensation. It based this conclusion on the following factors:

• *"Gifts" were made by the congregation.* The court concluded that the "gifts" were made by the congregation and not by individual donors, since: (1) "[t]he cash payments were gathered by congregation leaders in a routinized, highly structured program," and (2) "[i]ndividual church members contributed anonymously, and the regularly-scheduled payments were made to [the pastor] on behalf of the entire congregation."

• *Size of "gifts."* The court also noted that the gifts were a substantial portion of the pastor's overall compensation. It observed: "The congregation, collectively, knew that without these substantial, on-going cash payments, the church likely could not retain the services of a popular and successful minister at the relatively low salary it was paying. In other words, the congregation knew that its special occasion gifts enabled the church to pay a $15,000 salary for $30,000 worth of work. Regular, sizable payments made by persons to whom the taxpayer provides services are customarily regarded as a form of compensation and may therefore be treated as taxable compensation."

The IRS proposed that the court adopt the following test to determine whether transfers from church members to their minister represent nontaxable gifts:

> The feelings of love, admiration and respect that professedly motivated the parishioners to participate in the special occasion offerings arose from and were directly attributable to the services that [the pastor] performed for them as pastor of the church. Since the transfers were tied to the performance of services by [the pastor] they were, as a matter of law, compensation.

The court rejected this test as too broad, noting that

> it would include as taxable income every twenty dollar gift spontaneously given by a church member after an inspiring sermon, simply because the urge to give was tied to the minister's services. It would also include a departing church member's individual, unsolicited five hundred dollar gift to a long-tenured, highly respected priest, rabbi, or minister, a result that it totally at odds with the opinions of all nine [Supreme Court] Justices in Bogardus v. Commissioner:
>
> "Has [the payment] been made with the intention that services rendered in the past shall be requited more completely, though full acquittance has been given? If so, it bears a tax. *Has it been made to show good will, esteem, or kindliness toward persons who happen to have served, but who are paid without thought to make requital for the service? If so, it is exempt.*" Bogardus v. Commissioner, 302 U.S. 34, 45 (1936).

✎ **Key point: the court acknowledged that a twenty dollar gift spontaneously given by a church member to a pastor is a nontaxable gift rather than taxable compensation, despite the fact that the "urge to give" was tied to the pastor's services. The court also acknowledged that modest retirement gifts made by church members to a retiring minister can represent tax-free gifts.**

✎ **Key point: the court, in commenting on the Duberstein case, noted that "it is the rare donor who is completely 'detached and disinterested.'"**

There is one additional aspect of the court's ruling that is significant. The court noted that section 102(c) of the Code prohibits employers from treating as a tax-free gift "any amount transferred by or for an employer to, or for the benefit of, an employee." The court further noted that

> [a]lthough the legislative history suggests that [this section] was enacted to address other fact situations, its plain meaning may not be ignored in this case. That meaning seems far from plain, however. The church members are not [the pastor's] "employer," and the question whether their payments to the [pastor] were made "for" his employer seems little different than the traditional gift inquiry under *Duberstein* and *Bogardus.* We therefore decline the government's belated suggestion that we affirm on the alternative ground of section 102(c).

This is potentially significant observation, since it raises some doubt as to the relevance and applicability of Code section 102(c) to gifts made to clergy.

✎ **Key point: In 1995 the IRS issued audit guidelines for its agents to follow when auditing ministers. The guidelines cover a range of issues, including sources of ministerial income. The guidelines list "special gifts" as a source of taxable income. This makes it more likely that IRS agents will address such gifts when auditing ministers.**

Conclusions. Is it possible for a special occasion offering collected on behalf of a minister ever to be a tax-free gift rather than taxable compensation for services rendered? As suggested above, the answer is yes, so long as (1) the offering satisfies the definition of a gift announced by the Supreme Court in the *Duberstein* case, and (2) the offering consists of cash and checks made payable directly to the minister-recipient, donors are not given any charitable contribution credit for their "contributions," and the offering is not recorded as income in the church's books of account. Whether or not an offering will satisfy the *Duberstein* case will depend on several factors, including (1) the intent of the donors who contribute to the offering (e.g., if they are simply wanting to provide additional compensation to their minister in recognition of services rendered, then the transfer ordinarily will be taxable compensation rather than a tax-free gift); (2) whether or not a church adjusts its pastor's compensation on the basis of the special occasion offerings collected on his or her behalf; and (3) whether the contributions were spontaneous and voluntary as opposed to fixed amounts established under a "highly structured program" for transferring money to the minister on a regular basis.

Each case must be evaluated individually. There is no doubt that some transfers to clergy on special occasions will satisfy the definition of a tax-free gift. However, the cases summarized above illustrate that such a result will often be difficult to achieve.

The court in the *Goodwin* case (discussed above) conceded that individual gifts received directly from church members *can* represent tax-free gifts to a pastor. It observed that a "twenty dollar gift spontaneously given by a church member after an inspiring sermon" would constitute a nontaxable gift, as would a modest gift made by a member directly to a retiring minister.

☞ *Example.* The board of directors at First Church votes to award a "Christmas bonus" in the amount of $1,000 to Rev. C. The bonus is to be paid out of the church's general fund. Under these facts, Rev. C has clearly received taxable compensation of $1,000, and the W-2 or 1099 form issued by the church to Rev. C must reflect this fact.

☞ *Example.* A church collects an offering for its pastor once each year, at Christmas. This practice has occurred for more than 25 years. A member of the church board announces the offering during a worship service, and members are advised that their contributions will be receipted by the church. The Christmas gift made to the pastor under these circumstances is taxable compensation and should be added to the pastor's W-2 (or 1099).

☞ *Example.* Same facts as the previous example, except that a member of the board, in announcing the offering, informs church members that their contributions will not be receipted and will not be deductible. Members are informed that they will be making their gifts directly to the pastor, and accordingly are instructed to make checks payable directly to the pastor and not to the church. The church collects the offering and transfers it to the pastor without receipting any contributions. There are 2 ways to analyze this example. The conservative approach, based on the Goodwin case, would treat the "Christmas gift" to the pastor as taxable income. This was the view the IRS contended for in the Goodwin case, and presumably it reflects the IRS view on this issue. A more aggressive approach would be to treat the gift to the pastor as a tax-free gift rather than as taxable compensation. This view is based on the following considerations: (1) The members were not receipted for their contributions. (2) Members were informed that they were giving directly to the pastor. (3) Members did not deduct their contributions. (4) The church was acting merely as an intermediary. The gifts in reality were made by individual members directly to their pastor. (5) The church's minimal involvement in the arrangement (collecting and turning over the offering) did not amount to sufficient church involvement to prevent the offering from being characterized as an aggregate of individual gifts from members directly to their pastor. (6) Only 1 special occasion offering was collected each year. (7) Members were not pressured or coerced into making contributions. Participating in the offering was entirely voluntary. (8) The pastor was adequately compensated through salary and fringe benefits mutually agreed to between the pastor and church board. (9) Most members con-

tribute to such an offering out of sincere affection, respect, and admiration, and not out of a desire to compensate the pastor more fully for services rendered. Pastors and churches should not select the "aggressive approach" without the advice of a tax professional.

☞ *Example.* First Church collects an all-cash offering in commemoration of Rev. J's 25th year of service to the church. Donors are told to deposit currency or checks payable directly to Rev. J, and are informed that the proceeds of the offering will be given directly to Rev. J without being processed through the church's accounts, and that no charitable contribution credit will be received. See the previous example for the correct analysis to apply.

3. Retirement gifts

Often, a church will present a retiring minister with a retirement "gift." Sometimes, these gifts are very generous. Should a retiring minister treat such a gift as taxable compensation (reportable by the church on the minister's W-2 or 1099 and by the minister on Form 1040 or Schedule C), or treat it as a nontaxable gift (not reported by either the church or the minister)? Federal tax law requires all forms of compensation to be reported as income, but it permits bona fide gifts to be "excluded" (i.e., not reported) from taxable income. *IRC 102*. The question, then, is whether retirement "gifts" to clergy are more properly characterized as compensation (for services rendered) or as tax-free gifts? The answer to this question in a particular case is not always easy. In an important series of cases in the early 1950's, four federal appeals courts concluded that certain retirement gifts to clergy *were tax-free gifts rather than taxable compensation*. These 4 rulings are summarized below:

• *Schall v. Commissioner, 174 F.2d 893 (5th Cir. 1949).* A federal appeals court ruled that a church's retirement gift to its pastor represented a tax-free gift rather than taxable compensation. The pastor was forced to retire on the advice of his physician as a result of a long illness. He made no request of the congregation that any amount be paid to him after his resignation, and had no knowledge that the church would agree to do so. He did not agree to render any services in exchange for the gift and in fact did not do so. The court concluded:

> We are of opinion the Tax Court clearly erred in holding that the payments to [the pastor] were taxable income. Where, as here, all the facts and circumstances surrounding the adoption of the [gift] clearly prove an intent to make a gift, the mere use of the terms "salary" and "honorarium" do not convert the gift into a payment for services. Moreover, "a gift is none the less a gift because inspired by gratitude for past faithful service of the recipient . . . ." Manifestly, these payments to [the pastor] were non-taxable gifts, within the orbit of the rule defining same, as enunciated by this court in [another case]: "That only is a gift which is

purely such, not intended as a return of value or made because of any intent to repay another what is his due, but bestowed only because of personal affection or regard or pity, or from general motives of philanthropy or charity."

• *Mutch v. Commissioner, 209 F.2d 390 (3rd Cir. 1954).* A federal appeals court ruled that monthly retirement gifts made by a church to its retired pastor were tax-free gifts rather than taxable compensation. The court noted that the church's action in providing for the monthly honoraria "was motivated solely and sincerely by the congregation's love and affection for [the pastor]." The court described the church's action as a "free gift of a friendly, well-to-do group who as long as they were able and because they were, wished their old minister to live in a manner comparable to that which he had enjoyed while actively associated with them." The court also observed: "[The pastor] had been adequately compensated as far as money could for his services in the past. He was not being tied into any promise of services in the future. The installment gift, while it could be stopped or changed at any time by the trustees, had no conditions attached to its acceptance." The court concluded that no other ruling "justifies the taxing of this bona fide gift given [the pastor] with love and affection by his old congregation."

• *Kavanagh v. Hershman, 210 F.2d 654 (6th Cir. 1954).* A federal appeals court, in a one paragraph opinion, ruled that a distribution of funds to a minister was a tax-free gift rather than taxable compensation. The court based its decision on the *Mutch* decision (summarized above).

• *Abernathy v. Commissioner, 211 F.2d 651 (D.C. Cir. 1954).* The *Abernathy* case was a one paragraph decision issued by a federal appeals court in 1954. The ruling addressed the question of whether a $2,400 retirement gift paid by a church to its pastor "as a token of its gratitude and appreciation" and "in appreciation of his long and faithful service" represented taxable income or a tax-free gift. The federal court concluded that the transfer was a tax-free gift. It cited (without explanation) the *Schall*, *Mutch*, and *Kavanagh* decisions (summarized above) along with *Bogardus v. Commissioner, 302 U.S. 34 (1936)* (discussed in the previous below).

✎ **Key point: the Abernathy case was referred to, with approval, by a federal court in 1994 in a ruling addressing the tax status of congregational gifts to a minister. Goodwin v. United States, 94-2 U.S.T.C. ¶ 50,597 (S.D. Iowa 1994), affirmed, 67 F.3d 149 (8th Cir. 1995).**

IRS Revenue Ruling 55-422. In 1955, the IRS issued Revenue Ruling 55-422 in which it expressly agreed with these four federal appeals court decisions because of the following facts present in each case: (1) "the payments were not made in accordance with any enforceable agreement, established plan, or past practice"; (2) the minister "did not undertake to perform any further services for the congregation and was not expected to do so" following his retirement; (3) "there was a far closer personal

relationship between the [minister] and the congregation than is found in lay employment relationships"; and (4) "the available evidence indicated that the amount paid was determined in light of the financial position of the congregation and the needs of the recipient, who had been adequately compensated for his past services."

Commissioner v. Duberstein, 363 U.S. 278, 285 (1960). In this case the United States Supreme Court addressed the question of whether a $20,000 retirement gift made by a church to a retiring lay officer was taxable compensation or a tax-free gift. The church board had authorized the "gift" in a resolution characterizing the gift as a "gratuity" and specifying that it had been made "in appreciation for services rendered." The trial court concluded that the distribution was a tax-free gift, but a federal appeals court disagreed. The appeals court conceded that the courts had uniformly treated retirement gifts to clergy as tax-free gifts since "in such cases the parishioners are apt to be largely moved by gratitude for spiritual direction, kindness and affection and do not think in quantitative terms of whatever financial gains the pastor may have contributed to the [church]." *Stanton v. United States, 268 F.2d 727 (2nd Cir. 1959).* The case was appealed to the United States Supreme Court, which freely admitted the difficulty of distinguishing between tax-free gifts and taxable compensation. The Supreme Court did attempt to provide some guidance, however, by noting that "a gift in the statutory sense . . . proceeds from a detached and disinterested generosity . . . out of affection, respect, admiration, charity, or like impulses . . . . The most critical consideration . . . is the transferor's intention."

The Court also observed that "it doubtless is the exceptional payment by an employer to an employee that amounts to a gift," and that the church's characterization of the distribution as a "gift" is "not determinative—there must be an objective inquiry as to whether what is called a gift amounts to it in reality." Also relevant in resolving the issue of whether a particular distribution constitutes a tax-free gift or taxable compensation for services rendered is the following language from another Supreme Court decision: "What controls is the intention with which payment, however voluntary, has been made. Has it been made with the intention that services rendered in the past shall be requited more completely, though full acquittance has been given? If so, it bears a tax. Has it been made to show good will, esteem, or kindliness toward persons who happen to have served, but who are paid without thought to make requital for the service? If so, it is exempt." *Bogardus v. Commissioner, 302 U.S. 34, 45 (1936).*

Perkins v. Commissioner, 34 T.C. 117 (1960). In 1960 the Tax Court ruled that pension payments made by the United Methodist Church to retired clergy constituted taxable compensation rather than tax-free gifts. The court concluded that the pension payments could not be characterized as tax-free gifts since they did not satisfy all of the conditions specified by the IRS in Revenue Ruling 55-422 (discussed above). Specifically, the "pension payments were made in accordance with the established plan and past practice of the Methodist Church, there was no close relationship between the recipient [ministers] and the bulk of the contributing congregations, and the amounts paid were not determined in the light of the needs of the individual [ministers]."

Joyce v. Commissioner, 25 T.C.M. 914 (1966). In 1966 the Tax Court ruled that retirement payments made by the General Conference of Seventh-Day Adventists to the widow of a former minister represented taxable income and not tax-free gifts. Upon retirement ministers received monthly payments from the "sustentation fund" of the General Conference. Benefits were based upon the length of service of the minister. Benefits to the widow of a deceased minister were limited to three-quarters of the payment received by the deceased spouse. The General Conference issued the widow 1099 forms reporting the payments as taxable income. However, in reporting her taxes, the widow treated the payments as non-taxable gifts. The Court noted that "the ultimate criterion" in resolving such cases is "the basic or dominant reason that explains the action of the transferor." How is this "basis or dominant reason" to be determined? The Court listed the following considerations:

• To constitute a gift the benefits paid must proceed from a "detached and disinterested generosity" or "out of affection, respect, admiration, charity or like impulses."

• "The absence of a legal or moral obligation to make such payments . . . or the fact that payments are voluntary . . . do not [necessarily] establish that a gift was intended. However, payments which do proceed from a legal or moral obligation are not gifts."

• "Additional factors, which militate against a determination that gifts were intended, have been findings: (1) that a plan or past practice of payment was in existence; (2) that the needs of the widow were neither the prerequisite for, nor the measure of payment; and (3) that the transferor considered the payment as compensation, including the withholding of income tax."

The Court acknowledged that "in determining that certain payments constituted gifts, courts have seized upon the following: that payments were made directly to the widow rather than to the estate; that the widow performed no services for the transferor; that full compensation had been paid for the services of the deceased husband; and that the transferor derived no benefit from the payment."

The Court stressed that "[t]he determination of the transferor's dominant motive does not rest upon any single factor but is rather a conclusion reached after due consideration of all the relevant factors." It concluded that the payments made to the widow in this case represented taxable income on the basis of the following considerations: (1) Benefits payable to a minister, and to a surviving spouse, are fixed according to a computation based upon the length of service by the employee to the church. In other words, they are paid according to a formal plan. The Court concluded that "[t]he existence of a plan or practice is

most persuasive against the theory that a payment is a gift, and, we think it is decisive where a benefit to the [employer] is expected." The Court noted that the church benefited from the payments to widows by providing "an additional inducement for workers to enter the church's employ." (2) The church made payments to the widow "without any inquiry into her financial condition." (3) The amount of payments was "based on a computation which ignores financial condition, in that benefits are computed solely on the basis of length of service and the degree of major responsibility borne by the employee." The Court stressed that "[t]his lack of consideration of [the widow's] financial status is a highly relevant factor in determining that the motive of the transferor was not to make a gift to [her]." (4) The Court noted that the church itself treated the payments as taxable income to the widow and so reported them on 1099 forms. The Court observed that "[t]his factor, though not decisive, is, again, highly relevant to the determination that no gift was intended." (5) The Court noted that the church "recognized a moral obligation to make such payments to those employees, and their widows, who have loyally rendered service to the church. This fact alone has been held sufficient to prevent payments from constituting gifts."

The Court acknowledged that the payments were made directly to the widow and that she did not perform any services for the church. It rejected the widow's argument that this factor required the payments to be treated as gifts to her, since she had otherwise failed to overcome all of the other factors supporting the Court's decision that the payments were taxable.

✎ **Key point:** a federal appeals court mentioned "a departing church member's individual, unsolicited five hundred dollar gift to a long-tenured, highly respected priest, rabbi, or minister," as an example of a nontaxable gift. *Goodwin v. United States, 67 F.3d 149 (8th Cir. 1995).*

✎ **Key point:** the United States Supreme Court observed in a landmark 1936 case: "Has [the payment] been made with the intention that services rendered in the past shall be requited more completely, though full acquittance has been given? If so, it bears a tax. Has it been made to show good will, esteem, or kindliness toward persons who happen to have served, but who are paid without thought to make requital for the service? If so, it is exempt." *Bogardus v. Commissioner, 302 U.S. 34, 45 (1936).*

Conclusions. These cases, and Revenue Ruling 55-422, indicate that retirement gifts to clergy can under limited circumstances constitute tax-free gifts rather than taxable compensation so long as the conditions specified in Revenue Ruling 55-422 are satisfied. Significantly, the IRS has never officially revoked or even modified Revenue Ruling 55-422. However, there are three considerations that make such a conclusion questionable.

• Neither Revenue Ruling 55-422 nor any of the court decisions summarized above explained how a church can distribute any of its assets as a tax-free gift without jeopardizing its tax-exempt status. To be exempt from federal income taxation, a church must satisfy a number of requirements. One of these requirements is that none of its assets or income be distributed to any individual except as reasonable compensation for services rendered *or* for a charitable or religious purpose. IRC 501(c)(3). Treating a minister's retirement gift as a tax-free gift would appear to violate this requirement—at least if it is paid out of church funds. The effect of this would be to call into question the tax-exempt status of the church itself. Significantly, the courts have consistently ruled that *any* amount of income distributed to an individual (other than as reasonable compensation or in furtherance of charitable or religious purposes) will jeopardize a church's tax-exempt status. This problem is avoided completely by characterizing the retirement gift as taxable compensation—assuming that the "gift" is reasonable in amount (see the introduction to Section A of the present chapter). Churches wishing to take this more cautious position should include the amount of the "gift" as income on the retired minister's W-2 or 1099, and the minister should report the gift as compensation on Form 1040 (line 7) if an employee or on Schedule C if self-employed. Of course, as noted in the preceding section, payments made directly by a member to a minister may constitute a tax-free gift, but the donor ordinarily will not qualify for a charitable contribution deduction. Similarly, a church could collect an all-cash "retirement offering," with the express understanding that the entire proceeds will be paid directly to the minister, and that no contributions will be deductible. Such an offering, not processed through the church books or accounts, could in some cases qualify as a tax-free gift to the minister.

• A second problem with characterizing retirement gifts as tax-free gifts rather than taxable compensation is section 102(c) of the Internal Revenue Code. Section 102(c) (which was enacted in 1986) prohibits employers from characterizing payments to employees as tax-free gifts (with certain exceptions discussed in section A.2 of this chapter). Section 102(c) clearly prohibits a church from characterizing a retirement gift to its minister as a tax-free gift if the minister reports his or her federal income taxes as an employee (or is reclassified as an employee by the IRS).

✎ **Key point: a federal appeals court in 1995 made the following observation regarding Code section 102(c): "Although the legislative history suggests that [this section] was enacted to address other fact situations, its plain meaning may not be ignored in this case. That meaning seems far from plain, however. The church members are not [the pastor's] 'employer,' and the question whether their payments to the [pastor] were made 'for' his employer seems little different than the traditional gift inquiry under Duberstein and Bogardus. We therefore decline the government's belated suggestion that we affirm on the alternative ground of**

section 102(c). *Goodwin v. United States, 67 F.3d 149 (8th Cir. 1995)*.

• Finally, the IRS national office sent the author of this text a letter in 1990 stating that "Revenue Ruling 55-422 ceased to represent the Service's position on or before the date the Supreme Court decided *Commissioner v. Duberstein* [in 1960]." The IRS also informed that author that (1) "for years after 1986, section 102(c) ensures that [retirement] payments are not excludable" by clergy who are employees for income tax reporting purposes; and (2) retirement gifts to self-employed clergy are now evaluated under the *Duberstein* and *Stanton* cases (summarized above). While the IRS letter was an unofficial communication, it is our recommendation that clergy should report their taxes on the basis of the information contained in the letter.

One final point. As noted above, clergy who receive retirement gifts directly from members may be able to treat them as tax-free gifts (if they satisfy the definition of "gift" announced in the *Duberstein* case). Of course, the members receive no charitable contribution deduction since their contributions went directly to an individual.

4. Property purchased from an employer

If a church allows its minister to buy property at less than fair market value, the minister ordinarily must include in his or her church compensation the excess of the property's fair market value over the bargain sale price. This is so whether the minister is an employee or self-employed for income tax reporting purposes. *Treas. Reg. 1.61-2(d)(2)*.

☞ *Example. First Church sells its parsonage to Rev. B for a bargain price of $25,000 in cash. The parsonage has a fair market value of $75,000. Rev. B realizes income of $50,000 from this transaction, and this income must be reflected on Rev. B's W-2 or 1099 form and on her federal income tax return (Form 1040). Before making a bargain sale of church property to a minister, a church must also consider whether or not the resulting compensation may render the minister's total compensation unreasonable in amount. If it does, then the church's tax-exempt status (and the deductibility of contributions) is jeopardized.*

✎ **Key point: the IRS can impose "intermediate sanctions" (an excise tax) against an officer or director of a church or other charity, and in some cases against board members individually, if an officer or director is paid an excessive amount of compensation. The law clarifies that compensation may include property sold to an officer or director at an unreasonably low price. A rebuttable presumption arises that a sale is for a reasonable price if it is approved by an independent board on the basis of "comparability** data" and the basis for the board's decision is documented.

5. Sick pay

Amounts received by an employee for personal injuries or sickness are includable in income if paid directly by an employer or if they represent insurance proceeds from a policy paid for by an employer (and the insurance premiums paid by the employer were not included in the employee's income). *IRC 104.* However, such payments may be excluded from income under section 105 of the Code in the case of ministers who report their federal income taxes as employees (see chapter 5, section E).

6. Social security tax paid by church

Social security benefits are financed through two tax systems. Employers and employees each pay the "FICA" tax, which for 1997 amounts to 7.65% of an employee's taxable wages (a total tax of 15.3%). Self-employed persons pay the "self-employment tax," which for 1997 is 15.3% of net self-employment earnings. Clergy are always considered to be self-employed for social security purposes with respect to service performed in the exercise of ministry. This means that clergy never pay FICA taxes with respect to such services. Rather, they pay the self-employment tax (15.3%)—unless they have filed a timely application for exemption from self-employment taxes and have received written approval of their exemption from the IRS.

Because a minister pays a much higher social security tax than is required of employees, many churches agree to pay their minister an additional sum to cover a portion (i.e., one-half) of the minister's self-employment tax liability. This is perfectly appropriate. However, note that any amount paid to a minister to help him or her pay the higher self-employment tax must be reported as additional compensation on the minister's W-2 or 1099 form, and again on the minister's Form 1040. The amount paid by the church must be reported as compensation for social security purposes as well. *Revenue Ruling 68-507.*

✎ **Key point: IRS Publication 517 states that "if a church pays any amount toward your obligation for your income tax or self-employment tax, other than by withholding the amount from your salary, this amount is additional income to you and must be included in your gross income and self-employment income."**

Churches electing to pay "half" of a minister's self-employment tax may have a difficult time making this calculation, since it will not be clear what "half" of a minister's self-employment tax liability for the year will be until the minister completes a Form 1040 following the end of the current year. This topic is explained more fully in chapter 9. Churches desiring to pay a specified portion of a minister's self-employment tax should consider paying a fixed amount rather than "half" of the total self-employment tax liability. This will avoid the complexities involved in calculating "half" of a minister's self-employment tax.

7. Taxable fringe benefits

A **fringe benefit** is any material benefit provided by an employer to an employee (or self-employed person) apart from his or her stated compensation. Some fringe benefits must be valued and included in an employee's gross income for income tax and social security tax purposes, while others are specifically excluded from income. As a general rule, a fringe benefit must be valued and included in an employee's gross income unless it is specifically excluded by law. Excludable fringe benefits are discussed in chapter 5. This subsection will illustrate some taxable fringe benefits. One of the more common fringe benefits is an employer-provided car. Because of the complexity of valuing this benefit, it is addressed separately in the following subsection.

(1) Moving expenses paid by employing church. Employer reimbursements of an employee's moving expenses are treated as a tax-free fringe benefit if:

• the moving expenses would be deductible by the employee if paid directly by the employee (see chapter 7 for an explanation);

• the employee did not deduct the expenses in a prior year; and

• the employer only reimburses those moving expenses that are properly substantiated by the employee (under rules similar to an accountable expense reimbursement arrangement)

Employer reimbursements that satisfy these requirements are not reported in box 1 of the W-2 form, but must be reported in box 13. Code "P" is used to identify these nontaxable reimbursements in box 13. An employer's reimbursements of an employee's moving expenses are not excludable from the employee's income if the employee deducted the expenses in a prior year. A committee report explaining the moving expense rules specifies that an "employer [may] treat moving expenses as excludable unless it has actual knowledge that the employee deducted the expenses in a prior year. The employer has no obligation to determine whether the individual deducted the expenses."

Any reimbursements of moving expenses that do not satisfy the three requirements described above are treated as a taxable fringe benefit and are included in the employee's taxable wages.

❖ **New in 1998. Church leaders should be familiar with the following changes in moving expense reporting that take effect in 1998: (1) Form 4782, which is used by employers to report moving expense reimbursements made to employees, will be eliminated; (2) qualified moving expenses an employer pays to a third party on behalf of the employee (e.g. to a** moving company) will **not** be **reported on Form W-2; (3) qualified moving expenses reimbursements an employer pays directly to an employee will be reported in Box 13 of Form W-2 and will be identified using Code P (currently, all qualified moving expense reimbursements are identified with Code P, regardless of whether or not they were paid directly to the employee); (4) other moving expense reimbursements (nonqualified expenses) will continue to be included in wages (Form W-2, box 1) and are subject to income tax withholding and social security and Medicare taxes.**

(2) Employer-provided meals. Generally, if meals are provided to you by your employer as a means of increasing your compensation, and there is no business reason for providing them, their value is income to you. In some cases, however, the value of employer-provided meals is not included in your income. See chapter 5, section H, for details.

(3) Miscellaneous. Many of the other components of income discussed in this chapter could be considered "fringe benefits" (e.g., Christmas gifts from the church, social security taxes paid by the church on behalf of its minister, low-interest loans). In addition, some fringe benefits that ordinarily are excluded from gross income must in fact be valued and added to income if they do not satisfy various conditions discussed in chapter 5.

8. Personal use of a church-provided car

✎ **Key point: the personal use of a church-provided car is income to a minister, and must be valued and reported using one of 4 valuation methods**

One of the more common taxable fringe benefit for ministers is personal use of a church-owned car. If a church provides a car to its minister, the minister's personal use of the car is a taxable noncash fringe benefit. The church must determine the actual value of this fringe benefit so that it can be included in the minister's income and reported on his or her W-2 or 1099 form. The church may use either general valuation principles or one of three special valuation rules to value the personal use of the vehicle. You must use general valuation principles to value the personal use of the vehicle unless your employer chooses to use one of the three special valuation rules. If your employer uses a special valuation, you may use either that same valuation rule or the general valuation principles.

These four rules are summarized below:

(1) General valuation principles. Under the "general valuation principles," the amount to add to a worker's income equals (1) the amount a person would have to pay to lease a comparable vehicle on comparable terms in the same geographical area, multiplied times (2) the percentage of total vehicle miles for the period that were of a personal (rather than business) nature. You ordinarily cannot use a "cents-per-mile rate" to determine the value of the availability of an employer-provided car unless the same or comparable vehicle could be leased on a cents-per-mile basis for the same period of time that the vehicle was available to you (i.e., one year). In other words, if you have access to the car for an entire year, and a comparable vehicle in your community would not be leased at a cents-per-mile rate for a similar period of time, then you cannot use a cents-per-mile rule to value the availability of the car to you. You must use the general rule that is applied in your community to determine the lease value of a car (such as a fixed rate per week, month, or year).

(2) Special automobile lease valuation rule. Under this special rule, if your employer provides you with a car that is available to you for an entire calendar year, the value of the taxable benefit is the annual lease value ("ALV") of the car multiplied times the percentage of total miles driven during the year that are for personal use. The ALV is determined from an IRS table that is reproduced in Table 4-1. The ALV includes maintenance and insurance costs, but it does not include the cost of fuel. Therefore, if the employer provides fuel for the vehicle, this must be separately valued and reported as income. Employers may value the cost of fuel at 5.5 cents per mile. If the car is not available to you for an entire calendar year, the value is determined by using a prorated ALV (or a daily lease value, whichever applies). If you use the ALV method, you must continue to do so for all future years with respect to the same vehicle (unless the "commuting valuation rule, discussed below, is used).

TABLE 4-1

Annual Lease Value Table

automobile fair market value	annual lease value	automobile fair market value	annual lease value
$0 to 999	600	22,000 to 22,999	6,100
1,000 to 1,999	850	23,000 to 23,999	6,350
2,000 to 2,999	1,100	24,000 to 24,999	6,600
3,000 to 3,999	1,350	25,000 to 25,999	6,850
4,000 to 4,999	1,600	26,000 to 27,999	7,250
5,000 to 5,999	1,850	28,000 to 29,999	7,750
6,000 to 6,999	2,100	30,000 to 31,999	8,250
7,000 to 7,999	2,350	32,000 to 33,999	8,750
8,000 to 8,999	2,600	34,000 to 35,999	9,250
9,000 to 9,999	2,850	36,000 to 37,999	9,750
10,000 to 10,999	3,100	38,000 to 39,999	10,250
11,000 to 11,999	3,350	40,000 to 41,999	10,750
12,000 to 12,999	3,600	42,000 to 43,999	11,250
13,000 to 13,999	3,850	44,000 to 45,999	11,750
14,000 to 14,999	4,100	46,000 to 47,999	12,250
15,000 to 15,999	4,350	48,000 to 49,999	12,750
16,000 to 16,999	4,600	50,000 to 51,999	13,250
17,000 to 17,999	4,850	52,000 to 53,999	13,750
18,000 to 18,999	5,100	54,000 to 55,999	14,250
19,000 to 19,999	5,350	56,000 to 57,999	14,750
20,000 to 20,999	5,600	58,000 to 59,999	15,250
21,000 to 21,999	5,850		

Determine the fair market value of the employer-provided car as of the first date on which it is made available to you, and then find the corresponding

ALV from Table 4-1. A car's fair market value can be found in the "blue book," or an employer can use the price it paid for the car (assuming that it was an "arm's-length" transaction). Use the same ALV for four consecutive years. If you still are using the vehicle after four years, then determine the fair market value of the car at that time and find the ALV to be used for the next four years from Table 4-1. In other words, do not recompute the ALV each year based on the current fair market value of the car. The table is based on a four-year cycle.

☞ *Example. First Church purchases a car in 1997, and lets Rev. M use it for both personal and business use. The fair market value of the car in 1997 is $16,000. Rev. M uses the car 60% for business and 40% for personal use. If the church chooses to value the personal use of the car using the special lease valuation rule, the value would be $1,840 (ALV of $4,600 multiplied times the personal use percentage of 40%). This amount would be reported on Rev. M's W-2 (or 1099), and on his Form 1040. If Rev. M uses the same car in 1998, and 40% of total miles are for personal uses, then the church would again value the personal use of the car at $1,840. If Rev. M is using the same vehicle in 2001 (the fifth year), the church would recalculate the ALV by using the market value of the car for that year (as of January 1). This amount would be used for the fifth through the eighth year of use (the second four-year cycle).*

✎ **Key point: The income tax regulations contain a "total value inclusion" option for employer using the annual lease valuation method of valuing an employer-provided vehicle. Under this option, an employer may include in an employee's gross income the entire annual lease value of the automobile, and the employee then may claim the value of any business use of the vehicle by completing Form 2106 (for employees) or by deducting the amount on Schedule C (if self-employed). This "total value inclusion" rule is not available if an employer uses the general valuation rule or any of the other special valuation rules. Employers using the annual lease valuation rule may be forced into using the total value inclusion rule if an employee fails to maintain sufficient records to document the percentage of total miles that were driven for business as opposed to personal purposes. Treas. Reg. 1.132-5(b)(1)(iv).**

(3) Special cents-per-mile rule. Under this rule, the standard mileage rate, which for 1997 is 31.5 cents per mile, is multiplied by the number of miles you use the vehicle for personal purposes. If your employer does not provide the fuel for the vehicle, the mileage rate may be reduced by up to 5.5 cents per mile. Business miles must be substantiated and subtracted from total miles to determine personal miles. To qualify for use of this rule, the vehicle must be regularly used in the employer's trade or business throughout the calendar year (or for such shorter period of time as the vehicle may be owned or leased), or actually driven at least 10,000 miles in that year and used primarily by employees. *This rule cannot be used for an automobile if its fair market value when first provided to an employee is more than $15,700 (this figure is adjusted for inflation each year). Treas. Reg. 1.61-21(e)(1)(iii).* This limitation will prevent many clergy from using the "cents-per-mile" rule to value the personal use of an employer-provided car. It was imposed because of an IRS concern that the cents-per-mile rule would not adequately value the personal use of employer-provided "luxury cars." If you use the cents-per-mile method, you must continue to do so for all future years with respect to the same vehicle (unless the "commuting valuation rule," discussed below, is used).

☞ *Example. In 1997 First Church purchases a car and permits Rev. T to use it for both business and personal use. The car cost $16,500. The "cents-per-mile" method of valuing the personal use of the car cannot be used by either the church or Rev. T since the fair market value of the car when first provided to Rev. T was in excess of $15,700.*

☞ *Example. Same facts as the preceding example, except that the fair market value of the car when first provided to Rev. T (in 1997) was $12,500. The cents-per-mile method of valuing the personal use of the car by Rev. T can be used. If Rev. T drove the vehicle a total of 20,000 miles in 1997, of which 9,000 were for personal purposes, the church calculates the value of this personal use by multiplying 9,000 miles times the standard mileage rate of 31.5 cents for a total of $2,835. This amount would be added to the minister's W-2 or 1099, and Form 1040. This method should not be used if Rev. T cannot substantiate the number of personal miles the car was driven during the year.*

☞ *Example. Same facts as the previous example, except that the church required Rev. T to purchase his own gas. If the church uses the cents-per-mile special valuation rule, it can value the personal use of Rev. T's use of the car by multiplying all miles driven for personal purposes during the year times 26 cents (31.5 cents less 5.5 cents). This reduces the valuation of the personal miles to $2,340 (9,000 miles times 26 cents).*

(4) Special commuting valuation rule. If an employee is provided with an employer-provided vehicle, and is required to commute to and from work in the vehicle, then the value of the commuting miles (which are always deemed personal rather than business) can be computed at a rate of $3 per round-trip commute or $1.50 per one-way commute. The employer includes the value of all commuting on the employee's W-2. For this rule to apply, the following conditions must be satisfied:

• the vehicle is owned or leased by the church and is provided to an employee for use in connection with church business

- for "noncompensatory" business reasons (i.e., security) the church requires the employee to commute to and from work in the vehicle

- under a written policy statement adopted by the church board, no employee of the church can use the vehicle for personal purposes, except for commuting or "de minimis" (minimal) personal use (such as a stop for lunch between two business trips)

- the church reasonably believes that, except for commuting and de minimis use, no church employee uses the vehicle for any personal purpose

- the employee who is required by the church to commute to and from work in the vehicle is not a "control employee" (defined below)

- the church must be able to supply sufficient evidence to prove to the IRS that the preceding five conditions have been met

Control employee. The regulations define a *control employee* (for purposes of the commuting valuation rule) as an employee who satisfies any one or more of the following:

- a board appointed, confirmed, or elected officer with annual compensation of $66,000 or more

- a director (regardless of compensation)

- any employee with annual compensation of $135,000 or more

Obviously, senior ministers ordinarily will not be able to take advantage of this special commuting rule, since they typically are directors of their church, and in some cases they are appointed or confirmed by the church board and receive compensation of $66,000 or more during the year. In some cases, however, ministers may be eligible for the special commuting rule.

Alternate definition of a control employee. The income tax regulations give employers the option of using another definition of "control employee." *Treas. Reg. 1.61-21(f)(5).* The substitute definition adopts the definition of "highly compensated employee" that is set forth in "section 1.132-8(g)" of the income tax regulations. Unfortunately, there is no section 1.132-8(g). A definition of highly compensated employee does appear in section 1.132-8(f). This section adopts the definition of a "highly compensated employee" set forth in Code section 414(q). A highly compensated employee under this definition is an employee who (1) was a 5 percent owner of the employer at any time during the current or prior year (this definition will not apply to churches), or (2) had compensation for the previous year in excess of $80,000, and, if an employer elects, was in the top 20 percent of employees by compensation. In many cases it will be less likely that ministers will be control employees under the substitute definition, meaning that the special commuting rule will be available to them. This is because the substitute definition does

not include all directors (regardless of compensation) within the definition of the term highly compensated employee. Rather, it adopts a straight "income" test, which for 1997 is $80,000.

If a church would like to use the special rule for a minister (who is not a control employee under the substitute definition) it should specifically adopt the substitute definition by a church board resolution. The board should adopt a resolution stating simply that "for 1998 and future years unless otherwise provided, the board adopts the alternate definition of a control employee set forth in section 1.132-8(f) of the income tax regulations. Under this alternate definition, the definition of a highly compensated employee is substituted for the definition of a control employee."

Notification. In the past, employers had to *notify* employees if they used one of the three special valuation rules discussed above to determine the value of the personal use of an employer-provided vehicle. This notification requirement no longer applies.

Special conditions applicable to special valuation rules. An employer may not use any of the three special valuation rules unless *one or more* of the following four conditions is satisfied:

- the employer treats the value of the benefit as wages (for tax reporting purposes)

- the employee includes the value of the benefit in income

- the employee is not a *control employee* (defined above)

- the employer demonstrates a good faith effort to treat the benefit correctly for tax reporting purposes

If none of these conditions is satisfied, then the employer and employee must use the general valuation rule to value the personal use of an employer-provided car.

Reporting taxable income. The value of an employer-provided vehicle that is included in your income will be reported by your employer on your Form W-2 (or Form 1099 if you are self-employed). On Form W-2, the amount of the benefit should be included in box 1 (wages, tips, and other compensation), and in box 12 (which reports the value of taxable fringe benefits that were included in box 1).

Employee reimbursements. The income tax regulations specify that if the employer and employee use one of the special valuation rules, the amount of reportable income is decreased by "any amount reimbursed by the employee to the employer." The regulations further specify that "the employer and employee may use the special rules to determine the amount of the reimbursement due the employer by the employee. Thus, if an employee reimburses an employer for the value of a benefit as determined under a special valuation rule, no amount is includable in the employee's gross income with respect to the benefit." *Treas. Reg. 1.61-21(c)(2)(ii)(B).*

Tax withholding. Must a church withhold taxes on the personal use of an employer-provided vehicle? In answering this question, it is important to remember that clergy are exempt from income tax withholding unless they elect voluntary withholding of income taxes, and they are never subject to FICA tax withholding on their church income. Of course, nonminister employees generally are subject to income tax and FICA withholding. With respect to nonminister employees and ministers who have elected voluntary withholding, the law allows employers to elect not to withhold income tax on the value of the personal use of an employer-provided vehicle (FICA taxes generally must be withheld if applicable). An employer electing not to withhold income taxes on the personal use of an employer-provided vehicle must notify the employee (in writing) of this election by the later of (1) January 31 of the year of the election, or (2) within 30 days after the date the employer first provides the employee with the vehicle.

☞ *Example. First Church purchased a car early in 1997 that it provided to Rev. P for the year. The market value of the car at the time it was provided to Rev. P was $12,000. Rev. P drove the car 20,000 miles in 1997—8,000 miles being for personal and 12,000 miles for business purposes. In January of 1998 the church tries to determine the value of the personal miles to report on Rev. P's W-2 form. The employer selects the cents-per-mile method of valuing the personal use of the car and reports $2,520 of additional income on Rev. P's W-2 for 1997 (8,000 personal miles times 31.5 cents equals $2,520).*

☞ *Example. Same facts as the previous example, except that the church elects to use the general valuation rule. Under the general rule, the value of the personal use of an employer-provided vehicle equals (1) the amount a person would have to pay to lease a comparable vehicle on comparable terms in the same geographical area, multiplied times (2) the percentage of total vehicle miles for the period that were of a personal (rather than business) nature. The church must use the general rule that is applied in the community to determine the lease value of a car (such as a fixed rate per week, month, or year). If a comparable vehicle would lease for $4,000 per year, the church values the personal use of the car at $1,600 and reports this amount on Rev. P's W-2 ($4,000 lease value multiplied times the personal use percentage of 40%). This assumes that the minister has provided the church with adequate records substantiating personal miles.*

9. Below-market interest loans

✎ **Key point: churches that make low-interest or no-interest loans to clergy may be violating state nonprofit corporation law and generating taxable income**

Churches often make low-interest or no-interest loans (both are referred to as "below-market loans")

to ministers. These loans may result in additional compensation to the minister under the following rules:

(1) Demand loans. If you receive a below-market *demand loan* (a loan payable in full at any time upon the church's demand), you are treated as having received additional compensation from your church in an amount equal to the foregone interest, and then transferring the foregone interest back to the church. These additional transfers of compensation are deemed to occur annually, generally on December 31. The "lender" (church) must report this amount as interest income to the "borrower" (minister). Foregone interest for any period is the amount of interest that would be payable for that period if interest occurred at the applicable federal rate, over and above any interest actually payable on the loan for the same period. The applicable federal rate is established by the IRS each month in a revenue ruling. You can get this rate from any IRS office. A below-market demand loan of less than $10,000 is not subject to these rules (assuming one of its principal purposes was not the avoidance of tax).

(2) Term loans. If you receive a below-market *term loan* (any loan that is not a demand loan), you are treated as having received an additional payment of compensation on the date the loan was made. The amount of compensation (in effect a "discount") is the excess of the amount of the loan over the present value of all payments due under the loan. A below-market term loan of less than $10,000 is not subject to these rules (assuming one of its principal purposes is not the avoidance of tax).

The income tax regulations exempt certain loans from the tax on foregone interest. These include:

• Loans made by a charitable organization, if the primary purpose of the loan is to accomplish religious, charitable, or educational purposes. This exception ordinarily will not apply to below-market interest loans made by churches to ministers, since the purpose of such loans is to assist or compensate the minister rather than to fulfill specific exempt purposes.

• The regulations further specify that "[i]n the case of a compensation-related loan to an employee, where such loan is secured by a mortgage on the new principal residence . . . of the employee, acquired in connection with the transfer of that employee to a new principal place of work . . . the loan will be exempt from [tax] if the following conditions are satisfied: (a) The loan is a demand loan or is a term loan the benefits of the interest arrangements of which are not transferable by the employee and are conditioned on the future performance of substantial services by the employee; (b) the employee certifies to the employer that the employee reasonably expects to be entitled to and will itemize deductions for each year the loan is outstanding; and (c) the loan agreement requires that the loan proceeds be used only to purchase the new principal residence of the employee." *Treas. Reg. 1.7872-5T(c)(1).*

Other concerns. Low-interest or no-interest loans to clergy can create problems for a couple of other reasons. First, many state nonprofit corporation laws prohibit incorporated churches from making loans to officers and directors. No church should consider making any loan to a minister (even at a reasonable rate of interest) without first determining that such loans are permissible under state law. Second, no-interest or low-interest loans to clergy may be viewed as "inurement" of the church's income to a minister that can potentially jeopardize the church's tax-exempt status (see chapter 11, section F).

In summary, even if loans to clergy are allowed under your state's nonprofit corporation law, the church must recognize that no-interest and low-interest loans of $10,000 or more will result in income to a minister that must be valued and reported (on the minister's W-2 or 1099-MISC, and Form 1040). Failure to do so could result in prohibited "inurement" of the church's income to a private individual, and this could be disastrous for the church.

10. "In kind" transfers of property

Churches occasionally give clergy property without charge. Examples include automobiles, homes, and equipment. Such transfers result in taxable compensation to the minister that must be valued and reported on the minister's Form W-2 or 1099-MISC (and Form 1040). Generally, the amount to be included in income is the fair market value of the property less any amount paid by the minister for the property. For example, a federal court has ruled that a minister had to include in his gross income for federal income tax purposes the value of a boat and trailer received in payment for services as a minister. *Potito v. Commissioner, 534 F.2d 49 (5th Cir. 1976).*

11. Assignments of income

Ministers, like other taxpayers, occasionally attempt to "assign" income to a charity and thereby avoid income taxes on the assigned income. For example, Rev. G conducts services for two weeks at a church whose pastor is on vacation. The church wants to pay Rev. G income of $1,000 for these services, but Rev. G declines and requests that the money be applied to the church's building fund. Does Rev. G have to pay tax on the $1,000? In many cases, the answer will be yes. The United States Supreme Court addressed this issue in a landmark ruling in 1940. *Helvering v. Horst, 311 U.S. 112 (1940).* The *Horst* case addressed the question of whether or not a father could avoid taxation on bond interest coupons that he transferred to his son prior to the maturity date. The Supreme Court ruled that the father had to pay tax on the interest income even though he assigned all of his interest in the income to his son. It observed: "The power to dispose of income is the equivalent of ownership of it. The exercise of that power to procure the payment of income to another is the enjoyment and hence the realization of the income by him who exercises it." The Supreme Court reached the same conclusion in two other landmark cases. *Helvering v. Eubank, 311 U.S. 122 (1940), Lucas v. Earl, 281 U.S. 111 (1930).*

☞ *Example. A taxpayer earned an honorarium of $2,500 for speaking at a convention. He requested that the honorarium be distributed to a college. This request was honored, and the taxpayer assumed that he did not have to report the $2,500 as taxable income since he never received it. The IRS ruled that the taxpayer should have reported the $2,500 as taxable income. It noted that "the amount of the honorarium transferred to the educational institution at the taxpayer's request . . . is includible in the taxpayer's gross income [for tax purposes]. However, the taxpayer is entitled to a charitable contribution deduction . . . ." The IRS further noted that "the Supreme Court of the United States has held that a taxpayer who assigns or transfers compensation for personal services to another individual or entity fails to be relieved of federal income tax liability, regardless of the motivation behind the transfer" (citing the Horst case discussed above). Revenue Ruling 79-121.*

12. Refusal to accept full salary

Refusal to accept full salary. A related question is whether or not a minister is taxed on the full amount of a church-approved salary if he or she refuses to accept the full amount. The *constructive receipt doctrine*, set forth in income tax regulation 1.451-2(a), specifies:

> Income although not actually reduced to a taxpayer's possession is constructively received by him in the taxable year during which it is credited to his account, set apart for him, or otherwise made available so that he may draw upon it at any time, or so that he could have drawn upon it during the taxable year if notice of intention to withdraw had been given.

A number of courts have ruled that this principle requires employees to include in their taxable income any portion of their stated salary that they refuse to accept. On the other hand, some courts have reached an opposite conclusion. Perhaps the most notable case is *Giannini v. Commissioner, 129 F.2d 638 (9th Cir. 1942).* This case involved a corporate president whose annual compensation was 5 percent of the company's profits. In the middle of one year, the president informed members of his company's board of directors that he would not accept any further compensation for the year and suggested that the company "do something worthwhile" with the money. The company never credited to the president any further compensation for the year nor did it set any part of it aside for his use. The amount of salary refused by the president was nearly $1.5 million, and no part of this amount was reported by the president as taxable income in the year in question. The IRS audited the president and insisted that the $1.5 million should have been reported as taxable income. The taxpayer appealed, and a federal appeals court rejected the IRS position:

> [T]he taxpayer did not receive the money, and . . . did not direct its disposition. What he did was unqualifiedly refuse to accept any further com-

pensation for his services with the suggestion that the money be used for some worthwhile purpose. So far as the taxpayer was concerned, the corporation could have kept the money. . . . In these circumstances we cannot say as a matter of law that the money was beneficially received by the taxpayer and therefore subject to the income tax provisions . . . .

The court acknowledged that the United States Supreme Court has observed: "[O]ne who is entitled to receive, at a future date, interest or compensation for services and who makes a gift of it by an anticipatory assignment, realizes taxable income quite as much as if he had collected the income and paid it over to the object of his bounty." *Helvering v. Schaffner, 312 U. S. 579 (1941).* However, the court distinguished this language by observing that "the dominance over the fund and taxpayer's direction show that he beneficially received the money by exercising his right to divert it to a use." This was not true of the corporate president in the present case, the court concluded.

In summary, there is a reasonable basis for not treating as taxable income that portion of an employee's stated salary that is refused, particularly where the employee does not assign the income to a specified use but rather is content to leave the unpaid salary with the employer.

13. Discretionary funds

It is a fairly common practice for a congregation to set aside a sum of money in a "discretionary fund" and give a minister the sole authority to distribute the money in the fund. In some cases, the minister has no instructions regarding permissible distributions. In other cases, the congregation establishes some guidelines, but these often are oral and ambiguous. Consider the following examples.

☞ *Example. A congregation at an annual business meeting authorizes the creation of a "pastor's fund" in the amount of $10,000, with the understanding that Rev. T, the congregation's senior minister, will have the authority to distribute the fund for any purpose. Rev. T is not required to account to the congregation or church board for any distribution, and he is not prohibited from making distributions to himself. During 1997, Rev. T distributes the entire fund to members of the congregation who were in need. He did not distribute any portion of the fund to himself or to any family member.*

☞ *Example. Same facts as the previous example, except that Rev. T distributed $5,000 to himself in 1997.*

☞ *Example. The governing board of First Church sets aside $5,000 in a discretionary fund, and authorizes Rev. D, its senior minister, to distribute the funds for "benevolent purposes." Rev. D is required to account to the church board for*

all distributions and is prohibited from making any distributions to himself or to any family member.

Many clergy and church treasurers are unaware of the potential tax consequences of these arrangements. The tax consequences of some of the more common arrangements are summarized below.

Situation 1. The congregation (or governing board) establishes a discretionary fund and gives a minister full and unrestricted discretion to distribute it.

To the extent the minister has the authority to distribute any portion of the discretionary fund for any purpose, including a distribution to him or herself, without any oversight or control by the governing board, then the following consequences occur:

• *The entire fund must be reported as taxable income to the minister in the year it is funded.* This is so even if the minister in fact does not personally benefit from the fund. The mere fact that the minister *could* personally benefit from the fund is enough for the fund to constitute taxable income. The basis for this result is the "constructive receipt" rule, which is set forth in income tax regulation 1.451-2(a):

Income although not actually reduced to a taxpayer's possession is constructively received by him in the taxable year during which it is credited to his account, set apart for him, or otherwise made available so that he may draw upon it at any time, or so that he could have drawn upon it during the taxable year if notice of intention to withdraw had been given. However, income is not constructively received if the taxpayer's control of its receipt is subject to substantial limitations or restrictions.

For a discretionary fund to constitute taxable income to a minister, it is essential that the minister have the authority to "draw upon it at any time" for his or her own personal use. This means that the fund was established without any express prohibition against personal distributions.

• *Donations by members of the congregation to the fund would not be tax-deductible as charitable contributions since the fund is not subject to the full control of the congregation or its governing board.* For a charitable contribution to be tax-deductible, it must be subject to the full control of the church or other charity. The IRS stated the rule as follows in an important ruling: "The test in each case is whether the organization has full control of the donated funds, and discretion as to their use, so as to insure that they will be used to carry out its functions and purposes." If a church sets up a discretionary fund and authorizes a minister to make distributions from the fund for any purpose without any oversight or control by the church, this fundamental test is not met.

Situation 2. The congregation establishes a discretionary fund and gives a minister the discretion to distribute it for any purpose, but the congregation's governing board retains administrative control over the fund.

Under this scenario the fund would still constitute taxable income to the minister, but the donations of congregational members to the fund probably would be tax-deductible as charitable contributions since the congregational board exercises control over the funds. Board "control" could be established if the board simply reviewed all distributions to ensure consistency with the congregation's exempt purposes.

Situation 3. The congregation establishes a discretionary fund and gives a minister the discretion to distribute it only for specified purposes (such as relief of the needy) that are consistent with the congregation's exempt purposes. The minister does not qualify for distributions and in fact is prohibited from making distributions to him or herself. The congregation's governing board retains administrative control over the fund.

If a discretionary fund is set up by a resolution of a congregation's governing board that absolutely prohibits any distribution of the fund for the minister's personal use, then the constructive receipt rule is avoided and no portion of the fund represents taxable income to the minister. In the words of the income tax regulations, "income is not constructively received if the taxpayer's control of its receipt is subject to substantial limitations or restrictions." Accordingly, in order to avoid the reporting of the entire discretionary fund as taxable income to the minister, it is essential that the fund be established by means of a congregational or board resolution that absolutely prohibits any use of the fund by the minister for personal purposes.

In order to provide a reasonable basis for assuring donors that their contributions to the fund are deductible, the following steps should be taken: (1) The board resolution should specify that the fund may be distributed by the minister only for needs or projects that are consistent with the congregation's exempt purposes (as set forth in the congregation's charter); and (2) the congregational board must exercise control over the funds. As noted above, board "control" could be established if the board simply reviewed all distributions to ensure consistency with the congregation's exempt purposes.

➲ **Planning tip. Ministers can avoid the constructive receipt of taxable income and donors can be given reasonable assurance of the deductibility of their contributions if a discretionary fund**

• Gives a minister the discretion to distribute the fund only for specified purposes (such as relief of the needy) that are consistent with the congregation's exempt purposes.

• Prohibits (in writing) the minister from distributing any portion of the fund for him or herself or any family member.

• The congregation or its governing board retains administrative control over the fund to ensure that all distributions further the church's exempt purposes.

What is "charity"? Ministers who are authorized to distribute discretionary funds for benevolent purposes must recognize that the IRS interprets the term "charity" very strictly. More is required than a temporary financial setback or difficulty paying bills. Ministers should keep this important point in mind when making distributions from a discretionary fund. And, the church board should carefully scrutinize every distribution to ensure that this strict test is satisfied.

Should recipients receive a 1099? In general, a 1099-MISC form is issued only to self-employed workers who are paid compensation. Since most recipients of a minister's discretionary fund do not perform any services for their distribution, no 1099-MISC is required. *IRS Letter Ruling 9314014.*

14. Nonaccountable business expense reimbursements

A church's reimbursements of a minister's (or other staff member's) business expenses under a "nonaccountable" arrangement represent taxable income to the minister, whether the minister reports his or her income taxes as an employee or as self-employed. It is therefore important to recognize "nonaccountable" reimbursement arrangements. Reimbursed expenses are nonaccountable if the minister did not "account" to the employer for the expenses *or* did not return any "excess reimbursements" (employer reimbursements in excess of substantiated expenses) to the employer. Here are some examples of nonaccountable reimbursement arrangements:

• Your church pays a monthly "car allowance" to clergy or lay staff members, without requiring any accounting or substantiation.

• Your church reimburses business expenses without requiring adequate written substantiation (with receipts for all expenses of $25 or more) of the amount, date, place, and business purpose of each expense.

• Your church only reimburses business expenses once each year. Business expenses must be accounted for within a "reasonable time" under an accountable arrangement. Generally, this means within 60 days or less.

• Your church provides clergy or lay staff with travel advances and requires no accounting for the use of these funds.

In each of these cases the church's reimbursements are "nonaccountable," meaning that they must be reported by the church as income to the recipient.

☞ *Example. Rev. H receives a monthly "car allowance" of $300. Rev. H is not required to account for the use of any of these funds. This is an example of a nonaccountable reimbursement arrangement. The church is reimbursing business expenses (through a monthly car allowance) without requiring any accounting or substantiation. It must report all of the monthly allowances ($3,600) as income on Rev. H's W-2 form (or 1099 form if self-employed).*

✎ **Key point: a church's reimbursements of a minister's (or other staff member's) business expenses are not included in the recipient's income if the reimbursements are "accountable." See chapter 7 for details.**

✎ **Key point: the IRS audit guidelines for ministers that were released in 1995 define a minister's income to include "expense allowances for travel, transportation, or other business expenses received under a nonaccountable plan."**

15. Employer reimbursements of a spouse's travel expenses

As noted in chapter 7, a church must report reimbursements of the travel expenses of a spouse who accompanies a minister on a business trip as taxable income (ordinarily, to the minister) unless the spouse's presence on the trip serves a legitimate business purpose and the spouse's expenses are reimbursed under an accountable arrangement.

16. Forgiveness of debt

Churches often make loans to their ministers, often at no interest. Sadly, in some cases a minister never repays the debt. Church treasurers often are unsure of their obligations under these circumstances. Consider the following example:

☞ *Example. First Church hires Rev. B as a youth pastor. Rev. B is young and was recently married, and is in need of housing. Rev. B would like to buy a home but lacks the $10,000 needed for a down payment. The church board votes to loan Rev. B $10,000. Rev. B signs a no-interest $10,000 promissory note agreeing to pay the church back the $10,000 in 60 monthly installments of $166.67. Rev. B pays all of the monthly installments for the first year, but in the second and third year he pays only half of the required installments. He accepts another position and leaves First Church at the end of the third year. The balance due on his note is now $6,000. Over the next several months the church treasurer at First Church writes Rev. B on 3 occasions and requests that the note be paid in full. Rev. B does not respond to any of these requests. The church board eventually decides to forgive the debt and makes no further contact with Rev. B.*

What should a church treasurer do under these circumstances? Does the forgiven debt of $6,000 represent taxable income? The forgiveness of debt ordinarily represents taxable income to the debtor. *IRC 61(a)(12).* As a result, if a church makes a loan to a minister or other staff member and the debt is later forgiven by the church, the church should report the forgiven debt as income. Here are the rules to follow, using the same facts as in the example:

• If the church has not yet issued a W-2 or 1099 to Rev. B for his last year of employment, then reflect the forgiven debt on the W-2 or 1099.

• If the church already has issued a W-2 or 1099 to Rev. B for the last year of employment (within the past 3 years) then there are two options: (1) Issue a corrected W-2 or 1099, reporting the full amount of the forgiven debt as additional compensation for the last year of employment. A corrected W-2 is prepared on Form W-2c. Be sure to note the year of the Form W-2 that is being corrected. There is no separate form for a corrected 1099—simply fill out a new 1099 and check the box at the top of the form indicating that it is a "corrected" version. This approach correctly restates compensation for Rev. B's last year of employment. (2) Issue a 1099 reporting the full amount of the forgiven debt in the current year. It is preferable to report the forgiven debt as income in the year the debt is actually forgiven rather than restating Rev. B's compensation for his last year of employment, since taxable income does not actually occur until the year in which the debt is forgiven (the current year).

• In addition to the forgiven debt ($6,000) Rev. B received income because no interest was charged by the church on the loan. In essence, this additional "income" consists of the amount of interest Rev. B would have paid the church had the prevailing commercial interest rate been charged by the church on the loan. A below-market term loan of less than $10,000 is not subject to these rules (assuming one of its principal purposes is not the avoidance of tax). Check with a CPA or tax attorney for assistance in making this calculation. Different rules apply for "demand loans."

☞ *Example. An employer paid the moving expenses of newly hired employees to relocate them to the employer's city. Employees were required to reimburse the employer for a portion of the moving expenses paid by the employer if they terminated their employment within 1 year after being hired. An employee voluntarily terminated her employment within 1 year of being hired, and the employer was unsuccessful in collecting $5,000 in moving expenses from the employee. The employer eventually wrote this amount off as uncollectible. The IRS ruled that the employer had to report the forgiven debt as taxable income to the former employee. It observed: "It is well settled that where an employee's debt to his employer is satisfied by canceling such debt, income is realized by the employee. Therefore, the employee must include in gross income the total amount of the debt that was canceled by [the employer]. The income realized upon cancellation of indebtedness arose as a result of an employment relationship. Accordingly, Form W-2 should be used to report the amount of indebtedness canceled. This form should be used even if the debt is canceled in a year subsequent to the year of employment." IRS Letter Ruling 8315021.*

☞ *Example. A minister failed to report the discharge of an educational loan as income on his tax return. The Tax Court ruled that the forgiven loan balance should have been reported as income. The Court also upheld an IRS assessment of a negligence penalty against the minister. Parker v. Commissioner, 65 T.C.M. 1740 (1993).*

17. Severance pay

Many churches have entered into severance pay arrangements with a pastor or other staff member. Such arrangements can occur when a pastor or staff member is dismissed, retires, or voluntarily resigns. Consider the following examples:

☞ *Example. Rev. G is hired for a 3-year term at an annual salary of $45,000. After 2 years, the church membership votes to dismiss Rev. G. The church agrees to pay Rev. G "severance pay" in the amount of $45,000 (the full amount of the third year's salary).*

☞ *Example. Rev. C is called by a church for an indefinite term. After 10 years, Rev. C resigns to accept another position. The church board agrees to pay Rev. C "severance pay" of $20,000.*

☞ *Example. Rev. T accepts a call as a pastor of a local church. After 1 year, she is dismissed and is replaced by a male pastor. Rev. T believes that the church was guilty of sex discrimination. The church and Rev. T enter into a severance agreement in which Rev. T agrees to waive any claims she has against the church under state and federal law in exchange for its agreement to pay her "severance pay" of $40,000 (representing one year's salary).*

☞ *Example. K has served as bookkeeper of her church for 20 years. She is 68 years old. The church board decides that it is time for K to retire so that a younger person can take over her job. When the board learns that K has visited with an attorney, they offer her a severance pay of one year's full salary ($25,000).*

Is severance pay paid by a church taxable income to the recipient? In most cases, the answer is yes. The tax code imposes the income tax on "all income from whatever source derived," unless a specific exclusion applies. The severance pay described in the first and second examples (above) would be taxable under this general rule. There is one "exclusion" that will apply in some cases. Section 104 of the tax code excludes from taxable income "the amount of any damages received (whether by suit or agreement and whether as lump sums or as periodic payments) *on account of personal injuries or sickness.*" What does this language mean? Simply this—severance pay that is intended to settle personal injury claims may be nontaxable. The words "personal injuries" are defined broadly by the IRS and the courts, and include potential or threatened lawsuits based on discrimination and harassment. The severance pay

described in the third and fourth examples (above) *may* be nontaxable based on this section of the tax code.

✎ **Key point: the Tax Court has noted that "payments for terminating and canceling employment contracts are not payments for personal injuries." Matray v. Commissioner, 56 T.C.M. 1107 (1989).**

✎ **Key point: Congress enacted legislation in 1996 clarifying that all punitive damages, whether or not associated with personal injuries, are *included* in taxable income (there is a narrow exception in wrongful death cases if only punitive damages can be awarded under state law).**

The IRS and the courts have addressed the section 104 exclusion of severance pay based on personal injuries in several rulings. Here are a few examples.

☞ *Example. A company asked a female manager to resign because it was not satisfied with her management style. The employee retained an attorney who threatened to sue the company for sex discrimination. The employee's attorney worked out a severance agreement with the company in which the employee agreed to resign and release the company from all legal claims in exchange for a full year's salary plus other benefits. The employee assumed that the continuation of her salary for one year represented "damages received . . . on account of personal injuries" under section 104 of the code and accordingly was not taxable. The Tax Court disagreed, based on the following considerations: (1) the company paid the employee an additional year's salary "to reward her for her past services and to make her severance as amicable as possible"; (2) the severance agreement "contained no express reference to a sex discrimination claim, stating instead that the payment arose from the company's dissatisfaction with the employee's managerial style; (3) the company withheld taxes from the severance payments and issued the employee a W-2 reporting these payments as taxable income; (4) the company continued a number of employee benefits, including health insurance, for an additional year; and (5) the severance agreement was similar to other severance agreements the company executed with other officers who were asked to resign. Based on these considerations the Tax Court concluded that the severance pay that was paid to the former employee did not represent damages payable on account of a sex discrimination or other personal injury claim. Britell v. Commissioner, T.C Memo. 1995-264.*

☞ *Example. Example. An employee was dismissed by a company, and later threatened to sue the company for the emotional distress he had suffered. To avoid a lawsuit, the company entered into a severance agreement with the employee in which the employee released all legal claims* against the company in exchange for its promise to pay him a cash settlement. The agreement stated the company "intends to treat all payments made hereunder as wages for purposes of any withholding obligation the company may have in order to avoid any penalties and interest which might otherwise accrue." The Tax Court ruled that the severance pay was taxable income to the employee and not nontaxable damages payable as a result of personal injuries. The court noted that an employee's belief that he has "certain claims relating to personal injuries . . . does not establish that the [severance] payments were made on account of personal injuries." Further, the court pointed out that the company withheld taxes on the payments, and that such withholding "is a significant factor" in classifying the payments as taxable income. *Nagourney v. Commissioner, 57 T.C.M. 954 (1989).*

☞ **Example.** *Example. A company offered older workers an "early retirement" option. Under this option, older workers signed a severance agreement in which they agreed to resign and to release the company from any age discrimination claims in exchange for a continuation of their salary for one year and continued medical insurance. The IRS ruled that the amounts paid to workers who accepted the early retirement option were not excludable from taxable income as a settlement of a personal injury claim. The IRS based this decision on the following considerations: (1) Section 1.61-2(a)(1) of the income tax regulations specifies that severance pay "is income to the recipient unless excluded by law." (2) "Provisions that exempt income from taxation are to be construed narrowly." (3) "The burden of proof is on the taxpayer to show that the requirements imposed by the Code are met in order to be entitled to an exclusion from [taxable income]." (4) The existence of a severance agreement in which an employee waives any discrimination claims that he or she has against an employer does not by itself establish that amounts payable under the agreement represent nontaxable damages to settle a personal injury claim. The IRS pointed out that the employee "never filed a lawsuit or any other type of claim against [the employer] alleging age discrimination. A payment cannot be characterized as damages for personal injuries where there is no indication that personal injuries actually exist." IRS Letter Ruling 9331007.*

✎ **Key point: the Tax Court has ruled that "damages are not excludable under section 104 if . . . the damages were received upon the prosecution of economic rights arising out of a contract."** Guidry v. Commissioner, 67 T.C.M. 2507 (1994).

Conclusions. Here are some factors, based on the above cases, to assist in deciding whether a severance payment made to a former worker represents taxable compensation or nontaxable damages in settlement of a personal injury claim:

• *Purpose of the payment.* An amount paid to a former employee "to reward her for her past services and to make her severance as amicable as possible" is taxable compensation.

• *Reference to a discrimination claim.* An amount paid to a former employee under a severance agreement that contains no reference to a specific discrimination or other personal injury claim is taxable compensation.

• *Did the church issue a W-2?* If an employer pays a former employee severance pay, and reports the severance pay on a W-2 (or 1099), this is strong evidence that the amount represents taxable compensation.

• *Continuation of employee benefits.* If an employer continues one or more employee benefits (such as health insurance) as part of a severance agreement, this suggests that any amount payable under the agreement represents taxable compensation.

• *Similar to other agreements.* If a severance agreement is similar to other severance agreements an employer entered into with other employees, this suggests that amounts payable under the agreements represent taxable income.

• *Were taxes withheld?* If an employer withholds taxes from amounts paid under a severance agreement, this "is a significant factor" in classifying the payments as taxable income. Of course, this factor will not be relevant in the case of ministers whose wages are not subject to withholding (unless they elect voluntary withholding).

• *What is the payment called?* Referring to a payment as "severance pay" indicates that it is taxable compensation rather than nontaxable damages in settlement of a personal injury claim. Remember, section 1.61-2(a)(1) of the income tax regulations specifies that severance pay "is income to the recipient unless excluded by law."

• *Exclusions are narrowly interpreted.* The Supreme Court has ruled that "provisions that exempt income from taxation are to be narrowly construed." *United States v. Centennial Savings Bank, 111 S. Ct. 1510 (1001).* Any reasonable doubts about the correct classification of a particular payment should be resolved in favor of taxation rather than exclusion. Also remember this—the "burden of proof" is on the one claiming an exclusion.

• *Was severance pay based on salary?* Severance pay based on a former employee's salary (such as one year's salary) are more likely to be viewed as taxable compensation rather than nontaxable damages in settlement of a personal injury claim. As the IRS has noted, "where payments made by an employer to its employees are excludable from the employee's taxable income as damages for personal injury under section 104 of the Code, those payments are not remuneration for services performed by an employee for an employer, and therefore are not considered wages for purposes of the Code." *IRS Letter Ruling 9331007.*

• *An actual personal injury claim must exist.* To be nontaxable, severance pay must represent "damages" received in settlement of a personal injury claim. The income tax regulations defines the term "damages received" as "an amount received (other than workmen's compensation) through prosecution of a legal suit or action based upon tort or tort type rights, or through a settlement agreement entered into in lieu of such prosecution." *Treas. Reg. § 1.104-1(c).* The IRS has noted that this language requires more than a settlement agreement in which a former employee "waives" any discrimination or other personal injury claims he or she may have against an employer. If the employee "never filed a lawsuit or any other type of claim against [the employer] . . . the payment cannot be characterized as damages for personal injuries" since "there is no indication that personal injuries actually exist." *IRS Letter Ruling 9331007.*

✎ **Key point: church treasurers must determine whether severance pay is taxable so that it can be properly reported (on a W-2 and the church's 941 forms). Also, taxes must be withheld from severance pay that is paid to nonminister employees (and ministers who have elected voluntary withholding). Failure to properly report severance pay can result in substantial penalties for both a church and the recipient.**

What about a housing allowance? A related question is whether a church can designate any portion of severance pay as a housing allowance. This question has never been addressed by either the IRS or any court. However, an argument can be made that a church can designate a portion of severance pay as a housing allowance if the severance pay is treated as taxable compensation rather than as damages in settlement of a personal injury claim. If the severance pay represents taxable income, as the IRS will almost certainly insist in most cases, it is because the amount paid represents compensation based on services rendered. Since a housing allowance must be designated out of compensation paid to a minister for services rendered in the exercise of ministry, a reasonable case can be made that a housing allowance can be designated with respect to taxable severance pay.

Of course, a housing allowance can only be designated for ministers. And, the designation of a housing allowance will be of little value if the minister transfers immediately to another church that designates a timely housing allowance. But a designation of a housing allowance will be useful in the case of a minister who is not immediately employed by another church or religious organization. Note that there is no guaranty that this position will be accepted by either the IRS or the courts. All that can be said is that in many cases this position will have a reasonable basis and therefore no penalties will be assessed in the event the position is not allowed in an audit.

Also, note this—housing allowances are not reduced by the portion of a minister's compensation that represents vacation pay, even though the minister ordinarily is not performing services in the exercise of ministry during vacation. The same principle supports the availability of a housing allowance designated out of a minister's severance pay.

✎ **Key point: the Older Workers Benefit Protection Act of 1991, which applies to any employer with 20 or more employees that is engaged in interstate commerce, prohibits employees at least 40 years of age from "waiving" their rights under federal age discrimination law unless the waiver meets several specific requirements, including the following: (1) the waiver is in simple language; (2) the waiver specifically refers to rights arising under the federal Age Discrimination in Employment Act; (3) the employee does not waive rights or claims that may arise after the date the waiver is executed; (4) the employee must receive some benefit for signing the waiver in addition to salary; (5) the individual is advised in writing to consult with an attorney prior to executing the agreement; (6) the individual is given a period of at least 21 days within which to consider the agreement; and (7) the agreement provides that for a period of at least 7 days following the execution of such agreement, the individual may revoke the agreement. This law will not apply to most local churches, since they have fewer than 20 employees. Even churches with 20 or more employees are not subject to these requirements unless they are engaged in interstate commerce.**

18. Trips to the Holy Land

Many churches have presented their minister with an all-expense paid trip to the Holy Land for the minister and the minister's spouse. Ordinarily, such trips are provided in commemoration of some special occasion, such as a birthday or anniversary. In many cases, the value of such a trip is treated as a nontaxable "gift" to the minister. Is this correct? Unfortunately, the answer is no if either or both of the following statements is true:

(1) The trip is provided to honor the minister for his or her faithful services on behalf of the church.

(2) The trip is provided to enhance or enrich the minister's ministry. While a trip to the Holy Land can tangibly benefit one's ministry, such a trip is not a business expense under current law. The tax code provides that "no deduction shall be allowed . . . for expenses for travel as a form of education." *IRC 274(m)(2).* A committee report explaining this rule contains the following observations:

No deduction is allowed for costs of travel that would be deductible only on the ground that the travel itself constitutes a form of education (e.g., where a teacher of French travels to France to maintain general familiarity with the French language and culture, or where a social studies teacher travels to another state to learn about or photograph its people, customs, geography, etc.). . . .

The committee is concerned about deductions claimed for travel as a form of "education." The committee believes that any business purpose served by traveling for general educational purposes, in the absence of a specific need such as engaging in research which can only be performed at a particular facility, is at most indirect and insubstantial. By contrast, travel as a form of education may provide substantial personal benefits by permitting some individuals in particular professions to deduct the cost of a vacation, while most individuals must pay for vacation trips out of after-tax dollars, no matter how educationally stimulating the travel may be. Accordingly, the committee bill disallows deductions for travel that can be claimed only on the ground that the travel itself is "educational", but permits deductions for travel that is a necessary adjunct to engaging in an activity that gives rise to a business deduction relating to education.

As a result, the church's payment of the cost of such a trip is treated as the payment of personal "vacation" expenses, and the full amount must be included on the minister's W-2 or 1099. This includes transportation, meals, and lodging. It also includes all of the travel costs of the minister's spouse (and children) if these are paid by the church.

There are two very limited exceptions to the general rule summarized above.

• *Short-term missions trips.* If a church sends a minister to the Holy Land (or any other foreign country) for the sole purpose of engaging in religious activities, then the church's payment of the documented expenses incurred by the minister may be nontaxable as an accountable reimbursement of business expenses. This exception will be interpreted very narrowly, and the IRS will scrutinize such cases for evidence of abuse. A two-week vacation cannot be turned into a business trip because of a couple of speaking engagements. On the other hand, if a church sends a minister on a short-term missions trip to a foreign country, and the minister performs several religious services or engages in evangelistic activities or teaching at a seminary, then a reasonable basis exists for treating the trip as having a legitimate business purpose. In general, any element of personal pleasure (vacation, sight-seeing, etc.) must represent less than 25% of the total trip time.

• *Study at a foreign university.* If a minister travels to a university in a foreign country for an educational course that is reasonably necessary for the enhancement of his or her duties, then a church's reimbursement of the costs of such a trip may constitute a nontaxable reimbursement of business expenses if adequate substantiation is provided.

✎ **Key point: the IRS has ruled that the value of a free trip to a foreign country provided by a travel agency to a person who organizes a tour and solicits participants is taxable income.** *Revenue Ruling 64-154.*

19. Payment of personal expenses

Churches sometimes pay some of the personal expenses of their minister or other church employee. Such payments ordinarily represent taxable income to the minister.

✎ **Key point: the IRS can impose "intermediate sanctions" (an excise tax) against an officer or director of a church or other charity, and in some cases against board members individually, if an officer or director is paid an excessive amount of compensation. The law clarifies that the payment of personal expenses of an officer or director can be treated as compensation if it is clear that the employer intended the payments as compensation for services.**

20. Frequent flier miles

Do ministers and other church employees receive taxable income if they earn frequent flier miles for out-of-town business travel that they are not required to refund to the church? This is a controversial question that unfortunately has not been answered. There are four developments to note:

• *Charley v. Commissioner, T.C. Memo. 1993-558 (1993).* In this 1993 decision, the Tax Court ruled that frequent flier miles a company president earned while flying on company business were taxable income to him since he was not required to refund them to the company. The court concluded that "gross income includes all income from whatever source derived whether realized in the form of money, property, or services, unless otherwise excluded by law. . . . There is no indication in the record that [the president] could not use the accumulated travel credits for personal purposes nor, in fact, redeem the credits for cash on demand. There is no showing that [the company] had any rights, interest, or control over petitioners' personal travel account. . . . [T]he fact remains that [the president] was wealthier after the transaction than before. In such circumstances, the accretion of wealth is the receipt of income." The court upheld the assessment by the IRS of a negligence penalty against the president. Note that this ruling was a "memorandum" decision of the Tax Court, meaning that it was the opinion of only one judge. Such rulings have far less value as legal precedent than a "regular" decision by the entire Tax Court. In fact, the IRS routinely ignores memorandum decisions if it disagrees with the result.

• *IRS Letter Ruling 9547001.* In this private ruling in 1995, the IRS concluded that a company's travel policy of reimbursing employees' business air travel, but allowing employees to retain frequent flier miles earned as a result of such travel, was a "nonaccountable plan" since employees were not required to return amounts received in excess of expense reimbursements. As a result, the full amount of all airfare reimbursements had to be reported on the employees' W-2 forms as taxable income. Employees could then claim an employee business expense deduction on Schedule A (Form 1040) if they itemized their deductions, to the extent such expenses exceeded 2% of adjusted gross income.

• *IRS announcement.* IRS Letter Ruling 9547001 (summarized above), while not official precedent for anyone other than the company that requested it, unleashed a tidal wave of protest. The IRS announced later in 1995 that it was reconsidering the whole issue of the tax treatment of frequent flier miles employees are allowed to retain while on business travel. To date, no further clarification has been issued by the IRS.

• *Proposed legislation.* In the meantime, legislation has been introduced in Congress that would bar the IRS from taxing frequent flier miles. Any developments will be addressed in future editions of this tax guide.

21. Sabbatical pay

A sabbatical is an extended leave of absence during which a minister is free to pursue writing, education, or other activities. Churches that provide a minister with a sabbatical usually continue the minister's compensation in whole or in part during his or her absence. Sabbatical pay almost always represents taxable income to the minister. One exception would be sabbatical pay that could properly be characterized as a scholarship. Few sabbaticals will meet this test, as the following example illustrates.

☞ *Example. A professor was given a year off to pursue studies overseas. He was paid $27,000 during his sabbatical, and he treated this entire amount as a tax-free scholarship. The IRS ruled that the sabbatical income represented taxable income, and the Tax Court agreed The court noted that scholarships are nontaxable only if certain conditions are met. The recipient must be "a candidate for a degree at an educational organization" and the scholarship must be used for qualified tuition. The court noted that the professor's sabbatical income was not a nontaxable scholarship since he was not a candidate for a degree and failed to prove that he used any portion of the income for qualified tuition expenses. This ruling will be useful to church treasurers in evaluating the tax status of sabbatical income provided to pastors or other staff members. Kant v. Commissioner, T.C. Memo. 1997-217.*

B. Fees for Performing Marriages, Funerals, and Baptisms

Ministers often receive fees directly from church members for performing personal services such as marriages, funerals, or baptisms. Are these fees, which are paid directly from members to a minister, taxable income to the minister? The answer is yes. The income tax regulations specify that "marriage fees and other contributions received by a clergyman for services" are income to the minister. *Treas. Reg. 1.61-2(a)(1).* Note, however, that such fees ordinarily will be self-employment earnings to a minister if received directly from members, and not employee wages. As a result, they must be reported on a Schedule C (explained fully in Chapter 7).

C. Interest and Dividend Income

In general, any interest that you receive or that is credited to your account and can be withdrawn is taxable income. You do not need to have physical possession of it. Exceptions include interest you earn on (1) an IRA, Keogh account, or tax deferred annuity (until you begin making withdrawals), and (2) interest on obligations of a state or local government. Interest you receive in 1997 from bank accounts, loans which you make to others, and most other sources is taxable. The following are some other common sources of taxable interest: (1) dividends that are actually interest (e.g., distributions from credit unions and savings and loans); (2) interest paid at fixed intervals of one year or less on a money market or savings certificate (more complex rules apply if interest is deferred for more than one year); (3) the fair market value of gifts or services you receive for opening or making long-term deposits in savings instruments; (4) interest on treasury bills, bonds, and notes issued by any agency or instrumentality of the United States government (such interest is exempt from all state and local income taxes); (5) interest received on a tax refund; and (6) accrued interest on bonds that you sell between interest payment dates.

You can earn interest on U.S. savings bonds in one of two ways. On some bonds, interest is paid at stated intervals by interest checks or coupons. Other bonds are issued on a discount basis and the interest is the increase in their value over stated periods of time. Series HH bonds are issued at face value. Interest is paid twice each year by check. You must report interest on these bonds as income in the year you receive it. Series EE bonds are issued at a discount (i.e., your purchase price is *less* than the face amount of the bond). Only the face amount is payable at maturity. The difference between the purchase price and the redemption value is taxable interest. If you own Series EE bonds, you may defer reporting the interest until the earlier of the year you cash the bonds or the year in which they mature, or you may choose to report the increase in redemption value as interest in each year.

Taxable interest ordinarily is reported on Form 1040, line 8a. If your interest income is more than $400 in 1997, you must attach a Schedule B to your return and list each payer's name and the amount received from each. Taxpayers also must report nontaxable interest (from state or local governments) on line 8b (for informational purposes only).

Dividends are distributions of money, stock, or other property paid to you by a corporation. Most distributions that you receive are paid in cash. However, you may receive additional stock or other property. You may receive ordinary dividends, capital gain distributions, or nontaxable distributions. Ordinary dividends (taxable dividends) are the most common type of distribution from a corporation. They are paid out of the earnings and profits of a corporation and are ordinary income to you. Any dividend you receive is an ordinary dividend unless the paying corporation tells you otherwise. These dividends are reported on line 9 of Form 1040, and on Schedule B if over $400.

Capital gain distributions are paid by *mutual funds* from their net realized long-term capital gains. The mutual fund statement will tell you the amount you are to report as a capital gain distribution. These gains are not reported as dividends, but rather as capital gains. Report them on line 7 of Schedule B if over $400, and on Schedule D. If you do not use Schedule D for any other gains or losses, do not use it. Instead, show your capital gains distributions on line 14 of Form 1040.

✎ **Key point: for a discussion of the tax on capital gains, see section H of this chapter.**

A nontaxable distribution is a distribution that is not paid out of the earnings and profits of a corporation. It is a return of your investment in the stock of the company. These distributions are not treated as ordinary income or capital gains. Similarly, stock dividends and stock rights ordinarily are not taxable to you.

Be sure that each payer of interest income has your correct social security number. Otherwise, the payer may withhold a portion of the interest (so-called "backup withholding") and you may be subject to penalties.

D. Rental Income and Expenses

Ministers who accept a new position in another community occasionally retain ownership of their former residence, especially if they plan to return eventually to the previous location. The former residence is often rented. Other ministers acquire residential properties for investment purposes. In either case, ministers must be familiar with the basic rules that apply to rental income and expenses.

You generally must include in your gross income all amounts you receive as rent. In addition to normal rent payments, there are other amounts that may be considered rental income. For example, advance rental payments that you receive ordinarily must be reported as income in the year received (without reduction for expected expenses). Other examples include expenses paid by the tenant (you may be able to deduct the expenses), and payments made by a tenant to cancel a lease.

There are several expenses that you may deduct in computing you net rental income, including repairs (but not improvements, which must be depreciated), advertising, janitor services, utilities, fire and liability insurance (if you pay premiums for more than one year in advance, you must allocate this expense to the years the insurance is in effect), property taxes, mortgage interest, and commissions for the collection of rent.

You recover the cost you paid for a building that you use for rental purposes by taking deductions for *depreciation*. In effect, annual depreciation expenses are a means of spreading the cost of the building over its useful life. Depreciation reduces your cost or basis for figuring gain or loss on a later sale or exchange. You should claim the correct amount of depreciation each year. If you did not deduct depreciation in earlier years, you may not deduct the unclaimed depreciation in the current or any later tax year (though you may be able to claim the depreciation retroactively on amended tax returns). The total of all your yearly depreciation deductions cannot be more than your cost (or other basis) of the rental property.

Before figuring your depreciation, you must know: (1) what your basis in the property is; (2) when the property was placed in service; and (3) which method of depreciation you are permitted to use. Ordinarily, your basis in rental property is your cost plus any permanent improvements and less any depreciation that you have claimed (or could have claimed). Rental property is placed in service when it is ready and available for use.

Most property that you place in service after 1980 but before 1987 is "recovery property." In general, you figure your depreciation deductions for recovery property under the "accelerated cost recovery system" (ACRS). However, if you placed your property in service prior to 1981, you must continue to use the same method of figuring depreciation that you used in the past. You cannot use ACRS. In addition, ACRS is not available for property that you used for personal purposes before 1981 and that you later converted to rental property. Property that cannot be depreciated using ACRS must be depreciated under another method. The most common alternative is the "straight line" method. Under this method, your annual depreciation deduction is computed by dividing the basis of the property (less its salvage value) by the useful life of the property. Various "accelerated" depreciation methods exist which enable the taxpayer to claim larger depreciation deductions in the earlier years the property is rented.

☞ *Example. Rev. S purchased a home in 1976 and used it as his personal residence until 1984, when he moved and began renting it. Rev. S cannot use ACRS to figure depreciation deductions on the house. He may use the straight line method, or one of the accelerated depreciation methods.*

Under ACRS, rental property that you place in service after 1980 is depreciated over a period of 10, 15, 18, or 19 years. The 10 year rule applies to rented mobile homes; the 15 year rule applies to rental property placed in service before March 16, 1984; the 18 year rule applies to rental property placed in service after March 15, 1984, and before May 9, 1985; and the 19 year rule applies to rental property placed in service after May 9, 1985. The annual depreciation deduction under ACRS is figured by multiplying your unadjusted basis in the property by a percentage set forth in IRS Publication 534. An alternate ACRS method exists that in some cases may be simpler to apply (see Publication 534 for details).

The Tax Reform Act of 1986 introduced a "modified accelerated cost recovery system" (MACRS) which applies to most rental properties placed in service in or after 1987. If you began renting a home prior to 1987, continue using the same method of depreciation that you have used in the past. MACRS may be used by clergy for a home used as a personal residence prior to 1987 that was converted into a rental property after 1986. Residential rental property that you place in service after 1986 is depreciated over a 27.5 year period using the straight line method of depreciation (i.e., cost of the property less salvage value divided by its recovery period). Annual depreciation deductions are constant throughout the entire recovery period under the straight line method. A "mid-month" convention is employed, meaning that the property is deemed to be placed in service during the middle of the month (regardless of the actual date it was placed in service). Accordingly, one-half month's depreciation is allowed for the month the property is placed in service and for the month the property is disposed of during the recovery period. Nonresidential rental property (e.g., a commercial office building) placed in service after 1986 is depreciated over a 31.5 year recovery period using the straight line method and a mid-month convention (this increases to 39 years with respect to property placed in service on or after May 13, 1993). The accelerated depreciation allowable under ACRS is not available to rental properties placed in service after 1986 (you must use straight line depreciation), and the recovery periods are greatly increased.

In summary, if you began renting a home after 1980 and before 1987, continue to depreciate it using the ACRS method. If you began renting the home after 1986, use MACRS. This is so whether you purchased the home after 1986 for rental purposes, or converted a personal residence to rental use after 1986. If you began renting the home before 1981, continue using the same method of depreciation that you used in the past.

The post-1986 depreciation rules will result in significantly lower annual depreciation deductions for most rental properties. This is one way Congress is attempting to offset the effect of the dramatically reduced individual income tax rates that took effect in 1987.

Where you report rental income and expenses, including depreciation, depends on whether you provide certain services to your tenant. If you rent out a building, room, or apartment, and provide only heat, light, and trash collection, you normally report your rental income and expenses in Part 1 of Schedule E (Form 1040). If you provide additional services that are primarily for your tenant's convenience, such as regular cleaning or maid service, you report your rental income and expenses on Schedule C (Form 1040). If you are claiming depreciation on property you placed in service after 1980, you must show all the depreciation you are claiming on Form 4562.

Report rental income in the year you actually or constructively receive it. If you dispose of depreciable rental property at a profit, you will have to pay taxes on the gain (see IRS Publication 544).

More complex rules apply if you are renting out a portion of property that you use as a residence, or if you are renting out a vacation home.

Generally, losses from most "passive activities" can only be used to offset income from passive activities and not from any other form of income. Passive activities include rental activities regardless of whether the taxpayer materially or actively participates in the rental activity. However, beginning in 1994, certain taxpayers engaged in "real property trades or businesses" can claim losses from rental real estate as a deduction from nonpassive income (such as wages). Strict eligibility requirements apply. If you think this exception applies to you, be sure to consult with a local CPA or tax attorney.

E. Retirement Plans, Pensions, and Annuities

In general, if you did not pay part of the cost of your employee pension or annuity, or your employer did not withhold part of the cost of the contract from your pay while you worked, the amounts you receive each year are fully taxable and must be reported on your income tax return (Form 1040, line 16a). There is an exception to this rule—a portion of your retirement income may be excludable from income (for income tax purposes) if it is designated as a housing allowance by a church or denominational pension plan (see chapter 10 for details), and it is used by you to pay for housing-related expenses.

If both you and your employer paid part of the cost of your pension or annuity, you will not pay tax on the part of the pension or annuity you receive that represents a return of your cost. Any additional amount you receive will be taxable. Taxation of distributions under IRAs, Keogh plans, SEPs, and deferred compensation arrangements is discussed in chapter 10.

Generally, if you retire on disability, you must report your pension or annuity as income. However, you may be eligible to claim a credit for a portion of your disability payments. The credit is computed on Schedule R and reported on line 41 of Form 1040.

F. Social Security Benefits

✎ **Key point: clergy who are retired and who earn more than a specified amount of income may be taxed on some of their social security benefits**

❖ **New in 1997. Some higher-income retired taxpayers will begin paying taxes on a larger share of their social security benefits in 1997 than in prior years.**

If you received social security benefits other than supplemental security income benefits (SSI) in 1997, part of the amount you received may be taxable. If you received social security benefits during 1997, you will receive (before January 31, 1998) Form SSA-1099 showing the amount of benefits you received. Enclosed with the SSA-1099 will be IRS Notice 703. This notice contains a worksheet you can use to help determine if any of your benefits are taxable.

In determining whether or not your social security benefits received in 1997 are taxable, consider the following two rules.

1. In general, if the only income you received during 1997 was your social security benefits, your benefits probably will not be taxable and you probably will not have to file a return.

2. If you received other income in addition to social security benefits in 1997, your benefits generally will not be taxable unless your income is over a certain amount. Note the following:

• *Provisional income (adjusted gross income plus tax-exempt interest and some other forms of tax-exempt income plus half of the taxpayer's social security benefits) received during the year is less than $25,000 if you are single or $32,000 if you are married and file a joint return.* Under these circumstances, social security benefits ordinarily are not taxable.

• *Provisional income (defined above) received during the year is more than $25,000 but less than $34,000 if you are single or more than $32,000 but less than $44,000 if you are married and file a joint return.* Some of your social security benefits will be taxable. You are taxed on the lesser of (1) half of your social security benefits, or (2) half of the amount by which your provisional income exceeds $25,000 (if you are single) or $32,000 (if you are married and file jointly).

• *Provisional income (defined above) received during the year is more than $34,000 if you are single or more than $44,000 if you are married and file a joint return.* You must include in taxable income the *lesser* of (1) 85% of your social security benefits, or (2) the sum of 85% of the amount by which your provisional income (defined above) exceeds the applicable threshold amount ($34,000 if you are single, $44,000 if you are married filing jointly) plus the *lesser* of (a) the amount of benefits that would be taxed under pre-1994 law, or (b) $4,500 (if single) or $6,000 (married filing jointly).

How's that for simplicity! Maybe a few examples will help.

☞ **Example.** *Rev. E and his spouse are both over age 65 and file a joint return for 1997. They both received social security benefits during 1997. In January 1998, they received an SSA-1099 form showing that net social security benefits of $6,600 were received by Rev. E and $3,400 by his spouse in 1997 (for a total of $10,000). Rev. E and his spouse had adjusted gross income of $25,000 in 1997, plus tax-exempt interest of*

$1,000. *The benefits received by the Rev. E and his spouse are not taxable in 1997, since their provisional income (adjusted gross income plus tax-exempt interest and half of all social security benefits received) is less than $32,000.*

☞ **Example.** *Same facts as the previous example, except that Rev. E and his spouse had adjusted gross income of $35,000 in 1997. Under these facts, a portion of the social security benefits received by Rev. E and his spouse will be taxable, since their provisional income ($36,000) plus half of their social security benefits ($5,000) exceeds $32,000. Half of the excess (or $4,500) will be taxable.*

☞ **Example.** *Same facts as the previous example, except that Rev. E and his spouse had adjusted gross income of $50,000 in 1997. Under these facts, a portion of the social security benefits received by Rev. E and his spouse will be taxable, since their provisional income ($51,000) plus half of their social security benefits ($5,000) exceeds $44,000. The taxable amount is the lesser of (1) 85% of social security benefits (85% of $10,000 is $8,500), or (2) the sum of 85% of the amount by which provisional income exceeds the applicable threshold amount of $44,000 plus the lesser of (a) the amount of benefits that would be taxed under pre-1994 law, or (b) $6,000 (since Rev. E and his spouse are married filing jointly). This second limitation is harder to calculate. First, you take the amount by which provisional income ($51,000) exceeds $44,000— which is $7,000. You then multiply this amount times 85% to get $5,950, and then you add the lesser of the amount of benefits that would be taxable under pre-1994 law (half of benefits would be taxed, or $5,000), or $6,000—resulting in a total of $10,950. Since the first limitation ($8,500) is lower than the second limitation ($10,950), you use the first number. This means that $8,500 of social security benefits for 1997 will be taxable.*

G. Other Income

Section 61 of the Code defines gross income as "all income from whatever source derived." This is an expansive definition that results in the inclusion of several items not specifically itemized on lines 7-22 of Form 1040. Accordingly, line 21 requests that "other income" be reported. Several different kinds of income are reported on line 21. Some of the more common examples include

• a canceled debt, or a debt paid for you by another person (unless the person who canceled or paid your debt intended it to be a gift)

• the fair market value of a free tour you receive from a travel agency for organizing a group of tourists (in some cases this may be reported on Schedule C)

• most prizes and awards

- the amount by which your church-designated housing or parsonage allowance exceeds your actual expenses in owning or maintaining a home (assuming that your W-2 or 1099 form was reduced by the entire amount of the church-designated allowance).

H. Gains and Losses

Income ordinarily includes gains you realize from the sale or exchange of property. This section will summarize the rules that apply to the sale or exchange of investment property and your principal residence.

1. Sale of investment property

Sales and exchanges of assets generally result in taxable gains or deductible losses, although some exchanges of property are nontaxable. A sale is a transfer of property for money only or for a mortgage, note, or some other promise to pay money. An exchange (sometimes referred to as a trade) is a transfer of property for other property or services, and may be taxed in the same way as a sale. A transaction is not an exchange, ordinarily, when you voluntarily sell property for cash and immediately buy similar property to replace it. Such a sale and purchase are two separate transactions.

You figure your gain or loss on a sale or exchange of property by comparing the amount you realize with the adjusted basis of the property. Gain is the amount you realize from a sale or exchange minus the adjusted basis of the property you transfer. Loss is the adjusted basis of the property minus the amount you realize. The adjusted basis of property is your original cost plus such items as purchase commissions, legal fees, and improvements, and less accumulated depreciation. The amount you realize from a sale or exchange is the total of all money you receive plus the fair market value of all property or services you receive. If property you sell or exchange is subject to an indebtedness that the buyer assumes or pays off, then the amount of the debt must be included in the amount you realize from the sale or exchange. If you exchange properties and in addition pay cash, the amount you realize is the fair market value of the property you receive. However, you determine your gain or loss by subtracting the cash you paid and the adjusted basis of the property you exchanged.

Certain exchanges are nontaxable, meaning that any gain from the exchange is not taxed and any loss cannot be deducted. The most common types of nontaxable exchanges are (1) the exchange of property for the same kind of property ("like-kind" exchanges); (2) transfers of property between spouses, or to a former spouse if incident to a divorce; (3) exchanges of certain issues of U.S. Treasury obligations for certain other issues; (4) exchanges of life insurance contracts for other life insurance contracts or for an annuity contract; (5) exchanges of stock for other stock of the same company.

Special rules apply to the sale or exchange of property between "related persons." A loss on the sale or exchange of property is not deductible if the transaction is directly or indirectly between you and any of the following "related parties": (1) members of your family; (2) a corporation in which you own directly or indirectly more than 50% in value of the outstanding stock; or (3) an exempt charitable organization that is controlled in any manner, directly or indirectly, by you or any member of your family.

Capital gains tax rate reduction. Prior to 1997 the "capital gain" realized on the sale of a "capital asset" was taxed at ordinary income tax rates, except that individuals were subject to a maximum rate of 28 percent on the net capital gain. A capital asset generally means any property, with some exceptions (including depreciable real estate used in a taxpayer's trade or business, and property held for sale to customers). Common examples include real personal residences and investments. Congress enacted legislation in 1997 that modified the taxation of capital gains as follows:

- *Reduction in rate of tax.* The maximum rate of tax on net capital gain of individuals is reduced from 28 percent to 20 percent. This means that taxpayers who are in the 28 percent (or higher) income tax bracket will pay a capital gains tax of 20 percent. Lower-income taxpayers whose ordinary income is taxed at the 15 percent rate will pay a capital gains tax of 10 percent.

✎ **Key point: the lower capital gains tax rates apply to sales and exchanges of capital assets after July 28, 1997. For the lower tax rates to apply, the capital asset must have been held by the taxpayer for more than 18 months.**

✎ **Key point: for capital assets held for more than 1 year but not more than 18 months, the maximum capital gains tax rate is 28 percent.**

✎ **Key point: the capital gains rate on depreciable real estate used in a taxpayer's trade or business is reduced to 25 percent.**

- *Additional tax rate reduction in 2001.* Beginning in the year 2001, the maximum capital gains rates for assets which are held for more than 5 years are 18 percent (for persons in the 28 percent or higher ordinary income tax bracket) and 8 percent (for persons in the 15 percent ordinary income tax bracket). The 18 percent rate applies only to assets that are acquired on or after January 1, 2001.

☞ *Example. Rev. C is in the 28 percent ordinary income tax bracket. Rev. C sells securities in December of 1997 resulting in a capital gain of $10,000. The securities were purchased in 1995. The capital gains will be taxed at 28 percent ($2,800) since they were not held for more than 18 months beginning after July 28, 1997.*

☞ *Example. Same facts as the previous example, except that Rev. C waits until March of 1999 to sell the securities. If the gain remains $10,000, it will be taxed at the lower 20 percent rate ($2,000) since the securities were held for more than 18 months after July 28, 1997. If Rev. C waits until the year 2006 to sell the securities, the lower 18 percent tax rate will apply. Of course, by waiting for the lower capital gains tax rates to take effect, Rev. C assumes the risk that the value of the securities will decrease.*

✎ **Key point: securities with growth potential as opposed to high income (dividends and interest) are favored by the lower capital gains tax rates.**

2. Selling your home

Sales prior to May 7, 1997. There were two rules that permitted the deferral or exclusion of gain from the sale of a principal residence:

1. No gain was recognized on the sale of a "principal residence" if (1) a new residence was purchased that was at least equal in cost to the sales price of the old residence, and (2) the new residence was used as a principal residence of the taxpayer at some point within a "replacement period" that began two years prior to the sale of the old residence and ended two years after the sale.

2. A taxpayer could exclude on a one-time basis up to $125,000 of gain from the sale of a principal residence if the taxpayer (1) had attained age 55 before the sale, and (2) owned the property and used it as a principal residence for 3 or more of the 5 years preceding the sale.

Sales after May 6, 1997. The Taxpayer Relief Act eliminates these rules for sales of principal residences occurring after May 6, 1997. The new rules are much more liberal, and will greatly benefit many taxpayers. Here is breakdown of the new rules:

• *Higher nontaxable amounts.* Most importantly, after May 6, 1997 a married couple (who file a joint return) can exclude up to *$500,000* of gain from the sale or exchange of a principal residence. Single taxpayers can exclude up to $250,000.

• *Holding period.* To qualify for the full exclusion, a taxpayer must have owned and occupied the residence as a principal residence for at least 2 of the 5 years prior to the date of sale or exchange. But, unlike the former law, the tax benefit may not be lost completely if this "holding period" is not satisfied. Taxpayers who sell a home without meeting this requirement get a partial benefit if they had to sell their home on account of a change of place of employment, health, or other unforeseen circumstances. The partial benefit is the fraction of $500,000 (or $250,000 for single taxpayers) equal to the fraction of 2 years that the home was owned and occupied as a principal residence.

A special rule applies to persons who become physically or mentally incapable of self-care and who move into a licensed facility (including a nursing home). If they owned and occupied a residence for at least 1 year before moving into such a facility, the 2-year "holding period" rule will not apply to them.

• *Multiple sales allowed.* The old rule that permitted only one exclusion of up to $125,000 for taxpayers at least 55 years of age is out the window. Taxpayers can claim the $500,000 exclusion every two years, and there is no minimum age requirement!

• *Remarriages.* Assume that John is a single taxpayer who has never excluded gain from the sale of a home under the new rules. He marries Jane, who has used the exclusion within 2 years prior to their marriage. John can still claim up to a $250,000 exclusion of gain from the sale of residence. Once two years have passed since the last exclusion was allowed to either of them, they can exclude up to $500,000 of gain on a joint return.

☞ *Example. Rev. T is 60 years old, and is considering moving into a smaller and less expensive home. The new law permits Rev. T to do so without being concerned about whether this is the right time to exercise the once in a lifetime exclusion of up to $125,000 in gains from the sale of a residence. The gains Rev. T realizes from selling his current home and buying a less expensive home will be nontaxable gain under the new law—assuming that he lived in the old home for at least 2 years. And, if he later decides to relocate to another home (and at least 2 years have elapsed), he again can exclude the gain from tax.*

☞ *Example. Rev. R accepts a position at a church and purchases a new residence. One year later she accepts a position in another church in another state. She sells her former home and purchases a less expensive home resulting in a capital gain of $50,000. Since Rev. R owned and occupied her former home for less than 2 years on account of a change in employment location, she is eligible for a partial exclusion in capital gains. The exclusion is the same fraction as the fraction of 2 years that she owned and occupied her former home. Since she owned and occupied the former home for 1 year, the fraction is one-half. This means that she will pay capital gains tax on only half of her $50,000 gain.*

☞ *Example. Rev. G is a widower. In December of 1997 he sells his home and purchases a less expensive home. He excludes the capital gains from tax under the new rules. He remarries in 1998, and his wife sells her home after the marriage. She has never excluded gain from the sale of a residence under the new rules. They can claim an exclusion of up to $250,000 on their 1998 joint tax return.*

✎ **Key point: the new law does not "force" taxpayers to replace a current residence with a residence of equal or greater cost in order to avoid capital gains tax**

❖ **New in 1997.** Prior to 1997, persons who closed real estate transactions were required to file an information return (Form 1099S) with the IRS. This return reported the details of the transaction, and was designed to identify persons who owed capital gains tax. Congress enacted legislation in 1997 exempting sales of personal residences with a gross sales price of $500,000 or less ($250,000 or less for single taxpayers) from this reporting requirement, beginning after May 6, 1997. The purpose of this change is to relieve taxpayers of the reporting requirement on transactions that will be exempt from the capital gains tax under new rules that took effect after May 6, 1997. To qualify for this exemption, a home seller must provide the buyer with written assurance that no capital gain tax will be payable on the transaction. The IRS will issue further guidance on this requirement.

❖ **New in 1998.** Prior to 1998 a 10 percent "additional tax" applies to distributions from an IRA prior to age 59 and 1/2. Congress enacted legislation in 1997 that permits taxpayers to withdraw up to $10,000 from their IRA prior to age 59 and 1/2 for "first-time homebuyer expenses" without triggering the 10 percent penalty. The expenses must be incurred to buy or build a principal residence for yourself, or a child or grandchild. This new rule takes effect in 1998.

I. Splitting Income Between Spouses

Some ministers have attempted to "split" their church income with their spouse. This ordinarily is done to qualify the spouse for IRA (or pension) contributions, or to soften the impact of the social security "annual earnings test" (which reduces social security benefits to retired workers under 70 years of age who earn more than an amount prescribed by law). Do such arrangements work? That was the question addressed by the Tax Court in an important ruling. *Shelley v. Commissioner, T.C. Memo. 1994-432 (1994).* Rev. Shelley attempted to shift some of his church income to his wife so that she could make an annual IRA contribution. He also claimed his wife's "income" as a business expense deduction on his tax return. He explained that his wife performed a variety of services, including visiting members of the congregation who were in the hospital or unable to leave their homes, and assisting with weddings and funerals. Rev. Shelley acknowledged that his wife did not receive a paycheck, but simply had access to the couple's joint checking account. Mrs. Shelley was not employed elsewhere during the years in issue.

✎ **Key point: taxpayers have attempted to shift income to a spouse in 2 ways: (1) the tax-** payer pays a "salary," out of his or her own income, to a spouse; or (2) the taxpayer persuades the employer to pay a portion of his or her income to a spouse.

The IRS insisted that Rev. Shelley's "employment" of his wife was a "ruse" designed to generate compensation so that contributions to her IRA would be deductible. The IRS ruled that Mrs. Shelley's wages should be removed from the couple's joint tax return, and the deductions claimed for wages paid should not be allowed because Rev. Shelley failed to establish that an employment relationship existed between himself and his wife. Accordingly, the IRS concluded that Mrs. Shelley was not entitled to any IRA deductions and that the couple owed "excise taxes" for the "excess contributions" made to Mrs. Shelley's IRA.

The Tax Court noted that whether Mrs. Shelley was entitled to deduct IRA contributions "depends on whether she was employed and received wages during the years in issue." The Court continued:

Section 162 [of the Code] allows the deduction of "a reasonable allowance for salaries or other compensation for personal services actually rendered." Compensation is deductible only if it is: (1) reasonable in amount, (2) for services actually rendered, and (3) paid or incurred. When there is a family relationship, the facts require close scrutiny to determine whether there was in fact a bona fide employer-employee relationship or whether the payments were made on account of the family relationship.

We find that [Rev. Shelley has] failed to substantiate that wages were actually paid to Mrs. Shelley or that a bona fide employer-employee relationship existed. [He] did not issue Mrs. Shelley a paycheck, nor did he document any of the services she performed. [He] was unable to offer any explanation for how Mrs. Shelley's salary was determined, and there was no employment contract between [him] and Mrs. Shelley. [He] did not withhold income taxes from the alleged wages paid to his wife as required by [law] nor did he file employment tax returns (Forms 941). While we do not doubt that Mrs. Shelley contributed to church activities, there is little indication that this was done in the context of a employer-employee relationship. [Rev. Shelley's] testimony strongly suggested that the deductibility of Mrs. Shelley's IRA contributions was one of the principal reasons he employed her. [He] testified that he stopped employing her when she began working at Florida A & M University (FAMU) in 1990. He did not, however, hire anyone to replace her. Similarly, there is no indication that once employed at FAMU, Mrs. Shelley stopped performing the services for the church that she previously had performed. [Rev. Shelley has] failed to establish that the alleged wages were actually paid, that any employment contract existed, or that Mrs. Shelley was treated as an employee. Therefore, we sustain [the IRS position] on this issue.

The Tax Court concluded that the Shelley's improperly claimed an excess contribution to Mrs. Shelley's IRA, and that they were subject to the 6% excise tax on such contributions. It did concede that the Shelley's maximum allowable IRA contributions for the years under examination was $2,250 per year (the amount allowed for a married taxpayer whose spouse earns no income).

✎ **Key point:** many ministers have attempted to shift their church income to a spouse in order to achieve a tax benefit. These benefits include (1) rendering the spouse fully eligible for an IRA contribution; (2) reducing the impact on the minister of the "annual earnings test" that reduces the social security benefits of individuals between 62 and 70 years of age who earn more than specified amounts of annual income; (3) lower tax rates. Income shifting often does not work, because there is no "economic reality" to the arrangement. Ministers who have engaged in income shifting, or who are considering doing so, should carefully evaluate their circumstances in light of this ruling.

Conclusion. Ministers occasionally attempt to "shift" income to a spouse. This case illustrates one reason—to obtain a full $2,000 IRA contribution for the spouse. Another common reason is to divert income from the minister in order to avoid the annual social security earnings test. The courts have ruled consistently that the Social Security Administration may disregard "fictitious arrangements" among family members. As the Tax Court noted in the *Shelley* case, there must in fact be an employment relationship. In making this decision, the Court referred to several factors, which are summarized below:

Factors indicating an employment relationship:

The spouse performed meaningful services, including visiting members of the congregation who were in the hospital or unable to leave their homes, and assisting with weddings and funerals.

Factors indicating no employment relationship existed:

The spouse did not receive a paycheck, but rather had access to a joint bank account in the names of herself and her husband.

The spouse was not employed elsewhere.

The spouse's "compensation" was designed to provide a tax benefit (an IRA contribution), and lacked any economic reality.

The husband did not issue his wife a paycheck.

The husband did not document any of the services his spouse performed.

The husband could not explain how his wife's "salary" was determined.

There was no employment contract between the husband and his wife.

The husband did not withhold income taxes from the alleged wages paid to his wife.

The husband did not file employment tax returns (Forms 941).

While the spouse clearly performed services on behalf of the church, there was no evidence that these services were performed in the context of a employer-employee relationship.

The spouse's "salary" was discontinued when she obtained secular employment, though she continued to perform the same kinds of services on behalf of the church as she had done before.

The husband did not hire anyone to replace his wife when she accepted secular employment.

There was no evidence that the wife stopped performing the services for the church that she previously had performed.

There was no evidence that wages were actually paid to the spouse, or that any employment contract existed, or that the spouse was treated as an employee.

This aspect of the court's decision will be relevant to those ministers who seek to divert a portion of their church income to a spouse in order to achieve one or more of the benefits summarized above.

The courts generally have been skeptical of attempts by taxpayers to shift income to a spouse. Here is an excerpt from a typical ruling:

> Here the husband was in a position to control the business. His wife knew nothing about the duties of president of the company. The husband came into the office, he says to pay his own bills. But he also met with the company accountants. After he reached 70 years of age he admits he returned to work . . . . At that time he was exempted by regulation from any work deductions to his retirement benefits. *Both he and his wife admitted that his wife performed the same services both before and after she began to receive a salary.* She said she had drawn no salary prior to August 1977 so that her husband's social security contributions would be higher, enabling him to receive higher benefits. . . . *When the husband's salary was shifted to his wife that salary did not reflect an increase in her services to the company. It is a fair inference that the salary she received was intended as indirect compensation to her husband.* . . . Since the critical determination is whether the wife's wages reflected the services she rendered, and there is no evidence to explain or justify the dramatic increase in her salary from nothing to $22,400, the finding of the Social Security Administration is supported by substantial evidence. The determination of the Social Security Administration is affirmed. *Sutton v. Sullivan,* 1990 WL 48027 (E.D.N.Y. 1990).

The message is clear—ministers should not attempt to obtain tax benefits by shifting income to a spouse unless there is economic reality to the arrangement. The guidelines provided by the Tax Court in the *Shelley* decision will be very helpful in evaluating the likely success of such arrangements.

Chapter 5

EXCLUSIONS FROM GROSS INCOME

Chapter Highlights

- **Exclusions.** Some kinds of income are not taxable. These items are called "exclusions." Most exclusions apply in computing both income taxes and self-employment taxes. They generally are "claimed" by not reporting them as income on a tax return.

- **Housing allowance.** The housing allowance is an example of an exclusion that applies only to income taxes, and not to self-employment (social security) taxes. This exclusion is addressed fully in the next chapter.

- **Gifts.** "Gifts" are excludable from taxable income so long as they are not in fact compensation for services performed.

- **Life insurance and inheritances.** Life insurance proceeds and inheritances are excludable from taxable income.

- **Scholarships.** Qualified scholarships are excludable from taxable income.

- **Employer paid medical insurance premiums.** Medical insurance premiums paid by an employer for employees (and their spouses and dependents) are excludable from taxable income. This exclusion is not available to self-employed individuals.

- **Accident and health plans.** Amounts received by employees as reimbursements for medical care under an employer-financed accident and health plan are excludable from taxable income. This exclusion is not available to self-employed individuals.

- **Employer paid group life insurance.** Employees may exclude the cost of employer-provided group term life insurance so long as the amount of coverage does not exceed $50,000.

- **Tuition reductions.** Employees may exclude from their taxable income a "qualified tuition reduction" provided by their employer. A qualified tuition reduction is a reduction in tuition charged to employees or their spouses or dependent children by an employer that is an educational institution.

- **Lodging.** The value of lodging furnished to an employee on an employer's premises and for the employer's convenience may be excludable from taxable income if the employee is required to accept the lodging as a condition of employment. This exclusion is not available in the computation of self-employment taxes.

- **Educational assistance.** Amounts paid by an employer for an employee's tuition, fees, and books may be excludable from the employee's taxable income. The exclusion may not exceed $5,250.

- **Employer provided child care.** The value of free child care services provided by a church to its employees is excluded from employees' income so long as the benefit is based on a written plan that does not discriminate in favor of highly compensated employees. Other conditions apply.

- **Nondiscrimination rules.** Many of the exclusions are not available to employees who are either "highly compensated employees" or "key employees," if the same benefit is not available on a nondiscriminatory basis to lower-paid employees.

- **Employee status.** Some exclusions are available only to taxpayers who report their income taxes as employees and not as self-employed persons. Many, however, apply to both employees and self-employed persons.

✎ **Key point: some kinds of income are not taxable (they are called "exclusions")**

✎ **Key point: most exclusions reduce both income taxes and self-employment taxes (some apply only to one or the other)**

✎ **Key point: the housing allowance is the most important exclusion for clergy—because of its importance, the next chapter is devoted exclusively to this exclusion**

Certain kinds of income are not includable in gross income for federal income tax reporting purposes. These items are known as **exclusions**. Other income items are only partly excludable. The most important exclusions for clergy are the exclusions (for income tax purposes) of the fair rental value of a church-provided parsonage, and of a "housing allowance" provided to clergy who own or rent their homes. Because of the importance of these exclusions, they are discussed separately and in detail in the next chapter. This chapter will summarize a few other common exclusions. Note that exclusions are reductions from gross income. Since the Form 1040 begins with an itemization of various categories of gross income, there is no place on the return to list exclusions. Exclusions ordinarily should not be included in income on a minister's Form W-2 or 1099.

Social security. Are items of income that are excludable in computing income taxes also excludable in computing social security taxes? Recall that clergy are always treated as self-employed for social security purposes with respect to their ministerial services, and so they pay the so-called "self-employment tax" instead of "FICA" taxes. The income tax regulations specify that "income which is excludable from gross income under any provision of subtitle A of the Internal Revenue Code is not taken into account in determining net earnings from self-employment," with certain exceptions. *Treas. Reg. 1.1402(a)-2(a).* The exceptions, which *are* included in income for self-employment tax purposes, include

• the housing allowance

• the fair rental value of a church-provided home

• the foreign earned income exclusion

• meals and lodging provided for the convenience of an employer

But apart from these exceptions, the general rule is that the exclusions discussed in this chapter are excludable in computing *both* income taxes and self-employment taxes.

A. Gifts and Inheritances

✎ **Key point: "gifts" are excludable from taxable income so long as they are not in fact compensation for services performed**

Property received as a gift, or by inheritance, is not includable in gross income, although the income from such property is includable. Characterizing a particular payment as a gift as opposed to compensation for services rendered is often a difficult task. The United States Supreme Court has provided some clarification by noting the following characteristics of a gift:

A gift in the statutory sense . . . proceeds from a detached and disinterested generosity . . . out of affection, respect, admiration, charity, or like impulses. . . . The most critical consideration is the transferor's intention. *Commissioner v. Duberstein, 363 U.S. 285 (1960).*

☞ **Example.** Rev. C receives a Christmas card from a church member which contains a check in the amount of $100 (payable directly to Rev. C). The check probably is a gift and is accordingly excludable from income. *Goodwin v. United States, 67 F.3d 149 (8th Cir. 1995)* (the court described a nontaxable gift to include "an individual who chooses to send the pastor and his wife ten dollars on a birthday or during the Christmas season"). However, the donor will receive no charitable contribution deduction for such a transfer. As noted in chapter 4, checks made payable to the church for the minister (e.g., a Christmas offering) are taxable income to the minister. Churches cannot make "gifts" to private individuals without jeopardizing their tax-exempt status. See also IRC 102(c).

☞ **Example.** Rev. G received an inheritance of $100,000 in 1997 from the estate of a deceased relative. The $100,000 is not includable in Rev. G's income in 1997. However, any interest earned by Rev. G on the inheritance in 1997 will be included in income.

☞ **Example.** Rev. K performs ministerial services for a neighboring church that temporarily is without a minister. In recognition of his services, the congregation presents him with an "honorarium" of $500. The honorarium clearly represents compensation for services rendered, and is not a gift.

Be sure to consult chapter 4, sections A.2 and A.3, and chapter 10, section L, for a discussion of the tax treatment of retirement and other special occasion "gifts" to clergy.

B. Life Insurance Proceeds

✎ **Key point: life insurance proceeds and inheritances are excludable from taxable income**

Life insurance proceeds paid to you because of the death of an insured person ordinarily are not taxable income to you. However, if the proceeds are payable to you in installments, you must report as income the portion of each installment that represents earnings on the face amount of the policy. Generally, the taxable amount is that portion of each installment that exceeds the face amount of the policy divided by the number of annual installments you are to receive. For example, if the face amount of the policy is $100,000, and you are to receive 20 annual installments of $6,000, you would report as income $1,000 each year ($6,000 - $100,000/20). In addition, if your spouse died on or before October 22, 1986, and insurance proceeds are payable to you because of the death of your spouse and you receive them in installments, you may exclude up to $1,000 a year of the interest included in such installments. If you leave the proceeds from life insurance on deposit with an insurance company under an agreement to receive interest only (ordinarily not a good idea), all the interest you receive is taxable and the $1,000 annual exclusion mentioned above does not apply.

C. Scholarships and Fellowship Grants

✎ **Key point: qualified scholarships are excludable from taxable income**

Only amounts received as a *qualified scholarship* by a candidate for a degree may be excluded from gross income. A qualified scholarship is any amount that, in accordance with the conditions of the grant, is used for tuition and course-related expenses at a high school, college, or graduate school. Qualified tuition and related expenses are those used for (1) tuition and fees required for the enrollment or attendance at an educational institution, or (2) fees, books, supplies, and equipment required for courses of instruction at the educational institution. The scholarship need not specify that it is to be used only for qualified tuition and related expenses. All that is required is that the recipient uses the scholarship for such expenses, and that the scholarship does not specify that it is to be used for nonqualified expenses (such as room and board). However, that part of a "scholarship" received by a graduate student that represents compensation for required teaching or research responsibilities cannot be a characterized as a qualified scholarship.

Any amounts received in excess of the qualified tuition and related expenses (such as amounts received for room and board) are not eligible for this exclusion. Also, any amount received that represents payment for teaching, research, or other services required as a condition for receiving the qualified scholarship may not be excluded from gross income.

☞ *Example.* First Church establishes a scholarship fund for seminary students. Linda is a church member who is pursing a masters degree at a seminary. The church board votes to award her a scholarship of $1,500 for 1998. So long as Linda uses the scholarship award for tuition or other course-related expenses, she need not report it as income on her federal tax return, and the church need not issue her a 1099-MISC. The better practice would be for the church to stipulate that the scholarship is to be used for tuition or other course-related expenses (e.g., fees, books, supplies). This will ensure that the scholarship does not inadvertently become taxable income because its specific use was not designated and the recipient used it for nonqualified expenses. See chapter 8, section B.3, for a discussion of the deductibility of members' payments to the scholarship fund.

☞ *Example.* A professor was given a year off to pursue studies overseas. He was paid $27,000 during his sabbatical, and he treated this entire amount as a tax-free scholarship. The IRS ruled that the sabbatical income represented taxable income, and the Tax Court agreed The court noted that scholarships are nontaxable only if certain conditions are met. The recipient must be "a candidate for a degree at an educational organization" and the scholarship must be used for qualified tuition. The court noted that the professor's sabbatical income was not a nontaxable scholarship since he was not a candidate for a degree and failed to prove that he used any portion of the income for qualified tuition expenses. This ruling will be useful to church treasurers in evaluating the tax status of sabbatical income provided to pastors or other staff members. Kant v. Commissioner, T.C. Memo. 1997-217.

D. Medical Insurance Premiums

✎ **Key point: medical insurance premiums paid by an employer for employees (and their spouses and dependents) are excludable from taxable income (this exclusion is not available to self-employed individuals)**

Churches often provide ministers with accident or health insurance coverage, and pay some or all of the premiums for such coverage. Income tax regulation 1.106-1 specifies that the gross income of an *employee* does not include "contributions which his employer makes to an accident or health plan for compensation (through insurance or otherwise) to the employee for personal injuries or sickness incurred by him, his spouse, or his dependents . . . . The employer may contribute to an accident or health plan by paying the premium (or a portion of the premium) on a policy of accident or health insurance covering one or more of his employees, or by contributing to a separate trust or fund . . . ." The IRS has ruled that amounts furnished to a conference of churches by member churches to provide hospital and medical insurance coverage for clergy employees are excludable from clergy gross income under section 106. *Revenue Ruling 70-179.*

Section 106 excludes both (1) accident and health insurance premiums paid by an employer, *and* (2) payments made directly to employees by an employer to reimburse them for accident and health insurance premiums that they paid. However, the employer must require proof of prior payment of premiums as a condition of the reimbursement. *Revenue Ruling 85-44; Revenue Ruling 75-241; Revenue Ruling 67-360; Revenue Ruling 61-146; Adkins v. U.S., 882 F.2d 1078 (6th Cir. 1989).* Amounts can be excluded as employer contributions only if employees do not have any right to receive them in cash or any other form. An important exception is a "health flexible spending arrangement" under Code section 125 (discussed later in this chapter), under which an employee can elect to receive cash *or* an employer-paid premium under an accident and health plan.

In summary, three rules are clear:

• Church employees' health insurance premiums paid directly to the insurer by the church are excludable from the employees' gross income for federal tax reporting purposes.

• Church employees' health insurance premiums paid directly to employees are excludable from the employees' gross income for federal tax reporting purposes if the church requires proof that the employees in fact paid the premiums themselves. In other words, the church treats this arrangement like an "accountable" business expense reimbursement arrangement, and only reimburses those expenses for which it receives adequate substantiation.

• If a church provides employees with cash in lieu of paying their health insurance premiums, the exclusion does not apply and the amount of cash distributed to employees is fully taxable. However, the cash provided to the employees can be tax-free if the church adopts a type of "cafeteria plan" called a "health flexible spending arrangement" (discussed later in this chapter).

The exclusion of employer-paid medical insurance premiums is a significant tax-free benefit for clergy who report their income taxes as employees. In fact, it is one of the major reasons why clergy generally are "better off" reporting their income taxes as employees rather than as self-employed (see chapter 2). With the substantial increase in the cost of medical insurance over the past several years, this exclusion can reduce taxable income by thousands of dollars. For clergy (or any other church employee) to obtain the benefit of this exclusion, the church must adopt a written "plan." Section 106 of the Code does not define this term, but it is defined by several court decisions interpreting a related provision in Code section 105. Generally, these decisions indicate that a "plan" includes any commitment by an organization's board that is recorded in the board's minutes.

Clergy who report their federal income taxes as self-employed (using Form 1040, Schedule C) *are not eligible for this exclusion.* In other words, their Form 1099 and Schedule C must both report the amount of the employer-paid insurance premiums.

✎ **Key point: the Tax Court, in ruling that a Methodist minister had incorrectly been reporting his income taxes as self-employed, pointed out that by being reclassified as an employee the minister would be eligible for the exclusion of employer-paid medical insurance premiums that he incorrectly had been claiming in the past. Weber v. Commissioner 103 T.C. 378 (1994), aff'd 60 F.3d 1104 (4th Cir. 1995).**

Nondiscrimination rules. Prior to 1989, Code section 106(b) denied any exclusion to certain "highly compensated individuals." However, this exception did not apply to "church plans" or small employers (fewer than 20 employees). A "church plan" is defined as a plan maintained for its employees by a church or convention or association of churches exempt from federal income taxation under section 501(c)(3) of the Code. Section 106(b) expired at the end of 1988, and was replaced by Code section 4980B (new in 1989). Section 4980B specifies that if an employer-adopted group medical plan only covers "highly compensated employees" (defined in section H of this chapter), then the exclusion of employer-paid premiums may

be disallowed unless the employer permits employees to continue their coverage after discontinuing their employment. Like former section 106(b), this rule does not apply to churches or "small employers." Note further that the IRS has ruled an employee is entitled to exclude medical insurance premiums paid by his employer even though he is the only employee covered. *Revenue Ruling 58-90.*

Health insurance portability. While not directly related to church or clergy taxes, the Health Insurance Portability and Accountability Act of 1996 should be briefly mentioned in this context. The Act makes it easier for most workers to change jobs without losing their health insurance because of some preexisting medical condition that otherwise would make them uninsurable. Workers who leave their job do not take their health insurance coverage with them, but rather are permitted to enroll in their new employer's group medical plan regardless of a preexisting medical condition. Employers are permitted to exclude coverage for preexisting medical conditions (that were diagnosed or treated within 6 months prior a new employee's enrollment in the new plan) only for a period of up to 12 months. This 12-month "waiting period" can be reduced or eliminated if a new employee earned enough "creditable coverage" (a new term) through prior health insurance coverage under either a group plan or individual health insurance coverage. There are various ways to compute "creditable coverage." The Act prohibits group health plans from establishing rules for eligibility (including continued eligibility) based on any of the following health related factors in relation to the individual or a dependent: (1) health status; (2) medical condition (including both physical and mental illnesses); (3) claims experience; (4) receipt of health care; (5) medical history; (6) genetic information; (7) evidence of insurability; or (8) disability. The Act states that its portability provisions apply to church plans. There are substantial penalties for noncompliance. In some cases, these penalties are waived or reduced for church plans.

☞ *Example.* The board of directors of First Church adopts a written resolution agreeing to pay the medical insurance premiums of its minister and the minister's dependent family members (but not for any other church employee). For 1997, the premiums paid by the church were $3,000. If the minister reports income taxes as an employee, the $3,000 need not be reported on either Form W-2 or 1040. It does not matter that the same benefit is not made available to other church employees.

☞ *Example.* Same facts as the previous example except that the church also agrees to pay the $1,000 annual "deductible" under the health insurance policy. Is the $1,000 deductible paid by the church excluded from its minister's taxable income? See the next section (and examples) discussing amounts received under "accident and health plans."

☞ *Example.* A church adopts a plan under which it agrees to pay up to $1,500 of each employee's medical insurance premiums. Employee T is covered by the medical insurance plan of a spouse (who is employed by a secular employer), and so T requests a cash payment of $1,500 from the church. If the church agrees to do so, is this "cash payment in lieu of medical insurance premiums" excludable from T's taxable income? The answer is no. See Revenue Ruling 75-241; Adkins v. U.S., 882 F.2d 1078 (6th Cir. 1989); Marshall v. Commissioner, 56 T.C.M. 1006 (1989).

☞ **Example.** A church adopts a plan under which it agrees to pay up to $1,500 of each employee's medical insurance premiums. Employee G elects to receive $1,500 in cash in lieu of the church paying her medical insurance premiums for the year. However, G uses the $1,500 to pay her own medical insurance premiums, and can document this. The IRS ruled in 1990 that G is not entitled to exclude the $1,500 from her federal taxes. The IRS concluded that workers receive taxable compensation if they can choose to have their employer pay their medical insurance premiums or receive an equivalent amount in cash. It does not matter that employees in fact use the money to pay health insurance premiums, since they have the right to treat it as a cash benefit. This is all that is required to create taxable income under the "constructive receipt" rule (see chapter 10, section E). IRS Letter Ruling 9022060.

☞ **Example.** D is an employee at First Church. He pays his own health insurance premiums directly to an insurance company and is reimbursed by the church for the amount of the premiums. D does not have to report this amount as income for tax purposes so long as the church requires proof ("verification") that the insurance coverage exists and that the employee in fact paid the premium. IRS Letter Ruling 9022060.

☞ **Example.** Same facts as the previous example, except that D reports his federal income taxes as a self-employed person and is issued a 1099 form by the church each year. As a self-employed person, D is not eligible for the exclusion of the cost of employer-paid medical insurance premiums. D would have to report as additional income the church's reimbursement of his medical insurance premiums (and the church should add the amount of the reimbursement to D's 1099).

E. Amounts Received under Accident and Health Plans

✎ **Key point: amounts received by employees as reimbursements for medical care under an employer-financed accident and health plan generally are excludable from taxable income (this exclusion is not available to self-employed individuals)**

A minister who is an employee of his or her church (for federal income tax reporting purposes) can exclude from gross income amounts received under an employer-financed accident and health plan as payments for permanent injury or loss of bodily function, or as reimbursements of medical expenses. The payments can be made on behalf of a spouse or dependent of the minister. IRC 105(b). In addition, a personal injury lump-sum award you receive from a court judgment or insurance settlement is excludable from your gross income. More complex rules apply if you receive a "structured settlement" which provides for payments over a period of years or for your life.

This exclusion assumes that the church has established an "accident or health plan." The requirements for such a plan are not specified in the Code. The regulations simply state that "an accident or health plan is an arrangement for the payment of amounts of employees in the event of personal injuries or sickness." The regulations further specify that "an accident or health plan may be either insured or uninsured, and it is not necessary that the plan be in writing or that the employee's rights to benefits under the plan be enforceable." Ideally, a plan should be reflected in the minutes of the church board. The regulations do require that notice of a plan be "reasonably available" to employees (if employees' rights under the plan are not enforceable).

Nondiscrimination rules. Churches are free to reimburse employee medical expenses under a "self-insured" plan (e.g., reimbursements are paid out of the church's own funds rather than through an insurance policy) or an insured plan. However, if reimbursements are made under a self-insured plan, then nondiscrimination rules apply. IRC 105(h). Generally, these rules require that the plan not discriminate in favor of **highly compensated individuals** with regard to either amount of benefits or eligibility to participate. If it does, then highly compensated individuals ordinarily must report some or all of the amount of the church's reimbursements as taxable income. If a church reimbursement arrangement discriminates in favor of highly compensated individuals on the basis of the amount of benefits (e.g., highly compensated individuals receive a greater benefit than other participants in the plan), then such individuals must report the entire amount of the church's reimbursements as income. More complicated rules determine how to compute the taxable portion of church reimbursements if the plan discriminates on the basis of participation (rather than the amount of benefits). In general, a plan discriminates in favor of highly compensated individuals on the basis of eligibility to participate unless the plan benefits 70% or more of all employees (or 80% or more of all the employees who are eligible to benefit under the plan if 70% or more of all employees are eligible to benefit under the plan). Some employees can be disregarded in applying this test, including those who have not completed 3 years of service, or who have not attained age 25, or part-time or seasonal employees, if they are not participants in the employer's plan.

Who are highly compensated individuals? Any of the following: (1) one of the 5 highest paid officers;

(2) a shareholder who owns more than 10 percent in value of the stock of the employer (this definition will not apply to church employers); or (3) among the highest paid 25% of all employees (some employees are not considered, including those who have not completed 3 years of service, or who have not attained age 25, or part-time or seasonal employees—and who are not participants in the employer's plan). IRC 105(h)(5). Note that the definition of a highly compensated *individual* is different from the definition of a highly compensated *employee* (discussed later in this chapter).

The regulations specify that "benefits paid to participants who are not highly compensated individuals may be excluded from gross income . . . even if the plan is discriminatory." That is, the fact that highly compensated employees must report some or all of their reimbursements as income does not affect the ability of non-highly compensated employees to fully exclude employer reimbursements.

Severance pay. Section 104 of the tax code excludes from taxable income "the amount of any damages received (whether by suit or agreement and whether as lump sums or as periodic payments) *on account of personal injuries or sickness.*" As a result, severance pay that is intended to settle personal injury claims may be nontaxable. The tax treatment of severance pay arrangements is addressed in chapter 4, section A.17.

☞ *Example. Rev. M is a minister at First Church. She undergoes major surgery and incurs $15,000 of expenses that are not covered under any insurance policy. The church board decides to reimburse Rev. M for the full amount of $15,000. The church has no formal plan of reimbursing any employee's medical expenses. Since the church's actions constitute a reimbursement of medical expenses under a self-insured plan, the $15,000 is excludable from Rev. M's income only to the extent that the church's plan is not discriminatory. If Rev. M is one of the 5 highest paid officers, or is among the highest paid 25% of all employees, she may not exclude any of the $15,000 from her income for tax purposes if the same benefit is not available to non-highly compensated individuals.*

☞ *Example. First Church provides health insurance for Rev. G, who reports his income taxes as an employee. In order to reduce the cost of the insurance, the church elects a $1,000 deductible (e.g., the insurance pays for any expense only to the extent that it exceeds $1,000). The church established a "medical fund" for Rev. G in order to reimburse all of his medical expenses that are less than $1,000 (and not covered by insurance). The church does not provide health insurance, or a "medical fund," for any other employee. The church's "medical plan" is self-insured and discriminatory (in favor of Rev. G, a highly compensated individual), and accordingly all of Rev. G's medical expenses reimbursed by the church represent taxable income and must be included on his W-2 and Form 1040 (as wages). However,* the health insurance premiums paid by the church are not taxable to Rev. G.

☞ *Example. Rev. E is injured in an automobile accident. The accident was caused by another driver. Rev. E accepts a settlement offer of $50,000 from the other driver's insurance carrier. The lump-sum distribution of $50,000 is not reportable as income by Rev. E. The reason for this rule is that the settlement merely compensated Rev. E for his injuries, and did not provide him with any additional gain or benefits.*

F. Medical Savings Accounts (MSAs)

In general. The Health Insurance Portability and Accountability Act of 1996 was delayed for months in Congress because of a controversial proposal by Republican leaders to recognize "medical savings accounts" (MSAs). MSAs are not a new concept—they are recognized by several states. But they have never been recognized under federal law. The idea behind an MSA is simple—if people use their own money to pay for a portion of their medical expenses, they will be much more cost-conscious and they will shop around for the best deal. This in turn will drive down the escalating costs of medical care. Many in Congress opposed this free market approach to containing medical expenses, and eventually a compromise was reached that was passed overwhelmingly by Congress. The compromise restricts MSAs to self-employed workers and employees who work for "small employers," and it permits MSAs only for a limited number of individuals during a "trial period." The key elements of MSAs are summarized below.

Similar to IRAs. MSAs are similar to IRAs, except that they are used to pay for medical expenses. Like an IRA, an MSA has three main characteristics:

1. Contributions made to an MSA by an "eligible individual" are tax-deductible. An eligible individual is an employee covered under a "high deductible plan" of a "small employer," or a self-employed individual covered under a "high deductible plan." A "high deductible plan" is a health plan with an annual deductible of (1) at least $1,500 and no more than $2,250 in the case of individual coverage, or (2) at least $3,000 and no more than $4,500 in the case of family coverage. In addition, the maximum out-of-pocket expenses with respect to allowed costs (including the deductible) must be no more than $3,000 in the case of individual coverage and no more than $5,500 in the case of family coverage. An employer is a small employer if it employed no more than 50 employees during either the preceding year or the year before that.

✎ **Key point: Only employees who are employed by a small employer, and self-employed persons, are eligible to participate in an MSA—if they are covered under a high deductible health care plan.**

✎ **Key point: In order for an employee of an eligible employer to be eligible to make MSA contributions (or to have employer contributions made on his or her behalf), the employee must be covered under an employer-sponsored high deductible health plan and must not be covered under any other health plan.**

✎ **Key point: In the case of an employee, contributions can be made to an MSA either by the individual or by the individual's employer. However, an individual is not eligible to make contributions to an MSA for a year if any employer contributions are made to an MSA on behalf of the individual for the year.**

2. Employer contributions to an MSA are excluded from an eligible individual's taxable income. An employer's contributions to an eligible individual's MSA are excluded from the individual's taxable income.

3. Earnings not currently taxable. Like an IRA, earnings on an MSA are not currently taxable.

Other features of an MSA. There are a number of other aspects to an MSA that will be of interest to ministers and other church leaders. Some of these are summarized below:

1. Maximum contributions. The maximum annual contribution that can be made to an MSA for a year is 65 percent of the deductible under the high deductible plan in the case of individual coverage, and 75 percent of the deductible in the case of family coverage. No other dollar limits on the maximum contribution apply. Contributions for a year can be made until the due date for the individual's tax return for the year (determined without regard to extensions).

✎ **Key point: Contributions can be made to an MSA of an employee either by the employee or by his or her employer. However, an employee is not eligible to make contributions to an MSA for a year if any employer contributions are made to an MSA on behalf of the employee for the year.**

✎ **Key point: Employer contributions to an MSA are excludable from gross income and wages for employment tax purposes, but this exclusion does not apply to contributions made through a cafeteria plan.**

2. Limited coverage. In general, the number of taxpayers eligible to participate in an MSA is limited to 750,000 during a "trial period" (from 1997 through 2000).

✎ **Key point: How many people have enrolled in an MSA during the first year? The IRS reported that only 7,383 MSAs have been created as of April 30, 1997.**

3. Distributions for medical expenses. Another key concept is this—distributions from an MSA for the unreimbursed medical expenses of the taxpayer and his or her spouse or dependents are excludable from income. The exclusion applies regardless of whether the payment is made directly from the MSA to the medical service provider, the MSA distribution reimburses the individual for expenses already incurred, or the individual uses the MSA distribution to pay the medical service provider. Medical expenses generally are defined in the same way as the itemized deduction (Schedule A) for medical expenses, except that medical expenses do not include medical insurance premiums (with some exceptions).

✎ **Key point: Distributions that are not for medical expenses are included in income. In addition, such distributions are subject to an additional 10 percent tax unless made after age 59 1/2, death, or disability.**

4. Following the taxpayer's death. Upon death, if the beneficiary of the MSA is the individual's surviving spouse, the spouse may continue the MSA as his or her own. If the beneficiary is not the surviving spouse, the beneficiary must include the MSA balance in income in the year of death. If there is no beneficiary, the MSA balance includible on the final return of the decedent. In all cases, no estate tax applies.

5. How to set up an MSA. In general, an MSA is a trust or custodial account created exclusively for the benefit of the account holder, and is established in much the same way as an IRA. An MSA trustee (or custodian) may be a bank, insurance company, or other person who demonstrates to the satisfaction of the IRS that the manner in which such person will administer the trust will be consistent with the legal requirements. The MSA trustee (or custodian) is required to make such reports as may be required by the IRS.

☞ *Example. A church provides health insurance to its 10 employees, with deductibles of $1,000 for single employees and $2,000 for family coverage. Some employees have heard about MSAs, and they ask their church treasurer if they are eligible to participate. The answer is no. While the church is a "small employer," its employees are not "eligible individuals" since they are not covered under a "high deductible plan" (with deductibles of at least $1,500 and no more than $2,250 in the case of individual coverage, or at least $3,000 and no more than $4,500 in the case of family coverage).*

G. Group Term Life Insurance

✎ **Key point: employees may exclude the cost of employer-provided group term life insurance so long as the amount of coverage does not exceed $50,000**

The cost of group term life insurance bought by an employer for its employees ordinarily is not taxable to the employees so long as the amount of coverage does not exceed $50,000 per employee. *IRC 79.* Generally, term life insurance can qualify as group term life insurance only if it is available to at least ten full-time employees. However, there are some exceptions to this rule. For example, the ten full-time employee rule does not apply if (1) an employer provides the insurance to all full-time employees who provide satisfactory evidence of insurability, (2) insurance coverage is based on a uniform percentage of pay, and (3) evidence of insurability is limited to a medical questionnaire completed by the employee that does not require a physical examination.

The exclusion of the cost of up to $50,000 of group term life insurance paid for by an employer is not available to "key employees" if the plan discriminates in their favor. Generally, for 1997 a key employee of a church is an employee who is an officer and who receives annual compensation of at least $62,500 (this amount is adjusted each year for inflation). *IRC 79(d)(6), 416(i), IRS News Release IR-96-43.* A plan is not discriminatory simply because the amount of insurance provided to employees bears a direct relationship to the amount of their compensation.

There is no exclusion for any other kind of employer-provided life insurance. To illustrate, if a church pays the premiums on a "whole life" or universal life insurance policy on the life of its minister, which names the minister's spouse and children as beneficiaries, the premium amounts paid by the church must be included in the minister's income for tax purposes.

Further, you must include in your income the cost of group-term life insurance coverage provided to you by your employer that exceeds $50,000. The cost of group term life insurance coverage of up to $50,000 is excludable, but the cost of any additional coverage is taxable.

H. Certain Fringe Benefits

As noted in chapter 4, a fringe benefit is any material benefit provided by an employer to an employee (or self-employed person) apart from his or her stated compensation. Certain fringe benefits are generally includable in an employee's gross income for both income tax and social security tax purposes. Such "taxable" fringe benefits were discussed in chapter 4. Some fringe benefits are specifically excluded from income if certain requirements are satisfied. Several of these "nontaxable" fringe benefits are described in section 132 of the Code.

Before summarizing these fringe benefits, it is necessary to define two important terms—**highly compensated employee** and **key employee**. Many of the fringe benefits summarized below are excludable from taxable income only to the extent that the employee is not highly compensated or a key employee. These terms, for 1997, and in the context of religious organizations, are summarized below:

highly compensated employee

pre-1997 definition

Code section 414(q) defines the term "highly compensated employee" to include any employee who, during the year or the preceding year, was—(1) an officer who receives total annual compensation in excess of $60,000; (2) the highest paid officer if such person receives annual compensation below $60,000; (3) any employee who earns annual compensation in excess of $66,000 and who is in the "top-paid group" of employees (the top 20% of employees ranked by compensation); or (4) any employee earning compensation in excess of $100,000. *See also Treas. Reg. 1.132-8(f)(1).*

post-1996 definition

Amended section 414(q) defines a highly compensated employee as one who (1) was a 5 percent owner of the employer at any time during the current or prior year (this definition will not apply to churches), *or* (2) had compensation for the previous year in excess of $80,000, and, if an employer elects, was in the top 20 percent of employees by compensation. The $80,000 amount will be indexed annually for inflation. This revised definition repeals the pre-1997 rule requiring the highest paid officer be treated as highly compensated, no matter how little he or she was paid.

key employee

Code section 416(i)(1) defines the term "key employee" to include an employee who, at any time during the year or any of the 4 preceding plan years, is an officer of the employer having an annual compensation greater than $62,500. *IRS News Release IR-96-43.*

(1) No-additional-cost-service. If an employer offers an employee a service free of charge (or at a reduced price) that is the same service that it offers to the public in the ordinary course of its business, and the employer does not discriminate in favor of "highly compensated employees" in dispensing the service, the service is considered a "no-additional-cost" service and is excludable from the employee's income. In addition, the employer cannot incur substantial additional cost in providing the service to the employee. This exclusion ordinarily will not benefit clergy.

(2) Qualified employee discounts. A qualified employee discount is a reduction in price that an employer offers employees on certain property or services that it offers to the public in the ordinary course of its business. Such discounts cannot be excluded by highly compensated employees unless the same benefit is made available on substantially similar terms to lower-paid employees.

(3) Working condition fringe benefits. Employees do not include in income the value of a working condition fringe benefit. A working condition fringe benefit is any property or service provided to you by your employer to the extent that you could have deducted the cost of the property or service as *an employee business expense* had you paid for it yourself. Note that this exclusion generally does not apply to self-employed clergy. Perhaps the most common example of this exclusion for clergy is a church-provided car. If your church provides you with a car, the amount excludable as a working condition fringe benefit is the amount that would be allowable as an employee business expense deduction if you had to provide the car yourself. Your personal use of the car is a taxable noncash fringe benefit that your employer must value and include in your income for tax reporting purposes. See chapter 4, section A.8. The employer may either include the actual value of your personal use of the car, or include 100% of the value of the use of the car in your income (i.e., assume 100% personal use). If your employer elects the second alternative, you may be able to deduct the value of your business use of the car as a miscellaneous itemized deduction on Schedule A (use Form 2106 to compute the deduction).

IRS regulations specify that an employer's reimbursement of a nonemployee spouse's travel expenses incurred while accompanying an employee on a business trip qualifies as a nontaxable "working condition fringe benefit" so long as the following conditions are met:

• the employer has not treated such amounts as compensation

• the amounts would be deductible as a business expense without regard to the limitation on the deductibility of a spouse's travel expenses, meaning that the spouse's presence on the trip is for a legitimate business purpose, and

• the employee substantiates the expenses under an accountable arrangement (described above)

The tax treatment of a spouse's travel expenses is addressed fully in chapter 7.

(4) De minimis (minimal) fringe benefits. If your employer provides you with a fringe benefit that is so minimal in value that it would be unreasonable or administratively impractical to account for it, you will not have to include the value of such benefits in your income. Examples of de minimis fringe benefits that are **excludable** from taxable income include:

• occasional typing of personal letters (by yourself on church equipment, or on your behalf by another employee on church equipment)

• occasional personal use of the church duplicating machine

• occasional office parties and picnics for employees and their guests

• traditional holiday gifts of noncash property with low fair market value (such as turkeys and fruitcakes at Christmas time)

• coffee, donuts, and soft drinks furnished to employees

• local telephone calls

• subscriptions to professional publications paid for by the employer on behalf of an employee

Examples of fringe benefits that are **not excludable** from taxable income as de minimis fringe benefits include the following (these items must be valued and reported as income to the employee):

• season tickets to sporting or theatrical events

• the commuting use of a church-owned vehicle more than one day each month

• membership in a private country club or athletic facility

In determining whether a benefit is minimal, the frequency with which the benefit is provided must be considered. Therefore, if your employer provides you with a free lunch each day, such a benefit will not be de minimis even though the value of any one lunch would be.

☞ *Example. In 1997 a church paid for 2 dinners for staff members (and their spouses) at local restaurants. This common church practice has never been challenged or questioned by the IRS, and accordingly it may be assumed that the church's payment of the cost of such functions constitutes a nontaxable working condition fringe benefit.*

☞ *Example. In 1997 a church paid for 3 dinners for members of its governing board (and their spouses) at local restaurants. This is a common church practice, and few if any churches (or any other organization) ever report the cost of such meals as taxable income to the board members. The availability of the working condition fringe benefit exclusion is not clear, since this exclusion generally applies only to employees and self-employed workers (most board members are volunteers serving without pay). It is possible that the working condition fringe benefit exclusion could apply to uncompensated board members under 2 theories: (1) board members are "uncompensated workers," or (2) board members become "self-employed" workers by virtue of the "in kind" compensation (occasional meals) that is provided to them by the church, and this qualifies them for treating the meals as a working condition fringe benefit.*

For 1997, a transit pass (including tokens and fare cards) provided to you at a discount not exceeding $65 per month may be excluded as a de minimis fringe, as may employer-paid parking of up to $170 per month. Some employers provide meals to employees at less than fair market value (i.e., the employer subsidizes the cost of meals). Under a special de minimis fringe rule, if your employer operates a cafeteria or other eating facility on or near the business premises for employees, you will not have to include in income the excess of the value of the meals over the fees charged to you. To qualify for this rule, (1) the revenue received by the employer must generally equal or exceed its operating cost, (2) the employer must own or lease the facility, (3) substantially all of the use of the facility is by employees, (4) meals are provided during or immediately before or after the workday, and (5) access to the facility is not primarily for the benefit of officers, directors, or "highly compensated employees."

Some churches operate athletic facilities (such as a gym or pool) on church property, and make these facilities available to employees. You do not have to include in income the value of such a fringe benefit if substantially all of the use of the facility is by employees and their spouses and dependent children.

✎ **Key point: A high-level IRS official warned in 1996 that the whole issue of de minimis fringe benefits is being scrutinized more closely, and that employers should not assume that all relatively low-cost dinners and gifts provided to employees are tax-free. The official noted that gift certificates that can be exchanged for merchandise will not be considered de minimis if the cost of the merchandise is less than the value of the certificate and the employee receives the difference in cash. The official also cautioned against using any threshold amount (such as $25 or $75) to define "de minimis." The official noted that a de minimis gift is one that has a value that is so small that it would be unreasonable or administratively impractical to account for it. If the value of the gift is ascertainable, it is not a de minimis fringe benefit regardless of the value.**

(5) Cafeteria plans. A "cafeteria plan" is a written plan established by an employer for its employees that allows employees to choose between a taxable benefit (cash) and a menu of nontaxable "qualified" benefits. *IRC 125.* The idea is this—employees will not be taxed on the qualified noncash benefits they receive under the plan solely because they had the right to choose cash instead of any of the noncash benefits. As noted earlier in this chapter, it is a basic rule of tax law that employees who are given the choice of receiving a tax-free fringe benefit or cash must report the value of the fringe benefit as taxable income (assuming they choose the fringe benefit) because they had the right to receive a taxable benefit (cash). For example, the cost of employer-provided health insurance ordinarily is a tax-free fringe benefit to employees. However, employees cannot exclude the cost of this benefit from their taxable income if they had the right (whether it was exercised or not) to receive cash instead of having their employer pay their health insurance premiums. A cafeteria plan avoids this tax rule, and permits employees to receive certain tax-free fringe benefits from their employer even though they had the right to receive cash instead. However, note that a cafeteria plan must present employees with a choice between cash and one or more nontaxable fringe benefits. A plan that allows employees to choose among several non-cash fringe benefits is not a cafeteria plan.

Employer contributions to a cafeteria plan are not taxable, even if they are funded through salary reductions. This makes such plans very attractive to employees. The term "cafeteria" refers to the choice employees have under such plans, and not to an eating facility (as is commonly supposed). The requirements for a cafeteria plan are complex. Churches interested in establishing such a plan should consult with a tax attorney or CPA. Here are a few rules to keep in mind:

- Employees must be given the option to choose between cash and a menu of nontaxable "qualified" benefits. Qualified benefits available under a cafeteria plan include:

  ✓ employer-paid group term life insurance coverage up to $50,000

  ✓ employer-paid medical insurance premiums

  ✓ employer reimbursements of medical expenses under an accident or health plan

  ✓ employer-paid dependent care

- The only taxable benefit that a cafeteria plan may offer is *cash*. That is, employees can be given the option of choosing among any of the benefits listed above, or cash. The following benefits may *not* be offered—scholarships, educational assistance programs, de minimis fringe benefits, no-additional-cost services, employee discounts, and "working condition fringe benefits."

- A cafeteria plan must be set forth in a written agreement. The income tax regulations describe the required agreement in some detail as follows:

  The written document embodying a cafeteria plan must contain at least the following information: (i) a specific description of each of the benefits available under the plan, including the periods during which the benefits are provided (i.e., the periods of coverage), (ii) the plan's eligibility rules governing participation, (iii) the procedures governing participants' elections under the plan, including the period during which elections may be made, the extent to which elections are irrevocable, and the periods with respect to which elections are effective, (iv) the manner in which employer contributions may be made under the plan, such as by salary reduction agreement between the participant and the employer or by nonelective employer contributions to the plan, (v) the maximum amount of employer contributions available to any participant under the plan, and (vi) the plan year on which the cafeteria plan operates. *Proposed Treas. Reg. 1.125-1 (question and answers, answer A-3).*

- If a cafeteria plan discriminates in favor of "highly compensated employees" (defined above) then such employees lose the benefit of the exclusion and they generally are taxable on the value of the benefits received. Further, the exclusion is denied to "key employees" (defined above) if the qualified benefits provided to such employees exceed 25% of total nontaxable benefits provided to all employees under the plan. Special nondiscrimination rules apply to cafeteria plans that provide health benefits. *IRC 125(g)(2).*

• Every employer that adopts a cafeteria plan must comply with reporting and recordkeeping requirements. *IRC 6039D.* This means that a Form 5500 must be filed with the IRS. There is no exception for cafeteria plans maintained by churches. In addition, employers are required to keep such records as may be necessary to determine whether or not the requirements of a cafeteria plan are met. See section H, below, for more information.

• One popular type of cafeteria plan is the **flexible spending arrangement** ("FSA"). Many employees face the prospect of escalating medical costs and diminishing health benefits provided by their employer. FSAs were designed to address this predicament. Basically, a "health FSA" permits employees to pay for their medical expenses with pre-tax dollars (through a salary reduction). An FSA makes it easier for employees to pay for their medical expenses by eliminating federal taxes on the amount of the salary reductions. In addition to the other requirements for a cafeteria plan discussed above, a health FSA is subject to several additional rules and limitations, including the following: (1) An employee cannot receive amounts set aside in a health FSA as cash or any other benefit (in the event they are not needed to pay for medical expenses). (2) Amounts set aside in a health FSA must be used to offset medical expenses in the same year (any unused funds in the FSA at year-end are forfeited by the employee). In other words, you "use it or lose it." If an employee's salary is reduced too much during the year (salary reductions greatly exceed actual medical expenses), then the balance cannot be distributed back to the employee. The unused "salary" must remain in the account. If any unused balance is refundable to the employee, then the salary reductions are not tax-excludable (e.g., W-2 wages would *include* the amount of such salary reductions). (3) Changes in the amount of salary reductions contributed to the FSA are not permitted during the year (unless there are changes in family status or employment status). (4) An employee can be reimbursed for medical expenses at any time during the year up to the maximum amount of coverage (e.g., up to the total salary reductions for the year), even if actual payments to the FSA are less than this amount at a particular time of year.

(6) Qualified tuition reductions. Many churches operate private schools at the elementary or secondary level. In addition, most religious denominations operate private colleges or universities. Often, the church, denomination, or school will offer tuition discounts to school employees or to the spouses or dependent children of employees. Section 117(d) of the Code specifies that the amount of any "qualified tuition reduction" is excluded from an employee's gross income for income tax purposes so long as the following conditions are satisfied:

(1) The tuition reduction is for the education of

(a) an individual who currently is employed by the school

(b) an individual who ceased working at the school on account of retirement or disability

(c) a widow or widower of an individual who died while employed at the school

(d) a spouse or dependent child of any of the above-named individuals

(2) The school is an elementary, secondary, or undergraduate institution, and it normally maintains a regular faculty and curriculum and normally has a regularly enrolled body of pupils or students in attendance at the place where its educational activities are regularly carried on.

(3) "Highly compensated employees" (defined above) cannot exclude qualified tuition reductions from their gross income unless the same benefit is available on substantially similar terms to each member of a group of employees which is defined under a reasonable classification set up by the employer which does not discriminate in favor of highly compensated employees. The term "highly compensated employee" is a very technical one that is defined at the beginning of this section. Note that the fact that a highly compensated employee must report the value of a tuition reduction in his or her income for tax reporting purposes does not affect the right of employees who are *not* highly compensated to exclude the value of tuition reductions from their income.

✎ **Key point: employees may exclude from their taxable income a "qualified tuition reduction" provided by their employer**

There is some question whether this benefit would apply to employees of a *church* that operates a private school. To illustrate, assume that First Church employs 6 persons including 2 ministers, and in addition operates a private school that employs another 12 full-time persons (none of whom is "highly compensated"). The church provides 50% tuition discounts to employees of both the church and school, and a 100% discount to the children of the senior minister (who also serves as the administrator of the school, and receives an annual church salary of $42,000). There is little doubt that the 12 school employees qualify for the tuition reduction exclusion, and accordingly the value of the discount should not be reported on their W-2 or 1040 forms. This should be true even if these employees are paid by the church, since they work full-time for a school and therefore should be considered to be school employees.

But what about the senior minister, and the other church employees? Are they eligible for the exclusion? Code section 117(d) defines a "qualified tuition reduction" as "any reduction in tuition provided to an employee of an organization described in section 170(b)(1)(A)(ii) for the education (below the graduate level) at such organization (or another organization described in section 170(b)(1)(A)(ii)." Section 170(b)(1)(A)(ii) refers to educational institutions that "normally maintain a regular faculty and curriculum and normally have a regularly enrolled body of pupils or students in attendance at the place where its educational activities are regularly carried on." In other words, tuition reductions granted to the employees of an educational institution are tax-exempt, as are tuition reductions granted to employees of educational institutions for education they receive from another educational institution. But, it is unclear whether the IRS or the courts would consider an employee who works directly for a church to be an employee of an educational institution, even if the church operates a private school. The church still may be considered to be a religious rather than an educational institution. This conclusion is reinforced by the fact that Code section 170(b)(1)(A)(i) specifically lists "churches" as a separate category. The IRS may consider these persons to be employed by a church rather than by an educational institution. If so, they would not be eligible for the exclusion. The senior minister who serves as administrator of the school probably would be considered to be a highly compensated employee, even if all his compensation is for his services on behalf of the church, since he would be considered the highest paid officer of the school. In summary, while there is little doubt that the 12 school employees are eligible for the tuition reduction exclusion, it is doubtful whether the same would be true for the 6 church employees. Further, the senior minister would not be eligible for the exclusion even though he is an officer of the school, since he probably would be regarded as a highly compensated employee.

✎ **Key point: a federal appeals court rejected the claim of one church that its school employees were really church employees and therefore exempt from the Fair Labor Standards Act (minimum wage and overtime pay). The church pointed out that the school was "inextricably intertwined" with the church, that the church and school shared a common building and a common payroll account, and that school employees were required to subscribe to the church's statement of faith. The court rejected this reasoning without explanation. Dole v. Shenandoah Baptist Church, 899 F.2d 1389 (4th Cir. 1990).**

☞ *Example. A church operates a private religious school, and provides employees with a tuition discount of 50% off of the regular annual tuition of $3,000 (for any child who attends the school). An employee earns annual income of $20,000, and sends a child to the school. The employee pays tuition of $1,500 (the regular tuition of $3,000 reduced by 50%). The church would like to reduce the employee's taxable compensation by $1,500 in order to pay for the remaining tuition. In other words, can the employee pay for the remaining tuition ($1,500) with pre-tax dollars through a salary reduction arrangement? The*

answer is no. Salary reductions can reduce taxable income only if specifically authorized by law. For example, federal law specifically authorizes the payments of contributions to a 403(b) plan (tax-sheltered annuity) or to a "cafeteria plan" to be made through salary reductions. There is no authorization to pay for tuition expenses through salary reductions. Section 127 of the Internal Revenue Code permits employees, with certain limits, to exclude from taxable income the amounts paid by an employer for the employee's educational expenses. This benefit is available only to employees (not their children), and the education has to be at the college level. Obviously, this exclusion is not available to the children of church employees. Code section 117(a) provides for the exclusion of "qualified scholarships" from a recipient's taxable income. This benefit is available to students who are pursuing a degree at a school that is accredited by a nationally recognized accreditation agency. This exclusion would not be relevant in this example since it is benefit is only available to the student and not to the student's parents.

(7) Meals or lodging furnished for the convenience of the employer. Section 119(a) of the Code and the applicable regulations provide that (a) the value of **meals** furnished to an employee by his employer shall be excluded from the employee's gross income if the meals are furnished on the business premises of the employer and they are furnished for the convenience of the employer (e.g., for a substantial noncompensatory business reason of the employer), and (b) the value of **lodging** furnished to an employee by an employer shall be excluded from the gross income of the employee if three tests are met: (1) the lodging is furnished on the business premises of the employer, (2) the lodging is furnished for the convenience of the employer, and (3) the employee is required to accept such lodging as a condition of his employment. The third requirement means that the employee is required to accept such lodging in order to enable him properly to perform the duties of his employment. Lodging will be regarded as furnished to an employee to enable him to perform his duties properly when, for example, the lodging is furnished because the employee is required to be available for duty at all times or because the employee could not perform the services required of him unless he is furnished such lodging.

To illustrate, if a church located in a high-crime area hires a security guard and requires that he reside in a home located on the church's premises, the value of such lodging need not be included in the gross income of the employee if the tests described above are satisfied.

The Code specifies that ministers may not claim an exclusion for meals or lodging furnished for the convenience of an employer in computing their *self-employment tax* liability. *IRC 1402(a)(8).*

❖ New in 1998. Beginning in 1998, the operation by an employer of an eating facility for employees will be treated as a nontaxable fringe benefit if (1) the facility is located on or near the employer's premises, and (3) revenue from the facility normally equals or exceeds the operating costs of the facility.

☞ **Example.** *A religious organization required that certain of its executive officers live in houses that it owned, and use the houses as the primary place for performing their duties. The executives were not charged for their use or occupancy of the homes. The lodging was furnished on the business premises of the employer, it was furnished for the convenience of the employer, and the employees were required to accept such lodging as a condition of their employment. Accordingly, the value of such lodging was not includable in the gross income of the employees for income tax purposes. Revenue Ruling 77-80.*

☞ **Example.** *A religious college provided meals and lodging to its faculty and staff members. The value of such meals and lodging was not excludable from the employee's gross income. They were not furnished for the convenience of the employer since they were "not functionally related to the educational or religious goals of the institution." In addition, the employees were not required to accept such arrangements as a condition of their employment. Bob Jones University v. Commissioner, 670 F.2d 167 (Ct. Cl. 1982).*

☞ **Example.** *A religious secondary school furnished lodging to its teachers. The value of such lodging was includable in the employees' gross income since the lodging was not located on the business premises of the employer and was not the site of a significant portion of the employees' duties. Goldsboro Christian School, Inc. v. Commissioner, 436 F. Supp. 1314 (D.D.C. 1978), aff'd 103 S. Ct. 2017 (1983). See also IRS Letter Ruling 8213005.*

☞ **Example.** *Ten "church centers" were engaged in religious activities including praying, preaching the gospel, ministering to the spiritual needs of members, and teaching the Bible. The centers employed full-time ordained ministers and lay workers who were required as a condition of their employment to live at the assigned church center. The primary service required of the ministers and lay workers was prayer. In addition, the ministers conducted Sunday services, held prayer meetings, counseled and helped church members, and carried out evangelistic work. The lay workers taught Bible school, administered the church's business affairs, organized and ran annual conventions, and maintained the facilities. Although the ministers and lay workers were not paid a salary, they were provided with meals and lodging. The church centers asked the IRS for a ruling addressing the federal social security tax consequences of the meals and lodging provided to the full-time ordained ministers and full-time lay workers. With regard to the lay workers, the IRS concluded that the **lodging** was for the convenience of the employer and accordingly was not includable in gross income for either federal*

*income tax or social security (FICA) purposes. Similarly, the IRS concluded that the **meals** furnished on the church premises for the lay employees were for the convenience of the employer and accordingly were not includable in gross income for federal tax purposes. However, with regard to the ordained ministers who were employed by the churches, the IRS noted that such persons are self-employed for purposes of social security taxes with respect to service performed in the exercise of their ministries. Accordingly, they are not subject to FICA taxes, but rather pay the self-employment tax with respect to such services. The IRS further noted that section 1402(a)(8) of the Code prevents the section 119 exclusion for meals and lodging from reducing a minister's net earnings. Thus, the value of meals and lodging provided by the churches to their ordained ministers "must be included in the ministers' net earnings from self-employment" for self-employment tax purposes. On the other hand, the ordained ministers were entitled to exclude from their taxable income for federal income tax purposes the value of the housing provided to them on a cost-free basis (the parsonage exclusion). IRS Letter Ruling 9129037.*

On-campus housing. The courts generally have ruled that on-campus housing furnished to teachers or staff employees of educational institutions does not qualify for exclusion from income under Code section 119(a). Employees of educational institutions who are provided "qualified campus lodging" do not need to include the value of the lodging in their income if they pay rent equal to or exceeding the lesser of (1) 5% of the appraised value of the lodging, or (2) the average rents paid by individuals (other than employees or students) for comparable housing rented by the educational institution. The lodging must be appraised by an independent appraiser and the appraisal must be "reviewed" (although not necessarily repeated) annually. Qualified campus lodging is lodging located on or near a campus of an educational institution that is furnished by or on behalf of the institution to an employee or an employee's spouse or dependents, for use as a residence, and as to which the exclusion available under Code section 119(a) does not apply. In summary, if an employee of an educational institution resides in housing furnished by the institution, he or she should initially determine whether the exclusion available under section 119(a) (described above) applies. If it does, then the total value of the lodging is excluded from the employee's gross income. If, however, the section 119(a) exclusion does not apply for any reason, then the employee may be eligible for a partial exclusion under the new rule introduced by the Tax Reform Act of 1986. IRC 119(d).

☞ **Example.** *J is employed in an administrative capacity by a college. He rents a home from the college that is qualified campus lodging, but he is not required by the college to live in the home. The house is appraised at $50,000. The average rent paid for comparable college housing by persons other than employees or students is $5,000 per year. J pays an annual rent of $3,600. He cannot exclude the value of the housing under* *section 119(a) since he was not required to accept the lodging as a condition of his employment. However, under new section 119(d), he does not include in income any of the rental value of the lodging since the rent he pays is more than the lesser of 5% of the appraised value of the house (5% x $50,000 = $2,500) or the average rent paid for comparable college housing by persons other than employees or students ($5,000). If he paid rent of only $2,000, he would have to include $500 in income ($2,500 - $2,000).*

(8) Employer-provided educational assistance. In the past, an employee's taxable income did not include amounts paid by an employer for educational assistance if such amounts were paid pursuant to an educational assistance program that met certain requirements. This exclusion was limited to $5,250 of educational assistance per employee during a calendar year, and applied whether or not the education was job related. The exclusion expired for graduate education beginning after June 30, 1996, and for undergraduate education beginning after June 30, 1997. Congress enacted legislation in 1997 that extends this exclusion for undergraduate education for courses beginning before June 1, 2000. The exclusion does not apply to graduate-level courses.

❖ **New in 1997. Congress extended the exclusion for employer-provided educational assistance for undergraduate courses beginning before June 1, 2000.**

Under the terms of the exclusion, employees are limited to an exclusion of up to $5,250 of the benefits they receive during a calendar year. This exclusion applies to both income tax and social security taxes. A "qualified educational assistance program" in the context of church employers (1) is a separate written plan of an employer for the exclusive benefit of its employees to give them educational assistance; (2) cannot have eligibility requirements that discriminate in favor of officers or highly compensated employees or their dependents (as defined earlier in this chapter); (3) must not provide eligible employees with a choice between educational assistance and cash; and (4) must provide for reasonable notification of the availability and the terms of the program to eligible employees. *IRC 127.*

The term "employee" includes self-employed persons. Educational assistance provided by an employer includes payments for such expenses as tuition, fees, books, and equipment. It does not include payment for tools or supplies (other than books) that an employee may retain after the completion of a course; meals or lodging; or transportation.

Finally, note that any employer (including a church) that maintains an educational assistance plan must file an annual return (Form 5500, Schedule F) with the IRS. See section I, below, for more details.

✎ **Key point: even after this exclusion expires in 2000 it is still possible that some ministers and lay employees will be able to treat employer-paid educational expenses as a**

nontaxable **"working condition fringe benefit." A working condition fringe benefit is a benefit which, if the employee had paid for it, would have been deductible as a business expense. Working condition fringe benefits are discussed earlier in this chapter.**

(9) Employer-provided dependent care. Payments made by employers to their employees for child care may be excluded from income. *IRC 129.* The same applies to the value of child care services made available to employees on the employer's premises. This benefit will apply to many churches that maintain child care facilities and that offer child care services at reduced or no cost to employees. For the exclusion to be available, the following requirements must be satisfied:

• The child care payments, or the provision of child care services directly on the employer's premises, must be authorized by a written plan of the employer for the exclusive benefit of its employees.

• The employer must notify each employee of the availability and terms of the plan.

• The employer, by January 31 of each year, must furnish each employee a statement showing the amounts paid or expenses incurred by the employer in providing dependent care assistance to each employee during the previous year.

• The plan must not discriminate in favor of "highly compensated employees" (defined above).

If any of these rules is not met, only highly compensated employees are required to include the value of dependent care assistance in their gross income.

An employee may exclude the amount of child care payments made by an employer, or the value of child care services made available on the employer's premises, up to but not exceeding the lowest of the following three amounts: (1) the employee's earned income, (2) if an employee is married, the earned income of the employee's spouse, or (3) $5,000. In valuing child care services provided on an employer's premises, take into account how often an employee's dependents utilize the facility and the value of the services provided.

This exclusion is not available with respect to payments made directly to an employee's dependents. Further, the amount of the exclusion will reduce the dollar limit on work-related expenses used in computing the child care credit. Employers who reasonably believe that an employee will be able to exclude the entire value of employer-provided child care assistance are not required to withhold taxes on any portion of the value of this benefit.

To calculate the correct amount of the exclusion, an employee must complete IRS Form 2441. The name, address, and taxpayer identification number of the child care provider must be listed on the form. If the provider is a tax-exempt organization that does not have a federal taxpayer identification number, then only the name and address of the provider must be listed.

This exclusion is available to both employees and self-employed persons.

✎ **Key point: an employer's reimbursements of your moving expenses may be a tax-free fringe benefit if certain conditions are met.**

✎ **Key point: Persons who claim the dependent care credit must include on their tax return the name and social security number of each dependent. In the past, the IRS could assess a $50 penalty for each failure to provide a correct social security number for a dependent. The IRS now has the authority to deny both a dependency exemption and dependent care credit to any taxpayer who fails to provide the correct social security number of a dependent on his or her tax return.**

(10) Employer paid moving expenses. Employer reimbursements of an employee's moving expenses are treated as a tax-free fringe benefit if (1) the moving expenses would be deductible by the employee if paid directly by the employee (see chapter 7 for an explanation); (2) the employee did not deduct the expenses in a prior year; and (3) the employer only reimburses those moving expenses that are properly substantiated by the employee (under rules similar to an accountable expense reimbursement arrangement).

Employer reimbursements that satisfy these requirements are not reported in box 1 of the W-2 form, but must be reported in box 13. Code "P" is used to identify these nontaxable reimbursements in box 13. An employer's reimbursements of an employee's moving expenses are not excludable from the employee's income if the employee deducted the expenses in a prior year. A committee report explaining the new moving expense rules specifies that an "employer [may] treat moving expenses as excludable unless it has actual knowledge that the employee deducted the expenses in a prior year. The employer has no obligation to determine whether the individual deducted the expenses."

I. Reporting Requirements (Form 5500)

Federal law requires that "every employer maintaining a specified fringe benefit plan during any year . . . shall file a return . . . with respect to such plan showing for such year (1) the number of employees of the employer, (2) the number of employees of the employer eligible to participate under the plan, (3) the number of employees participating under the plan, (4) the total cost of the plan during the year, (5) the name, address, and taxpayer identification number of the employer and the type of business in which the employer is engaged, (6) the number of highly compensated employees among the employees described [above]." *IRC 6039D.* The term "specified fringe benefit plan" is defined to include

- employer paid group life insurance premiums

- accident and health plans

- employer paid medical insurance premiums

- employer-provided group legal services
- cafeteria plans

- employer-provided educational assistance

- employer-provided dependent care

As a result, any employer providing any of these types of fringe benefits to some or all of its employees must file an annual return with the IRS providing the kinds of information summarized above. The correct return is IRS Form 5500, Schedule F. The penalty for failing to file this return is up to $25 each day ($15,000 maximum).

However, in 1990 the IRS ruled that employers maintaining plans under Code sections 79 (employer paid group life insurance), 105 (accident and health plans), 106 (employer paid medical insurance premiums), or 129 (employer-provided dependent care) are not required to file Form 5500 (Schedule F) until the IRS publishes further guidance. *IRS Notice 90-24.* Thus far, the IRS has not issued the promised notice, and so churches and other employers that provide these kinds of fringe benefits need not file a 5500 form with the IRS. However, there are two kinds of fringe benefit for which a Form 5500 (Schedule F) must be filed annually—cafeteria plans and employer-provided educational assistance. These forms ordinarily are due by the last day of the seventh month after the plan year ends. For more information, see the instructions to Form 5500, Schedule F. There is no exemption of churches or church plans from this limited filing requirement. As a result, churches with either cafeteria plans under Code section 125 or employer-provided educational assistance plans under Code section 127 (both are described above) must file an annual Form 5500, Schedule F, with the IRS. Failure to do so may result in penalties.

The instructions to Form 5500 do exempt "church plans" from the requirement of filing a Form 5500 for employee benefit plans. This means that most churches need not file a Form 5500 with regard to some types of pension and retirement plans. See chapter 10 for more information about church retirement plans.

Chapter 6

MINISTERS' HOUSING AND PARSONAGE ALLOWANCES

Chapter Highlights

- **Parsonages.** Clergy can exclude from their income for federal income tax reporting purposes the fair rental value of a parsonage provided to them as compensation for ministerial services. The fair rental value of the parsonage is not "deducted" from the minister's income. Rather, it is not reported as additional income (as it generally would be by non-clergy workers).

- **Parsonage allowances.** Clergy who live in a parsonage can exclude from their income for federal income tax reporting purposes the portion of their ministerial compensation designated by their employer as a "parsonage allowance"—to the extent that it in fact is used to pay for parsonage-related expenses such as utilities, repairs, and furnishings.

- **Housing allowances.** Clergy who own or rent their homes can exclude from their income for federal income tax reporting purposes the portion of their ministerial income designated by their employer as a "housing" allowance—to the extent that the allowance is in fact used to pay for housing-related expenses such as rent, mortgage payments, utilities, repairs, furnishings, insurance, property taxes, additions, and maintenance. In addition, a housing allowance exclusion for clergy who own their homes may not exceed the fair rental value of their home (furnished, including utilities).

- **Designating an allowance.** Parsonage and housing "allowances" should be (1) adopted by the church board or congregation, (2) in writing, and (3) in advance of the calendar year. However, churches that fail to designate an allowance in advance of a calendar year should do so as soon as possible in the new year. The allowance will operate prospectively.

- **Safety net housing allowances.** Churches should consider adopting a "safety net" allowance to protect against the loss of this significant tax benefit due to the inadvertent failure by the church to designate an allowance.

- **Equity allowances.** Churches should consider adopting an appropriate "equity allowance" for clergy who live in church-owned parsonages.

- **Amending the allowance.** Churches can amend an allowance during the year if the original allowance proves to be too low. However, the amended allowance will only operate prospectively.

- **No retroactive application.** Under no circumstances can a minister exclude any portion of an allowance retroactively designated by a church.

- **Social security.** The fair rental value of a parsonage, and a housing allowance, are exclusions only for federal income tax reporting purposes. They must be included in a minister's self-employment earnings for purposes of the self-employment tax (the social security tax on self-employed persons).

- **Pension funds.** In some cases, a church pension plan may designate a housing allowance for retired clergy.

- **Reporting.** Housing allowances do not need to be reported by a church on a minister's W-2 or 1099. Further, a church does not need to issue two checks—one for salary and one for housing allowance.

- **Setting the allowance.** There is no "limit" on the amount of a minister's compensation that can be designated by a church as a housing allowance (assuming that the minister's compensation is reasonable in amount). However, for clergy who own their home, a church ordinarily should not designate a housing allowance significantly above the fair rental value of the home (plus utilities)—since clergy will not be able to exclude more than this amount.

Clergy typically find themselves in one of three housing arrangements. First, they may live in a church-provided parsonage. Second, they may be paid a "rental allowance" with which they rent a home. Third, they may be paid a "housing allowance" with which they purchase a home. Federal tax law enables clergy to exclude from their gross income for income tax purposes

- the fair rental value of a church-owned parsonage that they are permitted to occupy on a rent-free basis as part of their church compensation

- the portion of their church compensation that is designated in advance as a parsonage allowance to the extent that the minister's out-of-pocket expenses incurred in maintaining the parsonage (including furnishings and utilities) equal or exceed the allowance

- the portion of their church compensation that is designated in advance as a rental allowance to the extent that the minister's expenses incurred in renting a home equal or exceed the allowance

- the portion of their church compensation that is designated in advance as a housing allowance to the extent that the minister's expenses incurred in owning and maintaining the home equal or exceed the allowance and do not exceed the fair rental value of the home (furnished, including utilities).

These rules are summarized in Table 6-1. *They represent the most significant tax benefit enjoyed by clergy.* Yet, many ministers either fail to claim it or do not claim enough. In some cases, this results from tax advisers who are unfamiliar with ministers' taxes.

Because the rules for clergy living in church-owned parsonages differ from the rules that apply to clergy who own or rent their home, this chapter will be divided into two sections. Section A will summarize the requirements for obtaining the full benefit available to ministers who live in a church-owned parsonage. In section B, the rules that apply to ministers who rent or own their homes will be considered.

A. Parsonages

✎ **Key point: clergy can exclude from their federal income taxes the fair rental value of a parsonage provided to them as compensation for ministerial services. The fair rental value of the parsonage is not "deducted" from the minister's income. Rather, it is not reported as additional income (as it generally would be by non-clergy employees).**

✎ **Key point: clergy who live in a parsonage can exclude from their federal income taxes the portion of their ministerial compensation designated by their employer as a "parsonage allowance"—to the extent that it in fact is used to pay for parsonage-related expenses such as utilities, repairs, and furnishings.**

Since 1921, clergy have been permitted to exclude from their gross income for income tax purposes the fair rental value of a church-owned parsonage provided to them rent-free as part of their compensation for services rendered to the church. Congress has never explained the justification for this rule. Apparently, it is based on the principle that the rental value of lodging furnished rent-free to an employee on an employer's business premises should be ex-

Table 6-1
Tax Consequences of Different
Clergy Housing Arrangements

rule	explanation
parsonage	the exclusion (for federal income tax purposes) of the fair rental value of a church-owned parsonage provided rent-free to a minister
parsonage allowance	the exclusion (for federal income tax purposes) of that portion of a minister's compensation that a church designates as a *parsonage allowance*, to the extent that it is used for housing expenses by a minister who lives in a church-provided parsonage
housing allowance	the exclusion (for federal income tax purposes) of that portion of a minister's compensation that a church designates as a housing allowance, to the extent that it is used for housing expenses by a minister who owns his or her home and does not exceed the fair rental value of the home (furnished, including utilities)
rental allowance	the exclusion (for federal income tax purposes) of that portion of a minister's compensation that a church designates as a *rental allowance*, to the extent that it is used for housing expenses by a minister who rents his or her home

cluded from gross income if it is furnished "for the convenience of the employer" and the employee must accept such lodging in order to adequately perform his or her duties. *IRC 119.*

Section 107 of the Internal Revenue Code says simply that "in the case of a minister of the gospel, gross income does not include—(1) the rental value of a home furnished to him as part of his compensation; or (2) the rental allowance paid to him as part of his compensation, to the extent used by him to rent or provide a home." There are **four important considerations** to note in this section:

First: The exclusion of the "rental value" of a parsonage (and a parsonage allowance) is available only to a "minister of the gospel." This important term is defined fully in chapter 3.

Second: The exclusion of a parsonage allowance is available only with respect to compensation paid to the minister by the church. The income tax regulations (drafted by the Treasury Department and interpreting the Code) clarify this second requirement by requiring that the parsonage or parsonage allowance (to qualify for the exclusion) must be "provided as remuneration for services which are ordinarily the duties of a minister of the gospel." In other words, the parsonage (and parsonage allowance) exclusion is available only if (1) the recipient is a minister of the gospel, and (2) the benefit is made available to the minister as compensation for services which are ordinarily the duties of a minister of the gospel. These "eligibility" requirements are discussed fully in chapter 3, and they should be reviewed at this time.

Third: The annual fair rental value of a church-provided parsonage is an exclusion from gross income, rather than a deduction in computing or reducing adjusted gross income. As a result, it is not reported anywhere on Form 1040. In effect, the exclusion is "claimed" by not reporting the parsonage's fair rental value as income. Many ministers find this confusing, and think that they are not receiving a tax "benefit" unless they can "deduct" something on their tax return. In fact, some clergy erroneously "deduct" the fair rental value of a parsonage from their church compensation for tax reporting purposes. This practice clearly violates federal tax law. Keep in mind that virtually any other worker who receives rent-free use of an employer-provided home must include the fair rental value of the home in his or her gross income for both income tax and social security tax purposes. Ministers, however, do not include the fair rental value of a church-provided parsonage in their income for *income tax* purposes. This is a very real benefit. As noted below, the fair rental value of a parsonage (and any additional parsonage allowance designated by a church) must be included in self-employment earnings on Schedule SE (Form 1040) in computing a minister's *social security* tax liability.

☞ **Example.** Frank lives in Chicago and works for a large business company. His employer wants to transfer Frank to a Los Angeles office for two years, and then return him to Chicago. The company allows Frank to live in a home that it owns in Los Angeles for the two-year term. The fair rental value of the home provided to Frank rent-free is income to him for income tax and social security tax purposes. Accordingly, if Frank's annual salary is $50,000, and the annual rental value of the Los Angeles home is $15,000, Frank's employer must report compensation of $65,000 on Frank's W-2 form.

☞ **Example.** Same facts as the preceding example, except assume that Frank is a minister who leaves a church in Chicago to accept a pastorate in Los Angeles, and that the Los Angeles church provides him with rent-free use of a church-owned parsonage. Frank's W-2 income (assuming that he is an employee) would be only $50,000 (not $65,000). The fair rental value of the home is not reported as taxable income. This is a significant benefit compared to the previous example involving an employee who was not a minister, and it will result in a tax savings of several thousands of dollars. Some clergy erroneously "deduct" the rental value of their parsonage from their taxable income. For example, assume that Frank instructs his church treasurer to reduce his W-2 income by $15,000 so that only $35,000 is reported. This practice clearly violates federal law, and should be avoided. The tax benefit is that Frank does not have to report the fair rental value of the home ($15,000) as income in addition to his $50,000 salary. Finally, note that Frank would have to pay social security taxes on the rental value of the parsonage (assuming that he is not exempt from social security coverage).

Fourth: Section 107 excludes the fair rental value of a parsonage provided rent-free to a minister as well as an allowance paid to a minister to the extent used by him or her to pay expenses incurred in maintaining the parsonage (e.g., utilities, repairs, furnishings). Ministers who live in a church-owned parsonage do not report the fair rental value of the parsonage as income and the church is not required to declare an allowance in the amount of the fair rental value of the parsonage. The exclusion is automatic. However, if the minister incurs any expenses in living in the parsonage, then he or she may exclude them

---

Illustration 6-1
Parsonage Allowance Designation for Ministers Who Live in a Church-Owned Parsonage

The following resolution was duly adopted by the board of directors of First Church at a regularly scheduled meeting held on December 15, 1997, a quorum being present:

Whereas, section 107 of the Internal Revenue Code permits a minister of the gospel to exclude from gross income "the rental value of a home furnished to him as part of his compensation," or a church-designated allowance paid to him as part of his compensation to the extent used by him for actual expenses incurred in maintaining a church-owned parsonage; and

Whereas, Rev. John Smith is compensated by First Church exclusively for services as a minister of the gospel; and

Whereas First Church provides Rev. Smith with rent-free use of a church-owned parsonage as compensation for services that he renders to the church in the exercise of his ministry; and

Whereas, as additional compensation to Rev. Smith for services that he renders to the church in the exercise of his ministry, First

Church also desires to pay Rev. Smith for expenses that he incurs in maintaining the parsonage; therefore, it is hereby

Resolved, that the annual compensation paid to Rev. Smith for calendar year 1998 shall be $55,000, of which $5,000 is hereby designated to be a parsonage allowance pursuant to section 107 of the Internal Revenue Code; and it is further

Resolved, that the designation of $5,000 as a parsonage allowance shall apply to calendar year 1998 and all future years unless otherwise provided by this board; and it is further

Resolved, that as additional compensation to Rev. Smith for calendar year 1998 and for all future years unless otherwise provided by this board, Rev. Smith shall be permitted to live in the church-owned parsonage located at 123 Main St., and that no rent or other fee shall be payable by Rev. Smith for such occupancy and use.

only to the extent that they do not exceed a "parsonage allowance" declared in writing and in advance by the church board. See Illustration 6-1 for an example of a parsonage allowance designation.

☞ *Example. The IRS has ruled that a minister who lived in a church-owned parsonage could exclude from gross income that portion of his salary that was designated in advance by his employing church as a parsonage allowance. The IRS observed: "[A] minister of the gospel who is furnished a parsonage rent-free may exclude a rental allowance to the extent used by him to pay for utilities so long as the employing church or church organization designates a part of his remuneration as a rental allowance. . . . Accordingly, [if] a minister of the gospel who is provided a home rent-free by a church or other qualified organization as part of his compensation . . . pays for his utilities, [and] an amount of his compensation is designated as a 'rental allowance' to cover the cost of his utilities, he may exclude from his gross income not only the rental value of the home but also the amount of the 'rental allowance' to the extent used by him to pay for his utilities." Revenue Ruling 59-350.*

An additional requirement, not mentioned in section 107, is that the fair rental value of a parsonage (or a parsonage allowance declared by a church) must be **reasonable in amount**. *IRC 501(c)(3).* Providing a minister with a parsonage (or parsonage allowance) that is excessive in amount may constitute "unreasonable compensation." Such a finding could jeopardize the tax-exempt status of the church and lead to adverse tax consequences for the minister. See chapter 4, section A, for a discussion of unreasonable compensation.

The bankruptcy court presiding over the PTL bankruptcy acknowledged that clergy who live rent-free in a church-owned parsonage may exclude from income (for income tax purposes) the fair rental value of the parsonage. And, they may also exclude that part of their compensation designated by their employing church as a "parsonage allowance" to the extent it is actually used to pay parsonage-related expenses. However, the court noted that Jim Bakker not only lived in a parsonage rent-free, but also received a "housekeeping and maintenance allowance" (of about $28,000 each year) and a housing allowance (of $24,000 each year) despite the fact that PTL paid all of his utilities. Such payments clearly were above any reasonable parsonage-related expenses, in the court's judgment. *Heritage Village Church and Missionary Fellowship, Inc., 92 B.R. 1000 (D.S.C. 1988).* Obviously, clergy who live in a parsonage and who pay none of the expenses of maintaining the parsonage are not eligible for a parsonage allowance exclusion. Further, a "housing allowance" generally is not available to a minister who resides in a church-owned parsonage (on a rent-free basis). Housing (or rental) allowances are provided to clergy who do *not* live in a church-owned parsonage.

☞ *Example. Rev. W lives rent-free in a church-owned parsonage having a fair rental value of $6,000 in 1997. The church expects Rev. W to*

incur some expenses in living in the parsonage, and accordingly provides him with an allowance of $200 each month. His salary (not including the monthly allowance) was $30,000 in 1997. On his 1997 federal income tax return, Rev. W would not report the fair rental value of the parsonage ($6,000) as income, even though the church never designated that amount as a housing allowance. However, he would have to report the total monthly allowances ($2,400) as income unless the church board declared a "parsonage allowance" in writing and in advance of at least $2,400. Eden v. Commissioner, 41 T.C. 605 (1961). See also Revenue Ruling 59-350.

☞ *Example. Rev. R lives rent-free in a church-owned parsonage having a fair rental value of $6,000 in 1997. The church pays the utilities charged to the parsonage, which amount to $3,000 for 1997. While this specific issue has never been addressed by the IRS or the courts, it is reasonable to assume that parsonage utilities paid by a church would be excludable from a minister's gross income for income tax purposes. In effect, the church is designating this amount as a parsonage allowance each month by paying it. While the $3,000 does not represent taxable income to Rev. R for income tax reporting purposes, it is taxable for self-employment (social security) tax purposes and accordingly Rev. R must add the $3,000 to self-employment earnings in computing the self-employment tax.*

☞ *Example. IRS Publication 517 contains the following example: Rev. Amos Baker is a full-time minister at the Central Mission Church. The church allows him to use the parsonage that has an annual fair rental value of $4,800. The church pays him an annual salary of $13,200, of which $1,200 is designated for utility costs. During the year, his utility costs were $1,000. For income tax purposes, Rev. Baker excludes $5,800 from gross income (the fair rental value of the parsonage plus $1,000 from the allowance for utility costs). He will report $12,200 ($12,000 salary and $200 of unused utility allowance). His income for self-employment tax, however, is $18,000 ($13,200 S $4,800).*

☞ *Suggestion. Ministers living in parsonages should be sure to have the church board declare a "parsonage allowance" in advance of each calendar year to cover any miscellaneous expenses they may incur in living in the parsonage. The allowance should be declared in writing and be incorporated into the board's minutes. The allowance can be a portion of the minister's salary. For example, in the previous example, the church could have declared $2,400 of Rev. W's annual salary of $30,000 to be a parsonage allowance. The effect of this would have been to exclude the $2,400 from gross income (to the extent Rev. W incurred expenses of at least that amount). Churches failing to declare a parsonage allowance before January 1 should not wait until the following year to act. The declaration is effective from the date of its enactment. Therefore, a church* failing to declare a parsonage allowance until March can still provide its minister with an important tax benefit for the remainder of the year.

Rental value of a parsonage. The parsonage exclusion and parsonage allowance exclusion are exclusions for federal income tax purposes only. They cannot under any circumstances be excluded in computing a minister's social security (self-employment) tax liability. Therefore, in computing the social security tax on Schedule SE of Form 1040, a minister who lives in a church-owned parsonage must *include* the fair rental value of the parsonage as income on line 2 (of either the "short" or "long" Schedule SE, whichever applies). A minister must also include any parsonage allowance paid by the church to cover miscellaneous expenses in maintaining the parsonage. The rental value of a parsonage is a question of fact to be determined in each case on the basis of its particular circumstances. Some have suggested that a fair approximation of the monthly rental value of a home can be computed simply by taking 1% of the home's fair market value. For example, if a home has a fair market value of $80,000, then its monthly rental value would be $800 ($80,000 x 1%) and its annual rental value would be $9,600. Obviously, the most that can be said for this method is that it will yield accurate results in some cases, but very inaccurate results in others. Generally, however, this approach yields excessive rental values.

✎ **Key point: the IRS audit guidelines for ministers instruct agents that "[d]etermining the fair rental value [of a parsonage] is a question of all facts and circumstances based on the local market, but the church and minister have often already agreed on a figure and can provide documentary evidence."**

☞ **Example.** Rev. T lives in a church-owned parsonage. He is not exempt from social security coverage. In an effort to avoid any increase in Rev. T's social security tax liability, the church agrees to "rent" the parsonage to Rev. T for $1 each year. Rev. T then lists only $1 as the parsonage's rental value on his Schedule SE in computing his social security tax liability. This practice will not achieve its desired savings in social security taxes, since a minister must include the fair rental value of a church-provided parsonage as income on Schedule SE. The fair rental value of the parsonage is not $1. Rather, it is what houses of comparable size and quality in the same vicinity would rent for in an arm's-length transaction.

☞ **Example.** A minister was provided with a parsonage and in addition a portion of his annual compensation was designated a parsonage allowance to assist him in paying utilities, furnishings, and other miscellaneous expenses. The fair rental value of a parsonage is taxable in computing a minister's self-employment (social security) tax. The minister claimed that this amount "includes" any parsonage allowance designated by the church. As a result, he reduced his parsonage's fair rental value by the parsonage allowance designated by his church in computing his self-employment tax. The Tax Court ruled that this was improper, noting that the minister had "not proven that the stipulated fair rental value of the parsonage already includes amounts designated or received in cash relating to the utility and other household expenses of the parsonages." Radde v. Commissioner, T.C. Memo. 1997-490 (1997).

Some churches in high-cost areas purchase a parsonage in order to make housing available to their minister. However, the rental value of such parsonages often is very high, resulting in large increases in the minister's self-employment taxes. For

---

IRS "Tax Guide for Churches"

In 1994 the IRS released a "tax guide for churches." This short booklet contains summaries of several rules that apply to churches and ministers. The tax guide contains the following statements regarding parsonages and housing allowances:

A minister's gross income does not include the rental value of a home (a parsonage) provided, or the rental allowance paid, as part of his or her compensation for services performed that are ordinarily the duties of a minister.

A minister who is furnished a parsonage may exclude the fair rental value of a parsonage. A minister who receives a rental allowance may exclude the allowance to the extent it is used for expenses in providing a home. Generally, those expenses include rent, mortgage payments, utilities, repairs, and other expenses directly relating to providing a home.

Only one parsonage or rental allowance may be provided to a minister, and the parsonage or rental allowance must be reasonable in amount. The exclusion of the fair rental value of the parsonage or the rental allowance provided is for income tax purposes only. The amounts may not be excluded in calculating the minister's social security (self-employment) tax. The minister's employing organization must designate the rental allowance pursuant to official action taken in advance of the payment. If a minister is employed and paid by a local congregation, a resolution by a national church agency of the denomination will not be an effective designation. The designation must be made by the local congregation. A national church agency can make an effective designation for ministers it directly employs. . . . A minister who owns or is purchasing a home may exclude the parsonage allowance from gross income to the extent it is used for the down payment, mortgage payments, interest, real estate taxes, utilities, and repairs.

example, assume that church purchased a parsonage several years ago that currently is worth several hundreds of thousands of dollars, and that has an annual fair rental value of $25,000. A minister who lives in such a parsonage would need to add the full $25,000 fair rental value in computing his or her earnings subject to the self-employment tax (15.3% in 1997). This will result in an increase in self-employment taxes of nearly $4,000 (without taking into account any available deductions). While this is a significant tax increase, keep in mind the following considerations: (1) the minister is still receiving a significant income tax benefit (the $25,000 is not taxable for income tax purposes); (2) the additional taxes must be offset by the value of living in a home of substantial value; (3) clergy pay the full 15.3% self-employment rate only on earnings of up to $62,700 (they pay only the 2.9% medicare component of self-employment taxes on all net earnings from self-employment in excess of this amount)—so, to the extent that the fair rental value of the parsonage boosts the minister's earnings above $62,700 the excess is only partially taxable.

☞ *Example. Rev. H excluded a "parsonage allowance" from his reportable income though his employing church had never designated a portion of his compensation as a parsonage allowance. The Tax Court ruled that Rev. H was not entitled to exclude the allowance since it had not been designated by his church prior to the time of its payment. Hoelz v. Commissioner, 42 T.C.M. 1037 (1981).*

Equity allowances. Ministers who live in church-owned parsonages experience a significant disadvantage—they do not acquire any equity in a home. To illustrate, assume that Rev. E lives in church-owned parsonages throughout his 35-year career as a minister. When Rev. E retires, he must vacate the parsonage he is occupying, and he has no equity interest in any of the parsonages he has occupied that can be used to acquire a retirement home. If Rev. E had owned homes throughout his career, then he would have been accumulating equity in the amount of his combined principal mortgage payments plus any appreciation in the value of the homes that he owned. At retirement, not only would Rev. E have a home in which he could remain, but he also would have accumulated a significant equity interest. Some churches have helped ministers who live in parsonages avoid or at least reduce the adverse economic impact of this housing arrangement by providing them with an equity allowance over and above their stated compensation. This allowance is designed to partially or wholly compensate the minister for the "lost opportunity" of accumulating equity in a home. Since the purpose of such an allowance is to assist the minister in obtaining suitable housing at retirement, it is important that the allowance not be available to the minister until retirement. One way that churches can accomplish this is to deposit the annual equity allowance in a tax-favored retirement program not currently accessible to the minister. This is an excellent approach that can help to avoid a most unfortunate financial predicament for a minister who, often sacrificially, has devoted a lifetime to the church. However, since an equity allowance ordinarily

does not compensate a minister for actual costs incurred in living in a parsonage, it is not excludable from income as a parsonage allowance.

✎ **Key point: churches should consider adopting an appropriate "equity allowance" for clergy who live in church-owned parsonages**

IRS audit guidelines for ministers. The IRS issued audit guidelines in 1995 for its agents to follow when auditing ministers. The guidelines provide agents with the following information regarding parsonages and parsonage allowances:

Code section 107 provides an exclusion from gross income for a parsonage allowance . . . . The term parsonage allowance includes church provided parsonages, rental allowance with which the minister may rent a home and housing allowances with which the minister may purchase a home. The value of the parsonage allowance is not included in computing the minister's income subject to income tax and should not be included in W-2 wages. However, the parsonage allowance is subject to self-employment tax along with other earnings. If a church-owned parsonage is provided to the minister, instead of an allowance, the fair rental value of the housing must be determined. Determining the fair rental value is a question of all facts and circumstances based on the local market, but the church and minister have often already agreed on a figure and can provide documentary evidence. The exclusion under Code section 107 only applies if the employing church designates the amount of the parsonage allowance in advance of the tax year. The designation may appear in the minister's employment contract, the church minutes, the church budget, or any other document indicating official action. An additional requirement for purposes of Code section 107 is that the fair rental value of the parsonage or parsonage allowance must be reasonable in amount.

The audit guidelines contain the following example:

☞ *Example. A is an ordained minister. She receives an annual salary of $36,000 and use of a parsonage which has a fair rental value of $800 a month, including utilities. She has an accountable plan for other business expenses such as travel. A's gross income for arriving at taxable income for Federal income tax purposes is $36,000, but for self-employment tax purposes it is $45,600 ($36,000 salary + $9,600 fair rental value of parsonage).*

✎ **Key point: the audit guidelines assist IRS agents in the examination of ministers' tax returns. They alert agents to the key questions to ask, and provide background information along with the IRS position on a number of issues. It is therefore of utmost importance that ministers be familiar with these guidelines.**

✎ **Key point: the IRS audit guidelines for ministers, quoted above, specify that the parsonage allowance exclusion "only applies if** the employing church designates the amount of the parsonage allowance in advance of the tax year." This is an unfortunate statement since it is simply not true. It is true that a church's parsonage allowance designation may never be made retroactively, and only operates prospectively. But this does not mean that it has to be made in advance of a tax year. To illustrate, many churches fail to designate a parsonage allowance by the end of a calendar year and discover the omission a few months into the new year. The church can still designate a parsonage allowance for the minister for the remainder of the new year. Unfortunately, unless the guidelines are amended, agents may disallow unnecessarily any parsonage allowance exclusion under these facts.

Parsonages provided to retired ministers. The tax status of parsonages and parsonage allowances provided to retired ministers is addressed fully in chapter 10, section K, of this tax guide.

B. Owning or Renting Your Home

✎ **Key point: clergy who own or rent their homes can exclude from their federal income taxes the portion of their ministerial income designated by their employer as a "housing" allowance to the extent that the allowance is in fact used to pay for housing-related expenses and does not exceed the fair rental value of the home (furnished, including utilities).**

The previous section showed ministers who live in church-owned parsonages how to obtain the full benefit of a parsonage (and parsonage allowance) exclusion. In this section, the rules pertaining to ministers who own or rent their home will be considered. For simplicity, the "housing" and "rental" allowances will often be referred to simply as "housing" allowances.

Section 107 of the Internal Revenue Code provides that "in the case of a minister of the gospel, gross income does not include . . . [an] allowance paid to him as part of his compensation, to the extent used by him to rent or provide a home." There are **four important considerations** to note in this section:

First: The housing allowance is available only to a "minister of the gospel." This important term is defined fully in chapter 3.

Second: The exclusion of a housing allowance is available only with respect to compensation paid to a minister for service performed in the exercise of ministry. The income tax regulations (drafted by the Treasury Department and interpreting the Code) clarify this second requirement by requiring that the housing allowance (to qualify for the exclusion) must be "provided as remuneration for services which are ordinarily the duties of a minister of the gospel." In other words, the housing allowance exclusion is available only if (1) the recipient is a minister of the gospel, and (2) the benefit is made available to the minister as compensation for services which are ordinarily the duties of a minister of the gospel. These "eligibility" requirements are discussed fully in chapter 3, and they should be reviewed at this time.

Third: The housing allowance is an exclusion from gross income, rather than a deduction in computing or reducing adjusted gross income. As a result, it is not reported anywhere on Form 1040. In effect, the housing allowance is "claimed" by not reporting it as income. As will be explained later, if the actual housing allowance exclusion is less than the church-designated allowance, then the minister will need to report

---

TELEPHONE EXPENSES

Can clergy include the costs of both personal and business use of a home telephone in computing their housing allowance exclusion?

While neither the IRS nor a federal court has addressed this issue directly, a case can be made that local telephone expenses are properly includable in the housing allowance calculation. Here's why. Section 107 of the Code permits a minister to exclude a housing allowance "to the extent used by him to rent or provide a home." There is no requirement that the expenses be "business" related. All that is required is that the expenses be incurred to rent or provide a home. Clergy are permitted to exclude the full amount of their mortgage payments, insurance, taxes, electricity, natural gas, and water (assuming these expenses do not exceed the housing allowance)—despite the fact that the vast majority of such expenses are incurred for purely "personal" reasons having nothing to do with the conduct of the minister's profession. They are excludable not because they are business related, but because they are housing related. Under this analysis, telephone expenses would be includable in the housing allowance calculation so long as they are reasonably necessary to "provide a home." Clearly, the use of a telephone for local calls (the "base charge") is indispensable to a minister's home. Therefore, an argument could be made that such telephone expenses are includable in the housing allowance calculation (whether for business or personal use). Such expenses are like electricity expenses—they are reasonably necessary to "provide a home," and accordingly they are includable in their entirety in the housing allowance calculation despite the fact that a substantial portion of such expenses are not "business" related. Again, the IRS has not addressed this question, nor has any federal court. All that can be said is that local telephone expenses would appear to be no different than other housing expenses that are fully includable in the housing allowance calculation without regard to being "business" related. However, this same reasoning ordinarily would not apply to long-distance telephone calls.

the difference as additional income on his or her federal tax return. This assumes that the church reduced the minister's W-2 or 1099 income by the amount of the allowance. Note further that the actual housing allowance exclusion must be reported as "self-employment earnings" on a minister's Schedule SE (Form 1040) in computing social security taxes, assuming the minister has not applied for and received an approved exemption from social security coverage.

Fourth: The exclusion pertains only to an "allowance" declared by an employing church or church agency and used by a minister to "rent or provide a home." The income tax regulations define "provide a home" as including the purchase of a home or any expense directly related to owning or maintaining a home. Therefore, whether a minister owns or rents a home, it is essential that his or her employing church designate a housing allowance. The regulations require that the allowance be designated as a housing allowance by official board action taken in advance of payment. The designation need not be in advance of the calendar year, but it will only be effective from the date of its enactment. See Illustration 6-2 for an example of a church designated housing allowance.

✎ **Key point: parsonage and housing "allowances" should be (1) adopted by the church board or congregation, (2) in writing, and (3) in advance of the calendar year. However, churches that fail to designate an allowance in advance of a calendar year should do so as soon as possible in the new year. The allowance will operate prospectively.**

Designating the housing allowance. The income tax regulations specify that the designation of the allowance may be contained in "an employment contract, in minutes of or in a resolution by a church or other qualified organization or in its budget, or in any other appropriate instrument evidencing such official action." The regulations further provide that "the designation . . . is a sufficient designation if it permits a payment or a part thereof to be identified as a payment of rental allowance as distinguished from salary or other remuneration." *Treas. Reg. 1.107-1(b).* In other words, the designation must simply distinguish a part of the minister's compensation as a housing allowance. This can be done by giving a minister two separate checks—one designated as salary and the other as the housing or rental allowance. This approach is not necessary, since a church that has designated a portion of a minister's compensation as a housing or rental allowance has thereby made the required identification, and it is free to issue a minister one check per pay period that combines both salary and the housing or rental allowance.

The church's designation should be in writing, although if a board orally agrees to a specific allowance and neglects to make a written record of its action, it of course could draft an appropriate record of its action at a later time, dated as of the earlier meeting. *Kizer v. Commissioner, T.C. Memo. 1992-584.* The Tax Court has ruled that an oral designation is sufficient since "there is no requirement that the designation be in writing." *Libman v. Commissioner,*

HOUSING EXPENSES TO INCLUDE IN COMPUTING YOUR HOUSING ALLOWANCE EXCLUSION.

Clergy who own their homes should take the following expenses into account in computing their housing allowance exclusion:

- down payment on a home

- mortgage payments on a loan to purchase or improve your home (include both interest and principal)

- real estate taxes

- property insurance

- utilities (electricity, gas, water, trash pickup, local telephone charges)

- furnishings and appliances (purchase and repair)

- structural repairs and remodeling

- yard maintenance and improvements

- maintenance items (household cleansers, light bulbs, pest control, etc.)

- homeowners association dues

---

44 T.C.M. 370 (1982). This practice should be avoided, since it will always create problems of proof. For example, one traveling evangelist was denied any housing allowance exclusion despite his vigorous insistence that various churches in which he had conducted services had orally designated a portion of his compensation as a housing allowance. The Tax Court noted that there was no evidence of such designations, and that the minister's testimony was "marred by numerous inconsistencies." *Holland v. Commissioner, 47 T.C.M. 494 (1983).* In summary, if your church board did orally designate a portion of your compensation as a housing or rental allowance, you should go ahead and claim the exclusion. The church board could "memorialize" its earlier action in a written resolution if your return is audited and your allowance questioned. Such a practice is not recommended.

✎ **Key point: under no circumstances can a minister exclude any portion of an allowance retroactively designated by a church**

☞ **Example.** *In preparing his income tax return for 1997, Rev. H discovers that his church failed to designate a housing allowance for him in 1997. He asks his church board to pass a resolution retroactively granting the allowance for 1997. Such a resolution is ineffective, and Rev. H will not be eligible for any housing allowance in 1997. Hoelz v. Commissioner, 42 T.C.M. 1037 (1981); Ling v. Commissioner, 200 F. Supp. 282 (D.D.C. 1962).*

☞ *Example.* Rev. K was paid a salary by his church, but no portion of the salary was designated by the church as a housing allowance. The Tax Court ruled that Rev. K was not able to exclude any part of the expenses incurred in owning and maintaining his home as a housing allowance, since the church had not designated any portion of Rev. K's compensation as a housing allowance. *Eden v. Commissioner, 41 T.C. 605 (1964).*

☞ *Example.* A church board orally discussed a new minister's compensation package with him, and agreed to pay him a salary of $30,000 out of which $6,250 was designated as a housing allowance. The board's housing allowance designation was not recorded in the church minutes or in any other writing. The IRS audited the minister, and denied any housing allowance exclusion on the ground that no allowance had been properly designated. The Tax Court disagreed, and ruled that the minister was eligible for a housing allowance in the amount of $6,250. It observed: "It is clear that there was discussion about a parsonage allowance for [the minister], and that all of the members of the board of directors [of the church] who testified recollected that he was taking a cut in total compensation to come to their church. The recording secretary, the person whose obligation it was to keep the minutes of the various meetings, had a clear recollection of the discussion and thought that [the minister] was to receive the same amount as a parsonage allowance that he received at [his former church]." The court referred to a 1982 decision (Libman v. Commissioner) in which it ruled that "there is no requirement that the parsonage allowance designation be in writing. Rather, we held, the designation requirement is satisfied upon satisfactory proof of official action." In the present case, the court concluded that there was sufficient evidence of a proper designation, in advance of the year in question, though never committed to writing. Accordingly, the minister was entitled to the housing allowance exclusion. *Kizer v. Commissioner, T.C. Memo. 1992-584.*

Failure to designate a timely housing allowance. Unfortunately, many churches fail to designate a housing allowance for their ministers. This practice denies clergy an important tax benefit. If your church fails to designate a housing allowance prior to January 1 for the new year, it is not too late. For example, assume that Rev. B receives monthly compensation of $3,000 from First Church, that Rev. B owns or rents his home, that First Church fails to designate a housing allowance for Rev. B for 1997, and that the church board belatedly takes action on November 1, 1997 to designate Rev. B's entire remaining compensation for 1997 as a housing allowance. Under these facts, the question is how large a housing allowance exclusion Rev. B can claim. At the very least, he will be able to exclude housing expenses incurred in November and December. But can he also exclude housing expenses incurred in months prior to November? This important issue has never been addressed by the IRS or the courts. Section 107 of the Code provides that the housing al-

lowance exclusion covers "the rental allowance paid to [a minister] as part of his compensation *to the extent used by him to rent or provide a home.*" This language suggests that the housing expenses must be paid out of the designated allowance, meaning that Rev. B (in the above example) would only be able to exclude housing expenses incurred in November and December. Section 107 can be interpreted more broadly.

It could be argued that the critical event is the designation of a portion of Rev. B's salary as a housing allowance, and, that once an allowance is actually declared (even if belatedly), there is no reason why it should not be allocated to expenses incurred in prior months of the same year. Under this more liberal interpretation of section 107, the church's belated action would permit Rev. B to exclude his remaining salary of $4,000 from his gross income as a housing allowance exclusion (assuming his actual expenses in owning or maintaining his home are at least this amount), resulting in a substantial savings in income taxes. Ministers who adopt the more liberal interpretation must recognize that such a position has never been approved by the IRS or the courts, it may not be allowed, and it is an aggressive position. Clearly, the more reasonable interpretation of the regulation would be the first one given above.

☞ *Example.* An administrator of a Jewish synagogue was not eligible for a housing allowance since there was no evidence that a housing allowance had ever been properly designated for him. *Haimowitz v. Commissioner, T.C. Memo. 1997-40 (1997).*

Amending the housing allowance. What if a church designates $10,000 of a minister's 1997 compensation as a housing allowance based on reasonable estimates of the minister's anticipated expenses, and the minister trades homes later in the year and incurs much larger housing expenses? Can the church "amend" the minister's housing allowance designation? While neither the IRS nor the courts have addressed this question, it seems perfectly reasonable to conclude that the church *can* amend its housing allowance designation during the course of the year if changed circumstances render the allowance inadequate. Of course, any change would only operate prospectively.

✎ **Key point: churches can amend an allowance during the year if the original allowance proves to be too low. However, the amended allowance will only operate prospectively.**

Traveling evangelists. Traveling evangelists are entitled to a housing allowance exclusion if they maintain a permanent home and have local churches in which they conduct religious meetings declare in advance a portion of their compensation as a housing allowance. *See Revenue Ruling 64-326.* The requirement that each church designate a portion of an evangelist's compensation as a housing allowance is certainly an inconvenience, but it is well worth it. The Tax Court has rejected the contention of one evangelist that such a requirement impermissibly "discriminates" against evangelists. *Warnke v. Commissioner, 641 F. Supp. 1083 (D.C. Ky. 1986)*. Some evangelists have created nonprofit corporations. One of the justifications sometimes given for this procedure is to enable the evangelist to avoid the inconvenience of having each church designate a portion of his or her compensation as a housing or rental allowance—the idea being that the corporation can designate a portion of the evangelist's annual income as a housing allowance in a single action. See chapter 3 for a discussion of which organizations can designate housing allowances.

Other evangelists have churches during the first months of the year designate all of their compensation as a housing allowance and then do not bother with allowances for the last several months of the year. There is a potential problem with this arrangement. If evangelists have churches designate their entire compensation as a housing allowance, then there is no taxable income to report on a Form 1099 and an evangelist theoretically could avoid the reporting of any income. To ensure accountability, our recommendation is that churches issue evangelists and other guest speakers a Form 1099 if they are paid compensation (net of substantiated travel expenses) of $600 or more. Include a housing allowance designated by the church in computing the $600 amount, but also provide the evangelist or guest speaker with a written housing allowance designation on the church's stationary to confirm the housing allowance amount.

How much should a church designate as a housing allowance? Some churches simply declare a percentage (e.g., 40%) of a minister's salary as a housing allowance. Others declare a monetary amount based on a minister's projected expenses for the year. In either case, the church should make a separate designation for each minister on staff (churches can designate housing allowances for all ministers on staff). The allowance should be designated each year for each minister. General designations for several unspecified clergy are not adequate. In some cases, it is appropriate for a church to designate a minister's entire church compensation as a housing allowance. For example, assume that D is a minister of a small, mission church that is only able to pay him $5,000 per year. Assume further that D works a part-time secular job to support himself. If D has at least $5,000 of housing expenses, it would seem perfectly reasonable and appropriate for his church to designate his entire salary as a housing allowance. No court (or the IRS) has ever ruled that a housing allowance designated by a church cannot be fully claimed by a minister who has secular earnings. There is no current requirement that clergy allocate or apportion their housing expenses to their church and secular earnings on a prorata basis. Of course, the entire housing allowance would be taxable for self-employment tax purposes.

The Tax Court has suggested that a minister's entire compensation cannot be designated as a housing allowance, since this would leave the minister with no "compensation" for services rendered. The court observed: "The circumstance that [the minister's] entire compensation was artificially designated as a 'rental

---

Illustration 6-2
Housing Allowance Designation
For Ministers Who Own Or Rent
Their Homes

The following resolution was duly adopted by the board of directors of First Church at a regularly scheduled meeting held on December 15, 1997, a quorum being present:

Whereas, section 107 of the Internal Revenue Code permits a minister of the gospel to exclude from gross income (in computing federal income taxes) a church-designated allowance paid to him as part of his compensation to the extent used by him for <u>actual expenses in owning or renting a home</u>; and

Whereas, Rev. John Smith is compensated by First Church exclusively for services as a minister of the gospel; and

Whereas, First Church does not provide Rev. John Smith with a parsonage; therefore, it is hereby

Resolved, that the total compensation paid to Rev. John Smith for calendar year 1998 shall be $55,000, of which $12,500 is hereby designated to be a housing allowance pursuant to section 107 of the Internal Revenue Code; and it is further

Resolved, that the designation of $12,500 as a housing allowance shall apply to calendar year 1998 and all future years unless otherwise provided.

---

allowance' pursuant to the statement signed by the board of trustees of the church cannot in fact convert into a rental allowance that which was plainly compensation for services." *Marine v. Commissioner, 47 T.C. 609 (1967)*. This opinion is questionable, since the income tax regulations specify that a housing allowance exclusion is available only to the extent that it represents "remuneration for services which are ordinarily the duties of a minister of the gospel." Whether compensation paid by a church to a minister is in the form of a housing allowance, or "salary," is irrelevant.

Designating a housing allowance in the amount of a minister's actual expenses. This practice should be avoided, since it may not satisfy the requirement that housing allowances be designated "in advance." Quite to the contrary, under this approach there is no way to know how much of a minister's compensation is a housing allowance until *after* expenses are incurred. This simply is not consistent with the income tax regulations.

Is there a limit on how much their church can designate as an allowance? The IRS has stated that there are no limitations on how much of a minister's compensation can be designated by his or her employing church as a housing allowance. However, as noted above, this means very little since a minister cannot exclude the church designated allowance unless the conditions specified above are satisfied. *See Revenue Ruling 71-280.* Further, the IRS has ruled that a housing allowance may not be excluded by a minister to the extent that it represents "unreasonable compensation" for the minister's services. *Revenue Ruling 78-448.* For example, televangelists whose "ministries" designate hundreds of thousands of dollars of their compensation each year as a "housing allowance" would almost certainly have any corresponding exclusion challenged by the IRS if audited. *IRC 501(c)(3).* Providing a minister with a housing allowance (or parsonage) that is excessive in amount may constitute "unreasonable compensation." Such a finding could jeopardize the tax-exempt status of the church and lead to adverse tax consequences for the minister. See chapter 4, section A, for a discussion of unreasonable compensation.

✎ **Key point: there is no "limit" on the amount of a minister's compensation that can be designated by a church as a housing allowance (assuming that the minister's compensation is reasonable in amount). However, for clergy who own their home, a church ordinarily should not designate a housing allowance significantly above the fair rental value of the home (furnished, plus utilities)— since clergy will not be able to exclude more than this amount.**

How much may a minister claim as a housing allowance exclusion? First, it is important to note that ministers do not necessarily exclude the church-designated allowance. Section 107 restricts the exclusion to the *actual expenses* incurred by the minister in owning or renting a home, up to but not exceeding the amount of the church-designated allowance. For ministers who rent their homes, actual expenses may include rental payments, furnishings, and utilities. For ministers who own their homes, actual expenses include mortgage interest payments, down payments, real property taxes, insurance, utilities, furnishings, repairs, and improvements. If actual expenses exceed the church-designated allowance, the minister can only exclude the allowance. This illustrates why churches should always be liberal in designating housing allowances. Second, in 1971 the IRS imposed an additional limitation on ministers who own their homes: the housing allowance exclusion may not exceed the annual fair rental value of the minister's home (furnished) plus the cost of utilities. *See Revenue Ruling 71-280; IRS Letter Ruling 8825025.* Therefore, ministers who own their homes may only exclude actual expenses (that they can substantiate) to the extent such expenses do not exceed *either* the church-designated allowance *or* the fair rental value of the home plus the cost of utilities. In Publication 517, the IRS states the rule as follows: "If you are a minister who owns your home and you receive as part of your pay a housing or rental allowance, you may exclude from gross income the lowest of the following amounts: (1) the amount actually used to provide a home, (2) the amount officially designated as a rental allowance, or (3) the fair rental value of the home, including furnishings, utilities, garage, etc."

The "fair rental value" test makes it unlikely that ministers can exclude a down payment paid on a new residence, or any other extraordinary expenses. While the fair rental value test has never been challenged, it is questionable whether it represents a legitimate interpretation of the Code. Section 107 states that a minister can exclude an allowance paid to him to the extent that it is "used by him to rent or provide a home." Certainly a down payment on a home is an expense of "providing a home." Accordingly, some ministers have disregarded the fair rental value limitation, particularly in the year they purchase a new home and incur a large down payment that would not otherwise be excludable. Before making a decision to ignore the IRS position, you should consult with a local tax professional. Also note that the potentially adverse consequences of incurring a large down payment (in excess of a home's fair rental value) can be partially if not wholly offset by obtaining a loan for the amount of the down payment with payments spread out over several years. In such a case, no single large annual payment is incurred that might boost actual expenses over the fair rental value ceiling.

Note that the annual fair rental value test refers to the fair rental value of a *furnished* home. Accordingly, some ministers compute this test by adding the annual fair rental value of an unfurnished home, the annual fair rental value of furniture in such a home, plus the cost of utilities. By taking the fair rental value of furniture (as opposed to the fair rental value of a furnished home) this limitation on the housing allowance exclusion is increased substantially. Unfortunately, neither the IRS nor any court has addressed this issue. Clergy who include the annual fair rental value of furniture in computing this limitation must recognize that they are assuming an aggressive position that may not be accepted by the IRS (or the courts).

Home equity loans, second mortgage loans, and refinancing. What happens to ministers who own their homes after they pay off their home mortgage loan? Are they still eligible for a housing allowance, and if so, for what expenses? Can they include the "fair rental value" of their home in computing their housing allowance exclusion? Ministers who own their home may still claim a housing allowance exclusion (assuming they otherwise qualify), but since the exclusion may never exceed the actual expenses incurred in owning or maintaining a home, it will be reduced (often significantly) when the home mortgage loan is paid off. Clergy still will incur some expenses (e.g., utilities, repairs, improvements, furnishings, property taxes and insurance) that can be included in computing the housing allowance exclusion. However, since the "fair rental value" of the home is not an actual expense, it cannot be included in computing the exclusion. *Swaggart v. Commissioner, 48 T.C.M. 759 (1984).* Prior to 1991, some clergy who had paid off their homes obtained a "home equity loan" (secured by a new home mortgage) and included the mortgage payments (principal and interest) in computing their housing allowance exclusion. In 1991, the IRS ruled that this practice is not permissible unless the home equity loan was obtained for direct housing-related expenses. The fact that the loan is secured by a mortgage on the home is not enough. *IRS Letter Ruling 9115051.* The Tax Court agreed with this conclusion in a 1994 ruling. *Rasmussen v. Commissioner, T.C. Memo. 1994-311.* The court observed:

> Exemptions from gross income are to be construed narrowly . . . and [federal law does not] provide for the exclusion of payments on loans secured by a home if they are not used to "provide a home." The proceeds of the church loans were used to pay personal expenses of [the pastor and his wife] unrelated to their home. Thus, even assuming that the loans were secured by the [pastor's home, he has] not shown that the portion of the parsonage allowance used to repay the church loans was used for the maintenance or purchase of the home. On the record before us, we hold that [the pastor and his wife] have not proven that the portion of the parsonage allowance used to repay the church loans was used to provide a home as required by [federal law].

✎ **Key point: in 1994 the Tax Court agreed with a 1991 IRS private letter ruling that ministers cannot consider loan repayments as a housing expense in computing their housing allowance exclusion unless the loan is used for direct housing-related expenses. If the loan is for personal items such as a new car, a child's education, or medical expenses, it is not converted into a housing expense because it is secured by a mortgage on the minister's home.**

A related and more difficult question is how to calculate a housing allowance when a minister adds to an existing home mortgage. For example, assume that a minister refinances a home mortgage and increases the indebtedness, or obtains a second mortgage loan on top of an existing home mortgage loan, or obtains a "home equity" loan. What are the tax consequences in these cases if the additional mortgage debt is obtained to finance expenses not directly related to the home (for example, education, medical care, vacations, or a new car). In each of these cases, the minister has a pre-existing mortgage loan that was obtained solely to facilitate the purchase of the home. Unfortunately, neither the IRS nor any court has addressed this question. As noted above, both the IRS and the Tax Court have addressed what happens when a ministers home is paid off, and the minister obtains a subsequent home mortgage loan to finance personal expenses such as medical care and education. Obviously, these rulings provide a reasonable basis for concluding that some form of allocation would be required when a minister adds to an existing mortgage debt for non-housing expenses.

To illustrate, if a minister has an outstanding home mortgage loan in the amount of $50,000, and then obtains a second mortgage loan in the amount of $25,000 for various personal expenses, the mortgage interest payments allocable to the first loan could be considered in computing the ministers housing allowance exclusion, while the interest paid of the second mortgage loan would not. It would be easy to make such allocations in the case of a second mortgage loan or a home equity loan. The more difficult case involves refinancing. It is likely that the IRS and the courts would again apply some type of allocation rule. One possibility would be to make an allocation at the time of the refinancing. For example, if a minister with a $50,000 home mortgage debt refinances the indebtedness and increases it to $75,000, and the additional $25,000 debt is used for personal expenses, then two-thirds of the interest payments could be allocated to the home and be included in computing the housing allowance exclusion, while one-third of the interest payments would be allocated to personal expenses and would not be included. Future rulings may provide further clarification on such allocations.

The "double deduction." Ministers who own their homes and who itemize their deductions are eligible to deduct mortgage interest and property taxes on Schedule A even though such items were excluded as part of the housing allowance exclusion. This is the so-called "double deduction". *IRC 265.*

Housing expenses paid directly by a church. Some churches pay part or all of a minister's housing expenses directly. Can such payments be treated as a nontaxable "housing allowance"? Such a conclusion is possible, for by agreeing to pay for a minister's housing expenses a church could be viewed as having "designated" a housing allowance (in advance) in the amount of the expenses that it paid. On the other hand, the Tax Court has reached the opposition conclusion. A minister received a weekly "living allowance" from his church. He kept no records reflecting how these allowances were spent. In addition, his church paid his housing expenses (including mortgage payments, utilities, and furnishings). The Court ruled that the weekly allowances were taxable and could not be classified as a nontaxable housing allowance. It observed:

> [The minister and his spouse] have not substantiated that any of their weekly allowances were used "to rent or provide a home." In fact, the record reveals that [the church] directly paid for such expenses. Moreover, the regulations require that prior to payment of a rental allowance, the employing church must designate the rental allowance in an employment contract or other appropriate instrument so as to clearly identify the portion of the minister's salary that is the rental allowance. As [the minister and his spouse] had no written agreement with the church concerning this matter, they have failed to comply with the regulations. Accordingly, for the years in issue, we hold that the weekly allowances received by petitioners must be included in their gross incomes. *Pollard v. Commissioner, 48 T.C.M. 1303 (1984).*

"Safety net" allowances. It is wise not to limit an allowance to a particular calendar year. For example, if First Church intends to designate $7,500 of Rev. Smith's $40,000 salary in 1998 as a housing allowance, its designation should recite that it is effective for calendar year 1998 *and all future years unless otherwise provided.* This clause will protect Rev. Smith in the event that the board neglects to designate an allowance prior to the beginning of the next calendar year. It is also wise for a church to have a safety net designation to cover mid-year changes in personnel, delayed designations, and other unexpected contingencies. Such a designation could simply recite that "40 percent of the salary of every minister on staff, regardless of when hired, is hereby designated as a housing allowance for the current year and all future years, unless otherwise specifically provided." Such "safety net" designations should not be used as a substitute for annual housing allowance designations for each minister. They are simply a means of protecting ministers against inadvertent failures by the church board to designate a timely housing allowance.

✎ **Key point: churches should consider adopting a "safety net" allowance to protect against the loss of this significant tax benefit due to the inadvertent failure by the church to designate an allowance**

Retired ministers. Retired ministers are eligible for a housing allowance exclusion if certain conditions are met. See chapter 10, section K, for details. However, the surviving spouse of a deceased minister is not eligible for the exclusion, unless he or she is also a minister who otherwise qualifies. IRS Publication 517 states that "[t]he retirement allowances you receive as a retired minister are not earnings from self-employment for self-employment tax purposes."

Social security. The housing allowance is an exclusion for federal income tax purposes only. It cannot under any circumstances be excluded in computing a minister's social security (self-employment) tax liability. Therefore, in computing the social security tax on Schedule SE of Form 1040, a minister must include the actual housing allowance exclusion as income on line 2 of either the "short" or "long" Schedule SE (whichever applies). *IRC 1402(a)(8); Treas. Reg. 1.1402(a)-11(a); Flowers v. Commissioner, T.C. Memo. 1991-542.*

✎ **Key point: the fair rental value of a parsonage, and a housing allowance, are exclusions only for federal income tax reporting purposes. They must be included in a minister's self-employment earnings for purposes of the self-employment tax (the social security tax on self-employed persons).**

Impact on business expenses. A decision of the United States Tax Court may limit the deductibility of some business and professional expenses for ministers who exclude a portion of their church compensation from gross income as a housing or rental allowance. *Dalan v. Commissioner, T.C. Memo. 1988-106.* See chapter 7 for a full discussion of the potential ramifications of this decision.

☞ *Example. Rev. B purchases a new home in 1997. She makes a down payment of $12,000, and incurs other housing expenses (mortgage payments, utilities, furnishings, etc.) of $8,000 during the year. Her church compensation for the year is $35,000. Since Rev. B knew that she would be making a large down payment in 1997, she had the church board designate a housing allowance of $22,000 for the year. Assume that the annual fair rental value of the home (unfurnished) is $9,000, that Rev. B incurs $3,000 in utilities during 1997, and that it would cost an ad-*

ditional $4,000 to rent furniture for the entire home for 1997 (according to a local furniture store owner). Rev. B's housing allowance exclusion for 1997 is the lowest of the following three amounts: (1) her actual expenses (down payment of $12,000 plus other housing expenses of $8,000), (2) the church designated housing allowance ($22,000), and (3) the fair rental value of the home (furnished, including utilities). This third limitation can be interpreted to mean the fair rental value of the home (unfurnished), plus the cost to rent furniture, plus utilities. Under this interpretation, the third limitation would be $16,000. The other way to interpret this third limitation is to determine the annual fair rental value of the home assuming that is furnished, and then add utilities. Obviously, this interpretation will result in a lower amount. Both interpretations would appear to be reasonable. Neither the IRS nor any court has expressed a preference for either interpretation.

☞ *Example. Rev. D owns his home. First Church designated $8,000 of his $25,000 compensation in 1997 as a housing allowance. Rev. D's housing expenses for 1997 were utilities of $3,500, mortgage payments of $6,200, property taxes of $2,000, insurance payments of $500, repairs of $1,000, and furnishings of $750. The annual fair rental value of the home (including furnishings) is $7,500. Rev. D may exclude as a housing allowance his actual expenses up to but not exceeding the lesser of his church-designated allowance or the fair rental value of the home plus utilities. His actual expenses were $13,950, but he cannot exclude more than his church-designated allowance ($8,000) or the fair rental value of the home plus utilities ($11,000). As a result, he can only exclude $8,000 in 1997.*

☞ *Example. Rev. R rents a home. His church designated a rental allowance of $7,500 for 1997. Rev. R's actual expenses incurred in renting the home (he has receipts for all of them) are $8,200. The housing allowance of a minister who rents a home will be the lesser of (1) actual expenses incurred in renting the home, or (2) the church designated allowance. There is no "fair rental value" test for ministers who rent a home. Rev. R's housing allowance exclusion for 1997 will be $7,500 (the lesser of $7,500 or $8,200).*

☞ *Example. Rev. G, an ordained minister, purchased a home in 1997 for $50,000. During 1997 he paid $15,000 down on the home, and in addition paid $5,000 in principal and interest payments on his home loan, $2,000 for utilities, $1,000 for home furnishings, $750 for repairs, $500 for real property taxes, and $200 for homeowners insurance. Rev. G has receipts for all of these expenses. His church designated $10,000 of his salary of $30,000 as a housing allowance. The annual fair rental value of the home (including furnishings) is determined by an appraiser to be $6,500. As a homeowner, Rev. G is entitled to exclude only his actual expenses to the extent that they do not exceed the lower of the church designated allowance or the fair rental* value of the home (furnished, including the actual cost of utilities). Rev. G's actual expenses in providing the home for 1997 were $24,450. The church designated allowance is $10,000, and the fair rental value of the home (including utilities) is $8,500 ($6,500 + $2,000). As the IRS notes in Publication 517, a minister who owns a home can exclude the lowest of the following three amounts: (1) actual expenses incurred in providing a home; (2) church designated allowance; or (3) fair rental value of the home (furnished, including utilities). The lowest of these amounts is $8,500, and according to the IRS this is the amount that Rev. G can exclude.

☞ **Example.** Same facts as the preceding example, except that Rev. G's actual expenses are $10,000, his church designated allowance is $5,000, and the fair rental value of the home (furnished, including utilities) is $9,000. As noted above, a minister who owns a home can exclude as a housing allowance the lowest of the following amounts: (1) actual expenses incurred in providing a home; (2) church designated allowance; or (3) fair rental value of the home (furnished, including utilities). The lowest of these three amounts is $5,000. This example illustrates the adverse tax effect of a church designating an allowance that is too low. In this case, the low designation will have the effect of forcing Rev. G to unnecessarily include an additional $4,000 ($9,000 - $5,000) in gross income for 1997. Assuming that he is in the 15% tax bracket, this amounts to an additional tax liability of $600. The lesson is clear—churches should never designate an allowance for a homeowning minister that is less than the fair rental value of a minister's home (furnished, including utilities), and in some cases (i.e., a year in which the minister purchases a new home and incurs a large down payment) should designate an allowance in excess of this amount.

☞ **Example.** Rev. B owns a home. In February of 1997, Rev. B begins building a new home in the same community. He sells his home in June of 1997 and moves into the new home on July 1. Can he include the construction costs from February to July 1st in computing his housing allowance exclusion for 1997, in addition to the costs of maintaining his prior home? This is an interesting question that has not yet been addressed either by the IRS or the courts. There are two important considerations that are relevant in answering this question. First, the regulations interpreting section 107 of the Code specify that "for purposes of section 107, the term 'home' means a dwelling place." It is likely that the IRS and the courts would rule that a minister has only one "home"—his or her principal residence—and accordingly, that no expenses incurred in constructing a new home can be counted in computing the housing allowance exclusion until it in fact has become the minister's "dwelling." Revenue Ruling 72-588. Second, the existence of housing expenses on two homes ordinarily will increase a minister's actual expenses above the IRS ceilings on housing allowances (i.e., the exclusion cannot

exceed the annual fair rental value of the home, furnished, including utilities). A more difficult question is presented in a case where a minister is building a home while living in a church-owned parsonage. Even here, it would appear that the construction costs would not be excludable as a housing allowance until the minister actually moved into the home. Because of these uncertainties, it would be prudent for clergy who are contemplating building a new home to defer as much of the construction cost as is possible to the time when they will be occupying the new home.

☞ **Example.** First Church owned a home that it sold to its senior minister, Rev. D. The sales price was the home's fair market value at the time of the sale. Rev. D signed a promissory note and land contract agreeing to make monthly payments over a number of years until the sales price was paid in full. Title to the home remained in the name of the church until the note was paid in full. Under a "compensation agreement" adopted by the church, Rev. D was paid a salary (a portion of which was designated as a housing allowance by the church). The church also paid all of Rev. D's utility expenses. Principal and interest payments made by Rev. D to the church are properly included in computing his housing allowance exclusion, and he may also deduct the interest payments as an itemized deduction on Schedule A (if he is able to itemize deductions). IRS Letter Ruling 8937025.

☞ **Example.** The board of First Church adopts the following resolution: "The board of First Church authorizes a housing allowance for each member of the pastoral staff in the amount of their actual and substantiated housing expenses." This method of designating a housing allowance should be avoided, since the IRS and the courts may not consider this to be an advance designation of a portion of a minister's compensation as a housing allowance, as required by law. First Church will not know the amount of the housing allowance until the end of the year. Therefore, it seems doubtful that this would satisfy the advance designation requirement. It is not enough to agree in principle to pay a minister a "housing allowance," leaving to the future a determination of the amount of the allowance. A specific portion of a minister's compensation must be designated as a housing allowance.

☞ **Example.** A religious denomination seeks to relieve local churches of the burden of designating annual housing allowances for their ministers, and accordingly makes a designation for all ministers who have been ordained by the denomination. This general designation is not effective with respect to ministers of local churches, but it is effective with respect to minister-employees of the denomination. Revenue Ruling 62-117; Revenue Ruling 75-22.

☞ **Example.** The Tax Court ruled in 1981 that a "federation" of churches that supervised a police chaplain (who was an ordained minister) could designate a portion of his salary as a housing allowance, despite the fact that his salary was paid by the police department. *Boyd v. Commissioner, 42 T.C.M. 1136 (1981).*

☞ ***Example.*** The IRS has ruled that a regional denominational executive could not designate a portion of a state prison chaplain's salary as a housing allowance. The chaplain was an ordained minister with the Christian Church (Disciples of Christ). He excluded 45% of his wages as a housing allowance on the basis of a letter from a regional executive of the Christian Church which "endorsed" his ministry and stated that 45% of his annual salary constituted a housing allowance. The IRS noted that the income tax regulations specify that housing allowances must be declared "by the employing church or other qualified organization." The IRS concluded that the Christian Church was not actively involved in the day-to-day conduct of the state prison chaplain program. Its involvement was limited to sending a letter to the state endorsing the chaplain, and receiving annual reports from him. The IRS concluded that "we do not believe that this level of involvement is sufficient . . . to qualify the Church as an 'other qualified organization' . . . . . The Church is not closely involved with the state in the conduct of its chaplain program and the responsibilities of the Church are not similar to those of an employer." Accordingly, neither the Christian Church, nor any of its executives, could designate a housing allowance for the prison chaplain. The IRS disallowed the chaplain's exclusion of 45% of his salary as a housing allowance. *IRS Letter Ruling 9052001.*

☞ ***Example.*** Rev. C is paid salary of $30,000 for 1997 plus a housing allowance of $10,000. Rev. C has housing expenses of $10,000, consisting of mortgage payments on a conventional home loan of $6,000, utilities of $2,500, and property taxes and insurance of $1,500. Rev. C can claim the full church-designated housing allowance as an exclusion from taxable income for income tax reporting purposes since he has housing-related expenses of at least this amount.

☞ ***Example.*** Same facts as the previous example, except that Rev. C pays off his home mortgage loan. Rev. C is still eligible for a housing allowance, but it is excludable only to the extent of his actual housing-related expenses of $4,000. As a result, $6,000 of the housing allowance represents taxable income.

☞ ***Example.*** Same facts as the previous example, except that Rev. C obtains a loan, secured by mortgage on his home, to pay for various personal expenses (a car, a vacation, a child's college education, and various medical bills). The loan payments amount to $6,000 in 1997. Rev. C cannot include any portion of the $6,000 in computing his housing allowance exclusion for the year, since these are not an expense of providing a home. Rev. C's housing allowance exclusion

(the amount by which he can reduce his taxable income) is $4,000 (utilities, property taxes and insurance). The "excess housing allowance" of $6,000 must be reported as taxable income.

☞ ***Example.*** Same facts as the previous example, except that Rev. C obtains a loan, secured by a mortgage on his home, to pay for remodeling expenses and furnishings. The full amount of these loan payments can be considered in computing Rev. C's housing allowance for the year.

☞ ***Example.*** Rev. Y owns a home, and incurs housing expenses of $12,000 in 1997. These expenses include mortgage principal and interest, property taxes, utilities, insurance, property taxes, and repairs. The church designated (in advance) $12,000 of Rev. Y's 1997 compensation ($35,000) as a housing allowance. The church reports only $23,000 of taxable compensation on Rev. Y's W-2 for 1997 ($35,000 less $12,000). Rev. Y is able to itemize expenses on Schedule A (Form 1040). He is able to claim itemized deductions on Schedule A for both his mortgage interest and his property taxes, even though his taxable income was already reduced by these items because of their inclusion in the housing allowance. This is often referred to as the "double deduction." In reality, it represents an exclusion and a deduction.

☞ ***Example.*** A minister spent a portion of his church-designated housing allowance to purchase and install new floors, new carpet, and new cabinets in his home. The IRS ruled that a housing allowance can be used to pay for capital expenditures incurred for remodeling. *IRS Letter Ruling 8350005.*

IRS audit guidelines for ministers. The IRS issued audit guidelines in 1995 for its agents to follow when auditing ministers. The guidelines provide agents with the following information regarding housing allowances:

Code section 107 provides an exclusion from gross income for a "parsonage allowance," housing specifically provided to a minister of the gospel. This includes the rental value of a home furnished to him or her as part of compensation or a rental allowance, to the extent that the payment is used to rent or provide a home. The term "parsonage allowance" includes church provided parsonages, rental allowance with which the minister may rent a home and housing allowances with which the minister may purchase a home. A minister can receive a parsonage allowance for only one home.

The value of the parsonage allowance is not included in computing the minister's income subject to income tax and should not be included in W-2 wages. However, the parsonage allowance is subject to self-employment tax along with other earnings. . . .

The exclusion under Code section 107 only applies if the employing church designates the amount of the parsonage allowance in advance of the tax year. The designation may appear in the minister's employment contract, the church minutes, the church budget, or any other document indicating official action.

The amount of the parsonage allowance excludible from gross income is the least of: (1) The amount actually used to provide a home, (2) the amount officially designated as a housing allowance, or (3) the fair rental value of the home, including furnishings, utilities, garage, etc.

The IRS audit guidelines contain the following examples:

☞ **Example.** *B, an ordained minister, is vice president of academic affairs at Holy Bible Seminary. His compensation package includes a salary of $80,000 per year and a $30,000 housing allowance. His housing costs for the year included mortgage payments of $15,000, utilities of $3,000, and $3,600 for home maintenance and new furniture. The fair rental value of the home, as furnished, is $18,000 per year. The three amounts for comparison are: (a) Actual expenses of $21,600 ($15,000 mortgage payments + $3,000 utilities + $3,600 other costs); (b) designated housing allowance of $30,000; (c) fair rental value plus utilities of $21,000 ($18,000 + $3,000 utilities). B may exclude $21,000 from gross income but must include in income the other $9,000 of the housing allowance. The entire $30,000 will be considered in arriving at net self-employment income.*

☞ **Example.** *C is an ordained minister and has been in his church's employ for the last 20 years. His salary is $40,000 and his designated parsonage allowance is $15,000. C's mortgage was paid off last year. During the tax year he spent $2,000 on utilities, and $3,000 on real estate taxes and insurance. The fair rental value of his home, as furnished, is $750 a month. The three amounts for comparison are: (a) Actual housing costs of $5,000 ($2,000 utilities + $3,000 taxes and insurance); (b) designated housing allowance of $15,000; (c) fair rental value + utilities of $11,000 ($9,000 fair rental value + $2,000 utilities). C may only exclude his actual expenses of $5,000 for federal income tax purposes. He may not exclude the fair rental value of his home even though he has paid for it in previous years. $15,000 will be included in the computation of net self-employment income.*

☞ **Example.** *Assume the same facts as [the previous example], except that C takes out a home equity loan and uses the proceeds to pay for his daughter's college tuition. The payments are $300 per month. Even though he has a loan secured by his home, the money was not used to "provide a home" and can't be used to compute the excludible portion of the parsonage allowance. The results are the same as for [the previous example].*

☞ **Example.** *D is an ordained minister and received $40,000 in salary plus a designated housing allowance of $12,000. He spent $12,000 on mortgage payments, $2,400 on utilities, and $2,000 on new furniture. The fair rental value of his home as furnished is $16,000. D's exclusion is limited to $12,000 even though his actual cost ($16,400) and fair rental value and utilities ($18,400) are more. He may not deduct his housing costs in excess of the designated allowance.*

☞ **Example.** *E's designated housing allowance is $20,000. She and her husband live in one half of a duplex which they own. The other half is rented. Mortgage payments for the duplex are $1,500 per month. E's utilities run $1,800 per year, and her tenant pays his own from a separate meter. During the year E replaced carpeting throughout the structure at a cost of $6,500 and did minor repairs of $500. E must allocate her mortgage costs, carpeting, and repairs between her own unit and the rental unit in determining the amount of the excludible parsonage allowance. Amounts allocable to the rented portion for mortgage interest, taxes, etc., would be reported on Schedule E as usual. Her actual costs to provide a home were $14,300 ($9,000 mortgage payments, $1,800 utilities, and $3,500 for half the carpeting and repairs). The fair rental value for her unit is the same as the rent she charges for the other half, which is $750 a month, and she estimates that her furnishings add another $150 per month to the fair rental value. Her fair rental value plus utilities is $12,600 ($10,800 fair rental value + $1,800 utilities). E may exclude $12,600 for Federal income tax purposes. Even though a minister's home mortgage interest and real estate taxes have been paid with money excluded from income as a housing allowance, he or she may still claim itemized deductions for these items. The sale of the residence is treated the same as that of other taxpayers, even though it may have been completely purchased with funds excluded under Code section 107. A retired minister may receive part of his or her pension benefits as a designated parsonage allowance based on past services. If so, the "least of" rules apply.*

✎ **Key point: the audit guidelines assist IRS agents in the examination of ministers' tax returns. They alert agents to the key questions to ask, and provide background information along with the IRS position on a number of issues. It is therefore of utmost importance that ministers be familiar with these guidelines.**

C. Reporting of Housing Allowances

There are various ways for churches and clergy to report housing allowances for federal income tax purposes. Three methods are described below (for use in 1998) along with the advantages and disadvantages of each.

method 1: the "actual exclusion" method

This method consists of the following steps:

- The minister estimates his or her actual 1998 housing expenses by December of 1997 on a form provided by the church. See Illustrations 6-3, 6-4, and 6-5.

- The church board, in its December 1997 meeting, designates a portion of the minister's 1998 compensation as a housing allowance, based on the minister's estimated expenses (see Illustration 6-2).

- In January of 1999, the minister is required to substantiate actual housing expenses by submitting documentary evidence to the church treasurer.

- By the end of January of 1999, the church treasurer computes the minister's *actual housing allowance exclusion* for 1998 by applying the following rules:

- For clergy who own their home, take the *lowest* of the following 3 amounts

  ✓ actual housing expenses paid for by the minister during 1998, and properly substantiated

  ✓ the church-designated housing allowance for 1998

  ✓ the fair rental value of the home (furnished, including utilities)

- For clergy who rent their homes, take the *lower* of the following 2 amounts

  ✓ actual housing expenses paid for by the minister during 1998, and properly substantiated

  ✓ the church-designated housing allowance for 1998

- The church treasurer reduces the amount of compensation reported on the minister's 1998 W-2 (or 1099) form by the actual exclusion as determined above.

The *advantages* of this method include the following: (1) It ensures that clergy will not simply claim the church-designated allowance as their exclusion (often a lower amount applies). (2) It ensures that the church will not participate in the understatement of taxable income. (3) The church exercises appropriate fiscal control over compensation packages.

The primary *disadvantages* are: (1) Administrative inconvenience. It is difficult for some ministers to accumulate expenses and receipts by the due date of the church's W-2 (or 1099). And, this method imposes greater responsibilities on the church treasurer. For many churches, these inconveniences are well worth the cost. (2) Since a church's quarterly 941 forms will report a minister's wages net of the church-designated housing allowance, the 941 forms and

minister's W-2 form will not reconcile. This discrepancy can be addressed in an explanatory letter accompanying the W-2 form that is sent to the Social Security Administration (with the W-3 transmittal form).

method 2: the "estimated exclusion" method

This method consists of the following steps:

- The minister estimates his or her actual 1998 housing expenses by December of 1997 on a form provided by the church. See Illustrations 6-3, 6-4, and 6-5. Note that some modifications in these forms will be necessary since portions of them reflect method 1 (above).
- The church board, in its December 1997 meeting, designates a portion of the minister's 1998 compensation as a housing allowance, based on the minister's estimated expenses (see Illustration 6-2).

- In January of 1999, the church treasurer reduces the amount of compensation reported on the minister's 1998 W-2 (or 1099) form by the church-designated housing allowance.

- If the minister's actual exclusion is less than the church-designated allowance (according to the tests described under "method 1" above), then it is the minister's responsibility to report the "excess housing allowance" as additional income on line 21 of his or her Form 1040 (if an employee) or on Schedule C (if self-employed).

The primary *advantages* of this method are (1) It imposes slightly less administrative inconvenience on the church (than method 1). (2) It is the method illustrated by the IRS in Publication 517. This of course does not mean that the IRS prefers this method. On the contrary, there is little doubt that the IRS would prefer method 1 since it obviously contributes to a higher degree of tax compliance. (3) It avoids the lack of reconciliation between a church's 941 forms and W-2 forms noted as a disadvantage to method 1 (above).

The *disadvantages* of this method include: (1) It promotes the common practice of clergy simply claiming the church-designated housing allowance as their exclusion (though a lower amount may apply). (2) The church indirectly may contribute to the understatement of taxable income.

method 3: the "nonaccountable" method

This method consists of the following steps:

- The minister informs the church board during its December 1997 meeting of the appropriate housing allowance for 1998. No estimated expenses are discussed. The board simply designates an allowance in the amount requested by the minister (see Illustration 6-2).

- In January of 1999, the church treasurer reduces the amount of compensation reported on the minister's 1998 W-2 (or 1099) form by the church-designated housing allowance.

- If the minister's actual exclusion is less than the church-designated allowance (according to the tests described under "method 1" above), then it is the minister's responsibility to report the "excess housing allowance" as additional income on line 21 of his or her Form 1040 (if an employee) or on Schedule C (if self-employed).

There is no doubt that this is the most common method. It also is the worst, for the following reasons: (1) The church exercises no internal control whatever over the process of designating the allowance. It designates an amount without any assurance that it is reasonable in light of the minister's anticipated expenses for the new year. (2) It promotes the common practice of clergy simply claiming the church-designated housing allowance as their exclusion (though a lower amount may apply). (3) The church indirectly may contribute to the understatement of taxable income. There are no "advantages" to this approach, other than simplicity and convenience. It is not recommended.

ILLUSTRATION 6-3
HOUSING ALLOWANCE EXPENSE FORM
FOR CLERGY WHO OWN THEIR HOME

Ministers are permitted to exclude from their church income (for federal income tax purposes) a "housing allowance" designated by their employing church, to the extent that the allowance is used to pay housing expenses. To assist the church in designating an appropriate amount, please estimate on this form the housing expenses you expect to pay next year, and then return the form to the secretary of the church board not later than the board's December meeting.

CATEGORY OF EXPENSE	ESTIMATED AMOUNT FOR 1998
• down payment on a home	_____
• mortgage payments on a loan to purchase or improve your home (include both principal and interest)	_____
• real estate taxes	_____
• property insurance	_____
• utilities (electricity, gas, water, trash pickup, local telephone charges)	_____
• furnishings and appliances (purchase and repair)	_____
• structural repairs and remodeling	_____
• yard maintenance and improvements	_____
• maintenance items (household cleansers, light bulbs, pest control, etc.)	_____
• homeowners association dues	_____
• miscellaneous	_____
• TOTAL ESTIMATED EXPENSES FOR 1998	_____

The above listed expenses represent a reasonable estimate of my housing expenses for next year. I understand and agree that:

The church board will not designate a portion of my compensation as a housing allowance until I complete and return this form. Retroactive designations of housing allowances are not legally effective.

It is my responsibility to notify the church board in the event that these estimates prove to be materially inaccurate during the year.

My housing allowance exclusion is not the same as my estimated expenses. The actual housing allowance exclusion is the lowest of 3 amounts: (1) my actual housing expenses for the year, (2) the church-designated housing allowance, or (3) the annual fair rental value of my home (furnished, including utilities).

I will have to account to the church treasurer for my actual 1998 housing expenses not later than January 20, 1999. This means that I will have to present receipts substantiating my actual 1998 housing expenses. The church treasurer will then compute my actual housing allowance exclusion based on the information I have provided, and the test described in the previous paragraph. The church treasurer will then reduce the income reported on my W-2 form by the amount of the actual housing allowance exclusion. I understand that if I fail to account for my actual housing expenses by January 20, 1999, the church will report my entire compensation (including housing allowance) as income on my W-2 form, and that I will then be responsible for claiming the exclusion on my income tax return.

My housing allowance exclusion is an exclusion for federal income taxes only. I must add my housing allowance as income in reporting my self-employment taxes on Schedule SE (unless I am exempt from self-employment taxes).

_____

legible signature of minister

_____

date

I attest that I received this form from the above minister on _____, 19___.

_____

secretary of church board

ILLUSTRATION 6-4
HOUSING ALLOWANCE EXPENSE FORM
FOR CLERGY WHO RENT THEIR HOME

Ministers are permitted to exclude from their church income (for federal income tax purposes) a "housing allowance" designated by their employing church, to the extent that the allowance is used to pay housing expenses. To assist the church in designating an appropriate amount, please estimate on this form the housing expenses you expect to pay next year, and then return the form to the secretary of the church board not later than the board's December meeting.

CATEGORY OF EXPENSE	ESTIMATED AMOUNT FOR 1998
• rental payments	_____
• property insurance	_____
• utilities (electricity, gas, water, trash pickup, local telephone charges)	_____
• furnishings and appliances (purchase and repair)	_____
• structural repairs and remodeling	_____
• yard maintenance and improvements	_____
• maintenance items (household cleansers, light bulbs, pest control, etc.)	_____
• miscellaneous	_____
• TOTAL ESTIMATED EXPENSES FOR 1998	_____

The above listed expenses represent a reasonable estimate of my housing expenses for next year. I understand and agree that:

The church board will not designate a portion of my compensation as a housing allowance until I complete and return this form. Retroactive designations of housing allowances are not legally effective.

It is my responsibility to notify the church board in the event that these estimates prove to be materially inaccurate during the year.

My housing allowance exclusion is not the same as my estimated expenses. The actual housing allowance exclusion is the lower of 2 amounts: (1) my actual housing expenses for the year, or (2) the church-designated housing allowance.

I will have to account to the church treasurer for my actual 1998 housing expenses not later than January 20, 1999. This means that I will have to present receipts substantiating my actual 1998 housing expenses. The church treasurer will then compute my actual housing allowance exclusion based on the information I have provided, and the test described in the previous paragraph. The church treasurer will then reduce the income reported on my W-2 form by the amount of the actual housing allowance exclusion. I understand that if I fail to account for my actual housing expenses by January 20, 1999, the church will report my entire compensation (including housing allowance) as income on my W-2 form, and that I will then be responsible for claiming the exclusion on my income tax return.

My housing allowance exclusion is an exclusion for federal income taxes only. I must add my housing allowance as income in reporting my self-employment taxes on Schedule SE (unless I am exempt from self-employment taxes).

_____

legible signature of minister

_____

date

I attest that I received this form from the above minister on _____, 19___.

_____

secretary of church board

ILLUSTRATION 6-5
PARSONAGE ALLOWANCE EXPENSE FORM
FOR CLERGY WHO LIVE IN A CHURCH-OWNED PARSONAGE

Ministers are permitted to exclude from their church income (for federal income tax purposes) a "parsonage allowance" designated by their employing church, to the extent that the allowance is used to pay parsonage expenses. To assist the church in designating an appropriate amount, please estimate on this form the parsonage expenses you expect to pay next year, and then return the form to the secretary of the church board not later than the board's December meeting.

CATEGORY OF EXPENSE	ESTIMATED AMOUNT FOR 1998
• real estate taxes	_____
• property insurance	_____
• utilities (electricity, gas, water, trash pickup, local telephone charges)	_____
• furnishings and appliances (purchase and repair)	_____
• structural repairs and remodeling	_____
• yard maintenance and improvements	_____
• maintenance items (household cleansers, light bulbs, pest control, etc.)	_____
• miscellaneous	_____
• TOTAL ESTIMATED EXPENSES FOR 1998	_____

The above listed expenses represent a reasonable estimate of my parsonage expenses for next year. I understand and agree that:

The church board will not designate a portion of my compensation as a parsonage allowance until I complete and return this form. Retroactive designations of parsonage allowances are not legally effective.

It is my responsibility to notify the church board in the event that these estimates prove to be materially inaccurate during the year.

My parsonage allowance exclusion is not the same as my estimated expenses. The actual parsonage allowance exclusion is the lower of 2 amounts: (1) my actual parsonage expenses for the year, or (2) the church-designated parsonage allowance.

I will have to account to the church treasurer for my actual 1998 parsonage expenses not later than January 20, 1999. This means that I will have to present receipts substantiating my actual 1998 parsonage expenses. The church treasurer will then compute my actual parsonage allowance exclusion based on the information I have provided, and the test described in the previous paragraph. The church treasurer will then reduce the income reported on my W-2 form by the amount of the actual parsonage allowance exclusion. I understand that if I fail to account for my actual parsonage expenses by January 20, 1999, the church will report my entire compensation (including parsonage allowance) as income on my W-2 form, and that I will then be responsible for claiming the exclusion on my income tax return.

My parsonage allowance exclusion is an exclusion for federal income taxes only. I must add my parsonage allowance as income in reporting my self-employment taxes on Schedule SE (unless I am exempt from self-employment taxes).

_____

legible signature of minister

_____

date

I attest that I received this form from the above minister on _____, 19___.

_____

secretary of church board

Chapter 7

ADJUSTMENTS, DEDUCTIONS, AND CREDITS

Chapter Highlights

- **In general.** Most clergy can reduce their taxes by claiming various adjustments, deductions, and credits.

- **Adjustments.** An "adjustment" to gross income is a deduction that is available to most clergy whether or not they have enough expenses to itemize their deductions on Schedule A. Common adjustments for clergy include the new deduction of half their self-employment taxes, and IRA or Keogh contributions.

- **Deductibility of business expenses.** Most clergy have business expenses. The deductibility of these expenses depends on whether a minister is an employee or self-employed, whether or not the expenses are reimbursed by the church, and whether any reimbursed expenses are paid under an accountable or a nonaccountable reimbursement plan.

- **Unreimbursed business expenses.** Clergy who are employees for income tax reporting purposes claim their *unreimbursed business expenses* on Schedule A—if they are able to itemize, and only to the extent that such expenses exceed 2% of adjusted gross income. Unreimbursed expenses are those expenses paid out of a minister's own funds without any contribution from the church.

- **Employee business expenses reimbursed by a church under a *nonaccountable* arrangement.** Clergy who are employees for income tax reporting purposes claim any *business expenses reimbursed by their church under a "nonaccountable" reimbursement plan* on Schedule A—if they are able to itemize, and only to the extent that such expenses exceed 2% of adjusted gross income. The full amount of the church's reimbursements must be included in the minister's income whether or not the expenses are deductible. A church has a nonaccountable plan if it reimburses clergy (or other employees) for business expenses without requiring adequate substantiation of the amount, date, place, and business purpose of the expenses, or does not require excess reimbursements to be returned to the church.

- **Employee business expenses reimbursed by a church under an *accountable* arrangement.** The limitations on the deductibility of employee business expenses (summarized in the preceding 2 paragraphs) can be avoided if the church adopts an "accountable" reimbursement plan. An accountable plan is one that (1)

reimburses only those expenses that are substantiated (within 60 days of the expenses) as to the amount, date, place, and business purpose of the expenses, and (2) requires any excess reimbursements (reimbursements exceeding substantiated expenses) to be returned within 120 days to the church. Under an accountable plan, a minister reports to the church rather than to the IRS. The reimbursements are not reported as income to the minister, and the minister need not claim any deductions.

- **Self-employed ministers.** Clergy who report their income taxes as self-employed deduct their business expenses directly on Schedule C. They are not subject to the 2% limitation that applies to employees, and they may deduct their expenses even if they are not able to itemize deductions on Schedule A.

- **Examples of clergy business expenses.** Common business expenses for clergy include transportation, travel, entertainment, books and subscriptions, education, and vestments. In some cases, a home computer and a home office qualify as a business expense.

- **Commuting.** Commuting to and from work is never a business expense—unless you meet the rigid requirements of a home office. A recent Tax Court ruling seems to liberalize these rules.

- **Automobile expenses.** Automobile expenses are a major business expense for most clergy. These expenses can be deducted using either a standard mileage rate of 31.5 cents for all business miles (for 1997), or the actual costs of operating the car for business miles. Most clergy choose the standard mileage rate because of its simplicity. However, it is available only if it is selected for the first year a car is used in your trade or business.

- **Church-owned automobiles.** Clergy should consider the advantages of using a church-owned car for their business travel. This will eliminate most recordkeeping and reporting requirements. Some conditions apply.

- **Per diem rates.** Clergy can use new "per diem" rates to substantiate the amount of their lodging and meal expenses. If these rates are used, a minister need not retain receipts of actual meals and lodging expenses. Several conditions apply. These per diem rates can be

Chapter Highlights

used only in connection with an accountable reimbursement plan of the employer.

- **Home offices.** Most clergy have an office in their home. For the costs of such an office to be deductible as a business expense, several conditions must be satisfied. For example, the office must be used exclusively and regularly in the minister's trade or business. More stringent rules apply to clergy who are employees for income tax purposes.

- **Substantiation.** Business expenses must be substantiated by adequate evidence in order to support an income tax deduction *or* an expense reimbursement under an accountable reimbursement plan of an employer. Stricter substantiation rules apply to transportation, travel, and entertainment expenses.

- **The *Deason* rule.** The IRS has indicated that clergy must comply with the so-called *Deason* allocation rule. This rule requires clergy to re-duce their business expenses by the percentage of their total compensation that consists of a tax-exempt housing allowance. This reduction in business expenses does not apply to the computation of self-employment taxes (since the housing allowance is not deductible in computing these taxes).

- **Itemized deductions.** Clergy who have itemized deductions in excess of their standard deduction ($6,900 for married couples filing jointly, $4,150 for single persons) may deduct these expenses on Schedule A. Itemized deductions include medical expenses (in excess of 7.5% of adjusted gross income), certain taxes and interest payments, charitable contributions, casualty and theft losses (uncompensated by insurance), and miscellaneous expenses.

The preceding chapters have described several items that you must include in computing your gross income, and some of the "exclusions" that are not included in gross income. After your gross income is computed (and reported on Form 1040, line 22), you then compute your **adjusted gross income** by deducting various **adjustments** to gross income. Adjustments to gross income, and the more important itemized and business deductions, will be summarized in this chapter from both an employee and self-employed perspective.

A. Adjustments to Gross Income

✎ **Key point: most clergy can reduce their taxes by claiming various adjustments, deductions, and credits.**

✎ **Key point: an "adjustment" to gross income is a deduction that is available to most clergy whether or not they have enough expenses to itemize their deductions on Schedule A. Common adjustments for clergy include the deduction of half their self-employment taxes, and IRA or Keogh contributions.**

As noted above, you may deduct certain adjustments from gross income in computing your adjusted gross income. The adjustments are reported and deducted on Form 1040, lines 23-30. For 1997, these adjustments consist of the following:

- Your IRA deduction (including a spouse's contribution)—these rules are explained in chapter 10.

- Your medical savings account deduction.

- Moving expenses you pay that are not reimbursed by your employer.

- One-half of your self-employment tax.

- Self-employed workers' health insurance deduction. Self-employed persons can deduct 40 percent of the amount they paid in 1997 for health insurance for themselves as well as for their spouse and dependents. This deduction is not available for any month in which a self-employed person is eligible to participate in a subsidized health plan maintained by his or her employer (or his or her spouse's employer). Congress enacted legislation in 1997 that increases the deduction for health insurance coverage of self-employed persons as follows: the deduction is increased to 45 percent in 1998 and 1999; 50 percent in 2000 and 2001; 60 percent in 2002; 80 percent in 2003 through 2005; 90 percent in 2006; and 100 percent in 2007 and thereafter.

- Deduction of Keogh plan contributions—these rules are explained in chapter 10.

- A penalty incurred on an early withdrawal of funds from a time savings account.

- Alimony paid.

✎ **Key point: your unreimbursed moving expenses (and moving expenses reimbursed by your employer without an adequate accounting) can be deducted as an adjustment in computing your adjusted gross income. This means that the deduction is available even if you cannot itemize deductions on Schedule A.**

❖ **New in 1997. Congress enacted legislation increasing the health insurance deduction for self-employed workers. It increases to a de-**

duction for **100 percent of health insurance costs in the year 2007.**

B. Deductions—Introduction

After you have figured your adjusted gross income, you are ready to either (1) subtract itemized deductions, or (2) subtract your applicable standard deduction. For the most part, itemized deductions are deductions for various kinds of personal expenses that are grouped together on Schedule A (Form 1040). They include deductions for medical expenses, taxes and interest you pay, charitable contributions, nonbusiness casualty and theft losses, and various miscellaneous deductions (including certain employee business expenses). Many of these deductions will be summarized below. Ordinarily, you should itemize deductions *only if they total more than your standard deduction.* The standard deduction amounts for 1997 are set forth in Table 7-1.

Table 7-1

applicable status	standard deduction
• married filing joint return	$ 6,900
• married filing separately	3,450
• head of household	6,050
• single	4,150
• joint return, one spouse age 65 or older	7,700
• joint return, both spouses age 65 or older	8,500
• married filing separately, age 65 or older	4,250
• surviving spouse, age 65 or older	7,700
• head of household, age 65 or older	7,050
• single, age 65 or older	5,150

As Table 7-1 illustrates, if a single taxpayer is blind or age 65 or older the standard deduction is increased by an additional $1,000 (or by $2,000 if the taxpayer is both blind and at least age 65). If either married taxpayer (assuming they file a joint return) is blind or age 65 or older, the standard deduction is increased by an additional $800 ($1,600 if both).

C. Business and Professional Expenses

✎ **Key point: most clergy have business expenses. The deductibility of these expenses depends on whether a minister is an employee or self-employed, whether or not the expenses are reimbursed by the church, and whether any reimbursed expenses are paid under an accountable or a nonaccountable reimbursement arrangement.**

Section 162 of the Code authorizes taxpayers to deduct any ordinary and necessary expenses in-

curred in a trade or business. The exercise of one's ministry qualifies as a "trade or business," and accordingly ministers are free to deduct most of the expenses they incur in the exercise of their ministry, subject to certain conditions and limitations described below. The Code specifically lists travel expenses (including meals and lodging), compensation paid for services, and rent paid for business property or equipment, as examples of deductible business expenses. These certainly are not intended to be the only deductible business and professional expenses. Section 1.162-6 of the income tax regulations lists the following additional examples of business expenses:

- expenses paid or accrued in the operation and repair of an automobile used in making professional calls
- dues to professional societies
- subscriptions to professional journals
- rent paid or accrued for office rooms
- the cost of the fuel, light, water, telephone, etc., used in such offices
- the hiring of office assistants
- amounts currently paid or accrued for books, furniture, and professional instruments and equipment, the useful life of which is short, may be deducted

Other common examples of business expenses for ministers include:

- entertainment
- education
- convention expenses
- business gifts
- insurance
- vestments (including cleaning)

Ministers who perform their duties with no expectation of receiving compensation are not engaged in a "trade or business" and cannot claim any deduction for business expenses. However, they may be able to claim a charitable contribution deduction for expenses incurred in performing charitable activities. *Revenue Ruling 69-645; Thornton v. Commissioner, 57 T.C.M. 1119 (1989); Brydia v. Commissioner, 450 F.2d 954 (3rd Cir. 1971),*

clergy who report their income taxes as self-employed

As noted in chapter 2, clergy who are *self-employed* for income tax purposes compute their net earnings from self-employment on Schedule C by listing all self-employment earnings and then deducting all ordinary and necessary business and professional expenses. The resulting figure is then listed as a component of gross income on Form 1040, line 12.

Advantages to deducting business expenses on Schedule C. Reporting business and professional expenses on Schedule C has several benefits, including the following:

1. Business expenses are fully deductible. Since self-employed ministers list only their *net* self-employment earnings (i.e., after deducting all business and professional expenses) as a component of gross income on line 12 of Form 1040, they in effect are able to deduct 100% of their business and professional expenses (of course, self-employed persons, like employees, can deduct only 50% of business meals and entertainment). They are not subject to the "2% floor" that now applies to the deduction of employee business and professional expenses that are either unreimbursed, or reimbursed under a "nonaccountable" reimbursement plan—i.e., all of these expenses are now deductible only to the extent they exceed 2% of adjusted gross income.

2. Business expenses are deductible even if there are insufficient deductions to itemize on Schedule A. Business and professional expenses are deductible whether or not the minister itemizes deductions on Schedule A. Employees can claim unreimbursed business expenses (including travel and transportation expenses), and business expenses reimbursed by their church under a "nonaccountable" arrangement, only as miscellaneous itemized deductions on Schedule A (line 20), as explained below. Accordingly, employees who cannot itemize deductions will not be able to deduct any of these expenses. This is particularly unfortunate for employees whose business expenses are reimbursed under a nonaccountable plan—since they must include the full amount of all the expense reimbursements as taxable income, but they are denied any deduction of their expenses. This disadvantage can be minimized or eliminated if a minister who reports his or her federal income taxes as an employee enters into an "accountable" reimbursement arrangement with his or her employing church (fully explained below). Of course, self-employed ministers also may claim itemized deductions on Schedule A if their total deductions exceed the applicable standard deduction amount.

3. Lower adjusted gross income. Self-employed ministers who deduct reimbursed or unreimbursed business and professional expenses on Schedule C have a lower adjusted gross income than if these expenses were reported as miscellaneous itemized deductions on Schedule A. This will increase the amount of those itemized deductions that are available only to the extent they exceed a specified percentage of adjusted gross income (e.g., medical expenses and most miscellaneous expenses).

4. Possible reduction in self-employment tax. Reporting business and professional expenses on Schedule C may reduce a minister's self-employment (social security) tax liability, since this tax is based on net earnings from self-employment. Minister-employees often fail to deduct all of their business and professional expenses on Schedule SE in computing their self-employment tax, particularly if such expenses were not deductible for income tax purposes.

✎ **Key point: clergy who report their income taxes as self-employed deduct their business expenses directly on Schedule C. They are not subject to the 2% limitation that applies to employees, and they may deduct their expenses even if they are not able to itemize deductions on Schedule A.**

✎ **Key point: a simpler "Schedule C-EZ" can be used instead of Schedule C if several conditions are satisfied. These are explained later in this chapter. Some clergy will be able to use the simpler form.**

Now is good point to emphasize once again that *many ministers who report their federal income taxes as self-employed would be considered to be employees by the IRS—making these "benefits" of self-employed status illusory.* See chapter 2 for a full consideration of whether ministers are employees or self-employed for income tax reporting purposes.

clergy who report their income taxes as employees

✎ **Key point: ministers who report their income taxes as employees compute most of their employee business expenses on Form 2106 and then carry over the appropriate amount to Schedule A. Employees may be able to use a simplified Form 2106 to compute their business expense deduction. The simplified Form 2106-EZ is available to employees only if their employer does not reimburse business expenses and if they do not claim any depreciation for a car used in their work.**

The performance of services as an *employee* also constitutes a trade or business. However, as noted above, federal tax law now permits the deduction of *all unreimbursed employee business and professional expenses* (i.e., your employing church does not reimburse you for such expenses) *and* "nonaccountable" reimbursed business and professional expenses only as a miscellaneous itemized deduction on Schedule A. This means that only employees who itemize their deductions will be able to deduct their unreimbursed and nonaccountable reimbursed business and professional expenses. Also, most miscellaneous expenses are deductible only to the extent they exceed 2% of adjusted gross income (only 50% of business meals and entertainment are counted).

The restrictive rules that now apply to employee business expenses will result in more taxes for many minister-employees. However, the increased tax burden can be reduced if not eliminated if your employing church simply adopts an accountable reimbursement policy that requires an adequate accounting prior to the reimbursement of any expense and the return of any excess reimbursements. Failure to do so will needlessly result in the payment of additional taxes. All of these rules, and the more common examples of business and professional expenses, will be explained more fully below.

✎ **Key point: clergy who are employees for income tax reporting purposes claim their unreimbursed business expenses on Schedule A—if they are able to itemize, and only to the extent that such expenses exceed 2% of adjusted gross income.**

✎ **Key point:** clergy who are employees for income tax reporting purposes cannot claim any deduction for "unreimbursed" employee business expenses for which an employer reimbursement was available.

✎ **Key point:** clergy who are employees for income tax reporting purposes claim any business expenses reimbursed by their church under a "nonaccountable" reimbursement plan on Schedule A—if they are able to itemize, and only to the extent that such expenses exceed 2% of adjusted gross income.

✎ **Key point:** the limitations on the deductibility of employee business expenses (summarized in the preceding 3 paragraphs) can be avoided if the church adopts an "accountable" reimbursement plan. An accountable plan is one that (1) reimburses only those expenses that are substantiated (within 60 days of the expenses) as to the amount, date, place, and business purpose of the expenses, and (2) requires any excess reimbursements (reimbursements exceeding substantiated expenses) to be returned within 120 days to the church.

1. Transportation expenses

✎ **Key point:** automobile expenses are a major business expense for most clergy. These expenses can be deducted using either a standard mileage rate of 31.5 cents for all business miles (for 1997), or the actual costs of operating the car for business miles. Most clergy choose the standard mileage rate because of its simplicity. However, it is available only if it is selected for the first year a car is used in your trade or business.

Transportation expenses are the ordinary and necessary expenses of getting from one work place to another in the course of your work when you are not traveling away from home. Expenses for transportation while traveling away from home may be deductible as travel expenses. Travel expenses are discussed later in this section. This terminology is admittedly confusing. But you should recognize that transportation and travel expenses are completely distinct concepts for tax purposes. Generally, transportation expenses are all of the expenses associated with local transportation for business purposes (excluding commuting), while travel expenses are all of the expenses associated with travel (including meals and lodging) while away from home overnight for business purposes.

Commuting expenses. As mentioned above, the costs of commuting between your home and your regular place of work are *not* deductible as either transportation or travel expenses. They are considered to be nondeductible personal expenses. This is so even if you do work in your car while on the way to work. Ministers and church treasurers often are confused over the proper handling of commuting expenses. What if a pastor stops at the hospital to visit a member on the way home? Is this commuting?

What if a staff member makes more than one round-trip between home and the church in one day? Are both trips commuting? Are commuting expenses business expenses? Can they be reimbursed by the church? What is the best way for a church to treat these kinds of expenses? How should the church report reimbursements of commuting expenses?

● **Commuting—what is it?** Commuting refers to travel between one's home and regular place of work. The income tax regulations state that commuting expenses are personal expenses and do not qualify as business expenses. This is so even if a worker is required to make more than one round-trip between home and work in one day. For example, if a minister must return to the church in the evening for a board meeting, this trip is commuting. A commuting trip does not become a business expense just because work is done in the car.

☞ *Example.* Rev. H is the senior minister at First Church. He owns a home fifteen miles from the church. In order to utilize the time it takes to drive to and from work each day, Rev. H has a telephone installed in his car. He uses the telephone for mostly church-related calls. The fact that Rev. H makes business calls while commuting will not change the character of such trips from commuting to business. His commuting expenses remain nondeductible. The same rule applies if Rev. H commutes to and from First Church with an associate minister of the church and the two discuss church-related business during their commuting time. These rules do not violate a minister's constitutional guaranty of religious freedom. Hamblen v. Commissioner, 78 T.C. 53 (1981).

● **Trips between church and a second "business location."** Clergy and other church staff often travel between church and another business location in the community. For example, a pastor leaves the church to visit someone in a local hospital. Or, a church staff member travels from the church to a local store to purchase church supplies. These trips, from the church to a second business location, are business-related. This means that the expenses incurred in making such trips may be deductible as a business expense by the worker, or may be reimbursed by the church if it has established a business expense reimbursement arrangement.

● **Trips between a second business location and home.** What happens if a minister travels from church to a hospital to make a call, and then goes directly home from the hospital? Is this entire trip commuting, or simply a part of it? The miles from the church to the hospital are business-related, but the miles from the hospital to the minister's home are non-deductible commuting expenses.

☞ *Example.* Rev. C is an associate minister at her church. Her home is 5 miles from church. Her round-trip commutes between her home and the church are personal commuting miles, and are never deductible. If the church has adopted an accountable business expense reimbursement arrangement, these expenses are not reimbursable since they are not business-related. If the church reimburses these expenses anyway, the full amount of the reimbursements must be included on Rev. C's W-2 (or 1099) as taxable income. In the future, reimbursement of personal miles should be discouraged, even if the reimbursements are reported as taxable income.

☞ **Example.** Same facts as the previous example. Assume that Rev. C leaves work early one afternoon to call on several persons in a local hospital that is 3 miles from the church, and only 2 miles from Rev. C's home (the hospital is between Rev. C's home and the church). The miles between the church and hospital are business miles, and may be reimbursed by the church under a business expense reimbursement arrangement even though Rev. C has traveled 3 miles closer to her home. However, the remaining 2 miles between the hospital and Rev. C's home are personal miles and are not reimbursable as business expenses.

☞ **Example.** Same facts as the previous example, except that the hospital is 3 miles from the church and 8 miles from Rev. C's home. The entire 8 miles in traveling home from the hospital represent personal miles. On the other hand, if Rev. C returns to the church following her visit at the hospital, then these 3 miles would be business-related, and the only the remaining 5 miles to Rev. C's home would be personal.

• **Trips between home and a temporary business location.** Occasionally, a minister is called upon to travel to another city to perform a funeral or wedding. Are such occasional trips between a minister's home and the temporary "business location" non-deductible commuting expenses? The IRS ruled in 1990 that these kinds of trips are legitimate business activities rather than commuting, and the expenses associated with these trips can be deducted as a business expense (or reimbursed by the church under a business expense reimbursement arrangement).

☞ **Example.** Rev. G is senior minister at First Church. He is asked to perform a funeral service for a former church member in another community. He incurs $75 in auto expenses. These expenses are deductible business expenses rather than non-deductible commuting expenses since Rev. G was traveling to a temporary work location. The church can reimburse these expenses as business expenses. If it does not, Rev. G can deduct them as employee business expenses on Schedule A (if he is reports his income taxes as an employee) or on Schedule C (in the unlikely event that he is self-employed for income tax purposes).

☞ **Example.** Rev. B, while serving as senior minister of First Church, is asked to temporarily serve a small church 50 miles away by conducting services on Sunday afternoons until the church can find a minister. Rev. B's commitment is in addition to his duties at First Church, and it is

IRS CREATES AN EXCEPTION TO THE NONDE-DUCTIBILITY OF COMMUTING EXPENSES

The IRS ruled in 1990 that taxpayers can deduct their transportation expenses incurred in traveling between their home and a temporary work location. This is an exception to the general rule that "commuting expenses" between one's home and regular place of work are a non-deductible "personal expense." To qualify for the new rule, taxpayers must have a regular place of work and incur daily transportation expenses between their home and a *temporary* place of business. The temporary work location does not need to be in a different metropolitan area (as previously required). However, the temporary work site must in fact be temporary. Commuting expenses incurred in traveling between one's residence and a *regular* work site are still nondeductible.

The IRS warned that a taxpayer may be considered to be working at a particular location on a *regular* (rather than a temporary) basis "whether or not the taxpayer works or performs services at that location every week or on a set schedule." For example, the IRS noted that transportation expenses incurred by a doctor in traveling between his home and a local hospital are not deductible, since such a work site normally will be "regular" rather than temporary. The IRS defined a temporary work site as "any location at which the taxpayer performs services on an irregular or short-term (i.e., generally a matter of days or weeks) basis." How do this new rule affect clergy? Clearly, it will be of limited value. The important point to note is that expenses incurred in commuting between your home and regular place of work (the church) remain nondeductible personal expenses. This general rule is not affected by the new IRS position. Further, trips from home to local hospitals to visit parishioners generally will be nondeductible, since the hospitals ordinarily will not satisfy the definition of a temporary work site (your presence there is not irregular or short-term). In some larger cities, a minister will visit some hospitals very rarely. A minister's expenses incurred in traveling between his home and such a hospital will be deductible under the new rule. Further, visits to a parishioner's home for counseling or the performance of sacerdotal duties often will be deductible, if such visits (are irregular or short-term). One more point—trips between your church office and a local hospital remain tax-deductible, since they are not considered to be "commuting." If you incur expenses that are deductible under the new rule, you may deduct them according to the rules discussed in this chapter. Revenue Ruling 90-23.

expected to last for no more than two months. The round-trip transportation expenses incurred by Rev. B in "commuting" to and from the second assignment are deductible (assuming that he returns home each evening). Revenue Ruling 190, 1953-2 C.B. 303.

☞ *Example. You regularly work in an office in the city where you live. Your employer requires that you attend a one-week training session at a different office in the same city. You travel directly from your home to the training location and return each day. You can deduct the cost of your daily round-trip transportation between your home and the training location. IRS Publication 17.*

There are two ways for you to compute your transportation expenses:

method #1—standard mileage rate

By far the simpler method of computing your transportation expenses is to claim the applicable standard mileage rate for each business mile that you drive. Under this approach, you simply deduct a standard mileage rate for each mile that is driven during the year for church-related business. For 1997, the standard mileage rate (for business miles) is 31.5 cents per mile. The 31.5 cents per mile rate applies to *all* business miles. You may use the standard mileage rate instead of figuring your actual operating and fixed expenses, including depreciation, in computing your deductible costs in operating a car. You can use the standard mileage rate whether or not you are reimbursed by your church for your business expenses.

Three important limitations apply to the use of the standard mileage rate:

• **You must own your car.** If you lease your car, you cannot use the standard mileage rate to compute your transportation expenses. *Treas. Reg. 1.274(d)-1(a)(3).*

• **You must use the standard mileage rate in the first year you place a car in service in your business.** In later years you may use the standard mileage rate or actual expenses. If you do not choose the standard mileage rate in the first year, however, you may not use it for that car in any year. If you use the standard mileage rate in the first year, you are considered to have made an election not to use the accelerated cost recovery system (ACRS), discussed later. You also may not claim the section 179 deduction, discussed later. If you change to the actual cost method in later years, but before your car is fully depreciated, you have to estimate the useful life of the car and use straight line depreciation.

• **The standard mileage rate is not available to taxpayers who operate a "fleet of cars using two or more at the same time."** Some have interpreted this language to prohibit the standard mileage rate by clergy who own two cars that are used for business miles. On the other hand, in Publication 917 ("Business Use of a Car") the IRS seems to limit this language to organizations that own two or more vehicles that are used simultaneously for business purposes, and not to "alternating" use of two cars by one taxpayer. Publication 917 states that "if you use more than one car on an alternating basis, combine the total business miles of both cars" and multiply times the standard mileage rate.

If you elect the standard mileage rate, you still may deduct state and local personal property taxes (reduced proportionately by any non-business usage of the car) and parking fees and tolls. If you are reimbursed or receive an allowance for your car expenses, you may use the standard mileage rate to find the cost of operating your car. If you use the standard mileage rate, you are not required to keep any records of your actual transportation costs. However, you must maintain adequate records confirming the number of business miles you drove during the year (explained later).

☞ *Example. Rev. A purchased a car in 1997 for business use. He drove the car 20,000 miles for business purposes during the year, and elected to use the standard mileage rate to calculate his transportation expenses. Without considering any other rule or limitation, Rev. A is entitled to a deduction of $6,300 for the year (20,000 business miles x 31.5 cents).*

☞ *Example. Same facts as the previous example, except that Rev. A owns another car that he drove in 1997 for business purposes (accumulating 3,000 miles). According to IRS Publication 917, Rev. A is eligible to use the standard mileage rate for both vehicles, since he is using the vehicles on an alternating (rather than a simultaneous) basis.*

☞ *Example. Rev. W purchased a car in 1997 for business use. He drove the car 15,000 miles for business purposes during the year, and elected to use the actual expense method for computing his transportation expenses. Because of the complexity of this method, Rev. W would like to use the standard mileage rate for computing his transportation expenses in 1998. He may not do so, since he did not elect this method in the year he placed the car in service in his business.*

method #2—actual cost method

Alternatively, you can compute your transportation expenses by using your actual costs incurred in operating a car for business purposes. The remainder of this section summarizes the rules for claiming actual costs in lieu of the standard mileage rate. While using the actual cost method takes discipline and perseverance, several studies suggest you will have a higher deduction using this method than the standard mileage rate method, particularly if your car is relatively new. The question is whether you consider the potential savings in taxes worth the extra inconvenience. Most ministers prefer the convenience and simplicity of the standard mileage rate.

Your actual transportation expenses include the cost of local business travel by air, rail, bus, taxi, and the cost of driving and maintaining your car, but *not the cost of meals or lodging. You may not deduct the costs of commuting (e.g., by bus, subway, taxi, train, or car) between your home and your main or regular* place of work. These costs are nondeductible personal expenses. You may not deduct commuting expenses no matter what the distance is between your home and your regular place of work. Commuting expenses include parking fees paid to park your car at your place of work.

☞ *Example. Rev. F is a minister at First Church. She drives her car to and from work on most days, but occasionally takes a bus. The cost of traveling to and from work (whether by bus or in her own car) is a commuting expense that is not deductible by Rev. F whether she reports her income taxes as an employee or as a self-employed person.*

The most important element of transportation expense is your car. If you are required to use your car in your work, you can deduct the expenses associated with business use of the car. Deductible items include the cost of gas, oil, tires, repairs, tune-ups, batteries, car washes, insurance, depreciation, interest paid on a car loan, taxes, licenses, garage rent, parking fees, and tolls. If you use your car both for business and personal purposes, you must divide your expenses between business and personal use. For example, if you drive your car 20,000 miles during the year, 12,000 of which is for business and 8,000 of which is for personal use (including commuting), you can claim only 60% (12,000/20,000) of the cost of operating the car as a business expense.

☞ *Example. A church hired a pastor whose home was 70 miles from the church. The pastor chose to remain in his home, and commuted to and from work at the church every Sunday and Wednesday. The pastor claimed a business expense deduction for depreciation on the car he used in commuting to and from work. To substantiate this deduction he produced a letter signed by the six officers of the church stating that he was their pastor and containing a schedule of business miles traveled. The pastor claimed that he used his car to travel 12,643 business miles during the year under examination, which he claimed represented 70 percent of the total miles traveled during the year. The IRS disallowed the claimed depreciation deduction, and the Tax Court agreed. It noted that the evidence showed that 11,523 of the 12,643 miles traveled were commuting miles from the pastor's home to the church, and that "it is well settled that the cost of commuting between one's residence and regular place of employment is a nondeductible personal expense." The remaining 1,120 miles were used for business purposes since they represented travel to transport church members to various functions at other churches. Therefore, these miles qualified as business miles, and a depreciation deduction was allowable for the total amount of depreciation for the year multiplied times the "business use percentage" (the percentage of total miles that the car was used for business purposes, or 1,120 divided by 12,643). Clark v. Commissioner, 67 T.C.M. 2458 (1994).*

☞ *Example. The Tax Court refused to allow a minister to use the "actual expense method" to compute a deduction for the business use of his car since he could not prove the percentage of his total miles that the car was used for business purposes. A pastor often traveled by car in connection with his ministry, and reported travel expenses on his tax returns using the actual expense method. The IRS audited the minister and recalculated his expenses using the standard mileage rate. The IRS reasoned that the pastor must use the standard rate method to determine car expenses since he failed to prove the total miles driven each year. The IRS conceded that the pastor drove 13,170 business miles in one year under examination, and at least 12,274 business miles in the following year. These miles were not computed using a mileage log but instead by "reconstructing" the number of business miles by referring to actual receipts. However, the pastor kept no documentation during the years in question which showed the personal use of his car, or the total miles driven. The IRS claimed that without adequate substantiation of the total number of miles driven it was unable to determine a business use percentage of the miles and accordingly the pastor could not use the actual expense method for either year. In using the actual expense method, a taxpayer multiplies expenses incurred in owning and operating a car times the "business use percentage"—the percentage of total miles that the car is used for business purposes. If a taxpayer can prove business miles but not personal miles or total miles, then the business use percentage cannot be calculated and the actual expense method cannot be used. Rather, the taxpayer must use the standard mileage rate (multiplying business miles times the applicable standard mileage rate). Parker v. Commissioner, 65 T.C.M. 1740 (1994). See also Shelley v. Commissioner, T.C. Memo. 1994-432 (1994).*

Cars placed in service after 1986

❖ **New in 1997. The maximum "section 179 deduction" increased to $18,000 in 1997. It increases to $18,500 in 1998, $19,000 in 1999, $20,000 in 2000, and $24,000 in 2001 and 2002, and $25,000 in 2003.**

The biggest expense associated with a car is of course the purchase cost. However, since a car ordinarily will be used over a period of several years, it is not appropriate to claim the entire cost as a business deduction in the year of purchase. Rather, the purchase cost is allocated over the useful life of the vehicle, and an annual "depreciation" deduction is claimed each year. Computing a depreciation deduction is a complicated task, due to the application of three independent rules:

1. The MACRS deduction. You figure your annual depreciation deduction for cars placed in service after 1986 by using a *modified accelerated cost recovery system* (referred to as MACRS), or a permissible alternative. Under MACRS, a car used in business is depreciated over a *five-year* period using the so-called "200% declining balance method"—meaning that annual depreciation for each of the five years the car is in service is computed by multiplying 40% times the original cost of the car less accumulated depreciation. The newer method allows twice the "straight line" depreciation amount and tends to permit larger depreciation deductions in the first few years of a car's use.

The first year a car is placed in service, and the year after the final year of the five year service life, you deduct *half* the amount of depreciation that would be allowed for a full year. It does not matter when during the year you first began using the car. This rule is known as the "half-year" convention. If you place a car in service during the last three months of the tax year, and it is the only business asset you "place in service" during the year, then you must use a "mid-quarter convention" in computing your MACRS deduction. Further, if you place additional "business assets" in service during the year (e.g., a computer), you must use the mid-quarter convention if the total of all business assets placed in service in the final quarter of the year exceeds 40% of all property you placed in service during the year. Table 7-2 illustrates how to compute your annual depreciation deduction using MACRS under both the half-year and mid-quarter conventions.

Table 7-2
MACRS Depreciation Table

| year | half yr. convention | Mid-quarter convention Quarter car placed in service | | | | max. deprec. limit* |
		1st	2nd	3rd	4th	
1	20.00%	35.00%	25.00%	15.00%	5.00%	$3,160
2	32.00%	26.00%	30.00%	34.00%	38.00%	$5,000
3	19.20%	15.60%	18.00%	20.40%	22.80%	$3,050
4	11.52%	11.01%	11.37%	12.24%	13.68%	$1,775
5	11.52%	11.01%	11.37%	11.30%	10.94%	$1,775
6	5.76%	1.38%	4.26%	7.06%	9.58%	$1,775

* These amounts must be reduced if the car is used less than 100% for business purposes. Once you have determined the correct column to use, continue using it for later years. Multiply the unadjusted basis (defined below) of your car by the applicable percentage to determine your depreciation deduction.

A car's *unadjusted basis* (see Table 7-2) ordinarily is its cost less any section 179 deduction that you previously claimed. It is not reduced by any depreciation deduction. As noted below, there are limits on how much depreciation can be deducted in any year. If you use your car more than 50% for business, but less than 100%, you determine your depreciation deduction limits by multiplying the limit amount by the percentage of business use during the year.

If you choose, you may use an *alternate method of computing your depreciation.* This "alternate MACRS" method is based on the straight line method of depreciation and is used in place of the MACRS percentages discussed above. Under this method, you may choose a recovery period of either 3, 5, or 12 years. The straight line recovery percentages are shown in the regulations to section 168 of the Code.

2. The "section 179 deduction." Section 179 of the Code permits you to elect to deduct most if not all of the cost of business property in the year of pur-

chase if certain conditions are satisfied. Generally, the "section 179" deduction cannot exceed $18,000 for 1997. This amount increases to $18,500 for 1998, and increases further in future years as noted above. You must use business property, including a car, more than 50% for business in order to claim a section 179 deduction. Further, the deduction cannot exceed your professional income. The section 179 deduction is treated as a depreciation deduction for the tax year a car is placed in service.

3. The "luxury car" limitation. The first two rules have very little significance in most cases because of a third rule—there are "luxury car" limits on how much you can claim as either a section 179 deduction or as depreciation on a car used for business purposes. These limits are designed to prevent taxpayers from claiming "excessive" deductions for the cost of "luxury" cars. The problem with these limits is that they treat cars of moderate cost as luxury cars. The limits are summarized in Table 7-3. It is important to recognize that these limits are reduced proportionately if your business use of the car is more than 50% but less than 100%. For example, if you bought and placed in service on January 1, 1997 a car that you used 80% for business in 1997, your total section 179 deduction *and* depreciation cannot be more than $2,528 ($3,160 x 80%). If you do not use your car more than 50% in your work, no section 179 deduction is allowed. A section 179 election must be made in the year a car is placed in service (ordinarily, the year you begin using the car for business purposes).

Table 7-3
Cars Placed in Service After 1986—Maximum Limits[1]

Placed in service after	before	depreciation first year[2]	depreciation later years
12/31/86	1/1/89	2,560	4,100 (2nd yr) 2,450 (3rd yr) 1,475 (later yrs)
12/31/88	1/1/91	2,660	4,200 (2nd yr) 2,550 (3rd yr) 1,475 (later yrs)
12/31/90	1/1/92	2,660	4,300 (2nd yr) 2,550 (3rd yr) 1,575 (later yrs)
12/31/91	1/1/93	2,760	4,400 (2nd yr) 2,650 (3rd yr) 1,575 (later yrs)
12/31/92	1/1/94	2,860	4,600 (2nd yr) 2,750 (3rd yr) 1,675 (later yrs)
12/31/93	1/1/95	2,960	4,700 (2nd yr) 2,850 (3rd yr) 1,675 (later yrs)
12/31/94	1/1/96	3,060	4,900 (2nd yr) 2,950 (3rd yr) 1,675 (later yrs)
12/31/95	1/1/97	3,060	4,900 (2nd yr) 2,950 (3rd yr) 1,775 (later yrs)
12/31/96	1/1/98	3,160	5,000 (2nd yr) 3,050 (3rd yr) 1,775 (later yrs)

[1] These amounts must be reduced if the car is used less than 100% for business purposes.

[2] This is the maximum amount of your section 179 deduction and depreciation allowed for the tax year the car is placed in service.

☞ *Example. Rev. M purchased a car and began using it for business purposes in 1997. He uses it 80% for business purposes. His total depreciation deduction, including any section 179 deduction, for 1997 is limited to $2,528 ($3,160 x 80%). If* *the business use of the car remained at 80% for 1998, the depreciation deduction for that year would be limited to $4,000 (80% of $5,000).*

☞ ***Example.*** *Rev. T purchases an automobile for $18,000 which he places in service on May 4, 1997. He uses the automobile exclusively for business use. He does not claim a section 179 deduction for the automobile. Rev. T computes his depreciation expense for 1997 as follows: (1) multiply the car's "basis" (cost) of $18,000 times 40% (the double declining balance rate for cars) to yield $7,200; (2) since a half-year convention applies in the first year a car is placed in service, Rev. T can claim only half of the $7,200 depreciation expense, or a total of $3,600; (3) however, since the maximum amount of depreciation that a taxpayer can claim in the first year a car is placed in service is $3,160 for 1997, the depreciation deduction must be reduced from $3,600 to $3,160. For 1998 (the second year the car is in service), Rev. T computes his depreciation as follows: (1) subtract the $3,160 in depreciation claimed in 1997 from the original basis of $18,000 to yield an adjusted basis of $14,840; (2) multiply the adjusted basis of $14,840 times the double declining balance rate of 40% to yield $5,936 in depreciation; (3) however, the maximum depreciation deduction that Rev. T may claim for 1998 (the second year) is limited to $5,000. For 1999, follow the same procedure. Rev. T multiplies $9,840 ($14,840 - $5,000) times 40% to arrive at depreciation of $3,936. However, the maximum depreciation deduction for the third year the car is in service is $3,050. The same basic procedure would be followed for the fourth and fifth years the car is in service (note that the maximum depreciation deduction for the fourth and fifth years is $1,775).*

If you dispose of your car, you will have a gain or loss on the transaction. A gain will be treated as ordinary income to the extent of any depreciation (including any section 179 deduction) you claimed on the car. You ordinarily get no depreciation deduction for the year in which you dispose of a car. If you trade in a car you used entirely in your business for another car that will be used entirely in your business, the unadjusted basis of the new car is the adjusted basis of the old car, plus any additional amount you paid for the new car. If you trade in a car that you used only partly in your business, more complicated rules apply. See IRS Publication 917.

Less than 50% business use. You cannot take the section 179 deduction, and you must figure depreciation using the straight line method over a 5-year period (using the half-year convention), if you use your car *50% or less for business use.* The depreciation deduction under this rule is figured by multiplying the car's basis times 10% for the 1st and 6th years and 20% for the 2nd through 5th years. A qualified business use is any use in your trade or business. Any use of your car by another person is not treated as use in a trade or business unless that use (1) is directly connected with your business, (2) is properly reported by you as income to the other person, or (3) results in a payment of fair market rent.

You must allocate the use of your car that you use for more than one purpose during the tax year to the various uses. Allocate the use on the basis of mileage. The percentage of qualified business use is determined by dividing the number of miles you drive your car for business purposes during the year by the total number of miles you drive your car during the year for any purpose. You must meet the more than 50% business use test each year of the recovery period.

✎ **Key point: if you find these car depreciation rules confusing (they constitute some of the most complex tax rules in existence), then the standard mileage rate is for you.**

Leasing a car

If you lease a car that you use in your work, you may deduct the part of your lease payments that are for the use of the car in your work. You cannot deduct any part of the lease payments that are for commuting or other personal use of the car. You must spread any advance payments over the entire lease period. You may not deduct any payments you make to buy a car even if the payments are called lease payments. You may have to include in your gross income an amount called an *inclusion amount* if you leased car in 1997 that had a fair market value on the first day of the lease term exceeding $15,700 (e.g., a "luxury car"). These rules are designed to prevent taxpayers from avoiding the depreciation limitations (discussed above) by leasing a car. To compute the inclusion amount, refer to the tables reproduced in IRS Publication 917. *Treas. Reg. 1.280F-7T(a).*

☞ ***Example.*** *On May 1, 1997, Rev. J leased a new car for 3 years and immediately began using it both for personal and business purposes. The car had a fair market value of $20,000 on the first day of the lease term. For the remainder of 1997, Rev. J used the car 25% for personal use and 75% for business. Lease payments were $350 each month, or $2,800 for the eight months of 1997 that Rev. J leased the car. Rev. J can claim a business expense deduction of $2,100 (75% business use multiplied times total lease payments of $2,800). This deduction is available on Schedule A if Rev. J reports his income taxes as an employee (and is able to itemize), or on Schedule C (if self-employed). In addition, since the fair market value of the leased vehicle exceeds $15,700 (the 1997 amount) on the first day of the lease term, Rev. J must report an "inclusion amount" as taxable income on his tax return. This amount is computed on the basis of tables set forth in IRS Publication 917. According to these tables, Rev. J would have to report $10 as taxable income on his tax return for 1997. This is computed as follows: (1) First, find the dollar amount from the tables in IRS Publication 917 corresponding to a leased car with a fair market value of $20,000. The dollar amount is $38. (2) Next, prorate this amount based on the number of days the car was leased during the year (122/365 x $38 = $13). (3) Next, multiply the pro-*

Business Use of a Car:
A Comparison of the Major Tax Options

car owned by	method	characteristics	tax consequences
minister	actual expenses	• minister computes actual expenses of operating car for business use • actual expenses include gas, oil, tires, repairs, tune-ups, batteries, washes, insurance, depreciation, interest on car loans, taxes, licenses, garage rent, parking fees, tolls • annual depreciation deduction is limited by "luxury car" rules	• ministers can deduct expenses allocable to the business use of their car, and not reimbursed under an accountable plan, as an itemized deduction on Schedule A (for employees) or a Schedule C deduction (for self-employed) • deduction allowable only if records substantiate the amount, date, place, and business purpose of each expense • deduction allowable only if records substantiate the business use of the car • in many cases, a larger deduction will be available than with the standard mileage rate—but, the trade-off is that the recordkeeping requirements are much more complex
minister	standard mileage rate	• multiply current standard mileage rate (31.5 cents for 1997) times the number of miles driven for business use • must be used in first year a car is used for business purposes • cannot be used for leased vehicles	• ministers can deduct expenses allocable to the business use of their car, and not reimbursed under an accountable plan, as an itemized deduction on Schedule A (for employees) or a Schedule C deduction (for self-employed) • ministers must maintain records documenting the business nature of their business miles • can still deduct parking fees and tolls • most ministers use this method because of its simplicity
church	church-owned vehicle; no personal use permitted	• church owns vehicle • vehicle kept on church premises • written church policy prohibits personal use (including commuting) • minister using car does not live on church premises • church reasonably believes the vehicle is not used for any personal use	• no income to report (since no personal use allowed)
church	church-owned vehicle; no personal use allowed except for commuting (for security or other noncompensatory reasons)	• church owns vehicle • for "noncompensatory" reasons (such as vehicle security) the church requires the minister to commute • written church policy prohibits personal use (except commuting) • minister using car is not a "control employee" (defined in chapter 4, section A.8) • church reasonably believes the vehicle is not used for any personal use	• no income to report (since no personal use allowed)—except for $3 per round trip commute or $1.50 per one-way commute. • no recordkeeping required (since no personal use allowed) except number of commutes
church	church-owned vehicle; no restrictions as to personal use	none	• personal use must be valued and reported as income on the minister's W-2 or 1099 • use the general valuation method (discussed earlier) unless the church has elected one of the 3 special valuation rules

rated amount times the percentage of business use of the vehicle ($13 x 75% = $10). This is the inclusion amount that must be reported as taxable income on Rev. J's 1997 tax return. For 1998, the second year of the 3-year lease, the inclusion amount would be $63 ($84 from the tables multiplied times 75% business use). For 1999, the inclusion amount would be $94 ($125 from the tables multiplied times 75% business use). This example assumes that the percentage of business use remains the same for each year of the lease.

Employer-provided cars

✎ **Key point: clergy should consider the advantages of using a church-owned car for their business travel. This will eliminate most recordkeeping and reporting requirements. Some conditions apply.**

Many churches provide their minister with a church-owned car that the minister is free to use for both personal and business purposes. The minister's personal use of such a car must be valued and reported by both the church and minister as taxable income. The methods that can be used for computing the value of the personal use of the car are discussed in chapter 4, section A.8.

However, note that if the church board adopts a resolution restricting use of the car to church-related activities, then the minister reports no income or deductions (use of the car is a nontaxable, noncash "working condition fringe benefit"), and better yet, there are no accountings, reimbursements, allowances, or recordkeeping requirements. This assumes that the car is in fact used exclusively for church-related purposes. For churches and clergy to realize these tax benefits, the following conditions must be satisfied:

• The vehicle is owned or leased by the church and is provided to a minister (or other church employee) for use in connection with church business.

• When the vehicle is not being used for church business, it is kept on the church's premises (unless it is temporarily located elsewhere, such as a repair shop).

• No employee using the vehicle lives on the church's premises.

• Under a written policy statement adopted by the church board, no employee of the church can use the vehicle for personal purposes, except for "de minimis" (minimal) personal use (such as a stop for lunch between two business trips).

• The church reasonably believes that, except for de minimis use, no church employee uses the vehicle for any personal purpose.

• The church must be able to supply sufficient evidence to prove to the IRS that the preceding five conditions have been met (the church must complete Part III, Section C of IRS Form 4562 for each employee provided with a church-owned vehicle, specifying that it in fact satisfies the above requirements). *Treas. Reg. 1.274-6T(a)(2).*

Commuting is always considered to be personal use of a car, and accordingly the procedure discussed in the preceding paragraph would not be available if a church allowed its minister to commute to work in a church-owned vehicle. Fortunately, the regulations permit certain church employees who use a church-owned vehicle exclusively for business purposes *except for commuting* to receive all of the benefits associated with business use of a church-owned vehicle, if certain conditions are satisfied. These rules are explained fully in chapter 4, section A.8.

2. Travel expenses

Travel expenses are your ordinary and necessary expenses while traveling **away from home** for your work or business. You can deduct these expenses if you prove them, as explained below. However, you may not deduct expenses that are lavish or extravagant or that are for personal or vacation purposes. Travel expenses do not include expenses for transportation while not traveling away from home and expenses for entertainment. These expenses are discussed elsewhere in this chapter. Deductible travel expenses include:

• air, rail, and bus fares
• operating and maintaining your car
• taxi fares or other costs of transportation between the airport or station and your hotel, or from one work site to another
• meals and lodging while you are away from home on business
• cleaning and laundry expenses
• telephone and telegraph expenses
• tips

Your expenses must be for your travel or temporary living (including meals and lodging) while you are away from home. You are traveling away from home if your duties require you to be away from the general area of your tax home (defined below) substantially longer than an ordinary day's work and, during your time off while away, you need to get sleep or rest to meet the demands of your work. This does not mean napping in your car. You do not have to be away from your home from dusk to dawn as long as your relief from duty is long enough to get necessary sleep or rest. To satisfy these requirements, a trip ordinarily must be overnight.

☞ *Example. Rev. W travels to another city to conduct a funeral service for a former member of his congregation. He leaves at 7 AM and returns home that evening at 6 PM. Expenses incurred by Rev. W in making the trip are not travel expenses since he was not away from home overnight or for a sufficiently long period of time that required sleep or rest. Rev. W's car expenses constitute transportation expenses, but not the cost of meals. The de-*

ductibility of these expenses is explained fully elsewhere in this chapter.

☞ *Example. Same facts as the preceding example, except that Rev. W left home at 7 AM and did not return home until 11 AM the next day. Since this trip was overnight, the car, meals, and lodging expenses incurred by Rev. W are travel expenses. They are deductible according to the rules discussed at the beginning of this chapter.*

Instead of deducting the actual cost of your meals and lodging while you are traveling away from home for business, you may be able to deduct a "per diem" allowance provided by your employer. Per diem allowances are explained in section E of this chapter.

Your tax home. It is important to determine where your **tax home** is, since you may deduct travel expenses only to the extent that they are incurred while you are traveling away from your home. Generally, your tax home is your main place of employment or work. If you regularly work in two or more areas, your tax home is the general area where your main place of work is located. Although you regularly work within the city or general area of your tax home, you occasionally may have to work or conduct business at another location. It may not be practical to return home from this other location at the end of each day's work. You will be considered away from home, and your travel expenses (including meals and lodging) will constitute travel expenses, if you are away from home on a temporary rather than on an indefinite basis.

Your assignment or job away from your regular place of work is **temporary** if it lasts 1 year or less. In such a case, your tax home does not change and accordingly your travel expenses are incurred while away from home.

On the other hand, if your assignment or job away from home lasts more than 1 year, then you will be deemed to be away from home on an **indefinite** rather than a temporary basis. If your work at the new location is indefinite, then that location becomes your new tax home. A consequence of this change in tax home is that you cannot deduct your travel, meals, and lodging expenses while there (since they are not travel expenses incurred while "away from home"). Any reimbursements or advances you receive from an employer must be included in your income even if they are called travel allowances. Some persons move from one assignment to another and maintain no fixed tax home. Such transient workers (including some traveling evangelists) may not deduct travel, meals, or lodging expenses since they are never away from home.

☞ *Example. Rev. M is a minister at First Church. He accepts an assignment overseas for temporary missionary service. If the assignment overseas lasts for less than one year, then the assignment is temporary and Rev. M's tax home does not change. As a result, his expenses (including meals and lodging) incurred while traveling away from home on his temporary assignment constitute travel expenses.*

☞ *Example. Same facts as the preceding example, except that Rev. M's assignment lasts 18 months. Under these circumstances, Rev. M's foreign assignment will be considered indefinite. As a result, his tax home changes to the foreign location and no travel, meals, or lodging expenses are deductible. However, Rev. M may be eligible for a foreign earned income exclusion of up to $70,000 (in 1997) for any year in which he resides overseas for at least 330 days. This exclusion (claimed by filing IRS Form 2555) will eliminate any income tax liability in most cases, making the loss of any travel expense deduction irrelevant. See IRS Publication 463 for further details.*

Travel in the United States (including cruise ships)

If your trip was entirely for business, you may deduct your ordinary and necessary travel expenses. If your trip was primarily personal, you may not deduct any travel expenses even if you had some business activity at your destination. If your trip was primarily for business and, while away at your business destination you extend your stay for a vacation, make a nonbusiness side trip, or have other nonbusiness activities, you may deduct the travel expenses to and from your business destination.

☞ *Example. You work in Atlanta and make a business trip to New Orleans. On your way home, you stop in Mobile to visit relatives. You spend $450 for the 9 days you are away from home for travel, meals, lodging, and other travel expenses. If you had not stopped in Mobile, you would have been gone only 6 days and your total cost would have been $400. You may deduct $400 for your trip.*

If your trip was primarily for vacation, the entire cost of the trip is a nondeductible personal expense, except for any expenses incurred that are directly and properly allocable to your business. A trip can be a vacation even though a promoter advertises that a trip to a resort or on a cruise ship is primarily for business. The scheduling of incidental business activities during a trip, such as viewing video tapes or attending lectures, will not make what is intended to be a vacation into a business trip. The deduction for business travel on a cruise ship or other luxury water transportation cannot exceed twice the highest per diem travel amount paid by the federal government to its employees traveling in the United States multiplied times the number of days in transit.

☞ *Example. Rev. T lives in Minnesota. In January, she is invited by a pastor friend in Florida to visit for a week. While in Florida the pastor friend invites Rev. T to conduct a worship service on a Sunday morning. Rev. T does so. Rev. T's travel is not deductible as either a business expense or charitable contribution. IRS Publication 17 states: "If your trip was primarily for personal reasons, such as a vacation, the entire cost of the trip is a nondeductible personal expense."*

☞ **Example.** *Assume that Rev. T's pastor friend in Florida invited Rev. T to come to Florida for a weekend and conduct a worship service at his church. Rev. T's trip is for business purposes. If her travel expenses are unreimbursed, she can deduct them as a business expense. Alternatively, the church in Florida can reimburse Rev. T's travel expenses as a legitimate business expense. If adequate substantiation is provided, then the reimbursement is accountable and need not be reported as taxable income to Rev. T. IRS Publication 17 states that "[y]ou can deduct all your travel expenses if your trip was entirely business related."*

☞ **Example.** *Same facts as the previous example, except that following the worship service Rev. T decides to extend her trip by 5 days. IRS Publication 17 states: "If your trip was primarily for business and, while at your business destination, you extended your stay for a vacation, made a nonbusiness side trip, or had other nonbusiness activities, you can deduct your business-related travel expenses. These expenses include the travel costs of getting to and from your business destination, and you can deduct any business-related expenses at your business destination."*

You may deduct travel expenses for yourself, but ordinarily not those of your family, in attending a **convention** if you can show that your attendance benefits your own work or business. Ordinarily, no deduction will be allowed for expenses in attending a convention, seminar, or similar meeting that does not offer significant business-related activities, such as participation in meetings, workshops, lectures, or exhibits held during the day. Nonbusiness expenses, such as social or sightseeing expenses, are personal expenses and are not deductible, Your appointment or election as a delegate does not, in itself, entitle you to or deprive you of the deduction.

☞ **Example.** *Rev. O is senior minister of First Church. He and his spouse attend an annual church convention in another state. The trip lasts six days. Rev. O attends business sessions and visits an exhibit area during the day. His spouse spends most of her time visiting with friends and relatives, and occasionally attends business sessions and visits exhibits. She also assists her husband in entertaining friends. Rev. O can deduct the travel expenses he incurs in attending the convention, but not those of his spouse. This assumes, of course, that the deduction rules discussed elsewhere in this chapter are satisfied. If their hotel room costs $115 per night, but a single room would have cost $90, then Rev. O can deduct $90 per night as lodging expense. He may deduct the total cost of driving a car, however. If he and his spouse used public transportation, he may deduct only his fare.*

You may not deduct expenses paid by others. If your expenses are paid by reimbursement or allowance, certain limitations may apply (see sections D and E of this chapter).

No deduction will be allowed for travel or other costs of attending a convention, seminar, or similar meeting that is related to investment activities, financial planning, or other income-producing activities, and is not related to your trade or business.

You may deduct only 50% of your business-related meal expenses incurred while traveling away from home (as noted below, this rule can be avoided in many cases by an accountable reimbursement policy). You must show that the meal expense is directly related to the active conduct of your trade or business. Further, no deduction will be allowed for lavish or extravagant expenses.

✎ **Key point: the deductible portion of business meals and entertainment is limited to 50% of such expenses. This rule makes the adoption of an accountable business expense reimbursement arrangement very desirable, since employers can fully reimburse all of a worker's business meal and entertainment expenses under such an arrangement.**

The Deductibility Of A Spouse's Travel Expenses

✎ **Key point: the IRS issued regulations at the close of 1994 that make it easier for churches to treat reimbursements of a spouse's travel expenses incurred while accompanying a taxpayer on a business trip as a nontaxable fringe benefit.**

Most ministers attend conferences and conventions in the course of their ministry. Common examples include seminars and denominational meetings. In some cases ministers attend such events at their own expense, but often their travel expenses (including transportation, lodging, and meals) are reimbursed by their church. These expenses are legitimate business expenses so long as the primary purpose of the travel is in fact church business. This means that the expenses may be deductible by the minister depending on the circumstances. But what if the minister's spouse goes along? Can the church reimburse the spouse's travel expenses too? Are the tax consequences the same as for the minister, or do different rules apply? And what if the minister's children come too? These are important questions. Recently proposed IRS regulations provide some clarification.

Pre-1994 rules. For tax years prior to 1994, the tax status of expenses incurred by a taxpayer's spouse while accompanying the taxpayer on a business trip was addressed in the income tax regulations:

Where a taxpayer's wife accompanies him on a business trip, expenses attributable to her travel are not deductible unless it can be adequately shown that the wife's presence on the trip has a bona fide business purpose. The wife's performance of some incidental service does not cause her expenses to qualify as deductible business expenses. *Treas. Reg. 1.162-2(c).*

According to this language, a spouse's travel expenses incurred while accompanying a taxpayer were deductible "business expenses" only if they were reasonable and necessary to the conduct of the taxpayer's business. It often was difficult to determine whether a spouse's presence on a trip was necessary to the accomplishment of the taxpayer's business activities, or whether the spouse went along primarily for pleasure and social reasons. As the United States Tax Court observed, the proper tax treatment of spouses' travel expenses "has been a particularly troublesome question for the courts." This is "because of the likelihood of corporate payments of an essentially personal expense being disguised as a business expense."

There were hundreds of court rulings on this issue prior to 1994, with the vast majority of them concluding that a spouse's travel expense reimbursements were includable in taxable income and were *not deductible* as business expenses. However, in a few cases the courts concluded that the travel expenses of a spouse were deductible since the spouse's presence on a trip furthered the business of a taxpayer. Two illustrative cases are summarized below.

• *Case 1.* A federal appeals court (the second highest level of court in the nation) ruled that a wife's travel expenses were properly characterized as reasonable and necessary to the accomplishment of her husband's business. *United States v. Disney, 413 F.2d 783 (9th Cir. 1969).* The court observed that the taxpayer was a corporate executive, and that his duties on business trips included "the holding of meetings with the company's sales forces, the holding of screenings of the company's products to exhibitors, attendance at conferences dealing with marketing problems and attendance at trade conventions." He also was expected "to promote the public image of the company as one engaged in family-type entertainment, to enhance the morale and enthusiasm of company representatives, and to cultivate close and cordial relationships between his company and the exhibitors and other executives with whom the company dealt throughout the world. . . ." In order to fulfill these duties, the court concluded that "it was necessary for the taxpayer to have his wife with him at various luncheons, dinners, receptions, press conferences and on good-will visits. Not only was her presence at these events important, but her assistance in making arrangements for various functions was also necessary." The necessity for the wife's presence on the business trips was further established "by a long-standing company policy that the wives of company executives should accompany their husbands on such trips." The court emphasized that "the fact that an employer may prefer to have an executive take his wife along is not controlling if her presence does not serve the taxpayer-employee's business purpose in making the trip." Further, the court observed that "the fact that the wife spent much of her time on such trips attending to such [personal] duties as shopping, attending to laundry, answering the tele-

phone and the like, does not necessarily require the conclusion that her presence does not have a bona fide business purpose. The critical inquiries are whether the dominant purpose of the trip was to serve her husband's business purpose in making the trip and whether she actually spent a substantial amount of her time in assisting her husband in fulfilling that purpose."

• *Case 2.* In another case, the Tax Court concluded that the travel expenses incurred by a banker's wife in accompanying her husband on business trips were properly characterized as business expenses. *Bank of Stockton v. Commissioner, 36 T.C.M. 114 (1977).* The court observed that the employer-bank "required the officers who attended various annual conventions to be accompanied by their wives" who attended conventions "to assist their husbands in developing and renewing personal contacts with other bankers." The court further noted:

Wives of officers participated in the educational aspects of the convention and were instrumental to the success of the social activities. They both organized and hosted numerous convention activities and also entertained bankers with whom [the bank's] officers transacted business and from whom they sought advice. These activities aided [the bank's] officers in making new contacts and renewing old contacts. In addition, their presence and demeanor at the conventions enhanced the images of [the bank] and its officers. These activities, in turn, aided [the bank] in developing business relationships with other banks. Such relationships were of substantial benefit to [the bank]. We have also found that it was customary for wives of bankers to attend and participate in the [meetings and conventions].

These facts, concluded the court, "demonstrate that the wives' presence on the trips served a bona fide business purpose."

Conclusion. While the vast majority of courts prior to 1994 concluded that a spouse's travel expenses were not tax-deductible, this conclusion was not automatic. The two cases summarized above illustrate that it was possible for the travel expenses of a minister's spouse to be deductible if: (1) the minister was an executive officer; (2) the church (or other employer) had a "long-standing practice of defraying the travel expenses" of the minister's spouse; (3) one of the business objectives of the minister's travel was to "promote the public image" of the employing institution, and this task reasonably required the presence of the minister's spouse on at least some occasions; (4) the spouse's presence was necessary to assist the minister in "developing and renewing personal contacts"; (5) it was customary for the spouse to accompany the minister on some activities, and the spouse's absence would materially diminish the image that the minister was seeking to project of the employer. Obviously, clergy who were most likely to satisfy these criteria were those serving as presidents or senior executives of church-affiliated educational institutions and denominational agencies.

The 1993 tax law. In 1993 (for years beginning with 1994) Congress amended section 274 of the

Code to disallow any deduction (by employers or employees) for amounts "paid or incurred" with respect to a spouse, dependent, or other individual accompanying the taxpayer on business travel, unless the following three conditions are satisfied:

• the spouse, dependent, or other person is a bona fide employee of the organization that pays or reimburses the travel expenses

• the travel of the spouse, dependent, or other person is for a bona fide business purpose, and

• the expenses of the spouse, dependent, or other person would otherwise be deductible

This change denied a business expense deduction to for-profit employers that reimburse such expenses, as well as any deduction to the employee or spouse. The change was based on the conclusion of Congress that

in most cases, there will be a substantial personal component to any travel expense paid or incurred with respect to a family member who is accompanying an individual who is traveling on business. No deduction for these expenses should be allowed in light of the large element of personal consumption and the difficulties of enforcing the present-law rules.

This provision eliminated any possibility of a deduction for a spouse's (or child's) travel expenses in most cases, since a minister's spouse (or child) rarely is an employee of the church.

Not only did the new law prevent a deduction in most cases for the travel expenses incurred by a spouse or child accompanying a taxpayer on business travel, but it led many to conclude that the church's reimbursements of family members' travel expenses had to be treated as taxable income. Here's why. Section 132 of the Internal Revenue Code specifies that expenses paid by an employer on behalf of an employee represent a nontaxable "working condition fringe benefit" so long as the employee could have deducted the expense if he or she paid it directly. Since under the new law ministers cannot deduct the travel expenses of their spouses in most cases, the implication was that any reimbursement of these expenses by a church had to be reported as taxable income. In short—not only were the travel expenses incurred by a spouse or child not deductible, but a church's reimbursement of these expenses represented taxable income.

☞ *Example. Rev. C is a minister at First Church. Rev. C and his spouse attend a church convention. The spouse is not an employee of the church, and she has no official duties at the convention. The church reimburses the travel expenses of both Rev. C and his wife (including transportation, lodging, and meals). Under the new law, the travel expenses of Rev. C's spouse are not deductible (by either her or Rev. C) since she is not an employee and her presence at the convention did not serve a legitimate business purpose. Further, since her business expenses*

were not deductible, the church's reimbursements of her expenses represented taxable income.

The new regulations. The IRS issued regulations in 1994 clarifying that the 1993 law's denial of a deduction for a nonemployee spouse's travel expenses incurred while accompanying a taxpayer on a business trip does not prevent an employer's reimbursement of such expenses from qualifying as a nontaxable "working condition fringe benefit," so long as the following conditions are met:

• the employer has not treated such amounts as compensation

• the amounts would be deductible as a business expense without regard to the limitation on the deductibility of a spouse's travel expenses, meaning that the spouse's presence on the trip is for a legitimate business purpose, and

• the employee substantiates the expenses under an accountable arrangement (described above)

▲ **Caution. If any of these conditions is not met, then a church's reimbursement of a nonemployee spouse's travel expenses will represent taxable income to the minister. The same applies to children who accompany a minister on a business trip.**

✎ **Key point: the regulations clarify that ministers need not report as taxable income a church's reimbursement of their spouse's travel expenses, even though the spouse is not an employee and therefore cannot deduct such expenses. However, note that this result assumes that the church has not reported the reimbursement of the spouse's expenses as income, the spouse's presence on the trip is for a legitimate business purpose, and the spouse's expenses are reimbursed under an accountable arrangement. If any of these conditions is not met, then the church's reimbursement of the spouse's travel expenses represents taxable income to the minister.**

✎ **Key point: under the 1993 law, taxable employers cannot deduct their reimbursement of a spouse's travel expenses. However, the proposed regulations give them the option of deducting such reimbursements (as a business expense) if they report them as compensation to the employee. This of course prevents the reimbursements from qualifying as a nontaxable working condition fringe benefit. This rule will not apply to churches and other tax-exempt organizations, however some church treasurers and board members will be familiar with this rule based on their experience with secular employers.**

If a spouse is not a church employee, and the spouse's presence on a trip does not serve a legitimate business purpose, then that portion of the church's reimbursement of the travel expenses of the minister and spouse attributable to the spouse's travel represents taxable income to the minister. This is not simply a matter of splitting the combined expenses in half. Rather, the amount to add to the minister's taxable income is the actual amount of additional travel expenses attributable to the spouse's travel. For example, if the minister and spouse drive their car to a church convention, the travel expenses allocable to the spouse would include any additional hotel room charge based on double occupancy, and the spouse's meals. Of course, if the couple flies to their destination, then the spouse's airfare would be included.

✎ **Key point: ordinarily, no deduction will be allowed for expenses in attending a convention, seminar, or similar meeting that does not offer significant business-related activities, such as participation in meetings, workshops, lectures, or exhibits held during the day. Non-business expenses, such as social or sightseeing expenses, are personal expenses and are not deductible.**

✎ **Key point: some churches require that their minister be accompanied by his or her spouse while on business trips for accountability purposes. That is, the spouse's presence greatly reduces the risk of inappropriate conduct by the minister or false accusations that could be devastating to the minister's reputation and to the church as well. Many churches have been devastated by the sexual misconduct of their minister, and church leaders are justified in taking this risk seriously and in implementing procedures to prevent it. If the church board adopts a policy mandating a spouse's presence on the minister's business trips, and explains the "business rationale" for such a policy, an argument could be made that the spouse's presence on the minister's business trips serves a legitimate business purpose whether or not the spouse is engaged in any other business activities on the trip. This is an aggressive position that should not be adopted without the advice of a tax attorney or CPA. The strength of this position will be greatly reduced if (1) it is not consistently followed (that is, the church permits the spouse to accompany the minister on only selected business trips), or (2) one or more other church employees customarily accompany the minister on business trips and these individuals could share the same accommodations and otherwise provide the same accountability as the minister's spouse.**

Examples. The application of the new law and proposed regulations are illustrated by the following examples.

☞ **Example.** *Rev. B is senior minister of First Church. He attends a church convention in another city. He is accompanied by his spouse, who was selected by the church as an official delegate. The spouse is not an employee of the church. The spouse attends business meetings*

with her husband, and votes on matters addressed at the convention. Rev. B's travel expenses were $800 (transportation, lodging, meals), and travel expenses attributable to his spouse were an additional $400. The church reimburses fully those travel expenses of both Rev. B and his spouse that are adequately substantiated under an accountable arrangement. Since the spouse is not an employee of the church, her travel expenses ($400) are not deductible as a business expense. However, since her presence on the trip serves a legitimate business purpose, and her travel expenses were reimbursed under an accountable arrangement, the church's reimbursement of her travel expenses does not represent taxable income to either her or Rev. B.*

☞ **Example.** *Same facts as the previous example, except that the church issues Rev. B with a cash advance of $1,500 for all of the travel expenses that he and his spouse incur while attending the church convention. No substantiation of actual business expenses is required. The proposed regulations do not apply to this situation since the church is not reimbursing the spouse's travel expenses under an accountable arrangement. Accordingly, the full amount of the church's travel reimbursement represents taxable income and must be included on Rev. B's W-2 (or 1099). Rev. B will be able to deduct his travel expenses ($800) as an itemized deduction on Schedule A (or on Schedule C if self-employed), but the travel expenses incurred by his spouse ($400) are not deductible.*

☞ **Example.** *Same facts as the first example, except that Rev. B and his spouse must pay their own expenses in attending the church convention. Rev. B will be able to deduct his travel expenses ($800) as an itemized deduction on Schedule A (or on Schedule C if self-employed), but the travel expenses incurred by his spouse ($400) are not deductible since she is not an employee of the church.*

☞ **Example.** *Same facts as the first example, except that Rev. B's spouse is a church employee. Since the spouse is an employee of the church, and her presence on the trip serves a legitimate business purpose, her travel expenses ($400) are deductible as a business expense. Since the church reimbursed her expenses under an accountable arrangement, the reimbursement is not taxable income (it is not reported on her W-2) and there is no deduction to claim. As a church employee engaged in legitimate business travel, the treatment of the spouse is identical to that of Rev. B.*

☞ **Example.** *Same facts as the first example, except that Rev. B's spouse does not attend the convention as an official delegate of the church. She has no official duties at the convention, and does not attend or participate in business sessions. She spends most of her time with friends and relatives who are at the convention. Since* the spouse's presence on the trip does not serve a legitimate business purpose, the proposed regulations do not apply. As a result, her travel expenses reimbursed by the church ($400) represent taxable income to Rev. B.

☞ **Example.** Same facts as the preceding example, except that Rev. B's church board adopted the following resolution in 1997: "Whereas the scriptural qualifications for ministers include: above reproach, respectable, a good reputation (1 Timothy 3:2-7); and blameless, upright, and holy (Titus 1:7-8); and whereas the church has a significant interest in its minister adhering to these standards, since the church can be devastated if its minister violates them or is wrongfully accused of violating them; now therefore the official board resolves that its minister may not participate in any out-of-town business travel without the presence of his wife; and further resolves that the presence of the minister's wife on business trips serves the legitimate and essential business purpose of promoting and preserving the integrity of the minister's ministry and thereby protects the mission of the church; and further resolves that the substantiated travel expenses incurred by the minister's spouse in accompanying the minister on business trips as mandated by this policy shall be reimbursed by the church." It is possible that the spouse's travel expenses incurred as a result of such a policy would be viewed as serving a legitimate business purpose and accordingly that the church's reimbursement of such expenses would represent a nontaxable working condition fringe benefit under the new regulations (so long as the spouse's expenses are reimbursed under an accountable arrangement). This is an aggressive position, however, and should not be adopted without the advice of a tax attorney or CPA. Further, the strength of this position will be greatly reduced if (1) it is not consistently followed (that is, the church permits the spouse to accompany the minister on only selected business trips), or (2) one or more other church employees customarily accompany the minister on business trips and these individuals could share the same accommodations and otherwise provide the same accountability as the minister's spouse.

☞ **Example.** Rev. C is an executive with a denominational agency. One of Rev. C's functions is to attend church conferences and conventions, and to speak at local churches. Rev. C's spouse goes along on many of these trips. The denominational agency expects the spouse to accompany Rev. C on many of these trips, although the spouse performs no business function or purpose. The agency reimburses the travel expenses of both Rev. C and Rev. C's spouse under an accountable arrangement (only those expenses that are adequately substantiated are reimbursed). The spouse is not an employee of the agency. Since the spouse is not an employee of the agency, the spouse's travel expenses are not a business expense and cannot be deducted. However, it is possible that the agency's reimbursements of the spouse's expenses would not be included in Rev.

C's income—if the spouse's presence on Rev. C's trips serves a legitimate business purpose. While the likelihood that the spouse satisfies this condition is remote under these facts, it is possible. As noted earlier in this chapter, a few courts have suggested that a spouse's presence on a business trip can serve a business purpose if (1) the minister is an executive officer; (2) the church (or other employer) has a "long-standing practice of defraying the travel expenses" of the minister's spouse; (3) one of the business objectives of the minister's travel is to "promote the public image" of the employing institution, and this task reasonably required the presence of the minister's spouse on at least some occasions; (4) the spouse's presence is necessary to assist the minister in "developing and renewing personal contacts"; (5) it is customary for the spouse to accompany the minister on some activities, and the spouse's absence would materially diminish the image that the minister was seeking to project of the employer. There is little doubt that the IRS would challenge the business purpose of the spouse under these facts. Reliance on the proposed regulations to avoid recognizing the agency's reimbursement of the spouse's expenses as taxable income to the minister would be a highly aggressive position under these facts that should not be pursued without the advice of a tax attorney. Note, however, that this position may be strengthened by the adoption of an official policy (as explained above) requiring the spouse to accompany the minister on business trips in order to promote accountability and protect against unethical and unscriptural behavior that could have a negative impact on the finances and reputation of the denominational agency.

☞ **Example.** Same facts as the previous example, except that the spouse is a featured speaker at one or more special events held during the convention. Such responsibilities make it far more likely that the denomination's reimbursement of the spouse's travel expenses will be a nontaxable working condition fringe benefit, since the "business purpose" test is more likely satisfied. This assumes that the spouse's travel expenses are reimbursed under an accountable arrangement. If the denomination reimburses the spouse's expenses without adequate substantiation, or more than 60 days after incurring the travel expenses, then the reimbursements will represent taxable income to Rev. C and must be added to his W-2.

☞ **Example.** Rev. D is an associate minister at First Church. He travels to another city to interview for a pastoral position at Second Church. Rev. D's spouse goes along on the trip, but performs no specific business function. Rev. D and his spouse incur the following travel expenses in their trip to Second Church: airfare for Rev. D ($500); airfare for Rev. D's spouse ($500); hotel ($100 double occupancy; a single room would be $75); meals for Rev. D ($50); meals for Rev. D's spouse ($50). Second Church reimburses all of the travel expenses of both Rev. D and his spouse ($1,200) that they substantiate with receipts and other records. The reimbursement of Rev. D's expenses ($625) by Second Church does not represent taxable income to Rev. D, since it is an accountable reimbursement of legitimate business expenses incurred on behalf of the church. There is a reasonable basis for concluding that the church's reimbursement of the travel expenses allocable to Rev. D's spouse ($575) represents a nontaxable "working condition fringe benefit" under the proposed regulations, since (1) the spouse's presence on the trip served a legitimate business purpose, and (2) the spouse's expenses were reimbursed under an accountable arrangement. Accordingly, the church's reimbursement of the spouse's travel expenses ($575) would not be reported as income on Rev. D's 1099 or W-2. The basis for concluding that the spouse's presence on the trip serves a legitimate business purpose is the fact that many churches consider the spouse's presence during the interview process essential. The pastor and his or her spouse represent a model marital fidelity to many congregations, and the spouse typically serves a variety of volunteer roles within the church. It would be unthinkable for most churches to hire a pastoral candidate without meeting and interviewing the candidate's spouse. This is an aggressive position, and there is no assurance that it would be accepted by the IRS or the courts. Ministers should consult with a tax adviser before adopting this approach.

☞ *Example.* Same facts as the previous example, except that the couple brings their 2 minor children along on the trip at an additional cost of $1,100. Again, an argument can be made that the presence of the children on the trip serves a legitimate business function. The New Testament lists the following qualifications (among others) for a pastor: "He must manage his own family well and see that his children obey him with proper respect" (I Timothy 3:4); "an elder must be blameless, the husband of but one wife, a man whose children believe and are not open to the charge of being wild and disobedient" (Titus 1:6). According to these verses, an argument can be made that a church would be legitimately interested in meeting the pastor's entire family before making an employment decision. Obviously this will not be true for all churches, and would be less true for pastors with very young children. This is a highly aggressive position, and it is doubtful there is a reasonable basis for it. This means that ministers who take this position may be subject to penalties in addition to payment of back taxes and interest. Ministers should consult with a tax adviser before adopting this approach.

Charitable contributions. As noted in chapter 8, unreimbursed expenses incurred while performing donated labor for a church may constitute a deductible charitable contribution. The income tax regulations specify:

[U]nreimbursed expenditures made incident to the rendition of services to an organization contributions to which are deductible may constitute a de-

ductible contribution. For example, the cost of a uniform without general utility which is required to be worn in performing donated services is deductible. Similarly, out-of-pocket transportation expenses necessarily incurred in performing donated services are deductible. Reasonable expenditures for meals and lodging necessarily incurred while away from home in the course of performing donated services are also deductible. *Treas. Reg. 1.170A-1(g).*

Another way for travel expenses of a spouse to be nontaxable under the new rules would be if the spouse performed meaningful church-related business activities. Under these circumstances, the spouse's unreimbursed travel expenses could be claimed as a charitable contribution deduction. Consider the following examples:

☞ *Example.* A denomination's bylaws permit churches to send lay delegates to annual denominational meetings. These lay delegates, along with ordained ministers, comprise the eligible voters. Rev. G is an ordained minister who attends an annual meeting in another city. Rev. G's church selected his spouse to accompany him as an official delegate. Rev. G's spouse attends all business meetings, and exercises her voting privileges. The travel expenses of Rev. G's spouse are not reimbursed by the church. Rev. G's spouse can deduct her travel expenses as a charitable contribution. This conclusion is supported by the following language in the 1996 edition of IRS Publication 526 ("Charitable Contributions"): "If you are a chosen representative attending a convention of a qualified organization, you can deduct unreimbursed expenses for travel and transportation, including a reasonable amount for meals and lodging, while away from home overnight in connection with the convention." Alternatively, as noted above, the church's reimbursement of the spouse's expenses may represent a nontaxable "working condition fringe benefit" under the IRS newly proposed regulations.

☞ *Example.* Same facts as the previous example except that the church does not select Rev. G's spouse to attend the meeting as a church delegate. The spouse's unreimbursed expenses are not deductible as a charitable contribution. IRS Publication 526 states: "You cannot deduct your expenses in attending a church convention if you go only as a member of your church rather than as a chosen representative."

☞ *Example.* Same facts as the previous example except that after arriving at the location of the meeting Rev. G's spouse visits a religious music publisher to consider music for the church. Her unreimbursed expenses in making this side trip can be claimed as a charitable contribution. However, this does not convert her expenses incurred in traveling to the meeting site a deductible business expense. This conclusion is supported by the following language in IRS Publication 526: "You can deduct unreimbursed expenses that are *directly connected with giving services for your church during the convention."*

☞ ***Example.*** *Rev. H is invited to speak at a church in a different city. His spouse accompanies him on the trip, but she performs no specific duties on behalf of the church. Her unreimbursed travel expenses are not deductible as a charitable contribution.*

☞ ***Example.*** *Same facts as the previous example, except that Rev. H's spouse is asked to speak to a Sunday School class and sing a solo during the worship service at which her husband speaks. Her travel expenses are not reimbursed by either church. While not certain, it is possible that the spouse's activities during the trip represent sufficient charitable activity for her unreimbursed travel expenses to be deductible as a charitable contribution. If the church reimburses these expenses, then the expenses would not be deductible as a charitable contribution but as noted above the reimbursements may be nontaxable if they meet the requirements of a working condition fringe benefit.*

Travel outside the United States

If you travel outside the United States and the entire time is spent on business activities, you may deduct your travel expenses as if the travel had been entirely in the United States. Travel outside the United States does not include travel from one point in the United States to another point in the United States, even though you are on your way to a destination outside the United States. If travel was primarily for business, but there were some nonbusiness activities, you may have to allocate your expenses between business and nonbusiness expenses (on the basis of time spent on each). No allocation is required (i.e., travel will be considered entirely for business) if the trip is primarily for business and lasts less than a week or if the time spent on nonbusiness activities comprises less than 25% of the total time you are away from home. If the travel was primarily for vacation and some time was spent attending brief professional seminars or in a continuing education program, the entire cost of the trip is a nondeductible personal expense, except for registration fees and any other expenses incurred that are directly for and properly allocable to your trade or business. Generally, a trip will be considered entirely for business if you spend less than 25% of the total time you were outside the United States in nonbusiness activities (whether or not the trip lasts for more than one week).

As noted above, longer-term travel abroad for business-related purposes may qualify for a foreign earned income exclusion of up to $70,000 (in 1997) for any year in which you (1) have a tax home in a foreign country, and (2) satisfy either the "foreign residence" or "physical presence" tests. The "tax home" concept was discussed earlier in this chapter (the same principles apply here). The "foreign residence" test is satisfied if you demonstrate that you

were a bona fide resident of one or more foreign countries for an uninterrupted period which includes an entire taxable year. *IRC 911(d)(1)(A).* The "physical presence" test is satisfied if you were present in one or more foreign countries during at least 330 full days during any period of twelve consecutive months. These time limitations can be waived by the IRS in certain situations. *IRC 911(d)(1).* This exclusion (claimed by filing IRS Form 2555) may eliminate any tax liability in cases of extended foreign service, making the loss of any travel expense deduction irrelevant.

❖ **New in 1997. Congress enacted legislation in 1997 that increases the $70,000 annual foreign earned income exclusion by $2,000 per year beginning in 1998, until it reaches a maximum of $80,000 in the year 2002. In addition, the credit will be indexed for inflation beginning in 2008.**

Charitable travel

Treasury regulation 1.170A-1(g) provides:

[O]ut-of-pocket transportation expenses necessarily incurred in performing donated services are deductible. Reasonable expenditures for meals and lodging necessarily incurred while away from home in the course of performing donated services also are deductible.

Therefore, unreimbursed travel expenses incurred while away from home (whether within the United States or abroad) in the course of donated services to a tax-exempt religious or charitable organization are deductible as a charitable contribution.

The topic of charitable travel is addressed more fully in chapter 8.

3. Entertainment expenses

You may be able to deduct entertainment expenses you incur for your trade or business (i.e., your ministry). You may take the deduction only if you can demonstrate that the amounts spent are either (1) *directly related* to the active conduct of your ministry, or (2) *associated* with the active conduct of your ministry and the entertainment occurred directly before or after a substantial business discussion. These 2 tests are summarized below:

Directly related test. In order to show that entertainment was *directly related* to the active conduct of your business, you ordinarily must be able to demonstrate that (1) you had more than a general expectation of deriving income or some other specific business benefit at some indefinite future time; (2) you did engage in business during the entertainment period; and (3) the main purpose of the entertainment was the transaction of business.

Associated entertainment. In order to show that entertainment was *associated* with the active conduct of your ministry, you must be able to demonstrate that you had a clear business purpose in incurring the expense, and that the meal or entertainment directly preceded or followed a substantial business discussion.

Entertainment includes any activity generally considered to provide entertainment, amusement, or recreation. This covers entertaining guests at restaurants, social or athletic facilities, sporting events, or on hunting, fishing, vacation, or similar trips. Expenses are not deductible when a group of business acquaintances take turns picking up each other's entertainment checks without regard to whether any business purposes are served. Ministers incur entertainment expenses in a variety of situations. Common examples include entertaining denominational officials, guest speakers, church groups (youth, choir, the church board, etc.), or meeting with members at a restaurant for counseling purposes.

You may deduct only 50% of your business-related entertainment expenses, including meals. This 50% limitation is incorporated directly into the tax returns (line 9 of Form 2106, and line 24c of Schedule C). Note however that the 50% limitation *does not apply to expenses you incur that are reimbursed by your employer under an "accountable" reimbursement plan (described in section D of this chapter).* IRS Publication 463 ("Travel, Entertainment, and Gift Expenses") states: "As an employee, you are not subject to the 50% limit if your employer reimburses you under an accountable plan and does not treat your reimbursement as wages." Publication 463 states that the self-employed persons also can avoid

the 50% limitation through use of an accountable reimbursement arrangement.

Clergy who report their income taxes as employees (or who are reclassified as employees by the IRS in an audit) may deduct their unreimbursed and "non-accountable" reimbursed entertainment expenses only as a miscellaneous itemized deduction on Schedule A (you must be able to itemize deductions to claim them), and then only to the extent that all miscellaneous expenses exceed 2% of adjusted gross income. Further, only 50% of business meals and entertainment expenses would be deductible. These restrictive rules, which are explained fully in section D of this chapter, make the adoption of an accountable reimbursement policy essential. Clergy who truly are self-employed for income tax reporting purposes may deduct their unreimbursed and "non-accountable" reimbursed entertainment expenses directly on Schedule C whether or not they can itemize their deductions on Schedule A, and without regard to the 2% floor. However, they will be subject to the 50% limitation on business meals and entertainment.

Entertainment expenses incurred in your home are especially scrutinized by the IRS. You must be able to demonstrate that your expenses were not purely social but rather had a primary business purpose. Entertainment expenses of spouses may also be deductible if their presence serves a legitimate business purpose or if it would be impracticable under the circumstances to entertain the business associate with-

When Are Entertainment Expenses Deductible?	
General Rule	You can deduct ordinary and necessary expenses to entertain a client, customer, or employee if the expenses meet the directly-related test or the associated test.
Definitions	• *Entertainment* includes any activity generally considered to provide entertainment, amusement, or recreation, and includes meals provided to a customer or client. • An *ordinary* expense is one that is common and accepted in your field of business, trade, or profession. • A *necessary* expense is one that is helpful and appropriate, although not necessarily indispensible, for your business.
Tests to be met	Directly-related test • Entertainment took place in a clear business setting, **or** • Main purpose of entertainment was the active conduct of business, **and** You did engage in business with the person during the entertainment period, **and** You had more than a general expectation of getting income or some other specific business benefit. Associated Test • Entertainment is associated with your trade or business, **and** • Entertainment directly precedes or follows a substantial business discussion.
Other rules	• You cannot deduct the cost of your meal as an entertainment expense if you are claiming the meal as a travel expense. • You can deduct expenses only to the extent they are not lavish or extravagant under the circumstances. • You generally can deduct only 80% of your unreimbursed entertainment expenses.

out including his or her spouse. If a spouse's entertainment expenses are deductible because it is impracticable to entertain his or her spouse without the spouse being included, then your spouse's entertainment expenses incurred on the same occasion will also be deductible (where, for example, your spouse joins you because your business associate's spouse will be present).

You must meet certain requirements for proving the amount spent and the business nature of the expense (described below).

The IRS frequently challenges entertainment expenses, and so you should be prepared to fully substantiate such expenses as described below. The IRS also on occasion will challenge a minister's entertainment expenses on the ground that a minister is not engaged in any trade or business and accordingly no business or entertainment expense is permissible. This position is clearly unwarranted. The IRS itself has acknowledged that the term "trade or business" includes services performed in the exercise of ministry. See IRS Publication 517.

☞ **Example.** Rev. S invites the church's board of trustees to his home for dinner and a board meeting. The expenses incurred by Rev. S and his guests for food and beverages ordinarily will constitute entertainment expenses.

☞ **Example.** Rev. S invites a friend and fellow minister to his home for dinner. The friend resides in another state and is visiting Rev. S for the day. Ordinarily, such a visit will be a social visit and the expenses associated with it will not be deductible.

☞ **Example.** Rev. K is the senior minister of First Church. He takes an applicant for a ministerial staff position out to dinner, where they discuss the applicant's background and suitability for the position. The applicant's spouse comes along because it would be impractical to discuss the position solely with the applicant. Further, Rev. K's spouse accompanies her husband because the applicant's spouse is present. Rev. K pays everyone's meal expense. The cost of the meals of all four persons is a deductible entertainment expense. If Rev. K is not reimbursed by the church for the expense, he may deduct it on Schedule A as a miscellaneous expense if he reports his income taxes as an employee (and he is able to itemize), or on Schedule C if he is self-employed. If the church reimburses the expense but requires no substantiation of the amount or date of the expense, or the business purpose of the entertainment and business relationship of those entertained, then the expense is reimbursed under a "nonaccountable" plan. The result is that Rev. K may deduct the expense on Schedule A as a miscellaneous expense if he reports his income taxes as an employee (and he is able to itemize), or on Schedule C if he is self-employed. Further, the full amount of the reimbursement must be reported as income on his W-2 or 1099, and Form 1040. If Rev. K is reimbursed for the

expense under an "accountable" reimbursement plan, he reports neither the reimbursement nor the expense on his tax return.

☞ **Example.** Rev. S claimed a deduction for expenses incurred in entertaining guests who came to visit. He claimed that many of the guests were associated with the church where he previously had been the pastor. The IRS denied any deduction for these expenses, and the Tax Court agreed. It observed: "Entertainment expenses, like travel expenses, must be substantiated strictly . . . . While we understand that [Rev. S] may have wanted to maintain good relations with his former parishioners, he has not established any business purpose for the entertainment expenses, nor has he established the business relationship between himself and the guests. When asked whether the out-of-town guests were business guests, [his] testimony indicated that he regarded the guests as personal. We find that [he] has failed to meet his burden of proof and sustain [the IRS's] disallowance of these claimed deductions." Shelley v. Commissioner, T.C. Memo. 1994-432 (1994).

✎ **Key point:** the deductible portion of business meals and entertainment is only 50% of such expenses. This makes the adoption of an accountable business expense reimbursement arrangement very desirable, since employers can fully reimburse all of a worker's business meal and entertainment expenses under such an arrangement.

4. Business gifts

You may deduct the cost of business gifts. However, you cannot deduct more than $25 for business gifts you give, directly or indirectly, to any one individual during your tax year. Such gifts would include gifts made by a minister to church staff or board members.

☞ **Example.** The Tax Court ruled in 1994 that $2,300 in expenses incurred by a minister in one year to pay for plants, flowers, and other gifts to members and staff were a nondeductible personal expense rather than a deductible business expense. The court observed: "[The minister] testified that the gifts stemmed from a desire to foster goodwill among his parishioners and staff; however, [he has] not provided sufficient evidence to prove that these expenses were not personal. We find that [the minister] failed to prove that the gifts were not personal expenses; therefore, [he is] not entitled to deductions for these amounts." Shelley v. Commissioner, T.C. Memo. 1994-432 (1994).

5. Educational expenses

Certain educational expenses are deductible by ministers. Ministers who are self-employed for income tax purposes claim the deduction directly on

Schedule C. Employee-ministers may be able to claim certain educational expenses as an itemized deduction on Schedule A if they itemize their deductions.

You may deduct expenses you have for education, such as tuition, books, supplies, correspondence courses, and certain travel and transportation expenses, even though the education may lead to a degree, if the education: (1) is required by your employer, or by law or regulation, to keep your salary, status, or job, or (2) maintains or improves skills required in your present work. However, you may not deduct expenses incurred for education, even if one or both of the requirements mentioned above are met, if the education: (1) is required in order to meet the minimum educational requirements to qualify you in your trade or business, or (2) is part of a program of study that will lead to qualifying you in a new trade or business, even if you did not intend to enter that trade or business.

If your educational expenses are deductible, you may deduct transportation expenses (1) between the general area where you work and a school located beyond that general area, or (2) between your place of work and a school within the same general area. However, if you go home before going to school, you may deduct the expense of going from home to school only to the extent it is not more than the transportation expense you would have if you went directly from work to school. If you use your car, you may deduct your actual expenses, or you may use the standard mileage rate to figure the amount you can deduct (see transportation expenses, above). You may not deduct the cost of local transportation between your home and school on a nonworking day (this expense is a personal commuting expense).

If you travel away from home mainly to obtain qualifying education, you may deduct your expenses for travel, meals, and lodging while away from home. However, you may not deduct expenses for personal activities such as sightseeing or entertaining.

Educational expenses do not include travel as a form of education.

☞ *Example.* Rev. D is minister at First Church. She takes a counseling course at a local university. Expenses associated with the course are deductible educational expenses if the course maintains or improves job skills and is not a part of a program of study that will qualify Rev. D for a new trade or business.

☞ *Example.* Rev. D takes accounting courses at a local university in order to qualify for the CPA examination. Such courses are clearly part of a program of study that will qualify Rev. D for a new trade or business, and accordingly are not deductible as education expenses, even if Rev. D insists that she is pursuing her studies solely to improve her job skills as a minister.

☞ *Example.* A minister who is not a college graduate can claim as education expenses the costs of obtaining a college degree, if the degree will not qualify him for a new trade or business. Glasgow v. Commissioner, 31 T.C.M. 310 (1972).

☞ *Example.* Rev. B, a minister of music at First Church, enrolled in several music courses at a local college. Expenses associated with such courses were not deductible education expenses since the courses qualified the minister for a new trade or business of being a public school or junior college instructor. Burt v. Commissioner, 40 T.C.M. 1164 (1980).

☞ *Example.* J is a 23-year-old seminary student. She is not employed while attending school, and has never previously served as a minister of a church. Her educational expenses are not deductible, since they are (1) not related to a current job, (2) required in order to meet the minimum educational requirements to qualify her in her "trade or business," and (3) part of a program of study that will lead to qualifying her in a new trade or business.

☞ *Example.* The IRS ruled that a minister who served a local church without compensation could not deduct the cost of his educational expenses. The IRS concluded that the educational expenses were not a business expense since an uncompensated minister is not engaged in trade or business. IRS Letter Ruling 9431024.

Sometimes, educational expenses paid by your employer can be excluded from your income. See the discussion of "employer-provided educational assistance programs" in chapter 5, section H.

6. Subscriptions and books

Ministers often subscribe to a number of periodicals that are directly relevant to the performance of their professional duties. And clergy often purchase books that are directly related to the performance of their professional duties. The income tax regulations specify that "a professional man may claim as deductions the cost of . . . subscriptions to professional journals [and] amounts currently paid for books . . . the useful life of which is short." *Treas. Reg. 1.162-6.* Clearly, the cost of a subscription will be deductible as a business expense if it is related to the conduct of a minister's trade or business. Professional clergy journals (such as *Church Law & Tax Report*) and specialized clergy periodicals clearly satisfy this test. News magazines may also qualify if a minister can demonstrate that the information contained in such periodicals is related to his or her ministry (e.g., sources of illustrations for sermons). The cost of a general circulation daily newspaper is not deductible.

The unreimbursed cost of books that are related to one's ministry is a professional business expense and accordingly is deductible. Deduct the cost of any book that you acquired for use in your ministry and that has a useful life (not the same as its physical life) of less than one year. For example, the cost of a book that you purchase and read, but have no intention of using again, can be deducted in full in the year of purchase. On the other hand, commentaries or theological dictionaries and encyclopedias are purchased for extended reference use, and accordingly you may allocate the purchase price to the useful life of the books by means of annual depreciation deductions.

The cost of books that you acquire for extended use can be depreciated over the useful life of the books through annual depreciation deductions. Be sure to retain records demonstrating the cost of all such items, the dates of purchase, and the dates they were first used in your work. Your annual depreciation deduction is computed using a "modified" ACRS (or "MACRS") method. Multiply your unadjusted basis (original cost less any section 179 deduction) for each item times a specified percentage. For 5-year recovery property such as books, the annual percentages are 20% for the first year, 32% for the second year, 19.2% for the third year, 11.52% for the fourth and fifth years, and 5.76% for the sixth year (a "half-year convention" ordinarily applies). Property also may be depreciated under the straight line method assuming a useful life equal to the recovery period (e.g., 5 years) and no salvage value. IRS Publication 946 explains how to compute your depreciation deduction.

Alternatively, you may expense the entire cost of a business asset (including books) in the year of acquisition if the cost is less than $18,000 (for 1997). This alternative is referred to as the "section 179 deduction." Property must be used more than 50% for business purposes to be eligible for a section 179 deduction, or to use the MACRS method of computing depreciation. You must indicate on IRS Form 4562 that you have elected to claim the section 179 deduction in the year of acquisition. Form 4562 is submitted with your Form 1040 (you can obtain a copy from any IRS office).

Religious books generally are used exclusively in a minister's work and accordingly no allocation need be made between business and personal use.

Ministers who are self-employed for income tax purposes claim the deduction for book and subscription expenses directly on Schedule C. Employee-ministers (and "self-employed" clergy who are reclassified as employees by the IRS in an audit) may deduct these expenses only as an itemized deduction on Schedule A. This means that they cannot claim any deduction if they do not have sufficient deductions to itemize on Schedule A. Of course, this restrictive rule will not apply to clergy whose business expenses are reimbursed by their church under an "accountable" reimbursement plan (see section D of this chapter).

☞ *Example. Rev. S claimed deductions for the costs of publications used in his ministry. He claimed that he was reimbursed by the church for amounts he spent on business publications in excess of $1,600. He presented canceled checks and a summary of some of the publication expenses for each of the years in issue. The IRS disallowed the deductions in full, arguing that the evidence failed to establish that the publications were related to his business. The Tax Court disagreed, concluding that "[b]ased on [Rev. S's] testimony and notations made on the checks, we conclude that [he] has established that the expenses were related to his ministry and that he has substantiated the claimed deduction in each of the years in issue." Shelley v. Commissioner, T.C. Memo. 1994-432 (1994).*

7. Personal computers

Many ministers have purchased personal computers that they use at home for business as well as personal purposes. Since computers lend themselves to personal as well as business use, they are singled out for special treatment by Code section 280F (as "listed property").

If you report your income taxes as an employee (or you report as self-employed but are reclassified as an employee by the IRS in an audit) and you purchase a home computer that you use in connection with your work, you must meet the following tests to claim any depreciation or "section 179" deduction:

(1) Convenience of the employer. Your use of the computer in your home must be "for the convenience of your employer." For the convenience of your employer means that you can clearly demonstrate that you cannot perform your job without the home computer. The fact that the computer enables you to perform your work more easily and efficiently is not enough. Further, you must prove that the computers available at your place of employment are insufficient to enable you to properly perform your job. Obviously, this is a difficult test to satisfy.

(2) Condition of employment. Your use of the computer in your home must be required as a "condition of your employment." This means that you must not be able to properly perform your duties without the computer. It is not necessary that your employer explicitly requires you to use the computer. On the other hand, it is not enough that your employer merely states that your use of the home computer is a condition of your employment. If you are an employee and these tests are not met, you cannot deduct any of the cost of your home computer. *IRC 280F, Revenue Ruling 86-129.*

If you are an employee and you meet both tests described above, or if you are self-employed, then you can claim a depreciation deduction and a "section 179" deduction *if you use your home computer more than 50% of the time during the year in your work.* You can depreciate computers over a 5-year recovery period using the "modified" ACRS (MACRS) method. IRS Publication 534 explains the MACRS system and contains several tables to assist you in computing your depreciation deduction under a number of available alternatives.

Very few ministers depreciate their computers under the MACRS system. This is due to two considerations. First, computing depreciation is complex, and second, most clergy prefer to deduct the entire cost of a computer in the year of purchase (rather than deduct the cost over the 5-year life of the computer). Clergy can expense the entire cost of a computer in the year of acquisition if the cost is less than $18,000 (for 1997). This alternative is referred to as the section 179 deduction. It also is referred to as "first year expensing." A computer must be used more than 50% for business purposes to be eligible for the section 179 deduction. Obviously, it is essential that you keep records (such as a time log) documenting the percentage of business use if you plan to claim a section 179 deduction. Nonminister church employees are subject to these same rules.

You compute your depreciation or section 179 deduction on Form 4562. Section 4562 asks the following questions regarding personal computers: (1) date first placed in service as a business asset; (2) business use percentage for the year; (3) cost; (4) do you have evidence to support the business use claimed; and (5) is your evidence supporting the business use of the computer in writing?

If you use your computer 50% or less for business purposes, then you may not expense the cost in the year of purchase by claiming a section 179 deduction and MACRS depreciation is not available to you. Instead, you must depreciate the computer using the "straight line" method over the 5-year recovery period (i.e., the annual depreciation expense is the cost of the computer divided by 5 years). Using your computer to keep track of your personal investments does not count in determining whether or not you satisfy the "50% business use" test. On the other hand, if you meet the 50% business use test without considering use of the computer for investments, you may include your use of the computer for investments in computing your deduction.

Your section 179 deduction, or your annual depreciation deduction, of course is limited to the percentage of business use of the computer.

☞ *Example. An engineer who was an employee of a large company purchased a personal computer at a cost of $6,000, and deducted the entire amount in the year of purchase as a section 179 deduction. The IRS denied any deduction for the computer, and the taxpayer appealed. He claimed that he was entitled to deduct the costs he incurred in acquiring his computer because (1) it was essential to the performance of his duties as a professional engineer and employee, and (2) it was required by his employer. The IRS claimed that the engineer's expenses of purchasing his home computer, even though used in connection with the business of his employer, were personal in nature and not ordinary or necessary to his "trade or business" of being an employee (i.e., it was not placed in his home for the convenience of his employer or as a condition of his employment so he could properly perform his duties as an employee). The Tax Court agreed with the IRS and denied any deduction. It relied on a letter from the engineer's employer to the IRS acknowledging that the engineer "was not required as a necessary condition of his employment to purchase his own computer and/or use it in his home." This evidence convinced the court*

that the engineer "voluntarily undertook to purchase a computer, place it in his home, and use it for his convenience rather than the convenience of [his employer]. Accordingly, we find [the engineer] is not entitled to deduct any portion of the computer's cost, even if he could substantiate the cost, because it represents a nondeductible personal expense." This case illustrates the difficulty employees face in claiming a tax deduction for the cost of personal computers. Tavano v. Commissioner, T.C. Memo. 1991-237 (1991).

☞ *Example. Rev. R purchases a personal computer for $7,000 in 1997 that he uses 60% for business, 20% for investments, and 20% for personal activities. Since he uses it more than 50% for business purposes, he can take the accelerated MACRS depreciation deductions over the 5-year recovery period, or he can expense the cost of the computer in the year of purchase by claiming a section 179 deduction. Since costs incurred in investment activities ordinarily are deductible, Rev. R computes his annual depreciation deduction by multiplying the annual MACRS percentage (from tables in IRS Publication 534) times his unadjusted basis in the computer (original cost less any section 179 deduction) times the combined business and investment usage (80%).*

☞ *Example. Same facts as the preceding example, except that Rev. R uses the computer 40% for business, 30% for investments, and 30% for personal activities. Since his business usage is less than 50%, he is not eligible for the section 179 deduction or for MACRS depreciation deductions. He must use straight line depreciation over a 5-year period. However, in computing his annual depreciation deduction, the unadjusted basis of the computer is divided by 5 (years) and then multiplied by the combined business and investment usage (70%). Treas. Reg. 1.280F-6T(d)(5).*

☞ *Example. The Tax Court ruled that an employee could not claim any deduction for the business use of her personal computer since she failed to maintain any records demonstrating the percentage of total use that was for business purposes. Kelly v. Commissioner, T.C. Memo. 1997-185*

8. Clothing and laundry

You may be able to deduct the cost of clothing (including cleaning expenses) that you use in your ministry if the clothing (1) is of a type specifically required as a condition of employment, (2) is not adaptable to general or continued usage to the extent that it could take the place of ordinary clothing, and (3) is not so worn.

As with any professional or business expense, such an expense is deductible on Schedule C by a self-employed minister, and may be deductible on Schedule A by a minister-employee (to the extent that he or she itemizes deductions and then only to the extent that most miscellaneous expenses exceed 2% of adjusted gross income)—see section D of this chapter for further details. Ministers can avoid these restrictions by having their church adopt an "account-able" reimbursement policy (explained fully in section D).

☞ *Example. Rev. P is a minister at First Church. Ministers in his denomination wear ordinary cloth-ing (not vestments) in the performance of their ministerial duties. Rev. P believes that he should be able to claim the cost of his suits as a busi-ness expense, since he must wear suits in the performance of his duties. His position is in error and would not be upheld by the IRS or the courts, since he does not satisfy the second and third conditions discussed above, and may not be considered to have met the first.*

☞ *Example. A church pays a monthly clothing al-lowance to its minister. The Tax Court concluded that these amounts represented taxable income and were not deductible. The Court observed that the tax law "provides a comprehensive definition of gross income" and that this term "includes in-come realized in any form, whether in money, property, or services." Accordingly, "income may be realized in the form of clothing as well as in cash." In rejecting any deduction for the cost of the taxpayer's clothing, the court noted that "the cost of acquisition and maintenance of uniforms is deductible generally if (1) the clothing is of a type specifically required as a condition of em-ployment, (2) it is not adaptable to general usage as ordinary clothing, and (3) it is not so worn. There is no indication in this record that the amount of the clothing allowance is for uniforms or special clothing." Kalms v. Commissioner, T.C. Memo 1992-394.*

☞ *Example. Rev. S claimed laundry and dry clean-ing deductions of more than $300 per year. To support the deductions he presented canceled checks on which he had made notations. The IRS disallowed these deductions in full. The Tax Court mostly agreed: "Expenses of maintaining a professional wardrobe generally are nonde-ductible personal expenditures. Expenses for clothing are deductible only if the clothing is re-quired for the taxpayer's employment, is not suit-able for general and personal wear, and is not so worn. Thus [Rev. S] is permitted to deduct the cost of cleaning his robes and similar items. Only one check for $8 . . . bears a notation indicating that payment was for cleaning of [Rev. S's] robe and stole. Neither [Rev. S's] testimony, nor the notations on the other checks in evidence, are sufficient to establish that the remaining cleaning expenses claimed were not personal. Conse-quently, [Rev. S is] entitled to deduct only $8 for laundry expenses." Shelley v. Commissioner, T.C. Memo. 1994-432 (1994).*

9. Office in the home

✎ **Key point: most clergy have an office in their home. For the costs of such an office to be deductible as a business expense, several conditions must be satisfied. For example, the**

office must be used exclusively and regularly in the minister's trade or business. More stringent rules apply to clergy who are em-ployees for income tax purposes.

❖ **New in 1999. Congress enacted legislation in 1997 (which takes effect in 1999) that permits some taxpayers to claim a home office deduc-tion if they use their home office for largely administrative tasks—even if their income-generating activities occur at another loca-tion. As before, the home office must be used regularly and exclusively for business pur-poses.**

Many ministers maintain an office in their home. For some ministers, their "home office" is simply a desk or table in a corner of a bedroom. For others, it is a separate room that is used either exclusively or at least partially for business purposes. Can any of the expenses associated with such offices be de-ducted as a business or professional expense?

General rule—a housing allowance precludes a home office deduction. In 1964 the Tax Court ruled that section 265 of the Code (which denies a deduc-tion for any expense allocable to tax-exempt income) prevented a minister from deducting his unreim-bursed transportation expenses to the extent that they were allocable to his tax-exempt housing allow-ance. To illustrate, assume that a minister receives compensation of $15,000, of which $5,000 is an ex-cludable housing allowance, and incurs unreimbursed business expenses of $1,500. Since one-third of the minister's compensation is "tax-exempt," he should not be permitted to deduct one-third of his business expenses since they are "allocable" to tax-exempt in-come and their deduction would amount to a "double deduction." *Deason v. Commissioner, 41 T.C. 465 (1964).* The *Deason* ruling was reaffirmed by the Tax Court in 1992 in *McFarland v. Commissioner, T.C. Memo. 1992-440.* This same principle is commonly thought to apply to the home office expenses of a minister, meaning that ministers who claim a housing allowance or parsonage exclusion are not entitled to home office deduction. This is the view taken by the IRS in its audit guidelines for ministers.

✎ **Key point: the IRS audit guidelines for minis-ters (released in 1995) instruct IRS agents to take the position that a minister who excludes all of his or her housing expenses as a hous-ing allowance exclusion has in effect already "deducted" all of the expenses associated with an office in the home, and accordingly should not be able to claim any additional de-duction of such expenses as an itemized (home office) deduction on Schedule A.**

A limited exception. Not all ministers are able to claim all of their home expenses in computing their housing allowance exclusion. To illustrate, some churches designate an allowance that is less than ac-tual expenses. And other churches fail to designate an allowance at all. In these cases, a partial home office deduction (in some cases a full deduction) would be appropriate.

4 requirements for a home office deduction. Even if a minister elects to disregard the *Deason* allocation rule, or the limited exception applies, it is still unlikely that a home office deduction will be available because the requirements are so strict. For ministers to be eligible for a home office deduction, the following 4 requirements must be met:

(1) Exclusive use. The home office must be exclusively used in the minister's "trade or business." This means that the home office must not be used by other family members (for example, to watch television or do homework). The use of a part of your home for *both* personal and business purposes does not meet the exclusive use test. If, for example, you use the den of your home for personal purposes as well as a place where you prepare sermons and occasionally counsel church members, you may not deduct any expenses for the business use of that part of your home.

(2) Regular basis. The home office must be used on a regular basis in the minister's "trade or business." This means that the home office must be used on a continuous basis by the minister for professional purposes (e.g., preparing sermons, conducting counseling, doing research, contacting members, writing correspondence, preparing for board meetings). Occasional or incidental use of the office for such purposes is not enough, even if the office is used for no other purposes.

(3) Convenience of the employer. If the minister is an employee, the home office must be for the convenience of the employer. This means that the home office must do more than make the employee's job more easy or efficient—it must be essential to the performance of the employee's job. This is simply not the case when an office is available in the church. The courts and the IRS have ruled that if an employer provides employees access to an office on its premises for the performance of their duties, and an employee elects to conduct these duties at home as a matter of personal preference, then the employee's use of the home office is not for the "convenience of the employer" and there is no deduction allowed.

(4) Principal place of business. The home office must be the minister's principal place of business. You may have a principal place of business for each trade or business in which you engage. For example, as a minister, your principal place of business ordinarily will be your church. If, however, you also engage in a retail sales business and use part of your home as your principal place of business for retail selling, expenses for this business use of your home may be deductible. Investment activities on your own behalf do not constitute a trade or business.

The Soliman decision. In 1993 the United States Supreme Court announced a very narrow interpretation of a taxpayer's "principal place of business." *Commissioner v. Soliman, 113 S. Ct. 701 (1993).* The Court concluded that a physician did not qualify for a home office deduction even though he used his home office regularly and exclusively for business, because the "essence of his professional service" was performed in hospitals. It focused on the place where the primary income-generating functions were performed, and the amount of time spent at each location. Under this analysis, the only possible conclusion was that the physician's principal place of business was at the hospitals where he worked and performed income-generating functions, and not his home office where he performed largely administrative tasks.

Congress enacted legislation in 1997 repealing the *Soliman* decision. The new law, which takes effect in 1999, recognizes that some taxpayers will be eligible for a home office deduction if they use their home office for largely administrative tasks—even if their income-generating activities occur at another location. This is a major break for taxpayers with home offices. The new law provides that a home office qualifies as a principal place of business if:

---

29 Percent Of All Taxpayers Itemize Deductions On Schedule A

Only 29 percent (about 3 out of 10) taxpayers are able to itemize deductions on Schedule A. This interesting statistic is buried in the Spring 1994 *Statistics of Income Bulletin* issued by the IRS. This demonstrates that 7 out of 10 ministers and lay church workers who report their federal income taxes as employees (or who are reclassified as employees by the IRS) will be unable to deduct either their unreimbursed business expenses or business expenses reimbursed under a nonaccountable arrangement. Here's why. Employees can claim unreimbursed business expenses (including travel and transportation expenses), and business expenses reimbursed by their church under a nonaccountable arrangement, only as miscellaneous itemized deductions on Schedule A. Employees who cannot itemize deductions will not be able to deduct any of these expenses. This is particularly unfortunate for employees whose business expenses are reimbursed under a nonaccountable plan, since they must include the full amount of all the expense reimbursements as taxable income but they are denied any deduction of their expenses. Reimbursed expenses are nonaccountable if the employee was not required to or did not "account" to the employer for the expenses *or* was not required to or did not return any "excess reimbursements" (employer reimbursements in excess of substantiated expenses) to the employer. The most common form of nonaccountable reimbursement is a monthly car allowance paid to a church employee without any requirement that actual business expenses be substantiated. In addition, most miscellaneous expenses (including unreimbursed and unsubstantiated reimbursed employee business expenses) are deductible on Schedule A only to the extent they exceed 2% of adjusted gross income (only 50% of business meals and entertainment are counted). Ministers reporting their income taxes as employees can minimize if not eliminate the adverse effect of these rules by having their employing church adopt an accountable reimbursement policy.

(1) the office is used by the taxpayer to conduct administrative or management activities related to a trade or business, and

(2) there is no other fixed location where the taxpayer conducts substantial administrative and management activities of the trade or business

As before, the home office must be used regularly and exclusively for business purposes.

Taxpayers who meet these new requirements are eligible for a home office deduction even if they conduct some administrative and management activities at a fixed location of their business outside their home—so long as those activities are not substantial. For example, a taxpayer occasionally does minimal paperwork at another fixed location of the business. Further, taxpayers can claim a home office deduction even though they conduct substantial *non-administrative or non-management business activities* at a fixed location of their business outside their home. For example, a taxpayer meets with or provides services to customers or clients at a fixed location that is away from home. It is this rule that overturns the *Soliman* decision, and makes the home office deduction available to many more persons.

If a *self-employed* taxpayer in fact does not perform substantial administrative or management activities at any fixed location of the business away from home, then the second part of the new test is met whether or not the taxpayer elected not to use an office away from home that was available. However, for employees, the fact that they elect not to use an office on their employer's premises that is available to them for administrative activities will still be relevant in deciding whether or not they meet the "convenience of the employer" requirement.

Conclusions. Those ministers who satisfy the requirements summarized above will be permitted to deduct their home office expenses—assuming of course that they are either ignoring the *Deason* rule, or the limited exception applies. Perhaps even more importantly, they may be able to deduct their transportation costs from their home to their church. This is a significant development, since these transportation costs generally will far exceed the value of a home office deduction. However, ministers must recognize that few will be able to satisfy all of the requirements. After all, how many clergy have a home office that in fact is used exclusively and regularly for business purposes, and do not have an office in the church?

✎ **Key point: those few clergy who satisfy the requirements for a home office will be permitted to deduct their home office expenses. Perhaps even more importantly, they may be able to deduct their transportation costs from their home to their church. This is a significant development, since these transportation costs generally will far exceed the value of a home office deduction. However, clergy must recognize that few will be able to satisfy all four requirements.**

Computing the deduction. To figure the percentage of your home used for business, compare the square feet of space used for business to the total square feet in your home. Or, if the rooms in your home are approximately the same size, you may compare the number of rooms used for business to the total number of rooms in your home. You figure the business part of your expenses by applying the percentage to the total of each expense.

The deduction of home office expenses is limited to the gross income from that business use minus the sum of (1) the business percentage of the mortgage interest, real estate taxes, and casualty losses, and (2) the business expenses other than those related to the business use of a home. As a result, the deduction is limited to a modified net income from the business use of the home. Deductions in excess of the limit may be carried over to later years.

Deductible expenses include all the business portion of all operating expenses (utilities, repairs, mortgage payments, insurance, property taxes, etc.) plus depreciation.

Ministers who report their income taxes as employees (or who report as self-employed but are reclassified as employees by the IRS in an audit) report their home office expenses on Form 2106. However, if business use of your home was your only employee business expense for 1997, and your employer did not pay for any of these expenses, then enter your total expenses directly on line 20 of Schedule A (as an unreimbursed employee business expense). Self-employed clergy compute their home office deduction on Form 8829, and report the deduction on Schedule C (line 30).

IRS audit guidelines for ministers. In 1995 the IRS released audit guidelines for its agents to follow when auditing ministers. The guidelines provide IRS agents with the following information regarding the business use of a home:

In order for a home to qualify as a principal place of business . . . the functions performed and the time spent at each location where the trade or business is conducted are the primary considerations and must be compared to determine the relative importance of each. The church often provides an office on the premises for the minister, so the necessity of an office in the home should be questioned closely. Furthermore, since the total cost to provide the home is used in computing the exempt housing allowance, home office deductions for taxes, insurance, mortgage interest, etc. would be duplications. (Note that itemized deductions are allowable for mortgage interest and taxes.)

✎ **Key point: the guidelines instruct agents to "question closely" the necessity of a home office. This is a business expense that invites scrutiny. It should not be claimed unless there is a reasonable basis for it.**

☞ *Example. Rev. V reports his income taxes as an employee. He has an office at his church, but also maintains an office in his home where he* occasionally does research and other work-related activities. He also uses his home office to monitor investments, and assist his children with their homework. Rev. V is not eligible for a home office deduction for two reasons. First, his home office is not used exclusively for business purposes. And second, his home office is not for the convenience of his employer since an office is available at the church where Rev. V can perform all of his work-related duties.

☞ **Example.** Rev. H is pastor of a small congregation. He reports his income taxes as an employee. The church does not maintain an office for Rev. H, and so he performs all of his work-related administrative tasks at a home office that he uses regularly and exclusively in performing his duties. While H performs all of his non-administrative duties (preaching, sacraments) at the church, all of his administrative tasks (sermon preparation, business planning) at his home office. While Rev. H might not have qualified for a home office deduction under the Soliman ruling, he clearly qualifies under the new rules that take effect in 1999.

☞ **Example.** Rev. K has an office at the church, but she also has a home office which she uses regularly and exclusively to counsel with church members. Does she qualify for a home office deduction? While she uses her home office as a place for meeting with clients in the normal course of her activities, the home office still must be used for the convenience of her employer. This means that it is essential to use her home office to perform her duties. This is very unlikely if not impossible when an office is maintained in the church.

☞ **Example.** Rev. H had an office at the church (his principal place of work) and an office in his home where he prepared sermons and performed other ministerial duties. The Tax Court ruled that he could not deduct the costs of daily round trips by car between his home and church. The transportation was commuting. Hamblen v. Commissioner, 78 T.C. 53 (1981).

☞ **Example.** A minister claimed a deduction for a home office based on the fact that approximately 18% of his home was used for a home office. Accordingly, the minister claimed a deduction for 18% of the maintenance and repair expenses incurred with respect to his home. The IRS audited the minister and denied any home office deduction. The Tax Court agreed with the IRS. It noted that to deduct home office expenses a taxpayer must prove that a specific portion of his residence was used exclusively for business. However, in this case, the court concluded that the minister's "testimony makes clear that the office was used both as an office and as a guest room. Thus, [his] office fails the exclusive use test. Accordingly, we find that [the minister] cannot claim deductions attributable to a home office." Shelley v. Commissioner, T.C. Memo. 1994-432 (1994).

☞ **Example.** A minister claimed that he used 20 percent of his home as a "home office" associated with his counseling ministry. The minister did all of his counseling in another office, and used the office in his home (consisting of two rooms) to store his books and office equipment and to prepare for counseling sessions. He did not meet with or counsel clients at his home office but rather used his other office for that purpose. He claimed that he maintained his counseling books and accounting materials at the home office because the presence of these items in the other office would have "intimidated the clients." The Tax Court (relying on the Soliman case) concluded that the minister could not claim a business expense deduction for any portion of the expenses associated with his home office. Hairston v. Commissioner, T.C. Memo. Dec. 51,025(M) (1995).

10. Moving expenses

✎ **Key point: the moving expense deduction was overhauled in 1994. Some moving expenses no longer are deductible. On the other hand moving expenses are reported as an adjustment in computing adjusted gross income on line 25 of Form 1040. This change removes moving expenses from the category of a business expense. These expenses are deductible by employees and self-employed ministers alike whether or not they are able to itemize deductions on Schedule A.**

❖ **New in 1998. Church leaders should be familiar with the following changes in moving expense reporting that take effect in 1998: (1) Form 4782, which is used by employers to report moving expense reimbursements made to employees, will be eliminated; (2) qualified moving expenses an employer pays to a third party on behalf of the employee (e.g. to a moving company) will not be reported on Form W-2; (3) qualified moving expenses reimbursements an employer pays directly to an employee will be reported in Box 13 of Form W-2 and will be identified using Code P (currently, all qualified moving expense reimbursements are identified with Code P, regardless of whether or not they were paid directly to the employee); (4) other moving expense reimbursements (nonqualified expenses) will continue to be included in wages (Form W-2, box 1) and are subject to income tax withholding and social security and Medicare taxes.**

The moving expense deduction is now subject to the following rules: (1) the cost of pre-move house-hunting trips is excluded from the definition of moving expenses, as are the cost of meals incurred while traveling to a new home; (2) the cost of temporary living expenses for up to 30 days in the general location of the new job is excluded from the definition of moving expenses; (3) the mileage limit is increased from 35 miles to 50 miles (to claim any deduction, the taxpayer's new place of work must be at least 50 miles farther from the taxpayer's former residence than the former place of work); (4) "qualified" moving expenses not paid or reimbursed by the taxpayer's employer are allowable as a deduction in computing adjusted gross income (this is good news—they are now allowable whether or not the taxpayer is able to itemize expenses on Schedule A); (5) "qualified" moving expenses paid or reimbursed by the tax-payer's employer are excludable from gross income for tax purposes (if reimbursed, the reimbursements must be pursuant to an "accountable" arrangement) meaning that employer reimbursements are not re-ported as taxable income.

The moving expense deduction is discussed more fully in section G.6 of this chapter.

11. Telephone expenses

If you use your home telephone for business pur-poses, you may not deduct any of the basic local service charge (including taxes) for the first telephone line into your home.

Cellular phones. The use cellular telephones is increasing dramatically among church staff. Unfortu-nately, many ministers and church treasurers are not familiar with the strict tax rules that apply to the busi-ness use of such phones. Cellular telephones consti-tute "listed property" under Code section 280F. The result is that no deduction is allowed for the business use of such phones by an employee unless the fol-lowing 2 requirements are met:

(1) Convenience of the employer. Use of the cellu-lar phone is "for the convenience of the employer." This means that users can demonstrate that they cannot perform their job without the cellular phone. The fact that the phone enables them to perform their work more easily and efficiently is not enough. Fur-ther, users must be able to prove that the phones available at their place of employment are insufficient to enable them to properly perform their job.

(2) Condition of employment. Use of the cellular phone must be required as a "condition of employ-ment." This means that users must not be able to perform their duties without a cellular phone. It is not necessary that the employer explicitly requires use of cellular phones. On the other hand, it is not enough that the employer merely states that use of the cellu-lar phone is a condition of employment.

If you are an employee and these tests are not met, you cannot deduct any of the cost of your cellu-lar phone. *IRC 280F, Revenue Ruling 86-129.*

☞ *Example. A minister used his home phone to speak with members of his congregation or to deal with other church-related matters. He did not have a separate telephone line for business calls. He claimed a business deduction of 75% of his total telephone expenses (including both local and long distance charges) on his federal tax re-turns for 1985, 1986, and 1987. The IRS audited the minister and disallowed all of the deductions, but the Tax Court ruled in the minister's favor. The court observed: "No deduction is allowed for*

a taxpayer's telephone expenses if the primary purpose of the telephone is personal rather than business. . . . [The minister] presented canceled checks paid to the telephone company and testi-fied that approximately 75% of all local and long distance calls received at home were related to his business. [He] did not maintain a separate business telephone line. Due to the nature of [his] business and the hours devoted to his du-ties, we believe [his] approximation of the busi-ness use of his home phone. We hold that [he has] met [his] burden of proof as to the claimed telephone expenses and [is] entitled to the de-ductions claimed." Note that this case was de-cided before the tax law was changed to deny any deduction for basic local telephone service for the first telephone line into a home. However, even under the new rule, the minister's deduction for 75% of his long distance calls would have been upheld. Shelley v. Commissioner, T.C. Memo. 1994-432 (1994).

☞ *Example. A minister engaged in a counseling ministry from a downtown office, and also main-tained an office in his home. The minister claimed a business expense deduction for tele-phone expenses incurred at his downtown office and his home office. The IRS disallowed the por-tion of the telephone expenses attributable to the minister's home office. The Tax Court disagreed with this conclusion, noting that the minister clearly "incurred some telephone expenses at home in the course of conducting his trade or business as a counselor," and that the deductibil-ity of telephone expenses is not governed by the home office rules (the minister did not qualify for a home office deduction). The Court further noted that the tax code disallows a deduction for "basic local telephone service with respect to the first telephone line" to any residence of the taxpayer, regardless of any business use of the telephone. The Court added that "this section, however, does not apply in this case since [the minister has] not claimed local telephone service ex-penses." Hairston v. Commissioner, T.C. Memo. Dec. 51,025(M) (1995).*

12. Club dues

✎ **Key point: dues paid to clubs organized for business, pleasure, recreation, or social pur-poses cannot be claimed as a business ex-pense—other than dues paid to professional organizations such as bar associations and medical associations, and civic or public service organizations such as Kiwanis, Lions, and Rotary.**

Many ministers belong to local clubs, including fit-ness and golf clubs. Some churches agree to pay the annual dues or fees to these clubs as a fringe bene-fit. In some cases, the minister (or church) treats the club dues as a business expense because member-ship in the club will either contribute to the minister's health or expose the minister and church to the com-munity.

The issue of club dues was addressed by Congress in 1993, and by proposed regulations released by the IRS in 1994. Under the new tax law and IRS regulations dues paid for membership in any club organized for business, pleasure, recreation, or other social purposes cannot be claimed as a business expense—other than dues paid to professional organizations such as bar associations and medical associations, and civic or public service organizations such as Kiwanis, Lions, Rotary, chambers of commerce, and trade associations. As a result, dues paid to health and fitness clubs, golf clubs, airline and hotel clubs, and dinner clubs are no longer deductible as a business expense.

✎ **Key point: the fact that membership in a club may enhance a minister's health or length of ministry, or provide positive exposure of the church in the community, does not matter. These dues are not business expenses.**

There are two points to emphasize:

• *Reimbursements.* Since most club dues no longer can be treated as a business expense, a church cannot pay for or reimburse such dues under an accountable expense reimbursement arrangement. If a church pays for a minister's club dues, then the full amount must be added to the minister's W-2 or 1099 form as additional taxable compensation. It is not a business expense that is reimbursable under an accountable arrangement.

• *Deductions.* Second, ministers cannot claim a business expense deduction for unreimbursed club dues that they pay themselves.

Churches that in the past have paid their minister's club dues should re-evaluate this practice now in light of the new IRS regulations. If your church has an accountable business expense reimbursement arrangement, it cannot pay for or reimburse (under such an arrangement) dues it pays on behalf of a pastor to clubs organized for pleasure, recreation, or other social purposes. This includes dues paid to health and fitness clubs, golf clubs, airline and hotel clubs, and dinner clubs. If the church pays or reimburses these dues, then the full amount paid by the church must be reported as additional income on the pastor's W-2 or 1099.

Dues paid to professional organizations and civic or public service organizations (such as Kiwanis, Lions, and Rotary) can be treated as a business expense if they otherwise qualify.

☞ *Example. A church board adopts an accountable business expense reimbursement arrangement. The board agrees to pay its pastor's club dues at a local fitness club. These dues are $1,500 each year. Since the dues cannot be treated as a business expense, they cannot be reimbursed under an accountable expense reimbursement arrangement. As a result, the church must include the full $1,500 as additional income on the minister's W-2 at the end of the year, and the minister must report the full amount as additional income on*

Form 1040. However, note the possible "working condition fringe benefit" exception below.

☞ *Example. Same facts as the previous example, except that the minister's club dues were not reimbursed by the church. The key point to note here is that the minister will not be able to deduct any part of the dues as a business expense. They are a nondeductible personal expense.*

✎ **Key point: the IRS issued proposed regulations at the end of 1994 clarifying that employer reimbursements of an employee's club dues may qualify as a nontaxable "working condition fringe benefit" even as to those kinds of club dues that no longer can be treated as a business expenses if (1) the employer has not treated such amounts as compensation; (2) the amounts would be deductible as a business expense were it not for the new limitations on the deductibility of club dues; and (3) the employee substantiates the expenses under an accountable arrangement.**

☞ *Example. First Church provides Rev. R with a country club membership. The membership is valued at $15,000, which the church does not treat as compensation to Rev. R. Rev. R substantiates that he used the club membership 30% for business purposes. The church's payment of the business use of the club (30%) is a working condition fringe benefit. As a result, Rev. R may exclude from gross income $4,500 (30% percent of the club dues). Rev. R must include the other $11,500 in gross income as a fringe benefit (70% of the value of the club dues, which reflects Rev. R's personal use).*

13. Financial support paid by clergy to local churches or denominational agencies

Most ministers support their church with regular contributions. Some also make regular contributions to a denominational agency. Must this financial support be treated as a charitable contribution? Or, is it possible to treat it as "professional dues"? This question was addressed directly in an unpublished "small" Tax Court decision in 1992. *Forbes v. Commissioner, T.C. Sum. Op. 1992-167 (unpublished).*

A local church adopted a "tithing policy" requiring every employee to pay a tithe of ten percent of total compensation back to the church. The church strictly enforces the tithing policy. Tithing records are maintained on a computer and are periodically examined for all employees. Employees found to be delinquent in their tithes are required to become current. The church has dismissed several employees for failing to comply with the tithing requirement.

The church views its tithing policy as both moral and managerial. Morally, the church believes that "a church member whose wages are paid from the tithes of the parishioners, but refuses to participate in the support of the ministry, is dishonest and hypocritical." From a management standpoint, the church believes that an employee who disagrees with the its basic tenets and it unwilling to comply with its policies is not fulfilling his or her employment commitment.

One of the church's ministers received $24,600 in wages from the church in one year, which consisted of salary, housing allowance, and miscellaneous amounts received for services performed at weddings, funerals, and other occasions. She paid a tithe of $2,460 back to the church, as required by the tithing policy. In computing her self-employment (social security) taxes for the year she deducted this tithe as a "business expense."

The IRS audited the minister's tax return and claimed that she could only claim her tithe as a charitable contribution deduction and not as a business expense. As a result, the IRS concluded that it was improper for the minister to deduct the tithe in computing her social security taxes. While taxpayers can deduct business expenses in computing self-employment taxes, they cannot deduct charitable contributions. The minister appealed the IRS ruling to the Tax Court, claiming that her tithe was a business expense that she was entitled to deduct in computing her self-employment taxes.

The Tax Court concluded that the minister's tithes to the church represented a business or professional expense rather than a charitable contribution under the facts of this case. As a result, the minister properly deducted her tithes in computing her social security taxes. The court observed:

Under consideration of the record in this case, we agree with [the minister]. Tithing is required by [the church] as a matter of employment policy, and [the minister] must annually tithe ten percent of the income she receives as a result of her position as a minister. Since [the church's] tithing policy is rigorously enforced, [the minister's] employment is, in a very real sense, dependent upon her willingness to give. The fact that she is tithing to a charitable organization to which she belongs and to which she *might* tithe ten percent anyway is of little consequence given the facts in this case. Accordingly . . . we hold that [the minister] is entitled to compute her net earnings from self-employment by reducing her gross income from self-employment by the $2,460 she paid to [the church] during the year in issue as a tithe.

Federal tax law permits taxpayers to deduct business and professional expenses, which are defined as "all the ordinary and necessary expenses paid or incurred during the taxable year in carrying on any trade or business". The court concluded that the minister's tithes satisfied this definition and accordingly could be deducted as a business expense. It is significant that *the IRS conceded* that the minister's tithes could be deducted as a business or professional expense, except for a provision in federal law preventing taxpayers from claiming a business expense deduction for an item *that could be claimed as a charitable contribution.* The IRS claimed that this provision prevented the minister from deducting her

tithes as a business expense—since she could have claimed them as a charitable contribution. Not so, said the court. It concluded that "payments made as an integral part of a taxpayer's trade or business" are deductible as business or professional expenses even if "the recipient of the payment is a charitable organization." That is, the critical question to ask is whether or not a payment satisfies the definition of a business expense. Is it an ordinary and necessary expense paid or incurred in carrying on a trade or business? If so, it is deductible as a business expense even though it may be possible to characterize it as a charitable contribution.

Further, the court suggested that it would be unrealistic to treat the minister's tithe to the church as a voluntary charitable contribution, since in no sense was it a voluntary transfer of funds to the church. Rather, it was a mandatory payment, and as such it could not be characterized as a charitable contribution.

✎ **Key point: the United States Supreme Court has observed that a gift or charitable contribution "proceeds from a detached and disinterested generosity . . . out of affection, respect, admiration, charity, or like impulses." Surely, it would be inappropriate to classify mandatory financial support paid to a church by a minister or lay employee as a gift or contribution under this test, since in no sense does such support "proceed from a detached and disinterested generosity."**

Note the following additional considerations about this controversial decision:

• **This case suggests that in some cases mandatory contributions made by ministers and lay employees to a church can be treated as business expenses.** What is the practical effect of this result? Most importantly, it means that ministers may be able to deduct such contributions as a business expense in computing their self-employment (social security) tax on Schedule SE (of Form 1040). Remember, ministers always are considered to be self-employed for social security purposes with respect to their ministerial income. Consider the following examples:

☞ *Example. Rev. D receives compensation of $40,000 for 1997 from his church (of which $10,000 is designated as a housing allowance). Rev. D makes mandatory contributions of $4,000 to his church, and has other business expenses of $3,000. If the $4,000 in contributions to the church are mandatory, the Tax Court's ruling suggests that these can be deducted as a business expense in computing both income taxes and self-employment taxes. Rev. D would pay self-employment taxes on $33,000 (total compensation including housing allowance less the mandatory contributions and business expenses). Without taking into account any other facts or deductions (for the sake of simplicity) this would result in a tax of $5,049.*

☞ *Example. Same facts as the previous example, except that Rev. D's contributions to the church do not meet the Tax Court's definition of "mandatory". Rev. D would pay self-employment taxes on $37,000 (total compensation including housing allowance less business expenses but not less contributions). Without taking into account any other facts or deductions (for the sake of simplicity) this would result in a tax of $5,661. By not treating his contributions as a business expense Rev. D will pay $612 in additional self-employment taxes.*

• **The Tax Court concluded that mandatory contributions to a church by a church employee can be claimed as a business expense.** As a result, such expenses can be deducted as a miscellaneous itemized deduction on Schedule A (by church employees) or as a deduction on Schedule C (for self-employed workers). One problem—employees who do not have enough deductions to itemize on Schedule A (only 30% can do so) cannot claim any deduction for income tax purposes. This is true whether the contribution is treated as a charitable contribution or as a business expense. Note however that a mandatory contribution can still be deducted in computing self-employment taxes, even if the taxpayer cannot itemize income tax deductions on Schedule A. This is the primary reason why some ministers want to treat their church contributions as a business expense.

• **Reimbursing mandatory contributions**. Many church treasurers reimburse their minister's business expenses. If mandatory contributions to the church are considered to be business expenses for purposes of self-employment taxes, can a church treasurer reimburse them? This is a difficult question that the Tax Court's ruling did not address. Logically, if mandatory contributions are considered to be business expenses for self-employment tax purposes, they can be reimbursed under either an accountable or nonaccountable business expense reimbursement arrangement. There are two considerations to note: (1) Neither the IRS nor any court has directly addressed this issue. There is no clear precedent that can be cited in support of such a conclusion. This does not mean that the reimbursement of mandatory contributions would be wrong or illegal. It simply means that there is no direct precedent to support such a position. (2) Some would say there is a logical or theological inconsistency in a church reimbursing a minister's contributions, at least when the church's reimbursements come out of its own funds (as opposed to a salary reduction or restructuring). To illustrate, David refused to make a burnt offering to the Lord using donated oxen ("will I offer burnt offerings unto the Lord my God of that which cost me nothing?")

• **Contributions must be mandatory.** For contributions to a church to be treated by ministers and lay employees <u>as a business expense</u> rather than as a charitable contribution, they must be "mandatory" under the Tax Court's rigid definition. Note the following elements that were noted by the court:

• the church adopted a formal "tithing policy" that required every employee to pay a tithe (ten percent) of gross income to the church

• the church maintained tithing records on every employee

• the church periodically reviewed the tithing records of all employees and required delinquent employees to become current

• the church dismissed several employees for failing to comply with the tithing requirement

• the church clearly articulated both a theological and managerial basis for its tithing policy

☞ *Example. Rev. K would like to reduce the amount of social security taxes that he pays. He decides to deduct his church contributions as a business expense in computing his self-employment taxes. He claims that if he does not set an example to his congregation by making contributions to the church, he may be asked to resign. The church has never adopted a formal "tithing policy," and has never dismissed (or even suggested dismissing) a minister for inadequate contributions. These contributions are not mandatory, and are not deductible (for income tax or social security tax purposes) as a business expense.*

• **The IRS conceded that mandatory contributions could be treated as business expenses.** As noted above, it is important to recognize that *the IRS conceded* that the minister's tithes could be deducted as a business or professional expense except for a provision in federal law preventing taxpayers from claiming a business expense deduction for an item *that could be claimed as a charitable contribution.* Since the court concluded that this provision did not apply, the contributions were deductible as a business expense.

• **Denominational support.** Some denominations require ministers to make contributions for their support. If these contributions are mandatory, they can be treated as business expenses and deducted in computing self-employment taxes according to the Tax Court's decision. Once again, it is important to emphasize that the contributions must in fact be mandatory. For example, the denomination's governing documents specify that ministers can lose their ordained status for failure to pay the required support.

✎ **Key point: some ministers will prefer to report their mandatory contributions as a charitable contribution rather than as a business or professional expense. Some ministers will do so for theological reasons. Others will do so to reduce their audit risk, since the IRS may not accept the reasoning of the Tax Court in other cases.**

• **Effect of a "small Tax Court case".** The Tax Court's decision was a "small tax court case," meaning that it involved less than $10,000 and the taxpayer elected to pursue an expedited and simplified procedure authorized by section 7463 of the Internal Revenue Code. While small tax court cases are more quickly resolved, there is a trade-off—section 7463 specifies that "a decision entered in any case in which the proceedings are conducted under this section shall not be reviewed by any other court and shall not be treated as precedent for any other case." In other words, the decision of the Tax Court was final, and it cannot be cited as precedent in other cases. Obviously, this greatly limits the impact of the case. The IRS is free to completely ignore the decision in future cases.

IRS audit guidelines for ministers. In 1995 the IRS issued audit guidelines for its agents to follow when auditing ministers. The guidelines communicate the following information to agents regarding the tax treatment of ministers' financial support to a church or denominational agency:

Ministers often pay a small annual renewal fee to maintain their credentials, which constitutes a deductible expense. However, ministers' contributions to the church are not deductible as business expenses. They may argue that they are expected to donate generously to the church as part of their employment. This is not sufficient to convert charitable contributions to business expenses. The distinction is that charitable contributions are given to a qualifying organization (such as a church) for the furtherance of its charitable activities. Dues, on the other hand, are usually paid with the expectation that a financial benefit will result to the individual, as in a realtor's multilist dues or an electrician's union dues. A minister's salary and benefits are not likely to directly depend on the donations made to the church. They may still be deducted as contributions on Schedule A but may not be used as a business expense to reduce self-employment tax.

⊃ Observation. The guidelines acknowledge that annual renewal fees that are required to maintain a minister's credentials are deductible. This is an important clarification, since the IRS has challenged this proposition in several audits of ministers. There is no doubt that mandatory contributions to a denominational agency to maintain one's professional credentials represent a business expenses, whether the taxpayer is a minister or an attorney or any other professional.

⊃ Observation. The guidelines inform agents that ministers' contributions to an employing church are not deductible as business expenses. They can be claimed only as charitable contributions. The guidelines reject the conclusion reached by the Tax Court in the Forbes case (discussed above). Ministers who treat contributions to their employing church as a business expense are taking an aggressive position that is now more likely to be scrutinized and questioned.

D. Business and Professional Expenses—How to Report Them

Most clergy incur out-of-pocket business expenses during the course of the year for transportation, travel, entertainment, education, books, and similar items. These expenses can be handled and reported in any one of 3 ways—unreimbursed, nonaccountable reimbursements, or accountable reimbursements. These 3 methods are summarized below.

method #1—unreimbursed expenses

Many churches do not reimburse their minister's business and professional expenses. Such clergy have unreimbursed business expenses. Some churches reimburse their minister's business expenses only up to a specified amount. Such clergy have unreimbursed expenses to the extent that they incur expenses in excess of what the church is willing to reimburse.

Clergy who report their federal income taxes as employees (or who are reclassified as employees by the IRS) can deduct their business expenses only as a miscellaneous itemized deduction on Schedule A (of Form 1040), and then only to the extent that such expenses exceed 2% of adjusted gross income. These rules have resulted in the nondeductibility of unreimbursed business expenses for many clergy, since it is estimated that fewer than 30% of all taxpayers have sufficient expenses to be able to itemize deductions on Schedule A.

✎ Key point: clergy who are employees for income tax reporting purposes cannot claim any deduction for "unreimbursed" employee business expenses for which an employer reimbursement was available.

Those few clergy who are self-employed for federal income tax purposes can deduct their unreimbursed business expenses directly on Schedule C, whether or not they are able to itemize their deductions.

method #2—nonaccountable reimbursed expenses

It is very common for churches to reimburse a minister's business expenses without requiring any substantiation of actual expenses or a return of reimbursements in excess of substantiated expenses (e.g., "excess reimbursements"). The most common example is the monthly "car allowance." Many churches pay their minister a monthly allowance to cover business use of an automobile, without requiring any substantiation of actual expenses or a return of the amount by which the allowances exceed actual expenses. Such a reimbursement arrangement is called a nonaccountable reimbursement arrangement, since the minister is not required to "account" for (substantiate) the actual amount, date, place, and business purpose of each reimbursed expense.

A reimbursement arrangement is nonaccountable if it either (1) fails to require substantiation of the actual amount, date, place, and business purpose of each reimbursed expense within a reasonable time, or (2) fails to require excess reimbursements to be returned to the employer within a reasonable time.

What are the tax consequences of a nonaccountable plan? That depends on whether the minister is an employee or self-employed for federal income tax reporting purposes.

employees

For ministers who are employees for federal income tax reporting purposes (and this includes most ministers), the full amount of the church's reimbursements must be reported as income on the minister's W-2 (and 1040). The minister can deduct actual expenses only as a miscellaneous itemized deduction on Schedule A to the extent these expenses exceed 2% of adjusted gross income. These rules are especially harsh, since the church's reimbursements are fully reported as income to the minister who in many cases is unable to claim any deduction because of insufficient itemized expenses to use Schedule A.

self-employed

For those few clergy who are self-employed for federal income tax reporting purposes, the full amount of any church reimbursements must be reported as income on Form 1099 (and Schedule C). The minister is then able to deduct expenses on Schedule C whether or not he or she is able to itemize expenses on Schedule A. This is seen by some to be an "advantage" of reporting income taxes as self-employed. However, because the IRS would consider most clergy to be employees for income tax reporting purposes, clergy who report their income taxes as self-employed should not assume that they are unaffected by these harsh limitations on the deductibility of employee business expenses. *In fact, this is one of the primary reasons for IRS audits of clergy tax returns.* If the IRS succeeds in reclassifying "self-employed" clergy as employees, then their business expenses are shifted from Schedule C to Schedule A. For clergy who do not have enough deductions to itemize on Schedule A, this means that they receive no deduction for any of their business expenses.

This rule is especially harsh on clergy whose business expenses are reimbursed under a "nonaccountable" plan, since the full amount of all the reimbursements is included in their taxable income but they have no offsetting expenses to deduct. Those clergy who can use Schedule A can deduct their business expenses only to the extent that they exceed 2% of adjusted gross income. Either way, the IRS wins. Note, however, that the IRS has ruled that a minister may be able to deduct business expenses in computing self-employment taxes on Schedule SE even though the expenses were not deductible in computing income taxes because the minister could not use Schedule A. *Revenue Ruling 80-110.* Of course, those clergy who truly are self-employed for income tax reporting purposes are not affected by these limi-

tations, since they can deduct all of their business expenses (only 50% of business meals and entertainment) directly on Schedule C.

✎ **Key point: ministers who report their income taxes as employees (or who would be classified as employees by the IRS) cannot deduct any of their unreimbursed business expenses if they have insufficient itemized deductions to use Schedule A. However, these ministers are placed in an even worse position if their church reimburses some or all of their expenses under a nonaccountable arrangement, since all of the reimbursements are includable on the minister's W-2 as taxable income while the minister is unable to claim any offsetting deduction. This makes it critical for churches to avoid nonaccountable reimbursement arrangements.**

Examples of nonaccountable arrangements. Here are some common examples of nonaccountable reimbursement arrangements that should be avoided. Our recommendation—if you currently have any of these arrangements, immediately convert it to an accountable arrangement.

• Your church pays a monthly "car allowance" to clergy or lay staff members, without requiring any accounting or substantiation.

• Your church reimburses business expenses without requiring adequate written substantiation (with receipts for all expenses of $75 or more) of the amount, date, place, and business purpose of each expense.

• Your church only reimburses business expenses once each year. Business expenses must be accounted for within a "reasonable time" under an accountable arrangement. Generally, this means within 60 days or less.

• Your church provides clergy or lay staff with travel advances and requires no accounting for the use of these funds.

☞ *Example. Rev. B serves a senior minister of a church and reports his federal income taxes as an employee. The church expects Rev. B to pay business expenses out of his own salary, so it reimburses none of Rev. B's business expenses. In other words, all of Rev. B's business expenses are "unreimbursed." For 1997, Rev. B has total church compensation of $35,000, and incurs unreimbursed business expenses of $3,000. He does not have enough itemized deductions to use Schedule A. As an employee, the only way for Rev. B to deduct his unreimbursed business expenses is as an itemized deduction on Schedule A (to the extent that such expenses exceed 2% of his adjusted gross income). Since Rev. B does not have enough deductions to itemize on Schedule A, he cannot deduct any portion of his unreimbursed business expenses. According to the recent IRS report, 70% of all taxpayers cannot use Schedule A. This suggests that 7 out of 10 ministers who report their income taxes as* employees (or who would be classified as employees by the IRS in an audit) will be unable to deduct their unreimbursed business expenses. This unfortunate result can be avoided completely if a church simply adopts an accountable business expense reimbursement arrangement.

☞ *Example.* Rev. H receives a monthly "car allowance" of $300. Rev. H is not required to account for the use of any of these funds. This is an example of a nonaccountable reimbursement arrangement. The church is reimbursing business expenses (through a monthly car allowance) without requiring any accounting or substantiation. If Rev. H reports her income taxes as an employee (or as self-employed, but is reclassified as an employee by the IRS in an audit), and has insufficient itemized deductions to use Schedule A, the following reporting requirements apply: (1) the church must report all of the monthly allowances ($3,600) on Rev. H's W-2 form; (2) Rev. H must report all of the monthly allowances ($3,600) as income on her Form 1040; (3) Rev. H cannot deduct any of her car expenses since these are deductible only as itemized deductions on Schedule A. This result is even worse than the previous example, since in this case all of the monthly car allowances are includable on Rev. H's W-2 though she is unable to claim any offsetting deduction for her car expenses. As noted before, it can be assumed that 7 out of 10 clergy are not able to use Schedule A, and cannot deduct either unreimbursed business expenses or business expenses reimbursed under a nonaccountable arrangement. This harsh rule can be avoided if a church adopts an accountable reimbursement arrangement. This is especially critical if a church uses a nonaccountable reimbursement arrange-

ment, since not only are all of the expenses nondeductible under such an arrangement but all of the church's reimbursements are includable as taxable income on the minister's W-2.

method #3—accountable reimbursed expenses

The good news is that the adverse tax consequences of having both unreimbursed and nonaccountable reimbursed expenses can be eliminated entirely if a church simply adopts an accountable business expense reimbursement arrangement. *This is one of the most important components of an adequate clergy compensation package.* If a church adopts an accountable reimbursement arrangement, then none of the church's reimbursements needs to appear on an employee's W-2 (or 1040), and there are no expenses for the employee to deduct. The employee, in effect, reports to his or her employer rather than to the IRS. This is now the ideal way for churches to handle the business expenses of clergy and any other church worker.

To summarize, an **accountable reimbursement plan** is one that

• reimburses only those business expenses that an employee substantiates within a reasonable time as to the amount, date, place, and business purpose of each expense (in the case of entertainment expenses, you also must substantiate the business relationship of those persons you entertained), and

• requires any "excess reimbursements" (e.g., reimbursements in excess of substantiated business expenses) to be returned to the employer within a reasonable time *(see Treas. Reg. 1.62-2)*

ADVANTAGES OF AN ACCOUNTABLE REIMBURSEMENT PLAN

The implementation of an accountable reimbursement plan by a church is one of the most important components of a clergy compensation package. Consider the following benefits of such a plan:

• Clergy report their business expenses to the church rather than to the IRS.

• Clergy who report their income taxes as employees (or who report as self-employed and who are reclassified as employees by the IRS in an audit) avoid the limitations on the deductibility of employee business expenses. These include (1) the elimination of any deduction if the minister cannot itemize deductions on Schedule A (70% of all taxpayers cannot), and (2) the deductibility of business expenses on Schedule A as an itemized expense only to the extent that these expenses exceed 2% of the minister's adjusted gross income.

• The *Deason* allocation rule is avoided. Under this rule, clergy must reduce their business expense deduction by the percentage of their total compensation that consists of a tax-exempt housing allowance.

• The "50% limitation" that applies to the deductibility of business meals and entertainment expenses is avoided. Unless these expenses are reimbursed by an employer under an accountable arrangement, only 50% of them are deductible by either employees or the self-employed. See IRS Publication 463.

• Clergy who report their income taxes as self-employed avoid the shock of being reclassified as an employee by the IRS in an audit. Many clergy who report their income taxes as self-employed have been reclassified as employees by the IRS. The effect of this is to move their business expenses from Schedule C (where they are fully deductible), to Schedule A. The disadvantage of reporting these expenses on Schedule A is that no more than 30% of all taxpayers have sufficient itemized deductions to use Schedule A—meaning that the deduction of business expenses is lost completely. And, even if a minister is able to use Schedule A, the business expenses can be deducted only to the extent that they exceed 2% of adjusted gross income.

ILLUSTRATION 7-1
FULL "ACCOUNTABLE" REIMBURSEMENT POLICY
(monthly reimbursements)

The following resolution was duly adopted by the board of directors of _____ (the "Church") at a regularly scheduled meeting held on _____ (date), a quorum being present.

Whereas, income tax regulations 1.162-17 and 1.274-5T(f) provide that an employee "need not report on his tax return" expenses paid or incurred solely by him solely for the benefit of his employer for which he is required to account and does account to his employer and which are charged directly or indirectly to the employer; and

Whereas, income tax regulation 1.274-5T(f) further provides that "an adequate accounting means the submission to the employer of an account book, diary, statement of expense, or similar record maintained by the employee in which the information as to each element of expenditure (amount, date and place, business purpose, and business relationship) is recorded at or near the time of the expenditure, together with supporting documentary evidence, in a manner which conforms to all the "adequate records requirements" set forth in the regulation; and

Whereas, the Church desires to establish a reimbursement policy pursuant to the regulations mentioned above; be it therefore

Resolved, that the Church hereby adopts a reimbursement policy pursuant to income tax regulations 1.162-17 and 1.274-5T(f) upon the following terms and conditions:

1. Adequate accounting for reimbursed expenses. Any minister now or hereafter employed by the Church shall be reimbursed for any ordinary and necessary business and professional expense incurred on behalf of the Church, if the following conditions are satisfied: (1) the expenses are reasonable in amount; (2) the minister documents the amount, date, place, business purpose (and in the case of entertainment expenses, the business relationship of the person or persons entertained) of each such expense with the same kind of documentary evidence as would be required to support a deduction of the expense on the minister's federal tax return; and (3) the minister documents such expenses by providing the church treasurer with an accounting of such expenses no less frequently than monthly (in no event will an expense be reimbursed if substantiated more than 60 days after the expense is paid or incurred by a minister).

2. Cellular phones and personal computers. The Church will not reimburse cellular phone or personal computer expenses of a minister who is treated as an employee for federal income tax reporting purposes unless the minister's use of a cellular phone and personal computer meets the following two tests:

(1) Convenience of the employer. Use of the cellular phone or computer is "for the convenience of the employer." This means that the minister cannot perform his job without the cellular phone. The fact that the phone enables him to perform his work more easily and efficiently is not enough. Further, it must be demonstrated that the phones available at the Church are insufficient to enable the minister to properly perform his job.

(2) Condition of employment. Use of the cellular phone or computer must be required as a "condition of employment." It is not necessary that the Church specifically requires use of cellular phones. On the other hand, it is not enough that the Church merely states that use of the cellular phone is a condition of employment.

3. Reimbursements not funded out of salary reductions. Reimbursements shall be paid out of Church funds, and not by reducing pay checks by the amount of business expense reimbursements.

4. Reimbursable business expenses. Examples of reimbursable business expenses include local transportation, overnight travel (including lodging and meals), entertainment, books and subscriptions, education, vestments, and professional dues.

5. Tax reporting. The Church shall not include in a minister's W-2 form the amount of any business or professional expense properly substantiated and reimbursed according to this policy, and the minister should not report the amount of any such reimbursement as income on Form 1040.

6. Excess reimbursements. Any Church reimbursement that exceeds the amount of business or professional expenses properly accounted for by a minister pursuant to this policy must be returned to the Church within 120 days after the associated expenses are paid or incurred by the minister, and shall not be retained by the minister.

7. Expenses not fully reimbursed. If, for any reason, the Church's reimbursements are less than the amount of business and professional expenses properly substantiated by a minister, the Church will report no part of the reimbursements on the minister's W-2, and the minister may deduct the unreimbursed expenses as allowed by law.

8. Inadequate substantiation. Under no circumstances will the Church reimburse a minister for business or professional expenses incurred on behalf of the Church that are not properly substantiated according to this policy. Church and staff understand that this requirement is necessary to prevent our reimbursement plan from being classified as a nonaccountable plan.

9. Retention of records. All receipts and other documentary evidence used by a minister to substantiate business and professional expenses reimbursed under this policy shall be retained by the Church.

Attest:_____

_____
Secretary of the Board

207

✎ **Key point: the IRS issued audit guidelines for its agents to follow when auditing ministers. The guidelines state: "If [a reimbursement] arrangement meets all the requirements for an accountable plan, the amounts paid under the arrangement are excluded from the minister's gross income and are not required to be reported on his or her Form W-2. If, however, the arrangement does not meet one or more of the requirements, all payments under the arrangement are included in the minister's gross income and are reported as wages on the Form W-2, even though no withholding at the source is required."**

✎ **Key point: taxpayers must have sufficient documentary evidence to substantiate the amount, date, place, and business purpose of most business expenses, but they will not need a receipt for any expense of less than $75.**

Adequate accounting. Adequate substantiation or "accounting" under an accountable reimbursement plan generally means that the employee is required to substantiate (with reliable written evidence, including a receipt for any expense of $75 or more) the amount, date, place, and "business nature" of each expense before the church reimburses the expense. The information provided by the employee must be sufficient to enable the church to identify the specific nature of each reimbursed expense and to conclude that the expense is attributable to the employee's business (e.g., church-related) activities. It is not sufficient if an employee merely aggregates expenses into broad categories (such as "travel") or reports individual expenses through vague, nondescriptive terms (such as "miscellaneous business expense"). The income tax regulations specifically prohibit "accounting" to an employer by means of a taxpayer's own oral or written statements. Therefore, a minister will not adequately account to his or her church by orally informing the church treasurer of the amount of business expenses incurred during a particular month, or by signing a statement that merely recites what the minister's business expenses were. Note further that a minister's charging of business expenses to a church credit card will constitute a "reimbursement," but it does not in itself constitute an ade-

TABLE 7-4
Reporting Employee Business Expenses and Reimbursements

TYPE of reimbursement or other expense allowance arrangement	EMPLOYER Reports on Form W-2	EMPLOYEE Shows on Form 2106
ACCOUNTABLE Adequate accounting and excess returned	Not reported	Not shown
Adequate accounting and return of excess both required but excess not returned	Excess reported as wages in Box 1. Amount adequately accounted for is reported only in Box 13—it is *not* reported in Box 1.	All expenses, and reimbursements reported on Form W-2, Box 13, *only* if some or all of the unreturned excess expenses are claimed.[1] Otherwise, form is not filed.
Per diem or mileage allowance (up to federal rate) Adequate accounting and excess returned	Not reported	All expenses and reimbursements *only* if excess expenses are claimed.[1] Otherwise, form is not filed.
Per diem or mileage allowance (exceeds federal rate) Adequate accounting up to the federal rate only and excess not returned	Excess reported as wages in Box 1. Amount up to the federal rate is reported only in Box 13—it is *not* reported in Box 1.	All expenses, and reimbursements equal to the federal rate *only* if expenses in excess of the federal rate are claimed.[1] Otherwise, form is not filed.
NONACCOUNTABLE Either adequate accounting or return of excess, or both, not required	Entire amount is reported as wages in Box 1.	All expenses.[1]
No reimbursement	Normal reporting of wages, etc.	All expenses.[1]

[1] Any allowable expense is carried to line 20 of Schedule A and deducted as a miscellaneous itemized deduction.

quate "accounting" unless the minister periodically substantiates the amount, date, and business purpose of each expenditure with receipts or other written evidence.

The actual mechanics of an accountable reimbursement policy are set forth in sections 1.162-17 and 1.274-5T(f) of the income tax regulations. Section 1.162-17, which applies to all business and professional expenses *other than* transportation, travel, entertainment, and gift expenses, provides:

> The employee [or self-employed person] need not report on his tax return (either itemized or in total amount) expenses . . . paid or incurred by him solely for the benefit of his employer for which he is required to account and does account to his employer and which are charged directly or indirectly to the employer (for example, through credit cards) or for which the employee is paid through advances, reimbursements, or otherwise, provided the total amount of such advances, reimbursements, and charges is equal to such expenses. In such a case the taxpayer need only state in his return that the total of amounts charged directly or indirectly to his employer through credit cards or otherwise and received from the employer as advances or reimbursements did not exceed the ordinary and necessary business expenses paid or incurred by the employee. . . . To "account" to his employer . . . means to submit an expense account or other required written statement to the employer showing the business nature and the amount of all the employee's expenses (including those charged directly or indirectly to the employer through credit cards or otherwise) broken down into such broad categories as transportation, meals and lodging while away from home overnight, entertainment expenses, and other business expenses.

The corresponding rule with respect to transportation, travel, entertainment, and gift expenses is contained in regulation 1.274-5T(f):

> For purposes of computing tax liability, an employee [or self-employed person] need not report on his tax return business expenses for travel, transportation, entertainment, gifts, or with respect to listed property, paid or incurred by him solely for the benefit of his employer for which he is required to, and does, make an adequate accounting to his employer . . . and which are charged directly or indirectly to the employer (for example, through credit cards) or for which the employee is paid through advances, reimbursements, or otherwise, provided that the total amount of such advances, reimbursements, and charges is equal to such expenses. . . . [A]n adequate accounting means the submission to the employer of an account book, diary, log, statement of expense, trip sheet, or similar record maintained by the employee in which the information as to each element of an expenditure or use [amount, time and place, business purpose, and business relationship] is recorded at or near the time of the expenditure or use, together with supporting documentary evidence, in a manner which conforms to all the "adequate records" requirements [described in section E of this chapter]. An adequate accounting requires that the employee account for all amounts received from his employer during the taxable year

as advances, reimbursements, or allowances (including those charged directly or indirectly to the employer through credit cards or otherwise) for travel, entertainment, gifts, and the use of listed property.

Regulation 1.274-5T(f) goes on to provide that "[a]n employee who makes an adequate accounting to his employer . . . will not again be required to substantiate such expense account information," except in the following cases: (1) an employee whose business expenses exceed the total of amounts charged to his employer and amounts received through advances, reimbursements or otherwise and who claims a deduction on his return for such excess, or (2) employees in cases where it is determined that the accounting procedures used by the employer for the reporting and substantiation of expenses by such employees are not adequate, or where it cannot be determined that such procedures are adequate.

Accounting procedures will be considered inadequate to the extent that the employer does not require an adequate accounting from its employees or does not maintain such substantiation. The regulation cautions that "[t]o the extent an employer fails to maintain adequate accounting procedures it will thereby obligate its employees to substantiate separately their expense account information."

Most churches implement an accountable reimbursement plan by having the church board pass an appropriate resolution containing the requirements summarized above. A reimbursement policy should be in writing, and it should clearly specify what expenses the church will reimburse. It also should describe the documentation and reporting that will be required. The church should retain the records and receipts presented by a minister in documenting the business nature and amount of business expenses that he or she incurs (discussed more fully later). A sample resolution containing all of the most recent requirements is set forth in Illustration 7-1.

❖ **New in 1997: the IRS issued amended regulations in 1997 suggesting that the requirements for an accountable arrangement may be relaxed in the future.**

Changes in the requirements for an accountable arrangement? In 1997 the IRS amended the regulation (discussed below) that in the past has required employers to retain records and receipts submitted by employees to substantiate their expenses under an accountable arrangement. The new, amended regulation provides:

> The [IRS] Commissioner may, in his discretion, prescribe rules under which an employee may make an adequate accounting to his employer by submitting an account book, log, diary, etc., alone, without submitting documentary evidence.

This language is very important. It is saying that the IRS can issue new rules modifying the substantiation requirements for an adequate accounting by an employee to an employer under an accountable arrangement. The IRS explained this amendment as follows:

Under the amendment, the [IRS] could publish rules defining the circumstances (including the use of specified internal controls) under which an employee may make an adequate accounting to his employer by submitting an expense account alone, without the necessity of submitting documentary evidence (such as receipts). This change is expected to reduce the recordkeeping burden for employers and employees.

✎ **Key point. Why may the IRS issue rules allowing expense accounts (without supporting receipts or documentary evidence) to substantiate business expenses under an accountable arrangement? To relieve employers of the burden and cost of maintaining receipts and other documentary evidence supporting an employee's business expenses.**

✎ **Key point. The IRS has not yet issued rules permitting employees to substantiate business expenses under an accountable arrangement by submitting an expense account without any supporting receipts or documentary evidence. As soon as these rules are published, we will be addressing them in a future edition of this publication. Until they are issued, churches should continue to rely on the old rules.**

✎ **Key point. The IRS has warned that any relaxation in the substantiation requirements for accountable plans will not affect the deductibility of unreimbursed business expenses (or expenses reimbursed under a nonaccountable arrangement).**

The importance of this proposed change cannot be overstated. In the future, churches may be able to maintain an accountable business expense reimbursement arrangement by having employees submit an expense account or summary without any supporting receipts or other documentary evidence. This is a major development that we will be following closely.

☞ *Example. A church reimburses its pastor's business expenses upon receipt of an account book or log, without any receipts of other supporting documentary evidence. For 1997, the church reimbursed $4,000 of business expenses under this arrangement. Under present law, this arrangement is nonaccountable since it does not provide receipts for expenses of $75 or more. This means that the church should have reported the $4,000 as income on the pastor's W-2 for 1997. However, under the amended income tax regulations, the IRS may relax the requirements for an accountable plan. Depending on what (if anything) the IRS announces later, the church may be able to treat its reimbursement arrangement as accountable—meaning that reimbursed expenses would not be reported as income on the pastor's W-2. If the IRS does relax the rules for accountable plans, it likely will do so only if certain conditions are satisfied.*

☞ *Example. Same facts as the previous example, except that the church only reimburses those business expenses for which the pastor submits adequate documentation substantiating the amount, date, place, and business purpose of each expense. The church also requires receipts to support any individual expense of $75 or more. The pastor must substantiate expenses not later than two months after they are incurred. This is an accountable arrangement under present law, meaning that the church's reimbursements are not reported as income on the pastor's W-2. However, under the amended income tax regulations, the IRS may relax the requirements for accountable plans. Depending on what (if anything) the IRS announces later this year, the church may be able to continue to treat its reimbursement arrangement as accountable while requiring less substantiation of expenses. If the IRS does relax the rules for accountable plans, it likely will do so only if certain conditions are satisfied.*

When should employees account for their business expenses? The income tax regulations specify that under an accountable reimbursement arrangement an employee's "accounting" or substantiation of business expenses, and the return of any excess reimbursements, must occur within a **reasonable time**. The regulations state that "the determination of a reasonable period of time will depend on the facts and circumstances." However, the regulations provide the following 2 "safe harbors" that will satisfy the reasonable time requirement:

• Under the "fixed date method," business expenses will be deemed substantiated within a reasonable amount of time if done so *within 60 days* after the expenses are paid or incurred, and excess reimbursements will be deemed to have been returned to the employer within a reasonable amount of time if done so *within 120 days* after the expenses are paid or incurred.

• Under the alternative "periodic statement method," an employer gives employees a periodic statement (not less often than quarterly) setting forth the amount by which the employer's reimbursements exceed the amount of business expenses substantiated by the employee, and requesting the employee to either substantiate the difference or return it to the employer within 120 days of the statement. Expenses that are substantiated, or returned, during the 120 period satisfy the reasonable time requirement.

✎ **Key point: the regulations specify that if an employer has a plan or practice to provide amounts to employees in excess of expenses that properly substantiated and to avoid reporting and withholding on such amounts, the employer may not use either of the safe harbors for any years during which such plan or practice exists.**

Tax withholding. Churches must recognize that business expense reimbursements or allowances paid to employees must be included on the employees' W-2 forms, and are subject to income tax and FICA withholding when paid—*unless* the reimbursements are paid under an "accountable" reimbursement plan. The withholding requirements will not apply to clergy, who are exempt from tax withholding (unless they have elected voluntary withholding). Nonminister church employees will be covered by these same rules.

Expenses reimbursable under an accountable arrangement. All ordinary and necessary business and professional expenses (transportation, travel, entertainment, books, subscriptions, telephone, education, vestments, etc.) that you pay for out of your own funds can be reimbursed by your church through an accountable reimbursement arrangement. Do not limit your reimbursements to car expenses, since most ministers have a considerable amount of other business and professional expenses that they pay for out of their own funds. Churches occasionally reimburse clergy for non-business expenses. Such reimbursements, though they require an accounting, ordinarily must be included in the minister's wages for income tax reporting purposes, and they are not deductible by the minister. Such "personal, living, or family expenses" are not deductible, and the entire amount of a church's reimbursement must be included on the minister's W-2 and 1040.

Independent contractors. The income tax regulations permit independent contractors (i.e., self-employed persons) to be reimbursed for their business expenses, and such reimbursements need not be reported as income to the extent that the self-employed individual properly accounts to his or her "client or customer" for each expense that is reimbursed. Generally, the substantiation and "accounting" requirements described above for employees apply to self-employed as well. Since self-employed clergy are permitted to deduct their business expenses (whether unreimbursed or reimbursed under a nonaccountable plan) directly on Schedule C whether or not they can itemize deductions on Schedule A, there is less need for a reimbursement policy. However, an accountable reimbursement plan for self-employed persons would have the following advantages: (1) it would reduce the likelihood of additional taxes if the self-employed individual is audited by the IRS and reclassified as an employee; (2) it will reduce audit risk by permitting the individual to report to his or her church rather than to the IRS.

How churches pay for expense reimbursements. There are a variety of ways for a church to fund an accountable reimbursement plan. First, it can agree to reimburse all substantiated business expenses without limitation. Second, it can agree to reimburse substantiated expenses up to a fixed limit (e.g., $4,000 per year). Any business expenses incurred by the minister in excess of this amount would be unreimbursed. Third, prior to 1991 many churches agreed to reimburse a minister's substantiated business expenses out of his or her own compensation. This third approach was very popular since it did not "cost" the church anything. Under this approach, churches typically agreed to pay a minister's monthly business expenses out of the first weekly paycheck of the following month. Whatever was left after the substantiated expenses were reimbursed was classified as salary and reported on the minister's W-2.

Unfortunately, this rule has been repudiated by the IRS for 1991 and future years (see below).

Employer keeps employee records and receipts. Regulation 1.274-5T(f) (quoted above) specifies that a reimbursement arrangement will not satisfy the requirements of an accountable arrangement "to the extent that the employer . . . does not require an adequate accounting from its employees *or does not maintain such substantiation.* To the extent an employer fails to maintain adequate accounting procedures he will thereby obligate his employees to separately substantiate their expense account information."

According to this regulation churches and other employers are required to maintain the receipts and other records submitted by employees to substantiate their business expenses under an accountable expense reimbursement arrangement. Since employees are required to surrender their records and receipts to their employer after substantiating their business expenses, the regulations relieve employees of any further duty to produce these documents. The only exceptions to this rule are in cases where their expenses exceed their employer's reimbursements, or where it is determined that the accounting procedures used by the employer for the reporting and substantiation of expenses by employees are not adequate, or where it cannot be determined that such procedures are adequate. *Treas. Reg. 1.274-5T(f).*

In a 1963 ruling, the IRS observed that it was "studying the problems presented to employers regarding warehousing and retention of documentary evidence and intends to issue a Revenue Ruling on this matter in the near future." *Revenue Procedure 63-4.* For more than 30 years the promised ruling was delayed. Over the years, federal agencies and private employers alike have asked the IRS to provide relief from the administrative burden and cost of storing large quantities of paper receipts. Some employers asked the IRS to adopt a rule allowing employers to dispose of documentary evidence after an employee has made an adequate accounting—or return the documentary evidence to the employee for retention. Other employers asked the IRS to consider modifying the rules for accountable expense reimbursement arrangements to permit employees to substantiate their business expenses by submitting an expense voucher or summary without any receipts of documentary evidence. In 1997 the IRS responded to these concerns in the following two ways:

(1) It noted that with the increase in the receipt requirement to business expenses of $75 or more "the necessity for storing large quantities of paper records is significantly reduced."

(2) It amended the income tax regulation that in the past has required employers to retain records and receipts submitted by employees to substantiate their expenses under an accountable arrangement. The new, amended regulation is discussed above under the discussion of "adequate accounting."

Special rule for failure to return excess. The income tax regulations specify that if an employer establishes an accountable arrangement, but an employee fails to return within a reasonable period of time any reimbursements in excess of substantiated expenses, "only the amounts paid under the arrangement that are not in excess of the substantiated expenses are treated as paid under an accountable plan."

An employee cannot make a nonaccountable arrangement accountable. The regulations specify that "if a payor provides a nonaccountable plan, an employee who receives payments under the plan cannot compel the payor to treat the payments as paid under an accountable plan by voluntarily substantiating the expenses and returning any excess to the payor."

IRS Forbids Funding Accountable Reimbursements out of Salary Reductions

Section 1.62-2(d)(3) of the income tax regulations prohibits accountable plans from reimbursing employee business expenses through salary reductions. This regulation effectively put an end to a common church practice that allowed many clergy to enjoy the advantages of an accountable plan without any additional cost to the church. In the past, many churches adopted accountable plans under which a minister's substantiated business expenses were reimbursed out of his or her own salary. For example, assume that First Church pays Rev. G $500 each week, and also agrees to reimburse his substantiated business expenses for each month out of the first payroll check for the following month. Assume further that Rev. G substantiated $300 of business expenses for January. The church issued Rev. G his customary check of $500 for the first week of February, but only $200 of this check represents taxable salary while the remaining $300 represents a nontaxable reimbursement under an accountable plan. Only the $200 salary component of this check is included on Rev. G's W-2 (or 1099) form at the end of the year. This arrangement was practiced by many churches. In some cases, a church agreed to reimburse a minister's substantiated expenses up to a specified amount, with any additional expenses being reimbursed out of salary reductions.

Unfortunately, regulation 1.62-2(d)(3) prohibits this practice for accountable reimbursement plans. Such arrangements are not "illegal." They simply cannot be "accountable." Churches that continue to use this practice must recognize that all reimbursements paid through salary reduction will now be treated as paid under a nonaccountable plan. In explaining the regulation, the IRS observed:

Some practitioners have asked whether a portion of an employee's salary may be recharacterized as being paid under a reimbursement arrangement. The final regulations clarify that if [an employer] arranges to pay an amount to an employee regardless of whether the employee incurs . . . deductible business expenses . . . the arrangement does not meet the business connection requirement of [the regulations] and all amounts paid un-

der the arrangement are treated as paid under a nonaccountable plan. . . . Thus no part of an employee's salary may be recharacterized as being paid under a reimbursement arrangement or other expense allowance arrangement.

Regulation 1.62-2(d)(3) contains the following example:

Employer S pays its engineers $200 a day. On those days that an engineer travels away from home on business for Employer S, Employer S designates $50 of the $200 as paid to reimburse the engineer's travel expenses. Because Employer S would pay an engineer $200 a day regardless of whether the engineer was traveling away from home, the arrangement does not satisfy the reimbursement requirement of [the regulations]. Thus, no part of the $50 Employer S designated as a reimbursement is treated as paid under an accountable plan. Rather, all payments under the arrangement are treated as paid under a nonaccountable plan. Employer S must report the entire $200 as wages or other compensation on the employees' Forms W-2 and must withhold and pay employment taxes on the entire $200 when paid.

Regulation 1.62-2(d)(3) came as an unpleasant shock to many clergy, both because it conflicted with a very common practice among nonprofit and for-profit employers, and also because there was no advance warning whatever that the IRS was considering such a rule. Your editor contacted the IRS national office on numerous occasions, seeking clarification of the IRS position. The IRS responded in writing, confirming that the regulation prohibits churches from using salary reductions to fund business expense reimbursements under accountable reimbursement arrangements. In explaining its interpretation, the IRS noted that the tax benefits available to accountable reimbursement arrangements (i.e., the employer's reimbursements are not reportable as income to the employee) are based on the fact that the reimbursements are coming out of the employer's revenue and accordingly it "has an incentive to require sufficient substantiation to ensure that the allowance to the employee is limited to actual business expenditures incurred on the employer's behalf and for the employer's benefit." This justification simply does not apply when an employee's business expenses are reimbursed out of his or her own salary (through salary reductions). The IRS gave the following example:

For example, assume that an employee working for Corporation A is paid $40,000, designated as salary, and is not entitled to any additional amount under a nonaccountable plan. If the employee decides to incur $2,000 in employee business expenses, that amount is deductible only as a miscellaneous itemized deduction, subject to the two-percent floor. By contrast, assume that an employee working for Corporation B is paid $37,000, designated as salary, and is given an additional $4,000 for the year, designated as an expense allowance pursuant to a nonaccountable plan. Under the arrangement the employee may retain any part of the $3,000 whether or not the employee substantiates to the employer, regardless of the amount of employee business expenses. . . .

[T]here is no justification for different tax treatment of these two employees who receive (and are allowed to retain) identical dollar amounts from their employers and who make identical employee business expenditures.

The IRS concluded:

A salary reduction arrangement which "reimburses" an employee for employee business expenses by reducing the employee's salary will not be treated as an accountable plan because it does not meet the reimbursement requirement. This is the result regardless of whether a specific portion of the employee's compensation is designated for employee expenses . . . or the portion of the compensation to be treated as the expense allowance varies from pay period to pay period depending on the employee's expenses. As long as the employee is entitled to receive the full amount of annual compensation regardless of whether or not any employee business expenses are incurred during the taxable year, the arrangement does not meet the reimbursement requirement.

What is the effect of the regulation? Consider the following:

1. Regulation 1.62-2(d)(3), as interpreted by the IRS, will result in harsh tax treatment for clergy who report their income taxes as employees and who have unreimbursed business expenses or expenses reimbursed under a nonaccountable arrangement. Perhaps the most common type of nonaccountable arrangement is the monthly car allowance. It is imperative for churches that require clergy to pay for their own business expenses, or that pay clergy a monthly allowance (or otherwise reimburse expenses without proper substantiation) to consider seriously the adoption of an accountable reimbursement arrangement.

2. The harsh limitations on the deductibility of an employee's unreimbursed and nonaccountable reimbursed expenses are not avoided by classifying a minister as self-employed. Most clergy who report their income taxes as self-employed would be reclassified as employees by the IRS if audited and their reporting status questioned.

3. Can the restrictive regulation be avoided by proper drafting of a minister's compensation package? To illustrate, let's assume that First Church and Rev. K are discussing compensation for the next year, and that the church board proposes to pay Rev. K $30,000. However, since it will require Rev. K to pay his own business expenses, the church board decides to pay Rev. K a salary of $26,000, and establish a separate church account for $4,000 out of which substantiated business expenses will be reimbursed. At the end of the year, *any balance remaining in the reimbursement account would belong to the church, not Rev. K* (i.e., it would not be distributed to Rev. K as a "bonus" or as additional compensation). Since Rev. K has no right to any of the reimbursement account funds ($4,000) unless he adequately substantiates his business expenses, this arrangement should be permissible under the regulation. The church has not "agreed to pay an amount

to an employee regardless of whether the employee incurs deductible business expenses." Unfortunately, the IRS disagreed with this conclusion in a 1993 private letter ruling. The IRS was asked if the following arrangement could be considered to be accountable:

Company X proposes to modify the district manager's compensation arrangement to allow each district manager to elect on an annual basis and prior to the beginning of each calendar year to reduce the amount of gross commission payable to him for the upcoming calendar year. Under the arrangement, the district manager may elect to reduce his gross commissions by a percentage ranging from 0 to 40%. In exchange for the reduction in commissions, Company X will pay the district manager's business expenses for the calendar year up to a maximum amount equal to the amount by which the district manager elected to reduce his commissions. Company X will pay only for expenses that satisfy the business connection and substantiation requirements of . . . the income tax regulations. If the expenses a district manager incurs in a calendar year are less than the amount by which the gross commissions were reduced, the excess amounts will be forfeited and may not be carried over and used for expenses incurred in the next calendar year.

The IRS, in concluding that such an arrangement is not accountable, observed:

[A]n employer may not recharacterize a portion of an employee's salary as being paid under a reimbursement arrangement or other expense allowance arrangement. . . . [I]n order to have an accountable plan, section 62(c) of the Code and the regulations thereunder contemplate that the reimbursement or other expense allowance arrangement provided by an employer should be amounts paid to an employee in addition to salary. This conclusion is supported by the preamble to the final regulations . . . which provides that no part of an employee's salary may be recharacterized as being paid under a reimbursement arrangement or other expense allowance arrangement. *IRS Letter Ruling 9325023.*

✎ **Key Point: The IRS ruled in 1993 that a regulation prohibiting the funding of business expense reimbursements under accountable plans may not be avoided by "salary restructuring" agreements.**

Based on this most recent precedent, the best approach is for churches to adopt accountable reimbursement policies that reimburse clergy (and other church workers) out of church funds. Churches that are concerned with unlimited reimbursement arrangements can set a maximum amount that will be reimbursed per employee. A more aggressive approach would be for a church to designate a minister's salary and then set up a business expense reimbursement account in two separate actions, without any indication that the reimbursement account is being funded out of what otherwise would be the minister's salary. The IRS may view these separate actions as sufficiently unrelated to be consistent with an accountable reimbursement arrangement. There certainly is no guarantee that this approach will work, since the IRS may conclude that it constitutes a "restructuring" of the minister's salary and as such is incompatible with an accountable plan.

✎ **Key point: the IRS issued audit guidelines for its agents to follow when auditing ministers. The guidelines inform agents that if a church has a salary reduction arrangement which "reimburses" a minister for employee business expenses by reducing his or her salary, the arrangement will be treated as a nonaccountable plan. This is the result "regardless of whether a specific portion of the minister's compensation is designated for employee expenses or whether the portion of the compensation to be treated as the expense allowance varies from pay period to pay period depending on the minister's expenses. As long as the minister is entitled to receive the full amount of annual compensation, regardless of whether or not any employee business expenses are incurred during the taxable year, the arrangement does not meet the reimbursement requirement."**

⟲ Observation. The guidelines instruct IRS agents to be alert to salary reduction arrangements that are used to fund reimbursements under an "accountable" arrangement. According to the IRS, accountable plans cannot reimburse employee business expenses out of salary reductions. The important point is this—the guidelines are educating IRS agents as to this issue, and so it is now far more likely that salary restructuring and salary reduction arrangements will be discovered and questioned in an audit.

Sample Reimbursement Policy

The accountable reimbursement policy reproduced as Illustration 7-1 may have to be modified to fit your situation. For example, your church may issue you a credit card in the name of the church and request that you charge all employee business expenses to the card. The policy would not fit such a situation without some modification. Further, your church may agree to reimburse your business and professional expenses only up to a designated limit. Obviously, such a limitation should be clarified in the resolution. You also may want to specify that business use of a car will be reimbursed at the standard mileage rate "currently allowed by the IRS." Also, you can easily adapt the policy to cover non-clergy employees.

The reimbursement policy set forth in Illustration 7-1 can apply to clergy who are either employees or self-employed. *Treas. Reg. 1.274-5T(f)(6)(c).* However, as noted previously (see chapter 2), the reimbursement of business expenses is one of many factors to consider in deciding whether a particular worker is an employee rather than a self-employed person under the IRS 20 factor test (it suggests the individual is an employee).

Examples Illustrating Business Expense Reimbursements

These rules are summarized in Table 7-4, and illustrated in following examples.

nonaccountable arrangements

☞ *Example. Assume that Rev. B is senior minister at First Church, and that his church reimburses him for all of his business and professional expenses (by means of a credit card or cash reimbursements). However, Rev. B is not required to account for such expenses by providing the church treasurer with receipts documenting the amount, time and place, business purpose, and business relationship of each expense. Rev. B simply informs the treasurer at the end of each month of the total expenses incurred during that month. Assume further that Rev. B cannot itemize deductions on Schedule A (he does not have sufficient deductions), and that he is an employee for income tax reporting purposes. If Rev. B receives reimbursements of $4,000 in 1997: (1) the church would report the entire reimbursements ($4,000) as income on Rev. B's W-2, and Rev. B would report them as income (salary) on his Form 1040; (2) Rev. B cannot deduct the reimbursed expenses as adjustments to gross income (on Form 1040), since they are "nonaccountable" (i.e., he did not adequately account to the church for such expenses); (3) Rev. B cannot deduct the reimbursed expenses as a miscellaneous itemized deduction on Schedule A since he does not have sufficient expenses to itemize. In other words, all of Rev. B's business expense reimbursements are includable in his income for tax purposes, but he cannot offset any of this income by deducting any portion of his business expenses. Even if Rev. B could itemize deductions, his nonaccountable reimbursed expenses would be treated just like unreimbursed expenses—they are deductible only as miscellaneous itemized deductions, and then only to the extent that they (along with most other miscellaneous expenses) exceed 2% of Rev. B's adjusted gross income. Clearly, the tax impact of these reimbursement rules on many clergy will be disastrous if they do not account to their employing church for their business expenses. These rules make it absolutely essential for churches to adopt reimbursement policies that allow reimbursements of only those business and professional expenses for which a minister (or any other church employee) provides an adequate accounting. To illustrate, if First Church adopted an accountable reimbursement plan, and Rev. B was reimbursed for $4,000 of substantiated expenses, then the church would not report the $4,000 of reimbursements as income on Rev. B's W-2, and Rev. B would not have to report the reimbursements or claim the expenses on his Form 1040.*

☞ *Example. Same facts as the previous example, except that Rev. B is self-employed for income tax reporting purposes. The proper way to report* this arrangement would be as follows: (1) the church reports all of the reimbursements ($4,000) as income on Rev. B's 1099 form; (2) Rev. B includes the total reimbursements ($4,000) as compensation on his Schedule C (Form 1040); (3) Rev. B deducts his business expenses on Schedule C (whether or not he can itemize deductions no Schedule A, and not subject to the 2% floor). However, his Schedule C deductions are subject to the Deason rule (discussed below) and the limitation on business meals and entertainment expenses (only 50% are deductible).

☞ **Example.** In 1997, Rev. W incurred $3,500 in church related business expenses. He informed the church of this amount and received a full reimbursement. However, he did not document the business nature or amount of any of his expenses. The proper way to report this arrangement in 1997, assuming that Rev. W is an employee for income tax reporting purposes, is as follows: (1) the church reports all of the reimbursements ($3,500) as income on Rev. W's W-2 form; (2) Rev. W includes the total allowances ($3,500) as salary on his Form 1040; (3) Rev. W deducts the expenses on Schedule A as a miscellaneous itemized deduction (if he is able to use Schedule A, and then only to the extent that such expenses exceed 2% of adjusted gross income).

☞ **Example.** Same facts as the preceding example, except that Rev. W report his income taxes as a self-employed person. The proper way to report this arrangement would be as follows: (1) the church reports all of the reimbursements ($3,500) as income on Rev. W's 1099 form; (2) Rev. W includes the total allowances ($3,500) as compensation on his Schedule C (Form 1040); (3) Rev. W deducts the expenses on Schedule C (whether or not he can itemize deductions no Schedule A, and not subject to the 2% floor).

☞ **Example.** Rev. C brings all of his 1997 business expense receipts and records to the church treasurer on December 31, 1997, and adequately substantiates $4,150 of expenses. The church treasurer issues Rev. C a check for this amount. This is not an accountable plan since expenses are not substantiated within 60 days. Therefore, the church must report the $4,150 as income on Rev. C's W-2 (or 1099). If Rev. C reports his income taxes as an employee (or as self-employed, but is reclassified as an employee by the IRS in an audit), he may deduct his expenses only as miscellaneous itemized deductions on Schedule A, and then only to the extent that these expenses exceed 2% of adjusted gross income. If Rev. C is self-employed for income tax purposes, he may deduct his expenses on Schedule C—subject to the Deason rule and the limitation on business meals and entertainment expenses (only 50% are deductible).

expenses not reimbursed by the church

☞ **Example.** In 1997, Rev. D incurred $3,500 in church related business expenses. His church expected him to pay such expenses out of his salary and accordingly did not reimburse him for these expenses or pay him an allowance. Assuming that the IRS would regard Rev. D as an employee for income tax reporting purposes, he can deduct his business expenses only as a miscellaneous expense on Schedule A—if he itemizes his expenses and then only to the extent that they, together with most other miscellaneous expenses, exceed 2% of adjusted gross income. Because of the adverse tax impact of this method, churches should be discouraged from using it. A much better method is the adoption of an accountable reimbursement plan that requires periodic accounting of reimbursed expenses by the minister, as described above. It can cost the church nothing, yet may result in significant tax savings to the minister.

☞ **Example.** Rev. L reports his income taxes as a self-employed person. He has $2,000 of business expenses in 1997 that were not reimbursed by his church. He deducted all of them on Schedule C. He did not have enough expenses to itemize deductions on Schedule A. Rev. L is later audited by the IRS, and he is reclassified as an employee. He will not be able to deduct any of the $2,000 of business expenses since they are deductible, by an employee, only as an itemized deduction on Schedule A (this assumes that he does not have sufficient expenses to itemize on Schedule A even with the business expenses). However, all of the reimbursements ($2,000) must be reported as taxable income. This harsh result can be avoided if the church adopts an accountable reimbursement plan (see section D of this chapter for full details). This example illustrates one of the reasons why the IRS is focusing on self-employed taxpayers.

credit cards

☞ **Example.** Rev. G is senior minister of his church. The church reimburses him for all of his business expenses by means of a credit card (in the church's name). However, Rev. G is not required to account for such expenses by providing the church treasurer with receipts documenting the amount, time, place, business purpose (and, in the case of entertainment expenses, the business relationship) of each expense. Rev. G simply informs the treasurer at the end of each month of the total expenses incurred during that month. Assume further that Rev. G cannot itemize deductions on Schedule A (he does not have sufficient deductions), and that he is an employee for income tax reporting purposes. If Rev. G receives reimbursements of $4,000 in 1997: (1) the church would report the entire reimbursements ($4,000) as income on Rev. G's W-2, and Rev. G would report them as income (salary) on his Form 1040; (2) Rev. G cannot deduct the reimbursed expenses as adjustments to gross income (on Form 1040), since they are "nonaccountable" (i.e., he did not adequately account to the church for such expenses); (3) Rev. G cannot deduct the reimbursed expenses as a miscellaneous itemized deduction on Schedule A since he does not have sufficient expenses to itemize. In other words, all of Rev. G's business expense reimbursements are includable in his income for tax purposes, but he cannot offset any of this income by deducting any portion of his business expenses. Even if Rev. G could itemize deductions, his nonaccountable reimbursed expenses would be treated just like unreimbursed expenses—they are deductible only as miscellaneous itemized deductions, and then only to the extent that they (along with most other miscellaneous expenses) exceed 2 percent of Rev. G's adjusted gross income. These undesirable tax consequences could have been avoided had the church adopted an accountable reimbursement plan. Under these circumstances, the church would not have reported the $4,000 of reimbursements as income on Rev. G's W-2, and Rev. G would not have to report the reimbursements or claim the expenses on his Form 1040.

 Example. Rev. C is a minister at First Church. Rev. C has a church credit card on which he charges all church-related business expenses. Each month, Rev. C submits a statement of all charges to the church treasurer along with supporting receipts, documenting the amount, date, place, business relationship, and business nature of each expense. This is a proper reimbursement policy, and as a result Rev. C need not report any of the charges as income and he need not deduct any expenses, and the church need not report any of the reimbursements as compensation on Rev. C's W-2.

accountable arrangements

 Example. Rev. G is a minister at First Church. He is given a monthly allowance of $200 for business expenses. However, he is required to account for all business expenses incurred each month, and is only given credit for those expenses that are sufficiently documented (as to amount, time and place, business purpose, and business relationship) by adequate records that they would support a deduction on his income tax return. The proper reporting of this arrangement depends on whether or not Rev. G is required to return excess reimbursements to the church. If he is—and this requirement is stated in the church's written reimbursement policy, and the excess reimbursements must be returned within 120 days of the associated expensed—then the allowances need not be reported on Rev. G's W-2 (or 1099) or Form 1040, and they need not be deducted. If on the other hand Rev. G is not required to return excess reimbursements (the amount by which his allowances exceed his substantiated expenses), the plan is a "nonaccountable" one. The result is that the allowances must be reported as income on Rev. G's W-2 (or

1099) and Form 1040, and the deductibility of his business expenses will depend on whether the IRS would view him as an employee or as self-employed. If he is an employee for income tax reporting purposes, then he may deduct his expenses as miscellaneous itemized deductions on Schedule A (if he is able to itemize deductions, and subject to the 2% floor). If he is self-employed, then he may deduct his expenses on Schedule C.

car allowances

 Example. Rev. H is a minister at First Church. She is given a monthly "car allowance" of $300, and is not required to substantiate the business purpose or amount of any of her business expenses. This is a classic example of a "nonaccountable" reimbursement arrangement—the church is reimbursing business expenses without requiring the necessary substantiation. If Rev. H reports her income taxes as an employee (or as self-employed, but is reclassified as an employee by the IRS in an audit), the following reporting requirements apply: (1) the church must report all of the monthly allowances ($3,600) on Rev. H's W-2 form; (2) Rev. H must report all of the monthly allowances ($3,600) as income on her Form 1040; (3) Rev. H can deduct her actual expenses only as a miscellaneous itemized deduction on Schedule A (if she has sufficient itemized expenses to use Schedule A), and then only to the extent that such expenses exceed 2% of adjusted gross income.

salary reduction arrangements

 Example. First Church agreed to pay its minister, Rev. P, an annual salary for 1997 of $26,000, payable in weekly checks of $500. On February 1, 1997, Rev. P "accounts" to the church treasurer for $300 of business and professional expenses that he incurred in the performance of his ministry in January of 1997. Rev. P receives two checks for the first week in February—a check in the amount of $300 reimbursing him for the business and professional expenses that he accounted for, and a paycheck in the amount of $200. His weekly compensation remains $500, but $300 of this amount constitutes a business expense reimbursement. The same procedure is followed for every other month during the year. Because of the income tax regulation discussed in this chapter, this arrangement will constitute a nonaccountable plan in 1997 and future years. As a result: (1) Rev. P's W-2 (or 1099) for 1997 must include the full salary of $26,000; (2) Rev. P must report $26,000 as income on his Form 1040; (3) if Rev. P reports his income taxes as an employee (or as self-employed but is reclassified as an employee by the IRS in an audit) he can deduct his business expenses only as miscellaneous itemized deductions on Schedule A, to the extent they exceed 2% of adjusted gross income. The key point is this—accountable reimbursement arrangements no longer can fund business expense reimbursements out of an employee's salary.

This is perhaps the most unfortunate aspect of the regulations, since it will adversely affect the reimbursement arrangements of many churches. It is possible to avoid this restriction through an appropriate compensation package (as explained above).

mileage allowances

☞ **Example.** First Church adopts an accountable reimbursement arrangement for 1997, but it agrees to reimburse business miles at 37 cents per mile. Rev. S properly substantiates all of his business expenses for the year, including 7,000 miles that he drove his car for business use. The IRS approved standard mileage rate for 1997 is 31.5 cents per mile. The church does not require Rev. S to return to the church the amount by which his reimbursements exceed the IRS approved rate. The fact that the church reimburses Rev. S for his business miles at a rate in excess of the IRS approved rate will not render the church's entire reimbursement arrangement "nonaccountable." Rather, only the amount by which the church's reimbursement rate exceeds the IRS rate (6 cents per mile) is treated as nonaccountable. As a result, the church should add $385 (7,000 miles x 5.5 cents) to Rev. S's W-2 (or 1099), and Rev. S should report this amount as income on his Form 1040. The excess cannot be claimed as a deduction since it exceeds the IRS approved rate.

☞ **Example.** The IRS issued a ruling denying "accountable" status to an employer's reimbursements of employee business expenses. The employer reimbursed certain employees' business miles at a specified "per diem" (daily) rate or the standard mileage rate, whichever was greater. Odometer readings were not required on the employees' claim forms. The integrity of the claim was the responsibility of the employee. The IRS ruled that these employees were not reimbursed under an accountable arrangement. As a result, all of the employer's reimbursements of these expenses had to be reported as additional income on the employees' W-2 forms. The IRS observed: "To meet the substantiation requirement . . . of the regulations for passenger automobiles, an arrangement must require the submission of information sufficient to [demonstrate the amount, date, and business purpose of each reimbursed expense]. The supervisors auto arrangement does not require the submission of mileage records and, thus, does not meet the applicable substantiation requirements. In addition, the automobile arrangement provides for reimbursements at the rate of the greater of [a daily rate] or the applicable cents-per-mile rate without requiring the return of amounts in excess of actual or deemed substantiated expenses. Accordingly, the supervisors auto arrangement does not meet the substantiation or return of excess requirements of . . . the regulations. Therefore, the supervisors auto arrangement is a nonaccountable plan." IRS Letter Ruling 9547001.

☞ **Example.** A church pays a nonminister employee a mileage allowance at a rate of 35 cents per mile in 1997 (when the standard mileage rate is 31.5 cents per mile) to cover automobile business expenses. The church does not require the return of the portion of the mileage allowance (4 cents) that exceeds the standard mileage rate. In June, the employer advanced a nonminister employee $175 for 500 miles to be traveled by the employee during the month. In July, the employee substantiated to the church 500 business miles traveled. The amount deemed substantiated by the employee is $157.50 (500 miles x 31.5 cents per mile). The employee is not required to return the remaining $17.50 of the advance. No later than the first payroll period following the payroll period in which the business miles traveled are substantiated, the church must withhold and pay employment taxes on $17.50 (500 miles x 3.5 cents per mile). IRS Announcement 90-127.

failure to seek reimbursement of expenses

☞ **Example.** Reimbursement arrangements sometimes create an unexpected problem—employees cannot claim a deduction for business expenses for which they did not seek reimbursement. To illustrate, in one case a federal court refused to allow a taxpayer to claim a business expense deduction for several business expenses that could have been reimbursed under his employer's expense reimbursement arrangement. What is the rationale for this rule? A business expense, to be deductible, must be "ordinary and necessary." If an employee voluntarily chooses not to seek reimbursement for an expense from an employer, the presumption is that the expense was not "necessary." In re Williams, 95-2 USTC ¶50,349 (D. Ind. 1995).

cash allowances

☞ **Example.** First Church provides its minister, Rev. M, with a cash advance of $1,500 to attend a church convention. Rev. M's actual expenses in attending the convention were $1,200. He is not required to substantiate his expenses or return any excess reimbursement. This is a nonaccountable plan, meaning that the church must report the full $1,500 as income on Rev. M's W-2 (or 1099), and Rev. M must report the $1,500 as income on his Form 1040. Whether or not he can deduct any of his expenses depends on whether he is an employee or self-employed for income tax purposes (as explained above).

☞ **Example.** Same facts as the previous example, except that Rev. M is required to substantiate his expenses within 60 days after the convention and return excess reimbursements to the church. However, he is not required to return excess reimbursements within 120 days. Rev. M substantiates $1,200 of expenses, and fails to return the excess $300 within 120 days. According to the income tax regulations, only the $300 excess re-

imbursement is treated as paid under a nonaccountable plan, so only $300 (and not $1,500) is reported as income on Rev. M's W-2 (or 1099), and on his Form 1040.

E. Business and Professional Expenses—Substantiation and Recordkeeping Requirements

✎ **Key point: business expenses must be substantiated by adequate evidence in order to support an income tax deduction or an expense reimbursement under an accountable reimbursement plan of an employer. Stricter substantiation rules apply to transportation, travel, and entertainment expenses.**

It is absolutely essential that you retain records that will substantiate your business and professional expense deductions (and reimbursements). Section 274D of the Code (and the accompanying regulations) provide that no deduction for local business transportation, overnight travel (including meals and lodging), entertainment, or gift expenses will be allowed unless a taxpayer can substantiate the information summarized in Table 7-5.

You must be able to substantiate each of the elements mentioned above by *adequate records* or by *sufficient evidence corroborating your own statement*. For other business and professional expenses (other than those discussed above), you should be able to substantiate the amount, time (and place, if relevant), and business purpose of each expenditure. These requirements are discussed below.

Note that these requirements must be satisfied to adequately substantiate a deduction on your tax return, or an employer reimbursement of a business expense under an accountable business expense reimbursement arrangement (as explained in the preceding section).

adequate records

To meet the "adequate records" requirement, you must maintain an account book, diary, statement of expense or similar *written record*, that is maintained in such a way that each expense is recorded at or near the time the expense is incurred. A contemporaneous log (made at the time of each expense or use) is not required, but you should prepare and maintain the account book or similar record at or near the time of the expense while you can still remember it accurately. You ordinarily do not have to record information that duplicates information shown on a receipt. See Illustration 7-2 (end of chapter) for an example of a business mileage log prepared by the IRS (for illustrative purposes). The regulations specify that "documentary evidence, such as receipts, paid bills, or similar evidence sufficient to support an expenditure shall be required for . . . any expenditure of [$75] or more . . . ." *Treas. Reg. 1.274-5T(c)(2)(iii).*

An adequate record contains sufficient information for each element of every business use. The level of detail required to substantiate the use may vary depending on the facts and circumstances. For example, if one business use of your car is to make visits to a local hospital on an established route, you may satisfy the requirements by recording the length of the route once, and the date of each trip at or near the time of the trips. Or, you may establish the date of each trip with a receipt, record of a visit, or other documentary evidence.

✎ **Key point: From 1962 until October 1, 1995, taxpayers needed a receipt to substantiate most business expenses of $25 or more. In 1995 the IRS increased this amount from $25 to $75, effective October 1, 1995. Taxpayers must have sufficient documentary evidence to substantiate the amount, date, place, and business purpose of most business expenses, but they will not need a receipt for any individual expense of less than $75.**

Receipts. A receipt is ordinarily the best evidence to prove the amount of an expense. A receipt, paid bill, or other documentary evidence sufficient to substantiate an expense is required for any expense of $75 or more. A canceled check together with a bill from the payee will establish the cost. However, a canceled check alone does not prove a business expense without other evidence to show that it was for a business purpose. Some written statement of the business purpose of an expense is generally required. However, the degree of substantiation necessary to establish a business purpose will vary depending on the circumstances. For example, if the business purpose of an expenditure is evident from the surrounding facts and circumstances, a written explanation of such business purpose ordinarily is not required.

Estimating expenses. Under the so-called *Cohan* rule, if you do not have adequate records to substantiate an expense you may do so by (1) your own statement (written or oral) containing specific details, *and* (2) other supporting evidence. Under this rule, if the evidence indicates that a taxpayer incurred deductible business expenses but the exact amount of those expense cannot be determined, a court can make an approximation and not disallow the expenses entirely. The *Cohan* rule is not applied to the substantiation of transportation, travel, entertainment, and gift expenses under section 274 of the Code. Section 274 and the accompanying regulations directly overruled the *Cohan* rule by providing that no deduction is available for transportation, travel, entertainment, and gift expenses on the basis of approximations or unsupported testimony of the taxpayer.

You may prove an expense by reconstructing your expenses if you cannot produce a receipt for reasons beyond your control, such as fire, flood, or other casualty.

✎ **Key point: the IRS has prepared a sample expense record for use by taxpayers (it is not an "official form," however). It is reproduced as Illustration 7-3 at the end of this chapter.**

Sampling. You may maintain an adequate record for parts of a year and use that record to substantiate the amount of business expense for the entire year if you can demonstrate by other evidence that the periods for which an adequate record is kept are representative of your expenses throughout the entire year. The income tax regulations specify that "a taxpayer may maintain an adequate record for portions of a taxable year and use that record to substantiate the business use of listed property [such as a car] for all or a portion of the taxable year if the taxpayer can demonstrate by other evidence that the periods for which an adequate record is maintained are representative of the use for the taxable year or a portion thereof." *Treas. Reg. 1.274-5T(c)(3)(ii)(A).*

☞ *Example. Rev. M uses his car for local business transportation to visit members and make hospital calls. The car is also used by Rev. M and his family for personal purposes. Rev. M maintains adequate records during the first week of each month that show that 75% of the use of the car is for business. Invoices and bills show that business use of the car continued at the same rate during the later weeks of each month. Such weekly records are representative of the use of the car each month and are sufficient evidence to support the percentage of business use for the year. Treas. Reg. 1.274-5T(c)(3)(ii)(A).*

Standard mileage rate. There are two special rules for substantiating the amount of business expenses that should be considered, since they will be much easier to follow in many cases than accumulating receipts of actual expenses. These two special rules are the standard mileage rate for computing the amount of the business use of a car, and the "per diem rates" for determining the amount of travel expenses. You can account to your employer for the *amount* of your car expenses by documenting the business nature of your monthly mileage (or any other accounting period) and then multiplying business miles times the standard mileage rate (for 1997, 31.5 cents for all business miles driven during the year). *Revenue Ruling 84-127.* Alternatively, you can account for all of your actual expenses in the manner described in section C, above. In Revenue Ruling 87-93, the IRS announced that:

If an employer grants an allowance not exceeding [the standard mileage rate (31.5 cents a mile for all business miles in 1997)] to an employee for ordinary and necessary transportation expenses not involving travel away from home, such an arrangement will be considered to be an accounting to the employer . . . . However, an employer may grant an additional allowance for the parking fees and tolls attributable to the traveling and transportation expenses as separate items.

Per diem rates. The IRS allows taxpayers to substantiate the *amount* of their meals and lodging expenses by using "per diem" (daily) rates. *Revenue Procedure 89-67, Revenue Procedure 96-28.* In some cases using the per diem rates will simplify the

TABLE 7-5

Element to be proved (1)	Expense			
	Travel (2)	Entertainment (3)	Gift (4)	Transportation (car) (5)
Amount	Amount of each separate expense for travel, lodging, and meals. Incidental expenses may be totaled in reasonable categories, such as taxis, daily meals for traveler, etc.	Amount of each separate expense. Incidental expenses such as taxis, telephones, etc., may be totaled on a daily basis.	Cost of gift.	1) Amount of each separate expense including cost of the car, 2) Mileage for each business use of the car, and 3) Total miles for the tax year.
Time	Date you left and returned for each trip, and number of days for business.	Date of entertainment. For meals or entertainment directly before or after a business discussion, the date and duration of the business discussion.	Date of gift.	Date of the expense or use.
Place	Name of city or other designation.	Name and address or location of place of entertainment. Type of entertainment if not otherwise apparent. Place where business discussion was held if entertainment is directly before or after a business discussion.	Not applicable.	Name of city or other designation if applicable.
Description	Not applicable.	Not applicable.	Description of gift.	Not applicable.
Business Purpose	Business reason for travel or the business benefit gained or expected to be gained.	Business reason or the business benefit gained or expected to be gained. Nature of business discussion or activity.	Business reason for giving the gift or the business benefit gained or expected to be gained.	Business reason for the expense or use of the car.
Business Relationship	Not applicable.	Occupations or other information—such as names or other designations—about persons entertained that shows their business relationship to you. If all people entertained did not take part in business discussion, identify those who did. You must also prove that you or your employee was present if entertainment was a business meal.	Occupation or other information—such as name or other designation—about recipient that shows his or her business relationship to you.	Not applicable.

substantiation of meals and lodging expenses incurred while engaged in business travel. However, in recent years use of the per diem rates has become more complex. There is no doubt that many employers will discontinue using an increasingly complex process that was intended to make things easier. There are a number of points to keep in mind when considering the use of the per diem rates:

• the per diem rates are paid by the employer for expenses incurred (or which the employer reasonably believes will be incurred) by employees for travel away from home in the performance of their job

• there are per diem rates that apply to meals and incidental expenses only (M & IE), and to lodging plus meals and incidental expenses (lodging plus M & IE)—they are discussed below

• incidental expenses include, but are not limited to, expenses for laundry, cleaning and pressing of clothing, and fees and tips for services, such as for waiters and baggage handlers (it does not include taxicab fares or the costs of telegrams or telephone calls)

• the per diem rates can be used to substantiate the amount of meals and lodging expenses reimbursed by an employer only if the employer has adopted an *accountable reimbursement plan*

• persons who are self-employed for income tax reporting purposes may only use the per diem rates for meals (not lodging)

• the per diem rates only satisfy the substantiation requirements as to the *amount* of meals or lodging expenses—the employee still must substantiate the date, place, and business purpose of the expenses

• an employee who is reimbursed at a per diem rate for days of substantiated business travel, and who actually spends less than this amount, is not required to return the "excess reimbursement" to the employer (and failure to do so will not affect the "accountability" of the employer's reimbursement plan)

• use of the per diem rates is not mandatory—you can always deduct your actual expenses if you have adequate records

• if an employer pays an employee a per diem allowance that exceeds the federal or IRS rates described below, then only the excess is treated as a nonaccountable reimbursement (the reimbursements will be deemed to have been made under an accountable plan up to the amount of the federal or IRS per diem rates)

• the meal per diem rate can be used only if the employer pays the cost of the employee's lodging directly, or reasonably believes the employee will not incur any lodging costs

• employees who incur unreimbursed meals and incidental expenses can use the per diem rates for meals and incidental expenses to compute their business expense deduction on Schedule A; and this deduction is subject to the 50% reduction of meal and entertainment expenses as well as the 2% floor on the deductibility of miscellaneous itemized deductions

• self-employed persons who incur unreimbursed meals and incidental expenses can use the per diem rates for meals and incidental expenses to compute their business expense deduction on Schedule C; and this deduction is subject to the 50% reduction of meal and entertainment expenses

The meal per diem rates, and the lodging and meal rates, are summarized below:

Meals and incidental expenses (M & IE)

An employer that has adopted an accountable reimbursement plan can permit employees to substantiate the amount of their meal and incidental expenses incurred during business travel by using a per diem allowance. Incidental expenses include expenses for laundry and gratuities. The term does not include taxi fares or telephone calls. An employer uses the meals and incidental expense per diem rules when it pays an employee's lodging expenses directly, pays an employee the actual cost of lodging, or assumes that no lodging expenses will be incurred on a trip (for example, an employee will stay with friends).

The allowance must not exceed the lesser of the employer's actual per diem allowance or the per diem rate for federal travel in the continental United States (CONUS). The standard federal per diem rate for meals and incidental expenses for 1997 is $32 for most areas of the United States. Some locations are designated by the IRS as high-cost areas qualifying for higher standard meal allowances. For a listing of high-cost localities with the applicable per diem rates, see the current edition of IRS Publication 463.

Table 7-6: Per Diem Rates

Locality (destination) of overnight travel	Lodging per diem rate	Meals & incidental expense per diem rate	maximum per diem rate
high-cost localities*	$126	$40	$166
all other localities	$77	$32	$109

* note that the high-cost localities for the M & IE rate are not the same as the high-cost localities for the "lodging and M & IE" rate

The M & IE rate must be prorated if an employee travels for less than an entire day. Generally, you may use one-fourth the federal rate for each 6-hour segment of a day that you are traveling away from home in connection with your job.

☞ *Example. A church provides Rev. B with an advance per diem allowance for meal and incidental expenses of $200, based on 5 days of business travel at $40 per day to a locality for which the federal M & IE rate is $34 (the church pays lodging expenses directly). Rev. B is not required to return the portion of the allowance ($30) that exceeds the amount of the allowance deemed substantiated under the federal rate. However, the $30 excess must be treated as paid under a nonaccountable plan. Rev. B must report this amount as taxable income.*

☞ *Example. Rev. H makes an out-of-town business trip and pays her own expenses. Rev. H must keep receipts to prove the amount, date, place, and business nature of her meals expenses. She can claim the standard meal allowance for her destination city as a business expense in computing her taxes. However, she is subject to the 50% limit on business meals and entertainment expenses, as well as the 2% floor (miscellaneous business expenses are deductible by an employee only to the extent they exceed 2% of adjusted gross income).*

✎ **Key point: the IRS states in Publication 463: "You can use the standard meal allowance whether or not you are reimbursed for your traveling expenses. However, if you are not reimbursed for meal expenses, you can deduct only 50% of the standard meal allowance."**

✎ **Key point: four different per diem rates for meals and incidental expenses apply in 1997—a standard rate and three rates for "high-cost" localities.**

Lodging plus meals and incidental expenses (lodging plus M & IE)

An employer that has adopted an accountable reimbursement plan can permit employees to substantiate the amount of their lodging, meal and incidental expenses incurred during business travel by using a per diem allowance. If the per diem method is used, then employees do not need to keep receipts of their meals or lodging expenses. However, the employee still must be able to substantiate the date, place, and business purpose of these expenses. In many cases a receipt will be required to substantiate this items (though it is not required to substantiate the amount of the expense).

The amount of lodging, meals and incidental expenses that will be deemed substantiated is the lesser of the employer's per diem allowance, *or* one of the following two per diem rates that the employer chooses: (1) the "federal per diem rate" for the locality of travel, or (2) an "IRS rate" computed under the

"high-low" method. Once an employer chooses either the federal or IRS rate for a particular employee, this rate must be used for the remainder of the year for all other travel. The federal per diem rates (sometimes called the CONUS rates) are published periodically by the government, but these rates vary from city to city and can even change during the year and therefore cannot be relied upon unless you are certain you have the current rates.

The "high-low" per diem rates. A much simpler method of computing per diem rates is the "high-low" method which designates a standard per diem rate for lodging, meals and incidental expenses (lodging plus M & IE) for designated high-cost localities, and another rate for all other localities in the United States. For 1997, the per diem rate for high-cost localities is $166 and the rate for all other localities is $109 (see Table 7-6).

High-cost localities for purposes of computing the "M & IE" and "lodging and M & IE" rates are different.

✎ **Key point: for a listing of high-cost localities with the applicable per diem rates, see the current edition of IRS Publication 463.**

✎ **Key point: clergy whose churches have adopted an accountable reimbursement arrangement may use "per diem" rates to substantiate the amount of their lodging and meal expenses. If these rates are used, a minister need not retain receipts of actual meals and lodging expenses. Several conditions apply.**

☞ *Example. In 1997 Rev. N attends a church convention in another city for 4 days. The city has been designated by the IRS as a "high-cost" locality. Rev. N leaves at 9AM on Monday and returns at 9PM on Friday. His church has adopted an accountable reimbursement plan. The church provides Rev. N with a travel allowance of $190 per day to cover lodging and meals. Because the convention city is a high-cost locality, the amount deemed substantiated under the church's accountable reimbursement plan is $166. Assume that the high-low rate is higher than the federal per diem rate for the convention city, and so the church elects to use the higher amount. Accordingly, $166 of lodging and meal expenses are deemed substantiated each day under the per diem rules. The excess reimbursements of $24 per day are deemed nonaccountable, and must be reported as income on Rev. N's W-2 or 1099. However, this will not affect the accountability of the church's reimbursement plan. Note further that the M & IE rate must be prorated for the first day of travel, since Rev. N was in travel status for only three 6-hour quarters of the day. Therefore, the M & IE rate for Monday must be reduced by one-fourth and the daily per diem for lodging, meals and incidental expenses would be reduced correspondingly.*

☞ *Example. Rev. N (the same minister described in the previous example) goes on another business* *trip later the same year to another high-cost locality whose federal per diem rate is higher than $166. The church must use the "high-low" rate (though the federal per diem rate is higher) to substantiate Rev. N's lodging, meals and incidental expenses since it selected this method earlier in the year.*

☞ *Example. Rev. E leaves on a business trip at 5:30AM on Monday and returns home at 10PM on Wednesday. He travels to a high-cost locality. The church provides Rev. E with a per diem allowance equal to the high-low rate for high-cost localities. The church pays Rev. E a lodging rate of $126 for two nights, and a meals rate of $40 for three days (since he was in travel status for all four quarters of three days)—for a total reimbursement of $372. In fact, Rev. N only incurred expenses of $225. Rev. N is not required to report the difference as income. This rule assumes that he was in travel status for all of the days for which he received a travel allowance or reimbursement.*

Employer-provided vehicles

Churches can relieve clergy of the burdensome recordkeeping and substantiation requirements associated with business use of a car by simply purchasing a car for use by clergy. This approach merits serious consideration. However, for it to work, the income tax regulations require that certain conditions be satisfied. These conditions are discussed in section C.1 of this chapter.

F. Business and Professional Expenses—Reduction of Expenses if Housing Allowance Claimed: the Deason 'Allocation Rule

---

✎ **Key point: in 1995 the IRS has indicated that clergy must comply with the so-called *Deason* allocation rule. This rule requires clergy to reduce their business expenses by the percentage of their total compensation that consists of a tax-exempt housing allowance. This reduction in business expenses does not apply to the computation of self-employment taxes (since the housing allowance is not deductible in computing these taxes).**

Many ministers are still unaware that they may need to reduce their business expense deductions if they receive a housing allowance.

Let's begin with some important background information. In 1964, the Tax Court ruled that section 265 of the Code (which denies a deduction for any expense allocable to tax-exempt income) prevented a minister from deducting his unreimbursed transportation expenses to the extent that they were "allocable" to his tax-exempt housing allowance. *Deason v. Commissioner, 41 T.C. 465 (1964).* To illustrate, as-

sume that a minister receives compensation of $30,000, of which $10,000 is an excludable housing allowance, and incurs unreimbursed business expenses of $1,500. Since one-third of the minister's compensation is "tax-exempt," he should not be permitted to deduct one-third of his business expenses since they are "allocable" to tax-exempt income and their deduction would amount to a "double deduction." The IRS "acquiesced" (i.e., agreed) with the *Deason* ruling, but did not enforce it for several years. In fact, for years, the Internal Revenue Manual instructed agents not to raise the *Deason* allocation rule during an audit. Unfortunately, this position changed, in part due to a 1988 decision of the United States Tax Court reaffirming the *Deason* ruling. *Dalan v. Commissioner, T.C. Memo. 1988-106.* In 1992 the Tax Court reaffirmed its rulings in both the *Deason* and *Dalan* decisions. *McFarland v. Commissioner, T.C. Memo. 1992-440.*

✎ **Key point: the IRS issued audit guidelines for its agents to follow when auditing ministers. The guidelines instruct agents to apply the so-called *Deason* allocation rule. The guidelines explain this rule as follows: "A minister may deduct ordinary and necessary business expenses. However, if a minister's compensation includes a housing allowance which is exempt from income tax, then that portion of the expenses allocable to this tax-exempt income is not deductible. Before this allocation is made, the total amount of business expenses must be determined."**

✎ **Key point: the audit guidelines will instruct IRS agents in the examination of ministers' tax returns. They alert agents to the key questions to ask, and provide background information along with the IRS position on a number of issues. It is therefore of utmost importance that ministers be familiar with these guidelines.**

How do ministers reduce their business expenses to properly reflect this rule? The audit guidelines for ministers provide IRS agents with the following procedure:

• Determine a minister's total ministry income. The guidelines note that this amount includes salary, fees, expense allowances under nonaccountable plans, plus the housing allowance or parsonage annual fair rental value (FRV).

• Compute the "nontaxable income percentage" by dividing total ministry income into the minister's housing allowance exclusion (or the parsonage FRV).

• Multiply the minister's total business expenses times the nontaxable income percentage to yield the nondeductible portion of total business expenses.

• Subtract the nondeductible portion of business expenses from total business expenses to yield deductible business expenses.

⟳ **Observation. In a later section the audit guidelines instruct agents that business expenses**

need not be reduced in computing self-employment taxes, since the housing allowance or parsonage fair rental value are not tax-exempt in computing self-employment taxes.

The guidelines provide IRS agents with the following examples:

☞ **Example.** *F receives a salary of $36,000, an exempt housing allowance of $18,000 and an auto expense allowance of $6,000 for his services as an ordained minister. F incurs business expenses as follows: auto, $7,150; vestments, $350; dues, $120; publications and supplies, $300; totaling $7,920. His nondeductible expenses are computed as follows:*

total ministry income = $60,000 ($36,000 salary + $18,000 housing + $6,000 car allowance)

$18,000 housing allowance

30% nontaxable income percentage ($18,000/$60,000)

Total business expenses $7,920

Nontaxable income percentage (30%) x total expenses ($7,920) = nondeductible expenses ($2,376)

Total business expenses ($7,920) less nondeductible expenses (2,376) = deductible expenses of $5,544

F's deductible expenses are reported as Schedule A miscellaneous deductions since his church considers him an employee and issues a W-2. These expenses, along with any other miscellaneous deductions are subject to a further reduction of 2 percent of his adjusted gross income.

☞ **Example.** *G received a salary of $12,000, a housing allowance of $9,000, and earned $3,000 for various speaking engagements, weddings, funerals, etc., all related to her ministry. She reports her salary as "wages" on page 1 of her Form 1040 and her fees on Schedule C. Because her actual housing costs ($6,000) were less than her housing allowance and the FRV of her home for the year, she must include $3,000 of her housing allowance as "other income" for income tax purposes. Her total business expenses are $4,500. The computation of deductible expenses is shown below:*
$6,000 (housing allowance actually exempt from income tax)

total ministry income = $24,000 ($12,000 salary + $9,000 housing + $3,000 fees)

25% = nontaxable income percentage ($6,000/$24,000)

Total business expenses $4,500

Nontaxable income percentage (25%) x total expenses ($4,500) = nondeductible expenses ($1,125)

Total business expenses ($4,500) less nondeductible expenses ($1,125) = deductible expenses of $3,375

Note that this $3,375 would further be allocable between Schedule A miscellaneous deductions (related to salary) and Schedule C (related to other fees). However . . . this allocation will not change G's self-employment tax, since all ministry income and ministry expenses are included in the computation, regardless of where they are reported on the return for income tax purposes. The allocation between Schedule A and Schedule C will also affect any AGI-dependent computations.

There are 2 very important additional considerations that can save ministers a substantial amount of taxes:

• Since a housing allowance is not an exclusion for self-employment (social security) tax purposes, no "reduction" in business expenses is required in computing these taxes on Schedule SE.

• The adverse impact of the *Deason* ruling can be eliminated if a church simply adopts an accountable reimbursement arrangement (described in section D of this chapter). The reason for this interpretation is that section 265 reduces any *deduction* for business expenses allocable to tax-exempt income. Under an accountable reimbursement arrangement, however, there is no "deduction" claimed since the employer's reimbursements are not reported as income.

The *Dalan* and *McFarland* cases dealt only with the *unreimbursed* business and professional expenses of self-employed ministers. However, it is likely that the same reduction rule will apply to business expenses reimbursed by a church under a "nonaccountable" plan, and to all clergy whether they are self-employed or employees for income tax reporting purposes, since Code section 265, upon which these cases are based, prohibits a "deduction" for any amount otherwise allowable as a deduction which is allocable to income that is exempt from tax. Whether a minister is an employee or self-employed, and whether business and professional expenses are unreimbursed or reimbursed under a nonaccountable plan, the expenses are claimed as a "deduction"—on Schedule C for self-employed clergy, and on Schedule A for clergy who are employees.

Parsonages. What about clergy who live in church-owned parsonages? Are they affected by the *Deason* rule? The answer to this question is not clear. Logically, if the *Deason* rule is to be applied to clergy who own or rent their homes, then it should be applied to clergy who live in church-owned parsonages. However, applying the *Deason* rule to clergy who live in parsonages would involve unique difficulties. First, they would have to compute the fair rental value of their parsonage. Second, they would add this value to their other church compensation, and then determine the percentage of their total compensation consisting of "tax-exempt" income (the fair rental value of the parsonage). Third, they would reduce their business expense deduction by this percentage. As a practical matter, these computations are particularly difficult. The IRS "Tax Guide for Churches," which was issued in 1994, states: "A minister may be able to itemize deductions for ministerial trade or business expenses incurred while working as an employee. However, when a minister receives a tax free parsonage or rental allowance, the portion of expenses that are allocable to that tax free amount is not deductible." This statement indicates that the IRS will apply the *Deason* rule to ministers who live in church-owned parsonages.

Computing the reduction. Another ambiguity pertains to the proper manner of making the reduction in business and professional expenses called for by the *Deason* rule. IRS Publication 517 ("Social Security and other Information for Members of the Clergy") presents a full-page example of a schedule that ministers can use to compute the reduction in their business expense deduction required by the *Deason* rule. The comprehensive clergy tax illustrations set forth in chapter 12 of this tax guide contain schedules based on the IRS example.

Critique. The continuing reliance by the IRS and the Tax Court on the *Deason* decision is disturbing, because it perpetuates a completely erroneous position. A compelling argument can be made that the *Deason* ruling makes no sense. The IRS (and the Tax Court) are saying that clergy must reduce their business expenses by the percentage of their total compensation that consists of a tax-exempt housing allowance. This is nonsensical, since clergy cannot pay for business expenses out of such tax-exempt income *because the tax-exempt income is used entirely to pay for housing expenses.* The housing allowance is excludable, under section 107 of the Code, only "to the extent used to rent or provide a home." That is, the housing allowance is excludable only to the extent that it is in fact used to pay for housing-related expenses. This being the case, it is absolutely impossible for one cent of the "tax-exempt" housing allowance to be used for paying a minister's business and professional expenses. Business and professional expenses are neither directly nor indirectly "allocable" to a minister's tax-free housing allowance. In some cases, non-clergy taxpayers doubtless receive tax-exempt income, and use that income to pay business expenses. There may be some logic in requiring such taxpayers to reduce their business expense deductions by the percentage of their total compensation that is tax-free. However, this makes no sense in the case of a minister, whose "tax-exempt income" is tax-exempt *only if it in fact is used exclusively for housing-related expenses.*

G. Itemized Deductions

If your itemized deductions exceed your standard deduction (see section B of this chapter), you should report your itemized deductions on Schedule A (Form 1040). This section will summarize the itemized deductions.

Note that certain high-income taxpayers must reduce most of their itemized deductions. For 1997, taxpayers must reduce their itemized deductions by 3% of the amount of their adjusted gross income that exceeds $121,200 (this amount is indexed each year for inflation). However, in no event is the deduction reduced more than 80%. This limitation is applied to all itemized deductions except medical expenses, investment interest, and casualty losses. *It does apply to charitable contribution deductions.*

1. Medical expenses

You may deduct certain medical and dental expenses (for yourself, your spouse, and your dependents) if you itemize your deductions on Schedule A, but only to the extent that your expenses exceed 7.5% of your adjusted gross income. You must reduce your medical expenses by the amounts of any reimbursements you receive for those expenses before applying the 7.5% test. Reimbursements include amounts you receive from insurance or other sources for your medical expenses (including Medicare). It does not matter if the reimbursement is paid to the patient, the doctor, or the hospital.

Amounts you receive for personal injuries you sustain in an accident present special problems. Do not reduce your medical expenses by any repayments you receive for loss of earnings or damages for personal injury. However, you must reduce your medical expenses by the portion of any personal injury award (whether by settlement or court judgment) that repays you for hospitalization and medical care. If you receive a settlement or award after the year in which you were injured, then the part of the settlement or award that compensates you for medical expenses you incurred and deducted in the year of the accident must be included in your income in the year you receive the settlement or award. If a portion of the settlement or award is allocable to future medical expenses, then you must reduce any medical expenses you pay this year and in future years because of your injuries until the amount you receive in settlement has been completely used. You may include amounts you pay after that in your medical expenses.

The following expenses are deductible as medical expenses:

- fees for medical services
- fees for hospital services
- meals and lodging provided by a hospital during medical treatment
- medical and hospital insurance premiums that you pay
- special equipment
- special items (false teeth, artificial limbs, eyeglasses, hearing aids, crutches, etc.)
- transportation for necessary medical care
- medicines and drugs requiring a prescription
- the portion of a life-care fee or founder's fee paid either monthly or in a lump sum under an agreement with a retirement home that is allocable to medical care
- wages of an attendant who provides medical care
- the cost of home improvements if the main reason is for medical care

The following items are *not* deductible as medical expenses:

- funeral services

- health club dues
- household help
- life insurance
- maternity clothes
- medicare insurance (Medicare A—basic cost)
- non-prescription medicines and drugs
- nursing care for a healthy baby
- program to stop smoking
- toothpaste, cosmetics, toiletries
- trip for general improvement of health
- weight loss program

❖ **New in 1997. Congress enacted legislation in 1997 that increases the deduction for health insurance coverage of self-employed persons as follows: the deduction is increased to 45 percent in 1998 and 1999; 50 percent in 2000 and 2001; 60 percent in 2002; 80 percent in 2003 through 2005; 90 percent in 2006; and 100 percent in 2007 and thereafter.**

2. Taxes

If you itemize your taxes on Schedule A (Form 1040), you may deduct certain taxes you pay during the year. These include state and local income taxes, state and local real property taxes, and state and local personal property taxes. You can no longer deduct state and local general sales taxes as an itemized deduction. However, any sales tax paid or accrued on the purchase of property (e.g., depreciable business property) is added to the cost of the property. The three types of deductible taxes are summarized below.

a. income taxes

You may deduct state and local income taxes, including taxes on interest income that is exempt from federal income tax. You may not deduct state and local taxes on other exempt income. Deduct state and local income taxes withheld from your salary or paid by you on an estimated basis. However, estimated tax payments are not deductible if you later determine that no estimated taxes were necessary. If you receive a refund of state or local income taxes in a year after the year in which you paid them, you may have to include all or a part of the refund in your income in the year you receive it. If you did not itemize your deductions in the previous year, you do not have to include the refund.

b. real estate taxes

Real estate taxes are any taxes on real property levied for the general public welfare. They generally do not include taxes charged for local benefits and improvements that increase the value of your property. If you bought or sold real estate during 1997, the real estate taxes ordinarily must be divided between the buyer and seller according to the number of days in the real property tax year (the period to which the tax relates) that each owned the property. The seller pays the taxes up to the date of the sale, and the buyer pays the taxes beginning with the date of sale. If your monthly mortgage payment includes an amount placed in escrow for real estate taxes,

you may not deduct the total of these amounts included in your payments for the year. You may only deduct the amount of the tax that the lender actually paid to the taxing authority.

Ministers who own their homes and pay real property taxes can include the full amount of such taxes in computing their housing allowance exclusion, and may also fully deduct the amount of the taxes as an itemized deduction on Schedule A (if they itemize their deductions). For a full discussion of the housing allowance, see chapter 6.

c. personal property taxes

To qualify as a deductible personal property tax, a state or local tax must meet three tests: (1) the tax must be based solely on the value of the personal property; (2) the tax must be charged on a yearly basis, even if it is collected more than once a year, or less than once a year; and (3) the tax must be charged on personal property.

3. Interest

Interest is an amount paid for the use of borrowed money. To deduct interest on a debt, you must legally be liable for the debt. You may not deduct payments you make for someone else if you are not legally liable to make them. Both you and the lender must intend that the loan be repaid. In addition, there must be a debtor-creditor relationship between you and the lender.

For most ministers, the most significant interest deduction will be for mortgage interest they pay on the home they own. In most cases, you will be able to deduct all of the interest you pay on any loans secured by your main home, including first and second mortgages, home equity loans, and refinanced mortgages. Whether your home mortgage interest payments are deductible depends on the date you took out the mortgage, the amount of the mortgage, and your use of the proceeds. If all of your mortgages fit into one of the following categories, you can deduct *all* of your interest and report it on Schedule A (Form 1040): (1) mortgages you took out on your main home on or before October 13, 1987; (2) mortgages you took out on your main home after October 13, 1987, to buy, build or improve your home, but only if these mortgages (plus any mortgages in the preceding category) total $1 million or less throughout 1997, ($500,000 if married filing separately); (3) mortgages you took out after October 13, 1987, on your main home, other than to buy, build or improve your home, but only if these mortgages total $100,000 or less throughout 1997 ($50,000 if married filing separately). If you had a main home *and* a second home, the dollar limits explained in the second and third categories described above apply to the total mortgage on both homes.

Ministers who own their homes can deduct mortgage interest payments as an itemized deduction even though such payments were included in computing the housing allowance exclusion (the so-called **"double deduction"**). *IRC 265(a)(6)*. However, ministers are subject to the limitations on mortgage loans discussed in this section.

It is not always easy to determine whether an item is deductible as interest. Consider the following items:

a. *Late payment charges.* You may deduct a late payment charge if it was not for a specific service performed by your mortgage holder.

b. *Points.* The term "points" is sometimes used to describe certain charges paid by a borrower. They are also called loan origination fees, maximum loan charges, or premium charges. If the payment of any of these charges is *only* for the use of money, it ordinarily is interest paid in advance and must be deducted in installments over the life of the mortgage (not deducted in full in the year of payment). However, the IRS announced in 1992 that points are deductible in the year paid if the following 5 requirements are satisfied: (1) The points must be designated as "points," loan origination fees, discount points, or loan discount, on the Uniform Settlement Statement. (2) The amount must be computed as a percentage of the stated principal amount of the debt incurred by the taxpayer. (3) The amount paid must conform to the established business practice of charging points for loans for the acquisition of personal residences in the area where the residence is located, and the amount of points paid must not exceed the amount generally charged in the area. (4) The amount must be paid in connection with the acquisition of the taxpayer's principal residence, and the loan must be secured by that residence. (5) The amount must be paid directly by the taxpayer (e.g., they are withheld from the loan proceeds). *Revenue Procedure 92-12.*

c. *Mortgage prepayment penalty.* A penalty that you are assessed for paying off a loan early is deductible as interest.

d. *Service charges.* These amounts are not deductible as interest.

e. *Credit investigation fees.* These amounts are not deductible as interest.

f. *Credit card finance charges.* These amounts are deductible as interest. However, to the extent that they relate to personal items, they are not deductible.

Interest that you pay for personal reasons (i.e., interest on car loans, credit cards, and personal loans) no longer is deductible as an itemized deduction on Schedule A.

Interest you pay on a loan for income-producing rental property that is not used in your work is deducted on Schedule E (Form 1040). This type of interest is still fully deductible, and is available whether or not you itemize deductions on Schedule A. To illustrate, if you rent out part of your home and borrow money to make repairs, you may deduct the part of the interest payment representing the rented portion of the premises on Schedule E.

4. Charitable contributions

The rules that govern the deductibility of contributions are of vital concern to clergy and churches. Because of the significance of these rules, they are considered in detail in a separate chapter (chapter 8).

5. Casualty and theft losses

Most taxpayers have at some time suffered damage to their property as a result of hurricanes, earthquakes, tornadoes, fires, vandalism, car accidents, floods, or similar events. When property is damaged or destroyed by such events, it is called a *casualty.* If your property is stolen, you may also have a deductible theft loss. You must itemize your deductions on Schedule A (Form 1040) to be able to claim a casualty or theft loss to nonbusiness property. To determine your deduction, you must reduce the amount of your casualty and theft losses by any insurance or reimbursement you receive. No deduction is allowed for a casualty or theft loss that is covered by insurance unless a timely insurance claim for reimbursement has been filed. In addition, each individual loss must be reduced by $100, and your total losses are then reduced by 10% of your adjusted gross income.

In order to claim a casualty or theft loss, you must be able to show that the loss in fact occurred. In addition, the loss generally is defined as the lesser of (1) the decrease in fair market value of the property as a result of the casualty or theft, or (2) your adjusted basis in the property before the casualty or theft.

Calculate nonbusiness casualty and theft losses on Form 4684, and report them on Schedule A (Form 1040) as an itemized deduction.

6. Moving expenses

✎ **The treatment of moving expenses changed in the following ways for 1994 and future years: (1) the cost of pre-move househunting trips is excluded from the definition of moving expenses; (2) expenses incurred in the sale or purchase of a residence no longer are deductible; (3) the cost of temporary living expenses for up to 30 days in the general location of the new job is excluded from the definition of moving expenses; (4) the mileage limit is increased from 35 miles to 50 miles; (5) qualified moving expenses not paid or reimbursed by the taxpayer's employer are allowable as a deduction in computing adjusted gross income (this is good news—they are now allowable whether or not the taxpayer is able to itemize expenses on Schedule A); (6) moving expenses incurred and paid by the taxpayer's employer are excludable from gross income for tax purposes (if reimbursed, the reimbursements must be pursuant to an "accountable" arrangement).**

Moving expenses incurred and paid in 1994 and later years are subject to a number of important changes. In general, fewer moving expenses will be deductible. On the other hand, moving expenses reimbursed by an employer under an accountable arrangement are no longer reported as taxable income. And, the moving expense deduction is now an adjustment in computing adjusted gross income (on the front side of Form 1040). As such, it is available whether or not you can itemize deductions on Schedule A.

In general, you may deduct a portion of your moving expenses incurred because of a change of jobs or your acceptance of a new job, if you satisfy the following conditions:

(1) Your new job location is at least 50 miles farther from your former home than your old job location was. For example, if your old job was 3 miles from your former home, your new job must be at least 53 miles from that home (measured according to the shortest of the more commonly traveled routes between those points).

(2) If you report your income taxes as an **employee**, you must work full time for at least 39 weeks during the first 12 months after you arrive in the general area of your new job location. You do not have to work for one employer for the 39 weeks. However, you must work full time within the same general commuting area. If you report your income taxes as a **self-employed** person, you must work full time for at least 39 weeks during the first 12 months and for a total of at least 78 weeks during the first 24 months after you arrive in the area of your new job location. If you are married and file a joint return and both you and your spouse work full time, either of you may satisfy the full-time work test. However, you may not combine your weeks of work. You may deduct your moving expenses even if you have not met the time test by the due date of your 1997 return. You may do this if you expect to meet the 39-week test by the end of 1998 or the 78-week test by the end of 1999. If you do not meet the time test by then, you either must amend your 1997 return or report your moving expense deduction as other income on your Form 1040 for the tax year you cannot meet the test. These time tests do not apply in some situations that ordinarily are not relevant to clergy.

(3) Your move must be closely related, both in time and place, to the start of work at your new job location. In general, moving expenses incurred within one year from the date you first reported to work are considered closely related in time to the start of work at the new location. It is not necessary that you make arrangements to work before moving to a new location, as long as you actually do go to work. If you do not move within one year, you ordinarily may not deduct the expenses unless you can show that circumstances existed that prevented the move within that time. A move is generally not closely related in place to the start of work if the distance from your new home to the new job location is greater than the distance from your former home to the new job location.

Deductible moving expenses include the following:

(1) *Moving your household goods and personal effects.* You may deduct the cost of packing, crating and transporting your household goods and personal effects from your former home to your new one. You may also deduct the cost of storing and insuring household goods and personal effects within any consecutive 30-day period after the day your things are moved from your former home and before they are delivered to your new home.

(2) *Travel expenses.* You may deduct the cost of transportation and lodging (but not meals) for yourself and members of your household while traveling from your former home to your new home. You may deduct expenses of only one trip to your new home. However, all of the members of your household do not need to travel together.

You may not deduct any of the following expenses as moving expenses: pre-move househunting expenses, temporary living expenses, the expenses of disposing of your former home and obtaining your new home, home improvements to help you sell your former home, loss on the sale of your former home, mortgage penalties, any part of the purchase price of your new home, meal expenses incurred while moving to your new home, and real estate taxes.

If your allowable moving expenses (as defined above) are **reimbursed** by your employer under an accountable arrangement, then the reimbursements are not reportable as taxable income to you and there are no deductions to report. Employer reimbursements that are not pursuant to an accountable arrangement must be included in your taxable income. As noted previously in this chapter, an accountable arrangement is one by which an employer reimburses only those expenses that are deductible and that are properly substantiated.

✎ **Key point: the conference committee report to the new law states: "The conferees intend that the employer treat moving expenses as excludable unless it has actual knowledge that the employee deducted the expenses in a prior year. The employer has no obligation to determine whether the individual deducted the expenses."**

In summary, for moving expenses incurred and paid in 1994 or later, follow these rules: (1) First, determine your allowable business expenses under the new, restrictive rules summarized above; (2) if you are not reimbursed by your employer for your moving expenses, you may claim a deduction for your expenses as an adjustment in computing your adjusted gross income (this deduction is available whether or not you can itemize expenses on Schedule A); (3) if your employer reimburses your expenses under an accountable arrangement (that is, the employer reimburses your substantiated expenses), then none of the reimbursements should be reported as taxable income and you have no deductions to claim. If you are reimbursed for your moving expenses under a "nonaccountable" arrangement (you do not adequately account for your expenses), then your employer will need to report the full amount of the reimbursements as taxable income to you, and you can claim a deduction for those expenses you can adequately substantiate on line 24 of Form 1040.

Use Form 3903 to compute the moving expense deduction for unreimbursed moving expenses (or expenses reimbursed under a nonaccountable arrangement).

❖ **New in 1998. Church leaders should be familiar with the following changes in moving expense reporting that take effect in 1998: (1) Form 4782, which is used by employers to report moving expense reimbursements made to employees, will be eliminated; (2) qualified moving expenses an employer pays to a third party on behalf of the employee (e.g. to a moving company) will not be reported on Form W-2; (3) qualified moving expenses reimbursements an employer pays directly to an employee will be reported in Box 13 of Form W-2 and will be identified using Code P (currently, all qualified moving expense reimbursements are identified with Code P, regardless of whether or not they were paid directly to the employee); (4) other moving expense reimbursements (nonqualified expenses) will continue to be included in wages (Form W-2, box 1) and are subject to income tax withholding and social security and Medicare taxes.**

7. Miscellaneous deductions

You may deduct certain miscellaneous expenses on Schedule A (Form 1040). These deductions are in addition to the itemized deductions for medical expenses, taxes, interest, charitable contributions, and casualty and theft losses. As noted before, most miscellaneous itemized expenses are deductible only to the extent that they exceed 2% of adjusted gross income. Miscellaneous expenses subject to the 2% floor include:

- unreimbursed and "nonaccountable" reimbursed employee business expenses
- professional society dues
- safety deposit rental
- employee educational expenses
- tax counsel and assistance
- office in the home expenses
- work-related supplies
- expenses of looking for a new job
- investment counsel fees
- professional books and periodicals
- investment expenses
- 50% of unreimbursed business meals and entertainment
- IRA custodial fees

Certain miscellaneous expenses are not subject to the 2% floor. However, these expenses ordinarily are not available to ministers. Ministers who report their income taxes as self-employed ordinarily can deduct most if not all of their unreimbursed (and "nonaccountable" reimbursed) professional and business expenses on Schedule C (Form 1040) whether or not they are able to itemize deductions on Schedule A. See chapter 2 for a discussion of whether or not ministers are employees or self-employed for income tax reporting purposes.

H. Tax Credits

Unlike deductions, tax credits are subtracted directly from your tax liability, and therefore reduce your taxes dollar for dollar. Credits are reported on lines 40-46 of your Form 1040, immediately after you computed your actual tax liability (on line 39). For example, if your total tax liability amounted to $4,000 for 1997, and you have credits totaling $500, your tax liability is reduced to $3,500. The most common credits claimed by clergy include the child and dependent care credit and the earned income credit. These credits are summarized below.

1. Child and dependent care credit

If you pay someone to care for your dependent who is under 13 (or a disabled dependent) so that you can work or look for work, you may be able to claim a tax credit of up to 30% of the amount you pay. You may use up to $2,400 of these expenses to figure your credit if you have one qualifying dependent and up to $4,800 if you have two or more qualifying dependents. This means that your maximum credit for a single dependent is $720 ($2,400 x 30%) or $1,440 for two or more dependents ($4,800 x 30%). The credit is reduced by 1% for each $2,000 of adjusted gross income (or portion thereof) in excess of $10,000, until it decreases to 20% for taxpayers with adjusted gross income in excess of $28,000. To illustrate, if a taxpayer with $30,000 of adjusted gross income incurs $3,000 of qualifying child care expenses (for one child), the credit would be $480 (20% x $2,400).

To claim this credit, you must meet the following conditions: (1) your dependent care expenses must be incurred to allow you (and your spouse if you are married) to work or look for work; (2) you must have income from work during the year (your qualifying expenses ordinarily cannot exceed the earned income of the lower-compensated spouse); (3) you (and your spouse if married) must keep up a home that you live in with the qualifying dependent; (4) you must file a joint return if married; (5) you must have made payments for dependent care on behalf of a "qualifying person"; (6) you must report the name, address, and taxpayer identification number of the child care provider on your tax return; and (7) if you receive a reimbursement under an employer's dependent care assistance program, the dollar limit on expenses eligible for the child and dependent care credit ($2,400 for one dependent, $4,800 for two or more) is reduced dollar for dollar by any reimbursement excluded from your income.

Qualifying dependents include (1) your dependent under age 13 for whom you may claim an exemption deduction on your federal income tax return; (2) your dependent, or a person you could claim as a dependent except that the person has gross income of $2,650 or more (in 1997), who is physically or mentally not able to care for himself or herself; or (3) your spouse who is physically or mentally not able to care for himself or herself.

Only expenses incurred to enable you (and your spouse if married) to work are considered in computing the credit. Typically, such expenses include expenses for household services and expenses for the care of a qualifying person.

☞ *Example. Rev. A is single and has two children under age 13 who live with him. He has adjusted gross income of $19,000 in 1997. During the year, he paid $3,000 for a housekeeper to care for his children in his home so that he could work, and another $2,200 for child care at a nursery school. Rev. A's work-related expenses are $5,200 ($3,000 + $2,200). However, he is limited to $4,800 in expenses for two or more qualifying dependents. He computes his credit by taking 25% of $4,800 (i.e., $1,200). The 25% figure represents 30% reduced by a percentage point for each $2,000 (or portion thereof) of adjusted gross income in excess of $10,000 (i.e., 5%).*

The credit is computed on Form 2441, and reported on line 39 of Form 1040.

Persons who the dependent care credit must include on their tax return the name and social security number of each dependent. In the past, the IRS could assess a $50 penalty for each failure to provide a correct social security number for a dependent. The IRS has the authority to deny a dependent care credit to any taxpayer who fails to provide the correct social security number of a dependent on his or her tax return. If a person who you expect to claim as a dependent does not have a social security number, either you or that person should apply for one as soon as possible. You can apply for a number by filing IRS Form SS-5 with the Social Security Administration. You can obtain a Form SS-5 from any IRS or social security office. A penalty will not be applied for a failure to list a dependent's social security number on your 1997 tax return if the dependent was born after November 30, 1997.

2. Earned income credit

✎ Key point: the earned income credit is a significant tax benefit for lower-income families. Unfortunately, computing this benefit has become so complex that many eligible families do not claim it.

✎ Key point: no earned income credit will be available to taxpayers who do not list their social security number on their tax return. The social security number of a spouse also must be listed.

The earned income credit is a significant tax benefit for lower-income families. Unfortunately, computing this benefit has become so complex that many eligible families do not claim it. Here are the rules for 1997:

• For taxpayers with one qualifying child, the EIC is 34% of the first $6,500 of earned income in 1997. The maximum credit in 1997 is $2,210 and is reduced by 15.98% of earned income (or adjusted gross income, if greater) in excess of $11,930. The credit is phased out completely for income in excess of $25,760.

• For taxpayers with two or more qualifying children, the EIC is 40% of the first $9,140 of earned income in 1997. The maximum credit for 1997 is $3,656 and is reduced by 21.06% of earned income (or adjusted gross income, if greater) in excess of $11,930. The credit is phased out completely for income in excess of $29,290.

• The EIC is extended to certain qualifying taxpayers with no children, but only for taxpayers over age 25 and below age 65. For these taxpayers, the EIC will be 7.65% of the first $4,340 of earned income (for a maximum credit of $332 in 1997). The maximum credit will be reduced by 7.65% of earned income (or adjusted gross income, if greater) above $5,430. In 1997 the credit will be completely phased out for taxpayers with earned income (or adjusted gross income, if greater) over $9,770.

• The Internal Revenue Service (IRS) is required to provide notice to taxpayers with qualifying children who receive a refund on account of the EIC that the credit may be available on an advance payment basis. To prevent taxpayers from incurring an unexpectedly large tax liability due to receipt of the EIC on an advance payment basis, the amount of advance payment allowable in a taxable year is limited to 60% of the maximum credit available to a taxpayer with one qualifying child.

Note that the definition of earned income includes a housing allowance or the annual fair rental value of a church-provided parsonage. *Treas. Reg. 1.43-2(c)(2)(ii).*

Unfortunately, many taxpayers who qualify for the earned income credit do not claim it. As a result, Congress has ordered the IRS to establish a "public awareness program to inform the taxpaying public of the availability of the [earned income] credit. Such public awareness program shall be designed to assure that individuals who may be eligible are informed of the availability of such credit and filing procedures."

Denominational offices should advise younger clergy with dependent children of the availability of this important benefit.

As noted above, a credit is a direct dollar-for-dollar reduction in your tax liability. It is much more valuable than deductions and exclusions, which merely reduce taxable income.

No earned income credit is available to taxpayers earning more than $2,250 of "disqualified income" (in 1997). Disqualified income includes taxable interest and dividends, tax-exempt interest, and net capital gain income.

❖ **New in 1997.** Congress enacted legislation in 1997 that makes certain changes to the earned income credit, including the following: (1) *Fraud or recklessness.* A taxpayer who fraudulently claims an EIC is ineligible to claim the EIC for the next 10 years. A taxpayer who erroneously claims the EIC due to reckless or intentional disregard of the law is ineligible to claim the credit for the next 2 years. This provision took effect January 1, 1997. (2) *Definition of adjusted gross income.* The EIC is phased out for taxpayers with adjusted gross income above specified levels. The new law provides that tax-exempt interest and nontaxable distributions from pensions, annuities, and IRAs (if not rolled over into similar tax-favored products) are not counted in computing adjusted gross income for purposes of determining eligibility for the EIC. This provision takes effect in 1998.

3. Adoption Credit

❖ **New in 1997.** Taxpayers for the first time can claim a credit for certain expenses incurred in adopting a child.

Congress enacted legislation in 1996 giving taxpayers a maximum nonrefundable credit against income tax liability of $5,000 per child ($6,000 for children with special needs) for qualified adoption expenses paid or incurred by the taxpayer. Qualified adoption expenses are reasonable and necessary adoption fees, court costs, attorneys fees and other expenses that are directly related to the legal adoption of an eligible child. In the case of an international adoption, the credit is not available unless the adoption is finalized. In that case the credit is allowed for all prior qualified expenses in the year that the adoption becomes final. An eligible child is an individual (1) who has not attained age 18 as of the time of the adoption, or (2) who is physically or mentally incapable of caring for himself or herself. No credit is allowed for expenses incurred (1) in violation of state or federal law, (2) in carrying out any surrogate parenting arrangement, or (3) in connection with the adoption of a child of the taxpayer's spouse. The credit is phased out for taxpayers with modified adjusted gross income (AGI) above $75,000, and is fully phased out at $115,000 of modified AGI.

The $5,000 limit is a per child limit, not an annual limitation. For example, in the case of a domestic adoption if a taxpayer pays or incurs $3,000 of otherwise allowable qualified adoption expenses with respect to a child in year one and $3,000 of otherwise allowable qualified adoption expenses with respect to that same child in year two, then the taxpayer would receive a $3,000 credit with respect to year one and a $2,000 credit with respect to year two. The credit may be less than $5,000 because of other limitations.

The credit for adoption expenses takes effect in 1997. The credit for non-special needs adoptions is repealed for expenses paid or incurred after December 31, 2001.

4. Child Tax Credit

❖ **New in 1998.** Congress enacted legislation in 1997 creating a new "child tax credit." If you have one or more children under 17 years of age, and you earn less than a specified amount of income, then you will be able to claim a $400 credit on your 1998 tax return for each child. The credit increases to $500 in 1999 and thereafter.

Congress enacted legislation in 1997 that creates a new "child tax credit." Here is how it works. If you have one or more children under 17 years of age, and you earn less than a specified amount of income, then you will be able to claim a $400 credit on your 1998 tax return for each child. The credit increases to $500 in 1999. Here are some key considerations to note:

• *Qualifying child.* To qualify for the credit, you must have a child who (1) is under 17 years of age; (2) is your child, descendent, stepson or stepdaughter, or foster child; and (3) is claimed by you as a dependent on your tax return.

• *Phaseout for high-income taxpayers.* The child care credit is reduced by $50 for each $1,000 of adjusted gross income in excess of $110,000 for married couples filing jointly. For single persons, the credit is reduced by $50 for each $1,000 of adjusted gross income in excess of $75,000. These amounts are not adjusted for inflation.

• *Refundable child care credit.* Some lower income families will be eligible to receive a supplemental credit. To qualify, a family must be eligible to receive the earned income tax credit. Unfortunately, the amount of this credit is so difficult to compute that few eligible families will be able to claim it. Congress anticipated this problem, and has instructed the IRS to determine "whether a simplified method of calculating the credit can be achieved." We will report any progress in future issues of this newsletter. For now, here is a "ballpark test" that can be used—the supplemental credit will not be available unless you (1) qualify for the earned income credit, and (2) your earned income credit exceeds your share of FICA or self-employment taxes.

The child tax credit is in addition to the dependent care credit you can claim if you pay someone to care for your dependent child who is under 13 (or a disabled dependent) so that you can work.

5. HOPE Scholarship Tax Credit

❖ **New in 1998.** Beginning in 1998, taxpayers can claim a "HOPE" credit against federal income taxes of up to $1,500 per student per year for 50 percent of qualified tuition and related expenses (not including room, board, and books) paid during the first two years of the student's postsecondary, undergraduate education in a degree or certificate program.

Congress enacted legislation in 1997 that provides welcome relief to families with children in college or vocational training. Beginning in 1998, taxpayers can claim a "HOPE" credit against federal income taxes of up to $1,500 per student per year for 50 percent of qualified tuition and related expenses (not including room, board, and books) paid during the first two years of the student's postsecondary, undergraduate education in a degree or certificate program. Here are some of the key provisions:

• *Effective date.* HOPE scholarship credits are available for tuition expenses and academic fees paid after December 31, 1997, for education furnished in academic periods beginning after such date.

• *Eligible taxpayers.* Who qualifies for the HOPE scholarship credit? The law provides that the credit is available for tuition expenses incurred by a taxpayer, or the taxpayer's spouse or dependent child.

☞ *Example. A church member would like to claim a HOPE tax credit for monies he pays for scholarships on behalf of members of his church who are attending college. He is not eligible for the credit with respect to any student who is not his spouse or dependent.*

☞ *Example. A student attending a church-related college incurs $9,000 in tuition expenses for 1997. The student's mother pays this entire amount. She is not eligible for a HOPE credit, even if she claims her son as a dependent, since the credit is not available until 1998.*

☞ *Example. Same facts as the previous problem, except the year is 1998. The parent would be eligible for a HOPE credit in the amount of $1,500—assuming that she meets the conditions summarized below.*

☞ *Example. A parent pays $10,000 in tuition fees incurred by his son during 1998 while attending seminary as a full-time student. The parent is not eligible for a HOPE credit, since the tuition was not incurred during the first two years of postsecondary, undergraduate education.*

☞ *Example. A parent pays the full $5,000 tuition for 1998 on behalf of his daughter who attends a church-operated high school. The parent is not eligible for the HOPE credit, since the credit is limited to the first two years of postsecondary, undergraduate education.*

• *First two years of college.* The HOPE credit applies only to tuition incurred during the first two years of a college or vocational program leading to a degree or certificate.

• *Amount of credit.* The credit is 100 percent of the first $1,000 of tuition and fees, and 50 percent on the next $1,000 of tuition and fees—for a total available credit of $1,500. Remember that a credit is a direct dollar-for-dollar reduction in income taxes. It is

far more beneficial than a tax deduction which merely reduces taxable income.

☞ *Example. A student who incurs tuition of $1,000 is eligible for a $1,000 HOPE credit. A student who incurs tuition of $2,000 or more is eligible for a $1,500 HOPE credit.*

✎ **Key point. The amount of the HOPE credit is indexed for inflation after the year 2000.**

• *Eligible students.* To be eligible for a HOPE credit, a student must be enrolled at least half-time in a degree or certificate program leading to a recognized educational credential at an eligible educational institution.

• *What expenses are eligible for the credit?* The credit is available with respect to amounts paid for tuition and academic fees. It is not available with respect to amounts paid for books, meals, lodging, student activities, athletics, insurance, transportation, and similar personal expenses.

• *Phaseout for high-income taxpayers.* The HOPE credit is phased out for single taxpayers with adjusted gross income between $40,000 and $50,000. The credit is phased out for married taxpayers who file jointly with adjusted gross income between $80,000 and $100,000. These amounts will be indexed for inflation after 1999, although the first year when an adjustment can be made is 2001.

☞ *Example. A student incurs $5,000 in tuition expenses during her first semester of college in 1998. Her parents pay this entire amount. They have adjusted gross income of $50,000 for 1998. They are eligible to claim a HOPE credit of $1,500.*

☞ *Example. Same facts as the previous example, except that the parents have adjusted gross income of $100,000. They are not eligible for a HOPE credit because their income is too high.*

• *Which year is the credit claimed?* The HOPE credit is available in the year the tuition expenses are paid—so long as the education begins or continues during that year or during the first three months of the next year.

✎ **Key point. Congress gave the IRS authority to issue regulations providing that the HOPE credit will be "recaptured" if a student receives a refund of tuition for which a credit was previously claimed.**

• *What about loans?* Qualified tuition expenses paid with the proceeds of a loan are eligible for a HOPE credit. The credit is not applied to the repayment of the loan itself.

• *Reporting requirements.* The new law specifies that parents cannot claim the HOPE credit unless their tax return reports the name and social security number of the eligible student. Tax returns for 1998 and future years will allow parents to provide this information.

6. Lifetime Learning Credit

❖ **New in 1998. Congress enacted legislation in 1997 that allows taxpayers to claim a "lifetime learning credit" against federal income taxes equal to 20 percent of tuition and academic fees incurred during a year on behalf of the taxpayer, or the taxpayer's spouse or dependent child.**

Here's another break for parents with children in college—taxpayers are allowed a "lifetime learning credit" against federal income taxes equal to 20 percent of tuition and academic fees incurred during a year on behalf of the taxpayer, or the taxpayer's spouse or dependent child. Here are some of the details:

• *Effective date.* This credit applies to tuition expenses incurred after June 30, 1998, for education furnished in academic periods beginning after such date.

• *Eligible taxpayers.* The credit is available for tuition expenses incurred by a taxpayer, or the taxpayer's spouse or dependent child.

• *Amount of credit.* The credit is 20 percent of the first $5,000 of tuition and academic fees This means that the maximum credit will be $1,000 per year. However, for expenses paid after December 31, 2002, up to $10,000 of tuition and academic fees will be eligible for the 20 percent lifetime learning credit. This means that the maximum credit will increase to $2,000 per year.

• *No two-year limitation.* Unlike HOPE credits, the lifetime learning credit is not limited to the first two years of postsecondary, undergraduate education. It can be claimed for an unlimited number of years.

• *Multiple children.* The lifetime learning credit can be claimed in any one year on behalf of any number of eligible students.

☞ *Example. A church member has three dependent children who are attending college (one church-related college and two public universities). The parent may claim a credit of $1,000 for each of these three students, assuming that they each incur tuition expenses of at least $5,000 per year and all other conditions are met.*

✎ **Key point: the amount of the lifetime learning credit is indexed for inflation after the year 2000.**

• *Eligible students.* The lifetime learning credit is available to students at both undergraduate and graduate educational institutions (and postsecondary vocational schools). In addition, students need not be enrolled half-time or full-time.

There are important differences between students who qualify for HOPE credits and the lifetime learning credit. Consider the following: (1) HOPE credits are available only with respect to postsecondary, undergraduate education. Lifetime learning credits are available for both undergraduate and graduate education. (2) HOPE credits are available only for the first two years of undergraduate education. There is no limit on how often lifetime learning credits can be claimed. (3) HOPE credits cannot be claimed for more than two years for the same student. Lifetime learning credits are not subject to this limitation. (4) Like HOPE credits, lifetime learning credits are available with respect to education that is at least half-time. But unlike HOPE credits, lifetime learning credits also are available with respect to "any course of instruction at an eligible educational institution to acquire or improve job skills of the individual." In other words, many continuing education courses and professional seminars would qualify for the lifetime learning credit—if offered by an eligible educational institution.

☞ *Example. A parent incurs tuition expenses of $10,000 in 1998 for a child who attends seminary. The parent is eligible for a lifetime learning credit of $1,000 (unless phased out because of the parent's adjusted gross income).*

• *What expenses are eligible for the credit?* Same as for HOPE credits (see above).

• *Phaseout for high-income taxpayers.* Same as for HOPE credits (see above).

• *Which year is the credit claimed?* Same as for HOPE credits (see above).

• *What about loans?* Same as for HOPE credits (see above).

• *Choice of credit.* If a taxpayer claims a HOPE credit with respect to a student then the lifetime learning credit will not be available with respect to that same student for the year, although the lifetime learning credit may be available with respect to that student for other years. Also, taxpayers who claim an exclusion for distributions from an "education IRA" (explained later in this article) with respect to a student will not be able to claim a lifetime learning credit for that student during the same year.

Illustration 7-2: Daily Business Mileage and Expense Log

Date	Destination	Business Purpose	Start	Stop	Miles This Trip	Type of Expense	Amount
4/21							
4/22	Local (St. Louis)	visiting church members	8,097	8,188	91	Gas	$18.25
4/23	Indianapolis	Church conference	8,211	8,486	275	Parking	$2.00
4/24	Louisville	Seminary Board	8,486	8,599	113	Gas, Repair Flat Tire	$16.50 $8.00
4/25	Return to St. Louis		8,599	8,875	276	Gas	$17.25
4/26	Local	Hospital calls	8,914	9,005	91		
4/27							
Weekly Total					846		$62.00

ILLUSTRATION 7-3

THIS IS NOT AN OFFICIAL INTERNAL REVENUE FORM

Weekly Traveling Expense and Entertainment Record

From: August 7   To: August 13   Name: Bill Wilson

Expenses	Sunday	Monday	Tuesday	Wednesday	Thursday	Friday	Saturday	Total
1. Travel Expenses: Airlines								
Excess baggage								
Bus - Train								
Cab and Limousine								
Tips								
Porter								
2. Meals and Lodging: Breakfast			6 75	6 00	5 25	7 00		25 00
Lunch		9 75	10 00	9 25	8 25	8 50		45 75
Dinner		22 00	18 25	17 50				57 75
Hotel and Motel (Detail in Schedule B)		50 00	50 00	50 00	45 00			195 00
3. Entertainment (Detail in Schedule C)					50 00			50 00
4. Other Expenses: Postage								
Telephone & Telegraph		1 50				1 00		2 50
Stationery & Printing								
Stenographer								
Sample Room			15 00	15 00				30 00
Advertising								
Assistant(s) & Model(s)			20 00	20 00				40 00
Trade Shows								
5. Car Expenses: (List all car expenses - the division between business and personal expenses may be made at the end of the year.) (Detail mileage in Schedule A.)								
Gas, oil, lube, wash								
Repairs, parts								
Tires, supplies								
Parking fees, tolls		4 00			3 00	3 00		10 00
6. Other (Identify)								
Total		87 25	120 00	117 75	111 50	19 50		456 00

NOTE: Attach receipted bills for (1) ALL lodging and (2) any other expenses of $25.00 or more.

Schedule A - Car

Mileage: End		57,600	57,620	57,650	57,660	57,840	///////	
Start		57,445	57,600	57,620	57,650	57,660	///////	
Total		155	20	30	10	180		395
Business Mileage		155	20	30	10	170		385

Schedule B - Lodging

| Hotel or Motel | Name | | Bay Hotel | Bay Hotel | Bay Hotel | Modern Hotel | | | /////// |
| | City | | Albany | Albany | Albany | Troy | | | /////// |

Schedule C - Entertainment

Date	Item	Place	Amount	Business Purpose	Business Relationship
August 11	Bar	John's Steak House	15 00	Discuss purchases	Smith-Y Co.
	Dinner	Troy	35 00		

WEEKLY REIMBURSEMENTS:

Travel and transportation expenses .... N/A

Other reimbursements .... _____

TOTAL .... _____

Chapter 8

CHARITABLE CONTRIBUTIONS

Chapter Highlights

- **Introduction.** Every church is funded almost entirely by charitable contributions. This makes an understanding of charitable contributions very important. Further, there are many unique and sometimes technical legal rules that apply to charitable contributions that are not well understood by most donors or church leaders. Unfamiliarity with these rules can lead to unfortunate consequences, including the disallowance of charitable contribution deductions.

- **6 requirements.** Charitable contributions generally must satisfy 6 requirements:

  ✓ a gift of cash or property
  ✓ claimed as a deduction in the year in which the contribution is made
  ✓ the contribution is unconditional and without personal benefit to the donor
  ✓ the contribution is made "to or for the use of" a qualified charity
  ✓ the contribution is within the allowable legal limits
  ✓ the contribution is properly substantiated

- **Personal services.** The value of personal services is never deductible as a charitable contribution, but expenses incurred in performing services on behalf of a church or other charity may be.

- **Rent-free building space.** The value of rent-free building space made available to a church cannot be claimed as a charitable contribution.

- **Year of contribution.** Charitable contributions must be claimed in the year in which they are *delivered*. One exception is a check that is mailed to a charity—it is deductible in the year the check is mailed (and postmarked), even if it is received early in the next year.

- **If the donor receives a benefit.** Charitable contributions generally are deductible only to the extent they exceed the value of any premium or benefit received by the donor in return for the contribution.

- **"To or for the use of" a charity.** Charitable contributions must be made "to or for the use of" a qualified charitable organization.

- **Amount of deduction.** There are limits on the amount of a contribution that can be deducted. In some cases, contributions that exceed these limits can be "carried over" and claimed in future years.

- **Designated contributions.** "Designated contributions" are those that are made to a church with the stipulation that they be used for a specified purpose. If the purpose is an approved project or program of the church, the designation will not affect the deductibility of the contribution. However, if a donor stipulates that a contribution be spent on a designated individual, no deduction ordinarily is allowed unless the church exercises full administrative control over the donated funds to ensure that they are being spent in furtherance of the church's exempt purposes. However, contributions to a church or missions agency that specify a particular missionary may be tax-deductible if the church or missions agency exercises full administrative and accounting control over the contributions and ensures that they are spent in furtherance of the church's mission.

- **Direct contributions to an individual.** Direct contributions to missionaries, or any other individual, are not tax-deductible, even if they are used for religious or charitable purposes.

- **Substantiation.** Charitable contributions must be properly substantiated. New substantiation rules (that took effect in 1994) apply to individual contributions of cash or property of $250 or more and "quid pro quo" contributions in excess of $75. In addition, special substantiation procedures apply to contributions of noncash property valued by the donor at $500 or more. If the value is more than $5,000, then the donor must obtain a qualified appraisal of the property and attach an appraisal summary (IRS Form 8283) to the tax return on which the contribution is claimed. In some cases, a church that receives a donation of noncash property valued by the donor at more than $5,000 must submit an information return (IRS Form 8282) to the IRS if it disposes of the property within 2 years of the date of gift.

- **Church treasurers.** Church treasurers need to be familiar with the many legal requirements that apply to charitable contributions, so that they can determine the deductibility of contributions and properly advise donors.

- **Appraisals.** Churches are not appraisers, and they have no legal obligation to determine the value of donated property. They should provide donors with receipts or periodic summaries acknowledging receipt of cash or described property.

A. Introduction

The subject of charitable contributions is of vital significance to churches, clergy, and church members. Section 170 of the Code states that "there shall be allowed as a deduction any charitable contribution . . . payment of which is made within the taxable year." To be deductible, a contribution must meet the following 6 conditions:

✓ a gift of cash or other property
✓ made before the close of the tax year for which the contribution is claimed
✓ unconditional and without personal benefit to the contributor
✓ made "to or for the use of" a qualified organization
✓ not in excess of the amounts allowed by law
✓ properly substantiated

These conditions are summarized below.

1. Gift of cash or property

Generally, only contributions of cash or property are deductible. Virtually any kind of property can constitute a charitable contribution, including cash, charges to a bank credit card, real estate, promissory notes, stocks and bonds, automobiles, art objects, books, building materials, collections, jewelry, easements, insurance policies, and inventory.

Services. No deduction is allowed for a contribution of services. Accordingly, a church member who donates labor to his or her church may not deduct the value of the labor.

✎ **Key point: the value of personal services is never deductible as a charitable contribution, but expenses incurred in performing services on behalf of a church or other charity may be.**

☞ *Example. First Church begins a remodeling project. S, a church member, donates 30 hours of labor towards the project. S is a carpenter who ordinarily receives $15 per hour for his services on the open market. S asks the church treasurer for a receipt showing a contribution of $450 (30 hours times $15 per hour). The church may issue S a receipt documenting the hours of labor that were donated, but it should make no representation that this amount is deductible, since it is not.*

☞ *Example. Same facts as the preceding example, except that S asks the church to pay him for his services, and then he donates the payment back to the church in the form of a contribution. This is a permissible arrangement, but it ordinarily will not result in any tax advantage to S, since his deduction is offset by the inclusion of the same amount in his income for income tax reporting purposes. If S cannot itemize deductions on Schedule A, he will actually be worse off by having the church pay him the $450 for his services,*

since he will have additional income without any offsetting deduction.

☞ *Example. An attorney donates his time free of charge in representing a church. He is not entitled to a charitable contribution deduction for the value of his donated services. Grant v. Commissioner, 84 T.C. 809 (1986).*

☞ *Example. A commercial radio station broadcasts certain religious programs free of charge. It is not entitled to a charitable contribution deduction for the value of the free air time. Revenue Ruling 67-236.*

Unreimbursed expenses (including local transportation). While the value of labor or services can never be deducted as a charitable contribution, it is important to note that **unreimbursed expenses** incurred while performing donated labor for a church may constitute a deductible contribution. The income tax regulations specify:

[U]nreimbursed expenditures made incident to the rendition of services to an organization contributions to which are deductible may constitute a deductible contribution. For example, the cost of a uniform without general utility which is required to be worn in performing donated services is deductible. Similarly, out-of-pocket transportation expenses necessarily incurred in performing donated services are deductible. Reasonable expenditures for meals and lodging necessarily incurred while away from home in the course of performing donated services are also deductible. Treas. Reg. 1.170A-1(g).

❖ **New in 1998. The standard mileage rate for charitable travel increases to 14 cents per mile. The new rate is not indexed for inflation.**

Taxpayers may claim a deduction either for the actual costs of using a vehicle for charitable activities, or a standard mileage rate of 12 cents per mile (14 cents per mile beginning in 1998). Actual costs of using a vehicle for charitable services include any out-of-pocket cost of operating or maintaining a car. IRS Publication 526 ("Charitable Contributions") states that "you may deduct unreimbursed out-of-pocket expenses, such as the cost of gas and oil, that are directly related to the use of your car in giving services to a charitable organization. You may not deduct general repair and maintenance expenses, depreciation, or insurance. . . . You may deduct parking fees and tolls, whether you use your actual expenses or the standard rate." The Tax Court has confirmed that the actual cost of using a vehicle for charitable purposes does not include depreciation. The Tax Court has observed:

The regulations do not specifically refer to depreciation, but the [IRS] contends that the statute and the regulations do not authorize a deduction for depreciation. We agree. Depreciation is a "decrease in value." It is not a payment, or expenditure, or an out-of-pocket expense. Hence, it cannot be considered as a contribution, payment of which is made within the taxable year. We accordingly conclude that the [IRS] properly disallowed as a charitable contribution that portion of the amount claimed on the automobile which represented depreciation. *Mitchell v. Commissioner, 42 T.C. 953 (1964).*

Obviously, most volunteers use their vehicles for both charitable and personal purposes. These persons may claim a contribution deduction only for costs associated with their charitable services. In other words, they must determine the percentage of the total miles their vehicle is used during the year for both personal and charitable activities, respectively. They can then claim a deduction for their actual vehicle expenses multiplied times the percentage of their total miles that represent their charitable services. Of course, the volunteer must be able to substantiate each charitable travel expense with adequate written records. Further, the Tax Court has observed:

Unreimbursed amounts expended by a taxpayer to enable him to provide his own services to a charitable organization are deductible only if the charitable work is the cause of the payments. When the expenditures are incurred in an activity which also benefits the taxpayer personally, a charitable deduction has not been allowed, even though the charity also benefits. Therefore, travel expenditures which include a substantial, direct, personal benefit, in the form of a vacation or other recreational outing, are not deductible. The burden of proving that such expenditures qualify as charitable contributions rests with petitioner. *Tafralian v. Commissioner, T.C. Memo. 1991-33.*

☞ *Example. A church member used his car in performing lay religious activities. While he was denied a charitable contribution deduction for a portion of the depreciation and insurance expenses allocable to the car (they did not represent "payments"), he could deduct his out-of-pocket travel and transportation expenses.* Orr v. Commissioner, 343 F.2d 553 (5th Cir. 1965).

☞ *Example. A taxpayer was entitled to deduct as a charitable contribution his out-of-pocket expenses incurred in carrying out evangelistic work for his church.* Smith v. Commissioner, 60 T.C. 988 (1965).

☞ *Example. A taxpayer's unreimbursed out-of-pocket expenses for vestments, books, and transportation while participating in a "diaconate program" of his church, were deductible as charitable contributions.* Revenue Ruling 76-89.

☞ *Example. A taxpayer could not deduct as a charitable contribution transportation expenses incurred in attending choir rehearsals at his church. The court concluded that attendance at choir rehearsals was a form of religious worship that benefited the taxpayer directly, and that his participation in the choir only incidentally benefited the church.* Churukian v. Commissioner, 40 T.C.M. 475 (1980).

☞ *Example. A lay church member drove 2,000 miles in 1997 for charitable activities associated with her church. She has records to document the charitable nature of these 2,000 miles. She may either (1) claim the charitable standard mileage rate of 12 cents per mile (2,000 miles x 12 cents = $240), or (2) deduct her actual out-of-pocket expenses in operating the car for charitable purposes. IRS Publication 526 ("Charitable Contributions") states that "you may deduct unreimbursed out-of-pocket expenses, such as the cost of gas and oil, that are directly related to the use of your car in giving services to a charitable organization. You may not deduct general repair and maintenance expenses, depreciation, or insurance."* Revenue Procedure 80-32.

Charitable travel (out-of-town). Treasury regulation 1.170A-1(g) provides:

[O]ut-of-pocket transportation expenses necessarily incurred in performing donated services are deductible. Reasonable expenditures for meals and lodging necessarily incurred while away from home in the course of performing donated services also are deductible.

Therefore, unreimbursed travel expenses incurred while away from home (whether within the United States or abroad) in the course of donated services to a tax-exempt religious or charitable organization are deductible as a charitable contribution. Note two other important considerations regarding charitable travel:

(1) No significant element of personal pleasure, recreation, or vacation. No charitable deduction is allowed for travel expenses incurred while away from home in performing services for a religious or charitable organization unless there is no significant element of personal pleasure, recreation, or vacation involved in the travel. *IRC 170(j).* This rule also applies to a taxpayer's spouse and children. The purpose of this more restrictive rule is to deny a tax deduction to persons who perform only nominal services for a charity while traveling or who are not required to render services for significant portions of a trip. IRS Publication 526 ("Charitable Contributions") provides:

You can claim a charitable contribution deduction for travel expenses necessarily incurred while you are away from home performing services for a charitable organization only if there is no significant element of personal pleasure, recreation, or vacation in such travel. This applies whether you pay the expenses directly or indirectly. You are paying the expenses indirectly if you make a payment to the charitable organization and the organization pays for your travel expenses. The deduction will not be denied simply because you enjoy providing services to the charitable organization.

(2) Parents cannot deduct payments of their children's travel expenses. The United States Supreme Court ruled in 1990 that parents cannot deduct payments they make towards their missionary sons' travel expenses overseas. *Davis v. United States, 110 S. Ct. 2014 (1990).* The Court observed that "the plain language [of the regulation] indicates that tax-

payers may claim deductions only for expenditures made in connection with their own contributions of service to charities. . . . [A] taxpayer ordinarily reports his own income and takes his own expenses. . . . It would strain the language of the regulation to read it, as [the parents] suggest, as allowing a deduction for expenses made incident to a third party's rendition of services rather than to the taxpayer's own contribution of services."

The recordkeeping and reporting requirements for travel expenses, along with an explanation of the reimbursement method, are explained fully in sections D and E, below.

☞ *Example. A Presbyterian church planned a trip to the Holy Land for 27 of its high school students in order to "visit the places where Jesus lived and walked; visit and know young people of other backgrounds, cultures and religions; and share in an experience of Christian group living, understanding and friendship through work, travel, and worship." For various reasons the destination was changed to Italy, Greece, and Turkey. While in Greece the students assisted in a "farm school" that taught local farmers more advanced techniques. Their primary responsibility involved the construction of a new chicken coop for the school's chickens. The cost of the trip was $1,400 per student, and this cost was paid by several of the parents for their respective children. One of the parents claimed this payment as a charitable contribution, and this position was rejected by the IRS in an audit. The Tax Court agreed with the IRS. It observed: "We think it apparent that a deduction for expenses incident to the performance of services for the school is not allowable as a charitable contribution to [the church]. Although the church had a history of assisting the school, these are two distinctly separate organizations, and the services were not performed for the benefit of the church. That the trip increased the teenagers' interest in the church program, developed their leadership capabilities, and increased their religious understanding does not aid [the parent's] cause. If the trip, indeed, produced these results, the true beneficiaries were the teenagers themselves. . . . The evidence shows plainly that the 46-day expedition to Europe was primarily a vacation, sightseeing, and cultural trip for the teenagers. . . . Instead of the expenditures in question being incident to the rendition of services, we think the visit to the school and the work which was performed were only incidental to, or part of, a vacation trip. There is nothing to suggest that the expenses would have been less if the group had spent the entire trip solely for sightseeing. . . . While efforts to assist the teenagers in developing deeper religious involvement and concern for the needs of others are laudable, the tax laws do not permit parents to deduct sums which they expend for such purposes specifically on behalf of their own children. Tate v. Commissioner, 59 T.C. 543 (1973).*

☞ *Example. Rev. J elects to go on a 2-week preaching mission in Europe. He is in Europe for 10 days, and conducts 1-hour services on 4 of those days. Rev. J will not be able to claim a charitable contribution deduction for the travel expenses he incurs in making this trip. The same rule would apply if Rev. J's spouse or children go along on the trip.*

☞ *Example. Unreimbursed expenses of a delegate to a church conference qualify as deductible charitable contributions. Revenue Ruling 58-240.*

☞ *Example. Persons attending church conventions, assemblies, or other meetings in accordance with their rights, privileges, or obligations as members of the church (as opposed to attending such meetings as the duly chosen representative of a congregation or other official church body) are not, by their attendance, rendering gratuitous services to their church. Expenses incurred in attending such meetings do not constitute charitable contributions. Such expenses constitute nondeductible personal expenses under section 262 of the Code even if attendance is required or expected of them by the tenets of their particular religious group. However this does not preclude the deduction, as charitable contributions, of unreimbursed expenditures which are directly connected with and solely attributable to the rendition of gratuitous services performed for the church during the meeting. Revenue Ruling 61-46.*

✎ **Key point: IRS Publication 526 ("Charitable Contributions") states:**

• **"If you are a chosen representative attending a convention of a qualified organization, you can deduct unreimbursed expenses for travel and transportation, including a reasonable amount for meals and lodging, while away from home overnight in connection with the convention."**
• **"You cannot deduct your expenses in attending a church convention if you go only as a member of your church rather than as a chosen representative."**

☞ *Example. K is a music director at her church. She attends a church convention as a visitor (not as a delegate). After arriving at the location of the meeting K visits a religious music publisher to consider music for the church. Her unreimbursed expenses in making this side trip can be claimed as a charitable contribution. However, this does not convert her expenses incurred in traveling to the meeting site a deductible business expense. This conclusion is supported by the following language in IRS Publication 526: "You can deduct unreimbursed expenses that are directly connected with giving services for your church during the convention."*

Contributions of less than a donor's entire interest in property. Contributions of less than a donor's entire interest in property ordinarily are not deductible unless they fit within one of the following exceptions:

(1) A contribution (not in trust) of an irrevocable remainder interest in a personal residence or farm. To illustrate, a donor who wants to give his home or farm to his church, but who wants to retain possession during his life, can retain a "life estate" in the property and donate a "remainder interest" to the church. The donor may deduct the value of the remainder interest that he has conveyed to the church, though this interest represents less than the donor's entire interest in the property. The valuation of a remainder interest is a determined according to income tax regulation 1.170A-12.

(2) A contribution (not in trust) of an undivided interest in property. To illustrate, assume that Jane Reed owns a 100-acre tract of land, and that she donates one-half of this property to First Church. While this represents a gift of only a portion of the donor's interest in the property, it is nevertheless deductible. *Treas. Reg. 1.170A-7.*

(3) A contribution of an irrevocable remainder interest in property to a charitable remainder trust. A charitable remainder trust is a trust authorized by section 664 of the Code, which provides for a specified distribution, at least annually, to one or more non-charitable income beneficiaries for life or for a term of years (ordinarily not more than 20), with an irrevocable remainder interest to a charity. Many churches and other religious organizations have found such trusts to be an excellent means of raising funds, since they provide the donor with a current charitable contribution deduction plus a stream of income payments as well as assuring the charity that it will receive the trust property at some specified future date. Charitable remainder trusts can be either annuity trusts or unitrusts. The specified distribution to be paid at least annually must be a sum certain which is not less than 5% of the initial fair market value of all property placed in trust (in the case of a charitable remainder annuity trust) or a fixed percentage which is not less than 5% of the net fair market value of the trust assets, valued annually (in the case of a charitable remainder unitrust).

☞ *Example. In 1997, T creates a trust with property valued at $100,000. Annual trust income payments are to be made to T for 15 years, at which time the trust will terminate and the principal will be distributed to First Church. The trust provides that the annual payments to T must be 5% of the net fair market value of the trust's assets at the end of each year. If the trust assets are still valued at $100,000 at the end of 1997, T's annual trust distribution will be $5,000. If the value of the trust assets increases to $120,000 as of December 31, 1998, T's next annual payment will be $6,000 (5% x $120,000). In addition, T receives a charitable contribution deduction in 1997 (the year he established the trust) for the value of the remainder interest that he irrevocably vested in the church. Valuation of the charitable contribution deduction is a complex calculation described in the income tax regulations associated with section 664 of the Code.*

A contribution of a partial interest in property that does not fit within one of the three categories described above ordinarily is not deductible as a charitable contribution. To illustrate, an individual owning an office building who donates the **rent-free use** of a portion of the building to a charitable organization is not entitled to a charitable contribution deduction since the contribution consists of a partial interest in property that does not fit within one of the exceptions described above. This principle is illustrated in the income tax regulations with the following example: "A, an individual owning a 10-story office building, donates the rent-free use of the top floor of the building for the year 1971 to a charitable organization. Since A's contribution consists of a partial interest to which section 170(f)(3) applies, he is not entitled to a charitable contribution deduction for the contribution of such partial interest." Obviously, the same principle would apply to rent-free use of equipment. *IRC 170(f)(3)(A).*

✎ **Key point: the value of rent-free building space made available to a church cannot be claimed as a charitable contribution.**

Gift tax returns. Persons who donate more than $10,000 to any one person or organization in the same year are required to file a federal gift tax return with the IRS. Gifts to churches and other charities are exempted from this requirement. Congress enacted legislation in 1997 clarifying that this exemption applies only to gifts of a donor's *entire* interest in property to the church or charity. It does not apply to a gift of a *partial* interest in property. This provision applies to gifts made after August 5, 1997.

❖ **New in 1997. Congress clarified that donors who contribute property worth $10,000 or more are exempt from filing a gift tax return only if they donate their entire interest in the property.**

☞ *Example. John contributes $15,000 in cash to his church in 1998. He is not required to file a gift tax return with the IRS, because he has made a gift of his entire interest in the funds to his church.*

☞ *Example. Joan gives her home to her church in 1998. She is not required to file a gift tax return with the IRS, even though the home is worth more than $10,000, because she gave her entire interest in the property to the church.*

☞ *Example. Same facts as the previous example, except that Joan reserved a "life estate" in the home, which permits her to remain in the home for the rest of her life. Joan must file a gift tax return with the IRS, since she made only a partial gift of her property to the church.*

☞ *Example. Jack gives ten acres of land to a church in 1998. The deed provides that if the property ever ceases to be used for church purposes, then title will revert back to Jack or his heirs. Jack has retained a partial interest in the property (since title may revert to him or his heirs in the future). Jack's interest is known as a "possibility of reverter."*

Pledges. Pledges and subscriptions are commitments to contribute a fixed sum of money or designated property to a church or other charity in the future. Many churches base their annual budget, or the construction of a new facility, on the results of pledge campaigns. Are such commitments enforceable by a church? Traditionally, the courts refused to enforce such commitments on the basis of contract law. Since a donor typically receives nothing in exchange for his promise to make future contributions, the commitment was considered illusory and unenforceable. In recent years, however, several courts have enforced pledge commitments. In most cases, enforcement is based on the principle of detrimental reliance. That is, a church that relies to its detriment on a pledge in assuming debt or other legal obligation should be able to enforce the pledge. As one court has noted:

the consideration for a pledge to an eleemosynary [i.e., charitable] institution or organization is the accomplishment of the purposes for which such institution or organization was organized and created and in whose aid the pledge is made, and such consideration is sufficient. We therefore conclude that pledges made in writing to eleemosynary institutions and organizations are enforceable debts supported by consideration, unless the writing itself otherwise indicates or it is otherwise proved. *Hirsch v. Hirsch, 289 N.E.2d 386 (Ohio 1972). See also Estate of Timko v. Oral Roberts Evangelistic Association, 215 N.W.2d 750 (Mich. 1974).*

Another court observed that "the real basis for enforcing a charitable [pledge] is one of public policy—enforcement of a charitable pledge is a desirable social goal." The court continued: "Lightly to withhold judicial sanction from such obligations would be to destroy millions of assets of the most beneficent institutions in our land, and to render such institutions helpless to carry out the purposes of their organization." *Jewish Federation v. Barondess, 560 A.2d 1353 (N.J. Super. 1989).*

☞ *Example. A Georgia state court ruled that a person who promised to make a $25,000 contribution to a church could be compelled to honor his commitment. A church purchased property from an individual for $375,000. In the contract of sale the seller promised to donate $5,000 to the church each year for the next five years (for a total contribution of $25,000). When the promised donations were not made, the church sued the seller for breach of contract. The seller claimed that his promise to make the donations was unenforceable because of lack of "consideration" for his promise. A trial court ruled in favor of the seller, concluding that a commitment or promise is not enforceable unless the promisor receives something of value ("consideration") in return. The court concluded that the seller received no value for his promise to make the donations, and therefore the promise was not enforceable. The church appealed, and a state appeals court*

agreed with the church. It observed: "[A]lthough [the seller] asserts the promise to pay the church $25,000 was without consideration . . . nothing in the [record] shows that to be the case. [The sales contract] recites that the promise to pay $25,000 was made as additional consideration for the church to buy [the seller's] property." First Baptist Church v. King, 430 S.E.2d 635 (Ga. App. 1993).

Even in those states that consider pledges to be legally enforceable obligations, a cash-basis donor may claim a charitable contribution deduction only for the amount of the pledge actually paid during the year. *Mann v. Commissioner, 35 F.2d 873 (D.C. Cir. 1932).*

✎ **Key point: the issue of whether ministers should treat the financial support they pay to their church or denomination as a charitable contribution or as a business expense is addressed in chapter 7, section C.13.**

2. Time of contribution

✎ **Key point: charitable contributions must be claimed in the year in which they are delivered. One exception is a check that is mailed to a charity—it is deductible in the year the check is mailed (and postmarked), even if it is received early in the next year.**

Ordinarily, a contribution is made at the time of delivery. For example, a check that is mailed to a church (or other charity) is considered delivered on the date it is mailed. A contribution of real estate generally is deductible in the year that a deed to the property is delivered to the charity. A contribution of stock is deductible in the year that a properly endorsed stock certificate is mailed or otherwise delivered to the charity. A promissory note issued in favor of a charity (and delivered to the charity) does not constitute a contribution until note payments are made. Contributions charged to a bank credit card are deductible in the year the charge was made. Pledges are not deductible until actually paid.

Predated checks. The first Sunday in January often presents problems regarding the correct receipting of charitable contributions. For example, the first Sunday in January of 1998 falls on January 4th. Can a member who contributes a personal check to your church on Sunday, January 4th, deduct the check on his or her 1997 federal tax return if the check is backdated to read "December 31, 1997"? Many churches advise their congregations during worship services conducted on the first Sunday in January that checks contributed on that day can be credited to the previous year if they are dated December 31st of the previous year. Is this true? Unfortunately, *the answer is no.* Section 1.170A-1(b) of the income tax regulations specifies that "ordinarily, a contribution is made at the time delivery is effected. The unconditional delivery or mailing of a check which subsequently clears in due course will constitute an effective contribution on the date of delivery or mailing." According to this language, a check dated December 31, 1997 but physically delivered in

January of 1998 is deductible only on the donor's 1998 federal tax return. This is so whether a donor "predated" a check to read "December 31, 1997" during church services conducted in January of 1998, or in fact completed and dated the check on December 31, 1997 but deposited it on or after January 1, 1998.

The only exception to this rule is in the case of a check that is dated and mailed (and postmarked) in December of 1997. The fact that the church does not receive the check until January of 1998 does not prevent the donor from deducting it on his or her 1997 federal tax return.

Reporting End of Year Contributions

type of contribution	church reports as a 1997 contribution	church reports as a 1998 contribution
Checks written in December 1997 and deposited in church offering in January 1998.		X
Checks written and deposited in church offering in January 1998 but "back dated" to December 1997.		X
Checks written and deposited in church offering in December 1997 but "post dated" to January 1998.	X	
Checks written in December 1997 and deposited in the mail and postmarked in December 1997, but not received by the church until January 1998.	X	
Checks written in December 1997 and deposited in the mail in December 1997 but not postmarked until January 1998, and not received by the church until January 1998.		X

Postdated checks. At some time or other most churches receive a postdated check. A postdated check is a check that bears a future date. For example, Frank writes a check for $100 on March 1, 1998, that he dates April 15, 1998. Such checks often are received at the end of the year when some donors decide they will be better off for tax purposes if they delay their contribution until the following year. Other donors make gifts of postdated checks before leaving on an extended vacation or business trip. One court defined a postdated check as follows: "A postdated check is not a check immediately payable but is a promise to pay on the date shown. It is not a promise to pay presently and it does not mature until the day of its date, after which it is payable on demand the same as if it had not been issued until that date." In other words, a postdated check is treated like a promissory note. It is nothing more than a promise to pay a stated sum on or after a future date. It is not an enforceable obligation prior to the date specified.

Since a postdated check is no different than a promissory note, it should be treated the same way. If someone issues a note to a church, promising to pay $1,000 over the next year, no charitable contribution is made when the note is signed (assuming the donor is a "cash basis" taxpayer). Rather, a contribution is made when the note is paid. Until then, there is only a promise to pay. Like a promissory note, a church ordinarily should simply retain a postdated check until the date on the check occurs. There is no need to return it. A bank may be willing to accept such a check for deposit before the date on the check has occurred, with the understanding that the funds will not be available for withdrawal.

☞ *Example. Jane writes a check in the amount of $1,000 to her church during the last service of 1997, and drops it in the offering. She dates the check January 1, 1998, however, in order to claim a deduction in 1998 rather than in 1997. She does so because she believes her taxable income will be higher in 1998 and so the deduction will be "worth more" in that year. The check is a mere promise to pay on the day it is given to the church, and so no charitable contribution has occurred. The charitable contribution occurs on January 1, 1998. On that date the check becomes more than a mere promise to pay. It is a legally enforceable commitment. The church should record the check as a 1998 contribution.*

☞ *Example. Jack makes weekly contributions of $100 to his church. In anticipation of a month-long business trip, Jack issues four checks in the amount of $100 each that he postdates for the next four Sundays. He places the checks in the offering during a church service prior to leaving on his trip. The church should record each check as a contribution on or after the date specified on the check.*

☞ *Example. Lynn mails a check to her church on December 30, 1997 that is dated January 1, 1998 and that is received by the church on January 2, 1998. A contribution in the form of a check is effective on the date of delivery with one exception—a check that is mailed (and postmarked) in one year is deductible in that year even though it is not received by the church until the next year. This of course assumes that the check is accepted for deposit by the bank. In this case, however, the "mailbox rule" does not apply since the check was postdated. The church treasurer should record Lynn's check as a 1998 contribution.*

3. Unconditional and without personal benefit

The term **contribution** is synonymous with the term **gift**, and accordingly a contribution is not deductible unless it constitutes a valid gift. Since no gift exists in a legal sense unless a donor absolutely and irrevocably divests himself of title, dominion, and control over the gift, it follows that no charitable contribution deduction is available unless the contribution is **unconditional**. Similarly, no charitable contribution deduction is permitted if the donor receives a direct and material benefit for the contribution, since a gift by definition is a gratuitous transfer of property without consideration or benefit to the donor other than the feeling of satisfaction that it inspires. If a donor does receive a return benefit in exchange for a contribution, then a charitable contribution exists only to the extent that the cash or property transferred by the donor exceeds the fair market value of the benefit received in return. These two requirements of a charitable contribution—an unconditional transfer without personal benefit to the donor—are illustrated by the following examples:

✎ **Key point: charitable contributions generally are deductible only to the extent they exceed the value of any premium or benefit received by the donor in return for the contribution.**

☞ *Example. A church member purchases a church bond. No charitable contribution will be permitted for this purchase since the purchaser receives a return benefit. However, a charitable contribution will be available if the member gives the bond back to the church. Revenue Ruling 58-262.*

☞ *Example. A religious broadcaster offers a "gift" (a free book) to anyone who contributes $10 or more. Contributors who give $10 and who receive the book can claim a charitable contribution of only the amount by which their check exceeds the fair market value of the book.*

☞ *Example. A taxpayer was interested in purchasing a tract of land owned by a church. Accordingly, he offered to "donate" $5,000 to the church if the church would give him preferential consideration in the purchase of the land. It was also understood that if he did in fact purchase the land, the purchase price would be reduced by the amount of the $5,000 "contribution." A federal appeals court denied the taxpayer a charitable contribution deduction under these facts, since the $5,000 payment obviously was not unconditional and without personal benefit to the donor. Wineberg v. Commissioner, 326 F.2d 157 (9th Cir. 1964).*

☞ *Example. First Church charges a fee of $250 for each marriage occurring on its premises. The fee is designed to reimburse the church for utilities, wear and tear, custodial services, and other costs that it incurs as a result of the ceremony. A taxpayer's daughter was married at the church, and he paid the $250 fee. On his federal income tax return for that year, the taxpayer claimed a charitable contribution deduction for this fee. The Tax Court denied the deductibility of the fee, since it was not a charitable contribution. The court noted that the taxpayer received a material benefit in*

exchange for his fee that was of commensurate value. Summers v. Commissioner, 33 T.C.M. 696 (1974).

☞ *Example. First Church operates a religious school. A church member has a child who attends the school. Annual tuition at the school is $2,000. In 1998 the parent makes a check payable to the church for $2,000 in excess of her normal offerings, and in exchange the church permits the member's child to attend the school without charge. The member cannot claim the $2,000 as a charitable contribution since she received a material return benefit. If tuition were $1,000 per year, then the member would have made a contribution of $1,000. The subjects of tuition and scholarship gifts, and "quid pro quo" contributions, are discussed more fully later in this chapter.*

☞ *Example. A church trustee lived in the pastor's home. He did not pay rent or any of the expenses of the home. He claimed a charitable contribution deduction to the church that was disallowed by the IRS since the claimed deduction did not exceed the value of the free "room and board" received by the trustee. The Tax Court agreed. It observed: "It is further reasonable to infer that any 'contributions' made by [the trustee] to the [church] benefited him and were in anticipation of such housing or other benefits and, thus, did not proceed from 'detached and disinterested generosity.' Based on the record before us, we hold that [the trustee] has failed to prove that he made a 'contribution or gift' to the church. Williamson v. Commissioner, 62 T.C. 610 (1991).*

☞ *Example. First Church honors large donors to a building program by inscribing their names on a memorial plaque. Does the public disclosure, for many years to come, of the major donors' identity on a memorial plaque constitute a "benefit" received in exchange for the contributions that nullifies any charitable contribution deductions for these donors? In 1992, the IRS said no. The IRS observed: "Payments an exempt organization receives from donors are nontaxable contributions where there is no expectation that the organization will provide a substantial return benefit. Mere recognition of a . . . contributor as a benefactor normally is incidental to the contribution and not of sufficient value to the contributor to [preclude a charitable contribution deduction]. Examples of mere recognition [that do not nullify a charitable contribution deduction] are naming a . . . building after a benefactor . . . ." IRS News Release IR-92-4.*

☞ *Example. The Tax Court ruled that a woman who made contributions to a religious organization was not entitled to a charitable contribution deduction since the organization provided her with the necessities of life. Ohnmeiss v. Commissioner, T.C. Memo. 1991-594.*

For further discussion of the requirement that a contribution is deductible by a donor only to the extent that it exceeds the fair market value of any premium or merchandise received in exchange, see section C of this chapter.

The income tax regulations specify that if a contribution to a charity is dependent on the performance of some act or the happening of some event in order for it to be effective, then no deduction is allowable unless the possibility that the gift will not become effective is so remote as to be negligible. Further, if the contribution specifies that it will be voided if a specified future event occurs, then no deduction is allowable unless the possibility of the future event occurring is so remote as to be negligible. *Treas. Reg. 1.170A-1(e)*. To illustrate, if a donor transfers land to a church on the condition that the land will be used for church purposes and will revert to the donor if the land ever ceases to be so used, the donor is entitled to a charitable contribution deduction if on the date of the transfer the church does plan to use the property for church uses and the possibility that it will ever cease to so use the property is so remote as to be negligible. *IRS Letter Ruling 9443004*.

The United States Supreme Court has summarized these rules as follows:

The sine qua non of a charitable contribution is a transfer of money or property without adequate consideration. The taxpayer, therefore, must at a minimum demonstrate that he purposely contributed money or property in excess of any benefit he received in return. [A contribution is deductible] only if and to the extent it exceeds the market value of the benefit received . . . [and] only if the excess payment [was] made with the intention of making a gift. *United States v. American Bar Endowment, 106 S.Ct. 2426 (1986)*.

Returning contributions to a donor. Should church treasurers ever return a contribution to a donor? This is a question that nearly every church treasurer faces eventually. Such requests can arise in a variety of ways. Consider the following:

☞ *Example. A church member donates $1,000 to the church building fund in 1994. In 1998, the church abandons its plans to construct a new building. The member asks the church treasurer to return her $1,000 contribution.*

☞ *Example. A church member donates $2,500 to his church during the first six months of 1998. In July of 1998 he experiences a financial crisis and asks the church treasurer for a refund of his contributions.*

☞ *Example. A church member donates $2,000 to First Church during the first six months of 1998. In July of 1998 she becomes upset with First Church and begins attending Second Church. She later asks the treasurer of First Church for a refund of her contributions.*

A charitable contribution is a gift of money or property to a charitable organization. Like any gift, a charitable contribution is an irrevocable transfer of a donor's entire interest in the donated cash or property. Since the donor's entire interest in the donated property is transferred, it generally is impossible for the donor to recover the donated property. As we will see, there are a few exceptions to this general rule.

(1) Undesignated contributions

Most charitable contributions are undesignated, meaning that the donor does not specify how the contribution is to be spent. An example would be a church member's weekly contributions to a church's general fund. Undesignated contributions are unconditional gifts. A church has absolutely no legal obligation to return undesignated contributions to a donor under any circumstances. In fact, there are a number of problems associated with the return of undesignated contributions to a donor. These include:

• *Inconsistency.* As noted above, a return of a donor's contributions would be completely inconsistent with the church's prior characterization of the transfers as charitable contributions. As already noted, a charitable contribution is tax-deductible since it is an irrevocable gift to a charity. If a church complies with enough donors' requests to refund their contributions, then this raises a serious question as to the deductibility of any contribution made to the church. Contributions under these circumstances might be viewed as no-interest "demand loans"—that is, temporary transfers of funds that are recallable by donors at will. As such they would not be tax-deductible as charitable contributions.

• *Amended tax returns.* Donors who receive a "refund" of their contributions would have to be informed that they will need to file amended federal tax returns if they previously claimed a charitable contribution deduction for their "contributions". This would mean that donors would have to file a Form 1040X with the IRS. In most states, donors also would have to file amended state income tax returns.

• *Church liability.* In order to avoid the potential penalty for "aiding and abetting" a taxpayer in the substantial understatement of tax, the church could notify the IRS of the return of the contribution. This notification would need to include the donor's name, address, social security number, the date and amount of the earlier contribution, and the date the contribution was returned. Failure by the church to notify the IRS of the return of the contribution could result in a penalty under section 6701(b) of the Internal Revenue Code for "aiding and abetting" in the substantial understatement of tax. The church should inform the donor if it plans to notify the IRS of the returned contribution.

• *"Refund department".* Compliance with a donor's demand for the return of a contribution would morally compel a church to honor the demands of anyone wanting a return of a contribution. This would establish a terrible precedent.

Conclusion. Churches should resist appeals from donors to return their undesignated contributions. There is no legal basis for doing so, even in "emergencies". Honoring such requests can create serious problems, as noted above. Our recommendation—do not honor such requests without the recommendation of an attorney.

(2) Designated contributions

Often a donor will make a "designated" contribution to a church. That is, the donor designates how the contribution is to be spent. For example, a donor contributes a check in the amount of $500 and specifies that it be used for missions, or the building fund, or some other specific project. Designated contributions are held by the church "in trust" for the designated purpose. So long as the church honors the designation, or plans to do so in the foreseeable future, it has no legal obligation to return a donor's designated contribution. Quite to the contrary, returning a donor's designated contribution under these circumstances would create the same problems associated with the return of undesignated contributions (summarized above). Those problems should be reviewed again.

What if a donor contributes money to a church's building fund and the church later abandons its plans to construct a new facility? Such contributions are conditioned on the church pursuing its building program. When the condition fails, the contribution is revocable at the option of the donor. Should the church refund designated contributions to donors under these circumstances? There are a number of possibilities, including the following:

• *Donors can be identified.* If donors can be identified, they should be asked if they want their contributions returned or retained by the church and used for some other purpose. Ideally, donors should communicate their decision in writing to avoid any misunderstandings. Churches must provide donors with this option in order to avoid violating their legal duty to use "trust funds" only for the purposes specified. Of course, churches should advise these donors that they will need to file amended tax returns if they claimed a charitable contribution deduction for their contributions in a prior year. As noted above, the church may want to inform donors that it must notify the IRS of any return of a charitable contribution in order to avoid the potential penalty for "aiding and abetting" a taxpayer in the substantial understatement of tax.

✎ **Key point: often, donors prefer to let the church retain their designated contributions rather than go through the inconvenience of filing an amended tax return.**

• *Donors cannot be identified.* A church may not be able to identify all donors who contributed to the building fund. This is often true of donors who contributed small amounts, or donors who made anonymous cash offerings to the building fund. In some cases, designated contributions were made many years before the church abandoned its building plans, and there are no records that identify donors. Under these circumstances the church has a variety of options. One option would be to address the matter in a meeting of church members. Inform the membership of the amount of designated contributions in the

church building fund that cannot be associated with individual donors, and ask the church members to take an official action with regard to the disposition of the building fund. In most cases, the church membership will authorize the transfer of the funds to the general fund. Note that this procedure is appropriate only for that portion of the building fund that cannot be traced to specific donors. If donors can be identified, then use the procedure described above. Another option is to ask a court for authorization to transfer the building fund to another church fund. Many states have adopted the Uniform Management of Institutional Funds Act, and this Act permits churches to ask a civil court for authorization to remove a restriction on charitable contributions in some situations. The Act provides:

> If written consent of the donor cannot be obtained by reason of his death, disability, unavailability, or impossibility of identification, the governing board may apply in the name of the institution to the [appropriate] court for release of a restriction imposed by the applicable gift instrument on the use or investment of an institutional fund. . . . If the court finds that the restriction is obsolete, inappropriate, or impracticable, it may by order release the restriction in whole or in part.

Other options are available. Churches should be sure to consult with an attorney when deciding how to dispose of designated funds if the specified purpose has been abandoned.

• *Some donors can be identified, and some cannot.* In most cases, some of the building fund can be traced to specific donors, but some of it cannot. Both of the procedures summarized above would have to be used.

✎ **Key point: this section has focused on building funds. The same analysis is relevant to contributions that designate any other specific purpose or activity. Other examples include contributions designating a new organ, a missions activity, or a new vehicle.**

The Scientology case. In 1989, the Supreme Court ruled that "contributions" made to the Church of Scientology for "auditing" were not deductible as charitable contributions. *Hemandez v. Commissioner, 109 S. Ct. 2136 (1989).* Auditing involves a counseling session between a Church official and a counselee during which the counselor utilizes an electronic device (an "E-meter") to identify areas of spiritual difficulty by measuring skin responses during a question and answer session. Counselees are encouraged to attain spiritual awareness through a series of auditing sessions. The Church also offers members doctrinal courses known as "training." The Church charges fixed "donations" for auditing and training sessions (the charges are set forth in published schedules). For example, the published charges one year were $625 for a 12-hour basic auditing session, $750 for a 12-hour specialized auditing session, and $4,250 for a 100-hour package. A 5% "discount" was available to persons who paid their charges in advance, and the Church offered refunds of the unused portions of prepaid charges in the event that a person discontinued the services before their completion. The system of fixed charges was based on a tenet of Scientology (the doctrine of exchange) that requires persons to pay for any benefit received in order to avoid "spiritual decline."

The Supreme Court ruled that payments made to the Church of Scientology for auditing and training services are *not* deductible as charitable contributions. The Court emphasized that a charitable contribution is a payment made to a qualified charitable organization with no expectation of a return benefit. If a return benefit is received, then the payment is a contribution only to the extent that it exceeds the value of the benefit received in exchange. The Court concluded that payments made to the Church of Scientology for auditing and training sessions were a non-deductible reciprocal exchange since

the Church established fixed price schedules for auditing and training sessions in each branch church; it calibrated particular prices to auditing or training sessions of particular lengths and levels of sophistication; it returned a refund if auditing and training services went unperformed; it distributed account cards on which person who had paid money to the Church could monitor what prepaid services they had not yet claimed; and it categorically barred provision of auditing or training services for free. Each of these practices reveals the inherently reciprocal nature of the exchange.

In other words, "contributions" to the Church (1) were mandatory, in the sense that no benefits or services were available without the prescribed payment, and (2) represented a specified fee for a specified service.

The Court rejected the Church's claim that it would be unfair to permit members of more conventional churches to deduct contributions for which they undeniably receive benefits (i.e., sacraments, preaching, teaching, counseling) but deny Scientologists a deduction for payments they make for auditing and training. The Court disagreed with this contention, emphasizing that "the relevant inquiry in determining whether a payment is a [deductible] contribution is, as we have noted, *not whether the payment secures religious benefits or access to religious services, but whether the transaction in which the payment is involved is structured as a quid pro quo exchange.*" Scientologists clearly receive a specified benefit in exchange for a mandatory and specified fee, and this fact distinguishes payments by Scientologists for auditing and training from most voluntary contributions made by donors to more conventional churches. The typical contribution to a conventional church is voluntary (in the sense that religious benefits ordinarily are not withheld if the individual does not make a contribution) and specified religious benefits are not available only upon the payment of a specified fee. The typical church member receives a number of general benefits, none of which is associated with a prescribed fee, whether or not he or she contributes to the church. These facts demonstrate that the typical contribution to a conventional church does *not* constitute a "quid pro quo exchange" of a specified service for a specified and mandatory fee.

✎ **Key point: if a donor makes a "quid pro quo" contribution of more than $75 (that is, a payment that is partly a contribution and partly a payment for goods or services received in exchange), the church must provide a written statement to the donor that satisfies certain conditions. These are addressed in section C of this chapter.**

4. Contributions made to or for the use of a qualified organization

✎ **Key point: charitable contributions must be made "to or for the use of" a qualified charitable organization.**

Only those contributions made to qualified organizations are deductible. Section 170(c) of the Code defines *qualified organizations* to include, among others, any organization (1) created or organized in the United States (or a United States possession); (2) organized and operated exclusively for religious, educational, or other charitable purposes; (3) no part of the net earnings of which inures to the benefit of any private individual; and (4) not disqualified for tax-exempt status under section 501(c)(3) by reason of attempting to influence legislation, and which does not participate or intervene in any political campaign on behalf of any candidate for public office. IRS Publication 78 lists those organizations that have been recognized by the IRS to be qualified organizations. This listing is not exhaustive, however, since many organizations, including churches, are automatically exempt

---

CAN CONTRIBUTIONS BE RECOVERED BY A BANKRUPTCY COURT?

Section 548 of the bankruptcy code authorizes a bankruptcy trustee to "avoid" fraudulent transfers made by a debtor within a year of filing a bankruptcy petition. Fraudulent transfers include transfers made for less than "reasonably equivalent value". Does this provision give bankruptcy trustees the authority to demand that churches return contributions made by members within a year of filing a bankruptcy petition? A number of courts have said that it does. One notable exception was a federal appeals court ruling in 1996. The court conceded that a bankruptcy trustee ordinarily has the authority to recover a debtor's charitable contributions to a church. However, if making such contributions is an important religious practice to a debtor, then the Religious Freedom Restoration Act prevents a trustee from recovering these contributions. *In re Young, 82 F.3d 1407 (8th Cir. 1996).* The United States Supreme Court ruled in 1997 that the Religious Freedom Restoration Act is unconstitutional, and this ruling has the effect of repealing the federal appeals court decision. *City of Boerne v. Flores, 1997 WL 345322 (1997).* In summary, contributions made by church members to their church within a year before filing a bankruptcy petition are now subject to recovery by a bankruptcy court.

---

from federal income taxes without filing an exemption application and therefore their names ordinarily do not appear in the IRS listing. Some organizations are covered by a "group exemption ruling" (see chapter 11, section F).

To be deductible, a contribution must be made "to or for the use of" a qualified organization. Contributions and gifts made directly to individuals are not deductible. To illustrate, the courts have ruled that payments made directly to individual ministers, or to needy individuals, are not deductible. However, contributions to individuals will in some cases be deductible on the ground that they were "for the use of" a qualified organization. Contributions to foreign missionaries under the control and supervision of a religious organization often are considered to be deductible on this basis. The contribution is not made "to" the organization, but it is made "for the use of" the organization. Similarly, contributions are often made payable to a church, but with a stipulation that the funds be distributed to a specified individual. Common examples include Christmas gifts to a minister, scholarship gifts to a church school, and contributions to a church benevolence fund. The deductibility of these "designated contributions," along with contributions made to foreign missionaries, is considered in detail in Section B of this chapter.

Contributions to foreign charities. Church members sometimes make contributions directly to religious organizations or ministries overseas. Or, they make contributions to a United States religious organization for distribution to a foreign organization. Are these contributions tax-deductible? Federal law specifies that a charitable contribution, to be tax-deductible, must go to an organization "created or organized in the United States or in any possession thereof." In addition, the organization must be organized and operated exclusively for religious or other charitable purposes. This means that contributions made directly by church members to a foreign church or ministry are not tax-deductible in this country.

A related question, not addressed by the Court but addressed by the IRS in a 1963 ruling, is whether a donor can make a tax-deductible contribution to an American charity with the stipulation that it be transferred directly to a foreign charity. The IRS ruled that such a contribution is not deductible since it in effect is directly to the foreign charity. *Revenue Ruling 63-252.*

✎ **Key point: in its 1963 ruling, the IRS did concede that contributions to a United States charity are deductible even though they are earmarked for distribution to a foreign charity, so long as the foreign charity "was formed for purposes of administrative convenience and the [United States charity] controls every facet of its operations." The IRS concluded: "Since the foreign organization is merely an administrative arm of the [United States] organization, the fact that contributions are ultimately paid over to the foreign organization does not require a conclusion that the [United States] organization is not the real recipient of those contributions."**

☞ *Example. The Tax Court ruled that a taxpayer who sent contributions to a mosque in his family's home town in Iran was not entitled to a charitable contribution deduction. The Court noted that to be deductible a charitable contribution must go to a charity organized in the United States. Alisobhani v. Commissioner, T.C. Memo. 1994-629 (1994).*

5. Amount deductible

✎ **Key point: there are limits on the amount of a contribution that can be deducted. In some cases, contributions that exceed these limits can be "carried over" and claimed in future years.**

A taxpayer can deduct contributions to most charitable organizations up to 50% of his adjusted gross income. The 50% limit applies to contributions to all "public charities" including churches, church denominations, and religious organizations that receive a substantial part of their support (other than income from religious activities) from public contributions. Contributions to certain nonpublic charities are deductible only up to 20% of adjusted gross income. The IRS maintains that any contribution "for the use of" rather than "to" a qualified organization is deductible only up to 30% of adjusted gross income. To illustrate, out-of-pocket expenses incurred in the course of performing donated services for a church are deductible since such expenditures are incurred "for the use of" the church. While the church is a public charity, the donor can deduct such expenses only to the extent that they do not exceed 30% of adjusted gross income. Similarly, if a donor makes a payment to a missionary with the understanding that it will be used for missions work, such a contribution is "for the use of" rather than "to" a charitable organization and accordingly is deductible only up to 30% of adjusted gross income.

A 30% limit also applies to contributions of appreciated capital gain property to public charities unless the donor elects to have the 50% ceiling apply in which case the contribution is first reduced by the amount of gain that would have been long-term capital gain if the contributed property had been sold at the time of the contribution.

Contributions in excess of the 50% or 30% ceilings can be **carried over** and deducted in each of the five succeeding years until they are used up.

☞ *Example. A church member has adjusted gross income of $20,000 in 1997, and contributed $11,000 to her church in that year (she made no other contributions). If she itemizes her deductions, she may deduct $10,000 in 1997 ($20,000 x 50%) and may carry over the remaining $1,000 to 1998.*

Corporations may deduct charitable contributions of up to 10% of taxable income computed without regard to certain items. *IRC 170(b)(2).* They can carry over contributions in excess of this limit over the next five years, with some limitations. *IRC 170(d)(2).*

In order to apply the percentage limitations, the value of a charitable contribution must first be determined. Cash gifts obviously present no problem, and gifts of other property generally are valued at their fair market value at the time of the gift. If donated property is subject to a debt, the market value of the contribution must be reduced by the amount of the debt that is assumed by the charity.

Ordinary income property. If a donor contributes appreciated "ordinary income property" that would have resulted in ordinary income had the property been sold at its fair market value on the date of the gift, the amount of the contribution ordinarily is limited to the donor's basis (cost) in the property. Ordinary income property includes capital assets (including stock) held for one year or less. To illustrate, if a member purchases stock for $800, holds it for 9 months at which time it has increased in value to $1,000 and then donates it to his church, his deduction is limited to $800 (his cost). A charitable contribution deduction need not be reduced if the ordinary or capital gain income is included in the donor's gross income in the same year as the contribution.

Inventory. If a donor contributes inventory (property sold in the course of your business), the amount that can be claimed as a contribution deduction is the smaller of its fair market value on the day it was contributed or its "basis." The basis of donated inventory is any cost incurred for the inventory in an earlier year that would otherwise be included in opening inventory for the year of the contribution. The amount of any contribution deduction must be removed from opening inventory. It is not part of the cost of goods sold. If the cost of donated inventory is not included in opening inventory, the inventory's basis is zero and no charitable contribution deduction is available.

☞ *Example. In 1998, T, an individual using the calendar year as the taxable year and the accrual method of accounting, contributes property to a church from inventory having a fair market value of $600. The closing inventory at the end of 1997 included $400 of costs attributable to the acquisition of such property, and in 1997 T properly deducted under section 162 $50 of administrative and other expenses attributable to such property. The amount of the charitable contribution allowed for 1998 is $400 ($600 - [$600 -$400]). The cost of goods sold to be used in determining gross income for 1998 may not include the $400 which was included in opening inventory for that year. Treas. Reg. 1.170A-1(c)(4).*

☞ *Example. The facts are the same as the previous example except that the contributed property was acquired in 1998 at a cost of $400. The $400 cost of the property is included in determining the cost of goods sold for 1998, and $50 is allowed as a deduction for that year under section 162. T is not allowed any deduction for the contributed property, since the amount of the charitable con-*

tribution is reduced to zero ($600 - [$600 - $0]). Treas. Reg. 1.170A-1(c)(4).

Long-term capital gain property. If a donor contributes appreciated "capital gain property" that would have resulted in long-term capital gain had the property been sold for its fair market value on the date of the gift, the amount of the contribution is the property's fair market value. Such a contribution, however, is deductible only up to 30% of the donor's adjusted gross income. Donors who contribute capital gain property can elect to deduct their contribution up to 50% of adjusted gross income if they reduce the contribution by the gain that would have been long-term capital gain had the contributed property been sold on the date of the gift. Capital gain property includes capital assets (including stock) held for *more than one year*. In the illustration described in the preceding paragraph, if the stock donated to the church had been held for more than one year then the donor's contribution would have been the fair market value of the stock on the date of the contribution ($1,000), assuming that the donor's contributions of capital gain property did not exceed 30% of adjusted gross income (or 50% if the donor elects to reduce the value of the contribution by the capital gain that would have been realized had the property been sold). Unlike gifts of ordinary income property that must be reduced by the amount of the ordinary income that would have been realized had the property been sold for its fair market value on the date of the gift, gifts of long-term capital gain property made to churches and other public charities ordinarily do not have to be "reduced."

Bargain sales. A bargain sale is a sale of property to a charity at less than its fair market value. Many churches have received substantial contributions through this procedure. It is especially attractive to taxpayers who have property that has greatly appreciated in value. The church obtains property at a greatly reduced price, and the donor receives a significant charitable contribution deduction plus reduces the amount of taxable gain that he would have realized had he sold the property for its fair market value.

A bargain sale results in a transaction that is partly a sale and partly a charitable contribution. A special computation must be made to compute (1) the amount of any deductible charitable contribution, and (2) the taxable gain from the part of the transaction that is a sale. In general, the adjusted basis of the property must be allocated between the part sold and the part given to charity.

charitable contribution

Figure the amount of the charitable contribution in three steps.

(1) Subtract the amount the donor receives for the property from the property's fair market value at the time of sale. This gives the fair market value of the contributed part.

(2) Find the adjusted basis of the contributed part. This is computed by multiplying the adjusted basis of the property times the fair market value of the con-

tributed part, divided by the fair market value of the entire property.

(3) Determine whether the amount of your charitable contribution is the fair market value of the contributed part (step 1) or the adjusted basis of the contributed part (step 2). Generally, if the property sold was capital gain property, the charitable contribution is the fair market value of the contributed part. If it was ordinary income property, the charitable contribution is the adjusted basis of the contributed part. The terms "capital gain property" and "ordinary income property" are defined above.

taxable gain on sale

Part of a bargain sale may be a contribution, but part may be a sale that can result in a taxable gain to the donor. If a bargain sale results in a charitable contribution deduction, the adjusted basis of the property must be allocated between the part of the property sold and the part of the property given to charity. The *adjusted basis of the contributed part* is computed by multiplying the adjusted basis of the entire property times the fair market value of the contributed part, divided by the fair market value of the entire property. To determine the *fair market value of the contributed part*, the donor subtracts the amount received from the sale (the selling price) from the fair market value of the entire property. The *adjusted basis of the part sold* is computed by multiplying the selling price times the adjusted basis for the entire property, divided by the fair market value of the entire property.

Bargain sales are illustrated in the following examples:

☞ **Example.** *G sells ordinary income property with a fair market value of $10,000 to a church for $2,000. G's basis is $4,000 and his adjusted gross income is $20,000. G makes no other contributions during the year. The fair market value of the contributed part of the property is $8,000 ($10,000 - $2,000). The adjusted basis of the contributed part is $3,200 ($4,000 x [$8,000/$10,000]). Because the property is ordinary income property, G's charitable contribution deduction is limited to the adjusted basis of the contributed part. He can deduct $3,200.*

☞ **Example.** *A church member sells ordinary income property with a fair market value of $10,000 to his church for $4,000. If his basis (cost) in the property is $4,000 and his adjusted gross income is $30,000, the contribution from the sale is $6,000 ($10,000 fair market value less $4,000 selling price). But, since the amount of ordinary income that the donor would have received had he sold the property for its fair market value is $6,000 ($10,000 fair market value less $4,000 basis), and since the contribution must be reduced by this amount, the taxpayer is left with no charitable contribution deduction.*

☞ **Example.** *Same facts as the preceding example, except that the donated property was capital gain*

property held for more than one year. Unlike gifts of ordinary income property which must be reduced by the amount of ordinary income that would have been realized had the property been sold at its fair market value on the date of the contribution, gifts of long-term capital gain property made to a church ordinarily do not have to be reduced. Therefore, a deduction of $6,000 is permitted, assuming the percentage limitations discussed above are not exceeded.

Bargain sale contributions are limited to sales. There is no charitable contribution deduction available to persons who lease a building or property to a church at less than its fair rental value.

Itemized deductions. Charitable contributions are available only as an itemized deduction on Schedule A (Form 1040). This means that taxpayers who do not itemize deductions cannot claim a deduction for charitable contributions. No charitable contribution deduction is available to taxpayers who use Form 1040A or 1040EZ. As a result, most taxpayers are prevented from deducting any portion of their charitable contributions since it is estimated that about 70% of all taxpayers have insufficient deductions to use Schedule A. Efforts occasionally are initiated in Congress to resurrect the charitable contribution deduction for "nonitemizers." Any developments will be addressed in future editions of this tax guide.

Limitation on charitable contribution deductions for high-income taxpayers. In 1997, taxpayers must reduce their charitable contribution deductions by 3% of the amount of their adjusted gross income that exceeds $121,200. However, in no event is the deduction reduced more than 80%. This limitation is applied to all itemized deductions except medical expenses, investment interest, and casualty losses. There is no doubt that this rule makes charitable giving less attractive to higher-income individuals. The full impact on churches and other charities remains to be seen.

☞ **Example.** *Joan has adjusted gross income of $150,000 for 1997, and she made charitable contributions totaling $10,000 to her church that year. She will be allowed to deduct only $9,136 of her contributions. This amount represents $10,000 less 3% multiplied times the amount of adjusted gross income in excess of $121,200 ($28,800 x 3% = $864).*

☞ **Example.** *John has adjusted gross income of $250,000 for 1997, and he contributed $20,000 to his church that year. He will be allowed to deduct only $16,136 of his contributions. This amount represents $20,000 less 3% multiplied times the amount of adjusted gross income in excess of $121,200 ($128,800 x 3% = $3,864).*

6. Substantiation

Section 170 of the Code, which authorizes deductions for charitable contributions, states that a charitable contribution shall be allowable as a deduction only if verified. Because of the importance of this issue, it is addressed in a separate section of this chapter (see section C).

✎ **Key point: new requirements for substantiating charitable contributions took effect in 1994. It is essential for church treasurers to be familiar with these rules. They are explained fully in section C of this chapter.**

B. Designated Contributions

"Designated contributions" are contributions made to a church for a specified purpose. In most cases, a donor either designates a specific project (such as the church building fund) or a specific individual (such as a missionary, student, minister, or needy person). In this section, both kinds of designated contribution are addressed. More emphasis is given to contributions designating individuals, since this is the type of designated contribution that has caused the most confusion.

contributions designating a project or program

If the purpose is an approved *project or program* of the church, the designation ordinarily will not affect the deductibility of the contribution. An example is a contribution to a church building fund.

☞ *Example. A church establishes a "new building" fund. Bob donates $500 to his church, with the stipulation that the money be placed in the "new building" fund. This is a valid charitable contribution, and may be treated as such by the church treasurer.*

☞ *Example. A university owned several fraternity houses. Over the past several years, the physical condition of the fraternity houses declined to such an extent that student safety was jeopardized. As a result, university officials launched a fund-raising drive to help finance the cost of reconstructing and remodeling the fraternity houses. Donors were encouraged to contribute for the renovation of a specific fraternity house, and the university assured donors that it would "attempt" to honor their designations. However, the university made it clear to donors that it accepted their designated gifts with the understanding that the designations would not restrict or limit the university's full control over the contributions, and that the university could use the designated contributions for any purpose. The IRS cautioned that for a designated gift to be a tax-deductible charitable contribution, it "must be in reality a gift to the college and not a gift to the fraternity by using the college as a conduit. The college must have the attributes of ownership in respect of the donated property, and its rights as an owner must not, as a condition of the gift, be limited by conditions or restrictions which in effect make a private group the beneficiary of the donated property. . . . [The] university will accept gifts designated for the benefit of a particular fraternity only with the understanding that such designation will not restrict or limit uni-versity's full ownership rights in either the donated property or property acquired by use of the donated property. Accordingly, we conclude that contributions made to university for the purpose of reconstructing and remodeling fraternity housing will qualify for a charitable contribution deduction . . . ." Private Letter Ruling 9733015*

☞ *Example. Barb would like to help her church's music director buy a new home. She contributes $10,000 to her church, with the stipulation that it be used "for a new home for our music director." Neither the church board nor congregation has ever agreed to assist the music director in obtaining a home. Barb's gift is not a charitable contribution. As a result, the church treasurer should not accept it. Barb should be advised to make her gift directly to the music director. Of course, such a gift will not be tax-deductible by Barb. On the other hand, the music director may be able to treat it as a tax-free gift.*

contributions designating a specific individual

If a donor stipulates that a contribution be spent on a *designated individual*, no deduction ordinarily is allowed unless the church exercises full administrative control over the donated funds to ensure that they are being spent in furtherance of the church's exempt purposes. "Designated contributions" that typically are not deductible include contributions to church benevolence funds, scholarship funds, or contributions to an annual Christmas offering for church staff members. However, contributions to a church or missions agency for the benefit of a particular missionary may be tax-deductible if the church or missions agency exercises full administrative and accounting control over the contributions and ensures that they are spent in furtherance of the church's mission.

✎ **Key point: direct contributions to missionaries, or any other individual, are not tax-deductible, even if they are used for religious or charitable purposes.**

As noted above, a charitable contribution must be made "to or for the use of" a qualified organization. Contributions and gifts made directly to individuals are not deductible. However, contributions to individuals will in some cases be deductible on the ground that they were "for the use of" a qualified organization. Contributions to foreign missionaries under the control and supervision of a religious organization often are considered to be deductible on this basis. The contribution is not made "to" the organization, but it is made "for the use of" the organization. Similarly, contributions are often made payable to a church, but with a stipulation that the funds be distributed to a specified individual. Common examples include Christmas gifts to a minister, scholarship gifts to a church school, and contributions to a church benevolence fund. The deductibility of these "designated contributions," along with contributions made to foreign missionaries, is considered below. Of course, a donor can designate the specific charitable activity to which he would like his contribution applied. For example, a donor can contribute $500 to his church and specify that the entire proceeds be applied to foreign missions. Designating a charitable activity, as opposed to an individual, presents no legal difficulties.

1. Missionaries

Contributions made directly to a missionary may be deductible if it can be established that the contribution was "for the use of" a charitable organization (e.g., a church or religious denomination having control or supervision over the missionary). In 1962, the IRS clarified the application of this principle in a ruling upholding a donor's contribution to a church fund out of which missionaries, including his son, were compensated:

If contributions to the fund are earmarked by the donor for a particular individual, they are treated, in effect, as being gifts to the designated individual and are not deductible. However, a deduction will be allowable where it is established that a gift is intended by a donor for the use of the organization and not as a gift to an individual. The test in each case is whether the organization has full control of the donated funds, and discretion as to their use, so as to insure that they will be used to carry out its functions and purposes. In the instant case, the son's receipt of reimbursements from the fund is alone insufficient to require holding that this test is not met. Accordingly, unless the taxpayer's contributions to the fund are distinctly marked by him so that they may be used only for his son or are received by the fund pursuant to a commitment or understanding that they will be so used, they may be deducted by the taxpayer in computing his taxable income. *Revenue Ruling 62-113.*

This principle has been consistently applied by the courts in determining the deductibility of "designated" contributions to charitable organizations. Consider the following examples:

Peace v. Commissioner, 43 T.C.1 (1964). The Tax Court ruled that checks payable to the Sudan Interior Mission were deductible by a donor despite the listing of four missionaries' names on the lower left-hand corner of each check and a letter from the donor requesting that the checks be used for the missionaries. After analyzing all the facts, the court concluded that the donor knew and intended that his contributions would go into a common pool and be administered by the mission and distributed in accordance with stated policies regarding missionary support. As a result, the donor's designation of four individual missionaries "was no more than a manifestation of [his] desire" to have his donations credited to the support allowance of those individuals. The mission maintained "exclusive control, under its own policy, of both the administration and distribution of the funds."

Lesslie v. Commissioner, 36 T.C.M. 495 (1977). A taxpayer who sent a bank check to a missionary serving in Brazil with the express instruction that the funds be used for Presbyterian mission work was allowed a deduction by the Tax Court. The court noted that while the check was payable directly to the missionary, it was not a gift to him personally since it was given for the express purpose of "Presbyterian mission work." In substance, the court concluded, the funds were contributed "to or for the use of the church in its mission work, with the missionary receiving the funds as its agent."

Winn v. Commissioner, 595 F.2d 1060 (5th Cir. 1979). A federal appeals court upheld the deductibility of a contribution to a fund established by three Presbyterian churches for the support of a particular missionary, even though the contribution mentioned the missionary's name, since the contribution was "for the use of" an exempt missions organization. The court noted that a church officer received donated funds and distributed them for the missions work that the church intended.

Ratterman v. Commissioner, 11 T.C. 1140 (1948). A contribution given to a Jesuit priest was held to be deductible on the theory that members of the Jesuit Order are under a vow of poverty obligating them to give to the Order all property received by them, and accordingly a gift to a priest in reality is a gift "to or for the use of" the Order.

The Mormon missionary case. In a significant 1991 ruling, the United States Supreme Court gave its most detailed interpretation of the requirement that a charitable contribution must be "to or for the use of" a qualified charitable organization. *Davis v. United States, 110 S. Ct. 2014 (1991).* The case involved the question of whether the parents of Mormon missionaries can deduct (as charitable contributions) payments they make directly to their sons for travel expenses incurred in performing missionary activities. The parents conceded that their payments were not made "to" a qualified charity, since the monies went directly to the sons and not to the Mormon Church. However, they insisted that their payments were "for the use of" the Church, since the Church "had a reasonable ability to ensure that the contributions primarily served the organization's charitable purposes." They pointed to the Church's role in requesting the funds, setting the amount to be donated, and requiring weekly expense sheets from the missionaries. On the other hand, the IRS interpreted the wording "for the use of" much more narrowly to mean "in trust for." In other words, for a contribution to be "for the use of" a charity, it must be made to an individual or organization pursuant to a trust or similar legal arrangement for the benefit of the charity. Without such a legal and enforceable arrangement, a contribution to an individual cannot be considered "for the use of" the charity since there is no legal means of ensuring that the contribution in fact will be used for the exclusive benefit of the charity. An example of a contribution "for the use of" a qualified charity would be a contribution to a trustee who is required, under the terms of a trust agreement, to spend the trust income solely for the benefit of specified charities. Such a contribution is not "to" a charitable organization, but it should be deductible if made to a trustee who is required to distribute the funds to qualified charities. Obviously, the parents' transfer of funds to their missionary sons' personal checking accounts failed this definition.

The Court conceded that the words "for the use of" taken in isolation, could support the interpretation of either the parents or the IRS. However, it reviewed the events leading to the enactment of the phrase "for the use of" in 1921 and concluded that "it appears likely that in choosing the phrase 'for the use of' Congress was referring to donations made in trust or in a similar legal arrangement." The Court noted that the parents had presented no evidence supporting their claim that Congress intended the phrase "for the use of" to mean contributions directly to individual missionaries so long as the church "has a reasonable ability to supervise the use of the contributed funds." The Court further emphasized that the parents' interpretation "would tend to undermine the purposes of [federal tax law] by allowing taxpayers to claim deductions for funds transferred to children or other relatives for their own personal use. Because a recipient of donated funds need not have any legal relationship with a [church], the [IRS] would face virtually insurmountable administrative difficulties in verifying that any particular expenditure benefited a [church]. Although there is no suggestion whatsoever in this case that the transferred funds were used for an improper purpose, it is clear that [the parents'] interpretation would create an opportunity for tax evasion that others might be eager to exploit." The Court then referred to mail order ministries.

In conclusion, the Court concluded that the parents could not deduct the payments they made directly to their missionary sons because the payments were not made either "to or for the use of" a church or other qualified charity as required by federal law. The payments could not be considered "for the use of" a church since the parents "took no steps normally associated with creating a trust or similar legal arrangement. Although the sons may have promised to use the money in accordance with Church guidelines, they did not have any legal obligation to do so; there is no evidence that the [Church's] guidelines have any legally binding effect. . . . We conclude that because the [parents] did not donate the funds in trust for the Church, or in a similarly enforceable legal arrangement for the benefit of the Church, the funds were not donated 'for the use of' the Church . . . ."

✎ **Key point: the February 1992 "Tax Practitioner Newsletter" published by the IRS Salt Lake City District specifies: "The LDS Church initiated a new missionary funding program, on January 1, 1991. Under this new funding program, called the Equalized Funding Program, all missionary contributions are made directly to the Church. Contributions under the program then become the property of the Church and are under its control. The Church has the discretion to use those funds as the need appears in the various missions of the Church. By contrast, under the former missionary funding program of the Church, contributions sometimes were made directly to the individual missionaries. The Supreme Court held in Davis v. United States that such contributions were not deductible because they were not to or for the use of the Church. The IRS stated that contributions made directly to the Church under the new Equalized Funding Program**

qualify as deductible contributions under Internal Revenue Code section 170."

Contributions to churches or missions agencies that designate a particular missionary as the recipient of the contributed funds. Assume that a member of First Church makes a contribution of $500 to a denominational missions board, and designates on the check (or with a cover letter) that it is for a designated missionary. Is this common practice affected by the Supreme Court's decision in the *Davis* case (summarized above)? In many cases it will not be. In 1962, the IRS ruled that "designated contributions" are tax-deductible (assuming that all of the other legal requirements applicable to charitable contributions are satisfied) so long as the church or missions board "has full control of the donated funds, and discretion as to their use, so as to insure that they will be used to carry out its functions and purposes." In other words, if a donor contributes funds to a missions board, designating a particular missionary, the contribution will be deductible so long as the missions board retains *full administrative and accounting control* over the funds. What does this mean? Neither the IRS nor any federal court has addressed this issue directly. Presumably, this test could be satisfied if a missions agency adopts the following procedures:

• Require each missionary to complete a periodic (e.g., quarterly) "activity report" summarizing all missionary activities conducted for the previous period. This would include services conducted, teaching activities, and any other missionary activities. In each case, the summary should list the date and location of the activity.

• Require the missionary to complete a periodic "accounting" of the donated funds received from the missions agency. The agency should prepare an appropriate form. The form should account for all dollars distributed by the agency. Written receipts should be required for any expense of more than $25. This report should indicate the date, amount, location, and missionary purpose of each expense. It can be patterned after the expense report that is used for business travel. Keep in mind that "religious purposes" includes not only those expenses related directly to missionary activities, but also ordinary and necessary travel and living expenses while serving as a missionary.

• The missions agency must approve each missionary's ministry as a legitimate activity in furtherance of the church's religious mission.

• Prepare a letter of understanding that communicates these terms and conditions. The agency should specifically reserve the right to "audit" or otherwise verify the accuracy of any information provided to you. For example, you may on occasion wish to verify that the activity reports are accurate.

• Reconcile the expense summaries with the activity summaries. That is, confirm that the expenses claimed on the expense reports correspond to the missionary activities described in the activity reports.

Such procedures can be burdensome for a missions agency. This is the type of accounting and administrative control that the Mormon Church was attempting to avoid by its practice of direct person-to-person donations. However, such procedures (or similar ones) will be essential in order to demonstrate that the agency maintains administrative and accounting control over contributions designating specific missionaries.

Contributions to a local church designating a particular missionary not associated with any missions board or agency. Are these contributions tax-deductible? According to the IRS 1962 ruling, such contributions are deductible only if the church "has full control of the donated funds, and discretion as to their use, so as to insure that they will be used to carry out its functions and purposes." This means that the local church must assume the role of a missions board, and implement the kinds of procedures described above with regard to each such missionary. This is a significant responsibility that many churches will not be prepared to assume. The Supreme Court's decision in the *Davis* case (summarized above) ensures that contributions to local churches for independent missionaries and short-term "lay missionaries" from one's own church are not tax-deductible without such controls.

✎ **Key point: persons may still make direct contributions to individual missionaries or religious workers. Such contributions are not "illegal"—they merely are not tax-deductible as charitable contributions. The fact that taxpayers who cannot itemize their deductions on Schedule A (Form 1040) no longer may claim a charitable contribution deduction will reduce the impact of the Court's decision, since it is estimated that nearly 70% of all taxpayers no longer are able to itemize their deductions. This means that about 70% of all taxpayers will receive no tax benefit from making charitable contributions. It makes no difference whether such persons make their contributions to a missions board or directly to a missionary—the contributions are not deductible in either case.**

Hubert v. Commissioner, T.C. Memo. 1993-482 (1993). The Tax Court ruled that contributions to a church were deductible even though they were designated for the support of two missionaries. A member attended an inner-city Baptist church for many years. Due to a lack of funds, the church asked the member to sponsor two missionaries from the church. The member did so for a number of years. One of the missionaries worked in Peru, and was responsible for beginning 15 Baptist churches there. The other missionary worked in a variety of assignments overseas in missionary radio. The member was not related to either missionary or personally associated with them in any way other than the fact that he had taught one of them in his Sunday School class many years before.

In 1982 the member executed a last will and testament that created two trusts funded with $100,000 each. The income of each trust was to be paid to two missions organizations for the missionary work of the two missionaries during their lives, including support during retirement. The member died in 1986, and his estate claimed a charitable contribution deduction for the two $100,000 trusts. The IRS denied a deduction, arguing that the member intended to benefit the missionaries personally and that the missions organizations lacked full control over the use of the funds. The IRS relied in part on the Supreme Court's decision in the *Davis* case (the "Mormon missionary case" discussed above) denying a charitable contribution deduction to Mormon parents for contributions made directly to their missionary sons.

The Tax Court ruled that the estate *could* claim a charitable contribution deduction for the money placed in the two trusts despite the fact that the church member specified that the trusts were for the benefit of the two missionaries. The court noted that a charitable contribution, to be deductible, must be "to or for the use of" a charity. A contribution is "for the use of" a charity if it is transferred to a legally enforceable trust for the charity:

Under [the Supreme Court's decision in the Mormon missionary case] the test is not whether the charitable organization has full control of the funds, but rather is whether the charitable organization has a legally enforceable right to the funds. In [the Mormon missionary case] the charitable organization [did not] actually receive the funds, either directly or in trust. In the case before us, the income and later the principal are held in a legally enforceable trust for [the two missions] organizations which have control over the funds.

The court rejected the IRS argument that the charitable purpose failed because the intent and the actual effect of the gifts was to benefit the two missionaries rather than the church. The court acknowledged that the trusts focused on two specific missionaries. However, it concluded that "we are satisfied, on the facts before us, that decedent intended the bequests to be used to implement the missionary work of the [missions organizations] through the named missionaries, as well as through the building of foreign mission field medical clinics." The court explained:

The charities have complete discretion to use the funds in any manner which fits the stated purpose, including choosing the amounts of the funds to be used and the methods of using those funds. . . . On these facts, we conclude that decedent intended to benefit the general public, not the two named missionaries. Moreover, we find that the charitable organizations have substantial control over the use of the funds and were not meant to be mere conduits to funnel money to the missionaries. The fact that decedent directed the [missions organizations] to use the funds for specific purposes does not defeat the charitable nature of the bequests. Under general trust principles, the [missions organizations] have a fiduciary duty to use the funds as directed; however, they have complete discretion to determine the most appropriate ways to implement the directed purposes. We conclude that the charitable organizations had sufficient control and enforceable rights over the bequests to ensure that the funds were used for charitable purposes, as is required by [law]. The charitable nature of the bequests is further protected by the Attorneys General of Georgia and the State or States in which the charitable organizations are located. The Attorneys General are charged with ensuring that the charitable purposes of the trust are carried out.

The fact that the trusts were to continue distributing funds to the two missionaries following their retirements did not matter to the court. It observed:

The retirement provisions further decedent's charitable purpose by ensuring that the missionaries will be able to continue their work without concern for what will happen to them when the time comes to retire. During the retirement period, the [missions organizations] will continue to control the funds and may provide for the retirement of the missionaries as they see fit. Under the provisions of the will, upon retirement of the missionaries, the income and principal of the trusts are to be given to the charities "to provide for" the retirement of the missionaries and their wives.

The court did caution that "on different facts we might conclude that the charitable organization was a mere conduit to funnel money to an individual and, therefore, lacked sufficient control over the funds. In such a circumstance, because the bequest was intended to benefit one individual rather than the general public, the bequest would not qualify for a charitable deduction."

Conclusions. This case, along with the other precedent summarized above, suggests that contributions to a church or missions organization may be tax-deductible even though they designate a specific missionary in either of two situations:

Situation 1. In 1962, the IRS ruled that contributions to a church or missions organization are tax-deductible even though they designate a particular missionary so long as the church or missions organization "has full control of the donated funds, and discretion as to their use, so as to insure that they will be used to carry out its functions and purposes." *Revenue Ruling 62-113.* In other words, if a donor contributes funds to a church missions board and designates a particular missionary, the contribution will be deductible so long as the church or missions board

retains full administrative and accounting control over the funds.

Situation 2. Contributions "for the use of" a church or missions organization are tax-deductible even though they designate a particular missionary. The phrase "for the use of" means that a contribution is given to a trustee pursuant to a trust or similar legal arrangement for the benefit of a charitable organization. If this test is met, it does not matter that the trustee is directed to distribute funds to a church or missions organization for a specified individual. A contribution is deductible under these circumstances because the trustee has a legal duty to ensure that trust funds are used by the named beneficiary for religious or charitable purposes. This conclusion is reinforced by two additional considerations: (1) Churches and missions organizations have a "fiduciary duty" to distribute funds only for religious or charitable purposes. As a result, if a trust distributes funds to a church or missions organization for the missionary work of a specified individual, the church or missions organization has a fiduciary duty to ensure that trust distributions are used by the missionary for such purposes. Accordingly, such contributions are "for the use of" the church or missions organization even though they designate a specific recipient. (2) State attorneys general are empowered to ensure that the charitable purposes of charitable trusts are carried out.

2. Benevolence funds

Many churches have established benevolence funds to assist needy persons. Typical beneficiaries of such funds include the unemployed, persons with a catastrophic illness, accident victims, and the aged. There is no question that churches may establish benevolence funds. This is both a religious and a charitable function. Undesignated contributions to a church benevolence fund are deductible by the donor if he or she itemizes deductions on Schedule A (Form 1040). However, problems arise when a donor makes a contribution to a church benevolence fund and designates the intended recipient of the contribution. For example, assume that John Miller is a member of First Church, that the church has a benevolence fund, that Joan Green (another church member) is suffering from a catastrophic illness for which she has

---

ILLUSTRATION 8-1
Benevolence Fund Policy

First Church, in the exercise of its religious and charitable purposes, has established a benevolence fund to assist persons in financial need. The church welcomes contributions to the fund. Donors are free to suggest beneficiaries of the fund or of their contributions to the fund. However, such suggestions shall be deemed advisory rather than mandatory in nature. The administration of the fund, including all disbursements, is subject to the exclusive control and discretion of the church board. The church board may consider suggested designations, but in no event is it bound in any way to honor them, since they are accepted only on the condition that they are mere suggestions or recommendations. Donors wishing to make contributions to the benevolence fund subject to these conditions may be able to deduct their contributions if they itemize their deductions. Checks should be made payable to the church, with a notation that the funds are to be placed in the church benevolence fund. The church cannot guarantee this result, and recommends that donors who want assurance that their contributions are deductible seek the advice of a tax attorney or CPA.

The Official Board
First Church

inadequate medical insurance, and that Miller contributes $1,000 to the church benevolence fund with the instruction that his contribution be applied to Green's medical bills. Is Miller's contribution deductible? The answer to this question depends upon the following two considerations:

• **#1 — Contributions "to or for" a qualified charity.** As noted above, section 170 of the Code allows a charitable contribution deduction only with respect to donations "to or for the use of" charitable organizations. Contributions to an individual, however needy, are never deductible, since they can never (unlike certain contributions made to missionaries) be said to be "to or for the use of" a charitable organization.

• **#2 — The donor's intent.** The intent of the donor ordinarily determines whether the transfer should be characterized as a tax-deductible contribution to a church or a non-deductible transfer to an individual. The question to be asked whenever a donor makes a designated contribution to a church benevolence fund is this: Did the donor intend to make a contribution to the church, or did the donor only intend to benefit the designated individual (using the church as an intermediary in order to obtain a tax deduction for an otherwise non-deductible gift)? The fact that the payment was made to a church is not controlling, since taxpayers cannot obtain a deduction merely by funneling a payment through a church. As the IRS often asserts, it is the substance and not the form of a transaction that is controlling.

Let's apply these rules to some specific situations:

Contributions made directly to individuals. Obviously, contributions made directly to individuals are not deductible, no matter how needy the recipient may be. For example, the courts have repeatedly denied deductions for contributions made directly to relatives, clergy, students, military personnel, and needy persons.

Undesignated contributions made directly to a tax-exempt charitable organization. Contributions made directly to a tax-exempt charitable organization ordinarily are deductible. Accordingly, contributions to a church benevolence fund are deductible by donors who itemize deductions on Schedule A and who do *not* designate a recipient or beneficiary of their contribution. To illustrate, assume that First Church establishes a benevolence fund, and that a church member contributed $250 to the fund but made no reference (either orally or in writing) as to a desired recipient of the contribution. Such a contribution ordinarily will be deductible by the donor (assuming that he or she is able to itemize deductions on Schedule A), since it is clear that the contribution was made "to or for the use of" the church.

☞ *Example. In Notice 94-15 (1994) the IRS responded to the question of the deductibility of contributions made for the benefit of victims of the Los Angeles earthquake. The IRS noted that it had "received questions regarding the tax consequences of private efforts to provide relief to victims of the earthquake [in Los Angeles] includ-*

ing related disasters such as fires resulting from earthquake damage." The IRS concluded that "contributions earmarked for Los Angeles earthquake relief that are made to organizations currently recognized by the IRS as tax exempt . . . are fully deductible as charitable contributions." However, it cautioned that "the tax law does not allow taxpayers to deduct contributions earmarked for relief of any particular individual or family." What does this mean? The IRS is saying that donors can make tax-deductible contributions to a church or other charity even if those contributions specify that they are to be used for earthquake relief. Such contributions are deductible since the donor does not know who the ultimate recipient will be. Therefore, it is reasonable to assume that the intent of the donor is to contribute to the charity which in turn will make the decision of how the funds will be distributed. In other words, the charity in such a case exercises "full control of the donated funds, and discretion as to their use, so as to insure that they will be used to carry out its functions and purposes." On the other hand, if a donor contributes funds to a church for earthquake relief, but specifies a particular individual or family who is to receive the contributed funds, then this contribution is not tax-deductible since the church did not maintain "full control of the donated funds, and discretion as to their use, so as to insure that they will be used to carry out its functions and purposes."

Anonymous recommendations. First Church establishes a benevolence fund, and allows only undesignated contributions to the fund. However, donors and other church members are free to make anonymous recommendations (in writing) to the church board regarding desired recipients. Ordinarily, these contributions will be deductible as well. Alternatively, the board could appoint a benevolence committee to receive written or oral recommendations from the congregation regarding benevolence fund candidates, and to make recommendations to the church board. If the committee is not apprised of the identity of donors to the benevolence fund, and all church members are free to make recommendations to the committee regarding recipients of the fund, then donor contributions may be deductible. Of course, these procedures will not support the deductibility of contributions if the identity of benevolence fund donors is obvious to the board, and the board distributes such donations consistently with the expressed desires of the donors.

Contributions designating a specific beneficiary. The most difficult kind of benevolence fund contribution to evaluate (but by far the most common) is a contribution that designates a desired recipient. The designation may be written on the face of the check, on an envelope accompanying the contribution, in a letter, or it may be oral. To illustrate, a member contributes a check in the amount of $500 to a church's benevolence fund, and inserts a note requesting that a designated individual receive the proceeds. Is such a contribution deductible? Ordinarily, such "designated contributions" to a benevolence fund are *not* deductible, since the intent of the donor is to make a transfer of funds directly to a particular individual rather than to a charitable organization. This does not make them "illegal"—it simply makes them non-deductible by the donor. On the other hand, the recipient does not have to report the transfer as taxable income since it is excludable as a gift. Furthermore, the church ordinarily would hold such funds as the trustee of an implied trust, and accordingly could not divert them to any other purpose or use.

The IRS has stated that:

If contributions to the fund are earmarked by the donor for a particular individual, they are treated, in effect, as being gifts to the designated individual and are not deductible. However, a deduction will be allowable where it is established that a gift is intended by a donor for the use of the organization and not as a gift to an individual. The test in each case is whether the organization has full control of the donated funds, and discretion as to their use, so as to insure that they will be used to carry out its functions and purposes. *Revenue Ruling 62-113.*

This test suggests that in some cases it may be possible for a donor to deduct a designated contribution to a church benevolence fund if the circumstances clearly demonstrate that the donor's "designation" was a mere suggestion or recommendation and that the donor intended the contribution to be "to or for the use of" the church and subject to its control rather than to the designated individual. This was the conclusion the IRS reached in a 1987 private letter ruling. Here are the facts. A taxpayer contributed money to a philanthropic fund within a charitable organization. Once the taxpayer made the contribution, the charity had complete legal and equitable control over the fund. However, the donor could, from time to time, submit recommendations to the charity regarding recipients of the fund. Such recommendations, however, were advisory only, and the charity could accept or reject them. Under these facts, the IRS reached the following conclusion:

Although the term "contribution" is not defined either in the Internal Revenue Code or in the income tax regulations, it is well-established that in order to be deductible under section 170 of the Code, a contribution must qualify as a gift in the common sense of being a voluntary transfer of property without consideration.

Revenue Ruling 62-113 [quoted above] holds that contributions to a [tax-exempt] organization that are not earmarked by the donor for a particular individual, will be deductible if it is established that a gift is intended by the donor for the use of the organization and not as a gift to an individual. The test is whether the organization has full control of the donated funds and discretion as to their use, so as to insure that they will be used to carry out its functions and purposes.

From the information submitted and representations made, [the charity] is to have complete legal and equitable control over the funds contributed by [the donor]. [The donor's] right to suggest distributees will be advisory in nature and will not be binding on [the charity]. Moreover, the fund will be used in the furtherance of [the charity's] stated purposes. *IRS Letter Ruling 8752031.*

While private letter rulings apply only to the parties covered by the ruling and may not be used as precedent in support of a particular position, they reflect the thinking of the IRS on a particular issue and as a result can be of considerable relevance. The private letter ruling discussed above suggests that contributions to a church benevolence fund can be deductible even if the donor mentions a beneficiary, if the facts demonstrate that

• the donor's recommendation is advisory only

• the church retains "full control of the donated funds, and discretion as to their use," and

• the donor understands that his or her recommendation is advisory only and that the church retains full control over the donated funds, including the authority to accept or reject the donor's recommendations

How can these facts be established? One possible way would be for a church to adopt a "benevolence fund policy" making all distributions from a benevolence fund subject to the unrestricted control and discretion of the church board, and to communicate such a policy to all prospective donors. It can be argued that donors willing to make a designated contribution to a church benevolence fund under these conditions are manifesting an intent to make a contribution *to the church* rather than to the designated individual. A sample policy is printed in Illustration 8-1.

▲ **Warning. In light of IRS Letter Ruling 9405003 (discussed fully in the next section of this chapter) churches should not implement or rely on illustration 8-1 without the advice of a tax attorney or CPA.**

Churches adopting such a policy should make copies available to any person wanting to make a designated contribution to the church benevolence fund. There is no guaranty that such a policy will render a designated contribution deductible. Churches wishing to assure donors that their contributions to church benevolence funds will be deductible should use one of the more certain methods discussed above (e.g., undesignated contributions, or undesignated contributions and anonymous designations to the board).

Obviously, a church can administer a program in such a way as to jeopardize the deductibility of contributions. For example, a church can adopt the benevolence fund policy reproduced above, yet honor every "recommendation" made by a donor. Clearly, if this practice were known to the IRS, no contribution would be deductible since the church's alleged "control" over the donated funds does not in fact exist. Similarly, if a church receives only a few contributions to its benevolence fund each year, and at the time of each contribution receives a single anonymous recommendation regarding a recipient, it is reasonably clear that the contributions are associated with the recommendations, and the church's control over the funds will be compromised to the extent that it routinely honors such recommendations.

✎ **Key point: in 1994 the IRS ruled that donors could not deduct their contributions to a scholarship fund if they designated specific recipients. This ruling is discussed fully in the next section of this chapter. It is relevant to a consideration of benevolence fund policies since the IRS disregarded a religious organization's "scholarship policy" that purported to give the organization full control over contributions that designated specific scholarship recipients. The IRS concluded that the degree of control exercised by the organization over the contributions was insufficient to support a charitable contribution deduction. This ruling must be studied carefully by any church that has implemented a benevolence fund policy allowing donors to designate individual recipients. While it is still possible in some cases for a church to exercise sufficient control over designated benevolence fund contributions to support a charitable contribution deduction, this conclusion is now more in doubt as a result of the IRS ruling. One thing is clear—the degree of control exercised by the church over designated contributions must be real and substantial. Churches that merely "rubber stamp" every designated contribution to a benevolence fund will not demonstrate sufficient control. *IRS Letter Ruling 9405003*.**

Special appeals. There is one other possible exception to the general rule of nondeductibility of designated contributions to church benevolence funds. Many churches have made special appeals to raise funds for a particular benevolence need. For example, an offering is collected to assist a family with a child who has incurred substantial medical expenses. Are contributions made to such an offering tax-deductible? Unfortunately, neither the IRS nor any federal court has addressed this issue directly. However, it is possible that such contributions would be tax-deductible, if the following conditions are met: (1) the offering was preauthorized by the church board; (2) the recipient (or his or her family) is financially needy, and the uninsured medical expenses are substantial; (3) the offering is used exclusively to pay a portion of the medical expenses; (4) immediate family members are not the primary contributors; and (5) no more than one or two such offerings are collected for the same individual. In 1956, the IRS did issue a ruling acknowledging that charities can distribute funds for benevolent purposes, so long as certain conditions are satisfied:

Organizations privately established and funded as charitable foundations which are organized and actively operated to carry on one or more of the purposes specified in section 501(c)(3) of the Internal Revenue Code of 1954, and which otherwise meet the requirements for exemption from federal income tax *are not precluded from making distributions of their funds to individuals, provided such distributions are made on a true charitable basis in furtherance of the purposes for which they are organized.* However, organizations of this character which make such distributions should maintain

adequate records and case histories to show the name and address of each recipient of aid; the amount distributed to each; the purpose for which the aid was given; the manner in which the recipient was selected and the relationship, if any, between the recipient and (1) members, officers, or trustees of the organization, (2) a grantor or substantial contributor to the organization or a member of the family of either, and (3) a corporation controlled by a grantor or substantial contributor, in order that any or all distributions made to individuals can be substantiated upon request by the Internal Revenue Service. *Revenue Ruling 56-304.*

☞ *Example. How should the balance of a fund created to assist a cancer victim be distributed in the event of her death? That was the issue faced by a New Jersey appeals court. A woman was diagnosed as suffering from acute leukemia. After chemotherapy proved unsuccessful in treating the disease, her physicians recommended a bone marrow transplant. The woman's health insurance company refused to pay for the transplant on the ground that it was an experimental procedure. The woman's family launched a fund-raising campaign in their community, seeking private donations to defray the anticipated costs of the transplant. Their efforts included advertisements in newspapers urging readers to mail contributions to a fund established in the woman's name at a local bank. Nearly $21,000 was raised through these efforts. Unfortunately, the woman died before the transplant could be performed. The fund had a balance of nearly $8,000 at the time of the woman's death. A dispute arose as to the proper distribution of this fund balance. Family members insisted that the fund balance should be distributed to them, and they based their position on affidavits signed by several donors to the fund stating that had they known the leukemia victim would die before the bone marrow transplant they would have wanted the fund balance distributed to the woman's family. A court refused to distribute the balance to the family. Rather, it ordered the bank (in which the contributed funds were deposited) to distribute the remaining funds on a prorata basis among the donors. This ruling will be relevant to any church that has created a fund for the benefit of a specified individual or family (ordinarily for benevolent or charitable purposes). The important point is this—when the purpose of the fund no longer exists, then any fund balance should not necessarily be distributed to family members. Matter of Gonzalez, 621 A.2d 94 (N.J. Super. Ch. 1992).*

Conclusions. A few final remarks.

• **1099 forms.** Does the church need to give the recipient of the benevolence distributions a **1099 form** (if the distributions are $600 or more in any one year)? Ordinarily, the answer would be no, since the 1099 form is issued only to non-employees who receive *compensation* of $600 or more from the church during the year. *IRS Letter Ruling 9314014.* To the extent that benevolence distributions to a particular individual represent a legitimate charitable distribution by the church (consistently with its exempt purposes) then no 1099 would be required. It would be unrealistic to characterize such distributions as compensation for services rendered when in fact the individual performed no services whatever for the church.

• **How church treasurers should respond.** What should church treasurers do when a member attempts to contribute a check for a specified benevolence recipient and it is clear (on the basis of the above information) that the "contribution" is not tax-deductible? There are a number of alternatives, including the following:

(1) Simply refuse to accept the check. This is appropriate when the donor does not indicate on the face of the check that it is for the specified recipient (e.g., the designation is made orally or in an accompanying note or letter). The possibility in such cases is that the donor will deduct the "contribution," and that the IRS would not be able to question the deduction because the check is made payable to the church (without any reference to the designation). In order to prevent such potential abuse it is essential for church treasurers not to accept such checks.

(2) Accept the check but stamp it "NONDEDUCTIBLE" on its face in red ink. This would prevent the donor from claiming a charitable contribution deduction. Churches that choose this alternative should have an appropriate stamp made by a local printing company.

(3) Place an asterisk on the contribution summaries provided to church members by all contributions that are not deductible. This alternative is not sufficient, since a donor can substantiate a charitable contribution (of less than $250) with a canceled check. If a donor's designation does not appear on a check, and the check is accepted by the church and not stamped "NONDEDUCTIBLE," it is possible for the donor to claim a deduction with little risk of it being disallowed. The church would be contributing to the possibility of an impermissible charitable contribution deduction in such cases by adopting the third alternative.

• **Reviewing the church charter.** If your church has established a benevolence fund, you may wish to review your charter to be sure that your statement of purposes includes "charitable" as well as "religious" purposes. Some legal precedent suggests that benevolence activities are more properly characterized, for tax purposes, as charitable rather than religious.

• **No impact on nonitemizers.** With the significant increase in the standard deduction in recent years it is estimated that as few as 30% of all taxpayers are able to claim itemized deductions (including charitable contributions). This means that as many as 70% of all donors receive no tax benefit from a charitable contribution. Of course, this means that such individuals are able to designate contributions (or make direct gifts to needy individuals) without concern for the rules summarized in this section.

• **Definition of "charity".** Benevolence funds typically are established to assist persons in need. The income tax regulations define "charitable" to include relief of the poor and distressed or of the underprivileged." The regulations define "needy" as

being a person who lacks the necessities of life, involving physical, mental, or emotional well-being, as a result of poverty or temporary distress. Examples of needy persons include a person who is financially impoverished as a result of low income and lack of financial resources, a person who temporarily lacks food or shelter (and the means to provide for it), a person who is the victim of a natural disaster (such as fire or flood), a person who is the victim of a civil disaster (such as civil disturbance), a person who is temporarily not self sufficient as a result of a sudden and severe personal or family crisis (such as a person who is the victim of a crime of violence or who has been physically abused). *Treas. Reg. 1.170A-4A(b)(2)(ii)(D).*

The church board should carefully scrutinize every distribution to ensure that the recipient in fact meets this test.

☞ *Example. The IRS ruled that employee contributions to a nonprofit hospital's benevolence fund were tax-deductible. The IRS noted that the fund was established to assist financially needy persons who suffer economic hardship due to accident, loss, or disaster. Persons eligible for assistance include current employees of the hospital, retirees, former employees, volunteers and the spouses and children of such persons. It emphasized that employee contributions did not earmark specific recipients. Rather, all distributions from the fund were made by a committee consisting of employees of the hospital. The committee reviews a potential beneficiary's application to determine the need for emergency financial assistance and the availability of resources in the fund to meet that need. The IRS concluded that employee contributions to the fund were tax-deductible since the purpose of the fund was consistent with the hospital's charitable purposes and the class of potential beneficiaries was sufficiently large: "All awards of the fund are payable only after a determination of need in the discretion of the committee. Contributions may not be earmarked and there is no guarantee that funds will even be available for past contributors should they have a need arise and apply to the fund for assistance. Thus, contributions cannot be made to the fund with an expectation of procuring a financial benefit. The fund derives its income from voluntary contributions and no part of its income inures to the benefit of any individual. The class of potential beneficiaries consists of several thousand employees . . . . Such a class of beneficiaries is not so limited in size that the donee organization is considered to benefit specified individuals. Accordingly, we rule that contributions to the fund are deductible as charitable contributions . . . . The IRS cautioned that the hospital needed to comply with various recordkeeping requirements: "[A]dequate records and case histories should be maintained to show the name and address of each recipient, the amount distributed to each, the purpose for which the aid was given, the* manner in which the recipient was selected and the relationship, if any, between the recipient and members, officers, or trustees of the organization, in order that any or all distributions made to individuals can be substantiated upon request by the IRS." *Revenue Ruling 56-304 . IRS Letter Ruling 9741047.*

☞ **Example.** *The IRS ruled that a donor can deduct contributions to a charitable organization on behalf of needy persons in a foreign country. The charitable organization obtained a list of 5,000 needy families in the foreign country from a social welfare agency located in the country. From this list 25 families were randomly selected who were given $50 per month in support payments. The IRS stated the general rule that "contributions by an individual to a charitable organization that are for the benefit of a designated individual are not deductible under [federal tax law] even though the designated individual may be an appropriate beneficiary for a charitable organization. A gift for the benefit of a specific individual is a private gift, not a charitable gift." However, the IRS concluded that individual donors could deduct their contributions to the relief fund since the organization's "selection of beneficiaries is done in a way to assure objectivity and to preclude any influence by individual donors in the selection. Therefore, [the charity] is not acting as a conduit for private gifts from its contributors to other individuals. Accordingly, contributions to [the charity] for the relief of needy families in a foreign country will be deductible by donors under the provisions of section 170 of the Code." IRS Letter Ruling 8916041.*

3. Scholarship gifts

Many taxpayers have attempted to claim charitable contribution deductions for payments made to a church-operated private school (or to the church that operates the school) in which the taxpayer's child is enrolled. The IRS has emphasized that a charitable contribution is "a voluntary transfer of money or property that is made with no expectation of procuring a financial benefit commensurate with the amount of the transfer." *Revenue Ruling 83-104.* Therefore, payments made by a taxpayer on behalf of a child attending a church-operated school are not deductible as contributions either to the school or to the church if the payments are earmarked in any way for the child.

The fact that payments are not earmarked for a particular child does not necessarily mean that they are deductible. The IRS has held that the deductibility of undesignated payments by a taxpayer to a private school in which his child is enrolled depends upon

whether a reasonable person, taking all the facts and circumstances of the case in due account, would conclude that enrollment in the school was in no manner contingent upon making the payment, that the payment was not made pursuant to a plan (whether express or implied) to convert nondeductible tuition into charitable contributions,

and that receipt of the benefit was not otherwise dependent upon the making of the payment. *Revenue Ruling 83-104.*

In resolving this question, the IRS has stated that the presence of one or more of the following four factors creates a presumption that the payment is not a charitable contribution:

• the existence of a contract under which a taxpayer agrees to make a "contribution" and which contains provisions ensuring the admission of the taxpayer's child

• a plan allowing taxpayers either to pay tuition or to make "contributions" in exchange for schooling

• the earmarking of a contribution for the direct benefit of a particular individual, or

• the otherwise unexplained denial of admission or readmission to a school of children of taxpayers who are financially able, but who do not contribute. *Revenue Ruling 83-104.*

The IRS has observed that if none of these factors is determinative, a combination of several additional factors may indicate that a payment is not a charitable contribution. Such additional factors include but are not limited to the following: (1) the absence of a significant tuition charge; (2) substantial or unusual pressure to contribute applied to parents of children attending a school; (3) contribution appeals made as part of the admissions or enrollment process; (4) the absence of significant potential sources of revenue for operating the school other than contributions by parents of children attending the school; and (5) other factors suggesting that a contribution policy has been created as a means of avoiding the characterization of payments as tuition. If a combination of such factors is not present, payments by a parent will normally constitute deductible contributions, even if the actual cost of educating the child exceeds the amount of any tuition charged for the child's education.

An income tax regulation further specifies that the term "scholarship" does not include "any amount provided by an individual to aid a relative, friend, or other individual in pursuing his studies where the grantor is motivated by family or philanthropic considerations." *Treas. Reg. 1.117-(3)(a).*

The IRS has illustrated the application of these principles in the following examples (set forth in Revenue Ruling 83-104):

Situation 1. A school requests parents to contribute a designated amount (e.g., $400) for each child enrolled in the school. Parents who do not make the $400 contribution are required to pay tuition of $400 for each child. Parents who neither make the contribution nor pay the tuition cannot enroll their children in the school. A parent who pays $400 to the school is not entitled to a charitable contribution deduction because the parent must either make the contribution or pay the tuition in order for his child to attend the school. Therefore, admission to the school is contingent upon making a payment of $400. Such a payment is not voluntary.

Situation 2. A school solicits contributions from parents of applicants for admission during the school's solicitation for enrollment of students or while applications are pending. The solicitation materials are part of the application materials or are presented in a form indicating that parents of applicants have been singled out as a class for solicitation. Most parents who are financially able make a contribution or pledge to the school. No tuition is charged. The school suggests that parents make a payment of $400. A parent making a payment of $400 to the school is not entitled to a charitable contribution deduction. Because of the time and manner of the solicitation of contributions by the school, and the fact that no tuition is charged, it is not reasonable to expect that a parent can obtain the admission of his child to the school without making the suggested payments. Such payments are in the nature of tuition, not voluntary contributions.

Situation 3. A school admits a significantly larger percentage of applicants whose parents have made contributions to the school than applicants whose parents have not made contributions. Parents who make payments to the school are not entitled to a charitable contribution deduction. The IRS ordinarily will conclude that the parents of applicants are aware of the preference given to applicants whose parents have made contributions. The IRS therefore ordinarily will conclude that a parent could not reasonably expect to obtain the admission of his child to the school without making the payment.

Situation 4. A society for religious instruction has as its sole function the operation of a private school providing secular and religious education to the children of its members. No tuition is charged. The school is funded through the society's general account. Contributions to the account are solicited from all society members, as well as from local churches and nonmembers. Persons other than parents of children attending the school do not contribute a significant portion of the school's support. Funds normally come to the school from parents on a regular, established schedule. At times, parents are solicited by the school to contribute funds. No student is refused admittance because of the failure of his or her parents to contribute to the school. Under these circumstances, the IRS generally will conclude that payments to the society are nondeductible. Unless contributions from sources other than parents are of such magnitude that the school is not economically dependent upon parents' contributions, parents would ordinarily not be certain that the school could provide educational benefits without their payments. This conclusion is further evidenced by the fact that parents contribute on a regular, established schedule.

Situation 5. A private school charges a tuition of $300 per student. In addition, it solicits contributions from parents of students during periods other than the period of the school's solicitation for student enrollments. Solicitation materials indicate that parents of students have been singled out as a class for solicitation and the solicitation materials include a report

of the school's cost per student. Suggested amounts of contributions based on an individual's ability to pay are provided. No unusual pressure to contribute is placed upon individuals who have children in the school, and many parents do not contribute. In addition, the school receives contributions from many former students, parents of former students, and other individuals. A parent pays $100 to the school in addition to the $300 tuition payment. Under these circumstances, the IRS generally will conclude that the parent is entitled to claim a charitable contribution deduction of $100. Because a charitable organization normally solicits contributions from those known to have the greatest interest in the organization, the fact that parents are singled out for a solicitation will not in itself create an inference that future admissions or any other benefits depend upon a contribution from the parent.

Situation 6. A church operates a school providing secular and religious education that is attended both by children of parents who are members of the church and by children of nonmembers. The church receives contributions from all of its members. These contributions are placed in the church's general operating fund and are expended when needed to support church activities. A substantial portion of the other activities is unrelated to the school. Most church members do not have children in the school, and a major portion of the church's expenses are attributable to its nonschool functions. The methods of soliciting contributions from church members with children in the school are the same as the methods of soliciting contributions from members without children in the school. The church has full control over the use of the contributions that it receives. Members who have children enrolled in the school are not required to pay tuition for their children, but tuition is charged for the children of nonmembers. A church member whose child attends the school contributes $200 to the church for its general purposes. The IRS ordinarily will conclude that the parent is allowed a charitable contribution deduction of $200 to the church. Because the facts indicate that the church school is supported by the church, that most contributors to the church are not parents of children enrolled in the school, and that contributions from parent members are solicited in the same manner as contributions from other members, a parent's contributions will be considered charitable contributions, and not payments of tuition, unless there is a showing that the contributions by members with children in the school are significantly larger than those of other members. The absence of a tuition charge is not determinative in view of these facts.

The Scientology case. In a 1989 ruling the Supreme Court affirmed that tuition payments made to church or school are not tax-deductible as charitable contributions. The Court rejected the Church of Scientology's claim that *all* contributions for which the donor receives religious benefits and services are automatically deductible. *Hernandez v. Commissioner, 109 S. Ct. 2136 (1989).* It noted that if the Church's claim were accepted the effect would be to "expand the charitable contribution deduction far beyond what Congress has provided. Numerous forms of payments to eligible donees plausibly could be categorized as providing a religious benefit or as securing access to a religious service. For example, some taxpayers might regard their tuition payments to parochial schools as generating a religious benefit or as securing access to a religious service; such payments, however, have long been held not to be charitable contributions under [federal law]. Taxpayers might make similar claims about payments for church-sponsored counseling sessions or for medical care at church-affiliated hospitals that otherwise might not be deductible."

IRS Letter Ruling 9405003. A religious organization solicits contributions from family members and other interested persons to apply toward the tuition expenses of seminary students. Interested parents and family members send in contributions to the organization on behalf of a designated seminary student, and the organization transfers the funds to the student for his or her seminary expenses (less a nominal administrative fee). Most donors give a certain amount every month for the support of a particular student. Literature published by organization states that:

As with all Christian corporations for which donations qualify for tax-exempt status with the Internal Revenue Service, contributions must be directed to [the organization]. A check should not contain the name of the [student] for whose ministry it is given; instead the student's name should be designated on the envelope or a separate paper. *Although the disposition of all contributions rests with the board of directors, [the organization] honors the donor's designation whenever possible.* If it is not possible, [the organization] notifies the donor about the situation.

The organization's policy manual states that "because of the nonprofit status of [the organization] *the distribution of all contributions rests with the board of directors. However, [the organization] takes donors' designations into account as a matter of accountability and integrity."*

The organization claimed that donors' contributions for specified seminary students were fully deductible since the organizations' board of directors reserved the final authority to distribute all contributed funds. The IRS disagreed, noting that "an individual taxpayer is entitled to a deduction for charitable contributions or gifts to or for the use of qualified charitable organizations, payment of which is made during the taxable year." It added, "[i]n addition, a gift is not considered a contribution 'to' a charity if the facts show that the charity is merely a conduit to a particular person." The IRS then quoted from Revenue Ruling 62-113 (quoted above) in which it observed:

If contributions to the fund are earmarked by the donor for a particular individual, they are treated, in effect, as being gifts to the designated individual and are not deductible. However, a deduction will be allowable where it is established that a gift is intended by a donor for the use of the organization and not as a gift to an individual. The test in each case is whether the organization has full control of the donated funds, and discretion as to their use, so as to insure that they will be used to carry out

its functions and purposes. In the instant case, the son's receipt of reimbursements from the fund is alone insufficient to require holding that this test is not met. Accordingly, unless the taxpayer's contributions to the fund are distinctly marked by him so that they may be used only for his son or are received by the fund pursuant to a commitment or understanding that they will be so used, they may be deducted by the taxpayer in computing his taxable income.

The IRS concluded that contributions designating seminary students did not satisfy this test:

In the present case, the taxpayers' contributions to [the organization] were earmarked for the student not only through the use of account numbers which link donors to seminarians, but also by indicating the student's name on the contribution envelopes. Further, the organization's literature indicates that it will make every effort to use the contributions as the donor requests "as a matter of accountability and integrity." These facts indicate that the program is set up so that donors would expect that their contributions will go to the designated seminarian. Thus, the donor reasonably intends to benefit the individual recipient. In addition, taxpayers in this case have stated that they would not have made donations to this particular organization if their son had not been associated with it. Taxpayers' intended their donations to support their son and expected that their son would receive the contributions they made to the organization. It follows from these facts that the organization does not have full control of the donated funds. Thus, under the standard enunciated by Revenue Ruling 62-113 . . . the contributions made by taxpayers to the organization are not deductible . . . because they not only are earmarked but also are received subject to an understanding that the organization will use the funds as the donors designate and because the taxpayers intended to benefit the designated individual rather than the organization.

The IRS rejected the organization's claim that the parents' donations were deductible since the organization exercised "control" over their distribution. The IRS observed: "[T]he organization's statement in their literature that the disposition of all contributions rests with the board of directors is not sufficient to demonstrate control. In fact, the organization in this case refutes its own statement of control by going on to say that it considers designations by donors as a matter of accountability."

✎ **Key point: the IRS concluded that "contributions" on behalf of specific seminary students were not deductible because: (1) the contributions designated a specific student; (2) donors understood that their contributions would benefit the students they designated; and (3) the parents intended to benefit designated children rather than the school. This is a useful test for evaluating the deductibility of contributions to churches and schools that earmark a specific student.**

In conclusion, contributions by parents and others that designate a particular student are not deductible even if the school (or other organization) purports to retain full control over the distribution of those contributions. A mere statement that the school exercises control is not enough.

✎ **Key point: to be tax-deductible, a charitable contribution must be to (or for the use of) a charitable organization. Contributions that designate a specific *project or fund* (building fund, new organ) are tax-deductible since they clearly are made to a church.**

☞ *Example. A church operates a school and charges annual tuition of $2,000. A parent contributes $2,000 to the school's scholarship fund, and specifies that the contribution be used for his child's tuition (who attends the school). This "contribution" is not deductible. The church or school should so inform the parent at the time of the contribution, and should decline the check.*

☞ *Example. Same facts as the previous example, except that the donor is a neighbor rather than the student's parent. The result is the same.*

☞ *Example. A church establishes a scholarship fund to assist members who are attending seminary. A parent of a seminary student contributes $5,000 to the fund, with the stipulation that the contribution be applied toward her son's seminary tuition. Based on IRS Letter Ruling 9405003, this contribution would not be deductible if the parent understood that her contribution would benefit her son and the parent intended to benefit her son rather than the school (this can be established by asking the donor whether or not she would have contributed to the scholarship fund if her son were not a seminary student).*

☞ *Example. A member contributes $2,000 to a scholarship fund. The donor does not designate any student, but rather leaves the distribution of her contribution to the discretion of the school's scholarship committee. This contribution is tax-deductible.*

☞ *Example. A member contributes $1,000 to a church building fund. This contribution is tax-deductible since it is to a church rather than to a specific individual.*

☞ *Example. A donor made contributions to a college scholarship fund. The first contribution was accompanied by a letter stating, in part: "I am interested in the work that your college is doing and I am enclosing my check for [a stated amount], which as I understand it, represents tuition for one term, plus book requirements. Of late, I have been interested in the career of Mr. Robert Roble, who is a very promising young man in my opinion, and whose family lives close to my summer home. I believe he deserves all the help he can get toward his education. I am aware that a donation to a scholarship fund is only deductible if it is unspecified; however, if in*

your opinion and that of the authorities, it could be applied to the advantage of Mr. Robert Roble, I think it would be constructive." Subsequent contributions from the donor were marked "scholarship grants for Robert Roble." A federal appeals court concluded: "It is clear from the record that the [donor] intended to aid Roble in securing an education and that the payments to the college were earmarked for that purpose. . . . If a scholarship was involved, it was one the [donor], not the college, awarded Roble. . . . [The donor's payments] were for the sole benefit of one specified person, Robert Roble, rather than gifts to the college for the benefit of an indefinite number of persons . . . . The payments made were not to a general scholarship fund to be used as the college saw fit, but were to be applied to the educational expenses of Roble . . . . A contribution to an individual, no matter how worthy, does not qualify as a charitable deduction." Tripp v. Commissioner, 337 F.2d 432 (7th Cir. 1964).

☞ *Example. A donor contributed funds to the college scholarship funds at the colleges in which his son and daughter-in-law were enrolled. The contributions designated the donor's son and daughter-in-law as the intended recipients. The Tax Court, in denying the deductibility of these payments, observed: "The amounts paid to (the two colleges) were distributed by these institutions as scholarships to individuals specifically designated by [the donor] including [his] son and daughter-in-law. The payments were, in effect, tuition payments for specifically designated beneficiaries, and as such are nondeductible personal expenses." Lloyd v. Commissioner, T.C. Memo. 1970-95.*

☞ *Example. A prominent donor (who served in the state legislature) established a scholarship fund for the benefit of students in his district. Each year one senior student from each high school was selected by the high school principal on the basis of need and scholastic merit to receive proceeds from the scholarship fund. The donor did not participate in the selection of students to receive scholarships. Each check drawn on the scholarship fund was signed by the donor and made payable to a student and a college or university as joint payees. The donor claimed these payments as a deduction for charitable contributions. The IRS denied a charitable contribution deduction for these payments. It claimed that deductions should be disallowed because the identity of the recipient of the scholarship was made known to the donor prior to the time the funds were disbursed. A federal district court rejected the IRS position, and ruled that the donor was entitled to claim a charitable contribution deduction for his payments. The court observed: "I am unwilling to place the ultra-technical interpretation on Section 170 of the Internal Revenue Code which is urged upon us by the Government. Under the facts presented here, the [donor] had no voice in the selection of the individuals who would benefit from the scholarship donations; [the donor] instructed the principals of the various* high schools to select a student based upon need and merit. Any contributions which flow into a scholarship program result in benefit to both the educational institution and the individual recipients of those scholarships. No reason or authority is presented which would lead me to the conclusion that benefit by an individual scholarship recipient should defeat the deductibility of the gift; notwithstanding benefit by the individual student, the gift is nevertheless 'for the use of' an exempt entity. . . . The fact that the checks were made to the joint order of the student and the college or university is not inconsistent with plaintiffs' intention to further the educational purposes of the high schools and colleges in question." Bauer v. United States, 449 F. Supp. 755 (W.D. La. 1978).

☞ **Example.** A donor disbursed funds to various college scholarship funds to pay tuition and related educational expenses of certain individual students selected by the colleges. The IRS contended that the payments were in effect gifts to individual students rather than deductible charitable contributions. A federal appeals court disagreed and held: "Although [the government] contends that the scholarship awards by [the donor] were, in effect, mere gifts to individual students, the record clearly shows that the payments were made to the state teachers colleges themselves and that [the donor] had no part in the selection of any individual recipient of a scholarship." Sico Foundation v. United States, 295 F.2d 924 (Ct. Cl. 1961).

☞ **Example.** In 1968, the IRS approved a charitable contribution deduction for a corporation under the following facts: The corporation is a large employer that obtains its trained employees principally from graduates of accredited colleges and other educational institutions. To assure an adequate supply of trained young people who may seek employment with the corporation and to respond in a charitable manner to the financial needs of such educational institutions the corporation established a program for advancement of higher education. Under the program, amounts were made available to private and public educational institutions for their use in providing individuals with scholarships. The selection of these institutions was made on the following basis: (1) at least one scholarship was made available to each private institution that currently had twenty or more graduates employed by the corporation, and (2) further scholarships were made available to those public institutions from which the corporation drew a substantial number of graduates. No one institution was awarded more than five scholarships. Each educational institution involved selected the recipients of the scholarships. Upon a determination of the amount of each scholarship, based on the need of the recipient, payment was made to the educational institution which, in turn, made disbursements therefrom to or for the account of each student. Also, under this program, the corporation made grants-in-aid to private institutions in the form of unrestricted funds, the amounts of which were equivalent to the regular tuition charges made by the institutions for students. The recipients of the scholarships were not connected with the corporation in any manner and the educational benefits they derived from the corporation's expenditures could be utilized by them as they chose, free of any present or future obligations to the corporation. And, in turn, the corporation was free of any responsibility to offer employment to the students who derived these benefits. Revenue Ruling 68-484.

☞ **Example.** A donor established a scholarship fund with a large gift from his estate, with the stipulation that scholarships would be distributed to persons who bore the donor's family name and attended either of two specified colleges who bore the donor's family name. The IRS concluded that the scholarship gift was not tax-deductible as a charitable contribution since it did not benefit a large and indefinite class (as is required of a charitable distribution). Rather, "the class of beneficiaries . . . is necessarily limited to a private class of persons." This ruling will be relevant to those churches that have created scholarship funds for designated students (such as church members attending seminary). The smaller the pool of eligible recipients, the more likely that any contributions to the scholarship fund will be deemed non-deductible by the IRS since they will be seen as benefiting a private class of persons rather than serving a public and charitable purpose by designating a large and indefinite class of potential recipients. IRS Letter Ruling 9631004.

Recent legislation promoting education. Congress enacted legislation in 1997 that provides welcome relief to families with children in college or vocational training. This legislation will reduce the incentive for many parents to find a way to deduct contributions that are designated for their children's education. The new legislation introduces HOPE scholarships and lifetime learning credits (both are explained in chapter 7). It also makes significant changes in IRAs that are designed to favor education. These are addressed in chapter 10.

Conclusions. Be sure to review the "conclusions" at the end of the subsection on designated benevolence contributions (section B.2, above).

4. Gifts that designate clergy

Designated gifts to clergy can occur in various ways. For example, churches often collect an offering to honor a minister on his or her birthday or anniversary, at Christmas, or on some other special occasion. Sometimes members make gifts directly to a minister on such occasions. The deductibility of such "contributions" is discussed fully in chapter 4, section A.2, and chapter 10, section L.

It is also fairly common for individuals to attempt to "supplement" a minister's compensation by making "contributions" to a church that are designated for the benefit of a particular minister. To illustrate, assume that Rev. R is the youth pastor at First Church, that his annual compensation from the church is $20,000, and that his parents (who live in another state) want to supplement his income. Accordingly, they send $5,000 to First Church earmarked for their son, which is paid by the church to Rev. R in addition to his stated salary of $20,000. This contribution is not tax-deductible by the parents, since it clearly was their intent to benefit their son. The church acted simply as an intermediary through which the gift was funneled (in many cases, in an attempt to obtain a charitable contribution deduction).

But what if the church informed the parents that their $5,000 gift would be applied to reducing the church's obligation to pay a $20,000 salary? In other words, if the parents understand that their $5,000 gift will be applied toward the church's commitment to pay a $20,000 salary (leaving the church with an obligation of $15,000), does this make a difference? Does relieving the church of $5,000 of its $20,000 obligation warrant a charitable contribution deduction? This question was addressed directly by the Tax Court in a 1975 decision. *Davenport v. Commissioner, 34 T.C.M. 1585 (1975).* A couple paid $100 per month toward the housing expenses of their minister son, and they claimed a charitable contribution deduction for all of their payments. They argued that their payments were tax-deductible since they were relieving the church of an obligation to provide housing (or a housing allowance) for their son. In denying any charitable contribution deduction to the parents for their monthly payments, the court observed: "The cases are clear that the criteria for determining whether an amount is a charitable contribution is not whether the payment which is not made directly to the charity might incidentally relieve the charity of some cost but rather whether the payment is such that the contribution is 'for the use of' the charity in a meaning similar to 'in trust for.'"

The court referred to an earlier decision in which it denied a charitable contribution deduction for a payment made by a taxpayer directly to an educational institution for the education and maintenance of a child who was a ward of the Illinois Children's Home. *Thomason v. Commissioner, 2 T.C. 441 (1943).* In the prior case, the taxpayer had contended that since the Illinois Children's Home would have had to pay for the education and maintenance of this boy had he not done so, his payments were payments "for the use of" that charity and should be tax-deductible. In holding that the amount paid by the taxpayer in the *Thomason* case to the educational institution was not a charitable contribution, the court observed that these payments were earmarked "from the beginning not for a group or class of individuals, not to be used in any manner seen fit by the home, but for the use of a single individual" in whom the taxpayer "felt a keen fatherly and personal interest." The court further observed that "charity begins where certainty in beneficiaries ends," quoting from a Supreme Court case which held that the uncertainty of the objects of the donation is an essential element of charity. After reviewing this precedent, the court concluded:

Here, whether the [church] would have chosen to maintain a house . . . for the use of [the taxpayer's] son and his family as living quarters . . . is not shown by this record. It may have been that had the taxpayer paid the [$100 per month] directly to the church, that organization would have chosen to use the funds otherwise . . . . However, even were there something in this record to indicate that the church would have rented a house for the use of the taxpayer's son . . . it would not follow that the deduction would be allowable since by making the payments directly to the landlord the taxpayer took away the option of the church with respect to its use of the funds. As we have pointed out in several cases, the charity must have full control of the funds donated in order for a taxpayer to be entitled to a charitable deduction, and such is not the situation where the funds are designated by the donor for the use of a particular individual. In the instant case, in our view the evidence as a whole shows that it was the taxpayer's intent to benefit his son by insuring that his son had a place to live with his family . . . . Under these circumstances the payments were for the use or benefit of a particular individual, the taxpayer's son, and therefore are not charitable deductible contributions even though incidentally the payments . . . may have relieved the church of the necessity of paying for a place for the taxpayer's son to live.

Conclusions. Be sure to review the "conclusions" at the end of the subsection on designated benevolence contributions (section B.2, above).

C. Substantiation of Charitable Contributions

✎ **Key point: new requirements for substantiating charitable contributions took effect in 1994. It is essential for church treasurers to be familiar with these new rules. They are explained fully in section C of this chapter.**

✎ **Key point: if a donor makes a "quid pro quo" contribution of more than $75 (that is, a payment that is partly a contribution and partly a payment for goods or services received in exchange), the church must provide a written statement to the donor that satisfies 2 conditions:**

● **The statement must inform the donor that the amount of the contribution that is tax-deductible is limited to the excess of the amount of any money (or the value of any property other than money) contributed by the donor over the value of any goods or services provided by the church or other charity in return.**

● **The statement must provide the donor with a good faith estimate of the value of the goods or services furnished to the donor.**

A written statement need not be issued if only "token" goods or services are provided to the donor (generally, with a value of $69 or 2% of the amount of the contribution, whichever is less). Further, the rules do not apply to contributions in return for which the donor receives solely an intangible religious benefit that generally is not sold in a commercial context outside the donative context.

✎ **Key point: special substantiation procedures apply to contributions of noncash property valued by the donor at $500 or more. If the value is more than $5,000, then the donor must obtain a qualified appraisal of the property and attach an appraisal summary (IRS Form 8283) to the tax return on which the contribution is claimed. In some cases, a church that receives a donation of noncash property valued by the donor at more than $5,000 must submit an information return (IRS Form 8282) to the IRS if it disposes of the property within 2 years of the date of gift.**

✎ **Key point: church treasurers need to be familiar with the many legal requirements that apply to charitable contributions so that they can determine the deductibility of contributions and properly advise donors.**

✎ **Key point: churches are not appraisers, and they have no legal obligation to determine the value of donated property. They should provide donors with receipts or periodic summaries acknowledging receipt of cash or described property.**

As noted above, charitable contributions to churches and other tax-exempt organizations are deductible only if they satisfy certain conditions. One important condition is that the donor be able to *substantiate* the contribution. The substantiation requirements vary depending on the nature of the contribution. They are summarized below. Because of the complexity of the substantiation requirements, they are presented in the form of 10 rules. Simply find the rules that apply to a particular contribution, and follow the substantiation requirements described. The 10 rules are as follows:

Rule 1 — Individual cash contributions of less than $250

Rule 2 — Individual cash contributions of $250 or more

Rule 3 — Individual "quid pro quo" cash contributions of $75 or less

Rule 4 — Individual "quid pro quo" cash contributions of more than $75

Rule 5 — Individual contributions of property valued at less than $250

Rule 6 — Individual contributions of property valued at $250 or more

Rule 7 — Individual contributions of property valued at less than $5,000

Rule 8 — Individual contributions of property valued at more than $500

Rule 9 — Individual contributions of property valued at more than $5,000

Rule 10 — Quid Pro Quo Contributions of noncash property

✎ **Key point: the 10 rules for substantiating charitable contributions are summarized in Table 8-1.**

1. Contributions of Cash

Rule 1 — Individual cash contributions of less than $250

Donors making individual cash contributions of less than $250 must be able to substantiate such contributions with *one* of the following:

• canceled checks

• a receipt or letter from the donee church showing the church's name and the amounts and dates of the contributions, or

• any other reliable written record showing the name of the church and the amounts and dates of the contributions

If the donor has no canceled check or church receipt to support a contribution, then he or she has the burden of maintaining reliable written records supporting the contribution. It can no longer be assumed that oral testimony will be adequate substantiation. The IRS accepts any "reliable written records" as sufficient evidence supporting the contribution, whether or not offering envelopes are used. The income tax regulations specify that a written record will be considered "reliable" if it is made close to the time of the contribution, and it is part of a regular recordkeeping procedure. For example, the regulations state that "a contemporaneous diary entry stating the amount and date of the donation and the name of the donee charitable organization made by a taxpayer who regularly makes such diary entries would generally be considered reliable." If a donor makes a "quid pro quo" contribution (part contribution and part purchase of goods or services) then other requirements apply. These are discussed below.

To assist members in substantiating individual cash contributions of less than $250, churches should keep records showing the amount and date of every contribution (whether in the form of cash or check). Periodically (i.e., quarterly) the church should send contribution summaries to each member showing the amounts given and the respective dates. Such summaries will satisfy the definition of a church receipt, and will relieve cash donors (and donors who misplace canceled checks) of the necessity of substantiating their contributions through "reliable written records." Often donors will not have reliable written records of their own, and therefore a church's periodic contribution summaries will be of significant value. This is especially true for cash contributions, since members who contribute by check can always obtain a copy of a canceled check from their bank or credit union in the event that they misplace a canceled check. Of course, donors making cash contributions should be encouraged to use church envelopes. This will relieve them of the need to make diary entries or other written notations of the date and amount of each contribution.

Offering envelopes. Many churches use offering envelopes. This is an acceptable way to substantiate individual contributions of coins and currency of less than $250. Offering envelopes also reduce the risk of offering counters pocketing loose change. However, even with respect to coins and currency, offering envelopes are not required. The IRS permits donors to substantiate such contributions with any reliable written record (such as a notation on a personal calendar or in a diary).

☞ *Example. The IRS audits a taxpayer's 1997 federal income tax return, and questions an alleged contribution of $100 to First Church for which the taxpayer has no canceled check or church receipt. The taxpayer does maintain a daily diary. A diary entry on the alleged date of the contribution shows that a contribution of $100 was made to First Church. Such diary entries, if regularly made, will constitute reliable written records supporting the contribution.*

☞ *Example. A member of First Church ordinarily contributes cash (in church envelopes, and in individual amounts of less than $250) rather than checks. Since the member will have no canceled checks to support his contributions, he must rely upon the periodic receipts provided to him by his church. If First Church does not issue the member any receipt, then the member can only deduct his contributions to the extent that they can be substantiated by "reliable written records" in his possession.*

☞ *Example. The Tax Court ruled that a church member was not entitled to a charitable contribution deduction on her income tax return for the portion of her cash contributions to her church which were not supported by canceled checks, a receipt from the church, or other written records. The taxpayer did not keep any record of her alleged contributions but relied solely on her memory as to the amounts contributed. She was unable to obtain a receipt from her church because the records were not available due to a dissolution of the church. The IRS ruled that the taxpayer was entitled deductions of the amounts that she could document. The Tax Court agreed, relying on the income tax regulations requiring cash contributions to be supported by (1) a canceled check, (2) a receipt from the church showing the name of the church and the date and amount of each contribution, or (3) in the absence of a check or receipt from the church, "other reliable written records" showing the name of the church and the date and amount of each contribution. The court emphasized that (according to the income tax regulations) factors indicating that written records are reliable include (1) the "contemporaneous nature of the writing evidencing the contribution" (i.e., the written evidence supporting*

a contribution is dated at or near the time of the contribution), and (2) the "regularity of the taxpayer's recordkeeping procedures" (i.e., a diary entry stating the amount and date of a contribution by a taxpayer who "regularly makes such diary entries"). The Tax Court concluded that the taxpayer's memory or oral statements regarding the amounts of her contributions to the church failed to satisfy the substantiation requirements of the income tax regulations and accordingly her claimed contributions were not deductible to the extent they were based on such evidence. McFadden v. Commissioner, 57 T.C.M. 152 (1989).

☞ *Example. Will notations made on a kitchen calendar support a taxpayer's alleged contributions to her church? Yes, concluded the Tax Court. The donor attended a Baptist church, and regularly made cash contributions (of both checks and currency) to the church. The church maintained no formal record of the nature or amount of contributions made by any of its members, and accordingly the taxpayer in question received no receipts for her contributions. She did, however, maintain a kitchen calendar on which she made notations regarding her contributions to the church. The Tax Court ruled that the taxpayer was "entitled to deduct the amounts she recorded on her church calendar." It observed that "in addition to being documented on her calendar, [the taxpayer's] contributions to the church are substantiated by her own testimony, the testimony of the church's pastor, and records from another church verifying contributions of comparable amounts in subsequent years [the taxpayer changed churches in 1985]." Burns v. Commissioner, T.C.Memo. 1988-536.*

☞ *Example. A taxpayer claimed cash contributions of $3,500 to her church. She was audited and the IRS denied any deduction for these contributions. The IRS claimed that the woman had insufficient evidence to substantiate the contributions. The taxpayer claimed that these contributions were all made in cash, and so she had no canceled checks to substantiate them. She also claimed that she kept no records or receipts to prove her contributions. The only evidence she had was a letter from her church stating that the taxpayer made contributions of $3,500 to the church during the year in question "through tithes, offerings, and love donations." No church representative testified during the woman's trial. The Tax Court agreed with the IRS that the woman had failed to substantiate the $3,500 in charitable contributions to her church. It dismissed the church's letter by noting that "the letter from the church is very general and provides no information as to how and when [her] contributions were made. The evidence presented does not satisfy the court that [she] made the contributions to the church in the amount claimed." The Court was satisfied that the woman made some contributions to the church, and allowed her a deduction in the amount of $450. Witherspoon v. Commissioner,*

T.C. Memo. 1994-593. See also Brown v. Commissioner, T.C. Memo. Dec. 51,145(M) (1996).

Rule 2 — Individual cash contributions of $250 or more

Written acknowledgement. New substantiation rules taking effect in 1994 deny a deduction for individual contributions of $250 or more unless the donor "substantiates the contribution by a contemporaneous written acknowledgment of the contribution by the donee organization." *Donors cannot substantiate individual cash contributions of $250 or more with canceled checks.* They must receive a written acknowledgment from the church or other charity. The IRS announced in 1997 that "as long as it is in writing and contains the information required by law, a contemporaneous written acknowledgment may be in any format." The law specifies that a written acknowledgment must include the following information:

1. Name. The donor's name (a social security number is not required).

2. Value of any goods or services provided by charity. A statement indicating whether or not the church provided any goods or services to the donor in exchange for the contribution, and if so, a good faith estimate of the value of those goods or services.

3. If a charity provides no goods or services, or only "intangible religious benefits." If the church provides no goods or services to a donor in exchange for a contribution, or if the only goods or services the church provides are "intangible religious benefits," then the receipt must contain a statement to that effect. The term "intangible religious benefit" is defined by the new law as "any intangible religious benefit which is provided by an organization organized exclusively for religious purposes and which generally is not sold in a commercial transaction outside the donative context." The committee report to the new law states that the term *intangible religious benefit* includes "admission to a religious ceremony" or other insignificant "tangible benefits furnished to contributors that are incidental to a religious ceremony (such as wine)." However, the committee report clarifies that "this exception does apply, for example, to tuition for education leading to a recognized degree, travel services, or consumer goods."

The IRS issued regulations in 1994 specifying that if a church provides only goods or services with an insubstantial value in connection with a charitable contribution of $250 or more, its receipt need not identify or value those goods or services. Rather, the receipt can state that no goods or services were provided to the donor. In other words, when a donor makes a contribution to a charity and receives in return goods or services of insubstantial value, this is treated under the new regulations as though no goods or services were received. As a result, the charity's receipt should state that no goods or services were received (rather than identifying and valuing the goods or services with insubstantial value). The regulations define goods or services of insubstantial value to include:

• items such as bookmarks, calendars, key chains, mugs, posters, or tee shirts bearing the charity's name or logo and having a cost (as opposed to fair market value) of less than $6.90, or

• in other cases, the value of goods or services provided to the donor does not exceed the lesser of $69 or 2% of the amount of the contribution (note—the $69 and $6.90 amounts are adjusted annually for inflation and represent the 1997 amounts)

4. Receipt must be contemporaneous. The receipt must be "contemporaneous," meaning that it must be *received by the donor* on or before the *earlier* of the following two dates: (1) the date the donor files a tax return claiming a deduction for the contribution, or (2) the due date (including extensions) for filing the return.

⊃ **Recommendation. To avoid jeopardizing the tax deductibility of charitable contributions, churches should advise donors at the end of 1997 not to file their 1997 income tax returns until they have received a written acknowledgement of their contributions from the church. This communication should be in writing. To illustrate, the following statement could be placed in the church bulletin or newsletter for the last few weeks of 1997, or included in a letter to all donors: "IMPORTANT NOTICE: To ensure the deductibility of your church contributions, please do not file your 1997 income tax return until you have received a written acknowledgment of your contributions from the church. You may lose a deduction for some contributions if you file your tax return before receiving a written acknowledgement of your contributions from the church."**

Here are a few additional points to note concerning the new substantiation rules:

Donor's, not the church's, responsibility. The committee report to the new law states that the new substantiation requirement "does not impose an information reporting requirement upon charities; rather, it places the responsibility upon taxpayers who claim an itemized deduction for a contribution of $250 or more to request (and maintain in their records) substantiation from the charity of their contribution (and any good or service received in exchange)." While the sole risk of failing to comply with substantiation rules for contributions of $250 or more is upon the donor (who will not be able to substantiate a charitable contribution deduction), churches should take an active role in informing donors of the new rules to ensure the deductibility of contributions. The committee report to the new law instructed the IRS to issue a "notice or other announcement" urging charities "to assist taxpayers in meeting the substantiation requirements."

No reporting to the IRS. A church's written acknowledgments are issued to the donors. They are not sent to the IRS.

Why church contribution receipts are often inadequate. Most churches already provide some form of periodic written statement to donors acknowledging their contributions. However, any statements currently being used must be carefully reviewed to ensure compliance with the new requirements. *In some cases, they will need to be changed.* For example, many receipts do not specify whether the church provided any goods or services in exchange for each individual contribution of $250 or more. If goods or services were provided by the church to the donor in exchange for a particular contribution, then the church must include on its written acknowledgment a good faith estimate of the value of the goods or services that it provided to the donor. However, if such goods or services consist solely of *intangible religious benefits,* then the written acknowledgment must include a statement to that effect. The law specifies that the term "intangible religious benefit" means "any intangible religious benefit which is provided by an organization organized exclusively for religious purposes and which generally is not sold in a commercial transaction outside the donative context." Some churches issue receipts in February or March of the following year. Such a practice will jeopardize the deductibility of every individual contribution of $250 or more to the extent a receipt is received by a donor after a tax return is filed.

The $250 threshold. If a donor makes a $50 cash contribution each week to a church the new requirements do not apply even though the donor will have made $2,600 in contributions for the year. There has been no individual contribution of $250 or more. The donor in such a case can rely on canceled checks to substantiate the contributions, or on any acknowledgment provided by the church even if it does not comply with the new requirements.

Can separate contributions of $250 be combined? Let's say that a donor makes ten separate contributions to her church during 1997 of $250 or more. Must the church issue a written receipt that lists each of these contributions separately, or can the ten contributions be combined as one amount? The IRS addressed this question directly in regulations issued in 1997. The official comments to the regulations contain the following statement: "[F]or multiple contributions of $250 or more to one charity, one [receipt] that reflects the total amount of the taxpayer's contributions to the charity for the year is sufficient." In other words, the church is free to lump all of a donor's contributions together as one amount on its receipt.

✎ **Key point. Most churches currently itemize individual contributions on receipts provided to donors, and many will want to continue this practice even though it is not legally required. A receipt that merely provides donors with a lump sum of all their contributions will be of no value to a donor who wants to correct a discrepancy.**

✎ **Key point. The official comments to the final regulations also confirm that multiple contributions of less than $250 are not combined to trigger the substantiation rules applicable to contributions of $250 or more.**

✎ **Key point: this chapter (text, examples, and illustrations) shows receipts that separately list each contribution of $250 or more, because this is the most common church practice and it provides donors with information that will assist in detecting errors and reconciling discrepancies.**

Effect of noncompliance. There is no penalty imposed on the church (other than the $10 per contribution penalty for not complying with the quid pro quo reporting requirements, as explained below), but a donor will not be able to substantiate individual charitable contributions of $250 or more if audited and a deduction for such contributions will be denied. Accordingly, it is absolutely essential for church treasurers to be aware of these new rules, and issue sufficient "written acknowledgements" to any donor who has made one or more individual contributions to the church of $250 or more.

Multiple contributions on the same day. One topic that needs additional clarification is "multiple contributions". A committee report explaining the new contribution substantiation rules contains the following statement: "Separate payments generally will be treated as separate contributions and will not be aggregated for the purposes of applying the $250 threshold. . . . However, it is expected that the Treasury Department will issue anti-abuse rules to prevent avoidance of the substantiation requirement by a contributor simply writing multiple checks on the same date." It is not clear what this statement means. It would appear that the purpose is to prevent donors from avoiding the new substantiation requirements by simply contributing several checks on the same day (each less than $250) rather than contributing one large check. But, it is entirely possible for donors to contribute more than one check on the same day without any intent of abusing the system. Consider the following:

☞ *Example. A church has a morning and an evening service every Sunday. B makes a $200 contribution in the morning service and a $100 contribution in the evening service on the same Sunday. Is this abusive? Must the church aggregate these contributions so that they are subject to the new substantiation requirements?*

☞ *Example. D makes two $200 contributions in the same worship service.*

☞ *Example. E only makes larger contributions in multiples of $249 so that he will be able to use canceled checks to substantiate his contributions.*

☞ *Example. G customarily gives $100 weekly. She is away on a 6-week trip. At the first service following her return she contributes 6 $100 checks. Is this abusive? Must the church aggregate these contributions so that they are subject to the new substantiation requirements?*

It would seem reasonable to conclude that if there is "economic reality" to the making of multiple contributions of less than $250 then this should not be viewed as abusive and the new substantiation rules should not apply. To illustrate, there is a reasonable basis for "economic reality" to the first and fourth examples mentioned above. These are common practices that are ordinarily are not associated with any intent to avoid or abuse the substantiation rules. Even the second example may have economic reality in some situations. For example, if D made a $200 contribution to the general fund, and a separate $200 contribution to the building fund in the same service, this certainly has economic reality and is not abusive. Your author has filed comments with the IRS in an effort to have new regulations confirm this understanding.

Making contributions through payroll deductions. Regulations issued by the IRS address the issue of how to substantiate contributions made by payroll deduction. The regulations allow taxpayers to substantiate contributions made by payroll deduction by a combination of two documents: (1) a document furnished by the taxpayer's employer that reflects the amount withheld from the taxpayer's wages, and (2) a document prepared by the charity stating that it does not provide goods or services as "whole or partial consideration" for any contributions made by payroll deduction. The regulations also provide that "for purposes of applying the $250 threshold . . . to contributions made by payroll deduction, the amount withheld from each paycheck is treated as a separate contribution. Thus, the [new substantiation rules] will not apply to contributions made by payroll deduction unless the employer deducts $250 or more from a single paycheck for the purpose of payment to a donee organization."

Unreimbursed charitable travel. Many church members make short-term trips on behalf of their church. A common example is a short-term missions trip. Federal law permits church members to deduct their unreimbursed travel expenses while engaged in charitable travel. The income tax regulations specify:

[U]nreimbursed expenditures made incident to the rendition of services to an organization contributions to which are deductible may constitute a deductible contribution. . . . [O]ut-of-pocket transportation expenses necessarily incurred in performing donated services are deductible. Reasonable expenditures for meals and lodging necessarily incurred while away from home in the course of performing donated services are also deductible.

Do the new substantiation requirements apply to the deductibility of unreimbursed charitable travel expenses? To illustrate, assume that Greg, a member of First Church, participates in a short-term missions project and in the process incurs $300 of unreimbursed out-of-pocket travel expenses. The IRS has long acknowledged that such expenses are deductible as a charitable contribution. But what about the new rules for substantiating charitable contributions of $250 or more? Do they apply to this kind of contribution? Is the church responsible for keeping track of Greg's travel expenses in order to determine if they

are $250 or more? Must it issue a receipt that states the amount of travel expenses incurred?

Regulations issued by the IRS originally stated that where a taxpayer incurs unreimbursed expenses in the course of performing services for a charitable organization, the expenses may be substantiated by an "abbreviated written acknowledgment" provided by the charity containing the following information:

- a description of the services provided by the donor

- the dates when the services were provided

- whether or not the charity provided any goods or services in return, and

- if the charity provided any goods or services, a description and good faith estimate of the fair market value of those goods or services

In addition, the abbreviated written acknowledgment must be received by the taxpayer before the earlier of (1) the date he or she files a tax return claiming the contribution deduction, or (2) the due date (including extensions) for the tax return for that year.

In response to several comments, the IRS issued "final regulations" dropping the requirement that the abbreviated acknowledgment include the *specific dates* on which the volunteer services were performed. However, the final regulations keep the other requirements of the abbreviated acknowledgment summarized above.

☞ *Example. Here is an example of an abbreviated written acknowledgement that complies with the final regulations: "Greg Jones participated on a missions trip sponsored by First Church in the nation of Panama. His services included working in a medical clinic. The church provided no goods or services in return for these services." The church should be sure that Greg receives this receipt before the earlier of (1) the date he files a tax return claiming the contribution deduction, or (2) the due date (including extensions) for the tax return for that year.*

Good faith estimate of value. To substantiate an individual charitable contribution of $250 or more, a donor must obtain a receipt from the charity that states whether or not the charity provided any goods or services in exchange for a contribution of $250 or more (other than intangible religious benefits), and if so, a description and good faith estimate of the value of those goods and services. IRS regulations define a "good faith estimate" as an estimate of the fair market value of the goods or services provided by a charity in return for a donor's contribution. The fair market value of goods or services may differ from their cost to the charity. The charity may use any reasonable method that it applies in good faith in making the good faith estimate. However, a taxpayer is not required to determine how the charity made the estimate.

Reliance on a charity's estimate of value. IRS regulations specify that a taxpayer generally may treat an estimate of the value of goods or services as the fair market value for purposes of computing a charitable contribution deduction if the estimate is in a receipt issued by the charity. For example, if a charity provides a book in exchange for a $100 payment, and the book is sold at retail prices ranging from $18 to $25, the taxpayer may rely on any estimate of the charity that is within the $18 to $25 range (the charitable contribution deduction is limited to the amount by which the $100 donation exceeds the fair market value of the book that is provided to the donor). However, a taxpayer may not treat an estimate as the fair market value of the goods or services if the taxpayer knows, or has reason to know, that such treatment is unreasonable. For example, if the taxpayer is a dealer in the type of goods or services it receives from a charity or if the goods or services are readily valued, it is unreasonable for the taxpayer to treat the charity's estimate as the fair market value of the goods or services if that estimate is in error and the taxpayer knows, or has reason to know, the fair market value of the goods or services.

Alternative reporting procedure. The new law specifies that instead of providing written acknowledgments to donors, a church or other charity may elect to report the information directly to the IRS. Such a report would require a church to obtain donors' social security numbers, and in many cases the information would need to be transmitted to the IRS by means of magnetic tape. Few if any churches will opt for this alternative. We do not recommend it for the following reasons: (1) It is optional and not required. (2) Few if any churches will elect the optional procedure. (3) By requiring churches to obtain the social security numbers of donors making individual contributions of $250 or more, the alternative procedure is too intrusive and would offend many church members. (4) The alternative procedure requires churches to report directly to the IRS. We oppose any such reporting if not mandated by law, since it involves risks of computer errors, unresolved problems, and increased IRS scrutiny.

Why the new rules were enacted. Why were these new substantiation requirements enacted? For one reason—to raise additional federal revenue by reducing the number of unwarranted charitable contribution deductions. For example, assume that First Church operates a private school that charges annual tuition of $2,000, and that a parent makes a tuition check in the amount of $2,000 payable directly to the church. In the past, many parents claimed charitable contribution deductions for such "contributions" even though this was completely unjustified. Since the check was made payable to the church, it was often difficult for the IRS to ascertain the true nature of the "contribution" even if the donor were audited. Under the new rules, such abuses will be reduced substantially. In this example, the church will need to provide the donor with a written acknowledgment that specifies the nature and value of goods or services received in exchange for the contribution. This will easily place the IRS "on notice" of the true nature of the purported contribution. Many other examples could be cited.

☞ **Example.** B is a member of First Church. She makes 52 weekly contributions of $10 (for a total of $520) during 1997, and receives only "intangible religious benefits" in exchange for her contributions. The new substantiation rules do not affect either B or the church. She will be permitted to deduct her contributions (if she can itemize her deductions on Schedule A), and she can substantiate her contributions using canceled checks.

☞ **Example.** Same facts as the previous example, except that B made a one-time cash contribution of $1,000 to the church's mission fund on June 30, 1997. In order to ensure the deductibility of the $1,000 contribution, B must receive a written acknowledgment from the church not later than the date she files her tax return or the due date of her tax return, whichever is earlier, that (1) reports the date and amount of the $1,000 contribution, and (2) states that the only goods or services received by the donor in return for her $1,000 contribution were "intangible religious benefits." The $1,000 contribution may be aggregated with the weekly contributions for a total of $1,520, or all of the contributions can be separately itemized.

☞ **Example.** A member made weekly contributions to his church in 1997 that averaged $50 (none is for $250 or more). However, the member made a cash contribution of $500 to the missions fund and an additional cash contribution of $1,000 to the building fund. The church treasurer is aware of the new substantiation requirements, and plans to issue the member a written acknowledgment on April 15, 1998 (the due date of the 1997 tax return). The member files his tax return on February 1, 1998. The new law specifies that any contribution of $250 or more must be substantiated with a contemporaneous written acknowledgment, which is defined as an acknowledgment that is received by the donor by the earlier of (1) the date the donor files a tax return claiming a deduction for the contribution, or (2) the due date (including extensions) for filing the return. Since the member filed a tax return on February 1, 1998, a receipt issued by the church on April 15 is not contemporaneous and may re-

---

IRS SAYS MANY DONORS AND CHARITIES ARE NOT COMPLYING WITH SUBSTANTIATION RULES

In Announcement 90-25, issued in February 1990, the IRS announced that "a significant percentage of taxpayers fail to attach Form 8283 to their tax returns to support their noncash charitable contribution deduction." The IRS further observed that "charitable organizations that receive noncash contributions are failing to file Form 8282 when they dispose of the property." The purpose of the IRS announcement was "to remind taxpayers and charitable orhanizations of the filing requirements for these forms."

sult in a loss of a deduction for the $500 and $1,000 contributions. This example illustrates the importance of issuing proper receipts as soon as possible. In no event should a receipt (for one or more individual contributions of cash or property $250 or more) be issued after December 31st of the current year, since there is the possibility that some donors will file tax returns early in January. Church treasurers will need to be especially vigilant with respect to year-end contributions. Donors who make individual contributions of cash or property of $250 or more in the last few days of December must be issued a receipt promptly. Remember, if a donor files a tax return before the church issues a receipt, some of the donor's contributions may become non-deductible (since the church's written acknowledgment was not "contemporaneous").

☞ **Example.** The treasurer at First Church hears of the new substantiation requirements, but assumes that they will not affect her church since the church already issues annual contribution receipts to each donor. The church's receipts are issued by the end of January of the following year, and report the date and amount of each contribution of cash, and the date and a description of each contribution of property. The treasurer is in error in thinking that the new law will not affect the church's reporting. The church's current reporting is deficient in the following respects: (1) Since written acknowledgments are issued at the end of January, it is possible that they will be issued to some donors after they have filed their tax returns, meaning that the acknowledgments are not contemporaneous and may result in the non-deductibility of individual contributions of $250 or more (of either cash or property). (2) The church's written acknowledgment must specify whether the church provided any goods or services in exchange for contribution of $250 or more. If goods or services were provided by the church to the donor in exchange for a particular contribution, then the church must include on its written acknowledgment a good faith estimate of the value of the goods or services that it provided to the donor. If such goods or services consist solely of intangible religious benefits, then the written acknowledgment must include a statement to that effect. The church does not include this information on its current receipts, and accordingly they are insufficient with regard to individual contributions of $250 or more. (3) The church is not complying with the quid pro quo reporting requirements.

☞ **Example.** A church treasurer has heard that the new substantiation rules can be satisfied by filing reports with the IRS. Is this true, and if so is this option desirable? It is true that the new law permits charities to file information returns with the IRS (on forms to be developed by the IRS) reporting all of the information that must be included in a charity's written acknowledgment. In other words, a charity is permitted to report this information to the IRS instead of to individual donors directly. Few if any churches will elect this option, and we do not recommend it, for the following reasons: (1) It is optional and not required. (2) The alternative procedure would require a church to provide the IRS with the social security number of each donor who makes a contribution of $250 or more, along with the information required to be included in a charity's written acknowledgment under the new rules described above. By requiring churches to obtain the social security numbers of donors making individual contributions of $250 or more, the alternative procedure is too intrusive and would offend many church members. (3) The alternative procedure requires churches to report directly to the IRS. Instead of issuing individual donors (who make contributions of $250 or more) a written acknowledgment, a church would be reporting this same information (plus the donors' social security numbers) directly to the IRS. We oppose in principle any such reporting if not mandated by law, since it involves risks of computer errors, unresolved problems, and increased IRS scrutiny. (4) In many cases, a church would need to transmit the data to the IRS by means of magnetic tape. In summary, churches do not need to report contributions directly to the IRS, and we do not recommend this alternative.

☞ **Example.** M attends a fund-raising breakfast at her church. M makes a contribution of $300, and receives a free breakfast with a value of $4. The church has two options. First, it can issue a receipt separately identifying both the $300 contribution and the $4 value for the breakfast, and informing M that her tax deduction is limited to the amount by which her contribution exceeds the value of the breakfast ($296). Second, since the value of the breakfast meets the definition of "goods or services of insubstantial value" (since it is less than the lesser of $69 or 2% of the amount of the contribution), the church's receipt can simply state that no goods or services were provided in connection with the contribution.

☞ **Example.** Same facts as the previous example, except that the value of the breakfast is $10. The new regulations do not apply since the breakfast does not satisfy the definition of "goods or services of insubstantial value." The church's receipt may not state that "no goods or services" were provided in connection with the contribution. It must state a good faith value for the breakfast, and indicate on its receipt (or in a separate statement) that the contribution is deductible to the extent that it exceeds the value of the goods or services provided by the church.

☞ **Example.** A church conducts a fund-raising "auction". T buys a bicycle with a value of $200 for an offer of $100. The value of the bicycle does not satisfy the definition of "goods or services of insubstantial value." The church's receipt may not state that "no goods or services" were provided in connection with the contribution. It must state a good faith value for the bicycle, and indicate on its receipt (or in a separate statement) that the contribution is deductible to the extent that it ex-

*ceeds the value of the goods or services pro-
vided by the church.*

Rule 3 — Individual "quid pro quo" cash contributions of $75 or less

While the new quid pro quo rules (discussed below) do not apply to contributions of $75 or less, these contributions are still only deductible to the extent they exceed the value of the goods or services provided in exchange. To illustrate, a donor who contributes $50 to a charity and receives a "free" book with a market value of $10 is entitled to a deduction of only $40, since donors may only deduct the amount by which a contribution exceeds the value of any goods or services received in return. This is a fundamental rule of tax law. The new substantiation rules that took effect in 1994 simply impose a reporting requirement, backed up by penalties, upon charities as to quid pro quo contributions that exceed $75.

Rule 4 — Individual "quid pro quo" cash contributions of more than $75

In addition to providing a written acknowledgement for contributions of $250 or more (as discussed under Rule 2 above), a church has additional requirements with respect to *quid pro quo contributions* of more than $75. A quid pro quo contribution is a payment "made partly as a contribution and partly in consideration for goods or services" provided to the donor by the church. For example, a donor contributes $100 to her church, but in return receives a dinner worth $30. A church or other charity is required in connection with either the solicitation or receipt of a quid pro quo contribution to provide a **written statement** to the donor that

- informs the donor that the amount of the contribution that is tax-deductible is limited to the excess of the amount of any money (or the value of any property other than money) contributed by the donor over the value of any goods or services provided by the church or other charity in return, and

- provides the donor with a good faith estimate of the value of the goods or services furnished to the donor. This disclosure requirement applies to all quid pro quo contributions where the donor makes a payment of more than $75.

Exceptions to the quid pro quo reporting rule. A written statement need not be issued in either of the following situations:

(1) Only "de minimis" or token goods or services are given to the donor by the charity. Token goods or services are defined in either of the following 2 ways:

- items such as bookmarks, calendars, key chains, mugs, posters, or tee shirts *bearing the charity's name or logo* and having a cost (as opposed to fair market value) of less than $6.90

- in other cases, the value of goods or services provided to the donor does not exceed the lesser of $69 or 2% of the amount of the contribution); or

The $69 and $6.90 amounts are adjusted annually for inflation (and represent the 1997 amounts).

(2) Contributions in return for which the donor receives solely an *intangible religious benefit* that generally is not sold in a commercial context outside the donative context. The term "intangible religious benefit" is defined by the new law as "any intangible religious benefit which is provided by an organization organized exclusively for religious purposes and which generally is not sold in a commercial transaction outside the donative context." The committee report to the new law states that the term *intangible religious benefit* includes "admission to a religious ceremony" or other insignificant "tangible benefits furnished to contributors that are incidental to a religious ceremony (such as wine)." However, the committee report clarifies that "this exception does apply, for example, to tuition for education leading to a recognized degree, travel services, or consumer goods."

Penalties. The new law imposes a penalty of $10 per contribution (up to a maximum of $5,000 per fundraising event or mailing) upon charities that fail to make the required quid pro quo disclosures, unless a failure was due to reasonable cause. The penalties will apply if a charity either fails to make the required disclosure in connection with a quid pro quo contribution (as explained above) or makes a disclosure that is incomplete or inaccurate.

Intent to make a charitable contribution. For many years, the IRS has ruled that persons who receive goods or services in exchange for a payment to a charity are eligible for a charitable contribution deduction only with respect to the amount by which their payment that exceeds the fair rental value of the goods or services they received. Regulations issued by the IRS in 1997 add an additional condition—donors may not claim a charitable contribution in such a case unless they intended to make a payment in excess of the fair market value of the goods or services.

☞ *Example. A church sells tickets to a missions banquet. The cost of each ticket is $100, though the fair market value of the meal is only $20. Persons who purchase tickets are eligible to claim a charitable contribution deduction in the amount of $80—if they intended to make a payment in excess of the amount of the dinner.*

How will church treasurers know when donors intend to make a payment in excess of goods or services received in exchange? The final regulations aren't of much help here. They simply state that "the facts and circumstances" of each case must be considered.

✎ **Key point. One rule of thumb may help—the greater the amount by which a payment exceeds the market value of goods or services received in exchange, the more likely the donor intended to make a charitable contribution. In the previous example, it is clear that donors intend to make a contribution since the ticket price ($100) obviously exceeds the** value of the dinner. This is a good reason to set ticket prices at a level obviously higher than the value of a meal received at an appreciation banquet.

✎ Key point. Most persons who buy tickets to missions banquets, or who receive a free dinner in appreciation for a contribution, do not make their contribution in order to get a free meal. They would give the same amount whether or not the meal was received. As a result, an argument could be made that charitable contribution deductions should not be reduced by the value of appreciation meals. While there is much merit to this logic, the IRS has rejected it.

Refusal of benefits. What if a member purchases a $100 ticket to a church's missions banquet (in the above example), but has no intention of attending the banquet? Is the member entitled to a charitable contribution deduction of $100, or $80? In other words, must a charitable contribution be reduced by the amount of goods or services that a donor refuses to accept? The IRS issued regulations in 1997 noting that "a taxpayer who has properly rejected a benefit offered by a charitable organization may claim a deduction in the full amount of the payment to the charitable organization." How does a donor reject a benefit? The IRS suggested that charities create a form containing a "check-off box" that donors can check at the time they make a contribution if they want to refuse a benefit.

✎ Key point. The IRS distinguishes goods or services that were made available to a donor but not used, from those that were properly rejected. To illustrate, donors who purchase a ticket to a missions banquet for $100 must reduce their contribution by the value of the meal ($20 in the above example) even if they decide not to attend the banquet. However, if at the time a donor purchases a ticket he indicates unequivocally and in writing that he will not be attending the banquet, then the church treasurer can receipt the donor for the full value of the ticket ($100). And, the IRS has noted that in such a case the receipt issued by the church "need not reflect the value of the rejected benefit."

☞ *Example. A church conducts an auction to raise funds for missions. Members are asked to donate baked items which are then auctioned to other members at the highest price. A member donates a pie, which is "sold" to another member for $150 (assume that it has a "value" of $5). Do the new quid pro quo rules apply to the donor who bought the pie for $150? The answer is yes, since this member made a contribution of more than $75 in return for which she received goods or services other than token items or intangible religious benefits. The pie is not a "token" item, since its value ($5) exceeds the lesser of $69 or 2% of the contribution ($3).*

☞ *Example. A church conducts an auction of donated items. A member "purchases" a used bicycle (with a value of $50) for $250. This is a quid pro quo contribution, since it is part a contribution and part a purchase of goods or services. Accordingly, in addition to the substantiation requirements mentioned above, the church must issue the donor a written statement that (1) informs the donor that the amount of the contribution that is tax-deductible is limited to the excess of the amount of any money contributed by the donor over the value of any goods or services provided by the church in return, and (2) provides the donor with a good faith estimate of the value of the goods or services furnished to the donor. Accordingly, the church's written acknowledgment should report the contribution of $250, inform the donor that the contribution is deductible only to the extent that it exceeds the value of goods or services received in exchange, provide the donor with a description and good faith estimate of the value of the bicycle provided in return ($50), and then list the deductible portion of the contribution ($200).*

☞ *Example. A church-affiliated college conducts an annual banquet for persons who have contributed more than $1,000 during the year. The value of the meal provided is $30 per person. Do the quid pro quo reporting requirements apply? At first glance, the answer would appear to be yes, since donors are receiving a $30 benefit in exchange for their contributions. However, the new law defines a quid pro contribution as "a payment made partly as a contribution and partly in consideration for goods or services provided to the payor by the donee organization." When a donor makes a contribution of $1,000 to the college, does he or she do so in order to receive a free dinner? Is the dinner in any sense relevant to the donor in deciding whether or not to make the contribution? Obviously the answer in most if not all cases is no. The contribution is not made "in consideration for goods or services." Donors in such cases would have made their contributions even if no dinner were provided. Accordingly, an argument can be made that contributions to the college are not quid quo pro contributions. This conclusion is controversial, and may be addressed and rejected in the forthcoming IRS regulations. It should not be implemented without the advice of tax counsel.*

☞ *Example. A religious radio ministry offers a "free" book in exchange for contributions of $50 or more. The book has a value of $10. The quid pro quo rules apply to contributions in excess of $75, but not to contributions of $75 or less. Note, however, that while the new quid pro quo rules do not apply to contributions of $75 or less, these contributions are still only deductible to the extent they exceed the value of the goods or services provided in exchange.*

☞ *Example. Many churches conduct sales of merchandise to raise funds for various programs and activities. Examples include bake sales, auctions,* and bazaars. Should a church issue a 1099-MISC form to persons who purchase items at such events? No, ruled the IRS. Charities that sell items in the course of fund-raising events need not issue 1099 forms to purchasers since no compensation is being paid to them. Form 1099-MISC is issued to "non-employees" who are paid compensation of $600 or more during the year. IRS Letter Ruling 9517010.

2. Contributions of Noncash Property

The substantiation requirements for contributions of noncash property (e.g., land, equipment, stock, books, art, vehicles) are more stringent than for contributions of cash or checks. These rules are complex, but they are very important. It is important to note that more than one rule may apply to a particular contribution. For example, any contribution of property valued by the donor at less than $250 will trigger only Rule 5. But, contributions of property valued at $250 or more will trigger Rule 6, and possibly Rule 7 or Rule 8 (depending on the value of the donated property).

Your church could provide a significant benefit to its members by sharing the information contained in this chapter with donors who make contributions of noncash property.

Rule 5 — Individual contributions of property valued at less than $250

A taxpayer who makes a charitable contribution of noncash property valued at less than $250 must maintain a receipt from the church showing

• *Name.* The name of the donee church.

• *Date and location.* The date and location of the contribution.

• *Description of the donated property.* A description of the property in detail reasonably sufficient under the circumstances. Although the fair market value of the property is one of the circumstances to be taken into account in determining the amount of detail to be included on the receipt, *such value need not be stated on the receipt.*

The income tax regulations further provide:

A letter or other written communication from the donee [church] acknowledging receipt of the contribution, showing the date of the contribution, and containing the required description of the property contributed constitutes a receipt for purposes of this paragraph. A receipt is not required if the contribution is made in circumstances where it is impractical to obtain a receipt (e.g., by depositing property at a charity's unattended drop site). In such cases, however, the taxpayer shall maintain reliable written records with respect to each item of donated property that include the information required by [Rule 7, below]. *Treas. Reg. 1.170A-13(b)(1).*

In no case should a church act as an appraiser unless it is willing to assume the responsibility of proving the stated value of donated property in the event a donor is audited and the valuation of the contribution is questioned. A sample receipt for use by churches is set forth below.

Rule 6 — Individual contributions of property valued at $250 or more

✎ **Key point: new substantiation requirements apply to individual contribution of noncash property valued by the donor at $250 or more. These new requirements are in addition to the substantiation requirements that already exist with respect to contributions of noncash property valued by the donor at $500 or more.**

New requirements for substantiating contributions of noncash property valued by the donor at $250 or more took effect in 1994. These requirements are in addition to the other rules mentioned in this section. So, for example, if a donor contributes property valued at $750, Rules 7 and 8 would apply in addition to Rule 6.

Rule 6 is the same as Rule 2 (described fully above), with the following additional requirement—a church receipt must *describe* the property. No value should be stated. Be sure to review the requirements associated with Rule 2 at this time.

☞ *Example. A church member makes weekly contributions of $50 to her church in 1997, and in addition makes a one-time contribution of an automobile. The contribution of the automobile will need to be substantiated with a written receipt from the church that satisfies the requirements specified under Rule 2 above, and in addition that describes the automobile (though no value should be stated). The member will be able to substantiate her weekly contributions of $50 with canceled checks (since none is for $250 or more).*

Rule 7 — Individual contributions of property valued at less than $5,000

The income tax regulations require that *all* donors of noncash property valued at $5,000 or less maintain reliable written records with respect to each item

---

Illustration 8-2

Sample Receipt

First Church, of 123 Main Street, Chicago, Illinois, acknowledges receipt of a model ABC Acme bicycle from John Jones this 10th day of August, 1997, at Chicago, Illinois, in excellent condition. The donor has valued the property as of the date of the contribution at $200.

Rev. J. White

of donated property. The reliable written records must include the following information:

- the name and address of the church

- the date and location of the contribution

- a detailed description of the property

- the fair market value of the property at the time of the contribution, including a description of how the value was determined

- the cost or other basis of the property

- if less than the donor's entire interest in property is donated during the current year, an explanation of the total amount claimed as a deduction in the current year

- the terms of any agreement between the donor and church relating to the use, sale, or other disposition of the property.

Rule 8 — Individual contributions of property valued at more than $500

If the donated property is valued by the donor in excess of $500, the following *additional* written records must be maintained by the donor:

- an explanation of the manner of acquisition by the donor (such as by purchase, gift, inheritance, or exchange), and

- the cost or other basis of the property immediately preceding the date on which the contribution was made. These records are in addition to the requirements discussed above in connection with individual contributions of property valued by the donor at $250 or more.

Donors who contribute noncash property valued between $500 and $5,000 must complete Section A, Part I (and Part II if applicable) on the front side of IRS Form 8283, and then include the completed Form 8283 with the federal income tax return on which the contribution is claimed. This is an important requirement for churches to bear in mind, since many donors will be unaware of it. It would be an excellent practice for churches to write the IRS and request several copies of Form 8283, and then to provide donors of noncash property valued at more than $500 with a complimentary copy. The IRS will provide a church with several copies without charge. For your convenience, a copy of Form 8283 is reproduced at the end of this chapter.

☞ *Example. A donor contributes a vacant lot to First Church with a value of $4,000. What actions by the donor and church will ensure the deductibility of this contribution? The following steps should be followed: (1) The donor should provide the church with a deed to the property; (2) the church should issue the donor a written receipt satisfying the requirements of Rule 6 (explained above); (3) the donor must also maintain reliable written records containing the nine items of infor-*

mation required by Rules 7 and 8 (explained above); (4) the donor must complete Section A, Part I (and Part II if applicable) of IRS Form 8283 and include it with the Form 1040 on which the contribution is claimed. Different rules apply if the property is valued at more than $5,000 (see below).

Rule 9 — Individual contributions of property valued at more than $5,000

In this section, the rules for substantiating a contribution of property valued by the donor at more than $5,000 will be reviewed. These rules, which took effect in 1985, are still unknown to many church leaders and donors. This can lead to disastrous consequences, since IRS regulations warn that no deduction for any contribution of property valued by the donor at more than $5,000 will be allowed unless these requirements are satisfied. Churches are urged to share the information contained in this section with any donor contemplating a contribution of property (land, buildings, vehicles, equipment, books, art, etc.) to the church that might be valued by the donor at more than $5,000. The requirements discussed below ordinarily are triggered by a contribution of a single item of property valued by the donor at more than $5,000, but they also can be triggered by contributions of *similar items* within a calendar or fiscal year if the combined value claimed by the donor exceeds $5,000. Publicly traded stock is *not* subject to these requirements since its value is readily ascertainable. Contributions of nonpublicly traded stock (i.e., stock held by most small, family owned corporations) are subject to these requirements but only if the value claimed by the donor exceeds $10,000.

☞ *Example. Sarah S contributes a used automobile to First Church in September of 1998. The vehicle has a retail value of $4,000, but S believes $6,000 is a more accurate value and plans to deduct this amount as a charitable contribution on her 1998 federal income tax return. The substantiation rules discussed in this section apply.*

☞ *Example. Same facts as the preceding example, except that S plans to claim a contribution deduction of only $4,000. The rules discussed in the preceding section apply.*

☞ *Example. Joan B contributes a vacant lot and a used car to First Church in 1998. B plans to claim a charitable contribution deduction of $4,000 for each item. The substantiation rules discussed in this section (with respect to contributions of noncash property valued at more than $5,000) do not apply. If B had given two lots, and planned to claim a contribution deduction of $4,000 for each, the rules discussed in this section would apply since the lots are similar items whose values must be combined.*

The new substantiation requirements were enacted to make it more difficult for donors to improperly reduce taxable income by intentionally overvaluing contributed property and then claiming inflated charitable contribution deductions on their income tax returns.

a. the donor's obligations

Donors who contribute property valued at more than $5,000 to a church or other charity must satisfy each of the following requirements in order to claim a charitable contribution deduction:

(1) obtain a qualified appraisal

Qualified appraisal. A donor's first obligation is to obtain a qualified appraisal. The income tax regulations define a qualified appraisal as an appraisal made by a "qualified appraiser" no earlier than sixty days prior to the date of a contribution, and containing the following information:

• an adequate description of the donated property

• the physical condition of the property

• the date (or expected date) of the contribution

• the term of any agreement or understanding entered into by or on behalf of the donor pertaining to the use or disposition of the donated property

• the name, address, and social security number of the qualified appraiser

• the qualifications of the qualified appraiser who prepared and signed the qualified appraisal

• a statement that the appraisal was prepared for income tax purposes

• the date on which the property was valued

• the appraised fair market value of the property on the date (or expected date) of the contribution

• the method of valuation used to determine the fair market value

• the specific basis for the valuation

• a description of the fee arrangement between the donor and appraiser.

✎ **Key point: donors ordinarily should refrain from employing an appraiser who is unfamiliar with these requirements.**

Qualified appraiser. A qualified appraisal, as noted above, is one prepared by a *qualified appraiser*. The regulations define the term "qualified appraiser" as anyone meeting the following conditions:

• the individual holds himself or herself out to the public as an appraiser

• the individual is qualified to perform appraisals because of his or her education, experience, background, and membership, if any, in professional appraisal associations

• the appraiser is not the donor, the person from whom the donor obtained the property, the donee, any person employed by one of the foregoing persons, or any person whose relationship with any of the foregoing persons would cause a reasonable person to question his or her independence

• the appraiser understands that a false or fraudulent overvaluation of property may subject the appraiser to civil penalties

The regulations also provide that qualified appraisers cannot base their fee on a percentage of the appraised value.

The qualified appraisal must be received by the donor before the due date (including extensions) of the federal income tax return on which the deduction is claimed. Finally, note that a qualified appraisal must be obtained for each item of contributed property valued by the donor in excess of $5,000.

(2) prepare a qualified appraisal summary

A donor must also complete an *appraisal summary* and enclose it with the tax return on which the charitable contribution deduction is claimed. The appraisal summary is a summary of the qualified appraisal, and is made on Section B (side 2) of *IRS Form 8283.* Because of the importance of this form, one is reproduced at the end of this chapter. Please feel free to make copies of this form for persons who donate property to your church. Alternatively, you can obtain copies by contacting your nearest IRS office or by calling the toll-free IRS forms hotline at 1-800-829-3676. As noted in the preceding section, Section A (side 1) of Form 8283 is completed by donors who contribute property valued between $500 and $5,000.

Section B of Form 8283 contains four parts. Part I is completed by the donor or appraiser, and sets forth information from the qualified appraisal regarding the donated property, including its appraised value. Part II is completed by the donor and identifies individual items in groups of similar items having an appraised value of not more than $500. Part III contains the appraiser's certification that he or she satisfies the definition of a qualified appraiser. Part IV is a donee acknowledgment, which must be *completed by the church.* The church simply indicates the date on which it received the contribution, and agrees to file an information return (Form 8282) with the IRS if it disposes of the donated property within two years. The regulations specify that the church's acknowledgment "does not represent concurrence in the appraised value of the contributed property. Rather, it represents acknowledgment of receipt of the property described in the appraisal summary on the date specified in the appraisal summary . . . ."

The instructions to Form 8283 permit a church to complete part IV before the qualified appraisal is completed. They instruct the donor to "complete at least your name, identification number, and description of the donated property," along with Part II if applicable, before submitting the Form 8283 to the church (or other donee). In other words, the donor should fill in his or her name and social security number on the lines provided at the top of page 1 of the form, and also complete line 5(a) of Section B, Part I (on the back page of the form), before submitting the form to the church. After completing Section B, Part IV, the church returns the form to the donor, who then completes the remaining information required in Part I. The donor should also arrange to have the qualified appraiser complete Part III at this time.

If a donor fails to enclose a Form 8283 with a tax return on which a deduction is claimed for a charitable contribution of property valued at more than $5,000, the IRS may request that the donor submit the appraisal summary within ninety days of the request. If such a request is made and the donor complies with the request within the ninety day period, the deduction will not be disallowed for failure to comply with the appraisal summary requirement *if the donor's failure to enclose the summary was a good faith omission.*

(3) maintain records

The donor's third obligation is to maintain records containing the following information:

- the name and address of the church

- the date and location of the contribution

- a detailed description of the property

- the fair market value of the property at the time of the contribution, including a description of how the value was determined

- the cost or other basis of the property

- if less than the donor's entire interest in the property was given, an explanation of the total amount claimed as a deduction in the current year

- the terms of any agreement or understanding by or on behalf of the donor pertaining to the use or disposition of the property

Most of these items will be contained in the qualified appraisal, which should be retained by the donor.

b. the church's obligations

Churches receiving contributions of property valued by the donor at more than $5,000 have the following two obligations (assuming that the donor plans to claim a deduction for the contribution):

- as noted above, the church must complete and sign Part IV of Section B of the donor's Form 8283 appraisal summary, and

- the church must complete and return to the IRS an information return (IRS Form 8282) if it sells, exchanges, consumes, or otherwise disposes of the donated property within two years of the date of the contribution

The second requirement applies to the charity that received the donated property from the donor (the "original donee"), and, since July 5, 1988, to any "successor donee." A successor donee is any recipient of the donated property other than the "original donee." In other words, if a donor donates property to First Church on July 1, 1998, and on December 1, 1998 First Church transfers the property to Second Church, then it is Second Church that has the obligation to file a Form 8282 with the IRS in the event that it disposes of the property within 125 days of the original contribution to First Church (July 1, 1998). To assist Second Church in complying with the Form 8282 filing requirement, the income tax regulations require First Church to provide Second Church with a copy of the donor's qualified appraisal summary (Form 8283) within 15 days of the transfer.

A Form 8282 is reproduced at the end of this chapter for your convenience. Please feel free to make copies from this form for your use, or order original copies from the IRS. The church must file a Form 8282 within 125 days after it disposes of the donated property. A copy must also be sent to the donor. Form 8282 is very easy to complete. The IRS is primarily concerned with learning the amount received by the church in any sale or other disposition of the property as an additional means of verifying the valuation claimed by the donor.

There are two exceptions to this filing requirement. First, Form 8282 does not have to be filed if a church sells, consumes, or disposes of an item of donated property valued on the donor's Form 8283 at $500 or less. This exception will apply if a donor contributes several similar items of property (having a combined value in excess of $5,000) to a church during a calendar year, and the church disposes of or consumes one item that is separately valued at $500 or less. Second, Form 8282 does not need to be filed if a church consumes the donated property or distributes it without charge to another organization or individual. The consumption or distribution must be in furtherance of the church's tax-exempt purposes.

A new provision in the Internal Revenue Manual (the IRS administrative manual) states that the tax return of any donor who contributes property valued at more than $5,000 to a church should be selected for examination by the IRS if no Form 8282 is filed by the church. *IRM 4175.2.* Obviously, it is now more important than ever for churches to comply with this important filing obligation.

☞ *Example. A member contributes equipment to First Church valued at $15,000. The member asks an appraiser who attends the church to appraise the property. Such an appraiser may not satisfy the definition of a qualified appraiser since his relationship to the church might cause a reasonable person to question his independence.*

☞ *Example. A member contributes property to First Church in 1998 that is worth well in excess of $5,000. To assist the member in complying with the substantiation requirements, the church should: (1) acknowledge receipt of the contribution in a signed writing; (2) inform the member of the necessity of obtaining a qualified appraisal;*

and (3) inform the member of the obligation to complete an appraisal summary (Form 8283) prior to the due date for the 1998 income tax return (and as a convenience give the member a copy of the current form). The church is required to sign Section B, part 1, of the donor's Form 8283, and to complete and file with the IRS an information return (Form 8282) within 125 days of the date it disposes of the property (if it does so within two years of the date of the contribution).

☞ *Example.* A member contributes a house to First Church on October 10, 1997. The church sells the property in April of 1998. It must complete and file a Form 8282 information return with the IRS within 125 days of the date of sale, and also mail a copy to the donor.

☞ *Example.* The Tax Court ruled that a taxpayer who donated property to charity had substantially complied with the law even though a separate appraisal had not been obtained and the qualifications of the appraiser were omitted from the appraisal summary attached to the donor's tax return. The court noted that the donor had obtained an appraisal of the property prior to the time he decided to donate it to charity, and that this appraisal contained substantially all the information required by law. When the donor later decided to donate the property to charity, he simply enclosed a copy of this appraisal with the tax return on which a charitable contribution was claimed. The court concluded that the qualified appraisal rules are "directory, not mandatory," and therefore they could be met by substantial, rather than strict, compliance. The fact that the donor did not obtain a new appraisal did not preclude a charitable contribution deduction. Bond v. Commissioner, 100 T.C. 32 (1993).

☞ *Example.* A donor contributed "nonpublicly traded stock" worth more than $10,000 to a church, but obtained no qualified appraisal and attached no qualified appraisal summary to the tax return on which the charitable contribution deduction was claimed. The Tax Court ruled that the donor was not entitled to a charitable contribution deduction even though there was no dispute as to the value of the donated stock. Hewitt v. Commissioner, 109 T.C.12 (1997).

Rule 10 — Quid Pro Quo Contributions of Noncash Property

The quid pro quo rules are explained fully in the previous section dealing with cash contributions (see Rules 3 and 4). Those rules apply to contributions of property as well, and should be reviewed at this time.

How Church Treasurers Can Comply with the Substantiation Rules

There are a number of ways for church treasurers to comply with the new substantiation and quid pro quo reporting requirements. Some of the options are summarized below:

Option 1 — only cash contributions are received

In most churches, the only contributions that donors make are cash contributions. Illustration 8-3 is a receipt that acknowledges only cash contributions, and that takes into account the new substantiation rules. If a church only receives cash contributions, this form is all that will be required. Illustration 8-3 satisfies all of the new substantiation rules with the minimal complexity. However, it makes three very important assumptions:

• the church provided no goods or services in connection with any individual contribution of $250 or more other than intangible religious benefits

• no donor made any quid pro quo contribution

• only cash contributions were made (and not property)

Obviously, these assumptions will hold true for many if not most donors. However, if any one or more assumptions is not met, then appropriate adjustments will be required. For example, if a donor did make a quid pro quo contribution, then an appropriate statement would need to be issued separately by the church. And, if the church provides goods or services or more than insubstantial value in exchange for a contribution of $250 or more, it would need to adapt this form or include a separate statement with the form describing and valuing the goods or services that were provided. Illustration 8-4 can be used in conjunction with Illustration 8-3 to substantiate most contributions not covered by the simpler form.

✎ **Key point: the illustrations in this chapter separately list each contribution because this is the most common church practice and it provides donors with information that will assist in detecting errors and reconciling discrepancies. However, church treasurers are free to combine all contributions in a single amount.**

Option 2 — occasional contributions of property, or quid pro quo contributions, are received

Some churches receive occasional contributions of property, or quid pro quo contributions, in addition to cash contributions. Illustration 8-3 does not address these kinds of contributions. As a result, churches must either

• use Illustration 8-3 plus a second form that acknowledges contributions of property and quid pro quo contributions, or

• use a form that acknowledges cash contributions as well as contributions of property and quid pro quo contributions.

Illustration 8-4 is a form that churches can use to acknowledge contributions of property or quid pro quo contributions. It is designed to be used with Illustration 8-3 (the cash contributions receipt). Illustration 8-5 is a form that churches can use that acknowledges cash contributions as well as contributions of property and quid pro quo contributions.

Option 3 — the individual response approach

Another option is for church treasurers to continue to use the contribution receipts that the church has historically used for individual contributions of less than $250 (that do not constitute quid pro quo exchanges), and in addition to issue donors (1) individual written acknowledgments for each contribution (of cash or property) of $250 or more that comply with the new substantiation rules summarized in this chapter, and (2) individual quid pro quo statements for each quid pro quo contribution of more than $75. There are 2 advantages to this approach. First, it is more likely that the strict time ("contemporaneous") requirements under the new law will be met. And second, it permits churches to continue using their current receipting system for the vast majority of contributions that are not affected by the new law. For example, a donor who never gives an individual contribution of $250 or more or a quid pro quo contribution of more than $75 will continue to receive the same periodic contribution summary that he or she has received in the past from the church. For such individuals, nothing will change. The one disadvantage of this rule is inconvenience. In some churches, several individual receipts will have to be issued during the course of the year.

Option 4 — a unified acknowledgment

Some treasurers will prefer to consolidate all of the new requirements in one form. This approach is shown in Illustration 8-5. The advantage of this option is that donors will receive only one acknowledgment rather than 2 or 3 different acknowledgements. The disadvantage is that the unified form is more complicated, and may raise more questions from donors. For many donors, some sections of the unified form will not apply. *Note that in the case of contributions of noncash property a donor will have some additional recordkeeping requirements (see, for example, Rules 7 and 8, above).*

Comprehensive Example Illustrating Compliance with the Requirements

Assume the following facts:

(1) First Church issues quarterly contribution receipts to donors;

(2) John A. Doe made 13 weekly cash contributions of $30 to the church's general fund for the fourth quarter of 1997;

(3) Mr. Doe made a cash contribution of $500 on October 26 to the church's missions fund;

(4) Mr. Doe purchased a pie at a fund-raising raffle for $100 on October 15;

(5) Mr. Doe donated 10 shares of ABC stock (worth $50 per share) and an automobile (worth $6,000) to the church on November 16;

(6) Mr. Doe paid $100 for a dinner at a church event on December 8, but received a dinner having an estimated value of $30;

(7) on November 23 Mr. Doe made a cash contribution of $100 to the general fund and on December 21 made an additional contribution of $200 to the missions fund.

Option 1. The easiest way for church treasurers to respond to the new substantiation requirements would be to issue receipts for cash contributions, and then an additional receipt to cover those occasional contributions of cash or quid pro quo contributions. Illustrations 8-3 and 8-4 illustrate this approach. Note the following points:

• All of the cash contributions will be tax-deductible on Mr. Doe's 1997 tax return. All of the cash contributions of less than $250 are deductible even without a statement from the church. Canceled checks will be adequate substantiation for these. The cash contribution on October 26 of $500 is tax-deductible because it is acknowledged by the church's "contemporaneous" written statement.

• Mr. Doe purchased a pie at a fund-raising raffle on October 15 for $100. Assume that a good faith estimate of the value of the pie would be $5. Since Mr. Doe contributed more than $75 in a quid pro quo exchange, the church will need to (1) inform Mr. Doe that the amount of the contribution that is tax-deductible is limited to the excess of the cash donation over the value of the pie provided by the church in return, and (2) provide Mr. Doe with a good faith estimate of the value of the pie. The quid pro quo reporting rules do not apply if the church only provides goods or services whose value is insignificant (generally, with a value of the lesser of $69 or 2% of the amount of the contribution, whichever is less). But, this exception does not apply, since a good faith estimate of the value of a homemade pie is $5, which is more than the lesser of $69 or 2% of the amount of the contribution ($2).

• In order to substantiate the donation of the automobile, Mr. Doe will need to obtain a qualified appraisal from a qualified appraiser, and complete a qualified appraisal summary (IRS Form 8283) which must be attached to the tax return on which he claims a charitable contribution deduction for this contribution. This requirement applies to any contribution of noncash property valued by the donor at $5,000 or more.

• Illustration 8-3 allows the church to separately list multiple contributions made by a donor on the same day. To illustrate, on October 26 the donor made a contribution of $500 to the mission fund, and in addition made a separate contribution of $30 to the general fund. Separately identifying contributions on the same day can be important. For example, if a donor attends two scheduled services at the same church on the same day and makes a $150 contribution in each service, the church's receipt will either show two separate contributions of $150, or it will aggregate the contributions and show a single contribution of $300. This can be a very important distinction if the church's receipt does not comply with the new substantiation requirements, since those requirements are triggered by an individual contribution of at least $250. For this reason it is desirable to have the capacity to show separate contributions made on the same day. As noted above (in the discussion of Rule 2) this assumes that there is "economic reality" to making separate contributions on the same day (rather than an attempt to avoid the new substantiation rules).

• Illustrations 8-3 and 8-4 easily can be modified to correspond to semiannual or annual reporting periods.

Option 2. Illustration 8-5 combines all of the new substantiation and quid pro quo reporting requirements into one form. This form can be used to cover most kinds of contributions that will be made to a church. While it has the advantage of providing donors with a single form, it is far more complex and will confuse many donors. It contains information that is simply not necessary for the vast majority of donors who only make cash contributions to their church.

D. How to Claim the Deduction

Charitable contribution deductions are available only as itemized expenses on Schedule A. This means that taxpayers who do not itemize their deductions get no tax benefit from making charitable contributions. See section A.5 of this chapter for more details.

Table 8-1: Substantiation Requirements For Charitable Contributions
Under The New Rules Effective January 1, 1994

Note: *More than one rule may apply to a particular contribution. Follow each rule that applies.*

Rule	Form of contribution	Substantiation requirements
1	individual **cash** contributions of less than $250	new rules do not apply; substantiate with any *one* of the following: (1) a canceled check; (2) a receipt or letter from the donee church showing the church's name and the amounts and dates of the contributions, or (3) any other reliable written record showing the name of the church and the amounts and dates of the contributions
2	individual **cash** contributions of $250 or more	new rules apply; donors will not be allowed a tax deduction for individual cash contributions of $250 or more unless they receive a written receipt from the church or charity that satisfies the following requirements: (1) the receipt must be in writing; (2) the receipt must identify the donor by name (a social security number is not required); (3) the receipt may combine all contributions, even those that are for $250 or more, in a single amount or it can list each contribution separately to aid donors in resolving discrepancies; (4) the receipt must state whether or not the church provided any goods or services to the donor in exchange for the contribution, and if so, the receipt must include a good faith estimate of the value of those goods or services; (5) if the church provides no goods or services to a donor in exchange for a contribution, or if the only goods or services the church provides are "intangible religious benefits," then the receipt must contain a statement to that effect; (6) the written acknowledgment must be received by the donor on or before the *earlier* of the following two dates: the date the donor files a tax return claiming a deduction for the contribution, or the due date (including extensions) for filing the return
3	individual **cash** contributions of $75 or less that are part contribution and part payment for goods or services received in exchange ("quid pro quo" contributions)	the new quid pro quo rules (Rule 4) do not apply to contributions of $75 or less, these contributions are still only deductible to the extent they exceed the value of the goods or services provided in exchange
4	individual **cash** contributions of more than $75 that are part contribution and part payment for goods or services received in exchange ("quid pro quo" contributions)	new rules apply *(these are in addition to Rule 2)*; the church must provide a written statement to the donor that: (1) informs the donor that the amount of the contribution that is tax-deductible is limited to the excess of the amount of cash contributed by the donor over the value of any goods or services provided by the church in return; and (2) provides the donor with a good faith estimate of the value of the goods or services furnished to the donor *Note:* a written statement need not be issued if only token goods or services are provided to the donor (generally, with a value of $69 or 2% of the amount of the contribution, (whichever is less) or if the donor receives solely an intangible religious benefit that generally is not sold in a commercial context outside the donative context
5	individual contributions of **noncash property** valued at less than $250	new rules *do not* apply; substantiate with a receipt that lists the donor's name, the church's name, and date and location of the contribution, and description (but not value) of the property
6	individual contributions of **noncash property** valued at $250 or more	new rules apply; donors will not be allowed a tax deduction for individual contributions of property valued at $250 or more unless they receive a written receipt from the church or charity that satisfies the requirements of Rule 2 (above) and that describes the property (no value needs to be stated)
7	individual contributions of **noncash property** valued by the donor at $500 to $5,000	the income tax regulations require that *all* donors of noncash property valued at $5,000 or less maintain reliable written records with respect to each item of donated property; the reliable written records must include the following information: (1) the name and address of the church; (2) the date and location of the contribution; (3) a detailed description of the property; (4) the fair market value of the property at the time of the contribution, including a description of how the value was determined; (5) the cost or other basis of the property; (6) if less than the donor's entire interest in property is donated during the current year, an explanation of the total amount claimed as a deduction in the current year; (7) the terms of any agreement between the donor and church relating to the use, sale, or other disposition of the property *Note:* in addition to complying with Rule 6 (above), a donor must complete the front side (Section A, Part I, and Part II if applicable) of IRS Form 8283 and enclose the completed form with the Form 1040 on which the charitable contribution is claimed
8	individual contributions of **noncash property** valued at more than $500	if the donated property is valued by the donor in excess of $500, the following *additional* written records must be maintained by the donor: (1) an explanation of the manner of acquisition by the donor (such as by purchase, gift, inheritance, or exchange), and (2) the cost or other basis of the property immediately preceding the date on which the contribution was made; these records are in addition to the requirements discussed above in connection with individual contributions of property valued by the donor at $250 or more
9	individual contributions of **noncash property** valued at more than $5,000	in addition to complying with Rule 6 (above), a donor must obtain a qualified appraisal of the donated property from a qualified appraiser, and complete a qualified appraisal summary (the back side of Form 8283), and have the summary signed by the appraiser and a church representative; the completed Form 8283 is then enclosed with the Form 1040 on which the charitable contribution deduction is claimed
10	quid pro quo contributions of **noncash property**	new rules apply *(these are in addition to Rule 2)*; see Rules 3 and 4 (above)

Illustration 8-3: Cash Contributions Only

First Church
Chicago, Illinois
December 31, 1997
Contributions Statement for October through December of 1997
John A. Doe

Codes:

C = cash or check   10 = general fund   30 = missions
P = property   20 = building fund   40 = other

For the calendar quarter October through December of 1997, our records indicate that you made the following **cash contributions**. Should you have any questions about any amount reported or not reported on this statement, please notify the church treasurer within 90 days of the date of this statement. Statements that are not questioned within 90 days will be assumed to be accurate, and any supporting documentation (such as offering envelopes) retained by the church may be discarded. *No goods or services were provided to you by the church in connection with any contribution, or their value was insignificant or consisted entirely of intangible religious benefits.*

code	date	amount	code	date	amount	code	date	amount
10	Oct 5	30.00	10	Nov 2	30.00	10	Dec 7	30.00
10	Oct 12	30.00	10	Nov 9	30.00	10	Dec 14	30.00
10	Oct 19	30.00	10	Nov 16	30.00	10	Dec 21	30.00
30	Oct 26	500.00	10	Nov 23	30.00	30	Dec 21	200.00
10	Oct 26	30.00	10	Nov 23	100.00	10	Dec 28	30.00
				Nov 30	30.00			
Total	October	620.00		November	250.00		December	320.00
Grand Total	1190.00							

Illustration 8-4: Property and Quid Pro Quo Contributions

**First Church
Anytown, Illinois
December 31, 1997
Contributions Statement for October through December of 1997
John A. Doe**

For the calendar quarter October through December of 1997, our records indicate that you made the following individual property contributions and "quid pro quo" contributions. A quid pro quo contribution is a contribution that is in part a contribution and in part a purchase of goods or services. Should you have any questions about any amount reported or not reported on this statement, please notify the church treasurer within 90 days of the date of this statement. Statements that are not questioned within 90 days will be assumed to be accurate, and any supporting documentation (such as offering envelopes) retained by the church may be discarded. This statement includes a good faith estimate of the value of any goods or services you received in exchange for any individual contribution of more than $75. *If no value is listed, this means that no goods or services were provided, or their value was insignificant or consisted entirely of intangible religious benefits. If you received goods or services in return for your contribution, the deductible portion of your contribution is the amount by which it exceeds the value of the goods or services received in return (as noted below). This of course assumes that you otherwise qualify for a charitable contribution deduction.*

Codes:
C = cash or check   10 = general fund   30 = missions
P = property   20 = building fund   40 = other

code	form	date	gross amount	value and description of goods or services provided to you by the church (for contributions of more than $75)	net amount of contribution (tax-deductible amount)	description (for donated property valued by donor at $250 Or more)
10	C	Oct 15	100.00	5.00 pie	95.00	
30	P	Nov 16				10 shares of ABC stock
30	P	Nov 16				one 1988 Ford Taurus 4-door automobile; vehicle identification DLKJ4959034PJFG; 97,000 miles; excellent condition
30	C	Dec 8	100.00	30.00 dinner	70.00	
TOTAL					165.00	

281

Illustration 8-5: Cash, Property, and Quid Pro Quo Contributions

First Church
Anytown, Illinois
December 31, 1997
Contributions Statement for October through December of 1997
John A. Doe

Codes:
C = cash or check   10 = general fund   30 = missions
P = property   20 = building fund   40 = other

For the calendar quarter October through December of 1997 our records indicate that you made the following contributions. Should you have any questions about any amount reported or not reported on this statement, please notify the church treasurer within 90 days of the date of this statement. Statements that are not questioned within 90 days will be assumed to be accurate, and any supporting documentation (such as offering envelopes) retained by the church may be discarded. This statement includes a good faith estimate of the value of any goods or services you received in exchange for any individual contribution of more than $75. *If no value is listed, this means that no goods or services were provided, or their value was insignificant or consisted entirely of intangible religious benefits. If you received goods or services in return for your contribution, the deductible portion of your contribution is the amount by which it exceeds the value of the goods or services received in return (as noted below). This of course assumes that you otherwise qualify for a charitable contribution deduction.*

code	form	date	gross amount	value and description of goods or services provided to you by the church (for contributions of more than $75)	net amount of contribution (tax-deductible amount)	description (for donated property valued by donor at $250 Or more)
10	C	Oct 5	30.00		30.00	
10	C	Oct 12	30.00		30.00	
10	C	Oct 15	100.00	5.00 pie	95.00	
10	C	Oct 19	30.00		30.00	
30	C	Oct 26	500.00		500.00	
10	C	Oct 26	30.00		30.00	
10	C	Nov 2	30.00		30.00	
10	C	Nov 9	30.00		30.00	
30	P	Nov 16		10 shares of ABC stock		
30	P	Nov 16				one 1988 Ford Taurus 4-door automobile; vehicle identification DLKJ4959034PJFG; 97,000 miles; excellent condition
10	C	Nov 16	30.00		30.00	
10	C	Nov 23	100.00		100.00	
10	C	Nov 23	30.00		30.00	
10	C	Nov 30	30.00		30.00	
10	C	Dec 7	30.00		30.00	
30	C	Dec 8	100.00	30.00 dinner	70.00	
10	C	Dec 14	30.00		30.00	
10	C	Dec 21	30.00		30.00	
30	C	Dec 21	200.00		200.00	
10	C	Dec 28	30.00		30.00	
TOTAL					1355.00	

Form **8283**
(Rev. November 1992)

Department of the Treasury
Internal Revenue Service

Noncash Charitable Contributions

▶ Attach to your tax return if the total deduction claimed
for all property contributed exceeds $500.

▶ See separate instructions.

OMB No. 1545-0908
Expires 11-30-95

Attachment
Sequence No. **55**

Name(s) shown on your income tax return

Identifying number

Note: *Figure the amount of your contribution deduction before completing this form. See your tax return instructions.*

Section A—Include in this section **only** items (or groups of similar items) for which you claimed a deduction of $5,000 or less per item or group, and certain publicly traded securities (see instructions).

Part I — Information on Donated Property—If you need more space, attach a statement.

1	(a) Name and address of the donee organization	(b) Description of donated property
A		
B		
C		
D		
E		

Note: *If the amount you claimed as a deduction for an item is $500 or less, you do not have to complete columns (d), (e), and (f).*

	(c) Date of the contribution	(d) Date acquired by donor (mo., yr.)	(e) How acquired by donor	(f) Donor's cost or adjusted basis	(g) Fair market value	(h) Method used to determine the fair market value
A						
B						
C						
D						
E						

Part II — Other Information—If you gave less than an entire interest in property listed in Part I, complete lines 2a–2e. If restrictions were attached to a contribution listed in Part I, complete lines 3a–3c.

2 If less than the entire interest in the property is contributed during the year, complete the following:

a Enter letter from Part I that identifies the property _____. If Part II applies to more than one property, attach a separate statement.

b Total amount claimed as a deduction for the property listed in Part I: **(1)** For this tax year _____
(2) For any prior tax years _____

c Name and address of each organization to which any such contribution was made in a prior year (complete only if different than the donee organization above).

Name of charitable organization (donee)

Address (number, street, and room or suite no.)

City or town, state, and ZIP code

d For tangible property, enter the place where the property is located or kept _____

e Name of any person, other than the donee organization, having actual possession of the property _____

3 If conditions were attached to any contribution listed in Part I, answer the following questions and attach the required statement (see instructions):

		Yes	No
a	Is there a restriction, either temporary or permanent, on the donee's right to use or dispose of the donated property?		
b	Did you give to anyone (other than the donee organization or another organization participating with the donee organization in cooperative fundraising) the right to the income from the donated property or to the possession of the property, including the right to vote donated securities, to acquire the property by purchase or otherwise, or to designate the person having such income, possession, or right to acquire?		
c	Is there a restriction limiting the donated property for a particular use?		

For Paperwork Reduction Act Notice, see separate instructions.   Cat. No. 62299J   Form **8283** (Rev. 11-92)

Form 8283 (Rev. 11-92)　　　　　　　　　　　　　　　　　　　　　　　　　　　　Page **2**

Name(s) shown on your income tax return	Identifying number

Section B—Appraisal Summary—Include in this section only items (or groups of similar items) for which you claimed a deduction of more than $5,000 per item or group. Report contributions of certain publicly traded securities only in Section A.

If you donated art, you may have to attach the complete appraisal. See the **Note** in Part I below.

Part I　**Information on Donated Property**—To be completed by the taxpayer and/or appraiser.

4　Check type of property:

☐ Art* (contribution of $20,000 or more)　☐ Real Estate　☐ Gems/Jewelry　☐ Stamp Collections
☐ Art* (contribution of less than $20,000)　☐ Coin Collections　☐ Books　☐ Other

*Art includes paintings, sculptures, watercolors, prints, drawings, ceramics, antique furniture, decorative arts, textiles, carpets, silver, rare manuscripts, historical memorabilia, and other similar objects.

Note: *If your total art contribution deduction was $20,000 or more, you must attach a complete copy of the signed appraisal. See instructions.*

5	(a) Description of donated property (if you need more space, attach a separate statement)	(b) If tangible property was donated, give a brief summary of the overall physical condition at the time of the gift	(c) Appraised fair market value
A			
B			
C			
D			

	(d) Date acquired by donor (mo., yr.)	(e) How acquired by donor	(f) Donor's cost or adjusted basis	(g) For bargain sales, enter amount received	(h) Amount claimed as a deduction	(i) Average trading price of securities
					See Instructions	
A						
B						
C						
D						

Part II　**Taxpayer (Donor) Statement**—List each item included in Part I above that is separately identified in the appraisal as having a value of $500 or less. See instructions.

I declare that the following item(s) included in Part I above has to the best of my knowledge and belief an appraised value of not more than $500 (per item). Enter identifying letter from Part I and describe the specific item: _____

Signature of taxpayer (donor) ▶　　　　　　　　　　　　　　　　Date ▶

Part III　**Certification of Appraiser**

I declare that I am not the donor, the donee, a party to the transaction in which the donor acquired the property, employed by, married to, or related to any of the foregoing persons, or an appraiser regularly used by any of the foregoing persons and who does not perform a majority of appraisals during the taxable year for other persons.

Also, I declare that I hold myself out to the public as an appraiser or perform appraisals on a regular basis; and that because of my qualifications as described in the appraisal, I am qualified to make appraisals of the type of property being valued. I certify that the appraisal fees were not based upon a percentage of the appraised property value. Furthermore, I understand that a false or fraudulent overstatement of the property value as described in the qualified appraisal or this appraisal summary may subject me to the civil penalty under section 6701(a) (aiding and abetting the understatement of tax liability). I affirm that I have not been barred from presenting evidence or testimony by the Director of Practice.

Sign Here

Signature ▶	Title ▶	Date of appraisal ▶
Business address (including room or suite no.)		Identifying number
City or town, state, and ZIP code		

Part IV　**Donee Acknowledgment**—To be completed by the charitable organization.

This charitable organization acknowledges that it is a qualified organization under section 170(c) and that it received the donated property as described in Section B, Part I, above on _____
(Date)

Furthermore, this organization affirms that in the event it sells, exchanges, or otherwise disposes of the property (or any portion thereof) within 2 years after the date of receipt, it will file an information return (**Form 8282**, Donee Information Return) with the IRS and furnish the donor a copy of that return. This acknowledgment does not represent concurrence in the claimed fair market value.

Name of charitable organization (donee)	Employer identification number
Address (number, street, and room or suite no.)	City or town, state, and ZIP code
Authorized signature	Title	Date

*U.S. Government Printing Office: 1994 — 387-095/00260

Form **8282**

(Rev. Nov. 1992)

Department of the Treasury
Internal Revenue Service

Donee Information Return

(Sale, Exchange, or Other Disposition of Donated Property)

▶ See instructions on back.

OMB No. 1545-0908
Expires 11-30-95

Give Copy to Donor

Please Print or Type	Name of charitable organization (donee)	Employer identification number
	Address (number, street, and room or suite no.)	
	City or town, state, and ZIP code	

Note: If you are the original donee, **DO NOT** complete Part II or column (c) of Part III.

Part I — Information on ORIGINAL DONOR and DONEE You Gave the Property to

1a Name(s) of the original donor of the property	1b Identifying number

Note: Complete lines 2a–2d only if you gave this property to another charitable organization (successor donee).

2a Name of charitable organization	2b Employer identification number
2c Address (number, street, and room or suite no.)	
2d City or town, state, and ZIP code	

Part II — Information on PREVIOUS DONEES—Complete this part only if you were not the first donee to receive the property.

If you were the second donee, leave lines 4a–4d blank. If you were a third or later donee, complete lines 3a–4d. On lines 4a–4d, give information on the preceding donee (the one who gave you the property).

3a Name of original donee	3b Employer identification number
3c Address (number, street, and room or suite no.)	
3d City or town, state, and ZIP code	

4a Name of preceding donee	4b Employer identification number
4c Address (number, street, and room or suite no.)	
4d City or town, state, and ZIP code	

Part III — Information on DONATED PROPERTY

(a) Description of donated property sold, exchanged, or otherwise disposed of (if you need more space, attach a separate statement)	(b) Date you received the item(s)	(c) Date the first donee received the item(s) (if you weren't the first)	(d) Date item(s) sold, exchanged, or otherwise disposed of	(e) Amount received upon disposition

For Paperwork Reduction Act Notice, see instructions on back.   Cat. No. 62307Y   Form **8282** (Rev. 11-92)

Chapter 9

SOCIAL SECURITY FOR MINISTERS

Chapter Highlights

- **2 tax systems.** Social security taxes are paid under two tax systems. Employers and employees pay "FICA" taxes—which for 1996 and 1997 are 15.3% of each employee's wages (the employer and employee each pay half of this tax, or 7.65% apiece). Self-employed persons pay the "self-employment tax," which for 1996 and 1997 is 15.3% of net self-employment earnings.

- **Ministers self-employed.** Ministers always are self-employed for social security purposes with respect to their ministerial services. This means they pay the self-employment tax, not the "FICA" tax, with respect to such income. Churches must not treat clergy as employees for social security purposes, even if they treat them as employees for federal income tax purposes.

- **Exemption.** Clergy may exempt themselves from self-employment taxes with respect to their ministerial earnings, if several requirements are met. Among other things, the exemption must be filed within a limited time period, and it is available only to clergy who are opposed on the basis of *religious considerations* to the *acceptance* of social security benefits based on their ministerial services. The exemption is only effective upon its approval by the IRS.

- **Exemption applies only to ministerial services.** An exemption from self-employment taxes only applies to ministerial services. Clergy who have exempted themselves from self-employment taxes must pay social security taxes on any non-ministerial employment. And, they are eligible for social security benefits based on their non-ministerial services (assuming that they have worked enough quarters in non-ministerial employment).

- **Computing the self-employment tax.** The self-employment tax is computed by multiplying net self-employment earnings times the current self-employment tax rate. Net self-employment earnings consists of a minister's total church compensation, including the annual fair rental value of a parsonage or a housing allowance, but less most income tax exclusions and business expenses (whether unreimbursed, or reimbursed under a nonaccountable plan).

- **2 deductions.** Self-employed persons pay the combined FICA tax rate (15.3%) that is shared by employer and employee alike. To partly offset the tax burden that falls on self-employed persons, the law now allows them two deductions: (1) an amount equal to 7.65% multiplied times their net self-employment earnings (without regard to this deduction) may be deducted in computing earnings subject to the self-employment tax; (2) half their self-employment tax is deductible as an adjustment in computing income taxes, whether or not they can itemize deductions on Schedule A.

- **Maximum compensation subject to self-employment tax.** The self-employment tax rate of 15.3% consists of two components: (1) a Medicare hospital insurance tax of 2.9%, and (2) an "old-age, survivor and disability" ("social security") tax of 12.4%. All net income from self-employment, regardless of amount, is subject to the Medicare tax of 2.9%. However, for 1996 the 12.4% "social security" tax rate only applies to the first $62,700 of net self-employment income. Stated differently, self-employed persons who received compensation in excess of $62,700 in 1996 will pay the full 15.3% tax rate for net self-employment earnings up to $62,700, and the Medicare tax rate of 2.9% on all earnings above $62,700.

- **Maximum wages subject to FICA tax.** The FICA tax rate (7.65% for both employers and employees, or a combined tax of 15.3%) did not change in 1996. However, the amount of earnings subject to tax increased. The 7.65% tax rate is comprised of two components: (1) a Medicare hospital insurance tax of 1.45%, and (2) an "old-age, survivor and disability" ("social security") tax of 6.2%. For 1996 and future years there is no maximum amount of wages subject to the Medicare tax (the 1.45% tax rate). The tax is imposed on all wages regardless of amount. For 1996, the maximum wages subject to the 6.2% "social security" tax increases to $62,700. Stated differently, employees who received wages in excess of $62,700 in 1996 will pay the full 7.65% tax rate for wages up to $62,700, and the Medicare tax rate of 1.45% on all earnings above $62,700. Employers pay an identical amount.

- **For 1998.** The maximum earnings subject to the "social security" portion of FICA and self-employment taxes will be increased for 1998 to $68,400. All earnings are subject to the "Medicare" component of FICA and self-employment taxes.

- **Religious sects opposed to social security coverage.** Members of certain religious sects that are opposed to social security coverage, and that provide for the welfare and security of their members, may become exempt from social security coverage if several conditions are met.

A. Introduction

✎ **Key point: social security taxes are paid under two tax systems. Employers and employees pay "FICA" taxes—which for 1997 and 1998 are 15.3% of each employee's wages (the employer and employee each pay half of this tax, or 7.65% apiece). Self-employed persons pay the "self-employment tax," which for 1997 and 1998 is 15.3% of net self-employment earnings.**

The Social Security Act provides a variety of benefits that are designed to assist aged and disabled persons and their dependents. The **four major benefits** provided under the social security system are

- retirement benefits payable to a fully insured person

- survivors benefits payable to the surviving spouse or dependent children of a deceased worker

- disability benefits payable to a permanently disabled worker who is not able to engage in substantial gainful activity

- medical and hospital benefits payable at age 65 (the "medicare" program)

These important benefits are financed primarily through two separate tax systems. Under the Federal Insurance Contributions Act (FICA), a tax is levied against employers and employees, representing a percentage of an employee's wages. Under the Self-Employment Contributions Act (SECA), a tax is levied against the net earnings of self-employed persons. FICA taxes are withheld by an employer from an employee's wages and paid to the government, along with the employer's share of the FICA tax, according to the payroll tax procedures summarized later in this chapter and in chapter 11. Self-employment taxes are paid entirely by the self-employed worker, and ordinarily are paid to the government through the estimated tax procedure (Form 1040-ES).

B. Ministers Deemed Self-Employed

✎ **Key point: ministers always are self-employed for social security purposes with respect to their ministerial services. This means they pay the self-employment tax, not the "FICA" tax. Churches must not treat ministers as employees for social security purposes, even if they report their income taxes as employees.**

For social security purposes, a duly ordained, commissioned, or licensed minister of a church has always been treated as a **self-employed** person with respect to services performed in the exercise of ministry. This is true even if a minister is an employee for income tax purposes. Accordingly, a minister

CHECK YOUR SOCIAL SECURITY EARNINGS RECORD

Clergy should check their social security earnings record by submitting a Form SSA-7004 to the Social Security Administration at least every two years. Unfortunately, there is evidence that the Social Security Administration has been overcrediting the income earned by clergy who report their income taxes as employees. In some cases, this error is the fault of the Social Security Administration. But in other cases, the error apparently has been caused by the erroneous reporting of ministers as "employees" for social security purposes by many church treasurers. Since clergy are always "self-employed" for social security purposes with respect to their ministerial income, the effect of such an error can be the crediting of a minister's compensation as both employee "wages" and self-employment earnings for social security purposes. This has significantly inflated the monthly benefits paid to some clergy. Unfortunately, clergy usually are completely unaware of the problem—until they receive a demand from the Social Security Administration for repayment of the excess benefits. Obviously, this can create a significant hardship for clergy who have spent the excessive benefits, or who have become dependent on the level of erroneous benefits. To ensure that you are being credited with the correct amount of earnings, be sure to check your social security earnings record every one or two years, and immediately correct any errors. You can obtain a copy of Form SSA-7004 from any Social Security office, or by calling the Social Security toll-free telephone number 1-800-772-1213.

CORRECTING ERRORS IN YOUR SOCIAL SECURITY EARNINGS STATEMENT

The Social Security Act has been amended to enable employees to correct accidental underreporting of their wages by their employers. This is an important development for employees, since their social security benefits are based on the amount of wages that their employers report. Previously, incorrect wage information could be corrected by an employee only within three years after the year in which the wages were paid. Failure to correct an error within this period of time often meant that the employee had no further recourse, even though his or her social security benefits would be adversely affected due to the employer's inadvertent error. Nevertheless, it is still a good idea for employees to check their earnings record every year or two. Simply submit a copy of Form SSA-7004 to the Social Security Administration. You can obtain this form from any Social Security office, or by calling the Social Security toll-free telephone number 1-800-772-1213. Of course, clergy are self-employed for social security purposes with respect to their ministerial services, so the new law will not directly benefit them. Non-clergy church employees will be benefited (assuming the church has not exempted itself from the employer's share of FICA taxes), and they should be encouraged to periodically check their earnings record by submitting Form SSA-7004.

reports and pays his or her social security taxes as a self-employed person (and not as an employee) with respect to services performed in the exercise of ministry. *IRC 3121(b)(8)(A).* A large number of churches withhold FICA taxes from ministers compensation, and pay the employer's share of FICA taxes with respect to ministers income. Such reporting is incorrect.

It is important to emphasize that it is only with respect to **services performed in the exercise of ministry** that ministers are always deemed self-employed for social security purposes. This significant term is explained fully in chapter 3 (as is the definition of "minister").

The treatment of ministers as self-employed for social security purposes though they are in most cases employees for income tax purposes has generated considerable confusion. In explaining the reason for treating all ministers as self-employed for social security purposes (with respect to services performed in the exercise of ministry), the Tax Court has observed: "Congress chose not to place the onus of participation in the old-age and survivors insurance program upon the churches, but to permit ministers to be covered on an individual election basis, as self-employed, whether, in fact, they were employees or actually self-employed." *Silvey v. Commissioner, 35 T.C.M. 1812 (1976).* In other words, if ministers were treated as employees for social security purposes, then their employing churches would be required to pay the employer's share of the FICA tax, and this apparently was viewed as inappropriate. Of course, this justification is no longer relevant today in view of the coverage of church employees under the FICA system (absent a waiver by the employing church of its obligation to pay the employer's share of FICA taxes).

C. Exemption of Ministers from Social Security Coverage

✎ **Key point: ministers may exempt themselves from self-employment taxes with respect to their ministerial earnings, if several requirements are met. Among other things, the exemption must be filed within a limited time period, and it is available only to ministers who are opposed on the basis of *religious considerations* to the *acceptance* of social security benefits based on their ministerial services. The exemption is only effective upon its approval by the IRS. IRS Form 4361 is the exemption application form.**

Until 1968, services performed by a duly ordained, commissioned, or licensed minister of a church in the exercise of ministry were exempt from social security taxes. A minister could voluntarily elect to be covered under the social security program by filing a timely Form 2031 with the IRS.

Since January 1, 1968, however, ministers have been automatically covered under the social security system. But ministers are permitted to exempt themselves from coverage if they meet the following **six conditions**:

1. The minister must be an ordained, commissioned, or licensed minister of a church. Licensed ministers of a church or denomination that both licenses and ordains ministers are eligible for the exemption only if they perform substantially all the religious functions of an ordained minister under the tenets and practices of their church or denomination. *Revenue Ruling 78-301.* See chapter 3 for a complete explanation of what persons qualify as an "ordained, commissioned, or licensed minister."

2. The church or denomination that ordained, commissioned, or licensed the minister is a tax-exempt religious organization. *Revenue Ruling 80-59.* Form 4361 (the exemption application for ministers) specifies that : "You must establish that the body that ordained, commissioned, or licensed you . . . is exempt from federal income tax . . . as a religious organization described in section 501(c)(3) of the Internal Revenue Code. *You must also establish that the body is a church (or convention or association of churches) . . . .*"

3. The minister must file an exemption application (Form 4361) in triplicate with the IRS. A minister certifies on Form 4361 that "I am conscientiously opposed to, or because of my religious principles I am opposed to, the acceptance (for services I performed as a minister . . .) of any public insurance that makes payments in the event of death, disability, old age, or retirement, or that makes payments toward the cost of, or provides services for, medical care." The form states that "public insurance includes insurance systems established by the Social Security Act." There are three important factors to note.

a. Conscientious opposition based on religious belief. Code section 1402(e), and Form 4361, both specify that the exemption is available to a minister who is "conscientiously opposed to, or because of his religious principles is opposed to, the acceptance (with respect to services performed by him as such minister . . .) of any public insurance that makes payments in the event of death, disability, old age, or retirement, or that makes payments toward the cost of, or provides services for, medical care." However, the regulations interpreting this language specify that "ministers . . . requesting exemption from social security coverage must meet either of two alternative tests: (1) A **religious principles test** which refers to the institutional principles and discipline of the particular religious denomination to which he belongs, or (2) a **conscientious opposition test** which refers to the opposition because of religious considerations of individual ministers . . . (rather than opposition based upon the general conscience of any such individual or individuals)." *Treas. Reg. 1.1402(e)-2A(a)(2).* Under both the "religious principles" and "conscientious opposition" tests, a minister must have religion-based opposition to accepting social security benefits. The income tax regulations clearly reject the view that ministers can be eligible for exemption from social security coverage on the basis of "conscientious opposition" alone. The conscientious opposition must be rooted in religious belief. Code section

1402(e) specifically delegates to the Treasury Department the authority to adopt regulations prescribing the "form and manner" of filing exemption applications. Therefore, though the regulations' rejection of nonreligious conscientious opposition to social security benefits as a grounds for exemption seems to contradict the plain meaning of the Code, it is unlikely that a court would find the regulations to be invalid.

Clearly, economic or any other non-religious considerations are not a valid basis for the exemption. Regrettably, many ministers have been induced to exempt themselves from social security participation because of the recommendation of a financial counselor that they would be "better off financially." In many cases, counselors have recommended an alternative investment returning a commission or premium to themselves. Fortunately, such tactics will be significantly reduced because of a new requirement for exemption discussed later in this section.

The applicant qualifies for the exemption as long as he or she is *personally* opposed to accepting social security benefits on the basis of religious principles, even though his or her ordaining, commissioning, or licensing body is not officially opposed to social security participation (i.e., such an applicant would satisfy the "conscientious opposition" test described above).

b. Opposition to the acceptance of public insurance benefits. The exemption is available only if a minister is opposed on the basis of religious considerations to the *acceptance of social security benefits* rather than to payment of the tax. A minister may have religious opposition to payment of the tax, but this alone will not suffice. The individual must have religious opposition to accepting social security benefits upon his or her retirement or disability. This is an extraordinary claim that few ministers in good faith will be able to make.

c. Participation in private insurance programs permitted. The applicant's opposition must be to accepting benefits under the social security program (or any other "public insurance" system that provides retirement and other specified benefits). As a result, a minister who files the exemption application may still purchase life insurance or participate in retirement programs administered by non-governmental institutions (such as a life insurance company). *T.A.M. 8741002.* The income tax regulations specify that the term "public insurance" refers to "governmental, as distinguished from private, insurance and does not include insurance carried with a commercial insurance carrier." *Treas. Reg. 1.1402(e)-2A(a)(2); Revenue Ruling 77-78.* The regulation goes on to clarify that to qualify for the exemption a minister "need not be opposed to the acceptance of all public insurance" but he "must be opposed *on religious grounds* to the acceptance of any such payment which, in whole or in part, is based on, or measured by earnings from, services performed by him in his capacity as a minister."

4. The exemption application (Form 4361) must be filed on time. The deadline is the due date of the federal tax return for the second year in which a minister has net earnings from self-employment of $400 or more, any part of which derives from the performance of services in the exercise of ministry.

5. Notification of ordaining, commissioning, or licensing church or denomination. An applicant for exemption must inform "the ordaining, commissioning, or licensing body of the church or order that he is opposed" to social security coverage (the revised Form 4361 contains a statement that the applicant has satisfied this requirement), and presumably, that he or she intends to apply for an exemption from social security coverage. *IRC 1402(e)(1).* A new regulation specifies that a minister seeking exemption from social security coverage after December 31, 1986 "shall include with such application a statement to the effect that the individual making application for exemption has informed the ordaining, commissioning, or licensing body of the church that he or she is opposed to the acceptance (for services performed by a minister . . .)" of social security benefits. All of the newer exemption application forms contain such a statement. However, if a minister uses an older form that does not contain the statement, he or she must prepare such a statement independently and enclose it along with the Form 4361 exemption application. The statement must be to the effect that the applicant has informed the ordaining, commissioning, or licensing body of the church that he or she is opposed to the acceptance of social security benefits for services performed as a minister. Ministers who plan to apply for exemption from social security coverage must be sure to notify the church or denomination that ordained, commissioned, or licensed them regarding their opposition to social security coverage and presumably of their intention to file an exemption application. This notification must occur prior to the time the exemption application is filed.

Churches or religious denominations that ordain, commission, or license ministers should be aware that they now must be informed by applicants for exemption from social security coverage that they are applying for exemption. This new requirement apparently was designed to provide churches and denominations with an opportunity to counsel applicants regarding the desirability of seeking exemption. Further, knowledge that a particular minister has applied for exemption will assist the church or denomination in providing appropriate pension counseling to such a person. Churches and denominations should prepare standardized responses, setting forth in detail their response to a minister's claim of exemption. Ministers are free to obtain an exemption (assuming that they otherwise qualify) even if their church or denomination is officially opposed to ministers exemptions from social security coverage. Such churches and denominations should be sure to state, in detail, their reasons for urging an applicant to reconsider his or her decision to pursue exemption. At a minimum, a response should specify the various social security benefits that will be forfeited (i.e., retirement benefits, survivor benefits, disability benefits, and medicare). Some denominations have been threatened with lawsuits for failing to adequately counsel younger ministers regarding the financial disadvantages that may be associated with an exemption from social security. Churches and denominations may wish to have ministers applicants sign a form acknowledging that the church or denomination counseled the applicant against filing an exemption application, and releasing the church or denomination from any liability that may arise out of financial hardships associated with the applicant's decision. Of course, these procedures would not be as critical if a church or denomination has no position regarding social security exemptions. Even in such cases, however, it may be prudent to point out the benefits that are being forfeited, and the financial hardship that an exemption may create in some situations.

6. IRS verification. No application for exemption will be approved unless the IRS, or the Secretary of the Department of Health and Human Services (or a designated representative) "has verified that the individual applying for the exemption is aware of the grounds on which the individual may receive an exemption . . . and that the individual seeks an exemption on such grounds." *IRC 1402(e)(2).* This "verification" requirement was adopted to prevent the widespread practice of ministers exempting themselves from social security coverage solely on the basis of financial considerations. Prior to 1987, many ministers obtained exemption from social security coverage solely on account of financial opposition to the payment of self-employment taxes—even though this has never been an available basis for exemption. This was possible because the IRS did not verify that applicants were seeking exemption on the basis of the only ground available under federal law—opposition (based on religious convictions) to the acceptance of social security benefit. The IRS now must verify that ministers applicants in fact qualify for the exemption. A new regulation explains the required verification procedure as follows:

Upon receipt of an application for exemption from self-employment taxes . . . the IRS will mail to the applicant a statement that describes the grounds on which an individual may receive an exemption under [the law]. The individual filing the application shall certify that he or she has read the statement and that he or she seeks exemption from self-employment taxes on the grounds listed in the statement. The certification shall be made by signing a copy of the statement under penalties of perjury and mailing the signed copy to the IRS Service Center from which the statement was issued not later than 90 days after the date on which the statement was mailed to the individual. If the signed copy of the statement is not mailed to the IRS Service Center within 90 days of the date on which the statement was mailed to the individual, that individual's exemption will not be effective until the date that the signed copy of the statement is received at the Service Center. *Treas. Reg. 1.1402(e)-5A.*

In other words, the IRS satisfies the verification requirement by sending each applicant a statement reciting the grounds on which an exemption is available, and having the applicant sign the statement, certifying under penalty of perjury that he or she is seeking exemption on the basis of an available ground. The statement must then be returned to the IRS within 90 days from the date it was originally

sent by the IRS. Ministers who fail to return the signed statement within 90 days will delay recognition of their exemption until the date that the signed statement is received by the IRS.

Some common questions pertaining to the exemption from self-employment taxes are addressed below.

• **When is an exemption effective?** Filing a timely exemption application does *not* necessarily qualify a minister for exemption. The income tax regulations specify that "the filing of an application for exemption on Form 4361 by a minister . . . does not constitute an exemption from the tax on self-employment income . . . . The exemption is granted only if the application is approved by an appropriate internal revenue officer." In practice, an exemption is effective only when an applicant receives back one of the three 4361 forms (it is filed in triplicate) from the IRS marked "approved." Ministers should be careful not to lose an approved Form 4361. *Treadway v. Commissioner, 47 T.C.M. 1375 (1984).*

A federal court in Virginia ruled in 1991 that a minister was entitled to exemption from self-employment taxes *even though the IRS had no record of ever having received his exemption application (Form 4361). Eade v. United States, 92-1 USTC ¶ 50,017 (W.D. Va. 1991).* The minister was able to persuade a jury that he qualified for exemption, and that he in fact filed a timely exemption application. The court acknowledged that the income tax regulations specify that a minister's exemption is not effective until the IRS marks a copy of the exemption application "approved" and returns it to the minister. However, the court concluded that IRS approval of such applications is *a perfunctory act involving no discretion.* Accordingly, since the minister had done everything he was required to do in order to claim the exemption, and was in fact qualified for it, he was entitled to the exemption despite the apparent mistake of the Post Office or the Internal Revenue Service.

This case may resolve a dilemma for those many ministers who have submitted a timely application for exemption from self-employment taxes (Form 4361) but who have never received a reply from the IRS. Many of these ministers have assumed that they are exempt. They become alarmed when they discover that the income tax regulations state that the exemption is effective only when the IRS stamps their application "approved" and returns it to them.

The decision of the Virginia federal district court gives hope to these ministers. They will not necessarily be liable for self-employment taxes (plus penalties and interest) for previous years. However, to achieve this result, they must: (1) demonstrate that they were eligible for the exemption; (2) convince a jury that they in fact mailed a timely Form 4361; and (3) persuade the court to apply the same reasoning as the Virginia federal district court (i.e., that IRS "approval" of an exemption is a perfunctory, administrative act that is not a requirement for exemption). As the court itself noted, not every minister will be able to persuade a jury that he or she in fact mailed a timely Form 4361. There are a few other points to observe about this ruling. First, the decision does not provide any relief to those ministers who would like to exempt themselves from self-employment taxes after the "time limit" has expired. Ministers who are past the deadline are not given any relief or "extension" by the court's decision. Second, the decision in no way liberalizes the requirements for qualifying for exemption. To be eligible for the exemption from self-employment taxes, a minister must be opposed on the basis of religious considerations to the acceptance of social security benefits. This is indeed an extraordinary claim that very few ministers can satisfy. Nothing in the court's decision changes this. Finally, the court in no way was encouraging ministers to "opt out" of social security. Once again, very few ministers will be able to satisfy the extraordinary requirements for exempt status. This has not changed.

• **Can the period for filing an exemption application be extended or renewed?** This is a question that many ministers have asked. Consider the following rules:

(1) the general rule — no extension or renewal is allowed

A number of ministers have attempted to file exemption applications after the filing deadline (described above) expired. However, the courts have never permitted any exceptions to the filing deadline rules—except in one case that is discussed below. To illustrate, a number of ministers who failed to file a timely exemption application have argued that their constitutional right to freely exercise their religion is abridged by being forced to pay social security taxes against their will. This contention has been consistently rejected by the courts. The United States Supreme Court has observed that "[i]f we hold that ministers have a constitutional right to opt out of the social security system when participation conflicts with their religious beliefs, that same right should extend as well to persons with secular employment and to other taxes, since their right freely to exercise their religion is no less than that of ministers." *United States v. Lee, 455 U.S. 252 (1982)*. Other ministers have argued that they were unaware of the deadline, that they were certain (but could not prove) that they had filed a timely election, that they were given incorrect advice by IRS employees regarding the requirements for exemption, or that their opposition to participation in the social security program did not arise until after the deadline for filing an exemption application had passed. The courts have rejected all of these arguments (and every other theory ever devised to justify a tardy exemption application, except as noted below). *See, e.g., Ballinger v. Commissioner, 728 F.2d 1287 (10th Cir. 1984); Olsen v. Commissioner, 709 F.2d 278 (4th Cir. 1983); Keaton v. Commissioner, T.C. Memo. 1993-365; Paschall v. Commissioner, 46 T.C.M. 1197 (1983); Hess v. Commissioner, 40 T.C.M. 415 (1980).*

(2) a possible exception—a second ordination in another faith accompanied by a timely exemption application

In 1994, a federal appeals court for the tenth circuit (includes the states of Colorado, Kansas, New Mexico, Oklahoma, Utah, and Wyoming) ruled that the period of time during which a minister must file an application for exemption from social security started all over when he left the ministry for 5 years and was then reordained by another church. *Hall v. Commissioner, 94-2 USTC ¶ 50,392 (10th Cir. 1994).* The court reversed an earlier Tax Court ruling finding that the deadline for opting out of social security had expired. The court acknowledged that the deadline for filing an exemption application (Form 4361) is the due date of the federal tax return for the second year in which a minister has net earnings from self-employment of $400 or more, some of which comes from ministerial services. It disagreed with the Tax Court's view that the deadline for filing an exemption application is not renewed when a minister is reordained by another church. The court observed:

The plain language of the statute extends the exemption to "any individual who is . . . a duly ordained, commissioned, or licensed minister of a church . . . upon filing an application . . . together with a statement that either he is conscientiously opposed to, or because of religious principles he is opposed to, the acceptance . . . of any public insurance." Taxpayer fits that profile exactly. The Code also requires an applicant for exemption to file on or before "the due date of the return . . . for the second taxable year for which he has net earnings from self-employment [from his ministerial services] of $400 or more." As recited above, taxpayer filed during the first taxable year in which his self-employment income from his new ministry exceeded $400. When an individual enters the ministry anew in a new church, having adopted a new set of beliefs about the propriety of accepting public insurance, it is logical and inconsistent with the statutory language . . . to characterize that individual as a "new" minister for the purposes of seeking an exemption. The plain language does not preclude this sensible reading.

The court relied on the first amendment guaranty of religious freedom in support of its conclusion, noting that the Tax Court's narrow interpretation of the deadline for opting out of social security could interfere with the religious beliefs of ministers, like the minister in this case, who experience a profound change in their religious beliefs, change churches, are reordained, and attempt to opt out of social security.

The federal court's recent decision will not open the floodgates to other ministers. For the vast majority of ministers who fail to file an exemption application within this period of time, there is no second chance. They will never be able to exempt themselves from social security coverage.

The court's decision is a narrow one and applies only to those few ministers who

• change their church affiliation

• are reordained

• develop an opposition, based on their new religious convictions, to the acceptance of social security benefits, and

• submit an exemption application (Form 4361) by the due date of the federal tax return for the second year in which they have net self-employment earnings of $400 or more, any part of which comes from the performance of ministerial services in their new faith.

Few ministers will satisfy these requirements. The ruling will not apply to ministers who do not change their church affiliation or doctrine. Ministers who did not file an exemption application within the prescribed period, and who have served a local church for several years, are not given a second chance to opt out of social security by this ruling. The court itself agreed with its decision in an earlier case denying an exemption from social security to a minister who changed his religious beliefs, was reordained, and then waited five years before submitting an exemption application. *Ballinger v. Commissioner, 728 F.2d 1287 (10th Cir. 1984).*

(3) a change of faith accompanied by an untimely exemption application

The general rule applies and the period for filing an exemption application will not be renewed. In 1984, a federal appeals court ruled that the deadline for filing an application for exemption from self-employment taxes is not renewed or extended simply because a minister undergoes a change of faith. *Ballinger v. Commissioner, 728 F.2d 1287 (10th Cir. 1984).* In the *Ballinger* case a minister was ordained by a Baptist church in 1969 and served as a minister of that church from 1969 through 1972. He did not apply for an exemption from self-employment tax. He became a minister in another faith in 1973 and performed services as a minister of a church affiliated with his new faith in 1973, 1974 and 1975. He paid the appropriate self-employment tax on such earnings during each of these years. In 1978 the minister was formally ordained by his new church, and in the same year he submitted an exemption application (Form 4361) to the IRS, claiming that he followed his new church's teachings in opposition to accepting public or private insurance benefits, such as social security benefits in the event of death, disability or old-age. The IRS denied this application for exemption, and the Tax Court agreed. The Tax Court refused to interpret the time requirements for filing an exemption application as allowing an exemption after a second ordination. The minister appealed this decision to a federal appeals court, which agreed with the IRS and Tax Court. However, it insisted that it did not agree with the Tax Court's sweeping conclusion that an exemption is never permissible in cases of second ordinations. The court observed:

> The statute makes no distinction between a first ordination and subsequent ordinations. Not all churches or religions have a formally ordained ministry, whether because of the nature of their beliefs, the lack of a denominational structure or a variety of other reasons. Courts are not in a position to determine the merits of various churches nor an individual's conversion from one church to another. Thus, we cannot hold that an individual who functions as a minister in a church which does not ordain, license or commission that individual in a traditional or legally formal manner is

not entitled to the exemption. Nor can we hold that an individual who has a change of belief accompanied by a change to another faith is not entitled to the exemption. We interpret Congress' language providing an exemption for any individual who is "a duly ordained, commissioner or licensed minister of a church" to mean that the triggering event is the assumption of the duties and functions of a minister.

> Since the minister in this case began his duties with his new church in 1973, his deadline for filing an exemption application was April 15, 1975. It did not matter that he was not ordained until 1978, since the critical event according to this court is the date a person in fact begins performing the duties of a minister.

(4) a minister remains in the same church, but does not develop religious-based opposition to the acceptance of social security benefits until after the deadline has expired

The general rule applies and an exemption application will be denied. The federal appeals court in the *Ballinger* case observed:

> The more difficult question is whether an individual, who has already assumed the duties of a minister, belatedly acquires a belief in opposition to the acceptance of public insurance and that change in belief is not accompanied by a change in faiths, is entitled to the exemption if he files within the statutory time frame after acquiring his new belief. We find that the statute does not provide for an exemption in that situation. The triggering event for measuring the statutory time period is the assumption of ministerial duties, combined with earning a particular amount of income. Thus, the statute does not provide for an exemption where a minister belatedly acquires a belief in opposition to public insurance apart from conversion to another faith. The [minister] did not file for the exemption within the applicable time frame.

• **How far back can the IRS assess social security taxes?** This question is relevant whenever a minister has unreported or underreported self-employment taxes. This condition can occur in several ways, including the following:

• A minister submits a timely exemption application (Form 4361) but never receives back an approved copy. The minister assumes that he or she is exempt from self-employment taxes from the date the application is submitted, and does not pay self-employment taxes. The IRS rejects the *Eade* case (discussed above).

• Some ministers assume that they are "automatically" exempt from self-employment taxes, and accordingly they do not submit a Form 4361.

• Some ministers who have submitted a timely exemption application that has been approved by the IRS are later audited and the validity of their exemption is challenged.

• Many ministers underreport their self-employment taxes because they fail to include their housing allowance (or the fair rental value of a church-provided parsonage) in their taxable income for self-employment tax purposes.

Under any of these circumstances, can the IRS assess back taxes all the way back to the first year of the person's ministry? This question was answered in a 1982 ruling of the IRS. The ruling involved farmer who filed a timely Form 1040 for each year from 1973 through 1980, but who did not attach a Schedule SE or report or pay any self-employment tax (i.e., social security tax for self-employed persons) for any of those years. The question presented to the IRS was whether self-employment taxes could be assessed for *all* the years in question. The IRS noted that section 6501(a) of the Code specifies that taxes must be assessed within three years after a return is filed, though taxes may be assessed at any time in the case of failure to file a return. In other words, the IRS generally can assess back taxes only for the three years preceding a return, but there is no limit on how far back the IRS can assess taxes if no return is filed. The IRS concluded that "self-employment taxes are not separate and distinct from individual income taxes," but rather are "in all particulars an integral part of the income tax." Accordingly, "the filing of a Form 1040 that fully reports all income but contains no entry with respect to self-employment tax will be treated as the filing of a valid self-employment tax return," and therefore the "self-employment tax may not be assessed later than three years after the taxpayer files a Form 1040 and fully reports all income but makes no entry with respect to self-employment tax." *Revenue Ruling 82-185.*

☞ **Example.** *Rev. W was ordained in 1980, but never has paid social security taxes because of his belief that he submitted a timely exemption application (Form 4361) to the IRS. However, he does not have in his possession a copy of the exemption application, and he does not recall ever receiving back an "approved" copy from the IRS. In May of 1997 he learns that an exemption from social security is not effective unless the applicant receives back from the IRS an "approved" copy of the exemption application. Rev. W is afraid to contact the IRS or Social Security Administration to confirm his exemption out of a fear that he will be told that he is not exempt and that he will have to pay social security taxes all the way back to 1980 (with penalties and interest). According to Revenue Ruling 82-185, Rev. W will not be assessed social security taxes later than three years after he files a Form 1040 and fully reports all income (but makes no entry with respect to self-employment tax). This means that if Rev. W filed a Form 1040 for each year since 1980, and fully reported all income in each year, he cannot be assessed social security taxes for years prior to 1994 (i.e., three years from the filing deadline for Rev. W's 1993 income tax return would have been April 15, 1997—and so it is too late in May of 1997 for the IRS to assess taxes for 1993 or any preceding year).*

In 1993, the Tax Court ruled that a minister who had not paid self-employment taxes for the years 1983 through 1987 on the ground that the IRS had "improperly denied" his 1980 and 1983 applications for exemption from self-employment taxes, was liable for self-employment taxes for all of the years in question. It is unclear how the IRS could assess back taxes for 5 years, and for years that clearly were more than 3 years prior to the IRS audit. In fact, 1983 (one of the years for which the IRS was demanding back taxes) was a decade prior to the Court's decision, and nearly a decade prior to the IRS audit. *Reeder v. Commissioner, T.C. Memo. 1993-287.*

• **Is an exemption from social security coverage irrevocable?** The answer is yes, meaning that a minister who is exempt cannot later re-enter the program. The Tax Reform Act of 1986 gave ex-

---

CLERGY SELF-EMPLOYMENT EARNINGS

Clergy always are considered self-employed for social security purposes with respect to services performed in the exercise of ministry. Accordingly, they pay the "self-employment tax" rather than FICA taxes. The self-employment tax for 1997 is computed by multiplying net self-employment earnings (up to $65,400) times the self-employment tax rate of 15.3%. Only the Medicare component (2.9%) of self-employment taxes applies to self-employment earnings in excess of $65,400. Net self-employment earnings are computed as follows:

church salary

+ other items of church income (including taxable fringe benefits) described in chapter 4

+ self-employment earnings from outside businesses

+ annual fair rental value of parsonage, or housing allowance exclusion

+ business expenses reimbursements (under a nonaccountable plan)

+ the value of meals served on the church's premises for the convenience of the employer

– unreimbursed business expenses (disregard the *Deason* reduction rule)

– business expenses reimbursed under a nonaccountable plan (disregard the *Deason* reduction rule)

– most income tax exclusions (see chapter 5) other than the housing allowance, the fair rental value of a parsonage, meals or lodging furnished for the employer's convenience, and the foreign earned income exclusion

– net self-employment earnings (without regard to this deduction) multiplied times 7.65%

empt ministers a limited one-time opportunity to re-enter the system by waiving their exemption prior to April 15, 1988 (by filing a Form 2031). This opportunity was created in order to allow ministers to revoke an unverified "exemption" for which they were not in fact eligible. It is doubtful that Congress will ever again give exempt ministers an opportunity to revoke their exempt status, since the new conditions for exemption added by the Tax Reform Act of 1986 (and explained in detail above) make it much more likely that applicants for exemption in fact qualify.

❖ **New in 1997. A bill introduced in Congress would permit ministers who have opted out of social security to revoke their exemption. Representative English of Pennsylvania introduced House Bill 939, which if enacted would provide a limited opportunity for ministers to revoke an exemption from self-employment taxes.**

Several constitutional challenges have been brought against the exemption of ministers from social security coverage. Thus far, none has been successful. The courts have consistently held that the exemption of ministers who are opposed to participation on the basis of religious principles is mandated by the first amendment guaranty of religious freedom.

In 1995 the Tax Court upheld the revocation of a minister's exemption from social security on the ground that he did not qualify. This case is important, since it illustrates that while ministers cannot revoke an exemption from self-employment taxes, the IRS may do so if it can establish that a minister did not qualify for exemption. The Tax Court noted that a minister's exemption application had been filed on time, but it concluded that the minister was not eligible for exemption because of comments he made during his trial. Among other things, the minister made the following response when asked whether he was opposed to accepting social security benefits on the basis of religious principles (as required by law to qualify for the exemption): "No. I am not opposed to the—to that, as a religious issue, no. We were advised to—by our accountant, to file for an exemption with the state, providing the state would allow it. And we asked the state to allow it, which they did." This is an extraordinary ruling that is very significant for younger ministers who are trying to decide whether or not to file an application for exemption from self-employment taxes (Form 4361). The ruling indicates that filing a timely Form 4361—which contains a certification by the applicant that he or she meets all of the eligibility requirements—may not be enough. The IRS or the courts may later question whether or not the minister in fact was eligible for the exemption when the Form 4361 was filed. The court struggled with this conclusion. It acknowledged that the minister "signed an exemption application stating that he was opposed to public insurance because of his religious principles." However, it found the minister's "trial testimony to be more compelling." This conclusion was reinforced by the mistakes that appeared on the Form 4361, which suggested to the court that the minister had not read the form and was not aware that he was ineligible for exemption. Many ministers have filed a Form 4361 without being

eligible for the exemption from self-employment taxes. These ministers must recognize that the validity of their exemption may be questioned in an audit. *Hairston v. Commissioner, T.C. Memo. Dec. 51,025(M) (1995).*

These coverage rules are illustrated by the following examples.

☞ *Example. Rev. D, an ordained minister, is opposed to social security on the basis of economic considerations. He is not eligible for the exemption.*

☞ *Example. Rev. L is opposed on the basis of non-religious conscientious objection to the acceptance of social security benefits. He is not eligible for an exemption from social security coverage. Revenue Ruling 75-189.*

☞ *Example. Rev. G graduates from seminary in May of 1997, and accepts an associate pastoral position in July of the same year. Assuming that he earns at least $400 in self-employment earnings in 1997 and subsequent years, he must file an exemption application (Form 4361) no later than April 15, 1999 (the due date for the federal income tax return for the second year in which he had net earnings from self-employment of $400 or more, any part of which derived from ministry). If Rev. G obtains an automatic four-month extension for filing his 1999 income tax return, his Form 4361 is not due until August 15, 1999.*

☞ *Example. Rev. N is opposed on the basis of religious principles to paying social security taxes. He does not qualify for the exemption, since the opposition must be to the acceptance of benefits.*

☞ *Example. Rev. M accepts his first pastoral assignment in January of 1998. He has decided to exempt himself from self-employment taxes, but wants to be sure that all of the eligibility requirements are satisfied. He must obtain an exemption application (Form 4361) containing a statement that he has notified his ordaining, commissioning, or licensing body of his opposition to social security coverage. Also, his application will not be approved unless the IRS verifies that Rev. M is aware of the basis for the exemption and is claiming the exemption on that basis. This is done by sending Rev. M a statement reciting the grounds on which an exemption is available, and having him sign the statement, certifying under penalty of perjury that he is seeking exemption on the basis of an available ground. The statement must then be returned to the IRS within 90 days from the date it was originally sent by the IRS. If Rev. M fails to return the signed statement within 90 days, he will delay recognition of his exemption until the date that the signed statement is received by the IRS.*

☞ *Example. Rev. F is ordained in 1984 and does not apply for an exemption from social security coverage by the deadline on April 15, 1986. In*

1998, Rev. F becomes convinced, on the basis of religious principles, that he should not accept social security benefits. Accordingly, he submits an exemption. His exemption will not be accepted, and this will not violate Rev. F's constitutional rights.

☞ *Example*. Rev. S exempted herself from social security coverage in 1984 on the advice of a financial consultant who persuaded her that social security was a "bad investment." She would like to re-enter the system. She could have done so by submitting a waiver (Form 2031) no later that April 15, 1988. Her failure to do so renders her exemption irrevocable.

☞ *Example*. Rev. B is a licensed minister in a denomination that also ordains ministers. Rev. B is eligible for the exemption from social security coverage only if he is able to perform substantially the same religious duties as an ordained minister under the tenets and practices of his denomination. IRS Letter Ruling 9221025.

☞ *Example*. Rev. O filed an application (Form 4361) to the IRS within a year of his ordination in 1985. Accordingly, he quit paying social security taxes that year. Rev. O never received back a copy of his application marked "approved" by the IRS. Even though Rev. O is sure that he submitted the form, the income tax regulations specify that "the filing of an application for exemption on Form 4361 by a minister . . . does not constitute an exemption from the tax on self-employment income . . . . The exemption is granted only if the application is approved by an appropriate internal revenue officer." Accordingly, Rev. O never was exempted from social security coverage since he did not receive back a copy of his application marked "approved" by the IRS. Note, however, that a federal court in Virginia has concluded that ministers may qualify for exemption if they (1) demonstrate that they were eligible for the exemption when they submitted an exemption application; (2) convince a jury that they in fact mailed a timely Form 4361; and (3) persuade the IRS or a court to apply the same reasoning as the Virginia federal district court (i.e., that IRS "approval" of an exemption is a perfunctory, administrative act that is not a requirement for exemption). Eade v. United States, 92-1 USTC ¶ 50,017 (W.D. Va. 1991) (discussed above).

☞ *Example*. Rev. P became convinced that accepting social security benefits violated his understanding of the Bible. However, this conviction developed only after the deadline for filing an exemption application (Form 4361) had expired. He is not eligible for the exemption. Paschall v. Commissioner, 46 T.C.M. 1197 (1983).

☞ *Example*. Rev. H testified that he filed a timely exemption application, despite IRS assertions that the form was never received. Rev. H's wife testified that she distinctly remembered signing the application along with her husband. The Tax Court, in rejecting Rev. H's testimony, concluded that he had not been a "credible or convincing witness," and noted in particular that "his wife's signature was neither required nor provided for on the application form." Holland v. Commissioner, 47 T.C.M. 494 (1983).

IRS audit guidelines for ministers. In 1995 the IRS released audit guidelines for its agents to follow when auditing ministers. The guidelines inform agents that in order for ministers to claim exemption from self-employment tax they must satisfy the following requirements:

1. Be an ordained, commissioned or licensed minister of a church or denomination.

2. File Form 4361.

3. Be conscientiously opposed to public insurance (Medicare/Medicaid and Social Security benefits) because of religious beliefs.

4. File for exemption for reasons other than economic.

5. Notify the church or order that he or she is opposed to public insurance.

6. Establish that the organization that ordained, licensed, or commissioned the minister is a tax-exempt religious organization.

7. Establish that the organization is a church.

8. Sign and return the statement that the IRS mails to him or her to verify that he or she has requested an exemption based on the grounds listed on the statement.

⊃ **Observation. The guidelines fail to clarify that a minister must be opposed to the acceptance of benefits under a public insurance program. Opposition to the program is not sufficient.**

The guidelines further clarify that

Form 4361 must be filed by the due date of the Form 1040 (including extensions) for the second tax year in which at least $400 in self-employment ministerial earnings was received. The 2 years do not have to be consecutive. An approved Form 4361 is effective for all tax years after 1967 for which a minister received $400 or more of self-employed income for ministerial services.

The exemption from self-employment tax applies only to services performed as a minister. The exemption does not apply to other self-employment income. To determine if a minister is exempt from self-employment tax, request that he or she furnish a copy of the approved Form 4361 if it is not attached to the return. If the taxpayer cannot provide a copy, order a transcript for the year under examination. The ADP and IDRS Information handbook shows where the ministers' self-employment exemption codes are located on the transcripts and what the codes mean. Transcripts will not show exemption status prior to 1988. If the transcript does not show a MIN SE indicator and the taxpayer still claims that he or she is exempt from self-employment tax, the Taxpayer Relations Branch at the Service Center where the Form 4361 was filed can research this information and provide the taxpayer with a copy. The Social Security Administration in Baltimore also can provide the information on exemption for an individual.

⊃ **Observation. Many ministers who claim they are exempt from self-employment tax cannot prove that they are exempt. Ministers who file a timely application for exemption that is approved by the IRS will be sent a copy of their exemption application marked "approved." A surprisingly large number of ministers who have filed a timely exemption application cannot produce the approved copy of their application. In some cases they have mislaid the application, but in others they mistakenly believe they filed the application many years ago when in fact they did not. In either case, they may not pay self-employment taxes for several years. If they are audited and asked to verify their exemption from self-employment tax, they are unable to do so. The guidelines contain some helpful information for ministers in this situation, for they reveal the procedure that IRS agents are instructed to follow if a minister who claims to be exempt from self-employment taxes cannot produce an approved application. There are a number of recommendations that agents can pursue in verifying the exempt status of a minister who cannot produce a copy of an approved exemption application.**

The guidelines contain the following four examples:

☞ *Example. H has ministerial earnings of $400 in 1996 and $1800 in 1997. He has until April 15, 1998 (if no extension has been filed) to file Form 4361. If the approved Form 4361 is not received by the due date for the 1997 return, the self-employment tax for 1997 is still due by that date. If he later receives the approved 4361, he may amend his 1997 return.*

⊃ **Observation. This example illustrates an important point—most ministers who file an exemption application do so after a year or two of ministry during which they paid self-employment taxes. If they file a timely exemption application that is approved, they can file amended tax returns to claim a refund of self-employment taxes paid during the first year or two of ministry.**

☞ *Example. J earned $500 in 1995, $300 in 1996, and $6,000 in 1997 from her ministry. She has until April 15, 1998 (if no extension has been filed) to file Form 4361. If the approval of the exemption is not received by April 15, 1998, J must*

pay the self-employment tax with her 1997 return, but may amend it after the exemption is approved. J may file a claim for refund (an amended tax return) within 3 years from the time the return was filed or within 2 years from the time the tax was paid, whichever is later.

☞ *Example. K, ordained in 1996, has $7,500 in net earnings as a minister in both 1996 and 1997. He files Form 4361 on March 5, 1998. If the exemption is granted, it is effective for 1996 and all following years.*

☞ *Example. L, an ordained minister, has applied for and received exemption from self-employment tax for his services as a minister. In 1998 he has ministerial income of $12,000 and income from his shoe repair business, a sole proprietorship, of $9,000. He must compute self-employment tax on the $9,000.*

✎ **Key point: the audit guidelines will instruct IRS agents in the examination of ministers' tax returns. They alert agents to the key questions to ask, and provide background information along with the IRS position on a number of issues. It is therefore of utmost importance that ministers be familiar with these guidelines.**

D. Services to Which Exemption Applies

✎ **Key point: an exemption from self-employment taxes only applies to ministerial services. Ministers who have exempted themselves from self-employment taxes must pay social security taxes on any non-ministerial employment. And, they are eligible for social security benefits based on their non-ministerial services (assuming that they have worked enough quarters in non-ministerial employment).**

A minister whose exemption application is duly approved by the IRS is exempt from paying social security taxes on compensation earned from the performance of services in the exercise of ministry. The term "services performed in the exercise of ministry" is a technical one that is defined fully in chapter 3 of this text. Chapter 3 should be referred to at this time.

Secular employment. Some ministers who have exempted themselves from social security coverage have worked previously in secular employment. Does their exemption prevent them from ever receiving any social security benefits? The answer is no. An approved exemption only exempts a minister from social security participation with respect to services performed in the exercise of ministry. The exemption has no effect on services or employment not in the exercise of ministry. The income tax regulations specify that "a minister performing service in the exercise of his ministry may be eligible to file an application for exemption on Form 4361 even though he is not opposed to the acceptance of benefits under the Social Security Act with respect to service performed by him which is not in the exercise of his ministry." *Treas. Reg. 1.1402(e)-2A(a)(2).* As a result, a minister whose exemption application (Form 4361) has been approved by the IRS will be eligible to receive social security benefits based on earnings not covered by the exemption, assuming that such earnings are sufficient to entitle the minister to the benefits. Note also that the longer a minister is exempt from social security coverage, the lower his or her social security retirement benefits will tend to be.

E. Computation of Tax

✎ **Key point: the self-employment tax is computed by multiplying net self-employment earnings times the current self-employment tax rate. Net self-employment earnings consists of a minister's total church compensation, including the annual fair rental value of a parsonage or a housing allowance, but less most income tax exclusions and business expenses (whether unreimbursed, or reimbursed under a nonaccountable plan). Two deductions are allowed in computing net earnings from self-employment (see the next paragraph).**

✎ **Key point: self-employed persons pay the combined FICA tax rate (15.3%) that is shared by employer and employee alike. To partly offset the tax burden that falls on self-employed persons, the law now allows them two deductions: (1) an amount equal to 7.65% multiplied times their net self-employment earnings (without regard to this deduction) may be deducted in computing earnings subject to the self-employment tax; (2) half their self-employment tax is deductible as an adjustment in computing income taxes, whether or not they can itemize deductions on Schedule A.**

✎ **Key point: for 1997, the maximum earnings subject to self-employment taxes increases to $65,400. In addition, all self-employment earnings, regardless of amount, are subject to the 2.9% Medicare component of the self-employment tax.**

The social security tax for ministers who have not filed a timely exemption application is computed by multiplying the applicable self-employment tax rate times the minister's net earnings from self-employment. The net earnings from self-employment must be at least $400 for ministers. Net earnings from self-employment is defined as gross income derived from self-employment less certain deductions, including all unreimbursed ordinary and necessary business and professional expenses incurred in the exercise of ministry. Revenue Ruling 80-110, IRS Publication 517 ("Social Security and Other Information for Members of the Clergy"). Note that such expenses are deductible in computing net earnings from self-employment whether or not the minister actually deducts them as itemized expenses on Schedule A. For example, if a minister reports his or her income taxes

as an employee but is not able to itemize deductions, he or she may still reduce net earnings from self-employment for social security purposes by deducting unreimbursed business and professional expenses even though these items were not deductible for income tax purposes. In addition, IRS Publication 517 states that a minister may also deduct reimbursed employee business expenses that are included in a minister's gross income for income tax purposes (i.e., pursuant to a "nonaccountable" reimbursement policy—see chapter 7 for additional details). *IRC 1402.*

Note also that the IRS has acknowledged that the *Deason* reduction rule does not apply to the deductibility of business expenses on Schedule SE. This means that ministers do not need to reduce their business expense deduction on Schedule SE by the percentage of their total church compensation that consists of a housing allowance. The reason is that the housing allowance is not an exclusion in computing self-employment taxes on Schedule SE. See chapter 7, section F, for further details. This position is reflected in the current edition of IRS Publication 517 ("Social Security and Other Information for Members of the Clergy"), as well as in the IRS audit guidelines for ministers.

The income tax regulations specify that "income which is excludable from gross income under any provision of subtitle A of the Internal Revenue Code is not taken into account in determining net earnings from self-employment," with certain exceptions. *Treas. Reg. 1.1402(a)-2(a).* This means that most of the income tax exclusions (see chapter 5) are also excludable in computing self-employment tax. The exceptions, which *are* included in income for self-employment tax purposes, include (1) the housing allowance, (2) the fair rental value of a church-provided home, (3) the foreign earned income exclusion, and (4) meals and lodging provided for the convenience of an employer. But apart from these exceptions, the general rule is that the exclusions discussed chapter 5 are excludable in computing both income taxes and self-employment taxes.

☞ *Example. A church provided free meals to ministers who were required to reside in housing on the church's premises in order to fulfill their duties. The IRS concluded that the value of the meals represented taxable income to the ministers for self-employment (social security) tax purposes. It noted that section 1402(a)(8) of the Internal Revenue Code prevents the exclusion of meals "for the convenience of the employer" (under section 119) from reducing a minister's net earnings. Thus, the value of meals and cash reimbursements for groceries furnished by the church to its ministers "must be included in the ministers' net earnings from self-employment" for self-employment tax purposes. IRS Letter Ruling 9129037.*

Parsonages. As noted in the preceding paragraph, the law expressly *includes* within the definition of net earnings from self-employment the fair rental value of a church-owned parsonage provided without charge to a minister, as well as a housing allowance paid to a minister who owns or rents his or her home. The "fair rental value" of a parsonage is the fair rental value of a furnished parsonage. This is often a difficult computation to make. Ideally, it should be determined by qualified real estate appraisers. However, a rough approximation of monthly fair rental value that occasionally is used is 1% of the fair market value of the parsonage. To illustrate, if a parsonage has a fair rental value of $50,000, then its monthly fair rental value is $500 (1% of $50,000), and its annual fair rental value is $6,000. This method should be used with care. It has never been endorsed by the IRS, and often may give inflated values that result in unnecessary additions to self-employment tax liability. Also note that if a church pays the utilities of a minister who resides in a church-owned parsonage, the total amount paid by the church must be included in the minister's income for social security tax purposes.

Fringe benefits. Generally, the taxable fringe benefits discussed in chapter 4 are included in a minister's income for social security tax purposes.

Earnings subject to the self-employment tax. The 15.3% self-employment tax rate consists of two components: (1) a Medicare hospital insurance tax of 2.9%, and (2) an "old-age, survivor and disability" ("social security") tax of 12.4%. For 1997 the Medicare component of the self-employment tax (the 2.9% tax rate) applies to all net earnings from self-employment regardless of amount, while the "social security" component (the 12.4% tax rate) applies to net earnings from self-employment up to $65,400. As a result, persons who receive compensation in excess of $65,400 in 1997 will pay the full 15.3% tax rate for net self-employment earnings up to $65,400, and the Medicare rate of 2.9% on all net earnings regardless of amount. This provision directly impacts ministers who always are considered self-employed for social security purposes with respect to their ministerial services.

2 special deductions for the self-employed. Self-employed persons pay the *entire* FICA combined tax rate of 15.3% *without any offsetting credit*. Because of the unfair burden that this places on self-employed persons (who ordinarily have no "employer" to share half the tax) Congress amended the tax law to provide self-employed persons with 2 new deductions:

- Persons who are self-employed for social security purposes (including ministers with respect to their ministerial income) can reduce their taxable earnings by 7.65% (half the FICA tax rate). This is done by multiplying net earnings from self-employment times 0.9235 on line 4 of Schedule SE (Form 1040).

- Persons who are self-employed for social security purposes (including ministers with respect to their ministerial income) can deduct half of their actual self-employment taxes as an adjustment on line 25 of Form 1040, whether or not they are able to itemize deductions on Schedule A.

In explaining these changes Congress stated that its purpose was "to achieve parity between employees and the self-employed" for social security purposes. Unfortunately, many ministers fail to claim both of these deductions. Note the following additional considerations.

1. The calculation of estimated taxes in 1997 (and future years) should incorporate (1) the application of the Medicare component of the self-employment tax (the 2.9% tax rate) to all net earnings from self-employment regardless of amount, and (2) the 2 special deductions described above. Many ministers fail to take these rules into account in calculating their estimated taxes.

2. Churches that have paid "half" of their ministers' self-employment taxes in the past in order to "duplicate" the payment of half of a nonminister employee's FICA taxes will need to reassess this practice. The 2 special deductions make it difficult if not impossible to determine in advance what "half" of a minister's self-employment tax will be. It would be easier to simply agree to pay a designated dollar amount of a minister's self-employment taxes.

IRS audit guidelines for ministers. In 1995 the IRS released audit guidelines for its agents to follow when auditing ministers. The guidelines inform agents that "to compute self-employment tax, allowable trade or business expenses are subtracted from gross ministerial earnings, then the appropriate rate is applied." The guidelines instruct agents to include the following items in a minister's gross income for self-employment tax:

1. Salaries and fees for services, including offerings and honoraria received for funerals, baptisms, etc.

2. Any cash housing allowance or utility allowances.

3. Annual fair rental value (FRV) of a parsonage, if provided, including the cost of utilities and furnishings provided.

4. Any amounts received for business expenses treated as paid under a nonaccountable plan, such as an auto allowance.

The guidelines provide the following additional examples:

☞ *Example. M receives a salary from the church of $20,000. His parsonage allowance is $12,000. The church withholds federal income tax (by mutual agreement) and issues him a Form W-2. He has unreimbursed employee business expenses (before excluding nondeductible amounts attributable to his exempt income) of $5,200. His net earnings for self-employment tax are $26,800 ($20,000 + $12,000 - $5,200). Note that all of M's unreimbursed business expenses are deductible for self-employment tax purposes, although the portion attributable to the exempt housing allowance is not deductible for federal income tax purposes. Section 265 of the Internal Revenue Code regarding the allocation of business expenses related to exempt income relates to income* *tax computations but not self-employment tax computations.*

⟲ **Observation.** This example illustrates a very important point. Ministers' business expenses should not be reduced in computing their self-employment taxes, since the housing allowance does not represent tax-exempt income when computing self-employment taxes. The so-called Deason reduction rule applies only to the computation of income taxes.

☞ *Example. G received a salary of $12,000, a housing allowance of $9,000, and earned $3,000 for various speaking engagements, weddings, funerals, etc., all related to her ministry. . . . Her total business expenses are $4,500. G computes her self-employment taxable income as follows: $12,000 salary plus $9,000 housing allowance plus $3,000 Schedule C income less ($4,500) total business expenses equals $19,500 self-employment income.*

F. Working After You Retire

Persons who retire and begin receiving social security benefits may lose a portion of their benefits if they earn more than a specified amount of income. This limitation (called the "annual earning test") only applies to persons between 62 and 70 years of age. This rule has impacted a number of ministers and lay employees who want to work for a church without affecting the amount of their social security benefits.

The amount of annual income that retired persons (from age 65 to 70) may earn without losing some of their social security benefits was increased as a result of the Senior Citizens' Right to Work Act, enacted by Congress in 1996. This is good news for those churches that employ retired persons and would like to compensate them adequately without reducing their social security benefits. Under this law, workers from age 65 to 70 may earn up to $13,500 in 1997 without a reduction in their social security benefits. This is an increase of $1,000 over the prior law. It gets even better in future years. Workers can earn $14,500 in 1998 without a reduction in benefits; $15,500 in 1999; $17,000 in 2000; $25,000 in 2001; and $30,000 in 2002 and later years. These tests apply only to workers who are 65 to 70 years old. Social security benefits are reduced by $1 for every $3 of income above these limits. Workers 62 to 65 years of age were not addressed by the new law. For 1996, they can earn only $8,280 without a reduction in social security benefits (a $1 reduction for every $2 of income in excess of the limit). This amount is indexed for inflation in future years. There is no earnings limit for workers who have reached age 70.

G. Exemption of Members of Certain Religious Faiths

✎ **Key point: members of certain religious sects that are opposed to social security coverage, and that provide for the welfare and security of their members may become exempt from social security coverage if several conditions are met.**

As of 1988, section 1402(g) of the Internal Revenue Code permits self-employed *members* (whether ministers or laypersons) of certain religious faiths to exempt themselves from social security coverage if the following conditions are satisfied: (1) the member belongs to a recognized religious sect; (2) the sect is opposed to the acceptance of social security benefits on the basis of its established tenets or teachings; (3) the member adheres to the sect's tenets or teachings relating to social security coverage; (4) the member files an exemption application (Form 4029); (5) the member's exemption application is accompanied by evidence of his membership in and adherence to the tenets or teachings of the sect; (6) the member waives his right to all social security benefits; and (7) the Secretary of the Department of Health and Human Services finds that the sect (a) does in fact have established tenets or teachings in opposition to social security coverage, (b) makes provision for the financial support of its dependent members, and (c) has been in existence continually since December 31, 1950. Such an application, if granted, is irrevocable unless the member ceases to be a member of the sect or no longer adheres to the sect's tenets or teachings pertaining to participation in the social security system.

The regulations interpreting this statute specify that a member is not disqualified for the exemption because he is not opposed to obtaining personal liability or property insurance of a kind that will compensate other persons or property that are injured or damaged either by the member or while on the member's property.

The United States Supreme Court emphasized in a 1982 ruling that the exemption applied only to self-employed persons. Employers and employees who paid social security taxes under the FICA program were not eligible for the exemption (through 1988). Accordingly, an Amish employer who employed several persons to work on his farm and in his carpentry shop was not eligible for the exemption despite the fact that both he and his Amish employees were opposed to social security coverage on the basis of well-established Amish religious beliefs. *United States v. Lee, 455 U.S. 252 (1982).* The Court accepted the contention that compulsory participation in the social security program would interfere with the right of the Amish employer and employees to freely exercise their religion. This, however, was only the beginning and not the end of the Court's inquiry, since "[t]he state may justify a limitation on religious liberty by showing that it is essential to accomplish an overriding governmental interest." It concluded that the government's interest in "assuring mandatory and continuous participation in and contribution to the social security system" was an interest of sufficient magnitude to override the interest of Amish employers and employees in freely exercising their religion.

Congress amended the law in 1988 to extend this exemption to *employees* for tax years beginning in 1989 (in effect overruling the Supreme Court's decision in *United States v. Lee*). However, the exemption applies only if the employee and employer are both members of a qualifying religious sect (as described above). The exemption is available to both the employer and employee portion of the FICA tax. No time restriction is imposed on the filing of employee exemption applications, and the law prospectively amended (beginning in 1989) section 1402(g)(2) by eliminating the time restrictions on filing exemption applications by self-employed persons. *IRC 3127.*

The courts have strictly enforced the requirement that the member belong to a religious sect having established tenets or teachings in opposition to social security coverage and that provides for its dependent members. To illustrate, a Seventh-Day Adventist was denied an exemption despite his claim that he was personally opposed to social security coverage on the basis of religious beliefs, since the Seventh-Day Adventist Church had no established tenets or teachings against social security coverage and made no provision for the support of its dependent members. *Varga v. United States, 467 F. Supp. 1113 (D. Md. 1979).*

The exemption has been challenged on the ground that it unconstitutionally discriminates against persons who personally are opposed on the basis of religious beliefs to social security coverage but who are not members of a religious sect that has established tenets or teachings in opposition to social security coverage and that provides for its dependent members. Such challenges thus far have failed. One court has stated: "The limitation by Congress of the exemption of members of certain religious sects with established tenets opposed to insurance and which made reasonable provisions for their dependent members was in keeping with the overall welfare purpose of the Social Security Act. This provision provided assurance that those qualifying for the exemption would be otherwise provided for in the event of their dependency." *Palmer v. Commissioner, 52 T.C. 310 (1969). See also Bethel Baptist Church v. United States, 822 F.2d 1334 (3rd Cir. 1987); May v. Commissioner, T.C. Memo. Dec. 51,242(M) (1996).*

H. Is Social Security a "Good Investment"?

Is social security a good investment? Many ministers ask themselves this question, particularly when they are considering filing an exemption application with the government. Of course, the question is in one sense irrelevant, since ministers are automatically subject to social security taxes unless they are opposed to the acceptance of benefits on the basis of religious principles and they file a timely exemption application.

Historically, social security has been a good investment for most workers, including ministers. But it must be recognized that benefits received in the past were based on a larger percentage of workers and a smaller percentage of beneficiaries. In the future, there will be increasingly fewer workers supporting larger numbers of beneficiaries. Undoubtedly, changes will have to be made in the system. Taxes may increase. Benefits may be cut, or their rate of increase reduced, or they may be denied altogether to those in higher income brackets. The minimum retirement age may be increased. These potential changes suggest that social security should be viewed as a supplemental rather than an exclusive benefit plan.

As noted above, social security coverage provides several benefits—retirement, survivors, disability, hospitalization, and medical. While some ministers who have filed an exemption application conceivably could have duplicated the coverage social security provides, this is highly unlikely. Most exempt ministers only think of duplicating the retirement benefits through some form of retirement arrangement, forgetting that social security coverage provide far more than these benefits. Social security benefits have the additional advantages of being inflation-indexed and nontaxable (for most persons).

Form **4361**
(Rev. February 1997)

Department of the Treasury
Internal Revenue Service

Application for Exemption From Self-Employment Tax for Use by Ministers, Members of Religious Orders and Christian Science Practitioners

OMB No. 1545-0168

File Original and Two Copies

File original and two copies and attach supporting documents. This exemption is granted only if the IRS returns a copy to you marked "approved."

Please type or print

1 Name of taxpayer applying for exemption (as shown on Form 1040)

Social security number

Number and street (including apt. no.)

Telephone number (optional)
(   )

City or town, state, and ZIP code

2 Check ONE box:
☐ Christian Science practitioner
☐ Member of religious order not under a vow of poverty
☐ Ordained minister, priest, rabbi
☐ Commissioned or licensed minister (see line 6)

3 Date ordained, licensed, etc. (Attach supporting document. See instructions.)

/   /

4 Legal name of ordaining, licensing, or commissioning body or religious order

Number, street, and room or suite no.

Employer identification number

City or town, state, and ZIP code

5 Enter the first 2 years, after the date shown on line 3, that you had net self-employment earnings of $400 or more, any of which came from services as a minister, priest, rabbi, etc.; member of a religious order; or Christian Science practitioner ▶

6 If you apply for the exemption as a licensed or commissioned minister, and your denomination also ordains ministers, please indicate how your ecclesiastical powers differ from those of an ordained minister of your denomination. Attach a copy of your denomination's bylaws relating to the powers of ordained, commissioned, or licensed ministers.

- -

7 I certify that I am conscientiously opposed to, or because of my religious principles I am opposed to, the acceptance (for services I perform as a minister, member of a religious order not under a vow of poverty, or a Christian Science practitioner) of any public insurance that makes payments in the event of death, disability, old age, or retirement; or that makes payments toward the cost of, or provides services for, medical care. (Public insurance includes insurance systems established by the Social Security Act.)

I certify that as a duly ordained, commissioned, or licensed minister of a church or a member of a religious order not under a vow of poverty, I have informed the ordaining, commissioning, or licensing body of my church or order that I am conscientiously opposed to, or because of religious principles, I am opposed to the acceptance (for services I perform as a minister or as a member of a religious order) of any public insurance that makes payments in the event of death, disability, old age, or retirement; or that makes payments toward the cost of, or provides services for, medical care, including the benefits of any insurance system established by the Social Security Act.

I certify that I did not file an effective waiver certificate (Form 2031) electing social security coverage on earnings as a minister, member of a religious order not under a vow of poverty, or a Christian Science practitioner.

I request to be exempted from paying self-employment tax on my earnings from services as a minister, member of a religious order not under a vow of poverty, or a Christian Science practitioner, under section 1402(e) of the Internal Revenue Code. I understand that the exemption, if granted, will apply only to these earnings. Under penalties of perjury, I declare that I have examined this application and to the best of my knowledge and belief, it is true and correct.

Signature ▶   Date ▶

Caution: *Form 4361 is **not proof** of the right to an exemption from Federal income tax withholding or social security tax, the right to a parsonage allowance exclusion (section 107 of the Internal Revenue Code), assignment by your religious superiors to a particular job, or the exemption or church status of the ordaining, licensing, or commissioning body, or religious order.*

For Internal Revenue Service Use

☐ Approved for exemption from self-employment tax on ministerial earnings
☐ Disapproved for exemption from self-employment tax on ministerial earnings

By ....
(Director's signature)   (Date)

General Instructions

Section references are to the Internal Revenue Code.

Paperwork Reduction Act Notice.—We ask for the information on this form to carry out the Internal Revenue laws of the United States. You are required to give us the information. We need it to ensure that you are complying with these laws and to allow us to figure and collect the right amount of tax.

You are not required to provide the information requested on a form that is subject to the Paperwork Reduction Act unless the form displays a valid OMB control number. Books or records relating to a form or its instructions must be retained as long as their contents may become material in the administration of any Internal Revenue law. Generally, tax returns and return information are confidential, as required by section 6103.

The time needed to complete and file this form will vary depending on individual circumstances. The estimated average time is:

Recordkeeping, 7 min.; **Learning about the law or the form,** 20 min.; **Preparing the form,** 16 min.; **Copying, assembling, and sending the form to the IRS,** 17 min.

If you have comments concerning the accuracy of these time estimates or suggestions for making this form simpler, we would be happy to hear from you. You can write to the Tax Forms Committee, Western Area Distribution Center, Rancho Cordova, CA 95743-0001. **DO NOT** send the form to this address. Instead, see **Where To File** on page 2.

Purpose of Form.—File Form 4361 to apply for an exemption from self-employment tax if you are:

- An ordained, commissioned, or licensed minister of a church;
- A member of a religious order who has not taken a vow of poverty;
- A Christian Science practitioner; or
- A commissioned or licensed minister of a church or church denomination that ordains ministers, if you have authority to perform substantially all religious duties of your church or denomination.

This application must be based on your religious or conscientious opposition to the acceptance (for services performed as a minister, member of a religious order not under a vow of poverty, or Christian Science practitioner) of any public insurance that makes payments for death, disability, old age, or retirement; or that makes payments for the cost of, or provides services for, medical

(continued on page 2)

Form **4361** (Rev. 2-97)

Chapter 10

RETIREMENT PLANS

Chapter Highlights

- **Tax advantages.** There are several kinds of "tax-favored" retirement plans that are available to clergy and church employees. Contributions to such plans ordinarily are partially or fully deductible (or excludable) by the minister for income tax purposes, and taxation of interest earnings generally is deferred until a later date.

- **The value of early participation.** Clergy can accumulate substantial retirement funds by using tax-deferred retirement plans. How much is accumulated depends on three variables—the amount of the annual contributions to the plan, the interest earned, and the number of years of participation. Younger clergy should discipline themselves to participate in such plans at as early an age as possible, since the value of their contributions will be magnified over time.

- **Types of retirement plans.** Common retirement plans for clergy include:

  ✓ IRAs
  ✓ SEPs
  ✓ Keogh plans (for self-employed clergy)
  ✓ Nonqualified deferred compensation plans
  ✓ Tax-sheltered annuities ("403(b) plans")
  ✓ Church retirement income accounts

  ✓ Qualified pension plans
  ✓ 401(k) plans (established prior to July 2, 1986 or after 1996)
  ✓ "Rabbi trusts"

- **Legal requirements.** All tax-sheltered retirement plans require compliance with complex rules (summarized in this chapter).

- **Denominational retirement plans.** Most denominations offer retirement plans to their clergy (and sometimes to church employees). These ordinarily should be a minister's first choice, since they often involve unique advantages.

- **Housing allowances.** Denominational pensions can designate housing allowances for retired clergy if certain conditions are satisfied. This is a significant tax benefit for retired clergy. It is one of the advantages of a denominational plan.

- **Retirement gifts.** Church congregations often distribute a lump sum "retirement gift" to a retiring minister. Sometimes the "gift" is paid out in monthly installments. Ordinarily, these "gifts" constitute taxable compensation rather than a tax-free gift to the minister.

A. Introduction

✎ **Key point: many "tax-favored" retirement plan options are available to ministers and lay employees. Contributions to such plans are partly or fully tax-deductible (or excludable), and taxation of interest or earnings is deferred until distribution.**

✎ **Key point: ministers and lay staff members can accumulate substantial retirement funds by using tax-deferred retirement plans. How much is accumulated depends on 3 variables—the amount of the annual contributions to the plan, the rate of return, and the number of years of participation.**

A variety of retirement plans are available to ministers and lay church workers. The plans discussed in this chapter are **tax-favored**, meaning that contributions to the plans made by or on behalf of the worker ordinarily are partially or fully deductible for income tax purposes in the year of contribution, and the income (or appreciation) earned by the plan is not taxable until distributed. The deferral of tax on income generated by a retirement plan can result in sizable accumulations of wealth, especially if contributions begin early and are made systematically.

Before reviewing the various retirement options available to ministers and lay church workers, there are a few important observations that need to be made:

"Church plans." Federal law not only establishes a variety of tax-favored retirement arrangements, but heavily regulates those arrangements. Federal regulation derives primarily from the Internal Revenue Code, Department of Labor regulations, and "ERISA." ERISA is a comprehensive pension law enacted by Congress in 1974 that contains numerous provisions regulating pension plans (such as vesting of benefits, participation requirements, and nondiscrimination). "Church plans" are exempt from many of the legal requirements that apply to retirement plans. For example, church plans are exempt from the provisions of ERISA unless they voluntarily elect to be covered. Church plans also are exempt from the nondiscrimination rules that apply to tax-sheltered or "403(b)" annuities, and they are not required to file the annual Form 5500. Section 414(e) of the Internal Revenue Code defines the term *church plan* to include a plan "maintained for its employees by a church." The income tax regulations clarify that for the purpose of this definition the term *church* includes "a religious organization if such organization (1) is an integral part of a church, and (2) is engaged in carrying out the functions of a church, whether as a civil law corporation or otherwise." *Treas. Reg. § 1.414(e)-1(e).*

❖ **New in 1997. Ministers who report their income taxes as self-employed are permitted to participate as fully as employees in tax-favored retirement plans, including tax-sheltered or "403(b)" annuities.**

Self-employed ministers. Some ministers report their federal income taxes as self-employed persons rather than as employees. In the past, one of the disadvantages of self-employed status was ineligibility for a number of tax-favored retirement plans that are restricted by law to employees. Congress addressed this potential problem in two ways over the past few years:

(1) Contributions on behalf of self-employed ministers to church retirement plans. Congress enacted legislation in 1997 clarifying that in the case of contributions made on behalf of a minister who is self-employed to a church plan, the contribution is nontaxable to the extent that it would be if the minister were an employee of a church and the contribution were made to the plan. This provision takes effect in 1998.

(2) Self-employed ministers can participate in 403(b) tax-sheltered annuities. Congress enacted legislation in 1996 permitting self-employed ministers to participate in qualified retirement plans including 403(b) tax-sheltered annuities. This resolves a question that has plagued church plans for many years. In the past, there was much confusion over the eligibility of self-employed ministers and other church workers to participate in church retirement plans including 403(b) tax-sheltered annuities. This provision took effect in 1997.

Note that these provisions apply only to ministers. Self-employed lay church workers are not covered.

B. Individual Retirement Accounts

An individual retirement account (IRA) is a savings plan that lets you set aside money for your retirement. Contributions to the plan may be tax deductible, and earnings are not taxed until they are distributed to you. IRAs are available to you whether you report your income taxes as an employee or as self-employed person. Anyone who has compensation is eligible to set up or contribute to an IRA. Compensation includes an employee's salary or a self-employed person's earnings (less Keogh deductions), or any other amounts you receive for performing personal services. Compensation does *not* include rental income, interest income, dividend income, or any amount received as a pension, annuity, or deferred compensation. Further, compensation does not include a minister's housing allowance or the fair rental value of a church-provided parsonage.

Two kinds of IRAs are available—individual retirement accounts and individual retirement annuities. Only individual retirement accounts are discussed in this section since they are much more common and generally are preferable to annuities for most taxpayers. In addition, an employer can establish a simplified employee pension (SEP) which can be in the form of an individual retirement account (SEPs are discussed below).

As has been mentioned previously, you may be able to **deduct contributions** to your IRA. In general, if you do not participate in an employer's retirement plan, you may deduct IRA contributions of up to $2,000 or 100% of your compensation, whichever is less. If both you and your spouse have compensation, and neither participates in an employer-sponsored retirement plan, you each can set up a

Table 10-1

Annual contribution	years to retirement	annual rate of interest	value at retirement if		
			contribs. tax deductibleand and earnings tax deferred	contribs. not tax deductible and earnings taxable (28% tax bracket)	contribs. not tax deductible and earnings taxable (36% tax bracket)
$3000	20	4%	$93,000	$59,000	$51,000
$3,000	20	8%	$148,000	$82,000	$67,000
$3,000	20	12%	$242,000	$115,000	$91,000
$3,000	30	4%	$175,000	$104,000	$$87,000
$3,000	30	8%	$367,000	$173,000	$137,000
$3,000	30	12%	$811,000	$299,000	$221,000
$3,000	40	4%	$296,000	$163,000	$135,000
$3,000	40	8%	$839,000	$333,000	$251,000
$3,000	40	12%	$2,560,000	$720,000	$493,000

separate IRA and deduct IRS contributions of up to the lesser of $2,000 or 100% of your earned compensation. An employer-provided retirement plan includes a qualified pension plan, a "section 403(b)" tax-deferred annuity, or a simplified employee pension. An unfunded deferred compensation plan is not considered to be an employer-provided plan.

✎ **Key point: you can make 1997 contributions to your IRA at any time during 1997 or by April 15, 1998.**

If you do participate in an employer's retirement plan, or if you file a joint return and your spouse participates in such a plan, the dollar limit on your IRA deduction will be reduced according to the following rules:

IRA deductions for persons who participate in an employer retirement plan

(1) single persons: single persons who participate in an employer-provided retirement plan may deduct the lesser of $2,000 or 100% of compensation in 1997 if their "modified adjusted gross income" (i.e., adjusted gross income figured without any reduction for IRA contributions) is less than $25,000. If their modified adjusted gross income exceeds $35,000, they will not be eligible for any deduction for IRA contributions in 1997. Single persons whose modified adjusted gross income is between $25,000 and $35,000 are eligible for a partial deduction, computed according to the following equation:

maximum deduction = lesser of

1) actual IRA contributions for 1997

or

2) $\frac{(\$10,000 - \text{excess AGI}) \times \$2,000}{\$10,000}$

Excess AGI refers to the amount of modified adjusted gross income in excess of $25,000. The equation assumes that the individual's compensation exceeds $2,000. Note that the equation has a $200 "floor," meaning that a result of less than $200 is increased to $200 (if the result is 0 or less, no deduction is allowed). Round off the maximum deduction (computed according to the above formula) to the next highest multiple of $10. For example, a deduction amount of $611 is rounded up to $620. If your allowable deduction is less than your total IRA contributions for the year, you have nondeductible contributions and must submit a Form 8606 with your Form 1040, designating what portion of your 1997 IRA contributions is deductible and what portion is nondeductible.

☞ *Example.* Rev. M is single, and in 1997 had compensation of $23,000. He made a $2,000 IRA contribution, and also participated in an employer-sponsored retirement plan. Rev. Morris will be able to deduct the full $2,000 since his modified adjusted gross income (i.e., adjusted gross income figured without any deduction for IRA contributions) is less than $25,000. The same result is obtained by using the equation

reproduced above. No reduction in the amount of the deduction is required even though Rev. M participated in an employer-sponsored retirement plan, since his modified adjusted gross income was less than $25,000.

☞ *Example.* Same facts as the preceding example, except that Rev. M's modified adjusted gross income was $30,000. Since he participates in an employer-sponsored retirement plan, and his modified adjusted gross income is $25,000 or more, he is entitled to only a "partial" IRA deduction in 1997. According to the equation reproduced above, his 1997 deduction is limited to $1,000. Rev. Morris must inform the IRS, on Form 8606, what portion of his 1997 contributions he wishes to designate as deductible IRA contributions (up to a maximum of $1,000) and what portion he wishes to designate as nondeductible.

(2) married persons: a married person who participates in an employer-provided retirement plan (or whose spouse does, if they a file joint return) may deduct the lesser of $2,000 or 100% of compensation in 1997 if joint modified adjusted gross income is less than $40,000. If joint modified adjusted gross income exceeds $50,000, neither spouse will be eligible for any deduction for IRA contributions in 1997. Modified adjusted gross income, for purposes of determining the allowable IRA contribution, is computed without regard to any IRA contributions made during the year. If joint adjusted gross income is between $40,000 and $50,000, each spouse is eligible for a partial deduction, computed according to the equation set forth above, except that "excess AGI" refers to the amount of modified adjusted gross income in excess of $40,000. Note that the equation has a $200 "floor," meaning that a result of less than $200 is increased to $200 (if the result is 0 or less, no deduction is allowed). The $200 floor applies to each spouse. Round off the maximum deduction (computed according to the above formula) to the next highest multiple of $10. For example, a deduction amount of $611 is rounded up to $620. If your allowable deduction is less than your total IRA contributions for the year, you have nondeductible contributions and must submit a Form 8606 with your Form 1040, designating what portion of your 1997 IRA contributions is deductible and what portion is nondeductible.

☞ *Example.* Rev. S is a minister at First Church. His church provides a tax-sheltered annuity (a section 403(b) annuity) for him. He and his spouse file a joint return in 1997 on which they report adjusted gross income of $40,000 (including deductions of $2,000 for each spouse as their 1997 IRA contributions). Their "modified adjusted gross income" (adjusted gross income figured without any IRA deductions) is $44,000. Each spouse earned compensation of more than $2,000 in 1997. Since their modified adjusted gross income is $40,000 or more, they are each only entitled to a partial deduction of their 1997 IRA contribution, calculated as follows:

maximum deduction = lesser of

1) actual IRA contributions for 1997, or

2) *($10,000 - excess AGI) x $2,000*
   $10,000

According to this calculation, they are each eligible for a maximum 1997 IRA deduction of $1,200. Since a portion of their total 1997 IRA contributions is nondeductible, they must submit a Form 8606 with their Form 1040, designating what portion of their 1997 IRA contributions is deductible and what portion is nondeductible.

If Rev. S and his spouse reported modified adjusted gross income of less than $40,000, they both could deduct $2,000 as their IRA contribution in 1997.

☞ **Example.** Same facts, except that Rev. S's spouse contributed only $500 to an IRA in 1997. Under the calculation reproduced above, Rev. S would still be entitled to a maximum deduction of $1,200, but Rev. S's spouse would only be entitled to a maximum deduction in the amount of her IRA contributions of $500 (since $500 is less than $1,200).

☞ **Example.** Same facts except that neither Rev. S nor his spouse is a participant in an employer-sponsored retirement plan. Under these facts, Rev. S and his spouse can both deduct a full $2,000 as an IRA contribution in 1997, assuming that they each had at least $2,000 in compensation for the year.

❖ **New in 1998. An individual is not considered to be an active participant in an employer-sponsored retirement plan merely because his or her spouse is an active participant in such a plan; and the deductible IRA phaseout ranges are increased.**

Congress enacted legislation in 1997 containing two important modifications in these rules, effective in 1998:

(1) Spouse's participation not considered. An individual will not be considered to be an active participant in an employer-sponsored retirement plan merely because his or her spouse is an active participant in such a plan. However, the maximum deductible IRA contribution for an individual who is not an active participant, but whose spouse is, is phased out for taxpayers with adjusted gross income between $150,000 and $160,000.

(2) Phaseout limits increased. The deductible IRA phaseout ranges are increases as follows:

Joint Returns

tax year	phaseout range (adjusted gross income)
1998	$50,000-$60,000
1999	$51,000-$61,000
2000	$52,000-$62,000
2001	$53,000-$63,000
2002	$54,000-$64,000
2003	$60,000-$70,000
2004	$65,000-$75,000
2005	$70,000-$80,000
2006	$75,000-$85,000
2007 and thereafter	$80,000-$100,000

Single Taxpayers

tax year	phaseout range (adjusted gross income)
1998	$30,000-$40,000
1999	$31,000-$41,000
2000	$32,000-$42,000
2001	$33,000-$43,000
2002	$34,000-$44,000
2003	$40,000-$50,000
2004	$45,000-$55,000
2005 and thereafter	$50,000-$60,000

☞ **Example.** Rev. B is not a participant in an employer-sponsored retirement plan. Rev. B's spouse works for a secular employer, and is a participant in an employer-sponsored retirement plan. The combined adjusted gross income of the couple is $80,000. Neither can make a deductible contribution to an IRA during 1997.

☞ **Example.** Same facts as the previous example, except that the year is 1998. Rev. B is eligible to make a deductible $2,000 to an IRA. The fact that Rev. B's spouse is an active participant in an employer-sponsored retirement plan does not affect Rev. B's eligibility.

No effect on deferral of tax on earnings. The reduction rules summarized above apply to the amount of your annual IRA contribution that you can deduct in 1997. The earnings on *all* IRAs continue to be tax-deferred, whether or not your annual IRA contribution deduction is reduced or eliminated. You cannot claim a deduction for any contribution made to your IRA during or after the tax year in which you reach age 70 1/2. If both you and your spouse earn compensation, you each can set up a separate IRA. The deduction for each of you is figured separately.

Penalty on excess contributions. If the amount of an IRA owner's contributions exceed the amount he or she is allowed to contribute for that year, the owner will have to pay a 6% excise tax on the excess contribution each year it remains in the IRA (this tax is reported on Form 5329).

Distributions. Any money you receive from your IRA account is a distribution. In general, you must include distributions in your gross income in the year you receive them. Excepted from the general rule are tax-free rollovers (a distribution from your IRA which you reinvest in another IRA within 60 days). Special rules apply if both deductible and nondeductible contributions were previously made to the IRA. Unlike deductible contributions, nondeductible contributions are not taxed when they are distributed to the owner since they are considered to be a tax-free return of capital. If the owner has made both deductible and nondeductible contributions, part of the distribution is treated as a tax-free return of capital. The owner must determine how much of the distribution is not taxable, and how much is included in taxable income. See the instructions to Form 1040 for further information on making this allocation. An IRA owner must designate an annual contribution as either deductible or nondeductible by filing a Form 8606 by the due date of that year's federal income tax return. If nondeductible contributions to an IRA are not reported, all IRA contributions will be treated as deductible and all amounts of withdrawals from the IRA will be taxed unless it can be shown with satisfactory evidence that nondeductible contributions were in fact made.

You must begin receiving distributions from your IRA by April 1 of the year following the year in which you reach age 70 1/2. If you reach age 70 1/2 in 1997, you have until April 1, 1998 to start receiving distributions from your IRA. In addition, your IRA must distribute an amount at least equal to: (1) your entire interest; (2) an annuity that provides nonincreasing payments during your life expectancy or the life expectancy of you and your designated beneficiary; (3) approximately equal payments at least annually over a period of years that does not extend beyond your life expectancy; or (4) approximately equal payments at least annually over a period of years that does not extend beyond the combined life expectancy of you and your designated beneficiary.

If the actual distribution from your IRA during the year is less than the minimum amount that should be distributed, the difference is an "*excess accumulation.*" You may have to pay a 50% excise tax on the excess amount for that year and for any year the excess remains in the account. To figure the amount that should be distributed from an IRA, see IRS Form 5329. The institution with which you invest your IRA contributions ordinarily will explain the distribution requirements to you and assist you in making a decision.

Premature distributions are amounts you withdraw from your IRA before you are either age 59 1/2 or disabled. You must include premature distributions in your gross income and pay a penalty tax of 10% on the premature distribution. This penalty will not apply to portions of any distributions treated as a return of nondeductible contributions, or to distributions that are part of a series of substantially equal payments over the life or life expectancy of the owner or the owner and his or her beneficiary.

❖ **New in 1997. Under current law, a 15 percent tax is imposed on excess distributions from most types of retirement plans (including IRAs and tax-sheltered annuities). Excess distributions generally are those in excess of $160,000 for 1997, or $800,000 in the case of a lump-sum distribution. Congress had suspended this tax for the years 1997 through 1999. Congress enacted legislation in 1997 that repeals it permanently.**

❖ **New in 1997. The 10% penalty on early withdrawals from an IRA is waived if a withdrawal is used for medical expenses in excess of 7.5% of adjusted gross income.**

❖ **New in 1997. Congress enacted legislation permitting spouses who do not work outside the home to contribute up to $2,000 annually to their own IRA, if certain conditions are met.**

Spousal IRAs. In the past those persons who have chosen to remain at home to care for their children have been ineligible to participate fully in an IRA since they have no "compensation" from which to make contributions. This rule ignored the value of services rendered by these individuals, and in 1996 Congress recognized this inequity and enacted legislation allowing married persons who receive no compensation to contribute up to $2,000 annually to an IRA—if the compensation of their spouse is at least as much as the combined amount of their IRA contributions. This provision took effect in 1997.

❖ **New in 1998. Parents can contribute up to $500 each year to an "education IRA" on behalf of their child. Earnings on an education IRA generally accumulate tax-free—provided they are distributed for the post-secondary educational expenses of the beneficiary.**

Education IRAs. Taxpayers are given an important break for education expenses under a law enacted by Congress in 1997—they can contribute up to $500 each year to an "education IRA." Here is how it works. A taxpayer establishes an education IRA and designates a "beneficiary" (usually, the taxpayer's child). The taxpayer contributes up to $500 each year into the account, up until the beneficiary's 18th birthday. Earnings on an education IRA generally accumulate tax-free—provided they are distributed for the post-secondary educational expenses of the beneficiary. Here are some more specifics:

• *Effective date.* Parents can begin contributing to education IRAs on or after January 1, 1998.

• *Annual contribution limit.* Parents can contribute a maximum of $500 each year to an education IRA. This amount is phased out for higher income taxpayers. The phaseout begins at $95,000 of adjusted gross income for single parents, and is phased out completely at $110,000. The phaseout begins at $150,000 of adjusted gross income for married couples filing jointly, and is phased out completely at $160,000.

• *Qualified expenses.* Earnings must be distributed for "qualified expenses" in order to accumulate tax-free. Such expenses include post-secondary tuition, fees, books, supplies, equipment, and certain room and board expenses. Room and board expenses qualify only if the beneficiary is enrolled on at least a half-time basis. Further, "room and board expenses" are defined to mean the minimum room and board allowance as determined by the college or other academic institution in computing costs of attendance for federal financial aid programs.

✎ **Key point: expenses for elementary and secondary school expenses do not qualify.**

• *Termination of education IRAs.* Any balance remaining in an education IRA when a beneficiary attains 30 years of age must be distributed, and the earnings portion of such a distribution will be included in the beneficiary's taxable income and subject to an additional ten percent penalty tax because the distribution was not for educational purposes.

✎ **Key point: prior to a beneficiary reaching age 30, the balance in the education IRA may be "rolled over" (without penalty or tax) to another education IRA benefiting a different beneficiary—if the new beneficiary is a member of the family of the original beneficiary.**

• *Interaction with HOPE credits and lifetime learning credits.* In any year in which an exclusion is claimed for a distribution from an education IRA, neither a HOPE credit nor a lifetime learning credit may be claimed with respect to educational expenses incurred during that year on behalf of the same student. The HOPE credit and lifetime learning credit may be available in other years with respect to that beneficiary. These credits are addressed in chapter 7.

• *Qualified educational institutions.* Education IRAs can be distributed for the qualified educational expenses incurred by beneficiaries attending post-secondary undergraduate or graduate educational institutions. Some vocational institutions also qualify.

• *Tax treatment of distributions.* An education IRA will consist of two components—all annual contributions made to the account plus accumulated earnings. Distributions from the account likewise will consist of both contributions and earnings. The portion of an annual distribution that comes from annual contributions is always tax-free to the beneficiary, but the portion that comes from earnings may not be. Here are two rules to keep in mind:

(1) Qualified education expenses equal or exceed the annual distribution from an education IRA. The full amount of the distribution is tax-free to the beneficiary.

☞ *Example. A college student is the beneficiary of an education IRA established by her parents. The parents have made annual contributions of $500 for eight years (for a total of $4,000), and the account has accumulated an additional $1,000 in earnings, for a total account balance of $5,000. During one year the student incurs $10,000 of educational expenses, and $1,000 is distributed from the education IRA for these expenses. This distribution represents $800 of contributions and $200 of earnings. These amounts are computed on the basis of the ratio of total contributions ($4,000) to the total account balance ($5,000, representing contributions and earnings). Since the qualified educational expenses exceed the amount of the distribution, the full amount of the distribution is tax-free.*

(2) Qualified education expenses are less than the annual distribution from an education IRA. This scenario will be far less common, especially for the next several years. However, it may apply to students who are taking only a few courses. The earnings component of a distribution (see the previous example) will be partially tax-free and partially taxable. You compute these amounts by multiplying the earnings component of the distribution times the ratio of educational expenses to the total amount of the distribution.

☞ *Example. Same facts as the previous example, except that the student's educational expenses are only $600 for the year in question. Since her education expenses are less than the amount of the distribution, a portion of the distribution allocated to earnings will be tax-free and a portion will be taxable. The tax-free portion is computed by the ratio of educational expenses ($600) divided by the total distribution ($1,000)—or 60 percent. Taking 60 percent of the earnings component of the distribution ($200, as computed in the previous example) yields a tax-free earnings distribution of $120. This leaves a taxable portion of $80, which should be included in the beneficiary's taxable income.*

• *Technical requirements.* Parents cannot treat an existing IRA as an education IRA. You must establish a separate IRA that you specifically designate as an education IRA.

❖ **New in 1998. Withdrawals can be made from an IRA to pay for qualified higher education expenses of the taxpayer or the taxpayer's spouse, child, or grandchild—without triggering the 10 percent penalty that applies to early distributions from an IRA.**

Penalty-free withdrawals from an existing IRA to pay for educational expenses. Beginning in 1998, the 10 percent penalty that applies to early distributions from an IRA will not apply to amounts used for qualified higher education expenses (including graduate courses) of the taxpayer or the taxpayer's spouse, child, or grandchild. The penalty-free withdrawal is available for "qualified higher education expenses," meaning tuition, fees, books, supplies, equipment required for enrollment, and room and board. All expenses must be incurred at a post-secondary educational institution, including a graduate program.

❖ **New in 1998. Taxpayers can make annual *nondeductible* contributions of up to $2,000 to a Roth IRA. Distributions from such an IRA are not taxed if they are made after a five year holding period, and are made as a result of the account holder's attaining age 59 and 1/2 or older, death, disability, or purchase of a first home. Earnings on Roth IRAs accumulate tax-free.**

"Roth" ("backloaded") IRAs. Another new IRA that debuts in 1998 is the so-called "Roth" or "backloaded" IRA. It is named in honor of Senator William Roth (R-Del.), its chief advocate. Here is how it works. Taxpayers can make annual *nondeductible* contributions of up to $2,000 to a Roth IRA, and distributions from such an IRA are not taxed if they are made after a five year holding period, and are made as a result of the account holder's: (1) attaining age 59 and 1/2 or older, (2) death, (3) disability, or (4) purchase of a first home. Further, earnings on Roth IRAs accumulate tax-free. Here are some more details:

• *Phaseout for higher income taxpayers.* Roth IRAs are phased out for single taxpayers with adjusted gross income of $95,000 to $110,000, and for married taxpayers filing jointly with adjusted gross income of $150,000 to $160,000.

• *Rollovers.* A regular IRA may be rolled over to a Roth IRA. Only taxpayers with adjusted gross income of less than $100,000 are eligible for this provision.

✎ **Key point: if you roll over your regular IRA into a Roth IRA prior to 1999, the amount that would have been included in taxable income had the funds been withdrawn are included in your taxable income over a four-year period. The ten percent penalty on early withdrawals from an IRA does not apply.**

✎ **Key point: if you expect your income tax rate to drop when you retire, it ordinarily will not be advantageous to roll over your existing IRA into a Roth IRA. But if you are younger and a disciplined saver and investor, and expect your tax rate to increase when you retire, then a rollover should be considered. Discuss the specifics of your situation with a financial planner or CPA.**

• *Maximum IRA contribution.* Persons who cannot (or do not) make contributions to a deductible IRA or a Roth IRA can continue to make contributions to a nondeductible IRA, as under prior law. However, the new clarifies that in no case may contributions to all of a taxpayer's IRAs for the same year exceed $2,000.

• *No age limit on contributions.* Unlike a regular IRA, taxpayers can make contributions to a Roth IRA after they reach age 70 and 1/2.

• *Technical requirements.* A Roth IRA must be separately established, and it must be designated as a Roth IRA when it is created.

☞ *Example. Rev. G opens a Roth IRA. Contributions made by Rev. G each year are not tax-deductible. However, following a five-year holding period Rev. G may make tax-free distributions from the Roth IRA on account of any one or more of the following conditions: (1) attaining age 59 and 1/2 or older, (2) death, (3) disability, or (4) purchase of a first home.*

✎ **Key point: in summary, the advantage of a Roth IRA is that it is "backloaded." This means that annual contributions to the IRA are not tax-deductible, but that earnings and distributions are nontaxable if they meet the requirements mentioned above. This will be a major tax break for many taxpayers, and will make Roth IRAs preferable in some cases to ordinary IRAs.**

✎ **Key point: in general, a Roth IRA will be preferable to a regular IRA if your tax rate remains the same or increases during retirement. If your total effective tax rate drops during your retirement years, a regular IRA may be more attractive (though not significantly).**

Comparing Regular and Roth IRAs

	regular IRA	Roth IRA
annual contribution limit	$2,000	$2,000
both spouses can contribute	yes	yes
tax treatment of annual contributions	tax-deductible (phaseout rules apply to higher income taxpayers)	not tax-deductible
earnings	accumulate tax-free, but are taxed at distribution	accumulate tax free, and are *not* taxed at distribution (if on account of age, death, disability, or first-time homebuyer expenses)
distributions	taxed as ordinary income	not taxed (if on account of age, death, disability, or first-time homebuyer expenses)
how long can contributions be made	until age 70 and 1/2 (for deductible IRAs)	no limit

❖ **New in 1998. Taxpayers can withdraw up to $10,000 from their IRA prior to age 59 and 1/2 for "first-time homebuyer expenses" without triggering the 10 percent penalty that previously applied. The expenses must be incurred to buy or build a principal residence for yourself, or a child or grandchild.**

No penalty for early IRA withdrawals by first-time homebuyers. A 10 percent "additional tax" applies to distributions from an IRA prior to age 59 and 1/2. Congress enacted legislation in 1997 that permits taxpayers to withdraw up to $10,000 from their IRA prior to age 59 and 1/2 for "first-time homebuyer expenses" without triggering the 10 percent penalty. The expenses must be incurred to buy or build a principal residence for yourself, or a child or grandchild.

✎ **Key point: to avoid the 10 percent tax on premature IRA distributions, you must use the distribution within 120 days to build or buy a first-time home.**

✎ **Key point: to be considered a "first-time homebuyer," you must not have had an ownership interest in a principal residence during the 2-year period ending on the date of acquisition of the principal residence.**

C. Simplified Employee Pensions (SEPs)

A simplified employee pension is an individual retirement arrangement that permits your employer to contribute each year up to 15% of your compensation or $30,000, whichever is less, to your IRA. In addition, you may deduct up to $2,000 of your contributions to any IRAs you own or to the SEP-IRA. However, as noted in the preceding section, a deduction for IRA contributions may be reduced or eliminated if you (or your spouse) is covered by an employer retirement plan (including an SEP). Whether or not your deduction is affected depends on your filing status (single or married) and the amount of your income.

✎ **Key point: only compensation up to $160,000 is considered in applying the 15% test in 1997.**

SEPs were created in order to encourage employers to provide retirement benefits to employees without having to establish more formal and complex qualified plans. An SEP-IRA may be maintained by both employees and self-employed persons. All of the rules discussed above with respect to IRAs (deductions, tax-deferral, distributions) apply to SEP-IRAs. Additional requirements apply as well, and they are summarized below. Employee "compensation" *includes* salary reduction contributions to a tax-sheltered "section 403(b)" annuity. Special rules apply if an employer contributes to other retirement plans as well as an SEP. Compensation does not include a minister's housing allowance or the fair rental value of a church-provided parsonage.

Various conditions must be met in order for an SEP to qualify for tax-favored status. First, if an employer contributes to an SEP, it must make a contribution for *each* employee (including former employees) who has (1) attained age 21; (2) performed services for the employer in at least three of the preceding five calendar years; and (3) received annual compensation of at least $400 (during 1997) from the employer. Second, each employee's right to employer contributions must be 100% vested (i.e., the employer imposes no conditions on withdrawals by any employee). Third, employer contributions cannot discriminate in favor of "highly compensated employees" as defined in Code section 414(q). "Highly compensated employees" are defined in chapter 5, section H.

Amounts contributed to an SEP by an employer are excludable from gross income, meaning that the employee need not include them in gross income.

Employees of small employers (fewer than 25 employees) can fund their SEP through a salary reduction arrangement. This special provision, however, does not apply to tax-exempt organizations (including churches). *IRC 408(k)(6)(E).*

An employer can establish an SEP simply by completing and retaining IRS Form 5305-SEP. The form is not submitted to the IRS. In addition, the employer must provide each eligible employee with a copy of the completed Form 5305-SEP.

The potential disadvantages of SEPs for many churches will be the requirements that (1) employer contributions must be made on behalf of every employee; (2) contributions cannot be funded through salary reductions; and (3) the plan cannot favor highly compensated employees. If these disadvantages can be overcome, many churches will find that they can contribute significant amounts toward the retirement of their employees by using SEPs.

D. Keogh Plans

A minister who is **self-employed** for income tax reporting purposes (i.e., does not satisfy the "common law employee" test—see chapter 2) may establish and contribute to a Keogh plan. Keogh plans are not available to ministers who are employees for income tax purposes, and who have no self-employment earnings, even though they are considered self-employed for social security purposes with respect to services performed in the exercise of ministry. Like an IRA, a Keogh plan offers the dual benefits of tax deductible contributions and tax-deferred interest earnings.

Under the more common variety of Keogh plan (a "defined contribution" plan), the participant can deduct from gross income the lesser of $30,000 or 25% of net self-employment earnings (excluding Keogh contributions, or 20% *after* Keogh contributions). Since this is a deduction from gross income in computing adjusted gross income, it is available to all self-employed taxpayers whether or not they itemize their deductions. It is claimed as an adjustment to gross income on Form 1040, line 28. Generally, taxpayers receive larger contribution deductions under Keogh plans than under an IRA. As noted in the discussion of IRAs, a self-employed minister can contribute to a Keogh plan and to an IRA.

Complex rules apply to Keogh plans benefiting "owner-employees" (i.e., a self-employed person who owns more than 10% of his or her business). These rules ordinarily are of no relevance to ministers who establish their own Keogh plans, and accordingly they will not be considered.

Even if you are an employee for income tax reporting purposes, you are eligible to participate in a Keogh plan with respect to amounts received directly from members of your congregation in exchange for services you render to them, such as fees for performing marriages, baptisms, funerals, or other personal services, since such amounts typically represent self-employment earnings for all tax purposes.

Ministers may establish a Keogh plan through most banks, savings and loan institutions, insurance companies, and mutual funds. The Keogh plan administrator (or in some cases the minister) may be required to file an IRS Form 5500-C, Form 5500-R, or Form 5500EZ by the last day of the seventh month (i.e., July 31) after the end of each year. Ordinarily, this reporting requirement will not apply if a Keogh plan contains less than $100,000.

Like IRAs, Keogh plans are subject to certain limitations with respect to distributions. Ordinarily, you may not take distributions from your Keogh plan before age 59 1/2 (unless you become permanently disabled, or roll over the distribution into an IRA) without reporting the distribution as income and paying a 10% penalty. You *must* begin receiving distributions by April 1 of the year following the year you reach age 70 1/2. In addition, a Keogh plan *must* require that a participant's entire interest be distributed, beginning no later than the required commencement date over (1) the life of the participant, (2) the lives of the participant and a designated beneficiary, (3) a period not extending beyond the life expectancy of the participant, or (4) a period not extending beyond the life expectancy of the participant and a designated beneficiary. Annual recalculation of the life expectancy of a participant and his or her spouse is permitted in determining the required payback period. Alternatively, a participant may elect to receive a "lump-sum" distribution of his or her entire fund balance prior to the required commencement date. You are permitted to make a one-time election to use 5-year income averaging with respect to a single lump-sum distribution received on or after the date you attain age 59 1/2.

The Keogh rules are complex. Before choosing this alternative, self-employed ministers should discuss the applicable conditions, limitations, and reporting requirements with a tax attorney or CPA.

✎ **Key point: the IRS would consider most ministers to be employees for income tax reporting purposes (see chapter 2). Since such a conclusion would preclude eligibility for Keogh plans, it is essential that ministers not participate in a Keogh plan if there is any doubt as to their self-employed status.**

E. Deferred Compensation Plans

A "nonqualified" deferred compensation plan (sometimes called a "rabbi trust") is an arrangement whereby an employer promises to pay an employee (or self-employed person) compensation in the future in exchange for services performed currently. The term "nonqualified" means that the plan is not subject to the many conditions that apply to "qualified" benefit plans under section 401 of the Code. Nonqualified deferred compensation arrangements can be funded through salary reduction agreements or employer contributions, or they can be unfunded (a mere unsecured promise by the employer to pay future benefits). In either case, such arrangements ordinarily are attractive only if contributions made by or on behalf of an employee are not currently taxable and earnings can accumulate tax-free.

Prior to 1987, it often was difficult to determine whether such tax benefits were available in a particular case, since the IRS often asserted that contributions and earnings were currently taxable under either the "constructive receipt" or "economic benefit" doctrine.

Constructive receipt doctrine. The constructive receipt doctrine is set forth in income tax regulation 1.451-2(a): "Income although not actually reduced to a taxpayer's possession is constructively received by him in the taxable year during which it is credited to his account, set apart for him, or otherwise made available so that he may draw upon it at any time, or so that he could have drawn upon it during the taxable year if notice of intention to withdraw had been given. However, income is not constructively received if the taxpayer's control of its receipt is subject to substantial limitations or restrictions."

Economic benefit doctrine. The so-called economic benefit doctrine (Code section 83) provides that property transferred to a person as compensation for services (including deferred compensation) generally will be taxed at the first time that the property can be reasonably valued. For example, the economic benefit rule applied when assets were unconditionally and irrevocably paid into a fund or trust to be used for an employee's sole benefit. However, the IRS generally ruled that no income was includable currently in an employee's income (under the economic benefit doctrine) if the source of the deferred compensation remained subject to the general creditors of the employer, or was otherwise subject to a "substantial risk of forfeiture." To illustrate, in Revenue Ruling 72-25 the IRS ruled that an employee did not receive taxable income as a result of his employer's purchase of an insurance contract to provide a source of funds for deferred compensation because the insurance contract was the employer's asset and was subject to the claims of the employer's general creditors.

Section 457 of the Internal Revenue Code imposes special rules on the unfunded deferred compensation plans of state and local governments. This section once imposed these same rules upon the unfunded deferred compensation plans of churches and other religious organizations. However, in 1987 Congress amended section 457 to exempt the following organizations from the application of section 457: (1) a church; (2) a convention or association of churches; (3) an elementary or secondary school that is controlled, operated, or principally supported by a church or convention or association of churches; or (4) a "qualified church-controlled organization." *IRC 457(e)(13)*. A qualified church-controlled organization is defined in section 3121(w)(3)(B) of the Code as

> any church-controlled tax-exempt organization described in section 501(c)(3), other than an organization which (i) offers goods, services, or facilities for sale, other than on an incidental basis, to the general public, other than goods, services or facilities which are sold at a nominal charge which is substantially less than the cost of providing such goods, services, or facilities; and (ii) normally receives more than 25% of its support from either (I) governmental sources, or (II) receipts from admissions, sales of merchandise, performance of services, or furnishing of facilities, in activities which are not unrelated trades or businesses, or both.

Clearly, local churches, church denominations, and church-controlled elementary and secondary schools qualify as "church-controlled organizations." While it is less clear, it is reasonably certain that seminaries and Bible colleges would also qualify. The committee report on the Tax Reform Act of 1986, in construing the term "qualified church-controlled organization" in another context, noted that it included "the typical seminary, religious retreat center, or burial society, regardless of its funding sources, because it does not offer goods, services, or facilities for sale to the general public." The committee report also noted that the term "qualified church-controlled organization" included

> a church-run orphanage or old-age home, even if it is open to the general public, if not more than 25% of its support is derived from the receipts of admissions, sales of merchandise, performance of services, or furnishing of facilities (in other than unrelated trades or businesses) or from governmental sources. The committee specifically intends that the [term "qualified church-controlled organization" will not include] church-run universities (other than religious seminaries) and hospitals if both conditions (i) and (ii) exist.

A total "exemption" of churches and certain other religious organizations from section 457 creates its own problems. The effect of a total exemption is to determine the tax consequences of nonqualified deferred compensation plans of churches (and the other exempt organizations described above) under the pre-1987 "constructive receipt" and "economic benefit" doctrines rather than under the provisions of section 457. Generally, this should result in more liberal treatment for the deferred compensation arrangements of churches. Note, however, that the definition of "church" is rather narrow, and that a number of religious organizations will continue to be governed by section 457—meaning that their deferred compensation plans must meet the definition of an "eligible deferred compensation plan" in order to entitle employees to the limited tax benefits discussed above. Finally, the exemption applies only to "church employees." It is unclear whether this term will be defined to include ministers (or other church workers) who report their federal income taxes as self-employed persons.

The "Rabbi Trust"

✎ **Key point: a rabbi trust is an arrangement that can provide attractive, tax-sheltered retirement income for ministers and church workers. Employers that use the model rabbi trust published by the IRS in 1992 are assured that an employer's contributions to the trust will not be presently included in the employee's taxable income, and that income generated by the trust will be tax-deferred.**

In 1980, a synagogue asked the IRS whether its rabbi would realize taxable income if it funded a trust for his benefit. The synagogue proposed to create and fund the trust with a specified amount, and pay the net income from the trust to the rabbi at least quarter-annually. Upon his death, disability, retirement, or discharge, the trust would distribute the remaining principal and any accrued interest directly to the rabbi (or his estate). The trust was irrevocable, and the trust assets were subject to the claims of the synagogue's general creditors (as if they were any other general asset). Further, the trust specified that the rabbi's interest could not be assigned or used by him as collateral, and it was not subject to the claims of his creditors. In a landmark private letter ruling, the IRS concluded that the rabbi was *not* taxable on the funds transferred by the synagogue to the trust. *IRS Letter Ruling 8113107*.

The IRS concluded that the creation of the "rabbi trust" fund was not taxable to the rabbi under either the "economic benefit" or "constructive receipt" rules. These rules were devised by the IRS and the courts to tax income currently rather than in the future.

Economic benefit. The IRS acknowledged that under the *economic benefit doctrine*, the creation by an employer of a fund in which an employee has *vested rights* "will result in immediate inclusion" of the fund in the employee's taxable income. Such a taxable fund "is created when an amount is irrevocably placed with a third party, and a taxpayer's interest in the fund is vested if it is nonforfeitable." This rule did not require inclusion of the fund in the rabbi's income, since "the assets of the trust estate are subject to the claims of [the synagogue's] creditors." In other words, the creation of the trust did not result in any present "economic benefit" to the rabbi.

Constructive receipt. The IRS noted that under the *constructive receipt doctrine*, "income although not actually reduced to a taxpayer's possession is constructively received by him in the taxable year during which it is credited to his account, set apart for him, or otherwise made available so that he may draw upon it at any time, or so that he could have drawn upon it during the taxable year if notice of intention to withdraw had been given. However, income is not constructively received if the taxpayer's control of its receipt is subject to substantial limitations or restrictions." *Treas. Reg. 1.451-2(a)*. The IRS concluded that the trust fund was not presently taxable to the rabbi since "the assets of the trust estate are subject to the claims of [the synagogue's] creditors and are not paid or made available within the meaning of section 451 of the Code." The IRS further noted that "payments of income or principal under the terms of the trust agreement will be includable in [the rabbi's] gross income in the taxable year in which they are actually received or otherwise made available, whichever is earlier."

This ruling unleashed a whirlwind of requests by other taxpayers for similar IRS rulings (the rabbi's "private letter ruling" could not be relied upon by any other taxpayer). Hundreds of "rabbi trust" rulings were issued, primarily to business executives who immediately recognized the value of such a trust. In 1985, the IRS suspended the issuance of rabbi trust rulings, pending a reconsideration of its policy. The moratorium was lifted in 1986, and hundreds (if not thousands) of additional rabbi trust rulings have been issued by the IRS. All of these rulings are private letter rulings, meaning that they can be relied upon only by the individual taxpayers who requested them. Again, while a synagogue and its rabbi were responsible for the first such ruling, nearly all of the subsequent rulings were issued to business executives.

In 1992, the IRS acknowledged that it receives a flood of private ruling requests by employers seeking IRS approval of their rabbi trust arrangements. In response, the IRS published a "model" rabbi trust agreement. In the "revenue procedure" setting forth the model rabbi trust, the IRS noted:

The model trust provided in this revenue procedure is intended to serve as a safe harbor for taxpayers that adopt and maintain grantor trusts in connection with unfunded deferred compensation arrangements. If the model trust is used in accordance with this revenue procedure, an employee will not be in constructive receipt of income or incur an economic benefit solely on account of the adoption or maintenance of the trust. However, the desired tax effect will be achieved only if the nonqualified deferred compensation arrangement effectively defers compensation.

The IRS warned that it will not issue any rulings on unfunded deferred compensation arrangements that "use a trust other than the model trust." In other words, churches and other religious employers that have adopted rabbi trust arrangements in the past *should ensure that the language used in their trusts is identical to that in the model IRS form.* The IRS cautioned: "The model language must be adopted verbatim, except where substitute language is expressly permitted. . . . Of course, provisions may be renumbered if appropriate, language in brackets may be omitted, and blanks may be completed. In addition, the taxpayer may add sections to the model language provided that such additions are not inconsistent with the model language."

The IRS will continue to issue private letter rulings approving of rabbi trusts that are consistent with the model trust.

✎ **Key point: the model rabbi trust is reproduced at the end of this chapter.**

In summary, while the first "rabbi trust" involved a trust adopted by a synagogue for its rabbi, very few synagogues or churches have used these trusts. For the most part, they have been used by secular businesses as a component of executive compensation. However, a "rabbi trust" can be an effective tool for churches and religious organizations to bear in mind, particularly with regard to ministers receiving substantial compensation and who are nearing retirement age. Through proper drafting, it is possible for a church to set aside amounts in trust that would exceed the limits associated with other retirement plans. But, keep these points in mind:

• It is uncertain whether rabbi trusts can be used by religious organizations that are not synagogues, churches, denominations, or church-controlled.

• The trust must provide that the trust assets are subject to the general creditors of the employer under both federal and state law.

• The beneficiary (i.e., the minister) cannot have any legal interest in the trust fund until the trust assets are distributed. The trust should specify that the beneficiary's interest cannot be assigned, transferred, or used as collateral, and it is not subject to his or her creditors prior to distribution. The idea is this—the beneficiary cannot be taxed on the employer's transfer of funds to the rabbi trust, since the beneficiary has no interest in the funds and may never receive them should the employer become insolvent.

• The trust must be funded with the employer's assets. It is unclear whether or not a rabbi trust can be funded, in whole or in part, with an employee's own compensation (such as through a *salary reduction agreement).*

A properly drafted rabbi trust can provide several benefits, including the following: (1) the employer's transfer of funds to the trust will not be currently taxable under the "economic benefit" doctrine; (2) the employer's transfer of funds to the trust will not be currently taxable under the "constructive receipt" doctrine; (3) the trust will be considered a "grantor trust," meaning that all income and deductions attributable to the trust will be included in computing the taxable income, if any, of the employer (rather than the employee). In conclusion, those interested in pursuing this idea should consult with an attorney experienced in employee benefits.

F. Tax-Sheltered Annuities

✎ **Key point: one of the most popular retirement programs for ministers is the tax-sheltered annuity (TSA). Unfortunately, the rules associated with TSAs are complex, and often require professional assistance. However, the benefits provided under these plans are significant, and merit serious consideration.**

✎ **Key point: if you are a member of a denomination that offers you a tax-sheltered annuity as a retirement benefit option, your denomination will assist you with these rules to ensure that your contributions are within the applicable legal limits.**

✎ **Key point: the IRS has expressed concern over the failure of many 403(b) programs to comply with complex legal requirements. One IRS spokesman has stated that "we have made no secret of the fact that the IRS has yet to find a 403(b) plan fully in compliance," and that the overall noncompliance rate may be as high as 90%!**

➲ **Tip. One of the main areas of noncompliance for churches is excessive contributions (a church contributes more to a 403(b) on behalf of a pastor or other church employee than is permitted by law).**

A tax-sheltered annuity (more properly called a section 403(b) plan) is an excellent way for a tax-exempt church or religious organization to provide retirement benefits for some or all of its employees. The employer can fund contributions through "elective deferrals" (binding and irrevocable salary reduction agreements entered into between a church and an employee before the corresponding services are performed, and lasting for at least one year) or through "nonelective deferrals" (voluntary employer contributions not funded through salary reduction agreements), and it can make the program available only to selected employees. Contributions are not permitted out of compensation previously distributed to a participant. Whether an employee's annuity is funded through employer contributions or salary reductions, the employee's rights to the annuity must be nonforfeitable.

"Nondiscrimination" rules under Code section 403(b). Nondiscrimination rules apply to most 403(b) plans. These rules prohibit discrimination in favor of highly compensated employees. However, these rules do not apply to tax-sheltered annuity plans of (1) a church; (2) a convention or association of churches; (3) an elementary or secondary school that is controlled, operated, or principally supported by a church or convention or association of churches; or (4) a "qualified church-controlled organization." *IRC 403(b)(1)(D) and 403(b)(12)(B).* A qualified church-controlled organization is defined in section 3121(w)(3)(B) of the Code as

any church-controlled tax-exempt organization described in section 501(c)(3), other than an organization which (i) offers goods, services, or facilities for sale, other than on an incidental basis, to the general public, other than goods, services or facilities which are sold at a nominal charge which is substantially less than the cost of providing such goods, services, or facilities; and (ii) normally receives more than 25% of its support from either (I) governmental sources, or (II) receipts from admissions, sales of merchandise, performance of services, or furnishing of facilities, in activities which are not unrelated trades or businesses, or both.

Clearly, local churches, church denominations, and church-controlled elementary and secondary schools are qualify as "church-controlled organizations." While it is less clear, it is reasonably certain that seminaries and Bible colleges also qualify. The committee report on the Tax Reform Act of 1986, in construing the term "qualified church-controlled organization" in another context, noted that it included "the typical seminary, religious retreat center, or burial society, regardless of its funding sources, because it does not offer goods, services, or facilities for sale to the general public." The committee report also noted that the term "qualified church-controlled organization" includes

a church-run orphanage or old-age home, even if it is open to the general public, if not more than 25% of its support is derived from the receipts of admissions, sales of merchandise, performance of services, or furnishing of facilities (in other than unrelated trades or businesses) or from governmental sources. The committee specifically intends that the [term 'qualified church-controlled organization' will not include] church-run universities (other than religious seminaries) and hospitals if both conditions (i) and (ii) exist.

Federal law permits tax-exempt organizations that are not exempt from the antidiscrimination rules to disregard employees who are students not taken into account for employment tax purposes and part-time employees who work less than twenty hours per week.

All employees of a tax-exempt organization must be given the opportunity to make elective deferrals of compensation (through salary reduction agreements) if *any* employee may do so. However, this new nondiscrimination rule ordinarily will not apply to churches. *IRC 403(b)(12)(A) and 403(b)(1)(D).*

Application of pre-ERISA nondiscrimination rules to church plans. Church retirement plans are exempt from various requirements imposed by the Employee Retirement Income Security Act of 1974 ("ERISA") upon pension plans. For example, church plans are not subject to ERISA's vesting, coverage, and funding requirements. However, according to a comment in the conference committee's official report to the Small Business Job Protection Act of 1996, "in some cases" church plans will be "subject to provisions in effect before the enactment of ERISA" and that under these rules a church plan "cannot discriminate in favor of officers . . . [or] persons whose principal duties consist in supervising the work of other employees, or highly compensated employees." The Act clarifies that church plans subject to these pre-ERISA nondiscrimination rules may not discriminate in favor of "highly compensated employees" as defined under the new and simplified definition of that term contained in the Act, and this single nondiscrimination rule replaces the pre-ERISA rule banning discrimination in favor of officers or persons whose principal duties consist in supervising the work of other employees (unless they also satisfy the new definition of a highly compensated employee). The new definition of a highly compensated employee includes an employee who had compensation for the previous year in excess of $80,000, and, if an employer elects, was in the top 20 percent of employees by compensation. This provision took effect in 1997.

What church plans are subject to the pre-ERISA nondiscrimination rules? The general rule is that all church plans must satisfy the nondiscrimination rules contained in Code section 401(a)(4) as in effect prior to the enactment of ERISA in 1974—except for church plans that utilize section 403(b) tax-sheltered annuities. In summary, most church retirement plans utilize 403(b) annuities and such plans are fully exempt from the nondiscrimination rules. On the other hand, there are some church plans that do not utilize 403(b) annuities, and these are subject to the pre-ERISA nondiscrimination rules.

❖ **New in 1997. Self-employed ministers can participate in 403(b) plans.**

Employees or self-employed. A tax-sheltered annuity may be purchased *only* for common law employees subject to the will and control of the employer regarding both the work to be done and the manner in which it is to be performed. Congress enacted legislation in 1996 that permits self-employed ministers to participate in qualified retirement plans including 403(b) tax-sheltered annuities. This resolves a question that has plagued church plans for many years. In the past, there was much confusion over the eligibility of self-employed ministers to participate in church retirement plans including 403(b) tax-sheltered annuities. Section 403(b) of the tax code by its own language applies only to employees.

A provision in the Small Business Job Protection Act of 1996 permits participation (after 1996) in tax-sheltered annuities by "a duly ordained, commissioned, or licensed minister of a church, who in connection with the exercise of his or her ministry is a self-employed individual." The earned income of self-employed ministers becomes their "compensation" for purposes of calculating permissible contributions to a 403(b) tax-sheltered annuity, and a self-employed minister "shall be treated as his or her own employer which an organization described in section 501(c)(3) and exempt from tax . . . ."

✎ **Key point: This provision only benefits self-employed ministers. Self-employed lay church workers are not covered.**

☞ *Example. Rev. H is employed as the senior pastor of a church, has always reported his income taxes as self-employed, and participates in the church's 403(b) tax-sheltered annuity program. While Rev. H's participation in such a program has been questionable in the past, the new law specifically authorizes such participation beginning in 1997.*

☞ *Example. Rev. C is a self-employed itinerant evangelist. He will be eligible to establish and contribute to a 403(b) tax-sheltered annuity under the new rules beginning in 1997. Rev. C will be treated as his own employer that is presumed to be an exempt organization eligible to participate*

in a 403(b) tax-sheltered annuity. In addition, Rev. C will use his earned income as his "compensation" for purposes of computing the limits on contributions.

What about nonminister church workers who are self-employed for federal income tax reporting purposes? They are not helped by the new legislation. However, the Tax Court ruled in 1971 that a nonminister taxpayer who reported his federal income taxes as self-employed was an "employee" for purposes of eligibility for participating in a tax-sheltered annuity. *Haugen v. Commissioner, 30 T.C.M. 1247 (1971).* Churches should not allow self-employed workers (other than ministers) to participate in their tax-sheltered annuity programs without an opinion from legal counsel approving such participation.

❖ **New in 1997. Ministers who are employed by a non-exempt organization may participate in a tax-sheltered annuity so long as their duties consist of the exercise of ministry.**

Ministers employed by non-exempt organizations. Are tax-sheltered annuities available to ministers employed by organizations that are not exempt from tax under section 501(c)(3) of the tax code? Section 403(b) of the code limits participation in tax-sheltered annuities to employees of an employer "described in section 501(c)(3) which is exempt from tax." This includes religious, charitable, and educational organizations (and some others), but does not include government agencies and secular businesses. As a result, ministers employed by the government or a secular business (for example, as chaplains) generally have been deemed to be ineligible to participate in 403(b) tax-sheltered annuities. Congress enacted legislation in 1996 permitting ministers who are employed by a non-exempt organization to participate in a tax-sheltered annuity so long as their duties consist of the exercise of ministry.

☞ *Example. Rev. L is a chaplain employed by a state correctional facility. The correctional facility is not an exempt organization described in section 501(c)(3) of the tax code, and accordingly Rev. L was not permitted to participate in a 403(b) tax-sheltered annuity in the past (since only employees of 501(c)(3) employers could participate in such a retirement program). However, under the new law, Rev. L is allowed to participate since she is engaged in the exercise of her ministry while employed as a chaplain by the correctional facility.*

☞ *Example. Rev. M is an ordained minister who is temporarily working in a secular job as a salesman. In the past he has participated in a denominationally-sponsored 403(b) tax-sheltered annuity. The new rules do not permit Rev. M to continue contributing to his annuity since his present job does not constitute the exercise of ministry.*

Exclusion from gross income for income tax purposes. Payments made by your employer to a tax-sheltered annuity ordinarily are not taxable (i.e., they are excluded from income for tax purposes) provided they do not exceed the **least** of the following amounts:

- the annual "exclusion allowance"

- the annual employer contribution limitation

- a limitation of $9,500 on "elective deferrals" (contributions funded through salary reduction agreements)

All three of these limits are described below. Qualifying employer contributions are exclusions, and accordingly should not be reported as compensation on your federal income tax return. Note, however, that employers must list the amount of any "elective" contributions (i.e., through salary reductions) in box 13 of Form W-2 (i.e., put the letter "E" in box 13 along with the amount of the elective deferral). The employer also must check "deferred compensation" in box 15 of Form W-2. See chapter 11 for more details.

Social security. Elective contributions (e.g., salary reductions) to a tax-sheltered annuity are taxable for FICA purposes (social security for non-minister employees). However, they do not necessarily constitute self-employment earnings for purposes of determining self-employment tax liability (social security for self-employed persons). *See Revenue Ruling 68-395 and Revenue Ruling 78-6.* As noted previously, ministers are always treated as self-employed for social security purposes with respect to services performed in the exercise of ministry. IRS Publication 571 (1996 edition) specifies that "contributions for the minister toward a tax-sheltered annuity contract are not taken into account as net earnings from self-employment [for self-employment tax purposes] to the extent the contributions are not more than the exclusion allowance or employer contribution limit."

exclusion allowance

1. basic allowance. The basic exclusion allowance is the maximum employer contribution (or salary reduction amount) that an employee can exclude from gross income in any year (subject to the limitations on employer contributions discussed below). Generally, it is determined by multiplying 20% times your includable compensation for the year (generally, your gross income for the year excluding your **housing allowance** and any contributions by your employer to a tax-sheltered annuity plan) times your years of service (the number of years that you have worked for your present church employer plus any other related church organizations), and less all employer contributions to a tax-sheltered annuity that you excluded from gross income in prior years.

❖ **New in 1998. Congress enacted legislation in 1997 specifying that the term "includible compensation" shall not include elective deferrals (by salary reduction agreement) into a 403(b) annuity or a cafeteria plan. The effect of this change, which takes effect in the year 1998, will be to increase the** amount that some employees can contribute to their 403(b) annuity.

2. minimum exclusion allowance. Church employees with an adjusted gross income of not more than $17,000, are entitled to a *minimum exclusion allowance*. The minimum is your exclusion allowance as described above, but not less than the smaller of (1) $3,000, or (2) your includable compensation (ordinarily your gross income less a **housing allowance** and less any employer contributions to a tax-sheltered annuity). For purposes of this alternative rule, the term *church employee* includes any ordained, commissioned, or licensed minister, or a lay person, who is an employee of a church or church-controlled religious organization.

3. alternative exclusion allowance. Under a special alternative election, your employer may be able to contribute up to $10,000 for the year, even if this is more than 25% of your compensation for the year. The total contributions over your lifetime under this election may not exceed $40,000. *IRC 415(c)(7).* For more details, see the discussion of annual employer contribution limitations.

annual employer contribution limitations

1. general rule. The basic annual employer contribution limitation (Code section 415) for "defined contribution plans" (including most tax-sheltered annuities) is the **lesser of $30,000 or 25% of an employee's compensation**. Compensation, for purposes of the 25% test, does not include contributions toward a tax-sheltered annuity or a minister's **housing allowance**. *IRS Letter Ruling 8416003.* To illustrate, if a minister's annual church compensation is $30,000, and this amount includes a housing allowance of $6,000, the church's maximum contribution would be determined by multiplying the minister's church compensation of $30,000 less his housing allowance of $6,000 and less the amount of the tax-sheltered annuity contribution times 25%. This limit applies instead of the exclusion allowance (discussed above) if this limit is less than the exclusion allowance (but see the alternative rules for church employees, discussed below).

Some tax advisers prefer to say that the annual employer contribution limitation is **20%** of an employee's compensation *before* the contribution to his or her tax-sheltered annuity (but after deducting the housing allowance and other exclusions). The result is the same. For example, assume that a minister's total compensation is $50,000 (including a $10,000 housing allowance and an $8,000 contribution to a tax-sheltered annuity). For purposes of the limitation, the minister's "compensation" is $32,000 (total compensation less the housing allowance and less the tax-sheltered annuity contribution). Note that 20% of $40,000 (compensation *including* the tax-sheltered annuity contribution) is the same amount as 25% of $32,000 (compensation *less* the tax-sheltered annuity contribution). For many, the 20% figure is more easily applied. Just be sure that it is applied to "compensation" without any reduction for tax-sheltered annuity contributions. Also, note that this 20% rule only works for employees whose 403(b) contributions are funded entirely out of salary reductions.

❖ **New in 1998. Congress enacted legislation in 1996 that removes salary reduction contributions to both tax-sheltered annuities and cafeteria plans from the definition of "compensation" for computing permissible contributions to certain retirement plans including tax-sheltered annuities. This provision takes effect in 1998. The effect of the expanded definition of compensation is to increase the amount that some ministers, lay employees, and others may contribute to a variety of retirement plans including tax-sheltered annuities.**

☞ *Example. Rev. B earns $40,000 of compensation in 1997. He enters into a salary reduction agreement with his church whereby he agrees to contribute (through salary reductions) $6,000 to a tax-sheltered annuity maintained by his church and an additional $4,000 to a cafeteria plan. The church designates $10,000 of the total compensation as a housing allowance. Contributions to a tax-sheltered annuity using salary reductions cannot exceed a number of limits, including the lesser of $30,000 or 25% of compensation. Under the old rule, compensation was defined to exclude salary reduction contributions to both tax-sheltered annuities and cafeteria plans. Housing allowances are not included in the definition of compensation under either the old rule or the new rule. Therefore, Rev. B's compensation is $20,000 ($40,000 total compensation less the $10,000 salary reduction contributions to his tax-sheltered annuity and cafeteria plans and less the $10,000 housing allowance). Since 25% of $20,000 is $5,000, Rev. B's $6,000 contribution to his tax-sheltered annuity is excessive.*

☞ *Example. Same facts as the previous example, except that the year is 1998 (and the new definition of compensation applies). Rev. B has not made an excess contribution to his tax-sheltered annuity, since salary reduction contributions to both tax-sheltered annuities and cafeteria plans are now included in the definition of compensation. Rev. B's compensation is $30,000 (the housing allowance is still excluded), and 25% of this is $7,500.*

2. alternative rules for church employees. Church employees can elect to have the limitations imposed on employer contributions figured under one of three *alternative employer limitations*. These three rules occasionally are referred to as "catch-up" rules. Generally, the election to use one of the three alternative limitations will permit you to exclude from gross income a larger portion of your employer's contributions than allowed under the general rule (the lesser of $30,000 or 25% of your compensation). You may also choose to disregard the exclusion allowance (discussed above) that would otherwise apply. In explaining these favorable rules, the IRS has stated (in Publication 571) that "employees of these organizations [i.e., churches and certain other tax-exempt organizations] typically have a pattern of low employer contributions in the early stages of their careers and relatively high catch-up contributions later. Generally, the election to use one of the first two alternative limitations . . . will permit you to exclude from gross income a larger amount of your employer's contributions than allowed under the general rule that limits the contributions to 25% of your compensation."

The three alternative limitations are as follows: the year of separation from service limitation, the any year limitation, and the overall limitation. They are summarized below.

Year of separation from service limitation

You may elect to substitute your exclusion allowance (as computed above) in place of the 25% of compensation limitation in the year in which you separate from the service of your church employer. The $30,000 annual limitation still applies.

Any year limitation rule

You may elect to substitute for the 25% of compensation limitation the least of the following: (1) $4,000 plus 25% of your includable compensation; (2) your exclusion allowance for the year; or (3) $15,000. Because of the $15,000 maximum limitation, the $30,000 limitation cannot apply if you elect this limitation.

Overall limitation

You may elect to have the limitation on your employer's contributions and your exclusion allowance be equal to the lesser of 25% of includable compensation or $30,000. You are then free to disregard the computation of your exclusion allowance discussed earlier. In effect, your exclusion allowance and the maximum employer contribution are considered to be the same.

Ordinarily, you must make an election to use one of the three alternative limitations on the first tax return you file after you begin participating in a tax-sheltered annuity. You make the election for one of the three alternative limitations by figuring your tax using that one. However, the election is treated as made only when needed to support the exclusion allowance taken on the return. If you elect to use an alternative limitation, you cannot change the election and you may not elect to have any of the other alternative limitations apply for any future year with respect to any tax-sheltered annuity contract purchased for you by any employer.

Employer contributions in excess of the applicable limitation must be included in gross income for tax purposes.

3. special election for church employees. In addition to the "any year" or "overall" limitations, you can make a special election that allows your employer to contribute up to $10,000 for the year, even if this is more than 25% of your compensation for the year. The total contributions over your lifetime under this election may not exceed $40,000. In this situation, the exclusion allowance limit still applies, unless you also elect the "overall" limitation described earlier. You cannot make this election for a tax year for which you choose to use the "year of separation from service" limitation.

special $9,500 limitation on elective deferrals

In addition to the exclusion allowance limit and the annual employer contribution limitations that apply to tax-sheltered annuity contributions, there is an overall limit on combined "elective deferrals" (i.e., salary reduction agreements under which an employer and employee voluntarily agree that the employee's salary will be reduced by a designated amount, with the reduction being used to fund the annuity).

✎ **Key point: Congress enacted legislation in 1996 repealing a rule that permitted participants in a 403(b) annuity to make only one "salary reduction agreement" each year. The new rule, which took effect in 1996, specifies that a salary reduction agreement (and the ability to revoke such an agreement) may be entered into by participants in a tax-sheltered annuity on the basis of the same rules that apply to 401(k) plans.**

In general, church employees who are covered by only one tax-sheltered annuity can defer up to $9,500 each year (through elective deferrals). *IRC 402(g).* Employees who have completed at least **15 years of service** with a church (or certain other exempt organizations) have a higher "catch-up" limitation. *IRC 402(g)(8).* Basically, the $9,500 annual limitation is increased by the *smallest* of the following: (1) $3,000, (2) $15,000, reduced by increases to the $9,500 limit an employee was allowed in earlier years because of this rule, or (3) $5,000 multiplied times the number of years of service for the church, minus the total elective deferrals under the plan for earlier years. Elective deferrals in excess of the limit for the year must be included in gross income for tax purposes.

Special rules apply in determining the limitation on employer contributions on your behalf to a tax-sheltered annuity program if you also are covered under a qualified plan.

✎ **Key point: Congress enacted legislation in 1996 specifying that each tax-sheltered annuity contract (and not the tax-sheltered annuity plan itself) must provide that elective deferrals made under the contract may not exceed the annual limit on elective deferrals. If an employee's elective deferrals exceed the limits the only impact will be upon that employee rather than on the plan itself. This provision took effect in 1996.**

Application of elective deferral limits to 403(b) tax-sheltered annuity contracts. Currently, a tax-sheltered annuity plan must provide that elective deferrals made under the plan on behalf of an

employee may not exceed the annual limit on elective deferrals ($9,500 in 1997). Congress enacted legislation in 1996 specifying that each tax-sheltered annuity contract (and not the tax-sheltered annuity plan itself) must provide that elective deferrals made under the contract may not exceed the annual limit on elective deferrals. This change will affect the several thousand ministers and church employees who currently participate in these plans, to the extent their individual contracts do not contain this language. The new rule will benefit ministers and church employees. In the past, if a tax-sheltered annuity plan permitted an employee to make elective deferrals above the legal limit, the entire plan could lose its tax-exempt status and create disastrous consequences to all participants including those whose elective deferrals never exceeded the legal limits. Under the new rules, if an employee's elective deferrals exceed the limits the only impact will be upon that employee (who has violated the terms of his or her contract) rather than on the plan itself. There will be no impact on those employees whose elective deferrals are within the legal limits. This provision took effect in 1996.

✎ **Key point: Employees who temporarily are absent from work due to military service may make increased contributions to a tax-sheltered annuity.**

Reemployed veterans. Congress enacted legislation in 1996 that allows employees who temporarily are absent from work due to military service to make increased contributions to their employer's qualified retirement plan (including 403(b) tax-sheltered annuities) to "make up" for the contributions they missed while away from their job. Such "make-up contributions" will not affect the tax-favored status of the plan or the employee's account even though they exceed the limits that otherwise would apply. Of course, make-up contribution cannot exceed the amount the employee would have been permitted to contribute had he or she not been absent from work. Employers who do not allow employees who are away from work on military leave to make additional contributions to their retirement plan when they return may be in violation of the Uniformed Services Employment and Reemployment Rights Act ("USERRA"). This provision took effect on December 12, 1994.

Distributions. Distributions to an employee under a tax-sheltered annuity ordinarily are fully taxable to the employee upon receipt. In addition, the Code establishes various requirements with respect to when and how the accumulated annuity funds must be distributed. These requirements are set forth in section 401(a)(9). You need not begin receiving distributions from your tax-sheltered annuity until April 1st of the year following the later of the year of your retirement or the year in which you reach age 70 1/2.

Distributions to an employee from a tax-sheltered annuity attributable to contributions made pursuant to a salary reduction agreement may be made only when the employee attains age 59 1/2, separates from service, dies, becomes disabled, or experiences "hardship." *IRC 403(b)(11).* However, in the case of hardship, a tax-sheltered annuity cannot permit distribution of any *income attributable to salary reduction contributions*. The term "hardship" is not defined in section 403(b) of the Code. The same term is used in connection with premature distributions under a "401(k) plan" (discussed later in this chapter), and in that context is defined as a distribution that "is made on account of an immediate and heavy financial need of the employee and is necessary to satisfy the financial need. The determination of the existence of an immediate and heavy financial need and of the amount necessary to meet the need must be made in accordance with nondiscriminatory and objective standards set forth in the plan." *Treas. Reg. 1.401(k)-1(d)(2)(i)*. This definition probably will be relevant in construing the same term under Code section 403(b).

As originally worded, section 403(b) of the Code required tax-sheltered annuities to be **invested** in annuity contracts of life insurance companies. The term "annuity contract" has been liberalized over the years. Today, tax-sheltered annuity funds may be invested by the employer in a wide range of products, including mutual funds and face amount certificates.

Contributions in excess of the limitations described above are currently included in a participant's income for tax purposes, and may be subject to a 6% excise tax. The excise tax is not deductible. However, it can be avoided for a particular year if you return the excess contribution prior to the end of the year in which the contribution is made. Form 5330 is used to compute the tax. It must be filed by July 31 of the year following the year of contribution for taxpayers using a calendar year. A six month extension can be obtained by filing Form 5558.

The entity with which employer contributions are invested ordinarily will assist the employer in establishing the tax-sheltered annuity program. The establishment of such programs is quite simple, and ordinarily requires no IRS approval.

Form 5500. The instructions to the current IRS Form 5500 state that "church plans" not electing ERISA coverage under Code section 410(b) are not required to file 5500 forms. Code section 414(e) defines the term *church plan* to include a plan "maintained for its employees by a church." The income tax regulations clarify that for the purpose of this definition the term *church* includes "a religious organization if such organization (1) is an integral part of a church, and (2) is engaged in carrying out the functions of a church, whether as a civil law corporation or otherwise." *Treas. Reg. § 1.414(e)-1(e)*.

Conclusion. Tax-sheltered annuities involve some very complex rules. However, they provide very attractive tax benefits making them worthy of serious consideration. Persons wishing to pursue this subject further should consult with a CPA or tax attorney with experience in handling such arrangements, or with the staff of a denominational retirement plan.

G. Church Retirement Income Accounts

Section 403(b)(9) of the Code permits churches to place tax-sheltered annuity contributions in "retirement income accounts" subject to all of the benefits and limitations discussed above with respect to tax-sheltered annuities generally. The primary effect of this provision is to give churches greater flexibility in investing such funds. They are not restricted to annuity products, mutual funds, and face amount certificates. A separate retirement income account must be maintained by the church for each participating employee, although for investment purposes the funds may be commingled. However, it must at all times be possible to determine each employee's interest in the fund. In addition, the funds cannot be used for or diverted to any purpose other than the exclusive benefit of the employees and their beneficiaries.

H. Qualified Pension Plans

Some churches and religious denominations have established qualified pension plans to finance retirement benefits for their employees. Such plans enjoy several tax benefits, including the following: (1) the employer gets an immediate tax deduction for contributions to the plan (this benefit is not relevant to tax-exempt churches and religious organizations); (2) fund earnings are tax-exempt; (3) employees are not taxed on their share of the fund until they receive distributions; (4) qualifying lump-sum distributions are eligible for a one-time five-year forward averaging (through 1999); (5) qualifying distributions can be rolled over tax-free to another plan or IRA; and (6) an employee can elect to have benefits payable to a designated beneficiary after his or her death without incurring gift tax liability.

These various tax benefits are available only if the plan is qualified. Qualification means that the plan satisfies the several conditions enumerated in section 401 of the Code. Some of the more important requirements for qualification include the following: (1) the plan must be a written program that is communicated to employees; (2) the plan must be for the exclusive benefit of employees and their beneficiaries; (3) the plan must be properly funded; (4) the plan must begin making payments no later than a specified date; (5) contributions and benefits may not exceed specified limitations; (6) certain employees must be permitted to participate in the plan; (7) an employee's interest in the plan must vest within a specified time. Additional requirements apply to plans benefiting owner-employees and certain "top-heavy" plans (i.e., disproportionately benefit highly-compensated employees).

✎ **Key point:** "ERISA" is a comprehensive pension law enacted by Congress in 1974 containing numerous provisions regulating pension plans (such as vesting, participation, and nondiscrimination).

Church plans are exempted from the minimum participation, vesting, funding, and nondiscrimination requirements of ERISA unless they elect to be covered (Code section 410). Such an election is irrevocable. Code section 414(e) defines the term *church plan* to include a plan "maintained for its employees by a church." The income tax regulations clarify that for the purpose of this definition the term *church* includes "a religious organization if such organization (1) is an integral part of a church, and (2) is engaged in carrying out the functions of a church, whether as a civil law corporation or otherwise." *Treas. Reg. § 1.414(e)-1(e)*.

Qualified pension plans can be either defined benefit or defined contribution plans. In a defined benefit plan, each employee is promised specified benefits upon retirement either for a term of years or for life, based upon such factors as years of service and amount of compensation earned. Employer contributions are actuarially calculated to provide the promised benefits, and are not allocated to individual accounts for each employee. In a defined contribution plan, the employer does not promise specified benefits to the employees. Rather, the employer promises specified contributions on behalf of each employee. Such contributions must be allocated to individual accounts for each employee. Retirement benefits are whatever can be provided by the accumulated employer contributions plus any appreciation.

The establishment of a qualified pension plan obviously is a complex task that should be handled by an attorney having experience with employee benefits. While IRS approval is not necessary, it ordinarily is advisable. Often, employee pension plans are drafted using a master or prototype plan previously approved by the IRS.

The instructions to the current IRS Form 5500 state that church plans not electing ERISA coverage under Code section 410(b) are not required to file 5500 forms.

An employee can make voluntary contributions to a qualified pension plan if the plan permits. Such contributions are deductible by the employee up to the lesser of $2,000 or 100% of annual compensation paid by the employer. However, if the employee also contributes to an IRA, the $2,000 ceiling on contributions to the IRA is reduced by the amount of such voluntary contributions to the qualified pension plan.

A plan cannot be a qualified plan if it provides for contributions or benefits in excess of specified amounts. A defined benefit plan cannot provide annual benefits that exceed the lesser of $125,000 (for 1997) or 100% of an employee's average compensation for his or her highest 3 years. Contributions (and any other additions) to a defined contribution plan must not exceed the lesser of $30,000 or 25% of an employee's compensation.

✎ **Key point: Congress enacted legislation in 1996 replacing any "pre-ERISA" nondiscrimination rules that still apply to churches with a simplified nondiscrimination rule. The new law is addressed earlier in this section.**

I. 401(k) Plans ("cash or deferred arrangements")

❖ **New in 1997. Churches can establish 401(k) plans.**

A 401(k) retirement plan (also known as a "qualified cash or deferred arrangement") is one of the most popular forms of retirement plan in use today. Under a 401(k) plan an employee can elect to have an employer make contributions to an employee trust on his or her behalf, or to the employee directly in the form of cash. Section 401(k) of the Code specifies several conditions that must be satisfied in order for the employee to realize tax advantages. The Tax Reform Act of 1986 prohibited tax-exempt organizations (including churches) from establishing a 401(k) plan (other than plans adopted prior to July 2, 1986). This has not been a problem since these organizations can establish "tax-sheltered annuities" which contain many of the same features including generous employee contributions through tax-deferred "salary reduction agreements," and employer contributions. Congress enacted legislation in 1996 permitting churches to establish 401(k) plans.

Prior to 1996, tax-sheltered annuities were more attractive than 401(k) plans since an employee could contribute a slightly larger amount. The two kinds of plans are nearly identical today in terms of tax advantages, and so it is doubtful that many churches will create 401(k) plans as an alternative to tax-sheltered annuities. The provision allowing churches to establish 401(k) plans takes effect in 1997.

J. Denominational Plans

✎ **Key point: most denominations offer retirement plans to their ministers (and in some cases lay workers). These ordinarily should be a minister's first choice, since they often provide unique and proven advantages.**

Several religious denominations have established retirement plans for ministers and in some cases church employees. These plans generally fall into one of the above categories. Ministers ordinarily should participate in such programs if their employing church or organization pays some or all of the annual contribution. Even if the plan is entirely funded by the minister, such programs often are attractive. For example, most denominational pension plans declare housing allowances for retired ministers. This is a significant benefit (described below) that is not available with many alternative retirement programs. The availability of this one benefit can mean the elimination of income taxes on a significant portion of annual retirement distributions. Some ministers also may wish to consider providing additional retirement benefits by participating in one or more of the other tax-favored plans available to them. Of course, participation in more than one plan can affect the amount of your annual contributions to each, and may have other consequences some of which are summarized above. If you are considering participation in more than one program, be sure to consult with a tax attorney or CPA.

K. Housing Allowances

✎ **Key point: denominational pension plans can designate housing allowances for retired ministers if certain conditions are satisfied. This is a significant tax benefit, and is one of the main advantages of denominational pension plans.**

Are retired ministers eligible for a housing allowance? In 1989, the IRS announced that this is a question "under extensive study" and that it will "not issue rulings or determination letters on the question . . . until [it] resolves the issue through publication of a revenue ruling, revenue procedure, regulation, or otherwise." *Revenue Procedure 89-54.* Early in 1995 the IRS repeated that the issue of "whether amounts distributed to a retired minister from a pension or annuity plan should be excludable from the minister's gross income as a parsonage allowance" is "an area under extensive study in which rulings or determination letters will not be issued until the Service resolves the issue through publication of a revenue ruling, revenue procedure, regulations, or otherwise." *Revenue Procedure 96-3.* So far, the promised clarification has not been issued.

Consider the following precedent:

The income tax regulations. Section 1.107-1(b) if the income tax regulations specifies that ministers may exclude from their taxable income (for federal income tax reporting purposes) that portion of their compensation that is designated as a housing allowance "pursuant to official action taken *by the employing church or other qualified organization* before the payment is made."

Revenue Ruling 62-117. In 1962 the IRS ruled that a resolution of the executive committee of a national religious denomination could not effectively designate a portion of the salaries of ministers of local congregations as a housing allowance where each local congregation employed and compensated its own minister. The IRS concluded that the national church was not an "employing church or other qualified organization" eligible to designate a housing allowance for local ministers since local congregations were independent of the national church as to policy and conduct of their local affairs and ministers were hired and paid by the local congregations. Accordingly, "each congregation was the 'employing church' and only action taken by the individual church could effectively designate a portion of its minister's salary as a [housing allowance]." The IRS conceded that the national church could designate housing allowances for those ministers who were

Revenue Ruling 63-156. The IRS addressed the question of whether a retired minister of the gospel could exclude a housing allowance furnished to him "pursuant to official action taken by the employing qualified organization in recognition of his past services which were the duties of a minister of the

gospel in churches of his denomination." The IRS concluded that "the rental allowance paid to him as part of his compensation for past services is excludable . . . to the extent used by him for expenses directly related to providing a home."

Revenue Ruling 72-249. The IRS addressed the question of whether the widow of a retired minister could exclude as a rental allowance amounts she receives from her deceased husband's church. Prior to his retirement and death the husband was a minister of the gospel and pastor of a church. Shortly before he retired, in recognition of his years of past service, the church, through official action of its governing body, authorized the payment of a specific amount each month upon retirement, to be paid for so long as he lived with survivor benefits for his wife. The authorization designated a portion of the payment as a rental allowance. The wife was not a minister of the gospel and she did not perform any services for the church.

The IRS concluded that "until his death, and to the extent used to provide a home, the rental allowance paid to the retired minister was excludable from his gross income since it was paid as part of his compensation for past services and it was paid pursuant to official action of his church. However, the rental allowance exclusion does not apply to amounts paid to his widow since it does not represent compensation for services performed by her as a minister of the gospel."

✎ **Key point: this ruling suggests that local churches can designate housing allowances out of retirement distributions paid to a retired minister.**

Revenue Ruling 75-22. In 1975, the IRS addressed the question of whether the board of a denominational pension fund can designate a portion of a retired minister's pension distributions as a housing allowance. Could the pension board be deemed to be an "employing church or other qualified organization" eligible to designate housing allowances for retired ministers? The IRS concluded that it was. In reaching its decision, the IRS noted the following factors:

1. The general convention of a national denomination (consisting of representatives from affiliated churches) established a pension fund for retired ministers.

2. Pursuant to its bylaws and regulations the general convention proposed and duly enacted a resolution creating a fund for the purpose of establishing and maintaining a unified clergy pension system applicable to all of the retired clergy of that particular denomination compensating them for past services to its local churches or to the denomination.

3. The resolution provided that the fund is to be governed by a board of trustees who are elected by the general convention.

4. The trustees are empowered to establish such rules and regulations as are necessary to implement the purpose of the fund.

5. The trustees of the fund are the sole authority of the denomination's retirement program for its clergy.

6. The trustees have prescribed the eligibility requirements necessary to receive a pension.

7. They set the amount of the pension and the amount of the monthly assessment each local church must contribute to maintain the fund.

8. Neither the individual minister nor the local church can intervene in this process.

9. The trustees have designated a certain percentage of the pension that they pay to a retired minister as a rental allowance.

10. Ministers, as of their retirement, have severed their relationship with the local church and are reliant upon the fund for their pension.

Based on these factors the IRS concluded that the pension board met the requirement of being an "employing church":

[T]he fund was created by the general convention and specifically authorized by the formal actions of representatives of the local churches to make all determinations regarding the pensions paid to retired ministers compensating them for past services to the local churches of the denomination or to the denomination. *The trustees of the fund are, therefore, deemed to be acting on behalf of the local churches in matters affecting the unified pension system in compensating retired clergy for such past services.* (emphasis added)

The IRS noted that the facts in this case were distinguishable from those in Revenue Ruling 62-117 (summarized above) "in that the minister, effective with his retirement, has severed his relationship with the local church and is reliant upon the fund for his pension."

IRS Letter Ruling 7734028. The IRS addressed the question of whether the "financial board" of a denomination's pension fund could designate 40% of pensions paid to retired ministers as a housing allowance. The IRS concluded: "We feel that the facts in your case are similar to those presented in Revenue Ruling 75-22. In your situation, the Conference (or the Synod) is the sole authority in the area of retired ministers' pensions. It appears from the information furnished that the local church organizations have no direct control over the amount a retired minister will receive as a pension. Although the exact amount contributed by the local church organization is not specifically prescribed, each participating organization must contribute no less than the specific percentage. It may be stated that, pursuant to the authorization creating the Synod and the Conference, its Constitution and Bylaws, the participating church organizations have appointed the Synod and the Conference to act on their behalf, as their agent, in matters pertaining to the pensions of

retired ministers. Accordingly, we conclude that when the Synod or the Conference designates a portion of a retired minister's pension as a rental allowance, it will be considered that the local church or church organization that employed the minister made such designation . . . ."

✎ **Key point: The IRS has issued audit guidelines for its agents to follow when auditing ministers. The guidelines state that the "trustees of a minister's retirement plan may designate a portion of each pension distribution as a parsonage allowance excludable under Code section 107."**

Conclusion. The availability of a housing allowance exclusion for denominationally-sponsored pension plans has been a very attractive benefit for many retired ministers. In many instances, retired ministers are able to exclude some or all of their pension income by having the pension plan designate a portion of their income as a housing allowance.

Until further guidance is issued, retired ministers and denominational pension plans may continue to rely on the 1975 IRS ruling (its most recent official guidance) in evaluating whether or not the designation of housing allowances by denominational pension boards is appropriate.

☞ *Example. Rev. B was minister of First Church at the time of her retirement in 1997. She had been employed by First Church for 20 years, and prior to coming to First Church had been employed as a minister in 3 other churches, all of which were affiliated with Rev. B's denomination. The denomination operates a qualified pension plan for its ministers, and Rev. B was a participant in the plan for the last several years of her active ministry. The plan was designed to compensate retired ministers for their service to local churches, and is characterized by the same factors as were present in Revenue Ruling 75-22. The denomination may declare a portion of Rev. B's retirement income to be a housing allowance, and Rev. B can exclude her actual expenses in owning or providing a home to the extent that they do not exceed the designated allowance or, if Rev. B owns her home, the fair rental value of the home plus the actual cost of utilities. See chapter 6 for further details.*

Can local churches designate housing allowances for retired ministers? Some local churches establish their own retirement programs for retired ministers apart from a denominational plan. In some cases these churches are not affiliated with a denomination, and in others they simply choose not to participate in a denomination-sponsored plan. Can such churches designate a portion of the retirement distributions paid to retired ministers as a housing allowance? The answer would appear to be yes, based on the following:

(1) In Revenue Ruling 72-249 (summarized above) the IRS concluded that a local church could desig-

nate as a housing allowance a portion of the retirement distributions it made to a retired minister.

(2) In Revenue Ruling 75-22 the IRS concluded that a denominational pension fund could designate housing allowances out of the distributions paid to retired ministers since

[T]he fund was created by the general convention and specifically authorized by the formal actions of representatives of the local churches to make all determinations regarding the pensions paid to retired ministers compensating them for past services to the local churches of the denomination or to the denomination. *The trustees of the fund are, therefore, deemed to be acting on behalf of the local churches in matters affecting the unified pension system in compensating retired clergy for such past services.* (emphasis added)

The denominational pension plan could designate housing allowance because it was acting on behalf of local churches. The implication here is that local churches have the authority to designate housing allowances too if they maintain a retirement plan.

(3) In IRS Letter Ruling 7734028 the IRS reached the same result as in Revenue Ruling 75-22: "It may be stated that, pursuant to the authorization creating the Synod and the Conference, its Constitution and Bylaws, the participating church organizations have appointed the Synod and the Conference to act on their behalf, as their agent, in matters pertaining to the pensions of retired ministers. Accordingly, we conclude that when the Synod or the Conference designates a portion of a retired minister's pension as a rental allowance, it will be considered that the local church or church organization that employed the minister made such designation . . . ." Again, the implication is that local churches can designate housing allowances out of their own pension programs.

✎ **Key point: Congress enacted legislation in 1996 clarifying that housing allowances paid to retired ministers by church or denominational pension plans are not subject to self-employment tax.**

Self-employment tax. Should retired ministers pay self-employment (social security) taxes on that portion of their retirement distributions that are designated by their church or denominational retirement plan as a housing allowance? For many years, the IRS maintained that the answer to this question was "no." Unfortunately, the IRS reversed its position in audit guidelines it issued in 1995 for its agents to follow when auditing ministers. This came as a shock to many ministers and church retirement plan administrators, and it resulted in financial hardship to many retired ministers. Congress addressed this issue in 1996, and clarified that the self-employment tax does *not* apply to "the rental value of any parsonage or any parsonage allowance (whether or not excludable under section 107) provided after the individual retires, or any other retirement benefit received by such individual from a church plan . . . after the individual retires." *IRC 1402(a)(8).* This rule takes effect after December 31, 1994.

There are five things to note about the law enacted by Congress in 1996:

(1) That portion of a retired minister's retirement distributions designated as a housing allowance are not subject to self-employment taxes. This will require the IRS to modify its audit guidelines for ministers to comply with the new law.

(2) The fair rental value of a parsonage provided a retired minister is not subject to self-employment taxes. This will require the IRS to modify its audit guidelines for ministers to comply with the new law.

(3) The law affirmed that retirement benefits paid by a church plan to a retired minister are not subject to self-employment taxes.

(4) The law suggests that the exclusions from self-employment taxes of a housing allowance paid to a retired minister or the fair rental value of a parsonage provided to a retired minister only apply if these benefits are provided by a church retirement plan.

(5) The law specifies that the exclusions from self-employment tax of a housing allowance paid to a retired minister (and the fair rental value of a parsonage provided to a retired minister) apply "whether or not excludable under section 107." This is an interesting statement. Section 107 is the provision in the tax code that excludes housing allowances and the fair rental value of parsonages from *federal income tax.* Presumably, retired ministers can exclude housing allowances and the fair rental value of a parsonage in computing self-employment tax even though they could not exclude these items in computing federal income taxes. The meaning of this provision is not clear. In most cases, a housing allowance is not available under section 107 in computing income taxes because (1) a church failed to designate the allowance in advance, or (2) the minister has little if any actual housing expenses. Are church retirement plans able, under the new law, to retroactively designate housing allowances for retired ministers? Can they designate housing allowances in excess of a retired minister's actual housing expenses? The language of the Act suggests that the answers to these questions is "yes." However, this result is so extraordinary that church retirement plans and ministers should not rely upon it without the advice of legal counsel, or until clarification is provided by the IRS or the courts.

✎ **Key point: the new law took effect in 1995.**

☞ *Example.* In 1997 Rev. G retires from many years of ministry. He has participated in a church retirement plan that begins making monthly distributions to him in 1997, some of which are designated as a housing allowance by action of the church plan. Total retirement distributions total $9,000 for 1997, of which $5,000 represents a predesignated housing allowance and the remaining $4,00 represents undesignated retirement benefits. Under the new rules, Rev. G would not pay self-employment tax on either the undesignated retirement benefits ($4,000) or the housing allowance ($5,000).

☞ **Example.** Same facts as the previous problem, except that Rev. G retired in 1995. The answer is the same. However, Rev. G has already filed a tax return for 1995 on which he may have paid self-employment tax on the housing allowance. If so, he can file an amended tax return to claim this exclusion (which was made retroactive to 1995 by the Act).

☞ **Example.** Rev. T retires from many years of ministry. She is allowed to reside in a church parsonage without any rental charge. Under the new law, Rev. T does not pay self-employment taxes on the fair rental value of the parsonage.

✎ **Key point: Church and denominational retirement plans should notify retired ministers about this important change in the law, and advise them (1) that any portion of their retirement distributions designated in advance by the plan as a housing allowance in 1997 is not subject to self-employment taxes in computing 1997 taxes; (2) that if they are permitted to reside in a parsonage (without charge) during 1997 following their retirement, the fair rental value of the parsonage is not subject to self-employment taxes in computing 1997 taxes; (3) that these changes apply to future years as well; and (4) that they have a legal right to file an amended tax return for 1995 or 1996 if they paid self-employment tax on a housing allowance distribution or on the fair rental value of a parsonage provided to them after they retired.**

L. Retirement Distributions not Pursuant to a Formal Plan

Occasionally, a church that has made no financial provision for a minister's retirement will begin making payments to the minister after his or her retirement. For example, assume that Rev. T was employed by First Church for 30 years preceding his retirement in 1997, and that the church never established a retirement program for him. The church board, embarrassed that no provision had ever been made for Rev. T's retirement, enacted a resolution in 1997 agreeing to pay Rev. T a monthly sum of $500 until the time of his death. What is the tax effect of such distributions? Are they tax-free gifts to Rev. T, or taxable compensation for services rendered?

Prior to 1987, a number of courts ruled that payments to a retired minister constituted a tax-free gift to the minister rather than taxable compensation if all of the following conditions were satisfied: (1) the payments were made by a local church congregation with which the minister was associated; (2) the payments were not made in accordance with any enforceable agreement or established plan; (3) the pay-

ments were authorized at or about the time of the minister's retirement; (4) the minister did not perform any further services for the church and was not expected to do so; and (5) the minister was adequately compensated during his or her previous working relationship with the church. See, e.g., Abernathy v. Commissioner, 211 F.2d 651 (D.C. Cir. 1954); Hershman v. Kavanagh, 210 F.2d 654 (6th Cir. 1954); Mutch v. Commissioner, 209 F.2d 390 (3rd Cir. 1954). The IRS concurred with these decisions in a 1955 ruling. Revenue Ruling 55-422.

Similarly, a federal appeals court ruled that an annual sum paid to a minister by a former church from which he had to resign because of illness was a gift and not taxable compensation. The minister had served the church for several years when he was stricken with a severe heart attack. After a prolonged recovery, including eight months in a hospital, the minister was advised by his physician to move from Pennsylvania to Florida. The church congregation, aware of the physician's advice and of the minister's lack of funds to make the move, adopted the following resolution:

Whereas the pastor of this church . . . has become incapacitated for further service as pastor and has requested the congregation to join in a petition . . . to dissolve the pastoral relation; and whereas the congregation moved by affectionate regard for him and gratitude for his long and valued ministry among them, desire that he should continue to be associated with them in an honorary relation; now, therefore, be it resolved that . . . [the minister] be constituted pastor emeritus of this church with salary or honorarium amounting to two thousand dollars ($2,000) annually, payable in monthly installments, with no pastoral authority or duty, and that the session of this church be requested to report this action to the presbytery.

The minister made no request to the congregation for such payments, had no knowledge that the resolution would be adopted, did not agree to render any services in exchange for the payments, and in fact performed no pastoral services for the church following his resignation. Under these facts, the court concluded that the payments to the minister were nontaxable gifts rather than taxable compensation. Noting that "a gift is none the less a gift because inspired by gratitude for past faithful service," the court observed that the payments were gifts since they were "bestowed only because of personal affection or regard or pity and not with the intent to pay the minister what was due him." Schall v. Commissioner, 174 F.2d 893 (5th Cir. 1949). Another federal appeals court ruled that a $20,000 retirement payment by a church to its retiring minister was a tax-free gift rather than taxable compensation. Stanton v. Commissioner, 287 F.2d 876 (2d Cir. 1961).

However, the IRS no longer follows its 1955 ruling, and regards all retirement "gifts" to ministers to be taxable compensation on the basis of section 102(c) of the Internal Revenue Code (added in 1986). Section 102(c) generally prohibits employers from making tax-free gifts to employees (with a few insignificant exceptions). Accordingly, only ministers who are in fact self-employed for federal income tax reporting purposes have any chance of having a retirement distribution characterized as a tax-free gift by the IRS. This will be a very exceptional case, since the IRS no doubt would consider most ministers who currently report their income taxes as self-employed to be employees. Further, even if the IRS agreed that a retired minister had been self-employed, the retirement distribution still would have to satisfy the definition of a "gift" announced by the Supreme Court in the *Duberstein* case (discussed in chapter 4, section A.3). The IRS has stated that this test will determine whether a retirement distribution paid by a church to a retired minister (who was self-employed) is a tax-free gift or taxable compensation. See chapter 4, section A.3, for further details.

M. "SIMPLE" Retirement Plans

❖ **New in 1997. Congress has created an entirely new form of tax-favored retirement program, called SIMPLE.**

A new "simplified" retirement plan is now available to small businesses called the "savings incentive match plan for employees" (or "SIMPLE" for short). SIMPLE plans can be adopted by employers who employ 100 or fewer employees and who do not maintain another employer-sponsored retirement plan. A SIMPLE plan can be in the form of either an IRA or 401(k) plan.

✎ **Key point: Churches are neither specifically included nor excluded from participating in SIMPLE plans. Until further clarification, there appears to be no reason why churches cannot establish such a plan if they employ fewer than 100 persons and do not maintain another employer-sponsored retirement plan. Churches that would like to establish such a plan should consult with a local attorney or CPA.**

SIMPLE IRA plans

A SIMPLE retirement plan allows employees to make elective contributions to an IRA. Employee contributions have to be expressed as a percentage of the employee's compensation, and cannot exceed $6,000 per year. The $6,000 dollar limit is indexed for inflation in $500 increments. The employer is required to satisfy one of two contribution formulas:

(1) Under the matching contribution formula, the employer generally is required to match employee elective contributions on a dollar-for-dollar basis up to 3% of the employee's compensation. Under a special rule, the employer could elect a lower percentage matching contribution for all employees (but not less than 1% of each employee's compensation). In order for the employer to lower the matching percentage for any year, the employer has to notify employees of the applicable match within a reasonable time before the 60-day "election period" for the year (described below). In addition, a lower percentage cannot be elected for more than 2 out of any 5 years.

(2) Alternatively, for any year, an employer is permitted to elect, in lieu of making matching contributions, to make a 2% of compensation nonelective contribution on behalf of each eligible employee with at least $5,000 in compensation for such year. If such an election is made, the employer is required notify eligible employees of the change within a reasonable period before the 60-day election period for the year (described below). No contributions other than employee elective contributions and required employer matching contributions (or, alternatively, required employer nonelective contributions) can be made to a SIMPLE account.

✎ **Key point: The maximum employer contribution that can be made on behalf of any employee under the 2% of compensation nonelective contribution formula is $3,000. By contrast, the maximum employer contribution that can be made on behalf of any employee under the matching contribution formula is $6,000.**

✎ **Key point: Only employers who employ 100 or fewer employees and who do not currently maintain a "qualified plan" can establish SIMPLE retirement accounts for their employees. The term "qualified plan" is defined by the Act to include a qualified retirement plan, a 403(b) tax-sheltered annuity, or a simplified employee pension.**

Here are several other rules that apply to SIMPLE IRA plans:

• Each employee who received at least $5,000 in compensation from the employer during any 2 prior years and who is reasonably expected to receive at least $5,000 in compensation during the current year must be eligible to participate in the SIMPLE plan.

• Self-employed individuals can participate in a SIMPLE plan.

• All contributions to an employee's SIMPLE account have to be fully vested.

• Contributions to a SIMPLE account are excludable from the employee's income. SIMPLE accounts, like IRAs, are not subject to tax.

• Distributions from a SIMPLE account generally are taxed under the rules applicable to IRAs. They are includible in income when withdrawn. Tax-free rollovers can be made from one SIMPLE account to another. A SIMPLE account can be rolled over to an IRA on a tax-free basis after a two-year period has expired since the individual first participated in the SIMPLE plan. If an employee is no longer participating in a SIMPLE plan (for example, the employee has terminated employment), the employee's SIMPLE account will be treated as an IRA.

• Early withdrawals from a SIMPLE account generally are be subject to the 10-percent early withdrawal tax applicable to IRAs. However, withdrawals of contributions during the 2-year period beginning on the date the employee first participated in the SIMPLE plan are subject to a 25-percent early withdrawal tax (rather than 10%).

• Employer matching or nonelective contributions to a SIMPLE account are not treated as wages for employment tax purposes.

• Each eligible employee can elect, within the 60-day period before the beginning of any year (or the 60-day period before first becoming eligible to participate), to participate in the SIMPLE plan (that is, to make elective deferrals), and to modify any previous elections regarding the amount of contributions. An employer is required to contribute employees' elective deferrals to the employee's SIMPLE account within 30 days after the end of the month to which the contributions relate. Employees must be allowed to terminate participation in the SIMPLE plan at any time during the year. The plan can provide that an employee who terminates participation cannot resume participation until the following year. A plan can permit (but is not required to permit) an individual to make other changes to his or her salary reduction contribution election during the year (for example, reduce contributions).

• An employer is permitted to designate a SIMPLE account trustee to which contributions on behalf of eligible employees are made.

• Simplified reporting requirements apply to SIMPLE plans and so the employer will not be subject to fiduciary liability resulting from the employee exercising control over the assets in the SIMPLE account.

• The employer maintaining a SIMPLE plan is required to notify each employee of the employee's opportunity to make salary reduction contributions under the plan as well as the contribution alternative chosen by the employer immediately before the employee becomes eligible to make such election. This notice must include a copy of the summary description prepared by the trustee. An employer who fails to provide such notice will be subject to a penalty of $30 per day on which such failure continues, unless the failure is due to reasonable cause.

• The provisions relating to SIMPLE plans are effective for years beginning after December 31, 1996.

SIMPLE 401(k) plans

As noted elsewhere in this chapter, churches are permitted to establish 401(k) retirement plans for their employees beginning in 1997. These plans are one of the most popular kinds of retirement plan and it is likely that they will be adopted by some religious organizations.

The Act establishes SIMPLE 401(k) plans, and provides that they will satisfy the special nondiscrimination tests that apply to employee elective deferrals and employer matching contributions if the plan satisfies the contribution requirements applicable to SIMPLE plans (summarized above). In addition, the plan is not subject to the "top-heavy rules" for any year that (1) the employer does not maintain another

qualified retirement plans (including a 403(b) tax-sheltered annuity); (2) the employees' elective deferrals are limited to no more than $6,000; (3) the employer matches employees' elective deferrals up to 3% of compensation (or alternatively makes a 2% compensation nonelective contribution on behalf of all eligible employees having at least $5,000 of annual compensation); and (4) no other contributions are made to the plan.

The IRS Model Rabbi Trust Agreement

⟳ **Important: The model trust language contains a number of optional provisions, which are printed in italics and marked as "optional." The taxpayer may substitute language of its choice for any optional provision, provided that the substituted language is not inconsistent with the language of the model trust. The model trust language also contains several alternative provisions, which are printed in italics and marked as "alternative." The taxpayer must choose one of these alternatives. Items in brackets are explanatory.**

TRUST

OPTIONAL (a) This Agreement made this ___ day of ____, by and between (Company) and (Trustee).

OPTIONAL (b) WHEREAS, Company has adopted the nonqualified deferred compensation Plan(s) as listed in Appendix ____ .

OPTIONAL (c) WHEREAS, Company has incurred or expects to incur liability under the terms of such Plan(s) with respect to the individuals participating in such Plan(s).

(d) WHEREAS, Company wishes to establish a trust (hereinafter called "Trust") and to contribute to the Trust assets that shall be held therein, subject to the claims of Company's creditors in the event of Company's Insolvency, as herein defined, until paid to Plan participants and their beneficiaries in such manner and at such times as specified in the Plan(s).

(e) WHEREAS, it is the intention of the parties that this Trust shall constitute an unfunded arrangement and shall not affect the status of the Plan(s) as an unfunded plan maintained for the purpose of providing deferred compensation for a select group of management or highly compensated employees for purposes of Title I of the Employee Retirement Income Security Act of 1974.

(f) WHEREAS, it is the intention of Company to make contributions to the Trust to provide itself with a source of funds to assist it in the meeting of its liabilities under the Plan(s).

NOW, THEREFORE, the parties do hereby establish the Trust and agree that the Trust shall be comprised, held and disposed of as follows:

Section 1. Establishment Of Trust

(a) Company hereby deposits with Trustee in trust [insert amount deposited], which shall become the principal of the Trust to be held, administered and disposed of by Trustee as provided in this Trust Agreement.

ALTERNATIVES—Select one section (b):

(b) The Trust hereby established shall be revocable by Company.

(b) The Trust hereby established shall be irrevocable.

(b) The Trust hereby established is revocable by Company it shall become irrevocable upon a Change of Control, as defined herein.

(b) The Trust shall become irrevocable _____ [insert number] days following the issuance of a favorable private letter ruling regarding the Trust from the Internal Revenue Service.

(b) The Trust shall become irrevocable upon approval by the Board of Directors.

(c) The Trust is intended to be a grantor trust, of which Company is the grantor, within the meaning of subpart E, part I, subchapter J, chapter 1, subtitle A of the Internal Revenue Code of 1986, as amended, and shall be construed accordingly.

(d) The principal of the Trust, and any earnings thereon shall be held separate and apart from other funds of Company and shall be used exclusively for the uses and purposes of Plan participants and general creditors as herein set forth. Plan participants and their beneficiaries shall have no preferred claim on, or any beneficial ownership interest in, any assets of the Trust. Any rights created under the Plan(s) and this Trust Agreement shall be mere unsecured contractual rights of Plan participants and their beneficiaries against Company. Any assets held by the Trust will be subject to the claims of Company's general creditors under federal and state law in the event of Insolvency, as defined in Section 3(a) herein.

ALTERNATIVES—Select one or more of the following sections, as appropriate:

(e) Company, in its sole discretion, may at any time, or from time to time, make additional deposits of cash or other property in trust with Trustee to augment the principal to be held, administered and disposed of by Trustee as provided in this Trust Agreement. Neither Trustee nor any Plan participant or beneficiary shall have any right to compel such additional deposits.

(e) Upon a Change of Control, Company shall, as soon as possible, but in no event longer than _____ [fill in blank] days following the Change of Control, as defined herein, make an irrevocable contribution to the Trust in an amount that is sufficient to pay each Plan participant or beneficiary the benefits to which Plan participants or their beneficiaries would be entitled pursuant to the terms of the Plan(s) as of the date on which the Change of Control occurred.

(e) Within _____ [fill in blank] days following the end of the Plan year(s), ending after the Trust has become irrevocable pursuant to Section 1(b) hereof, Company shall be required to irrevocably deposit additional cash or other property to the Trust in an amount sufficient to pay each Plan participant or beneficiary the benefits payable pursuant to the terms of the Plan(s) as of the close of the Plan year(s).

Section 2. Payments to Plan Participants and Their Beneficiaries.

(a) Company shall deliver to Trustee a schedule (the "Payment Schedule") that indicates the amounts payable in respect of each Plan participant (and his or her beneficiaries), that provides a formula or other instructions acceptable to Trustee for determining the amounts so payable, the form in which such amount is to be paid (as provided for or available under the Plan(s)), and the time of commencement for payment of such amounts. Except as otherwise provided herein, Trustee shall make payments to the Plan participants and their beneficiaries in accordance with such Payment Schedule. The Trustee shall make provision for the reporting and withholding of any federal, state or local taxes that may be required to be withheld with respect to the payment of benefits pursuant to the terms of the Plan(s) and shall pay amounts withheld to the appropriate taxing authorities or determine that such amounts have been reported, withheld and paid by Company.

(b) The entitlement of a Plan participant or his or her beneficiaries to benefits under the Plan(s) shall be determined by Company or such party as it shall designate under the Plan(s), and any claim for Such benefits shall be considered and reviewed under the procedures set out in the Plan(s).

(c) Company may make payment of benefits directly to Plan participants or their beneficiaries as they become due under the terms of the Plan(s). Company shall notify Trustee of its decision to make payment of benefits directly prior to the time amounts are payable to participants or their beneficiaries. In addition, if the principal of the Trust, and any earnings thereon, are not sufficient to make payments of benefits in accordance with the terms of the Plan (s), Company shall make the balance of each such payment as it falls due. Trustee shall notify Company where principal and earnings are not sufficient.

Section 3. Trustee Responsibility Regarding Payments to Trust Beneficiary When Company Is Insolvent.

(a) Trustee shall cease payment of benefits to Plan participants and their beneficiaries if the Company is Insolvent. Company shall be considered "Insolvent" for purposes of this Trust Agreement if (i) Company is unable to pay its debts as they become due, or (ii) Company is subject to a pending proceeding as a debtor under the United States Bankruptcy Code.

OPTIONAL *or (iii) Company is determined to be insolvent by _____ [insert names of applicable federal and/or state regulatory agency].*

(b) At all times during the continuance of this Trust, as provided in Section 1(d) hereof, the principal and income of the Trust shall be subject to claims of general creditors of Company under federal and state law as set forth below.

(1) The Board of Directors and the Chief Executive Officer [or substitute the title of the highest ranking officer of the Company] of Company shall have the duty to inform Trustee in writing of Company's Insolvency. If a person claiming to be a creditor of Company alleges in writing to Trustee that Company has become Insolvent, Trustee shall determine whether Company is Insolvent and, pending such determination, Trustee shall discontinue payment of benefits to Plan participants or their beneficiaries.

(2) Unless Trustee has actual knowledge of Company's Insolvency, or has received notice from Company or a person claiming to be a creditor alleging that Company is Insolvent, Trustee shall have no duty to inquire whether Company is Insolvent. Trustee may in all events rely on such evidence concerning Company's solvency as may be furnished to Trustee and that provides Trustee with a reasonable basis for making a determination concerning Company's solvency.

(3) If at any time Trustee has determined that Company is Insolvent, Trustee shall discontinue payments to Plan participants or their beneficiaries and shall hold the assets of the Trust for the benefit of Company's general creditors. Nothing in this Trust Agreement shall in any way diminish any rights of Plan participants or their beneficiaries to pursue their rights as general creditors of Company with respect to benefits due under the Plan(s) or otherwise.

(4) Trustee shall resume the payment of benefits to Plan participants or their beneficiaries in accordance with Section 2 of this Trust Agreement only after Trustee has determined that Company is not Insolvent (or is no longer Insolvent).

(c) Provided that there are sufficient assets, if Trustee discontinues the payment of benefits from the Trust pursuant to Section 3(b) hereof and subsequently resumes such payments, the first payment following such discontinuance shall include the aggregate amount of all payments due to Plan participants or their beneficiaries under the terms of the Plan(s) for the period of such discontinuance, less the aggregate amount of any payments made to Plan participants or their beneficiaries by Company in lieu of the payments provided for hereunder during any such period of discontinuance.

Section 4. Payments to Company.

[The following need not be included if the first alternative under section 1(b) is selected.]

Except as provided in Section 3 hereof, after the Trust has become irrevocable, Company shall have no right or power to direct Trustee to return to Company or to divert to others any of the Trust assets before all payment of benefits have been made to Plan participants and their beneficiaries pursuant to the terms of the Plan(s).

Section 5. Investment Authority.

ALTERNATIVES—Select one section (a), as appropriate:

(a) In no event may Trustee invest in securities (including stock or rights to acquire stock) or obligations issued by Company, other than a de minimis amount held in common investment vehicles in which Trustee invests. All rights associated with assets of the Trust shall be exercised by Trustee or the person designated by Trustee, and shall in no event be exercisable by or rest with Plan participants.

(a) Trustee may invest in securities (including stock or rights to acquire stock) or obligations issued by Company. All rights associated with assets of the Trust shall be exercised by Trustee or the person designated by Trustee, and shall in no event be exercisable by or rest with Plan participants.

OPTIONAL: *, except that voting rights with respect to Trust assets will be exercised by Company.*

OPTIONAL: *, except that dividend rights with respect to Trust assets will rest with Company.*

OPTIONAL: *Company shall have the right, at anytime, and from time to time in its sole discretion, to substitute assets of equal fair market value for any asset held by the Trust.*

[If the second Alternative 5(a) is selected, the trust must provide either (1) that the trust is revocable under Alternative 1(b), or (2) the following provision must by included in the Trust]:

"Company shall have the right at anytime, and from time to time in its sole discretion, to substitute assets of equal fair market value for any asset held by the Trust. This right is exercisable by Company in a nonfiduciary capacity without the approval or consent of any person in a fiduciary capacity."

Section 6. Disposition of Income.

ALTERNATIVES—Select one section (a):

(a) During the term of this Trust, all income received by the Trust, net of expenses and taxes, shall be accumulated and reinvested.

(a) During the term of this Trust, all, or _____ [insert amount] part of the income received by the Trust, net of expenses and taxes, shall be returned to Company.

Section 7. Accounting by Trustee.

OPTIONAL: Trustee shall keep accurate and detailed records of all investments, receipts, disbursements, and all other transactions required to be made, including such specific records as shall be agreed upon in writing between Company and Trustee. Within ..... [insert number] days following the close of each calendar year and within _____ [insert number] days after the removal or resignation of Trustee, Trustee shall deliver to Company a written account of its administration of the Trust during such year or during the period from the close of the last preceding year to the date of such removal or resignation, setting forth all investments, receipts, disbursements and other transactions effected by it, including a description of all securities and investments purchased and sold with the cost or net proceeds of such purchases or sales (accrued interest paid or receivable being shown separately), and showing all cash, securities and other property held in the Trust at the end of such year or as of the date of such removal or resignation, as the case may be.

Section 8. Responsibility of Trustee.

OPTIONAL: (a) Trustee shall act with the care, skill, prudence and diligence under the circumstances then prevailing that a prudent person acting in like capacity and familiar with such matters would use in the conduct of an enterprise of a like character and with like aims, provided, however, that Trustee shall incur no liability to any person for any action taken pursuant to a direction, request or approval given by Company which is contemplated by, and in conformity with, the terms of the Plan(s) or this Trust and is given in writing by Company. In the event of a dispute between Company and a party, Trustee may apply to a court of competent jurisdiction to resolve the dispute.

OPTIONAL: (b) If Trustee undertakes or defends any litigation arising in connection with this Trust, Company agrees to indemnify Trustee against Trustee's costs, expenses and liabilities (including, without limitation, attorneys' fees and expenses) relating thereto and to be primarily liable for such payments. If Company does not pay such costs, expenses and liabilities in a reasonably timely manner, Trustee may obtain payment from the Trust.

OPTIONAL: (c) Trustee may consult with legal counsel (who may also be counsel for Company generally) with respect to any of its duties or obligations hereunder.

OPTIONAL: (d) Trustee may hire agents, accountants, actuaries, investment advisors, financial consultants or other professionals to assist it in performing any of its duties or obligations hereunder.

(e) Trustee shall have, without exclusion, all powers conferred on Trustees by applicable law, unless expressly provided otherwise herein, provided, however, that if an insurance policy is held as an asset of the Trust, Trustee shall have no power to name a beneficiary of the policy other than the Trust, to assign the policy (as distinct from conversion of the policy to a different form) other than to a successor Trustee, or to loan to any person the proceeds of any borrowing against such policy.

OPTIONAL: (f) However, notwithstanding the provisions of Section 8(e) above, Trustee may loan to Company the proceeds of any borrowing against an insurance policy held as an asset of the Trust.

(g) Notwithstanding any powers granted to Trustee pursuant to this Trust Agreement or to applicable law, Trustee shall not have any power that could give this Trust the objective of carrying on a business and dividing the gains therefrom, within the meaning of section 301.7701-2 of the Procedure and Administrative Regulations promulgated pursuant to the Internal Revenue Code.

Section 9. Compensation and Expenses of Trustee.

OPTIONAL: Company shall pay all administrative and Trustee's fees and expenses. If not so paid, the fees and expenses shall be paid from the Trust.

Section 10. Resignation and Removal of Trustee.

(a) Trustee may resign at any time by written notice to Company, which shall be effective _____ [insert number] days after receipt of such notice unless Company and Trustee agree otherwise.

OPTIONAL: (b) Trustee may be removed by Company on _____ [insert number] days notice or upon shorter notice accepted by Trustee.

OPTIONAL: (c) Upon a Change of Control, as defined herein, Trustee may not be removed by Company for _____ [insert number] year(s).

OPTIONAL: (d) If Trustee resigns within _____ [insert number] year(s) after a Change of Control, as defined herein, Company shall apply to a court of competent jurisdiction for the appointment of a successor Trustee or for instructions.

OPTIONAL: (e) If Trustee resigns or is removed within _____ [insert number] year(s) of a Change of Control, as defined herein, Trustee shall select a successor Trustee in accordance with the provisions of Section 11(b) hereof prior to the effective date of Trustee's resignation or removal.

(f) Upon resignation or removal of Trustee and appointment of a successor Trustee, all assets shall subsequently be transferred to the successor Trustee. The transfer shall be completed within—[insert number] days after receipt of notice of resignation, removal or transfer, unless Company extends the time limit.

(g) If Trustee resigns or is removed, a successor shall be appointed, in accordance with Section 11 hereof, by the effective date of resignation or removal under paragraph(s) (a) [or (b)] of this section. If no such appointment has been made, Trustee may apply to a court of competent jurisdiction for appointment of a successor or for instructions. All expenses of Trustee in connection with the proceeding shall be allowed as administrative expenses of the Trust.

Section 11. Appointment of Successor.

OPTIONAL: (a) If Trustee resigns [or is removed] in accordance with Section 10(a) [or (b)] hereof, Company may appoint any third party, such as a bank trust department or other party that may be granted corporate trustee powers under state law, as a successor to replace Trustee upon resignation or removal. The appointment shall be effective when accepted in writing by the new Trustee, who shall have all of the rights and powers of the former Trustee, including ownership rights in the Trust assets. The former Trustee shall execute any instrument necessary or reasonably requested by Company or the successor Trustee to evidence the transfer.

OPTIONAL: (b) If Trustee resigns or is removed pursuant to the provisions of Section 10(e) hereof and selects a successor Trustee, Trustee may appoint any third party such as a bank trust department or other party that may be granted corporate trustee powers under state law. The appointment of a successor Trustee shall be effective when accepted in writing by the new Trustee. The new Trustee shall have all the rights and powers of the former Trustee, including ownership rights in Trust assets. The former Trustee shall execute any instrument necessary or reasonably requested by the successor Trustee to evidence the transfer.

OPTIONAL: (c) The successor Trustee need not examine the records and acts of any prior Trustee and may retain or dispose of existing Trust assets, subject to Sections 7 and 8 hereof. The successor Trustee shall not be responsible for and Company shall indemnify and defend the successor Trustee from any claim or liability resulting from any action or inaction of any prior Trustee or from any other past event, or any condition existing at the time it becomes successor Trustee.

Section 12. Amendment or Termination.

(a) This Trust Agreement may be amended by a written instrument executed by Trustee and Company. [Unless the first alternative under 1(b) is selected, the following sentence must be included.] Notwithstanding the foregoing, no such amendment shall conflict with the terms of the Plan(s) or shall make the Trust revocable after it has become irrevocable in accordance with Section 1(b) hereof.

(b) The Trust shall not terminate until the date on which Plan participants and their beneficiaries are no longer entitled to benefits pursuant to the terms of the Plan(s) [unless the second alternative under 1(b) is selected, the following must be included:], "unless sooner revoked in accordance with Section 1(b) hereof." Upon termination of the Trust any assets remaining in the Trust shall be returned to Company.

OPTIONAL: (c) Upon written approval of participants or beneficiaries entitled to payment of benefits pursuant to the terms of the Plan(s), Company may terminate this Trust prior to the time all benefit payments under the Plan(s) have been made. All assets in the Trust at termination shall be returned to Company.

OPTIONAL: (d) Section(s)—[insert number(s)] of this Trust Agreement may not be amended by Company for—[insert number] year(s) following a Change of Control, as defined herein.

Section 13. Miscellaneous.

(a) Any provision of this Trust Agreement prohibited by law shall be ineffective to the extent of any such prohibition, without invalidating the remaining provisions hereof.

(b) Benefits payable to Plan participants and their beneficiaries under this Trust Agreement may not be anticipated, assigned (either at law or in equity), alienated, pledged, encumbered or subjected to attachment, garnishment, levy, execution or other legal or equitable process.

(c) This Trust Agreement shall be governed by and construed in accordance with the laws of _____ .

OPTIONAL: (d) For purposes of this Trust, Change of Control shall mean: [insert objective definition such as: "the purchase or other acquisition by any person, entity or group of persons, within the meaning of section 13(d) or 14(d) of the Securities Exchange Act of 1934 ("Act"), or any comparable successor provisions, of beneficial ownership (within the meaning of Rule 13d-3 promulgated under the Act) of 30% or more of either the outstanding shares of common stock or the combined voting power of Company's then outstanding voting securities entitled to vote generally, or the approval by the stockholders of Company of a reorganization, merger, or consolidation, in each case, with respect to which persons who were stockholders of Company immediately prior to such reorganization, merger or consolidation do not, immediately thereafter, own more than 50% of the combined voting power entitled to vote generally in the election of directors of the reorganized, merged or consolidated Company's then outstanding securities, or a liquidation or dissolution of Company or of the sale of all or substantially all of Company's assets"].

Chapter 11

REPORTING REQUIREMENTS

Chapter Highlights

- **Application to churches.** Federal law (and many states) requires churches to comply with several payroll tax reporting obligations. Almost every church will be subject to at least some of these rules.

- **Penalties.** Church leaders must take these rules seriously, since there are penalties for noncompliance. For example, church officers may be personally liable for a penalty equal to the amount of payroll taxes that were not withheld or deposited. It is essential for church leaders to understand these rules.

- **Churches not exempt.** The courts have rejected the argument that the application of the payroll tax reporting rules to churches violates the constitutional guaranty of religious freedom.

- **Clergy are self-employed for social security.** Clergy are always self-employed for social security purposes with respect to their ministerial services, and accordingly they pay the "self-employment tax" rather than the employee's share of FICA taxes—even if they report their federal income taxes as an employee. It is incorrect for churches to treat clergy as employees for social security purposes, and to withhold the employee's share of FICA taxes from their wages.

- **Clergy compensation not subject to withholding rules.** Clergy compensation is exempt from federal income tax withholding whether clergy report their income taxes as an employee or as self-employed.

- **Voluntary withholding.** Clergy who report their federal income taxes as an employee may elect "voluntary withholding." Under such an arrangement, the church withholds income taxes from a minister's wages as if he or she was subject to income tax withholding. Such an arrangement also may take into account the minister's self-employment taxes.

- **Exemption of some churches from FICA.** Federal law allowed churches that had nonminister employees as of July of 1984 to exempt themselves from the employer's share of FICA taxes by filing a Form 8274 with the IRS by October 30, 1984. Many churches did so. The effect of such an exemption is to treat all nonminister church employees as self-employed for social security purposes. Such employees must pay the self-employment tax (just like clergy).

- **10 payroll reporting requirements for churches.** The more common payroll tax reporting requirements that apply to churches include the following:

  ✓ obtain an employer identification number

  ✓ determine whether each worker is an employee or self-employed, and obtain each worker's social security number

  ✓ obtain a completed W-4 (withholding allowance certificate) from each employee

  ✓ the amount of employee wages (including many fringe benefits and other taxable items) must be computed

  ✓ the amount of federal income taxes a church must withhold from an employee's wages is easily determined from tables that appear in IRS Circular E (Publication 15)

  ✓ FICA taxes must be withheld from employee wages (unless the church filed a timely exemption from the employer's share of FICA taxes, in which case nonminister employees are treated as self-employed for social security purposes)

  ✓ withheld taxes (both income taxes and employees' share of FICA taxes) plus the employer's share of FICA taxes must be deposited with a bank if they exceed $500 at the end of any month

  ✓ a form 941 (employer's tax return) must be filed with the IRS quarterly if an employer has any employees who were paid wages or whose wages were subject to tax withholding

  ✓ issue a W-2 to every employee before February 1 of the following year (and send copies of all W-2s to the Social Security Administration before March 1 of the following year with a W-3 transmittal form)

  ✓ issue a 1099-MISC to any nonemployee worker (who was paid $600 or more) before February 1 of the following year (and send copies to the IRS before March 1 of the following year with a 1096 transmittal form)

- **These rules are illustrated with comprehensive examples (including completed forms) in this chapter.**

Introduction

While churches are exempt from federal income taxes as long as they satisfy the requirements for exemption set forth in section 501(c)(3) of the Internal Revenue Code, they still may be subject to certain taxes, including one or more of the following: (1) the employer's share of social security (FICA) taxes payable on the wages of nonminister employees; (2) the tax on unrelated business taxable income; (3) state sales tax; (4) property tax on property that is not used exclusively for exempt purposes; (5) state unemployment taxes (in at least one state). In addition, many churches are subject to one or more federal **reporting requirements**, including:

- the withholding of federal income taxes and social security (FICA) taxes from the wages of nonminister employees, and the reporting of withheld taxes to the IRS by filing a quarterly Form 941

- providing each employee with a wage and tax statement (Form W-2) each year

- providing each self-employed person (receiving compensation of $600 or more) with an annual statement of nonemployee compensation (Form 1099-MISC)

- providing each person to whom the church paid interest of $600 or more during the year a Form 1099-INT (a $10 rule applies in some cases)

- submitting a Form W-3 to the Social Security Administration each year (transmitting copies of all W-2 forms distributed to employees)

- submitting a Form 1096 (summary of 1099 forms) to the IRS each year

- completing Part V, Section C of Form 4562 if the church provides clergy or other employees with a car

- filing an annual unrelated business income tax return (Form 990-T) if the church earns unrelated business taxable income

- submitting a donee information return (Form 8282) to the IRS if donated property valued by the donor in excess of $5,000 is disposed of within two years of the date of contribution

- submitting to the IRS each year a certificate of racial nondiscrimination if the church operates a preschool, elementary or secondary school, or college (Form 5578)

Other federal tax returns and reports of relevance to churches and religious organizations include the application for recognition of tax-exempt status (Form 1023), the annual information return (Form 990), and the election to waive social security participation (Form 8274). All of these forms and reporting requirements are discussed below.

These certainly are not the only reporting requirements that apply to churches and religious organizations. To illustrate, churches and religious organizations that administer certain kinds of retirement plans have significant reporting obligations. The reporting requirements discussed in this chapter represent the most common federal reporting requirements for churches.

A. Payroll Tax Procedures for 1998

1. Why church leaders should take the payroll tax reporting rules seriously

✎ **Key point: federal law requires churches to comply with several payroll tax reporting obligations. Almost every church will be subject to at least some of these rules. Many states have similar provisions.**

✎ **Key point: church leaders must take these rules seriously, since there are penalties for noncompliance. For example, church officers may be personally liable for a penalty equal to the amount of payroll taxes that are not withheld or deposited. It is essential for church leaders to understand these rules.**

Without question, the most significant federal reporting obligation of most churches is the withholding and reporting of employee income taxes and social security (FICA) taxes. These requirements apply, in whole or in part, to almost every church. Yet, many churches do not comply with them because of unfamiliarity. This can lead to disastrous consequences. Consider the penalties summarized in Table 11-1.

One of the most serious penalties is found in **section 6672** of the Internal Revenue Code. This section specifies that

any person required to collect, truthfully account for, and pay over any [income tax or FICA tax] who willfully fails to collect such tax, or truthfully account for and pay over such tax, or willfully attempts in any manner to evade or defeat any such tax or the payment thereof, shall, in addition to other penalties provided by law, be liable for a penalty equal to the total amount of the tax evaded, or not collected, or not accounted for and paid over.

Stated simply, this section says that any corporate officer, director, or employee who is responsible for withholding taxes and paying them over to the government is liable for a penalty in the amount of 100% of such taxes if they are either not withheld or not paid over to the government. This penalty is of special relevance to church leaders, given the high rate of noncompliance by churches with the payroll reporting procedures.

Does the penalty imposed by section 6672 apply to churches and other nonprofit organizations? The answer is yes. Consider the following 3 points:

TABLE 11-1

SUMMARY OF PAYROLL TAX REPORTING PENALTIES

Code section	Action	Penalty
3403	• failure to withhold payroll taxes from employee wages	• employer liable for full amount of taxes (which can be deducted from future wages paid to the same employees)
3509	• failure to withhold payroll taxes from a "self-employed" worker the IRS later reclassifies as an employee	• (1) employer liable for 1.5% x wages paid to the worker (3% if no 1099 was filed) for income tax purposes, and 20% x employee's share of FICA taxes (40% if no 1099 was filed); (2) employer liable for full employer's share of FICA taxes; (3) employer generally liable for full amount of taxes if intentionally disregards withholding rules
6721	• failure to file a correct "information return" (1099, W-2) with IRS by due date (February 28 of following year) • failure to report all required information on a return • including incorrect information on a return	• *3-tier penalty:* $15 per return (if correct return filed within 30 days after due date); $30 per return (if correct return filed by August 1); $50 per return (if correct return not filed by August 1) • no penalty if failure due to reasonable cause (and not willful neglect) • no penalty applies if no more than 10 returns filed without full information or with incorrect information, and errors corrected by August 1 (and error not due to willful neglect) • in case of intentional disregard of filing requirement, penalty is larger of $100 per return or 10% of the total amount of items required to be reported correctly
6722	• failure to furnish a correct "payee statement" (1099, W-2) to workers, by due date (January 31 of following year) • failure to report all required information on a payee statement • including incorrect information on a payee statement	• penalty of $50 per statement • no penalty if failure due to reasonable cause (and not willful neglect)* • in case of intentional disregard of filing requirement, penalty is larger of $100 per return or 10% of the total amount of items required to be reported correctly
6723	• failure to insert taxpayer identification number (employer identification number) on any return or statement (e.g., W-2, 1099, W-3, 1096, 941)	• $50 per failure
6656	• failure to make timely deposits of payroll taxes in federal bank	• *4-tier penalty:* penalty equal to 2% of amount of underpayment if failure corrected not more than 5 days after due date; penalty equal to 5% of amount of underpayment if failure corrected after 5 days but not more than 15 days after due date; penalty equal to 10% of amount of underpayment if failure corrected after 15 days but not more than 10 days after date of first delinquency notice to taxpayer; penalty equal to 15% of amount of underpayment if failure not corrected within 10 days after date of first delinquency notice to taxpayer

TABLE 11-1 CONTINUED

SUMMARY OF PAYROLL TAX REPORTING PENALTIES

6672	• willful failure to withhold or deposit payroll taxes	• civil penalty equal to 100% of taxes not withheld or deposited assessed against either the employer, or its officers (including volunteer officers or directors of nonprofit organizations)
7201	• willful attempt to evade or defeat tax	• a felony, with a criminal penalty of up to $100,000 (up to $500,000 for a corporation), and imprisonment of up to 5 years (or both)
7202	• willful failure to withhold or deposit payroll taxes	• a felony, with a criminal penalty (in addition to the section 6672 civil penalty) of up to 5 years imprisonment or $10,000 fine (or both)—generally applies to officers
7203	• willful failure to file a return, pay a tax, or supply required information	• a misdemeanor, with a criminal penalty of up to $25,000 ($100,000 for a corporation), and imprisonment of up to 1 year (or both)
7204	• willful failure to provide a W-2 to employees, or willfully including false information in a W-2	• a misdemeanor, with a criminal penalty of up to $1,000, and imprisonment of up to 1 year (or both)
7207	• willfully providing the IRS with a false return or statement	• a misdemeanor, with a criminal penalty of up to $10,000 ($50,000 for a corporation), and imprisonment of up to 1 year (or both)

1. IRS Policy Statement P-5-60. In Policy Statement P-5-60 (part of the Internal Revenue Manual), the IRS states:

The 100% penalty (applicable to withheld income and social security taxes) will be used only as a collection device. If a corporation has willfully failed to collect or pay over income and employment taxes, or has willfully failed to pay over collected excise taxes, the 100% penalty may be asserted against responsible officers and employees of the corporation, *including volunteer members of boards of trustees of organizations referred to in section 501 of the Internal Revenue Code* [e.g., churches], whenever such taxes cannot be immediately collected from the corporation itself. . . . When the person responsible for withholding, collecting and paying over taxes cannot otherwise be determined, the Service will look to the president, secretary, and the treasurer of the corporation as responsible officers.

The IRS has been criticized for attempting to assess the 100% penalty against volunteer directors of charitable organizations having little if any control over finances. The IRS responded to this criticism by amending Policy Statement P-5-60 to include the following significant statements:

Determination of Responsible Persons

Responsibility is a matter of status, duty, and authority. Those performing ministerial acts without exercising independent judgment will not be deemed responsible. In general, non-owner employees of the business entity, who act solely under the dominion and control of others, and who are not in a position to make independent decisions on behalf of the business entity, will not be asserted the trust fund recovery penalty. *The penalty shall not be imposed on unpaid, volunteer members of any board of trustees or directors of an organization referred to in section 501 of the Internal Revenue Code to the extent such members are solely serving in an honorary capacity, do not participate in the day-to-day or financial operations of the organization, and/or do not have knowledge of the failure on which such penalty is imposed.*

In order to make accurate determinations all relevant issues should be thoroughly investigated. An individual will not be recommended for assertion if sufficient information is not available to demonstrate he or she was actively involved in the corporation at the time the liability was not being paid. However, this shall not apply if the potentially responsible individual intentionally makes information unavailable to impede the investigation.

This language indicates that the IRS will not assert the 100% penalty against uncompensated, volunteer board members of a church who (1) are solely serving in an honorary capacity, (2) do not participate in the day-to-day or financial operations of the organization, and (3) do not have knowledge of the failure to withhold or pay over withheld payroll taxes.

2. Court decisions. The courts have recognized that church officers can be liable for the section 6672 penalty. Consider the following two cases:

• **Carter v. United States, 717 F. Supp. 188 (S.D.N.Y. 1989).** A recent federal district court ruling in New York illustrates the importance of complying with the payroll tax procedures discussed in this chapter. A church-operated charitable organization failed to pay over to the IRS withheld income taxes and the employer's and employees' share of FICA taxes for a number of quarters in both 1984 and 1985. Accordingly, the IRS assessed a penalty in the amount of 100% of the unpaid taxes ($230,245.86) against *each* of the four officers of the organization pursuant to section 6672 of the Internal Revenue Code. The officers challenged the validity of the IRS actions. The court observed that federal law requires employers to withhold FICA and income taxes from the wages of their employees, and to hold the withheld taxes as a "special trust fund" for the benefit of the United States government until paid or deposited. If an employer fails to make the required payments, "the government may actually suffer a loss because the employees are given credit for the amount of the taxes withheld regardless of whether the employer ever pays the money to the government." Accordingly, "section 6672 of the Code supplies an alternative method for collecting the withheld taxes. Pursuant to this section, the government may assess a penalty, equal to the full amount of the unpaid tax, against a person responsible for paying over the money who willfully fails to do so." The court observed that a person is liable for the full amount of taxes under section 6672 if "(1) he or she was under a duty to collect, account for, and pay over the taxes (i.e., a 'responsible person'), and (2) the failure to pay the taxes was 'willful.'" The court concluded that the four officers of the church-related charitable organization satisfied both requirements, and accordingly that they were personally liable for the unpaid taxes under section 6672. The officers were "responsible persons" since (1) they were directors as well as officers, (2) they had the authority to sign checks (including payroll checks), and (3) they were involved in "routine business concerns such as corporate funding, bookkeeping, salaries, and hiring and firing." The fact that a nonprofit organization was involved, and that the officers donated their services without compensation, did not relieve them of liability. The court also ruled that the officers acted "willfully" and accordingly met the second requirement of section 6672. It defined "willful action" as "voluntary, conscious and intentional—as opposed to accidental—decisions not to remit funds properly withheld to the government." There need not be "an evil motive or an intent to defraud." The court specifically held that "the failure to investigate or to correct mismanagement after having notice that withheld taxes have not been remitted to the government is deemed to be willful conduct." Further, the court concluded that payment of employee wages and other debts with the knowledge that the payment of payroll taxes is "late" constitutes willful conduct.

• **In re Triplett, 115 B.R. 955 (N.D. Ill. 1990).** A federal bankruptcy court in Illinois ruled that a church treasurer was not personally liable for his church's failure to withhold and pay over to the IRS some

$100,000 in payroll taxes, *but that the pastor and chairman of the board of deacons might be.* The court concluded that the church treasurer did not have sufficient control over the finances of the church to be liable for the 100% penalty. It noted that the chairman of the board of deacons made all decisions regarding which bills would be paid, and he (and the pastor) were alone responsible day-to-day church operations. While the treasurer did not satisfy the definition of a "responsible person," the court suggested that the pastor and chairman of the deacon board would. It observed that "ample evidence exists to indicate that other church employees, like [the pastor and chairman of the deacon board] may be liable. It is fortuitous that the treasurer's assessment has been litigated before assessments against these other persons." This case illustrates that the IRS is committed to assessing the 100% penalty under Code section 6674 against church leaders in appropriate cases. While the treasurer in this case did not have sufficient control over church finances to be a "responsible person," there is little doubt that many church treasurers would satisfy the court's definition of a "responsible person."

✎ **Key point: Congress enacted legislation in 1996 creating important limitations on the authority of the IRS to assess the 100% civil penalty against church leaders who fail to withhold or deposit payroll taxes.**

Taxpayer Bill of Rights 2 (TBOR2). Congress enacted the Taxpayer Bill of Rights 2 in 1996. This law contains four important limitations on the application of the penalty under section 6672:

1. Notice requirement. The IRS must issue a notice to an individual the IRS had determined to be a responsible person with respect to unpaid payroll taxes at least 60 days prior to issuing a notice and demand for the penalty.

2. Disclosure of information if more than one person subject to penalty. TBOR2 requires the IRS, if requested in writing by a person considered by the IRS to be a responsible person, to disclose in writing to that person the name of any other person the IRS has determined to be a responsible person with respect to the tax liability. The IRS is required to disclose in writing whether it has attempted to collect this penalty from other responsible persons, the general nature of those collection activities, and the amount (if any) collected. Failure by the IRS to follow this provision does not absolve any individual from any liability for this penalty.

3. Contribution from other responsible parties. If more than one person is liable for this penalty, each person who paid the penalty is entitled to recover from other persons who are liable for the penalty an amount equal to the excess of the amount paid by such person over such person's proportionate share of the penalty. This proceeding is a federal cause of action and is separate from any proceeding involving IRS collection of the penalty from any responsible party.

4. Volunteer board members of churches and other charities. TBOR2 clarifies that the responsible person penalty is not to be imposed on volunteer, unpaid members of any board of trustees or directors of a tax-exempt organization to the extent such members are solely serving in an honorary capacity, do not participate in the day-to-day or financial activities of the organization, and do not have actual knowledge of the failure. However, this provision cannot operate in such a way as to eliminate all responsible persons from responsibility.

TBOR2 requires the IRS to develop materials to better inform board members of tax-exempt organizations (including voluntary or honorary members) that they may be treated as responsible persons. The IRS is required to make such materials routinely available to tax-exempt organizations. TBOR2 also requires the IRS to clarify its instructions to IRS employees on application of the responsible person penalty with regard to honorary or volunteer members of boards of trustees or directors of tax-exempt organizations.

☞ *Example. Bill serves as treasurer of his church. Due to financial difficulties, a decision is made by the pastor to use withheld payroll taxes to pay other debts. The IRS later asserts that the church owes $25,000 in unpaid payroll taxes. The church has no means of paying this debt. The IRS later insists that Bill and the other members of the church board are personally liable for the debt. It is likely that Bill is a responsible person who may be liable for the 100 percent penalty since he has authority over the day-to-day financial activities of the church. The new law will not protect him. However, the new law will protect those members of the church board who (1) are volunteer, unpaid members; (2) serve solely in an honorary capacity; (3) do not participate in the day-to-day or financial activities of the organization; and (4) do not have actual knowledge of the failure to pay over withheld taxes to the government.*

☞ *Example. A church board votes to use withheld taxes to pay other debts of the church. Over a three year period the church fails to deposit $100,000 in withheld taxes. The IRS claims that the board members are personally liable for the 100 percent penalty for failing to deposit withheld taxes. All of the members of the board claim they are protected by the provisions of the new law. They are not correct, since the new law specifies that its provisions cannot operate in such a way as to eliminate all responsible persons from responsibility.*

Conclusions. The precedent summarized above demonstrates that church officers and directors (and in some cases employees such as administrators or bookkeepers) can be *personally liable* for the payment of income taxes and FICA taxes that they fail to withhold, account for, or pay over to the government. It does not matter that they serve without compensation, so long as they satisfy the definition of a "responsible person" and act willfully. Many church officers and directors (and in some cases employees such as administrators or bookkeepers) will satisfy

the definition of a "responsible person," and such persons can be personally liable for unpaid payroll taxes if they act under the liberal definition of "willfully" described above. Clearly, church leaders must be knowledgeable regarding a church's payroll tax obligations, and insure that such obligations are satisfied.

2. Application of payroll reporting rules to clergy

✎ **Key point: there are 2 special rules that apply to clergy under the payroll reporting rules. Unfamiliarity with these 2 simple rules has created untold confusion. The rules are:**

(1) Clergy are always self-employed for social security purposes with respect to their ministerial services, and accordingly they pay the "self-employment tax" rather than the employee's share of FICA taxes—even if they report their federal income taxes as an employee.

(2) Clergy compensation is exempt from federal income tax withholding whether clergy report their income taxes as an employee or as self-employed.

The application of the payroll reporting rules to clergy has created considerable confusion because of 2 rather simple rules that are often misunderstood. These 2 rules are explained below.

Self-employed status for social security. The first special rule is that clergy always are self-employed for social security purposes with respect to services performed in the exercise of their ministry. Accordingly, clergy pay the "self-employment tax" rather than the employee's share of FICA taxes— even if they report their federal income taxes as an employee. It is incorrect for churches to treat clergy as employees for social security purposes, and to withhold the employee's share of FICA taxes from their wages. Yet, many do so. See chapter 9 for more details.

Exemption from income tax withholding. The second special rule is that clergy compensation is exempt from income tax withholding whether a minister reports his or her income taxes as an employee or as self-employed. While it is true that the Internal Revenue Code requires *every* employer, including churches and religious organizations, to withhold federal income taxes from employee wages, there are some exceptions to this rule. One exception is wages paid for "services performed by a duly ordained, commissioned, or licensed minister of a church in the exercise of his ministry." *IRC 3401(a)(9).* Therefore, a church need not withhold income taxes from the salary of a minister who is an employee for income tax reporting purposes. See chapter 3 for a complete explanation of the term "services performed by a duly ordained, commissioned, or licensed minister of a church in the exercise of his ministry." Further, since the withholding requirements only apply to the wages of *employees*, a church should not "withhold" taxes from the compensation of a minister (or any other worker, such as a part-time custodian) who reports his or her income taxes as a *self-employed* person.

The IRS maintains that a church and a minister-employee may agree voluntarily that federal income taxes be withheld from the minister's wages, but this is not required. Some ministers find **voluntary withholding** attractive since it eliminates the guesswork, quarterly reports, and penalties associated with the estimated tax procedure (which applies automatically if voluntary withholding is not elected). Use of voluntary withholding may help to avoid underpayment penalties that may apply to ministers and other taxpayers whose estimated tax payments are less than their actual tax liability. See chapter 1 for more information on the underpayment penalty. A minister-employee who elects to enter into a voluntary withholding arrangement with his or her church need only file a completed Form W-4 (employee's withholding allowance certificate) with the church. The filing of this form is deemed to be a request for voluntary withholding. Voluntary withholding arrangements can be terminated unilaterally by either a minister or the church, or by mutual consent. Alternatively, a minister can stipulate that the voluntary withholding arrangement will terminate on a specified date. In such a case, the minister must give the church a signed statement setting forth the date on which the voluntary withholding is to terminate; the minister's name and address; and a statement that he wishes to enter

into a voluntary withholding arrangement with his or her employer. This statement must be attached to a completed Form W-4. The voluntary withholding arrangement will terminate automatically on the date specified. Finally, either the church or the minister may terminate a voluntary withholding arrangement before a specified or mutually agreed upon termination date by providing a signed notice to the other. If a church and its minister voluntarily agree that income taxes will be withheld, a minister ordinarily will no longer be subject to the estimated tax requirements with respect to federal income taxes.

But what about a minister's self-employment taxes? Clergy who have not exempted themselves from social security coverage are required to pay the self-employment tax (social security tax for self-employed persons). Can a church "withhold" the self-employment tax from a minister-employee's wages? The answer is yes. IRS Publication 517 ("Social Security and Other Information for Members of the Clergy") states that "if you perform your services as an employee of the church (under the common law rules), you may be able to enter into a voluntary withholding agreement with your employer, the church, to cover any income *and self-employment tax* that may be due" (emphasis added). A church whose minister has elected voluntary withholding (and who is not exempt from social security taxes) simply withholds an additional amount from each paycheck to cover the minister's estimated self-employment tax liability for the year, and then reports this additional amount as additional *income tax* (not "FICA" tax) withheld on its quarterly 941 forms. The minister should amend his or her W-4 (withholding allowance certificate) by inserting on line 6 the additional amount of tax to be withheld. The excess income tax withheld is a credit against tax that the minister claims on his or her federal income tax return (Form 1040, line 54), and it in effect is applied against the minister's self-employment tax liability. Further, it is considered to be a timely payment of the minister's self-employment tax obligation, and so no penalties for late payment of the quarterly estimates will apply.

WHY CHURCHES OFTEN FAIL TO COMPLY FULLY WITH THE PAYROLL REPORTING RULES

The risks associated with Code section 6672 are aggravated by the widespread non-compliance on the part of churches with federal payroll tax reporting obligations. Churches all too often fail to comply with the payroll tax reporting obligations—either by failing to withhold taxes or by failing to pay withheld taxes over to the government. As one court indicated, "because these [withheld taxes] accrue on the withholding date but generally are paid on a quarterly basis, they can be a tempting source of available cash to [an employer]."

Why do so many churches fail to comply with these rules? There are many reasons. Certainly these include: (1) Payroll tax reporting rules are complex. (2) Unique rules apply to churches, including the exemption of clergy from income tax withholding, the treatment of clergy as self-employed for social security purposes, and the availability of an exemption from the employer's share of FICA taxes for some churches that file a timely application. Church treasurers cannot assume that a church can be treated like any secular business. (3) In many cases, church treasurers are volunteer, uncompensated individuals who serve for limited terms. It often is difficult for such individuals to adequately familiarize themselves with the application of federal payroll tax reporting obligations to churches.

✎ **Key point: clergy who report their federal income taxes as an employee may elect "voluntary withholding." Under such an arrangement, the church withholds income taxes from a minister's wages as if he or she was subject to income tax withholding. Such an arrangement also may take into account the minister's self-employment taxes.**

A **self-employed minister** is free to enter into an "unofficial" withholding arrangement whereby the church withholds a portion of his or her compensation each week and deposits it in a church account, and then distributes the balance to the minister in advance of each quarterly estimated tax payment due date. However, note that no W-4 form should be used to initiate such "unofficial" withholding arrangement, and none of the "withheld" taxes should be reported to the IRS on the church's 941 forms. Ministers who report their income taxes as self-employed persons should recognize that the use of a W-4 form will almost guaranty that they will be deemed to be an employee by the IRS. Only ministers who report their income taxes as employees should use a W-4 form to initiate (or amend) voluntary withholding.

3. Mandatory church compliance with the payroll tax reporting rules does not violate "separation of church and state"

✎ **Key point: the courts have rejected the argument that the application of the payroll tax reporting rules to churches violates the constitutional guaranty of religious freedom.**

There is no withholding exemption for any nonminister church employees. Accordingly, churches must be careful to follow the withholding requirements discussed below with respect to any nonminister employees (or to minister-employees who have elected voluntary withholding). Does the imposition of these requirements upon churches violate the constitutional principle of separation of church and state? Every court that has addressed this question has said no. In the most prominent case, a federal court rejected a local church's challenge to the constitutionality of the withholding requirements. *Eighth Street Baptist Church v. United States, 291 F. Supp. 603 (D. Kan. 1968); see also, Bethel Baptist Church v. United States, 822 F.2d 1334 (3rd Cir. 1987) Schultz v. Stark, 554 F. Supp. 1219 (D. Wis. 1983); Goldsboro Christian Schools, Inc. v. United States, 436 F. Supp. 1314 (D.S.C. 1976).* The church had raised the following five objections: (1) a church cannot be made a trustee or collection agent of the government against its will; (2) the first amendment prevents the IRS from requiring churches to withhold taxes from the wages of employees; (3) it was not the intent of Congress to require churches to withhold taxes from the wages of employees; (4) if withholding laws apply to churches, then churches would become "servants" of the federal government in violation of their constitutional right of religious freedom; and (5) church employees are exempt because they qualify for the exemption available to members of "religious orders."

A federal court summarily rejected the church's arguments. It observed that the law specified that *all* wages are subject to withholding with certain specified exceptions, and therefore one can assume that Congress intended wages of church members to be subject to withholding unless such wages fell within one of the exceptions. The court concluded that the wages of nonminister church employees were nowhere specifically exempted from the withholding requirements, and therefore were covered. It rejected the church's attempt to bring its employees under the exemption available to members of religious orders.

The court also rejected the church's constitutional arguments:

[A] taxing statute is not contrary to the provisions of the first amendment unless it directly restricts the free exercise by an individual of his religion. We think it clear that, within the intendment of the first amendment, the Internal Revenue Code, in imposing the income tax and requiring the filing of returns and the payment of the tax, is not to be considered as restricting an individual's free exercise of his religion.

In summary, the wages of nonminister church employees are subject to withholding. This obligation cannot be avoided by labeling a church employee as an independent contractor or self-employed person, unless the individual clearly does not satisfy the IRS "common law employee" test (discussed in chapter 2). Church secretaries, teachers, choir directors, preschool workers, and business managers almost always will satisfy the common law employee test and therefore will be employees of the church (unless they represent temporary help secured from a local temporary help service). Church custodians who work full-time similarly will almost always be employees subject to withholding. However, a custodian who is paid by the job rather than by the hour, who decides when to work and how to perform his or her services, who works substantially less than full-time, and who is not subject to the control of the church with respect to the performance of his or her services, often may properly be characterized as self-employed. The effect of this is that no income taxes or social security taxes are withheld from the worker's compensation. Rather, he or she uses the quarterly estimated tax procedure to prepay and report taxes.

If a church worker satisfies the common law employee definition, he or she will be an employee despite the church's characterization of the person as self-employed (although in a close case, such as the custodian described above, the written characterization of the worker as self-employed will be a relevant factor).

Obviously, if a church concludes that a particular worker is in fact self-employed, it is critical that it issue the person a 1099-MISC rather than a W-2 form at year end (assuming the person has received church compensation of at least $600 for the year). Churches should be careful in characterizing any worker as self-employed, since as noted above the Code (section 3509) imposes a penalty on any employer who fails to withhold income taxes or social security taxes from the compensation of a worker deemed to be self-employed but who the IRS later reclassifies as an employee.

4. The "10-step" approach to compliance with federal payroll tax reporting obligations

If a church has nonminister employees to whom it has paid wages, or if its minister is an employee for income tax purposes and has requested voluntary withholding, the following steps should be taken to comply with the withholding requirements. Reporting requirements for self-employed persons are also included.

STEP 1. Obtain an employer identification number (EIN) from the federal government if this has

not been done. This number must be listed on some of the returns listed below, and is used to reconcile a church's deposits of withheld taxes with the W-2 forms it issues to employees. The EIN is a nine-digit number that looks like this: 00-0246810.

✎ **Key point: the employer identification number is** *not* **a "tax exemption number," and has no relation to your nonprofit corporation status. It merely identifies you as an employer subject to tax withholding and reporting, and ensures that your church receives proper credit for payments of withheld taxes. You can obtain an EIN by submitting a Form SS-4 to the IRS.**

STEP 2. Determine whether each church worker is an employee or self-employed, and obtain the social security number of each worker. In some cases it is difficult to determine whether a worker is an employee or is self-employed. If in doubt, churches always should treat a worker as an employee, since substantial penalties can be assessed against a church for treating a worker as self-employed who the IRS later reclassifies as an employee.

In general, a self-employed worker is one who is not subject to the control of an employer with respect to how a job is to be done. Further, a self-employed person typically is engaged in a specific trade or business and offers his or her services to the general public. The IRS has developed 20 criteria to assist in classifying a worker as an employee or self-employed. These are reviewed in chapter 2 of this tax guide. Factors that tend to indicate employee status include the following:

• the worker is required to follow an employer's instructions regarding when, where, and how to work

• the worker receives "on-the-job" training from an experienced employee

• the worker is expected to perform the services personally, and not use a substitute

• the employer rather than the worker hires and pays any assistants

• the worker has a continuing working relationship with the employer

• the employer establishes set hours of work

• the worker is expected to work full time

• the work is done on the employer's premises

• the worker must submit regular oral or written reports to the employer

• the worker's business expenses are reimbursed by the employer

• the employer furnishes the worker's tools, supplies, and equipment

• the worker does not work for other employers

• the worker does not advertise his or her services to the general public

Not all of these factors must be present in order for a worker to be an employee. But if most of them apply, the worker is an employee. Once again—if in doubt, treat the worker as an employee.

The IRS and the courts have applied various tests in determining whether *ministers* are employees or self-employed for income tax reporting purposes. Those tests are reviewed in chapter 2. For nonminister workers, the 20 factor test summarized above generally should be applied although there is no reason why the tests applied to ministers could not be applied to lay church workers.

✎ **Key point: Congress enacted legislation in 1996 creating important limitations on the authority of the IRS to assess penalties against employers for misclassifying workers as self-employed. The new provision is discussed in section A.5 of this chapter ("section 530").**

✎ **Key point: churches must withhold 31% of the compensation paid to a self-employed person who fails to provide his or her social security number to the church. This is referred to as "backup withholding," and is designed to promote the reporting of taxable income.**

Backup withholding. After determining whether a worker is an employee or self-employed, you must obtain the worker's social security number. A worker who does not have a social security number can obtain one by filing Form SS-5. If a self-employed worker performs services for your church (and earns at least $600 for the year), but fails to provide you with his or her social security number, then the church is required by law to withhold 31% of the amount of compensation as "backup withholding". The 31% is reported on the church's 941 forms (discussed later). Of course, a self-employed person can stop backup withholding simply by providing the church with a correct social security number. The church will need the correct number to complete the worker's Form 1099-MISC (discussed later). Churches can be penalized if the social security number they report on a Form 1099-MISC is incorrect, *unless* they have exercised "due diligence." A church will be deemed to have exercised due diligence if it has self-employed persons provide their social security numbers using Form W-9. Accordingly, it is a good idea for churches to present self-employed workers (e.g., guest speakers, contract laborers) with a W-9 form, and then to withhold 31% of total compensation as "backup withholding" *unless* the worker returns the form. The church should retain each W-9 to demonstrate its "due diligence."

The backup withholding requirements were designed to ensure that self-employed persons fully report their income. Without backup reporting, self-employed persons can often underreport their true in-

TABLE 11-2

Ten Common Payroll Tax Reporting Errors

COMMON ERROR	**CORRECT REPORTING PROCEDURE**
1. Treating clergy as self-employed for income tax purposes	Most clergy are employees for federal income tax reporting tax purposes *but are exempt from fed. income tax withholding—see p. 335*
2. Treating clergy as employees for social security purposes	Clergy *always* are self-employed for social security purposes with respect to ministerial services
3. Withholding taxes from clergy pay without authorization	Clergy are exempt from income tax withholding whether they report their income taxes as employees or self-employed; clergy who report their income taxes as an employee can request voluntary withholding by submitting a Form W-4 to the church
4. Withholding payroll taxes from clergy who report their income taxes and social security taxes as self-employed	Do not withhold payroll taxes from self-employed persons
5. Giving W-2 forms to self-employed clergy	Provide self-employed workers who are paid $600 or more during the year with a Form 1099-MISC, not a W-2
6. Failure to provide 1099-MISC forms to nonemployee recipients of $600 or more of annual compensation	A Form 1099-MISC must be issued to such persons
7. Church employees failing to pay self-employment taxes if their employing church exempted itself from the employer's share of FICA taxes (by filing a Form 8274)	Such employees are treated as self-employed for social security with respect to their church compensation and must pay the self-employment tax
8. Not filing 941 forms	These forms must be filed quarterly by a church with any "employee"
9. Not issuing W-2 or 1099 forms	A W-2 must be issued to each employee; and a 1099-MISC must be issued to each nonemployee (who received compensation of at least $600 during the year)
10. Not complying with payroll tax deposit requirements	Submit directly to IRS payroll taxes of less than $500 at end of any calendar quarter with Form 941; if accumulate payroll taxes of $500 or more at end of any month, deposit with a bank by 15th day of next month

come (without detection) by simply refusing to provide their social security numbers to employers. Of course, to avoid backup withholding, some self-employed persons may consider providing you with a false social security number. The IRS will discover such a scheme when it receives the 1099-MISC containing the false number. At such time, the IRS will notify the church to commence backup withholding on any future payments to the individual (until a correct social security number is provided).

STEP 3. Have each employee complete a W-4 form. These forms are used by employees to claim withholding allowances. A church will need to know how many withholding allowances each nonminister employee claims in order to withhold the correct amount of federal income tax. A withholding allowance lowers the amount of tax that will be withheld from an employee's wages. Allowances generally are available for the employee, the employee's spouse, each of the employee's dependents, and in some cases for itemized deductions.

Ask all new employees to give you a signed W-4 when they start work. If an employee does not complete such a form, then the church must treat the employee as a single person without any withholding allowances or exemptions. Employers must put into effect any Form W-4 that replaces an existing certificate no later than the start of the first payroll period ending on or after the 30th day after the day on which you received the replacement W-4. Of course, you can put a W-4 into effect sooner, if you wish.

Employers are not responsible for verifying the withholding allowances that employees claim. However, employers must submit to the IRS any Form W-4 on which an employee claims more than 10 withholding allowances, *or* if an employee claims exemption from withholding and would normally receive wages in excess of $200 per week.

STEP 4. Compute each employee's taxable wages. The amount of taxes that a church should withhold from an employee's wages depends on the amount of the employee's wages and the information contained on his or her Form W-4. A church must determine the wages of each employee that are subject to withholding and FICA taxes. Wages subject to federal withholding include pay given to an employee for service performed. The pay may be in cash or in other forms. Measure pay that is not in money (such as property) by its fair market value. Wages include a number of items in addition to salary (see chapter 4 for more details). Some of these items include:

- bonuses
- Christmas and special occasion offerings
- retirement "gifts"
- the portion of an employee's social security tax paid by a church
- the personal use of a church-provided car
- purchases of church property for less than fair market value
- business expense reimbursements under a nonaccountable business expense reimbursement arrangement
- imputed interest on no-interest and low-interest church loans

- most reimbursements of a spouse's travel expenses
- forgiven debts
- noncash compensation

STEP 5. Determine the amount of income tax to withhold from each employee's wages. The amount of federal income tax the employer should withhold from an employee's wages may be computed in a number of ways. The most common methods are the *wage bracket method* and the *percentage method.*

• **Wage bracket method.** Under the wage bracket method, the employer simply locates an employee's taxable wages for the applicable payroll period (i.e., weekly, bi-weekly, monthly) on the wage bracket withholding tables in IRS Publication 15 ("Circular E"), and determines the tax to be withheld by using the column headed by the number of withholding allowances claimed by the employee. You can obtain a copy of IRS Publication 15 at any IRS office or by calling the IRS forms number (1-800-829-3676).

• **Percentage method.** Under the percentage method, the employer multiplies the value of one withholding allowance (derived from a table contained in Publication 15) by the number of allowances an employee claims on Form W-4, subtracts the total from the employee's wages, and determines the amount to be withheld from another table.

⊃ **Recommendation. Be sure to obtain a new IRS Publication 15 (Circular E) in January of each year. It will contain updated tables for computing the amount of income taxes to withhold from employees' wages, and other helpful information.**

Both of these methods are explained in detail in Publication 15. It is essential that a church obtain a copy of Publication 15 each year to ensure that the correct amount of taxes is being withheld.

STEP 6. Withhold FICA taxes from nonminister employees' wages. Churches and their nonminister employees are subject to social security (FICA) taxes. The combined FICA tax rate is 15.3% of each employee's wages. This rate is paid equally by the employer and employee, with each paying a tax of 7.65% of the employee's wages. Churches must withhold the employee's share of FICA taxes from the wages of nonminister employees, and in addition must pay the employer's share of FICA taxes. This 7.65% rate is comprised of two components: (1) a Medicare hospital insurance tax of 1.45%, and (2) an "old-age, survivor and disability" ("social security") tax of 6.2%. For 1998 the Medicare tax (the 1.45% tax rate) applies to all wages regardless of amount. The "social security" tax (the 6.2% tax rate) applies to wages only up to a specified amount. For 1998 this amount is $68,400 (up from $65,400 in 1997).

The church must withhold the employee's FICA tax from each wage payment. Simply multiply each wage payment by the applicable percentage above. Special tables in IRS Publication 15 help in making this computation. Wages of less than $108.28 per year paid to a church employee are exempt from FICA taxes.

✎ **Key point: federal law allowed churches that had nonminister employees as of July of 1984 to exempt themselves from the employer's share of FICA taxes by filing a Form 8274 with the IRS by October 30, 1984. Many churches did so. The exemption was available only to those churches that were opposed for religious reasons to the payment of social security taxes. The effect of such an exemption is to treat all nonminister church employees as self-employed for social security purposes. Such employees must pay the self-employment tax (just like clergy). They are not exempt from social security taxes, as some church leaders have assumed. Churches hiring their first nonminister employee after 1984 have until the day before the due date for their first quarterly 941 form to file the exemption application. Churches can revoke their exemption by filing a Form 941 accompanied by full payment of FICA taxes for that quarter.**

STEP 7. The church must deposit the taxes it withholds. Churches accumulate three kinds of federal payroll taxes:

- income taxes withheld from employees' wages
- employees' share of FICA taxes (withheld from employees' wages)
- the employer's share of FICA taxes

Most employers deposit withheld payroll taxes on a monthly or semiweekly basis. An employer's deposit status is determined by the total taxes reported in a four-quarter "lookback" period. For 1998 the lookback period will be July 1, 1996 through June 30, 1997.

Monthly depositor rule. Churches that reported payroll taxes of $50,000 or less in the lookback period will deposit their withheld taxes for 1998 on a *monthly basis* (payroll taxes withheld during each calendar month, along with the employer's share of FICA taxes, must be deposited by the 15th day of the following month).

Semiweekly depositor rule. Churches that reported payroll taxes of more than $50,000 in the lookback period must deposit their withheld taxes on a *semiweekly basis.* This means that for paydays falling on Wednesday, Thursday, or Friday, the payroll taxes must be deposited on or by the following Wednesday. For all other paydays, the payroll taxes must be deposited on the Friday following the payday.

In November of each year the IRS will notify employers of their deposit status for the coming year.

Employers accumulating $100,000 during a monthly or semiweekly period must deposit by the next banking day. Also, employers accumulating less than $500 in withheld payroll taxes during a calendar quarter may skip the deposit requirements altogether

and send the taxes in to the IRS with their quarterly 941 forms. Monthly depositors under the new rules complete a "monthly summary of federal tax liability" (on the Form 941). Semiweekly depositors report their tax liability on Schedule B of Form 941.

Use Form 8109 (Federal Tax Deposit Coupon) to deposit all employment taxes. The taxes may be deposited at any financial institution qualified to act as a depository for federal taxes or to the federal reserve bank serving your geographical area. Make the check or money order payable to the depository where you make the deposit. You can deposit taxes with a check drawn on another financial institution only if the depository is willing to accept that form of payment. However, depositories must accept checks drawn on and made payable to the depository itself. Deposits are timely if delivered on or before the deadline, or mailed on or before the second day before the due date. A penalty is charged when taxes are not deposited when due or when mailed or delivered to IRS offices rather than to authorized depositories. A penalty may be assessed when deposits are overstated. Both penalties can be waived if the late payment was due to reasonable cause rather than willful neglect.

❖ **New in 1998. Employers required to electronically deposit payroll taxes will not be assessed a penalty for noncompliance until July 1, 1998.**

Electronic deposits. In 1993 Congress enacted legislation requiring the IRS to develop a system for the electronic filing of payroll taxes. Congress wanted a simple, "paperless" way for employers to deposit their payroll taxes. In response the IRS came up with the Electronic Federal Tax Payment System (or EFTPS). The new electronic system is phased in over a period of years by increasing the percentage of total taxes subject to the new EFTPS system each year. For 1997, the target percentage was to be achieved by requiring all employers that deposited more than $50,000 in payroll taxes in 1995 to begin using EFTPS by January 1, 1997. Congress later postponed this deadline until July 1, 1997, and the IRS announced in 1997 that it would not impose penalties for noncompliance through the end of 1997—for employers that make timely deposits using paper forms while converting over to the EFTPS system. Congress enacted legislation in 1997 providing that no penalties will be assessed for failure to use the EFTPS system to deposit payroll taxes prior to July 1, 1998.

✎ **Key point: Congress enacted legislation in 1996 relieving some employers of the penalties the IRS may assess if payroll taxes are not deposited on time. The new rules are explained in section A.5 of this chapter.**

STEP 8. All employers subject to income tax withholding, social security taxes, or both, must file Form 941 quarterly. Form 941 reports the number of employees and amount of FICA taxes and withheld income taxes that are payable. Prior to 1994, churches that had waived their liability for the employer's share of FICA taxes (Form 8274) used a Form 941E. The Form 941E was discontinued in 1994. All churches (including those that exempted themselves from the employer's share of FICA taxes) now use Form 941. The new Form 941 contains a box on line 8 that is checked if "wages are not subject to social security and/or Medicare tax." This is true for churches that filed a timely Form 8274 exempting themselves from the employer's share of FICA taxes.

Form 941 is due on the last day of the month following the end of each calendar quarter:

Quarter	Ending	Due date of Form 941
Jan.-Feb.-Mar.	Mar. 31	Apr. 30
Apr.-May-June	June 30	July 31
July-Aug.-Sep.	Sep. 30	Oct. 31
Oct.-Nov.-Dec.	Dec. 31	Jan. 31

Churches with only one employee. Should a church with only one employee (its minister) file a Form 941? It is the position of the IRS national office that such a church need not file 941 forms. This position is based in part on an income tax regulation specifying that every employer shall file 941 forms for each calendar quarter in which it is "required to deduct and withhold" income taxes. Since a church with only one employee (its minister) is not required to withhold income taxes (ministers' wages are exempt from income tax withholding), there is no need for a church under such circumstances to file 941 forms. This assumes that the minister has not elected voluntary withholding. The same rule would apply to a church with more than one minister-employee, so long as there are no nonminister employees. Of course, issuing the minister a W-2 without filing quarterly 941 forms will present an apparent discrepancy that may trigger an IRS inquiry. On the other hand, submitting 941 forms that report a minister's wages but no FICA withholdings will also raise questions. In either case, the apparent discrepancy can be easily explained.

STEP 9. Prepare a W-2 form for every employee. A church reports each employee's wages and withheld income taxes and social security taxes on this form. Wages of a minister who reports his or her income taxes as an employee do not include the housing allowance exclusion. A church should provide triplicate copies of Form W-2 directly to employees before February 1 of the following year, and submit an additional copy for each employee to the Social Security Administration before March 1 (along with a Form W-3 transmittal form).

➲ **Magnetic media. If you are required to file 250 or more information returns (W-2 or 1099) you must use magnetic media rather than paper forms unless using magnetic media would be an undue hardship and you apply for a waiver on Form 8508 (waivers are effective for one year).**

➲ **Be sure to add cents to all amounts. Make all dollar entries without a dollar sign and comma, but with a decimal point and cents. For example, $1,000 should read "1000.00." Government scanning equipment assumes that the last 2 figures of any amount are cents. If you report $40,000 of income as "40000," the scanning equipment would interpret this as 400.00 ($400)!**

You may need some assistance with some of the boxes on the W-2. Here are some comments that will be useful to church treasurers in preparing W-2 forms. Note that the box numbers refer to the 1997 W-2 (since the 1998 form was not available at press time).

Box a. You do not need to put anything here. If you wish, you can use this box to assign your own codes to individual W-2 forms.

Box b. Insert your church's federal employer identification number (EIN). This is a 9-digit number that is assigned by the IRS. If you do not have one, you can obtain one by submitting a completed Form SS-4 to the IRS. Some churches have more than one EIN (for example, some churches that operate a private school have a number for both the church and the school). Be sure that the EIN listed on an employee's Form W-2 is the one associated with the employee's actual employer. Also, be sure that this box reports the same EIN that appears on the 941 forms on which the W-2 wages and withholdings are reported.

Box c. List your church's name and address.

Box d. Report the employee's social security number.

Box e. Identify the employee by name.

Box 1. Report all wages paid to workers who are treated as employees for federal income tax reporting purposes. Wages are defined in chapter 4 of this text. They include much more than a salary. Some of the more common items include:

• Salary

• Taxable fringe benefits (including imputed cost of employer provided group term life insurance coverage that exceeds $50,000 and spouse or dependent life insurance coverage that exceeds $2,000)

• The value of the personal use of an employer-provided car

• Bonuses

• Most Christmas gifts

• Business expense reimbursements paid under a "nonaccountable plan." A nonaccountable business expense reimbursement arrangement is one that does not require substantiation of business expenses, or does not require excess reimbursements to be returned to the church, or that reimburses expenses out of salary reductions. Also note that such reimbursements are subject to income tax and FICA withholding if paid to nonminister employees.

• If you reimburse employee travel expenses under an accountable plan using a "per diem" rate, you include in box 1 the amount by which your per diem rate reimbursements for the year *exceed* the IRS-approved per diem rates. Also note that such reimbursements are subject to income tax and FICA withholding if paid to nonminister employees. Use "Code L" in box 13 to report the amount equal to the IRS-approved rates.

• If you reimburse employee travel expenses under an accountable plan using a standard mileage rate in excess of the IRS-approved rate (31.5 cents for 1997), you include in box 1 the amount by which your standard mileage rate reimbursements for the year exceed the IRS-approved rate. Also note that such reimbursements are subject to income tax and FICA withholding if paid to nonminister employees.

• Employee contributions to a medical savings account if included in the employee's income

For ministers who report their income taxes as employees, do not report the annual fair rental value of a parsonage, and do not report any portion of a minister's compensation that was designated (in advance) as a housing allowance by the church. Also, some contributions made to certain retirement plans out of an employee's wages are not reported. But amounts distributed to an employee by the employer under a nonqualified deferred compensation plan are included in this box. See boxes 11 and 13.

Box 2. List all federal income taxes that you withhold from the employee's wages in 1998. The amounts reported in this box (for all employees) should correspond to the amount of withheld income taxes reported on your four 941 forms for 1998.

Box 3. Report an employee's wages subject to the "social security" component (the 6.2% rate) of FICA taxes. Box 3 should not list more than the maximum wage base for the "social security" component of FICA taxes ($68,400 for 1998). This box usually will be the same as box 1, but not always. For example, there are certain retirement contributions that are included in box 3 that are not included in box 1. To illustrate, contributions to a tax-sheltered annuity may be excludable from income and not reportable in box 1, but they are subject to FICA taxes and accordingly they represent FICA wages for nonminister employees. Remember, again, that all ministers (including those who report their income taxes as employees) are considered to be self-employed for social security purposes. Accordingly, they pay the self-employment tax, not FICA taxes.

✎ **Key point: for ministers, this box should be left blank with respect to services performed in the exercise or their ministry.**

Box 4. Report the "social security" component (6.2%) of FICA taxes that you withheld from the employee's wages. This tax is imposed on all wages up to a maximum of $68,400 in 1998. Do not report

the church's (the "employer's share") portion of FICA taxes. Ministers who report their income taxes as employees are still treated as self-employed for social security purposes with respect to their ministerial services.

✎ **Key point: for ministers, this box should be left blank with respect to services performed in the exercise or their ministry.**

Box 5. Report a nonminister employee's wages subject to the Medicare component (1.45%) of FICA taxes. All of an employee's wages are subject to the Medicare component of FICA taxes. There is no ceiling. For most workers (earning less than the maximum amount of wages subject to the "social security" component of FICA taxes) boxes 3 and 5 should show the same amount. For 1998 the maximum wages subject to the "social security" tax is $68,400.

✎ **Key point: for ministers, this box should be left blank with respect to services performed in the exercise or their ministry.**

Box 6. Report the "Medicare" component (1.45%) of FICA taxes that you withheld from the nonminister employee's wages in 1997. This tax is imposed on all wages regardless of amount.

✎ **Key point: for ministers, this box should be left blank with respect to services performed in the exercise or their ministry.**

Box 11. This box reports distributions made to an employee from a nonqualified deferred compensation plan, including a "section 457" retirement plan. Churches are exempt from the provisions of section 457. See chapter 10. However, some churches maintain nonqualified deferred compensation plans that are not "section 457" plans.

Box 12. Report the value of taxable fringe benefits that were included in box 1. This would include the value of the personal use of an employer-provided car. Do not report any amounts listed in box 13.

Box 13. Insert the appropriate code and dollar amount in this box. Insert the code letter followed by a space and then insert the dollar amount on the same line within the box. Do not enter more than 3 codes in this box. If more are needed, use another Form W-2. Use capital letters for the codes, and remember not to use dollar signs or commas but do include a decimal and cents (even for even dollars). For example, to report a $3,000 contribution to a section 403(b) tax-sheltered annuity, you would report "E 3000.00" in this box. The codes are as follows:

A—This will not apply to church employees.

B—This will not apply to church employees.

C—You (the church) provided your employee with more than $50,000 of group term life insurance. Report the cost of coverage in excess of $50,000. It should also be included in box 1 (and in boxes 3 and 5 for nonminister employees).

D—You (the church) made contributions to a "401(k)" retirement plan. Report the amount of your contributions.

E—You (the church) made contributions to a 403(b) tax-sheltered annuity pursuant to a "salary reduction agreement" on behalf of the employee. Report the amount of the contributions. While this amount ordinarily is not reported in box 1, it is included in boxes 3 and 5 for nonminister employees since it is subject to FICA taxes with respect to such workers.

F—Generally not applicable to churches.

G—Generally not applicable to churches since they are exempt from Code section 457.

H, I—Generally not applicable to churches.

J—You (the church) are reporting sick pay. Show the amount of any sick pay that is not includable in the employee's income because he or she contributed to the sick pay plan.

K—Generally not applicable to churches.

L—You (the church) reimbursed the employee for employee business expenses using the standard mileage rate or the per diem rates, and the amount you reimbursed exceeds the amounts allowed under these methods. Enter code "L" in box 13, followed by the amount of the reimbursements that equal the allowable standard mileage or per diem rates. Any excess reimbursements (above the per diem or standard mileage rates) should be included in box 1. For nonminister employees, report the excess in boxes 3 and 5 as well. *Do not* include any per diem or mileage allowance reimbursements for employee business expenses in box 13 if the total reimbursements are less than or equal to the amount deemed substantiated under the IRS-approved standard mileage rate or per diem rates.

M, N—Generally not applicable to churches.

P—You reimbursed an employee's moving expenses and your reimbursements are not includable in the employee's income (because they were adequately substantiated by the employee and the employee could have deducted them had they not been reimbursed).

Q—Generally not applicable to churches.

R—Report employer contributions to a medical savings account on behalf of the employee. Any portion that is not excluded from the employee's income also should be included in box 1.

S—Report employee salary reduction contributions to a SIMPLE retirement account. However, if the SIMPLE account is part of a 401(k) plan, use code D.

T—Report amounts paid (or expenses incurred) by an employer for qualified adoption expenses furnished to an employee under an adoption assistance program.

Box 14. This box is optional. You may use it to provide information to your employee. Some churches report a church-designated housing allowance in this box (for ministers who report their income taxes as employees). The IRS uses box 14 for this purpose in a comprehensive clergy tax example in the current edition of its Publication 517. The instructions to Form W-2 also list "parsonage allowances" as a type of entry that can be made in this box. This is not a requirement, however.

Box 15. Check the appropriate box.

statutory employee. Churches rarely if ever have statutory employees. These include certain drivers, insurance agents, and salespeople.

deceased. Check this box if the employee died during 1998.

pension plan. Check this box if the employee was an active participant in a retirement plan maintained by the church during 1998 (including a section 403(b) "tax-sheltered annuity" or a 401(k) plan). Do not check this box if you are reporting contributions made to a nonqualified deferred compensation plan.

legal representative. Churches generally will not check this box. This would apply only if the Form W-2 is being issued to a guardian or other legal representative on behalf of an employee.

household employee. Churches generally will not check this box. It applies to household workers.

subtotal. Do not check this box if you are submitting 41 or less W-2 forms. If you are submitting more than 41 W-2 forms, check this box and give subtotal figures for every 41 forms. Subtotal statements should be the last Form W-2 on a page. Some boxes are subtotaled, as are codes D, E, F, G, H and S of box 13.

deferred compensation. Check this box if the church made contributions on behalf of the employee (through salary reductions) in 1998 to certain kinds of retirement plans, including a section 403(b) "tax-sheltered annuity," or to a "401(k)" retirement plan. See also box 13. Do not check this box for nonqualified deferred compensation plans.

STEP 10. Prepare a Form 1099-MISC for every self-employed person receiving nonemployee compensation of $600 or more. The 1099-MISC form is one of the most important tax forms that most churches are required to issue. Yet, many church treasurers are unaware of this reporting requirement, or are unsure how to complete the form. The 1099-MISC form must be issued to any "non-employee" who is paid compensation of at least $600 during any year. It is designed to induce self-employed persons to report their full taxable income. The key point is this—the purpose of the 1099 reporting requirement is not to impose a "burden" on churches and other organizations. Rather, it is to insure that self-employed persons pay their fair share of taxes.

A church must issue a 1099 form to a person if the following five requirements are satisfied: (1) the church is "engaged in a trade or business"; (2) the church pays the person compensation of $600 or more during the calendar year; (3) the person is self-employed (a "non-employee"); (4) the payment is in the course of the church's "trade or business"; and (5) no exception exists. The income tax regulations specify that the term "person engaged in a trade or business" includes not only "those so engaged for gain or profit, but also organizations the activities of which are not for the purpose of gain or profit" including organizations exempt from federal income tax under section 501(c)(3) of the Code. This includes churches and other religious organizations. There is no doubt that churches are required to issue 1099 forms if the other requirements are satisfied.

A church should issue a 1099-MISC form to any person to whom it pays $600 or more in a year in the form of self-employment earnings. Self-employment earnings include compensation paid to any individual other than an employee. Examples include ministers who report their income as self-employed for income tax reporting purposes, some part-time custodians, and certain self-employed persons who perform miscellaneous services for the church (plumbers, carpenters, lawn maintenance, etc.) who are not incorporated. Churches also must issue a 1099-MISC to a self-employed person who is paid in property other than money. The regulations state that "if any payment required to be reported in Form 1099 is made in property other than money, the fair market value of the property at the time of payment is the amount to be included on such form." In other words, if a church pays a self-employed minister compensation in the form of a car or other property, the fair market value of the property must be reported on a 1099-MISC.

Exceptions. The income tax regulations specify that *no Form 1099-MISC is required* with respect to various kinds of payments, including the following:

1. *Payments of income required to be reported on Forms W-2 or 941.* This means that a church should not issue a 1099-MISC to any worker who is treated as an employee for income tax and payroll tax reporting purposes.

2. *Payments to a corporation.* Let's say that a church purchases supplies or equipment from a local business, or hires a local landscaping company to maintain the church grounds. In either case, there is no need for the church to issue a 1099-MISC if the company is a corporation. Note, however, that this exception only applies to corporations—and not to partnerships.

3. *Payments of bills for merchandise, telegrams, telephone, freight, storage, and similar charges.* According to this exception, a church need not issue a 1099-MISC to the telephone company, UPS, or to vendors from which it purchases merchandise.

4. *Travel expense reimbursements paid under an "accountable" reimbursement arrangement.* According to this exception, a church need not report on a 1099-MISC the amount of travel and other business expense reimbursements that it pays to a self-employed worker under an accountable reimburse-

ment arrangement (explained in chapter 7 of this tax guide). On the other hand, travel expense reimbursements (or advances) paid to a self-employed person under a "nonaccountable" plan must be reported as compensation on the 1099-MISC. An example of a nonaccountable reimbursement would be a monthly car allowance paid to a minister without any requirement that the minister substantiate that the allowances were used to pay for business expenses. Another common example of a nonaccountable reimbursement would be a church's reimbursement of a guest speaker's travel expenses based on the speaker's oral statement or estimate of the amount of the expenses (without any documentary substantiation).

The $600 requirement. Churches need not issue a person a 1099-MISC form unless the individual is paid *$600 or more* in compensation. There are two considerations to note. First, there is no need to issue a 1099-MISC to persons paid *less* than $600 in self-employment earnings during the year. Second, since reimbursements under an *accountable* business expense reimbursement arrangement are not included in the reportable income of self-employed persons, such reimbursements need not be considered in computing the $600 figure. Similarly, a portion of a minister's income that is designated as a *housing allowance* is not reportable as income, and accordingly it is reasonable to assume that such an allowance need not be taken into account in computing the $600 amount.

Completing the 1099-MISC. A 1099-MISC is easy to complete. A church (the "payer") should list its name, street address (no post office box numbers), and employer identification number on the form, as well as the name, address, and social security number (or other tax identification number) of the recipient. There are 12 numbered boxes on the 1099-MISC form. The key boxes are numbers 1, 3, 4, and 7. Let's look at these individually.

Box 1. Report in this box amounts paid to recipients for all types of "rents," such as real estate

---

FORM 1099-MISC CHECKLIST

The Form 1099-MISC is one of the most neglected church reporting requirements. Here is a simple test that may help. In general, a church must issue a 1099-MISC to an individual if all of the following five conditions are satisfied:

• the church is "engaged in a trade or business" (includes nonprofit activities)

• the church pays the person compensation of $600 or more during the calendar year

• the person is self-employed, rather than an employee

• the payment is in the course of the church's "trade or business"

• no exception exists

345

rentals paid for office space, machine rentals, and equipment rentals (e.g., hiring a bulldozer to clear land for a parking lot).

Box 3. Report compensation paid to a worker that is not subject to self-employment tax (and is not reported anywhere else on Form 1099).

Box 4. Report in this box "backup withholding"—which is explained under step 2 above.

Box 7. This is the most important box, since it reports all "nonemployee compensation." This box contains the compensation paid to a nonemployee (i.e., a self-employed person) in the course of the payer's "trade or business." For example, if Rev. G is the senior minister at Second Church, and reports his federal income taxes as a self-employed person, then the church reports his compensation in this box. And, if the church is required to issue a 1099-MISC to a contractor or other self-employed person who performs services on behalf of the church, the church reports the compensation in this box.

Canceled debts. The forgiveness or cancellation of a debt represents taxable income to the debtor (see chapter 4). However, the instructions to Form 1099 specify that "a canceled debt is not reportable on Form 1099." The instructions clarify that only "financial institutions" are required to report a canceled debt as income, and this is done on Form 1099-C. Of course, if the debtor is an employee, the forgiven debt represents taxable income that should be added to the debtor's compensation that is reported by the church on Form W-2 or Form 1099-MISC.

Repairs. The instructions to Form 1099-MISC clarify that "payment for services, including payment for parts or materials used to perform the services" are reportable as nonemployee compensation "if supplying the parts or materials was incidental to providing the service. For example, report the entire insurance company payments to an auto repair shop under a repair contract showing an amount for labor and another amount for parts, since furnishing parts was incidental to repairing the auto."

When to file. Federal law requires that the Form 1099-MISC be completed and submitted to the recipient of nonemployee compensation on or before January 31st of the following year. You may use substitute 1099 forms if they contain substantially similar language to the official forms and all IRS rulings pertaining to substitute forms are followed. In addition, "copy B" (for the recipient) must contain the following statement: "This important tax information is being furnished to the Internal Revenue Service. If you are required to file a return, a negligence penalty or other sanction will be imposed on you if this income is taxable and the IRS determines that it has not been reported." By February 28 of the following year, a church must transmit to the IRS a copy of each 1099 form that it issued for the prior year along with a transmittal Form 1096.

"Section 530" employees. Payments to section 530 employees should be reported as nonemployee compensation in box 7. Section 530 employees are defined later in this chapter.

Backup withholding. In order to issue a properly completed Form 1099-MISC, a church will need to obtain the recipient's name, address, and social security number. Churches should obtain this information at the time the person performs services, since it often can be difficult to obtain the necessary information at a later date. IRS Form W-9 can be used to obtain this information. If a self-employed person who is paid $600 or more during the course of a year by a church refuses to provide his or her social security number, then the church may be required to withhold 31% of the person's total compensation as "backup withholding." See "step 2," above.

⊃ **Be sure to add cents to all amounts. Make all dollar entries without a dollar sign and comma, but with a decimal point and cents. For example, $1,000 should read "1000.00." Government scanning equipment assumes that the last 2 figures of any amount are cents. If you report $40,000 of income as "40000," the scanning equipment would interpret this as 400.00 ($400)!**

❖ **New in 1997. All 1099 forms must contain the name, address, and telephone number of a "contact person" who can answer questions the recipient may have about the form. The purpose of this new requirement is to give recipients of 1099 forms the ability to contact a person who was responsible for preparing the form and who presumably has the ability to answer any questions the recipient may have. The instructions to Form 1099 specify that the contact person's telephone number should be inserted in the "filer name and address area" of the form.**

These 10 steps are illustrated in comprehensive examples at the end of this chapter.

5. Taxpayer Bill of Rights 2

✎ **Key point: Congress enacted legislation in 1996 containing a number of provisions pertaining to payroll reporting requirements.**

In 1988 Congress enacted the first "Taxpayer Bill of Rights." This legislation provided taxpayers with a number of important protections. In 1996 Congress enacted a second Taxpayer Bill of Rights that builds on what was accomplished in 1988. The new law contains a number of provisions pertaining to payroll reporting requirements. The more important provisions are summarized below.

Abatement of penalty for failure to deposit payroll taxes. Section 6656 of the tax code imposes a penalty on employers that fail to deposit payroll taxes on time. The penalty is 2 percent of the amount of the underpayment if the deposit is late by less than 5 days; 5 percent if the deposit is late by more than 5 days but not more than 15 days; and 10 percent if the deposit is late by more than 15 days. The penalty goes to 15 percent if the deposit is not made within 10 days of the date of the first delinquency notice sent by the IRS.

TBOR2 provides that the IRS may waive these penalties with respect to an inadvertent failure to deposit any employment tax if: (a) the employer's net worth is less than $7 million; (b) the failure to deposit occurs during the first quarter that the employer was required to deposit any employment tax; and (c) the return for the employment tax was filed on or before the due date.

TBOR2 also provides that the IRS may abate any penalty for failure to make deposits for the first time an employer makes a deposit if it inadvertently sends the deposit to the IRS instead of to the required government depository (ordinarily a bank).

The House Ways and Means Committee prepared the following example to illustrate this provision:

☞ **Example.** *Sally Essex is the new volunteer treasurer of a San Francisco charity called the Child Evangelism Fellowship, which provides services to inner-city children. Earlier this year, the first time Ms. Essex submitted the organization's payroll taxes of $644.34, she mistakenly mailed Form 941 and the check to the IRS, rather than to the Federal Reserve Bank as required by law. As a result of this innocent slip-up, the organization was assessed a penalty of $64.43 (10 percent of the payroll tax deposit). Under the new law, the IRS would have authority to abate the penalty.*

Civil damages for filing fraudulent 1099 forms. TBOR2 permits employers who issue fraudulent 1099 or W-2 forms to be sued by the person who receives them. Damages are the greater of $5,000, or actual damages plus attorney's fees. A committee report contains the following observation regarding this provision:

The committee does not want to open the door to unwarranted or frivolous actions or abusive litigation practices. The committee is concerned, for example, about the possibility that an unfounded or frivolous action might be brought under this section by a current or former employee of an employer who is not pleased with one or more items that his or her current or former employer has included on the employee's Form W-2. Therefore, actions brought under this section will be subject to Rule 11 of the Federal Rules of Civil Procedure, relating to the imposition of sanctions in the case of unfounded or frivolous claims, to the same extent as other civil actions.

☞ **Example.** *A church loans $15,000 to Rev. B, its youth pastor, to assist him in making a down payment on a home. Rev. B signs a $15,000 promissory note with a 5-year term. After two years Rev. B leaves the church to accept another position. He still owes the church $14,000 (unpaid principal and accrued interest), but does not respond to several requests by the church for*

repayment. *The church informs Rev. B that if he does not respond, it will have no option but to declare the entire balance due in full and include it on his W-2 form for the year. The church receives no response, and accordingly it issues Rev. B a W-2 at the end of the year reporting his wages and the $14,000 unpaid note. Rev. B threatens to sue the church for civil damages under TBOR2. Rev. B has no recourse under TBOR2, since the church's W-2 was not fraudulent. If Rev. B sues, he risks being assessed "sanctions" for filing a frivolous lawsuit.*

IRS must investigate disputed W-2s and 1099 forms. TBOR2 provides that, in any court proceeding, if a taxpayer asserts a reasonable dispute with respect to any item of income reported on an information return (Form 1099 or Form W-2) filed by an employer and the taxpayer has fully cooperated with the IRS, then the government has the burden of proving the deficiency (in addition to the information return itself). Fully cooperating with the IRS includes (but is not limited to) the following: bringing the reasonable dispute over the item of income to the attention of the IRS within a reasonable period of time, and providing (within a reasonable period of time) access to and inspection of all witnesses, information, and documents within the control of the taxpayer (as reasonably requested by the IRS).

☞ **Example.** *A church employee is issued a W-2 that incorrectly reports certain items as income. The employee refuses to pay tax on her full income, and this results in an IRS audit. The case is eventually appealed to a federal court where she insists that her employer erroneously included various items as wages on her W-2. Under TBOR2, the government has the burden of proving the deficiency, and cannot rely on the W-2 form itself—if the employee has fully cooperated with the IRS.*

Penalty for failure to pay withheld payroll taxes. This provision is discussed in section A.1 of this chapter.

"Section 530." In the late 1960s, the IRS began vigorously challenging employer attempts to classify workers as self-employed rather than as employees. Predictably, employers complained about what was seen as overreaching by the IRS. Employers also were concerned about being assessed large penalties if the IRS successfully reclassified workers as employees. Congress responded with "section 530" of the Revenue Act of 1978. Section 530 was designed to provide employers with relief from hostile IRS attempts to reclassify workers from self-employed to employees. It specifies that an employer can treat a worker as self-employed for employment tax purposes so long as three conditions are met:

(1) the employer has always treated the worker as self-employed

(2) all tax forms filed by the employer (1099, 941, etc.) since 1978 are consistent with self-employed status of the worker

(3) the employer has *"no reasonable basis"* for not treating the individual as an employee"

Stated differently, an employer can treat a worker as self-employed so long as it has a reasonable basis for doing so (and has consistently treated the worker as self-employed). Section 530 provides that an employer has a *reasonable basis* for treating a worker as self-employed if its position is based on any of the following:

(1) published IRS rulings or court decisions

(2) past IRS audit practice with respect to the employer

(3) a long-standing recognized practice of a significant segment of the industry in which the worker is engaged, or

(4) any other reasonable basis for treating a worker as self-employed

✎ **Key point: Section 530 relieves employers of penalties that otherwise may apply because of their treatment of certain workers as self-employed rather than as employees. It does not directly apply to a worker's personal tax reporting. To illustrate, section 530 can be used by a church to avoid employment tax penalties that otherwise might apply as a result of treating certain workers as self-employed. But, section 530 cannot be used by those workers in defending their self-employed status in reporting their own federal taxes.**

A congressional report explaining section 530, and which is an authoritative guide to its meaning, states that section 530 is to be "construed liberally in favor of taxpayers." Remember that the purpose of section 530 was to protect employers from zealous attempts by the IRS to reclassify millions of workers as employees, thereby subjecting employers to substantial penalties for incorrectly treating workers as self-employed.

Predictably, the IRS immediately set about to avoid the protections that section 530 had established. First, it asserted that the protections of section 530 only apply after a determination has been made that a worker is an employee under the so-called "common law employee" test (see chapter 2 of this tax guide). The IRS has continued to apply this interpretation despite its rejection by several courts.

Second, the IRS narrowly interpreted the availability of employer relief based on prior IRS audit practice. Section 530 specifies that an employer will be permitted to treat workers as self-employed for employment tax purposes on the basis of "a past Internal Revenue Service audit of the [employer] in which there was no assessment attributable to the treatment (for employment tax purposes) of the individuals holding positions substantially similar to the position held by [the worker]." This language does not require the prior audit to have addressed the employment tax status of any of the employer's

workers, but this is how the IRS has interpreted it. And, not only must the prior audit have addressed workers' employment status, but the IRS must have concluded that the workers were self-employed!

Third, the IRS has narrowly interpreted the provision in section 530 permitting an employer to treat workers as self-employed if such a position is based on a "long-standing recognized practice of a significant segment of the industry" in which the worker is engaged. The IRS interpreted a "long-standing recognized practice" as one that dates back at least ten years, and it defined a "significant segment of the industry" in which a worker is engaged as at least 50 percent of an industry.

Fourth, the IRS took the position that employers always have the final burden of proof in establishing the self-employed status of a worker.

The Act directly responds to these IRS interpretations of section 530 in the following ways:

Prior determination of employee status. The Act rejects the IRS position that the protections of section 530 only apply after a determination has been made that a worker is an employee under the so-called "common law employee" test.

Prior IRS audit. The Act agrees with the IRS interpretation of this provision. The prior IRS audit must have addressed the correct reporting status of the same workers, or workers in "substantially similar" positions.

Long-standing recognized practice of a significant segment of an industry. The Act rejects both of the narrow IRS interpretations of section 530. It specifies that a "long-standing recognized practice" shall not be construed "as requiring the practice to have continued for more than ten years." It further specifies that "in no event shall the significant segment requirement . . . be construed to require a reasonable showing of the practice of more than 25 percent of the industry."

Burden of proof. The Act provides that if an employer establishes a "prima facie case" that it was reasonable to treat a worker as self-employed on the basis of precedent (IRS or court rulings), prior audit practice, or a long-standing practice of a significant industry segment, then the burden of proof shifts to the IRS to prove that the worker is an employee. In order to shift the burden of proof to the IRS the employer must fully cooperate with reasonable requests by the IRS for information relevant to its treatment of the worker as self-employed.

✎ **Key point: What is a "prima facie case"? One court decision quoted in the committee report to the Act described a prima facie case as follows: "[T]his threshold burden is relatively low, and can be met with any reasonableness showing. Once the taxpayer has made this prima facie showing, the burden then shifts to the IRS to verify or refute the taxpayer's explanation." Mc-**

Clellan v. United States, 900 F. Supp. 101 (E.D. Mich. 1995).

Other provisions. The Act contains a few other provisions that will be of interest to church leaders.

(1) It clarifies that if an employer prospectively changes its treatment of workers from self-employed to employees for employment tax purposes, such a change cannot be considered in evaluating whether or not the workers were employees or self-employed for prior years.

(2) The IRS must, at or before the commencement of an audit involving worker classification issues, provide the employer with written notice of the provisions of section 530. However, a committee report explaining the Act contains the following clarification: "The conferees recognize that, in many cases, the portion of an audit involving worker classification issues will not arise until after the examination of the [employer] begins. In that case, the notice need only be given at the time the worker classification issue is first raised with the [employer]."

✎ **Key point: The amendments to section 530 take effect on January 1, 1997.**

☞ *Example. A church treats its ministers as self-employed for federal income tax reporting purposes. Section 530 will have limited relevance to such a church, since even if the IRS reclassifies the ministers as employees this will not result in the assessment of any penalties against the church since ministers' wages are exempt from income tax withholding and are not subject to FICA taxes even if the ministers are employees for income tax reporting purposes (ministers are self-employed for social security even if they are employees for income tax reporting purposes, and they pay their income taxes using the estimated quarterly tax procedure unless they elect voluntary tax withholding).*

☞ *Example. A minister reports his income taxes as a self-employed person rather than as an employee. He is audited by the IRS and his self-employed status is challenged. The minister will not be able to rely on section 530, since it only provides relief to employers from employment tax penalties that might otherwise apply because of their treatment of certain workers as self-employed rather than as employees. It offers no relief to individual taxpayers.*

☞ *Example. Approximately 25 percent of all churches continue to treat ministers as self-employed for federal income tax reporting purposes. A self-employed minister is audited, and the IRS challenges the minister's self-employed status. The minister will not be able to rely on the "significant segment" defense, since it only protects employers from employment tax penalties as a result of the classification of certain workers as self-employed.*

☞ *Example. A church has 3 ministers on staff, and has treated them as self-employed for at least 10 years. One of these ministers is audited, and the IRS challenges the minister's self-employed status. The minister will not be able to rely on the "long-standing recognized practice" defense, since it only protects employers from employment tax penalties as a result of the classification of certain workers as self-employed.*

☞ *Example. A church has treated its 3 custodians as self-employed for the past 20 years. The IRS attempts to reclassify the custodians as employees. The church can rely on the "long-standing recognized practice" provision of section 530 to defend against any employment tax penalties related to incorrectly treating the custodians as self-employed for employment tax purposes, so long as it can establish that this represents the practice of a significant segment of the industry in which the custodians were engaged.*

Including telephone numbers on 1099 forms. All 1099 forms issued after 1996 must contain the name, address, and telephone number of a "contact person" who can answer questions the recipient may have about the form. The purpose of this new requirement is to give recipients of 1099 forms the ability to contact a person who was responsible for preparing the form and who presumably has the ability to answer any questions the recipient may have.

The instructions to Form 1099 specify that the contact person's telephone number should be inserted in the "filer name and address area" of the form. In other words, the telephone number should accompany the church's name and address in the first box on the form.

✎ **Key point. For many churches, the "contact person" will be the church treasurer. This means that all 1099 forms issued by the church must contain the name, address, and telephone number of the treasurer. In other churches, the contact person will be a business administrator.**

B. Social Security Taxes

✎ **Key point: federal law allowed churches that had nonminister employees as of July of 1984 to exempt themselves from the employer's share of FICA taxes by filing a Form 8274 with the IRS by October 30, 1984. Many churches did so. The effect of such an exemption is to treat all nonminister church employees as self-employed for social security purposes. Such employees must pay the self-employment tax (just like clergy).**

Since the beginning of the social security program in 1937, the employees of churches and most other nonprofit organizations were exempted from mandatory coverage. The exemption was designed to encourage nonprofit organizations by freeing them from an additional tax burden that they ordinarily could not pass along to customers through price increases.

Churches and other nonprofit organizations were permitted to waive their exemption by filing Forms SS-15 and SS-15a with the IRS.

In 1983, Congress repealed the exemption for calendar years beginning with 1984. The repeal of the exemption was controversial for many church leaders because it required churches to report and pay the employer's share of FICA taxes. This "tax on churches" was denounced by some as a violation of the constitutional principle of separation of church and state.

A limited exemption. In the Tax Reform Act of 1984, Congress responded to such criticism by again amending the Social Security Act, this time to give churches a one-time irrevocable election to exempt themselves from social security coverage if they were opposed for religious reasons to the payment of the employer's share of FICA taxes and if they filed an election (Form 8274—reproduced at the end of this chapter) with the IRS prior to the deadline for filing the first required quarterly employer's tax return (Form 941) after July 17, 1984 on which the *employer's* share of FICA taxes is reported. Since a Form 941 is due on the last day of the month following the end of each calendar quarter (i.e., April 30, July 31, October 31, January 31), the election for churches in existence as of July of 1984 and having at least one nonminister employee was October 30, 1984 (the day before the deadline for filing Form 941 for the quarter ending September 30). Churches either not in existence as of July of 1984, or not having nonminister employees at that time, have until the day prior to the deadline for their first Form 941 to file an election (Form 8274).

To illustrate, a church organized in 1960, and hiring its first nonminister employee (a secretary) on September 1, 1997, had until October 30, 1997, to file the Form 8274. It must be emphasized that there is no deadline until a church has at least one nonminister employee, since the deadline corresponds to the next filing date of a church's quarterly tax return reporting the employer's share of social security taxes, and no tax or return is due until a church has nonminister employees.

What about a church with only one employee—its minister? As noted in the preceding section, the preferred practice would be for the church to file quarterly 941 forms reporting the minister's compensation, even though no taxes are withheld. But would the church thereby be prevented from filing a Form 8274 at a later date in the event that it hires nonminister employees (on the ground that it already has submitted 941 forms and accordingly the deadline for filing Form 8274 has expired)? The answer is no, since Code section 3121(w) defines the deadline for filing Form 8274 as anytime prior to the date of a church's first Form 941 "for the tax imposed under section 3111." Section 3111 pertains to the employer's share of FICA taxes, and therefore a church with no nonminister employees does not affect the deadline for filing a Form 8274 by filing 941 Forms for its minister.

A timely election relieves a church of the obligation to pay the employer's share of FICA taxes (7.65% of an employee's wages in 1997 and 1998), and relieves each nonminister employee of the obligation to pay the employee's share of FICA taxes (an additional 7.65% of wages in 1997 and 1998). However, the employee is not relieved of all social security tax liability. On the contrary, the nonminister employees of an electing church are required to report and pay their social security taxes as self-employed individuals (the "self-employment tax") if their annual compensation exceeds $108.28. And, this tax is significantly greater than the employee's share of FICA taxes. In 1998 for example the self-employment tax is 15.3% of net self-employment earnings. Therefore, a church employee receiving a salary of $10,000 in 1998 would pay $765 in FICA taxes if his or her church did not file an election on Form 8274 (the church would pay an additional $765). However, if the church filed the election to exempt itself from FICA taxes, the following consequences occur: (1) the church pays no FICA taxes; (2) the employee pays no FICA taxes; and (3) the employee must report and pay a self-employment tax liability of $1,530 (an additional $765 in taxes). However, the self-employment tax is offset by an income tax deduction of half the self-employment tax, and also by a similar deduction in computing self-employment taxes (explained fully in chapter 9).

The employees of an electing church ordinarily will be required to use the estimated tax procedure (Form 1040-ES) to report and pay their estimated self-employment tax in quarterly installments. Alternatively, an employee of an electing church can request that an additional amount be withheld from his or her wages each pay period to cover the estimated self-employment tax liability. The church simply withholds an additional amount from each paycheck to cover an employee's estimated self-employment tax liability for the year, and then reports this additional amount as additional *income tax* (not "FICA" tax) withheld on its quarterly 941 forms. The excess income tax withheld is a credit against tax that each employee may claim on his or her federal income tax return (Form 1040, line 54), and it in effect is applied against an employee's self-employment tax liability. A similar withholding arrangement has been approved by the IRS with respect to a minister-employee's self-employment tax (see IRS Publication 517). Unless an employee makes such a request, a church that has elected to exempt itself from the employer's share of FICA taxes has no obligation to withhold social security taxes from the wages of its employees.

Many churches and church employees consider this situation unfair. Churches are free to exempt themselves from social security taxes, but only at the cost of increasing the tax liability of their employees. In response, many electing churches have increased the salary of their employees to compensate for the increase in taxes. Of course, this leaves the church in essentially the same position as if it had not elected to be exempt—it in effect is paying social security taxes "indirectly." This dilemma, argued a church in Pennsylvania, unconstitutionally restricts the religious freedom of churches by forcing them (contrary to their religious convictions) to divert church resources away from religious and charitable functions in order to increase employee compensation (and thereby "indirectly" pay the social security tax). A federal appeals court rejected this contention. The court based its ruling on a 1982 Supreme Court decision that upheld the imposition of the social security tax to employees of Amish farmers though this directly violated the farmers' religious beliefs. The Supreme Court had observed that "tax systems could not function if denominations were allowed to challenge the tax systems because tax payments were spent in a manner that violates their religious belief." It concluded that the broad public interest in the maintenance of the federal tax systems was of such a high order that religious belief in conflict with the payment of the taxes provides no constitutional basis for resisting them. The appeals court found this precedent controlling in resolving the challenge to social security coverage of church employees. The appeals court also rejected the church's argument that the taxation of church employees violates the first amendment's nonestablishment of religion clause by creating an "excessive entanglement" between church and state. It also rejected the claim that the Internal Revenue Code was impermissibly discriminatory in granting clergy an exemption from social security coverage but not churches or church employees. *Bethel Baptist Church v. United States, 822 F.2d 1334 (3rd Cir. 1987).* Beginning in 1990, churches that elected to exempt themselves from the employer's share of FICA taxes will have less need to increase the compensation of nonminister employees, since such persons are now entitled to deduct half their self-employment taxes for income tax and self-employment tax purposes (this is supposed to offset the disadvantages of self-employed persons paying a self-employment tax at the combined FICA tax rate of 15.3%). See chapter 9 for details.

Churches that file a timely election application remain subject to income tax withholding and reporting requirements with respect to all nonminister employees and to ministers who have requested voluntary withholding. They must continue to issue W-2 forms to all nonminister employees and to ministers who are treated as employees for income tax purposes. In addition, they must file the employer's quarterly tax return (Form 941) with the IRS. The law specifies that the IRS can revoke a church's exemption from social security coverage if the church fails to issue W-2 forms for a period of two years or more to nonminister employees or ministers who report their federal income taxes as employees, and disregards an IRS request to furnish employees with such forms for the period during which its election has been in effect.

Only churches that are opposed "for religious reasons" to the payment of social security taxes are eligible for the exemption. Apparently, a local church will qualify for the exemption if it is opposed for religious reasons to the payment of social security taxes even if it is affiliated with a religious denomination that has no official position on the subject. Churches, conventions or association of churches, and elementary and secondary schools that are controlled, operated, or principally supported by a church are all eligible for the exemption. "Qualified church-controlled organizations" also are eligible for the exemption. Such organizations include most church-controlled tax-exempt organizations described in section 501(c)(3) of the Internal Revenue Code. See chapter 10, section E, for a full explanation of this term.

A number of churches having nonminister employees (e.g., an office secretary) apparently do not know whether or not they have elected to exempt themselves from the employer's share of social security (FICA) taxes by filing a timely Form 8274. Churches that filed a timely election but that nevertheless paid all employment taxes due from the effective date of their election through December 31, 1986 (a fairly common practice by churches that could not remember if they ever filed the election) are treated as if they never filed the election. *Internal Revenue News Release IR-87-94.*

Revoking the exemption. Churches that have elected to exempt themselves from the employer's share of FICA taxes (by filing a timely Form 8274) can revoke their exemption. Temporary regulations issued by the Treasury Department specify that churches can revoke their exemption (starting with any calendar quarter after December 31, 1986) by filing a Form 941 (employer's quarterly tax return) accompanied by full payment of social security taxes for that quarter. To illustrate, if a church with three employees elects in May of 1998 to revoke its previous election to be exempt from social security taxes, it should simply submit a Form 941 on or by July 31, 1998 (the deadline for filing a Form 941 for the second calendar quarter) along with the applicable FICA taxes for that quarter. Of course, if a church revokes its exemption, nonminister employees are no longer treated as self-employed for social security purposes and accordingly should no longer file quarterly estimated tax payments (their FICA taxes will be withheld from their wages).

The new social security reporting procedures. For many years the Social Security Administration has sent a "personal earnings and benefit estimate statement" (PEBES) to any person who requested one. This statement displays the person's earnings based on either self-employment income or information provided by employers on W-2 forms. The statement also provides an estimate of benefits that the person may be eligible for both now and in the future. Unfortunately, few workers ever request this information and this has led to many undetected problems. Here are some common examples:

• A nonminister church employee's social security benefits are reduced because the church failed to report one or more taxable fringe benefits on the employee's W-2 forms. To illustrate, a church fails to report the value of the personal use of a church-provided car as income on an employee's W-2. By understating the employee's wages subject to social security (FICA) taxes, the church is reducing the employee's social security benefits which are based on those earnings.

• A nonminister church employee's social security benefits are reduced because the church under-reported the wages paid to the employee on the W-2 forms it issued. To illustrate, a church paid an employee $20,000 in 1997, but it inadvertently reports $18,000 as wages on the employee's W-2. This clerical error will cause a reduction in the earnings reported to the Social Security Administration and this in turn may cause a reduction in the employee's social security benefits.

• A church incorrectly reports an employee's social security number on a W-2 form. This will prevent wages from being credited to the employee's record. Uncredited earnings can affect the employee's future benefits.

• A church incorrectly reports an employee's name on a W-2 form. To illustrate, a female employee is married and the church begins reporting her wage information (on Form W-2) under her new name. If the employee has not reported her name change to the Social Security Administration, then this can prevent wages from being credited to the employee's record. Uncredited earnings can affect the employee's future benefits.

⊃ **Tip. Church employees should be encouraged to immediately report to the Social Security Administration any change in their name. This will ensure that all wages are properly credited to the employee's record. Reporting a name change is easy. The employee simply submits a Form SS-5 (application for social security card) to the Social Security Administration. Church treasurers may want to keep some of these forms on hand, and give them to employees who have a name change. You can order a supply by calling 1-800-772-1213.**

⊃ **Observation. Many employees incorrectly assume that notifying their employer of a name change is all they need to do. Notifying an employer does not change the records of the Social Security Administration, and mismatches will occur until the government is notified.**

• A minister fails to include the fair rental value of a parsonage as earnings subject to the self-employment tax. Remember that all ministers are self-employed for social security purposes with respect to their ministerial income. As a result they pay the self-employment tax (the social security tax for self-employed workers) rather than FICA taxes (the social security tax for employers and employees).

• A minister fails to include a housing allowance as earnings subject to the self-employment tax.

Unfortunately, these kinds of errors are common, and they can disqualify workers from social security coverage or cause a needless reduction in benefits. Often, retired workers are not even aware that their benefits have been reduced because of one or more of these errors. Obviously, the solution to these problems is easy. The government should recognize that few workers ever take the time to obtain and review a PEBES statement from the Social Security Administration. The Social Security Administration should simply begin sending these statements automatically to all workers and encourage them to review the information for accuracy. This is exactly what Congress has required the Social Security Administration to do. Church treasurers need to be aware of the new rules, and be prepared for the questions they may soon receive.

Here are the new reporting procedures in a nutshell:

• *October 1995.* Beginning in October of 1995 and each year thereafter the Social Security Administration will send a PEBES statement to persons who reach age 60 during the year.

• *January 2000.* By January of the year 2000, some 123 million eligible workers age 25 and older will receive PEBES statements each year.

Each PEBES statement provides a year-by-year display of a worker's earnings as either a self-employed person or an employee, provides the worker with an estimate of future benefits, and asks the worker to carefully inspect the statement for errors. While many workers will contact the Social Security Administration directly if they have questions, many will be contacting their employers directly.

What steps can church treasurers take in response to the new reporting procedures? Consider the following:

Step 1: education

Church treasurers should inform any worker who attains age 60 during the current year that he or she will be receiving a PEBES statement from the Social Security Administration. Beginning in the year 2000, any worker who is 25 years of age or older will receive a PEBES statement. One way to inform workers is to provide them with an appropriate letter. Here is a sample letter prepared by the Social Security Administration (with appropriate editing):

[Employer's name] matches your Social Security and Medicare taxes dollar-for-dollar. This investment serves as a base for your retirement planning when you combine it with savings, in individual retirement account, or investments. To help you plan for your financial future, the Social Security Administration (SSA) can provide you with a Personal Earnings and Benefit Estimate Statement (PEBES) showing the earnings recorded under your Social Security number (SSN). The statement also provides an estimate of the Social Security benefits you and your family may qualify for now and in the future.

If you are age 60 or older and are not already receiving Social Security benefits, SSA will automatically send you a PEBES each year. By the year 2000, 123 million eligible individuals age 25 and older will receive an earnings statement each year.

Once you receive a statement, please carefully check the earnings to make sure they match your records. You don't need to do anything unless you believe the earnings information is incorrect. If the error involves recent earnings at your current job, report the discrepancy to Social Security's toll-free number, 1-800-772-1213. When you call, be sure to have your records of the correct earnings handy—such as W-2s, pay stubs, and tax returns. You should also call the toll-free number to report an SSA from properly crediting your earnings record which could affect future Social Security benefits payable to you and your family.

Step 2: corrections

Church workers who receive the PEBES statements may have questions for their church treasurers. In some cases errors will be detected. If it is clear that an error has occurred, church treasurers should do the following:

• *incorrect earnings.* If the church issued a W-2 form for a prior year that failed to report the correct amount of wages subject to social security taxes, then the church should file a Form W-2c (a corrected W-2) with the Social Security Administration. The Form W-2c reports the correct amounts of wages and social security taxes.

• *missing earnings.* If an employee was not issued a W-2 in a prior year, then a Form W-2 (original Copy A) should be filed for the missing year.

✎ **Key point: a church that files a W-2c form to correct a W-2 form that underreported an employee's earnings for a prior year may be responsible for paying back taxes plus interest.**

• *miscellaneous.* Here are some helpful hints when preparing correcting W-2 or W-2c forms: (1) Send W-2 and W-2c forms (with an accompanying W-3 or W-3c form) to the Social Security Administration, Data Operations Center, Wilkes-Barre, Pennsylvania 18769. (2) Never use a W-2 form to correct a previously submitted W-2 form. Use a Form W-2c instead—with a separate form for each year needing correction. (3) If the only correction needed is to an employee's name or social security number, file *only* Form W-2c (*not* a W-3c) and have the employee contact the Social Security Administration to obtain an SS-5 form to change his or her name on the government's records. However, if you need to correct the money amounts on a previous Form W-2 then a Form W-3c must be filed along with a Form W-2c. (4) If incorrect information reported on prior W-2 forms was also incorrectly reported on the church's 941 forms submitted to the IRS, then you may have to correct the corresponding 941 forms by filing a Form 941c with the IRS. (5) Be sure the church's employer identification number reported on your W-2c and W-3c forms (and 941c if applicable) is correct, and that you reported the same number on all of these forms.

Step 3: precautions

There are a number of steps that church treasurers can take to reduce the chance of reporting incorrect information on an employee's W-2 forms. Consider the following:

• *review social security cards.* Review the social security cards of new workers and be sure that church payroll records correctly report each worker's name and social security number.

• *reconcile W-2 and 941 forms.* Add up the total wages reported on your quarterly 941 forms for the year and compare this amount to the wages reported on all of the W-2 forms issued by the church.

• *the correct treatment of clergy.* Remember that clergy are self-employed for social security purposes with respect to their ministerial income. As a result, they pay self-employment taxes rather than FICA taxes—even though they may report their income taxes as employees. This rule has important applications that some church treasurers miss. For example, it means that no amount should be reported in boxes 3 (social security wages), 4 (social security tax withheld), 5 (Medicare wages and tips), and 6 (Medicare tax withheld) on a minister's Form W-2. A similar rule applies to nonminister employees who are employed by churches that have exempted themselves from the employer's share of FICA taxes by filing a timely Form 8274 with the IRS. Such employees, like clergy, are treated as self-employed with regard to their church compensation.

• *name changes.* Encourage workers who change their names to promptly notify the Social Security Administration. Provide them with an SS-5 form to simplify the process.

• *annual check of payroll records.* Each year have employees check the accuracy of their names and social security numbers on the church's payroll records.

C. Unemployment Taxes

Congress enacted the Federal Unemployment Tax Act (FUTA) in 1935 in response to the widespread unemployment that accompanied the great depression. The Act called for a cooperative federal-state program of benefits to unemployed workers. It is financed by a federal excise tax on wages paid by employers in covered employment. An employer, however, is allowed a credit of up to 90% of the federal tax for "contributions" paid to a state fund established under a federally approved state unemployment compensation law. All fifty states have employment security laws implementing the federal mandatory minimum standards of coverage. States are free to expand their coverage beyond the federal minimum.

From 1960 to 1970, the Act excluded from the definition of covered employment all "service performed in the employ of a religious, charitable, educational, or other organization described in section 501(c)(3) which is exempt from income tax under

353

section 501(a)." A 1970 amendment in effect narrowed this broad exemption of nonprofit organizations by conditioning federal approval of state compensation plans on the coverage of all nonprofit organizations except those specifically exempted. The Act was then amended to exempt service performed

(1) in the employ of (A) a church or convention or association of churches, or (B) an organization which is operated primarily for religious purposes and which is operated, supervised, controlled, or principally supported by a church or convention or association of churches; (2) a duly ordained, commissioned, or licensed minister of a church in the exercise of his ministry or by a member of a religious order in the exercise of duties required by such order; (3) in the employ of a school which is not an institution of higher education. *IRC 3309(b).*

The Act continues the exemption of "service performed in the employ of a religious . . . organization" from the federal tax. Thus, while the exemption of religious organizations under federal law remains broad, the requirement imposed on states has been significantly narrowed.

In 1976, Congress eliminated the exemption of services performed "in the employ of a school which is not an institution of higher education" from the categories of employment that could be exempted from coverage under state programs without loss of federal approval.

In 1978 the Secretary of the Department of Labor announced that the elimination of this exemption required mandatory coverage of all the employees of church-related schools. This ruling was followed by many states, prompting a number of lawsuits.

In 1981, the United States Supreme Court ruled that the elimination of service performed "in the employ of a school which is not an institution of higher education" did not require the coverage of the employees of unincorporated church-related schools, since the continuing exemption of church employees was broad enough to cover the employees of unincorporated church-controlled elementary and secondary schools. *St. Martin Evangelical Lutheran Church v. South Dakota, 451 U.S. 772 (1981).* The Court concluded that the employees of separately incorporated church schools are exempt from coverage only if the school is operated primarily for religious purposes and is operated, supervised, controlled, or principally supported by a church or convention or association of churches.

In summary, the following activities ordinarily are exempt from state unemployment taxes:

1. Service performed in the employ of a church, a convention or association of churches, or an organization that is operated primarily for religious purposes and that is operated, supervised, controlled, or principally supported by a church or convention or association of churches. The exemption is not limited to employees performing strictly "religious" duties.

2. Service performed in the employ of an unincorporated church-controlled elementary or secondary school.

3. Service performed in the employ of an incorporated religious elementary or secondary school if it is operated primarily for religious purposes and is operated, supervised, controlled, or principally supported by a church or a convention or association of churches.

4. Service performed by a duly ordained, commissioned, or licensed minister of a church in the exercise of his ministry or by a member of a religious order in the exercise of duties required by such order.

❖ **New in 1997. Congress enacted legislation that expanded the list of exceptions to include work performed in an elementary or secondary school that is operated primarily for religious purposes, even if it is not operated, supervised, controlled, or principally supported by a church or a convention or association of churches.**

✎ **Key point: some churches that operate private schools have separately incorporated them in order to reduce the church's risk of liability. Unfortunately, separate incorporation will have little effect on the church's liability for the obligations of the school—unless the church relinquishes control of the school. If a church is willing to relinquish control, then the school becomes largely independent. This has a number of consequences, including the following: (1) liability of the church is reduced; and (2) employees of the school are not covered by federal or state unemployment law in most states.**

Oregon Supreme Court ruling. In a highly controversial decision the Oregon Supreme Court ruled in 1989 that all religious organizations, including churches, are subject to state unemployment taxes. *Employment Division v. Rogue Valley Youth for Christ, 770 P.2d 588 (Ore. 1989).* As noted above, the Federal Unemployment Tax Act contains a set of guidelines that a state's unemployment tax program must meet in order to avoid federal unemployment taxes. Although compliance with the federal guidelines is optional, states normally comply in order to avoid subjecting local employers to double taxation (under both federal and state law). One of the federal guidelines with which states must comply exempts services performed in the employ of a church, a convention or association of churches, or certain church-controlled organizations from unemployment tax. There is no exemption for religious organizations not affiliated with a church or convention or association of churches. Accordingly, under FUTA, states *must* subject non-church-affiliated religious organizations to state unemployment tax or risk losing their exemption from federal unemployment tax.

However, the Oregon Supreme Court previously had ruled that the state could *not* make distinctions between church-affiliated and non-church-affiliated religious organizations, since such a distinction "contravenes the equality among pluralistic faiths and kinds of religious organizations embodied in the Oregon constitution's guarantees of religious freedom." How should these conflicting provisions be reconciled? The Employment Division of the Oregon Department of Human Resources (the agency responsible for enforcing the Oregon unemployment law) took the position that it had to assess unemployment taxes against *all* religious organizations—including churches—in order to keep Oregon in compliance with the FUTA guidelines and the Oregon constitution. The Oregon Supreme Court agreed. It emphasized that in order to satisfy the state constitution's requirement of "treating all religious organizations similarly" it had two options: (1) completely exempt all religious organizations (whether or not church-affiliated), or (2) eliminate the exemption of all religious organizations (including churches). The court elected the second alternative, since the other option would have led to a broader exemption then permitted by FUTA and accordingly would have subjected Oregon employers to double unemployment tax under both state and federal law.

The court acknowledged that taxing all religious organizations "creates potential constitutional problems involving the free exercise of religion." However, it concluded that its decision did not violate the constitutional guaranty of religious freedom. The Oregon Supreme Court's decision remains an unfortunate precedent that has not been followed by any other court.

New York. A New York state court ruled that a state law exempting "persons employed at a place of religious worship" from unemployment benefits *did not violate the first amendment's "nonestablishment of religion" clause. Claim of Klein, 563 N.Y.S.2d 132 (Sup. Ct. 1990).* A teacher who had been employed by a religious school sought unemployment benefits. Benefits were denied on the ground that she had been employed by a religious school. The teacher claimed that the state law exempting religious employees from unemployment coverage was unconstitutional. A state appeals court disagreed. It applied a 3-part test announced in 1971 by the United States Supreme Court. Under this test, a law that appears to favor religion will be struck down unless it satisfies 3 conditions—it has a secular purpose, it has a primary effect that neither advances nor inhibits religion, and it does not create an "excessive entanglement" between church and state. The court concluded that the New York law exempting religious employees from unemployment benefits satisfied this test. It further noted that the Supreme Court has ruled that "government policies with secular objectives may incidentally benefit religion." Such was the case here.

Rhode Island. A federal court in Rhode Island ruled that the exemption of churches from unemployment tax did not violate the first amendment's nonestablishment of religion clause. *Rojas v. Fitch, 928 F. Supp. 155 (D.R.I. 1996).* The Salvation Army dismissed an employee for budgetary reasons. The employee applied for unemployment benefits, and was informed that she was not eligible since her former employer was a religious organization that was exempt from unemployment tax. The employee filed a lawsuit claiming that the exemption of religious organizations from the unemployment law violated the first amendment. A federal court disagreed in an important decision that reaffirms the historic exemption of churches from unemployment taxes. The court applied the United States Supreme Court's so-called *Lemon* test in determining whether the exemption of churches from the Rhode Island unemployment law constituted an impermissible establishment of religion. Under this test, first announced in a 1971 decision *(Lemon v. Kurtzman)*, a law challenged as an establishment of religion will be valid only if it satisfies the following three conditions—a secular purpose, a primary effect that neither advances nor inhibits religion, and no excessive entanglement between church and state. The court concluded that all of these tests were met.

D. Form 990 (Annual Information Returns)

"Information returns" are financial reports that provide information to the IRS other than an amount of tax due. Some common types of information returns have already been discussed in this chapter (Forms W-2, 1099, and 941). This section will describe another type of information return that must be filed annually by certain kinds of tax-exempt organizations.

Section 6033 of the Internal Revenue Code requires every organization that is exempt from federal income taxes to file an annual return (Form 990) with the IRS. Form 990 consists of more than one hundred questions requesting detailing information about the finances, services, and administration of the exempt organization. However, section 6033 exempts several organizations from the reporting requirements, including:

(1) a church, an interchurch organization of local units of a church, a convention or association of churches, an integrated auxiliary of a church (such as a men's or women's organization, religious school, missions society, or youth group), and certain church-controlled organizations *(see Revenue Procedure 86-23)*

(2) a school below college level affiliated with a church (or operated by a religious order)

(3) a mission society sponsored by or affiliated with one or more churches or church denominations, if more than one-half of the society's activities are conducted in, or directed at persons in, foreign countries

(4) an exclusively religious activity of any religious order

(5) a religious or apostolic organization described in section 501(d) of the Code

(6) an exempt organization whose annual gross receipts are normally $25,000 or less

Some members of Congress are suggesting that churches (and most of the other currently exempt organizations mentioned above) be required to file 990 forms each year as a means of avoiding financial impropriety and fraud. At this time, such efforts are merely suggestions.

E. Proof of Racial Nondiscrimination

Churches and other religious organizations that operate, supervise, or control a private school must file a certificate of racial nondiscrimination (Form 5578) each year with the IRS. The certificate is due by the 15th day of the fifth month following the end of the organization's fiscal year. This is *May 15th* of the following year for organizations that operate on a calendar year basis. This means that the Form 5578 for 1997 is due May 15, 1998.

A "private school" is defined as an educational organization that normally maintains a regular faculty and curriculum and normally has a regularly enrolled body of pupils or students in attendance at the place where its educational activities are regularly conducted. The term includes primary, secondary, preparatory, or high schools, and colleges and universities, whether operated as a separate legal entity or an activity of a church.

✎ **Key point: the term "school" also includes preschools, and this is what makes the reporting requirement relevant for many churches. As many as 25 percent of all churches operate a preschool program. Private religious schools that are not affiliated with or controlled by a church also must file the form.**

Form 5578 is easy to complete. A church official simply identifies the church and the school, and certifies that the school has "satisfied the applicable requirements of section 4.01 through 4.05 of Revenue Procedure 75-50." This reference is to the following requirements:

• The school has a statement in its charter, bylaws, or other governing instrument, or in a resolution of its governing body, that it has a racially nondiscriminatory policy toward students.

• The school has a statement of its racially nondiscriminatory policy toward students in all its brochures and catalogs dealing with student admissions, programs, and scholarships.

• The school makes its racially nondiscriminatory policy known to all segments of the general community served by the school through the publication of a notice of its racially nondiscriminatory policy at least annually in a newspaper of general circulation or through utilization of the broadcast media. However, such notice is not required if one or more exceptions apply. These include: (1) During the preceding three years the enrollment consists of students at least 75 percent of whom are members of the sponsoring church or religious denomination and the school publicizes its nondis-

criminatory policy in religious periodicals distributed in the community; (2) the school draws its students from local communities and follows a racially nondiscriminatory policy toward students and demonstrates that it follows a racially nondiscriminatory policy by showing that it currently enrolls students of racial minority groups in meaningful numbers.

• The school can demonstrate that all scholarships or other comparable benefits are offered on a racially nondiscriminatory basis.

Filing the certificate of racial nondiscrimination is one of most commonly ignored federal reporting requirements. Churches that operate a private school (including a preschool), as well as independent schools, may obtain copies of Form 5578 by calling the IRS forms number (1-800-829-3676).

A sample Form 5578 is reproduced at the end of this chapter.

F. Application for Recognition of Tax-Exempt Status (Form 1023)

Before 1969, there was no legal requirement that an organization file with the IRS an application for tax-exempt status. Rather, an organization was automatically exempt if it met the requirements set forth in section 501(c)(3) of the Code. In general, those requirements are as follows: (1) the organization is organized exclusively for exempt purposes (e.g., religious, charitable, educational) purposes; (2) the organization is operated exclusively for exempt purposes; (3) none of the organization's net earnings inures to the benefit of any private individuals; (4) the organization does not engage in substantial efforts to influence legislation; and (5) the organization does not intervene or participate in political campaigns. Although many organizations voluntarily applied for IRS recognition of exempt status by filing a Form 1023 (Application for Recognition of Exemption under Section 501(c)(3) of the Internal Revenue Code), many did not.

The Tax Reform Act of 1969 added section 508 to the Code. This section stipulated that after October 9, 1969, no organization, with a few exceptions, would be treated as exempt unless it gave notice to the IRS, in the manner prescribed by regulation, that it was applying for recognition of exempt status under section 501(c)(3). This is commonly referred to as the "508(a) notice." The income tax regulations state that the 508(a) notice is given by submitting a properly completed Form 1023 to the appropriate IRS district director.

Section 508(c) and the income tax regulations state that the following organizations are exempted from the 508(a) notice requirement and therefore are not required to file a Form 1023 to be exempt from federal income tax:

1. Churches, interchurch organizations of local units of a church, conventions and associations of churches, or integrated auxiliaries of a church, such

as a men's or women's organization, religious seminary, mission society, or youth group.

2. Any organization that is not a private foundation and the gross receipts of which in each taxable year are normally not more than $5,000.

3. Subordinate organizations covered by a group exemption letter.

The recognition of the exempt status of an organization without the need for complying with the section 508(a) notice requirement of course assumes that all of the prerequisites contained in section 501(c)(3) of the Code have been satisfied.

The IRS maintains that although such organizations are not required to file a Form 1023 to be exempt from federal income taxes or to receive tax-deductible charitable contributions, they may "find it advantageous to obtain recognition of exemption." IRS Publication 557. Presumably, such organizations might voluntarily wish to obtain IRS recognition of tax-exempt status in order to assure contributors who itemize their deductions that donations will be tax deductible.

The IRS publishes a cumulative listing (Publication 78) of organizations that have been determined to be exempt from federal income tax, contributions to which are tax-deductible. Contributions made to an organization whose name does not appear in Publication 78 may be questioned by the IRS, in which case the contributor would have to substantiate the deductibility of his or her contributions by demonstrating that the donee met the requirements of section 501(c)(3) and was exempt from the notice requirements. Similarly, some potential contributors may be reluctant to contribute to a religious organization not listed in Publication 78.

Group exemptions. Recognition of exemption under section 501(c)(3) may be obtained on a group basis for "subordinate organizations" affiliated with and under the supervision or control of a "central organization." This procedure relieves each of the subordinates covered by a group exemption of the necessity of filing an individual application for recognition of exemption. The group exemption procedure has been used by many religious denominations to obtain recognition of the exempt status of each affiliated church and agency. The procedure is set forth in Revenue Procedure 80-27. Unfortunately, the current group exemption procedure technically is available only to "connectional" or "hierarchical" church organizations consisting of a "central organization" that exerts "general supervision or control" over "subordinate" churches and church agencies. There are many religious denominations, however, that exert little if any "general supervision or control" over "subordinate" churches. Up until now, these "congregational" church organizations have had to construe the group exemption requirements very loosely in order to obtain the benefits of a group exemption. Many have done so. The current group exemption procedure, granting favored status only to connectional church organizations, is suspect under the Supreme Court's interpretation of the first amendment's nonestablishment of religion clause. In 1982, the Court ruled that "when we are presented with a . . . law granting a denominational preference, our precedents demand that we treat the law as suspect and that we apply strict scrutiny in adjudging its constitutionality." *Larson v. Valente, 102 S. Ct. 1673 (1982).* The Court concluded that any law granting a denominational preference must be "invalidated unless it is closely fitted to further that interest." There is no conceivable governmental interest that would justify the government's stated preference for connectional church organizations in the present group exemption procedure. This issue is more than one of administrative convenience, since a congregational church organization that is forced to conform itself to the current "connectional" group exemption procedure may increase thereby its legal liability for the misconduct and improprieties of affiliated churches and agencies because of its representation that it exercises "general supervision and control" over affiliated organizations. Such a representation could serve as a possible basis of legal liability unless the denomination could demonstrate that it pursued the group exemption as a matter of expedience and that it construed the "supervision or control" language very loosely. Courts should recognize the dilemma that congregational church organizations face under the current group exemption procedure, and reject any attempt to use their compliance with the procedure as a basis for increased legal liability for the wrongs of affiliated organizations. Efforts are underway to amend the group exemption procedure to take into account congregational as well as connectional church organizations.

Loss of a church's exempt status would have a variety of negative consequences, including (1) the church's net income would be subject to federal (and possibly state) income taxation; (2) donors no longer could deduct contributions to the church; (3) ineligibility to establish "403(b)" tax-sheltered annuities; (4) possible loss of property and sales tax exemptions; (5) loss of preferential mailing rates; (6) possible loss of a housing allowance exclusion for ministers serving the church; (7) possible inapplicability of a minister's exemption from social security taxes to compensation received from the church; and (8) clergy compensation might not be exempt from federal income tax withholding. Clearly, any activity that jeopardizes a church's exemption from federal income taxation, and correspondingly the benefits summarized above, is a matter that must be taken very seriously.

Integrated auxiliaries. As noted above (in this section and section D) "integrated auxiliaries" are exempt from filing an annual information returns (Form 990) and an application for exemption from income tax (Form 1023). The term "integrated auxiliary" was defined originally in section 1.6033-2(5)(i) of the income tax regulations to include an organization "(a) which is exempt from taxation as an organization described in section 501(c)(3); (b) which is affiliated . . . with a church; and (c) whose principal activity is exclusively religious." The regulations further clarified that an organization's principal activity will not be considered exclusively religious if that activity is educational, literary, charitable, or of another nature (other than religious) that would serve as a basis for exemption under section 501(c)(3). In *Lutheran Social Services of Minnesota v. United States, 758 F.2d 1283 (8th Cir. 1985)*, a federal appeals court ruled that this "exclusively religious" test was inconsistent with the tax code (section 6033) and therefore was invalid. This conclusion was adopted by another federal court in 1986. *Lutheran Children and Family Service of Eastern Pennsylvania v. United States, 58 A.F.T.R.2d ¶86-5662 (E.D. Pa. 1986)*.

The IRS responded to these court rulings by issuing Revenue Procedure 86-23 in 1986. In this procedure, the IRS announced that it would regard organizations as integrated auxiliaries if the following requirements are met: (a) the organization must be described in sections 501(c)(3) of the Code; (b) the organization must be affiliated with a church or convention or association of churches; and (c) the organization must meet an "internal support test."

An organization meets the **"affiliation" test** in any one of the following three ways: (1) it is covered by a group exemption letter (see above); (2) it is operated, supervised, or controlled by or in connection with, a church or convention or association of churches; or (3) relevant facts and circumstances show that it is so affiliated. The factors to be considered include:

(a) The organization's enabling instrument (corporate charter, trust instrument, articles of association, constitution, or similar document) or bylaws affirm that the organization shares common religious doctrines, principles, disciplines, or practices with the church or convention or association of churches.

(b) The church or convention or association of churches has authority to appoint or remove or to control the appointment or removal of at least one of the organization's officers or directors.

(c) The church or convention or association of churches receives reports, at least annually, on the financial and general operations of the organization.

(d) The corporate name of the organization indicates an institutional relationship, which relationship is affirmed by the church or convention or association of churches or a designee thereof; or if the corporate name of the organization does not indicate an institutional relationship, this institutional relationship is affirmed by the church, or convention or association of churches, or designee thereof.

(e) In the event of dissolution, the assets are required to be distributed to the church or convention or association of churches or to an affiliate thereof within the meeting of this revenue procedure.

(f) Any other relevant fact or circumstance.

The absence of one or more of the above factors does not necessarily preclude classification of an organization as being affiliated with a church or convention or association of churches.

An organization meets the **internal support test** unless it both (1) offers admissions, goods, services, or facilities for sale, other than on an incidental basis,

to the general public (except goods, services, or facilities sold at a nominal charge or substantially less than cost), and (2) normally receives more than 50 percent of its support from a combination of governmental sources, public solicitation of contributions (such as through a community fund drive), and receipts from the sale of admissions, goods, performance of services, or furnishing of facilities in activities that are not unrelated trades or businesses. In general, the philosophy of the IRS is that if an organization is "internally supported" by a church or religious denomination then there is no compelling reason why that organization should file annual information returns (Form 990) or an application for exemption from federal income tax (Form 1023). On the other hand, if an organization is not internally supported by a church or denomination, and is supported through public donations or the sale of products or services, then there is a compelling interest in having the public accountability that annual information returns and applications for exemption can provide (both of these forms are available for public inspection).

IRS regulations issued in 1994 incorporate the rules set forth in Revenue Ruling 86-23. The following examples are contained in the regulations, and they illustrate the new integrated auxiliary rules.

☞ *Example. Organization B is a retirement home described in sections 501(c)(3) and 509(a)(2). Organization B is affiliated (within the meaning of this paragraph (h)) with a church. Admission to Organization B is open to all members of the community for a fee. Organization B advertises in publications of general distribution appealing to the elderly and maintains its name on non-denominational listings of available retirement homes. Therefore, Organization B offers its services for sale to the general public on more than an incidental basis. Organization B receives a cash contribution of $50,000 annually from the church. Fees received by Organization B from its residents total $100,000 annually. Organization B does not receive any government support or contributions from the general public. Total support is $150,000 ($100,000 + $50,000), and $100,000 of that total is from receipts from the performance of services (66-2/3% of total support). Therefore, Organization B receives more than 50 percent of its support from receipts from the performance of services. Organization B is not internally supported and is not an integrated auxiliary.*

☞ *Example. Organization C is a hospital that is described in sections 501(c)(3) and 509(a)(1). Organization C is affiliated (within the meaning of this paragraph (h)) with a church. Organization C is open to all persons in need of hospital care in the community, although most of Organization C's patients are members of the same denomination as the church with which Organization C is affiliated. Organization C maintains its name on hospital listings used by the general public, and participating doctors are allowed to admit all patients. Therefore, Organization C offers its services for sale to the general public on more than an incidental basis. Organization C annually* receives $250,000 in support from the church, $1,000,000 in payments from patients and third party payors (including Medicare, Medicaid and other insurers) for patient care, $100,000 in contributions from the public, $100,000 in grants from the federal government (other than Medicare and Medicaid payments) and $50,000 in investment income. Total support is $1,500,000 ($250,000 + $1,000,000 + $100,000 + $100,000 + $50,000), and $1,200,000 ($1,000,000 + $100,000 + $100,000) of that total is support from receipts from the performance of services, government sources, and public contributions (80% of total support). Therefore, Organization C receives more than 50 percent of its support from receipts from the performance of services, government sources, and public contributions. Organization C is not internally supported and is not an integrated auxiliary.

☞ **Example.** Organization D is a seminary for training ministers of a church and is described in sections 501(c)(3) and 509(a)(1). Organization D is affiliated (within the meaning of this paragraph (h)) with a church. Organization D is open only to members of the denomination of the church with which it is affiliated. Organization D annually receives $100,000 in support from the church with which it is affiliated and $300,000 in tuition payments from students. Therefore, Organization D is internally supported (even though more than 50 percent of its total support comes from receipts from the performance of services) because it does not offer admissions, goods, services, or facilities for sale, other than on an incidental basis, to the general public. Organization D is an integrated auxiliary.

G. Unrelated Business Income Tax Return

Section 511 of the Code imposes a tax on the "unrelated business taxable income" of every tax-exempt organization, including churches, as a means of placing the business activities of exempt organizations on the same tax basis as the taxable business endeavors with which they compete. Churches that generate unrelated business taxable income must report such income on Form 990-T (due on the 15th day of the fifth month following the end of a church's fiscal year). Section 512 defines *unrelated business taxable income* as "the gross income derived by any organization from any unrelated trade or business regularly carried on by it" less certain deductions. Section 513 defines the term *unrelated trade or business* as "any trade or business the conduct of which is not substantially related (aside from the need of such organization for income or funds or the use it makes of the profits derived) to the exercise or performance by such organization of its charitable, educational, or other purpose or function constituting the basis for its exemption under section 501 . . . ."

Accordingly, the following three conditions must be met before an activity of an exempt organization may be classified as an unrelated trade or business and the gross income of such activity subjected to the tax

on unrelated business taxable income: (1) the activity must be a trade or business, (2) the trade or business must be regularly carried on, and (3) the trade or business must not be substantially related to exempt purposes. The term *trade or business* generally includes any activity carried on for the production of income from the sale of goods or the performance of services. Whether or not an activity is *regularly carried on* requires a comparison of similar activities conducted by taxable organizations. For example, if a particular income-producing activity is of a kind normally conducted by commercial organizations on a year-round basis, the conduct of such activities by an exempt organization over a period of a few days or weeks does not constitute the regular carrying on of a trade or business. To illustrate, the operation of a sandwich stand for a few days each year at a county fair is not a trade or business that is "regularly carried on" since such a stand would not unfairly compete with commercial restaurants that operate on a year-round basis. The regulations state that certain intermittent income-producing activities occur so infrequently (e.g., a few days each year) that they will not be regarded as a trade or business that is regularly carried on.

An activity constituting a trade or business that is substantially related to the exempt purposes of an organization is not an unrelated trade or business. The regulations stipulate that for the conduct of a trade or business to be substantially related to an organization's exempt purposes, the activity must "contribute importantly to the accomplishment of those purposes." Note, however, that the accomplishment of an organization's exempt purposes does not include a church's need for income or its ultimate use of income. In other words, the tax on unrelated business taxable income cannot be avoided by devoting all net earnings from an unrelated trade or business to an exempt activity.

Section 513(a) of the Code specifically states that the term *unrelated trade or business* does not include (1) activities in which substantially all the work is performed by unpaid volunteers, (2) activities carried on by a church or other charitable organization primarily for the convenience of its members, students, or employees, or (3) selling merchandise substantially all of which has been received by the exempt organization as gifts or contributions. Many income-producing activities of churches are exempt from the tax on unrelated business income on the basis of one or more of these exemptions. To illustrate, church bake sales ordinarily are exempt because they are not regularly carried on and because they involve volunteer labor and donated merchandise. Car washes, fundraising dinners, bazaars, and many similar income-producing activities of churches are similarly exempt.

In addition, section 512(b) exempts dividends, interest, annuities, royalties, and rents from real property from the tax on unrelated business taxable income. However, section 514 of the Code states that the exclusion of dividends, interest, annuities, royalties, and rents from the definition of unrelated business income does not apply in the case of unrelated "debt-financed property." *Debt-financed property* is defined as any property held to produce income and that is subject to an "acquisition indebtedness," such as a mortgage, at any time during the year. Income derived from debt-financed property generally constitutes unrelated business taxable income unless the property falls within one of the following three exceptions:

1. Substantially all (85% or more) of the property is used for exempt purposes. Property is not used for exempt purposes merely because income derived from the property is expended for exempt purposes. If less than 85% of the use of the property is devoted to exempt purposes, only that part of the property that is not used to further exempt purposes is treated as unrelated debt-financed property.

2. Income from debt-financed property is otherwise taken into account in computing the gross income of any unrelated trade or business.

3. The property is used in a trade or business that is substantially supported by volunteer workers, that is carried on primarily for the convenience of its members, students, or employees; or that involves the selling of merchandise substantially all of which has been received by the organization as gifts or contributions.

In addition, the Code specifies that if a church acquires real property for the principal purpose of using it substantially for exempt purposes within fifteen years of the time of acquisition, the property is not treated as unrelated debt-financed property even though it may otherwise meet the definition. Furthermore, contrary to the rule that applies to other exempt organizations, the property need not be in the immediate vicinity of the church. *IRC 514(b)(3)(E).* However, this rule will apply with respect to any structure on the land when acquired by the church only so long as the intended future use of the land in furtherance of the church's exempt purpose requires that the structure be demolished or removed in order to use the land in such a manner. This rule will apply after the first five years of the 15-year period only if the church demonstrates to the IRS that use of the land in furtherance of the church's exempt purposes before the expiration of the 15-year period is reasonably certain. *IRS Letter Ruling 9603019.*

If a tax-exempt organization "controls" another exempt or non-exempt organization (a "controlled" organization), the interest, annuities, royalties, dividends, and rent received by the controlling organization from the controlled organization may be taxable as unrelated business taxable income at a specific ratio depending on whether the controlled organization is exempt or non-exempt. *IRC 512(b)(13).*

Exempt organizations that have unrelated business taxable income pay the corporate income tax rates on such income. The tax is levied on income after the deduction of all expenses, modifications and a $1,000 exclusion.

☞ **Example.** The IRS ruled that income received by a church from selling tickets to gospel concerts at its facilities does not result in unrelated business *taxable income. The concerts were not advertised in any commercial publications but were mentioned in the church section of a local newspaper, in local church bulletins, and on a religious television program. Tickets were sold for the concerts to limit the size of the audience to the capacity of the church. Gospel singers and musicians who perform the concerts receive either a predetermined fixed fee or voluntary donations that are collected at the concerts. The singers and musicians are allowed to sell items during the concerts, including cassette tapes of gospel music, T-shirts, books, and Bibles. The IRS concluded: "Your exempt purpose is to spread the Gospel of Jesus Christ through Christian television broadcasting, missionary, and humanitarian efforts. Music is an integral part of most of these activities. Gospel singers regularly perform on your programs and are part of many of your other missionary and humanitarian efforts. The music presented in these activities helps to spread the Gospel message. The concerts, which you will host, will not be an end unto themselves but will simply be another means of accomplishing your exempt purposes. In some cases, you will be reaching people with Gospel music who would not otherwise be able to attend such concerts. Therefore, the activity of hosting the concerts will be substantially related to your exempt purposes. Based on the discussion set forth above, we rule that income received by you from the sale of tickets for Gospel concerts, which you will host at your facilities, will not be unrelated business taxable income." IRS Letter Ruling 9325062.*

☞ **Example.** *The IRS ruled that gains realized by a charity from the sale of land were not taxable as unrelated business income. An owner of timberland proposed to donate portions of the property to a charity over a number of years. The charity's board of directors wanted to sell the timberland upon receipt in order to satisfy its fiduciary duty under state law to avoid speculative and nonproductive investments. The board planned to use real estate brokers to sell the donated land in parcels at a price sufficient to satisfy the board's fiduciary duty. The board was concerned that gains realized from the sale of donated timberland would be taxable to the charity. As a result, the board asked the IRS if the gains would be taxable. The IRS ruled that any gain realized by the charity from the sale of donated timberland would not be taxable. The IRS noted that federal law imposes a tax on the "unrelated business income" of tax-exempt organizations (including churches). However, "all gains or losses from the sale, exchange, or other disposition of property" are excluded from this tax, other than gains from the sale of property "held primarily for sale to customers in the ordinary course of the trade or business." The IRS referred to a Supreme Court ruling addressing the standard to be applied in determining whether property is held "primarily" for sale to customers in the ordinary course of business. The Court interpreted the word "primarily" to mean "of first importance" or "principally." The IRS concluded that "by this stand-*

ard, ordinary income would not result unless a sales purpose is dominant." IRS Letter Ruling 9412039.

☞ **Example.** The IRS issued a private letter ruling addressing the application of the tax on unrelated business income to various items sold in a charity's gift shop. While the ruling involved a museum rather than a church, it will be of interest to any church that conducts similar activities. The museum sells a wide variety of merchandise at retail, wholesale, and by mail order. Items for sale include everything from replicas of artwork to gum and candy. The IRS noted that exempt organizations must pay an unrelated business income tax on net earnings generated from an unrelated trade or business that is not substantially related to the organization's exempt purposes. The IRS concluded that the museum's various sales activities constituted a trade or business, and that some sales were exempt from the unrelated business income tax since they were substantially related to the museum's exempt purposes. This category included sales of replicas of artwork; sales of books and tapes relating to the museum and its collections; sales of miscellaneous products such as film, batteries, and umbrellas which are sold for the convenience of visitors and enable them to devote a greater portion of their time to viewing the museum. On the other hand, the sale of other items was not sufficiently related to the museum's exempt purposes to be exempt from the tax on unrelated business income. These items included the sales of newspapers, magazines, candy, pain relievers, toothpaste, golf clothing and accessories, neckties, caps, shirts and books, which do not relate to museum collections; sales of souvenirs and mementos; and, sales of items that were mere "interpretations" rather than reproductions of items in the museum's collections (such as the depiction of artwork on furniture, dinnerware, silverware, rugs, lamps, jewelry, place mats, and tote bags). IRS Letter Ruling 9550003.

☞ **Example.** A charity operated a catering service that provided meals to members of the general public. The IRS ruled that income generated from this activity was not taxable as "unrelated business income" since the activity was operated by volunteer workers. This same exception applies to many church fund-raising activities, including bake sales and car washes. Income from these activities almost always will be exempt from the tax on unrelated business income because they are conducted by volunteer workers. Other exceptions also may apply in some cases. IRS Letter Ruling 9605001.

☞ **Example.** The IRS ruled that income generated by a charity from various "vocational training" programs was not subject to the unrelated business income tax (UBIT). The IRS concluded that the charity's proposed activities "are being undertaken to further the goals of the existing programs for residents, and not for the production of income. The proposed activities are a natural extension of existing programs for resi-

dents. The scale of the operations is no larger than is necessary for the organization to accomplish its charitable purposes. This is evidenced by the fact that the individuals providing labor for these facilities are residents who are employed as part of your rehabilitation program, and your staff. Supervision will be provided by members of your staff who will not receive additional pay for performing this duty." Therefore, income generated from the sale of products is not subject to UBIT. IRS Letter Ruling 9718034.

☞ **Example.** The sale of charity-owned property was not subject to the unrelated business income tax, ruled the IRS. A school was given land by a donor with the understanding that it would use the land for school purposes and not sell it unless absolutely necessary. The school attempted to lease the property for many years, but the school's trustees eventually decided that the land had to be sold. The school asked the IRS if the sales proceeds would be subject to the unrelated business income tax (UBIT). The IRS said no. UBIT is imposed on earnings generated by exempt organizations from an "unrelated trade or business" that is regularly carried on. There are a number of exceptions. For example, the tax code specifically exempts from this tax "all gains from the sale of property" other than "property held primarily for sale to customers in the ordinary course of the trade or business." The IRS ruled that taxable income would not result "unless a sales purpose is dominant." The IRS concluded that this standard had not been met in this case because of the following factors: (1) the land was held for "a significant period of time" before it was sold (contrary to the "short turn around period experienced by a typical buyer and seller of property"); (2) the school did not "regularly sell real estate"; (3) the school's "management activities with respect to the property have been minimal," and have consisted of collecting rents and providing routine maintenance and repairs; and (4) the school had not been "involved in any way with improving the land or providing services to tenants". The IRS concluded that "these facts distinguish [this sale] from the sale of property held primarily for sale to customers in the ordinary course of business." Therefore "income from the sale of this property is excluded from the computation of unrelated business taxable income." IRS Letter Ruling 9651014.

☞ **Example.** The IRS ruled that revenue generated from a fund-raising concert was subject to UBIT. A charity conducted two concerts each year to raise funds. The concerts in no way furthered the charity's exempt purposes, other than the raising of revenue. The IRS acknowledged that "intermittent" activities are not "regularly carried on," and therefore cannot be a taxable unrelated trade or business. However, it insisted that the "preparatory time for an event must be taken into account in determining whether an activity is regularly carried on." Since the charity in this case spent up to six months preparing for each concert, the concerts were "regularly carried on." IRS Letter Ruling 9712001.

☞ *Example.* A charity's rental income was subject to UBIT, said the IRS. A charity rented a portion of its premises to another charity with similar purposes. The IRS noted that rental income received by a charity from "debt-financed" property generally is subject to UBIT. However, an exception applies to rental agreements that are substantially related to the charity's exempt purposes. This test was met, the IRS concluded, because the rental agreement "will contribute importantly to the accomplishment of [the charity's] purposes" and will help further its "charitable goals." The IRS noted that a rental agreement will be "substantially related" to a charity's exempt purposes if it meets any one or more of the following conditions: (1) it has a "causal relationship to the achievement of exempt purposes (other than through the production of income)"; (2) it contributes importantly to the accomplishment of those purposes; (3) the entire property is devoted to the charity's exempt purposes at least 85 percent of the time, or (4) at least 85 percent of the property (in terms of physical area) is used for the charity's exempt purposes. IRS Letter Ruling 9726005.

Bingo games. The income tax regulations provide that bingo games conducted by a church do not constitute an unrelated trade or business so long as such games are legal under state or local law and bingo games are ordinarily not carried out on a commercial basis by for-profit organizations in the same state. The regulations further specify that

[n]ormally, the entire state will constitute the appropriate jurisdiction for determining whether bingo games are ordinarily carried out on a commercial basis. However, if state law permits local jurisdictions to determine whether bingo games may be conducted by for-profit organizations, or if state law limits or confines the conduct of bingo games by for-profit organizations to specific local jurisdictions, then the local jurisdiction will constitute the appropriate jurisdiction for determining whether bingo games are ordinarily carried out on a commercial basis.

The regulations give the following example, which is preceded by the comment that "it is assumed that the bingo games referred to are operated by individuals who are compensated for their services. Accordingly, none of the bingo games would be excluded from the term 'unrelated trade or business' under section 513(a)(1)."

☞ *Example.* Church Z, a tax-exempt organization, conducts weekly bingo games in State O. State and local laws in State O expressly provide that bingo games may be conducted by tax-exempt organizations. Bingo games are not conducted in State O by any for-profit businesses. Since Z's bingo games are not conducted in violation of State or local law and are not the type of activity ordinarily carried out on a commercial basis in State O, Z's bingo games do not constitute unrelated trade or business.

H. Charitable Contributions

There are a number of reporting requirements under federal law that are associated with charitable contributions. These are all discussed fully in chapter 8 of this tax guide. Some of these rules involve specific obligations on the part of churches as recipients of charitable contributions. These include:

1. Substantiation of Contributions of $250 or More

Donors will not be allowed a tax deduction for any individual cash (or property) contribution of $250 or more unless they receive a written acknowledgment from the church or charity that satisfies the following requirements:

• The receipt must be in writing.

• The receipt must identify the donor by name (a social security number is not required).

• For contributions of noncash property valued by the donor at $250 or more, the receipt must describe the property. No value should be stated.

• The receipt must state whether or not the church provided any goods or services to the donor in exchange for the contribution, and if so, the receipt must include a good faith estimate of the value of those goods or services.

• If the church provides no goods or services to a donor in exchange for a contribution, or if the only goods or services the church provides are "intangible religious benefits," then the receipt must contain a statement to that effect.

• The written acknowledgment must be received by the donor on or before the *earlier* of the following two dates: (1) the date the donor files a tax return claiming a deduction for the contribution, or (2) the due date (including extensions) for filing the return.

While the sole risk of failing to comply with these substantiation rules is upon the donor (who will not be able to substantiate a charitable contribution deduction), churches should take an active role in informing donors of the new rules to ensure the deductibility of contributions. The committee report to the new law instructs the IRS to issue a "notice or other announcement" urging charities "to assist taxpayers in meeting the substantiation requirements."

2. Quid Pro Quo Contributions

If a donor makes a "quid pro quo" contribution of more than $75 (that is, a payment that is partly a contribution and partly a payment for goods or services received in exchange), the church must provide a written statement to the donor that satisfies 2 conditions:

• The statement must inform the donor that the amount of the contribution that is tax-deductible is limited to the excess of the amount of any money (or the value of any property other than money) contributed by the donor over the value of any goods or services provided by the church or other charity in return.

• The statement must provide the donor with a good faith estimate of the value of the goods or services furnished to the donor.

A written statement need not be issued if only "token" goods or services are provided to the donor (generally, with a value of $67 or 2% of the amount of the contribution, whichever is less). Further, the rules do not apply to contributions in return for which the donor receives solely an intangible religious benefit that generally is not sold in a commercial context outside the donative context.

3. Donee Information Return (Form 8282)

Churches receiving contributions of property valued by the donor at more than $5,000 have the following two obligations (assuming that the donor plans to claim a deduction for the contribution): (1) as noted in chapter 8, the church must complete and sign part 1 of the donor's Form 8283 appraisal summary, and (2) the church must complete and return to the IRS an information return (IRS Form 8282) if it sells, exchanges, consumes, or otherwise disposes of the donated property within two years of the date of the contribution. This filing requirement applies to the charity that received the donated property from the donor (the "original donee"), and, since July 5, 1988, to any "successor donee." A successor donee is any recipient of the donated property other than the "original donee." In other words, if a donor donates property to First Church on July 1, 1998 and on December 1, 1998 First Church transfers the property to Second Church, then it is Second Church that has the obligation to file a Form 8282 with the IRS in the event that it disposes of the property within 125 days of the original contribution to First Church. To assist Second Church in complying with the Form 8282 filing requirement, the income tax regulations require First Church to provide Second Church with a copy of the donor's qualified appraisal summary (Form 8283) within 15 days of the transfer.

A Form 8282 is reproduced at the end of this chapter for your convenience. Please feel free to make copies from this form for your use, or order original copies from the IRS. The church must file a Form 8282 within 125 days after it disposes of the donated property. A copy must also be sent to the donor. Form 8282 is very easy to complete. The IRS is primarily concerned with learning the amount received by the church in any sale or other disposition of the property as an additional means of verifying the valuation claimed by the donor.

There are two exceptions to this filing requirement. First, Form 8282 does not have to be filed if a church sells, consumes, or disposes of an item of donated property valued on the donor's Form 8283 at $500 or less. This exception will apply if a donor contributes several similar items of property (having a combined value in excess of $5,000) to a church during a calendar year, and the church disposes of or consumes one item that is separately valued at $500 or

less. Second, Form 8282 does not need to be filed if a church consumes the donated property or distributes it without charge to another organization or individual. The consumption or distribution must be in furtherance of the church's tax-exempt purposes.

The Internal Revenue Manual (the IRS administrative manual) states that the tax return of any donor who contributes property valued at more than $5,000 to a church should be selected for examination by the IRS if no Form 8282 is filed by the church. *IRM 4175.2*. Obviously, it is now more important than ever for churches to comply with this important filing obligation.

I. Comprehensive Illustration of Tax Withholding and Reporting Requirements (2 minister-employees; 5 nonminister employees; 1 self-employed custodian; church operated preschool)

Note: Since the 1998 payroll tax forms were not available when this book was published, this illustration uses the 1997 forms and reflects the reporting requirements for the fourth quarter of 1997. When appropriate, comments are made regarding changes that take effect in 1998. By studying this illustration, you should have no difficulty completing the corresponding 1998 forms (which will be substantially similar to the 1997 forms).

Assume the following facts:

First Church was organized in 1940 in Anytown, Illinois. Rev. Jacob Ellis has served as senior minister of the church since 1976, and Rev. James Milton has served as associate minister since 1983. Both ministers are ordained, and both report their federal income taxes as employees. However, Rev. Ellis has requested voluntary withholding of his federal income taxes and self-employment taxes, while Rev. Milton has not. Neither minister is exempt from social security coverage.

Rev. Ellis received $45,000 in compensation from the church in 1997, of which $10,000 was designated by the church board (in December of 1996) as a housing allowance for 1997. In 1997, the church adopted an "accountable" business expense reimbursement arrangement for Rev. Ellis. It reimbursed only those business expenses for which Rev. Ellis provided a timely and adequate accounting (substantiating the amount, date, place, and business nature of each expense). The church reimbursed $4,000 of business expenses in 1997.

Rev. Ellis's total church compensation was $50,000 in 1997, and consisted of salary of $40,000 and housing allowance of $10,000.

Rev. Milton received $40,000 in compensation from the church in 1997, and in addition was permitted to live in the church's parsonage (the parsonage has a fair rental value of $6,000 in 1997). Rev. Milton was expected to pay utilities and other miscellaneous expenses associated with living in the parsonage, and accordingly the church board declared $4,000 of Rev. Milton's 1997 compensation as a parsonage allowance. Rev. Milton was also paid a monthly car allowance of $300 in 1997, and was not required to account for any of these reimbursements. As a result, this allowance arrangement was nonaccountable and resulted in additional income of $3,600 for 1997. Rev. Milton's total church compensation was $43,600, broken down as follows: salary of $36,000; parsonage allowance of $4,000; and car allowance of $3,600.

First Church did not file an election (Form 8274) to exempt itself from FICA taxes.

In 1980, the church hired a full-time secretary, Joan Reed, who has worked for the church ever since. Her yearly salary in 1997 was $18,000. In 1988, the church hired a full-time bookkeeper, Janice Guerra, who is paid an annual salary of $20,000 in 1997. The church also pays John Rhodes $200 each month to perform all necessary custodial duties. Mr. Rhodes chooses his own hours, and performs his duties in the manner he chooses (using his own equipment) without any supervision on the part of the church. The church treats Mr. Rhodes as a self-employed person.

In 1970, the church obtained an employer identification number (00-0238457) by filing an SS-4 form with the IRS.

On July 1, 1997, a member of the congregation donated a van to the church. The vehicle had an appraised value of $10,000 (the donor claimed a charitable contribution deduction on his 1997 federal income tax return). The church sold the van in December of 1997 for $9,000.

Rev. Lane conducted two weeks of special services at the church in November of 1997, for which the church paid him $800. In addition, the church paid Rev. Lane's travel expenses which were adequately accounted for under an "accountable" reimbursement plan.

Finally, the church began operating a child-care facility in 1985. In 1997, the facility has 20 preschool-age children. The church has employed two workers to operate the preschool—Susan Peck and Sharon Adams. Both are treated as employees by the church, and each receives a yearly salary of $14,000.

Aside from Mr. Rhodes, all workers are paid on a weekly basis. Gross weekly compensation for each worker is as follows: Rev. Ellis—$961.54 including salary, housing allowance, and car allowance, or $769.23 net of the allowance; Rev. Milton—$819.23 including salary, the parsonage allowance, and car allowance, or $742.31 net of the allowance; Joan Reed—$346.15; Janice Guerra—$384.62; Susan Peck—$269.23; Sharon Adams—$269.23.

Filing requirements—the "10-step approach":

For 1997, the church would have the following filing and reporting requirements. The "10-step" system for complying with a church's federal payroll tax reporting obligations (discussed in this chapter) is applied.

STEP 1. Employer identification number. The church obtained an employer identification number (00-0238457) in 1970.

STEP 2. Workers' status, and social security numbers. The church determines that each worker is an employee for income tax reporting purposes, except for custodian John Rhodes and guest speaker Rev. Lane (both of whom are self-employed). The church obtains the social security numbers for all workers (employees and self-employed).

STEP 3. W-4 forms. To enable the church to withhold the proper amount of federal income taxes and FICA taxes from employee wages, the church should be sure that each employee has completed and signed a W-4. Each employee did in fact prepare a

Table 11-3

Employee	Withholding Allowances	Weekly Pay	Income tax withheld	FICA withheld[1]	FICA employer's[2]
Ellis	3	$769.23[3]	$220 [4]	$0 [5]	$0
Milton	4	761.54[6]	0 [7]	0	0
Reed	3	346.15	10	26.48	26.48
Peck	2	269.23	17	20.60	20.60
Adams	1	269.23	24	20.60	20.60
Guerra	3	384.62	16	29.42	29.42
TOTAL		$2,800.00	$287	$97.10	$97.10

1. Includes both the social security and Medicare tax (combined rate of 7.65%).
2. Includes both the social security and Medicare tax (combined rate of 7.65%).
3. Wages subject to income tax withholding (Rev. Ellis requested voluntary withholding), net of the housing allowance.
4. $73 per week (from Circular E tax bracket tables) plus an additional $147 per week pursuant to Rev. Ellis's revised W-4 (line 6).
5. Clergy, unless exempt, pay self-employment taxes (SECA) rather than FICA taxes.
6. Wages subject to income tax withholding (net of housing allowance), including an average of $69.23 per week ($300 per month) for business expenses under a nonaccountable arrangement.
7. Rev. Milton is exempt from income tax withholding and did not elect voluntary withholding.

W-4 form that was effective for 1997, and their forms are set forth below. Note that Rev. Ellis submitted a revised W-4 in 1997 which requested an additional amount of $147 to be withheld from his salary each week. This amount is to cover his self-employment tax liability. Rev. Ellis estimated that his net self-employment earnings for 1997 would be $50,000 (his total salary of $40,000 plus his housing allowance of $10,000). Note that he properly included his housing allowance in computing his estimated self-employment tax liability. He multiplied his net self-employment earnings of $50,000 by the self-employment tax rate for 1997 (15.3%) to obtain his estimated tax liability of $7,650. He divided this amount by 52 to determine the additional amount to be withheld from his salary in 1997 to cover this liability ($147 per week).

STEP 4. Taxable wages. The church computes the wages of all employees.

STEP 5. Determine income tax to be withheld. The church uses the wage bracket method of computing the amount of income taxes to withhold from each employee's wages. Based on the withholding allowances claimed on the employees' W-4 forms, and the wage bracket withholding tables in IRS Circular E (1997 edition) the church withheld the amounts listed in Table 11-3. Note that Ellis, Milton, Reed, and Guerra are married, and Peck and Adams are single. Based on this data, the church accumulates $481.20 in taxes each week, consisting of withheld taxes of $384.10 ($287 of income taxes, and $97.10 representing the employee's share of FICA taxes) and the employer's share of FICA taxes ($97.10), or approximately $1,924.80 each month. The church does not withhold any taxes from the wages of Rev. Milton, but it should advise him of his obligation to report and prepay his federal income taxes and social security taxes through use of the estimated tax procedure (Form 1040-ES). Remember that *clergy compensation is exempt from federal payroll tax withholding—even if they report their income taxes as employees.* However, clergy who report their income taxes as employees are permitted to elect voluntary withholding (as Rev. Ellis has done). This is not mandatory, and so Rev. Milton is free to avoid the withholding rules completely.

STEP 6. Withhold FICA taxes from nonminister employees' wages. First Church must withhold from each nonminister employee's wages his or her share of FICA taxes (7.65%) and in addition must pay the employer's share of FICA taxes (an additional 7.65%). The amount of social security tax to be withheld from a particular employee's wages is determined by multiplying the current FICA tax rate (7.65%) times the employee's taxable wage base. See Table 11-3.

STEP 7. The church must deposit the taxes it withholds. According to the rules discussed in the text, the church deposits these taxes by the 15th day of the following month with a qualified financial institution (along with a Form 8109). The forms set forth below illustrate the final deposit of 1997 taxes on January 15, 1998. If an employer reported withheld taxes of $50,000 or less during the most recent

lookback period (for 1997, the lookback period is July 1, 1995 through June 30, 1996), the taxes are deposited monthly with a bank (by the 15th day of the following month). Assuming that the total payroll taxes paid by First Church during the lookback period were less than $50,000, then the church deposits its payroll taxes for each calendar month in 1997 by the 15th day of the following month.

STEP 8. File quarterly Form 941. The church files 941 forms each quarter by April 30, July 31, October 31, and January 31. The January 31, 1998 Form 941 (for the final calendar quarter of 1997) is set forth below. Note the following:

• Line 1 is completed only on Form 941 for the first calendar quarter of the year (due April 30).

✎ **Key point: the IRS national office has informed your author that churches with only one employee (the minister) need not file 941 forms. This opinion was based on the following two considerations: (1) The general instructions to Form 941 state, under a section entitled "who must file," that "employers who withhold income tax, and both social security and Medicare taxes, must file Form 941 quarterly." This language exempts churches from filing 941 forms if their only employee is their minister and it supersedes the seemingly conflicting instructions to line 2. (2) Section 31.6011(a)(4) of the income tax regulations specifies that every employer shall file 941 forms for each calendar quarter in which it is "required to deduct and withhold" income taxes. Since a church with only one employee (its minister) is not required to withhold income taxes (ministers' wages are exempt from income tax withholding), there is no need for a church under such circumstances to file 941 forms.**

• Rev. Milton's wages are included on line 2. A case could be made that Rev. Milton's wages need not appear on line 2. It is true that the instructions to Form 941 specify that an employer must list on line 2 the total of all wages and other compensation paid to an employee "even if you do not have to withhold income or social security taxes on it." This language suggests that Rev. Milton's wages must be reported on line 2, even though these wages are exempt from income tax withholding and he did not elect voluntary withholding. Of course, since Rev. Milton's wages are exempt from income tax withholding, and as a minister he is treated as self-employed for social security purposes with respect to his church employment, the church's 941 forms will only show the amount of wages paid to him. There will be no entry for income taxes withheld (line 3), taxable social security wages (line 6a), taxable Medicare wages (line 7), or total social security and Medicare taxes (line 8). Reporting only Rev. Milton's wages seems absurd, since the purpose of the 941 form is to ensure that employers are properly withholding payroll taxes. Clearly, the objective that the 941 form is designed to achieve would not be furthered by requiring the church to list Rev. Milton's wages on line 2.

Of course, issuing a minister a W-2 form without including his wages on line 2 of the church's quarterly 941 forms will present an apparent discrepancy that may trigger an IRS inquiry. On the other hand, submitting 941 forms that report his wages on line 2 but no FICA withholdings will also raise questions. In either case, the apparent discrepancy can be easily explained. The IRS did not specifically address the issue of whether a church that files 941 forms for its nonminister employees should include on line 2 the wages paid to a minister. The rationale presented above does not appear to apply if a church must file 941 forms because it has nonminister employees. As a result, this illustration reports Rev. Milton's wages on line 2.

• Rev. Ellis's wages are included on line 2.

• The amount on line 2 equals the combined weekly payroll of all employees for the thirteen payroll periods in the fourth quarter.

• The amount on line 3 equals the total amount of all federal income taxes withheld during the thirteen payroll periods in the fourth quarter.

• Line 6 includes all wages paid during the quarter that are subject to FICA taxes. Since clergy (Rev. Ellis and Rev. Milton) always are self-employed for social security purposes with respect to services performed in the exercise of their ministry, this line includes only those wages paid to nonminister employees during the quarter.

STEP 9. Issue W-2 forms. Before February 1, 1998, the church issues a W-2 form to each employee. It also submits an additional copy along with a W-3 transmittal form to the Social Security Administration before March 1, 1998. *Publication 517 states that clergy who report their income taxes as employees should receive a W-2 from their church even though they did not elect voluntary withholding.* The church included the "car allowances" ($3,600) on the W-2 form of Rev. Milton. The amounts were included with salary in box 1 of Form W-2. The income tax regulations now require withholding on all business expense reimbursements paid under a "nonaccountable" plan (i.e., expenses are reimbursed without any substantiation or accounting by the employee). However, since Rev. Milton wages are not subject to income tax withholding, and he did not elect voluntary withholding, the church is not required to withhold any tax from these reimbursements.

Note that the amount of Rev. Ellis's housing allowance was reported in box 14 of his W-2. The annual fair rental value of Rev. Milton's parsonage, plus the parsonage allowance designated by the church, are reported in box 14 of his W-2. While such reporting is not required, this is the approach taken by the IRS in Publication 517.

STEP 10. Issue 1099 forms. The church issues a 1099-MISC form to Mr. Rhodes before February 1, 1998. It also sends an additional copy to the IRS before March 1, 1998 along with a Form 1096 transmittal form. The church also must issue Rev. Lane (the guest speaker) a Form 1099-MISC before February 1, 1998, reporting the $800 in "nonemployee compensation." It is incorrect to assume that the church has no obligation to issue Rev. Lane a Form 1099-MISC because it characterized the payment as an "honorarium" or "gift." The church obtained Rev. Lane's social security number by providing him with a W-9 form.

All 1099 forms issued after 1996 must contain the name, address, and telephone number of a "contact person" who can answer questions the recipient may have about the form. The IRS has revised Form 1099-MISC for 1997 by asking for the telephone number of a contact person in the box that asks for the employer's (payer's) name and address. The 1099 forms in this chapter follow this approach.

Miscellaneous reporting requirements. In addition to the payroll tax reporting obligations, First Church must comply with other federal reporting rules. These include:

• The church must file a Form 5578 (proof of racial nondiscrimination) by May 15, 1998.

• The church must file with the IRS a Form 8282 (donee information return) within 90 days of the day on which it sold the donated vehicle.

The church also may wish to remind Rev. Ellis that his housing allowance must be included in income for purposes of computing his self-employment tax liability. Similarly, the church may wish to remind Rev. Milton that the fair rental value of the church-owned parsonage, and the parsonage allowance designated by the church, must be included in income for purposes of computing his self-employment tax liability.

All of these requirements are illustrated below.

--- Cut here and give the certificate to your employer. Keep the top portion for your records. ---

| Form **W-4** Department of the Treasury Internal Revenue Service | **Employee's Withholding Allowance Certificate** ▶ For Privacy Act and Paperwork Reduction Act Notice, see reverse. | OMB No. 1545-0010 **1997** |

1 Type or print your first name and middle initial | Last name | 2 Your social security number
Jacob C. Ellis | | 011 22 0001

Home address (number and street or rural route)
12 Main St.

3 ☐ Single ☒ Married ☐ Married, but withhold at higher Single rate.
Note: If married, but legally separated, or spouse is a nonresident alien, check the Single box.

City or town, state, and ZIP code
Anytown, IL 61600

4 If your last name differs from that on your social security card, check here and call 1-800-772-1213 for a new card ▶ ☐

5 Total number of allowances you are claiming (from line G above or from the worksheets on page 2 if they apply) | 5 | 3
6 Additional amount, if any, you want withheld from each paycheck | 6 | $ 147
7 I claim exemption from withholding for 1997, and I certify that I meet BOTH of the following conditions for exemption:
• Last year I had a right to a refund of ALL Federal income tax withheld because I had NO tax liability; AND
• This year I expect a refund of ALL Federal income tax withheld because I expect to have NO tax liability.
If you meet both conditions, enter "EXEMPT" here | 7

Under penalties of perjury, I certify that I am entitled to the number of withholding allowances claimed on this certificate or entitled to claim exempt status.

Employee's signature ▶ Jacob C. Ellis | Date ▶ Jan. 5, 1997

8 Employer's name and address (Employer: Complete 8 and 10 only if sending to the IRS) | 9 Office code (optional) | 10 Employer identification number

Cat. No. 10220Q

--- Cut here and give the certificate to your employer. Keep the top portion for your records. ---

| Form **W-4** Department of the Treasury Internal Revenue Service | **Employee's Withholding Allowance Certificate** ▶ For Privacy Act and Paperwork Reduction Act Notice, see reverse. | OMB No. 1545-0010 **1997** |

1 Type or print your first name and middle initial | Last name | 2 Your social security number
Janice L. Guerra | | 203 11 0010

Home address (number and street or rural route)
17 Birch Drive

3 ☐ Single ☒ Married ☐ Married, but withhold at higher Single rate.
Note: If married, but legally separated, or spouse is a nonresident alien, check the Single box.

City or town, state, and ZIP code
Anytown, IL 61600

4 If your last name differs from that on your social security card, check here and call 1-800-772-1213 for a new card ▶ ☐

5 Total number of allowances you are claiming (from line G above or from the worksheets on page 2 if they apply) | 5 | 3
6 Additional amount, if any, you want withheld from each paycheck | 6 | $
7 I claim exemption from withholding for 1997, and I certify that I meet BOTH of the following conditions for exemption:
• Last year I had a right to a refund of ALL Federal income tax withheld because I had NO tax liability; AND
• This year I expect a refund of ALL Federal income tax withheld because I expect to have NO tax liability.
If you meet both conditions, enter "EXEMPT" here | 7

Under penalties of perjury, I certify that I am entitled to the number of withholding allowances claimed on this certificate or entitled to claim exempt status.

Employee's signature ▶ Janice L. Guerra | Date ▶ Jan. 4, 1997

8 Employer's name and address (Employer: Complete 8 and 10 only if sending to the IRS) | 9 Office code (optional) | 10 Employer identification number

Cat. No. 10220Q

--- Cut here and give the certificate to your employer. Keep the top portion for your records. ---

| Form **W-4** Department of the Treasury Internal Revenue Service | **Employee's Withholding Allowance Certificate** ▶ For Privacy Act and Paperwork Reduction Act Notice, see reverse. | OMB No. 1545-0010 **1997** |

1 Type or print your first name and middle initial | Last name | 2 Your social security number
Joan A. Reed | | 101 22 1000

Home address (number and street or rural route)
15 Maple Avenue

3 ☐ Single ☒ Married ☐ Married, but withhold at higher Single rate.
Note: If married, but legally separated, or spouse is a nonresident alien, check the Single box.

City or town, state, and ZIP code
Anytown, IL 61600

4 If your last name differs from that on your social security card, check here and call 1-800-772-1213 for a new card ▶ ☐

5 Total number of allowances you are claiming (from line G above or from the worksheets on page 2 if they apply) | 5 | 3
6 Additional amount, if any, you want withheld from each paycheck | 6 | $
7 I claim exemption from withholding for 1997, and I certify that I meet BOTH of the following conditions for exemption:
• Last year I had a right to a refund of ALL Federal income tax withheld because I had NO tax liability; AND
• This year I expect a refund of ALL Federal income tax withheld because I expect to have NO tax liability.
If you meet both conditions, enter "EXEMPT" here | 7

Under penalties of perjury, I certify that I am entitled to the number of withholding allowances claimed on this certificate or entitled to claim exempt status.

Employee's signature ▶ Joan A. Reed | Date ▶ Jan. 4, 1997

8 Employer's name and address (Employer: Complete 8 and 10 only if sending to the IRS) | 9 Office code (optional) | 10 Employer identification number

Cat. No. 10220Q

--- Cut here and give the certificate to your employer. Keep the top portion for your records. ---

| Form **W-4** Department of the Treasury Internal Revenue Service | **Employee's Withholding Allowance Certificate** ▶ For Privacy Act and Paperwork Reduction Act Notice, see reverse. | OMB No. 1545-0010 **1997** |

1 Type or print your first name and middle initial | Last name | 2 Your social security number
Sharon M. Adams | | 222 00 111

Home address (number and street or rural route)
1400 Lynn St., Apt. H

3 ☒ Single ☐ Married ☐ Married, but withhold at higher Single rate.
Note: If married, but legally separated, or spouse is a nonresident alien, check the Single box.

City or town, state, and ZIP code
Anytown, IL 61600

4 If your last name differs from that on your social security card, check here and call 1-800-772-1213 for a new card ▶ ☐

5 Total number of allowances you are claiming (from line G above or from the worksheets on page 2 if they apply) | 5 |
6 Additional amount, if any, you want withheld from each paycheck | 6 | $
7 I claim exemption from withholding for 1997, and I certify that I meet BOTH of the following conditions for exemption:
• Last year I had a right to a refund of ALL Federal income tax withheld because I had NO tax liability; AND
• This year I expect a refund of ALL Federal income tax withheld because I expect to have NO tax liability.
If you meet both conditions, enter "EXEMPT" here | 7

Under penalties of perjury, I certify that I am entitled to the number of withholding allowances claimed on this certificate or entitled to claim exempt status.

Employee's signature ▶ Sharon M. Adams | Date ▶ Jan. 4, 1997

8 Employer's name and address (Employer: Complete 8 and 10 only if sending to the IRS) | 9 Office code (optional) | 10 Employer identification number

Cat. No. 10220Q

Form W-2 Wage and Tax Statement 1997
Copy A For Social Security Administration

Form (top-right) — Joan A. Reed

a Control number	22222
b Employer's identification number	00-0238457
c Employer's name, address, and ZIP code	First Church, 423 Able Avenue, Anytown, IL 61000
d Employee's social security number	101-22-1000
e Employee's name (first, middle initial, last)	Joan A. Reed
Address	15 Maple Avenue, Anytown, IL 61000
1 Wages, tips, other compensation	18000.00
2 Federal income tax withheld	520.00
3 Social security wages	18000.00
4 Social security tax withheld	1116.00
5 Medicare wages and tips	18000.00
6 Medicare tax withheld	261.00

For Official Use Only ▶ OMB No. 1545-0008
Cat. No. 10134D
Department of the Treasury—Internal Revenue Service
For Paperwork Reduction Act Notice, see separate instructions.

Form W-2 Wage and Tax Statement 1997
Copy A For Social Security Administration

Form (bottom-right) — Sharon M. Adams

a Control number	22222
b Employer's identification number	00-0238457
c Employer's name, address, and ZIP code	First Church, 423 Able Avenue, Anytown, IL 61000
d Employee's social security number	222-00-1111
e Employee's name (first, middle initial, last)	Sharon M. Adams
Address	1400 Lynn St., Apt. H, Anytown, IL 61000
1 Wages, tips, other compensation	14000.00
2 Federal income tax withheld	1248.00
3 Social security wages	14000.00
4 Social security tax withheld	868.00
5 Medicare wages and tips	14000.00
6 Medicare tax withheld	203.00

For Official Use Only ▶ OMB No. 1545-0008
Cat. No. 10134D
Department of the Treasury—Internal Revenue Service
For Paperwork Reduction Act Notice, see separate instructions.

Form W-2 Wage and Tax Statement 1997
Copy A For Social Security Administration

Form (top-left) — Janice L. Guerra

a Control number	22222
b Employer's identification number	00-0238457
c Employer's name, address, and ZIP code	First Church, 423 Able Avenue, Anytown, IL 61000
d Employee's social security number	203-11-0010
e Employee's name (first, middle initial, last)	Janice L. Guerra
Address	17 Birch Drive, Anytown, IL 61000
1 Wages, tips, other compensation	20000.00
2 Federal income tax withheld	832.00
3 Social security wages	20000.00
4 Social security tax withheld	1240.00
5 Medicare wages and tips	20000.00
6 Medicare tax withheld	290.00

For Official Use Only ▶ OMB No. 1545-0008
Cat. No. 10134D
Department of the Treasury—Internal Revenue Service
For Paperwork Reduction Act Notice, see separate instructions.
Do NOT Cut or Separate Forms on This Page

Form W-2 Wage and Tax Statement 1997
Copy A For Social Security Administration

Form (bottom-left) — Jacob C. Ellis

a Control number	22222
b Employer's identification number	00-0238457
c Employer's name, address, and ZIP code	First Church, 423 Able Avenue, Anytown, IL 61000
d Employee's social security number	011-22-0001
e Employee's name (first, middle initial, last)	Jacob C. Ellis
Address	112 Main St., Anytown, IL 61000
1 Wages, tips, other compensation	40000.00
2 Federal income tax withheld	1248.00
3 Social security wages	
14 Other	10000.00 — housing allowance

For Official Use Only ▶ OMB No. 1545-0008
Cat. No. 10134D
Department of the Treasury—Internal Revenue Service
For Paperwork Reduction Act Notice, see separate instructions.
Do NOT Cut or Separate Forms on This Page

a Control number	22222	Void ☐	For Official Use Only ▶ OMB No. 1545-0008		
b Employer's identification number 00-0238457				1 Wages, tips, other compensation 14000.00	2 Federal income tax withheld 884.00
c Employer's name, address, and ZIP code First Church 423 Able Avenue Anytown, IL 61000				3 Social security wages 14000.00	4 Social security tax withheld 868.00
				5 Medicare wages and tips 14000.00	6 Medicare tax withheld 203.00
				7 Social security tips	8 Allocated tips
d Employee's social security number 010-11-2222				9 Advance EIC payment	10 Dependent care benefits
e Employee's name (first, middle initial, last) Susan L. Peck 501 Elm St. Anytown, IL 61000				11 Nonqualified plans	12 Benefits included in box 1
				13 See Instrs. for box 13	14 Other
				15 Statutory employee ☐ Deceased ☐ Pension plan ☐ Legal rep. ☐ Hshld. emp. ☐ Subtotal ☐ Deferred compensation	
f Employee's address and ZIP code					

16 State Employer's state I.D. No.	17 State wages, tips, etc.	18 State income tax	19 Locality name	20 Local wages, tips, etc.	21 Local income tax

Form **W-2** Wage and Tax Statement **1997**

Copy A For Social Security Administration

Cat. No. 10134D

Department of the Treasury—Internal Revenue Service

For Paperwork Reduction Act Notice, see separate instructions.

---

a Control number	22222	Void ☐	For Official Use Only ▶ OMB No. 1545-0008		
b Employer's identification number 00-0238457				1 Wages, tips, other compensation 39600.00	2 Federal income tax withheld
c Employer's name, address, and ZIP code First Church 423 Able Avenue Anytown, IL 61000				3 Social security wages	4 Social security tax withheld
				5 Medicare wages and tips	6 Medicare tax withheld
				7 Social security tips	8 Allocated tips
d Employee's social security number 100-20-0020				9 Advance EIC payment	10 Dependent care benefits
e Employee's name (first, middle initial, last) James D. Milton 201 Oak St. Anytown, IL 61000				11 Nonqualified plans	12 Benefits included in box 1
				13 See Instrs. for box 13	14 Other 4000.00-parsonage allowance 6000.00-parsonage rental value
				15 Statutory employee ☐ Deceased ☐ Pension plan ☐ Legal rep. ☐ Hshld. emp. ☐ Subtotal ☐ Deferred compensation	
f Employee's address and ZIP code					

16 State Employer's state I.D. No.	17 State wages, tips, etc.	18 State income tax	19 Locality name	20 Local wages, tips, etc.	21 Local income tax

Form **W-2** Wage and Tax Statement **1997**

Copy A For Social Security Administration

Cat. No. 10134D

Department of the Treasury—Internal Revenue Service

For Paperwork Reduction Act Notice, see separate instructions.

Do NOT Cut or Separate Forms on This Page

Form **941**
(Rev. January 1997)
Department of the Treasury
Internal Revenue Service

Employer's Quarterly Federal Tax Return
▶ See separate instructions for information on completing this return.

Please type or print.

OMB No. 1545-0029

4141

Enter state code for state in which deposits made (see page 3 of instructions).

If address is different from prior return, check here ▶ ☐

Name (as distinguished from trade name)
First Church

Date quarter ended
Dec. 31, 1997

Trade name, if any

Employer identification number
00-0238457

Address (number and street)
423 Able Avenue

City, state, and ZIP code
Anytown, IL 61000

| | T | FF | FD | FP | I | T |

IRS Use

If you do not have to file returns in the future, check here ▶ ☐ and enter date final wages paid ▶
If you are a seasonal employer, see **Seasonal employers** on page 1 of the instructions and check here ▶ ☐

1	Number of employees (except household) employed in the pay period that includes March 12th ▶	1	
2	Total wages and tips, plus other compensation	2	36,400 00
3	Total income tax withheld from wages, tips, and sick pay	3	3731 00
4	Adjustment of withheld income tax for preceding quarters of calendar year .	4	
5	Adjusted total of income tax withheld (line 3 as adjusted by line 4—see instructions) .	5	3731 00
6	Taxable social security wages .	6a $ 16,500 00	× 12.4% (.124) =	6b	2,046 00
	Taxable social security tips .	6c $	× 12.4% (.124) =	6d	
7	Taxable Medicare wages and tips .	7a $ 16,500 00	× 2.9% (.029) =	7b	479 00
8	Total social security and Medicare taxes (add lines 6b, 6d, and 7b). Check here if wages are not subject to social security and/or Medicare tax. ▶ ☐	8	2525 00
9	Adjustment of social security and Medicare taxes (see instructions for required explanation). Sick Pay $ ___ ± Fractions of Cents $ ___ ± Other $ ___ =	9	
10	Adjusted total of social security and Medicare taxes (line 8 as adjusted by line 9—see instructions) .	10	2525 00
11	Total taxes (add lines 5 and 10)	11	6256 00
12	Advance earned income credit (EIC) payments made to employees . .	12	
13	Net taxes (subtract line 12 from line 11). **This should equal line 17, column (d) below** (or line D of Schedule B (Form 941))	13	6256 00
14	Total deposits for quarter, including overpayment applied from a prior quarter .	14	6256 00
15	**Balance due** (subtract line 14 from line 13). See instructions . . .	15	

16 **Overpayment,** if line 14 is more than line 13, enter excess here ▶ $ ___ and check if to be: ☐ Applied to next return OR ☐ Refunded.

• **All filers:** If line 13 is less than $500, you need not complete line 17 or Schedule B.
• **Semiweekly schedule depositors:** Complete Schedule B (Form 941) and check here . . ▶ ☐
• **Monthly schedule depositors:** Complete line 17, columns (a) through (d), and check here . . ▶ ☒

17	Monthly Summary of Federal Tax Liability			
	(a) First month liability	(b) Second month liability	(c) Third month liability	(d) Total liability for quarter
	2406.00	1925.00	1925.00	6256.00

Sign Here
Under penalties of perjury, I declare that I have examined this return, including accompanying schedules and statements, and to the best of my knowledge and belief, it is true, correct, and complete.

Signature ▶ *Jacob C. Ellis*   Print Your Name and Title ▶ *Jacob C. Ellis President*   Date ▶ *Jan. 24, 1998*

For Paperwork Reduction Act Notice, see page 1 of separate instructions.   Cat. No. 17001Z   Form **941** (Rev. 1-97)

DO NOT STAPLE

a Control number   **33333**   For Official Use Only ▶   OMB No. 1545-0008

b Kind of Payer	941 ☒	Military ☐	943 ☐
	CT-1 ☐	Hshld. ☐	Medicare govt. emp. ☐
d Establishment number			

c Total number of statements   **6**

e Employer's identification number
00-0238457

f Employer's name
First Church

g Employer's address and ZIP code
423 Able Avenue
Anytown, IL 61000

h Other EIN used this year

1 Wages, tips, other compensation	2 Federal income tax withheld
145,600.00	14,924.00
3 Social security wages	4 Social security tax withheld
66,000.00	4,092.00
5 Medicare wages and tips	6 Medicare tax withheld
66,000.00	957.00
7 Social security tips	8 Allocated tips
9 Advance EIC payments	10 Dependent care benefits
11 Nonqualified plans	12 Deferred compensation
13	14
15 Income tax withheld by third-party payer	

Employer's state I.D. No.

Under penalties of perjury, I declare that I have examined this return and accompanying documents, and, to the best of my knowledge and belief, they are true, correct, and complete.

Signature ▶ *Jacob C. Ellis*   Title ▶ *President*   Date ▶ *Feb. 15, 1998*

Telephone number (*314*) *555-4444*

Form **W-3** Transmittal of Wage and Tax Statements **1997**   Department of the Treasury Internal Revenue Service

Form 1099-MISC (left)

9595 ☐ VOID ☐ CORRECTED

PAYER'S name, street address, city, state, ZIP code, and telephone no.

First Church
423 Able Avenue
Anytown, IL 61000
319-555-3333

PAYER'S Federal identification number	RECIPIENT'S identification number
00-0238457	001-10-1230

RECIPIENT'S name

John C. Rhodes

Street address (including apt. no.)

321 South St.

City, state, and ZIP code

Anytown, IL 61000

Account number (optional)

OMB No. 1545-0115

1997 Form 1099-MISC

Miscellaneous Income

Copy A
For
Internal Revenue
Service Center

File with Form 1096.

For Paperwork Reduction Act Notice and instructions for completing this form, see Instructions for Forms 1099, 1098, 5498, and W-2G.

Box	Amount
1 Rents	$
2 Royalties	$
3 Other income	$
4 Federal income tax withheld	$
5 Fishing boat proceeds	$
6 Medical and health care payments	$
7 Nonemployee compensation	$ 2400
8 Substitute payments in lieu of dividends or interest	$
9 Payer made direct sales of $5,000 or more of consumer products to a buyer (recipient) for resale ▶	☐
10 Crop insurance proceeds	$
11 State income tax withheld	
12 State/Payer's state number	
13	$

2nd TIN Not. ☐

Cat. No. 14425J

Do NOT Cut or Separate Forms on This Page

Department of the Treasury - Internal Revenue Service

Form 1099-MISC

Form 1099-MISC (right)

9595 ☐ VOID ☐ CORRECTED

PAYER'S name, street address, city, state, ZIP code, and telephone no.

First Church
423 Able Avenue
Anytown, IL 61000
319-555-3333

PAYER'S Federal identification number	RECIPIENT'S identification number
00-0238457	202-22-3030

RECIPIENT'S name

James E. Lane

Street address (including apt. no.)

1225 Willow

City, state, and ZIP code

Anytown, IL 61000

Account number (optional)

OMB No. 1545-0115

1997 Form 1099-MISC

Miscellaneous Income

Copy A
For
Internal Revenue
Service Center

File with Form 1096.

For Paperwork Reduction Act Notice and instructions for completing this form, see Instructions for Forms 1099, 1098, 5498, and W-2G.

Box	Amount
1 Rents	$
2 Royalties	$
3 Other income	$
4 Federal income tax withheld	$
5 Fishing boat proceeds	$
6 Medical and health care payments	$
7 Nonemployee compensation	$ 800
8 Substitute payments in lieu of dividends or interest	$
9 Payer made direct sales of $5,000 or more of consumer products to a buyer (recipient) for resale ▶	☐
10 Crop insurance proceeds	$
11 State income tax withheld	
12 State/Payer's state number	
13	$

2nd TIN Not. ☐

Cat. No. 14425J

Do NOT Cut or Separate Forms on This Page

Department of the Treasury - Internal Revenue Service

Form 1099-MISC

Form 1096

DO NOT STAPLE 6969

Form **1096**	Annual Summary and Transmittal of U.S. Information Returns	OMB No. 1545-0108
Department of the Treasury Internal Revenue Service		**1997**

FILER'S name

First Church

Street address (including room or suite number)

423 Able Avenue

City, state, and ZIP code

Anytown, IL 61000

If you are not using a preprinted label, enter in box 1 or 2 below the identification number you used as the filer on the information returns being transmitted. Do not fill in both boxes 1 and 2.

Name of person to contact if the IRS needs more information

Jacob C. Ellis

Telephone number

(319) 555-4444

For Official Use Only

1 Employer identification number	2 Social security number	3 Total number of forms	4 Federal income tax withheld	5 Total amount reported with this Form 1096
00-0238457		2	$	$ 3200.00

Enter an "X" in only one box below to indicate the type of form being filed.   If this is your FINAL return, enter an "X" here ▶ ☐

W-2G 32	1098 81	1099-A 80	1099-B 79	1099-C 85	1099-DIV 91	1099-G 86	1099-INT 92	1099-LTC 93	1099-MISC 95	1099-MSA 94	1099-OID 96	1099-PATR 97	1099-R 98
☐	☐	☐	☐	☐	☐	☐	☐	☐	☒	☐	☐	☐	☐

1099-S 75	5498 28	5498-MSA 27
☐	☐	☐

Please return this entire page to the Internal Revenue Service. Photocopies are NOT acceptable.

Under penalties of perjury, I declare that I have examined this return and accompanying documents, and, to the best of my knowledge and belief, they are true, correct, and complete.

Signature ▶ Jacob C. Ellis   Title ▶ President   Date ▶ Feb. 3, 1998

Form 5578 (Rev. December 1996)

Annual Certification of Racial Nondiscrimination for a Private School Exempt From Federal Income Tax

Department of the Treasury
Internal Revenue Service

(For use by organizations that do not file Form 990 or Form 990-EZ)

OMB No. 1545-0213

For IRS use ONLY ▶

For the period beginning **Jan. 1** , 19 **97** and ending **Dec. 31** , 19 **97**

1a Name of organization that operates, supervises, and/or controls school(s).

First Church

Address (number and street or P.O. box no. if mail is not delivered to street address). Room/suite

423 Able Avenue

City, town or post office, state, and ZIP + 4

Anytown, IL 61000

1b Employer identification number

00 0238457

2a Name of central organization holding group exemption letter covering the school(s). (If same as 1a above, write "Same" and complete 2c if the organization in 1a above holds an individual exemption letter, write "Not Applicable -

not applicable

Address (number and street or P.O. box no. if mail is not delivered to street address) Room/suite

2b Employer identification number

City, town or post office, state, and ZIP + 4

2c Group exemption number (see instructions under **Definitions**)

3a Name of school (If more than one school, write "See Attached." and attach list of the names, addresses, ZIP codes, and employer identification numbers of the schools) (If same as 1a above, write "Same.")

Evergreen Preschool

Address (number and street or P.O. box no. if mail is not delivered to street address)

423 Able Avenue

3b Employer identification number, if any

City, town or post office, state, and ZIP + 4

Anytown, IL 61000

Under penalties of perjury, I hereby certify that I am authorized to take official action on behalf of the above school(s) and that to the best of my knowledge and belief the school(s) has (have) satisfied the applicable requirements of sections 4.01 through 4.05 of Rev. Proc. 75-50, 1975-2 C.B. 587, for the period covered by this certification.

Jacob C. Ellis (Signature)

Jacob C. Ellis, **President** (Type or print name and title)

May 1, 1998 (Date)

General Instructions

Section references are to the Internal Revenue Code.

This form is open to public inspection.

Paperwork Reduction Act Notice.—We ask for the information on this form to carry out the Internal Revenue laws of the United States. You are required to give us the information. We need it to ensure that you are complying with these laws.

The organization is not required to provide the information requested on a form that is subject to the Paperwork Reduction Act unless the form displays a valid OMB control number. Books or records relating to a form or its instructions must be retained as long as their contents may become material in the administration of any Internal Revenue law. The rules governing the confidentiality of this form are covered in Code section 6104.

The time needed to complete and file this form will vary depending on individual circumstances. The estimated average time is 4 hours and 44 minutes. If you have comments concerning the accuracy of this time estimate or suggestions for making this form simpler, we would be happy to hear from you. You can write to the Tax Forms Committee, Western Area Distribution Center, Rancho Cordova, CA 95743-0001. **DO NOT** send the form to this address. Instead, see **Where To File** below.

Purpose of Form

Form 5578 may be used by organizations that operate tax-exempt private schools to provide the Internal Revenue Service with the annual certification of racial nondiscrimination required by Rev. Proc. 75-50 (the relevant part of which is reproduced on page 2).

Who Must File

Every organization that claims exemption from Federal income tax under section 501(c)(3) of the Internal Revenue Code and that operates, supervises, or controls a private school or schools must file a certification of racial nondiscrimination. If an organization is required to file Form 990, Return of Organization Exempt From Income Tax, or Form 990-EZ, Short Form Return of Organization Exempt From Income Tax, either as a separate return or as part of a group return, the certification must be made on Schedule A (Form 990), Organization Exempt Under Section 501(c)(3), rather than on this form.

An authorized official of a central organization may file one form to certify for the school or schools, and activities of subordinate organizations that would otherwise be required to file on an individual basis, but only if the central organization has enough control over the schools listed on the form to ensure that the schools maintain a racially nondiscriminatory policy as to students.

Definitions

A racially nondiscriminatory policy as to students means that the school admits the students of any race to all the rights, privileges, programs, and activities generally accorded or made available to students at that school and that the school does not discriminate on the basis of race in the administration of its educational policies, admissions policies, scholarship and loan programs, and other school administered programs.

The IRS considers discrimination on the basis of race to include discrimination on the basis of color or national or ethnic origin.

A school is an educational organization that normally maintains a regular faculty and curriculum and normally has a regularly enrolled body of pupils or students in attendance at the place where its educational activities are regularly carried on. The term includes primary, secondary, preparatory, or high schools and colleges and universities, whether operated as a separate legal entity or as an activity of a church or other organization described in Code section 501(c)(3). The term also includes preschools and any other organization that is a school as defined in Code section 170(b)(1)(A)(ii).

A central organization is an organization that has one or more subordinates under its general supervision or control. A subordinate is a chapter, local, post, or other unit of a central organization. A central organization may also be a subordinate, as in the case of a state organization that has subordinate units and is itself affiliated with a national organization.

The group exemption number (GEN) is a four-digit number issued to a central organization by the IRS. It identifies a central organization that has received a ruling from the IRS recognizing on a group basis the exemption from Federal income tax of the central organization and its covered subordinates.

When To File

Under Rev. Proc. 75-50, a certification of racial nondiscrimination must be filed annually by the 15th day of the 5th month following the end of the organization's calendar year or fiscal period

Where To File

Mail Form 5578 to the Internal Revenue Service Center, Ogden, UT 84201-0027.

Cat. No. 42658A

Form **5578** (Rev. 12-96)

Form 8282 (Rev. September 1995)

Donee Information Return

(Sale, Exchange, or Other Disposition of Donated Property)

Department of the Treasury
Internal Revenue Service

▶ See instructions on back.

▶ Give Copy to Donor

OMB No. 1545-0908

Please Print or Type	Name of charitable organization (donee)	Employer identification number
	First Church	**00 0238457**
	Address (number, street, and room or suite no.)	
	423 Able Avenue	
	City or town, state, and ZIP code	
	Anytown, IL 61000	

Part I — Information on the ORIGINAL DONOR and DONEE Receiving the Property

1a Name(s) of the original donor of the property

James Kay

1b Identifying number

220-33-3110

2a Name of charitable organization

2b Employer identification number

Address (number, street, and room or suite no.)

City or town, state, and ZIP code

Note: Complete lines 2a-2d only if you gave this property to another charitable organization (successor donee).

Part II — Information on PREVIOUS DONEES—Complete this part only if you were not the first donee to receive the property. If you were the second donee, leave lines 4a-4d blank. If you were a third or later donee, complete lines 3a-4d. On lines 3a-3d, give information on the preceding donee (the one who gave you the property).

Note: If you are the original donee, skip Part II and go to Part III now.

3a Name of original donee

3b Employer identification number

Address (number, street, and room or suite no.)

City or town, state, and ZIP code

4a Name of preceding donee

4b Employer identification number

Address (number, street, and room or suite no.)

City or town, state, and ZIP code

Part III — Information on DONATED PROPERTY—If you are the original donee, leave column (c) blank.

(a) Description of donated property sold, exchanged, or otherwise disposed of (if you need more space, attach a separate statement)	(b) Date you received the item(s)	(c) Date the item(s) was exchanged or otherwise disposed of	(d) Date item(s) sold, exchanged, or otherwise disposed of	(e) Amount received upon disposition
1943 Dodge Caravan Vehicle No. 82RT15FV5S26K95	**7-1-96**		**12-15-96**	**9000 00**

For Paperwork Reduction Act Notice, see instructions on back.

Cat. No. 62307Y

Form **8282** (Rev. 9-95)

372

J. Illustration #2—Tax Withholding and Reporting Requirements (1 self-employed minister; 1 secretary; 1 self-employed custodian; church has exempted itself from FICA coverage)

Note: *Since the 1998 payroll tax forms were not available when this book was published, this illustration uses the 1997 forms and reflects the reporting requirements for the fourth quarter of 1997. When appropriate, comments are made regarding changes that take effect in 1998. By studying this illustration, you should have no difficulty completing the corresponding 1998 forms (which will be substantially similar to the 1998 forms).*

Assume that Second Church (of Anytown, Illinois) has one minister, Rev. Adam M. Hoyle, who has served since 1990, and one office secretary, Anna H. Todd, who was hired in 1993. Rev. Hoyle reports his federal income taxes as a self-employed person, and Anna Todd reports as an employee. The church filed a Form 8274 in October of 1984, waiving the church's obligation to pay the employer's portion of social security (FICA) taxes. The effect of this election is that the church is not liable for the employer's share of any FICA taxes, and nonminister employees are treated as self-employed for social security purposes (just like ministers). This means that Mrs. Todd must pay the self-employment tax (15.3%) rather than the employee's share of FICA taxes (7.65%).

Rev. Hoyle's annual church compensation for 1997 is $45,000 (which includes a housing allowance of ($8,000), and Mrs. Todd's compensation is $17,000 ($326.92 per week). The church also has a self-employed custodian, John Bridges, who receives a lump sum of $200 each month. The church submitted an application (SS-4) for an employer identification number in 1974 (00-0019283).

The church adopted a reimbursement policy early in 1997 whereby it agreed to reimburse Rev. Hoyle for any business expense that he incurred on behalf of the church and that he substantiated with adequate records within one month of incurring each expense, up to a maximum of $4,000 per year. For 1997, Rev. Hoyle incurred and substantiated $3,600 in actual business expenses on behalf of the church, and he was reimbursed by the church for all of these expenses.

Filing requirements—the "10-step approach":

For 1997, the church would have the following filing and reporting requirements. The "10-step" system for complying with a church's federal payroll tax reporting obligations (discussed in this chapter) is applied.

STEP 1. Employer identification number. The church obtained an employer identification number (00-0019283) in 1983.

STEP 2. Workers' status, and social security numbers. The church determines that Rev. Hoyle and custodian John Bridges are self-employed, and Mrs. Todd is an employee. The church obtains the social security numbers for all workers.

STEP 3. W-4 forms. To enable the church to withhold the proper amount of federal income taxes from the wages of its sole employee (Anna Todd), the church had Mrs. Todd complete and sign an updated W-4 form early in 1997. Mrs. Todd's new W-4 requested the church to withhold an additional amount of taxes ($50) from her wages to cover her self-employment tax liability. The church honored this request beginning with the first payroll period of 1997. Since the other church workers (Rev. Hoyle and Mr. Bridges) are self-employed, they do not complete a W-4 form.

STEP 4. Taxable wages. The church computes the wages of its employee (Mrs. Todd).

STEP 5. Determine income tax to be withheld. The church uses the wage bracket method of computing the amount of income taxes to withhold from Mrs. Todd's wages. Based on the two withholding allowances claimed on her W-4 form, and a weekly salary of $326.92, the church withheld $15 each week from her wages (she is married). This amount is determined according to a table in IRS Publication 15 (Circular E).

STEP 6. Withhold additional income taxes from nonminister employees' wages. Since the church filed a Form 8274 waiving participation in the FICA program, it does not withhold any social security (FICA) taxes from Mrs. Todd's wages. Similarly, the church is not responsible for the employer's share of FICA taxes. However, the law requires that Mrs. Todd be treated as self-employed for social security purposes (because the church filed the Form 8274). Rather than pay her self-employment taxes using the quarterly estimated tax procedure, Mrs. Todd decides to have the church withhold an additional amount *of income taxes* from her wages in 1997 to cover her expected self-employment tax liability. She requests that an additional $50 be withheld (total wages of $17,000 multiplied times the self-employment tax rate for 1997 of 15.3% and divided by 52 weeks). Mrs. Todd will still have to complete a Schedule SE (long form) to report her self-employment tax liability for 1997. However, the excess withheld income taxes reported on line 54 (Form 1040) will offset the self-employment tax liability.

STEP 7. The church must deposit the taxes it withholds. Since the church does not withhold any income taxes or FICA taxes, it is not subject to the deposit rules.

STEP 8. File quarterly Form 941. The church files 941 forms each quarter by April 30, July 31, October 31, and January 31. The January 31, 1998 Form 941 (for the final calendar quarter of 1997) is set forth with the forms below. Note that Form 941E (for churches that have waived FICA coverage by filing Form 8274) was discontinued in 1995. All churches now use Form 941, whether or not they have filed a timely Form 8274 electing to exempt themselves from the employer's share of FICA taxes on their nonminister employees.

STEP 9. Issue W-2 forms. Before February 1, 1998, the church issues a W-2 form to its sole employee, Mrs. Todd. It also submits an additional copy along with a W-3 transmittal form to the Social Security Administration before March 1, 1998.

STEP 10. Issue 1099 forms. Similarly, the church issues a 1099-MISC form to Rev. Hoyle and Mr. Bridges before February 1, 1998. It also sends an additional copy to the IRS before March 1, 1998 along with a form 1096 transmittal form. Note that Rev. Hoyle's 1099-MISC form does not include the amount of the church-designated housing allowance. If the church-designated housing allowance exceeds the actual expenses incurred by Rev. Hoyle in owning or maintaining a home in 1997 (or any other applicable limitation), the excess should be reported as "other income" (i.e., excess housing allowance) on Rev. Hoyle's Schedule C (Form 1040). Note that the church does not include on Rev. Hoyle's 1099-MISC form any of the business expense reimbursements that it paid to him in 1997, since the reimbursements

were all paid pursuant to an "accountable" reimbursement arrangement. See chapter 7 for details.

All 1099 forms issued after 1996 must contain the name, address, and telephone number of a "contact person" who can answer questions the recipient may have about the form.

All 1099 forms issued after 1996 must contain the name, address, and telephone number of a "contact person" who can answer questions the recipient may have about the form. The IRS has revised Form 1099-MISC for 1997 by asking for the telephone number of a contact person in the box that asks for the employer's (payer's) name and address. The 1099 forms in this chapter follow this approach.

Miscellaneous reporting requirements. In addition to the payroll tax reporting obligations, First Church may wish to remind Rev. Hoyle that his housing allowance must be included in his income for purposes of computing his self-employment tax liability.

All these requirements are illustrated in the forms that follow.

Form **8274** (Rev. September 1994) Department of the Treasury Internal Revenue Service	**Certification by Churches and Qualified Church-Controlled Organizations Electing Exemption From Employer Social Security and Medicare Taxes**	**File Two Copies**
Full name of organization Second Church		Employer identification number 00-0019283
Address (number and street or P.O. box number if mail is not delivered to street address) 867 Alton Road		
City, state, and ZIP code Anytown, IL 61000		Date wages first paid
If exemption is based on a group ruling, give full name of central organization		Group exemption number

Sign Here ► I certify that the above named organization is a church or qualified church-controlled organization which, as defined in section 3121(w) of the Internal Revenue Code, is opposed for religious reasons to the payment of employer social security and Medicare taxes, and elects not to be subject to such taxes.

A. Hoyle (Signature of authorized official)   President (Title)   Oct. 20 1984 (Date)

- - - - - - - - - - - - ► **Cut here and give the certificate to your employer. Keep the top portion for your records.** - - - - - - - - - - -

Form **W-4**
Department of the Treasury
Internal Revenue Service

Employee's Withholding Allowance Certificate

► **For Privacy Act and Paperwork Reduction Act Notice, see reverse.**

OMB No. 1545-0010

1997

1 Type or print your first name and middle initial	Last name	2 Your social security number
Anna H. Todd		003 20 3111

Home address (number and street or rural route)
301 Estes Avenue

City or town, state, and ZIP code
Anytown, IL 61000

3 ☐ Single ☒ Married ☐ Married, but withhold at higher Single rate.
Note: If married, but legally separated, or spouse is a nonresident alien, check the Single box.

4 If your last name differs from that on your social security card, check here and call 1-800-772-1213 for a new card . . . ► ☐

5	Total number of allowances you are claiming (from line G above or from the worksheets on page 2 if they apply) .	5	2
6	Additional amount, if any, you want withheld from each paycheck	6 $	50
7	I claim exemption from withholding for 1997, and I certify that I meet **BOTH** of the following conditions for exemption:		

- Last year I had a right to a refund of **ALL** Federal income tax withheld because I had **NO** tax liability; **AND**
- This year I expect a refund of **ALL** Federal income tax withheld because I expect to have **NO** tax liability.

If you meet both conditions, enter "EXEMPT" here . . . . ► | 7 |

Under penalties of perjury, I certify that I am entitled to the number of withholding allowances claimed on this certificate or entitled to claim exempt status.

Employee's signature ► **Anna H. Todd**   Date ► **Jan. 2** , 19**97**

8 Employer's name and address (Employer: Complete 8 and 10 only if sending to the IRS)	9 Office code (optional)	10 Employer identification number

Cat. No. 10220Q

Form **941**
(Rev. January 1997)
Department of the Treasury
Internal Revenue Service

4141

Employer's Quarterly Federal Tax Return

► **See separate instructions for information on completing this return.**

Please type or print.

OMB No. 1545-0029

Enter state code for state in which deposits made . ► ☐

Name (as distinguished from trade name)
Second Church

Trade name, if any

Address (number and street)
867 Alton Road

Date quarter ended
Dec. 31, 1997

Employer identification number
00-0019283

City, state, and ZIP code
Anytown, IL 61000

T	
FF	
FD	
FP	
I	
T	

If address is different from prior return, check here ►

IRS Use

| 1 1 1 1 1 1 1 1 1 | 2 | 3 3 3 3 3 | 4 4 4 |
| 5 5 5 | 6 | 7 | 8 8 8 8 8 | 9 9 | 10 10 10 10 10 10 10 10 |

If you do not have to file returns in the future, check here ► ☐ and enter date final wages paid ►

If you are a seasonal employer, see **Seasonal employers** on page 1 of the instructions and check here ► ☐

1	Number of employees (except household) employed in the pay period that includes March 12th ►	1	
2	Total wages and tips, plus other compensation	2	4250 00
3	Total income tax withheld from wages, tips, and sick pay	3	845 00
4	Adjustment of withheld income tax for preceding quarters of calendar year . . .	4	
5	Adjusted total of income tax withheld (line 3 as adjusted by line 4—see instructions) . .	5	845 00

6	Taxable social security wages	6a $	× 12.4% (.124) =	6b	
	Taxable social security tips	6c $	× 12.4% (.124) =	6d	
7	Taxable Medicare wages and tips . . .	7a $	× 2.9% (.029) =	7b	

8	Total social security and Medicare taxes (add lines 6b, 6d, and 7b). Check here if wages are not subject to social security and/or Medicare tax . . . . ► ☒	8	
9	Adjustment of social security and Medicare taxes (see instructions for required explanation) Sick Pay $ _____ ± Fractions of Cents $ _____ ± Other $ _____ =	9	
10	Adjusted total of social security and Medicare taxes (line 8 as adjusted by line 9—see instructions)	10	
11	**Total taxes** (add lines 5 and 10)	11	845 00
12	Advance earned income credit (EIC) payments made to employees	12	
13	Net taxes (subtract line 12 from line 11). **This should equal line 17, column (d) below** (or line D of Schedule B (Form 941))	13	845 00
14	Total deposits for quarter, including overpayment applied from a prior quarter	14	845 00
15	**Balance due** (subtract line 14 from line 13). See instructions	15	
16	**Overpayment,** if line 14 is more than line 13, enter excess here ► $ _____		

and check if to be: ☐ Applied to next return **OR** ☐ Refunded.

- **All filers:** If line 13 is less than $500, you need not complete line 17 or Schedule B.
- **Semiweekly schedule depositors:** Complete Schedule B and check here . . . . ► ☐
- **Monthly schedule depositors:** Complete line 17, columns (a) through (d), and check here . . . . ► ☐

17	Monthly Summary of Federal Tax Liability			
	(a) First month liability	**(b)** Second month liability	**(c)** Third month liability	**(d)** Total liability for quarter
	325	260	260	845

Sign Here

Under penalties of perjury, I declare that I have examined this return, including accompanying schedules and statements, and to the best of my knowledge and belief, it is true, correct, and complete.

Signature ► **A. Hoyle**   Print Your Name and Title ► **Adam Hoyle President**   Date ► **Jan. 20 1998**

For Paperwork Reduction Act Notice, see page 1 of separate instructions.   Cat. No. 17001Z   Form **941** (Rev. 1-97)

a Control number	22222	Void ☐	For Official Use Only ▶ OMB No. 1545-0008	

b Employer's identification number 00-0019283		1 Wages, tips, other compensation 17000.00	2 Federal income tax withheld 3380.00
c Employer's name, address, and ZIP code Second Church 867 Alton Road Anytown, IL 61000		3 Social security wages	4 Social security tax withheld
		5 Medicare wages and tips	6 Medicare tax withheld
		7 Social security tips	8 Allocated tips
d Employee's social security number 003-21-3111		9 Advance EIC payment	10 Dependent care benefits
e Employee's name (first, middle initial, last) Anna H. Todd 301 Estes Avenue Anytown, IL 61000		11 Nonqualified plans	12 Benefits included in box 1
		13 See Instrs. for box 13	14 Other

15 Statutory employee ☐	Deceased ☐	Pension plan ☐	Legal rep. ☐	Hshld. emp. ☐	Subtotal ☐	Deferred compensation ☐

f Employee's address and ZIP code

16 State	Employer's state I.D. No.	17 State wages, tips, etc.	18 State income tax	19 Locality name	20 Local wages, tips, etc.	21 Local income tax

Cat. No. 10134D

Form **W-2** Wage and Tax Statement **1997**

Copy A For Social Security Administration

Department of the Treasury—Internal Revenue Service
For Paperwork Reduction Act Notice, see separate instructions.

DO NOT STAPLE

a Control number	33333	For Official Use Only ▶ OMB No. 1545-0008	

b Kind of Payer ▶ 941 ☒	Military ☐	943 ☐	1 Wages, tips, other compensation 17000.00	2 Federal income tax withheld 3380.00
CT-1 ☐	Hshld. ☐	Medicare govt. emp. ☐	3 Social security wages	4 Social security tax withheld
c Total number of statements	d Establishment number		5 Medicare wages and tips	6 Medicare tax withheld
e Employer's identification number 00-0019283			7 Social security tips	8 Allocated tips
f Employer's name Second Church			9 Advance EIC payments	10 Dependent care benefits
			11 Nonqualified plans	12 Deferred compensation
867 Alton Road Anytown, IL 61000			13	
g Employer's address and ZIP code			14	
h Other EIN used this year			15 Income tax withheld by third-party payer	
i Employer's state I.D. No.				

Under penalties of perjury, I declare that I have examined this return and accompanying documents, and, to the best of my knowledge and belief, they are true, correct, and complete.

Signature ▶ A. Hoyle   Title ▶ President   Date ▶ Feb. 15 1998

Telephone number (319) 444-2222

Form **W-3** Transmittal of Wage and Tax Statements **1997**   Department of the Treasury Internal Revenue Service

Form 1099-MISC (1997) — Copy A

□ VOID   □ CORRECTED

9595

OMB No. 1545-0115   **1997**   Form 1099-MISC   Miscellaneous Income

Copy A
For
Internal Revenue Service Center

File with Form 1096.

For Paperwork Reduction Act Notice and instructions for completing this form, see Instructions for Forms 1099, 1098, 5498, and W-2G.

PAYER'S name, street address, city, state, ZIP code, and telephone no.
Second Church
867 Alton Road
Anytown, IL 61000
319-444-2222

PAYER'S Federal identification number: 00-0019283
RECIPIENT'S identification number: 260-03-0010

RECIPIENT'S name: John L. Bridges
Street address (including apt. no.): 1700 National Avenue
City, state, and ZIP code: Anytown, IL 61000

Account number (optional):

1 Rents $
2 Royalties $
3 Other income $
4 Federal income tax withheld $
5 Fishing boat proceeds $
6 Medical and health care payments $
7 Nonemployee compensation $ 2,400.00
8 Substitute payments in lieu of dividends or interest $
9 Payer made direct sales of $5,000 or more of consumer products to a buyer (recipient) for resale ► □
10 Crop insurance proceeds $
11 State income tax withheld $
12 State/Payer's state number
13
2nd TIN Not.

Cat. No. 14425J   Department of the Treasury - Internal Revenue Service

Do NOT Cut or Separate Forms on This Page

Form 1099-MISC

Form 1099-MISC (1997) — Copy A

□ VOID   □ CORRECTED

9595

OMB No. 1545-0115   **1997**   Form 1099-MISC   Miscellaneous Income

Copy A
For
Internal Revenue Service Center

File with Form 1096.

For Paperwork Reduction Act Notice and instructions for completing this form, see Instructions for Forms 1099, 1098, 5498, and W-2G.

PAYER'S name, street address, city, state, ZIP code, and telephone no.
Second Church
867 Alton Road
Anytown, IL 61000
319-444-2222

PAYER'S Federal identification number: 00-0019283
RECIPIENT'S identification number: 303-30-0003

RECIPIENT'S name: Adam M. Hoyle
Street address (including apt. no.): 641 Eastgate Blvd.
City, state, and ZIP code: Anytown, IL 61000

Account number (optional):

1 Rents $
2 Royalties $
3 Other income $
4 Federal income tax withheld $
5 Fishing boat proceeds $
6 Medical and health care payments $
7 Nonemployee compensation $ 37000.00
8 Substitute payments in lieu of dividends or interest $
9 Payer made direct sales of $5,000 or more of consumer products to a buyer (recipient) for resale ► □
10 Crop insurance proceeds $
11 State income tax withheld $
12 State/Payer's state number
13
2nd TIN Not.

Cat. No. 14425J   Department of the Treasury - Internal Revenue Service

Do NOT Cut or Separate Forms on This Page

Form 1099-MISC

Form 1096 — Annual Summary and Transmittal of U.S. Information Returns

DO NOT STAPLE   6969

Form **1096**   Department of the Treasury Internal Revenue Service

Annual Summary and Transmittal of U.S. Information Returns

OMB No. 1545-0108   **1997**

FILER'S name: Second Church
Street address (including room or suite number): 867 Alton Road
City, state, and ZIP code: Anytown, IL 61000

If you are not using a preprinted label, enter in box 1 or 2 below the identification number you used as the filer on the information returns being transmitted. Do not fill in both boxes 1 and 2.

Name of person to contact if the IRS needs more information: Adam Hoyle
Telephone number: (319) 444-2222

For Official Use Only

1 Employer identification number	2 Social security number	3 Total number of forms	4 Federal income tax withheld	5 Total amount reported with this Form 1096
00-0019283		2	$	$ 39400.00

Enter an "X" in only one box below to indicate the type of form being filed.   If this is your FINAL return, enter an "X" here . . ► □

W-2G 32	1098 81	1099-A 80	1099-B 79	1099-C 85	1099-DIV 91	1099-G 86	1099-INT 92	1099-LTC 93	1099-MISC 95	1099-MSA 94	1099-OID 96	1099-PATR 97	1099-R 98
□	□	□	□	□	□	□	□	□	☒	□	□	□	□

1099-S 75	5498 28	5498-MSA 27
□	□	□

Please return this entire page to the Internal Revenue Service. Photocopies are NOT acceptable.

Under penalties of perjury, I declare that I have examined this return and accompanying documents, and, to the best of my knowledge and belief, they are true, correct, and complete.

Signature ► A. Hoyle   Title ► President   Date ► Feb. 1, 1998

377

K. Illustration #3—Tax Withholding and Reporting Requirements (1 self-employed minister; no other compensated church workers)

Assume that Third Church (of Anytown, Illinois) has one minister, Rev. Jane Frank, who reports her income taxes as a self-employed person. The church has no other compensated workers. Rev. Frank lives in a church-owned parsonage. Under these facts, the church has only one reporting obligation—it must issue a 1099-MISC form to Rev. Frank before February 1, 1998 (assuming she receives at least $600 in compensation from the church). The 1099-MISC reports compensation paid to Rev. Frank (do not include the fair rental value of the parsonage). The church also sends an additional copy to the IRS before March 1, 1998 with a Form 1096 transmittal form. The church has no other reporting obligations. Rev. Frank uses the estimated tax procedure (Form 1040-ES) to report both her federal income taxes and self-employment taxes. Note that the fair rental value of the parsonage *is* included in her earnings for purposes of determining her self-employment tax liability, as would be any "parsonage allowance" designated by the church. The church may wish to so advise Rev. Frank.

Chapter 12

COMPREHENSIVE ILLUSTRATION OF CLERGY TAX REPORTING

Rev. Jerome L. Scott is senior minister at First Church. He has served in that position for the past five years. He is married to Jane Scott, who is employed as an accountant by a local firm. The Scotts have two children, Andrew and Amy, aged 15 and 13, respectively. Rev. Scott has not exempted himself from social security coverage. He and his wife file a joint federal income tax return. Listed below are several facts concerning Rev. Scott's income and expenses for 1997, along with several pertinent items of information. Thereafter, the Scott's federal tax return for 1997 is reproduced under two separate assumptions: (1) Rev. Scott is an *employee* for income tax reporting purposes, and (2) Rev. Scott is *self-employed* for income tax reporting purposes.

Rev. Jerome L. and Mrs. Jane Scott

Income

Rev. Scott
* Church salary $40,000.00
* Church designated
  housing allowance
  (separate from church salary) 12,000.00
* Honoraria for speaking
  at other churches 1,500.00
* Honoraria for performing
  weddings, funerals, etc. 600.00
* Christmas gift
  from the church 500.00
* monthly "car expense"
  allowance from the
  church of $300 .... 3,600.00

Jane Scott
* salary as accountant 30,000.00
* interest earnings at
  First United Bank 500.00

Housing Expenses
* monthly mortgage payments
  of $500 .... 6,000.00
* utilities (paid by the Scotts) 2,800.00
* home insurance 500.00
* real property taxes 810.00
* new furniture 1,000.00
* repairs 500.00
* TOTAL 11,610.00

*Individual retirement account
(IRA) contributions*
* each spouse
  contributed $2,000 .... 4,000.00

Rev. Scott's business and professional expenses
* business use of car
  (31.5 cents x 8,730
  business miles) 2,750.00
* subscriptions 200.00

* travel expenses (to church convention)
  * meals 320.00
  * lodging 300.00
  * airline tickets 600.00
* seminary course to improve skills 500.00
* business supplies 200.00
* Total 4,870.00

Medical expenses
* Combined expenses 1,500.00

Taxes
* state income taxes 1,200.00
* real estate taxes 810.00

Interest
* mortgage interest on home 4,000.00
* interest on credit cards
  and a car loan 500.00

Charitable Contributions
* Cash contributions to First Church 4,500.00
* Miscellaneous cash contributions 800.00

The Scotts have written receipts substantiating each individual contribution of $250 or more. The receipts comply with the new substantiation rules that apply to charitable contributions.

*Travel expenses associated
with Rev. Scott's honoraria*
* $230 travel and lodging
  plus $100 meals 330.00

Miscellaneous data

1. Employee Filing Example: Rev. Scott reports his federal income taxes as an employee. However, note that:

(A) All clergy, including those who report their federal income taxes as employees, are considered to be **self-employed for social security** purposes with respect to their ministerial services. *IRC 3121(b)(8)(B), 1402(c)*. There is nothing that Rev. Scott, or the church, can do to change this. As a result, the church should *not* withhold the employee's share of FICA taxes (7.65% of wages) from his compensation, and there are no employer contributions that the church is required to make. Rather, Rev. Scott must pay the "self-employment tax"—the social security tax for those considered self-employed for social security purposes. Rev. Scott must use Schedule SE to compute his self-employment tax.

(B) Clergy who report their income taxes as employees are **exempt by law from the income tax withholding requirements**. They must use the quarterly estimated tax procedure to prepay their income taxes and self-employment taxes. Alternatively, they can elect "voluntary withholding." Since Rev. Scott reports his federal income taxes as an employee, his wages are exempt from income tax withholding and he uses the quarterly estimated tax procedure to prepay his taxes. For 1997, he did not request voluntary withholding. Total estimated tax payments for 1997 were $8,000 ($2,000 per quarter).

Jane Scott had $6,000 in federal taxes withheld from her wages as an accountant. Total withholdings (Form 1040, line 54) equal $6,000.

First Church issued Rev. Scott a W-2 on January 28, 1998, listing compensation of $44,100 computed as follows: salary of $40,000 (not including the church-designated housing allowance), Christmas gift of $500, and monthly business expense allowances ($3,600 for the year). The housing allowance is an exclusion so it was not reported.

Self-employed Filing Example: Rev. Scott prepaid his federal income taxes in 1997 by means of the estimated tax procedure. Rev. Scott's fourth quarterly voucher (from Form 1040-ES), which he sent to the IRS January 10, 1998, is set forth below. Total estimated tax payments for 1997 were $8,000 ($2,000 per quarter).

Jane Scott had $3,500 in federal taxes withheld from her wages as an accountant.

First Church issued Rev. Scott a Form 1099-MISC on January 28, 1998, listing compensation of $34,100 computed as follows: salary of $30,000 (not including the church-designated housing allowance), Christmas gift of $500, and monthly business expense allowances ($3,600 for the year). The housing allowance is an exclusion so it was not reported.

2. Housing. Rev. Scott is not furnished a parsonage by First Church. However, the church does designate a housing allowance each year to enable Rev. Scott to pay for his own home. In December of 1996, the official board of First Church determined that Rev. Scott's 1997 church compensation would be $52,000, of which $12,000 was designated as a housing allowance and an additional $40,000 was designated as salary. Assume that the fair rental value of Rev. Scott's home (furnished, plus the cost of utilities) is $12,500. The Scott's monthly house payment is $500, or a total of $6,000 for 1997. Of this amount, $4,000 represents mortgage interest and $2,000 represents payment of principal.

3. Business expenses. Rev. Scott is not required to account to the church for any of his business and professional expenses. Accordingly, the church has a **nonaccountable** reimbursement plan. Such a plan has the following consequences: (1) the total reimbursements are included on the minister's W-2 (or 1099-MISC) form, and on his income tax return (as wages on line 7 of Form 1040 if an employee, or on Schedule C if self-employed). The expenses themselves can be deducted by an employee only as miscellaneous itemized deductions on Schedule A, and then only to the extent that they (along with most other miscellaneous expenses) exceed 2% of adjusted gross income. Self-employed persons are not subject to this limitation. Rev. Scott has records

to substantiate $4,870 of business and professional expenses. Note that this result could have been avoided had the church adopted an **accountable** reimbursement plan. Such a plan reimburses only those expenses that are adequately substantiated within 60 days (as to amount, date, place, and business purpose), and requires any excess reimbursements to be returned to the church. Reimbursements under an accountable plan do not need to be included in a worker's income, and there are no expenses to deduct. The failure of the church to adopt such a plan will result in the nondeductibility of a portion of Rev. Scott's business expenses. The difference often is not significant if a minister is able to itemize expenses on Schedule A (like Rev. Scott). This limitation does not apply to self-employed persons. For those clergy who do not have sufficient expenses to use Schedule A, the difference can be much more substantial—all the church's business expense reimbursements are included in the minister's taxable income, yet the minister cannot claim any offsetting deductions since these can be claimed only as a miscellaneous itemized deduction on Schedule A.

Rev. Scott computes his business transportation expenses by using the standard mileage rate (31.5 cents in 1997 for all business miles).

Only 50% of business meals and entertainment expenses are deductible in 1997. This is taken into account in computing Rev. Scott's business expenses on Schedule C as well as Form 2106.

4. Records. The Scotts have adequate receipts and other documentary evidence to support each expense listed above.

5. IRA accounts. Rev. Scott and Jane Scott each contribute to an IRA account. Since neither is covered under an employer retirement plan, neither is affected by the limitations on the deductibility of IRA contributions.

6. The "Deason" reduction rule. Both illustrations apply the "reduction rule" announced in the Tax Court's *Deason* ruling. The effect of this ruling is to reduce the amount of business expenses that Rev. Scott is able to deduct. However, note that the reduction rule is not applied to Rev. Scott's *self-employment taxes*, since the housing allowance is not an exclusion in computing such taxes. For more information on the *Deason* rule, see chapter 7, section F. The application of the *Deason* rule is reflected in a schedule at the end of each comprehensive example. The schedules are in substantially the same form as the schedule suggested by the IRS in the current edition of Publication 517, as well as in the audit guidelines for ministers issued by the IRS in 1995.

7. Personal interest. None of the Scotts' interest on credit cards and their car loan is tax-deductible.

Form 1040 (1997) — Page 2

33	Amount from line 32 (adjusted gross income)	69061 00
34a	Check if: ☐ You were 65 or older. ☐ Blind. ☐ Spouse was 65 or older. ☐ Blind. ▶ 34a	
b	If you are married filing separately and your spouse itemizes deductions or you were a dual-status alien, see page 18 and check here ▶ 34b ☐	
35	Enter the larger of your: Itemized deductions from Schedule A, line 28, OR Standard deduction shown below for your filing status. But see page 18 if you checked any box on line 34a or 34b or someone can claim you as a dependent. ● Single—$4,150 ● Married filing jointly or Qualifying widow(er)—$6,900 ● Head of household—$6,050 ● Married filing separately—$3,450	13650 00
36	Subtract line 35 from line 33	55411 00
37	If line 33 is $90,900 or less, multiply $2,650 by the total number of exemptions claimed on line 6d. If line 33 is over $90,900, see the worksheet on page 19 for the amount to enter	10600 00
38	Taxable income. Subtract line 37 from line 36. If line 37 is more than line 36, enter -0-	44811 00
39	Tax. See page 19. Check if any tax is from a ☐ Form(s) 8814 b ☐ Form 4972	7195 00

Credits

40	Credit for child and dependent care expenses. Attach Form 2441	
41	Credit for the elderly or the disabled. Attach Schedule R.	
42	Adoption credit. Attach Form 8839	
43	Foreign tax credit. Attach Form 1116	
44	Other. Check if from a ☐ Form 3800 b ☐ Form 8396 c ☐ Form 8801 d ☐ Form (specify)	
45	Add lines 40 through 44	7195 00
46	Subtract line 45 from line 39. If line 45 is more than line 39, enter -0-	7518 00

Other Taxes

47	Self-employment tax. Attach Schedule SE	
48	Alternative minimum tax. Attach Form 6251	
49	Social security and Medicare tax on tip income not reported to employer. Attach Form 4137	
50	Tax on qualified retirement plans (including IRAs) and MSAs. Attach Form 5329 if required	
51	Advance earned income credit payments from Form(s) W-2	
52	Household employment taxes. Attach Schedule H.	
53	Add lines 46 through 52. This is your total tax.	14713 00

Payments

Line	Description	Amount
54	Federal income tax withheld from Forms W-2 and 1099	6000
55	1997 estimated tax payments and amount applied from 1996 return.	8000
56a	Earned income credit. Attach Schedule EIC. If you have a qualifying child b Nontaxable earned income amount ▶ and type ▶	
57	Amount paid with Form 4868 (request for extension)	
58	Excess social security and RRTA tax withheld (see page 27)	
59	Other payments. Check if from a ☐ Form 2439 b ☐ Form 4136	
60	Add lines 54, 55, 56a, 57, 58, and 59. These are your total payments	14000 00

Refund

61	If line 60 is more than line 53, subtract line 53 from line 60. This is the amount you OVERPAID	
62a	Amount of line 61 you want REFUNDED TO YOU.	
b	Routing number	
c	Type: ☐ Checking ☐ Savings	
d	Account number	
63	Amount of line 61 you want APPLIED TO YOUR 1998 ESTIMATED TAX ▶	

Amount You Owe

Line	Description	Amount
64	If line 53 is more than line 60, subtract line 60 from line 53. This is the AMOUNT YOU OWE. For details on how to pay, see page 27.	713
65	Estimated tax penalty. Also include on line 64	

Sign Here — Under penalties of perjury, I declare that I have examined this return and accompanying schedules and statements, and to the best of my knowledge and belief, they are true, correct, and complete. Declaration of preparer (other than taxpayer) is based on all information of which preparer has any knowledge.

Your signature: Jerome L. Scott   Date: Mar. 1, 1998   Your occupation: minister
Spouse's signature. If a joint return, BOTH must sign.: Jane T. Scott   Date: Mar. 1, 1998   Spouse's occupation: accountant

Paid Preparer's Use Only

Form 1040 (1997)

Form 1040 — U.S. Individual Income Tax Return 1997

Department of the Treasury—Internal Revenue Service

For the year Jan. 1–Dec. 31, 1997, or other tax year beginning , 1997, ending , 19

OMB No. 1545-0074

Label

Your first name and initial: Jerome L.   Last name: Scott
If a joint return, spouse's first name and initial: Jane T.   Last name: Scott
Home address (number and street). If you have a P.O. box, see page 10.: 418 Walnut   Apt. no
City, town or post office, state, and ZIP code. If you have a foreign address, see page 10.: Anytown, FL 33322

Your social security number: 100 22 1234
Spouse's social security number: 101 22 2345

Presidential Election Campaign (See page 10) — Do you want $3 to go to this fund? Yes ☐ No ☒ / If a joint return, does your spouse want $3 to go to this fund? Yes ☐ No ☒

Filing Status

1. ☐ Single
2. ☒ Married filing joint return (even if only one had income)
3. ☐ Married filing separate return. Enter spouse's social security no. above and full name here ▶
4. ☐ Head of household (with qualifying person). (See page 10.) If the qualifying person is a child but not your dependent, enter this child's name here ▶
5. ☐ Qualifying widow(er) with dependent child (year spouse died ▶ 19). (See page 10.)

Exemptions

	(2) Dependent's social security number	(3) Dependent's relationship to you	(4) No. of months lived in your home in 1997
6a ☒ Yourself.			
b ☒ Spouse			
c Dependents: Andrew Scott	001 11 0123	son	12
Amy Scott	001 12 1234	daughter	12

No. of boxes checked on 6a and 6b: 2
No. of your children on 6c who lived with you: 2
d Total number of exemptions claimed: 4

Income

Line	Description	Amount
7	Wages, salaries, tips, etc. Attach Form(s) W-2.	74100 00
8a	Taxable interest. Attach Schedule B if required	500 00
b	Tax-exempt interest. DO NOT include on line 8a.	
9	Dividends. Attach Schedule B if required	
10	Taxable refunds, credits, or offsets of state and local income taxes (see page 12)	
11	Alimony received	1820 00
12	Business income or (loss). Attach Schedule C or C-EZ	
13	Capital gain or (loss). Attach Schedule D	
14	Other gains or (losses). Attach Form 4797	
15a	Total IRA distributions. 15a b Taxable amount (see page 13)	
16a	Total pensions and annuities. 16a b Taxable amount (see page 13)	
17	Rental real estate, royalties, partnerships, S corporations, trusts, etc. Attach Schedule E	
18	Farm income or (loss). Attach Schedule F	
19	Unemployment compensation	
20a	Social security benefits. 20a b Taxable amount (see page 14)	
21	Other income. List type and amount—see page 15 excess housing allowance	400 00
22	Add the amounts in the far right column for lines 7 through 21. This is your total income ▶	76820 00

Adjusted Gross Income

Line	Description	Amount
23	IRA deduction (see page 16)	4000 00
24	Medical savings account deduction. Attach Form 8853	
25	Moving expenses. Attach Form 3903 or 3903-F	3759 00
26	One-half of self-employment tax. Attach Schedule SE	
27	Self-employed health insurance deduction (see page 17)	
28	Keogh and self-employed SEP and SIMPLE plans	
29	Penalty on early withdrawal of savings	
30a	Alimony paid b Recipient's SSN ▶	
31	Add lines 23 through 30a	7759 00
32	Subtract line 31 from line 22. This is your adjusted gross income	69061 00

For Privacy Act and Paperwork Reduction Act Notice, see page 38.   Cat. No. 11320B   Form 1040 (1997)

SCHEDULES A&B (Form 1040)

Department of the Treasury
Internal Revenue Service (99)

Schedule A—Itemized Deductions

(Schedule B is on back)

▶ Attach to Form 1040. ▶ See Instructions for Schedules A and B (Form 1040).

OMB No. 1545-0074

1997

Attachment Sequence No. 07

Name(s) shown on Form 1040: Jerome L. and Jane T. Scott

Your social security number: 100 22 1234

Medical and Dental Expenses		Caution: Do not include expenses reimbursed or paid by others.			
(See page A-2.)	1	Medical and dental expenses (see page A-1)	1	1500 00	
	2	Enter amount from Form 1040, line 33.	2	61661	
	3	Multiply line 2 above by 7.5% (.075)	3	5180 00	
	4	Subtract line 3 from line 1. If line 3 is more than line 1, enter -0-			4 0

Taxes You Paid	5	State and local income taxes	5	1200 00	
(See page A-2.)	6	Real estate taxes (see page A-2)	6	810 00	
	7	Personal property taxes	7		
	8	Other taxes. List type and amount ▶	8		
	9	Add lines 5 through 8.			9 2010 00

Interest You Paid	10	Home mortgage interest and points reported to you on Form 1098	10	4000 00	
(See page A-3.)	11	Home mortgage interest not reported to you on Form 1098. If paid to the person from whom you bought the home, see page A-3 and show that person's name, identifying no., and address ▶	11		
Note: Personal interest is not deductible.	12	Points not reported to you on Form 1098. See page A-3 for special rules.	12		
	13	Investment interest. Attach Form 4952 if required. (See page A-3.)	13		
	14	Add lines 10 through 13.			14 4000 00

Gifts to Charity	15	Gifts by cash or check. If you made any gift of $250 or more, see page A-3	15	5300 00	
If you made a gift and got a benefit for it, see page A-3.	16	Other than by cash or check. If any gift of $250 or more, see page A-3. You MUST attach Form 8283 if over $500	16		
	17	Carryover from prior year	17		
	18	Add lines 15 through 17.			18 5300 00

Casualty and Theft Losses	19	Casualty or theft loss(es). Attach Form 4684. (See page A-4.)			19

Job Expenses and Most Other Miscellaneous Deductions	20	Unreimbursed employee expenses—job travel, union dues, job education, etc. You MUST attach Form 2106 or 2106-EZ if required. (See page A-5.) ▶	20	3721 00	
(See page A-5 for expenses to deduct here.)	21	Tax preparation fees	21		
	22	Other expenses—investment, safe deposit box, etc. List type and amount ▶	22		
	23	Add lines 20 through 22	23	3721 00	
	24	Enter amount from Form 1040, line 33.	24	61661	
	25	Multiply line 24 above by 2% (.02)	25	1381 00	
	26	Subtract line 25 from line 23. If line 25 is more than line 23, enter -0-			26 2340 00

Other Miscellaneous Deductions	27	Other—from list on page A-5. List type and amount ▶			27

Total Itemized Deductions	28	Is Form 1040, line 33, over $121,200 (over $60,600 if married filing separately)?			28 13650 00
		NO. Your deduction is not limited. Add the amounts in the far right column for lines 4 through 27. Also, enter on Form 1040, line 35, the **larger** of this amount or your standard deduction.			
		YES. Your deduction may be limited. See page A-5 for the amount to enter.			

✳ See attached notes

For Paperwork Reduction Act Notice, see Form 1040 instructions.   Cat. No. 11330X   Schedule A (Form 1040) 1997

Schedules A&B (Form 1040) 1997

Name(s) shown on Form 1040. Do not enter name and social security number if shown on other side.

Jerome L. and Jane T. Scott

OMB No. 1545-0074   Page 2

Your social security number: 100 22 1234

Schedule B—Interest and Dividend Income

Attachment Sequence No. 08

Part I Interest Income				Amount
(See pages 12 and B-1.)	1	List name of payer. If any interest is from a seller-financed mortgage and the buyer used the property as a personal residence, see page B-1 and list this interest first. Also, show that buyer's social security number and address ▶ First United Bank, Anytown, FL		500 00
Note: If you received a Form 1099-INT, Form 1099-OID, or substitute statement from a brokerage firm, list the firm's name as the payer and enter the total interest shown on that form.			1	
	2	Add the amounts on line 1	2	500 00
	3	Excludable interest on series EE U.S. savings bonds issued after 1989 from Form 8815. You MUST attach Form 8815 to Form 1040	3	
	4	Subtract line 3 from line 2. Enter the result here and on Form 1040, line 8a ▶	4	500 00

Part II Dividend Income				Amount
(See pages 12 and B-1.)	5	List name of payer. Include gross dividends and/or other distributions on stock here. Any capital gain distributions and nontaxable distributions will be deducted on lines 7 and 8 ▶	5	500 00
Note: If you received a Form 1099-DIV or substitute statement from a brokerage firm, list the firm's name as the payer and enter the total dividends shown on that form.				
	6	Add the amounts on line 5	6	500 00
	7	Capital gain distributions. Enter here and on Schedule D	7	
	8	Nontaxable distributions. (See the inst. for Form 1040, line 9.)	8	
	9	Add lines 7 and 8 ▶	9	
	10	Subtract line 9 from line 6. Enter the result here and on Form 1040, line 9 ▶	10	

Part III Foreign Accounts and Trusts			Yes	No
(See page B-2.)		You must complete this part if you **(a)** had over $400 of interest or dividends; **(b)** had a foreign account; or **(c)** received a distribution from, or were a grantor of, or a transferor to, a foreign trust.		
	11a	At any time during 1997, did you have an interest in or a signature or other authority over a financial account in a foreign country, such as a bank account, securities account, or other financial account? See page B-2 for exceptions and filing requirements for Form TD F 90-22.1.		X
	b	If "Yes," enter the name of the foreign country ▶		
	12	During 1997, did you receive a distribution from, or were you the grantor of, or transferor to, a foreign trust? If "Yes," you may have to file Form 3520 or 926. See page B-2.		X

For Paperwork Reduction Act Notice, see Form 1040 instructions.   Schedule B (Form 1040) 1997

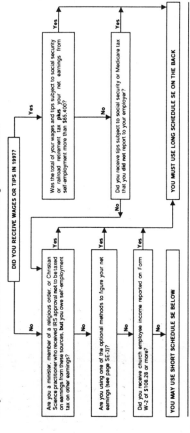

SCHEDULE C-EZ (Form 1040)

Department of the Treasury
Internal Revenue Service (99)

Net Profit From Business
(Sole Proprietorship)

► Partnerships, joint ventures, etc., must file Form 1065.
► Attach to Form 1040 or Form 1041. ► See instructions on back.

OMB No. 1545-0074

1997

Attachment Sequence No. 09A

Name of proprietor: Jerome L. Scott

Social security number (SSN): 100 22 1234

Part I General Information

You May Use This Schedule Only If You:
- Had business expenses of $2,500 or less.
- Use the cash method of accounting.
- Did not have an inventory at any time during the year.
- Did not have a net loss from your business.
- Had only one business as a sole proprietor.

And You:
- Had no employees during the year.
- Are not required to file Form 4562, Depreciation and Amortization, for this business. See the instructions for Schedule C, line 13, on page C-3 to find out if you must file.
- Do not deduct expenses for business use of your home.
- Do not have prior year unallowed passive activity losses from this business.

A Principal business or profession, including product or service: Minister

B Enter principal business code (see page C-6) ► 8 1 7 1

C Business name. If no separate business name, leave blank.

D Employer ID number (EIN), if any

E Business address (including suite or room no.). Address not required if same as on Form 1040, page 1.
First Church, 103 Carl Avenue
City, town or post office, state, and ZIP code: Anytown, FL 33322

Part II Figure Your Net Profit

1 Gross receipts. Caution: If this income was reported to you on Form W-2 and the "Statutory employee" box on that form was checked, see Statutory Employees in the instructions for Schedule C, line 1, on page C-2 and check here ► ☐ | **1** | 2160 | 00

2 Total expenses. If more than $2,500, you must use Schedule C. See instructions | **2** | 280 | 00

3 Net profit. Subtract line 2 from line 1. If less than zero, you must use Schedule C. Enter on Form 1040, line 12, and ALSO on Schedule SE, line 2. (Statutory employees do not report this amount on Schedule SE, line 2. Estates and trusts, enter on Form 1041, line 3.) | **3** | 1820 | 00

Part III Information on Your Vehicle. Complete this part ONLY if you are claiming car or truck expenses on line 2.

4 When did you place your vehicle in service for business purposes? (month, day, year) ► / /

5 Of the total number of miles you drove your vehicle during 1997, enter the number of miles you used your vehicle for:

a Business _____ b Commuting _____ c Other _____

6 Do you (or your spouse) have another vehicle available for personal use? ☐ Yes ☐ No

7 Was your vehicle available for use during off-duty hours? ☐ Yes ☐ No

8a Do you have evidence to support your deduction? ☐ Yes ☐ No

b If "Yes," is the evidence written? ☐ Yes ☐ No

For Paperwork Reduction Act Notice, see Form 1040 instructions. Cat. No. 14374D Schedule C-EZ (Form 1040) 1997

SCHEDULE SE (Form 1040)

Department of the Treasury
Internal Revenue Service (99)

Self-Employment Tax

► See Instructions for Schedule SE (Form 1040).
► Attach to Form 1040.

OMB No. 1545-0074

1997

Attachment Sequence No. 17

Name of person with self-employment income (as shown on Form 1040): Jerome L. Scott

Social security number of person with self-employment income ► 100 22 1234

Who Must File Schedule SE

You must file Schedule SE if:

- You had net earnings from self-employment from other than church employee income (line 4 of Long Schedule SE) of $400 or more, OR
- You had church employee income of $108.28 or more. Income from services you performed as a minister or a member of a religious order is not church employee income. See page SE-1.

Note: Even if you had a loss or a small amount of income from self-employment, it may be to your benefit to file Schedule SE and use either "optional method" in Part II of Long Schedule SE. See page SE-3.

Exception. If your only self-employment income was from earnings as a minister, member of a religious order, or Christian Science practitioner and you filed Form 4361 and received IRS approval not to be taxed on those earnings, do not file Schedule SE. Instead, write "Exempt–Form 4361" on Form 1040, line 47.

May I Use Short Schedule SE or MUST I Use Long Schedule SE?

DID YOU RECEIVE WAGES OR TIPS IN 1997?

Are you a minister, member of a religious order, or Christian Science practitioner who received IRS approval not to be taxed on earnings from these sources, but you owe self-employment tax on other earnings? → No

Are you using one of the optional methods to figure your net earnings (see page SE-3)? → No

Did you receive church employee income reported on Form W-2 of $108.28 or more? → No

YOU MAY USE SHORT SCHEDULE SE BELOW

Was the total of your wages and tips subject to social security or railroad retirement tax plus your net self-employment more than $65,400? → Yes

Did you receive tips subject to social security or Medicare tax that you did not report to your employer? → Yes

YOU MUST USE LONG SCHEDULE SE ON THE BACK

Section A—Short Schedule SE. Caution: Read above to see if you can use Short Schedule SE.

1 Net farm profit or (loss) from Schedule F, line 36, and farm partnerships, Schedule K-1 (Form 1065), line 15a | **1** |

2 Net profit or (loss) from Schedule C, line 31; Schedule C-EZ, line 3; and Schedule K-1 (Form 1065), line 15a (other than farming). Ministers and members of religious orders, see page SE-1 for amounts to report on this line. See page SE-2 for other income to report. | **2** | 53210 | 00

3 Combine lines 1 and 2 | **3** | 53210 | 00

4 Net earnings from self-employment. Multiply line 3 by 92.35% (.9235). If less than $400, do not file this schedule; you do not owe self-employment tax | **4** | 49139 | 00

5 Self-employment tax. If the amount on line 4 is:

- $65,400 or less, multiply line 4 by 15.3% (.153). Enter the result here and on Form 1040, line 47.
- More than $65,400, multiply line 4 by 2.9% (.029). Then, add $8,109.60 to the result. Enter the total here and on Form 1040, line 47. | **5** | 7518 | 00

6 Deduction for one-half of self-employment tax. Multiply line 5 by 50% (.5). Enter the result here and on Form 1040, line 26 | **6** | 3759 |

For Paperwork Reduction Act Notice, see Form 1040 instructions. Cat. No. 11358Z Schedule SE (Form 1040) 1997

Form **2106**

Department of the Treasury
Internal Revenue Service (99)

Employee Business Expenses

▶ See separate instructions.
▶ Attach to Form 1040.

OMB No. 1545-0139

1997

Attachment
Sequence No. **54**

Your name: *Jerome L. Scott*

Social security number: 100 | 22 | 1234

Occupation in which you incurred expenses: *Minister*

Part I Employee Business Expenses and Reimbursements

STEP 1 Enter Your Expenses

		Column A Other Than Meals and Entertainment		Column B Meals and Entertainment	
1	Vehicle expense from line 22 or line 29	1	2750 00		
2	Parking fees, tolls, and transportation, including train, bus, etc., that **did not** involve overnight travel or commuting to and from work	2			
3	Travel expense while away from home overnight, including lodging, airplane, car rental, etc. **Do not** include meals and entertainment	3	900 00		
4	Business expenses not included on lines 1 through 3. **Do not** include meals and entertainment	4	900 00		
5	Meals and entertainment expenses (see instructions)	5		320 00	
6	**Total expenses.** In Column A, add lines 1 through 4 and enter the result. In Column B, enter the amount from line 5	6	4550 00	320 00	

Note: *If you were not reimbursed for any expenses in Step 1, skip line 7 and enter the amount from line 6 on line 8.*

STEP 2 Enter Reimbursements Received From Your Employer for Expenses Listed in STEP 1

7	Enter reimbursements received from your employer that were **not** reported to you in box 1 of Form W-2. Include any reimbursements reported under code "L" in box 13 of your Form W-2 (see instructions)	7			

STEP 3 Figure Expenses To Deduct on Schedule A (Form 1040)

8	Subtract line 7 from line 6	8	4550 00	320 00	

Note: *If both columns of line 8 are zero, **stop here.** If Column A is less than zero, report the amount as income on Form 1040, line 7.*

9	In Column A, enter the amount from line 8. In Column B, multiply the amount on line 8 by 50% (.50). (If either column is zero or less, enter -0- in that column.)	9	4550 00	160 00	
10	Add the amounts on line 9 of both columns and enter the total here. **Also, enter the total on Schedule A (Form 1040), line 20.** (Fee-basis state or local government officials, qualified performing artists, and individuals with disabilities: See the instructions for special rules on where to enter the total.) ▶	10		3721 00	※

For Paperwork Reduction Act Notice, see instructions.

Cat. No. 11700N

Form **2106** (1997)

※ *See attached notes*

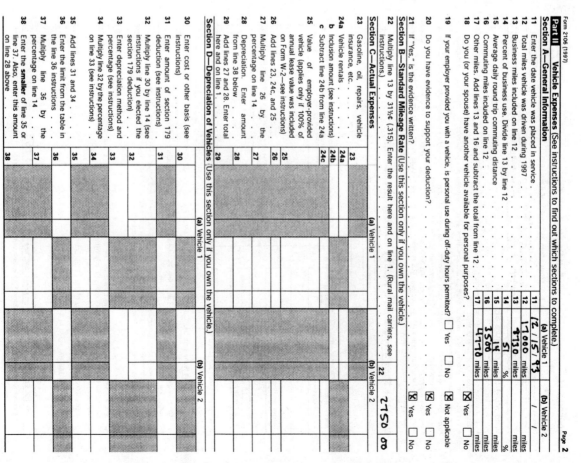

Form 2106 (1997)

Page **2**

Part II Vehicle Expenses (See instructions to find out which sections to complete.)

Section A—General Information

		(a) Vehicle 1	(b) Vehicle 2
11	Enter the date vehicle was placed in service	11	12 / 15 / 93	/ /
12	Total miles vehicle was driven during 1997	12	17,000 miles	miles
13	Business miles included on line 12	13	7130 miles	miles
14	Percent of business use. Divide line 13 by line 12	14	51 %	%
15	Average daily round trip commuting distance	15	14 miles	miles
16	Commuting miles included on line 12	16	3500 miles	miles
17	Other miles. Add lines 13 and 16 and subtract the total from line 12	17	4770 miles	miles
18	Do you (or your spouse) have another vehicle available for personal purposes?		☒ Yes ☐ No
19	If your employer provided you with a vehicle, is personal use during off-duty hours permitted?		☐ Yes ☐ No ☒ Not applicable
20	Do you have evidence to support your deduction?		☒ Yes ☐ No
21	If "Yes," is the evidence written?		☒ Yes ☐ No

Section B—Standard Mileage Rate (Use this section only if you own the vehicle.)

			(a) Vehicle 1	(b) Vehicle 2
22	Multiply line 13 by 31½¢ (.315). (Rural mail carriers, see instructions.)		22	2750 00	

Section C—Actual Expenses

		(a) Vehicle 1		(b) Vehicle 2	
23	Gasoline, oil, repairs, vehicle insurance, etc.	23				
24a	Vehicle rentals	24a				
b	Inclusion amount (see instructions)	24b				
c	Subtract line 24b from line 24a	24c				
25	Value of employer-provided vehicle (applies only if 100% of annual lease value was included on Form W-2—see instructions)	25				
26	Add lines 23, 24c, and 25	26				
27	Multiply line 26 by the percentage on line 14	27				
28	Depreciation. Enter amount from line 38 below	28				
29	Add lines 27 and 28. Enter total here and on line 1	29				

Section D—Depreciation of Vehicles (Use this section only if you own the vehicle.)

		(a) Vehicle 1		(b) Vehicle 2	
30	Enter cost or other basis (see instructions)	30				
31	Enter amount of section 179 deduction (see instructions)	31				
32	Multiply line 30 by line 14 (see instructions if you elected the section 179 deduction)	32				
33	Enter depreciation method and percentage (see instructions)	33				
34	Multiply line 32 by the percentage on line 33 (see instructions)	34				
35	Add lines 31 and 34	35				
36	Enter the limit from the table in the line 36 instructions	36				
37	Multiply line 36 by the percentage on line 14	37				
38	Enter the **smaller** of line 35 or line 37. Also, enter this amount on line 28 above	38				

✪

Form 4562 — Depreciation and Amortization (Including Information on Listed Property)

OMB No. 1545-0172
1997
Attachment Sequence No. 67

Department of the Treasury Internal Revenue Service (99)

▶ See separate instructions. ▶ Attach this form to your return.

Name(s) shown on return: Jerome L. and Jane T. Scott

Business or activity to which this form relates: minister

Identifying number: 100-22-1234

Part I — Election To Expense Certain Tangible Property (Section 179) (Note: If you have any "listed property," complete Part V before you complete Part I.)

1	Maximum dollar limitation. If an enterprise zone business, see page 2 of the instructions	1	$18,000
2	Total cost of section 179 property placed in service. See page 2 of the instructions	2	
3	Threshold cost of section 179 property before reduction in limitation	3	$200,000
4	Reduction in limitation. Subtract line 3 from line 2. If zero or less, enter -0-	4	
5	Dollar limitation for tax year. Subtract line 4 from line 1. If zero or less, enter -0-. If married filing separately, see page 2 of the instructions	5	

6 (a) Description of property	(b) Cost (business use only)	(c) Elected cost

7	Listed property. Enter amount from line 27	7	
8	Total elected cost of section 179 property. Add amounts in column (c), lines 6 and 7	8	
9	Tentative deduction. Enter the smaller of line 5 or line 8	9	
10	Carryover of disallowed deduction from 1996. See page 3 of the instructions	10	
11	Business income limitation. Enter the smaller of business income (not less than zero) or line 5 (see instructions)	11	
12	Section 179 expense deduction. Add lines 9 and 10, but do not enter more than line 11	12	
13	Carryover of disallowed deduction to 1998. Add lines 9 and 10, less line 12 ▶	13	

Note: Do not use Part II or Part III below for listed property (automobiles, certain other vehicles, cellular telephones, certain computers, or property used for entertainment, recreation, or amusement). Instead, use Part V for listed property.

Part II — MACRS Depreciation For Assets Placed in Service ONLY During Your 1997 Tax Year (Do Not Include Listed Property.)

Section A—General Asset Account Election

14 If you are making the election under section 168(i)(4) to group any assets placed in service during the tax year into one or more general asset accounts check this box. See page 3 of the instructions ▶ ☐

Section B—General Depreciation System (GDS) (See page 3 of the instructions.)

(a) Classification of property	(b) Month and year placed in service	(c) Basis for depreciation (business/investment use only—see instructions)	(d) Recovery period	(e) Convention	(f) Method	(g) Depreciation deduction
15a 3-year property						
b 5-year property						
c 7-year property						
d 10-year property						
e 15-year property						
f 20-year property						
g 25-year property			25 yrs.		S/L	
h Residential rental property			27.5 yrs.	MM	S/L	
			27.5 yrs.	MM	S/L	
i Nonresidential real property			39 yrs.	MM	S/L	
				MM	S/L	

Section C—Alternative Depreciation System (ADS) (See page 6 of the instructions.)

16a Class life					S/L	
b 12-year			12 yrs.		S/L	
c 40-year			40 yrs.	MM	S/L	

Part III — Other Depreciation (Do Not Include Listed Property.) (See page 6 of the instructions.)

17	GDS and ADS deductions for assets placed in service in tax years beginning before 1997	17	
18	Property subject to section 168(f)(1) election	18	
19	ACRS and other depreciation	19	

Part IV — Summary (See page 7 of the instructions.)

20	Listed property. Enter amount from line 26	20	
21	Total. Add deductions on line 12, lines 15 and 16 in column (g), and lines 17 through 20. Enter here and on the appropriate lines of your return. Partnerships and S corporations—see instructions	21	
22	For assets shown above and placed in service during the current year, enter the portion of the basis attributable to section 263A costs	22	

Form 4562 (1997) Page 2

Part V — Listed Property—Automobiles, Certain Other Vehicles, Cellular Telephones, Certain Computers, and Property Used for Entertainment, Recreation, or Amusement

Note: For any vehicle for which you are using the standard mileage rate or deducting lease expense, complete only 23a, 23b, columns (a) through (c) of Section A, all of Section B, and Section C if applicable.

Section A—Depreciation and Other Information (Caution: See page 8 of the instructions for limits for passenger automobiles.)

23a Do you have evidence to support the business/investment use claimed? ☒ Yes ☐ No 23b If "Yes," is the evidence written? ☒ Yes ☐ No

(a) Type of property (list vehicles first)	(b) Date placed in service	(c) Business/ investment use percentage	(d) Cost or other basis	(e) Basis for depreciation (business/investment use only)	(f) Recovery period	(g) Method/ Convention	(h) Depreciation deduction	(i) Elected section 179 cost
24 Property used more than 50% in a qualified business use (See page 7 of the instructions):								
car	12-15-93	51 %	12,000					
		%						
25 Property used 50% or less in a qualified business use (See page 7 of the instructions):								
		%			S/L –			
		%			S/L –			
		%			S/L –			

26	Add amounts in column (h). Enter the total here and on line 20, page 1	26	
27	Add amounts in column (i). Enter the total here and on line 7, page 1	27	

Section B—Information on Use of Vehicles

Complete this section for vehicles used by a sole proprietor, partner, or other "more than 5% owner," or related person.
If you provided vehicles to your employees, first answer the questions in Section C to see if you meet an exception to completing this section for those vehicles.

	(a) Vehicle 1		(b) Vehicle 2		(c) Vehicle 3		(d) Vehicle 4		(e) Vehicle 5		(f) Vehicle 6	
28 Total business/investment miles driven during the year (DO NOT include commuting miles)	8130											
29 Total commuting miles driven during the year	3500											
30 Total other personal (noncommuting) miles driven	4770											
31 Total miles driven during the year. Add lines 28 through 30	17000											
	Yes	No	Yes	No	Yes	No	Yes	No	Yes	No	Yes	No
32 Was the vehicle available for personal use during off-duty hours?	✗											
33 Was the vehicle used primarily by a more than 5% owner or related person?		✗										
34 Is another vehicle available for personal use?		✗										

Section C—Questions for Employers Who Provide Vehicles for Use by Their Employees

Answer these questions to determine if you meet an exception to completing Section B for vehicles used by employees who are not more than 5% owners or related persons.

	Yes	No
35 Do you maintain a written policy statement that prohibits all personal use of vehicles, including commuting, by your employees?		
36 Do you maintain a written policy statement that prohibits personal use of vehicles, except commuting, by your employees? See page 9 of the instructions for vehicles used by corporate officers, directors, or 1% or more owners		
37 Do you treat all use of vehicles by employees as personal use?		
38 Do you provide more than five vehicles to your employees, obtain information from your employees about the use of the vehicles, and retain the information received?		
39 Do you meet the requirements concerning qualified automobile demonstration use? See page 9 of the instructions	Yes	No

Note: If your answer to 35, 36, 37, 38, or 39 is "Yes," you need not complete Section B for the covered vehicles.

Part VI — Amortization

(a) Description of costs	(b) Date amortization begins	(c) Amortizable amount	(d) Code section	(e) Amortization period or percentage	(f) Amortization for this year
40 Amortization of costs that begins during your 1997 tax year:					
41 Amortization of costs that began before 1997					41	

Notes and Schedules
Jerome L. and Jane T. Scott
1997 tax returns

Form 1040
line 7:

Rev. Scott's church salary*	$40,000
Christmas gift from church	500
Business expense allowances	3,600
Jane Scott's salary	30,000
TOTAL	$74,100

* housing allowance ($12,000) not included in church wages since it is an exclusion from gross income

line 22:

A minister's housing allowance exclusion is the lowest of:
1) actual expenses incurred in
   owning or maintaining a home $11,600
2) church designated allowance 12,000
3) fair rental value of home
   (furnished, including utilities) 12,500

The lowest of these three amounts is Rev. Scott's actual expenses of $11,600. This represents the amount that can be excluded from gross income. However, since Rev. Scott's W-2 and Form 1040 (line 7) were reduced by the amount of the church designated housing allowance ($12,000), Rev. Scott reports as "other income" on Form 1040 (line 21) the excess by which the church designated housing allowance exceeds his actual housing expenses:

	church designated allowance	$12,000
-	actual expenses incurred in owning and maintaining a home	11,600
=	excess allowance reported as income	$400

Schedule A
Lines 6 and 9a:

Ministers are permitted to fully deduct real estate and mortgage interest payments as itemized expenses on Schedule A even though both items were included in computing the housing allowance exclusion. *IRC 265(a)(6)(B).*

Schedule SE
line 2:

Church salary		$40,000
Christmas gift from church	+	500
Business expenses allowances	+	3,600
Housing allowance exclusion	+	11,600
Schedule C net earnings	+	1,820
Employee business expenses (only 50% of business meals are included)	-	4,710*
TOTAL		$52,810

* not reduced under the *Deason* rule, since the housing
allowance is not tax-exempt for self-employment tax purposes

Form 2106

line 3: airline tickets ($600) plus lodging ($300) incurred in attending church convention

line 4: subscriptions ($200) plus seminary course ($500) plus business supplies ($200)

line 5: meals ($320) incurred in attending church convention; this amount must be reduced by 50% (see line 10)

line 10: IRC section 265 — Computation of Unallowed Part of Deduction

The Tax Court has ruled that actual business expenses (not reimbursed under an accountable plan) must be reduced by the percentage of total church compensation that is tax-exempt. See *Deason v. Commissioner,* 41 T.C. 465 (1964). Deductible business expenses are computed as follows:

Total ministry income (salary, housing allowance exclusion, car allowances, Christmas gift)	$55,700
Housing allowance exclusion (lowest of actual housing expenses church designated allowance, or fair rental value of furnished home including utilities)	11,600
Nontaxable income percentage (11,600/45,600)	21%
Total business expenses	4,710
Nondeductible business expenses—nontaxable income percentage (21%) x total business expenses ($4,710)	989
Deductible business expenses—total business expenses ($4,710) less nondeductible business expenses ($989)—report on Form 2106, line 10	3,721

Schedule C-EZ

line 2: meals ($100) must be reduced by 50% leaving $50, plus lodging expenses of $230, totals $280.

Form 1040 — Department of the Treasury—Internal Revenue Service
U.S. Individual Income Tax Return 1997

For the year Jan. 1–Dec. 31, 1997, or other tax year beginning , 1997, ending , 19 · OMB No. 1545-0074

Label
Your first name and initial: Jerome L. — Last name: Scott
Your social security number: 100 : 22 : 1234

If a joint return, spouse's first name and initial: Jane T. — Last name: Scott
Spouse's social security number: 101 : 22 : 2345

Home address (number and street). If you have a P.O. box, see page 10: 418 Walnut — Apt. no.

City, town or post office, state, and ZIP code. If you have a foreign address, see page 10: Anytown, FL 33522

Presidential Election Campaign (See page 10)
Do you want $3 to go to this fund? — Yes [X] No
If a joint return, does your spouse want $3 to go to this fund? — Yes [X] No

Filing Status
2 [X] Married filing joint return (even if only one had income)

Exemptions
6a [X] Yourself. 6b [X] Spouse

Dependents:
(1) First name	Last name	(2) social security number	(3) relationship	(4) No. of months
Andrew	Scott	00:11:0123	son	12
Amy	Scott	001:12:1234	daughter	12

No. of boxes checked on 6a and 6b: 2
No. of your children on 6c who lived with you: 2
Add numbers entered on lines above: 4

Income

Line	Description	Amount
7	Wages, salaries, tips, etc. Attach Form(s) W-2	30000 00
8a	Taxable interest. Attach Schedule B if required	500 00
12	Business income or (loss). Attach Schedule C or C-EZ	42658 00
22	Add the amounts in the far right column for lines 7 through 21. This is your **total income**	4000 00 (23)
26	One-half of self-employment tax. Attach Schedule SE	3759 00
31	Add lines 23 through 30a	7759 00
32	Subtract line 31 from line 22. This is your **adjusted gross income**	64899 00

Cat. No. 11320B   Form **1040** (1997)

Form 1040 (1997) — Page 2

Tax Computation

Line	Description	Amount
33	Amount from line 32 (adjusted gross income)	64899 00
35	Itemized deductions or Standard deduction	11300 00
36	Subtract line 35 from line 33	53599 00
37	Multiply $2,650 by the total number of exemptions claimed on line 6d	10600 00
38	Taxable income	42999 00
39	Tax. See page 19	6677 00

Credits

Other Taxes

Line	Description	Amount
45	Add lines 40 through 44	6677 00
46	Subtract line 45 from line 39	1518 00
47	Self-employment tax. Attach Schedule SE	7518 00
53	Add lines 46 through 52. This is your **total tax**	14195 00

Payments

Line	Description	Amount
54	Federal income tax withheld from Forms W-2 and 1099	6000 00
55	1997 estimated tax payments	8000 00
60	Add lines 54, 55, 56a, 57, 58, and 59. These are your **total payments**	14000 00

Amount You Owe

Line	Description	Amount
64	AMOUNT YOU OWE	195 00

Sign Here
Your signature: Jerome L. Scott — Date: Mar. 1, 1998 — Your occupation: Minister
Spouse's signature: Jane T. Scott — Date: Mar. 1, 1998 — Spouse's occupation: accountant

Form **1040** (1997)

SCHEDULE A&B (Form 1040)

Department of the Treasury
Internal Revenue Service (99)

Schedule A—Itemized Deductions

(Schedule B is on back)

▶ Attach to Form 1040. ▶ See Instructions for Schedules A and B (Form 1040).

OMB No. 1545-0074

1997

Attachment Sequence No. 07

Name(s) shown on Form 1040: Jerome L. and Jane T. Scott

Your social security number: 100 22 1234

Section		Line		Amount
Medical and Dental Expenses	Caution: Do not include expenses reimbursed or paid by others.			
	1 Medical and dental expenses (see page A-1)	1	1500 00	
	2 Enter amount from Form 1040, line 33. 2	24,849		
	3 Multiply line 2 above by 7.5% (.075)	3	1848 00	
	4 Subtract line 3 from line 1. If line 3 is more than line 1, enter -0-			4	0
Taxes You Paid (See page A-2.)	5 State and local income taxes	5	1200 00	
	6 Real estate taxes (see page A-2)	6	800 00	
	7 Personal property taxes	7		
	8 Other taxes. List type and amount ▶	8		
	9 Add lines 5 through 8			9	2000 00
Interest You Paid (See page A-2.) Note: Personal interest is not deductible.	10 Home mortgage interest and points reported to you on Form 1098	10	4000 00	
	11 Home mortgage interest not reported to you on Form 1098. If paid to the person from whom you bought the home, see page A-3 and show that person's name, identifying no., and address ▶	11		
	12 Points not reported to you on Form 1098. See page A-3 for special rules	12		
	13 Investment interest. Attach Form 4952 if required. (See page A-3.)	13		
	14 Add lines 10 through 13			14	4000 00
Gifts to Charity If you made a gift and got a benefit for it, see page A-3.	15 Gifts by cash or check. If you made any gift of $250 or more, see page A-3	15	5300 00	
	16 Other than by cash or check. If any gift of $250 or more, see page A-3. You MUST attach Form 8283 if over $500	16		
	17 Carryover from prior year	17		
	18 Add lines 15 through 17			18	5300 00
Casualty and Theft Losses	19 Casualty or theft loss(es). Attach Form 4684. (See page A-4.)			19	
Job Expenses and Most Other Miscellaneous Deductions (See page A-5 for expenses to deduct here.)	20 Unreimbursed employee expenses—job travel, union dues, job education, etc. You MUST attach Form 2106 or 2106-EZ if required. (See page A-4.) ▶	20		
	21 Tax preparation fees	21		
	22 Other expenses—investment, safe deposit box, etc. List type and amount ▶	22		
	23 Add lines 20 through 22	23		
	24 Enter amount from Form 1040, line 33. 24		25 Multiply line 24 above by 2% (.02)	25	
	26 Subtract line 25 from line 23. If line 25 is more than line 23, enter -0-			26	
Other Miscellaneous Deductions	27 Other—from list on page A-5. List type and amount ▶			27	
Total Itemized Deductions	28 Is Form 1040, line 33, over $121,200 (over $60,600 if married filing separately)? **NO.** Your deduction is not limited. Add the amounts in the far right column for lines 4 through 27. Also, enter on Form 1040, line 35, the **larger of** this amount or your standard deduction. **YES.** Your deduction may be limited. See page A-5 for the amount to enter.			28	11300 00

For Paperwork Reduction Act Notice, see Form 1040 instructions.   Cat. No. 11330X   Schedule A (Form 1040) 1997

Schedules A&B (Form 1040) 1997

Name(s) shown on Form 1040. Do not enter name and social security number if shown on other side.
Jerome L. and Jane T. Scott

OMB No. 1545-0074   Page 2

Your social security number: 100 22 1234

Attachment Sequence No. 08

Schedule B—Interest and Dividend Income

**Part I
Interest Income**

(See pages 12 and B-1.)

Note: If you received a Form 1099-INT, Form 1099-OID, or substitute statement from a brokerage firm, list the firm's name as the payer and enter the total interest shown on that form.

	Amount
1 List name of payer. If any interest is from a seller-financed mortgage and the buyer used the property as a personal residence, see page B-1 and list this interest first. Also, show that buyer's social security number and address ▶ First United Bank, Anytown, FL	500 00
2 Add the amounts on line 1	2	500 00
3 Excludable interest on series EE U.S. savings bonds issued after 1989 from Form 8815, line 14. You MUST attach Form 8815 to Form 1040	3	
4 Subtract line 3 from line 2. Enter the result here and on Form 1040, line 8a ▶	4	500 00

Note: If you had over $400 in taxable interest income, you must also complete Part III.

**Part II
Dividend Income**

(See pages 12 and B-1.)

Note: If you received a Form 1099-DIV or substitute statement from a brokerage firm, list the firm's name as the payer and enter the total dividends shown on that form.

	Amount
5 List name of payer. Include gross dividends and/or other distributions on stock here. Any capital gain distributions and nontaxable distributions will be deducted on lines 7 and 8 ▶	500 00
6 Add the amounts on line 5	6	500 00
7 Capital gain distributions. Enter here and on Schedule D	7	
8 Nontaxable distributions. (See the inst. for Form 1040, line 9)	8	
9 Add lines 7 and 8	9	
10 Subtract line 9 from line 6. Enter the result here and on Form 1040, line 9 ▶	10	500 00

Note: If you had over $400 in gross dividends and/or other distributions on stock, you must also complete Part III.

**Part III
Foreign Accounts and Trusts**

(See page B-2.)

	Yes	No
11a At any time during 1997, did you have an interest in or a signature or other authority over a financial account in a foreign country, such as a bank account, securities account, or other financial account? See page B-2 for exceptions and filing requirements for Form TD F 90-22.1 . . .		X
b If "Yes," enter the name of the foreign country ▶		
12 During 1997, did you receive a distribution from, or were you the grantor of, or transferor to, a foreign trust? If "Yes," you may have to file Form 3520 or 926. See page B-2 . . .		X

For Paperwork Reduction Act Notice, see Form 1040 instructions.   Schedule B (Form 1040) 1997

SCHEDULE C (Form 1040)

Department of the Treasury
Internal Revenue Service (99)

Profit or Loss From Business
(Sole Proprietorship)

▶ Partnerships, joint ventures, etc., must file Form 1065.

▶ Attach to Form 1040 or Form 1041. ▶ See Instructions for Schedule C (Form 1040).

OMB No. 1545-0074

1997

Attachment Sequence No. 09

Name of proprietor: Jerome L. Scott

Social security number (SSN): 100 22 1234

A Principal business or profession, including product or service (see page C-1): Minister

B Enter principal business code (see page C-6) ▶ 8 7 1 1

C Business name. If no separate business name, leave blank.

D Employer ID number (EIN), if any

E Business address (including suite or room no.) ▶ First Church, 103 Coral Avenue
City, town or post office, state, and ZIP code ▶ Anytown, FL 33322

F Accounting method: (1) ☒ Cash (2) ☐ Accrual (3) ☐ Other (specify) ▶

G Did you "materially participate" in the operation of this business during 1997? If "No," see page C-2 for limit on losses. ☒ Yes ☐ No

H If you started or acquired this business during 1997, check here ▶ ☐

Part I — Income

1	Gross receipts or sales. Caution: If this income was reported to you on Form W-2 and the "Statutory employee" box on that form was checked, see page C-2 and check here ▶ ☐	1
2	Returns and allowances	2
3	Subtract line 2 from line 1	3
4	Cost of goods sold (from line 42 on page 2)	4
5	Gross profit. Subtract line 4 from line 3	5	46600 00
6	Other income, including Federal and state gasoline or fuel tax credit or refund (see page C-2)	6	
7	Gross income. Add lines 5 and 6 ▶	7	46600 00

Part II — Expenses. Enter expenses for business use of your home only on line 30.

8	Advertising	8		
9	Bad debts from sales or services (see page C-3)	9		
10	Car and truck expenses (see page C-3)	10	2750 00	
11	Commissions and fees	11		
12	Depletion	12		
13	Depreciation and section 179 expense deduction (not included in Part III) (see page C-3)	13		
14	Employee benefit programs (other than on line 19)	14		
15	Insurance (other than health)	15		
16	Interest:			
16a	Mortgage (paid to banks, etc.)	16a		
16b	Other	16b		
17	Legal and professional services	17		
18	Office expense	18		
19	Pension and profit-sharing plans	19		
20	Rent or lease (see page C-4):			
20a	Vehicles, machinery, and equipment	20a		
20b	Other business property	20b		
21	Repairs and maintenance	21	200 00	
22	Supplies (not included in Part III)	22		
23	Taxes and licenses	23		
24	Travel, meals, and entertainment:			
24a	Travel	24a	1130 00	
24b	Meals and entertainment		420	
24c	Enter 50% of line 24b subject to limitations (see page C-4)		210	
24d	Subtract line 24c from line 24b	24d	210 00	
25	Utilities	25		
26	Wages (less employment credits)	26		
27	Other expenses (from line 48 on page 2)	27	700 00	
28	Total expenses before expenses for business use of home. Add lines 8 through 27 in columns ▶	28	3942 00	

29	Tentative profit (loss). Subtract line 28 from line 7	29	42658 00
30	Expenses for business use of your home. Attach Form 8829	30	
31	Net profit or (loss). Subtract line 30 from line 29.	31	42658 00
	• If a profit, enter on Form 1040, line 12, and ALSO on Schedule SE, line 2 (statutory employees, see page C-5). Estates and trusts, enter on Form 1041, line 3.		
	• If a loss, you MUST go on to line 32.		
32	If you have a loss, check the box that describes your investment in this activity (see page C-5).	32a ☐ All investment is at risk.
	• If you checked 32a, enter the loss on Form 1040, line 12, and ALSO on Schedule SE, line 2 (statutory employees, see page C-5). Estates and trusts, enter on Form 1041, line 3.	32b ☐ Some investment is not at risk.
	• If you checked 32b, you MUST attach Form 6198.	

For Paperwork Reduction Act Notice, see Form 1040 instructions.   Cat. No. 11334P   Schedule C (Form 1040) 1997

Schedule C (Form 1040) 1997   Page 2

Part III — Cost of Goods Sold (see page C-5)

33	Method(s) used to value closing inventory: a ☐ Cost b ☐ Lower of cost or market c ☐ Other (attach explanation)	
34	Was there any change in determining quantities, costs, or valuations between opening and closing inventory? If "Yes," attach explanation	☐ Yes ☐ No
35	Inventory at beginning of year. If different from last year's closing inventory, attach explanation	35
36	Purchases less cost of items withdrawn for personal use	36
37	Cost of labor. Do not include salary paid to yourself	37
38	Materials and supplies	38
39	Other costs	39
40	Add lines 35 through 39	40
41	Inventory at end of year	41
42	Cost of goods sold. Subtract line 41 from line 40. Enter the result here and on page 1, line 4	42

Part IV — Information on Your Vehicle. Complete this part ONLY if you are claiming car or truck expenses on line 10 and are not required to file Form 4562 for this business. See the instructions for line 13 on page C-3 to find out if you must file.

43	When did you place your vehicle in service for business purposes? (month, day, year) ▶ / /	
44	Of the total number of miles you drove your vehicle during 1997, enter the number of miles you used your vehicle for:	
a	Business ____ b Commuting ____ c Other ____	
45	Do you (or your spouse) have another vehicle available for personal use?	☐ Yes ☐ No
46	Was your vehicle available for use during off-duty hours?	☐ Yes ☐ No
47a	Do you have evidence to support your deduction?	☐ Yes ☐ No
b	If "Yes," is the evidence written?	☐ Yes ☐ No

Part V — Other Expenses. List below business expenses not included on lines 8–26 or line 30.

education (seminary course)	500 00
professional subscriptions	200 00
48	Total other expenses. Enter here and on page 1, line 27	48	700 00

389

SCHEDULE SE
(Form 1040)

Department of the Treasury
Internal Revenue Service (99)

Self-Employment Tax

▶ See Instructions for Schedule SE (Form 1040).

▶ Attach to Form 1040.

OMB No. 1545-0074

1997

Attachment
Sequence No. **17**

Name of person with **self-employment** income (as shown on Form 1040)

Jerome L. Scott

Social security number of person
with **self-employment** income ▶ *100 22 1234*

Who Must File Schedule SE

You must file Schedule SE if:

- You had net earnings from self-employment from **other than** church employee income (line 4 of Short Schedule SE or line 4c of Long Schedule SE) of $400 or more, **OR**

- You had church employee income of $108.28 or more. Income from services you performed as a minister or a member of a religious order **is not** church employee income. See page SE-1.

Note: *Even if you had a loss or a small amount of income from self-employment, it may be to your benefit to file Schedule SE and use either "optional method" in Part II of Long Schedule SE. See page SE-3.*

Exception. If your only self-employment income was from earnings as a minister, member of a religious order, or Christian Science practitioner **and** you filed Form 4361 and received IRS approval not to be taxed on those earnings, **do not** file Schedule SE. Instead, write "Exempt–Form 4361" on Form 1040, line 47.

May I Use Short Schedule SE or MUST I Use Long Schedule SE?

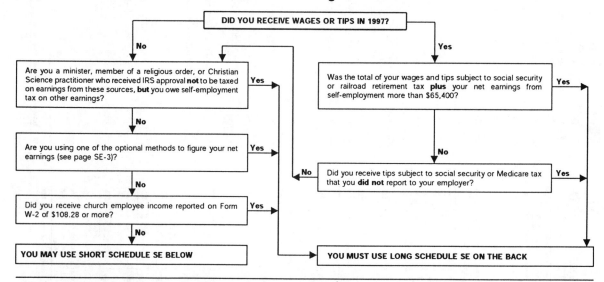

Section A—Short Schedule SE. Caution: *Read above to see if you can use Short Schedule SE.*

1	Net farm profit or (loss) from Schedule F, line 36, and farm partnerships, Schedule K-1 (Form 1065), line 15a	**1**	
2	Net profit or (loss) from Schedule C, line 31; Schedule C-EZ, line 3; and Schedule K-1 (Form 1065), line 15a (other than farming). Ministers and members of religious orders, see page SE-1 for amounts to report on this line. See page SE-2 for other income to report	**2**	53210 00 *
3	Combine lines 1 and 2	**3**	53210 00
4	**Net earnings from self-employment.** Multiply line 3 by 92.35% (.9235). If less than $400, **do not** file this schedule; you do not owe self-employment tax . . . . ▶	**4**	49139 00
5	**Self-employment tax.** If the amount on line 4 is: • $65,400 or less, multiply line 4 by 15.3% (.153). Enter the result here and on **Form 1040, line 47.** • More than $65,400, multiply line 4 by 2.9% (.029). Then, add $8,109.60 to the result. Enter the total here and on **Form 1040, line 47.**	**5**	7518 00
6	**Deduction for one-half of self-employment tax.** Multiply line 5 by 50% (.5). Enter the result here and on **Form 1040, line 26**	**6**	3759

For Paperwork Reduction Act Notice, see Form 1040 instructions.   Cat. No. 11358Z   **Schedule SE (Form 1040) 1997**

✳ *see attached notes*

Form 4562 — Depreciation and Amortization (Including Information on Listed Property)

OMB No. 1545-0172
1997
Attachment Sequence No. 67

Department of the Treasury
Internal Revenue Service (99)

► See separate instructions. ► Attach this form to your return.

Name(s) shown on return: Jerome L. and Jane T. Scott
Business or activity to which this form relates: minister
Identifying number: 100-22-1234

Part I — Election To Expense Certain Tangible Property (Section 179) (Note: If you have any "listed property," complete Part V before you complete Part I.)

1 Maximum dollar limitation. If an enterprise zone business, see page 2 of the instructions	1	$18,000
2 Total cost of section 179 property placed in service. See page 2 of the instructions	2	
3 Threshold cost of section 179 property before reduction in limitation	3	$200,000
4 Reduction in limitation. Subtract line 3 from line 2. If zero or less, enter -0-	4	
5 Dollar limitation for tax year. Subtract line 4 from line 1. If zero or less, enter -0-. If married filing separately, see page 2 of the instructions	5	

(a) Description of property	(b) Cost (business use only)	(c) Elected cost
6		

7 Listed property. Enter amount from line 27	7	
8 Total elected cost of section 179 property. Add amounts in column (c), lines 6 and 7	8	
9 Tentative deduction. Enter the smaller of line 5 or line 8	9	
10 Carryover of disallowed deduction from 1996. See page 3 of the instructions	10	
11 Business income limitation. Enter the smaller of business income (not less than zero) or line 5 (see instructions)	11	
12 Section 179 expense deduction. Add lines 9 and 10, but do not enter more than line 11	12	
13 Carryover of disallowed deduction to 1998. Add lines 9 and 10, less line 12 ►	13	

Note: Do not use Part II or Part III below for listed property (automobiles, certain other vehicles, cellular telephones, certain computers, or property used for entertainment, recreation, or amusement). Instead, use Part V for listed property.

Part II — MACRS Depreciation For Assets Placed in Service ONLY During Your 1997 Tax Year (Do Not Include Listed Property)

Section A—General Asset Account Election

14 If you are making the election under section 168(i)(4) to group any assets placed in service during the tax year into one or more general asset accounts, check this box. See page 3 of the instructions ► ☐

Section B—General Depreciation System (GDS) (See page 3 of the instructions.)

(a) Classification of property	(b) Month and year placed in service	(c) Basis for depreciation (business/investment use only—see instructions)	(d) Recovery period	(e) Convention	(f) Method	(g) Depreciation deduction
15a 3-year property						
b 5-year property						
c 7-year property						
d 10-year property						
e 15-year property						
f 20-year property						
g 25-year property			25 yrs.		S/L	
h Residential rental property			27.5 yrs.	MM	S/L	
			27.5 yrs.	MM	S/L	
i Nonresidential real property			39 yrs.	MM	S/L	
				MM	S/L	

Section C—Alternative Depreciation System (ADS) (See page 6 of the instructions.)

16a Class life					S/L	
b 12-year			12 yrs.		S/L	
c 40-year			40 yrs.	MM	S/L	

Part III — Other Depreciation (Do Not Include Listed Property) (See page 6 of the instructions.)

17 GDS and ADS deductions for assets placed in service in tax years beginning before 1997	17	
18 Property subject to section 168(f)(1) election	18	
19 ACRS and other depreciation	19	

Part IV — Summary (See page 7 of the instructions.)

20 Listed property. Enter amount from line 26	20	
21 Total. Add deductions on line 12, lines 15 and 16 in column (g), and lines 17 through 20. Enter here and on the appropriate lines of your return. Partnerships and S corporations—see instructions	21	
22 For assets shown above and placed in service during the current year, enter the portion of the basis attributable to section 263A costs	22	

For Paperwork Reduction Act Notice, see the separate instructions.   Cat. No. 12906N   Form 4562 (1997)

Form 4562 (1997)   Page 2

Part V — Listed Property—Automobiles, Certain Other Vehicles, Cellular Telephones, Certain Computers, and Property Used for Entertainment, Recreation, or Amusement

Note: For any vehicle for which you are using the standard mileage rate or deducting lease expense, complete only 23a, 23b, columns (a) through (c) of Section A, all of Section B, and Section C if applicable.

Section A—Depreciation and Other Information (Caution: See page 8 of the instructions for limits for passenger automobiles.)

23a Do you have evidence to support the business/investment use claimed? ☒ Yes ☐ No   23b If "Yes," is the evidence written? ☒ Yes ☐ No

(a) Type of property (list vehicles first)	(b) Date placed in service	(c) Business/investment use percentage	(d) Cost or other basis	(e) Basis for depreciation (business/investment use only)	(f) Recovery period	(g) Method/Convention	(h) Depreciation deduction	(i) Elected section 179 cost
24 Property used more than 50% in a qualified business use (See page 7 of the instructions):								
Car	12-15-97	51 %	12,000					
		%						
		%						
25 Property used 50% or less in a qualified business use (See page 7 of the instructions):								
		%			S/L –			
		%			S/L –			
		%			S/L –			

26 Add amounts in column (h). Enter the total here and on line 20, page 1	26	
27 Add amounts in column (i). Enter the total here and on line 7, page 1	27	

Section B—Information on Use of Vehicles

Complete this section for vehicles used by a sole proprietor, partner, or other "more than 5% owner," or related person.
If you provided vehicles to your employees, first answer the questions in Section C to see if you meet an exception to completing this section for those vehicles.

	(a) Vehicle 1		(b) Vehicle 2		(c) Vehicle 3		(d) Vehicle 4		(e) Vehicle 5		(f) Vehicle 6	
28 Total business/investment miles driven during the year (DO NOT include commuting miles)	5130											
29 Total commuting miles driven during the year	3500											
30 Total other personal (noncommuting) miles driven	4770											
31 Total miles driven during the year. Add lines 28 through 30	11600											
	Yes	No	Yes	No	Yes	No	Yes	No	Yes	No	Yes	No
32 Was the vehicle available for personal use during off-duty hours?	X											
33 Was the vehicle used primarily by a more than 5% owner or related person?		X										
34 Is another vehicle available for personal use?		X										

Section C—Questions for Employers Who Provide Vehicles for Use by Their Employees

Answer these questions to determine if you meet an exception to completing Section B for vehicles used by employees who are not more than 5% owners or related persons.

	Yes	No
35 Do you maintain a written policy statement that prohibits all personal use of vehicles, including commuting, by your employees?		
36 Do you maintain a written policy statement that prohibits personal use of vehicles, except commuting, by your employees? See page 9 of the instructions for vehicles used by corporate officers, directors, or 1% or more owners		
37 Do you treat all use of vehicles by employees as personal use?		
38 Do you provide more than five vehicles to your employees, obtain information from your employees about the use of the vehicles, and retain the information received?		
39 Do you meet the requirements concerning qualified automobile demonstration use? See page 9 of the instructions		

Note: If your answer to 35, 36, 37, 38, or 39 is "Yes," you need not complete Section B for the covered vehicles.

Part VI — Amortization

(a) Description of costs	(b) Date amortization begins	(c) Amortizable amount	(d) Code section	(e) Amortization period or percentage	(f) Amortization for this year
40 Amortization of costs that begins during your 1997 tax year:					
41 Amortization of costs that began before 1997					41

Form 4562 (1997)

Notes and Schedules
Jerome L. and Jane T. Scott
1997 tax returns

Schedule A

Lines 6 and 9a:

Ministers are permitted to fully deduct real estate and mortgage interest payments as itemized expenses on Schedule A even though both items were included in computing the housing allowance exclusion. *IRC 265(a)(6)(B).*

Schedule C (for work at First Church)

line 6:

Rev. Scott's church compensation	$40,000*
Christmas gift from church	500
Business expense allowances	3,600
Honoraria	2,100
Excess of church designated housing allowance over actual expenses	400**
TOTAL	$46,600

* housing allowance ($12,000) not included in church wages since it is an exclusion from gross income

** A minister's housing allowance exclusion is the lowest of:

1) actual expenses incurred in owning or maintaining a home	$11,600
2) church designated allowance	12,000
3) fair rental value of home (furnished, including utilities)	12,500

The lowest of these three amounts is Rev. Scott's actual expenses of $11,600. This represents the amount that can be excluded from gross income. However, since Rev. Scott's 1099-MISC and Schedule C (line 6) were reduced by the full amount of the church designated housing allowance ($12,000), Rev. Scott reports as "other income" on Schedule C (line 6) the excess by which the church designated housing allowance exceeds his actual housing expenses:

	church designated allowance	$12,000
-	actual expenses incurred in owning and maintaining a home	11,600
=	excess allowance reported as income	$ 400

line 28: IRC section 265 — Computation of Unallowed Part of Deduction

The Tax Court has ruled that actual business expenses (not reimbursed under an accountable plan) must be reduced by the percentage of total church compensation that is tax-exempt. See *Deason v. Commis*sioner, 41 T.C. 465 (1964). Deductible business expenses are computed as follows:

Total ministry income	$55,700
Housing allowance exclusion (lowest of actual housing expenses, church designated allowance, or fair rental value of furnished home including utilities)	11,600
Nontaxable income percentage (11,600/55,700)	21%
Total business expenses	4,990
Nondeductible business expenses—nontaxable income percentage (21%) x total business expenses ($4,990)	1,048
Deductible business expenses—total business expenses ($4,990) less nondeductible business expenses ($1,048)—report on Schedule C, line 28	3,942

Schedule SE

line 2:

Housing allowance exclusion.	$11,600
Schedule C net earnings without regard to Deason reduction rule	41,610*
TOTAL	$53,210

* not reduced under the *Deason* rule, since the housing allowance is not tax-exempt for self-employment tax purposes

1997 Tax Table

Use if your taxable income is less than $100,000. If $100,000 or more, use the Tax Rate Schedules.

Example. Mr. and Mrs. Brown are filing a joint return. Their taxable income on line 38 of Form 1040 is $25,300. First, they find the $25,300–25,350 income line. Next, they find the column for married filing jointly and read down the column. The amount shown where the income line and filing status column meet is $3,799. This is the tax amount they should enter on line 39 of their Form 1040.

Sample Table

At least	But less than	Single	Married filing jointly *	Married filing sepa-rately	Head of a house-hold
		Your tax is—			
25,200	25,250	3,859	3,784	4,385	3,784
25,250	25,300	3,873	3,791	4,399	3,791
25,300	25,350	3,887	(3,799)	4,413	3,799
25,350	25,400	3,901	3,806	4,427	3,806

If line 38 (taxable income) is— At least	But less than	And you are— Single	Married filing jointly *	Married filing sepa-rately	Head of a house-hold
		Your tax is—			
$0	$5	$0	$0	$0	$0
5	15	2	2	2	2
15	25	3	3	3	3
25	50	6	6	6	6
50	75	9	9	9	9
75	100	13	13	13	13
100	125	17	17	17	17
125	150	21	21	21	21
150	175	24	24	24	24
175	200	28	28	28	28
200	225	32	32	32	32
225	250	36	36	36	36
250	275	39	39	39	39
275	300	43	43	43	43
300	325	47	47	47	47
325	350	51	51	51	51
350	375	54	54	54	54
375	400	58	58	58	58
400	425	62	62	62	62
425	450	66	66	66	66
450	475	69	69	69	69
475	500	73	73	73	73
500	525	77	77	77	77
525	550	81	81	81	81
550	575	84	84	84	84
575	600	88	88	88	88
600	625	92	92	92	92
625	650	96	96	96	96
650	675	99	99	99	99
675	700	103	103	103	103
700	725	107	107	107	107
725	750	111	111	111	111
750	775	114	114	114	114
775	800	118	118	118	118
800	825	122	122	122	122
825	850	126	126	126	126
850	875	129	129	129	129
875	900	133	133	133	133
900	925	137	137	137	137
925	950	141	141	141	141
950	975	144	144	144	144
975	1,000	148	148	148	148
1,000					
1,000	1,025	152	152	152	152
1,025	1,050	156	156	156	156
1,050	1,075	159	159	159	159
1,075	1,100	163	163	163	163
1,100	1,125	167	167	167	167
1,125	1,150	171	171	171	171
1,150	1,175	174	174	174	174
1,175	1,200	178	178	178	178
1,200	1,225	182	182	182	182
1,225	1,250	186	186	186	186
1,250	1,275	189	189	189	189
1,275	1,300	193	193	193	193

If line 38 (taxable income) is— At least	But less than	And you are— Single	Married filing jointly *	Married filing sepa-rately	Head of a house-hold
		Your tax is—			
1,300	1,325	197	197	197	197
1,325	1,350	201	201	201	201
1,350	1,375	204	204	204	204
1,375	1,400	208	208	208	208
1,400	1,425	212	212	212	212
1,425	1,450	216	216	216	216
1,450	1,475	219	219	219	219
1,475	1,500	223	223	223	223
1,500	1,525	227	227	227	227
1,525	1,550	231	231	231	231
1,550	1,575	234	234	234	234
1,575	1,600	238	238	238	238
1,600	1,625	242	242	242	242
1,625	1,650	246	246	246	246
1,650	1,675	249	249	249	249
1,675	1,700	253	253	253	253
1,700	1,725	257	257	257	257
1,725	1,750	261	261	261	261
1,750	1,775	264	264	264	264
1,775	1,800	268	268	268	268
1,800	1,825	272	272	272	272
1,825	1,850	276	276	276	276
1,850	1,875	279	279	279	279
1,875	1,900	283	283	283	283
1,900	1,925	287	287	287	287
1,925	1,950	291	291	291	291
1,950	1,975	294	294	294	294
1,975	2,000	298	298	298	298
2,000					
2,000	2,025	302	302	302	302
2,025	2,050	306	306	306	306
2,050	2,075	309	309	309	309
2,075	2,100	313	313	313	313
2,100	2,125	317	317	317	317
2,125	2,150	321	321	321	321
2,150	2,175	324	324	324	324
2,175	2,200	328	328	328	328
2,200	2,225	332	332	332	332
2,225	2,250	336	336	336	336
2,250	2,275	339	339	339	339
2,275	2,300	343	343	343	343
2,300	2,325	347	347	347	347
2,325	2,350	351	351	351	351
2,350	2,375	354	354	354	354
2,375	2,400	358	358	358	358
2,400	2,425	362	362	362	362
2,425	2,450	366	366	366	366
2,450	2,475	369	369	369	369
2,475	2,500	373	373	373	373
2,500	2,525	377	377	377	377
2,525	2,550	381	381	381	381
2,550	2,575	384	384	384	384
2,575	2,600	388	388	388	388
2,600	2,625	392	392	392	392
2,625	2,650	396	396	396	396
2,650	2,675	399	399	399	399
2,675	2,700	403	403	403	403

If line 38 (taxable income) is— At least	But less than	And you are— Single	Married filing jointly *	Married filing sepa-rately	Head of a house-hold
		Your tax is—			
2,700	2,725	407	407	407	407
2,725	2,750	411	411	411	411
2,750	2,775	414	414	414	414
2,775	2,800	418	418	418	418
2,800	2,825	422	422	422	422
2,825	2,850	426	426	426	426
2,850	2,875	429	429	429	429
2,875	2,900	433	433	433	433
2,900	2,925	437	437	437	437
2,925	2,950	441	441	441	441
2,950	2,975	444	444	444	444
2,975	3,000	448	448	448	448
3,000					
3,000	3,050	454	454	454	454
3,050	3,100	461	461	461	461
3,100	3,150	469	469	469	469
3,150	3,200	476	476	476	476
3,200	3,250	484	484	484	484
3,250	3,300	491	491	491	491
3,300	3,350	499	499	499	499
3,350	3,400	506	506	506	506
3,400	3,450	514	514	514	514
3,450	3,500	521	521	521	521
3,500	3,550	529	529	529	529
3,550	3,600	536	536	536	536
3,600	3,650	544	544	544	544
3,650	3,700	551	551	551	551
3,700	3,750	559	559	559	559
3,750	3,800	566	566	566	566
3,800	3,850	574	574	574	574
3,850	3,900	581	581	581	581
3,900	3,950	589	589	589	589
3,950	4,000	596	596	596	596
4,000					
4,000	4,050	604	604	604	604
4,050	4,100	611	611	611	611
4,100	4,150	619	619	619	619
4,150	4,200	626	626	626	626
4,200	4,250	634	634	634	634
4,250	4,300	641	641	641	641
4,300	4,350	649	649	649	649
4,350	4,400	656	656	656	656
4,400	4,450	664	664	664	664
4,450	4,500	671	671	671	671
4,500	4,550	679	679	679	679
4,550	4,600	686	686	686	686
4,600	4,650	694	694	694	694
4,650	4,700	701	701	701	701
4,700	4,750	709	709	709	709
4,750	4,800	716	716	716	716
4,800	4,850	724	724	724	724
4,850	4,900	731	731	731	731
4,900	4,950	739	739	739	739
4,950	5,000	746	746	746	746

Continued on next page

* This column must also be used by a qualifying widow(er).

1997 Tax Table—*Continued*

If line 38 (taxable income) is— At least	But less than	And you are— Single	Married filing jointly *	Married filing sepa-rately	Head of a house-hold
		Your tax is—			
5,000					
5,000	5,050	754	754	754	754
5,050	5,100	761	761	761	761
5,100	5,150	769	769	769	769
5,150	5,200	776	776	776	776
5,200	5,250	784	784	784	784
5,250	5,300	791	791	791	791
5,300	5,350	799	799	799	799
5,350	5,400	806	806	806	806
5,400	5,450	814	814	814	814
5,450	5,500	821	821	821	821
5,500	5,550	829	829	829	829
5,550	5,600	836	836	836	836
5,600	5,650	844	844	844	844
5,650	5,700	851	851	851	851
5,700	5,750	859	859	859	859
5,750	5,800	866	866	866	866
5,800	5,850	874	874	874	874
5,850	5,900	881	881	881	881
5,900	5,950	889	889	889	889
5,950	6,000	896	896	896	896
6,000					
6,000	6,050	904	904	904	904
6,050	6,100	911	911	911	911
6,100	6,150	919	919	919	919
6,150	6,200	926	926	926	926
6,200	6,250	934	934	934	934
6,250	6,300	941	941	941	941
6,300	6,350	949	949	949	949
6,350	6,400	956	956	956	956
6,400	6,450	964	964	964	964
6,450	6,500	971	971	971	971
6,500	6,550	979	979	979	979
6,550	6,600	986	986	986	986
6,600	6,650	994	994	994	994
6,650	6,700	1,001	1,001	1,001	1,001
6,700	6,750	1,009	1,009	1,009	1,009
6,750	6,800	1,016	1,016	1,016	1,016
6,800	6,850	1,024	1,024	1,024	1,024
6,850	6,900	1,031	1,031	1,031	1,031
6,900	6,950	1,039	1,039	1,039	1,039
6,950	7,000	1,046	1,046	1,046	1,046
7,000					
7,000	7,050	1,054	1,054	1,054	1,054
7,050	7,100	1,061	1,061	1,061	1,061
7,100	7,150	1,069	1,069	1,069	1,069
7,150	7,200	1,076	1,076	1,076	1,076
7,200	7,250	1,084	1,084	1,084	1,084
7,250	7,300	1,091	1,091	1,091	1,091
7,300	7,350	1,099	1,099	1,099	1,099
7,350	7,400	1,106	1,106	1,106	1,106
7,400	7,450	1,114	1,114	1,114	1,114
7,450	7,500	1,121	1,121	1,121	1,121
7,500	7,550	1,129	1,129	1,129	1,129
7,550	7,600	1,136	1,136	1,136	1,136
7,600	7,650	1,144	1,144	1,144	1,144
7,650	7,700	1,151	1,151	1,151	1,151
7,700	7,750	1,159	1,159	1,159	1,159
7,750	7,800	1,166	1,166	1,166	1,166
7,800	7,850	1,174	1,174	1,174	1,174
7,850	7,900	1,181	1,181	1,181	1,181
7,900	7,950	1,189	1,189	1,189	1,189
7,950	8,000	1,196	1,196	1,196	1,196

If line 38 (taxable income) is— At least	But less than	And you are— Single	Married filing jointly *	Married filing sepa-rately	Head of a house-hold
		Your tax is—			
8,000					
8,000	8,050	1,204	1,204	1,204	1,204
8,050	8,100	1,211	1,211	1,211	1,211
8,100	8,150	1,219	1,219	1,219	1,219
8,150	8,200	1,226	1,226	1,226	1,226
8,200	8,250	1,234	1,234	1,234	1,234
8,250	8,300	1,241	1,241	1,241	1,241
8,300	8,350	1,249	1,249	1,249	1,249
8,350	8,400	1,256	1,256	1,256	1,256
8,400	8,450	1,264	1,264	1,264	1,264
8,450	8,500	1,271	1,271	1,271	1,271
8,500	8,550	1,279	1,279	1,279	1,279
8,550	8,600	1,286	1,286	1,286	1,286
8,600	8,650	1,294	1,294	1,294	1,294
8,650	8,700	1,301	1,301	1,301	1,301
8,700	8,750	1,309	1,309	1,309	1,309
8,750	8,800	1,316	1,316	1,316	1,316
8,800	8,850	1,324	1,324	1,324	1,324
8,850	8,900	1,331	1,331	1,331	1,331
8,900	8,950	1,339	1,339	1,339	1,339
8,950	9,000	1,346	1,346	1,346	1,346
9,000					
9,000	9,050	1,354	1,354	1,354	1,354
9,050	9,100	1,361	1,361	1,361	1,361
9,100	9,150	1,369	1,369	1,369	1,369
9,150	9,200	1,376	1,376	1,376	1,376
9,200	9,250	1,384	1,384	1,384	1,384
9,250	9,300	1,391	1,391	1,391	1,391
9,300	9,350	1,399	1,399	1,399	1,399
9,350	9,400	1,406	1,406	1,406	1,406
9,400	9,450	1,414	1,414	1,414	1,414
9,450	9,500	1,421	1,421	1,421	1,421
9,500	9,550	1,429	1,429	1,429	1,429
9,550	9,600	1,436	1,436	1,436	1,436
9,600	9,650	1,444	1,444	1,444	1,444
9,650	9,700	1,451	1,451	1,451	1,451
9,700	9,750	1,459	1,459	1,459	1,459
9,750	9,800	1,466	1,466	1,466	1,466
9,800	9,850	1,474	1,474	1,474	1,474
9,850	9,900	1,481	1,481	1,481	1,481
9,900	9,950	1,489	1,489	1,489	1,489
9,950	10,000	1,496	1,496	1,496	1,496
10,000					
10,000	10,050	1,504	1,504	1,504	1,504
10,050	10,100	1,511	1,511	1,511	1,511
10,100	10,150	1,519	1,519	1,519	1,519
10,150	10,200	1,526	1,526	1,526	1,526
10,200	10,250	1,534	1,534	1,534	1,534
10,250	10,300	1,541	1,541	1,541	1,541
10,300	10,350	1,549	1,549	1,549	1,549
10,350	10,400	1,556	1,556	1,556	1,556
10,400	10,450	1,564	1,564	1,564	1,564
10,450	10,500	1,571	1,571	1,571	1,571
10,500	10,550	1,579	1,579	1,579	1,579
10,550	10,600	1,586	1,586	1,586	1,586
10,600	10,650	1,594	1,594	1,594	1,594
10,650	10,700	1,601	1,601	1,601	1,601
10,700	10,750	1,609	1,609	1,609	1,609
10,750	10,800	1,616	1,616	1,616	1,616
10,800	10,850	1,624	1,624	1,624	1,624
10,850	10,900	1,631	1,631	1,631	1,631
10,900	10,950	1,639	1,639	1,639	1,639
10,950	11,000	1,646	1,646	1,646	1,646

If line 38 (taxable income) is— At least	But less than	And you are— Single	Married filing jointly *	Married filing sepa-rately	Head of a house-hold
		Your tax is—			
11,000					
11,000	11,050	1,654	1,654	1,654	1,654
11,050	11,100	1,661	1,661	1,661	1,661
11,100	11,150	1,669	1,669	1,669	1,669
11,150	11,200	1,676	1,676	1,676	1,676
11,200	11,250	1,684	1,684	1,684	1,684
11,250	11,300	1,691	1,691	1,691	1,691
11,300	11,350	1,699	1,699	1,699	1,699
11,350	11,400	1,706	1,706	1,706	1,706
11,400	11,450	1,714	1,714	1,714	1,714
11,450	11,500	1,721	1,721	1,721	1,721
11,500	11,550	1,729	1,729	1,729	1,729
11,550	11,600	1,736	1,736	1,736	1,736
11,600	11,650	1,744	1,744	1,744	1,744
11,650	11,700	1,751	1,751	1,751	1,751
11,700	11,750	1,759	1,759	1,759	1,759
11,750	11,800	1,766	1,766	1,766	1,766
11,800	11,850	1,774	1,774	1,774	1,774
11,850	11,900	1,781	1,781	1,781	1,781
11,900	11,950	1,789	1,789	1,789	1,789
11,950	12,000	1,796	1,796	1,796	1,796
12,000					
12,000	12,050	1,804	1,804	1,804	1,804
12,050	12,100	1,811	1,811	1,811	1,811
12,100	12,150	1,819	1,819	1,819	1,819
12,150	12,200	1,826	1,826	1,826	1,826
12,200	12,250	1,834	1,834	1,834	1,834
12,250	12,300	1,841	1,841	1,841	1,841
12,300	12,350	1,849	1,849	1,849	1,849
12,350	12,400	1,856	1,856	1,856	1,856
12,400	12,450	1,864	1,864	1,864	1,864
12,450	12,500	1,871	1,871	1,871	1,871
12,500	12,550	1,879	1,879	1,879	1,879
12,550	12,600	1,886	1,886	1,886	1,886
12,600	12,650	1,894	1,894	1,894	1,894
12,650	12,700	1,901	1,901	1,901	1,901
12,700	12,750	1,909	1,909	1,909	1,909
12,750	12,800	1,916	1,916	1,916	1,916
12,800	12,850	1,924	1,924	1,924	1,924
12,850	12,900	1,931	1,931	1,931	1,931
12,900	12,950	1,939	1,939	1,939	1,939
12,950	13,000	1,946	1,946	1,946	1,946
13,000					
13,000	13,050	1,954	1,954	1,954	1,954
13,050	13,100	1,961	1,961	1,961	1,961
13,100	13,150	1,969	1,969	1,969	1,969
13,150	13,200	1,976	1,976	1,976	1,976
13,200	13,250	1,984	1,984	1,984	1,984
13,250	13,300	1,991	1,991	1,991	1,991
13,300	13,350	1,999	1,999	1,999	1,999
13,350	13,400	2,006	2,006	2,006	2,006
13,400	13,450	2,014	2,014	2,014	2,014
13,450	13,500	2,021	2,021	2,021	2,021
13,500	13,550	2,029	2,029	2,029	2,029
13,550	13,600	2,036	2,036	2,036	2,036
13,600	13,650	2,044	2,044	2,044	2,044
13,650	13,700	2,051	2,051	2,051	2,051
13,700	13,750	2,059	2,059	2,059	2,059
13,750	13,800	2,066	2,066	2,066	2,066
13,800	13,850	2,074	2,074	2,074	2,074
13,850	13,900	2,081	2,081	2,081	2,081
13,900	13,950	2,089	2,089	2,089	2,089
13,950	14,000	2,096	2,096	2,096	2,096

* This column must also be used by a qualifying widow(er).

Continued on next page

1997 Tax Table—*Continued*

If line 38 (taxable income) is— At least	But less than	And you are— Single	Married filing jointly *	Married filing separately	Head of a household
		Your tax is—			
14,000					
14,000	14,050	2,104	2,104	2,104	2,104
14,050	14,100	2,111	2,111	2,111	2,111
14,100	14,150	2,119	2,119	2,119	2,119
14,150	14,200	2,126	2,126	2,126	2,126
14,200	14,250	2,134	2,134	2,134	2,134
14,250	14,300	2,141	2,141	2,141	2,141
14,300	14,350	2,149	2,149	2,149	2,149
14,350	14,400	2,156	2,156	2,156	2,156
14,400	14,450	2,164	2,164	2,164	2,164
14,450	14,500	2,171	2,171	2,171	2,171
14,500	14,550	2,179	2,179	2,179	2,179
14,550	14,600	2,186	2,186	2,186	2,186
14,600	14,650	2,194	2,194	2,194	2,194
14,650	14,700	2,201	2,201	2,201	2,201
14,700	14,750	2,209	2,209	2,209	2,209
14,750	14,800	2,216	2,216	2,216	2,216
14,800	14,850	2,224	2,224	2,224	2,224
14,850	14,900	2,231	2,231	2,231	2,231
14,900	14,950	2,239	2,239	2,239	2,239
14,950	15,000	2,246	2,246	2,246	2,246
15,000					
15,000	15,050	2,254	2,254	2,254	2,254
15,050	15,100	2,261	2,261	2,261	2,261
15,100	15,150	2,269	2,269	2,269	2,269
15,150	15,200	2,276	2,276	2,276	2,276
15,200	15,250	2,284	2,284	2,284	2,284
15,250	15,300	2,291	2,291	2,291	2,291
15,300	15,350	2,299	2,299	2,299	2,299
15,350	15,400	2,306	2,306	2,306	2,306
15,400	15,450	2,314	2,314	2,314	2,314
15,450	15,500	2,321	2,321	2,321	2,321
15,500	15,550	2,329	2,329	2,329	2,329
15,550	15,600	2,336	2,336	2,336	2,336
15,600	15,650	2,344	2,344	2,344	2,344
15,650	15,700	2,351	2,351	2,351	2,351
15,700	15,750	2,359	2,359	2,359	2,359
15,750	15,800	2,366	2,366	2,366	2,366
15,800	15,850	2,374	2,374	2,374	2,374
15,850	15,900	2,381	2,381	2,381	2,381
15,900	15,950	2,389	2,389	2,389	2,389
15,950	16,000	2,396	2,396	2,396	2,396
16,000					
16,000	16,050	2,404	2,404	2,404	2,404
16,050	16,100	2,411	2,411	2,411	2,411
16,100	16,150	2,419	2,419	2,419	2,419
16,150	16,200	2,426	2,426	2,426	2,426
16,200	16,250	2,434	2,434	2,434	2,434
16,250	16,300	2,441	2,441	2,441	2,441
16,300	16,350	2,449	2,449	2,449	2,449
16,350	16,400	2,456	2,456	2,456	2,456
16,400	16,450	2,464	2,464	2,464	2,464
16,450	16,500	2,471	2,471	2,471	2,471
16,500	16,550	2,479	2,479	2,479	2,479
16,550	16,600	2,486	2,486	2,486	2,486
16,600	16,650	2,494	2,494	2,494	2,494
16,650	16,700	2,501	2,501	2,501	2,501
16,700	16,750	2,509	2,509	2,509	2,509
16,750	16,800	2,516	2,516	2,516	2,516
16,800	16,850	2,524	2,524	2,524	2,524
16,850	16,900	2,531	2,531	2,531	2,531
16,900	16,950	2,539	2,539	2,539	2,539
16,950	17,000	2,546	2,546	2,546	2,546
17,000					
17,000	17,050	2,554	2,554	2,554	2,554
17,050	17,100	2,561	2,561	2,561	2,561
17,100	17,150	2,569	2,569	2,569	2,569
17,150	17,200	2,576	2,576	2,576	2,576
17,200	17,250	2,584	2,584	2,584	2,584
17,250	17,300	2,591	2,591	2,591	2,591
17,300	17,350	2,599	2,599	2,599	2,599
17,350	17,400	2,606	2,606	2,606	2,606
17,400	17,450	2,614	2,614	2,614	2,614
17,450	17,500	2,621	2,621	2,621	2,621
17,500	17,550	2,629	2,629	2,629	2,629
17,550	17,600	2,636	2,636	2,636	2,636
17,600	17,650	2,644	2,644	2,644	2,644
17,650	17,700	2,651	2,651	2,651	2,651
17,700	17,750	2,659	2,659	2,659	2,659
17,750	17,800	2,666	2,666	2,666	2,666
17,800	17,850	2,674	2,674	2,674	2,674
17,850	17,900	2,681	2,681	2,681	2,681
17,900	17,950	2,689	2,689	2,689	2,689
17,950	18,000	2,696	2,696	2,696	2,696
18,000					
18,000	18,050	2,704	2,704	2,704	2,704
18,050	18,100	2,711	2,711	2,711	2,711
18,100	18,150	2,719	2,719	2,719	2,719
18,150	18,200	2,726	2,726	2,726	2,726
18,200	18,250	2,734	2,734	2,734	2,734
18,250	18,300	2,741	2,741	2,741	2,741
18,300	18,350	2,749	2,749	2,749	2,749
18,350	18,400	2,756	2,756	2,756	2,756
18,400	18,450	2,764	2,764	2,764	2,764
18,450	18,500	2,771	2,771	2,771	2,771
18,500	18,550	2,779	2,779	2,779	2,779
18,550	18,600	2,786	2,786	2,786	2,786
18,600	18,650	2,794	2,794	2,794	2,794
18,650	18,700	2,801	2,801	2,801	2,801
18,700	18,750	2,809	2,809	2,809	2,809
18,750	18,800	2,816	2,816	2,816	2,816
18,800	18,850	2,824	2,824	2,824	2,824
18,850	18,900	2,831	2,831	2,831	2,831
18,900	18,950	2,839	2,839	2,839	2,839
18,950	19,000	2,846	2,846	2,846	2,846
19,000					
19,000	19,050	2,854	2,854	2,854	2,854
19,050	19,100	2,861	2,861	2,861	2,861
19,100	19,150	2,869	2,869	2,869	2,869
19,150	19,200	2,876	2,876	2,876	2,876
19,200	19,250	2,884	2,884	2,884	2,884
19,250	19,300	2,891	2,891	2,891	2,891
19,300	19,350	2,899	2,899	2,899	2,899
19,350	19,400	2,906	2,906	2,906	2,906
19,400	19,450	2,914	2,914	2,914	2,914
19,450	19,500	2,921	2,921	2,921	2,921
19,500	19,550	2,929	2,929	2,929	2,929
19,550	19,600	2,936	2,936	2,936	2,936
19,600	19,650	2,944	2,944	2,944	2,944
19,650	19,700	2,951	2,951	2,951	2,951
19,700	19,750	2,959	2,959	2,959	2,959
19,750	19,800	2,966	2,966	2,966	2,966
19,800	19,850	2,974	2,974	2,974	2,974
19,850	19,900	2,981	2,981	2,981	2,981
19,900	19,950	2,989	2,989	2,989	2,989
19,950	20,000	2,996	2,996	2,996	2,996
20,000					
20,000	20,050	3,004	3,004	3,004	3,004
20,050	20,100	3,011	3,011	3,011	3,011
20,100	20,150	3,019	3,019	3,019	3,019
20,150	20,200	3,026	3,026	3,026	3,026
20,200	20,250	3,034	3,034	3,034	3,034
20,250	20,300	3,041	3,041	3,041	3,041
20,300	20,350	3,049	3,049	3,049	3,049
20,350	20,400	3,056	3,056	3,056	3,056
20,400	20,450	3,064	3,064	3,064	3,064
20,450	20,500	3,071	3,071	3,071	3,071
20,500	20,550	3,079	3,079	3,079	3,079
20,550	20,600	3,086	3,086	3,086	3,086
20,600	20,650	3,094	3,094	3,097	3,094
20,650	20,700	3,101	3,101	3,111	3,101
20,700	20,750	3,109	3,109	3,125	3,109
20,750	20,800	3,116	3,116	3,139	3,116
20,800	20,850	3,124	3,124	3,153	3,124
20,850	20,900	3,131	3,131	3,167	3,131
20,900	20,950	3,139	3,139	3,181	3,139
20,950	21,000	3,146	3,146	3,195	3,146
21,000					
21,000	21,050	3,154	3,154	3,209	3,154
21,050	21,100	3,161	3,161	3,223	3,161
21,100	21,150	3,169	3,169	3,237	3,169
21,150	21,200	3,176	3,176	3,251	3,176
21,200	21,250	3,184	3,184	3,265	3,184
21,250	21,300	3,191	3,191	3,279	3,191
21,300	21,350	3,199	3,199	3,293	3,199
21,350	21,400	3,206	3,206	3,307	3,206
21,400	21,450	3,214	3,214	3,321	3,214
21,450	21,500	3,221	3,221	3,335	3,221
21,500	21,550	3,229	3,229	3,349	3,229
21,550	21,600	3,236	3,236	3,363	3,236
21,600	21,650	3,244	3,244	3,377	3,244
21,650	21,700	3,251	3,251	3,391	3,251
21,700	21,750	3,259	3,259	3,405	3,259
21,750	21,800	3,266	3,266	3,419	3,266
21,800	21,850	3,274	3,274	3,433	3,274
21,850	21,900	3,281	3,281	3,447	3,281
21,900	21,950	3,289	3,289	3,461	3,289
21,950	22,000	3,296	3,296	3,475	3,296
22,000					
22,000	22,050	3,304	3,304	3,489	3,304
22,050	22,100	3,311	3,311	3,503	3,311
22,100	22,150	3,319	3,319	3,517	3,319
22,150	22,200	3,326	3,326	3,531	3,326
22,200	22,250	3,334	3,334	3,545	3,334
22,250	22,300	3,341	3,341	3,559	3,341
22,300	22,350	3,349	3,349	3,573	3,349
22,350	22,400	3,356	3,356	3,587	3,356
22,400	22,450	3,364	3,364	3,601	3,364
22,450	22,500	3,371	3,371	3,615	3,371
22,500	22,550	3,379	3,379	3,629	3,379
22,550	22,600	3,386	3,386	3,643	3,386
22,600	22,650	3,394	3,394	3,657	3,394
22,650	22,700	3,401	3,401	3,671	3,401
22,700	22,750	3,409	3,409	3,685	3,409
22,750	22,800	3,416	3,416	3,699	3,416
22,800	22,850	3,424	3,424	3,713	3,424
22,850	22,900	3,431	3,431	3,727	3,431
22,900	22,950	3,439	3,439	3,741	3,439
22,950	23,000	3,446	3,446	3,755	3,446

* This column must also be used by a qualifying widow(er).

Continued on next page

1997 Tax Table—*Continued*

If line 38 (taxable income) is— At least	But less than	And you are— Single	Married filing jointly *	Married filing separately	Head of a household
		Your tax is—			
23,000					
23,000	23,050	3,454	3,454	3,769	3,454
23,050	23,100	3,461	3,461	3,783	3,461
23,100	23,150	3,469	3,469	3,797	3,469
23,150	23,200	3,476	3,476	3,811	3,476
23,200	23,250	3,484	3,484	3,825	3,484
23,250	23,300	3,491	3,491	3,839	3,491
23,300	23,350	3,499	3,499	3,853	3,499
23,350	23,400	3,506	3,506	3,867	3,506
23,400	23,450	3,514	3,514	3,881	3,514
23,450	23,500	3,521	3,521	3,895	3,521
23,500	23,550	3,529	3,529	3,909	3,529
23,550	23,600	3,536	3,536	3,923	3,536
23,600	23,650	3,544	3,544	3,937	3,544
23,650	23,700	3,551	3,551	3,951	3,551
23,700	23,750	3,559	3,559	3,965	3,559
23,750	23,800	3,566	3,566	3,979	3,566
23,800	23,850	3,574	3,574	3,993	3,574
23,850	23,900	3,581	3,581	4,007	3,581
23,900	23,950	3,589	3,589	4,021	3,589
23,950	24,000	3,596	3,596	4,035	3,596
24,000					
24,000	24,050	3,604	3,604	4,049	3,604
24,050	24,100	3,611	3,611	4,063	3,611
24,100	24,150	3,619	3,619	4,077	3,619
24,150	24,200	3,626	3,626	4,091	3,626
24,200	24,250	3,634	3,634	4,105	3,634
24,250	24,300	3,641	3,641	4,119	3,641
24,300	24,350	3,649	3,649	4,133	3,649
24,350	24,400	3,656	3,656	4,147	3,656
24,400	24,450	3,664	3,664	4,161	3,664
24,450	24,500	3,671	3,671	4,175	3,671
24,500	24,550	3,679	3,679	4,189	3,679
24,550	24,600	3,686	3,686	4,203	3,686
24,600	24,650	3,694	3,694	4,217	3,694
24,650	24,700	3,705	3,701	4,231	3,701
24,700	24,750	3,719	3,709	4,245	3,709
24,750	24,800	3,733	3,716	4,259	3,716
24,800	24,850	3,747	3,724	4,273	3,724
24,850	24,900	3,761	3,731	4,287	3,731
24,900	24,950	3,775	3,739	4,301	3,739
24,950	25,000	3,789	3,746	4,315	3,746
25,000					
25,000	25,050	3,803	3,754	4,329	3,754
25,050	25,100	3,817	3,761	4,343	3,761
25,100	25,150	3,831	3,769	4,357	3,769
25,150	25,200	3,845	3,776	4,371	3,776
25,200	25,250	3,859	3,784	4,385	3,784
25,250	25,300	3,873	3,791	4,399	3,791
25,300	25,350	3,887	3,799	4,413	3,799
25,350	25,400	3,901	3,806	4,427	3,806
25,400	25,450	3,915	3,814	4,441	3,814
25,450	25,500	3,929	3,821	4,455	3,821
25,500	25,550	3,943	3,829	4,469	3,829
25,550	25,600	3,957	3,836	4,483	3,836
25,600	25,650	3,971	3,844	4,497	3,844
25,650	25,700	3,985	3,851	4,511	3,851
25,700	25,750	3,999	3,859	4,525	3,859
25,750	25,800	4,013	3,866	4,539	3,866
25,800	25,850	4,027	3,874	4,553	3,874
25,850	25,900	4,041	3,881	4,567	3,881
25,900	25,950	4,055	3,889	4,581	3,889
25,950	26,000	4,069	3,896	4,595	3,896
26,000					
26,000	26,050	4,083	3,904	4,609	3,904
26,050	26,100	4,097	3,911	4,623	3,911
26,100	26,150	4,111	3,919	4,637	3,919
26,150	26,200	4,125	3,926	4,651	3,926
26,200	26,250	4,139	3,934	4,665	3,934
26,250	26,300	4,153	3,941	4,679	3,941
26,300	26,350	4,167	3,949	4,693	3,949
26,350	26,400	4,181	3,956	4,707	3,956
26,400	26,450	4,195	3,964	4,721	3,964
26,450	26,500	4,209	3,971	4,735	3,971
26,500	26,550	4,223	3,979	4,749	3,979
26,550	26,600	4,237	3,986	4,763	3,986
26,600	26,650	4,251	3,994	4,777	3,994
26,650	26,700	4,265	4,001	4,791	4,001
26,700	26,750	4,279	4,009	4,805	4,009
26,750	26,800	4,293	4,016	4,819	4,016
26,800	26,850	4,307	4,024	4,833	4,024
26,850	26,900	4,321	4,031	4,847	4,031
26,900	26,950	4,335	4,039	4,861	4,039
26,950	27,000	4,349	4,046	4,875	4,046
27,000					
27,000	27,050	4,363	4,054	4,889	4,054
27,050	27,100	4,377	4,061	4,903	4,061
27,100	27,150	4,391	4,069	4,917	4,069
27,150	27,200	4,405	4,076	4,931	4,076
27,200	27,250	4,419	4,084	4,945	4,084
27,250	27,300	4,433	4,091	4,959	4,091
27,300	27,350	4,447	4,099	4,973	4,099
27,350	27,400	4,461	4,106	4,987	4,106
27,400	27,450	4,475	4,114	5,001	4,114
27,450	27,500	4,489	4,121	5,015	4,121
27,500	27,550	4,503	4,129	5,029	4,129
27,550	27,600	4,517	4,136	5,043	4,136
27,600	27,650	4,531	4,144	5,057	4,144
27,650	27,700	4,545	4,151	5,071	4,151
27,700	27,750	4,559	4,159	5,085	4,159
27,750	27,800	4,573	4,166	5,099	4,166
27,800	27,850	4,587	4,174	5,113	4,174
27,850	27,900	4,601	4,181	5,127	4,181
27,900	27,950	4,615	4,189	5,141	4,189
27,950	28,000	4,629	4,196	5,155	4,196
28,000					
28,000	28,050	4,643	4,204	5,169	4,204
28,050	28,100	4,657	4,211	5,183	4,211
28,100	28,150	4,671	4,219	5,197	4,219
28,150	28,200	4,685	4,226	5,211	4,226
28,200	28,250	4,699	4,234	5,225	4,234
28,250	28,300	4,713	4,241	5,239	4,241
28,300	28,350	4,727	4,249	5,253	4,249
28,350	28,400	4,741	4,256	5,267	4,256
28,400	28,450	4,755	4,264	5,281	4,264
28,450	28,500	4,769	4,271	5,295	4,271
28,500	28,550	4,783	4,279	5,309	4,279
28,550	28,600	4,797	4,286	5,323	4,286
28,600	28,650	4,811	4,294	5,337	4,294
28,650	28,700	4,825	4,301	5,351	4,301
28,700	28,750	4,839	4,309	5,365	4,309
28,750	28,800	4,853	4,316	5,379	4,316
28,800	28,850	4,867	4,324	5,393	4,324
28,850	28,900	4,881	4,331	5,407	4,331
28,900	28,950	4,895	4,339	5,421	4,339
28,950	29,000	4,909	4,346	5,435	4,346
29,000					
29,000	29,050	4,923	4,354	5,449	4,354
29,050	29,100	4,937	4,361	5,463	4,361
29,100	29,150	4,951	4,369	5,477	4,369
29,150	29,200	4,965	4,376	5,491	4,376
29,200	29,250	4,979	4,384	5,505	4,384
29,250	29,300	4,993	4,391	5,519	4,391
29,300	29,350	5,007	4,399	5,533	4,399
29,350	29,400	5,021	4,406	5,547	4,406
29,400	29,450	5,035	4,414	5,561	4,414
29,450	29,500	5,049	4,421	5,575	4,421
29,500	29,550	5,063	4,429	5,589	4,429
29,550	29,600	5,077	4,436	5,603	4,436
29,600	29,650	5,091	4,444	5,617	4,444
29,650	29,700	5,105	4,451	5,631	4,451
29,700	29,750	5,119	4,459	5,645	4,459
29,750	29,800	5,133	4,466	5,659	4,466
29,800	29,850	5,147	4,474	5,673	4,474
29,850	29,900	5,161	4,481	5,687	4,481
29,900	29,950	5,175	4,489	5,701	4,489
29,950	30,000	5,189	4,496	5,715	4,496
30,000					
30,000	30,050	5,203	4,504	5,729	4,504
30,050	30,100	5,217	4,511	5,743	4,511
30,100	30,150	5,231	4,519	5,757	4,519
30,150	30,200	5,245	4,526	5,771	4,526
30,200	30,250	5,259	4,534	5,785	4,534
30,250	30,300	5,273	4,541	5,799	4,541
30,300	30,350	5,287	4,549	5,813	4,549
30,350	30,400	5,301	4,556	5,827	4,556
30,400	30,450	5,315	4,564	5,841	4,564
30,450	30,500	5,329	4,571	5,855	4,571
30,500	30,550	5,343	4,579	5,869	4,579
30,550	30,600	5,357	4,586	5,883	4,586
30,600	30,650	5,371	4,594	5,897	4,594
30,650	30,700	5,385	4,601	5,911	4,601
30,700	30,750	5,399	4,609	5,925	4,609
30,750	30,800	5,413	4,616	5,939	4,616
30,800	30,850	5,427	4,624	5,953	4,624
30,850	30,900	5,441	4,631	5,967	4,631
30,900	30,950	5,455	4,639	5,981	4,639
30,950	31,000	5,469	4,646	5,995	4,646
31,000					
31,000	31,050	5,483	4,654	6,009	4,654
31,050	31,100	5,497	4,661	6,023	4,661
31,100	31,150	5,511	4,669	6,037	4,669
31,150	31,200	5,525	4,676	6,051	4,676
31,200	31,250	5,539	4,684	6,065	4,684
31,250	31,300	5,553	4,691	6,079	4,691
31,300	31,350	5,567	4,699	6,093	4,699
31,350	31,400	5,581	4,706	6,107	4,706
31,400	31,450	5,595	4,714	6,121	4,714
31,450	31,500	5,609	4,721	6,135	4,721
31,500	31,550	5,623	4,729	6,149	4,729
31,550	31,600	5,637	4,736	6,163	4,736
31,600	31,650	5,651	4,744	6,177	4,744
31,650	31,700	5,665	4,751	6,191	4,751
31,700	31,750	5,679	4,759	6,205	4,759
31,750	31,800	5,693	4,766	6,219	4,766
31,800	31,850	5,707	4,774	6,233	4,774
31,850	31,900	5,721	4,781	6,247	4,781
31,900	31,950	5,735	4,789	6,261	4,789
31,950	32,000	5,749	4,796	6,275	4,796

* This column must also be used by a qualifying widow(er).

Continued on next page

1997 Tax Table—*Continued*

If line 38 (taxable income) is— At least	But less than	And you are— Single	Married filing jointly *	Married filing sepa-rately	Head of a house-hold
		Your tax is—			
32,000					
32,000	32,050	5,763	4,804	6,289	4,804
32,050	32,100	5,777	4,811	6,303	4,811
32,100	32,150	5,791	4,819	6,317	4,819
32,150	32,200	5,805	4,826	6,331	4,826
32,200	32,250	5,819	4,834	6,345	4,834
32,250	32,300	5,833	4,841	6,359	4,841
32,300	32,350	5,847	4,849	6,373	4,849
32,350	32,400	5,861	4,856	6,387	4,856
32,400	32,450	5,875	4,864	6,401	4,864
32,450	32,500	5,889	4,871	6,415	4,871
32,500	32,550	5,903	4,879	6,429	4,879
32,550	32,600	5,917	4,886	6,443	4,886
32,600	32,650	5,931	4,894	6,457	4,894
32,650	32,700	5,945	4,901	6,471	4,901
32,700	32,750	5,959	4,909	6,485	4,909
32,750	32,800	5,973	4,916	6,499	4,916
32,800	32,850	5,987	4,924	6,513	4,924
32,850	32,900	6,001	4,931	6,527	4,931
32,900	32,950	6,015	4,939	6,541	4,939
32,950	33,000	6,029	4,946	6,555	4,946
33,000					
33,000	33,050	6,043	4,954	6,569	4,954
33,050	33,100	6,057	4,961	6,583	4,965
33,100	33,150	6,071	4,969	6,597	4,979
33,150	33,200	6,085	4,976	6,611	4,993
33,200	33,250	6,099	4,984	6,625	5,007
33,250	33,300	6,113	4,991	6,639	5,021
33,300	33,350	6,127	4,999	6,653	5,035
33,350	33,400	6,141	5,006	6,667	5,049
33,400	33,450	6,155	5,014	6,681	5,063
33,450	33,500	6,169	5,021	6,695	5,077
33,500	33,550	6,183	5,029	6,709	5,091
33,550	33,600	6,197	5,036	6,723	5,105
33,600	33,650	6,211	5,044	6,737	5,119
33,650	33,700	6,225	5,051	6,751	5,133
33,700	33,750	6,239	5,059	6,765	5,147
33,750	33,800	6,253	5,066	6,779	5,161
33,800	33,850	6,267	5,074	6,793	5,175
33,850	33,900	6,281	5,081	6,807	5,189
33,900	33,950	6,295	5,089	6,821	5,203
33,950	34,000	6,309	5,096	6,835	5,217
34,000					
34,000	34,050	6,323	5,104	6,849	5,231
34,050	34,100	6,337	5,111	6,863	5,245
34,100	34,150	6,351	5,119	6,877	5,259
34,150	34,200	6,365	5,126	6,891	5,273
34,200	34,250	6,379	5,134	6,905	5,287
34,250	34,300	6,393	5,141	6,919	5,301
34,300	34,350	6,407	5,149	6,933	5,315
34,350	34,400	6,421	5,156	6,947	5,329
34,400	34,450	6,435	5,164	6,961	5,343
34,450	34,500	6,449	5,171	6,975	5,357
34,500	34,550	6,463	5,179	6,989	5,371
34,550	34,600	6,477	5,186	7,003	5,385
34,600	34,650	6,491	5,194	7,017	5,399
34,650	34,700	6,505	5,201	7,031	5,413
34,700	34,750	6,519	5,209	7,045	5,427
34,750	34,800	6,533	5,216	7,059	5,441
34,800	34,850	6,547	5,224	7,073	5,455
34,850	34,900	6,561	5,231	7,087	5,469
34,900	34,950	6,575	5,239	7,101	5,483
34,950	35,000	6,589	5,246	7,115	5,497
35,000					
35,000	35,050	6,603	5,254	7,129	5,511
35,050	35,100	6,617	5,261	7,143	5,525
35,100	35,150	6,631	5,269	7,157	5,539
35,150	35,200	6,645	5,276	7,171	5,553
35,200	35,250	6,659	5,284	7,185	5,567
35,250	35,300	6,673	5,291	7,199	5,581
35,300	35,350	6,687	5,299	7,213	5,595
35,350	35,400	6,701	5,306	7,227	5,609
35,400	35,450	6,715	5,314	7,241	5,623
35,450	35,500	6,729	5,321	7,255	5,637
35,500	35,550	6,743	5,329	7,269	5,651
35,550	35,600	6,757	5,336	7,283	5,665
35,600	35,650	6,771	5,344	7,297	5,679
35,650	35,700	6,785	5,351	7,311	5,693
35,700	35,750	6,799	5,359	7,325	5,707
35,750	35,800	6,813	5,366	7,339	5,721
35,800	35,850	6,827	5,374	7,353	5,735
35,850	35,900	6,841	5,381	7,367	5,749
35,900	35,950	6,855	5,389	7,381	5,763
35,950	36,000	6,869	5,396	7,395	5,777
36,000					
36,000	36,050	6,883	5,404	7,409	5,791
36,050	36,100	6,897	5,411	7,423	5,805
36,100	36,150	6,911	5,419	7,437	5,819
36,150	36,200	6,925	5,426	7,451	5,833
36,200	36,250	6,939	5,434	7,465	5,847
36,250	36,300	6,953	5,441	7,479	5,861
36,300	36,350	6,967	5,449	7,493	5,875
36,350	36,400	6,981	5,456	7,507	5,889
36,400	36,450	6,995	5,464	7,521	5,903
36,450	36,500	7,009	5,471	7,535	5,917
36,500	36,550	7,023	5,479	7,549	5,931
36,550	36,600	7,037	5,486	7,563	5,945
36,600	36,650	7,051	5,494	7,577	5,959
36,650	36,700	7,065	5,501	7,591	5,973
36,700	36,750	7,079	5,509	7,605	5,987
36,750	36,800	7,093	5,516	7,619	6,001
36,800	36,850	7,107	5,524	7,633	6,015
36,850	36,900	7,121	5,531	7,647	6,029
36,900	36,950	7,135	5,539	7,661	6,043
36,950	37,000	7,149	5,546	7,675	6,057
37,000					
37,000	37,050	7,163	5,554	7,689	6,071
37,050	37,100	7,177	5,561	7,703	6,085
37,100	37,150	7,191	5,569	7,717	6,099
37,150	37,200	7,205	5,576	7,731	6,113
37,200	37,250	7,219	5,584	7,745	6,127
37,250	37,300	7,233	5,591	7,759	6,141
37,300	37,350	7,247	5,599	7,773	6,155
37,350	37,400	7,261	5,606	7,787	6,169
37,400	37,450	7,275	5,614	7,801	6,183
37,450	37,500	7,289	5,621	7,815	6,197
37,500	37,550	7,303	5,629	7,829	6,211
37,550	37,600	7,317	5,636	7,843	6,225
37,600	37,650	7,331	5,644	7,857	6,239
37,650	37,700	7,345	5,651	7,871	6,253
37,700	37,750	7,359	5,659	7,885	6,267
37,750	37,800	7,373	5,666	7,899	6,281
37,800	37,850	7,387	5,674	7,913	6,295
37,850	37,900	7,401	5,681	7,927	6,309
37,900	37,950	7,415	5,689	7,941	6,323
37,950	38,000	7,429	5,696	7,955	6,337
38,000					
38,000	38,050	7,443	5,704	7,969	6,351
38,050	38,100	7,457	5,711	7,983	6,365
38,100	38,150	7,471	5,719	7,997	6,379
38,150	38,200	7,485	5,726	8,011	6,393
38,200	38,250	7,499	5,734	8,025	6,407
38,250	38,300	7,513	5,741	8,039	6,421
38,300	38,350	7,527	5,749	8,053	6,435
38,350	38,400	7,541	5,756	8,067	6,449
38,400	38,450	7,555	5,764	8,081	6,463
38,450	38,500	7,569	5,771	8,095	6,477
38,500	38,550	7,583	5,779	8,109	6,491
38,550	38,600	7,597	5,786	8,123	6,505
38,600	38,650	7,611	5,794	8,137	6,519
38,650	38,700	7,625	5,801	8,151	6,533
38,700	38,750	7,639	5,809	8,165	6,547
38,750	38,800	7,653	5,816	8,179	6,561
38,800	38,850	7,667	5,824	8,193	6,575
38,850	38,900	7,681	5,831	8,207	6,589
38,900	38,950	7,695	5,839	8,221	6,603
38,950	39,000	7,709	5,846	8,235	6,617
39,000					
39,000	39,050	7,723	5,854	8,249	6,631
39,050	39,100	7,737	5,861	8,263	6,645
39,100	39,150	7,751	5,869	8,277	6,659
39,150	39,200	7,765	5,876	8,291	6,673
39,200	39,250	7,779	5,884	8,305	6,687
39,250	39,300	7,793	5,891	8,319	6,701
39,300	39,350	7,807	5,899	8,333	6,715
39,350	39,400	7,821	5,906	8,347	6,729
39,400	39,450	7,835	5,914	8,361	6,743
39,450	39,500	7,849	5,921	8,375	6,757
39,500	39,550	7,863	5,929	8,389	6,771
39,550	39,600	7,877	5,936	8,403	6,785
39,600	39,650	7,891	5,944	8,417	6,799
39,650	39,700	7,905	5,951	8,431	6,813
39,700	39,750	7,919	5,959	8,445	6,827
39,750	39,800	7,933	5,966	8,459	6,841
39,800	39,850	7,947	5,974	8,473	6,855
39,850	39,900	7,961	5,981	8,487	6,869
39,900	39,950	7,975	5,989	8,501	6,883
39,950	40,000	7,989	5,996	8,515	6,897
40,000					
40,000	40,050	8,003	6,004	8,529	6,911
40,050	40,100	8,017	6,011	8,543	6,925
40,100	40,150	8,031	6,019	8,557	6,939
40,150	40,200	8,045	6,026	8,571	6,953
40,200	40,250	8,059	6,034	8,585	6,967
40,250	40,300	8,073	6,041	8,599	6,981
40,300	40,350	8,087	6,049	8,613	6,995
40,350	40,400	8,101	6,056	8,627	7,009
40,400	40,450	8,115	6,064	8,641	7,023
40,450	40,500	8,129	6,071	8,655	7,037
40,500	40,550	8,143	6,079	8,669	7,051
40,550	40,600	8,157	6,086	8,683	7,065
40,600	40,650	8,171	6,094	8,697	7,079
40,650	40,700	8,185	6,101	8,711	7,093
40,700	40,750	8,199	6,109	8,725	7,107
40,750	40,800	8,213	6,116	8,739	7,121
40,800	40,850	8,227	6,124	8,753	7,135
40,850	40,900	8,241	6,131	8,767	7,149
40,900	40,950	8,255	6,139	8,781	7,163
40,950	41,000	8,269	6,146	8,795	7,177

* This column must also be used by a qualifying widow(er).

Continued on next page

1997 Tax Table—*Continued*

If line 38 (taxable income) is— At least	But less than	And you are— Single	Married filing jointly *	Married filing sepa-rately	Head of a house-hold
		Your tax is—			
41,000					
41,000	41,050	8,283	6,154	8,809	7,191
41,050	41,100	8,297	6,161	8,823	7,205
41,100	41,150	8,311	6,169	8,837	7,219
41,150	41,200	8,325	6,176	8,851	7,233
41,200	41,250	8,339	6,187	8,865	7,247
41,250	41,300	8,353	6,201	8,879	7,261
41,300	41,350	8,367	6,215	8,893	7,275
41,350	41,400	8,381	6,229	8,907	7,289
41,400	41,450	8,395	6,243	8,921	7,303
41,450	41,500	8,409	6,257	8,935	7,317
41,500	41,550	8,423	6,271	8,949	7,331
41,550	41,600	8,437	6,285	8,963	7,345
41,600	41,650	8,451	6,299	8,977	7,359
41,650	41,700	8,465	6,313	8,991	7,373
41,700	41,750	8,479	6,327	9,005	7,387
41,750	41,800	8,493	6,341	9,019	7,401
41,800	41,850	8,507	6,355	9,033	7,415
41,850	41,900	8,521	6,369	9,047	7,429
41,900	41,950	8,535	6,383	9,061	7,443
41,950	42,000	8,549	6,397	9,075	7,457
42,000					
42,000	42,050	8,563	6,411	9,089	7,471
42,050	42,100	8,577	6,425	9,103	7,485
42,100	42,150	8,591	6,439	9,117	7,499
42,150	42,200	8,605	6,453	9,131	7,513
42,200	42,250	8,619	6,467	9,145	7,527
42,250	42,300	8,633	6,481	9,159	7,541
42,300	42,350	8,647	6,495	9,173	7,555
42,350	42,400	8,661	6,509	9,187	7,569
42,400	42,450	8,675	6,523	9,201	7,583
42,450	42,500	8,689	6,537	9,215	7,597
42,500	42,550	8,703	6,551	9,229	7,611
42,550	42,600	8,717	6,565	9,243	7,625
42,600	42,650	8,731	6,579	9,257	7,639
42,650	42,700	8,745	6,593	9,271	7,653
42,700	42,750	8,759	6,607	9,285	7,667
42,750	42,800	8,773	6,621	9,299	7,681
42,800	42,850	8,787	6,635	9,313	7,695
42,850	42,900	8,801	6,649	9,327	7,709
42,900	42,950	8,815	6,663	9,341	7,723
42,950	43,000	8,829	6,677	9,355	7,737
43,000					
43,000	43,050	8,843	6,691	9,369	7,751
43,050	43,100	8,857	6,705	9,383	7,765
43,100	43,150	8,871	6,719	9,397	7,779
43,150	43,200	8,885	6,733	9,411	7,793
43,200	43,250	8,899	6,747	9,425	7,807
43,250	43,300	8,913	6,761	9,439	7,821
43,300	43,350	8,927	6,775	9,453	7,835
43,350	43,400	8,941	6,789	9,467	7,849
43,400	43,450	8,955	6,803	9,481	7,863
43,450	43,500	8,969	6,817	9,495	7,877
43,500	43,550	8,983	6,831	9,509	7,891
43,550	43,600	8,997	6,845	9,523	7,905
43,600	43,650	9,011	6,859	9,537	7,919
43,650	43,700	9,025	6,873	9,551	7,933
43,700	43,750	9,039	6,887	9,565	7,947
43,750	43,800	9,053	6,901	9,579	7,961
43,800	43,850	9,067	6,915	9,593	7,975
43,850	43,900	9,081	6,929	9,607	7,989
43,900	43,950	9,095	6,943	9,621	8,003
43,950	44,000	9,109	6,957	9,635	8,017
44,000					
44,000	44,050	9,123	6,971	9,649	8,031
44,050	44,100	9,137	6,985	9,663	8,045
44,100	44,150	9,151	6,999	9,677	8,059
44,150	44,200	9,165	7,013	9,691	8,073
44,200	44,250	9,179	7,027	9,705	8,087
44,250	44,300	9,193	7,041	9,719	8,101
44,300	44,350	9,207	7,055	9,733	8,115
44,350	44,400	9,221	7,069	9,747	8,129
44,400	44,450	9,235	7,083	9,761	8,143
44,450	44,500	9,249	7,097	9,775	8,157
44,500	44,550	9,263	7,111	9,789	8,171
44,550	44,600	9,277	7,125	9,803	8,185
44,600	44,650	9,291	7,139	9,817	8,199
44,650	44,700	9,305	7,153	9,831	8,213
44,700	44,750	9,319	7,167	9,845	8,227
44,750	44,800	9,333	7,181	9,859	8,241
44,800	44,850	9,347	7,195	9,873	8,255
44,850	44,900	9,361	7,209	9,887	8,269
44,900	44,950	9,375	7,223	9,901	8,283
44,950	45,000	9,389	7,237	9,915	8,297
45,000					
45,000	45,050	9,403	7,251	9,929	8,311
45,050	45,100	9,417	7,265	9,943	8,325
45,100	45,150	9,431	7,279	9,957	8,339
45,150	45,200	9,445	7,293	9,971	8,353
45,200	45,250	9,459	7,307	9,985	8,367
45,250	45,300	9,473	7,321	9,999	8,381
45,300	45,350	9,487	7,335	10,013	8,395
45,350	45,400	9,501	7,349	10,027	8,409
45,400	45,450	9,515	7,363	10,041	8,423
45,450	45,500	9,529	7,377	10,055	8,437
45,500	45,550	9,543	7,391	10,069	8,451
45,550	45,600	9,557	7,405	10,083	8,465
45,600	45,650	9,571	7,419	10,097	8,479
45,650	45,700	9,585	7,433	10,111	8,493
45,700	45,750	9,599	7,447	10,125	8,507
45,750	45,800	9,613	7,461	10,139	8,521
45,800	45,850	9,627	7,475	10,153	8,535
45,850	45,900	9,641	7,489	10,167	8,549
45,900	45,950	9,655	7,503	10,181	8,563
45,950	46,000	9,669	7,517	10,195	8,577
46,000					
46,000	46,050	9,683	7,531	10,209	8,591
46,050	46,100	9,697	7,545	10,223	8,605
46,100	46,150	9,711	7,559	10,237	8,619
46,150	46,200	9,725	7,573	10,251	8,633
46,200	46,250	9,739	7,587	10,265	8,647
46,250	46,300	9,753	7,601	10,279	8,661
46,300	46,350	9,767	7,615	10,293	8,675
46,350	46,400	9,781	7,629	10,307	8,689
46,400	46,450	9,795	7,643	10,321	8,703
46,450	46,500	9,809	7,657	10,335	8,717
46,500	46,550	9,823	7,671	10,349	8,731
46,550	46,600	9,837	7,685	10,363	8,745
46,600	46,650	9,851	7,699	10,377	8,759
46,650	46,700	9,865	7,713	10,391	8,773
46,700	46,750	9,879	7,727	10,405	8,787
46,750	46,800	9,893	7,741	10,419	8,801
46,800	46,850	9,907	7,755	10,433	8,815
46,850	46,900	9,921	7,769	10,447	8,829
46,900	46,950	9,935	7,783	10,461	8,843
46,950	47,000	9,949	7,797	10,475	8,857
47,000					
47,000	47,050	9,963	7,811	10,489	8,871
47,050	47,100	9,977	7,825	10,503	8,885
47,100	47,150	9,991	7,839	10,517	8,899
47,150	47,200	10,005	7,853	10,531	8,913
47,200	47,250	10,019	7,867	10,545	8,927
47,250	47,300	10,033	7,881	10,559	8,941
47,300	47,350	10,047	7,895	10,573	8,955
47,350	47,400	10,061	7,909	10,587	8,969
47,400	47,450	10,075	7,923	10,601	8,983
47,450	47,500	10,089	7,937	10,615	8,997
47,500	47,550	10,103	7,951	10,629	9,011
47,550	47,600	10,117	7,965	10,643	9,025
47,600	47,650	10,131	7,979	10,657	9,039
47,650	47,700	10,145	7,993	10,671	9,053
47,700	47,750	10,159	8,007	10,685	9,067
47,750	47,800	10,173	8,021	10,699	9,081
47,800	47,850	10,187	8,035	10,713	9,095
47,850	47,900	10,201	8,049	10,727	9,109
47,900	47,950	10,215	8,063	10,741	9,123
47,950	48,000	10,229	8,077	10,755	9,137
48,000					
48,000	48,050	10,243	8,091	10,769	9,151
48,050	48,100	10,257	8,105	10,783	9,165
48,100	48,150	10,271	8,119	10,797	9,179
48,150	48,200	10,285	8,133	10,811	9,193
48,200	48,250	10,299	8,147	10,825	9,207
48,250	48,300	10,313	8,161	10,839	9,221
48,300	48,350	10,327	8,175	10,853	9,235
48,350	48,400	10,341	8,189	10,867	9,249
48,400	48,450	10,355	8,203	10,881	9,263
48,450	48,500	10,369	8,217	10,895	9,277
48,500	48,550	10,383	8,231	10,909	9,291
48,550	48,600	10,397	8,245	10,923	9,305
48,600	48,650	10,411	8,259	10,937	9,319
48,650	48,700	10,425	8,273	10,951	9,333
48,700	48,750	10,439	8,287	10,965	9,347
48,750	48,800	10,453	8,301	10,979	9,361
48,800	48,850	10,467	8,315	10,993	9,375
48,850	48,900	10,481	8,329	11,007	9,389
48,900	48,950	10,495	8,343	11,021	9,403
48,950	49,000	10,509	8,357	11,035	9,417
49,000					
49,000	49,050	10,523	8,371	11,049	9,431
49,050	49,100	10,537	8,385	11,063	9,445
49,100	49,150	10,551	8,399	11,077	9,459
49,150	49,200	10,565	8,413	11,091	9,473
49,200	49,250	10,579	8,427	11,105	9,487
49,250	49,300	10,593	8,441	11,119	9,501
49,300	49,350	10,607	8,455	11,133	9,515
49,350	49,400	10,621	8,469	11,147	9,529
49,400	49,450	10,635	8,483	11,161	9,543
49,450	49,500	10,649	8,497	11,175	9,557
49,500	49,550	10,663	8,511	11,189	9,571
49,550	49,600	10,677	8,525	11,203	9,585
49,600	49,650	10,691	8,539	11,217	9,599
49,650	49,700	10,705	8,553	11,231	9,613
49,700	49,750	10,719	8,567	11,245	9,627
49,750	49,800	10,733	8,581	11,259	9,641
49,800	49,850	10,747	8,595	11,274	9,655
49,850	49,900	10,761	8,609	11,289	9,669
49,900	49,950	10,775	8,623	11,305	9,683
49,950	50,000	10,789	8,637	11,320	9,697

* This column must also be used by a qualifying widow(er).

Continued on next page

1997 Tax Table—Continued

50,000

If line 38 (taxable income) is—		And you are—			
At least	But less than	Single	Married filing jointly	Married filing separately	Head of a household
		Your tax is—			

51,000

52,000

* This column must also be used by a qualifying widow(er).

- 45 -

1997 Tax Table—Continued

53,000

If line 38 (taxable income) is—		And you are—			
At least	But less than	Single	Married filing jointly	Married filing separately	Head of a household
		Your tax is—			

54,000

55,000

56,000

57,000

58,000

Continued on next page

1997 Tax Table—Continued

59,000

If line 38 (taxable income) is—		And you are—			
At least	But less than	Single	Married filing jointly	Married filing separately	Head of a household
		Your tax is—			

60,000

61,000

* This column must also be used by a qualifying widow(er).

- 46 -

62,000

63,000

64,000

65,000

66,000

67,000

Continued on next page

1997 Tax Table—*Continued*

If line 38 (taxable income) is— At least	But less than	And you are— Single	Married filing jointly *	Married filing separately	Head of a household
		Your tax is—			
68,000					
68,000	68,050	16,091	13,691	16,916	14,751
68,050	68,100	16,106	13,705	16,931	14,765
68,100	68,150	16,122	13,719	16,947	14,779
68,150	68,200	16,137	13,733	16,962	14,793
68,200	68,250	16,153	13,747	16,978	14,807
68,250	68,300	16,168	13,761	16,993	14,821
68,300	68,350	16,184	13,775	17,009	14,835
68,350	68,400	16,199	13,789	17,024	14,849
68,400	68,450	16,215	13,803	17,040	14,863
68,450	68,500	16,230	13,817	17,055	14,877
68,500	68,550	16,246	13,831	17,071	14,891
68,550	68,600	16,261	13,845	17,086	14,905
68,600	68,650	16,277	13,859	17,102	14,919
68,650	68,700	16,292	13,873	17,117	14,933
68,700	68,750	16,308	13,887	17,133	14,947
68,750	68,800	16,323	13,901	17,148	14,961
68,800	68,850	16,339	13,915	17,164	14,975
68,850	68,900	16,354	13,929	17,179	14,989
68,900	68,950	16,370	13,943	17,195	15,003
68,950	69,000	16,385	13,957	17,210	15,017
69,000					
69,000	69,050	16,401	13,971	17,226	15,031
69,050	69,100	16,416	13,985	17,241	15,045
69,100	69,150	16,432	13,999	17,257	15,059
69,150	69,200	16,447	14,013	17,272	15,073
69,200	69,250	16,463	14,027	17,288	15,087
69,250	69,300	16,478	14,041	17,303	15,101
69,300	69,350	16,494	14,055	17,319	15,115
69,350	69,400	16,509	14,069	17,334	15,129
69,400	69,450	16,525	14,083	17,350	15,143
69,450	69,500	16,540	14,097	17,365	15,157
69,500	69,550	16,556	14,111	17,381	15,171
69,550	69,600	16,571	14,125	17,396	15,185
69,600	69,650	16,587	14,139	17,412	15,199
69,650	69,700	16,602	14,153	17,427	15,213
69,700	69,750	16,618	14,167	17,443	15,227
69,750	69,800	16,633	14,181	17,458	15,241
69,800	69,850	16,649	14,195	17,474	15,255
69,850	69,900	16,664	14,209	17,489	15,269
69,900	69,950	16,680	14,223	17,505	15,283
69,950	70,000	16,695	14,237	17,520	15,297
70,000					
70,000	70,050	16,711	14,251	17,536	15,311
70,050	70,100	16,726	14,265	17,551	15,325
70,100	70,150	16,742	14,279	17,567	15,339
70,150	70,200	16,757	14,293	17,582	15,353
70,200	70,250	16,773	14,307	17,598	15,367
70,250	70,300	16,788	14,321	17,613	15,381
70,300	70,350	16,804	14,335	17,629	15,395
70,350	70,400	16,819	14,349	17,644	15,409
70,400	70,450	16,835	14,363	17,660	15,423
70,450	70,500	16,850	14,377	17,675	15,437
70,500	70,550	16,866	14,391	17,691	15,451
70,550	70,600	16,881	14,405	17,706	15,465
70,600	70,650	16,897	14,419	17,722	15,479
70,650	70,700	16,912	14,433	17,737	15,493
70,700	70,750	16,928	14,447	17,753	15,507
70,750	70,800	16,943	14,461	17,768	15,521
70,800	70,850	16,959	14,475	17,784	15,535
70,850	70,900	16,974	14,489	17,799	15,549
70,900	70,950	16,990	14,503	17,815	15,563
70,950	71,000	17,005	14,517	17,830	15,577
71,000					
71,000	71,050	17,021	14,531	17,846	15,591
71,050	71,100	17,036	14,545	17,861	15,605
71,100	71,150	17,052	14,559	17,877	15,619
71,150	71,200	17,067	14,573	17,892	15,633
71,200	71,250	17,083	14,587	17,908	15,647
71,250	71,300	17,098	14,601	17,923	15,661
71,300	71,350	17,114	14,615	17,939	15,675
71,350	71,400	17,129	14,629	17,954	15,689
71,400	71,450	17,145	14,643	17,970	15,703
71,450	71,500	17,160	14,657	17,985	15,717
71,500	71,550	17,176	14,671	18,001	15,731
71,550	71,600	17,191	14,685	18,016	15,745
71,600	71,650	17,207	14,699	18,032	15,759
71,650	71,700	17,222	14,713	18,047	15,773
71,700	71,750	17,238	14,727	18,063	15,787
71,750	71,800	17,253	14,741	18,078	15,801
71,800	71,850	17,269	14,755	18,094	15,815
71,850	71,900	17,284	14,769	18,109	15,829
71,900	71,950	17,300	14,783	18,125	15,843
71,950	72,000	17,315	14,797	18,140	15,857
72,000					
72,000	72,050	17,331	14,811	18,156	15,871
72,050	72,100	17,346	14,825	18,171	15,885
72,100	72,150	17,362	14,839	18,187	15,899
72,150	72,200	17,377	14,853	18,202	15,913
72,200	72,250	17,393	14,867	18,218	15,927
72,250	72,300	17,408	14,881	18,233	15,941
72,300	72,350	17,424	14,895	18,249	15,955
72,350	72,400	17,439	14,909	18,264	15,969
72,400	72,450	17,455	14,923	18,280	15,983
72,450	72,500	17,470	14,937	18,295	15,997
72,500	72,550	17,486	14,951	18,311	16,011
72,550	72,600	17,501	14,965	18,326	16,025
72,600	72,650	17,517	14,979	18,342	16,039
72,650	72,700	17,532	14,993	18,357	16,053
72,700	72,750	17,548	15,007	18,373	16,067
72,750	72,800	17,563	15,021	18,388	16,081
72,800	72,850	17,579	15,035	18,404	16,095
72,850	72,900	17,594	15,049	18,419	16,109
72,900	72,950	17,610	15,063	18,435	16,123
72,950	73,000	17,625	15,077	18,450	16,137
73,000					
73,000	73,050	17,641	15,091	18,466	16,151
73,050	73,100	17,656	15,105	18,481	16,165
73,100	73,150	17,672	15,119	18,497	16,179
73,150	73,200	17,687	15,133	18,512	16,193
73,200	73,250	17,703	15,147	18,528	16,207
73,250	73,300	17,718	15,161	18,543	16,221
73,300	73,350	17,734	15,175	18,559	16,235
73,350	73,400	17,749	15,189	18,574	16,249
73,400	73,450	17,765	15,203	18,590	16,263
73,450	73,500	17,780	15,217	18,605	16,277
73,500	73,550	17,796	15,231	18,621	16,291
73,550	73,600	17,811	15,245	18,636	16,305
73,600	73,650	17,827	15,259	18,652	16,319
73,650	73,700	17,842	15,273	18,667	16,333
73,700	73,750	17,858	15,287	18,683	16,347
73,750	73,800	17,873	15,301	18,698	16,361
73,800	73,850	17,889	15,315	18,714	16,375
73,850	73,900	17,904	15,329	18,729	16,389
73,900	73,950	17,920	15,343	18,745	16,403
73,950	74,000	17,935	15,357	18,760	16,417
74,000					
74,000	74,050	17,951	15,371	18,776	16,431
74,050	74,100	17,966	15,385	18,791	16,445
74,100	74,150	17,982	15,399	18,807	16,459
74,150	74,200	17,997	15,413	18,822	16,473
74,200	74,250	18,013	15,427	18,838	16,487
74,250	74,300	18,028	15,441	18,853	16,501
74,300	74,350	18,044	15,455	18,869	16,515
74,350	74,400	18,059	15,469	18,884	16,529
74,400	74,450	18,075	15,483	18,900	16,543
74,450	74,500	18,090	15,497	18,915	16,557
74,500	74,550	18,106	15,511	18,931	16,571
74,550	74,600	18,121	15,525	18,946	16,585
74,600	74,650	18,137	15,539	18,962	16,599
74,650	74,700	18,152	15,553	18,977	16,613
74,700	74,750	18,168	15,567	18,993	16,627
74,750	74,800	18,183	15,581	19,008	16,641
74,800	74,850	18,199	15,595	19,024	16,655
74,850	74,900	18,214	15,609	19,039	16,669
74,900	74,950	18,230	15,623	19,055	16,683
74,950	75,000	18,245	15,637	19,070	16,697
75,000					
75,000	75,050	18,261	15,651	19,086	16,711
75,050	75,100	18,276	15,665	19,101	16,725
75,100	75,150	18,292	15,679	19,117	16,739
75,150	75,200	18,307	15,693	19,132	16,753
75,200	75,250	18,323	15,707	19,148	16,767
75,250	75,300	18,338	15,721	19,163	16,781
75,300	75,350	18,354	15,735	19,179	16,795
75,350	75,400	18,369	15,749	19,194	16,809
75,400	75,450	18,385	15,763	19,210	16,823
75,450	75,500	18,400	15,777	19,225	16,837
75,500	75,550	18,416	15,791	19,241	16,851
75,550	75,600	18,431	15,805	19,256	16,865
75,600	75,650	18,447	15,819	19,272	16,879
75,650	75,700	18,462	15,833	19,287	16,893
75,700	75,750	18,478	15,847	19,303	16,907
75,750	75,800	18,493	15,861	19,318	16,921
75,800	75,850	18,509	15,875	19,334	16,935
75,850	75,900	18,524	15,889	19,349	16,949
75,900	75,950	18,540	15,903	19,367	16,963
75,950	76,000	18,555	15,917	19,385	16,977
76,000					
76,000	76,050	18,571	15,931	19,403	16,991
76,050	76,100	18,586	15,945	19,421	17,005
76,100	76,150	18,602	15,959	19,439	17,019
76,150	76,200	18,617	15,973	19,457	17,033
76,200	76,250	18,633	15,987	19,475	17,047
76,250	76,300	18,648	16,001	19,493	17,061
76,300	76,350	18,664	16,015	19,511	17,075
76,350	76,400	18,679	16,029	19,529	17,089
76,400	76,450	18,695	16,043	19,547	17,103
76,450	76,500	18,710	16,057	19,565	17,117
76,500	76,550	18,726	16,071	19,583	17,131
76,550	76,600	18,741	16,085	19,601	17,145
76,600	76,650	18,757	16,099	19,619	17,159
76,650	76,700	18,772	16,113	19,637	17,173
76,700	76,750	18,788	16,127	19,655	17,187
76,750	76,800	18,803	16,141	19,673	17,201
76,800	76,850	18,819	16,155	19,691	17,215
76,850	76,900	18,834	16,169	19,709	17,229
76,900	76,950	18,850	16,183	19,727	17,243
76,950	77,000	18,865	16,197	19,745	17,257

* This column must also be used by a qualifying widow(er).

Continued on next page

1997 Tax Table—*Continued*

If line 38 (taxable income) is— At least	But less than	And you are— Single	Married filing jointly *	Married filing separately	Head of a household
		Your tax is—			
77,000					
77,000	77,050	18,881	16,211	19,763	17,271
77,050	77,100	18,896	16,225	19,781	17,285
77,100	77,150	18,912	16,239	19,799	17,299
77,150	77,200	18,927	16,253	19,817	17,313
77,200	77,250	18,943	16,267	19,835	17,327
77,250	77,300	18,958	16,281	19,853	17,341
77,300	77,350	18,974	16,295	19,871	17,355
77,350	77,400	18,989	16,309	19,889	17,369
77,400	77,450	19,005	16,323	19,907	17,383
77,450	77,500	19,020	16,337	19,925	17,397
77,500	77,550	19,036	16,351	19,943	17,411
77,550	77,600	19,051	16,365	19,961	17,425
77,600	77,650	19,067	16,379	19,979	17,439
77,650	77,700	19,082	16,393	19,997	17,453
77,700	77,750	19,098	16,407	20,015	17,467
77,750	77,800	19,113	16,421	20,033	17,481
77,800	77,850	19,129	16,435	20,051	17,495
77,850	77,900	19,144	16,449	20,069	17,509
77,900	77,950	19,160	16,463	20,087	17,523
77,950	78,000	19,175	16,477	20,105	17,537
78,000					
78,000	78,050	19,191	16,491	20,123	17,551
78,050	78,100	19,206	16,505	20,141	17,565
78,100	78,150	19,222	16,519	20,159	17,579
78,150	78,200	19,237	16,533	20,177	17,593
78,200	78,250	19,253	16,547	20,195	17,607
78,250	78,300	19,268	16,561	20,213	17,621
78,300	78,350	19,284	16,575	20,231	17,635
78,350	78,400	19,299	16,589	20,249	17,649
78,400	78,450	19,315	16,603	20,267	17,663
78,450	78,500	19,330	16,617	20,285	17,677
78,500	78,550	19,346	16,631	20,303	17,691
78,550	78,600	19,361	16,645	20,321	17,705
78,600	78,650	19,377	16,659	20,339	17,719
78,650	78,700	19,392	16,673	20,357	17,733
78,700	78,750	19,408	16,687	20,375	17,747
78,750	78,800	19,423	16,701	20,393	17,761
78,800	78,850	19,439	16,715	20,411	17,775
78,850	78,900	19,454	16,729	20,429	17,789
78,900	78,950	19,470	16,743	20,447	17,803
78,950	79,000	19,485	16,757	20,465	17,817
79,000					
79,000	79,050	19,501	16,771	20,483	17,831
79,050	79,100	19,516	16,785	20,501	17,845
79,100	79,150	19,532	16,799	20,519	17,859
79,150	79,200	19,547	16,813	20,537	17,873
79,200	79,250	19,563	16,827	20,555	17,887
79,250	79,300	19,578	16,841	20,573	17,901
79,300	79,350	19,594	16,855	20,591	17,915
79,350	79,400	19,609	16,869	20,609	17,929
79,400	79,450	19,625	16,883	20,627	17,943
79,450	79,500	19,640	16,897	20,645	17,957
79,500	79,550	19,656	16,911	20,663	17,971
79,550	79,600	19,671	16,925	20,681	17,985
79,600	79,650	19,687	16,939	20,699	17,999
79,650	79,700	19,702	16,953	20,717	18,013
79,700	79,750	19,718	16,967	20,735	18,027
79,750	79,800	19,733	16,981	20,753	18,041
79,800	79,850	19,749	16,995	20,771	18,055
79,850	79,900	19,764	17,009	20,789	18,069
79,900	79,950	19,780	17,023	20,807	18,083
79,950	80,000	19,795	17,037	20,825	18,097
80,000					
80,000	80,050	19,811	17,051	20,843	18,111
80,050	80,100	19,826	17,065	20,861	18,125
80,100	80,150	19,842	17,079	20,879	18,139
80,150	80,200	19,857	17,093	20,897	18,153
80,200	80,250	19,873	17,107	20,915	18,167
80,250	80,300	19,888	17,121	20,933	18,181
80,300	80,350	19,904	17,135	20,951	18,195
80,350	80,400	19,919	17,149	20,969	18,209
80,400	80,450	19,935	17,163	20,987	18,223
80,450	80,500	19,950	17,177	21,005	18,237
80,500	80,550	19,966	17,191	21,023	18,251
80,550	80,600	19,981	17,205	21,041	18,265
80,600	80,650	19,997	17,219	21,059	18,279
80,650	80,700	20,012	17,233	21,077	18,293
80,700	80,750	20,028	17,247	21,095	18,307
80,750	80,800	20,043	17,261	21,113	18,321
80,800	80,850	20,059	17,275	21,131	18,335
80,850	80,900	20,074	17,289	21,149	18,349
80,900	80,950	20,090	17,303	21,167	18,363
80,950	81,000	20,105	17,317	21,185	18,377
81,000					
81,000	81,050	20,121	17,331	21,203	18,391
81,050	81,100	20,136	17,345	21,221	18,405
81,100	81,150	20,152	17,359	21,239	18,419
81,150	81,200	20,167	17,373	21,257	18,433
81,200	81,250	20,183	17,387	21,275	18,447
81,250	81,300	20,198	17,401	21,293	18,461
81,300	81,350	20,214	17,415	21,311	18,475
81,350	81,400	20,229	17,429	21,329	18,489
81,400	81,450	20,245	17,443	21,347	18,503
81,450	81,500	20,260	17,457	21,365	18,517
81,500	81,550	20,276	17,471	21,383	18,531
81,550	81,600	20,291	17,485	21,401	18,545
81,600	81,650	20,307	17,499	21,419	18,559
81,650	81,700	20,322	17,513	21,437	18,573
81,700	81,750	20,338	17,527	21,455	18,587
81,750	81,800	20,353	17,541	21,473	18,601
81,800	81,850	20,369	17,555	21,491	18,615
81,850	81,900	20,384	17,569	21,509	18,629
81,900	81,950	20,400	17,583	21,527	18,643
81,950	82,000	20,415	17,597	21,545	18,657
82,000					
82,000	82,050	20,431	17,611	21,563	18,671
82,050	82,100	20,446	17,625	21,581	18,685
82,100	82,150	20,462	17,639	21,599	18,699
82,150	82,200	20,477	17,653	21,617	18,713
82,200	82,250	20,493	17,667	21,635	18,727
82,250	82,300	20,508	17,681	21,653	18,741
82,300	82,350	20,524	17,695	21,671	18,755
82,350	82,400	20,539	17,709	21,689	18,769
82,400	82,450	20,555	17,723	21,707	18,783
82,450	82,500	20,570	17,737	21,725	18,797
82,500	82,550	20,586	17,751	21,743	18,811
82,550	82,600	20,601	17,765	21,761	18,825
82,600	82,650	20,617	17,779	21,779	18,839
82,650	82,700	20,632	17,793	21,797	18,853
82,700	82,750	20,648	17,807	21,815	18,867
82,750	82,800	20,663	17,821	21,833	18,881
82,800	82,850	20,679	17,835	21,851	18,895
82,850	82,900	20,694	17,849	21,869	18,909
82,900	82,950	20,710	17,863	21,887	18,923
82,950	83,000	20,725	17,877	21,905	18,937
83,000					
83,000	83,050	20,741	17,891	21,923	18,951
83,050	83,100	20,756	17,905	21,941	18,965
83,100	83,150	20,772	17,919	21,959	18,979
83,150	83,200	20,787	17,933	21,977	18,993
83,200	83,250	20,803	17,947	21,995	19,007
83,250	83,300	20,818	17,961	22,013	19,021
83,300	83,350	20,834	17,975	22,031	19,035
83,350	83,400	20,849	17,989	22,049	19,049
83,400	83,450	20,865	18,003	22,067	19,063
83,450	83,500	20,880	18,017	22,085	19,077
83,500	83,550	20,896	18,031	22,103	19,091
83,550	83,600	20,911	18,045	22,121	19,105
83,600	83,650	20,927	18,059	22,139	19,119
83,650	83,700	20,942	18,073	22,157	19,133
83,700	83,750	20,958	18,087	22,175	19,147
83,750	83,800	20,973	18,101	22,193	19,161
83,800	83,850	20,989	18,115	22,211	19,175
83,850	83,900	21,004	18,129	22,229	19,189
83,900	83,950	21,020	18,143	22,247	19,203
83,950	84,000	21,035	18,157	22,265	19,217
84,000					
84,000	84,050	21,051	18,171	22,283	19,231
84,050	84,100	21,066	18,185	22,301	19,245
84,100	84,150	21,082	18,199	22,319	19,259
84,150	84,200	21,097	18,213	22,337	19,273
84,200	84,250	21,113	18,227	22,355	19,287
84,250	84,300	21,128	18,241	22,373	19,301
84,300	84,350	21,144	18,255	22,391	19,315
84,350	84,400	21,159	18,269	22,409	19,329
84,400	84,450	21,175	18,283	22,427	19,343
84,450	84,500	21,190	18,297	22,445	19,357
84,500	84,550	21,206	18,311	22,463	19,371
84,550	84,600	21,221	18,325	22,481	19,385
84,600	84,650	21,237	18,339	22,499	19,399
84,650	84,700	21,252	18,353	22,517	19,413
84,700	84,750	21,268	18,367	22,535	19,427
84,750	84,800	21,283	18,381	22,553	19,441
84,800	84,850	21,299	18,395	22,571	19,455
84,850	84,900	21,314	18,409	22,589	19,469
84,900	84,950	21,330	18,423	22,607	19,483
84,950	85,000	21,345	18,437	22,625	19,497
85,000					
85,000	85,050	21,361	18,451	22,643	19,511
85,050	85,100	21,376	18,465	22,661	19,525
85,100	85,150	21,392	18,479	22,679	19,539
85,150	85,200	21,407	18,493	22,697	19,553
85,200	85,250	21,423	18,507	22,715	19,567
85,250	85,300	21,438	18,521	22,733	19,581
85,300	85,350	21,454	18,535	22,751	19,595
85,350	85,400	21,469	18,549	22,769	19,609
85,400	85,450	21,485	18,563	22,787	19,625
85,450	85,500	21,500	18,577	22,805	19,640
85,500	85,550	21,516	18,591	22,823	19,656
85,550	85,600	21,531	18,605	22,841	19,671
85,600	85,650	21,547	18,619	22,859	19,687
85,650	85,700	21,562	18,633	22,877	19,702
85,700	85,750	21,578	18,647	22,895	19,718
85,750	85,800	21,593	18,661	22,913	19,733
85,800	85,850	21,609	18,675	22,931	19,749
85,850	85,900	21,624	18,689	22,949	19,764
85,900	85,950	21,640	18,703	22,967	19,780
85,950	86,000	21,655	18,717	22,985	19,795

* This column must also be used by a qualifying widow(er).

Continued on next page

1997 Tax Table—Continued

If line 38 (taxable income) is—		And you are—			
At least	But less than	Single	Married filing jointly	Married filing separately	Head of a household
		Your tax is—			

86,000

At least	But less than	Single	Married filing jointly	Married filing separately	Head of a household
86,000	86,050	21,677	18,731	23,003	19,811
86,050	86,100	21,688	18,745	23,021	19,826
86,100	86,150	21,702	18,759	23,039	19,842
86,150	86,200	21,717	18,773	23,057	19,857
86,200	86,250	21,733	18,787	23,075	19,873
86,250	86,300	21,744	18,801	23,088	19,888
86,300	86,350	21,758	18,815	23,111	19,904
86,350	86,400	21,773	18,829	23,122	19,919
86,400	86,450	21,795	18,844	23,147	19,935
86,450	86,500	21,810	18,857	23,160	19,950
86,500	86,550	21,826	18,871	23,183	19,966
86,550	86,600	21,841	18,885	23,195	19,981
86,600	86,650	21,857	18,899	23,219	19,997
86,650	86,700	21,888	18,913	23,232	20,012
86,700	86,750	21,903	18,927	23,255	20,028
86,750	86,800	21,919	18,941	23,273	20,043
86,800	86,850	21,934	18,969	23,239	20,059
86,850	86,900	21,950	18,983	23,322	20,074
86,900	86,950	21,965	18,997	23,345	20,105

87,000

At least	But less than	Single	Married filing jointly	Married filing separately	Head of a household
87,000	87,050	21,981	19,011	23,363	20,121
87,050	87,100	21,996	19,025	23,381	20,136
87,100	87,150	22,027	19,053	23,393	20,152
87,200	87,250	22,043	19,081	23,435	20,183

1997 Tax Table—Continued

95,000 / 96,000 / 97,000 / 98,000 / 99,000

If line 38 (taxable income) is—		And you are—			
At least	But less than	Single	Married filing jointly	Married filing separately	Head of a household
		Your tax is—			

$100,000 or over — use the Tax Rate Schedules on page 51

* This column must also be used by a qualifying widow(er).

Continued on next page

398

INDEX

Accelerated cost recovery system (ACRS), 127-128, 178-179, 194

"Accountable" business expense reimbursement arrangements (see "Reimbursements of business expenses—accountable plans")

Accounting, for business expenses (see "Reimbursements of business expenses—accountable plans")

Accuracy related penalties, 31-32

Address, change of, 46-47

Adjusted gross income, 29-30, 50, 100, 172-173

Adjustments to gross income, 172-173

Adoption expenses, 230

Allowances, car (see "Reimbursements of business expenses—nonaccountable plans")

Amended returns, 30

Anniversary gifts, 106-109, 114, 136, 143, 248, 261-262, 340, 342

Annual earnings test, 299

Annual information returns (Form 990), 355-356

Annuities, tax-sheltered, 50, 312-318

Apostolic associations, 27, 355

Appraisals, 32, 234, 262-285

Assignments, of clergy, 95-98

Assignments of income, 118

Audits, 31, 40-42, 50, 206
28-29, 37-38, 47, 195

Audit risk, 31, 50, 206

Automobiles
    Automobile allowances, 120, 204-206, 223
    Commuting, 115-116, 143, 171, 175-177, 181, 182, 193
    Employer-provided, personal use, 114-117, 143
    Employer-provided, no personal use, 181, 182, 222
    Leasing, 180, 182
    Luxury cars, 179-180
    Reporting business expenses, 204-218
    Standard mileage rate, business travel, 177, 181, 217
    Transportation expenses, 175-182
    Travel expenses, 182-190

Avoidance of taxes, 46

Backup withholding, 338, 340, 346

Bankruptcy court, recovery of contributions, 244

Bargain sales, 246-247

Below-market interest loans, 117-118

Benevolence funds, 252-257

Bill of rights (see "Taxpayer bill of rights")

Birthday gifts, 106-109, 114, 136, 143, 248, 261-262, 340, 342

Bonuses, 106

Books (see "Business and professional expenses")

Business and professional expenses
    Accounting for, 204-218
    Automobile (see separate topic "Automobile")
    Books, 193-194
    Business gifts, 192, 219
    Clothing, 195-196
    Computers, 194-195
    Dalan allocation rule (see "*Deason* allocation rule")
    Deason allocation rule, 196, 215, 222-224, 297
    Denominational support, 201-204
    Dues, 200-201
    Educational expenses, 192-193
    Entertainment expenses, 190-192
    Home office, 196-199
    In general, 173-224
    Moving expenses, 113-114, 149, 172, 199-200, 226-228, 344
    Office in the home, 196-199
    Professional dues, 200-204
    Recordkeeping requirements, 218-222

Reimbursements, of business expenses, (see separate topic "Reimbursements of business expenses" in this index)
    Reporting of, 204-218
    Salary reductions, use of to fund reimbursements, 212-214
    Salary "restructuring," use of to fund reimbursements, 212-214
    Spouses' travel expenses, 184-190
    Subscriptions and books, 193-194
    Substantiation, 218-222
    Telephone, 200
    Tithes or financial support, 201-204
    Transportation expenses, 175-182, 219
    Travel expenses, 182-190, 219
    Unreimbursed expenses (see separate topic "Reimbursements of business expenses" in this index)

Cafeteria plans, 144-145, 149

Campus lodging, 147-148

Capital gains, 130-132

Cars (see "Automobiles")

Cellular telephones, 200

Change of address, 46-47

Chaplains, 86, 89, 91, 94, 163-164

Charitable contributions
    Amount deductible, 245-247
    Bankruptcy court, recovery of contributions, 244
    Basic requirements, 235-248
    Benevolence funds, 252-257
    Checks, postdated, 240
    Checks, predated, 239-240
    Designated contributions, 248-262
    Foreign charities, 245
    Foreign missionaries, 249-252
    In general, 234-285
    Inventory, 246
    Pledges, 239
    Postdated checks, 240
    Predated checks, 239-240
    Returning to the donor, 242-243
    Scholarship gifts, 257-261
    Services, 235-236
    Substantiation, 247-248, 262-278
    Travel and transportation expenses, 190, 235-236

Child care credit, 228-229

Christmas gifts, 106-109, 114, 136, 143, 248, 261-262, 340, 342

Circular "E," 340

Churches, reporting requirements
    Application for tax exemption, 356-359
    Common payroll tax reporting errors, 339
    Comprehensive illustrations (with forms), 363-379
    Donee information returns, 275-276, 283, 363
    Information returns (Form 990), 355-356
    In general, 330-379
    Payroll tax procedures, 331-349
    Proof of nondiscrimination, 356
    Social security (FICA), 349-353
    Ten-step approach, 337-346
    Unemployment taxes, 353-355
    Unrelated business income, 359-362

Church plans, 313-314

Clergy (see "Ministers")

Clothing (see "Business and professional expenses")

Club dues, 200-201

Commuting expenses, 115-116, 143, 171, 175-177, 181, 182, 193

Commuting valuation rule, 115-116

Compensation (see "Income")

Computers, 194-195

Constructive receipt of income, 118-120, 139, 310-312

Contributions (see "Charitable contributions")

Credits

Adoption credit, 230

Child and dependent care, 228-229

Earned income credit, 229-230

Dalan rule (see "Deason allocation rule")

Deason rule, 196, 215, 222-224, 297

Debt, cancellation or forgiveness of, 121-122

Deductions, itemized, 224-228

Deferred compensation (see "Retirement plans")

Dependent care assistance, employer provided, 148-149, 228

Dependents (see "Personal exemptions")

Deposit requirements (payroll taxes), 341

Depreciation (see "Accelerated cost recovery system" and "Modified accelerated cost recovery system")

Designated contributions

Benevolence funds, 252-257

Christmas gifts, 106-109, 114, 136, 143, 248, 261-262, 340, 342

Foreign missionaries, 249-252

Scholarships, 257-261

Discretionary funds, pastors', 119-120

"Double deduction," 161, 225-226

Earned income credit, 229-230

Earnings test, social security, 299

Economic benefit doctrine, 310-312

Education

Business expense, 192-193

Employer-provided educational assistance, 148

Employee or self-employed, 49-72, 138, 144, 173-175, 204-218, 287-288, 309-310, 314, 335-337

Employer identification number, 148, 229, 337-338, 342

Entertainment expenses, 190-192, 219

Equity allowances, 155

ERISA, 313-314

Estimated taxes, 38-40, 335-337

Evangelists, 52, 67, 68, 158-159, 183

Evasion of taxes (see "Penalties")

Exclusions

Accident insurance proceeds, 139-140

Dependent care, employer provided, 148-149, 228

Education assistance, employer provided, 148

Fringe benefits, 142-149

Gifts and inheritances, 136

Group term life insurance, 141-142

Health insurance premiums paid by employer, 50, 63, 137-139

Health insurance, self-employed, 172

In general, 135-149

Life insurance, 136-137, 141-142

Meals and lodging, employer provided, 146-148

Scholarships, 137

Severance pay, 122-124, 140

Tuition reductions, 145-146

Exemptions

Federal income taxes, churches, 356-359

Group exemptions, 357

Loss of exempt status, 357

Personal exemptions, 35-36

Social security taxes, ministers (see "Social security—ministers")

Extensions of time to file returns, 30

FICA taxes, 287-288, 335-337, 339, 340-341, 349-353

Filing requirements (who must file a tax return), 27-28

Filing status, 35

Flexible spending arrangement (FSA), 145

Foreign charities, contributions to, 245

Foreign earned income exclusion, 136, 183, 190, 297

Foreign travel expenses, 190

Forgiveness of debt, 121-122

Form 990, 355-356

Form 5500, 145, 148, 149, 318, 319

Forms, IRS (reproduced in text)

941: 370, 375

1040: 381, 387

1096: 371, 377

1099-MISC: 371, 377

2106: 384

4361: 301

4562: 385, 391

5578: 372

8274: 374

8282: 285, 372

8283: 283-284

8822: 47

Schedule A: 382, 388

Schedule B: 382, 388

Schedule C: 389

Schedule C-EZ: 383

Schedule SE: 383, 390

W-2: 368-369, 376

W-3: 370, 376

W-4: 349-350, 358

Forms, legal (see "Legal forms")

Fraud, penalty, 33

Freedom of religion

Exemption of ministers from self-employment tax, 291, 294, 337, 351

No basis for a church exemption from tax withholding rules, 337

No basis for a minister not paying taxes, 27

Unemployment tax, 353-355

Frequent flier miles, 125-126

Fringe benefits, 113-114, 142-149

Frivolous tax returns, penalty, 33

Gains and losses, 130-132

Gifts, 106-112, 114, 136, 143, 248, 261-262, 340, 342

Gross income (see "Income")

Group exemptions, churches, 357

Health insurance premiums paid by employer, 50, 63, 137-139

Highly compensated employees, 142

Holy Land, trips to, 124-125

Home, office in, 196-199

Home, sale of, 131-132

Housing allowances (see also "Parsonages and parsonage allowances")

Amending the allowance, 158

Designations, 156-162

"Double deduction," 161, 225-226

Eligibility, 73-99, 156

Evangelists, 158-159

Exclusion for income taxes only, 162

Expenses, 157

How much, 159, 160

How to declare and report, 156-170

In general, 150, 156-165

Limitations, 156-161

Retired clergy, 162, 320-323

Retroactive designations prohibited, 157-158

Safety net designations, 161-162

Sample church designation, 159

Sample form for estimating expenses, 168-169

Severance pay, 124

Social security taxes—no exclusion, 150, 162

Telephone expenses, 156

Husbands and wives, splitting income, 132-134
Income
    Bonuses, 106
    Christmas and other special occasion "gifts" to clergy, 106-109, 114, 136, 143, 248, 261-262, 340, 342
    In general, 100-126
    Employer provided cars (personal use), 114-117, 143
    Frequent flier miles, 125-126
    Gains and losses, 130-132
    Fringe benefits, 113-114
    Holy Land, trips to, 124-125
    Interest and dividends, 126-127
    Loans to clergy, 117-118
    Payment of personal expenses, 125
    Percentage of income, compensation based on, 103
    Property purchased from employer, 112-113
    Refusal to accept full salary, 118-119
    Rental income, 127-128
    Retirement gifts, 109-112, 323-324
    Salary, 101-106
    Severance pay, 122-124
    Sick pay, 113
    Social security benefits, 128-129
    Social security paid by church, 113
    Unreasonable compensation, 101-105
    Wages, salaries, earnings, 101-126
Integral agencies of a church, 94-95
Integrated auxiliaries, 357-358
Interest and dividends, 126-127
Intermediate sanctions, 103-105
Inventory, gifts of, 246
IRAs (see "Retirement plans")
Israel, trips to, 124-125
Itemized deductions
    Casualty and theft losses, 226
    Charitable contributions, 234-285
    Interest, 225-226
    Medical expenses, 224-225
    Miscellaneous deductions, 228
    Taxes, 225
Keogh plans (see "Retirement plans")
Key employees, 142
Knight v. Commissioner, 76-77, 81, 82-84
Leasing a car, 180-182
Legal forms
    Accountable reimbursement policy, 207
    Benevolence fund policy, 252
    Charitable contribution receipt, 272, 280-282
    Contract clause designating minister as self-employed, 53
    Housing allowance designation, 159
    Housing allowance expense form (for clergy who own their home), 168
    Housing allowance expense form (for clergy who rent their home), 169
    Housing allowance expense form (for clergy who live in a parsonage), 170
    Parsonage allowance designation, 152
    Parsonage allowance expense form (for clergy who live in a church-owned parsonage), 170
Life insurance, 136-137, 141-142
Limitations period, 34, 292-293
Loans to clergy, 117-118
Lodging, employer-provided, 146-148, 151-156
Luxury car, 179-180
Magazines, 193-194
"Mail order" ministerial credentials, 27
Meals and lodging, employer provided, 146-147
Medical insurance (see "Health insurance")

Medical savings accounts (MSAs), 140-141
Mileage (see "Standard mileage rate")
Ministers (see topics throughout index)
    Assignments of, 95-98
    Christmas gifts, 106-109, 114, 136, 143, 248, 261-262, 340, 342
    Defined, 75-86
    Duty to pay taxes, 27
    Employee or self-employed, 49-72, 138, 144, 173-175, 204-218, 287-288, 309-310, 314, 335-337
    Exemption from social security (see "Social security—ministers")
    Housing allowance, 150, 158-170
    Ordained, commissioned, licensed, 74, 75-86
    Parsonages, 151-156, 297-298
    Payroll tax reporting, 331-349
    Retirement gifts, 109-112, 323-324
    Services performed in the exercise of ministry, 86-98, 296-297, 335-337
    Social security (see "Social security—ministers")
    Withholding, 36-38, 335-337
Missionaries, 249-252
Modified accelerated cost recovery system (MACRS), 127-128, 178-179, 194
Mortgage points, 226
Moving expenses, 113-114, 149, 172, 199-200, 226-228, 344
Negligence, penalty, 32, 33-34
Newspapers, 193-194
Offers in compromise, 41-42
Office in the home, 196-199
Orders, religious, 98-99
Parsonage allowance (see also "Housing allowances")
    Eligibility, 73-99, 151-152
    Equity allowances, 155
    Exclusion for income tax only, 154
    How to report, 151-156, 170
    In general, 151-156
    Retired ministers, 156, 320-323
    Sample church designation, 152
    Sample form for estimating expenses, 170
    Social security taxes—no exclusion, 154
Parsonages, 151-156, 170
Pastors (see "Ministers")
Payroll reporting requirements, churches, 331-349
Penalties
    Churches, 331-335
    Individuals, 31-34
Percentage of income, compensation based on, 103
Per diem rates, 219-222
Personal exemptions, 35-36
Pledges, 239
Postdated checks, 240
Predated checks, 239-240
Preparing your own tax returns, 34-35
Professional expenses (see "Business and professional expenses")
Qualified appraisals, 273-276, 284-285
Qualified church-controlled organization, 311, 313, 351
Qualified tuition reductions, 145-146
Rabbi trusts, 310, 311-312, 325-329
Recordkeeping
    Business and professional expenses, 218-222
    Charitable contributions, 247-248, 262-285
    In general, 29
Reductions of salary to fund reimbursements, 212-214
Refunds, 30
Reimbursements of business expenses—accountable plan
    Advantages of an accountable plan, 206
    In general, 51, 174-175, 206-218
    Salary reductions, use of prohibited, 212-214

Salary "restructuring", use of prohibited, 212-214
Reimbursements of business expenses—nonaccountable plan, 51, 174-175, 204-206, 214-218
Religious orders, 98-99
Rental allowance (see "Housing allowances")
Rental income, 127-128
Rent-free use of building, 238
Reporting requirements, churches, 330-379
Retired ministers, annual earnings test, 299
Retired ministers, housing allowances, 162, 320-323
Retired ministers, parsonages, 156, 320-323
Retirement gifts to clergy, 109-112, 323-324
Retirement plans
    401(k) plans, 319
    Church retirement income accounts, 318
    Deferred compensation plans, 310-312
    Denominational plans, 319-320
    Housing allowances, 320-323

    IRAs, 303-309
    In general, 128-129, 302-329
    Keogh plans, 309-310
    Qualified pension plans, 318-319
    Rabbi trusts, 310, 311-312, 325-329
    Retirement gifts, 109-112, 323-324
    SEPs (simplified employee pension plans), 309
    SIMPLE retirement plans, 324-325
    Tax-sheltered annuities—section 403(b) plans, 50, 312-318
Salary reductions, use of to fund reimbursements, 212-214
Salary "restructuring," use of to fund reimbursements, 212-214
Sanctions, intermediate, 103-105
Scholarships, 137, 148, 257-261
Schools
    Campus lodging, 147-148
    Proof of racial nondiscrimination, 356
    Scholarships, 137, 148, 257-261
    Tuition reductions, 145-146
Section 179, 179, 194-195
Self-employment earnings, 293, 297-299
Self-employed status (see "Employee or self-employed")
Self-employment tax (see "Social security—ministers")
"Services performed by a minister of a church in the exercise of his ministry," 86-98, 296-297, 335-337
Severance pay, 122-124, 140
Shelley v. Commissioner, 64-66, 72
Social security benefits, taxability, 128-129
Social security—churches, 349-353
Social security—ministers
    Annual earnings test, 299
    Computation of tax, 293, 297-299
    Exemption of members of certain religious faiths, 299-300
    Exemption of ministers, 288-296
    Form 4361 (see "Forms, IRS")
    Housing allowance—no exclusion, 150, 154, 162
    In general, 286-301
    Retirement, working after, 299
    Self-employed status, 287-288, 335-337
    Self-employment tax, 287-288, 335-337
    Services to which exemption applies, 86-99, 287-288, 335-337
    Tax paid by church, 113
    Working after you retire, 299
Spouses
    Splitting income with, 132-134
    Travel expenses, 121, 143, 184-190
Standard deduction, 27-30, 173, 224
Standard mileage rate, business travel, 177, 181, 217
Standard mileage rate, charitable travel, 235-236
Statute of limitations, 34, 292-293

Subscriptions, 193-194
Substantiation
    Business and professional expenses, 218-222
    Charitable contributions, 247-248, 262-278
Taxable income, 29-30
Taxpayer Bill of Rights, 42-46
Tax protestors, 27
Tax return
    Who must file (see "Filing requirements")
    When to file, 30
Tax-sheltered annuities (see "Retirement plans")
Tax Tables, 393-398
Telephone expenses, 156, 200
Tithes or financial support to a church, 201-204
Transportation expenses (see "Business and professional expenses")
Travel expense (see "Business and professional expenses")
Tuition reductions (see "Qualified tuition reductions")
Underpayment penalty, 40
Unemployment taxes, 353-355
Unreasonable compensation, 101-105
Unreimbursed business expenses, 174-175, 204
Unrelated business income, 359-362
Voluntary withholding, 36-38, 335-337
Weber v. Commissioner, 60-64, 72
When to file a return
    Form 1040, 30
    Extensions, 30
    Amended returns, 30
Withholding (of income and social security taxes)
    Backup withholding, 338, 340, 346
    Deposit requirements, 341
    Exemption of clergy, 36-38, 335-337
    In general, 36-38, 335-337, 340-341
    Ministers, 36-38, 335-337
    Personal use of employer-provided car, 114-117, 143
    Voluntary withholding, 36-38, 335-337

Church Law & Tax Report
1998 Resource Guide

New! Church Treasurer Alert!—A **monthly newsletter for church treasurers, financial secretaries and church bookkeepers.** It's like having the nation's leading accounting, tax, and financial experts helping your church each month. Covers topics such as filing IRS forms, federal tax law, employee benefits, charitable contributions, planned and deferred giving, staff compensation, church accounting, computer software, IRS developments, plus much more! Price: $29.95—*now only $24.95 through this special offer!*

The Church Guide to Planning and Budgeting. Provides a comprehensive step-by-step guide to the budgeting process in the local church. You'll receive practical help on a variety of budgeting approaches including incremental budgeting, program budgeting, and zero-based budgeting. Plus, you'll discover how to effectively use a cash budget, capital-spending budget, and debt-retirement budget. Price: $12.95.

The Church Guide to Financial Reporting. An invaluable resource for every church treasurer! Financial reports provide the vital information needed to plan, budget, and control church finances. *The Church Guide to Financial Reporting* provides practical examples of effective financial reporting techniques for each level of congregational life. Discover how to prepare reports for congregational members, church leaders, and other decision makers within the congregation. Price: $9.95.

The Church Guide to Internal Controls. Few churches implement effective procedures to protect church assets. All too often, church money is handled in a casual way. *The Church Guide to Internal Controls* presents 50 practical steps that any church can easily implement to reduce the risk of theft or mismanagement of church funds. Price: $12.95.

NEW! Legal and Tax Update for Church Treasurers—Audio Tape. This new audio tape by Richard Hammar and James Cobble provides church treasurers with an annual review of important legal, tax, and financial developments that affect the church. You'll get vital information you need to stay informed on key developments that impact your responsibilities as church treasurer. Price: $9.95.

Church Guide to Employment Law. Practical, down-to-earth information on one of the most problematic legal areas facing churches today. Every major employment issue facing churches is covered. If your church has employees, then you need this vital reference book by Julie L. Bloss, J.D., CEBS. 152 pages. Price: $12.95.

Church Guide to Copyright Law-2nd ed. 190 page reference book. A complete and practical copyright reference designed for churches, clergy, and church musicians. Covers dozens of issues, including overhead transparencies, computer programs, chorus booklets, audio tapes, radio broadcasts, educational activities, and performances. Price: $12.95

The New Minister's Guide to Legal and Tax Issues audio tape. A one-hour tape covering the following vital topics: estimated tax obligations, minister's housing allowance, social security options, professional record keeping requirements, and confidentiality. Helps to orient clergy who are just beginning the ministry. A must for new ministers. Price: $9.95

Federal Reporting Requirements for Churches audio tape, updated annually. A clear presentation of church filing requirements. Covers forms W-4, W-2, W-3, 941, 941E, 1099-MISC, 1096, 5578, and more. Price: $9.95

Income and Expenses for Church Staff audio tape, updated annually. A one-hour tape discussing the major tax issues confronting clergy and other church staff. Coverage includes employee or self-employed status, housing allowances, car allowances, gifts, social security options, plus much more. Price: $9.95

Housing and Parsonage Allowances for Clergy audio tape. The housing allowance is the most important tax benefit available to clergy, and the most misunderstood. On this 60-minute tape, Richard Hammar explains the requirements for claiming the full advantage of this benefit, whether you live in a parsonage, or you own or rent your home. Price: $9.95

Charitable Contributions and Designated Offerings audio tape. A clear and concise explanation of the law of charitable contributions. Here it is. In one 90-minute tape, Richard Hammar explores those issues that are of the most importance to church treasurers and bookkeepers—including the 6 requirements of a deductible contribution, whether churches must ever "appraise" a donor's gift, the deductibility of "designated offerings," and the IRS requirements on substantiating contributions of property. Price $9.95

What Every Church Member Should Know About Charitable Contributions bulletin insert, 100 per set. Helps church members to take full advantage of tax laws concerning charitable giving. Also explains the most important tax laws that affect giving to the church. Price: $7.95

1998 Compensation Handbook for Church Staff. Complete compensation profiles for 9 staff positions. 148 pages. The best book available! Price: $19.95.

Use the Order Form found on back page

Use this Discount Certificate to order your 1999 edition of the Church and Clergy Tax Guide and the Order Form for additional resources

Church and Clergy Tax Guide—1999 Edition Discount Certificate

The ***Church and Clergy Tax Guide*** is revised and updated every year. This certificate is good towards $3 off the regular price for the 1999 edition of t**he *Church and Clergy Tax Guide*,** available after January 1, 1999. To qualify, orders must be placed by December 1, 1998. To order, return a copy of this certificate along with your payment of $11.95 (regular price $14.95) to: **Christian Ministry Resources, PO Box 1098, Matthews, NC 28106.** Add $5 for postage & handling. Please indicate your mailing information below:

Note: *Payment of $11.95 plus $5 for shipping must be included with order to qualify for the discount.*

Quantity _____   Amount Enclosed $_____

Name _____

Address_____

City _____

State _____ Zipcode _____

Signature_____

Order Form for Additonal Resources (see previous page)
For fast orders call 1-800-222-1840 between 8AM and 4:30 PM EST.

Please send me the following items:

	Price	Quantity	Total
1. The Church Guide to Planning and Budgeting	$12.95		
2. The Church Guide to Financial Reporting	$9.95		
3. The Church Guide to Internal Controls	$12.95		
4. Complete Financial Management Set (Numbers 1, 2 & 3 above)	$26.89		
5. Church Treasurer Alert! (monthly newsletter)	$24.95		
6. Church Guide to Copyright Law Kit	$29.95		
7. The Church Guide to Employment Law	$12.95		
8. The 1998 Compensation Handbook for Church Staff	$19.95		
9. Orientation and Training for Board Member (audio cassette)	$9.95		
10. What Church Members Should Know (bulletin inserts)	$7.95		
11. New Minister's Guide to Legal and Tax Issues (audio cassette)	$9.95		
12. Risk Management for Churches: A Self-Directed Audit	$9.95		
13. NEW! Legal and Tax Update for Church Treasurers—audio tape	$9.95		
14. Other			
15. Other _____			

Church_____

Name_____

Address_____

City_____

State____ Zipcode_____ Phone_____

Shipping (see table) _____

NC residents add 6% tax _____

Total Due _____

Return Payment To:
Christian Ministry Resources
PO Box 1098
Matthews, NC 28106

Shipping Charges

$4 for orders of $20 or less
$5 for orders more than $20